U.S. History

Table of Contents

Preface

Welcome to *U.S. History*, an OpenStax resource. This textbook has been created with several goals in mind: accessibility, customization, and student engagement—all while encouraging students toward high levels of academic scholarship. Instructors and students alike will find that this textbook offers a strong foundation in U.S. history in an accessible format.

About OpenStax

OpenStax is a non-profit organization committed to improving student access to quality learning materials. Our free textbooks go through a rigorous editorial publishing process. Our texts are developed and peer-reviewed by educators to ensure they are readable, accurate, and meet the scope and sequence requirements of today's college courses. Unlike traditional textbooks, OpenStax resources live online and are owned by the community of educators using them. Through our partnerships with companies and foundations committed to reducing costs for students, OpenStax is working to improve access to higher education for all. OpenStax is an initiative of Rice University and is made possible through the generous support of several philanthropic foundations. Since our launch in 2012 our texts have been used by millions of learners online and over 1,200 institutions worldwide.

About OpenStax's Resources

OpenStax resources provide quality academic instruction. Three key features set our materials apart from others: they can be customized by instructors for each class, they are a "living" resource that grows online through contributions from educators, and they are available free or for minimal cost.

Customization

OpenStax learning resources are designed to be customized for each course. Our textbooks are developed to meet the scope and sequence of a typical course and; therefore, provide a solid foundation on which instructors can build, and our resources are conceived and written with flexibility in mind. Instructors can select the sections most relevant to their curricula and create a textbook that speaks directly to the needs of their classes and student body. Teachers are encouraged to expand on existing examples by adding unique context via geographically localized applications and topical connections.

U.S. History can be easily customized using our online platform (http://legacy.cnx.org/content/col11740/latest/). Simply select the content most relevant to your current semester and create a textbook that speaks directly to the needs of your class. U.S. History is organized as a collection of sections that can be rearranged, modified, and enhanced through localized examples or to incorporate a specific theme of your course. This customization feature will ensure that your textbook truly reflects the goals of your course.

Cost

Our textbooks are available for free online, and also in low-cost print and iBook textbook editions.

About *U.S. History*

U.S. History has been developed to meet the scope and sequence of most introductory U.S. History courses. At the same time, the book includes a number of innovative features designed to enhance student learning. Instructors can also customize the book, adapting it to the approach that works best in their classroom.

Coverage and Scope

To develop *U.S. History*, we solicited ideas from historians at all levels of higher education, from community colleges to Ph.D.-granting universities. They told us about their courses, students, challenges, resources, and how a textbook can best meet their and their students' needs.

The result is a book that covers the breadth of the chronological history of the United States and also provides the necessary depth to ensure the course is manageable for instructors and students alike. *U.S. History* explores the key forces and major developments that together form the American experience, with particular attention paid to considering issues of race, class, and gender.

The pedagogical choices, chapter arrangements, and learning objective fulfillment were developed and vetted with feedback from educators dedicated to the project. They thoroughly read the material and offered critical and detailed commentary. Reviewer feedback centered around achieving equilibrium between the various political, social, and cultural dynamics that permeate history. The outcome is a balanced approach to U.S. history, considering the people, events, and ideas that have shaped the United States from both the top down (politics, economics, diplomacy) and bottom up (eyewitness accounts, lived experience).

While the book is organized primarily chronologically, as needed, material treating different topics or regions over the same time period is spread over multiple chapters. For example, chapters 9, 11, and 12 look at economic, political, social, and cultural developments during the first half of the eighteenth century in the North, West, and South respectively, while chapters 18 to 20 closely examine industrialization, urbanization, and politics in the period after Reconstruction.

Pedagogical Foundation

Throughout the OpenStax version of U.S. History, you will find featured material that engage the students in historical inquiry by taking selected topics a step further. Our features include:

Americana: This feature explores the significance of artifacts from American pop culture and considers what values, views, and philosophies are reflected in these objects.

Defining "American": This feature analyzes primary sources, including documents, speeches, and other writings, to consider important issues of the day and present varying points of view on them, while keeping a focus on the theme of what it means to be American.

My Story: This feature presents first-person accounts (diaries, interviews, letters) of significant or exceptional events from the American experience.

Link It Up: This feature is a very brief introduction to a website with an interactive experience, video, or primary sources that help improve student understanding of the material.

Questions for Each Level of Learning

The OpenStax version of *U.S. History* offers two types of end-of-module questions for students.

Review Questions are simple recall questions from each module in the chapter and are in either multiple-choice or open-response format. The answers can be looked up in the text.

Critical Thinking Questions are higher-level, conceptual questions that ask students to *demonstrate their understanding by applying* what they have learned in each module to the whole of the chapter. They ask for outside-the-box thinking, for *reasoning* about the concepts. They push the student to places they wouldn't have thought of going themselves.

About Our Team

Our team is a diverse mix of historians representing various institutions across the nation. We'd like to extend a special thanks to our senior contributors who worked tirelessly to ensure the coverage and level is appropriate for students.

Senior Contributing Authors

P. Scott Corbett, PhD—Ventura College

Dr. Corbett's major fields of study are recent American history and American diplomatic history. He teaches a variety of courses at Ventura College, and he serves as an instructor at California State University's Channel Islands campus. A passionate educator, Scott has also taught history to university students in Singapore and China.

Volker Janssen, PhD—California State University–Fullerton

Born and raised in Germany, Dr. Janssen received his BA from the University of Hamburg and his MA and PhD from the University of California, San Diego. He is a former Fulbright scholar and an active member of Germany's advanced studies foundation "Studienstiftung des Deutschen Volkes." Volker currently serves as Associate Professor at California State University's Fullerton campus, where he specializes in the social, economic, and institutional history of California, and more recently, the history of technology.

John M. Lund, PhD—Keene State College

Dr. Lund's primary research focuses on early American history, with a special interest in oaths, Colonial New England, and Atlantic legal cultures. John has over 20 years of teaching experience. In addition to working with students at Keene State College, he lectures at Franklin Pierce University, and serves the online learning community at Southern New Hampshire University.

Todd Pfannestiel, PhD—Clarion University

Dr. Pfannestiel is a Professor in the history department of Clarion University in Pennsylvania, where he also holds the position of Dean of the College of Arts and Sciences. Todd has a strong history of service to his institution, its students, and the community that surrounds it.

Paul Vickery, PhD—Oral Roberts University

Educating others is one of Dr. Vickery's delights, whether in the classroom, through authoring books and articles, or via informal teaching during his travels. He is currently Professor of History at Oral Roberts University, where his emphasis is on the history of ideas, ethics, and the role of the church and theology in national development. Paul reads Portuguese, Italian, French, and Hebrew, and has taught on five continents.

Sylvie Waskiewicz, PhD—Lead Editor

Dr. Waskiewicz received her BSBA from Georgetown University and her MA and PhD from the Institute of French Studies at New York University. With over 10 years of teaching experience in English and French history and language, Sylvie left academia to join the ranks of higher education publishing. She has spent the last eight years editing college textbooks and academic journals.

Reviewers

Amy Bix	Iowa State University
Edward Bond	Alabama A&M University
Tammy Byron	Dalton State College
Benjamin Carp	Brooklyn College, CUNY
Sharon Deubreau	Rhodes State College
Gene Fein	Fordham University
Joel Franks	San Jose State University
Raymond Frey	Centenary College
Richard Gianni	Indiana University Northwest
Larry Gragg	Missouri University of Science and Technology
Laura Graves	South Plains College
Elisa Guernsey	Monroe Community College
Thomas Chase Hagood	University of Georgia
Charlotte Haller	Worcester State University
David Head	Spring Hill College
Tamora Hoskisson	Salt Lake Community College
Jean Keller	Palomar College

Kathleen Kennedy	Missouri State University
Mark Klobas	Scottsdale Community College
Ann Kordas	Johnson & Wales University
Stephanie Laffer	Miami International University of Art and Design
Jennifer Lang	Delgado Community College
Jennifer Lawrence	Tarrant County College
Wendy Maier-Sarti	Oakton Community College
Jim McIntyre	Moraine Valley Community College
Marianne McKnight	Salt Lake Community College
Brandon Morgan	Central New Mexico Community College
Caryn Neumann	Miami University of Ohio
Michelle Novak	Houston Community College
Lisa Ossian	Des Moines Area Community College
Paul Ringel	High Point University
Jason Ripper	Everett Community College
Silvana Siddali	Saint Louis University
Brooks Simpson	Arizona State University
Steven Smith	California State University, Fullerton
David Trowbridge	Marshall University
Eugene Van Sickle	University of North Georgia
Hubert van Tuyll	Augusta State University

Ancillaries

OpenStax projects offer an array of ancillaries for students and instructors. Please visit http://openstaxcollege.org and view the learning resources for this title.

CHAPTER 1

The Americas, Europe, and Africa Before 1492

Figure 1.1 In *Europe supported by Africa and America* (1796), artist William Blake, who was an abolitionist, depicts the interdependence of the three continents in the Atlantic World; however, he places gold armbands on the Indian and African women, symbolizing their subjugation. The strand binding the three women may represent tobacco.

Chapter Outline

1.1 The Americas
1.2 Europe on the Brink of Change
1.3 West Africa and the Role of Slavery

Introduction

Globalization, the ever-increasing interconnectedness of the world, is not a new phenomenon, but it accelerated when western Europeans discovered the riches of the East. During the Crusades (1095–1291), Europeans developed an appetite for spices, silk, porcelain, sugar, and other luxury items from the East, for which they traded fur, timber, and Slavic people they captured and sold (hence the word *slave*). But when the Silk Road, the long overland trading route from China to the Mediterranean, became costlier and more dangerous to travel, Europeans searched for a more efficient and inexpensive trade route over water, initiating the development of what we now call the Atlantic World.

In pursuit of commerce in Asia, fifteenth-century traders unexpectedly encountered a "New World" populated by millions and home to sophisticated and numerous peoples. Mistakenly believing they had reached the East Indies, these early explorers called its inhabitants Indians. West Africa, a diverse and culturally rich area, soon entered the stage as other nations exploited its slave trade and brought its peoples to the New World in chains. Although Europeans would come to dominate the New World, they could not have done so without Africans and native peoples (Figure 1.1).

1.1 The Americas

By the end of this section, you will be able to:
- Locate on a map the major American civilizations before the arrival of the Spanish
- Discuss the cultural achievements of these civilizations
- Discuss the differences and similarities between lifestyles, religious practices, and customs among the native peoples

Between nine and fifteen thousand years ago, some scholars believe that a land bridge existed between Asia and North America that we now call **Beringia**. The first inhabitants of what would be named the Americas migrated across this bridge in search of food. When the glaciers melted, water engulfed Beringia, and the Bering Strait was formed. Later settlers came by boat across the narrow strait. (The fact that Asians and American Indians share genetic markers on a Y chromosome lends credibility to this migration theory.) Continually moving southward, the settlers eventually populated both North and South America, creating unique cultures that ranged from the highly complex and urban Aztec civilization in what is now Mexico City to the woodland tribes of eastern North America. Recent research along the west coast of South America suggests that migrant populations may have traveled down this coast by water as well as by land.

Researchers believe that about ten thousand years ago, humans also began the domestication of plants and animals, adding agriculture as a means of sustenance to hunting and gathering techniques. With this agricultural revolution, and the more abundant and reliable food supplies it brought, populations grew and people were able to develop a more settled way of life, building permanent settlements. Nowhere in the Americas was this more obvious than in Mesoamerica (Figure 1.3).

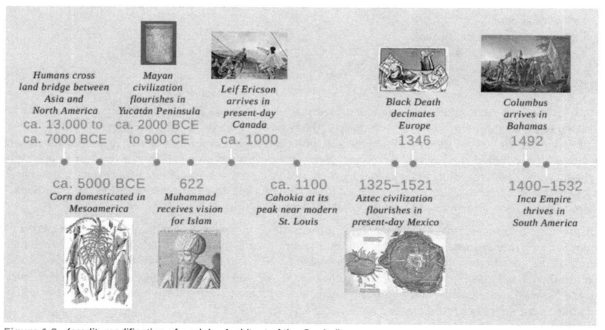

Figure 1.2   (credit: modification of work by Architect of the Capitol)

Download for free at http://cnx.org/content/col11740/latest/

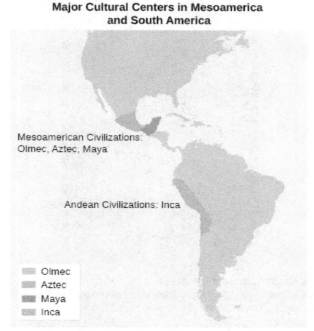

Figure 1.3 This map shows the extent of the major civilizations of the Western Hemisphere. In South America, early civilizations developed along the coast because the high Andes and the inhospitable Amazon Basin made the interior of the continent less favorable for settlement.

THE FIRST AMERICANS: THE OLMEC

Mesoamerica is the geographic area stretching from north of Panama up to the desert of central Mexico. Although marked by great topographic, linguistic, and cultural diversity, this region cradled a number of civilizations with similar characteristics. Mesoamericans were polytheistic; their gods possessed both male and female traits and demanded blood sacrifices of enemies taken in battle or ritual bloodletting. Corn, or maize, domesticated by 5000 BCE, formed the basis of their diet. They developed a mathematical system, built huge edifices, and devised a calendar that accurately predicted eclipses and solstices and that priest-astronomers used to direct the planting and harvesting of crops. Most important for our knowledge of these peoples, they created the only known written language in the Western Hemisphere; researchers have made much progress in interpreting the inscriptions on their temples and pyramids. Though the area had no overarching political structure, trade over long distances helped diffuse culture. Weapons made of obsidian, jewelry crafted from jade, feathers woven into clothing and ornaments, and cacao beans that were whipped into a chocolate drink formed the basis of commerce. The mother of Mesoamerican cultures was the Olmec civilization.

Flourishing along the hot Gulf Coast of Mexico from about 1200 to about 400 BCE, the Olmec produced a number of major works of art, architecture, pottery, and sculpture. Most recognizable are their giant head sculptures (Figure 1.4) and the pyramid in La Venta. The Olmec built aqueducts to transport water into their cities and irrigate their fields. They grew maize, squash, beans, and tomatoes. They also bred small domesticated dogs which, along with fish, provided their protein. Although no one knows what happened to the Olmec after about 400 BCE, in part because the jungle reclaimed many of their cities, their culture was the base upon which the Maya and the Aztec built. It was the Olmec who worshipped a rain god, a maize god, and the feathered serpent so important in the future pantheons of the Aztecs (who called him Quetzalcoatl) and the Maya (to whom he was Kukulkan). The Olmec also developed a system of trade throughout Mesoamerica, giving rise to an elite class.

Figure 1.4   The Olmec carved heads from giant boulders that ranged from four to eleven feet in height and could weigh up to fifty tons. All these figures have flat noses, slightly crossed eyes, and large lips. These physical features can be seen today in some of the peoples indigenous to the area.

THE MAYA

After the decline of the Olmec, a city rose in the fertile central highlands of Mesoamerica. One of the largest population centers in pre-Columbian America and home to more than 100,000 people at its height in about 500 CE, Teotihuacan was located about thirty miles northeast of modern Mexico City. The ethnicity of this settlement's inhabitants is debated; some scholars believe it was a multiethnic city. Large-scale agriculture and the resultant abundance of food allowed time for people to develop special trades and skills other than farming. Builders constructed over twenty-two hundred apartment compounds for multiple families, as well as more than a hundred temples. Among these were the Pyramid of the Sun (which is two hundred feet high) and the Pyramid of the Moon (one hundred and fifty feet high). Near the Temple of the Feathered Serpent, graves have been uncovered that suggest humans were sacrificed for religious purposes. The city was also the center for trade, which extended to settlements on Mesoamerica's Gulf Coast.

The Maya were one Mesoamerican culture that had strong ties to Teotihuacan. The Maya's architectural and mathematical contributions were significant. Flourishing from roughly 2000 BCE to 900 CE in what is now Mexico, Belize, Honduras, and Guatemala, the Maya perfected the calendar and written language the Olmec had begun. They devised a written mathematical system to record crop yields and the size of the population, and to assist in trade. Surrounded by farms relying on primitive agriculture, they built the city-states of Copan, Tikal, and Chichen Itza along their major trade routes, as well as temples, statues of gods, pyramids, and astronomical observatories (Figure 1.5). However, because of poor soil and a drought that lasted nearly two centuries, their civilization declined by about 900 CE and they abandoned their large population centers.

Figure 1.5 El Castillo, located at Chichen Itza in the eastern Yucatán peninsula, served as a temple for the god Kukulkan. Each side contains ninety-one steps to the top. When counting the top platform, the total number of stairs is three hundred and sixty-five, the number of days in a year. (credit: Ken Thomas)

The Spanish found little organized resistance among the weakened Maya upon their arrival in the 1520s. However, they did find Mayan history, in the form of glyphs, or pictures representing words, recorded in folding books called codices (the singular is *codex*). In 1562, Bishop Diego de Landa, who feared the converted natives had reverted to their traditional religious practices, collected and burned every codex he could find. Today only a few survive.

Click and Explore

Visit the **University of Arizona Library Special Collections** (http://openstaxcollege.org/l/mayancodex) to view facsimiles and descriptions of two of the four surviving Mayan codices.

THE AZTEC

When the Spaniard Hernán Cortés arrived on the coast of Mexico in the sixteenth century, at the site of present-day Veracruz, he soon heard of a great city ruled by an emperor named Moctezuma. This city was tremendously wealthy—filled with gold—and took in tribute from surrounding tribes. The riches and complexity Cortés found when he arrived at that city, known as Tenochtitlán, were far beyond anything he or his men had ever seen.

According to legend, a warlike people called the Aztec (also known as the Mexica) had left a city called Aztlán and traveled south to the site of present-day Mexico City. In 1325, they began construction of Tenochtitlán on an island in Lake Texcoco. By 1519, when Cortés arrived, this settlement contained upwards of 200,000 inhabitants and was certainly the largest city in the Western Hemisphere at that time and probably larger than any European city (Figure 1.6). One of Cortés's soldiers, Bernal Díaz del Castillo, recorded his impressions upon first seeing it: "When we saw so many cities and villages built in the water and other great towns on dry land we were amazed and said it was like the enchantments . . . on account of the great towers and cues and buildings rising from the water, and all built of masonry. And some of our soldiers even asked whether the things that we saw were not a dream? . . . I do not know how to describe it, seeing things as we did that had never been heard of or seen before, not even dreamed about."

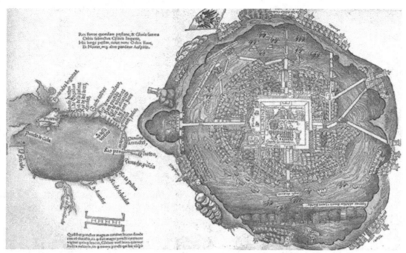

Figure 1.6 This rendering of the Aztec island city of Tenochtitlán depicts the causeways that connected the central city to the surrounding land. Envoys from surrounding tribes brought tribute to the Emperor.

Unlike the dirty, fetid cities of Europe at the time, Tenochtitlán was well planned, clean, and orderly. The city had neighborhoods for specific occupations, a trash collection system, markets, two aqueducts bringing in fresh water, and public buildings and temples. Unlike the Spanish, Aztecs bathed daily, and wealthy homes might even contain a steam bath. A labor force of slaves from subjugated neighboring tribes had built the fabulous city and the three causeways that connected it to the mainland. To farm, the Aztec constructed barges made of reeds and filled them with fertile soil. Lake water constantly irrigated these *chinampas*, or "floating gardens," which are still in use and can be seen today in Xochimilco, a district of Mexico City.

Each god in the Aztec pantheon represented and ruled an aspect of the natural world, such as the heavens, farming, rain, fertility, sacrifice, and combat. A ruling class of warrior nobles and priests performed ritual human sacrifice daily to sustain the sun on its long journey across the sky, to appease or feed the gods, and to stimulate agricultural production. The sacrificial ceremony included cutting open the chest of a criminal or captured warrior with an obsidian knife and removing the still-beating heart (**Figure 1.7**).

Figure 1.7 In this illustration, an Aztec priest cuts out the beating heart of a sacrificial victim before throwing the body down from the temple. Aztec belief centered on supplying the gods with human blood—the ultimate sacrifice—to keep them strong and well.

Click and Explore

Explore **Aztec-History.com (http://openstaxcollege.org/l/azteccreation)** to learn more about the Aztec creation story.

MY STORY

❂ *The Aztec Predict the Coming of the Spanish*

The following is an excerpt from the sixteenth-century Florentine Codex of the writings of Fray Bernardino de Sahagun, a priest and early chronicler of Aztec history. When an old man from Xochimilco first saw the Spanish in Veracruz, he recounted an earlier dream to Moctezuma, the ruler of the Aztecs.

> Said Quzatli to the sovereign, "Oh mighty lord, if because I tell you the truth I am to die, nevertheless I am here in your presence and you may do what you wish to me!" He narrated that mounted men would come to this land in a great wooden house [ships] this structure was to lodge many men, serving them as a home; within they would eat and sleep. On the surface of this house they would cook their food, walk and play as if they were on firm land. They were to be white, bearded men, dressed in different colors and on their heads they would wear round coverings.

Ten years before the arrival of the Spanish, Moctezuma received several omens which at the time he could not interpret. A fiery object appeared in the night sky, a spontaneous fire broke out in a religious temple and could not be extinguished with water, a water spout appeared in Lake Texcoco, and a woman could be heard wailing, "O my children we are about to go forever." Moctezuma also had dreams and premonitions of impending disaster. These foretellings were recorded after the Aztecs' destruction. They do, however, give us insight into the importance placed upon signs and omens in the pre-Columbian world.

THE INCA

In South America, the most highly developed and complex society was that of the Inca, whose name means "lord" or "ruler" in the Andean language called Quechua. At its height in the fifteenth and sixteenth centuries, the Inca Empire, located on the Pacific coast and straddling the Andes Mountains, extended some twenty-five hundred miles. It stretched from modern-day Colombia in the north to Chile in the south and included cities built at an altitude of 14,000 feet above sea level. Its road system, kept free of debris and repaired by workers stationed at varying intervals, rivaled that of the Romans and efficiently connected the sprawling empire. The Inca, like all other pre-Columbian societies, did not use axle-mounted wheels for transportation. They built stepped roads to ascend and descend the steep slopes of the Andes; these would have been impractical for wheeled vehicles but worked well for pedestrians. These roads enabled the rapid movement of the highly trained Incan army. Also like the Romans, the Inca were effective administrators. Runners called *chasquis* traversed the roads in a continuous relay system, ensuring quick communication over long distances. The Inca had no system of writing, however. They communicated and kept records using a system of colored strings and knots called the *quipu* (Figure 1.8).

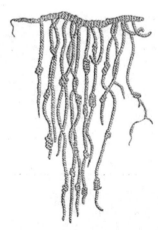

Figure 1.8 The Inca had no written language. Instead, they communicated and kept records by means of a system of knots and colored strings called the *quipu*. Each of these knots and strings possessed a distinct meaning intelligible to those educated in their significance.

The Inca people worshipped their lord who, as a member of an elite ruling class, had absolute authority over every aspect of life. Much like feudal lords in Europe at the time, the ruling class lived off the labor of the peasants, collecting vast wealth that accompanied them as they went, mummified, into the next life. The Inca farmed corn, beans, squash, quinoa (a grain cultivated for its seeds), and the indigenous potato on terraced land they hacked from the steep mountains. Peasants received only one-third of their crops for themselves. The Inca ruler required a third, and a third was set aside in a kind of welfare system for those unable to work. Huge storehouses were filled with food for times of need. Each peasant also worked for the Inca ruler a number of days per month on public works projects, a requirement known as the *mita*. For example, peasants constructed rope bridges made of grass to span the mountains above fast-flowing icy rivers. In return, the lord provided laws, protection, and relief in times of famine.

The Inca worshipped the sun god Inti and called gold the "sweat" of the sun. Unlike the Maya and the Aztecs, they rarely practiced human sacrifice and usually offered the gods food, clothing, and coca leaves. In times of dire emergency, however, such as in the aftermath of earthquakes, volcanoes, or crop failure, they resorted to sacrificing prisoners. The ultimate sacrifice was children, who were specially selected and well fed. The Inca believed these children would immediately go to a much better afterlife.

In 1911, the American historian Hiram Bingham uncovered the lost Incan city of Machu Picchu (Figure 1.9). Located about fifty miles northwest of Cusco, Peru, at an altitude of about 8,000 feet, the city had been built in 1450 and inexplicably abandoned roughly a hundred years later. Scholars believe the city was used for religious ceremonial purposes and housed the priesthood. The architectural beauty of this city is unrivaled. Using only the strength of human labor and no machines, the Inca constructed walls and buildings of polished stones, some weighing over fifty tons, that were fitted together perfectly without the use of mortar. In 1983, UNESCO designated the ruined city a World Heritage Site.

Figure 1.9 Located in today's Peru at an altitude of nearly 8,000 feet, Machu Picchu was a ceremonial Incan city built about 1450 CE.

Click and Explore

Browse the British Museum's World Cultures collection (http://openstaxcollege.org/l/inca) to see more examples and descriptions of Incan (as well as Aztec, Mayan, and North American Indian) art.

NORTH AMERICAN INDIANS

With few exceptions, the North American native cultures were much more widely dispersed than the Mayan, Aztec, and Incan societies, and did not have their population size or organized social structures. Although the cultivation of corn had made its way north, many Indians still practiced hunting and gathering. Horses, first introduced by the Spanish, allowed the Plains Indians to more easily follow and hunt the huge herds of bison. A few societies had evolved into relatively complex forms, but they were already in decline at the time of Christopher Columbus's arrival.

In the southwestern part of today's United States dwelled several groups we collectively call the Pueblo. The Spanish first gave them this name, which means "town" or "village," because they lived in towns or villages of permanent stone-and-mud buildings with thatched roofs. Like present-day apartment houses, these buildings had multiple stories, each with multiple rooms. The three main groups of the Pueblo people were the Mogollon, Hohokam, and Anasazi.

The Mogollon thrived in the Mimbres Valley (New Mexico) from about 150 BCE to 1450 CE. They developed a distinctive artistic style for painting bowls with finely drawn geometric figures and wildlife, especially birds, in black on a white background. Beginning about 600 CE, the Hohokam built an extensive irrigation system of canals to irrigate the desert and grow fields of corn, beans, and squash. By 1300, their crop yields were supporting the most highly populated settlements in the southwest. The Hohokam decorated pottery with a red-on-buff design and made jewelry of turquoise. In the high desert of New Mexico, the Anasazi, whose name means "ancient enemy" or "ancient ones," carved homes from steep cliffs accessed by ladders or ropes that could be pulled in at night or in case of enemy attack (Figure 1.10).

Figure 1.10 To access their homes, the cliff-dwelling Anasazi used ropes or ladders that could be pulled in at night for safety. These pueblos may be viewed today in Canyon de Chelly National Monument (above) in Arizona and Mesa Verde National Park in Colorado.

Roads extending some 180 miles connected the Pueblos' smaller urban centers to each other and to Chaco Canyon, which by 1050 CE had become the administrative, religious, and cultural center of their civilization. A century later, however, probably because of drought, the Pueblo peoples abandoned their cities. Their present-day descendants include the Hopi and Zuni tribes.

The Indian groups who lived in the present-day Ohio River Valley and achieved their cultural apex from the first century CE to 400 CE are collectively known as the Hopewell culture. Their settlements, unlike those of the southwest, were small hamlets. They lived in wattle-and-daub houses (made from woven lattice branches "daubed" with wet mud, clay, or sand and straw) and practiced agriculture, which they supplemented by hunting and fishing. Utilizing waterways, they developed trade routes stretching from Canada to Louisiana, where they exchanged goods with other tribes and negotiated in many different languages. From the coast they received shells; from Canada, copper; and from the Rocky Mountains, obsidian. With these materials they created necklaces, woven mats, and exquisite carvings. What remains of their culture today are huge burial mounds and earthworks. Many of the mounds that were opened by archaeologists contained artworks and other goods that indicate their society was socially stratified.

Perhaps the largest indigenous cultural and population center in North America was located along the Mississippi River near present-day St. Louis. At its height in about 1100 CE, this five-square-mile city, now called Cahokia, was home to more than ten thousand residents; tens of thousands more lived on farms surrounding the urban center. The city also contained one hundred and twenty earthen mounds or pyramids, each dominating a particular neighborhood and on each of which lived a leader who exercised authority over the surrounding area. The largest mound covered fifteen acres. Cahokia was the hub of political and trading activities along the Mississippi River. After 1300 CE, however, this civilization declined—possibly because the area became unable to support the large population.

INDIANS OF THE EASTERN WOODLAND

Encouraged by the wealth found by the Spanish in the settled civilizations to the south, fifteenth- and sixteenth-century English, Dutch, and French explorers expected to discover the same in North America. What they found instead were small, disparate communities, many already ravaged by European diseases brought by the Spanish and transmitted among the natives. Rather than gold and silver, there was an abundance of land, and the timber and fur that land could produce.

The Indians living east of the Mississippi did not construct the large and complex societies of those to the west. Because they lived in small autonomous clans or tribal units, each group adapted to the specific environment in which it lived (Figure 1.11). These groups were by no means unified, and warfare among tribes was common as they sought to increase their hunting and fishing areas. Still, these tribes shared some common traits. A chief or group of tribal elders made decisions, and although the chief was male, usually the women selected and counseled him. Gender roles were not as fixed as they were in the patriarchal societies of Europe, Mesoamerica, and South America.

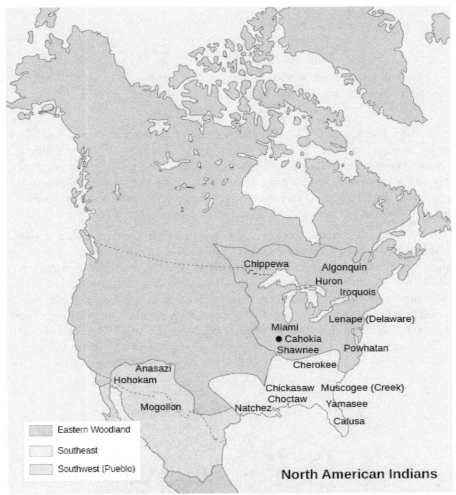

Figure 1.11 This map indicates the locations of the three Pueblo cultures the major Eastern Woodland Indian tribes, and the tribes of the Southeast, as well as the location of the ancient city of Cahokia.

Women typically cultivated corn, beans, and squash and harvested nuts and berries, while men hunted, fished, and provided protection. But both took responsibility for raising children, and most major Indian societies in the east were matriarchal. In tribes such as the Iroquois, Lenape, Muscogee, and Cherokee, women had both power and influence. They counseled the chief and passed on the traditions of the tribe. This **matriarchy** changed dramatically with the coming of the Europeans, who introduced, sometimes forcibly, their own customs and traditions to the natives.

Clashing beliefs about land ownership and use of the environment would be the greatest area of conflict with Europeans. Although tribes often claimed the right to certain hunting grounds—usually identified by some geographical landmark—Indians did not practice, or in general even have the concept of, private ownership of land. There were tribal hunting grounds, usually identified by some geographical landmark, but there was no private ownership of land. A person's possessions included only what he or she had made, such as tools or weapons. The European Christian worldview, on the other hand, viewed land as the source of wealth. According to the Christian Bible, God created humanity in his own image with the command to use and subdue the rest of creation, which included not only land, but also all animal life.

Upon their arrival in North America, Europeans found no fences, no signs designating ownership. Land, and the game that populated it, they believed, were there for the taking.

1.2 Europe on the Brink of Change

By the end of this section, you will be able to:
- Describe the European societies that engaged in conversion, conquest, and commerce
- Discuss the motives for and mechanisms of early European exploration

The fall of the Roman Empire (476 CE) and the beginning of the European Renaissance in the late fourteenth century roughly bookend the period we call the Middle Ages. Without a dominant centralized power or overarching cultural hub, Europe experienced political and military discord during this time. Its inhabitants retreated into walled cities, fearing marauding pillagers including Vikings, Mongols, Arabs, and Magyars. In return for protection, they submitted to powerful lords and their armies of knights. In their brief, hard lives, few people traveled more than ten miles from the place they were born.

The Christian Church remained intact, however, and emerged from the period as a unified and powerful institution. Priests, tucked away in monasteries, kept knowledge alive by collecting and copying religious and secular manuscripts, often adding beautiful drawings or artwork. Social and economic devastation arrived in 1340s, however, when Genoese merchants returning from the Black Sea unwittingly brought with them a rat-borne and highly contagious disease, known as the bubonic plague. In a few short years, it had killed many millions, about one-third of Europe's population. A different strain, spread by airborne germs, also killed many. Together these two are collectively called the **Black Death** (Figure 1.12). Entire villages disappeared. A high birth rate, however, coupled with bountiful harvests, meant that the population grew during the next century. By 1450, a newly rejuvenated European society was on the brink of tremendous change.

Figure 1.12   This image depicts the bodily swellings, or buboes, characteristic of the Black Death.

Click and Explore

Visit **EyeWitness to History (http://openstaxcollege.org/l/plague)** to learn more about the Black Death.

LIFE IN FEUDAL EUROPE

During the Middle Ages, most Europeans lived in small villages that consisted of a manorial house or castle for the lord, a church, and simple homes for the peasants or **serfs**, who made up about 60 percent of western Europe's population. Hundreds of these castles and walled cities remain all over Europe (Figure 1.13).

Figure 1.13 One of the most beautifully preserved medieval walled cities is Carcassonne, France. Notice the use of a double wall.

Europe's **feudal society** was a mutually supportive system. The lords owned the land; knights gave military service to a lord and carried out his justice; serfs worked the land in return for the protection offered by the lord's castle or the walls of his city, into which they fled in times of danger from invaders. Much land was communally farmed at first, but as lords became more powerful they extended their ownership and rented land to their subjects. Thus, although they were technically free, serfs were effectively bound to the land they worked, which supported them and their families as well as the lord and all who depended on him. The Catholic Church, the only church in Europe at the time, also owned vast tracts of land and became very wealthy by collecting not only tithes (taxes consisting of 10 percent of annual earnings) but also rents on its lands.

A serf's life was difficult. Women often died in childbirth, and perhaps one-third of children died before the age of five. Without sanitation or medicine, many people perished from diseases we consider inconsequential today; few lived to be older than forty-five. Entire families, usually including grandparents, lived in one- or two-room hovels that were cold, dark, and dirty. A fire was kept lit and was always a danger to the thatched roofs, while its constant smoke affected the inhabitants' health and eyesight. Most individuals owned no more than two sets of clothing, consisting of a woolen jacket or tunic and linen undergarments, and bathed only when the waters melted in spring.

In an agrarian society, the seasons dictate the rhythm of life. Everyone in Europe's feudal society had a job to do and worked hard. The father was the unquestioned head of the family. Idleness meant hunger. When the land began to thaw in early spring, peasants started tilling the soil with primitive wooden plows and crude rakes and hoes. Then they planted crops of wheat, rye, barley, and oats, reaping small yields that barely sustained the population. Bad weather, crop disease, or insect infestation could cause an entire village to starve or force the survivors to move to another location.

Early summer saw the first harvesting of hay, which was stored until needed to feed the animals in winter. Men and boys sheared the sheep, now heavy with wool from the cold weather, while women and children washed the wool and spun it into yarn. The coming of fall meant crops needed to be harvested and prepared for winter. Livestock was butchered and the meat smoked or salted to preserve it. With the harvest in and the provisions stored, fall was also the time for celebrating and giving thanks to God. Winter brought the people indoors to weave yarn into fabric, sew clothing, thresh grain, and keep the fires going. Everyone celebrated the birth of Christ in conjunction with the winter solstice.

THE CHURCH AND SOCIETY

After the fall of Rome, the Christian Church—united in dogma but unofficially divided into western and eastern branches—was the only organized institution in medieval Europe. In 1054, the eastern branch of Christianity, led by the Patriarch of Constantinople (a title that because roughly equivalent to the western Church's pope), established its center in Constantinople and adopted the Greek language for its services. The western branch, under the pope, remained in Rome, becoming known as the Roman Catholic Church and continuing to use Latin. Following this split, known as the Great Schism, each branch of Christianity maintained a strict organizational hierarchy. The pope in Rome, for example, oversaw a huge bureaucracy led by cardinals, known as "princes of the church," who were followed by archbishops, bishops, and then priests. During this period, the Roman Church became the most powerful international organization in western Europe.

Just as agrarian life depended on the seasons, village and family life revolved around the Church. The sacraments, or special ceremonies of the Church, marked every stage of life, from birth to maturation, marriage, and burial, and brought people into the church on a regular basis. As Christianity spread throughout Europe, it replaced pagan and animistic views, explaining supernatural events and forces of nature in its own terms. A benevolent God in heaven, creator of the universe and beyond the realm of nature and the known, controlled all events, warring against the force of darkness, known as the Devil or Satan, here on earth. Although ultimately defeated, Satan still had the power to trick humans and cause them to commit evil or sin.

All events had a spiritual connotation. Sickness, for example, might be a sign that a person had sinned, while crop failure could result from the villagers' not saying their prayers. Penitents confessed their sins to the priest, who absolved them and assigned them penance to atone for their acts and save themselves from eternal damnation. Thus the parish priest held enormous power over the lives of his parishioners.

Ultimately, the pope decided all matters of theology, interpreting the will of God to the people, but he also had authority over temporal matters. Because the Church had the ability to excommunicate people, or send a soul to hell forever, even monarchs feared to challenge its power. It was also the seat of all knowledge. Latin, the language of the Church, served as a unifying factor for a continent of isolated regions, each with its own dialect; in the early Middle Ages, nations as we know them today did not yet exist. The mostly illiterate serfs were thus dependent on those literate priests to read and interpret the Bible, the word of God, for them.

CHRISTIANITY ENCOUNTERS ISLAM

The year 622 brought a new challenge to Christendom. Near Mecca, Saudi Arabia, a prophet named Muhammad received a revelation that became a cornerstone of the Islamic faith. The **Koran**, which Muhammad wrote in Arabic, contained his message, affirming monotheism but identifying Christ not as

God but as a prophet like Moses, Abraham, David, and Muhammad. Following Muhammad's death in 632, Islam spread by both conversion and military conquest across the Middle East and Asia Minor to India and northern Africa, crossing the Straits of Gibraltar into Spain in the year 711 (Figure 1.14).

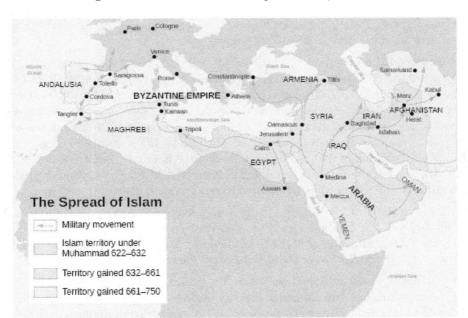

Figure 1.14 In the seventh and eighth centuries, Islam spread quickly across North Africa and into the Middle East. The religion arrived in Europe via Spain in 711 and remained there until 1492, when Catholic monarchs reconquered the last of Muslim-held territory after a long war.

The Islamic conquest of Europe continued until 732. Then, at the Battle of Tours (in modern France), Charles Martel, nicknamed the Hammer, led a Christian force in defeating the army of Abdul Rahman al-Ghafiqi. Muslims, however, retained control of much of Spain, where Córdoba, known for leather and wool production, became a major center of learning and trade. By the eleventh century, a major Christian holy war called the **Reconquista**, or reconquest, had begun to slowly push the Muslims from Spain. This drive was actually an extension of the earlier military conflict between Christians and Muslims for domination of the Holy Land (the Biblical region of Palestine), known as the **Crusades**.

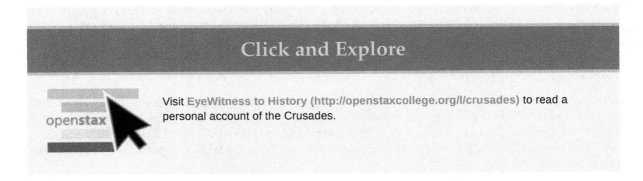

Visit EyeWitness to History (http://openstaxcollege.org/l/crusades) to read a personal account of the Crusades.

JERUSALEM AND THE CRUSADES

The city of Jerusalem is a holy site for Jews, Christians, and Muslims. It was here King Solomon built the Temple in the tenth century BCE. It was here the Romans crucified Jesus in 33 CE, and from here, Christians maintain, he ascended into heaven, promising to return. From here, Muslims believe,

Muhammad traveled to heaven in 621 to receive instructions about prayer. Thus claims on the area go deep, and emotions about it run high, among followers of all three faiths. Evidence exists that the three religions lived in harmony for centuries. In 1095, however, European Christians decided not only to retake the holy city from the Muslim rulers but also to conquer what they called the Holy Lands, an area that extended from modern-day Turkey in the north along the Mediterranean coast to the Sinai Peninsula and that was also held by Muslims. The Crusades had begun.

Religious zeal motivated the knights who participated in the four Crusades. Adventure, the chance to win land and a title, and the Church's promise of wholesale forgiveness of sins also motivated many. The Crusaders, mostly French knights, retook Jerusalem in June 1099 amid horrific slaughter. A French writer who accompanied them recorded this eyewitness account: "On the top of Solomon's Temple, to which they had climbed in fleeing, many were shot to death with arrows and cast down headlong from the roof. Within this Temple, about ten thousand were beheaded. If you had been there, your feet would have been stained up to the ankles with the blood of the slain. What more shall I tell? Not one of them was allowed to live. They did not spare the women and children." A Muslim eyewitness also described how the conquerors stripped the temple of its wealth and looted private homes.

In 1187, under the legendary leader Saladin, Muslim forces took back the city. Reaction from Europe was swift as King Richard I of England, the Lionheart, joined others to mount yet another action. The battle for the Holy Lands did not conclude until the Crusaders lost their Mediterranean stronghold at Acre (in present-day Israel) in 1291 and the last of the Christians left the area a few years later.

The Crusades had lasting effects, both positive and negative. On the negative side, the wide-scale persecution of Jews began. Christians classed them with the infidel Muslims and labeled them "the killers of Christ." In the coming centuries, kings either expelled Jews from their kingdoms or forced them to pay heavy tributes for the privilege of remaining. Muslim-Christian hatred also festered, and intolerance grew.

On the positive side, maritime trade between East and West expanded. As Crusaders experienced the feel of silk, the taste of spices, and the utility of porcelain, desire for these products created new markets for merchants. In particular, the Adriatic port city of Venice prospered enormously from trade with Islamic merchants. Merchants' ships brought Europeans valuable goods, traveling between the port cities of western Europe and the East from the tenth century on, along routes collectively labeled the Silk Road. From the days of the early adventurer Marco Polo, Venetian sailors had traveled to ports on the Black Sea and established their own colonies along the Mediterranean Coast. However, transporting goods along the old Silk Road was costly, slow, and unprofitable. Muslim middlemen collected taxes as the goods changed hands. Robbers waited to ambush the treasure-laden caravans. A direct water route to the East, cutting out the land portion of the trip, had to be found. As well as seeking a water passage to the wealthy cities in the East, sailors wanted to find a route to the exotic and wealthy Spice Islands in modern-day Indonesia, whose location was kept secret by Muslim rulers. Longtime rivals of Venice, the merchants of Genoa and Florence also looked west.

THE IBERIAN PENINSULA

Although Norse explorers such as Leif Ericson, the son of Eric the Red who first settled Greenland, had reached and established a colony in northern Canada roughly five hundred years prior to Christopher Columbus's voyage, it was explorers sailing for Portugal and Spain who traversed the Atlantic throughout the fifteenth century and ushered in an unprecedented age of exploration and permanent contact with North America.

Located on the extreme western edge of Europe, Portugal, with its port city of Lisbon, soon became the center for merchants desiring to undercut the Venetians' hold on trade. With a population of about one million and supported by its ruler Prince Henry, whom historians call "the Navigator," this independent kingdom fostered exploration of and trade with western Africa. Skilled shipbuilders and navigators who took advantage of maps from all over Europe, Portuguese sailors used triangular sails and built lighter vessels called caravels that could sail down the African coast.

Just to the east of Portugal, King Ferdinand of Aragon married Queen Isabella of Castile in 1469, uniting two of the most powerful independent kingdoms on the Iberian peninsula and laying the foundation for the modern nation of Spain. Isabella, motivated by strong religious zeal, was instrumental in beginning the **Inquisition** in 1480, a brutal campaign to root out Jews and Muslims who had seemingly converted to Christianity but secretly continued to practice their faith, as well as other heretics. This powerful couple ruled for the next twenty-five years, centralizing authority and funding exploration and trade with the East. One of their daughters, Catherine of Aragon, became the first wife of King Henry VIII of England.

AMERICANA

⚙ *Motives for European Exploration*

Historians generally recognize three motives for European exploration—God, glory, and gold. Particularly in the strongly Catholic nations of Spain and Portugal, religious zeal motivated the rulers to make converts and retake land from the Muslims. Prince Henry the Navigator of Portugal described his "great desire to make increase in the faith of our Lord Jesus Christ and to bring him all the souls that should be saved."

Sailors' tales about fabulous monsters and fantasy literature about exotic worlds filled with gold, silver, and jewels captured the minds of men who desired to explore these lands and return with untold wealth and the glory of adventure and discovery. They sparked the imagination of merchants like Marco Polo, who made the long and dangerous trip to the realm of the great Mongol ruler Kublai Khan in 1271. The story of his trip, printed in a book entitled *Travels*, inspired Columbus, who had a copy in his possession during his voyage more than two hundred years later. Passages such as the following, which describes China's imperial palace, are typical of the *Travels*:

> You must know that it is the greatest Palace that ever was. . . . The roof is very lofty, and the walls of the Palace are all covered with gold and silver. They are also adorned with representations of dragons [sculptured and gilt], beasts and birds, knights and idols, and sundry other subjects. And on the ceiling too you see nothing but gold and silver and painting. [On each of the four sides there is a great marble staircase leading to the top of the marble wall, and forming the approach to the Palace.]

> The hall of the Palace is so large that it could easily dine 6,000 people; and it is quite a marvel to see how many rooms there are besides. The building is altogether so vast, so rich, and so beautiful, that no man on earth could design anything superior to it. The outside of the roof also is all colored with vermilion and yellow and green and blue and other hues, which are fixed with a varnish so fine and exquisite that they shine like crystal, and lend a resplendent lustre to the Palace as seen for a great way round. This roof is made too with such strength and solidity that it is fit to last forever.

Why might a travel account like this one have influenced an explorer like Columbus? What does this tell us about European explorers' motivations and goals?

The year 1492 witnessed some of the most significant events of Ferdinand and Isabella's reign. The couple oversaw the final expulsion of North African Muslims (Moors) from the Kingdom of Granada, bringing the nearly eight-hundred-year Reconquista to an end. In this same year, they also ordered all unconverted Jews to leave Spain.

Also in 1492, after six years of lobbying, a Genoese sailor named Christopher Columbus persuaded the monarchs to fund his expedition to the Far East. Columbus had already pitched his plan to the rulers of Genoa and Venice without success, so the Spanish monarchy was his last hope. Christian zeal was the prime motivating factor for Isabella, as she imagined her faith spreading to the East. Ferdinand, the more practical of the two, hoped to acquire wealth from trade.

Most educated individuals at the time knew the earth was round, so Columbus's plan to reach the East by sailing west was plausible. Though the calculations of Earth's circumference made by the Greek geographer Eratosthenes in the second century BCE were known (and, as we now know, nearly accurate), most scholars did not believe they were dependable. Thus Columbus would have no way of knowing when he had traveled far enough around the Earth to reach his goal—and in fact, Columbus greatly underestimated the Earth's circumference.

In August 1492, Columbus set sail with his three small caravels (Figure 1.15). After a voyage of about three thousand miles lasting six weeks, he landed on an island in the Bahamas named Guanahani by the native Lucayans. He promptly christened it San Salvador, the name it bears today.

Figure 1.15 Columbus sailed in three caravels such as these. The *Santa Maria*, his largest, was only 58 feet long.

1.3 West Africa and the Role of Slavery

At the end of this section, you will be able to:
- Locate the major West African empires on a map
- Discuss the roles of Islam and Europe in the slave trade

It is difficult to generalize about West Africa, which was linked to the rise and diffusion of Islam. This geographical unit, central to the rise of the Atlantic World, stretches from modern-day Mauritania to the Democratic Republic of the Congo and encompasses lush rainforests along the equator, savannas on either side of the forest, and much drier land to the north. Until about 600 CE, most Africans were hunter-gatherers. Where water was too scarce for farming, herders maintained sheep, goats, cattle, or camels. In the more heavily wooded area near the equator, farmers raised yams, palm products, or plantains. The savanna areas yielded rice, millet, and sorghum. Sub-Saharan Africans had little experience in maritime matters. Most of the population lived away from the coast, which is connected to the interior by five main rivers—the Senegal, Gambia, Niger, Volta, and Congo.

Although there were large trading centers along these rivers, most West Africans lived in small villages and identified with their extended family or their clan. Wives, children, and dependents (including slaves) were a sign of wealth among men, and **polygyny**, the practice of having more than one wife at a time, was widespread. In time of need, relatives, however far away, were counted upon to assist in supplying food or security. Because of the clannish nature of African society, "we" was associated with the village and family members, while "they" included everyone else. Hundreds of separate dialects emerged; in modern Nigeria, nearly five hundred are still spoken.

Click and Explore

Read **The Role of Islam in African Slavery (http://openstaxcollege.org/l/ islamslavery)** to learn more about the African slave trade.

THE MAJOR AFRICAN EMPIRES

Following the death of the prophet Muhammad in 632 CE, Islam continued to spread quickly across North Africa, bringing not only a unifying faith but a political and legal structure as well. As lands fell under the control of Muslim armies, they instituted Islamic rule and legal structures as local chieftains converted, usually under penalty of death. Only those who had converted to Islam could rule or be engaged in trade. The first major empire to emerge in West Africa was the Ghana Empire (Figure 1.16). By 750, the Soninke farmers of the sub-Sahara had become wealthy by taxing the trade that passed through their area. For instance, the Niger River basin supplied gold to the Berber and Arab traders from west of the Nile Valley, who brought cloth, weapons, and manufactured goods into the interior. Huge Saharan salt mines supplied the life-sustaining mineral to the Mediterranean coast of Africa and inland areas. By 900, the monotheistic Muslims controlled most of this trade and had converted many of the African ruling elite. The majority of the population, however, maintained their tribal animistic practices, which gave living attributes to nonliving objects such as mountains, rivers, and wind. Because Ghana's king controlled the gold supply, he was able to maintain price controls and afford a strong military. Soon, however, a new kingdom emerged.

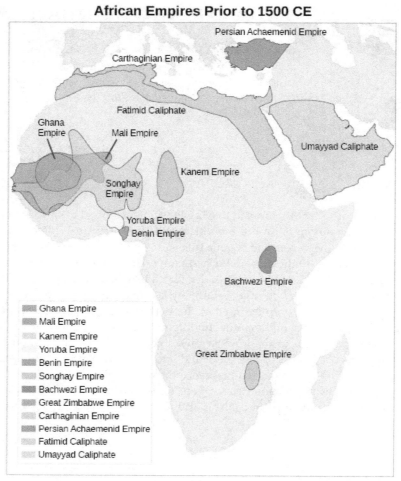

Figure 1.16 This map shows the locations of the major West African empires before 1492. Along the Mediterranean coast, Muslim states prevailed.

By 1200 CE, under the leadership of Sundiata Keita, Mali had replaced Ghana as the leading state in West Africa. After Sundiata's rule, the court converted to Islam, and Muslim scribes played a large part in administration and government. Miners then discovered huge new deposits of gold east of the Niger River. By the fourteenth century, the empire was so wealthy that while on a *hajj*, or pilgrimage to the holy city of Mecca, Mali's ruler Mansu Musa gave away enough gold to create serious price inflation in the cities along his route. Timbuktu, the capital city, became a leading Islamic center for education, commerce and the slave trade. Meanwhile, in the east, the city of Gao became increasingly strong under the leadership of Sonni Ali and soon eclipsed Mali's power. Timbuktu sought Ali's assistance in repelling the Tuaregs from the north. By 1500, however, the Tuareg empire of Songhay had eclipsed Mali, where weak and ineffective leadership prevailed.

THE ROLE OF SLAVERY

The institution of slavery is not a recent phenomenon. Most civilizations have practiced some form of human bondage and servitude, and African empires were no different (Figure 1.17). Famine or fear of stronger enemies might force one tribe to ask another for help and give themselves in a type of bondage in exchange. Similar to the European serf system, those seeking protection, or relief from starvation, would become the servants of those who provided relief. Debt might also be worked off through a form of servitude. Typically, these servants became a part of the extended tribal family. There is some evidence of **chattel slavery**, in which people are treated as personal property to be bought and sold, in the Nile Valley. It appears there was a slave-trade route through the Sahara that brought sub-Saharan Africans to Rome, which had slaves from all over the world.

Figure 1.17 Traders with a group of slaves. Note how the slaves are connected at the neck. Muslim traders brought slaves to the North African coast, where they might be sent to Europe or other parts of Africa.

Arab slave trading, which exchanged slaves for goods from the Mediterranean, existed long before Islam's spread across North Africa. Muslims later expanded this trade and enslaved not only Africans but also Europeans, especially from Spain, Sicily, and Italy. Male captives were forced to build coastal fortifications and serve as galley slaves. Women were added to the harem.

The major European slave trade began with Portugal's exploration of the west coast of Africa in search of a trade route to the East. By 1444, slaves were being brought from Africa to work on the sugar plantations of the Madeira Islands, off the coast of modern Morocco. The slave trade then expanded greatly as European colonies in the New World demanded an ever-increasing number of workers for the extensive plantations growing tobacco, sugar, and eventually rice and cotton (Figure 1.18).

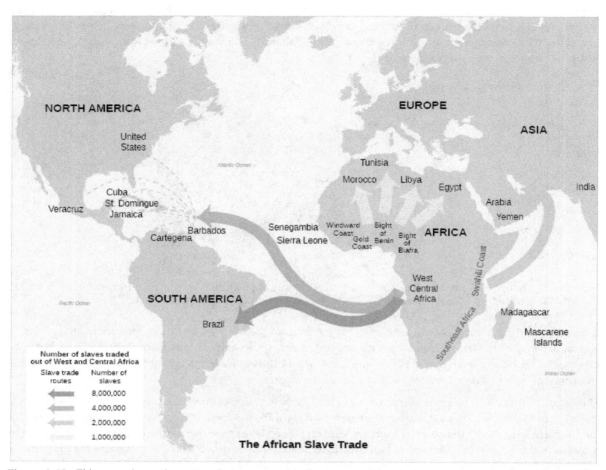

Figure 1.18 This map shows the routes that were used in the course of the slave trade and the number of enslaved people who traveled each route. As the figures indicate, most African slaves were bound for Brazil and the Caribbean. While West Africans made up the vast majority of the enslaved, the east coast of Africa, too, supplied slaves for the trade.

In the New World, the institution of slavery assumed a new aspect when the mercantilist system demanded a permanent, identifiable, and plentiful labor supply. African slaves were both easily identified (by their skin color) and plentiful, because of the thriving slave trade. This led to a race-based slavery system in the New World unlike any bondage system that had come before. Initially, the Spanish tried to force Indians to farm their crops. Most Spanish and Portuguese settlers coming to the New World were gentlemen and did not perform physical labor. They came to "serve God, but also to get rich," as noted by Bernal Díaz del Castillo. However, enslaved natives tended to sicken or die from disease or from the overwork and cruel treatment they were subjected to, and so the indigenous peoples proved not to be a dependable source of labor. Although he later repented of his ideas, the great defender of the Indians, Bartolomé de Las Casas, seeing the near extinction of the native population, suggested the Spanish send black (and white) laborers to the Indies. These workers proved hardier, and within fifty years, a change took place: The profitability of the African slave trade, coupled with the seemingly limitless number of potential slaves and the Catholic Church's denunciation of the enslavement of Christians, led race to become a dominant factor in the institution of slavery.

In the English colonies along the Atlantic coast, indentured servants initially filled the need for labor in the North, where family farms were the norm. In the South, however, labor-intensive crops such as tobacco, rice, and indigo prevailed, and eventually the supply of indentured servants was insufficient to meet the demand. These workers served only for periods of three to seven years before being freed; a more permanent labor supply was needed. Thus, whereas in Africa permanent, inherited slavery was unknown, and children of those bound in slavery to the tribe usually were free and intermarried with their captors, this changed in the Americas; slavery became permanent, and children born to slaves became slaves. This development, along with slavery's identification with race, forever changed the institution and shaped its unique character in the New World.

AMERICANA

✧ *The Beginnings of Racial Slavery*

Slavery has a long history. The ancient Greek philosopher Aristotle posited that some peoples were *homunculi*, or humanlike but not really people—for instance, if they did not speak Greek. Both the Bible and the Koran sanction slavery. Vikings who raided from Ireland to Russia brought back slaves of all nationalities. During the Middle Ages, traders from the interior of Africa brought slaves along well-established routes to sell them along the Mediterranean coast. Initially, slavers also brought European slaves to the Caribbean. Many of these were orphaned or homeless children captured in the cities of Ireland. The question is, when did slavery become based on race? This appears to have developed in the New World, with the introduction of gruelingly labor-intensive crops such as sugar and coffee. Unable to fill their growing need from the ranks of prisoners or indentured servants, the European colonists turned to African laborers. The Portuguese, although seeking a trade route to India, also set up forts along the West African coast for the purpose of exporting slaves to Europe. Historians believe that by the year 1500, 10 percent of the population of Lisbon and Seville consisted of black slaves. Because of the influence of the Catholic Church, which frowned on the enslavement of Christians, European slave traders expanded their reach down the coast of Africa.

When Europeans settled Brazil, the Caribbean, and North America, they thus established a system of racially based slavery. Here, the need for a massive labor force was greater than in western Europe. The land was ripe for growing sugar, coffee, rice, and ultimately cotton. To fulfill the ever-growing demand for these crops, large plantations were created. The success of these plantations depended upon the availability of a permanent, plentiful, identifiable, and skilled labor supply. As Africans were already familiar with animal husbandry as well as farming, had an identifying skin color, and could be readily supplied by the existing African slave trade, they proved the answer to this need. This process set the stage for the expansion of New World slavery into North America.

Key Terms

Beringia an ancient land bridge linking Asia and North America

Black Death two strains of the bubonic plague that simultaneously swept western Europe in the fourteenth century, causing the death of nearly half the population

chasquis Incan relay runners used to send messages over great distances

chattel slavery a system of servitude in which people are treated as personal property to be bought and sold

chinampas floating Aztec gardens consisting of a large barge woven from reeds, filled with dirt and floating on the water, allowing for irrigation

Crusades a series of military expeditions made by Christian Europeans to recover the Holy Land from the Muslims in the eleventh, twelfth, and thirteenth centuries

feudal society a social arrangement in which serfs and knights provided labor and military service to noble lords, receiving protection and land use in return

Inquisition a campaign by the Catholic Church to root out heresy, especially among converted Jews and Muslims

Koran the sacred book of Islam, written by the prophet Muhammad in the seventh century

matriarchy a society in which women have political power

mita the Incan labor tax, with each family donating time and work to communal projects

polygyny the practice of taking more than one wife

quipu an ancient Incan device for recording information, consisting of variously colored threads knotted in different ways

Reconquista Spain's nearly eight-hundred-year holy war against Islam, which ended in 1492

serf a peasant tied to the land and its lord

Summary

1.1 The Americas

Great civilizations had risen and fallen in the Americas before the arrival of the Europeans. In North America, the complex Pueblo societies including the Mogollon, Hohokam, and Anasazi as well as the city at Cahokia had peaked and were largely memories. The Eastern Woodland peoples were thriving, but they were soon overwhelmed as the number of English, French, and Dutch settlers increased.

Mesoamerica and South America had also witnessed the rise and fall of cultures. The once-mighty Mayan population centers were largely empty. In 1492, however, the Aztecs in Mexico City were at their peak. Subjugating surrounding tribes and requiring tribute of both humans for sacrifice and goods for consumption, the island city of Tenochtitlán was the hub of an ever-widening commercial center and the equal of any large European city until Cortés destroyed it. Further south in Peru, the Inca linked one of the largest empires in history through the use of roads and disciplined armies. Without the use of the wheel, they cut and fashioned stone to build Machu Picchu high in the Andes before abandoning the city for unknown reasons. Thus, depending on what part of the New World they explored, the Europeans encountered peoples that diverged widely in their cultures, traditions, and numbers.

1.2 Europe on the Brink of Change

One effect of the Crusades was that a larger portion of western Europe became familiar with the goods of the East. A lively trade subsequently developed along a variety of routes known collectively as the Silk Road to supply the demand for these products. Brigands and greedy middlemen made the trip along this route expensive and dangerous. By 1492, Europe—recovered from the Black Death and in search of new products and new wealth—was anxious to improve trade and communications with the rest of the world. Venice and Genoa led the way in trading with the East. The lure of profit pushed explorers to seek new trade routes to the Spice Islands and eliminate Muslim middlemen.

Portugal, under the leadership of Prince Henry the Navigator, attempted to send ships around the continent of Africa. Ferdinand of Aragon and Isabella of Castile hired Columbus to find a route to the East by going west. As strong supporters of the Catholic Church, they sought to bring Christianity to the East and any newly found lands, as well as hoping to find sources of wealth.

1.3 West Africa and the Role of Slavery

Before 1492, Africa, like the Americas, had experienced the rise and fall of many cultures, but the continent did not develop a centralized authority structure. African peoples practiced various forms of slavery, all of which differed significantly from the racial slavery that ultimately developed in the New World. After the arrival of Islam and before the Portuguese came to the coast of West Africa in 1444, Muslims controlled the slave trade out of Africa, which expanded as European powers began to colonize the New World. Driven by a demand for labor, slavery in the Americas developed a new form: It was based on race, and the status of slave was both permanent and inherited.

Review Questions

1. Which of the following Indian peoples built homes in cliff dwellings that still exist?
- A. Anasazi
- B. Cherokee
- C. Aztec
- D. Inca

2. Which culture developed the only writing system in the Western Hemisphere?
- A. Inca
- B. Iroquois
- C. Maya
- D. Pueblo

3. Which culture developed a road system rivaling that of the Romans?
- A. Cherokee
- B. Inca
- C. Olmec
- D. Anasazi

4. What were the major differences between the societies of the Aztec, Inca, and Maya and the Indians of North America?

5. The series of attempts by Christian armies to retake the Holy Lands from Muslims was known as _____.
- A. the Crusades
- B. the Reconquista
- C. the Black Death
- D. the Silk Road

6. _____ became wealthy trading with the East.
- A. Carcassonne
- B. Jerusalem
- C. Rome
- D. Venice

7. In 1492, the Spanish forced these two religious groups to either convert or leave.

A. Jews and Muslims
B. Christians and Jews
C. Protestants and Muslims
D. Catholics and Jews

8. How did European feudal society operate? How was this a mutually supportive system?

9. Why did Columbus believe he could get to the Far East by sailing west? What were the problems with this plan?

10. The city of _____ became a leading center for Muslim scholarship and trade.
A. Cairo
B. Timbuktu

C. Morocco
D. Mali

11. Which of the following does *not* describe a form of slavery traditionally practiced in Africa?
A. a system in which those in need of supplies or protection give themselves in servitude
B. a system in which debtors repay those whom they owe by giving themselves in servitude
C. a system in which people are treated as chattel—that is, as personal property to be bought and sold
D. a system in which people are enslaved permanently on account of their race

Critical Thinking Questions

12. The Inca were able to control an empire that stretched from modern Colombia to southern Chile. Which of their various means for achieving such control do you think were most effective, and why?

13. How did the Olmec, Aztec, Inca, Maya, and North American Indians differ in their ways of life and cultural achievements? How did their particular circumstances—geography, history, or the accomplishments of the societies that had preceded them, for example—serve to shape their particular traditions and cultures?

14. What were the lasting effects of the Crusades? In what ways did they provide opportunities—both negative and positive—for cross-cultural encounters and exchanges?

15. Was race identified with slavery before the era of European exploration? Why or why not? How did slavery's association with race change the institution's character?

16. What are the differences between the types of slavery traditionally practiced in Africa and the slavery that developed in the New World? How did other types of servitude, such as European serfdom, compare to slavery?

CHAPTER 2

Early Globalization: The Atlantic World, 1492–1650

Figure 2.1 After Christopher Columbus "discovered" the New World, he sent letters home to Spain describing the wonders he beheld. These letters were quickly circulated throughout Europe and translated into Italian, German, and Latin. This woodcut is from the first Italian verse translation of the letter Columbus sent to the Spanish court after his first voyage, *Lettera delle isole novamente trovata* by Giuliano Dati.

Chapter Outline

2.1 Portuguese Exploration and Spanish Conquest
2.2 Religious Upheavals in the Developing Atlantic World
2.3 Challenges to Spain's Supremacy
2.4 New Worlds in the Americas: Labor, Commerce, and the Columbian Exchange

Introduction

The story of the Atlantic World is the story of global migration, a migration driven in large part by the actions and aspirations of the ruling heads of Europe. Columbus is hardly visible in this illustration of his ships making landfall on the Caribbean island of Hispaniola (Figure 2.1). Instead, Ferdinand II of Spain (in the foreground) sits on his throne and points toward Columbus's landing. As the ships arrive, the Arawak people tower over the Spanish, suggesting the native population density of the islands.

This historic moment in 1492 sparked new rivalries among European powers as they scrambled to create New World colonies, fueled by the quest for wealth and power as well as by religious passions. Almost continuous war resulted. Spain achieved early preeminence, creating a far-flung empire and growing rich with treasures from the Americas. Native Americans who confronted the newcomers from Europe suffered unprecedented losses of life, however, as previously unknown diseases sliced through their populations. They also were victims of the arrogance of the Europeans, who viewed themselves as uncontested masters of the New World, sent by God to bring Christianity to the "Indians."

2.1 Portuguese Exploration and Spanish Conquest

By the end of this section, you will be able to:
- Describe Portuguese exploration of the Atlantic and Spanish exploration of the Americas, and the importance of these voyages to the developing Atlantic World
- Explain the importance of Spanish exploration of the Americas in the expansion of Spain's empire and the development of Spanish Renaissance culture

Portuguese colonization of Atlantic islands in the 1400s inaugurated an era of aggressive European expansion across the Atlantic. In the 1500s, Spain surpassed Portugal as the dominant European power. This age of exploration and the subsequent creation of an Atlantic World marked the earliest phase of globalization, in which previously isolated groups—Africans, Native Americans, and Europeans—first came into contact with each other, sometimes with disastrous results.

PORTUGUESE EXPLORATION

Portugal's Prince Henry the Navigator spearheaded his country's exploration of Africa and the Atlantic in the 1400s. With his support, Portuguese mariners successfully navigated an eastward route to Africa, establishing a foothold there that became a foundation of their nation's trade empire in the fifteenth and sixteenth centuries.

Portuguese mariners built an Atlantic empire by colonizing the Canary, Cape Verde, and Azores Islands, as well as the island of Madeira. Merchants then used these Atlantic outposts as debarkation points for subsequent journeys. From these strategic points, Portugal spread its empire down the western coast of Africa to the Congo, along the western coast of India, and eventually to Brazil on the eastern coast of South America. It also established trading posts in China and Japan. While the Portuguese didn't rule over

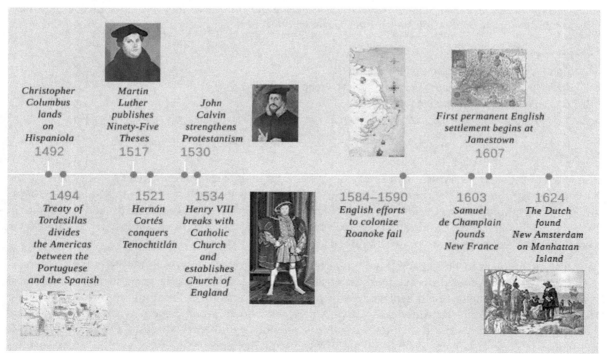

Figure 2.2

an immense landmass, their strategic holdings of islands and coastal ports gave them almost unrivaled control of nautical trade routes and a global empire of trading posts during the 1400s.

The travels of Portuguese traders to western Africa introduced them to the African slave trade, already brisk among African states. Seeing the value of this source of labor in growing the profitable crop of sugar on their Atlantic islands, the Portuguese soon began exporting African slaves along with African ivory and gold. Sugar fueled the Atlantic slave trade, and the Portuguese islands quickly became home to sugar plantations. The Portuguese also traded these slaves, introducing much-needed human capital to other European nations. In the following years, as European exploration spread, slavery spread as well. In time, much of the Atlantic World would become a gargantuan sugar-plantation complex in which Africans labored to produce the highly profitable commodity for European consumers.

AMERICANA

✪ Elmina Castle

In 1482, Portuguese traders built Elmina Castle (also called São Jorge da Mina, or Saint George's of the Mine) in present-day Ghana, on the west coast of Africa (Figure 2.3). A fortified trading post, it had mounted cannons facing out to sea, not inland toward continental Africa; the Portuguese had greater fear of a naval attack from other Europeans than of a land attack from Africans. Portuguese traders soon began to settle around the fort and established the town of Elmina.

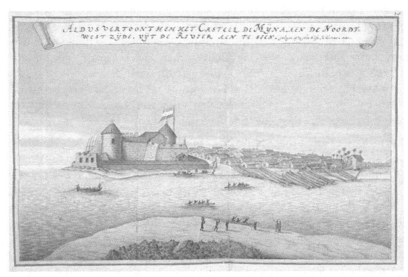

Figure 2.3 Elmina Castle on the west coast of Ghana was used as a holding pen for slaves before they were brought across the Atlantic and sold. Originally built by the Portuguese in the fifteenth century, it appears in this image as it was in the 1660s, after being seized by Dutch slave traders in 1637.

Although the Portuguese originally used the fort primarily for trading gold, by the sixteenth century they had shifted their focus. The dungeon of the fort now served as a holding pen for African slaves from the interior of the continent, while on the upper floors Portuguese traders ate, slept, and prayed in a chapel. Slaves lived in the dungeon for weeks or months until ships arrived to transport them to Europe or the Americas. For them, the dungeon of Elmina was their last sight of their home country.

SPANISH EXPLORATION AND CONQUEST

The Spanish established the first European settlements in the Americas, beginning in the Caribbean and, by 1600, extending throughout Central and South America. Thousands of Spaniards flocked to the Americas seeking wealth and status. The most famous of these Spanish adventurers are Christopher Columbus (who, though Italian himself, explored on behalf of the Spanish monarchs), Hernán Cortés, and Francisco Pizarro.

The history of Spanish exploration begins with the history of Spain itself. During the fifteenth century, Spain hoped to gain advantage over its rival, Portugal. The marriage of Ferdinand of Aragon and Isabella of Castile in 1469 unified Catholic Spain and began the process of building a nation that could compete for worldwide power. Since the 700s, much of Spain had been under Islamic rule, and King Ferdinand II and Queen Isabella I, arch-defenders of the Catholic Church against Islam, were determined to defeat the Muslims in Granada, the last Islamic stronghold in Spain. In 1492, they completed the Reconquista: the centuries-long Christian conquest of the Iberian Peninsula. The Reconquista marked another step forward in the process of making Spain an imperial power, and Ferdinand and Isabella were now ready to look further afield.

Their goals were to expand Catholicism and to gain a commercial advantage over Portugal. To those ends, Ferdinand and Isabella sponsored extensive Atlantic exploration. Spain's most famous explorer, Christopher Columbus, was actually from Genoa, Italy. He believed that, using calculations based on other mariners' journeys, he could chart a westward route to India, which could be used to expand European trade and spread Christianity. Starting in 1485, he approached Genoese, Venetian, Portuguese, English, and Spanish monarchs, asking for ships and funding to explore this westward route. All those he petitioned—including Ferdinand and Isabella at first—rebuffed him; their nautical experts all concurred that Columbus's estimates of the width of the Atlantic Ocean were far too low. However, after three years of entreaties, and, more important, the completion of the Reconquista, Ferdinand and Isabella agreed to finance Columbus's expedition in 1492, supplying him with three ships: the *Nina*, the *Pinta*, and the *Santa Maria*. The Spanish monarchs knew that Portuguese mariners had reached the southern tip of Africa and sailed the Indian Ocean. They understood that the Portuguese would soon reach Asia and, in this competitive race to reach the Far East, the Spanish rulers decided to act.

Columbus held erroneous views that shaped his thinking about what he would encounter as he sailed west. He believed the earth to be much smaller than its actual size and, since he did not know of the existence of the Americas, he fully expected to land in Asia. On October 12, 1492, however, he made landfall on an island in the Bahamas. He then sailed to an island he named **Hispaniola** (present-day Dominican Republic and Haiti) (Figure 2.4). Believing he had landed in the East Indies, Columbus called the native Taínos he found there "Indios," giving rise to the term "Indian" for any native people of the New World. Upon Columbus's return to Spain, the Spanish crown bestowed on him the title of Admiral of the Ocean Sea and named him governor and viceroy of the lands he had discovered. As a devoted Catholic, Columbus had agreed with Ferdinand and Isabella prior to sailing west that part of the expected wealth from his voyage would be used to continue the fight against Islam.

Figure 2.4 This sixteenth-century map shows the island of Hispaniola (present-day Haiti and Dominican Republic). Note the various fanciful elements, such as the large-scale ships and sea creatures, and consider what the creator of this map hoped to convey. In addition to navigation, what purpose would such a map have served?

Columbus's 1493 letter—or ***probanza de mérito*** (proof of merit)—describing his "discovery" of a New World did much to inspire excitement in Europe. *Probanzas de méritos* were reports and letters written by Spaniards in the New World to the Spanish crown, designed to win royal patronage. Today they highlight the difficult task of historical work; while the letters are primary sources, historians need to understand the context and the culture in which the conquistadors, as the Spanish adventurers came to be called, wrote them and distinguish their bias and subjective nature. While they are filled with distortions and fabrications, *probanzas de méritos* are still useful in illustrating the expectation of wealth among the explorers as well as their view that native peoples would not pose a serious obstacle to colonization.

In 1493, Columbus sent two copies of a *probanza de mérito* to the Spanish king and queen and their minister of finance, Luis de Santángel. Santángel had supported Columbus's voyage, helping him to obtain funding from Ferdinand and Isabella. Copies of the letter were soon circulating all over Europe, spreading news of the wondrous new land that Columbus had "discovered." Columbus would make three more voyages over the next decade, establishing Spain's first settlement in the New World on the island of Hispaniola. Many other Europeans followed in Columbus's footsteps, drawn by dreams of winning wealth by sailing west. Another Italian, Amerigo Vespucci, sailing for the Portuguese crown, explored the South American coastline between 1499 and 1502. Unlike Columbus, he realized that the Americas were not part of Asia but lands unknown to Europeans. Vespucci's widely published accounts of his voyages fueled speculation and intense interest in the New World among Europeans. Among those who read Vespucci's reports was the German mapmaker Martin Waldseemuller. Using the explorer's first name as a label for the new landmass, Waldseemuller attached "America" to his map of the New World in 1507, and the name stuck.

DEFINING "AMERICAN"

✪ *Columbus's Probanza de mérito of 1493*

The exploits of the most famous Spanish explorers have provided Western civilization with a narrative of European supremacy and Indian savagery. However, these stories are based on the self-aggrandizing efforts of conquistadors to secure royal favor through the writing of *probanzas de méritos* (proofs of merit). Below are excerpts from Columbus's 1493 letter to Luis de Santángel, which illustrates how fantastic reports from European explorers gave rise to many myths surrounding the Spanish conquest and the New World.

> This island, like all the others, is most extensive. It has many ports along the sea-coast excelling any in Christendom—and many fine, large, flowing rivers. The land there is elevated, with many mountains and peaks incomparably higher than in the centre isle. They are most beautiful, of a thousand varied forms, accessible, and full of trees of endless varieties, so high that they seem to touch the sky, and I have been told that they never lose their foliage. . . . There is honey, and there are many kinds of birds, and a great variety of fruits. Inland there are numerous mines of metals and innumerable people. Hispaniola is a marvel. Its hills and mountains, fine plains and open country, are rich and fertile for planting and for pasturage, and for building towns and villages. The seaports there are incredibly fine, as also the magnificent rivers, most of which bear gold. The trees, fruits and grasses differ widely from those in Juana. There are many spices and vast mines of gold and other metals in this island. They have no iron, nor steel, nor weapons, nor are they fit for them, because although they are well-made men of commanding stature, they appear extraordinarily timid. The only arms they have are sticks of cane, cut when in seed, with a sharpened stick at the end, and they are afraid to use these. Often I have sent two or three men ashore to some town to converse with them, and the natives came out in great numbers, and as soon as they saw our men arrive, fled without a moment's delay although I protected them from all injury.

What does this letter show us about Spanish objectives in the New World? How do you think it might have influenced Europeans reading about the New World for the first time?

The 1492 Columbus landfall accelerated the rivalry between Spain and Portugal, and the two powers vied for domination through the acquisition of new lands. In the 1480s, Pope Sixtus IV had granted Portugal the right to all land south of the Cape Verde islands, leading the Portuguese king to claim that the lands discovered by Columbus belonged to Portugal, not Spain. Seeking to ensure that Columbus's finds would remain Spanish, Spain's monarchs turned to the Spanish-born Pope Alexander VI, who issued two papal decrees in 1493 that gave legitimacy to Spain's Atlantic claims at the expense of Portugal. Hoping to salvage Portugal's Atlantic holdings, King João II began negotiations with Spain. The resulting Treaty of Tordesillas in 1494 drew a north-to-south line through South America (Figure 2.5); Spain gained territory west of the line, while Portugal retained the lands east of the line, including the east coast of Brazil.

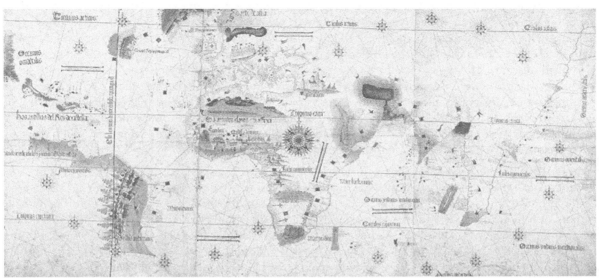

Figure 2.5 This 1502 map, known as the Cantino World Map, depicts the cartographer's interpretation of the world in light of recent discoveries. The map shows areas of Portuguese and Spanish exploration, the two nations' claims under the Treaty of Tordesillas, and a variety of flora, fauna, figures, and structures. What does it reveal about the state of geographical knowledge, as well as European perceptions of the New World, at the beginning of the sixteenth century?

Columbus's discovery opened a floodgate of Spanish exploration. Inspired by tales of rivers of gold and timid, malleable natives, later Spanish explorers were relentless in their quest for land and gold. Hernán Cortés hoped to gain hereditary privilege for his family, tribute payments and labor from natives, and an annual pension for his service to the crown. Cortés arrived on Hispaniola in 1504 and took part in the conquest of that island. In anticipation of winning his own honor and riches, Cortés later explored the Yucatán Peninsula. In 1519, he entered Tenochtitlán, the capital of the Aztec (Mexica) Empire. He and his men were astonished by the incredibly sophisticated causeways, gardens, and temples in the city, but they were horrified by the practice of human sacrifice that was part of the Aztec religion. Above all else, the Aztec wealth in gold fascinated the Spanish adventurers.

Hoping to gain power over the city, Cortés took Moctezuma, the Aztec ruler, hostage. The Spanish then murdered hundreds of high-ranking Mexica during a festival to celebrate Huitzilopochtli, the god of war. This angered the people of Tenochtitlán, who rose up against the interlopers in their city. Cortés and his people fled for their lives, running down one of Tenochtitlán's causeways to safety on the shore. Smarting from their defeat at the hands of the Aztec, Cortés slowly created alliances with native peoples who resented Aztec rule. It took nearly a year for the Spanish and the tens of thousands of native allies who joined them to defeat the Mexica in Tenochtitlán, which they did by laying siege to the city. Only by playing upon the disunity among the diverse groups in the Aztec Empire were the Spanish able to capture the grand city of Tenochtitlán. In August 1521, having successfully fomented civil war as well as fended off rival Spanish explorers, Cortés claimed Tenochtitlán for Spain and renamed it Mexico City.

The traditional European narrative of exploration presents the victory of the Spanish over the Aztec as an example of the superiority of the Europeans over the savage Indians. However, the reality is far more complex. When Cortés explored central Mexico, he encountered a region simmering with native conflict. Far from being unified and content under Aztec rule, many peoples in Mexico resented it and were ready to rebel. One group in particular, the Tlaxcalan, threw their lot in with the Spanish, providing as many as 200,000 fighters in the siege of Tenochtitlán. The Spanish also brought smallpox into the valley of Mexico. The disease took a heavy toll on the people in Tenochtitlán, playing a much greater role in the city's demise than did Spanish force of arms.

Cortés was also aided by a Nahua woman called Malintzin (also known as La Malinche or Doña Marina, her Spanish name), whom the natives of Tabasco gave him as tribute. Malintzin translated for Cortés in his dealings with Moctezuma and, whether willingly or under pressure, entered into a physical relationship with him. Their son, Martín, may have been the first mestizo (person of mixed indigenous American and European descent). Malintzin remains a controversial figure in the history of the Atlantic World; some people view her as a traitor because she helped Cortés conquer the Aztecs, while others see her as a victim of European expansion. In either case, she demonstrates one way in which native peoples responded to the arrival of the Spanish. Without her, Cortés would not have been able to communicate, and without the language bridge, he surely would have been less successful in destabilizing the Aztec Empire. By this and other means, native people helped shape the conquest of the Americas.

Spain's acquisitiveness seemingly knew no bounds as groups of its explorers searched for the next trove of instant riches. One such explorer, Francisco Pizarro, made his way to the Spanish Caribbean in 1509, drawn by the promise of wealth and titles. He participated in successful expeditions in Panama before following rumors of Inca wealth to the south. Although his first efforts against the Inca Empire in the 1520s failed, Pizarro captured the Inca emperor Atahualpa in 1532 and executed him one year later. In 1533, Pizarro founded Lima, Peru. Like Cortés, Pizarro had to combat not only the natives of the new worlds he was conquering, but also competitors from his own country; a Spanish rival assassinated him in 1541.

Spain's drive to enlarge its empire led other hopeful conquistadors to push further into the Americas, hoping to replicate the success of Cortés and Pizarro. Hernando de Soto had participated in Pizarro's conquest of the Inca, and from 1539 to 1542 he led expeditions to what is today the southeastern United States, looking for gold. He and his followers explored what is now Florida, Georgia, the Carolinas, Tennessee, Alabama, Mississippi, Arkansas, Oklahoma, Louisiana, and Texas. Everywhere they traveled, they brought European diseases, which claimed thousands of native lives as well as the lives of the explorers. In 1542, de Soto himself died during the expedition. The surviving Spaniards, numbering a little over three hundred, returned to Mexico City without finding the much-anticipated mountains of gold and silver.

Francisco Vásquez de Coronado was born into a noble family and went to Mexico, then called New Spain, in 1535. He presided as governor over the province of Nueva Galicia, where he heard rumors of wealth to the north: a golden city called Quivira. Between 1540 and 1542, Coronado led a large expedition of Spaniards and native allies to the lands north of Mexico City, and for the next several years, they explored the area that is now the southwestern United States (Figure 2.6). During the winter of 1540–41, the explorers waged war against the Tiwa in present-day New Mexico. Rather than leading to the discovery of gold and silver, however, the expedition simply left Coronado bankrupt.

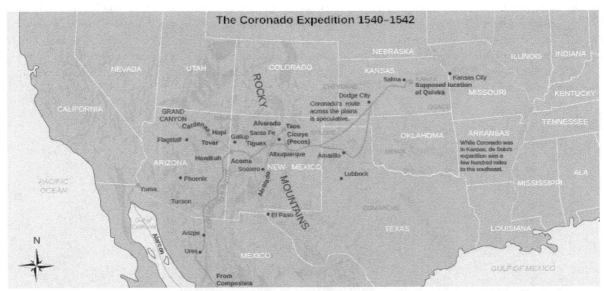

Figure 2.6 This map traces Coronado's path through the American Southwest and the Great Plains. The regions through which he traveled were not empty areas waiting to be "discovered": rather, they were populated and controlled by the groups of native peoples indicated. (credit: modification of work by National Park Service)

THE SPANISH GOLDEN AGE

The exploits of European explorers had a profound impact both in the Americas and back in Europe. An exchange of ideas, fueled and financed in part by New World commodities, began to connect European nations and, in turn, to touch the parts of the world that Europeans conquered. In Spain, gold and silver from the Americas helped to fuel a golden age, the Siglo de Oro, when Spanish art and literature flourished. Riches poured in from the colonies, and new ideas poured in from other countries and new lands. The Hapsburg dynasty, which ruled a collection of territories including Austria, the Netherlands, Naples, Sicily, and Spain, encouraged and financed the work of painters, sculptors, musicians, architects, and writers, resulting in a blooming of Spanish Renaissance culture. One of this period's most famous works is the novel *The Ingenious Gentleman Don Quixote of La Mancha*, by Miguel de Cervantes. This two-volume book (1605 and 1618) told a colorful tale of an *hidalgo* (gentleman) who reads so many tales of chivalry and knighthood that he becomes unable to tell reality from fiction. With his faithful sidekick Sancho Panza, Don Quixote leaves reality behind and sets out to revive chivalry by doing battle with what he perceives as the enemies of Spain.

Click and Explore

Explore the collection at The Cervantes Project (http://openstaxcollege.org/l/cervantes) for images, complete texts, and other resources relating to Cervantes's works.

Spain attracted innovative foreign painters such as El Greco, a Greek who had studied with Italian Renaissance masters like Titian and Michelangelo before moving to Toledo. Native Spaniards created equally enduring works. *Las Meninas (The Maids of Honor)*, painted by Diego Velázquez in 1656, is one of the best-known paintings in history. Velázquez painted himself into this imposingly large royal portrait (he's shown holding his brush and easel on the left) and boldly placed the viewer where the king and queen would stand in the scene (Figure 2.7).

Figure 2.7 *Las Meninas (The Maids of Honor)*, painted by Diego Velázquez in 1656, is unique for its time because it places the viewer in the place of King Philip IV and his wife, Queen Mariana.

2.2 Religious Upheavals in the Developing Atlantic World

By the end of this section, you will be able to:
- Explain the changes brought by the Protestant Reformation and how it influenced the development of the Atlantic World
- Describe Spain's response to the Protestant Reformation

Until the 1500s, the Catholic Church provided a unifying religious structure for Christian Europe. The Vatican in Rome exercised great power over the lives of Europeans; it controlled not only learning and scholarship but also finances, because it levied taxes on the faithful. Spain, with its New World wealth, was the bastion of the Catholic faith. Beginning with the reform efforts of Martin Luther in 1517 and John Calvin in the 1530s, however, Catholic dominance came under attack as the **Protestant Reformation**, a split or schism among European Christians, began.

During the sixteenth century, Protestantism spread through northern Europe, and Catholic countries responded by attempting to extinguish what was seen as the Protestant menace. Religious turmoil between Catholics and Protestants influenced the history of the Atlantic World as well, since different nation-states competed not only for control of new territories but also for the preeminence of their religious beliefs there. Just as the history of Spain's rise to power is linked to the Reconquista, so too is the history of early globalization connected to the history of competing Christian groups in the Atlantic World.

MARTIN LUTHER

Martin Luther (Figure 2.8) was a German Catholic monk who took issue with the Catholic Church's practice of selling **indulgences**, documents that absolved sinners of their errant behavior. He also objected to the Catholic Church's taxation of ordinary Germans and the delivery of Mass in Latin, arguing that it failed to instruct German Catholics, who did not understand the language.

Figure 2.8 Martin Luther, a German Catholic monk and leader of the Protestant Reformation, was a close friend of the German painter Lucas Cranach the Elder. Cranach painted this and several other portraits of Luther.

Many Europeans had called for reforms of the Catholic Church before Martin Luther did, but his protest had the unintended consequence of splitting European Christianity. Luther compiled a list of what he viewed as needed Church reforms, a document that came to be known as *The Ninety-Five Theses*, and nailed it to the door of a church in Wittenberg, Germany, in 1517. He called for the publication of the Bible in everyday language, took issue with the Church's policy of imposing tithes (a required payment to the Church that appeared to enrich the clergy), and denounced the buying and selling of indulgences. Although he had hoped to reform the Catholic Church while remaining a part of it, Luther's action instead triggered a movement called the Protestant Reformation that divided the Church in two. The Catholic Church condemned him as a heretic, but a doctrine based on his reforms, called Lutheranism, spread through northern Germany and Scandinavia.

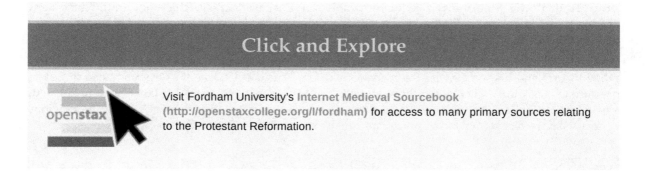

Click and Explore

Visit Fordham University's Internet Medieval Sourcebook (http://openstaxcollege.org/l/fordham) for access to many primary sources relating to the Protestant Reformation.

JOHN CALVIN

Like Luther, the French lawyer John Calvin advocated making the Bible accessible to ordinary people; only by reading scripture and reflecting daily about their spiritual condition, he argued, could believers begin to understand the power of God. In 1535, Calvin fled Catholic France and led the Reformation movement from Geneva, Switzerland.

Calvinism emphasized human powerlessness before an omniscient God and stressed the idea of predestination, the belief that God selected a few chosen people for salvation while everyone else was predestined to damnation. Calvinists believed that reading scripture prepared sinners, if they were among the elect, to receive God's grace. In Geneva, Calvin established a Bible commonwealth, a community of believers whose sole source of authority was their interpretation of the Bible, not the authority of any prince or monarch. Soon Calvin's ideas spread to the Netherlands and Scotland.

PROTESTANTISM IN ENGLAND

Protestantism spread beyond the German states and Geneva to England, which had been a Catholic nation for centuries. Luther's idea that scripture should be available in the everyday language of worshippers inspired English scholar William Tyndale to translate the Bible into English in 1526. The seismic break with the Catholic Church in England occurred in the 1530s, when Henry VIII established a new, Protestant state religion.

A devout Catholic, Henry had initially stood in opposition to the Reformation. Pope Leo X even awarded him the title "Defender of the Faith." The tides turned, however, when Henry desired a male heir to the Tudor monarchy. When his Spanish Catholic wife, Catherine (the daughter of Ferdinand and Isabella), did not give birth to a boy, the king sought an annulment to their marriage. When the Pope refused his request, Henry created a new national Protestant church, the Church of England, with himself at its head. This left him free to annul his own marriage and marry Anne Boleyn.

Anne Boleyn also failed to produce a male heir, and when she was accused of adultery, Henry had her executed. His third wife, Jane Seymour, at long last delivered a son, Edward, who ruled for only a short time before dying in 1553 at the age of fifteen. Mary, the daughter of Henry VIII and his discarded first wife Catherine, then came to the throne, committed to restoring Catholicism. She earned the nickname "Bloody Mary" for the many executions of Protestants, often by burning alive, that she ordered during her reign.

Religious turbulence in England was finally quieted when Elizabeth, the Protestant daughter of Henry VIII and Anne Boleyn, ascended the throne in 1558. Under Elizabeth, the Church of England again became the state church, retaining the hierarchical structure and many of the rituals of the Catholic Church. However, by the late 1500s, some English members of the Church began to agitate for more reform. Known as **Puritans**, they worked to erase all vestiges of Catholicism from the Church of England. At the time, the term "puritan" was a pejorative one; many people saw Puritans as holier-than-thou frauds who used religion to swindle their neighbors. Worse still, many in power saw Puritans as a security threat because of their opposition to the national church.

Under Elizabeth, whose long reign lasted from 1558 to 1603, Puritans grew steadily in number. After James I died in 1625 and his son Charles I ascended the throne, Puritans became the target of increasing state pressure to conform. Many crossed the Atlantic in the 1620s and 1630s instead to create a New England, a haven for reformed Protestantism where Puritan was no longer a term of abuse. Thus, the religious upheavals that affected England so much had equally momentous consequences for the Americas.

RELIGIOUS WAR

By the early 1500s, the Protestant Reformation threatened the massive Spanish Catholic empire. As the preeminent Catholic power, Spain would not tolerate any challenge to the Holy Catholic Church. Over the course of the 1500s, it devoted vast amounts of treasure and labor to leading an unsuccessful effort to eradicate Protestantism in Europe.

Spain's main enemies at this time were the runaway Spanish provinces of the North Netherlands. By 1581, these seven northern provinces had declared their independence from Spain and created the Dutch Republic, also called Holland, where Protestantism was tolerated. Determined to deal a death blow to Protestantism in England and Holland, King Philip of Spain assembled a massive force of over thirty thousand men and 130 ships, and in 1588 he sent this navy, the Spanish Armada, north. But English sea power combined with a maritime storm destroyed the fleet.

The defeat of the Spanish Armada in 1588 was but one part of a larger but undeclared war between Protestant England and Catholic Spain. Between 1585 and 1604, the two rivals sparred repeatedly. England launched its own armada in 1589 in an effort to cripple the Spanish fleet and capture Spanish treasure. However, the foray ended in disaster for the English, with storms, disease, and the strength of the Spanish Armada combining to bring about defeat.

The conflict between Spain and England dragged on into the early seventeenth century, and the newly Protestant nations, especially England and the Dutch Republic, posed a significant challenge to Spain (and also to Catholic France) as imperial rivalries played out in the Atlantic World. Spain retained its mighty American empire, but by the early 1600s, the nation could no longer keep England and other European rivals—the French and Dutch—from colonizing smaller islands in the Caribbean (Figure 2.9).

Figure 2.9   This portrait of Elizabeth I of England, painted by George Gower in about 1588, shows Elizabeth with her hand on a globe, signifying her power over the world. The pictures in the background show the English defeat of the Spanish Armada.

Religious intolerance characterized the sixteenth and seventeenth centuries, an age of powerful state religions with the authority to impose and enforce belief systems on the population. In this climate, religious violence was common. One of the most striking examples is the St. Bartholomew's Day Massacre of 1572, in which French Catholic troops began to kill unarmed French Protestants (Figure 2.10). The murders touched off mob violence that ultimately claimed nine thousand lives, a bloody episode that highlights the degree of religious turmoil that gripped Europe in the aftermath of the Protestant Reformation.

Figure 2.10 *Saint Bartholomew's Day Massacre* (1772-84), by François Dubois, shows the horrific violence of the St. Bartholomew's Day Massacre. In this scene, French Catholic troops slaughter French Protestant Calvinists.

2.3 Challenges to Spain's Supremacy

By the end of this section, you will be able to:
- Identify regions where the English, French, and Dutch explored and established settlements
- Describe the differences among the early colonies
- Explain the role of the American colonies in European nations' struggles for domination

For Europeans, the discovery of an Atlantic World meant newfound wealth in the form of gold and silver as well as valuable furs. The Americas also provided a new arena for intense imperial rivalry as different European nations jockeyed for preeminence in the New World. The religious motives for colonization spurred European expansion as well, and as the Protestant Reformation gained ground beginning in the 1520s, rivalries between Catholic and Protestant Christians spilled over into the Americas.

ENGLISH EXPLORATION

Disruptions during the Tudor monarchy—especially the creation of the Protestant Church of England by Henry VIII in the 1530s, the return of the nation to Catholicism under Queen Mary in the 1550s, and the restoration of Protestantism under Queen Elizabeth—left England with little energy for overseas projects. More important, England lacked the financial resources for such endeavors. Nonetheless, English monarchs carefully monitored developments in the new Atlantic World and took steps to assert England's claim to the Americas. As early as 1497, Henry VII of England had commissioned John Cabot, an Italian mariner, to explore new lands. Cabot sailed from England that year and made landfall somewhere along the North American coastline. For the next century, English fishermen routinely crossed the Atlantic to fish the rich waters off the North American coast. However, English colonization efforts in the 1500s were closer to home, as England devoted its energy to the colonization of Ireland.

Queen Elizabeth favored England's advance into the Atlantic World, though her main concern was blocking Spain's effort to eliminate Protestantism. Indeed, England could not commit to large-scale colonization in the Americas as long as Spain appeared ready to invade Ireland or Scotland. Nonetheless,

Elizabeth approved of English **privateers**, sea captains to whom the home government had given permission to raid the enemy at will. These skilled mariners cruised the Caribbean, plundering Spanish ships whenever they could. Each year the English took more than £100,000 from Spain in this way; English privateer Francis Drake first made a name for himself when, in 1573, he looted silver, gold, and pearls worth £40,000.

Elizabeth did sanction an early attempt at colonization in 1584, when Sir Walter Raleigh, a favorite of the queen's, attempted to establish a colony at **Roanoke**, an island off the coast of present-day North Carolina. The colony was small, consisting of only 117 people, who suffered a poor relationship with the local Indians, the Croatans, and struggled to survive in their new land (Figure 2.11). Their governor, John White, returned to England in late 1587 to secure more people and supplies, but events conspired to keep him away from Roanoke for three years. By the time he returned in 1590, the entire colony had vanished. The only trace the colonists left behind was the word *Croatoan* carved into a fence surrounding the village. Governor White never knew whether the colonists had decamped for nearby Croatoan Island (now Hatteras) or whether some disaster had befallen them all. Roanoke is still called "the lost colony."

Figure 2.11 In 1588, a promoter of English colonization named Thomas Hariot published *A Briefe and True Report of the New Found Land of Virginia*, which contained many engravings of the native peoples who lived on the Carolina coast in the 1580s. This print, "The brovvyllinge of their fishe ouer the flame" (1590) by Theodor de Bry, shows the ingenuity and wisdom of the "savages" of the New World. (credit: UNC Chapel Hill)

English promoters of colonization pushed its commercial advantages and the religious justification that English colonies would allow the establishment of Protestantism in the Americas. Both arguments struck a chord. In the early 1600s, wealthy English merchants and the landed elite began to pool their resources to form **joint stock companies**. In this novel business arrangement, which was in many ways the precursor to the modern corporation, investors provided the capital for and assumed the risk of a venture in order to reap significant returns. The companies gained the approval of the English crown to establish colonies, and their investors dreamed of reaping great profits from the money they put into overseas colonization.

The first permanent English settlement was established by a joint stock company, the Virginia Company. Named for Elizabeth, the "virgin queen," the company gained royal approval to establish a colony on the east coast of North America, and in 1606, it sent 144 men and boys to the New World. In early 1607, this group sailed up Chesapeake Bay. Finding a river they called the James in honor of their new king, James I, they established a ramshackle settlement and named it Jamestown. Despite serious struggles, the colony survived.

Many of Jamestown's settlers were desperate men; although they came from elite families, they were younger sons who would not inherit their father's estates. The Jamestown adventurers believed they would find instant wealth in the New World and did not actually expect to have to perform work. Henry Percy, the eighth son of the Earl of Northumberland, was among them. His account, excerpted below, illustrates the hardships the English confronted in Virginia in 1607.

MY STORY

☸ *George Percy and the First Months at Jamestown*

The 144 men and boys who started the Jamestown colony faced many hardships; by the end of the first winter, only 38 had survived. Disease, hunger, and poor relationships with local natives all contributed to the colony's high death toll. George Percy, who served twice as governor of Jamestown, kept records of the colonists' first months in the colony. These records were later published in London in 1608. This excerpt is from his account of August and September of 1607.

> The fourth day of September died Thomas Jacob Sergeant. The fifth day, there died Benjamin Beast. Our men were destroyed with cruel diseases, as Swellings, Fluxes, Burning Fevers, and by wars, and some departed suddenly, but for the most part they died of mere famine. There were never Englishmen left in a foreign Country in such misery as we were in this new discovered Virginia. . . . Our food was but a small Can of Barley sod* in water, to five men a day, our drink cold water taken out of the River, which was at a flood very salty, at a low tide full of slime and filth, which was the destruction of many of our men. Thus we lived for the space of five months in this miserable distress, not having five able men to man our Bulwarks upon any occasion. If it had not pleased God to have put a terror in the Savages' hearts, we had all perished by those wild and cruel Pagans, being in that weak estate as we were; our men night and day groaning in every corner of the Fort most pitiful to hear. If there were any conscience in men, it would make their hearts to bleed to hear the pitiful murmurings and outcries of our sick men without relief, every night and day, for the space of six weeks, some departing out of the World, many times three or four in a night; in the morning, their bodies trailed out of their Cabins like Dogs to be buried. In this sort did I see the mortality of diverse of our people.
>
> *soaked

According to George Percy's account, what were the major problems the Jamestown settlers encountered? What kept the colony from complete destruction?

By any measure, England came late to the race to colonize. As Jamestown limped along in the 1610s, the Spanish Empire extended around the globe and grew rich from its global colonial project. Yet the English persisted, and for this reason the Jamestown settlement has a special place in history as the first permanent colony in what later became the United States.

After Jamestown's founding, English colonization of the New World accelerated. In 1609, a ship bound for Jamestown foundered in a storm and landed on Bermuda. (Some believe this incident helped inspire Shakespeare's 1611 play *The Tempest*.) The admiral of the ship, George Somers, claimed the island for the English crown. The English also began to colonize small islands in the Caribbean, an incursion into the Spanish American empire. They established themselves on small islands such as St. Christopher (1624), Barbados (1627), Nevis (1628), Montserrat (1632), and Antigua (1632).

From the start, the English West Indies had a commercial orientation, for these islands produced cash crops: first tobacco and then sugar. Very quickly, by the mid-1600s, Barbados had become one of the most important English colonies because of the sugar produced there. Barbados was the first English colony dependent on slaves, and it became a model for other English slave societies on the American mainland. These differed radically from England itself, where slavery was not practiced.

English Puritans also began to colonize the Americas in the 1620s and 1630s. These intensely religious migrants dreamed of creating communities of reformed Protestantism where the corruption of England would be eliminated. One of the first groups of Puritans to remove to North America, known as **Pilgrims** and led by William Bradford, had originally left England to live in the Netherlands. Fearing their children were losing their English identity among the Dutch, however, they sailed for North America in 1620 to settle at Plymouth, the first English settlement in New England. The Pilgrims differed from other Puritans in their insistence on separating from what they saw as the corrupt Church of England. For this reason, Pilgrims are known as **Separatists**.

Like Jamestown, Plymouth occupies an iconic place in American national memory. The tale of the 102 migrants who crossed the Atlantic aboard the *Mayflower* and their struggle for survival is a well-known narrative of the founding of the country. Their story includes the signing of the Mayflower Compact, a written agreement whereby the English voluntarily agreed to help each other. Some interpret this 1620 document as an expression of democratic spirit because of the cooperative and inclusive nature of the agreement to live and work together. In 1630, a much larger contingent of Puritans left England to escape conformity to the Church of England and founded the Massachusetts Bay Colony. In the following years, thousands more arrived to create a new life in the rocky soils and cold climates of New England.

In comparison to Catholic Spain, however, Protestant England remained a very weak imperial player in the early seventeenth century, with only a few infant colonies in the Americas in the early 1600s. The English never found treasure equal to that of the Aztec city of Tenochtitlán, and England did not quickly grow rich from its small American outposts. The English colonies also differed from each other; Barbados and Virginia had a decidedly commercial orientation from the start, while the Puritan colonies of New England were intensely religious at their inception. All English settlements in America, however, marked the increasingly important role of England in the Atlantic World.

FRENCH EXPLORATION

Spanish exploits in the New World whetted the appetite of other would-be imperial powers, including France. Like Spain, France was a Catholic nation and committed to expanding Catholicism around the globe. In the early sixteenth century, it joined the race to explore the New World and exploit the resources of the Western Hemisphere. Navigator Jacques Cartier claimed northern North America for France, naming the area New France. From 1534 to 1541, he made three voyages of discovery on the Gulf of St. Lawrence and the St. Lawrence River. Like other explorers, Cartier made exaggerated claims of mineral wealth in America, but he was unable to send great riches back to France. Due to resistance from the native peoples as well as his own lack of planning, he could not establish a permanent settlement in North America.

Explorer Samuel de Champlain occupies a special place in the history of the Atlantic World for his role in establishing the French presence in the New World. Champlain explored the Caribbean in 1601 and then the coast of New England in 1603 before traveling farther north. In 1608 he founded Quebec, and he made numerous Atlantic crossings as he worked tirelessly to promote New France. Unlike other imperial powers, France—through Champlain's efforts—fostered especially good relationships with native peoples, paving the way for French exploration further into the continent: around the Great Lakes, around Hudson Bay, and eventually to the Mississippi. Champlain made an alliance with the Huron confederacy and the Algonquins and agreed to fight with them against their enemy, the Iroquois (Figure 2.12).

Figure 2.12 In this engraving, titled *Defeat of the Iroquois* and based on a drawing by explorer Samuel de Champlain, Champlain is shown fighting on the side of the Huron and Algonquins against the Iroquois. He portrays himself in the middle of the battle, firing a gun, while the native people around him shoot arrows at each other. What does this engraving suggest about the impact of European exploration and settlement on the Americas?

The French were primarily interested in establishing commercially viable colonial outposts, and to that end, they created extensive trading networks in New France. These networks relied on native hunters to harvest furs, especially beaver pelts, and to exchange these items for French glass beads and other trade goods. (French fashion at the time favored broad-brimmed hats trimmed in beaver fur, so French traders had a ready market for their North American goods.) The French also dreamed of replicating the wealth of Spain by colonizing the tropical zones. After Spanish control of the Caribbean began to weaken, the French turned their attention to small islands in the West Indies, and by 1635 they had colonized two, Guadeloupe and Martinique. Though it lagged far behind Spain, France now boasted its own West Indian colonies. Both islands became lucrative sugar plantation sites that turned a profit for French planters by relying on African slave labor.

Click and Explore

To see how cartographers throughout history documented the exploration of the Atlantic World, browse the hundreds of digitized historical maps that make up the collection American Shores: Maps of the Middle Atlantic Region to 1850 (http://openstaxcollege.org/l/nypl) at the New York Public Library.

DUTCH COLONIZATION

Dutch entrance into the Atlantic World is part of the larger story of religious and imperial conflict in the early modern era. In the 1500s, Calvinism, one of the major Protestant reform movements, had found adherents in the northern provinces of the Spanish Netherlands. During the sixteenth century, these provinces began a long struggle to achieve independence from Catholic Spain. Established in 1581 but not recognized as independent by Spain until 1648, the Dutch Republic, or Holland, quickly made itself a powerful force in the race for Atlantic colonies and wealth. The Dutch distinguished themselves as commercial leaders in the seventeenth century (Figure 2.13), and their mode of colonization relied on powerful corporations: the Dutch East India Company, chartered in 1602 to trade in Asia, and the Dutch West India Company, established in 1621 to colonize and trade in the Americas.

Figure 2.13 Amsterdam was the richest city in the world in the 1600s. In *Courtyard of the Exchange in Amsterdam*, a 1653 painting by Emanuel de Witt, merchants involved in the global trade eagerly attend to news of shipping and the prices of commodities.

While employed by the Dutch East India Company in 1609, the English sea captain Henry Hudson explored New York Harbor and the river that now bears his name. Like many explorers of the time, Hudson was actually seeking a northwest passage to Asia and its wealth, but the ample furs harvested from the region he explored, especially the coveted beaver pelts, provided a reason to claim it for the Netherlands. The Dutch named their colony New Netherlands, and it served as a fur-trading outpost for the expanding and powerful Dutch West India Company. With headquarters in New Amsterdam on the island of Manhattan, the Dutch set up several regional trading posts, including one at Fort Orange—named for the royal Dutch House of Orange-Nassau—in present-day Albany. (The color orange remains significant to the Dutch, having become particularly associated with William of Orange, Protestantism, and the Glorious Revolution of 1688.) A brisk trade in furs with local Algonquian and Iroquois peoples brought the Dutch and native peoples together in a commercial network that extended throughout the Hudson River Valley and beyond.

The Dutch West India Company in turn established colonies on Aruba, Bonaire, and Curaçao, St. Martin, St. Eustatius, and Saba. With their outposts in New Netherlands and the Caribbean, the Dutch had established themselves in the seventeenth century as a commercially powerful rival to Spain. Amsterdam became a trade hub for all the Atlantic World.

2.4 New Worlds in the Americas: Labor, Commerce, and the Columbian Exchange

By the end of this section, you will be able to:
- Describe how Europeans solved their labor problems
- Describe the theory of mercantilism and the process of commodification
- Analyze the effects of the Columbian Exchange

European promoters of colonization claimed the Americas overflowed with a wealth of treasures. Burnishing national glory and honor became entwined with carving out colonies, and no nation wanted to be left behind. However, the realities of life in the Americas—violence, exploitation, and particularly the need for workers—were soon driving the practice of slavery and forced labor. Everywhere in America a stark contrast existed between freedom and slavery. The Columbian Exchange, in which Europeans transported plants, animals, and diseases across the Atlantic in both directions, also left a lasting impression on the Americas.

LABOR SYSTEMS

Physical power—to work the fields, build villages, process raw materials—is a necessity for maintaining a society. During the sixteenth and seventeenth centuries, humans could derive power only from the wind, water, animals, or other humans. Everywhere in the Americas, a crushing demand for labor beddeviled Europeans because there were not enough colonists to perform the work necessary to keep the colonies going. Spain granted *encomiendas*—legal rights to native labor—to conquistadors who could prove their service to the crown. This system reflected the Spanish view of colonization: the king rewarded successful conquistadors who expanded the empire. Some native peoples who had sided with the conquistadors, like the Tlaxcalan, also gained *encomiendas*; Malintzin, the Nahua woman who helped Cortés defeat the Mexica, was granted one.

The Spanish believed native peoples would work for them by right of conquest, and, in return, the Spanish would bring them Catholicism. In theory the relationship consisted of reciprocal obligations, but in practice the Spaniards ruthlessly exploited it, seeing native people as little more than beasts of burden. Convinced of their right to the land and its peoples, they sought both to control native labor and to impose what they viewed as correct religious beliefs upon the land's inhabitants. Native peoples everywhere resisted both the labor obligations and the effort to change their ancient belief systems. Indeed, many retained their religion or incorporated only the parts of Catholicism that made sense to them.

The system of *encomiendas* was accompanied by a great deal of violence (Figure 2.14). One Spaniard, Bartolomé de Las Casas , denounced the brutality of Spanish rule. A Dominican friar, Las Casas had been one of the earliest Spanish settlers in the Spanish West Indies. In his early life in the Americas, he owned Indian slaves and was the recipient of an *encomienda*. However, after witnessing the savagery with which *encomenderos* (recipients of *encomiendas*) treated the native people, he reversed his views. In 1515, Las Casas released his native slaves, gave up his *encomienda*, and began to advocate for humane treatment of native peoples. He lobbied for new legislation, eventually known as the New Laws, which would eliminate slavery and the *encomienda* system.

Figure 2.14 In this startling image from the Kingsborough Codex (a book written and drawn by native Mesoamericans), a well-dressed Spaniard is shown pulling the hair of a bleeding, severely injured native. The drawing was part of a complaint about Spanish abuses of their *encomiendas*.

Las Casas's writing about the Spaniards' horrific treatment of Indians helped inspire the so-called **Black Legend**, the idea that the Spanish were bloodthirsty conquerors with no regard for human life. Perhaps not surprisingly, those who held this view of the Spanish were Spain's imperial rivals. English writers and others seized on the idea of Spain's ruthlessness to support their own colonization projects. By demonizing the Spanish, they justified their own efforts as more humane. All European colonizers, however, shared a disregard for Indians.

MY STORY

✵ *Bartolomé de Las Casas on the Mistreatment of Indians*

Bartolomé de Las Casas's *A Short Account of the Destruction of the Indies*, written in 1542 and published ten years later, detailed for Prince Philip II of Spain how Spanish colonists had been mistreating natives.

> Into and among these gentle sheep, endowed by their Maker and Creator with all the qualities aforesaid, did creep the Spaniards, who no sooner had knowledge of these people than they became like fierce wolves and tigers and lions who have gone many days without food or nourishment. And no other thing have they done for forty years until this day, and still today see fit to do, but dismember, slay, perturb, afflict, torment, and destroy the Indians by all manner of cruelty—new and divers and most singular manners such as never before seen or read or heard of—some few of which shall be recounted below, and they do this to such a degree that on the Island of Hispaniola, of the above three millions souls that we once saw, today there be no more than two hundred of those native people remaining. . . .

> Two principal and general customs have been employed by those, calling themselves Christians, who have passed this way, in extirpating and striking from the face of the earth those suffering nations. The first being unjust, cruel, bloody, and tyrannical warfare. The other—after having slain all those who might yearn toward or suspire after or think of freedom, or consider escaping from the torments that they are made to suffer, by which I mean all the native-born lords and adult males, for it is the Spaniards' custom in their wars to allow only young boys and females to live—being to oppress them with the hardest, harshest, and most heinous bondage to which men or beasts might ever be bound into.

How might these writings have been used to promote the "black legend" against Spain as well as subsequent English exploration and colonization?

Indians were not the only source of cheap labor in the Americas; by the middle of the sixteenth century, Africans formed an important element of the labor landscape, producing the cash crops of sugar and tobacco for European markets. Europeans viewed Africans as non-Christians, which they used as a justification for enslavement. Denied control over their lives, slaves endured horrendous conditions. At every opportunity, they resisted enslavement, and their resistance was met with violence. Indeed, physical, mental, and sexual violence formed a key strategy among European slaveholders in their effort to assert mastery and impose their will. The Portuguese led the way in the evolving transport of slaves across the Atlantic; slave "factories" on the west coast of Africa, like Elmina Castle in Ghana, served as holding pens for slaves brought from Africa's interior. In time, other European imperial powers would follow in the footsteps of the Portuguese by constructing similar outposts on the coast of West Africa.

The Portuguese traded or sold slaves to Spanish, Dutch, and English colonists in the Americas, particularly in South America and the Caribbean, where sugar was a primary export. Thousands of African slaves found themselves growing, harvesting, and processing **sugarcane** in an arduous routine of physical labor. Slaves had to cut the long cane stalks by hand and then bring them to a mill, where the cane juice was extracted. They boiled the extracted cane juice down to a brown, crystalline sugar, which then had to be cured in special curing houses to have the molasses drained from it. The result was refined sugar, while the leftover molasses could be distilled into rum. Every step was labor-intensive and often dangerous.

Las Casas estimated that by 1550, there were fifty thousand slaves on Hispaniola. However, it is a mistake to assume that during the very early years of European exploration all Africans came to America as slaves; some were free men who took part in expeditions, for example, serving as conquistadors alongside Cortés in his assault on Tenochtitlán. Nonetheless, African slavery was one of the most tragic outcomes in the emerging Atlantic World.

Click and Explore

Browse the PBS collection Africans in America: Part 1 (http://openstaxcollege.org/l/afinam) to see information and primary sources for the period 1450 through 1750.

COMMERCE IN THE NEW WORLD

The economic philosophy of **mercantilism** shaped European perceptions of wealth from the 1500s to the late 1700s. Mercantilism held that only a limited amount of wealth, as measured in gold and silver bullion, existed in the world. In order to gain power, nations had to amass wealth by mining these precious raw materials from their colonial possessions. During the age of European exploration, nations employed conquest, colonization, and trade as ways to increase their share of the bounty of the New World. Mercantilists did not believe in free trade, arguing instead that the nation should control trade to create wealth. In this view, colonies existed to strengthen the colonizing nation. Mercantilists argued against allowing their nations to trade freely with other nations.

Spain's mercantilist ideas guided its economic policy. Every year, slaves or native workers loaded shipments of gold and silver aboard Spanish treasure fleets that sailed from Cuba for Spain. These ships groaned under the sheer weight of bullion, for the Spanish had found huge caches of silver and gold in the New World. In South America, for example, Spaniards discovered rich veins of silver ore in the mountain called Potosí and founded a settlement of the same name there. Throughout the sixteenth century, Potosí was a boom town, attracting settlers from many nations as well as native people from many different cultures.

Colonial mercantilism, which was basically a set of protectionist policies designed to benefit the nation, relied on several factors: colonies rich in raw materials, cheap labor, colonial loyalty to the home government, and control of the shipping trade. Under this system, the colonies sent their raw materials, harvested by slaves or native workers, back to their mother country. The mother country sent back finished materials of all sorts: textiles, tools, clothing. The colonists could purchase these goods *only* from their mother country; trade with other countries was forbidden.

The 1500s and early 1600s also introduced the process of **commodification** to the New World. American silver, tobacco, and other items, which were used by native peoples for ritual purposes, became European commodities with a monetary value that could be bought and sold. Before the arrival of the Spanish, for example, the Inca people of the Andes consumed *chicha*, a corn beer, for ritual purposes only. When the Spanish discovered chicha, they bought and traded for it, turning it into a commodity instead of a ritual substance. Commodification thus recast native economies and spurred the process of early commercial capitalism. New World resources, from plants to animal pelts, held the promise of wealth for European imperial powers.

THE COLUMBIAN EXCHANGE

As Europeans traversed the Atlantic, they brought with them plants, animals, and diseases that changed lives and landscapes on both sides of the ocean. These two-way exchanges between the Americas and Europe/Africa are known collectively as the **Columbian Exchange** (Figure 2.15).

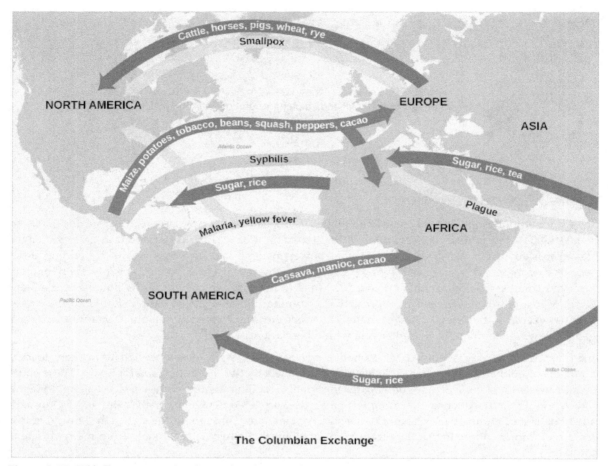

Figure 2.15 With European exploration and settlement of the New World, goods and diseases began crossing the Atlantic Ocean in both directions. This "Columbian Exchange" soon had global implications.

Of all the commodities in the Atlantic World, sugar proved to be the most important. Indeed, sugar carried the same economic importance as oil does today. European rivals raced to create sugar plantations in the Americas and fought wars for control of some of the best sugar production areas. Although refined sugar was available in the Old World, Europe's harsher climate made sugarcane difficult to grow, and it was not plentiful. Columbus brought sugar to Hispaniola in 1493, and the new crop was growing there by the end of the 1490s. By the first decades of the 1500s, the Spanish were building sugar mills on the island. Over the next century of colonization, Caribbean islands and most other tropical areas became centers of sugar production.

Though of secondary importance to sugar, tobacco achieved great value for Europeans as a cash crop as well. Native peoples had been growing it for medicinal and ritual purposes for centuries before European contact, smoking it in pipes or powdering it to use as snuff. They believed tobacco could improve concentration and enhance wisdom. To some, its use meant achieving an entranced, altered, or divine state; entering a spiritual place.

Tobacco was unknown in Europe before 1492, and it carried a negative stigma at first. The early Spanish explorers considered natives' use of tobacco to be proof of their savagery and, because of the fire and smoke produced in the consumption of tobacco, evidence of the Devil's sway in the New World. Gradually, however, European colonists became accustomed to and even took up the habit of smoking, and they brought it across the Atlantic. As did the Indians, Europeans ascribed medicinal properties to tobacco, claiming that it could cure headaches and skin irritations. Even so, Europeans did not import tobacco in great quantities until the 1590s. At that time, it became the first truly global commodity; English, French, Dutch, Spanish, and Portuguese colonists all grew it for the world market.

Native peoples also introduced Europeans to chocolate, made from cacao seeds and used by the Aztec in Mesoamerica as currency. Mesoamerican Indians consumed unsweetened chocolate in a drink with chili peppers, vanilla, and a spice called achiote. This chocolate drink—*xocolatl*—was part of ritual ceremonies like marriage and an everyday item for those who could afford it. Chocolate contains theobromine, a stimulant, which may be why native people believed it brought them closer to the sacred world.

Spaniards in the New World considered drinking chocolate a vile practice; one called chocolate "the Devil's vomit." In time, however, they introduced the beverage to Spain. At first, chocolate was available only in the Spanish court, where the elite mixed it with sugar and other spices. Later, as its availability spread, chocolate gained a reputation as a love potion.

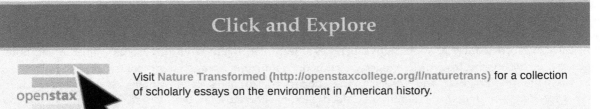

Click and Explore

Visit **Nature Transformed (http://openstaxcollege.org/l/naturetrans)** for a collection of scholarly essays on the environment in American history.

The crossing of the Atlantic by plants like cacao and tobacco illustrates the ways in which the discovery of the New World changed the habits and behaviors of Europeans. Europeans changed the New World in turn, not least by bringing Old World animals to the Americas. On his second voyage, Christopher Columbus brought pigs, horses, cows, and chickens to the islands of the Caribbean. Later explorers followed suit, introducing new animals or reintroducing ones that had died out (like horses). With less vulnerability to disease, these animals often fared better than humans in their new home, thriving both in the wild and in domestication.

Europeans encountered New World animals as well. Because European Christians understood the world as a place of warfare between God and Satan, many believed the Americas, which lacked Christianity, were home to the Devil and his minions. The exotic, sometimes bizarre, appearances and habits of animals in the Americas that were previously unknown to Europeans, such as manatees, sloths, and poisonous snakes, confirmed this association. Over time, however, they began to rely more on observation of the natural world than solely on scripture. This shift—from seeing the Bible as the source of all received wisdom to trusting observation or empiricism—is one of the major outcomes of the era of early globalization.

Travelers between the Americas, Africa, and Europe also included microbes: silent, invisible life forms that had profound and devastating consequences. Native peoples had no immunity to diseases from across the Atlantic, to which they had never been exposed. European explorers unwittingly brought with them chickenpox, measles, mumps, and **smallpox**, which ravaged native peoples despite their attempts to treat the diseases, decimating some populations and wholly destroying others (**Figure 2.16**).

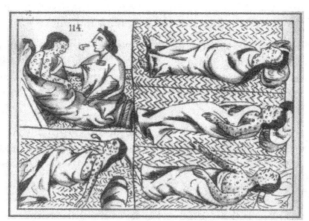

Figure 2.16 This sixteenth-century Aztec drawing shows the suffering of a typical victim of smallpox. Smallpox and other contagious diseases brought by European explorers decimated Indian populations in the Americas.

In eastern North America, some native peoples interpreted death from disease as a hostile act. Some groups, including the Iroquois, engaged in raids or "**mourning wars**," taking enemy prisoners in order to assuage their grief and replace the departed. In a special ritual, the prisoners were "requickened"—assigned the identity of a dead person—and adopted by the bereaved family to take the place of their dead. As the toll from disease rose, mourning wars intensified and expanded.

Key Terms

Black Legend Spain's reputation as bloodthirsty conquistadors

Calvinism a branch of Protestantism started by John Calvin, emphasizing human powerlessness before an omniscient God and stressing the idea of predestination

Columbian Exchange the movement of plants, animals, and diseases across the Atlantic due to European exploration of the Americas

commodification the transformation of something—for example, an item of ritual significance—into a commodity with monetary value

encomienda legal rights to native labor as granted by the Spanish crown

Hispaniola the island in the Caribbean, present-day Haiti and Dominican Republic, where Columbus first landed and established a Spanish colony

indulgences documents for purchase that absolved sinners of their errant behavior

joint stock company a business entity in which investors provide the capital and assume the risk in order to reap significant returns

mercantilism the protectionist economic principle that nations should control trade with their colonies to ensure a favorable balance of trade

mourning wars raids or wars that tribes waged in eastern North America in order to replace members lost to smallpox and other diseases

Pilgrims Separatists, led by William Bradford, who established the first English settlement in New England

privateers sea captains to whom the British government had given permission to raid Spanish ships at will

probanza de mérito proof of merit: a letter written by a Spanish explorer to the crown to gain royal patronage

Protestant Reformation the schism in Catholicism that began with Martin Luther and John Calvin in the early sixteenth century

Puritans a group of religious reformers in the sixteenth and seventeenth centuries who wanted to "purify" the Church of England by ridding it of practices associated with the Catholic Church and advocating greater purity of doctrine and worship

Roanoke the first English colony in Virginia, which mysteriously disappeared sometime between 1587 and 1590

Separatists a faction of Puritans who advocated complete separation from the Church of England

smallpox a disease that Europeans accidentally brought to the New World, killing millions of Indians, who had no immunity to the disease

sugarcane one of the primary crops of the Americas, which required a tremendous amount of labor to cultivate

Summary

2.1 Portuguese Exploration and Spanish Conquest

Although Portugal opened the door to exploration of the Atlantic World, Spanish explorers quickly made inroads into the Americas. Spurred by Christopher Columbus's glowing reports of the riches to be found in the New World, throngs of Spanish conquistadors set off to find and conquer new lands. They accomplished this through a combination of military strength and strategic alliances with native peoples. Spanish rulers Ferdinand and Isabella promoted the acquisition of these new lands in order to strengthen and glorify their own empire. As Spain's empire expanded and riches flowed in from the Americas, the Spanish experienced a golden age of art and literature.

2.2 Religious Upheavals in the Developing Atlantic World

The sixteenth century witnessed a new challenge to the powerful Catholic Church. The reformist doctrines of Martin Luther and John Calvin attracted many people dissatisfied with Catholicism, and Protestantism spread across northern Europe, spawning many subgroups with conflicting beliefs. Spain led the charge against Protestantism, leading to decades of undeclared religious wars between Spain and England, and religious intolerance and violence characterized much of the sixteenth and seventeenth centuries. Despite the efforts of the Catholic Church and Catholic nations, however, Protestantism had taken hold by 1600.

2.3 Challenges to Spain's Supremacy

By the beginning of the seventeenth century, Spain's rivals—England, France, and the Dutch Republic—had each established an Atlantic presence, with greater or lesser success, in the race for imperial power. None of the new colonies, all in the eastern part of North America, could match the Spanish possessions for gold and silver resources. Nonetheless, their presence in the New World helped these nations establish claims that they hoped could halt the runaway growth of Spain's Catholic empire. English colonists in Virginia suffered greatly, expecting riches to fall into their hands and finding reality a harsh blow. However, the colony at Jamestown survived, and the output of England's islands in the West Indies soon grew to be an important source of income for the country. New France and New Netherlands were modest colonial holdings in the northeast of the continent, but these colonies' thriving fur trade with native peoples, and their alliances with those peoples, helped to create the foundation for later shifts in the global balance of power.

2.4 New Worlds in the Americas: Labor, Commerce, and the Columbian Exchange

In the minds of European rulers, colonies existed to create wealth for imperial powers. Guided by mercantilist ideas, European rulers and investors hoped to enrich their own nations and themselves, in order to gain the greatest share of what was believed to be a limited amount of wealth. In their own individual quest for riches and preeminence, European colonizers who traveled to the Americas blazed new and disturbing paths, such as the *encomienda* system of forced labor and the use of tens of thousands of Africans as slaves.

All native inhabitants of the Americas who came into contact with Europeans found their worlds turned upside down as the new arrivals introduced their religions and ideas about property and goods. Europeans gained new foods, plants, and animals in the Columbian Exchange, turning whatever they could into a commodity to be bought and sold, and Indians were introduced to diseases that nearly destroyed them. At every turn, however, Indians placed limits on European colonization and resisted the newcomers' ways.

Review Questions

1. Which country initiated the era of Atlantic exploration?
    A. France
    B. Spain
    C. England
    D. Portugal

2. Which country established the first colonies in the Americas?
    A. England
    B. Portugal
    C. Spain
    D. the Netherlands

3. Where did Christopher Columbus first land?
    A. Hispaniola
    B. the Bahamas
    C. Jamestown
    D. Mexico

4. Why did the authors of *probanzas de méritos* choose to write in the way that they did? What should we consider when we interpret these documents today?

5. Where did the Protestant Reformation begin?
    A. Northern Europe
    B. Spain
    C. England
    D. the American colonies

6. What was the chief goal of the Puritans?
    A. to achieve a lasting peace with the Catholic nations of Spain and France
    B. to eliminate any traces of Catholicism from the Church of England
    C. to assist Henry VIII in his quest for an annulment to his marriage
    D. to create a hierarchy within the Church of England modeled on that of the Catholic Church

7. What reforms to the Catholic Church did Martin Luther and John Calvin call for?

8. Why didn't England make stronger attempts to colonize the New World before the late sixteenth to early seventeenth century?

A. English attention was turned to internal struggles and the encroaching Catholic menace to Scotland and Ireland.
B. The English monarchy did not want to declare direct war on Spain by attempting to colonize the Americas.
C. The English military was occupied in battling for control of New Netherlands.
D. The English crown refused to fund colonial expeditions.

9. What was the main goal of the French in colonizing the Americas?
    A. establishing a colony with French subjects
    B. trading, especially for furs
    C. gaining control of shipping lanes
    D. spreading Catholicism among native peoples

10. What were some of the main differences among the non-Spanish colonies?

11. How could Spaniards obtain *encomiendas*?
    A. by serving the Spanish crown
    B. by buying them from other Spaniards
    C. by buying them from native chiefs
    D. by inheriting them

12. Which of the following best describes the Columbian Exchange?
    A. the letters Columbus and other conquistadors exchanged with the Spanish crown
    B. an exchange of plants, animals, and diseases between Europe and the Americas
    C. a form of trade between the Spanish and natives
    D. the way in which explorers exchanged information about new lands to conquer

13. Why did diseases like smallpox affect Indians so badly?
    A. Indians were less robust than Europeans.
    B. Europeans deliberately infected Indians.
    C. Indians had no immunity to European diseases.
    D. Conditions in the Americas were so harsh that Indians and Europeans alike were devastated by disease.

Critical Thinking Questions

14. What were the consequences of the religious upheavals of the sixteenth and seventeenth centuries?

15. What types of labor systems were used in the Americas? Did systems of unfree labor serve more than an economic function?

16. What is meant by the Columbian Exchange? Who was affected the most by the exchange?

17. What were the various goals of the colonial European powers in the expansion of their empires? To what extent were they able to achieve these goals? Where did they fail?

18. On the whole, what was the impact of early European explorations on the New World? What was the impact of the New World on Europeans?

CHAPTER 3

Creating New Social Orders: Colonial Societies, 1500–1700

Figure 3.1 John Smith's famous map of Virginia (1622) illustrates many geopolitical features of early colonization. In the upper left, Powhatan, who governed a powerful local confederation of Algonquian communities, sits above other local chiefs, denoting his authority. Another native figure, Susquehannock, who appears in the upper right, visually reinforces the message that the English did not control the land beyond a few outposts along the Chesapeake.

Chapter Outline

3.1 Spanish Exploration and Colonial Society
3.2 Colonial Rivalries: Dutch and French Colonial Ambitions
3.3 English Settlements in America
3.4 The Impact of Colonization

Introduction

By the mid-seventeenth century, the geopolitical map of North America had become a patchwork of imperial designs and ambitions as the Spanish, Dutch, French, and English reinforced their claims to parts of the land. Uneasiness, punctuated by violent clashes, prevailed in the border zones between the Europeans' territorial claims. Meanwhile, still-powerful native peoples waged war to drive the invaders from the continent. In the Chesapeake Bay and New England colonies, conflicts erupted as the English pushed against their native neighbors (Figure 3.1).

The rise of colonial societies in the Americas brought Native Americans, Africans, and Europeans together for the first time, highlighting the radical social, cultural, and religious differences that hampered their ability to understand each other. European settlement affected every aspect of the land and its people, bringing goods, ideas, and diseases that transformed the Americas. Reciprocally, Native American practices, such as the use of tobacco, profoundly altered European habits and tastes.

3.1 Spanish Exploration and Colonial Society

By the end of this section, you will be able to:
- Identify the main Spanish American colonial settlements of the 1500s and 1600s
- Discuss economic, political, and demographic similarities and differences between the Spanish colonies

During the 1500s, Spain expanded its colonial empire to the Philippines in the Far East and to areas in the Americas that later became the United States. The Spanish dreamed of mountains of gold and silver and imagined converting thousands of eager Indians to Catholicism. In their vision of colonial society, everyone would know his or her place. Patriarchy (the rule of men over family, society, and government) shaped the Spanish colonial world. Women occupied a lower status. In all matters, the Spanish held themselves to be atop the social pyramid, with native peoples and Africans beneath them. Both Africans and native peoples, however, contested Spanish claims to dominance. Everywhere the Spanish settled, they brought devastating diseases, such as smallpox, that led to a horrific loss of life among native peoples. European diseases killed far more native inhabitants than did Spanish swords.

The world native peoples had known before the coming of the Spanish was further upset by Spanish colonial practices. The Spanish imposed the *encomienda* system in the areas they controlled. Under this system, authorities assigned Indian workers to mine and plantation owners with the understanding that the recipients would defend the colony and teach the workers the tenets of Christianity. In reality, the *encomienda* system exploited native workers. It was eventually replaced by another colonial labor system, the *repartimiento*, which required Indian towns to supply a pool of labor for Spanish overlords.

ST. AUGUSTINE, FLORIDA

Spain gained a foothold in present-day Florida, viewing that area and the lands to the north as a logical extension of their Caribbean empire. In 1513, Juan Ponce de León had claimed the area around today's St. Augustine for the Spanish crown, naming the land Pascua Florida (Feast of Flowers, or Easter) for the nearest feast day. Ponce de León was unable to establish a permanent settlement there, but by 1565, Spain was in need of an outpost to confront the French and English privateers using Florida as a base from which

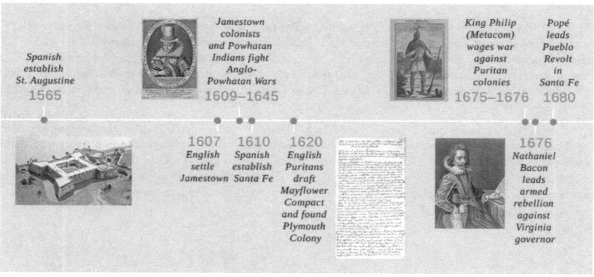

Figure 3.2

to attack treasure-laden Spanish ships heading from Cuba to Spain. The threat to Spanish interests took a new turn in 1562 when a group of French Protestants (Huguenots) established a small settlement they called Fort Caroline, north of St. Augustine. With the authorization of King Philip II, Spanish nobleman Pedro Menéndez led an attack on Fort Caroline, killing most of the colonists and destroying the fort. Eliminating Fort Caroline served dual purposes for the Spanish—it helped reduce the danger from French privateers and eradicated the French threat to Spain's claim to the area. The contest over Florida illustrates how European rivalries spilled over into the Americas, especially religious conflict between Catholics and Protestants.

In 1565, the victorious Menéndez founded St. Augustine, now the oldest European settlement in the Americas. In the process, the Spanish displaced the local **Timucua** Indians from their ancient town of Seloy, which had stood for thousands of years (Figure 3.3). The Timucua suffered greatly from diseases introduced by the Spanish, shrinking from a population of around 200,000 pre-contact to fifty thousand in 1590. By 1700, only one thousand Timucua remained. As in other areas of Spanish conquest, Catholic priests worked to bring about a spiritual conquest by forcing the surviving Timucua, demoralized and reeling from catastrophic losses of family and community, to convert to Catholicism.

Figure 3.3 In this drawing by French artist Jacques le Moyne de Morgues, Timucua flee the Spanish settlers, who arrive by ship. Le Moyne lived at Fort Caroline, the French outpost, before the Spanish destroyed the colony in 1562.

Spanish Florida made an inviting target for Spain's imperial rivals, especially the English, who wanted to gain access to the Caribbean. In 1586, Spanish settlers in St. Augustine discovered their vulnerability to attack when the English pirate Sir Francis Drake destroyed the town with a fleet of twenty ships and one hundred men. Over the next several decades, the Spanish built more wooden forts, all of which were burnt by raiding European rivals. Between 1672 and 1695, the Spanish constructed a stone fort, Castillo de San Marcos (Figure 3.4), to better defend St. Augustine against challengers.

Figure 3.4 The Spanish fort of Castillo de San Marcos helped Spanish colonists in St. Augustine fend off marauding privateers from rival European countries.

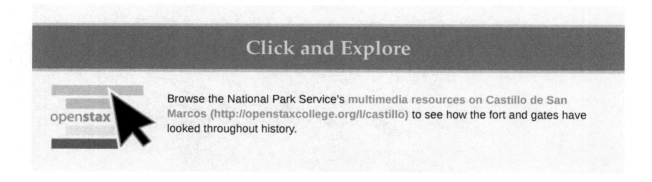

Click and Explore

Browse the National Park Service's multimedia resources on Castillo de San Marcos (http://openstaxcollege.org/l/castillo) to see how the fort and gates have looked throughout history.

SANTA FE, NEW MEXICO

Further west, the Spanish in Mexico, intent on expanding their empire, looked north to the land of the Pueblo Indians. Under orders from King Philip II, Juan de Oñate explored the American southwest for Spain in the late 1590s. The Spanish hoped that what we know as New Mexico would yield gold and silver, but the land produced little of value to them. In 1610, Spanish settlers established themselves at Santa Fe—originally named La Villa Real de la Santa Fe de San Francisco de Asís, or "Royal City of the Holy Faith of St. Francis of Assisi"—where many Pueblo villages were located. Santa Fe became the capital of the Kingdom of New Mexico, an outpost of the larger Spanish Viceroyalty of New Spain, which had its headquarters in Mexico City.

As they had in other Spanish colonies, Franciscan missionaries labored to bring about a spiritual conquest by converting the Pueblo to Catholicism. At first, the Pueblo adopted the parts of Catholicism that dovetailed with their own long-standing view of the world. However, Spanish priests insisted that natives discard their old ways entirely and angered the Pueblo by focusing on the young, drawing them away from their parents. This deep insult, combined with an extended period of drought and increased attacks by local Apache and Navajo in the 1670s—troubles that the Pueblo came to believe were linked to the Spanish presence—moved the Pueblo to push the Spanish and their religion from the area. Pueblo leader Popé demanded a return to native ways so the hardships his people faced would end. To him and to thousands of others, it seemed obvious that "when Jesus came, the Corn Mothers went away." The expulsion of the Spanish would bring a return to prosperity and a pure, native way of life.

In 1680, the Pueblo launched a coordinated rebellion against the Spanish. The Pueblo Revolt killed over four hundred Spaniards and drove the rest of the settlers, perhaps as many as two thousand, south toward Mexico. However, as droughts and attacks by rival tribes continued, the Spanish sensed an opportunity to regain their foothold. In 1692, they returned and reasserted their control of the area. Some of the Spanish explained the Pueblo success in 1680 as the work of the Devil. Satan, they believed, had stirred up the Pueblo to take arms against God's chosen people—the Spanish—but the Spanish, and their God, had prevailed in the end.

3.2 Colonial Rivalries: Dutch and French Colonial Ambitions

By the end of this section, you will be able to:
- Compare and contrast the development and character of the French and Dutch colonies in North America
- Discuss the economies of the French and Dutch colonies in North America

Seventeenth-century French and Dutch colonies in North America were modest in comparison to Spain's colossal global empire. New France and New Netherland remained small commercial operations focused on the fur trade and did not attract an influx of migrants. The Dutch in New Netherland confined their operations to Manhattan Island, Long Island, the Hudson River Valley, and what later became New Jersey. Dutch trade goods circulated widely among the native peoples in these areas and also traveled well into the interior of the continent along preexisting native trade routes. French *habitants*, or farmer-settlers, eked out an existence along the St. Lawrence River. French fur traders and missionaries, however, ranged far into the interior of North America, exploring the Great Lakes region and the Mississippi River. These pioneers gave France somewhat inflated imperial claims to lands that nonetheless remained firmly under the dominion of native peoples.

FUR TRADING IN NEW NETHERLAND

The Dutch Republic emerged as a major commercial center in the 1600s. Its fleets plied the waters of the Atlantic, while other Dutch ships sailed to the Far East, returning with prized spices like pepper to be sold in the bustling ports at home, especially Amsterdam. In North America, Dutch traders established themselves first on Manhattan Island.

One of the Dutch directors-general of the North American settlement, Peter Stuyvesant, served from 1647 to 1664 and expanded the fledgling outpost of New Netherland east to present-day Long Island and for many miles north along the Hudson River. The resulting elongated colony served primarily as a fur-trading post, with the powerful Dutch West India Company controlling all commerce. Fort Amsterdam, on the southern tip of Manhattan Island, defended the growing city of New Amsterdam. In 1655, Stuyvesant took over the small outpost of New Sweden along the banks of the Delaware River in present-day New Jersey, Pennsylvania, and Delaware. He also defended New Amsterdam from Indian attacks by ordering African slaves to build a protective wall on the city's northeastern border, giving present-day Wall Street its name (Figure 3.5).

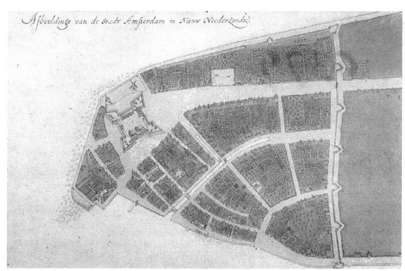

Figure 3.5 The Castello Plan is the only extant map of 1660 New Amsterdam (present-day New York City). The line with spikes on the right side of the colony is the northeastern wall for which Wall Street was named.

New Netherland failed to attract many Dutch colonists; by 1664, only nine thousand people were living there. Conflict with native peoples, as well as dissatisfaction with the Dutch West India Company's trading practices, made the Dutch outpost an undesirable place for many migrants. The small size of the population meant a severe labor shortage, and to complete the arduous tasks of early settlement, the Dutch West India Company imported some 450 African slaves between 1626 and 1664. (The company had involved itself heavily in the slave trade and in 1637 captured Elmina, the slave-trading post on the west coast of Africa, from the Portuguese.) The shortage of labor also meant that New Netherland welcomed non-Dutch immigrants, including Protestants from Germany, Sweden, Denmark, and England, and embraced a degree of religious tolerance, allowing Jewish immigrants to become residents beginning in the 1650s. Thus, a wide variety of people lived in New Netherland from the start. Indeed, one observer claimed eighteen different languages could be heard on the streets of New Amsterdam. As new settlers arrived, the colony of New Netherland stretched farther to the north and the west (Figure 3.6).

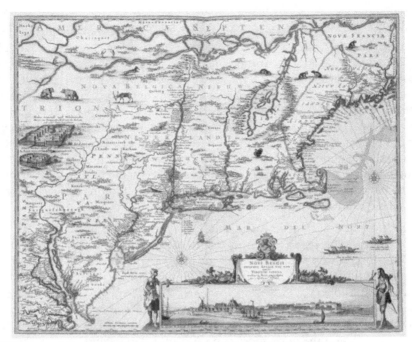

Figure 3.6   This 1684 map of New Netherland shows the extent of Dutch settlement.

The Dutch West India Company found the business of colonization in New Netherland to be expensive. To share some of the costs, it granted Dutch merchants who invested heavily in it **patroonships**, or large tracts of land and the right to govern the tenants there. In return, the shareholder who gained the patroonship promised to pay for the passage of at least thirty Dutch farmers to populate the colony. One of the largest patroonships was granted to Kiliaen van Rensselaer, one of the directors of the Dutch West India Company; it covered most of present-day Albany and Rensselaer Counties. This pattern of settlement created a yawning gap in wealth and status between the tenants, who paid rent, and the wealthy patroons.

During the summer trading season, Indians gathered at trading posts such as the Dutch site at Beverwijck (present-day Albany), where they exchanged furs for guns, blankets, and alcohol. The furs, especially beaver pelts destined for the lucrative European millinery market, would be sent down the Hudson River to New Amsterdam. There, slaves or workers would load them aboard ships bound for Amsterdam.

Click and Explore

Explore an interactive map of New Amsterdam in 1660 (http://openstaxcollege.org/l/WNET) that shows the city plan and the locations of various structures, including houses, businesses, and public buildings. Rolling over the map reveals relevant historical details, such as street names, the identities of certain buildings and businesses, and the names of residents of the houses (when known).

COMMERCE AND CONVERSION IN NEW FRANCE

After Jacques Cartier's voyages of discovery in the 1530s, France showed little interest in creating permanent colonies in North America until the early 1600s, when Samuel de Champlain established Quebec as a French fur-trading outpost. Although the fur trade was lucrative, the French saw Canada as an inhospitable frozen wasteland, and by 1640, fewer than four hundred settlers had made their home there. The sparse French presence meant that colonists depended on the local native Algonquian people; without them, the French would have perished. French fishermen, explorers, and fur traders made extensive contact with the Algonquian. The Algonquian, in turn, tolerated the French because the colonists supplied them with firearms for their ongoing war with the Iroquois. Thus, the French found themselves escalating native wars and supporting the Algonquian against the Iroquois, who received weapons from their Dutch trading partners. These seventeenth-century conflicts centered on the lucrative trade in beaver pelts, earning them the name of the Beaver Wars. In these wars, fighting between rival native peoples spread throughout the Great Lakes region.

A handful of French Jesuit priests also made their way to Canada, intent on converting the native inhabitants to Catholicism. The **Jesuits** were members of the Society of Jesus, an elite religious order founded in the 1540s to spread Catholicism and combat the spread of Protestantism. The first Jesuits arrived in Quebec in the 1620s, and for the next century, their numbers did not exceed forty priests. Like the Spanish Franciscan missionaries, the Jesuits in the colony called New France labored to convert the native peoples to Catholicism. They wrote detailed annual reports about their progress in bringing the faith to the Algonquian and, beginning in the 1660s, to the Iroquois. These documents are known as the *Jesuit Relations* (Figure 3.7), and they provide a rich source for understanding both the Jesuit view of the Indians and the Indian response to the colonizers.

One native convert to Catholicism, a Mohawk woman named Katherine Tekakwitha, so impressed the priests with her piety that a Jesuit named Claude Chauchetière attempted to make her a saint in the Church. However, the effort to canonize Tekakwitha faltered when leaders of the Church balked at elevating a "savage" to such a high status; she was eventually canonized in 2012. French colonizers pressured the native inhabitants of New France to convert, but they virtually never saw native peoples as their equals.

DEFINING "AMERICAN"

✦ *A Jesuit Priest on Indian Healing Traditions*

The *Jesuit Relations* (Figure 3.7) provide incredible detail about Indian life. For example, the 1636 edition, written by the Catholic priest Jean de Brébeuf, addresses the devastating effects of disease on native peoples and the efforts made to combat it.

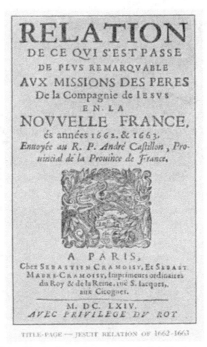

Figure 3.7 French Jesuit missionaries to New France kept detailed records of their interactions with—and observations of—the Algonquian and Iroquois that they converted to Catholicism. (credit: Project Gutenberg).

> Let us return to the feasts. The *Aoutaerohi* is a remedy which is only for one particular kind of disease, which they call also *Aoutaerohi*, from the name of a little Demon as large as the fist, which they say is in the body of the sick man, especially in the part which pains him. They find out that they are sick of this disease, by means of a dream, or by the intervention of some Sorcerer. . . .
>
> Of three kinds of games especially in use among these Peoples,—namely, the games of crosse [lacrosse], dish, and straw,—the first two are, they say, most healing. Is not this worthy of compassion? There is a poor sick man, fevered of body and almost dying, and a miserable Sorcerer will order for him, as a cooling remedy, a game of crosse. Or the sick man himself, sometimes, will have dreamed that he must die unless the whole country shall play crosse for his health; and, no matter how little may be his credit, you will see then in a beautiful field, Village contending against Village, as to who will play crosse the better, and betting against one another Beaver robes and Porcelain collars, so as to excite greater interest.

According to this account, how did Indians attempt to cure disease? Why did they prescribe a game of lacrosse? What benefits might these games have for the sick?

3.3 English Settlements in America

By the end of this section, you will be able to:
- Identify the first English settlements in America
- Describe the differences between the Chesapeake Bay colonies and the New England colonies
- Compare and contrast the wars between native inhabitants and English colonists in both the Chesapeake Bay and New England colonies
- Explain the role of Bacon's Rebellion in the rise of chattel slavery in Virginia

At the start of the seventeenth century, the English had not established a permanent settlement in the Americas. Over the next century, however, they outpaced their rivals. The English encouraged emigration far more than the Spanish, French, or Dutch. They established nearly a dozen colonies, sending swarms of immigrants to populate the land. England had experienced a dramatic rise in population in the sixteenth century, and the colonies appeared a welcoming place for those who faced overcrowding and grinding poverty at home. Thousands of English migrants arrived in the Chesapeake Bay colonies of Virginia and Maryland to work in the tobacco fields. Another stream, this one of pious Puritan families, sought to live as they believed scripture demanded and established the Plymouth, Massachusetts Bay, New Haven, Connecticut, and Rhode Island colonies of New England (Figure 3.8).

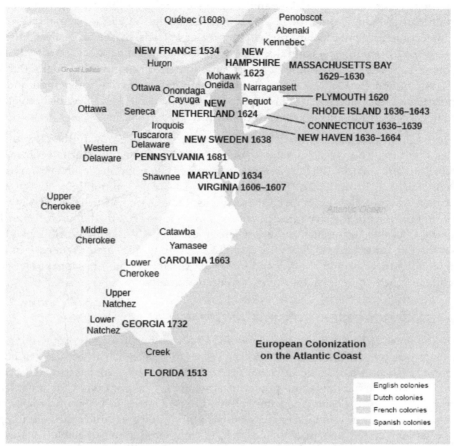

Figure 3.8 In the early seventeenth century, thousands of English settlers came to what are now Virginia, Maryland, and the New England states in search of opportunity and a better life.

THE DIVERGING CULTURES OF THE NEW ENGLAND AND CHESAPEAKE COLONIES

Promoters of English colonization in North America, many of whom never ventured across the Atlantic, wrote about the bounty the English would find there. These boosters of colonization hoped to turn a profit—whether by importing raw resources or providing new markets for English goods—and spread Protestantism. The English migrants who actually made the journey, however, had different goals. In Chesapeake Bay, English migrants established Virginia and Maryland with a decidedly commercial orientation. Though the early Virginians at Jamestown hoped to find gold, they and the settlers in Maryland quickly discovered that growing tobacco was the only sure means of making money. Thousands of unmarried, unemployed, and impatient young Englishmen, along with a few Englishwomen, pinned their hopes for a better life on the tobacco fields of these two colonies.

A very different group of English men and women flocked to the cold climate and rocky soil of New England, spurred by religious motives. Many of the Puritans crossing the Atlantic were people who brought families and children. Often they were following their ministers in a migration "beyond the seas," envisioning a new English Israel where reformed Protestantism would grow and thrive, providing a model for the rest of the Christian world and a counter to what they saw as the Catholic menace. While the English in Virginia and Maryland worked on expanding their profitable tobacco fields, the English in New England built towns focused on the church, where each congregation decided what was best for itself. The Congregational Church is the result of the Puritan enterprise in America. Many historians believe the fault lines separating what later became the North and South in the United States originated in the profound differences between the Chesapeake and New England colonies.

The source of those differences lay in England's domestic problems. Increasingly in the early 1600s, the English state church—the Church of England, established in the 1530s—demanded conformity, or compliance with its practices, but Puritans pushed for greater reforms. By the 1620s, the Church of England began to see leading Puritan ministers and their followers as outlaws, a national security threat because of their opposition to its power. As the noose of conformity tightened around them, many Puritans decided to remove to New England. By 1640, New England had a population of twenty-five thousand. Meanwhile, many loyal members of the Church of England, who ridiculed and mocked Puritans both at home and in New England, flocked to Virginia for economic opportunity.

The troubles in England escalated in the 1640s when civil war broke out, pitting Royalist supporters of King Charles I and the Church of England against Parliamentarians, the Puritan reformers and their supporters in Parliament. In 1649, the Parliamentarians gained the upper hand and, in an unprecedented move, executed Charles I. In the 1650s, therefore, England became a republic, a state without a king. English colonists in America closely followed these events. Indeed, many Puritans left New England and returned home to take part in the struggle against the king and the national church. Other English men and women in the Chesapeake colonies and elsewhere in the English Atlantic World looked on in horror at the mayhem the Parliamentarians, led by the Puritan insurgents, appeared to unleash in England. The turmoil in England made the administration and imperial oversight of the Chesapeake and New England colonies difficult, and the two regions developed divergent cultures.

THE CHESAPEAKE COLONIES: VIRGINIA AND MARYLAND

The Chesapeake colonies of Virginia and Maryland served a vital purpose in the developing seventeenth-century English empire by providing tobacco, a cash crop. However, the early history of Jamestown did not suggest the English outpost would survive. From the outset, its settlers struggled both with each other and with the native inhabitants, the powerful Powhatan, who controlled the area. Jealousies and infighting among the English destabilized the colony. One member, John Smith, whose famous map begins this chapter, took control and exercised near-dictatorial powers, which furthered aggravated the squabbling. The settlers' inability to grow their own food compounded this unstable situation. They were essentially employees of the Virginia Company of London, an English joint-stock company, in which investors provided the capital and assumed the risk in order to reap the profit, and they had to make a profit for their shareholders as well as for themselves. Most initially devoted themselves to finding gold and silver instead of finding ways to grow their own food.

Early Struggles and the Development of the Tobacco Economy

Poor health, lack of food, and fighting with native peoples took the lives of many of the original Jamestown settlers. The winter of 1609–1610, which became known as "the starving time," came close to annihilating the colony. By June 1610, the few remaining settlers had decided to abandon the area; only the last-minute arrival of a supply ship from England prevented another failed colonization effort. The supply ship brought new settlers, but only twelve hundred of the seventy-five hundred who came to Virginia between 1607 and 1624 survived.

MY STORY

✪ *George Percy on "The Starving Time"*

George Percy, the youngest son of an English nobleman, was in the first group of settlers at the Jamestown Colony. He kept a journal describing their experiences; in the excerpt below, he reports on the privations of the colonists' third winter.

> Now all of us at James Town, beginning to feel that sharp prick of hunger which no man truly describe but he which has tasted the bitterness thereof, a world of miseries ensued as the sequel will express unto you, in so much that some to satisfy their hunger have robbed the store for the which I caused them to be executed. Then having fed upon horses and other beasts as long as they lasted, we were glad to make shift with vermin as dogs, cats, rats, and mice. All was fish that came to net to satisfy cruel hunger as to eat boots, shoes, or any other leather some could come by, and, those being spent and devoured, some were enforced to search the woods and to feed upon serpents and snakes and to dig the earth for wild and unknown roots, where many of our men were cut off of and slain by the savages. And now famine beginning to look ghastly and pale in every face that nothing was spared to maintain life and to do those things which seem incredible as to dig up dead corpses out of graves and to eat them, and some have licked up the blood which has fallen from their weak fellows.
>
> —George Percy, "A True Relation of the Proceedings and Occurances of Moment which have happened in Virginia from the Time Sir Thomas Gates shipwrecked upon the Bermudes anno 1609 until my departure out of the Country which was in anno Domini 1612," London 1624

What is your reaction to George Percy's story? How do you think Jamestown managed to survive after such an experience? What do you think the Jamestown colonists learned?

By the 1620s, Virginia had weathered the worst and gained a degree of permanence. Political stability came slowly, but by 1619, the fledgling colony was operating under the leadership of a governor, a council, and a House of Burgesses. Economic stability came from the lucrative cultivation of tobacco. Smoking tobacco was a long-standing practice among native peoples, and English and other European consumers soon adopted it. In 1614, the Virginia colony began exporting tobacco back to England, which earned it a sizable profit and saved the colony from ruin. A second tobacco colony, Maryland, was formed in 1634, when King Charles I granted its charter to the Calvert family for their loyal service to England. Cecilius Calvert, the second Lord Baltimore, conceived of Maryland as a refuge for English Catholics.

Growing tobacco proved very labor-intensive (Figure 3.9), and the Chesapeake colonists needed a steady workforce to do the hard work of clearing the land and caring for the tender young plants. The mature leaf of the plant then had to be cured (dried), which necessitated the construction of drying barns. Once cured, the tobacco had to be packaged in hogsheads (large wooden barrels) and loaded aboard ship, which also required considerable labor.

Figure 3.9 In this 1670 painting by an unknown artist, slaves work in tobacco-drying sheds.

To meet these labor demands, early Virginians relied on indentured servants. An **indenture** is a labor contract that young, impoverished, and often illiterate Englishmen and occasionally Englishwomen signed in England, pledging to work for a number of years (usually between five and seven) growing tobacco in the Chesapeake colonies. In return, indentured servants received paid passage to America and food, clothing, and lodging. At the end of their indenture servants received "freedom dues," usually food and other provisions, including, in some cases, land provided by the colony. The promise of a new life in America was a strong attraction for members of England's underclass, who had few if any options at home. In the 1600s, some 100,000 indentured servants traveled to the Chesapeake Bay. Most were poor young men in their early twenties.

Life in the colonies proved harsh, however. Indentured servants could not marry, and they were subject to the will of the tobacco planters who bought their labor contracts. If they committed a crime or disobeyed their masters, they found their terms of service lengthened, often by several years. Female indentured servants faced special dangers in what was essentially a bachelor colony. Many were exploited by unscrupulous tobacco planters who seduced them with promises of marriage. These planters would then sell their pregnant servants to other tobacco planters to avoid the costs of raising a child.

Nonetheless, those indentured servants who completed their term of service often began new lives as tobacco planters. To entice even more migrants to the New World, the Virginia Company also implemented the **headright system**, in which those who paid their own passage to Virginia received fifty acres plus an additional fifty for each servant or family member they brought with them. The headright system and the promise of a new life for servants acted as powerful incentives for English migrants to hazard the journey to the New World.

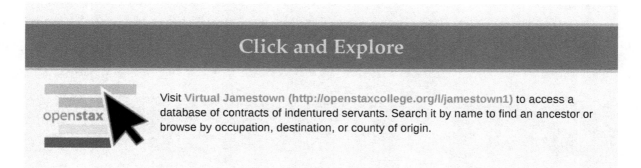

Click and Explore

Visit **Virtual Jamestown (http://openstaxcollege.org/l/jamestown1)** to access a database of contracts of indentured servants. Search it by name to find an ancestor or browse by occupation, destination, or county of origin.

The Anglo-Powhatan Wars

By choosing to settle along the rivers on the banks of the Chesapeake, the English unknowingly placed themselves at the center of the Powhatan Empire, a powerful Algonquian confederacy of thirty native groups with perhaps as many as twenty-two thousand people. The territory of the equally impressive Susquehannock people also bordered English settlements at the north end of the Chesapeake Bay.

Tensions ran high between the English and the Powhatan, and near-constant war prevailed. The First Anglo-Powhatan War (1609–1614) resulted not only from the English colonists' intrusion onto Powhatan land, but also from their refusal to follow native protocol by giving gifts. English actions infuriated and insulted the Powhatan. In 1613, the settlers captured Pocahontas (also called Matoaka), the daughter of a Powhatan headman named Wahunsonacook, and gave her in marriage to Englishman John Rolfe. Their union, and her choice to remain with the English, helped quell the war in 1614. Pocahontas converted to Christianity, changing her name to Rebecca, and sailed with her husband and several other Powhatan to England where she was introduced to King James I (Figure 3.10). Promoters of colonization publicized Pocahontas as an example of the good work of converting the Powhatan to Christianity.

Figure 3.10   This 1616 engraving by Simon van de Passe, completed when Pocahontas and John Rolfe were presented at court in England, is the only known contemporary image of Pocahontas. Note her European garb and pose. What message did the painter likely intend to convey with this portrait of Pocahontas, the daughter of a powerful Indian chief?

Click and Explore

Explore the interactive exhibit Changing Images of Pocahontas (http://openstaxcollege.org/l/pocahontas) on PBS's website to see the many ways artists have portrayed Pocahontas over the centuries.

Peace in Virginia did not last long. The Second Anglo-Powhatan War (1620s) broke out because of the expansion of the English settlement nearly one hundred miles into the interior, and because of the continued insults and friction caused by English activities. The Powhatan attacked in 1622 and succeeded in killing almost 350 English, about a third of the settlers. The English responded by annihilating every Powhatan village around Jamestown and from then on became even more intolerant. The Third Anglo-Powhatan War (1644–1646) began with a surprise attack in which the Powhatan killed around five hundred English colonists. However, their ultimate defeat in this conflict forced the Powhatan to acknowledge King Charles I as their sovereign. The Anglo-Powhatan Wars, spanning nearly forty years, illustrate the degree of native resistance that resulted from English intrusion into the Powhatan confederacy.

The Rise of Slavery in the Chesapeake Bay Colonies

The transition from indentured servitude to slavery as the main labor source for some English colonies happened first in the West Indies. On the small island of Barbados, colonized in the 1620s, English planters first grew tobacco as their main export crop, but in the 1640s, they converted to sugarcane and began increasingly to rely on African slaves. In 1655, England wrestled control of Jamaica from the Spanish and quickly turned it into a lucrative sugar island, run on slave labor, for its expanding empire. While slavery was slower to take hold in the Chesapeake colonies, by the end of the seventeenth century, both Virginia and Maryland had also adopted chattel slavery—which legally defined Africans as property and not people—as the dominant form of labor to grow tobacco. Chesapeake colonists also enslaved native people.

When the first Africans arrived in Virginia in 1619, slavery—which did not exist in England—had not yet become an institution in colonial America. Many Africans worked as servants and, like their white counterparts, could acquire land of their own. Some Africans who converted to Christianity became free landowners with white servants. The change in the status of Africans in the Chesapeake to that of slaves occurred in the last decades of the seventeenth century.

Bacon's Rebellion, an uprising of both whites and blacks who believed that the Virginia government was impeding their access to land and wealth and seemed to do little to clear the land of Indians, hastened the transition to African slavery in the Chesapeake colonies. The rebellion takes its name from Nathaniel Bacon, a wealthy young Englishman who arrived in Virginia in 1674. Despite an early friendship with Virginia's royal governor, William Berkeley, Bacon found himself excluded from the governor's circle of influential friends and councilors. He wanted land on the Virginia frontier, but the governor, fearing war with neighboring Indian tribes, forbade further expansion. Bacon marshaled others, especially former indentured servants who believed the governor was limiting their economic opportunities and denying them the right to own tobacco farms. Bacon's followers believed Berkeley's frontier policy didn't protect English settlers enough. Worse still in their eyes, Governor Berkeley tried to keep peace in Virginia by signing treaties with various local native peoples. Bacon and his followers, who saw all Indians as an obstacle to their access to land, pursued a policy of extermination.

Tensions between the English and the native peoples in the Chesapeake colonies led to open conflict. In 1675, war broke out when Susquehannock warriors attacked settlements on Virginia's frontier, killing English planters and destroying English plantations, including one owned by Bacon. In 1676, Bacon and other Virginians attacked the Susquehannock without the governor's approval. When Berkeley ordered Bacon's arrest, Bacon led his followers to Jamestown, forced the governor to flee to the safety of Virginia's eastern shore, and then burned the city. The civil war known as Bacon's Rebellion, a vicious struggle between supporters of the governor and those who supported Bacon, ensued. Reports of the rebellion traveled back to England, leading Charles II to dispatch both royal troops and English commissioners to restore order in the tobacco colonies. By the end of 1676, Virginians loyal to the governor gained the upper hand, executing several leaders of the rebellion. Bacon escaped the hangman's noose, instead dying of dysentery. The rebellion fizzled in 1676, but Virginians remained divided as supporters of Bacon continued to harbor grievances over access to Indian land.

Bacon's Rebellion helped to catalyze the creation of a system of racial slavery in the Chesapeake colonies. At the time of the rebellion, indentured servants made up the majority of laborers in the region. Wealthy whites worried over the presence of this large class of laborers and the relative freedom they enjoyed, as well as the alliance that black and white servants had forged in the course of the rebellion. Replacing indentured servitude with black slavery diminished these risks, alleviating the reliance on white indentured servants, who were often dissatisfied and troublesome, and creating a caste of racially defined laborers whose movements were strictly controlled. It also lessened the possibility of further alliances between black and white workers. Racial slavery even served to heal some of the divisions between wealthy and poor whites, who could now unite as members of a "superior" racial group.

While colonial laws in the tobacco colonies had made slavery a legal institution before Bacon's Rebellion, new laws passed in the wake of the rebellion severely curtailed black freedom and laid the foundation for racial slavery. Virginia passed a law in 1680 prohibiting free blacks and slaves from bearing arms, banning blacks from congregating in large numbers, and establishing harsh punishments for slaves who assaulted Christians or attempted escape. Two years later, another Virginia law stipulated that all Africans brought to the colony would be slaves for life. Thus, the increasing reliance on slaves in the tobacco colonies—and the draconian laws instituted to control them—not only helped planters meet labor demands, but also served to assuage English fears of further uprisings and alleviate class tensions between rich and poor whites.

DEFINING "AMERICAN"

✿ Robert Beverley on Servants and Slaves

Robert Beverley was a wealthy Jamestown planter and slaveholder. This excerpt from his *History and Present State of Virginia*, published in 1705, clearly illustrates the contrast between white servants and black slaves.

> Their Servants, they distinguish by the Names of Slaves for Life, and Servants for a time. Slaves are the Negroes, and their Posterity, following the condition of the Mother, according to the Maxim, partus sequitur ventrem [status follows the womb]. They are call'd Slaves, in respect of the time of their Servitude, because it is for Life.
>
> Servants, are those which serve only for a few years, according to the time of their Indenture, or the Custom of the Country. The Custom of the Country takes place upon such as have no Indentures. The Law in this case is, that if such Servants be under Nineteen years of Age, they must be brought into Court, to have their Age adjudged; and from the Age they are judg'd to be of, they must serve until they reach four and twenty: But if they be adjudged upwards of Nineteen, they are then only to be Servants for the term of five Years.
>
> The Male-Servants, and Slaves of both Sexes, are employed together in Tilling and Manuring the Ground, in Sowing and Planting Tobacco, Corn, &c. Some Distinction indeed is made between them in their Cloaths, and Food; but the Work of both, is no other than what the Overseers, the Freemen, and the Planters themselves do.
>
> Sufficient Distinction is also made between the Female-Servants, and Slaves; for a White Woman is rarely or never put to work in the Ground, if she be good for any thing else: And to Discourage all Planters from using any Women so, their Law imposes the heaviest Taxes upon Female Servants working in the Ground, while it suffers all other white Women to be absolutely exempted: Whereas on the other hand, it is a common thing to work a Woman Slave out of Doors; nor does the Law make any Distinction in her Taxes, whether her Work be Abroad, or at Home.

According to Robert Beverley, what are the differences between servants and slaves? What protections did servants have that slaves did not?

PURITAN NEW ENGLAND

The second major area to be colonized by the English in the first half of the seventeenth century, New England, differed markedly in its founding principles from the commercially oriented Chesapeake tobacco colonies. Settled largely by waves of Puritan families in the 1630s, New England had a religious orientation from the start. In England, reform-minded men and women had been calling for greater changes to the English national church since the 1580s. These reformers, who followed the teachings of John Calvin and other Protestant reformers, were called Puritans because of their insistence on "purifying" the Church of England of what they believed to be un-scriptural, especially Catholic elements that lingered in its institutions and practices.

Many who provided leadership in early New England were learned ministers who had studied at Cambridge or Oxford but who, because they had questioned the practices of the Church of England, had been deprived of careers by the king and his officials in an effort to silence all dissenting voices. Other Puritan leaders, such as the first governor of the Massachusetts Bay Colony, John Winthrop, came from the privileged class of English gentry. These well-to-do Puritans and many thousands more left their English homes not to establish a land of religious freedom, but to practice their own religion without persecution. Puritan New England offered them the opportunity to live as they believed the Bible demanded. In their "New" England, they set out to create a model of reformed Protestantism, a new English Israel.

The conflict generated by Puritanism had divided English society, because the Puritans demanded reforms that undermined the traditional festive culture. For example, they denounced popular pastimes like bear-baiting—letting dogs attack a chained bear—which were often conducted on Sundays when people had a few leisure hours. In the culture where William Shakespeare had produced his masterpieces, Puritans called for an end to the theater, censuring playhouses as places of decadence. Indeed, the Bible itself became part of the struggle between Puritans and James I, who headed the Church of England. Soon after ascending the throne, James commissioned a new version of the Bible in an effort to stifle Puritan reliance on the Geneva Bible, which followed the teachings of John Calvin and placed God's authority above the monarch's. The King James Version, published in 1611, instead emphasized the majesty of kings.

During the 1620s and 1630s, the conflict escalated to the point where the state church prohibited Puritan ministers from preaching. In the Church's view, Puritans represented a national security threat, because their demands for cultural, social, and religious reforms undermined the king's authority. Unwilling to conform to the Church of England, many Puritans found refuge in the New World. Yet those who emigrated to the Americas were not united. Some called for a complete break with the Church of England, while others remained committed to reforming the national church.

Plymouth: The First Puritan Colony

The first group of Puritans to make their way across the Atlantic was a small contingent known as the Pilgrims. Unlike other Puritans, they insisted on a complete separation from the Church of England and had first migrated to the Dutch Republic seeking religious freedom. Although they found they could worship without hindrance there, they grew concerned that they were losing their Englishness as they saw their children begin to learn the Dutch language and adopt Dutch ways. In addition, the English Pilgrims (and others in Europe) feared another attack on the Dutch Republic by Catholic Spain. Therefore, in 1620, they moved on to found the Plymouth Colony in present-day Massachusetts. The governor of Plymouth, William Bradford, was a Separatist, a proponent of complete separation from the English state church. Bradford and the other Pilgrim Separatists represented a major challenge to the prevailing vision of a unified English national church and empire. On board the *Mayflower*, which was bound for Virginia but landed on the tip of Cape Cod, Bradford and forty other adult men signed the Mayflower Compact (**Figure 3.11**), which presented a religious (rather than an economic) rationale for colonization. The compact expressed a community ideal of working together. When a larger exodus of Puritans established the Massachusetts Bay Colony in the 1630s, the Pilgrims at Plymouth welcomed them and the two colonies cooperated with each other.

AMERICANA

✺ *The Mayflower Compact and Its Religious Rationale*

The Mayflower Compact, which forty-one Pilgrim men signed on board the *Mayflower* in Plymouth Harbor, has been called the first American governing document, predating the U.S. Constitution by over 150 years. But was the Mayflower Compact a constitution? How much authority did it convey, and to whom?

Figure 3.11   The original Mayflower Compact is no longer extant; only copies, such as this ca.1645 transcription by William Bradford, remain.

In the name of God, Amen. We, whose names are underwritten, the loyal subjects of our dread Sovereign Lord King James, by the Grace of God, of Great Britain, France, and Ireland, King, defender of the Faith, etc.

Having undertaken, for the Glory of God, and advancements of the Christian faith and honor of our King and Country, a voyage to plant the first colony in the Northern parts of Virginia, do by these presents, solemnly and mutually, in the presence of God, and one another, covenant and combine ourselves together into a civil body politic; for our better ordering, and preservation and furtherance of the ends aforesaid; and by virtue hereof to enact, constitute, and frame, such just and equal laws, ordinances, acts, constitutions, and offices, from time to time, as shall be thought most meet and convenient for the general good of the colony; unto which we promise all due submission and obedience.

In witness whereof we have hereunto subscribed our names at Cape Cod the 11th of November, in the year of the reign of our Sovereign Lord King James, of England, France, and Ireland, the eighteenth, and of Scotland the fifty-fourth, 1620

Different labor systems also distinguished early Puritan New England from the Chesapeake colonies. Puritans expected young people to work diligently at their calling, and all members of their large families, including children, did the bulk of the work necessary to run homes, farms, and businesses. Very few migrants came to New England as laborers; in fact, New England towns protected their disciplined homegrown workforce by refusing to allow outsiders in, assuring their sons and daughters of steady employment. New England's labor system produced remarkable results, notably a powerful maritime-based economy with scores of oceangoing ships and the crews necessary to sail them. New England mariners sailing New England–made ships transported Virginian tobacco and West Indian sugar throughout the Atlantic World.

"A City upon a Hill"

A much larger group of English Puritans left England in the 1630s, establishing the Massachusetts Bay Colony, the New Haven Colony, the Connecticut Colony, and Rhode Island. Unlike the exodus of young males to the Chesapeake colonies, these migrants were families with young children and their university-trained ministers. Their aim, according to John Winthrop (Figure 3.12), the first governor of Massachusetts Bay, was to create a model of reformed Protestantism—a "city upon a hill," a new English Israel. The idea of a "city upon a hill" made clear the religious orientation of the New England settlement, and the charter of the Massachusetts Bay Colony stated as a goal that the colony's people "may be soe religiously, peaceablie, and civilly governed, as their good Life and orderlie Conversacon, maie wynn and incite the Natives of Country, to the Knowledg and Obedience of the onlie true God and Saulor of Mankinde, and the Christian Fayth." To illustrate this, the seal of the Massachusetts Bay Company (Figure 3.12) shows a half-naked Indian who entreats more of the English to "come over and help us."

(a)   (b)

Figure 3.12 In the 1629 seal of the Massachusetts Bay Colony (a), an Indian is shown asking colonists to "Come over and help us." This seal indicates the religious ambitions of John Winthrop (b), the colony's first governor, for his "city upon a hill."

Puritan New England differed in many ways from both England and the rest of Europe. Protestants emphasized literacy so that everyone could read the Bible. This attitude was in stark contrast to that of Catholics, who refused to tolerate private ownership of Bibles in the vernacular. The Puritans, for their part, placed a special emphasis on reading scripture, and their commitment to literacy led to the establishment of the first printing press in English America in 1636. Four years later, in 1640, they published the first book in North America, the Bay Psalm Book. As Calvinists, Puritans adhered to the doctrine of predestination, whereby a few "elect" would be saved and all others damned. No one could be sure whether they were predestined for salvation, but through introspection, guided by scripture, Puritans hoped to find a glimmer of redemptive grace. Church membership was restricted to those Puritans who were willing to provide a conversion narrative telling how they came to understand their spiritual estate by hearing sermons and studying the Bible.

Although many people assume Puritans escaped England to establish religious freedom, they proved to be just as intolerant as the English state church. When dissenters, including Puritan minister Roger Williams and Anne Hutchinson, challenged Governor Winthrop in Massachusetts Bay in the 1630s, they were banished. Roger Williams questioned the Puritans' taking of Indian land. Williams also argued for a complete separation from the Church of England, a position other Puritans in Massachusetts rejected, as well as the idea that the state could not punish individuals for their beliefs. Although he did accept that nonbelievers were destined for eternal damnation, Williams did not think the state could compel true orthodoxy. Puritan authorities found him guilty of spreading dangerous ideas, but he went on to found Rhode Island as a colony that sheltered dissenting Puritans from their brethren in Massachusetts. In Rhode Island, Williams wrote favorably about native peoples, contrasting their virtues with Puritan New England's intolerance.

Anne Hutchinson also ran afoul of Puritan authorities for her criticism of the evolving religious practices in the Massachusetts Bay Colony. In particular, she held that Puritan ministers in New England taught a shallow version of Protestantism emphasizing hierarchy and actions—a "covenant of works" rather than a "covenant of grace." Literate Puritan women like Hutchinson presented a challenge to the male ministers' authority. Indeed, her major offense was her claim of direct religious revelation, a type of spiritual experience that negated the role of ministers. Because of Hutchinson's beliefs and her defiance of authority in the colony, especially that of Governor Winthrop, Puritan authorities tried and convicted her of holding false beliefs. In 1638, she was excommunicated and banished from the colony. She went to Rhode Island and later, in 1642, sought safety among the Dutch in New Netherland. The following year, Algonquian warriors killed Hutchinson and her family. In Massachusetts, Governor Winthrop noted her death as the righteous judgment of God against a heretic.

Like many other Europeans, the Puritans believed in the supernatural. Every event appeared to be a sign of God's mercy or judgment, and people believed that witches allied themselves with the Devil to carry out evil deeds and deliberate harm such as the sickness or death of children, the loss of cattle, and other catastrophes. Hundreds were accused of witchcraft in Puritan New England, including townspeople whose habits or appearance bothered their neighbors or who appeared threatening for any reason. Women, seen as more susceptible to the Devil because of their supposedly weaker constitutions, made up the vast majority of suspects and those who were executed. The most notorious cases occurred in Salem Village in 1692. Many of the accusers who prosecuted the suspected witches had been traumatized by the Indian wars on the frontier and by unprecedented political and cultural changes in New England. Relying on their belief in witchcraft to help make sense of their changing world, Puritan authorities executed nineteen people and caused the deaths of several others.

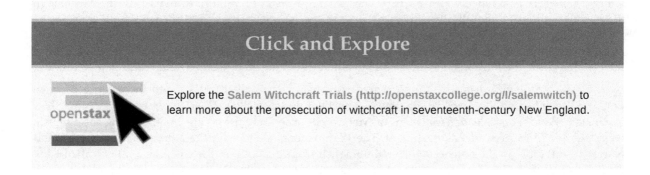

Click and Explore

Explore the Salem Witchcraft Trials (http://openstaxcollege.org/l/salemwitch) to learn more about the prosecution of witchcraft in seventeenth-century New England.

Puritan Relationships with Native Peoples

Like their Spanish and French Catholic rivals, English Puritans in America took steps to convert native peoples to their version of Christianity. John Eliot, the leading Puritan missionary in New England, urged natives in Massachusetts to live in "praying towns" established by English authorities for converted

Indians, and to adopt the Puritan emphasis on the centrality of the Bible. In keeping with the Protestant emphasis on reading scripture, he translated the Bible into the local Algonquian language and published his work in 1663. Eliot hoped that as a result of his efforts, some of New England's native inhabitants would become preachers.

Tensions had existed from the beginning between the Puritans and the native people who controlled southern New England (Figure 3.13). Relationships deteriorated as the Puritans continued to expand their settlements aggressively and as European ways increasingly disrupted native life. These strains led to King Philip's War (1675–1676), a massive regional conflict that was nearly successful in pushing the English out of New England.

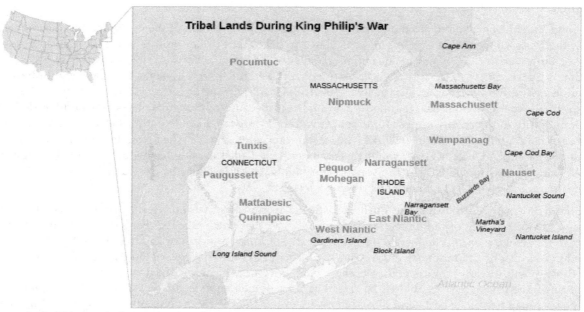

Figure 3.13   This map indicates the domains of New England's native inhabitants in 1670, a few years before King Philip's War.

When the Puritans began to arrive in the 1620s and 1630s, local Algonquian peoples had viewed them as potential allies in the conflicts already simmering between rival native groups. In 1621, the Wampanoag, led by Massasoit, concluded a peace treaty with the Pilgrims at Plymouth. In the 1630s, the Puritans in Massachusetts and Plymouth allied themselves with the Narragansett and Mohegan people against the Pequot, who had recently expanded their claims into southern New England. In May 1637, the Puritans attacked a large group of several hundred Pequot along the Mystic River in Connecticut. To the horror of their native allies, the Puritans massacred all but a handful of the men, women, and children they found.

By the mid-seventeenth century, the Puritans had pushed their way further into the interior of New England, establishing outposts along the Connecticut River Valley. There seemed no end to their expansion. Wampanoag leader Metacom or Metacomet, also known as King Philip among the English, was determined to stop the encroachment. The Wampanoag, along with the Nipmuck, Pocumtuck, and Narragansett, took up the hatchet to drive the English from the land. In the ensuing conflict, called King Philip's War, native forces succeeded in destroying half of the frontier Puritan towns; however, in the end, the English (aided by Mohegans and Christian Indians) prevailed and sold many captives into slavery in the West Indies. (The severed head of King Philip was publicly displayed in Plymouth.) The war also forever changed the English perception of native peoples; from then on, Puritan writers took great pains to vilify the natives as bloodthirsty savages. A new type of racial hatred became a defining feature of Indian-English relationships in the Northeast.

MY STORY

☼ *Mary Rowlandson's Captivity Narrative*

Mary Rowlandson was a Puritan woman whom Indian tribes captured and imprisoned for several weeks during King Philip's War. After her release, she wrote *The Narrative of the Captivity and the Restoration of Mrs. Mary Rowlandson*, which was published in 1682 (Figure 3.14). The book was an immediate sensation that was reissued in multiple editions for over a century.

(a) (b)

Figure 3.14   Puritan woman Mary Rowlandson wrote her captivity narrative, the front cover of which is shown here (a), after her imprisonment during King Philip's War. In her narrative, she tells of her treatment by the Indians holding her as well as of her meetings with the Wampanoag leader Metacom (b), shown in a contemporary portrait.

> But now, the next morning, I must turn my back upon the town, and travel with them into the vast and desolate wilderness, I knew not whither. It is not my tongue, or pen, can express the sorrows of my heart, and bitterness of my spirit that I had at this departure: but God was with me in a wonderful manner, carrying me along, and bearing up my spirit, that it did not quite fail. One of the Indians carried my poor wounded babe upon a horse; it went moaning all along, "I shall die, I shall die." I went on foot after it, with sorrow that cannot be expressed. At length I took it off the horse, and carried it in my arms till my strength failed, and I fell down with it. Then they set me upon a horse with my wounded child in my lap, and there being no furniture upon the horse's back, as we were going down a steep hill we both fell over the horse's head, at which they, like inhumane creatures, laughed, and rejoiced to see it, though I thought we should there have ended our days, as overcome with so many difficulties. But the Lord renewed my strength still, and carried me along, that I might see more of His power; yea, so much that I could never have thought of, had I not experienced it.

What sustains Rowlandson her during her ordeal? How does she characterize her captors? What do you think made her narrative so compelling to readers?

Click and Explore

Access the entire text of Mary Rowlandson's captivity narrative (http://openstaxcollege.org/l/captivenarr) at the Gutenberg Project.

3.4 The Impact of Colonization

By the end of this section, you will be able to:
- Explain the reasons for the rise of slavery in the American colonies
- Describe changes to Indian life, including warfare and hunting
- Contrast European and Indian views on property
- Assess the impact of European settlement on the environment

As Europeans moved beyond exploration and into colonization of the Americas, they brought changes to virtually every aspect of the land and its people, from trade and hunting to warfare and personal property. European goods, ideas, and diseases shaped the changing continent.

As Europeans established their colonies, their societies also became segmented and divided along religious and racial lines. Most people in these societies were not free; they labored as servants or slaves, doing the work required to produce wealth for others. By 1700, the American continent had become a place of stark contrasts between slavery and freedom, between the haves and the have-nots.

THE INSTITUTION OF SLAVERY

Everywhere in the American colonies, a crushing demand for labor existed to grow New World cash crops, especially sugar and tobacco. This need led Europeans to rely increasingly on Africans, and after 1600, the movement of Africans across the Atlantic accelerated. The English crown chartered the Royal African Company in 1672, giving the company a monopoly over the transport of African slaves to the English colonies. Over the next four decades, the company transported around 350,000 Africans from their homelands. By 1700, the tiny English sugar island of Barbados had a population of fifty thousand slaves, and the English had encoded the institution of chattel slavery into colonial law.

This new system of African slavery came slowly to the English colonists, who did not have slavery at home and preferred to use servant labor. Nevertheless, by the end of the seventeenth century, the English everywhere in America—and particularly in the Chesapeake Bay colonies—had come to rely on African slaves. While Africans had long practiced slavery among their own people, it had not been based on race. Africans enslaved other Africans as war captives, for crimes, and to settle debts; they generally used their slaves for domestic and small-scale agricultural work, not for growing cash crops on large plantations. Additionally, African slavery was often a temporary condition rather than a lifelong sentence, and, unlike New World slavery, it was typically not heritable (passed from a slave mother to her children).

The growing slave trade with Europeans had a profound impact on the people of West Africa, giving prominence to local chieftains and merchants who traded slaves for European textiles, alcohol, guns, tobacco, and food. Africans also charged Europeans for the right to trade in slaves and imposed taxes on slave purchases. Different African groups and kingdoms even staged large-scale raids on each other to meet the demand for slaves.

Once sold to traders, all slaves sent to America endured the hellish **Middle Passage**, the transatlantic crossing, which took one to two months. By 1625, more than 325,800 Africans had been shipped to the New World, though many thousands perished during the voyage. An astonishing number, some four million, were transported to the Caribbean between 1501 and 1830. When they reached their destination in America, Africans found themselves trapped in shockingly brutal slave societies. In the Chesapeake colonies, they faced a lifetime of harvesting and processing tobacco.

Everywhere, Africans resisted slavery, and running away was common. In Jamaica and elsewhere, runaway slaves created **maroon communities**, groups that resisted recapture and eked a living from the land, rebuilding their communities as best they could. When possible, they adhered to traditional ways, following spiritual leaders such as Vodun priests.

CHANGES TO INDIAN LIFE

While the Americas remained firmly under the control of native peoples in the first decades of European settlement, conflict increased as colonization spread and Europeans placed greater demands upon the native populations, including expecting them to convert to Christianity (either Catholicism or Protestantism). Throughout the seventeenth century, the still-powerful native peoples and confederacies that retained control of the land waged war against the invading Europeans, achieving a degree of success in their effort to drive the newcomers from the continent.

At the same time, European goods had begun to change Indian life radically. In the 1500s, some of the earliest objects Europeans introduced to Indians were glass beads, copper kettles, and metal utensils. Native people often adapted these items for their own use. For example, some cut up copper kettles and refashioned the metal for other uses, including jewelry that conferred status on the wearer, who was seen as connected to the new European source of raw materials.

As European settlements grew throughout the 1600s, European goods flooded native communities. Soon native people were using these items for the same purposes as the Europeans. For example, many native inhabitants abandoned their animal-skin clothing in favor of European textiles. Similarly, clay cookware gave way to metal cooking implements, and Indians found that European flint and steel made starting fires much easier (Figure 3.15).

Figure 3.15   In this 1681 portrait, the Niantic-Narragansett chief Ninigret wears a combination of European and Indian goods. Which elements of each culture are evident in this portrait?

The abundance of European goods gave rise to new artistic objects. For example, iron awls made the creation of shell beads among the native people of the Eastern Woodlands much easier, and the result was an astonishing increase in the production of **wampum**, shell beads used in ceremonies and as jewelry and currency. Native peoples had always placed goods in the graves of their departed, and this practice escalated with the arrival of European goods. Archaeologists have found enormous caches of European trade goods in the graves of Indians on the East Coast.

Native weapons changed dramatically as well, creating an arms race among the peoples living in European colonization zones. Indians refashioned European brassware into arrow points and turned axes used for chopping wood into weapons. The most prized piece of European weaponry to obtain was a **musket**, or light, long-barreled European gun. In order to trade with Europeans for these, native peoples intensified their harvesting of beaver, commercializing their traditional practice.

The influx of European materials made warfare more lethal and changed traditional patterns of authority among tribes. Formerly weaker groups, if they had access to European metal and weapons, suddenly gained the upper hand against once-dominant groups. The Algonquian, for instance, traded with the French for muskets and gained power against their enemies, the Iroquois. Eventually, native peoples also used their new weapons against the European colonizers who had provided them.

Click and Explore

Explore the complexity of **Indian-European relationships** **(http://openstaxcollege.org/l/NHC)** in the series of primary source documents on the National Humanities Center site.

ENVIRONMENTAL CHANGES

The European presence in America spurred countless changes in the environment, setting into motion chains of events that affected native animals as well as people. The popularity of beaver-trimmed hats in Europe, coupled with Indians' desire for European weapons, led to the overhunting of beaver in the Northeast. Soon, beavers were extinct in New England, New York, and other areas. With their loss came the loss of beaver ponds, which had served as habitats for fish as well as water sources for deer, moose, and other animals. Furthermore, Europeans introduced pigs, which they allowed to forage in forests and other wildlands. Pigs consumed the foods on which deer and other indigenous species depended, resulting in scarcity of the game native peoples had traditionally hunted.

European ideas about owning land as private property clashed with natives' understanding of land use. Native peoples did not believe in private ownership of land; instead, they viewed land as a resource to be held in common for the benefit of the group. The European idea of usufruct—the right to common land use and enjoyment—comes close to the native understanding, but colonists did not practice usufruct widely in America. Colonizers established fields, fences, and other means of demarcating private property. Native peoples who moved seasonally to take advantage of natural resources now found areas off limits, claimed by colonizers because of their insistence on private-property rights.

The Introduction of Disease

Perhaps European colonization's single greatest impact on the North American environment was the introduction of disease. Microbes to which native inhabitants had no immunity led to death everywhere Europeans settled. Along the New England coast between 1616 and 1618, epidemics claimed the lives of 75 percent of the native people. In the 1630s, half the Huron and Iroquois around the Great Lakes died of smallpox. As is often the case with disease, the very young and the very old were the most vulnerable and had the highest mortality rates. The loss of the older generation meant the loss of knowledge and tradition, while the death of children only compounded the trauma, creating devastating implications for future generations.

Some native peoples perceived disease as a weapon used by hostile spiritual forces, and they went to war to exorcise the disease from their midst. These "mourning wars" in eastern North America were designed to gain captives who would either be adopted ("requickened" as a replacement for a deceased loved one) or ritually tortured and executed to assuage the anger and grief caused by loss.

The Cultivation of Plants

European expansion in the Americas led to an unprecedented movement of plants across the Atlantic. A prime example is tobacco, which became a valuable export as the habit of smoking, previously unknown in Europe, took hold (Figure 3.16). Another example is sugar. Columbus brought sugarcane to the Caribbean on his second voyage in 1494, and thereafter a wide variety of other herbs, flowers, seeds, and roots made the transatlantic voyage.

Figure 3.16 Adriaen van Ostade, a Dutch artist, painted *An Apothecary Smoking in an Interior* in 1646. The large European market for American tobacco strongly influenced the development of some of the American colonies.

Just as pharmaceutical companies today scour the natural world for new drugs, Europeans traveled to America to discover new medicines. The task of cataloging the new plants found there helped give birth to the science of botany. Early botanists included the English naturalist Sir Hans Sloane, who traveled to Jamaica in 1687 and there recorded hundreds of new plants (Figure 3.17). Sloane also helped popularize the drinking of chocolate, made from the cacao bean, in England.

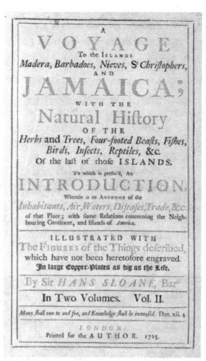

Figure 3.17 English naturalist Sir Hans Sloane traveled to Jamaica and other Caribbean islands to catalog the flora of the new world.

Indians, who possessed a vast understanding of local New World plants and their properties, would have been a rich source of information for those European botanists seeking to find and catalog potentially useful plants. Enslaved Africans, who had a tradition of the use of medicinal plants in their native land, adapted to their new surroundings by learning the use of New World plants through experimentation or from the native inhabitants. Native peoples and Africans employed their knowledge effectively within their own communities. One notable example was the use of the peacock flower to induce abortions: Indian and enslaved African women living in oppressive colonial regimes are said to have used this herb to prevent the birth of children into slavery. Europeans distrusted medical knowledge that came from African or native sources, however, and thus lost the benefit of this source of information.

Key Terms

headright system a system in which parcels of land were granted to settlers who could pay their own way to Virginia

indenture a labor contract that promised young men, and sometimes women, money and land after they worked for a set period of years

Jesuits members of the Society of Jesus, an elite Catholic religious order founded in the 1540s to spread Catholicism and to combat the spread of Protestantism

maroon communities groups of runaway slaves who resisted recapture and eked a living from the land

Middle Passage the perilous, often deadly transatlantic crossing of slave ships from the African coast to the New World

musket a light, long-barreled European gun

patroonships large tracts of land and governing rights granted to merchants by the Dutch West India Company in order to encourage colonization

repartimiento a Spanish colonial system requiring Indian towns to supply workers for the colonizers

Timucua the native people of Florida, whom the Spanish displaced with the founding of St. Augustine, the first Spanish settlement in North America

wampum shell beads used in ceremonies and as jewelry and currency

Summary

3.1 Spanish Exploration and Colonial Society

In their outposts at St. Augustine and Santa Fe, the Spanish never found the fabled mountains of gold they sought. They did find many native people to convert to Catholicism, but their zeal nearly cost them the colony of Santa Fe, which they lost for twelve years after the Pueblo Revolt. In truth, the grand dreams of wealth, conversion, and a social order based on Spanish control never came to pass as Spain envisioned them.

3.2 Colonial Rivalries: Dutch and French Colonial Ambitions

The French and Dutch established colonies in the northeastern part of North America: the Dutch in present-day New York, and the French in present-day Canada. Both colonies were primarily trading posts for furs. While they failed to attract many colonists from their respective home countries, these outposts nonetheless intensified imperial rivalries in North America. Both the Dutch and the French relied on native peoples to harvest the pelts that proved profitable in Europe.

3.3 English Settlements in America

The English came late to colonization of the Americas, establishing stable settlements in the 1600s after several unsuccessful attempts in the 1500s. After Roanoke Colony failed in 1587, the English found more success with the founding of Jamestown in 1607 and Plymouth in 1620. The two colonies were very different in origin. The Virginia Company of London founded Jamestown with the express purpose of making money for its investors, while Puritans founded Plymouth to practice their own brand of Protestantism without interference.

Both colonies battled difficult circumstances, including poor relationships with neighboring Indian tribes. Conflicts flared repeatedly in the Chesapeake Bay tobacco colonies and in New England, where a massive uprising against the English in 1675 to 1676—King Philip's War—nearly succeeded in driving the intruders back to the sea.

3.4 The Impact of Colonization

The development of the Atlantic slave trade forever changed the course of European settlement in the Americas. Other transatlantic travelers, including diseases, goods, plants, animals, and even ideas like the concept of private land ownership, further influenced life in America during the sixteenth and seventeenth centuries. The exchange of pelts for European goods including copper kettles, knives, and guns played a significant role in changing the material cultures of native peoples. During the seventeenth century, native peoples grew increasingly dependent on European trade items. At the same time, many native inhabitants died of European diseases, while survivors adopted new ways of living with their new neighbors.

Review Questions

1. Which of the following was a goal of the Spanish in their destruction of Fort Caroline?
   A. establishing a foothold from which to battle the Timucua
   B. claiming a safe place to house the New World treasures that would be shipped back to Spain
   C. reducing the threat of French privateers
   D. locating a site for the establishment of Santa Fe

2. Why did the Spanish build Castillo de San Marcos?
   A. to protect the local Timucua
   B. to defend against imperial challengers
   C. as a seat for visiting Spanish royalty
   D. to house visiting delegates from rival imperial powers

3. How did the Pueblo attempt to maintain their autonomy in the face of Spanish settlement?

4. What was patroonship?
   A. a Dutch ship used for transporting beaver furs
   B. a Dutch system of patronage that encouraged the arts
   C. a Dutch system of granting tracts of land in New Netherland to encourage colonization
   D. a Dutch style of hat trimmed with beaver fur from New Netherland

5. Which religious order joined the French settlement in Canada and tried to convert the natives to Christianity?
   A. Franciscans
   B. Calvinists
   C. Anglicans
   D. Jesuits

6. How did the French and Dutch colonists differ in their religious expectations? How did both compare to Spanish colonists?

7. What was the most lucrative product of the Chesapeake colonies?
   A. corn
   B. tobacco
   C. gold and silver
   D. slaves

8. What was the primary cause of Bacon's Rebellion?
   A. former indentured servants wanted more opportunities to expand their territory
   B. African slaves wanted better treatment
   C. Susquahannock Indians wanted the Jamestown settlers to pay a fair price for their land
   D. Jamestown politicians were jockeying for power

9. The founders of the Plymouth colony were:
   A. Puritans
   B. Catholics

C. Anglicans

D. Jesuits

10. Which of the following is *not* true of the Puritan religion?

A. It required close reading of scripture.

B. Church membership required a conversion narrative.

C. Literacy was crucial.

D. Only men could participate.

11. How did the Chesapeake colonists solve their labor problems?

12. What was the Middle Passage?

A. the fabled sea route from Europe to the Far East

B. the land route from Europe to Africa

C. the transatlantic journey that African slaves made to America

D. the line between the northern and southern colonies

13. Which of the following is *not* an item Europeans introduced to Indians?

A. wampum

B. glass beads

C. copper kettles

D. metal tools

14. How did European muskets change life for native peoples in the Americas?

15. Compare and contrast European and Indian views on property.

Critical Thinking Questions

16. Compare and contrast life in the Spanish, French, Dutch, and English colonies, differentiating between the Chesapeake Bay and New England colonies. Who were the colonizers? What were their purposes in being there? How did they interact with their environments and the native inhabitants of the lands on which they settled?

17. Describe the attempts of the various European colonists to convert native peoples to their belief systems. How did these attempts compare to one another? What were the results of each effort?

18. How did chattel slavery differ from indentured servitude? How did the former system come to replace the latter? What were the results of this shift?

19. What impact did Europeans have on their New World environments—native peoples and their communities as well as land, plants, and animals? Conversely, what impact did the New World's native inhabitants, land, plants, and animals have on Europeans? How did the interaction of European and Indian societies, together, shape a world that was truly "new"?

CHAPTER 4

Rule Britannia! The English Empire, 1660–1763

Figure 4.1 Isaac Royall and his family, seen here in a 1741 portrait by Robert Feke, moved to Medford, Massachusetts, from the West Indian island of Antigua, bringing their slaves with them. They were an affluent British colonial family, proud of their success and the success of the British Empire.

Chapter Outline

4.1 Charles II and the Restoration Colonies
4.2 The Glorious Revolution and the English Empire
4.3 An Empire of Slavery and the Consumer Revolution
4.4 Great Awakening and Enlightenment
4.5 Wars for Empire

Introduction

The eighteenth century witnessed the birth of Great Britain (after the union of England and Scotland in 1707) and the expansion of the British Empire. By the mid-1700s, Great Britain had developed into a commercial and military powerhouse; its economic sway ranged from India, where the British East India Company had gained control over both trade and territory, to the West African coast, where British slave traders predominated, and to the British West Indies, whose lucrative sugar plantations, especially in Barbados and Jamaica, provided windfall profits for British planters. Meanwhile, the population rose dramatically in Britain's North American colonies. In the early 1700s the population in the colonies had reached 250,000. By 1750, however, over a million British migrants and African slaves had established a near-continuous zone of settlement on the Atlantic coast from Maine to Georgia.

During this period, the ties between Great Britain and the American colonies only grew stronger. Anglo-American colonists considered themselves part of the British Empire in all ways: politically, militarily, religiously (as Protestants), intellectually, and racially. The portrait of the Royall family (Figure 4.1) exemplifies the colonial American gentry of the eighteenth century. Successful and well-to-do, they display fashions, hairstyles, and furnishings that all speak to their identity as proud and loyal British subjects.

4.1 Charles II and the Restoration Colonies

By the end of this section, you will be able to:
- Analyze the causes and consequences of the Restoration
- Identify the Restoration colonies and their role in the expansion of the Empire

When Charles II ascended the throne in 1660, English subjects on both sides of the Atlantic celebrated the restoration of the English monarchy after a decade of living without a king as a result of the English Civil Wars. Charles II lost little time in strengthening England's global power. From the 1660s to the 1680s, Charles II added more possessions to England's North American holdings by establishing the Restoration colonies of New York and New Jersey (taking these areas from the Dutch) as well as Pennsylvania and the Carolinas. In order to reap the greatest economic benefit from England's overseas possessions, Charles II enacted the mercantilist Navigation Acts, although many colonial merchants ignored them because enforcement remained lax.

CHARLES II

The chronicle of Charles II begins with his father, Charles I. Charles I ascended the English throne in 1625 and soon married a French Catholic princess, Henrietta Maria, who was not well liked by English Protestants because she openly practiced Catholicism during her husband's reign. The most outspoken Protestants, the Puritans, had a strong voice in Parliament in the 1620s, and they strongly opposed the king's marriage and his ties to Catholicism. When Parliament tried to contest his edicts, including the king's efforts to impose taxes without Parliament's consent, Charles I suspended Parliament in 1629 and ruled without one for the next eleven years.

The ensuing struggle between the king and Parliament led to the outbreak of war. The English Civil War lasted from 1642 to 1649 and pitted the king and his Royalist supporters against Oliver Cromwell and his Parliamentary forces. After years of fighting, the Parliamentary forces gained the upper hand, and in 1649, they charged Charles I with treason and beheaded him. The monarchy was dissolved, and England

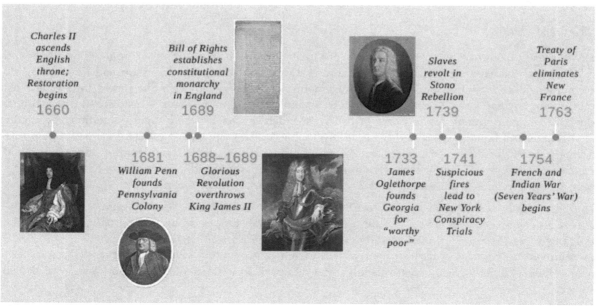

Figure 4.2

became a republic: a state without a king. Oliver Cromwell headed the new English Commonwealth, and the period known as the **English interregnum**, or the time between kings, began.

Though Cromwell enjoyed widespread popularity at first, over time he appeared to many in England to be taking on the powers of a military dictator. Dissatisfaction with Cromwell grew. When he died in 1658 and control passed to his son Richard, who lacked the political skills of his father, a majority of the English people feared an alternate hereditary monarchy in the making. They had had enough and asked Charles II to be king. In 1660, they welcomed the son of the executed king Charles I back to the throne to resume the English monarchy and bring the interregnum to an end (Figure 4.3). The return of Charles II is known as the Restoration.

(a)   (b)

Figure 4.3 The monarchy and Parliament fought for control of England during the seventeenth century. Though Oliver Cromwell (a), shown here in a 1656 portrait by Samuel Cooper, appeared to offer England a better mode of government, he assumed broad powers for himself and disregarded cherished English liberties established under Magna Carta in 1215. As a result, the English people welcomed Charles II (b) back to the throne in 1660. This portrait by John Michael Wright was painted ca. 1660–1665, soon after the new king gained the throne.

Charles II was committed to expanding England's overseas possessions. His policies in the 1660s through the 1680s established and supported the **Restoration colonies**: the Carolinas, New Jersey, New York, and Pennsylvania. All the Restoration colonies started as **proprietary colonies**, that is, the king gave each colony to a trusted individual, family, or group.

THE CAROLINAS

Charles II hoped to establish English control of the area between Virginia and Spanish Florida. To that end, he issued a royal charter in 1663 to eight trusted and loyal supporters, each of whom was to be a feudal-style proprietor of a region of the province of Carolina.

These proprietors did not relocate to the colonies, however. Instead, English plantation owners from the tiny Caribbean island of Barbados, already a well-established English sugar colony fueled by slave labor, migrated to the southern part of Carolina to settle there. In 1670, they established Charles Town (later Charleston), named in honor of Charles II, at the junction of the Ashley and Cooper Rivers (Figure 4.4). As the settlement around Charles Town grew, it began to produce livestock for export to the West Indies. In the northern part of Carolina, settlers turned sap from pine trees into turpentine used to waterproof wooden ships. Political disagreements between settlers in the northern and southern parts of Carolina escalated in the 1710s through the 1720s and led to the creation, in 1729, of two colonies, North and South Carolina. The southern part of Carolina had been producing rice and indigo (a plant that yields a dark blue dye used by English royalty) since the 1700s, and South Carolina continued to depend on these main crops.

North Carolina continued to produce items for ships, especially turpentine and tar, and its population increased as Virginians moved there to expand their tobacco holdings. Tobacco was the primary export of both Virginia and North Carolina, which also traded in deerskins and slaves from Africa.

Figure 4.4 The port of colonial Charles Towne, depicted here on a 1733 map of North America, was the largest in the South and played a significant role in the Atlantic slave trade.

Slavery developed quickly in the Carolinas, largely because so many of the early migrants came from Barbados, where slavery was well established. By the end of the 1600s, a very wealthy class of rice planters who relied on slaves had attained dominance in the southern part of the Carolinas, especially around Charles Town. By 1715, South Carolina had a black majority because of the number of slaves in the colony. The legal basis for slavery was established in the early 1700s as the Carolinas began to pass slave laws based on the Barbados slave codes of the late 1600s. These laws reduced Africans to the status of property to be bought and sold as other commodities.

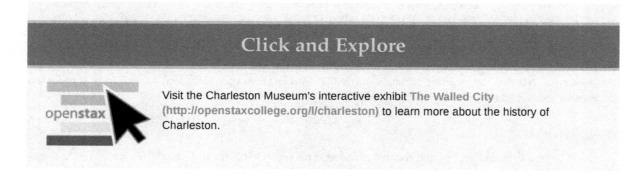

Click and Explore

Visit the Charleston Museum's interactive exhibit The Walled City (http://openstaxcollege.org/l/charleston) to learn more about the history of Charleston.

As in other areas of English settlement, native peoples in the Carolinas suffered tremendously from the introduction of European diseases. Despite the effects of disease, Indians in the area endured and, following the pattern elsewhere in the colonies, grew dependent on European goods. Local Yamasee and Creek tribes built up a trade deficit with the English, trading deerskins and captive slaves for European guns. English settlers exacerbated tensions with local Indian tribes, especially the Yamasee, by expanding their rice and tobacco fields into Indian lands. Worse still, English traders took native women captive as payment for debts.

The outrages committed by traders, combined with the seemingly unstoppable expansion of English settlement onto native land, led to the outbreak of the Yamasee War (1715–1718), an effort by a coalition of local tribes to drive away the European invaders. This native effort to force the newcomers back across the

Atlantic nearly succeeded in annihilating the Carolina colonies. Only when the Cherokee allied themselves with the English did the coalition's goal of eliminating the English from the region falter. The Yamasee War demonstrates the key role native peoples played in shaping the outcome of colonial struggles and, perhaps most important, the disunity that existed between different native groups.

NEW YORK AND NEW JERSEY

Charles II also set his sights on the Dutch colony of New Netherland. The English takeover of New Netherland originated in the imperial rivalry between the Dutch and the English. During the Anglo-Dutch wars of the 1650s and 1660s, the two powers attempted to gain commercial advantages in the Atlantic World. During the Second Anglo-Dutch War (1664–1667), English forces gained control of the Dutch fur trading colony of New Netherland, and in 1664, Charles II gave this colony (including present-day New Jersey) to his brother James, Duke of York (later James II). The colony and city were renamed New York in his honor. The Dutch in New York chafed under English rule. In 1673, during the Third Anglo-Dutch War (1672–1674), the Dutch recaptured the colony. However, at the end of the conflict, the English had regained control (Figure 4.5).

Figure 4.5 "View of New Amsterdam" (ca. 1665), a watercolor by Johannes Vingboons, was painted during the Anglo-Dutch wars of the 1660s and 1670s. New Amsterdam was officially reincorporated as New York City in 1664, but alternated under Dutch and English rule until 1674.

The Duke of York had no desire to govern locally or listen to the wishes of local colonists. It wasn't until 1683, therefore, almost 20 years after the English took control of the colony, that colonists were able to convene a local representative legislature. The assembly's 1683 Charter of Liberties and Privileges set out the traditional rights of Englishmen, like the right to trial by jury and the right to representative government.

The English continued the Dutch patroonship system, granting large estates to a favored few families. The largest of these estates, at 160,000 acres, was given to Robert Livingston in 1686. The Livingstons and the other manorial families who controlled the Hudson River Valley formed a formidable political and economic force. Eighteenth-century New York City, meanwhile, contained a variety of people and religions—as well as Dutch and English people, it held French Protestants (Huguenots), Jews, Puritans, Quakers, Anglicans, and a large population of slaves. As they did in other zones of colonization, native peoples played a key role in shaping the history of colonial New York. After decades of war in the 1600s, the powerful Five Nations of the Iroquois, composed of the Mohawk, Oneida, Onondaga, Cayuga, and Seneca, successfully pursued a policy of neutrality with both the English and, to the north, the French in Canada during the first half of the 1700s. This native policy meant that the Iroquois continued to live in their own villages under their own government while enjoying the benefits of trade with both the French and the English.

PENNSYLVANIA

The Restoration colonies also included Pennsylvania, which became the geographic center of British colonial America. Pennsylvania (which means "Penn's Woods" in Latin) was created in 1681, when Charles II bestowed the largest proprietary colony in the Americas on William Penn (Figure 4.6) to settle the large debt he owed the Penn family. William Penn's father, Admiral William Penn, had served the English crown by helping take Jamaica from the Spanish in 1655. The king personally owed the Admiral money as well.

Figure 4.6 Charles II granted William Penn the land that eventually became the Commonwealth of Pennsylvania in order to settle a debt the English crown owed to Penn's father.

Like early settlers of the New England colonies, Pennsylvania's first colonists migrated mostly for religious reasons. William Penn himself was a Quaker, a member of a new Protestant denomination called the Society of Friends. George Fox had founded the Society of Friends in England in the late 1640s, having grown dissatisfied with Puritanism and the idea of predestination. Rather, Fox and his followers stressed that everyone had an "inner light" inside him or her, a spark of divinity. They gained the name Quakers because they were said to quake when the inner light moved them. Quakers rejected the idea of worldly rank, believing instead in a new and radical form of social equality. Their speech reflected this belief in that they addressed all others as equals, using "thee" and "thou" rather than terms like "your lordship" or "my lady" that were customary for privileged individuals of the hereditary elite.

The English crown persecuted Quakers in England, and colonial governments were equally harsh; Massachusetts even executed several early Quakers who had gone to proselytize there. To avoid such persecution, Quakers and their families at first created a community on the sugar island of Barbados. Soon after its founding, however, Pennsylvania became the destination of choice. Quakers flocked to Pennsylvania as well as New Jersey, where they could preach and practice their religion in peace. Unlike New England, whose official religion was Puritanism, Pennsylvania did not establish an official church. Indeed, the colony allowed a degree of religious tolerance found nowhere else in English America. To help encourage immigration to his colony, Penn promised fifty acres of land to people who agreed to come to Pennsylvania and completed their term of service. Not surprisingly, those seeking a better life came in large numbers, so much so that Pennsylvania relied on indentured servants more than any other colony.

One of the primary tenets of Quakerism is pacifism, leading William Penn to establish friendly relationships with local native peoples. He formed a covenant of friendship with the Lenni Lenape (Delaware) tribe, buying their land for a fair price instead of taking it by force. In 1701, he also signed a treaty with the Susquehannocks to avoid war. Unlike other colonies, Pennsylvania did not experience war on the frontier with native peoples during its early history.

Chapter 4 | Rule Britannia! The English Empire, 1660–1763

101

As an important port city, Philadelphia grew rapidly. Quaker merchants there established contacts throughout the Atlantic world and participated in the thriving African slave trade. Some Quakers, who were deeply troubled by the contradiction between their belief in the "inner light" and the practice of slavery, rejected the practice and engaged in efforts to abolish it altogether. Philadelphia also acted as a magnet for immigrants, who came not only from England, but from all over Europe by the hundreds of thousands. The city, and indeed all of Pennsylvania, appeared to be the best country for poor men and women, many of whom arrived as servants and dreamed of owning land. A very few, like the fortunate Benjamin Franklin, a runaway from Puritan Boston, did extraordinarily well. Other immigrant groups in the colony, most notably Germans and Scotch-Irish (families from Scotland and England who had first lived in Ireland before moving to British America), greatly improved their lot in Pennsylvania. Of course, Africans imported into the colony to labor for white masters fared far worse.

AMERICANA

✪ *John Wilson Offers Reward for Escaped Prisoners*

The *American Weekly Mercury*, published by William Bradford, was Philadelphia's first newspaper. This advertisement from "John Wilson, *Goaler*" (jailer) offers a reward for anyone capturing several men who escaped from the jail.

> BROKE out of the Common Goal of Philadelphia, the 15th of this Instant February, 1721, the following Persons:
>
> John Palmer, also Plumly, *alias* Paine, *Servant to Joseph Jones, run away and was lately taken up at New-York. He is fully described in the* American Mercury, Novem. 23, 1721. *He has a Cinnamon coloured Coat on, a middle sized fresh coloured Man. His Master will give a Pistole Reward to any who Shall Secure him, besides what is here offered.*
>
> Daniel Oughtopay, *A Dutchman, aged about 24 Years, Servant to Dr. Johnston in Amboy. He is a thin Spare man, grey Drugget Waistcoat and Breeches and a light-coloured Coat on.*
>
> Ebenezor Mallary, *a New-England, aged about 24 Years, is a middle-sized thin Man, having on a Snuff colour'd Coat, and ordinary Ticking Waistcoat and Breeches. He has dark brown strait Hair.*
>
> Matthew Dulany, *an Irish Man, down-look'd Swarthy Complexion, and has on an Olive-coloured Cloth Coat and Waistcoat with Cloth Buttons.*
>
> John Flemming, *an Irish Lad, aged about 18, belonging to Mr. Miranda, Merchant in this City. He has no Coat, a grey Drugget Waistcoat, and a narrow brim'd Hat on.*
>
> John Corbet, *a Shropshire Man, a Runaway Servant from Alexander Faulkner of Maryland, broke out on the 12th Instant. He has got a double-breasted Sailor's Jacket on lined with red Bays, pretends to be a Sailor, and once taught School at Josephs Collings's in the Jerseys. Whoever takes up and secures all, or any One of these Felons, shall have a Pistole Reward for each of them and reasonable Charges, paid them by* John Wilson, *Goaler*
>
> —Advertisement from the *American Weekly Mercury*, 1722

What do the descriptions of the men tell you about life in colonial Philadelphia?

Click and Explore

Browse a number of issues of the American Weekly Mercury (http://openstaxcollege.org/l/philly1) that were digitized by New Jersey's Stockton University. Read through several to get a remarkable flavor of life in early eighteenth-century Philadelphia.

THE NAVIGATION ACTS

Creating wealth for the Empire remained a primary goal, and in the second half of the seventeenth century, especially during the Restoration, England attempted to gain better control of trade with the American colonies. The mercantilist policies by which it tried to achieve this control are known as the **Navigation Acts**.

The 1651 Navigation Ordnance, a product of Cromwell's England, required that only English ships carry goods between England and the colonies, and that the captain and three-fourths of the crew had to be English. The ordnance further listed "enumerated articles" that could be transported only to England or to English colonies, including the most lucrative commodities like sugar and tobacco as well as indigo, rice, molasses, and naval stores such as turpentine. All were valuable goods not produced in England or in demand by the British navy. After ascending the throne, Charles II approved the 1660 Navigation Act, which restated the 1651 act to ensure a monopoly on imports from the colonies.

Other Navigation Acts included the 1663 Staple Act and the 1673 Plantation Duties Act. The Staple Act barred colonists from importing goods that had not been made in England, creating a profitable monopoly for English exporters and manufacturers. The Plantation Duties Act taxed enumerated articles exported from one colony to another, a measure aimed principally at New Englanders, who transported great quantities of molasses from the West Indies, including smuggled molasses from French-held islands, to make into rum.

In 1675, Charles II organized the Lords of Trade and Plantation, commonly known as the Lords of Trade, an administrative body intended to create stronger ties between the colonial governments and the crown. However, the 1696 Navigation Act created the Board of Trade, replacing the Lords of Trade. This act, meant to strengthen enforcement of customs laws, also established vice-admiralty courts where the crown could prosecute customs violators without a jury. Under this act, customs officials were empowered with warrants known as "writs of assistance" to board and search vessels suspected of containing smuggled goods.

Despite the Navigation Acts, however, Great Britain exercised lax control over the English colonies during most of the eighteenth century because of the policies of Prime Minister Robert Walpole. During his long term (1721–1742), Walpole governed according to his belief that commerce flourished best when it was not encumbered with restrictions. Historians have described this lack of strict enforcement of the Navigation Acts as **salutary neglect**. In addition, nothing prevented colonists from building their own fleet of ships to engage in trade. New England especially benefited from both salutary neglect and a vibrant maritime culture made possible by the scores of trading vessels built in the northern colonies. The case of the 1733 Molasses Act illustrates the weaknesses of British mercantilist policy. The 1733 act placed a sixpence-per-gallon duty on raw sugar, rum, and molasses from Britain's competitors, the French and the Dutch, in order to give an advantage to British West Indian producers. Because the British did not enforce the 1733 law, however, New England mariners routinely smuggled these items from the French and Dutch West Indies more cheaply than they could buy them on English islands.

4.2 The Glorious Revolution and the English Empire

By the end of this section, you will be able to:
- Identify the causes of the Glorious Revolution
- Explain the outcomes of the Glorious Revolution

During the brief rule of King James II, many in England feared the imposition of a Catholic absolute monarchy by the man who modeled his rule on that of his French Catholic cousin, Louis XIV. Opposition to James II, spearheaded by the English Whig party, overthrew the king in the Glorious Revolution of

1688–1689. This paved the way for the Protestant reign of William of Orange and his wife Mary (James's Protestant daughter).

JAMES II AND THE GLORIOUS REVOLUTION

King James II (Figure 4.7), the second son of Charles I, ascended the English throne in 1685 on the death of his brother, Charles II. James then worked to model his rule on the reign of the French Catholic King Louis XIV, his cousin. This meant centralizing English political strength around the throne, giving the monarchy absolute power. Also like Louis XIV, James II practiced a strict and intolerant form of Roman Catholicism after he converted from Protestantism in the late 1660s. He had a Catholic wife, and when they had a son, the potential for a Catholic heir to the English throne became a threat to English Protestants. James also worked to modernize the English army and navy. The fact that the king kept a standing army in times of peace greatly alarmed the English, who believed that such a force would be used to crush their liberty. As James's strength grew, his opponents feared their king would turn England into a Catholic monarchy with absolute power over her people.

Figure 4.7 James II (shown here in a painting ca. 1690) worked to centralize the English government. The Catholic king of France, Louis XIV, provided a template for James's policies.

In 1686, James II applied his concept of a centralized state to the colonies by creating an enormous colony called the **Dominion of New England**. The Dominion included all the New England colonies (Massachusetts, New Hampshire, Plymouth, Connecticut, New Haven, and Rhode Island) and in 1688 was enlarged by the addition of New York and New Jersey. James placed in charge Sir Edmund Andros, a former colonial governor of New York. Loyal to James II and his family, Andros had little sympathy for New Englanders. His regime caused great uneasiness among New England Puritans when it called into question the many land titles that did not acknowledge the king and imposed fees for their reconfirmation. Andros also committed himself to enforcing the Navigation Acts, a move that threatened to disrupt the region's trade, which was based largely on smuggling.

In England, opponents of James II's efforts to create a centralized Catholic state were known as Whigs. The Whigs worked to depose James, and in late 1688 they succeeded, an event they celebrated as the **Glorious Revolution** while James fled to the court of Louis XIV in France. William III (William of Orange) and his wife Mary II ascended the throne in 1689.

The Glorious Revolution spilled over into the colonies. In 1689, Bostonians overthrew the government of the Dominion of New England and jailed Sir Edmund Andros as well as other leaders of the regime (Figure 4.8). The removal of Andros from power illustrates New England's animosity toward the English overlord who had, during his tenure, established Church of England worship in Puritan Boston and vigorously enforced the Navigation Acts, to the chagrin of those in port towns. In New York, the same year that Andros fell from power, Jacob Leisler led a group of Protestant New Yorkers against the dominion government. Acting on his own authority, Leisler assumed the role of King William's governor and organized intercolonial military action independent of British authority. Leisler's actions usurped the crown's prerogative and, as a result, he was tried for treason and executed. In 1691, England restored control over the Province of New York.

Figure 4.8 This broadside, signed by several citizens, demands the surrender of Sir Edmund (spelled here "Edmond") Andros, James II's hand-picked leader of the Dominion of New England.

The Glorious Revolution provided a shared experience for those who lived through the tumult of 1688 and 1689. Subsequent generations kept the memory of the Glorious Revolution alive as a heroic defense of English liberty against a would-be tyrant.

ENGLISH LIBERTY

The Glorious Revolution led to the establishment of an English nation that limited the power of the king and provided protections for English subjects. In October 1689, the same year that William and Mary took the throne, the 1689 Bill of Rights established a constitutional monarchy. It stipulated Parliament's independence from the monarchy and protected certain of Parliament's rights, such as the right to freedom of speech, the right to regular elections, and the right to petition the king. The 1689 Bill of Rights also guaranteed certain rights to all English subjects, including trial by jury and habeas corpus (the requirement that authorities bring an imprisoned person before a court to demonstrate the cause of the imprisonment).

John Locke (1632–1704), a doctor and educator who had lived in exile in Holland during the reign of James II and returned to England after the Glorious Revolution, published his *Two Treatises of Government* in 1690. In it, he argued that government was a form of contract between the leaders and the people, and that representative government existed to protect "life, liberty and property." Locke rejected the divine right of kings and instead advocated for the central role of Parliament with a limited monarchy. Locke's political philosophy had an enormous impact on future generations of colonists and established the paramount importance of representation in government.

Click and Explore

Visit the Digital Locke Project (http://openstaxcollege.org/l/jlocke) to read more of John Locke's writings. This digital collection contains over thirty of his philosophical texts.

The Glorious Revolution also led to the English Toleration Act of 1689, a law passed by Parliament that allowed for greater religious diversity in the Empire. This act granted religious tolerance to **nonconformist** Trinitarian Protestants (those who believed in the Holy Trinity of God the Father, Son, and Holy Ghost), such as Baptists (those who advocated adult baptism) and Congregationalists (those who followed the Puritans' lead in creating independent churches). While the Church of England remained the official state religious establishment, the Toleration Act gave much greater religious freedom to nonconformists. However, this tolerance did not extend to Catholics, who were routinely excluded from political power. The 1689 Toleration Act extended to the British colonies, where several colonies—Pennsylvania, Rhode Island, Delaware, and New Jersey—refused to allow the creation of an established colonial church, a major step toward greater religious diversity.

4.3 An Empire of Slavery and the Consumer Revolution

By the end of this section, you will be able to:
- Analyze the role slavery played in the history and economy of the British Empire
- Explain the effects of the 1739 Stono Rebellion and the 1741 New York Conspiracy Trials
- Describe the consumer revolution and its effect on the life of the colonial gentry and other settlers

Slavery formed a cornerstone of the British Empire in the eighteenth century. Every colony had slaves, from the southern rice plantations in Charles Town, South Carolina, to the northern wharves of Boston. Slavery was more than a labor system; it also influenced every aspect of colonial thought and culture. The uneven relationship it engendered gave white colonists an exaggerated sense of their own status. English liberty gained greater meaning and coherence for whites when they contrasted their status to that of the unfree class of black slaves in British America. African slavery provided whites in the colonies with a shared racial bond and identity.

SLAVERY AND THE STONO REBELLION

The transport of slaves to the American colonies accelerated in the second half of the seventeenth century. In 1660, Charles II created the Royal African Company (Figure 4.9) to trade in slaves and African goods. His brother, James II, led the company before ascending the throne. Under both these kings, the Royal African Company enjoyed a monopoly to transport slaves to the English colonies. Between 1672 and 1713, the company bought 125,000 captives on the African coast, losing 20 percent of them to death on the Middle Passage, the journey from the African coast to the Americas.

Figure 4.9 The 1686 English guinea shows the logo of the Royal African Company, an elephant and castle, beneath a bust of King James II. The coins were commonly called guineas because most British gold came from Guinea in West Africa.

The Royal African Company's monopoly ended in 1689 as a result of the Glorious Revolution. After that date, many more English merchants engaged in the slave trade, greatly increasing the number of slaves being transported. Africans who survived the brutal Middle Passage usually arrived in the West Indies, often in Barbados. From there, they were transported to the mainland English colonies on company ships. While merchants in London, Bristol, and Liverpool lined their pockets, Africans trafficked by the company endured a nightmare of misery, privation, and dislocation.

Slaves strove to adapt to their new lives by forming new communities among themselves, often adhering to traditional African customs and healing techniques. Indeed, the development of families and communities formed the most important response to the trauma of being enslaved. Other slaves dealt with the trauma of their situation by actively resisting their condition, whether by defying their masters or running away. Runaway slaves formed what were called "maroon" communities, groups that successfully resisted recapture and formed their own autonomous groups. The most prominent of these communities lived in the interior of Jamaica, controlling the area and keeping the British away.

Slaves everywhere resisted their exploitation and attempted to gain freedom. They fully understood that rebellions would bring about massive retaliation from whites and therefore had little chance of success. Even so, rebellions occurred frequently. One notable uprising that became known as the Stono Rebellion took place in South Carolina in September 1739. A literate slave named Jemmy led a large group of slaves in an armed insurrection against white colonists, killing several before militia stopped them. The militia suppressed the rebellion after a battle in which both slaves and militiamen were killed, and the remaining slaves were executed or sold to the West Indies.

Jemmy is believed to have been taken from the Kingdom of Kongo, an area where the Portuguese had introduced Catholicism. Other slaves in South Carolina may have had a similar background: Africa-born and familiar with whites. If so, this common background may have made it easier for Jemmy to communicate with the other slaves, enabling them to work together to resist their enslavement even though slaveholders labored to keep slaves from forging such communities.

In the wake of the Stono Rebellion, South Carolina passed a new slave code in 1740 called An Act for the Better Ordering and Governing of Negroes and Other Slaves in the Province, also known as the Negro Act of 1740. This law imposed new limits on slaves' behavior, prohibiting slaves from assembling, growing their own food, learning to write, and traveling freely.

THE NEW YORK CONSPIRACY TRIALS OF 1741

Eighteenth-century New York City contained many different ethnic groups, and conflicts among them created strain. In addition, one in five New Yorkers was a slave, and tensions ran high between slaves and the free population, especially in the aftermath of the Stono Rebellion. These tensions burst forth in 1741.

That year, thirteen fires broke out in the city, one of which reduced the colony's Fort George to ashes. Ever fearful of an uprising among enslaved New Yorkers, the city's whites spread rumors that the fires were part of a massive slave revolt in which slaves would murder whites, burn the city, and take over the colony. The Stono Rebellion was only a few years in the past, and throughout British America, fears of similar incidents were still fresh. Searching for solutions, and convinced slaves were the principal danger, nervous British authorities interrogated almost two hundred slaves and accused them of conspiracy. Rumors that Roman Catholics had joined the suspected conspiracy and planned to murder Protestant inhabitants of the city only added to the general hysteria. Very quickly, two hundred people were arrested, including a large number of the city's slave population.

After a quick series of trials at City Hall, known as the New York Conspiracy Trials of 1741, the government executed seventeen New Yorkers. Thirteen black men were publicly burned at the stake, while the others (including four whites) were hanged (Figure 4.10). Seventy slaves were sold to the West Indies. Little evidence exists to prove that an elaborate conspiracy, like the one white New Yorkers imagined, actually existed.

Figure 4.10   In the wake of a series of fires throughout New York City, rumors of a slave revolt led authorities to convict and execute thirty people, including thirteen black men who were publicly burned at the stake.

The events of 1741 in New York City illustrate the racial divide in British America, where panic among whites spurred great violence against and repression of the feared slave population. In the end, the Conspiracy Trials furthered white dominance and power over enslaved New Yorkers.

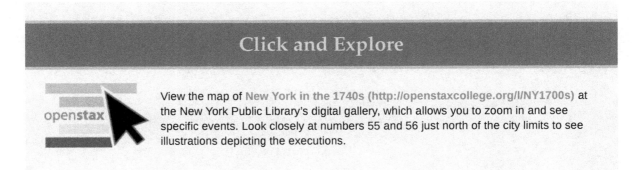

Click and Explore

View the map of New York in the 1740s (http://openstaxcollege.org/l/NY1700s) at the New York Public Library's digital gallery, which allows you to zoom in and see specific events. Look closely at numbers 55 and 56 just north of the city limits to see illustrations depicting the executions.

COLONIAL GENTRY AND THE CONSUMER REVOLUTION

British Americans' reliance on indentured servitude and slavery to meet the demand for colonial labor helped give rise to a wealthy colonial class—the gentry—in the Chesapeake tobacco colonies and elsewhere. To be "genteel," that is, a member of the gentry, meant to be refined, free of all rudeness. The British American gentry modeled themselves on the English aristocracy, who embodied the ideal of refinement and gentility. They built elaborate mansions to advertise their status and power. William Byrd II of Westover, Virginia, exemplifies the colonial gentry; a wealthy planter and slaveholder, he is known for founding Richmond and for his diaries documenting the life of a gentleman planter (Figure 4.11).

Figure 4.11   This painting by Hans Hysing, ca. 1724, depicts William Byrd II. Byrd was a wealthy gentleman planter in Virginia and a member of the colonial gentry.

Chapter 4 | Rule Britannia! The English Empire, 1660–1763

109

MY STORY

✸ *William Byrd's Secret Diary*

The diary of William Byrd, a Virginia planter, provides a unique way to better understand colonial life on a plantation (Figure 4.12). What does it show about daily life for a gentleman planter? What does it show about slavery?

August 27, 1709

I rose at 5 o'clock and read two chapters in Hebrew and some Greek in Josephus. I said my prayers and ate milk for breakfast. I danced my dance. I had like to have whipped my maid Anaka for her laziness but I forgave her. I read a little geometry. I denied my man G-r-l to go to a horse race because there was nothing but swearing and drinking there. I ate roast mutton for dinner. In the afternoon I played at piquet with my own wife and made her out of humor by cheating her. I read some Greek in Homer. Then I walked about the plantation. I lent John H-ch £7 [7 English pounds] in his distress. I said my prayers and had good health, good thoughts, and good humor, thanks be to God Almighty.

September 6, 1709

About one o'clock this morning my wife was happily delivered of a son, thanks be to God Almighty. I was awake in a blink and rose and my cousin Harrison met me on the stairs and told me it was a boy. We drank some French wine and went to bed again and rose at 7 o'clock. I read a chapter in Hebrew and then drank chocolate with the women for breakfast. I returned God humble thanks for so great a blessing and recommended my young son to His divine protection. . . .

September 15, 1710

I rose at 5 o'clock and read two chapters in Hebrew and some Greek in Thucydides. I said my prayers and ate milk and pears for breakfast. About 7 o'clock the negro boy [*or* Betty] that ran away was brought home. My wife against my will caused little Jenny to be burned with a hot iron, for which I quarreled with her. . . .

Figure 4.12   This photograph shows the view down the stairway from the third floor of Westover Plantation, home of William Byrd II. What does this image suggest about the lifestyle of the inhabitants—masters and servants—of this house?

One of the ways in which the gentry set themselves apart from others was through their purchase, consumption, and display of goods. An increased supply of consumer goods from England that became available in the eighteenth century led to a phenomenon called the consumer revolution. These products linked the colonies to Great Britain in real and tangible ways. Indeed, along with the colonial gentry, ordinary settlers in the colonies also participated in the frenzy of consumer spending on goods from Great Britain. Tea, for example, came to be regarded as the drink of the Empire, with or without fashionable tea sets.

The consumer revolution also made printed materials more widely available. Before 1680, for instance, no newspapers had been printed in colonial America. In the eighteenth century, however, a flood of journals, books, pamphlets, and other publications became available to readers on both sides of the Atlantic. This shared trove of printed matter linked members of the Empire by creating a community of shared tastes and ideas.

Cato's Letters, by Englishmen John Trenchard and Thomas Gordon, was one popular series of 144 pamphlets. These Whig circulars were published between 1720 and 1723 and emphasized the glory of England, especially its commitment to liberty. However, the pamphlets cautioned readers to be ever vigilant and on the lookout for attacks upon that liberty. Indeed, *Cato's Letters* suggested that there were constant efforts to undermine and destroy it.

Another very popular publication was the English gentlemen's magazine the *Spectator*, published between 1711 and 1714. In each issue, "Mr. Spectator" observed and commented on the world around him. What made the *Spectator* so wildly popular was its style; the essays were meant to persuade, and to cultivate among readers a refined set of behaviors, rejecting deceit and intolerance and focusing instead on the polishing of genteel taste and manners.

Novels, a new type of literature, made their first appearance in the eighteenth century and proved very popular in the British Atlantic. Daniel Defoe's *Robinson Crusoe* and Samuel Richardson's *Pamela: Or, Virtue Rewarded* found large and receptive audiences. Reading also allowed female readers the opportunity to interpret what they read without depending on a male authority to tell them what to think. Few women beyond the colonial gentry, however, had access to novels.

4.4 Great Awakening and Enlightenment

By the end of this section, you will be able to:
* Explain the significance of the Great Awakening
* Describe the genesis, central ideas, and effects of the Enlightenment in British North America

Two major cultural movements further strengthened Anglo-American colonists' connection to Great Britain: the Great Awakening and the Enlightenment. Both movements began in Europe, but they advocated very different ideas: the Great Awakening promoted a fervent, emotional religiosity, while the Enlightenment encouraged the pursuit of reason in all things. On both sides of the Atlantic, British subjects grappled with these new ideas.

THE FIRST GREAT AWAKENING

During the eighteenth century, the British Atlantic experienced an outburst of Protestant revivalism known as the **First Great Awakening**. (A Second Great Awakening would take place in the 1800s.) During the First Great Awakening, evangelists came from the ranks of several Protestant denominations: Congregationalists, Anglicans (members of the Church of England), and Presbyterians. They rejected what appeared to be sterile, formal modes of worship in favor of a vigorous emotional religiosity. Whereas Martin Luther and John Calvin had preached a doctrine of predestination and close reading of scripture, new evangelical ministers spread a message of personal and experiential faith that rose above mere book learning. Individuals could bring about their own salvation by accepting Christ, an especially welcome message for those who had felt excluded by traditional Protestantism: women, the young, and people at the lower end of the social spectrum.

The Great Awakening caused a split between those who followed the evangelical message (the "New Lights") and those who rejected it (the "Old Lights"). The elite ministers in British America were firmly

Old Lights, and they censured the new revivalism as chaos. Indeed, the revivals did sometimes lead to excess. In one notorious incident in 1743, an influential New Light minister named James Davenport urged his listeners to burn books. The next day, he told them to burn their clothes as a sign of their casting off the sinful trappings of the world. He then took off his own pants and threw them into the fire, but a woman saved them and tossed them back to Davenport, telling him he had gone too far.

Another outburst of Protestant revivalism began in New Jersey, led by a minister of the Dutch Reformed Church named Theodorus Frelinghuysen. Frelinghuysen's example inspired other ministers, including Gilbert Tennent, a Presbyterian. Tennent helped to spark a Presbyterian revival in the Middle Colonies (Pennsylvania, New York, and New Jersey), in part by founding a seminary to train other evangelical clergyman. New Lights also founded colleges in Rhode Island and New Hampshire that would later become Brown University and Dartmouth College.

In Northampton, Massachusetts, Jonathan Edwards led still another explosion of evangelical fervor. Edwards's best-known sermon, "Sinners in the Hands of an Angry God," used powerful word imagery to describe the terrors of hell and the possibilities of avoiding damnation by personal conversion (Figure 4.13). One passage reads: "The wrath of God burns against them [sinners], their damnation don't slumber, the pit is prepared, the fire is made ready, the furnace is now hot, ready to receive them, the flames do now rage and glow. The glittering sword is whet, and held over them, and the pit hath opened her mouth under them." Edwards's revival spread along the Connecticut River Valley, and news of the event spread rapidly through the frequent reprinting of his famous sermon.

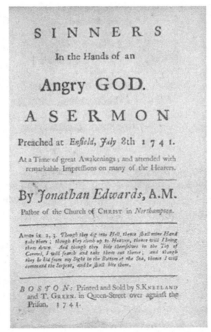

Figure 4.13 This image shows the frontispiece of *Sinners in the Hands of an Angry God, A Sermon Preached at Enfield, July 8, 1741* by Jonathan Edwards. Edwards was an evangelical preacher who led a Protestant revival in New England. This was his most famous sermon, the text of which was reprinted often and distributed widely.

The foremost evangelical of the Great Awakening was an Anglican minister named George Whitefield. Like many evangelical ministers, Whitefield was itinerant, traveling the countryside instead of having his own church and congregation. Between 1739 and 1740, he electrified colonial listeners with his brilliant oratory.

AMERICANA

✪ *Two Opposing Views of George Whitefield*

Not everyone embraced George Whitefield and other New Lights. Many established Old Lights decried the way the new evangelical religions appealed to people's passions, rather than to traditional religious values. The two illustrations below present two very different visions of George Whitefield (Figure 4.14).

(a)   (b)

Figure 4.14   In the 1774 portrait of George Whitefield by engraver Elisha Gallaudet (a), Whitefield appears with a gentle expression on his face. Although his hands are raised in exultation or entreaty, he does not look particularly roused or rousing. In the 1763 British political cartoon to the right, "Dr. Squintum's Exaltation or the Reformation" (b), Whitefield's hands are raised in a similar position, but there the similarities end.

Compare the two images above. On the left is an illustration for Whitefield's memoirs, while on the right is a cartoon satirizing the circus-like atmosphere that his preaching seemed to attract (Dr. Squintum was a nickname for Whitefield, who was cross-eyed). How do these two artists portray the same man? What emotions are the illustration for his memoirs intended to evoke? What details can you find in the cartoon that indicate the artist's distaste for the preacher?

The Great Awakening saw the rise of several Protestant denominations, including Methodists, Presbyterians, and Baptists (who emphasized adult baptism of converted Christians rather than infant baptism). These new churches gained converts and competed with older Protestant groups like Anglicans (members of the Church of England), Congregationalists (the heirs of Puritanism in America), and Quakers. The influence of these older Protestant groups, such as the New England Congregationalists, declined because of the Great Awakening. Nonetheless, the Great Awakening touched the lives of thousands on both sides of the Atlantic and provided a shared experience in the eighteenth-century British Empire.

THE ENLIGHTENMENT

The **Enlightenment**, or the Age of Reason, was an intellectual and cultural movement in the eighteenth century that emphasized reason over superstition and science over blind faith. Using the power of the press, Enlightenment thinkers like John Locke, Isaac Newton, and Voltaire questioned accepted knowledge and spread new ideas about openness, investigation, and religious tolerance throughout

Europe and the Americas. Many consider the Enlightenment a major turning point in Western civilization, an age of light replacing an age of darkness.

Several ideas dominated Enlightenment thought, including rationalism, empiricism, progressivism, and cosmopolitanism. Rationalism is the idea that humans are capable of using their faculty of reason to gain knowledge. This was a sharp turn away from the prevailing idea that people needed to rely on scripture or church authorities for knowledge. Empiricism promotes the idea that knowledge comes from experience and observation of the world. Progressivism is the belief that through their powers of reason and observation, humans could make unlimited, linear progress over time; this belief was especially important as a response to the carnage and upheaval of the English Civil Wars in the seventeenth century. Finally, cosmopolitanism reflected Enlightenment thinkers' view of themselves as citizens of the world and actively engaged in it, as opposed to being provincial and close-minded. In all, Enlightenment thinkers endeavored to be ruled by reason, not prejudice.

The **Freemasons** were a fraternal society that advocated Enlightenment principles of inquiry and tolerance. Freemasonry originated in London coffeehouses in the early eighteenth century, and Masonic lodges (local units) soon spread throughout Europe and the British colonies. One prominent Freemason, Benjamin Franklin, stands as the embodiment of the Enlightenment in British America (Figure 4.15). Born in Boston in 1706 to a large Puritan family, Franklin loved to read, although he found little beyond religious publications in his father's house. In 1718 he was apprenticed to his brother to work in a print shop, where he learned how to be a good writer by copying the style he found in the *Spectator*, which his brother printed. At the age of seventeen, the independent-minded Franklin ran away, eventually ending up in Quaker Philadelphia. There he began publishing the *Pennsylvania Gazette* in the late 1720s, and in 1732 he started his annual publication *Poor Richard: An Almanack*, in which he gave readers much practical advice, such as "Early to bed, early to rise, makes a man healthy, wealthy, and wise."

Figure 4.15 In this 1748 portrait by Robert Feke, a forty-year-old Franklin wears a stylish British wig, as befitted a proud and loyal member of the British Empire.

Franklin subscribed to **deism**, an Enlightenment-era belief in a God who created, but has no continuing involvement in, the world and the events within it. Deists also advanced the belief that personal morality—an individual's moral compass, leading to good works and actions—is more important than strict church doctrines. Franklin's deism guided his many philanthropic projects. In 1731, he established a reading library that became the Library Company of Philadelphia. In 1743, he founded the American Philosophical Society to encourage the spirit of inquiry. In 1749, he provided the foundation for the University of Pennsylvania, and in 1751, he helped found Pennsylvania Hospital.

His career as a printer made Franklin wealthy and well-respected. When he retired in 1748, he devoted himself to politics and scientific experiments. His most famous work, on electricity, exemplified Enlightenment principles. Franklin observed that lightning strikes tended to hit metal objects and reasoned that he could therefore direct lightning through the placement of metal objects during an electrical storm. He used this knowledge to advocate the use of lightning rods: metal poles connected to wires directing lightning's electrical charge into the ground and saving wooden homes in cities like Philadelphia from catastrophic fires. He published his findings in 1751, in *Experiments and Observations on Electricity*.

Franklin also wrote of his "rags to riches" tale, his *Memoir*, in the 1770s and 1780s. This story laid the foundation for the American Dream of upward social mobility.

Click and Explore

Visit the **Worldly Ways section (http://openstaxcollege.org/l/bfranklin1)** of PBS's Benjamin Franklin site to see an interactive map showing Franklin's overseas travels and his influence around the world. His diplomatic, political, scientific, and business achievements had great effects in many countries.

THE FOUNDING OF GEORGIA

The reach of Enlightenment thought was both broad and deep. In the 1730s, it even prompted the founding of a new colony. Having witnessed the terrible conditions of debtors' prison, as well as the results of releasing penniless debtors onto the streets of London, James Oglethorpe, a member of Parliament and advocate of social reform, petitioned King George II for a charter to start a new colony. George II, understanding the strategic advantage of a British colony standing as a buffer between South Carolina and Spanish Florida, granted the charter to Oglethorpe and twenty like-minded proprietors in 1732. Oglethorpe led the settlement of the colony, which was called Georgia in honor of the king. In 1733, he and 113 immigrants arrived on the ship *Anne*. Over the next decade, Parliament funded the migration of twenty-five hundred settlers, making Georgia the only government-funded colonial project.

Oglethorpe's vision for Georgia followed the ideals of the Age of Reason, seeing it as a place for England's "worthy poor" to start anew. To encourage industry, he gave each male immigrant fifty acres of land, tools, and a year's worth of supplies. In Savannah, the Oglethorpe Plan provided for a utopia: "an agrarian model of sustenance while sustaining egalitarian values holding all men as equal."

Oglethorpe's vision called for alcohol and slavery to be banned. However, colonists who relocated from other colonies, especially South Carolina, disregarded these prohibitions. Despite its proprietors' early vision of a colony guided by Enlightenment ideals and free of slavery, by the 1750s, Georgia was producing quantities of rice grown and harvested by slaves.

4.5 Wars for Empire

By the end of this section, you will be able to:
- Describe the wars for empire
- Analyze the significance of these conflicts

Wars for empire composed a final link connecting the Atlantic sides of the British Empire. Great Britain fought four separate wars against Catholic France from the late 1600s to the mid-1700s. Another war, the War of Jenkins' Ear, pitted Britain against Spain. These conflicts for control of North America also helped colonists forge important alliances with native peoples, as different tribes aligned themselves with different European powers.

GENERATIONS OF WARFARE

Generations of British colonists grew up during a time when much of North America, especially the Northeast, engaged in war. Colonists knew war firsthand. In the eighteenth century, fighting was seasonal. Armies mobilized in the spring, fought in the summer, and retired to winter quarters in the fall. The British army imposed harsh discipline on its soldiers, who were drawn from the poorer classes, to ensure they did not step out of line during engagements. If they did, their officers would kill them. On the battlefield, armies dressed in bright uniforms to advertise their bravery and lack of fear. They stood in tight formation and exchanged volleys with the enemy. They often feared their officers more than the enemy.

Click and Explore

Read the diary of a provincial soldier who fought in the French and Indian War on the Captain David Perry Web Site (http://openstaxcollege.org/l/DPerry) hosted by Rootsweb. David Perry's journal, which includes a description of the 1758 campaign, provides a glimpse of warfare in the eighteenth century.

Most imperial conflicts had both American and European fronts, leaving us with two names for each war. For instance, King William's War (1688–1697) is also known as the War of the League of Augsburg. In America, the bulk of the fighting in this conflict took place between New England and New France. The war proved inconclusive, with no clear victor (Figure 4.16).

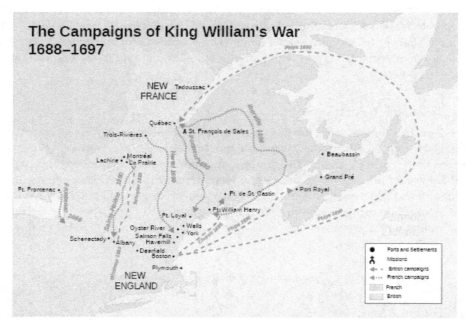

Figure 4.16 This map shows the French and British armies' movements during King William's War, in which there was no clear victor.

Queen Anne's War (1702–1713) is also known as the War of Spanish Succession. England fought against both Spain and France over who would ascend the Spanish throne after the last of the Hapsburg rulers died. In North America, fighting took place in Florida, New England, and New France. In Canada, the French prevailed but lost Acadia and Newfoundland; however, the victory was again not decisive because the English failed to take Quebec, which would have given them control of Canada.

This conflict is best remembered in the United States for the French and Indian raid against Deerfield, Massachusetts, in 1704. A small French force, combined with a native group made up of Catholic Mohawks and Abenaki (Pocumtucs), attacked the frontier outpost of Deerfield, killing scores and taking 112 prisoners. Among the captives was the seven-year-old daughter of Deerfield's minister John Williams, named Eunice. She was held by the Mohawks for years as her family tried to get her back, and became assimilated into the tribe. To the horror of the Puritan leaders, when she grew up Eunice married a Mohawk and refused to return to New England.

In North America, possession of Georgia and trade with the interior was the focus of the War of Jenkins' Ear (1739–1742), a conflict between Britain and Spain over contested claims to the land occupied by the fledgling colony between South Carolina and Florida. The war got its name from an incident in 1731 in which a Spanish Coast Guard captain severed the ear of British captain Robert Jenkins as punishment for raiding Spanish ships in Panama. Jenkins fueled the growing animosity between England and Spain by presenting his ear to Parliament and stirring up British public outrage. More than anything else, the War of Jenkins' Ear disrupted the Atlantic trade, a situation that hurt both Spain and Britain and was a major reason the war came to a close in 1742. Georgia, founded six years earlier, remained British and a buffer against Spanish Florida.

King George's War (1744–1748), known in Europe as the War of Austrian Succession (1740–1748), was fought in the northern colonies and New France. In 1745, the British took the massive French fortress at Louisbourg on Cape Breton Island, Nova Scotia (Figure 4.17). However, three years later, under the terms of the Treaty of Aix-la-Chapelle, Britain relinquished control of the fortress to the French. Once again, war resulted in an incomplete victory for both Britain and France.

Download for free at http://cnx.org/content/col11740/latest/

Figure 4.17 In this 1747 painting by J. Stevens, *View of the landing of the New England forces in ye expedition against Cape Breton*, British forces land on the island of Cape Breton to capture Fort Louisbourg.

THE FRENCH AND INDIAN WAR

The final imperial war, the **French and Indian War** (1754–1763), known as the Seven Years' War in Europe, proved to be the decisive contest between Britain and France in America. It began over rival claims along the frontier in present-day western Pennsylvania. Well-connected planters from Virginia faced stagnant tobacco prices and hoped expanding into these western lands would stabilize their wealth and status. Some of them established the Ohio Company of Virginia in 1748, and the British crown granted the company half a million acres in 1749. However, the French also claimed the lands of the Ohio Company, and to protect the region they established Fort Duquesne in 1754, where the Ohio, Monongahela, and Allegheny Rivers met.

The war began in May 1754 because of these competing claims between Britain and France. Twenty-two-year-old Virginian George Washington, a surveyor whose family helped to found the Ohio Company, gave the command to fire on French soldiers near present-day Uniontown, Pennsylvania. This incident on the Pennsylvania frontier proved to be a decisive event that led to imperial war. For the next decade, fighting took place along the frontier of New France and British America from Virginia to Maine. The war also spread to Europe as France and Britain looked to gain supremacy in the Atlantic World.

The British fared poorly in the first years of the war. In 1754, the French and their native allies forced Washington to surrender at Fort Necessity, a hastily built fort constructed after his attack on the French. In 1755, Britain dispatched General Edward Braddock to the colonies to take Fort Duquesne. The French, aided by the Potawotomis, Ottawas, Shawnees, and Delawares, ambushed the fifteen hundred British soldiers and Virginia militia who marched to the fort. The attack sent panic through the British force, and hundreds of British soldiers and militiamen died, including General Braddock. The campaign of 1755 proved to be a disaster for the British. In fact, the only British victory that year was the capture of Nova Scotia. In 1756 and 1757, Britain suffered further defeats with the fall of Fort Oswego and Fort William Henry (Figure 4.18).

Figure 4.18 This schematic map depicts the events of the French and Indian War. Note the scarcity of British victories.

The war began to turn in favor of the British in 1758, due in large part to the efforts of William Pitt, a very popular member of Parliament. Pitt pledged huge sums of money and resources to defeating the hated Catholic French, and Great Britain spent part of the money on bounties paid to new young recruits in the colonies, helping invigorate the British forces. In 1758, the Iroquois, Delaware, and Shawnee signed the Treaty of Easton, aligning themselves with the British in return for some contested land around Pennsylvania and Virginia. In 1759, the British took Quebec, and in 1760, Montreal. The French empire in North America had crumbled.

The war continued until 1763, when the French signed the Treaty of Paris. This treaty signaled a dramatic reversal of fortune for France. Indeed, New France, which had been founded in the early 1600s, ceased to exist. The British Empire had now gained mastery over North America. The Empire not only gained New France under the treaty; it also acquired French sugar islands in the West Indies, French trading posts in India, and French-held posts on the west coast of Africa. Great Britain's victory in the French and Indian War meant that it had become a truly global empire. British colonists joyously celebrated, singing the refrain of "Rule, Britannia! / Britannia, rule the waves! / Britons never, never, never shall be slaves!"

In the American colonies, ties with Great Britain were closer than ever. Professional British soldiers had fought alongside Anglo-American militiamen, forging a greater sense of shared identity. With Great Britain's victory, colonial pride ran high as colonists celebrated their identity as British subjects.

This last of the wars for empire, however, also sowed the seeds of trouble. The war led Great Britain deeply into debt, and in the 1760s and 1770s, efforts to deal with the debt through imperial reforms would have the unintended consequence of causing stress and strain that threatened to tear the Empire apart.

Key Terms

deism an Enlightenment-era belief in the existence of a supreme being—specifically, a creator who does not intervene in the universe—representing a rejection of the belief in a supernatural deity who interacts with humankind

Dominion of New England James II's consolidated New England colony, made up of all the colonies from New Haven to Massachusetts and later New York and New Jersey

English interregnum the period from 1649 to 1660 when England had no king

Enlightenment an eighteenth-century intellectual and cultural movement that emphasized reason and science over superstition, religion, and tradition

First Great Awakening an eighteenth-century Protestant revival that emphasized individual, experiential faith over church doctrine and the close study of scripture

Freemasons a fraternal society founded in the early eighteenth century that advocated Enlightenment principles of inquiry and tolerance

French and Indian War the last eighteenth-century imperial struggle between Great Britain and France, leading to a decisive British victory; this war lasted from 1754 to 1763 and was also called the Seven Years' War

Glorious Revolution the overthrow of James II in 1688

Navigation Acts a series of English mercantilist laws enacted between 1651 and 1696 in order to control trade with the colonies

nonconformists Protestants who did not conform to the doctrines or practices of the Church of England

proprietary colonies colonies granted by the king to a trusted individual, family, or group

Restoration colonies the colonies King Charles II established or supported during the Restoration (the Carolinas, New York, New Jersey, and Pennsylvania)

salutary neglect the laxness with which the English crown enforced the Navigation Acts in the eighteenth century

Summary

4.1 Charles II and the Restoration Colonies

After the English Civil War and interregnum, England began to fashion a stronger and larger empire in North America. In addition to wresting control of New York and New Jersey from the Dutch, Charles II established the Carolinas and Pennsylvania as proprietary colonies. Each of these colonies added immensely to the Empire, supplying goods not produced in England, such as rice and indigo. The Restoration colonies also contributed to the rise in population in English America as many thousands of Europeans made their way to the colonies. Their numbers were further augmented by the forced migration of African slaves. Starting in 1651, England pursued mercantilist policies through a series of Navigation Acts designed to make the most of England's overseas possessions. Nonetheless, without proper enforcement of Parliament's acts and with nothing to prevent colonial traders from commanding their own fleets of ships, the Navigation Acts did not control trade as intended.

Chapter 4 | Rule Britannia! The English Empire, 1660–1763

121

4.2 The Glorious Revolution and the English Empire

The threat of a Catholic absolute monarchy prompted not only the overthrow of James II but also the adoption of laws and policies that changed English government. The Glorious Revolution restored a Protestant monarchy and at the same time limited its power by means of the 1689 Bill of Rights. Those who lived through the events preserved the memory of the Glorious Revolution and the defense of liberty that it represented. Meanwhile, thinkers such as John Locke provided new models and inspirations for the evolving concept of government.

4.3 An Empire of Slavery and the Consumer Revolution

The seventeenth and eighteenth centuries saw the expansion of slavery in the American colonies from South Carolina to Boston. The institution of slavery created a false sense of superiority in whites, while simultaneously fueling fears of slave revolt. White response to such revolts, or even the threat of them, led to gross overreactions and further constraints on slaves' activities. The development of the Atlantic economy also allowed colonists access to more British goods than ever before. The buying habits of both commoners and the rising colonial gentry fueled the consumer revolution, creating even stronger ties with Great Britain by means of a shared community of taste and ideas.

4.4 Great Awakening and Enlightenment

The eighteenth century saw a host of social, religious, and intellectual changes across the British Empire. While the Great Awakening emphasized vigorously emotional religiosity, the Enlightenment promoted the power of reason and scientific observation. Both movements had lasting impacts on the colonies. The beliefs of the New Lights of the First Great Awakening competed with the religions of the first colonists, and the religious fervor in Great Britain and her North American colonies bound the eighteenth-century British Atlantic together in a shared, common experience. The British colonist Benjamin Franklin gained fame on both sides of the Atlantic as a printer, publisher, and scientist. He embodied Enlightenment ideals in the British Atlantic with his scientific experiments and philanthropic endeavors. Enlightenment principles even guided the founding of the colony of Georgia, although those principles could not stand up to the realities of colonial life, and slavery soon took hold in the colony.

4.5 Wars for Empire

From 1688 to 1763, Great Britain engaged in almost continuous power struggles with France and Spain. Most of these conflicts originated in Europe, but their engagements spilled over into the colonies. For almost eighty years, Great Britain and France fought for control of eastern North America. During most of that time, neither force was able to win a decisive victory, though each side saw occasional successes with the crucial help of native peoples. It was not until halfway through the French and Indian War (1754–1763), when Great Britain swelled its troops with more volunteers and native allies, that the balance of power shifted toward the British. With the 1763 Treaty of Paris, New France was eliminated, and Great Britain gained control of all the lands north of Florida and east of the Mississippi. British subjects on both sides of the Atlantic rejoiced.

Review Questions

1. To what does the term "Restoration" refer?
    A. the restoration of New York to English power
    B. the restoration of Catholicism as the official religion of England
    C. the restoration of Charles II to the English throne
    D. the restoration of Parliamentary power in England

2. What was the predominant religion in Pennsylvania?

   A. Quakerism

   B. Puritanism

   C. Catholicism

   D. Protestantism

3. What sorts of labor systems were used in the Restoration colonies?

4. Which of the following represents a concern that those in England and her colonies maintained about James II?

   A. that he would promote the spread of Protestantism

   B. that he would reduce the size of the British army and navy, leaving England and her colonies vulnerable to attack

   C. that he would advocate for Parliament's independence from the monarchy

   D. that he would institute a Catholic absolute monarchy

5. What was the Dominion of New England?

   A. James II's overthrow of the New England colonial governments

   B. the consolidated New England colony James II created

   C. Governor Edmund Andros's colonial government in New York

   D. the excise taxes New England colonists had to pay to James II

6. What was the outcome of the Glorious Revolution?

7. The Negro Act of 1740 was a reaction to _____.

   A. fears of a slave conspiracy in the setting of thirteen fires in New York City

   B. the Stono Rebellion

   C. the Royal African Company's monopoly

   D. the growing power of maroon communities

8. What was the "conspiracy" of the New York Conspiracy Trials of 1741?

   A. American patriots conspiring to overthrow the royal government

   B. indentured servants conspiring to overthrow their masters

   C. slaves conspiring to burn down the city and take control

   D. Protestants conspiring to murder Catholics

9. What was the First Great Awakening?

   A. a cultural and intellectual movement that emphasized reason and science over superstition and religion

   B. a Protestant revival that emphasized emotional, experiential faith over book learning

   C. a cultural shift that promoted Christianity among slave communities

   D. the birth of an American identity, promoted by Benjamin Franklin

10. Which of the following is not a tenet of the Enlightenment?

   A. atheism

   B. empiricism

   C. progressivism

   D. rationalism

11. Who were the Freemasons, and why were they significant?

12. What was the primary goal of Britain's wars for empire from 1688 to 1763?

   A. control of North America

   B. control of American Indians

   C. greater power in Europe and the world

   D. defeat of Catholicism

13. Who were the main combatants in the French and Indian War?

   A. France against Indians

   B. Great Britain against Indians

   C. Great Britain against France

   D. Great Britain against the French and their Indian allies

14. What prompted the French and Indian War?

Critical Thinking Questions

15. How did Pennsylvania's Quaker beginnings distinguish it from other colonies in British America?

16.   What were the effects of the consumer revolution on the colonies?

17.   How did the ideas of the Enlightenment and the Great Awakening offer opposing outlooks to British Americans? What similarities were there between the two schools of thought?

18.   What was the impact of the wars for empire in North America, Europe, and the world?

19.   What role did Indians play in the wars for empire?

20.   What shared experiences, intellectual currents, and cultural elements drew together British subjects on both sides of the Atlantic during this period? How did these experiences, ideas, and goods serve to strengthen those bonds?

124

Chapter 4 | Rule Britannia! The English Empire, 1660–1763

CHAPTER 5

Imperial Reforms and Colonial Protests, 1763-1774

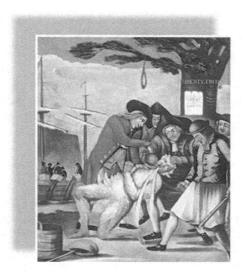

Figure 5.1 *The Bostonians Paying the Excise-man, or Tarring and Feathering* (1774), attributed to Philip Dawe, depicts the most publicized tarring and feathering incident of the American Revolution. The victim is John Malcolm, a customs official loyal to the British crown.

Chapter Outline

5.1 Confronting the National Debt: The Aftermath of the French and Indian War
5.2 The Stamp Act and the Sons and Daughters of Liberty
5.3 The Townshend Acts and Colonial Protest
5.4 The Destruction of the Tea and the Coercive Acts
5.5 Disaffection: The First Continental Congress and American Identity

Introduction

The Bostonians Paying the Excise-man, or Tarring and Feathering (Figure 5.1), shows five Patriots tarring and feathering the Commissioner of Customs, John Malcolm, a sea captain, army officer, and staunch **Loyalist**. The print shows the Boston Tea Party, a protest against the Tea Act of 1773, and the Liberty Tree, an elm tree near Boston Common that became a rallying point against the Stamp Act of 1765. When the crowd threatened to hang Malcolm if he did not renounce his position as a royal customs officer, he reluctantly agreed and the protestors allowed him to go home. The scene represents the animosity toward those who supported royal authority and illustrates the high tide of unrest in the colonies after the British government imposed a series of imperial reform measures during the years 1763–1774.

The government's formerly lax oversight of the colonies ended as the architects of the British Empire put these new reforms in place. The British hoped to gain greater control over colonial trade and frontier settlement as well as to reduce the administrative cost of the colonies and the enormous debt left by the French and Indian War. Each step the British took, however, generated a backlash. Over time, imperial reforms pushed many colonists toward separation from the British Empire.

5.1 Confronting the National Debt: The Aftermath of the French and Indian War

By the end of this section, you will be able to:
- Discuss the status of Great Britain's North American colonies in the years directly following the French and Indian War
- Describe the size and scope of the British debt at the end of the French and Indian War
- Explain how the British Parliament responded to the debt crisis
- Outline the purpose of the Proclamation Line, the Sugar Act, and the Currency Act

Great Britain had much to celebrate in 1763. The long and costly war with France had finally ended, and Great Britain had emerged victorious. British subjects on both sides of the Atlantic celebrated the strength of the British Empire. Colonial pride ran high; to live under the British Constitution and to have defeated the hated French Catholic menace brought great joy to British Protestants everywhere in the Empire. From Maine to Georgia, British colonists joyously celebrated the victory and sang the refrain of "Rule, Britannia! Britannia, rule the waves! Britons never, never, never shall be slaves!"

Despite the celebratory mood, the victory over France also produced major problems within the British Empire, problems that would have serious consequences for British colonists in the Americas. During the war, many Indian tribes had sided with the French, who supplied them with guns. After the 1763 Treaty of Paris that ended the French and Indian War (or the Seven Years' War), British colonists had to defend the frontier, where French colonists and their tribal allies remained a powerful force. The most organized resistance, Pontiac's Rebellion, highlighted tensions the settlers increasingly interpreted in racial terms.

The massive debt the war generated at home, however, proved to be the most serious issue facing Great Britain. The frontier had to be secure in order to prevent another costly war. Greater enforcement of imperial trade laws had to be put into place. Parliament had to find ways to raise revenue to pay off the crippling debt from the war. Everyone would have to contribute their expected share, including the British subjects across the Atlantic.

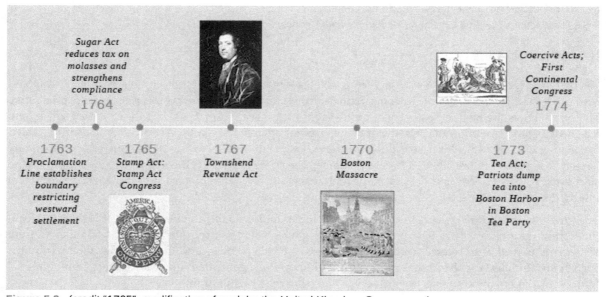

Figure 5.2   (credit "1765": modification of work by the United Kingdom Government)

Download for free at http://cnx.org/content/col11740/latest/

PROBLEMS ON THE AMERICAN FRONTIER

With the end of the French and Indian War, Great Britain claimed a vast new expanse of territory, at least on paper. Under the terms of the Treaty of Paris, the French territory known as New France had ceased to exist. British territorial holdings now extended from Canada to Florida, and British military focus shifted to maintaining peace in the king's newly enlarged lands. However, much of the land in the American British Empire remained under the control of powerful native confederacies, which made any claims of British mastery beyond the Atlantic coastal settlements hollow. Great Britain maintained ten thousand troops in North America after the war ended in 1763 to defend the borders and repel any attack by their imperial rivals.

British colonists, eager for fresh land, poured over the Appalachian Mountains to stake claims. The western frontier had long been a "middle ground" where different imperial powers (British, French, Spanish) had interacted and compromised with native peoples. That era of accommodation in the "middle ground" came to an end after the French and Indian War. Virginians (including George Washington) and other land-hungry colonists had already raised tensions in the 1740s with their quest for land. Virginia landowners in particular eagerly looked to diversify their holdings beyond tobacco, which had stagnated in price and exhausted the fertility of the lands along the Chesapeake Bay. They invested heavily in the newly available land. This westward movement brought the settlers into conflict as never before with Indian tribes, such as the Shawnee, Seneca-Cayuga, Wyandot, and Delaware, who increasingly held their ground against any further intrusion by white settlers.

The treaty that ended the war between France and Great Britain proved to be a significant blow to native peoples, who had viewed the conflict as an opportunity to gain additional trade goods from both sides. With the French defeat, many Indians who had sided with France lost a valued trading partner as well as bargaining power over the British. Settlers' encroachment on their land, as well as the increased British military presence, changed the situation on the frontier dramatically. After the war, British troops took over the former French forts but failed to court favor with the local tribes by distributing ample gifts, as the French had done. They also significantly reduced the amount of gunpowder and ammunition they sold to the Indians, worsening relationships further.

Indians' resistance to colonists drew upon the teachings of Delaware (Lenni Lenape) prophet Neolin and the leadership of Ottawa war chief Pontiac. Neolin was a spiritual leader who preached a doctrine of shunning European culture and expelling Europeans from native lands. Neolin's beliefs united Indians from many villages. In a broad-based alliance that came to be known as Pontiac's Rebellion, Pontiac led a loose coalition of these native tribes against the colonists and the British army.

Pontiac started bringing his coalition together as early as 1761, urging Indians to "drive [the Europeans] out and make war upon them." The conflict began in earnest in 1763, when Pontiac and several hundred Ojibwas, Potawatomis, and Hurons laid siege to Fort Detroit. At the same time, Senecas, Shawnees, and Delawares laid siege to Fort Pitt. Over the next year, the war spread along the backcountry from Virginia to Pennsylvania. Pontiac's Rebellion (also known as Pontiac's War) triggered horrific violence on both sides. Firsthand reports of Indian attacks tell of murder, scalping, dismemberment, and burning at the stake. These stories incited a deep racial hatred among colonists against all Indians.

The actions of a group of Scots-Irish settlers from Paxton (or Paxtang), Pennsylvania, in December 1763, illustrates the deadly situation on the frontier. Forming a mob known as the Paxton Boys, these frontiersmen attacked a nearby group of Conestoga of the Susquehannock tribe. The Conestoga had lived peacefully with local settlers, but the Paxton Boys viewed all Indians as savages and they brutally murdered the six Conestoga they found at home and burned their houses. When Governor John Penn put the remaining fourteen Conestoga in protective custody in Lancaster, Pennsylvania, the Paxton Boys broke into the building and killed and scalped the Conestoga they found there (Figure 5.3). Although Governor Penn offered a reward for the capture of any Paxton Boys involved in the murders, no one ever identified the attackers. Some colonists reacted to the incident with outrage. Benjamin Franklin described the Paxton Boys as "the barbarous Men who committed the atrocious act, in Defiance of Government, of all Laws human and divine, and to the eternal Disgrace of their Country and Colour," stating that "the Wickedness cannot be covered, the Guilt will lie on the whole Land, till Justice is done on the Murderers. The blood of the innocent will cry to heaven for vengeance." Yet, as the inability to bring the perpetrators to justice clearly indicates, the Paxton Boys had many more supporters than critics.

Figure 5.3 This nineteenth-century lithograph depicts the massacre of Conestoga in 1763 at Lancaster, Pennsylvania, where they had been placed in protective custody. None of the attackers, members of the Paxton Boys, were ever identified.

Click and Explore

Visit **Explore PAhistory.com (http://openstaxcollege.org/l/paxton)** to read the full text of Benjamin Franklin's "Benjamin Franklin, An Account of the Paxton Boys' Murder of the Conestoga Indians, 1764."

Pontiac's Rebellion and the Paxton Boys' actions were examples of early American race wars, in which both sides saw themselves as inherently different from the other and believed the other needed to be eradicated. The prophet Neolin's message, which he said he received in a vision from the Master of Life, was: "Wherefore do you suffer the whites to dwell upon your lands? Drive them away; wage war against them." Pontiac echoed this idea in a meeting, exhorting tribes to join together against the British: "It is important for us, my brothers, that we exterminate from our lands this nation which seeks only to destroy us." In his letter suggesting "gifts" to the natives of smallpox-infected blankets, Field Marshal Jeffrey Amherst said, "You will do well to inoculate the Indians by means of blankets, as well as every other method that can serve to extirpate this execrable race." Pontiac's Rebellion came to an end in 1766, when it became clear that the French, whom Pontiac had hoped would side with his forces, would not be returning. The repercussions, however, would last much longer. Race relations between Indians and whites remained poisoned on the frontier.

Well aware of the problems on the frontier, the British government took steps to try to prevent bloodshed and another costly war. At the beginning of Pontiac's uprising, the British issued the Proclamation of 1763, which forbade white settlement west of the **Proclamation Line**, a borderline running along the spine of the Appalachian Mountains (**Figure 5.4**). The Proclamation Line aimed to forestall further conflict on the frontier, the clear flashpoint of tension in British North America. British colonists who had hoped to move west after the war chafed at this restriction, believing the war had been fought and won to ensure the right to settle west. The Proclamation Line therefore came as a setback to their vision of westward expansion.

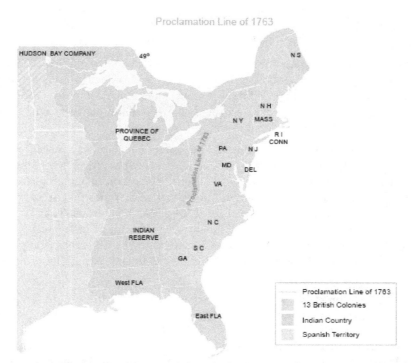

Figure 5.4 This map shows the status of the American colonies in 1763, after the end of the French and Indian War. Although Great Britain won control of the territory east of the Mississippi, the Proclamation Line of 1763 prohibited British colonists from settling west of the Appalachian Mountains. (credit: modification of work by the National Atlas of the United States)

THE BRITISH NATIONAL DEBT

Great Britain's newly enlarged empire meant a greater financial burden, and the mushrooming debt from the war was a major cause of concern. The war nearly doubled the British national debt, from £75 million in 1756 to £133 million in 1763. Interest payments alone consumed over half the national budget, and the continuing military presence in North America was a constant drain. The Empire needed more revenue to replenish its dwindling coffers. Those in Great Britain believed that British subjects in North America, as the major beneficiaries of Great Britain's war for global supremacy, should certainly shoulder their share of the financial burden.

The British government began increasing revenues by raising taxes at home, even as various interest groups lobbied to keep their taxes low. Powerful members of the aristocracy, well represented in Parliament, successfully convinced Prime Minister John Stuart, third earl of Bute, to refrain from raising taxes on land. The greater tax burden, therefore, fell on the lower classes in the form of increased import duties, which raised the prices of imported goods such as sugar and tobacco. George Grenville succeeded Bute as prime minister in 1763. Grenville determined to curtail government spending and make sure that, as subjects of the British Empire, the American colonists did their part to pay down the massive debt.

IMPERIAL REFORMS

The new era of greater British interest in the American colonies through imperial reforms picked up in pace in the mid-1760s. In 1764, Prime Minister Grenville introduced the Currency Act of 1764, prohibiting the colonies from printing additional paper money and requiring colonists to pay British merchants in gold and silver instead of the colonial paper money already in circulation. The Currency Act aimed to standardize the currency used in Atlantic trade, a logical reform designed to help stabilize the Empire's economy. This rule brought American economic activity under greater British control. Colonists relied on their own paper currency to conduct trade and, with gold and silver in short supply, they found their finances tight. Not surprisingly, they grumbled about the new imperial currency regulations.

Grenville also pushed Parliament to pass the Sugar Act of 1764, which actually lowered duties on British molasses by half, from six pence per gallon to three. Grenville designed this measure to address the problem of rampant colonial smuggling with the French sugar islands in the West Indies. The act attempted to make it easier for colonial traders, especially New England mariners who routinely engaged in illegal trade, to comply with the imperial law.

To give teeth to the 1764 Sugar Act, the law intensified enforcement provisions. Prior to the 1764 act, colonial violations of the Navigation Acts had been tried in local courts, where sympathetic colonial juries refused to convict merchants on trial. However, the Sugar Act required violators to be tried in **vice-admiralty courts**. These crown-sanctioned tribunals, which settled disputes that occurred at sea, operated without juries. Some colonists saw this feature of the 1764 act as dangerous. They argued that trial by jury had long been honored as a basic right of Englishmen under the British Constitution. To deprive defendants of a jury, they contended, meant reducing liberty-loving British subjects to political slavery. In the British Atlantic world, some colonists perceived this loss of liberty as parallel to the enslavement of Africans.

As loyal British subjects, colonists in America cherished their Constitution, an unwritten system of government that they celebrated as the best political system in the world. The British Constitution prescribed the roles of the King, the House of Lords, and the House of Commons. Each entity provided a check and balance against the worst tendencies of the others. If the King had too much power, the result would be tyranny. If the Lords had too much power, the result would be oligarchy. If the Commons had the balance of power, democracy or mob rule would prevail. The British Constitution promised representation of the will of British subjects, and without such representation, even the **indirect tax** of the Sugar Act was considered a threat to the settlers' rights as British subjects. Furthermore, some American colonists felt the colonies were on equal political footing with Great Britain. The Sugar Act meant they were secondary, mere adjuncts to the Empire. All subjects of the British crown knew they had liberties under the constitution. The Sugar Act suggested that some in Parliament labored to deprive them of what made them uniquely British.

5.2 The Stamp Act and the Sons and Daughters of Liberty

By the end of this section, you will be able to:
- Explain the purpose of the 1765 Stamp Act
- Describe the colonial responses to the Stamp Act

In 1765, the British Parliament moved beyond the efforts during the previous two years to better regulate westward expansion and trade by putting in place the Stamp Act. As a **direct tax** on the colonists, the Stamp Act imposed an internal tax on almost every type of printed paper colonists used, including newspapers, legal documents, and playing cards. While the architects of the Stamp Act saw the measure as a way to defray the costs of the British Empire, it nonetheless gave rise to the first major colonial protest against British imperial control as expressed in the famous slogan "no taxation without representation." The Stamp Act reinforced the sense among some colonists that Parliament was not treating them as equals of their peers across the Atlantic.

THE STAMP ACT AND THE QUARTERING ACT

Prime Minister Grenville, author of the Sugar Act of 1764, introduced the Stamp Act in the early spring of 1765. Under this act, anyone who used or purchased anything printed on paper had to buy a revenue stamp (Figure 5.5) for it. In the same year, 1765, Parliament also passed the Quartering Act, a law that attempted to solve the problems of stationing troops in North America. The Parliament understood the Stamp Act and the Quartering Act as an assertion of their power to control colonial policy.

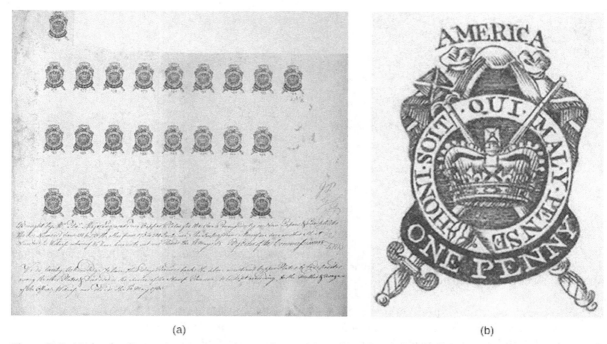

(a)   (b)

Figure 5.5 Under the Stamp Act, anyone who used or purchased anything printed on paper had to buy a revenue stamp for it. Image (a) shows a partial proof sheet of one-penny stamps. Image (b) provides a close-up of a one-penny stamp. (credit a: modification of work by the United Kingdom Government; credit b: modification of work by the United Kingdom Government)

The Stamp Act signaled a shift in British policy after the French and Indian War. Before the Stamp Act, the colonists had paid taxes to their colonial governments or indirectly through higher prices, not directly to the Crown's appointed governors. This was a time-honored liberty of representative legislatures of the colonial governments. The passage of the Stamp Act meant that starting on November 1, 1765, the colonists would contribute £60,000 per year—17 percent of the total cost—to the upkeep of the ten thousand British soldiers in North America (Figure 5.6). Because the Stamp Act raised constitutional issues, it triggered the first serious protest against British imperial policy.

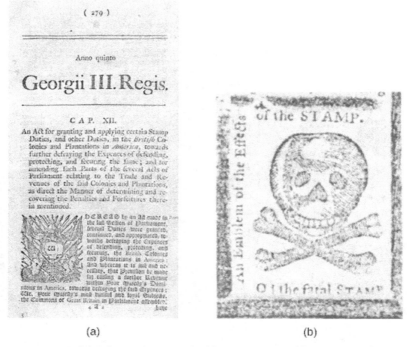

(a)   (b)

Figure 5.6   The announcement of the Stamp Act, seen in this newspaper publication (a), raised numerous concerns among colonists in America. Protests against British imperial policy took many forms, such as this mock stamp (b) whose text reads "An Emblem of the Effects of the STAMP. O! the Fatal STAMP."

Parliament also asserted its prerogative in 1765 with the Quartering Act. The Quartering Act of 1765 addressed the problem of housing British soldiers stationed in the American colonies. It required that they be provided with barracks or places to stay in public houses, and that if extra housing were necessary, then troops could be stationed in barns and other uninhabited private buildings. In addition, the costs of the troops' food and lodging fell to the colonists. Since the time of James II, who ruled from 1685 to 1688, many British subjects had mistrusted the presence of a standing army during peacetime, and having to pay for the soldiers' lodging and food was especially burdensome. Widespread evasion and disregard for the law occurred in almost all the colonies, but the issue was especially contentious in New York, the headquarters of British forces. When fifteen hundred troops arrived in New York in 1766, the New York Assembly refused to follow the Quartering Act.

COLONIAL PROTEST: GENTRY, MERCHANTS, AND THE STAMP ACT CONGRESS

For many British colonists living in America, the Stamp Act raised many concerns. As a direct tax, it appeared to be an unconstitutional measure, one that deprived freeborn British subjects of their liberty, a concept they defined broadly to include various rights and privileges they enjoyed as British subjects, including the right to representation. According to the unwritten British Constitution, only representatives for whom British subjects voted could tax them. Parliament was in charge of taxation, and although it was a representative body, the colonies did not have "actual" (or direct) representation in it. Parliamentary members who supported the Stamp Act argued that the colonists had virtual representation, because the architects of the British Empire knew best how to maximize returns from its possessions overseas. However, this argument did not satisfy the protesters, who viewed themselves as having the same right as all British subjects to avoid taxation without their consent. With no representation in the House of Commons, where bills of taxation originated, they felt themselves deprived of this inherent right.

The British government knew the colonists might object to the Stamp Act's expansion of parliamentary power, but Parliament believed the relationship of the colonies to the Empire was one of dependence, not equality. However, the Stamp Act had the unintended and ironic consequence of drawing colonists from very different areas and viewpoints together in protest. In Massachusetts, for instance, James Otis, a lawyer and defender of British liberty, became the leading voice for the idea that "Taxation without representation is tyranny." In the Virginia House of Burgesses, firebrand and slaveholder Patrick Henry introduced the Virginia Stamp Act Resolutions, which denounced the Stamp Act and the British crown in language so strong that some conservative Virginians accused him of treason (Figure 5.7). Henry replied that Virginians were subject only to taxes that they themselves—or their representatives—imposed. In short, there could be **no taxation without representation**.

Figure 5.7 *Patrick Henry Before the Virginia House of Burgesses* (1851), painted by Peter F. Rothermel, offers a romanticized depiction of Henry's speech denouncing the Stamp Act of 1765. Supporters and opponents alike debated the stark language of the speech, which quickly became legendary.

The colonists had never before formed a unified political front, so Grenville and Parliament did not fear true revolt. However, this was to change in 1765. In response to the Stamp Act, the Massachusetts Assembly sent letters to the other colonies, asking them to attend a meeting, or congress, to discuss how to respond to the act. Many American colonists from very different colonies found common cause in their opposition to the Stamp Act. Representatives from nine colonial legislatures met in New York in the fall of 1765 to reach a consensus. Could Parliament impose taxation without representation? The members of this first congress, known as the Stamp Act Congress, said no. These nine representatives had a vested interest in repealing the tax. Not only did it weaken their businesses and the colonial economy, but it also threatened their liberty under the British Constitution. They drafted a rebuttal to the Stamp Act, making clear that they desired only to protect their liberty as loyal subjects of the Crown. The document, called the Declaration of Rights and Grievances, outlined the unconstitutionality of taxation without representation and trials without juries. Meanwhile, popular protest was also gaining force.

Click and Explore

Browse the collection of the Massachusetts Historical Society (http://openstaxcollege.org/l/masshist1) to examine digitized primary sources of the documents that paved the way to the fight for liberty.

MOBILIZATION: POPULAR PROTEST AGAINST THE STAMP ACT

The Stamp Act Congress was a gathering of landowning, educated white men who represented the political elite of the colonies and was the colonial equivalent of the British landed aristocracy. While these gentry were drafting their grievances during the Stamp Act Congress, other colonists showed their distaste for the new act by boycotting British goods and protesting in the streets. Two groups, the **Sons of Liberty** and the **Daughters of Liberty**, led the popular resistance to the Stamp Act. Both groups considered themselves British patriots defending their liberty, just as their forebears had done in the time of James II.

Forming in Boston in the summer of 1765, the Sons of Liberty were artisans, shopkeepers, and small-time merchants willing to adopt extralegal means of protest. Before the act had even gone into effect, the Sons of Liberty began protesting. On August 14, they took aim at Andrew Oliver, who had been named the Massachusetts Distributor of Stamps. After hanging Oliver in effigy—that is, using a crudely made figure as a representation of Oliver—the unruly crowd stoned and ransacked his house, finally beheading the effigy and burning the remains. Such a brutal response shocked the royal governmental officials, who hid until the violence had spent itself. Andrew Oliver resigned the next day. By that time, the mob had moved on to the home of Lieutenant Governor Thomas Hutchinson who, because of his support of Parliament's actions, was considered an enemy of English liberty. The Sons of Liberty barricaded Hutchinson in his home and demanded that he renounce the Stamp Act; he refused, and the protesters looted and burned his house. Furthermore, the Sons (also called "True Sons" or "True-born Sons" to make clear their commitment to liberty and distinguish them from the likes of Hutchinson) continued to lead violent protests with the goal of securing the resignation of all appointed stamp collectors (Figure 5.8).

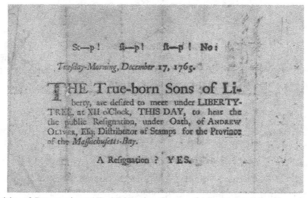

Figure 5.8 With this broadside of December 17, 1765, the Sons of Liberty call for the resignation of Andrew Oliver, the Massachusetts Distributor of Stamps.

Starting in early 1766, the Daughters of Liberty protested the Stamp Act by refusing to buy British goods and encouraging others to do the same. They avoided British tea, opting to make their own teas with local herbs and berries. They built a community—and a movement—around creating homespun cloth instead of buying British linen. Well-born women held "spinning bees," at which they competed to see who could spin the most and the finest linen. An entry in *The Boston Chronicle* of April 7, 1766, states that on March 12, in Providence, Rhode Island, "18 Daughters of Liberty, young ladies of good reputation, assembled at the house of Doctor Ephraim Bowen, in this town. . . . There they exhibited a fine example of industry, by spinning from sunrise until dark, and displayed a spirit for saving their sinking country rarely to be found among persons of more age and experience." At dinner, they "cheerfully agreed to omit tea, to render their conduct consistent. Besides this instance of their patriotism, before they separated, they unanimously resolved that the Stamp Act was unconstitutional, that they would purchase no more British manufactures unless it be repealed, and that they would not even admit the addresses of any gentlemen should they have the opportunity, without they determined to oppose its execution to the last extremity, if the occasion required."

The Daughters' **non-importation movement** broadened the protest against the Stamp Act, giving women a new and active role in the political dissent of the time. Women were responsible for purchasing goods for the home, so by exercising the power of the purse, they could wield more power than they had in the past. Although they could not vote, they could mobilize others and make a difference in the political landscape.

From a local movement, the protests of the Sons and Daughters of Liberty soon spread until there was a chapter in every colony. The Daughters of Liberty promoted the boycott on British goods while the Sons enforced it, threatening retaliation against anyone who bought imported goods or used stamped paper. In the protest against the Stamp Act, wealthy, lettered political figures like John Adams supported the goals of the Sons and Daughters of Liberty, even if they did not engage in the Sons' violent actions. These men, who were lawyers, printers, and merchants, ran a propaganda campaign parallel to the Sons' campaign of violence. In newspapers and pamphlets throughout the colonies, they published article after article outlining the reasons the Stamp Act was unconstitutional and urging peaceful protest. They officially condemned violent actions but did not have the protesters arrested; a degree of cooperation prevailed, despite the groups' different economic backgrounds. Certainly, all the protesters saw themselves as acting in the best British tradition, standing up against the corruption (especially the extinguishing of their right to representation) that threatened their liberty (Figure 5.9).

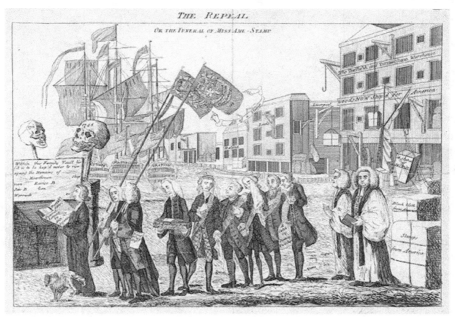

Figure 5.9 This 1766 illustration shows a funeral procession for the Stamp Act. Reverend William Scott leads the procession of politicians who had supported the act, while a dog urinates on his leg. George Grenville, pictured fourth in line, carries a small coffin. What point do you think this cartoon is trying to make?

THE DECLARATORY ACT

Back in Great Britain, news of the colonists' reactions worsened an already volatile political situation. Grenville's imperial reforms had brought about increased domestic taxes and his unpopularity led to his dismissal by King George III. While many in Parliament still wanted such reforms, British merchants argued strongly for their repeal. These merchants had no interest in the philosophy behind the colonists' desire for liberty; rather, their motive was that the non-importation of British goods by North American colonists was hurting their business. Many of the British at home were also appalled by the colonists' violent reaction to the Stamp Act. Other Britons cheered what they saw as the manly defense of liberty by their counterparts in the colonies.

In March 1766, the new prime minister, Lord Rockingham, compelled Parliament to repeal the Stamp Act. Colonists celebrated what they saw as a victory for their British liberty; in Boston, merchant John Hancock treated the entire town to drinks. However, to appease opponents of the repeal, who feared that it would weaken parliamentary power over the American colonists, Rockingham also proposed the Declaratory Act. This stated in no uncertain terms that Parliament's power was supreme and that any laws the colonies may have passed to govern and tax themselves were null and void if they ran counter to parliamentary law.

Click and Explore

Visit USHistory.org (http://openstaxcollege.org/l/decact) to read the full text of the Declaratory Act, in which Parliament asserted the supremacy of parliamentary power.

5.3 The Townshend Acts and Colonial Protest

By the end of this section, you will be able to:
- Describe the purpose of the 1767 Townshend Acts
- Explain why many colonists protested the 1767 Townshend Acts and the consequences of their actions

Colonists' joy over the repeal of the Stamp Act and what they saw as their defense of liberty did not last long. The Declaratory Act of 1766 had articulated Great Britain's supreme authority over the colonies, and Parliament soon began exercising that authority. In 1767, with the passage of the Townshend Acts, a tax on consumer goods in British North America, colonists believed their liberty as loyal British subjects had come under assault for a second time.

THE TOWNSHEND ACTS

Lord Rockingham's tenure as prime minister was not long (1765–1766). Rich landowners feared that if he were not taxing the colonies, Parliament would raise their taxes instead, sacrificing them to the interests of merchants and colonists. George III duly dismissed Rockingham. William Pitt, also sympathetic to the colonists, succeeded him. However, Pitt was old and ill with gout. His chancellor of the exchequer, Charles Townshend (Figure 5.10), whose job was to manage the Empire's finances, took on many of his duties. Primary among these was raising the needed revenue from the colonies.

Figure 5.10 Charles Townshend, chancellor of the exchequer, shown here in a 1765 painting by Joshua Reynolds, instituted the Townshend Revenue Act of 1767 in order to raise money to support the British military presence in the colonies.

Townshend's first act was to deal with the unruly New York Assembly, which had voted not to pay for supplies for the garrison of British soldiers that the Quartering Act required. In response, Townshend proposed the Restraining Act of 1767, which disbanded the New York Assembly until it agreed to pay for the garrison's supplies, which it eventually agreed to do.

The Townshend Revenue Act of 1767 placed duties on various consumer items like paper, paint, lead, tea, and glass. These British goods had to be imported, since the colonies did not have the manufacturing base to produce them. Townshend hoped the new duties would not anger the colonists because they were external taxes, not internal ones like the Stamp Act. In 1766, in arguing before Parliament for the repeal of the Stamp Act, Benjamin Franklin had stated, "I never heard any objection to the right of laying duties to regulate commerce; but a right to lay internal taxes was never supposed to be in parliament, as we are not represented there."

The Indemnity Act of 1767 exempted tea produced by the British East India Company from taxation when it was imported into Great Britain. When the tea was re-exported to the colonies, however, the colonists had to pay taxes on it because of the Revenue Act. Some critics of Parliament on both sides of the Atlantic saw this tax policy as an example of corrupt politicians giving preferable treatment to specific corporate interests, creating a monopoly. The sense that corruption had become entrenched in Parliament only increased colonists' alarm.

In fact, the revenue collected from these duties was only nominally intended to support the British army in America. It actually paid the salaries of some royally appointed judges, governors, and other officials whom the colonial assemblies had traditionally paid. Thanks to the Townshend Revenue Act of 1767, however, these officials no longer relied on colonial leadership for payment. This change gave them a measure of independence from the assemblies, so they could implement parliamentary acts without fear that their pay would be withheld in retaliation. The Revenue Act thus appeared to sever the relationship between governors and assemblies, drawing royal officials closer to the British government and further away from the colonial legislatures.

The Revenue Act also gave the customs board greater powers to counteract smuggling. It granted "writs of assistance"—basically, search warrants—to customs commissioners who suspected the presence of contraband goods, which also opened the door to a new level of bribery and trickery on the waterfronts of colonial America. Furthermore, to ensure compliance, Townshend introduced the Commissioners of Customs Act of 1767, which created an American Board of Customs to enforce trade laws. Customs enforcement had been based in Great Britain, but rules were difficult to implement at such a distance, and smuggling was rampant. The new customs board was based in Boston and would severely curtail smuggling in this large colonial seaport.

Townshend also orchestrated the Vice-Admiralty Court Act, which established three more vice-admiralty courts, in Boston, Philadelphia, and Charleston, to try violators of customs regulations without a jury. Before this, the only colonial vice-admiralty court had been in far-off Halifax, Nova Scotia, but with three local courts, smugglers could be tried more efficiently. Since the judges of these courts were paid a percentage of the worth of the goods they recovered, leniency was rare. All told, the Townshend Acts resulted in higher taxes and stronger British power to enforce them. Four years after the end of the French and Indian War, the Empire continued to search for solutions to its debt problem and the growing sense that the colonies needed to be brought under control.

REACTIONS: THE NON-IMPORTATION MOVEMENT

Like the Stamp Act, the Townshend Acts produced controversy and protest in the American colonies. For a second time, many colonists resented what they perceived as an effort to tax them without representation and thus to deprive them of their liberty. The fact that the revenue the Townshend Acts raised would pay royal governors only made the situation worse, because it took control away from colonial legislatures that otherwise had the power to set and withhold a royal governor's salary. The Restraining Act, which had been intended to isolate New York without angering the other colonies, had the opposite effect, showing the rest of the colonies how far beyond the British Constitution some members of Parliament were willing to go.

The Townshend Acts generated a number of protest writings, including "Letters from a Pennsylvania Farmer" by John Dickinson. In this influential pamphlet, which circulated widely in the colonies, Dickinson conceded that the Empire could regulate trade but argued that Parliament could not impose either internal taxes, like stamps, on goods or external taxes, like customs duties, on imports.

AMERICANA

✪ "Address to the Ladies" Verse from The Boston Post-Boy and Advertiser

This verse, which ran in a Boston newspaper in November 1767, highlights how women were encouraged to take political action by boycotting British goods. Notice that the writer especially encourages women to avoid British tea (Bohea and Green Hyson) and linen, and to manufacture their own homespun cloth. Building on the protest of the 1765 Stamp Act by the Daughters of Liberty, the non-importation movement of 1767–1768 mobilized women as political actors.

Young ladies in town, and those that live round,
Let a friend at this season advise you:
Since money's so scarce, and times growing worse
Strange things may soon hap and surprize you:
First then, throw aside your high top knots of pride
Wear none but your own country linnen;
of economy boast, let your pride be the most
What, if homespun they say is not quite so gay
As brocades, yet be not in a passion,
For when once it is known this is much wore in town,
One and all will cry out, 'tis the fashion!
And as one, all agree that you'll not married be
To such as will wear London Fact'ry:
But at first sight refuse, tell'em such you do chuse
As encourage our own Manufact'ry.
No more Ribbons wear, nor in rich dress appear,
Love your country much better than fine things,
Begin without passion, 'twill soon be the fashion
To grace your smooth locks with a twine string.
Throw aside your Bohea, and your Green Hyson Tea,
And all things with a new fashion duty;
Procure a good store of the choice Labradore,
For there'll soon be enough here to suit ye;
These do without fear and to all you'll appear
Fair, charming, true, lovely, and cleaver;
Tho' the times remain darkish, young men may be sparkish.
And love you much stronger than ever. !O!

In Massachusetts in 1768, Samuel Adams wrote a letter that became known as the **Massachusetts Circular**. Sent by the Massachusetts House of Representatives to the other colonial legislatures, the letter laid out the unconstitutionality of taxation without representation and encouraged the other colonies to again protest the taxes by boycotting British goods. Adams wrote, "It is, moreover, [the Massachusetts House of Representatives] humble opinion, which they express with the greatest deference to the wisdom of the Parliament, that the acts made there, imposing duties on the people of this province, with the sole and express purpose of raising a revenue, are infringements of their natural and constitutional rights; because, as they are not represented in the Parliament, his Majesty's Commons in Britain, by those acts, grant their property without their consent." Note that even in this letter of protest, the humble and submissive tone shows the Massachusetts Assembly's continued deference to parliamentary authority. Even in that hotbed of political protest, it is a clear expression of allegiance and the hope for a restoration of "natural and constitutional rights."

Great Britain's response to this threat of disobedience served only to unite the colonies further. The colonies' initial response to the Massachusetts Circular was lukewarm at best. However, back in Great

Britain, the secretary of state for the colonies—Lord Hillsborough—demanded that Massachusetts retract the letter, promising that any colonial assemblies that endorsed it would be dissolved. This threat had the effect of pushing the other colonies to Massachusetts's side. Even the city of Philadelphia, which had originally opposed the Circular, came around.

The Daughters of Liberty once again supported and promoted the boycott of British goods. Women resumed spinning bees and again found substitutes for British tea and other goods. Many colonial merchants signed non-importation agreements, and the Daughters of Liberty urged colonial women to shop only with those merchants. The Sons of Liberty used newspapers and circulars to call out by name those merchants who refused to sign such agreements; sometimes they were threatened by violence. For instance, a broadside from 1769–1770 reads:

> WILLIAM JACKSON,
> an IMPORTER;
> at the BRAZEN HEAD,
> North Side of the TOWN-HOUSE,
> and Opposite the Town-Pump, [in]
> Corn-hill, BOSTON
> It is desired that the SONS
> and DAUGHTERS of LIBERTY,
> would not buy any one thing of
> him, for in so doing they will bring
> disgrace upon themselves, and their
> Posterity, for ever and ever, AMEN.

The boycott in 1768–1769 turned the purchase of consumer goods into a political gesture. It mattered what you consumed. Indeed, the very clothes you wore indicated whether you were a defender of liberty in homespun or a protector of parliamentary rights in superfine British attire.

Click and Explore

For examples of the types of luxury items that many American colonists favored, visit the National Humanities Center (http://openstaxcollege.org/l/britlux) to see pictures and documents relating to home interiors of the wealthy.

TROUBLE IN BOSTON

The Massachusetts Circular got Parliament's attention, and in 1768, Lord Hillsborough sent four thousand British troops to Boston to deal with the unrest and put down any potential rebellion there. The troops were a constant reminder of the assertion of British power over the colonies, an illustration of an unequal relationship between members of the same empire. As an added aggravation, British soldiers moonlighted as dockworkers, creating competition for employment. Boston's labor system had traditionally been closed, privileging native-born laborers over outsiders, and jobs were scarce. Many Bostonians, led by the Sons of Liberty, mounted a campaign of harassment against British troops. The Sons of Liberty also helped protect the smuggling actions of the merchants; smuggling was crucial for the colonists' ability to maintain their boycott of British goods.

John Hancock was one of Boston's most successful merchants and prominent citizens. While he maintained too high a profile to work actively with the Sons of Liberty, he was known to support their aims, if not their means of achieving them. He was also one of the many prominent merchants who had made their fortunes by smuggling, which was rampant in the colonial seaports. In 1768, customs officials seized the *Liberty*, one of his ships, and violence erupted. Led by the Sons of Liberty, Bostonians rioted against customs officials, attacking the customs house and chasing out the officers, who ran to safety at Castle William, a British fort on a Boston harbor island. British soldiers crushed the riots, but over the next few years, clashes between British officials and Bostonians became common.

Conflict turned deadly on March 5, 1770, in a confrontation that came to be known as the **Boston Massacre**. On that night, a crowd of Bostonians from many walks of life started throwing snowballs, rocks, and sticks at the British soldiers guarding the customs house. In the resulting scuffle, some soldiers, goaded by the mob who hectored the soldiers as "lobster backs" (the reference to lobster equated the soldiers with bottom feeders, i.e., aquatic animals that feed on the lowest organisms in the food chain), fired into the crowd, killing five people. Crispus Attucks, the first man killed—and, though no one could have known it then, the first official casualty in the war for independence—was of Wampanoag and African descent. The bloodshed illustrated the level of hostility that had developed as a result of Boston's occupation by British troops, the competition for scarce jobs between Bostonians and the British soldiers stationed in the city, and the larger question of Parliament's efforts to tax the colonies.

The Sons of Liberty immediately seized on the event, characterizing the British soldiers as murderers and their victims as martyrs. Paul Revere, a silversmith and member of the Sons of Liberty, circulated an engraving that showed a line of grim redcoats firing ruthlessly into a crowd of unarmed, fleeing civilians. Among colonists who resisted British power, this view of the "massacre" confirmed their fears of a tyrannous government using its armies to curb the freedom of British subjects. But to others, the attacking mob was equally to blame for pelting the British with rocks and insulting them.

It was not only British Loyalists who condemned the unruly mob. John Adams, one of the city's strongest supporters of peaceful protest against Parliament, represented the British soldiers at their murder trial. Adams argued that the mob's lawlessness required the soldiers' response, and that without law and order, a society was nothing. He argued further that the soldiers were the tools of a much broader program, which transformed a street brawl into the injustice of imperial policy. Of the eight soldiers on trial, the jury acquitted six, convicting the other two of the reduced charge of manslaughter.

Adams argued: "Facts are stubborn things; and whatever may be our wishes, our inclinations, or the dictates of our passions, they cannot alter the state of facts and evidence: nor is the law less stable than the fact; if an assault was made to endanger their lives, the law is clear, they had a right to kill in their own defense; if it was not so severe as to endanger their lives, yet if they were assaulted at all, struck and abused by blows of any sort, by snow-balls, oyster-shells, cinders, clubs, or sticks of any kind; this was a provocation, for which the law reduces the offence of killing, down to manslaughter, in consideration of those passions in our nature, which cannot be eradicated. To your candour and justice I submit the prisoners and their cause."

AMERICANA

✹ *Propaganda and the Sons of Liberty*

Long after the British soldiers had been tried and punished, the Sons of Liberty maintained a relentless propaganda campaign against British oppression. Many of them were printers or engravers, and they were able to use public media to sway others to their cause. Shortly after the incident outside the customs house, Paul Revere created "The bloody massacre perpetrated in King Street Boston on March 5th 1770 by a party of the 29th Regt." (Figure 5.11), based on an image by engraver Henry Pelham. The picture—which represents only the protesters' point of view—shows the ruthlessness of the British soldiers and the helplessness of the crowd of civilians. Notice the subtle details Revere uses to help convince the viewer of the civilians' innocence and the soldiers' cruelty. Although eyewitnesses said the crowd started the fight by throwing snowballs and rocks, in the engraving they are innocently standing by. Revere also depicts the crowd as well dressed and well-to-do, when in fact they were laborers and probably looked quite a bit rougher.

Figure 5.11   The Sons of Liberty circulated this sensationalized version of the events of March 5, 1770, in order to promote the rightness of their cause. The verses below the image begin as follows: "Unhappy Boston! see thy Sons deplore, Thy hallowed Walks besmeared with guiltless Gore."

Newspaper articles and pamphlets that the Sons of Liberty circulated implied that the "massacre" was a planned murder. In the *Boston Gazette* on March 12, 1770, an article describes the soldiers as striking first. It goes on to discuss this version of the events: "On hearing the noise, one Samuel Atwood came up to see what was the matter; and entering the alley from dock square, heard the latter part of the combat; and when the boys had dispersed he met the ten or twelve soldiers aforesaid rushing down the alley towards the square and asked them if they intended to murder people? They answered Yes, by God, root and branch! With that one of them struck Mr. Atwood with a club which was repeated by another; and being unarmed, he turned to go off and received a wound on the left shoulder which reached the bone and gave him much pain."

What do you think most people in the United States think of when they consider the Boston Massacre? How does the propaganda of the Sons of Liberty still affect the way we think of this event?

PARTIAL REPEAL

As it turned out, the Boston Massacre occurred after Parliament had partially repealed the Townshend Acts. By the late 1760s, the American boycott of British goods had drastically reduced British trade. Once again, merchants who lost money because of the boycott strongly pressured Parliament to loosen its restrictions on the colonies and break the non-importation movement. Charles Townshend died suddenly in 1767 and was replaced by Lord North, who was inclined to look for a more workable solution with the colonists. North convinced Parliament to drop all the Townshend duties except the tax on tea. The administrative and enforcement provisions under the Townshend Acts—the American Board of Customs Commissioners and the vice-admiralty courts—remained in place.

To those who had protested the Townshend Acts for several years, the partial repeal appeared to be a major victory. For a second time, colonists had rescued liberty from an unconstitutional parliamentary measure. The hated British troops in Boston departed. The consumption of British goods skyrocketed after the partial repeal, an indication of the American colonists' desire for the items linking them to the Empire.

5.4 The Destruction of the Tea and the Coercive Acts

By the end of this section, you will be able to:
- Describe the socio-political environment in the colonies in the early 1770s
- Explain the purpose of the Tea Act of 1773 and discuss colonial reactions to it
- Identify and describe the Coercive Acts

The Tea Act of 1773 triggered a reaction with far more significant consequences than either the 1765 Stamp Act or the 1767 Townshend Acts. Colonists who had joined in protest against those earlier acts renewed their efforts in 1773. They understood that Parliament had again asserted its right to impose taxes without representation, and they feared the Tea Act was designed to seduce them into conceding this important principle by lowering the price of tea to the point that colonists might abandon their scruples. They also deeply resented the East India Company's monopoly on the sale of tea in the American colonies; this resentment sprang from the knowledge that some members of Parliament had invested heavily in the company.

SMOLDERING RESENTMENT

Even after the partial repeal of the Townshend duties, however, suspicion of Parliament's intentions remained high. This was especially true in port cities like Boston and New York, where British customs agents were a daily irritant and reminder of British power. In public houses and squares, people met and discussed politics. Philosopher John Locke's *Two Treatises of Government*, published almost a century earlier, influenced political thought about the role of government to protect life, liberty, and property. The Sons of Liberty issued propaganda ensuring that colonists remained aware when Parliament overreached itself.

Violence continued to break out on occasion, as in 1772, when Rhode Island colonists boarded and burned the British revenue ship *Gaspée* in Narragansett Bay (Figure 5.12). Colonists had attacked or burned British customs ships in the past, but after the Gaspée Affair, the British government convened a Royal Commission of Inquiry. This Commission had the authority to remove the colonists, who were charged with treason, to Great Britain for trial. Some colonial protestors saw this new ability as another example of the overreach of British power.

Figure 5.12 This 1883 engraving, which appeared in *Harper's New Monthly Magazine*, depicts the burning of the *Gaspée*. This attack provoked the British government to convene a Royal Commission of Inquiry; some regarded the Commission as an example of excessive British power and control over the colonies.

Samuel Adams, along with Joseph Warren and James Otis, re-formed the Boston **Committee of Correspondence**, which functioned as a form of shadow government, to address the fear of British overreach. Soon towns all over Massachusetts had formed their own committees, and many other colonies followed suit. These committees, which had between seven and eight thousand members in all, identified enemies of the movement and communicated the news of the day. Sometimes they provided a version of events that differed from royal interpretations, and slowly, the committees began to supplant royal governments as sources of information. They later formed the backbone of communication among the colonies in the rebellion against the Tea Act, and eventually in the revolt against the British crown.

THE TEA ACT OF 1773

Parliament did not enact the Tea Act of 1773 in order to punish the colonists, assert parliamentary power, or even raise revenues. Rather, the act was a straightforward order of economic protectionism for a British tea firm, the East India Company, that was on the verge of bankruptcy. In the colonies, tea was the one remaining consumer good subject to the hated Townshend duties. Protest leaders and their followers still avoided British tea, drinking smuggled Dutch tea as a sign of patriotism.

The Tea Act of 1773 gave the British East India Company the ability to export its tea directly to the colonies without paying import or export duties and without using middlemen in either Great Britain or the colonies. Even with the Townshend tax, the act would allow the East India Company to sell its tea at lower prices than the smuggled Dutch tea, thus undercutting the smuggling trade.

This act was unwelcome to those in British North America who had grown displeased with the pattern of imperial measures. By granting a monopoly to the East India Company, the act not only cut out colonial merchants who would otherwise sell the tea themselves; it also reduced their profits from smuggled foreign tea. These merchants were among the most powerful and influential people in the colonies, so their dissatisfaction carried some weight. Moreover, because the tea tax that the Townshend Acts imposed remained in place, tea had intense power to symbolize the idea of "no taxation without representation."

COLONIAL PROTEST: THE DESTRUCTION OF THE TEA

The 1773 act reignited the worst fears among the colonists. To the Sons and Daughters of Liberty and those who followed them, the act appeared to be proof positive that a handful of corrupt members of Parliament were violating the British Constitution. Veterans of the protest movement had grown accustomed to interpreting British actions in the worst possible light, so the 1773 act appeared to be part of a large conspiracy against liberty.

As they had done to protest earlier acts and taxes, colonists responded to the Tea Act with a boycott. The Committees of Correspondence helped to coordinate resistance in all of the colonial port cities, so up and down the East Coast, British tea-carrying ships were unable to come to shore and unload their wares. In Charlestown, Boston, Philadelphia, and New York, the equivalent of millions of dollars' worth of tea was held hostage, either locked in storage warehouses or rotting in the holds of ships as they were forced to sail back to Great Britain.

In Boston, Thomas Hutchinson, now the royal governor of Massachusetts, vowed that radicals like Samuel Adams would not keep the ships from unloading their cargo. He urged the merchants who would have accepted the tea from the ships to stand their ground and receive the tea once it had been unloaded. When the *Dartmouth* sailed into Boston Harbor in November 1773, it had twenty days to unload its cargo of tea and pay the duty before it had to return to Great Britain. Two more ships, the *Eleanor* and the *Beaver*, followed soon after. Samuel Adams and the Sons of Liberty tried to keep the captains of the ships from paying the duties and posted groups around the ships to make sure the tea would not be unloaded.

On December 16, just as the *Dartmouth*'s deadline approached, townspeople gathered at the Old South Meeting House determined to take action. From this gathering, a group of Sons of Liberty and their followers approached the three ships. Some were disguised as Mohawks. Protected by a crowd of spectators, they systematically dumped all the tea into the harbor, destroying goods worth almost $1 million in today's dollars, a very significant loss. This act soon inspired further acts of resistance up and down the East Coast. However, not all colonists, and not even all Patriots, supported the dumping of the tea. The wholesale destruction of property shocked people on both sides of the Atlantic.

Click and Explore

To learn more about the Boston Tea Party, explore the extensive resources in the Boston Tea Party Ships and Museum collection (http://openstaxcollege.org/l/teapartyship) of articles, photos, and video. At the museum itself, you can board replicas of the *Eleanor* and the *Beaver* and experience a recreation of the dumping of the tea.

PARLIAMENT RESPONDS: THE COERCIVE ACTS

In London, response to the destruction of the tea was swift and strong. The violent destruction of property infuriated King George III and the prime minister, Lord North (Figure 5.13), who insisted the loss be repaid. Though some American merchants put forward a proposal for restitution, the Massachusetts Assembly refused to make payments. Massachusetts's resistance to British authority united different factions in Great Britain against the colonies. North had lost patience with the unruly British subjects in Boston. He declared: "The Americans have tarred and feathered your subjects, plundered your merchants, burnt your ships, denied all obedience to your laws and authority; yet so clement and so long forbearing has our conduct been that it is incumbent on us now to take a different course. Whatever may be the consequences, we must risk something; if we do not, all is over." Both Parliament and the king agreed that Massachusetts should be forced to both pay for the tea and yield to British authority.

Figure 5.13 Lord North, seen here in *Portrait of Frederick North, Lord North* (1773–1774), painted by Nathaniel Dance, was prime minister at the time of the destruction of the tea and insisted that Massachusetts make good on the loss.

In early 1774, leaders in Parliament responded with a set of four measures designed to punish Massachusetts, commonly known at the **Coercive Acts**. The Boston Port Bill shut down Boston Harbor until the East India Company was repaid. The Massachusetts Government Act placed the colonial government under the direct control of crown officials and made traditional town meetings subject to the governor's approval. The Administration of Justice Act allowed the royal governor to unilaterally move any trial of a crown officer out of Massachusetts, a change designed to prevent hostile Massachusetts juries from deciding these cases. This act was especially infuriating to John Adams and others who emphasized the time-honored rule of law. They saw this part of the Coercive Acts as striking at the heart of fair and equitable justice. Finally, the Quartering Act encompassed all the colonies and allowed British troops to be housed in occupied buildings.

At the same time, Parliament also passed the Quebec Act, which expanded the boundaries of Quebec westward and extended religious tolerance to Roman Catholics in the province. For many Protestant colonists, especially Congregationalists in New England, this forced tolerance of Catholicism was the most objectionable provision of the act. Additionally, expanding the boundaries of Quebec raised troubling questions for many colonists who eyed the West, hoping to expand the boundaries of their provinces. The Quebec Act appeared gratuitous, a slap in the face to colonists already angered by the Coercive Acts.

American Patriots renamed the Coercive and Quebec measures the **Intolerable Acts**. Some in London also thought the acts went too far; see the cartoon "The Able Doctor, or America Swallowing the Bitter Draught" (Figure 5.14) for one British view of what Parliament was doing to the colonies. Meanwhile, punishments designed to hurt only one colony (Massachusetts, in this case) had the effect of mobilizing all the colonies to its side. The Committees of Correspondence had already been active in coordinating an approach to the Tea Act. Now the talk would turn to these new, intolerable assaults on the colonists' rights as British subjects.

Figure 5.14   The artist of "The Able Doctor, or America Swallowing the Bitter Draught" (*London Magazine*, May 1, 1774) targets select members of Parliament as the perpetrators of a devilish scheme to overturn the constitution; this is why Mother Britannia weeps. Note that this cartoon came from a British publication; Great Britain was not united in support of Parliament's policies toward the American colonies.

5.5 Disaffection: The First Continental Congress and American Identity

By the end of this section, you will be able to:
- Describe the state of affairs between the colonies and the home government in 1774
- Explain the purpose and results of the First Continental Congress

Disaffection—the loss of affection toward the home government—had reached new levels by 1774. Many colonists viewed the Intolerable Acts as a turning point; they now felt they had to take action. The result was the First Continental Congress, a direct challenge to Lord North and British authority in the colonies. Still, it would be a mistake to assume there was a groundswell of support for separating from the British Empire and creating a new, independent nation. Strong ties still bound the Empire together, and colonists did not agree about the proper response. Loyalists tended to be property holders, established residents who feared the loss of their property. To them the protests seemed to promise nothing but mob rule, and the violence and disorder they provoked were shocking. On both sides of the Atlantic, opinions varied.

After the passage of the Intolerable Acts in 1774, the Committees of Correspondence and the Sons of Liberty went straight to work, spreading warnings about how the acts would affect the liberty of all colonists, not just urban merchants and laborers. The Massachusetts Government Act had shut down the colonial government there, but resistance-minded colonists began meeting in extralegal assemblies. One of these assemblies, the Massachusetts Provincial Congress, passed the **Suffolk Resolves** in September 1774, which laid out a plan of resistance to the Intolerable Acts. Meanwhile, the First Continental Congress was convening to discuss how to respond to the acts themselves.

The First Continental Congress was made up of elected representatives of twelve of the thirteen American colonies. (Georgia's royal governor blocked the move to send representatives from that colony, an indication of the continued strength of the royal government despite the crisis.) The representatives met in Philadelphia from September 5 through October 26, 1774, and at first they did not agree at all about the appropriate response to the Intolerable Acts. Joseph Galloway of Pennsylvania argued for a conciliatory approach; he proposed that an elected Grand Council in America, like the Parliament in Great Britain, should be paired with a royally appointed President General, who would represent the authority of the Crown. More radical factions argued for a move toward separation from the Crown.

In the end, Paul Revere rode from Massachusetts to Philadelphia with the Suffolk Resolves, which became the basis of the Declaration and Resolves of the First Continental Congress. In the Declaration and Resolves, adopted on October 14, the colonists demanded the repeal of all repressive acts passed since 1773 and agreed to a non-importation, non-exportation, and non-consumption pact against all British goods until the acts were repealed. In the "Petition of Congress to the King" on October 24, the delegates adopted a further recommendation of the Suffolk Resolves and proposed that the colonies raise and regulate their own militias.

The representatives at the First Continental Congress created a Continental Association to ensure that the full boycott was enforced across all the colonies. The Continental Association served as an umbrella group for colonial and local committees of observation and inspection. By taking these steps, the First Continental Congress established a governing network in opposition to royal authority.

Click and Explore

Visit the Massachusetts Historical Society (http://openstaxcollege.org/l/ firstcongress) to see a digitized copy and read the transcript of the First Continental Congress's petition to King George.

DEFINING "AMERICAN"

⚙ *The First List of Un-American Activities*

In her book *Toward A More Perfect Union: Virtue and the Formation of American Republics*, historian Ann Fairfax Withington explores actions the delegates to the First Continental Congress took during the weeks they were together. Along with their efforts to bring about the repeal of the Intolerable Acts, the delegates also banned certain activities they believed would undermine their fight against what they saw as British corruption.

In particular, the delegates prohibited horse races, cockfights, the theater, and elaborate funerals. The reasons for these prohibitions provide insight into the state of affairs in 1774. Both horse races and cockfights encouraged gambling and, for the delegates, gambling threatened to prevent the unity of action and purpose they desired. In addition, cockfighting appeared immoral and corrupt because the roosters were fitted with razors and fought to the death (Figure 5.15).

Figure 5.15   Cockfights, as depicted in *The Cockpit* (1759) by British artist and engraver William Hogarth, were among the entertainments the First Continental Congress sought to outlaw, considering them un-American.

The ban on the theater aimed to do away with another corrupt British practice. Critics had long believed that theatrical performances drained money from working people. Moreover, they argued, theatergoers learned to lie and deceive from what they saw on stage. The delegates felt banning the theater would demonstrate their resolve to act honestly and without pretense in their fight against corruption.

Finally, eighteenth-century mourning practices often required lavish spending on luxury items and even the employment of professional mourners who, for a price, would shed tears at the grave. Prohibiting these practices reflected the idea that luxury bred corruption, and the First Continental Congress wanted to demonstrate that the colonists would do without British vices. Congress emphasized the need to be frugal and self-sufficient when confronted with corruption.

The First Continental Congress banned all four activities—horse races, cockfights, the theater, and elaborate funerals—and entrusted the Continental Association with enforcement. Rejecting what they saw as corruption coming from Great Britain, the delegates were also identifying themselves as standing apart from their British relatives. They cast themselves as virtuous defenders of liberty against a corrupt Parliament.

In the Declaration and Resolves and the Petition of Congress to the King, the delegates to the First Continental Congress refer to George III as "Most Gracious Sovereign" and to themselves as "inhabitants of the English colonies in North America" or "inhabitants of British America," indicating that they still considered themselves British subjects of the king, not American citizens. At the same time, however, they were slowly moving away from British authority, creating their own de facto government in the First Continental Congress. One of the provisions of the Congress was that it meet again in one year to mark its progress; the Congress was becoming an elected government.

Key Terms

Boston Massacre a confrontation between a crowd of Bostonians and British soldiers on March 5, 1770, which resulted in the deaths of five people, including Crispus Attucks, the first official casualty in the war for independence

Coercive Acts four acts (Administration of Justice Act, Massachusetts Government Act, Port Bill, Quartering Act) that Lord North passed to punish Massachusetts for destroying the tea and refusing to pay for the damage

Committees of Correspondence colonial extralegal shadow governments that convened to coordinate plans of resistance against the British

Daughters of Liberty well-born British colonial women who led a non-importation movement against British goods

direct tax a tax that consumers pay directly, rather than through merchants' higher prices

indirect tax a tax imposed on businesses, rather than directly on consumers

Intolerable Acts the name American Patriots gave to the Coercive Acts and the Quebec Act

Loyalists colonists in America who were loyal to Great Britain

Massachusetts Circular a letter penned by Son of Liberty Samuel Adams that laid out the unconstitutionality of taxation without representation and encouraged the other colonies to boycott British goods

no taxation without representation the principle, first articulated in the Virginia Stamp Act Resolutions, that the colonists needed to be represented in Parliament if they were to be taxed

non-importation movement a widespread colonial boycott of British goods

Proclamation Line a line along the Appalachian Mountains, imposed by the Proclamation of 1763, west of which British colonists could not settle

Sons of Liberty artisans, shopkeepers, and small-time merchants who opposed the Stamp Act and considered themselves British patriots

Suffolk Resolves a Massachusetts plan of resistance to the Intolerable Acts that formed the basis of the eventual plan adopted by the First Continental Congress for resisting the British, including the arming of militias and the adoption of a widespread non-importation, non-exportation, and non-consumption agreement

vice-admiralty courts British royal courts without juries that settled disputes occurring at sea

Summary

5.1 Confronting the National Debt: The Aftermath of the French and Indian War
The British Empire had gained supremacy in North America with its victory over the French in 1763. Almost all of the North American territory east of the Mississippi fell under Great Britain's control, and British leaders took this opportunity to try to create a more coherent and unified empire after decades of lax oversight. Victory over the French had proved very costly, and the British government attempted to better regulate their expanded empire in North America. The initial steps the British took in 1763 and 1764

raised suspicions among some colonists about the intent of the home government. These suspicions would grow and swell over the coming years.

5.2 The Stamp Act and the Sons and Daughters of Liberty

Though Parliament designed the 1765 Stamp Act to deal with the financial crisis in the Empire, it had unintended consequences. Outrage over the act created a degree of unity among otherwise unconnected American colonists, giving them a chance to act together both politically and socially. The crisis of the Stamp Act allowed colonists to loudly proclaim their identity as defenders of British liberty. With the repeal of the Stamp Act in 1766, liberty-loving subjects of the king celebrated what they viewed as a victory.

5.3 The Townshend Acts and Colonial Protest

Like the Stamp Act in 1765, the Townshend Acts led many colonists to work together against what they perceived to be an unconstitutional measure, generating the second major crisis in British Colonial America. The experience of resisting the Townshend Acts provided another shared experience among colonists from diverse regions and backgrounds, while the partial repeal convinced many that liberty had once again been defended. Nonetheless, Great Britain's debt crisis still had not been solved.

5.4 The Destruction of the Tea and the Coercive Acts

The colonial rejection of the Tea Act, especially the destruction of the tea in Boston Harbor, recast the decade-long argument between British colonists and the home government as an intolerable conspiracy against liberty and an excessive overreach of parliamentary power. The Coercive Acts were punitive in nature, awakening the worst fears of otherwise loyal members of the British Empire in America.

5.5 Disaffection: The First Continental Congress and American Identity

The First Continental Congress, which comprised elected representatives from twelve of the thirteen American colonies, represented a direct challenge to British authority. In its Declaration and Resolves, colonists demanded the repeal of all repressive acts passed since 1773. The delegates also recommended that the colonies raise militias, lest the British respond to the Congress's proposed boycott of British goods with force. While the colonists still considered themselves British subjects, they were slowly retreating from British authority, creating their own de facto government via the First Continental Congress.

Review Questions

1. Which of the following was a cause of the British National Debt in 1763?
  A. drought in Great Britain
  B. the French and Indian War
  C. the continued British military presence in the American colonies
  D. both B and C

2. What was the main purpose of the Sugar Act of 1764?
  A. It raised taxes on sugar.
  B. It raised taxes on molasses.

  C. It strengthened enforcement of molasses smuggling laws.
  D. It required colonists to purchase only sugar distilled in Great Britain.

3. What did British colonists find so onerous about the acts that Prime Minister Grenville passed?

4. Which of the following was *not* a goal of the Stamp Act?
  A. to gain control over the colonists

B. to raise revenue for British troops stationed in the colonies

C. to raise revenue to pay off British debt from the French and Indian War

D. to declare null and void any laws the colonies had passed to govern and tax themselves

5. For which of the following activities were the Sons of Liberty responsible?

A. the Stamp Act Congress

B. the hanging and beheading of a stamp commissioner in effigy

C. the massacre of Conestoga in Pennsylvania

D. the introduction of the Virginia Stamp Act Resolutions

6. Which of the following was *not* one of the goals of the Townshend Acts?

A. higher taxes

B. greater colonial unity

C. greater British control over the colonies

D. reduced power of the colonial governments

7. Which event was most responsible for the colonies' endorsement of Samuel Adams's Massachusetts Circular?

A. the Townshend Duties

B. the Indemnity Act

C. the Boston Massacre

D. Lord Hillsborough's threat to dissolve the colonial assemblies that endorsed the letter

8. What factors contributed to the Boston Massacre?

9. Which of the following is true of the Gaspée affair?

A. Colonists believed that the British response represented an overreach of power.

B. It was the first time colonists attacked a revenue ship.

C. It was the occasion of the first official death in the war for independence.

D. The ship's owner, John Hancock, was a respectable Boston merchant.

10. What was the purpose of the Tea Act of 1773?

A. to punish the colonists for their boycotting of British tea

B. to raise revenue to offset the British national debt

C. to help revive the struggling East India Company

D. to pay the salaries of royal appointees

11. What was the significance of the Committees of Correspondence?

12. Which of the following was decided at the First Continental Congress?

A. to declare war on Great Britain

B. to boycott all British goods and prepare for possible military action

C. to offer a conciliatory treaty to Great Britain

D. to pay for the tea that was dumped in Boston Harbor

13. Which colony provided the basis for the Declarations and Resolves?

A. Massachusetts

B. Philadelphia

C. Rhode Island

D. New York

Critical Thinking Questions

14. Was reconciliation between the American colonies and Great Britain possible in 1774? Why or why not?

15. Look again at the painting that opened this chapter: *The Bostonians Paying the Excise-man, or Tarring and Feathering* (Figure 5.1). How does this painting represent the relationship between Great Britain and the American colonies in the years from 1763 to 1774?

16. Why did the colonists react so much more strongly to the Stamp Act than to the Sugar Act? How did the principles that the Stamp Act raised continue to provide points of contention between colonists and the British government?

17.   History is filled with unintended consequences. How do the British government's attempts to control and regulate the colonies during this tumultuous era provide a case in point? How did the aims of the British measure up against the results of their actions?

18.   What evidence indicates that colonists continued to think of themselves as British subjects throughout this era? What evidence suggests that colonists were beginning to forge a separate, collective "American" identity? How would you explain this shift?

CHAPTER 6

America's War for Independence, 1775-1783

Figure 6.1 This famous 1819 painting by John Trumbull shows members of the committee entrusted with drafting the Declaration of Independence presenting their work to the Continental Congress in 1776. Note the British flags on the wall. Separating from the British Empire proved to be very difficult as the colonies and the Empire were linked with strong cultural, historical, and economic bonds forged over several generations.

Chapter Outline

6.1 Britain's Law-and-Order Strategy and Its Consequences

6.2 The Early Years of the Revolution

6.3 War in the South

6.4 Identity during the American Revolution

Introduction

By the 1770s, Great Britain ruled a vast empire, with its American colonies producing useful raw materials and profitably consuming British goods. From Britain's perspective, it was inconceivable that the colonies would wage a successful war for independence; in 1776, they appeared weak and disorganized, no match for the Empire. Yet, although the Revolutionary War did indeed drag on for eight years, in 1783, the thirteen colonies, now the United States, ultimately prevailed against the British.

The Revolution succeeded because colonists from diverse economic and social backgrounds united in their opposition to Great Britain. Although thousands of colonists remained loyal to the crown and many others preferred to remain neutral, a sense of community against a common enemy prevailed among Patriots. The signing of the Declaration of Independence (Figure 6.1) exemplifies the spirit of that common cause. Representatives asserted: "That these United Colonies are, and of Right ought to be Free and Independent States; that they are Absolved from all Allegiance to the British Crown, . . . And for the support of this Declaration, . . . we mutually pledge to each other our Lives, our Fortunes and our sacred Honor."

6.1 Britain's Law-and-Order Strategy and Its Consequences

By the end of this section, you will be able to:
- Explain how Great Britain's response to the destruction of a British shipment of tea in Boston Harbor in 1773 set the stage for the Revolution
- Describe the beginnings of the American Revolution

Great Britain pursued a policy of law and order when dealing with the crises in the colonies in the late 1760s and 1770s. Relations between the British and many American Patriots worsened over the decade, culminating in an unruly mob destroying a fortune in tea by dumping it into Boston Harbor in December 1773 as a protest against British tax laws. The harsh British response to this act in 1774, which included sending British troops to Boston and closing Boston Harbor, caused tensions and resentments to escalate further. The British tried to disarm the insurgents in Massachusetts by confiscating their weapons and ammunition and arresting the leaders of the patriotic movement. However, this effort faltered on April 19, when Massachusetts militias and British troops fired on each other as British troops marched to Lexington and Concord, an event immortalized by poet Ralph Waldo Emerson as the "shot heard round the world." The American Revolution had begun.

ON THE EVE OF REVOLUTION

The decade from 1763 to 1774 was a difficult one for the British Empire. Although Great Britain had defeated the French in the French and Indian War, the debt from that conflict remained a stubborn and seemingly unsolvable problem for both Great Britain and the colonies. Great Britain tried various methods of raising revenue on both sides of the Atlantic to manage the enormous debt, including instituting a tax on tea and other goods sold to the colonies by British companies, but many subjects resisted these taxes. In the colonies, Patriot groups like the Sons of Liberty led boycotts of British goods and took violent measures that stymied British officials.

Boston proved to be the epicenter of protest. In December 1773, a group of Patriots protested the Tea Act passed that year—which, among other provisions, gave the East India Company a monopoly on tea—by boarding British tea ships docked in Boston Harbor and dumping tea worth over $1 million (in current

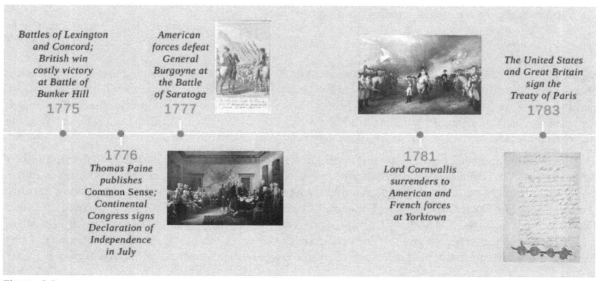

Figure 6.2

Download for free at http://cnx.org/content/col11740/latest/

prices) into the water. The destruction of the tea radically escalated the crisis between Great Britain and the American colonies. When the Massachusetts Assembly refused to pay for the tea, Parliament enacted a series of laws called the Coercive Acts, which some colonists called the Intolerable Acts. Parliament designed these laws, which closed the port of Boston, limited the meetings of the colonial assembly, and disbanded all town meetings, to punish Massachusetts and bring the colony into line. However, many British Americans in other colonies were troubled and angered by Parliament's response to Massachusetts. In September and October 1774, all the colonies except Georgia participated in the First Continental Congress in Philadelphia. The Congress advocated a boycott of all British goods and established the Continental Association to enforce local adherence to the boycott. The Association supplanted royal control and shaped resistance to Great Britain.

AMERICANA

⚙ *Joining the Boycott*

Many British colonists in Virginia, as in the other colonies, disapproved of the destruction of the tea in Boston Harbor. However, after the passage of the Coercive Acts, the Virginia House of Burgesses declared its solidarity with Massachusetts by encouraging Virginians to observe a day of fasting and prayer on May 24 in sympathy with the people of Boston. Almost immediately thereafter, Virginia's colonial governor dissolved the House of Burgesses, but many of its members met again in secret on May 30 and adopted a resolution stating that "the Colony of Virginia will concur with the other Colonies in such Measures as shall be judged most effectual for the preservation of the Common Rights and Liberty of British America."

After the First Continental Congress in Philadelphia, Virginia's Committee of Safety ensured that all merchants signed the non-importation agreements that the Congress had proposed. This British cartoon (Figure 6.3) shows a Virginian signing the Continental Association boycott agreement.

Figure 6.3 In "The Alternative of Williams-Burg" (1775), a merchant has to sign a non-importation agreement or risk being covered with the tar and feathers suspended behind him.

Note the tar and feathers hanging from the gallows in the background of this image and the demeanor of the people surrounding the signer. What is the message of this engraving? Where are the sympathies of the artist? What is the meaning of the title "The Alternative of Williams-Burg?"

In an effort to restore law and order in Boston, the British dispatched General Thomas Gage to the New England seaport. He arrived in Boston in May 1774 as the new royal governor of the Province of

Massachusetts, accompanied by several regiments of British troops. As in 1768, the British again occupied the town. Massachusetts delegates met in a Provincial Congress and published the Suffolk Resolves, which officially rejected the Coercive Acts and called for the raising of colonial militias to take military action if needed. The Suffolk Resolves signaled the overthrow of the royal government in Massachusetts.

Both the British and the rebels in New England began to prepare for conflict by turning their attention to supplies of weapons and gunpowder. General Gage stationed thirty-five hundred troops in Boston, and from there he ordered periodic raids on towns where guns and gunpowder were stockpiled, hoping to impose law and order by seizing them. As Boston became the headquarters of British military operations, many residents fled the city.

Gage's actions led to the formation of local rebel militias that were able to mobilize in a minute's time. These **minutemen**, many of whom were veterans of the French and Indian War, played an important role in the war for independence. In one instance, General Gage seized munitions in Cambridge and Charlestown, but when he arrived to do the same in Salem, his troops were met by a large crowd of minutemen and had to leave empty-handed. In New Hampshire, minutemen took over Fort William and Mary and confiscated weapons and cannons there. New England readied for war.

THE OUTBREAK OF FIGHTING

Throughout late 1774 and into 1775, tensions in New England continued to mount. General Gage knew that a powder magazine was stored in Concord, Massachusetts, and on April 19, 1775, he ordered troops to seize these munitions. Instructions from London called for the arrest of rebel leaders Samuel Adams and John Hancock. Hoping for secrecy, his troops left Boston under cover of darkness, but riders from Boston let the militias know of the British plans. (Paul Revere was one of these riders, but the British captured him and he never finished his ride. Henry Wadsworth Longfellow memorialized Revere in his 1860 poem, "Paul Revere's Ride," incorrectly implying that he made it all the way to Concord.) Minutemen met the British troops and skirmished with them, first at Lexington and then at Concord (Figure 6.4). The British retreated to Boston, enduring ambushes from several other militias along the way. Over four thousand militiamen took part in these skirmishes with British soldiers. Seventy-three British soldiers and forty-nine Patriots died during the British retreat to Boston. The famous confrontation is the basis for Emerson's "Concord Hymn" (1836), which begins with the description of the "shot heard round the world." Although propagandists on both sides pointed fingers, it remains unclear who fired that shot.

Figure 6.4 Amos Doolittle was an American printmaker who volunteered to fight against the British. His engravings of the battles of Lexington and Concord—such as this detail from *The Battle of Lexington, April 19th 1775*—are the only contemporary American visual records of the events there.

After the battles of Lexington and Concord, New England fully mobilized for war. Thousands of militias from towns throughout New England marched to Boston, and soon the city was besieged by a sea of rebel forces (Figure 6.5). In May 1775, Ethan Allen and Colonel Benedict Arnold led a group of rebels against

Fort Ticonderoga in New York. They succeeded in capturing the fort, and cannons from Ticonderoga were brought to Massachusetts and used to bolster the Siege of Boston.

Figure 6.5 This 1779 map shows details of the British and Patriot troops in and around Boston, Massachusetts, at the beginning of the war.

In June, General Gage resolved to take Breed's Hill and Bunker Hill, the high ground across the Charles River from Boston, a strategic site that gave the rebel militias an advantage since they could train their cannons on the British. In the Battle of Bunker Hill (Figure 6.6), on June 17, the British launched three assaults on the hills, gaining control only after the rebels ran out of ammunition. British losses were very high—over two hundred were killed and eight hundred wounded—and, despite his victory, General Gage was unable to break the colonial forces' siege of the city. In August, King George III declared the colonies to be in a state of rebellion. Parliament and many in Great Britain agreed with their king. Meanwhile, the British forces in Boston found themselves in a terrible predicament, isolated in the city and with no control over the countryside.

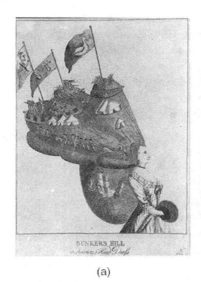

(a)   (b)

Figure 6.6 The British cartoon "Bunkers Hill or America's Head Dress" (a) depicts the initial rebellion as an elaborate colonial coiffure. The illustration pokes fun at both the colonial rebellion and the overdone hairstyles for women that had made their way from France and Britain to the American colonies. Despite gaining control of the high ground after the colonial militias ran out of ammunition, General Thomas Gage (b), shown here in a painting made in 1768–1769 by John Singleton Copley, was unable to break the siege of the city.

In the end, General George Washington, commander in chief of the Continental Army since June 15, 1775, used the Fort Ticonderoga cannons to force the evacuation of the British from Boston. Washington had positioned these cannons on the hills overlooking both the fortified positions of the British and Boston Harbor, where the British supply ships were anchored. The British could not return fire on the colonial positions because they could not elevate their cannons. They soon realized that they were in an untenable position and had to withdraw from Boston. On March 17, 1776, the British evacuated their troops to Halifax, Nova Scotia, ending the nearly year-long siege.

By the time the British withdrew from Boston, fighting had broken out in other colonies as well. In May 1775, Mecklenburg County in North Carolina issued the **Mecklenburg Resolves**, stating that a rebellion against Great Britain had begun, that colonists did not owe any further allegiance to Great Britain, and that governing authority had now passed to the Continental Congress. The resolves also called upon the formation of militias to be under the control of the Continental Congress. Loyalists and Patriots clashed in North Carolina in February 1776 at the Battle of Moore's Creek Bridge.

In Virginia, the royal governor, Lord Dunmore, raised Loyalist forces to combat the rebel colonists and also tried to use the large slave population to put down the rebellion. In November 1775, he issued a decree, known as **Dunmore's Proclamation**, promising freedom to slaves and indentured servants of rebels who remained loyal to the king and who pledged to fight with the Loyalists against the insurgents. Dunmore's Proclamation exposed serious problems for both the Patriot cause and for the British. In order for the British to put down the rebellion, they needed the support of Virginia's landowners, many of whom owned slaves. (While Patriot slaveholders in Virginia and elsewhere proclaimed they acted in defense of liberty, they kept thousands in bondage, a fact the British decided to exploit.) Although a number of slaves did join Dunmore's side, the proclamation had the unintended effect of galvanizing Patriot resistance to Britain. From the rebels' point of view, the British looked to deprive them of their slave property and incite a race war. Slaveholders feared a slave uprising and increased their commitment to the cause against Great Britain, calling for independence. Dunmore fled Virginia in 1776.

COMMON SENSE

With the events of 1775 fresh in their minds, many colonists reached the conclusion in 1776 that the time had come to secede from the Empire and declare independence. Over the past ten years, these colonists had argued that they deserved the same rights as Englishmen enjoyed in Great Britain, only to find themselves relegated to an intolerable subservient status in the Empire. The groundswell of support for their cause of independence in 1776 also owed much to the appearance of an anonymous pamphlet, first published in January 1776, entitled *Common Sense*. Thomas Paine, who had emigrated from England to Philadelphia in 1774, was the author. Arguably the most radical pamphlet of the revolutionary era, *Common Sense* made a powerful argument for independence.

Paine's pamphlet rejected the monarchy, calling King George III a "royal brute" and questioning the right of an island (England) to rule over America. In this way, Paine helped to channel colonial discontent toward the king himself and not, as had been the case, toward the British Parliament—a bold move that signaled the desire to create a new political order disavowing monarchy entirely. He argued for the creation of an American republic, a state without a king, and extolled the blessings of **republicanism**, a political philosophy that held that elected representatives, not a hereditary monarch, should govern states. The vision of an American republic put forward by Paine included the idea of **popular sovereignty**: citizens in the republic would determine who would represent them, and decide other issues, on the basis of majority rule. Republicanism also served as a social philosophy guiding the conduct of the Patriots in their struggle against the British Empire. It demanded adherence to a code of virtue, placing the public good and community above narrow self-interest.

Paine wrote *Common Sense* (Figure 6.7) in simple, direct language aimed at ordinary people, not just the learned elite. The pamphlet proved immensely popular and was soon available in all **thirteen colonies**, where it helped convince many to reject monarchy and the British Empire in favor of independence and a republican form of government.

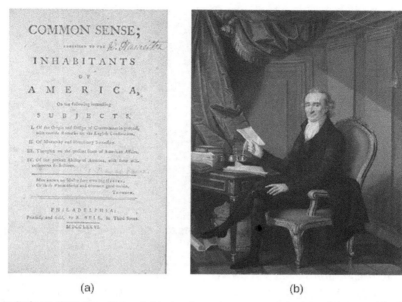

(a)   (b)

Figure 6.7 Thomas Paine's *Common Sense* (a) helped convince many colonists of the need for independence from Great Britain. Paine, shown here in a portrait by Laurent Dabos (b), was a political activist and revolutionary best known for his writings on both the American and French Revolutions.

THE DECLARATION OF INDEPENDENCE

In the summer of 1776, the Continental Congress met in Philadelphia and agreed to sever ties with Great Britain. Virginian Thomas Jefferson and John Adams of Massachusetts, with the support of the Congress, articulated the justification for liberty in the Declaration of Independence (Figure 6.8). The Declaration, written primarily by Jefferson, included a long list of grievances against King George III and laid out the foundation of American government as a republic in which the consent of the governed would be of paramount importance.

Figure 6.8 The Dunlap Broadsides, one of which is shown here, are considered the first published copies of the Declaration of Independence. This one was printed on July 4, 1776.

The preamble to the Declaration began with a statement of Enlightenment principles about universal human rights and values: "We hold these Truths to be self-evident, that all Men are created equal, that they are endowed by their Creator with certain unalienable Rights, that among these are Life, Liberty, and the pursuit of Happiness—That to secure these Rights, Governments are instituted among Men, deriving their just Powers from the Consent of the Governed, that whenever any Form of Government becomes destructive of these Ends, it is the Right of the People to alter or abolish it." In addition to this statement of principles, the document served another purpose: Patriot leaders sent copies to France and Spain in hopes of winning their support and aid in the contest against Great Britain. They understood how important foreign recognition and aid would be to the creation of a new and independent nation.

The Declaration of Independence has since had a global impact, serving as the basis for many subsequent movements to gain independence from other colonial powers. It is part of America's civil religion, and thousands of people each year make pilgrimages to see the original document in Washington, DC.

The Declaration also reveals a fundamental contradiction of the American Revolution: the conflict between the existence of slavery and the idea that "all men are created equal." One-fifth of the population in 1776 was enslaved, and at the time he drafted the Declaration, Jefferson himself owned more than one hundred slaves. Further, the Declaration framed equality as existing only among white men; women and nonwhites were entirely left out of a document that referred to native peoples as "merciless Indian savages" who indiscriminately killed men, women, and children. Nonetheless, the promise of equality for all planted the seeds for future struggles waged by slaves, women, and many others to bring about its full realization. Much of American history is the story of the slow realization of the promise of equality expressed in the Declaration of Independence.

Click and Explore

Visit **Digital History (http://openstaxcollege.org/l/fcombatants)** to view "The Female Combatants." In this 1776 engraving by an anonymous artist, Great Britain is depicted on the left as a staid, stern matron, while America, on the right, is shown as a half-dressed American Indian. Why do you think the artist depicted the two opposing sides this way?

6.2 The Early Years of the Revolution

By the end of this section, you will be able to:
- Explain the British and American strategies of 1776 through 1778
- Identify the key battles of the early years of the Revolution

After the British quit Boston, they slowly adopted a strategy to isolate New England from the rest of the colonies and force the insurgents in that region into submission, believing that doing so would end the conflict. At first, British forces focused on taking the principal colonial centers. They began by easily capturing New York City in 1776. The following year, they took over the American capital of Philadelphia. The larger British effort to isolate New England was implemented in 1777. That effort ultimately failed when the British surrendered a force of over five thousand to the Americans in the fall of 1777 at the Battle of Saratoga.

The major campaigns over the next several years took place in the middle colonies of New York, New Jersey, and Pennsylvania, whose populations were sharply divided between Loyalists and Patriots. Revolutionaries faced many hardships as British superiority on the battlefield became evident and the difficulty of funding the war caused strains.

THE BRITISH STRATEGY IN THE MIDDLE COLONIES

After evacuating Boston in March 1776, British forces sailed to Nova Scotia to regroup. They devised a strategy, successfully implemented in 1776, to take New York City. The following year, they planned to end the rebellion by cutting New England off from the rest of the colonies and starving it into submission. Three British armies were to move simultaneously from New York City, Montreal, and Fort Oswego to converge along the Hudson River; British control of that natural boundary would isolate New England.

General William Howe (Figure 6.9), commander in chief of the British forces in America, amassed thirty-two thousand troops on Staten Island in June and July 1776. His brother, Admiral Richard Howe, controlled New York Harbor. Command of New York City and the Hudson River was their goal. In August 1776, General Howe landed his forces on Long Island and easily routed the American Continental Army there in the Battle of Long Island (August 27). The Americans were outnumbered and lacked both military experience and discipline. Sensing victory, General and Admiral Howe arranged a peace conference in September 1776, where Benjamin Franklin, John Adams, and South Carolinian John Rutledge represented the Continental Congress. Despite the Howes' hopes, however, the Americans demanded recognition of their independence, which the Howes were not authorized to grant, and the conference disbanded.

Figure 6.9 General William Howe, shown here in a 1777 portrait by Richard Purcell, led British forces in America in the first years of the war.

On September 16, 1776, George Washington's forces held up against the British at the Battle of Harlem Heights. This important American military achievement, a key reversal after the disaster on Long Island, occurred as most of Washington's forces retreated to New Jersey. A few weeks later, on October 28, General Howe's forces defeated Washington's at the Battle of White Plains and New York City fell to the British. For the next seven years, the British made the city the headquarters for their military efforts to defeat the rebellion, which included raids on surrounding areas. In 1777, the British burned Danbury, Connecticut, and in July 1779, they set fire to homes in Fairfield and Norwalk. They held American prisoners aboard ships in the waters around New York City; the death toll was shocking, with thousands perishing in the holds. Meanwhile, New York City served as a haven for Loyalists who disagreed with the effort to break away from the Empire and establish an American republic.

GEORGE WASHINGTON AND THE CONTINENTAL ARMY

When the Second Continental Congress met in Philadelphia in May 1775, members approved the creation of a professional Continental Army with Washington as commander in chief (Figure 6.10). Although sixteen thousand volunteers enlisted, it took several years for the Continental Army to become a truly professional force. In 1775 and 1776, militias still composed the bulk of the Patriots' armed forces, and these soldiers returned home after the summer fighting season, drastically reducing the army's strength.

Figure 6.10 This 1775 etching shows George Washington taking command of the Continental Army at Cambridge, Massachusetts, just two weeks after his appointment by the Continental Congress.

That changed in late 1776 and early 1777, when Washington broke with conventional eighteenth-century military tactics that called for fighting in the summer months only. Intent on raising revolutionary morale after the British captured New York City, he launched surprise strikes against British forces in their winter quarters. In Trenton, New Jersey, he led his soldiers across the Delaware River and surprised an encampment of **Hessians**, German mercenaries hired by Great Britain to put down the American rebellion. Beginning the night of December 25, 1776, and continuing into the early hours of December 26, Washington moved on Trenton where the Hessians were encamped. Maintaining the element of surprise by attacking at Christmastime, he defeated them, taking over nine hundred captive. On January 3, 1777, Washington achieved another much-needed victory at the Battle of Princeton. He again broke with eighteenth-century military protocol by attacking unexpectedly after the fighting season had ended.

DEFINING "AMERICAN"

Thomas Paine on "The American Crisis"

During the American Revolution, following the publication of *Common Sense* in January 1776, Thomas Paine began a series of sixteen pamphlets known collectively as *The American Crisis* (Figure 6.11). He wrote the first volume in 1776, describing the dire situation facing the revolutionaries at the end of that hard year.

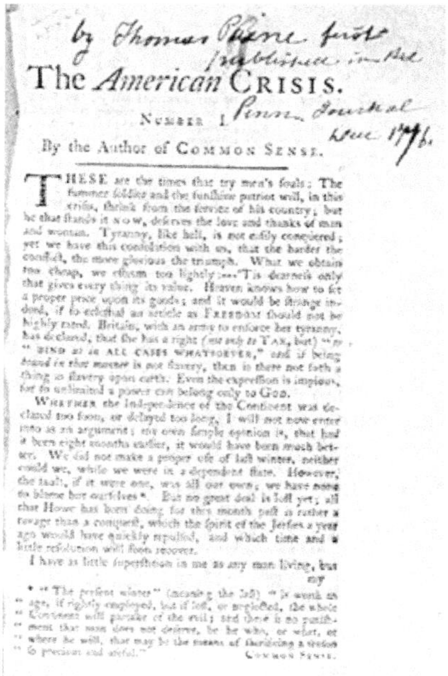

by Thomas Paine first published in the Penn. Journal Dec 1776.

The *American* CRISIS.

NUMBER I.

By the Author of COMMON SENSE.

THESE are the times that try men's souls: The summer soldier and the sunshine patriot will, in this crisis, shrink from the service of his country; but he that stands it NOW, deserves the love and thanks of man and woman. Tyranny, like hell, is not easily conquered; yet we have this consolation with us, that the harder the conflict, the more glorious the triumph. What we obtain too cheap, we esteem too lightly:—'Tis dearness only that gives every thing its value. Heaven knows how to set a proper price upon its goods; and it would be strange indeed, if so celestial an article as FREEDOM should not be highly rated. Britain, with an army to enforce her tyranny, has declared, that she has a right (*not only to* TAX, but) "*to* BIND *us in* ALL CASES WHATSOEVER," and if being *bound in that manner* is not slavery, then is there not such a thing as slavery upon earth. Even the expression is impious, for so unlimited a power can belong only to GOD.

WHETHER the Independence of the Continent was declared too soon, or delayed too long, I will not now enter into as an argument; my own simple opinion is, that had it been eight months earlier, it would have been much better. We did not make a proper use of last winter, neither could we, while we were in a dependent state. However, the fault, if it were one, was all our own; we have none to blame but ourselves*. But no great deal is lost yet; all that Howe has been doing for this month past is rather a ravage than a conquest, which the spirit of the Jersies a year ago would have quickly repulsed, and which time and a little resolution will soon recover.

I have as little superstition in me as any man living, but my

* "The present winter" (meaning the last) "is worth an "age, if rightly employed, but if lost, or neglected, the whole "Continent will partake of the evil; and there is no punish-"ment that man does not deserve, be he who, or what, or "where he will, that may be the means of sacrificing a season "so precious and useful." COMMON SENSE.

Figure 6.11 Thomas Paine wrote the pamphlet *The American Crisis*, the first page of which is shown here, in 1776.

> These are the times that try men's souls. The summer soldier and the sunshine patriot will, in this crisis, shrink from the service of their country; but he that stands it now, deserves the love and thanks of man and woman. . . . Britain, with an army to enforce her tyranny, has declared that she has a right (not only to tax) but "to bind us in all cases whatsoever," and if being bound in that manner, is not slavery, then is there not such a thing as slavery upon earth. Even the expression is impious; for so unlimited a power can belong only to God. . . .
> I shall conclude this paper with some miscellaneous remarks on the state of our affairs; and shall begin with asking the following question, Why is it that the enemy have left the New England provinces, and made these middle ones the seat of war? The answer is easy: New England is not infested with Tories, and we are. I have been tender in raising the cry against these men, and used numberless arguments to show them their danger, but it will not do to sacrifice a world either to their folly or their baseness. The period is now arrived, in which either they or we must change our sentiments, or one or both must fall. . . .
> By perseverance and fortitude we have the prospect of a glorious issue; by cowardice and submission, the sad choice of a variety of evils—a ravaged country—a depopulated city—habitations without safety, and slavery without hope—our homes turned into barracks and bawdy-houses for Hessians, and a future race to provide for, whose fathers we shall doubt of. Look on this picture and weep over it! and if there yet remains one thoughtless wretch who believes it not, let him suffer it unlamented.
> —Thomas Paine, "The American Crisis," December 23, 1776

What topics does Paine address in this pamphlet? What was his purpose in writing? What does he write about Tories (Loyalists), and why does he consider them a problem?

Click and Explore

Visit Wikisource (http://openstaxcollege.org/l/amcrisis) to read the rest of Thomas Paine's first *American Crisis* pamphlet, as well as the other fifteen in the series.

PHILADELPHIA AND SARATOGA: BRITISH AND AMERICAN VICTORIES

In August 1777, General Howe brought fifteen thousand British troops to Chesapeake Bay as part of his plan to take Philadelphia, where the Continental Congress met. That fall, the British defeated Washington's soldiers in the Battle of Brandywine Creek and took control of Philadelphia, forcing the Continental Congress to flee. During the winter of 1777–1778, the British occupied the city, and Washington's army camped at Valley Forge, Pennsylvania.

Washington's winter at Valley Forge was a low point for the American forces. A lack of supplies weakened the men, and disease took a heavy toll. Amid the cold, hunger, and sickness, soldiers deserted in droves. On February 16, Washington wrote to George Clinton, governor of New York: "For some days past, there has been little less than a famine in camp. A part of the army has been a week without any kind of flesh & the rest three or four days. Naked and starving as they are, we cannot enough admire the incomparable patience and fidelity of the soldiery, that they have not been ere [before] this excited by their sufferings to a general mutiny and dispersion." Of eleven thousand soldiers encamped at Valley Forge, twenty-five hundred died of starvation, malnutrition, and disease. As Washington feared, nearly one hundred soldiers deserted every week. (Desertions continued, and by 1780, Washington was executing recaptured deserters every Saturday.) The low morale extended all the way to Congress, where some wanted to replace Washington with a more seasoned leader.

Assistance came to Washington and his soldiers in February 1778 in the form of the Prussian soldier Friedrich Wilhelm von Steuben (Figure 6.12). Baron von Steuben was an experienced military man, and he implemented a thorough training course for Washington's ragtag troops. By drilling a small corps of soldiers and then having them train others, he finally transformed the Continental Army into a force capable of standing up to the professional British and Hessian soldiers. His drill manual—*Regulations for the Order and Discipline of the Troops of the United States*—informed military practices in the United States for the next several decades.

Figure 6.12 Prussian soldier Friedrich Wilhelm von Steuben, shown here in a 1786 portrait by Ralph Earl, was instrumental in transforming Washington's Continental Army into a professional armed force.

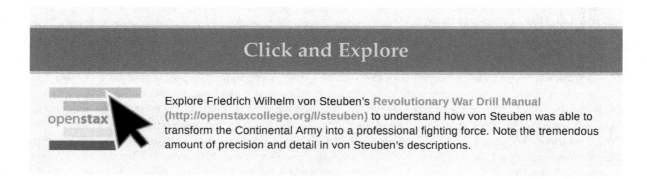

Click and Explore

Explore Friedrich Wilhelm von Steuben's Revolutionary War Drill Manual (http://openstaxcollege.org/l/steuben) to understand how von Steuben was able to transform the Continental Army into a professional fighting force. Note the tremendous amount of precision and detail in von Steuben's descriptions.

Meanwhile, the campaign to sever New England from the rest of the colonies had taken an unexpected turn during the fall of 1777. The British had attempted to implement the plan, drawn up by Lord George Germain and Prime Minister Lord North, to isolate New England with the combined forces of three armies. One army, led by General John Burgoyne, would march south from Montreal. A second force, led by Colonel Barry St. Leger and made up of British troops and Iroquois, would march east from Fort Oswego on the banks of Lake Ontario. A third force, led by General Sir Henry Clinton, would march north from New York City. The armies would converge at Albany and effectively cut the rebellion in two by isolating New England. This northern campaign fell victim to competing strategies, however, as General Howe had meanwhile decided to take Philadelphia. His decision to capture that city siphoned off troops that would have been vital to the overall success of the campaign in 1777.

The British plan to isolate New England ended in disaster. St. Leger's efforts to bring his force of British regulars, Loyalist fighters, and Iroquois allies east to link up with General Burgoyne failed, and he retreated to Quebec. Burgoyne's forces encountered ever-stiffer resistance as he made his way south from Montreal, down Lake Champlain and the upper Hudson River corridor. Although they did capture Fort Ticonderoga when American forces retreated, Burgoyne's army found themselves surrounded by a sea of colonial militias in Saratoga, New York. In the meantime, the small British force under Clinton that left New York City to aid Burgoyne advanced slowly up the Hudson River, failing to provide the much-needed support for the troops at Saratoga. On October 17, 1777, Burgoyne surrendered his five thousand soldiers to the Continental Army (Figure 6.13).

Figure 6.13 This German engraving, created by Daniel Chodowiecki in 1784, shows British soldiers laying down their arms before the American forces.

The American victory at the Battle of Saratoga was the major turning point in the war. This victory convinced the French to recognize American independence and form a military alliance with the new nation, which changed the course of the war by opening the door to badly needed military support from France. Still smarting from their defeat by Britain in the Seven Years' War, the French supplied the United States with gunpowder and money, as well as soldiers and naval forces that proved decisive in the defeat of Great Britain. The French also contributed military leaders, including the Marquis de Lafayette, who arrived in America in 1777 as a volunteer and served as Washington's aide-de-camp.

The war quickly became more difficult for the British, who had to fight the rebels in North America as well as the French in the Caribbean. Following France's lead, Spain joined the war against Great Britain in 1779, though it did not recognize American independence until 1783. The Dutch Republic also began to support the American revolutionaries and signed a treaty of commerce with the United States in 1782.

Great Britain's effort to isolate New England in 1777 failed. In June 1778, the occupying British force in Philadelphia evacuated and returned to New York City in order to better defend that city, and the British then turned their attention to the southern colonies.

6.3 War in the South

By the end of this section, you will be able to:
- Outline the British southern strategy and its results
- Describe key American victories and the end of the war
- Identify the main terms of the Treaty of Paris (1783)

By 1778, the war had turned into a stalemate. Although some in Britain, including Prime Minister Lord North, wanted peace, King George III demanded that the colonies be brought to obedience. To break the deadlock, the British revised their strategy and turned their attention to the southern colonies, where they could expect more support from Loyalists. The southern colonies soon became the center of the fighting. The southern strategy brought the British success at first, but thanks to the leadership of George Washington and General Nathanael Greene and the crucial assistance of French forces, the Continental Army defeated the British at Yorktown, effectively ending further large-scale operations during the war.

GEORGIA AND SOUTH CAROLINA

The British architect of the war strategy, Lord George Germain, believed Britain would gain the upper hand with the support of Loyalists, slaves, and Indian allies in the South, and indeed, this southern strategy initially achieved great success. The British began their southern campaign by capturing Savannah, the capital of Georgia, in December 1778. In Georgia, they found support from thousands of slaves who ran to the British side to escape their bondage. As the British regained political control in Georgia, they forced the inhabitants to swear allegiance to the king and formed twenty Loyalist regiments. The Continental Congress had suggested that slaves be given freedom if they joined the Patriot army against the British, but revolutionaries in Georgia and South Carolina refused to consider this proposal. Once again, the Revolution served to further divisions over race and slavery.

After taking Georgia, the British turned their attention to South Carolina. Before the Revolution, South Carolina had been starkly divided between the backcountry, which harbored revolutionary partisans, and the coastal regions, where Loyalists remained a powerful force. Waves of violence rocked the backcountry from the late 1770s into the early 1780s. The Revolution provided an opportunity for residents to fight over their local resentments and antagonisms with murderous consequences. Revenge killings and the destruction of property became mainstays in the savage civil war that gripped the South.

In April 1780, a British force of eight thousand soldiers besieged American forces in Charleston (Figure 6.14). After six weeks of the Siege of Charleston, the British triumphed. General Benjamin Lincoln, who led the effort for the revolutionaries, had to surrender his entire force, the largest American loss during the entire war. Many of the defeated Americans were placed in jails or in British prison ships anchored in Charleston Harbor. The British established a military government in Charleston under the command of General Sir Henry Clinton. From this base, Clinton ordered General Charles Cornwallis to subdue the rest of South Carolina.

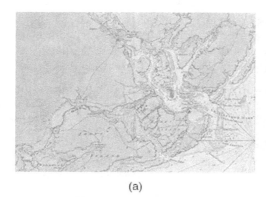

(a)   (b)

Figure 6.14   This 1780 map of Charleston (a), which shows details of the Continental defenses, was probably drawn by British engineers in anticipation of the attack on the city. The Siege of Charleston was one of a series of defeats for the Continental forces in the South, which led the Continental Congress to place General Nathanael Greene (b), shown here in a 1783 portrait by Charles Wilson Peale, in command in late 1780. Greene led his troops to two crucial victories.

The disaster at Charleston led the Continental Congress to change leadership by placing General Horatio Gates in charge of American forces in the South. However, General Gates fared no better than General Lincoln; at the Battle of Camden, South Carolina, in August 1780, Cornwallis forced General Gates to retreat into North Carolina. Camden was one of the worst disasters suffered by American armies during the entire Revolutionary War. Congress again changed military leadership, this time by placing General Nathanael Greene (Figure 6.14) in command in December 1780.

As the British had hoped, large numbers of Loyalists helped ensure the success of the southern strategy, and thousands of slaves seeking freedom arrived to aid Cornwallis's army. However, the war turned in the Americans' favor in 1781. General Greene realized that to defeat Cornwallis, he did not have to win a single battle. So long as he remained in the field, he could continue to destroy isolated British forces. Greene therefore made a strategic decision to divide his own troops to wage war—and the strategy worked. American forces under General Daniel Morgan decisively beat the British at the Battle of Cowpens in South Carolina. General Cornwallis now abandoned his strategy of defeating the backcountry rebels in South Carolina. Determined to destroy Greene's army, he gave chase as Greene strategically retreated north into North Carolina. At the Battle of Guilford Courthouse in March 1781, the British prevailed on the battlefield but suffered extensive losses, an outcome that paralleled the Battle of Bunker Hill nearly six years earlier in June 1775.

YORKTOWN

In the summer of 1781, Cornwallis moved his army to **Yorktown**, Virginia. He expected the Royal Navy to transport his army to New York, where he thought he would join General Sir Henry Clinton. Yorktown was a tobacco port on a peninsula, and Cornwallis believed the British navy would be able to keep the coast clear of rebel ships. Sensing an opportunity, a combined French and American force of sixteen thousand men swarmed the peninsula in September 1781. Washington raced south with his forces, now a disciplined army, as did the Marquis de Lafayette and the Comte de Rochambeau with their French troops. The French Admiral de Grasse sailed his naval force into Chesapeake Bay, preventing Lord Cornwallis from taking a seaward escape route.

In October 1781, the American forces began the battle for Yorktown, and after a siege that lasted eight days, Lord Cornwallis capitulated on October 19 (Figure 6.15). Tradition says that during the surrender of his troops, the British band played "The World Turned Upside Down," a song that befitted the Empire's unexpected reversal of fortune.

Figure 6.15 The 1820 painting above, by John Trumbull, is titled *Surrender of Lord Cornwallis*, but Cornwallis actually sent his general, Charles O'Hara, to perform the ceremonial surrendering of the sword. The painting depicts General Benjamin Lincoln holding out his hand to receive the sword. General George Washington is in the background on the brown horse, since he refused to accept the sword from anyone but Cornwallis himself.

DEFINING "AMERICAN"

✲ *"The World Turned Upside Down"*

"The World Turned Upside Down," reputedly played during the surrender of the British at Yorktown, was a traditional English ballad from the seventeenth century. It was also the theme of a popular British print that circulated in the 1790s (Figure 6.16).

Figure 6.16   In many of the images in this popular print, entitled "The World Turned Upside Down or the Folly of Man," animals and humans have switched places. In one, children take care of their parents, while in another, the sun, moon, and stars appear below the earth.

Why do you think these images were popular in Great Britain in the decade following the Revolutionary War? What would these images imply to Americans?

Click and Explore

Visit the Public Domain Review (http://openstaxcollege.org/l/worldupside) to explore the images in an eighteenth-century British chapbook (a pamphlet for tracts or ballads) titled "The World Turned Upside Down." The chapbook is illustrated with woodcuts similar to those in the popular print mentioned above.

THE TREATY OF PARIS

The British defeat at Yorktown made the outcome of the war all but certain. In light of the American victory, the Parliament of Great Britain voted to end further military operations against the rebels and to begin peace negotiations. Support for the war effort had come to an end, and British military forces began to evacuate the former American colonies in 1782. When hostilities had ended, Washington resigned as commander in chief and returned to his Virginia home.

In April 1782, Benjamin Franklin, John Adams, and John Jay had begun informal peace negotiations in Paris. Officials from Great Britain and the United States finalized the treaty in 1783, signing the Treaty of Paris (Figure 6.17) in September of that year. The treaty recognized the independence of the United

States; placed the western, eastern, northern, and southern boundaries of the nation at the Mississippi River, the Atlantic Ocean, Canada, and Florida, respectively; and gave New Englanders fishing rights in the waters off Newfoundland. Under the terms of the treaty, individual states were encouraged to refrain from persecuting Loyalists and to return their confiscated property.

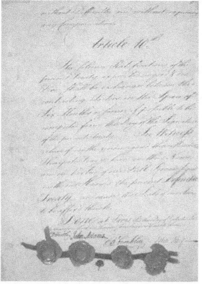

Figure 6.17 The last page of the Treaty of Paris, signed on September 3, 1783, contained the signatures and seals of representatives for both the British and the Americans. From right to left, the seals pictured belong to David Hartley, who represented Great Britain, and John Adams, Benjamin Franklin, and John Jay for the Americans.

6.4 Identity during the American Revolution

By the end of this section, you will be able to:
- Explain Loyalist and Patriot sentiments
- Identify different groups that participated in the Revolutionary War

The American Revolution in effect created multiple civil wars. Many of the resentments and antagonisms that fed these conflicts predated the Revolution, and the outbreak of war acted as the catalyst they needed to burst forth. In particular, the middle colonies of New York, New Jersey, and Pennsylvania had deeply divided populations. Loyalty to Great Britain came in many forms, from wealthy elites who enjoyed the prewar status quo to runaway slaves who desired the freedom that the British offered.

LOYALISTS

Historians disagree on what percentage of colonists were Loyalists; estimates range from 20 percent to over 30 percent. In general, however, of British America's population of 2.5 million, roughly one-third remained loyal to Great Britain, while another third committed themselves to the cause of independence. The remaining third remained apathetic, content to continue with their daily lives as best they could and preferring not to engage in the struggle.

Many Loyalists were royal officials and merchants with extensive business ties to Great Britain, who viewed themselves as the rightful and just defenders of the British constitution. Others simply resented local business and political rivals who supported the Revolution, viewing the rebels as hypocrites and schemers who selfishly used the break with the Empire to increase their fortunes. In New York's Hudson Valley, animosity among the tenants of estates owned by Revolutionary leaders turned them to the cause of King and Empire.

During the war, all the states passed **confiscation acts**, which gave the new revolutionary governments in the former colonies the right to seize Loyalist land and property. To ferret out Loyalists, revolutionary governments also passed laws requiring the male population to take oaths of allegiance to the new states. Those who refused lost their property and were often imprisoned or made to work for the new local revolutionary order.

William Franklin, Benjamin Franklin's only surviving son, remained loyal to Crown and Empire and served as royal governor of New Jersey, a post he secured with his father's help. During the war, revolutionaries imprisoned William in Connecticut; however, he remained steadfast in his allegiance to Great Britain and moved to England after the Revolution. He and his father never reconciled.

As many as nineteen thousand colonists served the British in the effort to put down the rebellion, and after the Revolution, as many as 100,000 colonists left, moving to England or north to Canada rather than staying in the new United States (Figure 6.18). Eight thousand whites and five thousand free blacks went to Britain. Over thirty thousand went to Canada, transforming that nation from predominately French to predominantly British. Another sizable group of Loyalists went to the British West Indies, taking their slaves with them.

Figure 6.18 *The Coming of the Loyalists*, a ca. 1880 work that artist Henry Sandham created at least a century after the Revolution, shows Anglo-American colonists arriving by ship in New Brunswick, Canada.

MY STORY

⚙ *Hannah Ingraham on Removing to Nova Scotia*

Hannah Ingraham was eleven years old in 1783, when her Loyalist family removed from New York to Ste. Anne's Point in the colony of Nova Scotia. Later in life, she compiled her memories of that time.

> [Father] said we were to go to Nova Scotia, that a ship was ready to take us there, so we made all haste to get ready. . . . Then on Tuesday, suddenly the house was surrounded by rebels and father was taken prisoner and carried away. . . . When morning came, they said he was free to go.
>
> We had five wagon loads carried down the Hudson in a sloop and then we went on board the transport that was to bring us to Saint John. I was just eleven years old when we left our farm to come here. It was the last transport of the season and had on board all those who could not come sooner. The first transports had come in May so the people had all the summer before them to get settled. . . .
>
> We lived in a tent at St. Anne's until father got a house ready. . . . There was no floor laid, no windows, no chimney, no door, but we had a roof at least. A good fire was blazing and mother had a big loaf of bread and she boiled a kettle of water and put a good piece of butter in a pewter bowl. We toasted the bread and all sat around the bowl and ate our breakfast that morning and mother said: "Thank God we are no longer in dread of having shots fired through our house. This is the sweetest meal I ever tasted for many a day."

What do these excerpts tell you about life as a Loyalist in New York or as a transplant to Canada?

SLAVES AND INDIANS

While some slaves who fought for the Patriot cause received their freedom, revolutionary leaders—unlike the British—did not grant such slaves their freedom as a matter of course. Washington, the owner of more than two hundred slaves during the Revolution, refused to let slaves serve in the army, although he did allow free blacks. (In his will, Washington did free his slaves.) In the new United States, the Revolution largely reinforced a racial identity based on skin color. Whiteness, now a national identity, denoted freedom and stood as the key to power. Blackness, more than ever before, denoted servile status. Indeed, despite their class and ethnic differences, white revolutionaries stood mostly united in their hostility to both blacks and Indians.

MY STORY

✪ *Boyrereau Brinch and Boston King on the Revolutionary War*

In the Revolutionary War, some blacks, both free and enslaved, chose to fight for the Americans (Figure 6.19). Others chose to fight for the British, who offered them freedom for joining their cause. Read the excerpts below for the perspective of a black veteran from each side of the conflict.

Figure 6.19   Jean-Baptiste-Antoine de Verger created this 1781 watercolor, which depicts American soldiers at the Siege of Yorktown. Verger was an officer in Rochambeau's army, and his diary holds firsthand accounts of his experiences in the campaigns of 1780 and 1781. This image contains one of the earliest known representations of a black Continental soldier.

Boyrereau Brinch was captured in Africa at age sixteen and brought to America as a slave. He joined the Patriot forces and was honorably discharged and emancipated after the war. He told his story to Benjamin Prentiss, who published it as *The Blind African Slave* in 1810.

> Finally, I was in the battles at Cambridge, White Plains, Monmouth, Princeton, Newark, Frog's Point, Horseneck where I had a ball pass through my knapsack. All which battels [sic] the reader can obtain a more perfect account of in history, than I can give. At last we returned to West Point and were discharged [1783], as the war was over. Thus was I, a slave for five years fighting for liberty. After we were disbanded, I returned to my old master at Woodbury [Connecticut], with whom I lived one year, my services in the American war, having emancipated me from further slavery, and from being bartered or sold. . . . Here I enjoyed the pleasures of a freeman; my food was sweet, my labor pleasure: and one bright gleam of life seemed to shine upon me.

Boston King was a Charleston-born slave who escaped his master and joined the Loyalists. He made his way to Nova Scotia and later Sierra Leone, where he published his memoirs in 1792. The excerpt below describes his experience in New York after the war.

> When I arrived at New-York, my friends rejoiced to see me once more restored to liberty, and joined me in praising the Lord for his mercy and goodness. . . . [In 1783] the horrors and devastation of war happily terminated, and peace was restored between America and Great Britain, which diffused universal joy among all parties, except us, who had escaped from slavery and taken refuge in the English army; for a report prevailed at New-York, that all the slaves, in number 2000, were to be delivered up to their masters, altho' some of them had been three or four years among the English. This dreadful rumour filled us all with inexpressible anguish and terror, especially when we saw our old masters coming from Virginia, North-Carolina, and other parts, and seizing upon their slaves in the streets of New-York, or even dragging them out of their beds. Many of the slaves had very cruel masters, so that the thoughts of returning home with them embittered life to us. For some days we lost our appetite for food, and sleep departed from our eyes. The English had compassion upon us in the day of distress, and issued out a Proclamation, importing, That all slaves should be free, who had taken refuge in the British lines, and claimed the sanction and privileges of

the Proclamations respecting the security and protection of Negroes. In consequence of this, each of us received a certificate from the commanding officer at New-York, which dispelled all our fears, and filled us with joy and gratitude.

What do these two narratives have in common, and how are they different? How do the two men describe freedom?

For slaves willing to run away and join the British, the American Revolution offered a unique occasion to escape bondage. Of the half a million slaves in the American colonies during the Revolution, twenty thousand joined the British cause. At Yorktown, for instance, thousands of black troops fought with Lord Cornwallis. Slaves belonging to George Washington, Thomas Jefferson, Patrick Henry, and other revolutionaries seized the opportunity for freedom and fled to the British side. Between ten and twenty thousand slaves gained their freedom because of the Revolution; arguably, the Revolution created the largest slave uprising and the greatest emancipation until the Civil War. After the Revolution, some of these African Loyalists emigrated to Sierra Leone on the west coast of Africa. Others removed to Canada and England. It is also true that people of color made heroic contributions to the cause of American independence. However, while the British offered slaves freedom, most American revolutionaries clung to notions of black inferiority.

Powerful Indian peoples who had allied themselves with the British, including the Mohawk and the Creek, also remained loyal to the Empire. A Mohawk named Joseph Brant, whose given name was Thayendanegea (Figure 6.20), rose to prominence while fighting for the British during the Revolution. He joined forces with Colonel Barry St. Leger during the 1777 campaign, which ended with the surrender of General Burgoyne at Saratoga. After the war, Brant moved to the Six Nations reserve in Canada. From his home on the shores of Lake Ontario, he remained active in efforts to restrict white encroachment onto Indian lands. After their defeat, the British did not keep promises they'd made to help their Indian allies keep their territory; in fact, the Treaty of Paris granted the United States huge amounts of supposedly British-owned regions that were actually Indian lands.

(a)

(b)

Figure 6.20 What similarities can you see in these two portraits of Joseph Brant, one by Gilbert Stuart in 1786 (a) and one by Charles Wilson Peale in 1797 (b)? What are the differences? Why do you think the artists made the specific choices they did?

PATRIOTS

The American revolutionaries (also called Patriots or Whigs) came from many different backgrounds and included merchants, shoemakers, farmers, and sailors. What is extraordinary is the way in which the struggle for independence brought a vast cross-section of society together, animated by a common cause.

During the war, the revolutionaries faced great difficulties, including massive supply problems; clothing, ammunition, tents, and equipment were all hard to come by. After an initial burst of enthusiasm in 1775 and 1776, the shortage of supplies became acute in 1777 through 1779, as Washington's difficult winter at Valley Forge demonstrates.

Funding the war effort also proved very difficult. Whereas the British could pay in gold and silver, the American forces relied on paper money, backed by loans obtained in Europe. This first American money was called **Continental currency**; unfortunately, it quickly fell in value. "Not worth a Continental" soon became a shorthand term for something of no value. The new revolutionary government printed a great amount of this paper money, resulting in runaway inflation. By 1781, inflation was such that 146 Continental dollars were worth only one dollar in gold. The problem grew worse as each former colony, now a revolutionary state, printed its own currency.

WOMEN

In colonial America, women shouldered enormous domestic and child-rearing responsibilities. The war for independence only increased their workload and, in some ways, solidified their roles. Rebel leaders required women to produce articles for war—everything from clothing to foodstuffs—while also keeping their homesteads going. This was not an easy task when their husbands and sons were away fighting. Women were also expected to provide food and lodging for armies and to nurse wounded soldiers.

The Revolution opened some new doors for women, however, as they took on public roles usually reserved for men. The Daughters of Liberty, an informal organization formed in the mid-1760s to oppose British revenue-raising measures, worked tirelessly to support the war effort. Esther DeBerdt Reed of Philadelphia, wife of Governor Joseph Reed, formed the Ladies Association of Philadelphia and led a fundraising drive to provide sorely needed supplies to the Continental Army. In "The Sentiments of an American Woman" (1780), she wrote to other women, "The time is arrived to display the same sentiments which animated us at the beginning of the Revolution, when we renounced the use of teas, however agreeable to our taste, rather than receive them from our persecutors; when we made it appear to them that we placed former necessaries in the rank of superfluities, when our liberty was interested; when our republican and laborious hands spun the flax, prepared the linen intended for the use of our soldiers; when exiles and fugitives we supported with courage all the evils which are the concomitants of war." Reed and other elite women in Philadelphia raised almost $300,000 in Continental money for the war.

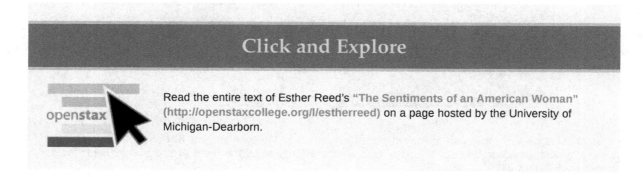

Read the entire text of Esther Reed's "The Sentiments of an American Woman" (http://openstaxcollege.org/l/estherreed) on a page hosted by the University of Michigan-Dearborn.

Women who did not share Reed's elite status nevertheless played key economic roles by producing homespun cloth and food. During shortages, some women formed mobs and wrested supplies from those who hoarded them. Crowds of women beset merchants and demanded fair prices for goods; if a merchant refused, a riot would ensue. Still other women accompanied the army as "camp followers," serving as cooks, washerwomen, and nurses. A few also took part in combat and proved their equality with men through violence against the hated British.

Key Terms

confiscation acts state-wide acts that made it legal for state governments to seize Loyalists' property

Continental currency the paper currency that the Continental government printed to fund the Revolution

Dunmore's Proclamation the decree signed by Lord Dunmore, the royal governor of Virginia, which proclaimed that any slaves or indentured servants who fought on the side of the British would be rewarded with their freedom

Hessians German mercenaries hired by Great Britain to put down the American rebellion

Mecklenburg Resolves North Carolina's declaration of rebellion against Great Britain

minutemen colonial militias prepared to mobilize and fight the British with a minute's notice

popular sovereignty the practice of allowing the citizens of a state or territory to decide issues based on the principle of majority rule

republicanism a political philosophy that holds that states should be governed by representatives, not a monarch; as a social philosophy, republicanism required civic virtue of its citizens

thirteen colonies the British colonies in North America that declared independence from Great Britain in 1776, which included Connecticut, Delaware, Georgia, Maryland, the province of Massachusetts Bay, New Hampshire, New Jersey, New York, North Carolina, Pennsylvania, Rhode Island and Providence Plantations, South Carolina, and Virginia

Yorktown the Virginia port where British General Cornwallis surrendered to American forces

Summary

6.1 Britain's Law-and-Order Strategy and Its Consequences
Until Parliament passed the Coercive Acts in 1774, most colonists still thought of themselves as proud subjects of the strong British Empire. However, the Coercive (or Intolerable) Acts, which Parliament enacted to punish Massachusetts for failing to pay for the destruction of the tea, convinced many colonists that Great Britain was indeed threatening to stifle their liberty. In Massachusetts and other New England colonies, militias like the minutemen prepared for war by stockpiling weapons and ammunition. After the first loss of life at the battles of Lexington and Concord in April 1775, skirmishes continued throughout the colonies. When Congress met in Philadelphia in July 1776, its members signed the Declaration of Independence, officially breaking ties with Great Britain and declaring their intention to be self-governing.

6.2 The Early Years of the Revolution
The British successfully implemented the first part of their strategy to isolate New England when they took New York City in the fall of 1776. For the next seven years, they used New York as a base of operations, expanding their control to Philadelphia in the winter of 1777. After suffering through a terrible winter in 1777–1778 in Valley Forge, Pennsylvania, American forces were revived with help from Baron von Steuben, a Prussian military officer who helped transform the Continental Army into a professional fighting force. The effort to cut off New England from the rest of the colonies failed with the General Burgoyne's surrender at Saratoga in October 1777. After Saratoga, the struggle for independence gained a powerful ally when France agreed to recognize the United States as a new nation and began to send much-

needed military support. The entrance of France—Britain's archrival in the contest of global empire—into the American fight helped to turn the tide of the war in favor of the revolutionaries.

6.3 War in the South

The British gained momentum in the war when they turned their military efforts against the southern colonies. They scored repeated victories in the coastal towns, where they found legions of supporters, including slaves escaping bondage. As in other colonies, however, control of major seaports did not mean the British could control the interior. Fighting in the southern colonies devolved into a merciless civil war as the Revolution opened the floodgates of pent-up anger and resentment between frontier residents and those along the coastal regions. The southern campaign came to an end at Yorktown when Cornwallis surrendered to American forces.

6.4 Identity during the American Revolution

The American Revolution divided the colonists as much as it united them, with Loyalists (or Tories) joining the British forces against the Patriots (or revolutionaries). Both sides included a broad cross-section of the population. However, Great Britain was able to convince many slaves to join its forces by promising them freedom, something the southern revolutionaries would not agree to do. The war provided new opportunities, as well as new challenges, for slaves, free blacks, women, and Indians. After the war, many Loyalists fled the American colonies, heading across the Atlantic to England, north to Canada, or south to the West Indies.

Review Questions

1. How did British General Thomas Gage attempt to deal with the uprising in Massachusetts in 1774?
   A. He offered the rebels land on the Maine frontier in return for loyalty to England.
   B. He allowed for town meetings in an attempt to appease the rebels.
   C. He attempted to seize arms and munitions from the colonial insurgents.
   D. He ordered his troops to burn Boston to the ground to show the determination of Britain.

2. Which of the following was *not* a result of Dunmore's Proclamation?
   A. Slaves joined Dunmore to fight for the British.
   B. A majority of slaves in the colonies won their freedom.
   C. Patriot forces increased their commitment to independence.
   D. Both slaveholding and non-slaveholding whites feared a slave rebellion.

3. Which of the following is *not* true of a republic?

   A. A republic has no hereditary ruling class.
   B. A republic relies on the principle of popular sovereignty.
   C. Representatives chosen by the people lead the republic.
   D. A republic is governed by a monarch and the royal officials he or she appoints.

4. What are the main arguments that Thomas Paine makes in his pamphlet *Common Sense*? Why was this pamphlet so popular?

5. Which city served as the base for British operations for most of the war?
   A. Boston
   B. New York
   C. Philadelphia
   D. Saratoga

6. What battle turned the tide of war in favor of the Americans?
   A. the Battle of Saratoga
   B. the Battle of Brandywine Creek
   C. the Battle of White Plains
   D. the Battle of Valley Forge

7. Which term describes German soldiers hired by Great Britain to put down the American rebellion?

    A. Patriots

    B. Royalists

    C. Hessians

    D. Loyalists

8. Describe the British strategy in the early years of the war and explain whether or not it succeeded.

9. How did George Washington's military tactics help him to achieve success?

10. Which American general is responsible for improving the American military position in the South?

    A. John Burgoyne

    B. Nathanael Greene

    C. Wilhelm Frederick von Steuben

    D. Charles Cornwallis

11. Describe the British southern strategy and its results.

12. Which of the following statements best represents the division between Patriots and Loyalists?

    A. Most American colonists were Patriots, with only a few traditionalists remaining loyal to the King and Empire.

    B. Most American colonists were Loyalists, with only a few firebrand revolutionaries leading the charge for independence.

    C. American colonists were divided among those who wanted independence, those who wanted to remain part of the British Empire, and those who were neutral.

    D. The vast majority of American colonists were neutral and didn't take a side between Loyalists and Patriots.

13. Which of the following is *not* one of the tasks women performed during the Revolution?

    A. holding government offices

    B. maintaining their homesteads

    C. feeding, quartering, and nursing soldiers

    D. raising funds for the war effort

Critical Thinking Questions

14. How did the colonists manage to triumph in their battle for independence despite Great Britain's military might? If any of these factors had been different, how might it have affected the outcome of the war?

15. How did the condition of certain groups, such as women, blacks, and Indians, reveal a contradiction in the Declaration of Independence?

16. What was the effect and importance of Great Britain's promise of freedom to slaves who joined the British side?

17. How did the Revolutionary War provide both new opportunities and new challenges for slaves and free blacks in America?

18. Describe the ideology of republicanism. As a political philosophy, how did republicanism compare to the system that prevailed in Great Britain?

19. Describe the backgrounds and philosophies of Patriots and Loyalists. Why did colonists with such diverse individual interests unite in support of their respective causes? What might different groups of Patriots and Loyalists, depending upon their circumstances, have hoped to achieve by winning the war?

CHAPTER 7

Creating Republican Governments, 1776–1790

Figure 7.1 John Trumbull, Washington's aide-de-camp, painted this wartime image of Washington on a promontory above the Hudson River. Just behind Washington, his slave William "Billy" Lee has his eyes firmly fixed on his master. In the far background, British warships fire on an American fort.

Chapter Outline

7.1 Common Sense: From Monarchy to an American Republic
7.2 How Much Revolutionary Change?
7.3 Debating Democracy
7.4 The Constitutional Convention and Federal Constitution

Introduction

After the Revolutionary War, the ideology that "all men are created equal" failed to match up with reality, as the revolutionary generation could not solve the contradictions of freedom and slavery in the new United States. Trumbull's 1780 painting of George Washington (Figure 7.1) hints at some of these contradictions. What attitude do you think Trumbull was trying to convey? Why did Trumbull include Washington's slave Billy Lee, and what does Lee represent in this painting?

During the 1770s and 1780s, Americans took bold steps to define American equality. Each state held constitutional conventions and crafted state constitutions that defined how government would operate and who could participate in political life. Many elite revolutionaries recoiled in horror from the idea of majority rule—the basic principle of democracy—fearing that it would effectively create a "mob rule" that would bring about the ruin of the hard-fought struggle for independence. Statesmen everywhere believed that a republic should replace the British monarchy: a government where the important affairs would be entrusted only to representative men of learning and refinement.

7.1 Common Sense: From Monarchy to an American Republic

By the end of this section, you will be able to:
- Compare and contrast monarchy and republican government
- Describe the tenets of republicanism

While monarchies dominated eighteenth-century Europe, American revolutionaries were determined to find an alternative to this method of government. Radical pamphleteer Thomas Paine, whose enormously popular essay *Common Sense* was first published in January 1776, advocated a republic: a state without a king. Six months later, Jefferson's Declaration of Independence affirmed the break with England but did not suggest what form of government should replace monarchy, the only system most English colonists had ever known. In the late eighteenth century, republics were few and far between. Genoa, Venice, and the Dutch Republic provided examples of states without monarchs, but many European Enlightenment thinkers questioned the stability of a republic. Nonetheless, after their break from Great Britain, Americans turned to republicanism for their new government.

REPUBLICANISM AS A POLITICAL PHILOSOPHY

Monarchy rests on the practice of dynastic succession, in which the monarch's child or other relative inherits the throne. Contested dynastic succession produced chronic conflict and warfare in Europe. In the eighteenth century, well-established monarchs ruled most of Europe and, according to tradition, were obligated to protect and guide their subjects. However, by the mid-1770s, many American colonists believed that George III, the king of Great Britain, had failed to do so. Patriots believed the British monarchy under George III had been corrupted and the king turned into a tyrant who cared nothing for the traditional liberties afforded to members of the British Empire. The disaffection from monarchy explains why a republic appeared a better alternative to the revolutionaries.

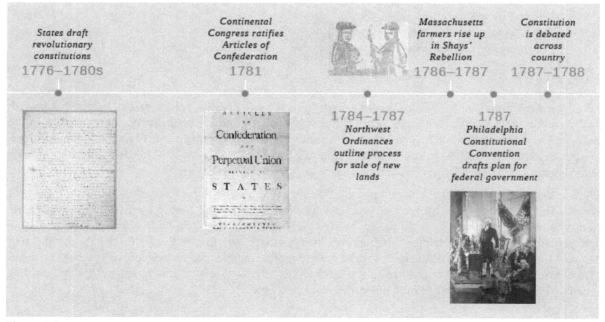

Figure 7.2

American revolutionaries looked to the past for inspiration for their break with the British monarchy and their adoption of a republican form of government. The Roman Republic provided guidance. Much like the Americans in their struggle against Britain, Romans had thrown off monarchy and created a republic in which Roman citizens would appoint or select the leaders who would represent them.

Click and Explore

Visit the Metropolitan Museum of Art (http://openstaxcollege.org/l/ceracchi) to see a Roman-style bust of George Washington, complete with toga. In 1791, Italian sculptor Giuseppe Ceracchi visited Philadelphia, hoping the government might commission a monument of his creation. He did not succeed, but the bust of Washington, one of the ones he produced to demonstrate his skill, illustrates the connection between the American and Roman republics that revolutionaries made.

While republicanism offered an alternative to monarchy, it was also an alternative to **democracy**, a system of government characterized by **majority rule**, where the majority of citizens have the power to make decisions binding upon the whole. To many revolutionaries, especially wealthy landowners, merchants, and planters, democracy did not offer a good replacement for monarchy. Indeed, **conservative Whigs** defined themselves in opposition to democracy, which they equated with anarchy. In the tenth in a series of essays later known as *The Federalist Papers*, Virginian James Madison wrote: "Democracies have ever been spectacles of turbulence and contention; have ever been found incompatible with personal security or the rights of property; and have in general been as short in their lives as they have been violent in their deaths." Many shared this perspective and worked hard to keep democratic tendencies in check. It is easy to understand why democracy seemed threatening: majority rule can easily overpower minority rights, and the wealthy few had reason to fear that a hostile and envious majority could seize and redistribute their wealth.

While many now assume the United States was founded as a democracy, history, as always, is more complicated. Conservative Whigs believed in government by a patrician class, a ruling group composed of a small number of privileged families. **Radical Whigs** favored broadening the popular participation in political life and pushed for democracy. The great debate after independence was secured centered on this question: Who should rule in the new American republic?

REPUBLICANISM AS A SOCIAL PHILOSOPHY

According to political theory, a republic requires its citizens to cultivate virtuous behavior; if the people are virtuous, the republic will survive. If the people become corrupt, the republic will fall. Whether republicanism succeeded or failed in the United States would depend on civic virtue and an educated citizenry. Revolutionary leaders agreed that the ownership of property provided one way to measure an individual's virtue, arguing that property holders had the greatest stake in society and therefore could be trusted to make decisions for it. By the same token, non-property holders, they believed, should have very little to do with government. In other words, unlike a democracy, in which the mass of non-property holders could exercise the political right to vote, a republic would limit political rights to property holders. In this way, republicanism exhibited a bias toward the elite, a preference that is understandable given the colonial legacy. During colonial times, wealthy planters and merchants in the American colonies had looked to the British ruling class, whose social order demanded deference from those of lower rank, as a model of behavior. Old habits died hard.

DEFINING "AMERICAN"

✳ *Benjamin Franklin's Thirteen Virtues for Character Development*

In the 1780s, Benjamin Franklin carefully defined thirteen virtues to help guide his countrymen in maintaining a virtuous republic. His choice of thirteen is telling since he wrote for the citizens of the thirteen new American republics. These virtues were:

1. Temperance. Eat not to dullness; drink not to elevation.
2. Silence. Speak not but what may benefit others or yourself; avoid trifling conversation.
3. Order. Let all your things have their places; let each part of your business have its time.
4. Resolution. Resolve to perform what you ought; perform without fail what you resolve.
5. Frugality. Make no expense but to do good to others or yourself; i.e., waste nothing.
6. Industry. Lose no time; be always employ'd in something useful; cut off all unnecessary actions.
7. Sincerity. Use no hurtful deceit; think innocently and justly, and, if you speak, speak accordingly.
8. Justice. Wrong none by doing injuries, or omitting the benefits that are your duty.
9. Moderation. Avoid extremes; forbear resenting injuries so much as you think they deserve.
10. Cleanliness. Tolerate no uncleanliness in body, cloaths, or habitation.
11. Tranquillity. Be not disturbed at trifles, or at accidents common or unavoidable.
12. Chastity. Rarely use venery but for health or offspring, never to dullness, weakness, or the injury of your own or another's peace or reputation.
13. Humility. Imitate Jesus and Socrates.

Franklin's thirteen virtues suggest that hard work and good behavior will bring success. What factors does Franklin ignore? How would he likely address a situation in which children inherit great wealth rather than working for it? How do Franklin's values help to define the notion of republican virtue?

Click and Explore

Check how well you are demonstrating all thirteen of Franklin's virtues (http://openstaxcollege.org/l/13virtues) on thirteenvirtues.com, where you can register to track your progress.

George Washington served as a role model par excellence for the new republic, embodying the exceptional talent and public virtue prized under the political and social philosophy of republicanism. He did not seek to become the new king of America; instead he retired as commander in chief of the Continental Army and returned to his Virginia estate at Mount Vernon to resume his life among the planter elite. Washington modeled his behavior on that of the Roman aristocrat Cincinnatus, a representative of the patrician or ruling class, who had also retired from public service in the Roman Republic and returned to his estate to pursue agricultural life.

The aristocratic side of republicanism—and the belief that the true custodians of public virtue were those who had served in the military—found expression in the Society of the Cincinnati, of which Washington was the first president general (Figure 7.3). Founded in 1783, the society admitted only officers of the Continental Army and the French forces, not militia members or minutemen. Following the rule of primogeniture, the eldest sons of members inherited their fathers' memberships. The society still exists today and retains the motto *Omnia relinquit servare rempublicam* ("He relinquished everything to save the Republic").

Figure 7.3 This membership certificate for the Society of the Cincinnati commemorates "the great Event which gave Independence to North America."

7.2 How Much Revolutionary Change?

By the end of this section, you will be able to:
- Describe the status of women in the new republic
- Describe the status of nonwhites in the new republic

Elite republican revolutionaries did not envision a completely new society; traditional ideas and categories of race and gender, order and decorum remained firmly entrenched among members of their privileged class. Many Americans rejected the elitist and aristocratic republican order, however, and advocated radical changes. Their efforts represented a groundswell of sentiment for greater equality, a part of the democratic impulse unleashed by the Revolution.

THE STATUS OF WOMEN

In eighteenth-century America, as in Great Britain, the legal status of married women was defined as **coverture**, meaning a married woman (or *feme covert*) had no legal or economic status independent of her husband. She could not conduct business or buy and sell property. Her husband controlled any property she brought to the marriage, although he could not sell it without her agreement. Married women's status as *femes covert* did not change as a result of the Revolution, and wives remained economically dependent on their husbands. The women of the newly independent nation did not call for the right to vote, but some, especially the wives of elite republican statesmen, began to agitate for equality under the law between husbands and wives, and for the same educational opportunities as men.

Some women hoped to overturn coverture. From her home in Braintree, Massachusetts, Abigail Adams (Figure 7.4) wrote to her husband, Whig leader John Adams, in 1776, "In the new code of laws which I suppose it will be necessary for you to make, I desire you would remember the ladies and be more generous and favorable to them than your ancestor. Do not put such unlimited power in the husbands. Remember, all men would be tyrants if they could." Abigail Adams ran the family homestead during the Revolution, but she did not have the ability to conduct business without her husband's consent. Elsewhere in the famous 1776 letter quoted above, she speaks of the difficulties of running the homestead when her husband is away. Her frustration grew when her husband responded in an April 1776 letter: "As to your extraordinary Code of Laws, I cannot but laugh. We have been told that our Struggle has loosened the bands of Government every where. That Children and Apprentices were disobedient—that schools and Colledges were grown turbulent—that Indians slighted their Guardians and Negroes grew insolent to their Masters. But your Letter was the first Intimation that another Tribe more numerous and powerfull than all the rest were grown discontented. . . . Depend on it, We know better than to repeal our Masculine systems."

              (a)   (b)

Figure 7.4 Abigail Adams (a), shown here in a 1766 portrait by Benjamin Blythe, is best remembered for her eloquent letters to her husband, John Adams (b), who would later become the second president of the United States.

Another privileged member of the revolutionary generation, Mercy Otis Warren, also challenged gender assumptions and traditions during the revolutionary era (Figure 7.5). Born in Massachusetts, Warren actively opposed British reform measures before the outbreak of fighting in 1775 by publishing anti-British works. In 1812, she published a three-volume history of the Revolution, a project she had started in the late 1770s. By publishing her work, Warren stepped out of the female sphere and into the otherwise male-dominated sphere of public life.

Inspired by the Revolution, Judith Sargent Murray of Massachusetts advocated women's economic independence and equal educational opportunities for men and women (Figure 7.5). Murray, who came from a well-to-do family in Gloucester, questioned why boys were given access to education as a birthright while girls had very limited educational opportunities. She began to publish her ideas about educational equality beginning in the 1780s, arguing that God had made the minds of women and men equal.

Figure 7.5 John Singleton Copley's 1772 portrait of Judith Sargent Murray (a) and 1763 portrait of Mercy Otis Warren (b) show two of America's earliest advocates for women's rights. Notice how their fine silk dresses telegraph their privileged social status.

Murray's more radical ideas championed woman's economic independence. She argued that a woman's education should be extensive enough to allow her to maintain herself—and her family—if there was no male breadwinner. Indeed, Murray was able to make money of her own from her publications. Her ideas were both radical and traditional, however: Murray also believed that women were much better at raising children and maintaining the morality and virtue of the family than men.

Adams, Murray, and Warren all came from privileged backgrounds. All three were fully literate, while many women in the American republic were not. Their literacy and station allowed them to push for new roles for women in the atmosphere of unique possibility created by the Revolution and its promise of change. Female authors who published their work provide evidence of how women in the era of the American Revolution challenged traditional gender roles.

Overall, the Revolution reconfigured women's roles by undermining the traditional expectations of wives and mothers, including subservience. In the home, the separate domestic sphere assigned to women, women were expected to practice republican virtues, especially frugality and simplicity. Republican motherhood meant that women, more than men, were responsible for raising good children, instilling in them all the virtue necessary to ensure the survival of the republic. The Revolution also opened new doors to educational opportunities for women. Men understood that the republic needed women to play a substantial role in upholding republicanism and ensuring the survival of the new nation. Benjamin Rush, a Whig educator and physician from Philadelphia, strongly advocated for the education of girls and young women as part of the larger effort to ensure that republican virtue and republican motherhood would endure.

THE MEANING OF RACE

By the time of the Revolution, slavery had been firmly in place in America for over one hundred years. In many ways, the Revolution served to reinforce the assumptions about race among white Americans. They viewed the new nation as a white republic; blacks were slaves, and Indians had no place. Racial hatred of blacks increased during the Revolution because many slaves fled their white masters for the freedom offered by the British. The same was true for Indians who allied themselves with the British; Jefferson wrote in the Declaration of Independence that separation from the Empire was necessary because George

III had incited "the merciless Indian savages" to destroy the white inhabitants on the frontier. Similarly, Thomas Paine argued in *Common Sense* that Great Britain was guilty of inciting "the Indians and Negroes to destroy us." For his part, Benjamin Franklin wrote in the 1780s that, in time, alcoholism would wipe out the Indians, leaving the land free for white settlers.

MY STORY

⚙ *Phillis Wheatley: "On Being Brought from Africa to America"*

Phillis Wheatley (Figure 7.6) was born in Africa in 1753 and sold as a slave to the Wheatley family of Boston; her African name is lost to posterity. Although most slaves in the eighteenth century had no opportunities to learn to read and write, Wheatley achieved full literacy and went on to become one of the best-known poets of the time, although many doubted her authorship of her poems because of her race.

Figure 7.6   This portrait of Phillis Wheatley from the frontispiece of *Poems on various subjects, religious and moral* shows the writer at work. Despite her status as a slave, her poems won great renown in America and in Europe.

Wheatley's poems reflected her deep Christian beliefs. In the poem below, how do her views on Christianity affect her views on slavery?

> Twas mercy brought me from my Pagan land,
> Taught my benighted soul to understand
> That there's a God, that there's a Saviour too:
> Once I redemption neither sought nor knew.
> Some view our sable race with scornful eye,
> "Their colour is a diabolic dye."
> Remember, Christians, Negroes, black as Cain,
> May be refin'd, and join th' angelic train.
> —Phillis Wheatley, "On Being Brought from Africa to America"

Slavery

Slavery offered the most glaring contradiction between the idea of equality stated in the Declaration of Independence ("all men are created equal") and the reality of race relations in the late eighteenth century.

Racism shaped white views of blacks. Although he penned the Declaration of Independence, Thomas Jefferson owned more than one hundred slaves, of whom he freed only a few either during his lifetime or in his will (Figure 7.7). He thought blacks were inferior to whites, dismissing Phillis Wheatley by arguing,

"Religion indeed has produced a Phillis Wheatley; but it could not produce a poet." White slaveholders took their female slaves as mistresses, as most historians agree that Jefferson did with one of his slaves, Sally Hemings. Together, they had several children.

Figure 7.7   This page, taken from one of Thomas Jefferson's record books from 1795, lists his slaves.

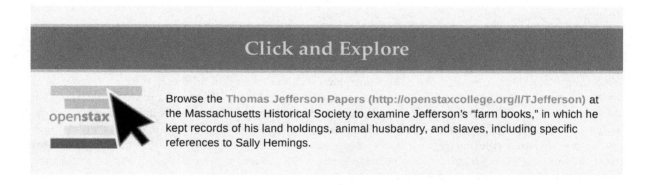

Click and Explore

Browse the Thomas Jefferson Papers (http://openstaxcollege.org/l/TJefferson) at the Massachusetts Historical Society to examine Jefferson's "farm books," in which he kept records of his land holdings, animal husbandry, and slaves, including specific references to Sally Hemings.

Jefferson understood the contradiction fully, and his writings reveal hard-edged racist assumptions. In his *Notes on the State of Virginia* in the 1780s, Jefferson urged the end of slavery in Virginia and the removal of blacks from that state. He wrote: "It will probably be asked, Why not retain and incorporate the blacks into the state, and thus save the expense of supplying, by importation of white settlers, the vacancies they will leave? Deep rooted prejudices entertained by the whites; ten thousand recollections, by the blacks, of the injuries they have sustained; new provocations; the real distinctions which nature has made; and many other circumstances, will divide us into parties, and produce convulsions which will probably never end but in the extermination of the one or the other race. —To these objections, which are political, may be added others, which are physical and moral." Jefferson envisioned an "empire of liberty" for white farmers and relied on the argument of sending blacks out of the United States, even if doing so would completely destroy the slaveholders' wealth in their human property.

Southern planters strongly objected to Jefferson's views on abolishing slavery and removing blacks from America. When Jefferson was a candidate for president in 1796, an anonymous "Southern Planter" wrote, "If this wild project succeeds, under the auspices of Thomas Jefferson, President of the United States, and three hundred thousand slaves are set free in Virginia, farewell to the safety, prosperity, the importance, perhaps the very existence of the Southern States" (Figure 7.8). Slaveholders and many other Americans protected and defended the institution.

Figure 7.8 This 1796 broadside to "the Citizens of the Southern States" by "a Southern Planter" argued that Thomas Jefferson's advocacy of the emancipation of slaves in his *Notes on the State of Virginia* posed a threat to the safety, the prosperity, and even the existence of the southern states.

Freedom

While racial thinking permeated the new country, and slavery existed in all the new states, the ideals of the Revolution generated a movement toward the abolition of slavery. Private **manumissions**, by which slaveholders freed their slaves, provided one pathway from bondage. Slaveholders in Virginia freed some ten thousand slaves. In Massachusetts, the Wheatley family manumitted Phillis in 1773 when she was twenty-one. Other revolutionaries formed societies dedicated to abolishing slavery. One of the earliest efforts began in 1775 in Philadelphia, where Dr. Benjamin Rush and other Philadelphia Quakers formed what became the Pennsylvania Abolition Society. Similarly, wealthy New Yorkers formed the New York Manumission Society in 1785. This society worked to educate black children and devoted funds to protect free blacks from kidnapping.

Slavery persisted in the North, however, and the example of Massachusetts highlights the complexity of the situation. The 1780 Massachusetts constitution technically freed all slaves. Nonetheless, several hundred individuals remained enslaved in the state. In the 1780s, a series of court decisions undermined slavery in Massachusetts when several slaves, citing assault by their masters, successfully sought their freedom in court. These individuals refused to be treated as slaves in the wake of the American Revolution. Despite these legal victories, about eleven hundred slaves continued to be held in the New England states in 1800. The contradictions illustrate the difference between the letter and the spirit of the laws abolishing slavery in Massachusetts. In all, over thirty-six thousand slaves remained in the North, with the highest concentrations in New Jersey and New York. New York only gradually phased out slavery, with the last slaves emancipated in the late 1820s.

Indians

The 1783 Treaty of Paris, which ended the war for independence, did not address Indians at all. All lands held by the British east of the Mississippi and south of the Great Lakes (except Spanish Florida) now belonged to the new American republic (Figure 7.9). Though the treaty remained silent on the issue, much of the territory now included in the boundaries of the United States remained under the control of native peoples. Earlier in the eighteenth century, a "middle ground" had existed between powerful native groups in the West and British and French imperial zones, a place where the various groups interacted and accommodated each other. As had happened in the French and Indian War and Pontiac's Rebellion, the Revolutionary War turned the middle ground into a battle zone that no one group controlled.

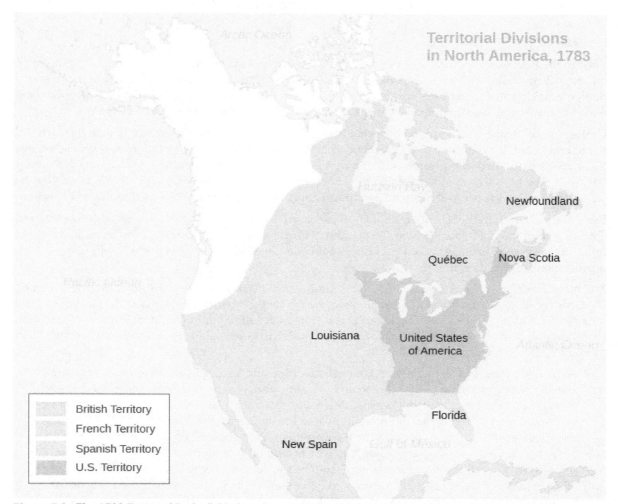

Figure 7.9 The 1783 Treaty of Paris divided North America into territories belonging to the United States and several European countries, but it failed to address Indian lands at all.

During the Revolution, a complex situation existed among Indians. Many villages remained neutral. Some native groups, such as the Delaware, split into factions, with some supporting the British while other Delaware maintained their neutrality. The Iroquois Confederacy, a longstanding alliance of tribes, also split up: the Mohawk, Cayuga, Onondaga, and Seneca fought on the British side, while the Oneida and Tuscarora supported the revolutionaries. Ohio River Valley tribes such as the Shawnee, Miami, and Mungo had been fighting for years against colonial expansion west; these groups supported the British. Some native peoples who had previously allied with the French hoped the conflict between the colonies and Great Britain might lead to French intervention and the return of French rule. Few Indians sided with the American revolutionaries, because almost all revolutionaries in the middle ground viewed them as an enemy to be destroyed. This racial hatred toward native peoples found expression in the American massacre of ninety-six Christian Delawares in 1782. Most of the dead were women and children.

After the war, the victorious Americans turned a deaf ear to Indian claims to what the revolutionaries saw as their hard-won land, and they moved aggressively to assert control over western New York and Pennsylvania. In response, Mohawk leader Joseph Brant helped to form the Western Confederacy, an alliance of native peoples who pledged to resist American intrusion into what was then called the Northwest. The Northwest Indian War (1785–1795) ended with the defeat of the Indians and their claims. Under the Treaty of Greenville (1795), the United States gained dominion over land in Ohio.

RELIGION AND THE STATE

Prior to the Revolution, several colonies had official, tax-supported churches. After the Revolution, some questioned the validity of state-authorized churches; the limitation of public office-holding to those of a particular faith; and the payment of taxes to support churches. In other states, especially in New England where the older Puritan heritage cast a long shadow, religion and state remained intertwined.

During the colonial era in Virginia, the established church had been the Church of England, which did not tolerate Catholics, Baptists, or followers or other religions. In 1786, as a revolutionary response against the privileged status of the Church of England, Virginia's lawmakers approved the Virginia Statute for Religious Freedom, which ended the Church of England's hold and allowed religious liberty. Under the statute, no one could be forced to attend or support a specific church or be prosecuted for his or her beliefs.

Pennsylvania's original constitution limited officeholders in the state legislature to those who professed a belief in both the Old and the New Testaments. This religious test prohibited Jews from holding that office, as the New Testament is not part of Jewish belief. In 1790, however, Pennsylvania removed this qualification from its constitution.

The New England states were slower to embrace freedom of religion. In the former Puritan colonies, the Congregational Church (established by seventeenth-century Puritans) remained the church of most inhabitants. Massachusetts, Connecticut, and New Hampshire all required the public support of Christian churches. Article III of the Massachusetts constitution blended the goal of republicanism with the goal of promoting Protestant Christianity. It reads:

> As the happiness of a people, and the good order and preservation of civil government, essentially depend upon piety, religion and morality; and as these cannot be generally diffused through a community, but by the institution of the public worship of GOD, and of public instructions in piety, religion and morality: Therefore, to promote their happiness and to secure the good order and preservation of their government, the people of this Commonwealth have a right to invest their legislature with power to authorize and require, and the legislature shall, from time to time, authorize and require, the several towns, parishes, precincts, and other bodies-politic, or religious societies, to make suitable provision, at their own expense, for the institution of the public worship of GOD, and for the support and maintenance of public protestant teachers of piety, religion and morality, in all cases where such provision shall not be made voluntarily. . . .
>
> And every denomination of Christians, demeaning themselves peaceably, and as good subjects of the Commonwealth, shall be equally under the protection of the law: And no subordination of any one sect or denomination to another shall ever be established by law.

Download for free at http://cnx.org/content/col11740/latest/

Click and Explore

Read more about religion and state governments at the Religion and the Founding of the American Republic (http://openstaxcollege.org/l/farmbook1) exhibition page on the Library of Congress site. What was the meaning of the term "nursing fathers" of the church?

7.3 Debating Democracy

By the end of this section, you will be able to:
* Explain the development of state constitutions
* Describe the features of the Articles of Confederation
* Analyze the causes and consequences of Shays' Rebellion

The task of creating republican governments in each of the former colonies, now independent states, presented a new opportunity for American revolutionaries to define themselves anew after casting off British control. On the state and national levels, citizens of the new United States debated who would hold the keys to political power. The states proved to be a laboratory for how much democracy, or majority rule, would be tolerated.

THE STATE CONSTITUTIONS

In 1776, John Adams urged the thirteen independent colonies—soon to be states—to write their own state constitutions. Enlightenment political thought profoundly influenced Adams and other revolutionary leaders seeking to create viable republican governments. The ideas of the French philosopher Montesquieu, who had advocated the separation of powers in government, guided Adams's thinking. Responding to a request for advice on proper government from North Carolina, Adams wrote *Thoughts on Government*, which influenced many state legislatures. Adams did not advocate democracy; rather, he wrote, "there is no good government but what is republican." Fearing the potential for tyranny with only one group in power, he suggested a system of **checks and balances** in which three separate branches of government—executive, legislative, and judicial—would maintain a balance of power. He also proposed that each state remain sovereign, as its own republic. The state constitutions of the new United States illustrate different approaches to addressing the question of how much democracy would prevail in the thirteen republics. Some states embraced democratic practices, while others adopted far more aristocratic and republican ones.

Click and Explore

Visit the Avalon Project (http://openstaxcollege.org/l/statecons) to read the constitutions of the seven states (Virginia, New Jersey, North Carolina, Maryland, Connecticut, Pennsylvania, and Delaware) that had written constitutions by the end of 1776.

The 1776 Pennsylvania constitution and the 1784 New Hampshire constitution both provide examples of democratic tendencies. In Pennsylvania, the requirement to own property in order to vote was eliminated, and if a man was twenty-one or older, had paid taxes, and had lived in the same location for one year, he could vote (Figure 7.10). This opened voting to most free white male citizens of Pennsylvania. The 1784 New Hampshire constitution allowed every small town and village to send representatives to the state government, making the lower house of the legislature a model of democratic government.

Figure 7.10 The 1776 Pennsylvania constitution, the first page of which is shown here, adhered to more democratic principles than some other states' constitutions did initially.

Conservative Whigs, who distrusted the idea of majority rule, recoiled from the abolition of property qualifications for voting and office holding in Pennsylvania. Conservative Whig John Adams reacted with horror to the 1776 Pennsylvania constitution, declaring that it was "so democratical that it must produce confusion and every evil work." In his mind and those of other conservative Whigs, this constitution simply put too much power in the hands of men who had no business exercising the right to vote. Pennsylvania's constitution also eliminated the executive branch (there was no governor) and the upper house. Instead, Pennsylvania had a one-house—a **unicameral**—legislature.

The Maryland and South Carolina constitutions provide examples of efforts to limit the power of a democratic majority. Maryland's, written in 1776, restricted office holding to the wealthy planter class. A man had to own at least £5,000 worth of personal property to be the governor of Maryland, and possess an estate worth £1,000 to be a state senator. This latter qualification excluded over 90 percent of the white males in Maryland from political office. The 1778 South Carolina constitution also sought to protect the interests of the wealthy. Governors and lieutenant governors of the state had to have "a settled plantation or freehold in their and each of their own right of the value of at least ten thousand pounds currency, clear of debt." This provision limited high office in the state to its wealthiest inhabitants. Similarly, South Carolina state senators had to own estates valued at £2,000.

John Adams wrote much of the 1780 Massachusetts constitution, which reflected his fear of too much democracy. It therefore created two legislative chambers, an upper and lower house, and a strong governor with broad veto powers. Like South Carolina, Massachusetts put in place office-holding requirements: To be governor under the new constitution, a candidate had to own an estate worth at least £1,000. To serve in the state senate, a man had to own an estate worth at least £300 and have at least £600 in total wealth. To vote, he had to be worth at least sixty pounds. To further keep democracy in check, judges were appointed, not elected. One final limit was the establishment of the state capitol in the commercial center of Boston, which made it difficult for farmers from the western part of the state to attend legislative sessions.

THE ARTICLES OF CONFEDERATION

Most revolutionaries pledged their greatest loyalty to their individual states. Recalling the experience of British reform efforts imposed in the 1760s and 1770s, they feared a strong national government and took some time to adopt the Articles of Confederation, the first national constitution. In June 1776, the Continental Congress prepared to announce independence and began to think about the creation of a new government to replace royal authority. Reaching agreement on the Articles of Confederation proved difficult as members of the Continental Congress argued over western land claims. Connecticut, for example, used its colonial charter to assert its claim to western lands in Pennsylvania and the Ohio Territory (Figure 7.11).

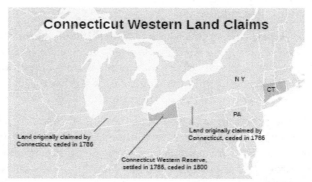

Figure 7.11 Connecticut, like many other states, used its state constitution to stake claims to uncharted western lands.

Members of the Continental Congress also debated what type of representation would be best and tried to figure out how to pay the expenses of the new government. In lieu of creating a new federal government, the Articles of Confederation created a "league of friendship" between the states. Congress readied the Articles in 1777 but did not officially approve them until 1781 (Figure 7.12). The delay of four years illustrates the difficulty of getting the thirteen states to agree on a plan of national government. Citizens viewed their respective states as sovereign republics and guarded their prerogatives against other states.

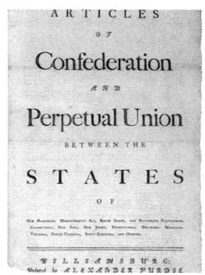

Figure 7.12   The first page of the 1777 Articles of Confederation, printed by Alexander Purdie, emphasized the "perpetual union" between the states.

The Articles of Confederation authorized a unicameral legislature, a continuation of the earlier Continental Congress. The people could not vote directly for members of the national Congress; rather, state legislatures decided who would represent the state. In practice, the national Congress was composed of state delegations. There was no president or executive office of any kind, and there was no national judiciary (or Supreme Court) for the United States.

Passage of any law under the Articles of Confederation proved difficult. It took the consensus of nine states for any measure to pass, and amending the Articles required the consent of all the states, also extremely difficult to achieve. Further, any acts put forward by the Congress were non-binding; states had the option to enforce them or not. This meant that while the Congress had power over Indian affairs and foreign policy, individual states could choose whether or not to comply.

The Congress did not have the power to tax citizens of the United States, a fact that would soon have serious consequences for the republic. During the Revolutionary War, the Continental Congress had sent requisitions for funds to the individual former colonies (now revolutionary states). These states already had an enormous financial burden because they had to pay for militias as well as supply them. In the end, the states failed to provide even half the funding requested by the Congress during the war, which led to a national debt in the tens of millions by 1784.

By the 1780s, some members of the Congress were greatly concerned about the financial health of the republic, and they argued that the national government needed greater power, especially the power to tax. This required amending the Articles of Confederation with the consent of all the states. Those who called for a stronger federal government were known as nationalists. The nationalist group that pushed for the power to tax included Washington's chief of staff, Alexander Hamilton; Virginia planter James Madison; Pennsylvania's wealthy merchant Robert Morris (who served under the Confederation government as superintendent of finance in the early 1780s); and Pennsylvania lawyer James Wilson. Two New Yorkers, Gouverneur Morris and James Duane, also joined the effort to address the debt and the weakness of the Confederation government.

These men proposed a 5 percent tax on imports coming into the United States, a measure that would have yielded enough revenue to clear the debt. However, their proposal failed to achieve unanimous support from the states when Rhode Island rejected it. Plans for a national bank also failed to win unanimous support. The lack of support illustrates the Americans' deep suspicion of a powerful national government, a suspicion that originated from the unilateral and heavy-handed reform efforts that the British Parliament imposed on the colonies in the 1760s and 1770s. Without revenue, the Congress could not pay back American creditors who had lent it money. However, it did manage to make interest payments to foreign creditors in France and the Dutch Republic, fearful that defaulting on those payments would destroy the republic's credit and leave it unable to secure loans.

One soldier in the Continental Army, Joseph Plumb Martin, recounted how he received no pay in paper money after 1777 and only one month's payment in specie, or hard currency, in 1781. Like thousands of other soldiers, Martin had fought valiantly against the British and helped secure independence, but had not been paid for his service. In the 1780s and beyond, men like Martin would soon express their profound dissatisfaction with their treatment. Their anger found expression in armed uprisings and political divisions.

Establishing workable foreign and commercial policies under the Articles of Confederation also proved difficult. Each state could decide for itself whether to comply with treaties between the Congress and foreign countries, and there were no means of enforcement. Both Great Britain and Spain understood the weakness of the Confederation Congress, and they refused to make commercial agreements with the United States because they doubted they would be enforced. Without stable commercial policies, American exporters found it difficult to do business, and British goods flooded U.S. markets in the 1780s, in a repetition of the economic imbalance that existed before the Revolutionary War.

The Confederation Congress under the Articles did achieve success through a series of directives called land ordinances, which established rules for the settlement of western lands in the public domain and the admission of new states to the republic. The ordinances were designed to prepare the land for sale to citizens and raise revenue to boost the failing economy of the republic. In the land ordinances, the Confederation Congress created the Mississippi and Southwest Territories and stipulated that slavery would be permitted there. The system of dividing the vast domains of the United States stands as a towering achievement of the era, a blueprint for American western expansion.

The Ordinance of 1784, written by Thomas Jefferson and the first of what were later called the Northwest Ordinances, directed that new states would be formed from a huge area of land below the Great Lakes, and these new states would have equal standing with the original states. The Ordinance of 1785 called for the division of this land into rectangular plots in order to prepare for the government sale of land. Surveyors would divide the land into townships of six square miles, and the townships would be subdivided into thirty-six plots of 640 acres each, which could be further subdivided. The price of an acre of land was set at a minimum of one dollar, and the land was to be sold at public auction under the direction of the Confederation.

The Ordinance of 1787 officially turned the land into an incorporated territory called the Northwest Territory and prohibited slavery north of the Ohio River (Figure 7.13). The map of the 1787 Northwest Territory shows how the public domain was to be divided by the national government for sale. Townships of thirty-six square miles were to be surveyed. Each had land set aside for schools and other civic purposes. Smaller parcels could then be made: a 640-acre section could be divided into quarter-sections of 160 acres, and then again into sixteen sections of 40 acres. The geometric grid pattern established by the ordinance is still evident today on the American landscape. Indeed, much of the western United States, when viewed from an airplane, is composed of an orderly grid system.

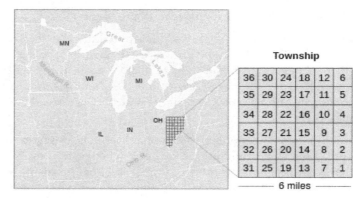

Key Points of the Northwest Ordinance of 1787

- Territory divided into 3–5 states

- Eligible for statehood with 60,000 settlers

- Religious freedom, the right of trial by jury, free access to the major rivers of the region

- Banned slavery north of the Ohio River

- Township = 6 miles square

- 6 miles square = 36 plots

- 1 plot = 640 acres (1 mile square)

- The Northwest Territory eventually became the states of Ohio, Indiana, Illinois, Michigan, and Wisconsin

Figure 7.13 The Northwest Ordinance of 1787 created territories and an orderly method for the admission of new states.

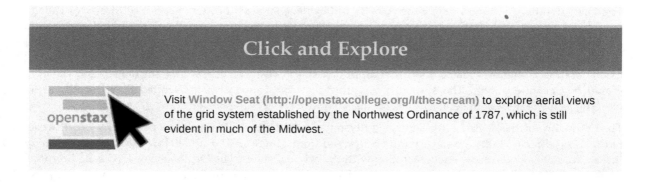

Click and Explore

Visit Window Seat (http://openstaxcollege.org/l/thescream) to explore aerial views of the grid system established by the Northwest Ordinance of 1787, which is still evident in much of the Midwest.

The land ordinances proved to be the great triumph of the Confederation Congress. The Congress would appoint a governor for the territories, and when the population in the territory reached five thousand free adult settlers, those citizens could create their own legislature and begin the process of moving toward statehood. When the population reached sixty thousand, the territory could become a new state.

SHAYS' REBELLION

Despite Congress's victory in creating an orderly process for organizing new states and territories, land sales failed to produce the revenue necessary to deal with the dire economic problems facing the new country in the 1780s. Each state had issued large amounts of paper money and, in the aftermath of the Revolution, widespread internal devaluation of that currency occurred as many lost confidence in the value of state paper money and the Continental dollar. A period of extreme inflation set in. Added to this dilemma was American citizens' lack of specie (gold and silver currency) to conduct routine business. Meanwhile, demobilized soldiers, many of whom had spent their formative years fighting rather than learning a peacetime trade, searched desperately for work.

The economic crisis came to a head in 1786 and 1787 in western Massachusetts, where farmers were in a difficult position: they faced high taxes and debts, which they found nearly impossible to pay with the worthless state and Continental paper money. For several years after the peace in 1783, these indebted citizens had petitioned the state legislature for redress. Many were veterans of the Revolutionary War who had returned to their farms and families after the fighting ended and now faced losing their homes.

Download for free at http://cnx.org/content/col11740/latest/

Their petitions to the state legislature raised economic and political issues for citizens of the new state. How could people pay their debts and state taxes when paper money proved unstable? Why was the state government located in Boston, the center of the merchant elite? Why did the 1780 Massachusetts constitution cater to the interests of the wealthy? To the indebted farmers, the situation in the 1780s seemed hauntingly familiar; the revolutionaries had routed the British, but a new form of seemingly corrupt and self-serving government had replaced them.

In 1786, when the state legislature again refused to address the petitioners' requests, Massachusetts citizens took up arms and closed courthouses across the state to prevent foreclosure (seizure of land in lieu of overdue loan payments) on farms in debt. The farmers wanted their debts forgiven, and they demanded that the 1780 constitution be revised to address citizens beyond the wealthy elite who could serve in the legislature.

Many of the rebels were veterans of the war for independence, including Captain Daniel Shays from Pelham (Figure 7.14). Although Shays was only one of many former officers in the Continental Army who took part in the revolt, authorities in Boston singled him out as a ringleader, and the uprising became known as Shays' Rebellion. The Massachusetts legislature responded to the closing of the courthouses with a flurry of legislation, much of it designed to punish the rebels. The government offered the rebels clemency if they took an oath of allegiance. Otherwise, local officials were empowered to use deadly force against them without fear of prosecution. Rebels would lose their property, and if any militiamen refused to defend the state, they would be executed.

Figure 7.14 This woodcut, from Bickerstaff's Boston Almanack of 1787, depicts Daniel Shays and Job Shattuck. Shays and Shattuck were two of the leaders of the rebels who rose up against the Massachusetts government in 1786 to 1787. As Revolutionary War veterans, both men wear the uniform of officers of the Continental Army.

Despite these measures, the rebellion continued. To address the uprising, Governor James Bowdoin raised a private army of forty-four hundred men, funded by wealthy Boston merchants, without the approval of the legislature. The climax of Shays' Rebellion came in January 1787, when the rebels attempted to seize the federal armory in Springfield, Massachusetts. A force loyal to the state defeated them there, although the rebellion continued into February.

Shays' Rebellion resulted in eighteen deaths overall, but the uprising had lasting effects. To men of property, mostly conservative Whigs, Shays' Rebellion strongly suggested the republic was falling into anarchy and chaos. The other twelve states had faced similar economic and political difficulties, and continuing problems seemed to indicate that on a national level, a democratic impulse was driving the population. Shays' Rebellion convinced George Washington to come out of retirement and lead the convention called for by Alexander Hamilton to amend the Articles of Confederation in order to deal with insurgencies like the one in Massachusetts and provide greater stability in the United States.

7.4 The Constitutional Convention and Federal Constitution

By the end of this section, you will be able to:
- Identify the central issues of the 1787 Constitutional Convention and their solutions
- Describe the conflicts over the ratification of the federal constitution

The economic problems that plagued the thirteen states of the Confederation set the stage for the creation of a strong central government under a federal constitution. Although the original purpose of the convention was to amend the Articles of Confederation, some—though not all—delegates moved quickly to create a new framework for a more powerful national government. This proved extremely controversial. Those who attended the convention split over the issue of robust, centralized government and questions of how Americans would be represented in the federal government. Those who opposed the proposal for a stronger federal government argued that such a plan betrayed the Revolution by limiting the voice of the American people.

THE CONSTITUTIONAL CONVENTION

There had been earlier efforts to address the Confederation's perilous state. In early 1786, Virginia's James Madison advocated a meeting of states to address the widespread economic problems that plagued the new nation. Heeding Madison's call, the legislature in Virginia invited all thirteen states to meet in Annapolis, Maryland, to work on solutions to the issue of commerce between the states. Eight states responded to the invitation. But the resulting 1786 Annapolis Convention failed to provide any solutions because only five states sent delegates. These delegates did, however, agree to a plan put forward by Alexander Hamilton for a second convention to meet in May 1787 in Philadelphia. Shays' Rebellion gave greater urgency to the planned convention. In February 1787, in the wake of the uprising in western Massachusetts, the Confederation Congress authorized the Philadelphia convention. This time, all the states except Rhode Island sent delegates to Philadelphia to confront the problems of the day.

The stated purpose of the Philadelphia Convention in 1787 was to amend the Articles of Confederation. Very quickly, however, the attendees decided to create a new framework for a national government. That framework became the United States Constitution, and the Philadelphia convention became known as the Constitutional Convention of 1787. Fifty-five men met in Philadelphia in secret; historians know of the proceedings only because James Madison kept careful notes of what transpired. The delegates knew that what they were doing would be controversial; Rhode Island refused to send delegates, and New Hampshire's delegates arrived late. Two delegates from New York, Robert Yates and John Lansing, left the convention when it became clear that the Articles were being put aside and a new plan of national government was being drafted. They did not believe the delegates had the authority to create a strong national government.

Click and Explore

Read "Reasons for Dissent from the Proposed Constitution" (http://openstaxcollege.org/l/YatesLansing) in order to understand why Robert Yates and John Lansing, New York's delegates to the 1787 Philadelphia Convention, didn't believe the convention should draft a new plan of national government.

THE QUESTION OF REPRESENTATION

One issue that the delegates in Philadelphia addressed was the way in which representatives to the new national government would be chosen. Would individual citizens be able to elect representatives? Would representatives be chosen by state legislatures? How much representation was appropriate for each state?

James Madison put forward a proposition known as the Virginia Plan, which called for a strong national government that could overturn state laws (Figure 7.15). The plan featured a **bicameral** or two-house legislature, with an upper and a lower house. The people of the states would elect the members of the lower house, whose numbers would be determined by the population of the state. State legislatures would send delegates to the upper house. The number of representatives in the upper chamber would also be based on the state's population. This **proportional representation** gave the more populous states, like Virginia, more political power. The Virginia Plan also called for an executive branch and a judicial branch, both of which were absent under the Articles of Confederation. The lower and upper house together were to appoint members to the executive and judicial branches. Under this plan, Virginia, the most populous state, would dominate national political power and ensure its interests, including slavery, would be safe.

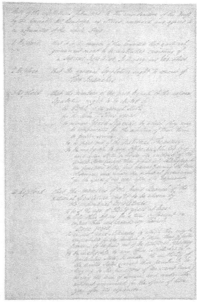

Figure 7.15 James Madison's Virginia Plan, shown here, proposed a strong national government with proportional state representation.

The Virginia Plan's call for proportional representation alarmed the representatives of the smaller states. William Paterson introduced a New Jersey Plan to counter Madison's scheme, proposing that all states have equal votes in a unicameral national legislature. He also addressed the economic problems of the day by calling for the Congress to have the power to regulate commerce, to raise revenue though taxes on imports and through postage, and to enforce Congressional requisitions from the states.

Roger Sherman from Connecticut offered a compromise to break the deadlock over the thorny question of representation. His **Connecticut Compromise**, also known as the Great Compromise, outlined a different bicameral legislature in which the upper house, the Senate, would have equal representation for all states; each state would be represented by two senators chosen by the state legislatures. Only the lower house, the House of Representatives, would have proportional representation.

THE QUESTION OF SLAVERY

The question of slavery stood as a major issue at the Constitutional Convention because slaveholders wanted slaves to be counted along with whites, termed "free inhabitants," when determining a state's total population. This, in turn, would augment the number of representatives accorded to those states in the lower house. Some northerners, however, such as New York's Gouverneur Morris, hated slavery and did not even want the term included in the new national plan of government. Slaveholders argued that slavery imposed great burdens upon them and that, because they carried this liability, they deserved special consideration; slaves needed to be counted for purposes of representation.

The issue of counting or not counting slaves for purposes of representation connected directly to the question of taxation. Beginning in 1775, the Second Continental Congress asked states to pay for war by collecting taxes and sending the tax money to the Congress. The amount each state had to deliver in tax revenue was determined by a state's total population, including both free and enslaved individuals. States routinely fell far short of delivering the money requested by Congress under the plan. In April 1783, the Confederation Congress amended the earlier system of requisition by having slaves count as three-fifths of the white population. In this way, slaveholders gained a significant tax break. The delegates in Philadelphia adopted this same three-fifths formula in the summer of 1787.

Under the **three-fifths compromise** in the 1787 Constitution, each slave would be counted as three-fifths of a white person. Article 1, Section 2 stipulated that "Representatives and direct Taxes shall be apportioned among the several states . . . according to their respective Number, which shall be determined by adding to the whole number of free Persons, including those bound for service for a Term of Years [white servants], and excluding Indians not taxed, three fifths of all other persons." Since representation in the House of Representatives was based on the population of a state, the three-fifths compromise gave extra political power to slave states, although not as much as if the total population, both free and slave, had been used. Significantly, no direct federal income tax was immediately imposed. (The Sixteenth Amendment, ratified in 1913, put in place a federal income tax.) Northerners agreed to the three-fifths compromise because the Northwest Ordinance of 1787, passed by the Confederation Congress, banned slavery in the future states of the northwest. Northern delegates felt this ban balanced political power between states with slaves and those without. The three-fifths compromise gave an advantage to slaveholders; they added three-fifths of their human property to their state's population, allowing them to send representatives based in part on the number of slaves they held.

THE QUESTION OF DEMOCRACY

Many of the delegates to the Constitutional Convention had serious reservations about democracy, which they believed promoted anarchy. To allay these fears, the Constitution blunted democratic tendencies that appeared to undermine the republic. Thus, to avoid giving the people too much direct power, the delegates made certain that senators were chosen by the state legislatures, not elected directly by the people (direct elections of senators came with the Seventeenth Amendment to the Constitution, ratified in 1913). As an additional safeguard, the delegates created the **Electoral College**, the mechanism for choosing the president. Under this plan, each state has a certain number of electors, which is its number of senators (two) plus its number of representatives in the House of Representatives. Critics, then as now, argue that this process prevents the direct election of the president.

THE FIGHT OVER RATIFICATION

The draft constitution was finished in September 1787. The delegates decided that in order for the new national government to be implemented, each state must first hold a special ratifying convention. When nine of the thirteen had approved the plan, the constitution would go into effect.

When the American public learned of the new constitution, opinions were deeply divided, but most people were opposed. To salvage their work in Philadelphia, the architects of the new national government began a campaign to sway public opinion in favor of their blueprint for a strong central government. In the fierce debate that erupted, the two sides articulated contrasting visions of the American republic and of democracy. Supporters of the 1787 Constitution, known as **Federalists**, made the case that a centralized republic provided the best solution for the future. Those who opposed it, known as **Anti-Federalists**, argued that the Constitution would consolidate all power in a national government, robbing the states of the power to make their own decisions. To them, the Constitution appeared to mimic the old corrupt and centralized British regime, under which a far-off government made the laws. Anti-Federalists argued that wealthy aristocrats would run the new national government, and that the elite would not represent ordinary citizens; the rich would monopolize power and use the new government to formulate policies that benefited their class—a development that would also undermine local state elites. They also argued that the Constitution did not contain a bill of rights.

New York's ratifying convention illustrates the divide between the Federalists and Anti-Federalists. When one Anti-Federalist delegate named Melancton Smith took issue with the scheme of representation as being too limited and not reflective of the people, Alexander Hamilton responded:

> It has been observed by an honorable gentleman [Smith], that a pure democracy, if it were practicable, would be the most perfect government. Experience has proven, that no position in politics is more false than this. The ancient democracies, in which the people themselves deliberated, never possessed one feature of good government. Their very character was tyranny; their figure deformity: When they assembled, the field of debate presented an ungovernable mob, not only incapable of deliberation, but prepared for every enormity. In these assemblies, the enemies of the people brought forward their plans of ambition systematically. They were opposed by their enemies of another party; and it became a matter of contingency, whether the people subjected themselves to be led blindly by one tyrant or by another.

The Federalists, particularly John Jay, Alexander Hamilton, and James Madison, put their case to the public in a famous series of essays known as *The Federalist Papers*. These were first published in New York and subsequently republished elsewhere in the United States.

DEFINING "AMERICAN"

✪ *James Madison on the Benefits of Republicanism*

The tenth essay in *The Federalist Papers*, often called Federalist No. 10, is one of the most famous. Written by James Madison (Figure 7.16), it addresses the problems of political parties ("factions"). Madison argued that there were two approaches to solving the problem of political parties: a republican government and a democracy. He argued that a large republic provided the best defense against what he viewed as the tumult of direct democracy. Compromises would be reached in a large republic and citizens would be represented by representatives of their own choosing.

Figure 7.16   John Vanderlyn's 1816 portrait depicts James Madison, one of the leading Federalists who supported the 1787 Constitution.

From this view of the subject, it may be concluded, that a pure Democracy, by which I mean a Society consisting of a small number of citizens, who assemble and administer the Government in person, can admit of no cure for the mischiefs of faction. A common passion or interest will, in almost every case, be felt by a majority of the whole; a communication and concert result from the form of Government itself; and there is nothing to check the inducements to sacrifice the weaker party, or an obnoxious individual. Hence it is, that such Democracies have ever been spectacles of turbulence and contention; have ever been found incompatible with personal security, or the rights of property; and have in general been as short in their lives, as they have been violent in their deaths. Theoretic politicians, who have patronized this species of Government, have erroneously supposed, that by reducing mankind to a perfect equality in their political rights, they would, at the same time, be perfectly equalized and assimilated in their possessions, their opinions, and their passions.

A Republic, by which I mean a Government in which the scheme of representation takes place, opens a different prospect, and promises the cure for which we are seeking. Let us examine the points in which it varies from pure Democracy, and we shall comprehend both the nature of the cure, and the efficacy which it must derive from the Union.

The two great points of difference, between a Democracy and a Republic, are, first, the delegation of the Government, in the latter, to a small number of citizens elected by the rest: Secondly, the greater number of citizens, and greater sphere of country, over which the latter may be extended.

Does Madison recommend republicanism or democracy as the best form of government? What arguments does he use to prove his point?

Download for free at http://cnx.org/content/col11740/latest/

Click and Explore

Read the full text of Federalist No. 10 (http://openstaxcollege.org/l/federalist10) on Wikisource. What do you think are Madison's most and least compelling arguments? How would different members of the new United States view his arguments?

Including all the state ratifying conventions around the country, a total of fewer than two thousand men voted on whether to adopt the new plan of government. In the end, the Constitution only narrowly won approval (Figure 7.17). In New York, the vote was thirty in favor to twenty-seven opposed. In Massachusetts, the vote to approve was 187 to 168, and some claim supporters of the Constitution resorted to bribes in order to ensure approval. Virginia ratified by a vote of eighty-nine to seventy-nine, and Rhode Island by thirty-four to thirty-two. The opposition to the Constitution reflected the fears that a new national government, much like the British monarchy, created too much centralized power and, as a result, deprived citizens in the various states of the ability to make their own decisions.

Figure 7.17   The first page of the 1787 United States Constitution, shown here, begins: "We the People of the United States, in Order to form a more perfect Union, establish Justice, insure domestic Tranquility, provide for the common defence, promote the general Welfare, and secure the Blessings of Liberty to ourselves and our Posterity, do ordain and establish this Constitution for the United States of America."

Key Terms

Anti-Federalists those who opposed the 1787 Constitution and favored stronger individual states

bicameral having two legislative houses, an upper and a lower house

checks and balances the system that ensures a balance of power among the branches of government

Connecticut Compromise also known as the Great Compromise, Roger Sherman's proposal at the Constitutional Convention for a bicameral legislature, with the upper house having equal representation for all states and the lower house having proportional representation

conservative Whigs the politically and economically elite revolutionary class that wanted to limit political participation to a few powerful families

coverture the legal status of married women in the United States, which included complete legal and economic dependence on husbands

democracy a system of government in which the majority rules

Electoral College the mechanism by which electors, based on the number of representatives from each state, choose the president

Federalists those who supported the 1787 Constitution and a strong central government; these advocates of the new national government formed the ruling political party in the 1790s

majority rule a fundamental principle of democracy, providing that the majority should have the power to make decisions binding upon the whole

manumission the freeing of a slave by his or her owner

monarchy a form of government with a monarch at its head

proportional representation representation that gives more populous states greater political power by allowing them more representatives

radical Whigs revolutionaries who favored broadening participation in the political process

three-fifths compromise the agreement at the Constitutional Convention that each slave would count as three-fifths of a white person for purposes of representation

unicameral having a single house (of legislative government)

Summary

7.1 Common Sense: From Monarchy to an American Republic

The guiding principle of republicanism was that the people themselves would appoint or select the leaders who would represent them. The debate over how much democracy (majority rule) to incorporate in the governing of the new United States raised questions about who was best qualified to participate in government and have the right to vote. Revolutionary leaders argued that property holders had the greatest stake in society and favored a republic that would limit political rights to property holders. In this way, republicanism exhibited a bias toward the elite. George Washington served as a role model for the new republic, embodying the exceptional talent and public virtue prized in its political and social philosophy.

7.2 How Much Revolutionary Change?

After the Revolution, the balance of power between women and men and between whites, blacks, and Indians remained largely unchanged. Yet revolutionary principles, including the call for universal equality in the Declaration of Independence, inspired and emboldened many. Abigail Adams and others pressed for greater rights for women, while the Pennsylvania Abolition Society and New York Manumission Society worked toward the abolition of slavery. Nonetheless, for blacks, women, and native peoples, the revolutionary ideals of equality fell far short of reality. In the new republic, full citizenship—including the right to vote—did not extend to nonwhites or to women.

7.3 Debating Democracy

The late 1770s and 1780s witnessed one of the most creative political eras as each state drafted its own constitution. The Articles of Confederation, a weak national league among the states, reflected the dominant view that power should be located in the states and not in a national government. However, neither the state governments nor the Confederation government could solve the enormous economic problems resulting from the long and costly Revolutionary War. The economic crisis led to Shays' Rebellion by residents of western Massachusetts, and to the decision to revise the Confederation government.

7.4 The Constitutional Convention and Federal Constitution

The economic crisis of the 1780s, shortcomings of the Articles of Confederation, and outbreak of Shays' Rebellion spurred delegates from twelve of the thirteen states to gather for the Constitutional Convention of 1787. Although the stated purpose of the convention was to modify the Articles of Confederation, their mission shifted to the building of a new, strong federal government. Federalists like James Madison and Alexander Hamilton led the charge for a new United States Constitution, the document that endures as the oldest written constitution in the world, a testament to the work done in 1787 by the delegates in Philadelphia.

Review Questions

1. To what form of government did the American revolutionaries turn after the war for independence?
   A. republicanism
   B. monarchy
   C. democracy
   D. oligarchy

2. Which of the following was not one of Franklin's thirteen virtues?
   A. sincerity
   B. temperance
   C. mercy
   D. tranquility

3. What defined republicanism as a social philosophy?

4. Which of the following figures did *not* actively challenge the status of women in the early American republic?
   A. Abigail Adams
   B. Phillis Wheatley
   C. Mercy Otis Warren
   D. Judith Sargent Murray

5. Which state had the clearest separation of church and state?
   A. New Hampshire
   B. Pennsylvania
   C. Virginia
   D. New York

6. How would you characterize Thomas Jefferson's ideas on race and slavery?

7. Which of the following states had the most democratic constitution in the 1780s?
   A. Pennsylvania
   B. Massachusetts
   C. South Carolina
   D. Maryland

8. Under the Articles of Confederation, what power did the national Confederation Congress have?
   A. the power to tax
   B. the power to enforce foreign treaties
   C. the power to enforce commercial trade agreements
   D. the power to create land ordinances

9. What were the primary causes of Shays' Rebellion?

10. Which plan resolved the issue of representation for the U.S. Constitution?
   A. the Rhode Island Agreement
   B. the New Jersey Plan
   C. the Connecticut Compromise
   D. the Virginia Plan

11. How was the U.S. Constitution ratified?
   A. by each state at special ratifying conventions
   B. at the Constitutional Convention of 1787
   C. at the Confederation Convention
   D. by popular referendum in each state

12. Explain the argument that led to the three-fifths rule and the consequences of that rule.

Critical Thinking Questions

13. Describe the state constitutions that were more democratic and those that were less so. What effect would these different constitutions have upon those states? Who could participate in government, whether by voting or by holding public office? Whose interests were represented, and whose were compromised?

14. In what ways does the United States Constitution manifest the principles of both republican and democratic forms of government? In what ways does it deviate from those principles?

15. In this chapter's discussion of New York's ratifying convention, Alexander Hamilton takes issue with Anti-Federalist delegate Melancton Smith's assertion that (as Hamilton says) "a pure democracy, if it were practicable, would be the most perfect government." What did Smith—and Hamilton—mean by "a pure democracy"? How does this compare to the type of democracy that represents the modern United States?

16. Describe popular attitudes toward African Americans, women, and Indians in the wake of the Revolution. In what ways did the established social and political order depend upon keeping members of these groups in their circumscribed roles? If those roles were to change, how would American society and politics have had to adjust?

17. How did the process of creating and ratifying the Constitution, and the language of the Constitution itself, confirm the positions of African Americans, women, and Indians in the new republic? How did these roles compare to the stated goals of the republic?

18. What were the circumstances that led to Shays' Rebellion? What was the government's response? Would this response have confirmed or negated the grievances of the participants in the uprising? Why?

CHAPTER 8

Growing Pains: The New Republic, 1790–1820

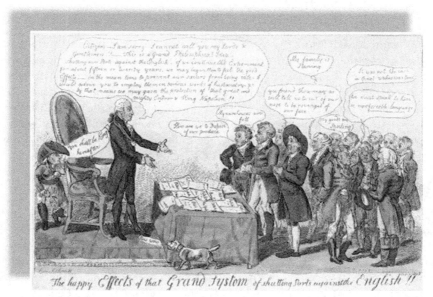

Figure 8.1 "The happy Effects of the Grand Systom [sic] of shutting Ports against the English!!" appeared in 1808. Less than a year earlier, Thomas Jefferson had recommended (and Congress had passed) the Embargo Act of 1807, which barred American ships from leaving their ports.

Chapter Outline

8.1 Competing Visions: Federalists and Democratic-Republicans
8.2 The New American Republic
8.3 Partisan Politics
8.4 The United States Goes Back to War

Introduction

The partisan political cartoon above (Figure 8.1) lampoons Thomas Jefferson's 1807 Embargo Act, a move that had a devastating effect on American commerce. American farmers and merchants complain to President Jefferson, while the French emperor Napoleon Bonaparte whispers to him, "You shall be King hereafter." This image illustrates one of many political struggles in the years after the fight for ratification of the Constitution. In the nation's first few years, no organized political parties existed. This began to change as U.S. citizens argued bitterly about the proper size and scope of the new national government. As a result, the 1790s witnessed the rise of opposing political parties: the Federalists and the Democratic-Republicans. Federalists saw unchecked democracy as a dire threat to the republic, and they pointed to the excesses of the French Revolution as proof of what awaited. Democratic-Republicans opposed the Federalists' notion that only the wellborn and well educated were able to oversee the republic; they saw it as a pathway to oppression by an aristocracy.

8.1 Competing Visions: Federalists and Democratic-Republicans

By the end of this section, you will be able to:
- Describe the competing visions of the Federalists and the Democratic-Republicans
- Identify the protections granted to citizens under the Bill of Rights
- Explain Alexander Hamilton's financial programs as secretary of the treasury

In June 1788, New Hampshire became the ninth state to ratify the federal Constitution, and the new plan for a strong central government went into effect. Elections for the first U.S. Congress were held in 1788 and 1789, and members took their seats in March 1789. In a reflection of the trust placed in him as the personification of republican virtue, George Washington became the first president in April 1789. John Adams served as his vice president; the pairing of a representative from Virginia (Washington) with one from Massachusetts (Adams) symbolized national unity. Nonetheless, political divisions quickly became apparent. Washington and Adams represented the Federalist Party, which generated a backlash among those who resisted the new government's assertions of federal power.

FEDERALISTS IN POWER

Though the Revolution had overthrown British rule in the United States, supporters of the 1787 federal constitution, known as Federalists, adhered to a decidedly British notion of social hierarchy. The Federalists did not, at first, compose a political party. Instead, Federalists held certain shared assumptions. For them, political participation continued to be linked to property rights, which barred many citizens from voting or holding office. Federalists did not believe the Revolution had changed the traditional social roles between women and men, or between whites and other races. They did believe in clear distinctions in rank and intelligence. To these supporters of the Constitution, the idea that all were equal appeared ludicrous. Women, blacks, and native peoples, they argued, had to know their place as secondary to white male citizens. Attempts to impose equality, they feared, would destroy the republic. The United States was not created to be a democracy.

The architects of the Constitution committed themselves to leading the new republic, and they held a majority among the members of the new national government. Indeed, as expected, many assumed the

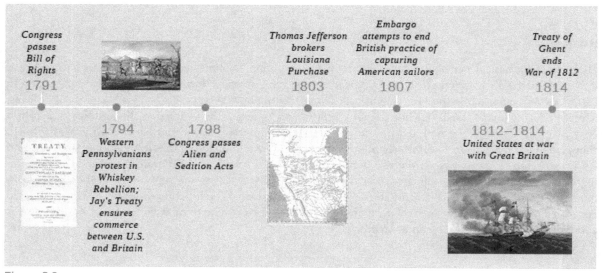

Figure 8.2

new executive posts the first Congress created. Washington appointed Alexander Hamilton, a leading Federalist, as secretary of the treasury. For secretary of state, he chose Thomas Jefferson. For secretary of war, he appointed Henry Knox, who had served with him during the Revolutionary War. Edmond Randolph, a Virginia delegate to the Constitutional Convention, was named attorney general. In July 1789, Congress also passed the Judiciary Act, creating a Supreme Court of six justices headed by those who were committed to the new national government.

Congress passed its first major piece of legislation by placing a duty on imports under the 1789 Tariff Act. Intended to raise revenue to address the country's economic problems, the act was a victory for nationalists, who favored a robust, powerful federal government and had worked unsuccessfully for similar measures during the Confederation Congress in the 1780s. Congress also placed a fifty-cent-per-ton duty (based on materials transported, not the weight of a ship) on foreign ships coming into American ports, a move designed to give the commercial advantage to American ships and goods.

THE BILL OF RIGHTS

Many Americans opposed the 1787 Constitution because it seemed a dangerous concentration of centralized power that threatened the rights and liberties of ordinary U.S. citizens. These opponents, known collectively as Anti-Federalists, did not constitute a political party, but they united in demanding protection for individual rights, and several states made the passing of a bill of rights a condition of their acceptance of the Constitution. Rhode Island and North Carolina rejected the Constitution because it did not already have this specific bill of rights.

Federalists followed through on their promise to add such a bill in 1789, when Virginia Representative James Madison introduced and Congress approved the **Bill of Rights** (Table 8.1). Adopted in 1791, the bill consisted of the first ten amendments to the Constitution and outlined many of the personal rights state constitutions already guaranteed.

Table 8.1 Rights Protected by the First Ten Amendments

Amendment 1	Right to freedoms of religion and speech; right to assemble and to petition the government for redress of grievances
Amendment 2	Right to keep and bear arms to maintain a well-regulated militia
Amendment 3	Right not to house soldiers during time of war
Amendment 4	Right to be secure from unreasonable search and seizure
Amendment 5	Rights in criminal cases, including to due process and indictment by grand jury for capital crimes, as well as the right not to testify against oneself
Amendment 6	Right to a speedy trial by an impartial jury
Amendment 7	Right to a jury trial in civil cases
Amendment 8	Right not to face excessive bail or fines, or cruel and unusual punishment
Amendment 9	Rights retained by the people, even if they are not specifically enumerated by the Constitution
Amendment 10	States' rights to powers not specifically delegated to the federal government

The adoption of the Bill of Rights softened the Anti-Federalists' opposition to the Constitution and gave the new federal government greater legitimacy among those who otherwise distrusted the new centralized power created by men of property during the secret 1787 Philadelphia Constitutional Convention.

Click and Explore

Visit the National Archives (http://openstaxcollege.org/l/BillRights) to consider the first ten amendments to the Constitution as an expression of the fears many citizens harbored about the powers of the new federal government. What were these fears? How did the Bill of Rights calm them?

ALEXANDER HAMILTON'S PROGRAM

Alexander Hamilton, Washington's secretary of the treasury, was an ardent nationalist who believed a strong federal government could solve many of the new country's financial ills. Born in the West Indies, Hamilton had worked on a St. Croix plantation as a teenager and was in charge of the accounts at a young age. He knew the Atlantic trade very well and used that knowledge in setting policy for the United States. In the early 1790s, he created the foundation for the U.S. financial system. He understood that a robust federal government would provide a solid financial foundation for the country.

The United States began mired in debt. In 1789, when Hamilton took up his post, the federal debt was over $53 million. The states had a combined debt of around $25 million, and the United States had been unable to pay its debts in the 1780s and was therefore considered a credit risk by European countries. Hamilton wrote three reports offering solutions to the economic crisis brought on by these problems. The first addressed public credit, the second addressed banking, and the third addressed raising revenue.

The Report on Public Credit

For the national government to be effective, Hamilton deemed it essential to have the support of those to whom it owed money: the wealthy, domestic creditor class as well as foreign creditors. In January 1790, he delivered his "Report on Public Credit" (Figure 8.3), addressing the pressing need of the new republic to become creditworthy. He recommended that the new federal government honor all its debts, including all paper money issued by the Confederation and the states during the war, at face value. Hamilton especially wanted wealthy American creditors who held large amounts of paper money to be invested, literally, in the future and welfare of the new national government. He also understood the importance of making the new United States financially stable for creditors abroad. To pay these debts, Hamilton proposed that the federal government sell bonds—federal interest-bearing notes—to the public. These bonds would have the backing of the government and yield interest payments. Creditors could exchange their old notes for the new government bonds. Hamilton wanted to give the paper money that states had issued during the war the same status as government bonds; these federal notes would begin to yield interest payments in 1792.

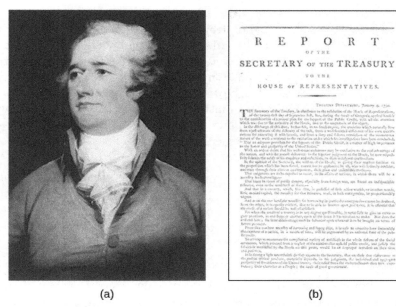

Figure 8.3 As the first secretary of the treasury, Alexander Hamilton (a), shown here in a 1792 portrait by John Trumbull, released the "Report on Public Credit" (b) in January 1790.

Hamilton designed his "Report on Public Credit" (later called "First Report on Public Credit") to ensure the survival of the new and shaky American republic. He knew the importance of making the United States financially reliable, secure, and strong, and his plan provided a blueprint to achieve that goal. He argued that his plan would satisfy creditors, citing the goal of "doing justice to the creditors of the nation." At the same time, the plan would work "to promote the increasing respectability of the American name; to answer the calls for justice; to restore landed property to its due value; to furnish new resources both to agriculture and commerce; to cement more closely the union of the states; to add to their security against foreign attack; to establish public order on the basis of upright and liberal policy."

Hamilton's program ignited a heated debate in Congress. A great many of both Confederation and state notes had found their way into the hands of speculators, who had bought them from hard-pressed veterans in the 1780s and paid a fraction of their face value in anticipation of redeeming them at full value at a later date. Because these speculators held so many notes, many in Congress objected that Hamilton's plan would benefit them at the expense of the original note-holders. One of those who opposed Hamilton's 1790 report was James Madison, who questioned the fairness of a plan that seemed to cheat poor soldiers.

Not surprisingly, states with a large debt, like South Carolina, supported Hamilton's plan, while states with less debt, like North Carolina, did not. To gain acceptance of his plan, Hamilton worked out a compromise with Virginians Madison and Jefferson, whereby in return for their support he would give up New York City as the nation's capital and agree on a more southern location, which they preferred. In July 1790, a site along the Potomac River was selected as the new "federal city," which became the District of Columbia.

Hamilton's plan to convert notes to bonds worked extremely well to restore European confidence in the U.S. economy. It also proved a windfall for creditors, especially those who had bought up state and Confederation notes at far less than face value. But it immediately generated controversy about the size and scope of the government. Some saw the plan as an unjust use of federal power, while Hamilton argued that Article 1, Section 8 of the Constitution granted the government "implied powers" that gave the green light to his program.

The Report on a National Bank

As secretary of the treasury, Hamilton hoped to stabilize the American economy further by establishing a national bank. The United States operated with a flurry of different notes from multiple state banks and no coherent regulation. By proposing that the new national bank buy up large volumes of state bank notes and demanding their conversion into gold, Hamilton especially wanted to discipline those state banks that issued paper money irresponsibly. To that end, he delivered his "Report on a National Bank" in December 1790, proposing a Bank of the United States, an institution modeled on the Bank of England. The bank would issue loans to American merchants and bills of credit (federal bank notes that would circulate as money) while serving as a repository of government revenue from the sale of land. Stockholders would own the bank, along with the federal government.

Like the recommendations in his "Report on Public Credit," Hamilton's bank proposal generated opposition. Jefferson, in particular, argued that the Constitution did not permit the creation of a national bank. In response, Hamilton again invoked the Constitution's implied powers. President Washington backed Hamilton's position and signed legislation creating the bank in 1791.

The Report on Manufactures

The third report Hamilton delivered to Congress, known as the "Report on Manufactures," addressed the need to raise revenue to pay the interest on the national debt. Using the power to tax as provided under the Constitution, Hamilton put forth a proposal to tax American-made whiskey. He also knew the importance of promoting domestic manufacturing so the new United States would no longer have to rely on imported manufactured goods. To break from the old colonial system, Hamilton therefore advocated tariffs on all foreign imports to stimulate the production of American-made goods. To promote domestic industry further, he proposed federal subsidies to American industries. Like all of Hamilton's programs, the idea of government involvement in the development of American industries was new.

With the support of Washington, the entire Hamiltonian economic program received the necessary support in Congress to be implemented. In the long run, Hamilton's financial program helped to rescue the United States from its state of near-bankruptcy in the late 1780s. His initiatives marked the beginning of an American capitalism, making the republic creditworthy, promoting commerce, and setting for the nation a solid financial foundation. His policies also facilitated the growth of the stock market, as U.S. citizens bought and sold the federal government's interest-bearing certificates.

THE DEMOCRATIC-REPUBLICAN PARTY AND THE FIRST PARTY SYSTEM

James Madison and Thomas Jefferson felt the federal government had overstepped its authority by adopting the treasury secretary's plan. Madison found Hamilton's scheme immoral and offensive. He argued that it turned the reins of government over to the class of speculators who profited at the expense of hardworking citizens.

Jefferson, who had returned to the United States in 1790 after serving as a diplomat in France, tried unsuccessfully to convince Washington to block the creation of a national bank. He also took issue with what he perceived as favoritism given to commercial classes in the principal American cities. He thought urban life widened the gap between the wealthy few and an underclass of landless poor workers who, because of their oppressed condition, could never be good republican property owners. Rural areas, in contrast, offered far more opportunities for property ownership and virtue. In 1783 Jefferson wrote, "Those who labor in the earth are the chosen people of God, if ever he had a chosen people." Jefferson believed that self-sufficient, property-owning republican citizens or yeoman farmers held the key to the success and longevity of the American republic. (As a creature of his times, he did not envision a similar role for either women or nonwhite men.) To him, Hamilton's program seemed to encourage economic inequalities and work against the ordinary American yeoman.

Opposition to Hamilton, who had significant power in the new federal government, including the ear of President Washington, began in earnest in the early 1790s. Jefferson turned to his friend Philip Freneau to help organize the effort through the publication of the *National Gazette* as a counter to the Federalist press, especially the *Gazette of the United States* (Figure 8.4). From 1791 until 1793, when it ceased publication, Freneau's partisan paper attacked Hamilton's program and Washington's administration. "Rules for Changing a Republic into a Monarchy," written by Freneau, is an example of the type of attack aimed at the national government, and especially at the elitism of the Federalist Party. Newspapers in the 1790s became enormously important in American culture as partisans like Freneau attempted to sway public opinion. These newspapers did not aim to be objective; instead, they served to broadcast the views of a particular party.

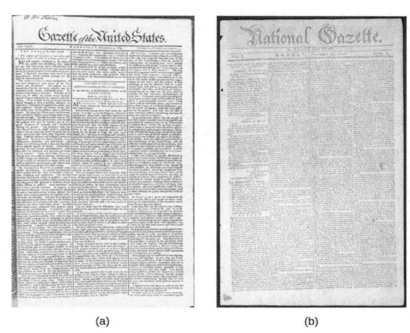

(a)   (b)

Figure 8.4   Here, the front page of the Federalist *Gazette of the United States* from September 9, 1789 (a), is shown beside that of the oppositional *National Gazette* from November 14, 1791 (b). The *Gazette of the United States* featured articles, sometimes written pseudonymously or anonymously, from leading Federalists like Alexander Hamilton and John Adams. The *National Gazette* was founded two years later to counter their political influence.

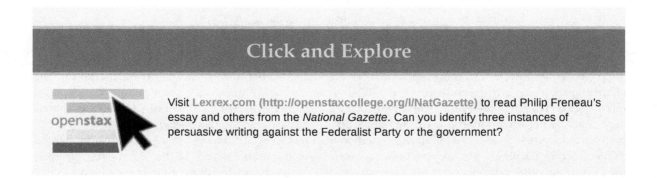

Click and Explore

Visit **Lexrex.com (http://openstaxcollege.org/l/NatGazette)** to read Philip Freneau's essay and others from the *National Gazette*. Can you identify three instances of persuasive writing against the Federalist Party or the government?

Opposition to the Federalists led to the formation of Democratic-Republican societies, composed of men who felt the domestic policies of the Washington administration were designed to enrich the few while ignoring everyone else. **Democratic-Republicans** championed limited government. Their fear of centralized power originated in the experience of the 1760s and 1770s when the distant, overbearing, and seemingly corrupt British Parliament attempted to impose its will on the colonies. The 1787 federal constitution, written in secret by fifty-five wealthy men of property and standing, ignited fears of a similar menacing plot. To opponents, the Federalists promoted aristocracy and a monarchical government—a betrayal of what many believed to be the goal of the American Revolution.

While wealthy merchants and planters formed the core of the Federalist leadership, members of the Democratic-Republican societies in cities like Philadelphia and New York came from the ranks of artisans. These citizens saw themselves as acting in the spirit of 1776, this time not against the haughty British but by what they believed to have replaced them—a commercial class with no interest in the public good. Their political efforts against the Federalists were a battle to preserve republicanism, to promote the public good against private self-interest. They published their views, held meetings to voice their opposition, and sponsored festivals and parades. In their strident newspapers attacks, they also worked to undermine the traditional forms of deference and subordination to aristocrats, in this case the Federalist elites. Some members of northern Democratic-Republican clubs denounced slavery as well.

DEFINING CITIZENSHIP

While questions regarding the proper size and scope of the new national government created a divide among Americans and gave rise to political parties, a consensus existed among men on the issue of who qualified and who did not qualify as a citizen. The 1790 Naturalization Act defined citizenship in stark racial terms. To be a citizen of the American republic, an immigrant had to be a "free white person" of "good character." By excluding slaves, free blacks, Indians, and Asians from citizenship, the act laid the foundation for the United States as a republic of white men.

Full citizenship that included the right to vote was restricted as well. Many state constitutions directed that only male property owners or taxpayers could vote. For women, the right to vote remained out of reach except in the state of New Jersey. In 1776, the fervor of the Revolution led New Jersey revolutionaries to write a constitution extending the right to vote to unmarried women who owned property worth £50. Federalists and Democratic-Republicans competed for the votes of New Jersey women who met the requirements to cast ballots. This radical innovation continued until 1807, when New Jersey restricted voting to free white males.

8.2 The New American Republic

By the end of this section, you will be able to:
- Identify the major foreign and domestic uprisings of the early 1790s
- Explain the effect of these uprisings on the political system of the United States

The colonies' alliance with France, secured after the victory at Saratoga in 1777, proved crucial in their victory against the British, and during the 1780s France and the new United States enjoyed a special relationship. Together they had defeated their common enemy, Great Britain. But despite this shared experience, American opinions regarding France diverged sharply in the 1790s when France underwent its own revolution. Democratic-Republicans seized on the French revolutionaries' struggle against monarchy as the welcome harbinger of a larger republican movement around the world. To the Federalists, however, the French Revolution represented pure anarchy, especially after the execution of the French king in 1793. Along with other foreign and domestic uprisings, the French Revolution helped harden the political divide in the United States in the early 1790s.

THE FRENCH REVOLUTION

The French Revolution, which began in 1789, further split American thinkers into different ideological camps, deepening the political divide between Federalists and their Democratic-Republican foes. At first, in 1789 and 1790, the revolution in France appeared to most in the United States as part of a new chapter in the rejection of corrupt monarchy, a trend inspired by the American Revolution. A constitutional monarchy replaced the absolute monarchy of Louis XVI in 1791, and in 1792, France was declared a republic. Republican liberty, the creed of the United States, seemed to be ushering in a new era in France. Indeed, the American Revolution served as an inspiration for French revolutionaries.

The events of 1793 and 1794 challenged the simple interpretation of the French Revolution as a happy chapter in the unfolding triumph of republican government over monarchy. The French king was executed in January 1793 (Figure 8.5), and the next two years became known as **the Terror**, a period of extreme violence against perceived enemies of the revolutionary government. Revolutionaries advocated direct representative democracy, dismantled Catholicism, replaced that religion with a new philosophy known as the Cult of the Supreme Being, renamed the months of the year, and relentlessly employed the guillotine against their enemies. Federalists viewed these excesses with growing alarm, fearing that the radicalism of the French Revolution might infect the minds of citizens at home. Democratic-Republicans interpreted the same events with greater optimism, seeing them as a necessary evil of eliminating the monarchy and aristocratic culture that supported the privileges of a hereditary class of rulers.

Figure 8.5 An image from a 1791 Hungarian journal depicts the beheading of Louis XVI during the French Revolution. The violence of the revolutionary French horrified many in the United States—especially Federalists, who saw it as an example of what could happen when the mob gained political control and instituted direct democracy.

The controversy in the United States intensified when France declared war on Great Britain and Holland in February 1793. France requested that the United States make a large repayment of the money it had borrowed from France to fund the Revolutionary War. However, Great Britain would judge any aid given to France as a hostile act. Washington declared the United States neutral in 1793, but Democratic-Republican groups denounced neutrality and declared their support of the French republicans. The Federalists used the violence of the French revolutionaries as a reason to attack Democratic-Republicanism in the United States, arguing that Jefferson and Madison would lead the country down a similarly disastrous path.

Click and Explore

Visit Liberty, Equality, Fraternity (http://openstaxcollege.org/l/revolution) for images, texts, and songs relating to the French Revolution. This momentous event's impact extended far beyond Europe, influencing politics in the United States and elsewhere in the Atlantic World.

THE CITIZEN GENÊT AFFAIR AND JAY'S TREATY

In 1793, the revolutionary French government sent Edmond-Charles Genêt to the United States to negotiate an alliance with the U.S. government. France empowered Genêt to issue **letters of marque**—documents authorizing ships and their crews to engage in piracy—to allow him to arm captured British ships in American ports with U.S. soldiers. Genêt arrived in Charleston, South Carolina, amid great Democratic-Republican fanfare. He immediately began commissioning American privateer ships and organizing volunteer American militias to attack Spanish holdings in the Americas, then traveled to Philadelphia, gathering support for the French cause along the way. President Washington and Hamilton denounced Genêt, knowing his actions threatened to pull the United States into a war with Great Britain. The **Citizen Genêt affair**, as it became known, spurred Great Britain to instruct its naval commanders in the West Indies to seize all ships trading with the French. The British captured hundreds of American ships and their cargoes, increasing the possibility of war between the two countries.

In this tense situation, Great Britain worked to prevent a wider conflict by ending its seizure of American ships and offered to pay for captured cargoes. Hamilton saw an opportunity and recommended to Washington that the United States negotiate. Supreme Court Justice John Jay was sent to Britain, instructed by Hamilton to secure compensation for captured American ships; ensure the British leave the Northwest outposts they still occupied despite the 1783 Treaty of Paris; and gain an agreement for American trade in the West Indies. Even though Jay personally disliked slavery, his mission also required him to seek compensation from the British for slaves who left with the British at the end of the Revolutionary War.

The resulting 1794 agreement, known as Jay's Treaty, fulfilled most of his original goals. The British would turn over the frontier posts in the Northwest, American ships would be allowed to trade freely in the West Indies, and the United States agreed to assemble a commission charged with settling colonial debts U.S. citizens owed British merchants. The treaty did not address the important issue of **impressment**, however—the British navy's practice of forcing or "impressing" American sailors to work and fight on British warships. Jay's Treaty led the Spanish, who worried that it signaled an alliance between the United States and Great Britain, to negotiate a treaty of their own—Pinckney's Treaty—that allowed American commerce to flow through the Spanish port of New Orleans. Pinckney's Treaty allowed American farmers, who were moving in greater numbers to the Ohio River Valley, to ship their products down the Ohio and Mississippi Rivers to New Orleans, where they could be transported to East Coast markets.

Jay's Treaty confirmed the fears of Democratic-Republicans, who saw it as a betrayal of republican France, cementing the idea that the Federalists favored aristocracy and monarchy. Partisan American newspapers tried to sway public opinion, while the skillful writing of Hamilton, who published a number of essays on the subject, explained the benefits of commerce with Great Britain.

THE FRENCH REVOLUTION'S CARIBBEAN LEGACY

Unlike the American Revolution, which ultimately strengthened the institution of slavery and the powers of American slaveholders, the French Revolution inspired slave rebellions in the Caribbean, including a 1791 slave uprising in the French colony of Saint-Domingue (modern-day Haiti). Thousands of slaves joined together to overthrow the brutal system of slavery. They took control of a large section of the island, burning sugar plantations and killing the white planters who had forced them to labor under the lash.

In 1794, French revolutionaries abolished slavery in the French empire, and both Spain and England attacked Saint-Domingue, hoping to add the colony to their own empires. Toussaint L'Ouverture, a former domestic slave, emerged as the leader in the fight against Spain and England to secure a Haiti free of slavery and further European colonialism. Because revolutionary France had abolished slavery, Toussaint aligned himself with France, hoping to keep Spain and England at bay (Figure 8.6).

Figure 8.6 An 1802 portrait shows Toussaint L'Ouverture, *"Chef des Noirs Insurgés de Saint Domingue"* ("Leader of the Black Insurgents of Saint Domingue"), mounted and armed in an elaborate uniform.

Events in Haiti further complicated the partisan wrangling in the United States. White refugee planters from Haiti and other French West Indian islands, along with slaves and free people of color, left the Caribbean for the United States and for Louisiana, which at the time was held by Spain. The presence of these French migrants raised fears, especially among Federalists, that they would bring the contagion of French radicalism to the United States. In addition, the idea that the French Revolution could inspire a successful slave uprising just off the American coastline filled southern whites and slaveholders with horror.

THE WHISKEY REBELLION

While the wars in France and the Caribbean divided American citizens, a major domestic test of the new national government came in 1794 over the issue of a tax on whiskey, an important part of Hamilton's financial program. In 1791, Congress had authorized a tax of 7.5 cents per gallon of whiskey and rum. Although most citizens paid without incident, trouble erupted in four western Pennsylvania counties in an uprising known as the Whiskey Rebellion.

Farmers in the western counties of Pennsylvania produced whiskey from their grain for economic reasons. Without adequate roads or other means to transport a bulky grain harvest, these farmers distilled their grains into gin and whiskey, which were more cost-effective to transport. Since these farmers depended on the sale of whiskey, some citizens in western Pennsylvania (and elsewhere) viewed the new tax as further proof that the new national government favored the commercial classes on the eastern seaboard at the expense of farmers in the West. On the other hand, supporters of the tax argued that it helped stabilize the economy and its cost could easily be passed on to the consumer, not the farmer-distiller.

However, in the spring and summer months of 1794, angry citizens rebelled against the federal officials in charge of enforcing the federal excise law. Like the Sons of Liberty before the American Revolution, the whiskey rebels used violence and intimidation to protest policies they saw as unfair. They tarred and feathered federal officials, intercepted the federal mail, and intimidated wealthy citizens. The extent of their discontent found expression in their plan to form an independent western commonwealth, and they even began negotiations with British and Spanish representatives, hoping to secure their support for independence from the United States. The rebels also contacted their backcountry neighbors in Kentucky and South Carolina, circulating the idea of secession.

With their emphasis on personal freedoms, the whiskey rebels aligned themselves with the Democratic-Republican Party. They saw the tax as part of a larger Federalist plot to destroy their republican liberty and, in its most extreme interpretation, turn the United States into a monarchy. The federal government lowered the tax, but when federal officials tried to subpoena those distillers who remained intractable, trouble escalated. Washington responded by creating a thirteen-thousand-man militia, drawn from several states, to put down the rebellion (Figure 8.7). This force made it known, both domestically and to the European powers that looked on in anticipation of the new republic's collapse, that the national government would do everything in its power to ensure the survival of the United States.

Figure 8.7   This painting, attributed to Frederick Kemmelmeyer ca. 1795, depicts the massive force George Washington led to put down the Whiskey Rebellion of the previous year. Federalists made clear they would not tolerate mob action.

DEFINING "AMERICAN"

✪ *Alexander Hamilton: "Shall the majority govern or be governed?"*

Alexander Hamilton frequently wrote persuasive essays under pseudonyms, like "Tully," as he does here. In this 1794 essay, Hamilton denounces the whiskey rebels and majority rule.

It has been observed that the means most likely to be employed to turn the insurrection in the western country to the detriment of the government, would be artfully calculated among other things 'to divert your attention from the true question to be decided.'

Let us see then what is this question. It is plainly this—shall the majority govern or be governed? shall the nation rule, or be ruled? shall the general will prevail, or the will of a faction? shall there be government, or no government? . . .

The Constitution *you* have ordained for yourselves and your posterity contains this express clause, 'The Congress *shall have power* to lay and collect taxes, duties, imposts, and *Excises*, to pay the debts, and provide for the common defence and general welfare of the United States.' You have then, by a solemn and deliberate act, the most important and sacred that a nation can perform, pronounced and decreed, that your Representatives in Congress shall have power to lay Excises. You have done nothing since to reverse or impair that decree. . . .

But the four western counties of Pennsylvania, undertake to rejudge and reverse your decrees, you have said, 'The Congress *shall have power* to lay *Excises*.' They say, 'The Congress *shall not have* this power.' . . .

There is no road to *despotism* more sure or more to be dreaded than that which begins at *anarchy*."

—Alexander Hamilton's "Tully No. II" for the *American Daily Advertiser*, Philadelphia, August 26, 1794

What are the major arguments put forward by Hamilton in this document? Who do you think his audience is?

WASHINGTON'S INDIAN POLICY

Relationships with Indians were a significant problem for Washington's administration, but one on which white citizens agreed: Indians stood in the way of white settlement and, as the 1790 Naturalization Act made clear, were not citizens. After the War of Independence, white settlers poured into lands west of the Appalachian Mountains. As a result, from 1785 to 1795, a state of war existed on the frontier between these settlers and the Indians who lived in the Ohio territory. In both 1790 and 1791, the Shawnee and Miami had defended their lands against the whites who arrived in greater and greater numbers from the East. In response, Washington appointed General Anthony Wayne to bring the Western Confederacy—a loose alliance of tribes—to heel. In 1794, at the Battle of Fallen Timbers, Wayne was victorious. With the 1795 Treaty of Greenville (Figure 8.8), the Western Confederacy gave up their claims to Ohio.

Figure 8.8   Notice the contrasts between the depictions of federal and native representatives in this painting of the signing of the Treaty of Greenville in 1795. What message or messages did the artist intend to convey?

8.3 Partisan Politics

By the end of this section, you will be able to:
* Identify key examples of partisan wrangling between the Federalists and Democratic-Republicans
* Describe how foreign relations affected American politics
* Assess the importance of the Louisiana Purchase

George Washington, who had been reelected in 1792 by an overwhelming majority, refused to run for a third term, thus setting a precedent for future presidents. In the presidential election of 1796, the two parties—Federalist and Democratic-Republican—competed for the first time. Partisan rancor over the French Revolution and the Whiskey Rebellion fueled the divide between them, and Federalist John Adams defeated his Democratic-Republican rival Thomas Jefferson by a narrow margin of only three electoral votes. In 1800, another close election swung the other way, and Jefferson began a long period of Democratic-Republican government.

THE PRESIDENCY OF JOHN ADAMS

The war between Great Britain and France in the 1790s shaped U.S. foreign policy. As a new and, in comparison to the European powers, extremely weak nation, the American republic had no control over European events, and no real leverage to obtain its goals of trading freely in the Atlantic. To Federalist president John Adams, relations with France posed the biggest problem. After the Terror, the French Directory ruled France from 1795 to 1799. During this time, Napoleon rose to power.

AMERICANA

❂ *The Art of Ralph Earl*

Ralph Earl was an eighteenth-century American artist, born in Massachusetts, who remained loyal to the British during the Revolutionary War. He fled to England in 1778, but he returned to New England in the mid-1780s and began painting portraits of leading Federalists.

His portrait of Connecticut Federalist Oliver Ellsworth and his wife Abigail conveys the world as Federalists liked to view it: an orderly landscape administered by men of property and learning. His portrait of dry goods merchant Elijah Boardman shows Boardman as well-to-do and highly cultivated; his books include the works of Shakespeare and Milton (Figure 8.9).

(a)   (b)

Figure 8.9   Ralph Earl's portraits are known for placing their subjects in an orderly world, as seen here in the 1801 portrait of Oliver and Abigail Wolcott Ellsworth (a) and the 1789 portrait of Elijah Boardman (b).

What similarities do you see in the two portraits by Ralph Earl? What do the details of each portrait reveal about the sitters? About the artist and the 1790s?

Because France and Great Britain were at war, the French Directory issued decrees stating that any ship carrying British goods could be seized on the high seas. In practice, this meant the French would target American ships, especially those in the West Indies, where the United States conducted a brisk trade with the British. France declared its 1778 treaty with the United States null and void, and as a result, France and the United States waged an undeclared war—or what historians refer to as the Quasi-War—from 1796 to 1800. Between 1797 and 1799, the French seized 834 American ships, and Adams urged the buildup of the U.S. Navy, which consisted of only a single vessel at the time of his election in 1796 (Figure 8.10).

Figure 8.10 This 1799 print, entitled "Preparation for WAR to defend Commerce," shows the construction of a naval ship, part of the effort to ensure the United States had access to free trade in the Atlantic world.

In 1797, Adams sought a diplomatic solution to the conflict with France and dispatched envoys to negotiate terms. The French foreign minister, Charles-Maurice de Talleyrand, sent emissaries who told the American envoys that the United States must repay all outstanding debts owed to France, lend France 32 million guilders (Dutch currency), and pay a £50,000 bribe before any negotiations could take place. News of the attempt to extract a bribe, known as the **XYZ affair** because the French emissaries were referred to as X, Y, and Z in letters that President Adams released to Congress, outraged the American public and turned public opinion decidedly against France (Figure 8.11). In the court of public opinion, Federalists appeared to have been correct in their interpretation of France, while the pro-French Democratic-Republicans had been misled.

Figure 8.11 This anonymous 1798 cartoon, *Property Protected à la Françoise*, satirizes the XYZ affair. Five Frenchmen are shown plundering the treasures of a woman representing the United States. One man holds a sword labeled "French Argument" and a sack of gold and riches labeled "National Sack and Diplomatic Perquisites," while the others collect her valuables. A group of other Europeans look on and commiserate that France treated them the same way.

Click and Explore

Read the "transcript" of the above cartoon in the America in Caricature, 1765–1865 (http://openstaxcollege.org/l/cartoon) collection at Indiana University's Lilly Library.

The complicated situation in Haiti, which remained a French colony in the late 1790s, also came to the attention of President Adams. The president, with the support of Congress, had created a U.S. Navy that now included scores of vessels. Most of the American ships cruised the Caribbean, giving the United States the edge over France in the region. In Haiti, the rebellion leader Toussaint, who had to contend with various domestic rivals seeking to displace him, looked to end an U.S. embargo on France and its colonies, put in place in 1798, so that his forces would receive help to deal with the civil unrest. In early 1799, in order to capitalize upon trade in the lucrative West Indies and undermine France's hold on the island, Congress ended the ban on trade with Haiti—a move that acknowledged Toussaint's leadership, to the horror of American slaveholders. Toussaint was able to secure an independent black republic in Haiti by 1804.

THE ALIEN AND SEDITION ACTS

The surge of animosity against France during the Quasi-War led Congress to pass several measures that in time undermined Federalist power. These 1798 war measures, known as the Alien and Sedition Acts, aimed to increase national security against what most had come to regard as the French menace. The Alien Act and the Alien Enemies Act took particular aim at French immigrants fleeing the West Indies by giving the president the power to deport new arrivals who appeared to be a threat to national security. The act expired in 1800 with no immigrants having been deported. The Sedition Act imposed harsh penalties—up to five years' imprisonment and a massive fine of $5,000 in 1790 dollars—on those convicted of speaking or writing "in a scandalous or malicious" manner against the government of the United States. Twenty-five men, all Democratic-Republicans, were indicted under the act, and ten were convicted. One of these was Congressman Matthew Lyon (Figure 8.12), representative from Vermont, who had launched his own newspaper, *The Scourge Of Aristocracy and Repository of Important Political Truth*.

Figure 8.12 This 1798 cartoon, "Congressional Pugilists," shows partisan chaos in the U.S. House of Representatives as Matthew Lyon, a Democratic-Republican from Vermont, holds forth against his opponent, Federalist Roger Griswold.

The Alien and Sedition Acts raised constitutional questions about the freedom of the press provided under the First Amendment. Democratic-Republicans argued that the acts were evidence of the Federalists' intent to squash individual liberties and, by enlarging the powers of the national government, crush states' rights. Jefferson and Madison mobilized the response to the acts in the form of statements known as the Virginia and Kentucky Resolutions, which argued that the acts were illegal and unconstitutional. The resolutions introduced the idea of nullification, the right of states to nullify acts of Congress, and advanced the argument of states' rights. The resolutions failed to rally support in other states, however. Indeed, most other states rejected them, citing the necessity of a strong national government.

The Quasi-War with France came to an end in 1800, when President Adams was able to secure the Treaty of Mortefontaine. His willingness to open talks with France divided the Federalist Party, but the treaty reopened trade between the two countries and ended the French practice of taking American ships on the high seas.

THE REVOLUTION OF 1800 AND THE PRESIDENCY OF THOMAS JEFFERSON

The **Revolution of 1800** refers to the first transfer of power from one party to another in American history, when the presidency passed to Democratic-Republican Thomas Jefferson (Figure 8.13) in the 1800 election. The peaceful transition calmed contemporary fears about possible violent reactions to a new party's taking the reins of government. The passing of political power from one political party to another without bloodshed also set an important precedent.

Figure 8.13 Thomas Jefferson's victory in 1800 signaled the ascendency of the Democratic-Republicans and the decline of Federalist power.

The election did prove even more divisive than the 1796 election, however, as both the Federalist and Democratic-Republican Parties waged a mudslinging campaign unlike any seen before. Because the Federalists were badly divided, the Democratic-Republicans gained political ground. Alexander Hamilton, who disagreed with President Adams's approach to France, wrote a lengthy letter, meant for people within his party, attacking his fellow Federalist's character and judgment and ridiculing his handling of foreign affairs. Democratic-Republicans got hold of and happily reprinted the letter.

Jefferson viewed participatory democracy as a positive force for the republic, a direct departure from Federalist views. His version of participatory democracy only extended, however, to the white yeoman farmers in whom Jefferson placed great trust. While Federalist statesmen, like the architects of the 1787 federal constitution, feared a pure democracy, Jefferson was far more optimistic that the common American farmer could be trusted to make good decisions. He believed in majority rule, that is, that the majority of yeoman should have the power to make decisions binding upon the whole. Jefferson had cheered the French Revolution, even when the French republic instituted the Terror to ensure the monarchy would not return. By 1799, however, he had rejected the cause of France because of his opposition to Napoleon's seizure of power and creation of a dictatorship.

Over the course of his two terms as president—he was reelected in 1804—Jefferson reversed the policies of the Federalist Party by turning away from urban commercial development. Instead, he promoted agriculture through the sale of western public lands in small and affordable lots. Perhaps Jefferson's most lasting legacy is his vision of an "empire of liberty." He distrusted cities and instead envisioned a rural republic of land-owning white men, or yeoman republican farmers. He wanted the United States to be the breadbasket of the world, exporting its agricultural commodities without suffering the ills of urbanization and industrialization. Since American yeomen would own their own land, they could stand up against those who might try to buy their votes with promises of property. Jefferson championed the rights of states and insisted on limited federal government as well as limited taxes. This stood in stark contrast to the Federalists' insistence on a strong, active federal government. Jefferson also believed in fiscal austerity. He pushed for—and Congress approved—the end of all internal taxes, such as those on whiskey and rum. The most significant trimming of the federal budget came at the expense of the military; Jefferson did not believe in maintaining a costly military, and he slashed the size of the navy Adams had worked to build up. Nonetheless, Jefferson responded to the capture of American ships and sailors by pirates off the coast of North Africa by leading the United States into war against the Muslim Barbary States in 1801, the first conflict fought by Americans overseas.

The slow decline of the Federalists, which began under Jefferson, led to a period of one-party rule in national politics. Historians call the years between 1815 and 1828 the "Era of Good Feelings" and highlight the "Virginia dynasty" of the time, since the two presidents who followed Jefferson—James Madison and James Monroe—both hailed from his home state. Like him, they owned slaves and represented the Democratic-Republican Party. Though Federalists continued to enjoy popularity, especially in the Northeast, their days of prominence in setting foreign and domestic policy had ended.

PARTISAN ACRIMONY

The earliest years of the nineteenth century were hardly free of problems between the two political parties. Early in Jefferson's term, controversy swirled over President Adams's judicial appointments of many Federalists during his final days in office. When Jefferson took the oath of office, he refused to have the commissions for these Federalist justices delivered to the appointed officials.

One of Adams's appointees, William Marbury, had been selected to be a justice of the peace in the District of Columbia, and when his commission did not arrive, he petitioned the Supreme Court for an explanation from Jefferson's secretary of state, James Madison. In deciding the case, *Marbury v. Madison*, in 1803, Chief Justice John Marshall agreed that Marbury had the right to a legal remedy, establishing that individuals had rights even the president of the United States could not abridge. However, Marshall also found that Congress's Judicial Act of 1789, which would have given the Supreme Court the power to grant Marbury remedy, was unconstitutional because the Constitution did not allow for cases like Marbury's to come directly before the Supreme Court. Thus, Marshall established the principle of judicial review, which strengthened the court by asserting its power to review (and possibly nullify) the actions of Congress and the president. Jefferson was not pleased, but neither did Marbury get his commission.

The animosity between the political parties exploded into open violence in 1804, when Aaron Burr, Jefferson's first vice president, and Alexander Hamilton engaged in a duel. When Democratic-Republican Burr lost his bid for the office of governor of New York, he was quick to blame Hamilton, who had long hated him and had done everything in his power to discredit him. On July 11, the two antagonists met in Weehawken, New Jersey, to exchange bullets in a duel in which Burr shot and mortally wounded Hamilton.

THE LOUISIANA PURCHASE

Jefferson, who wanted to expand the United States to bring about his "empire of liberty," realized his greatest triumph in 1803 when the United States bought the Louisiana territory from France. For $15 million—a bargain price, considering the amount of land involved—the United States doubled in size. Perhaps the greatest real estate deal in American history, the **Louisiana Purchase** greatly enhanced the Jeffersonian vision of the United States as an agrarian republic in which yeomen farmers worked the land. Jefferson also wanted to bolster trade in the West, seeing the port of New Orleans and the Mississippi River (then the western boundary of the United States) as crucial to American agricultural commerce. In his mind, farmers would send their produce down the Mississippi River to New Orleans, where it would be sold to European traders.

The purchase of Louisiana came about largely because of circumstances beyond Jefferson's control, though he certainly recognized the implications of the transaction. Until 1801, Spain had controlled New Orleans and had given the United States the right to traffic goods in the port without paying customs duties. That year, however, the Spanish had ceded Louisiana (and New Orleans) to France. In 1802, the United States lost its right to deposit goods free in the port, causing outrage among many, some of whom called for war with France.

Jefferson instructed Robert Livingston, the American envoy to France, to secure access to New Orleans, sending James Monroe to France to add additional pressure. The timing proved advantageous. Because black slaves in the French colony of Haiti had successfully overthrown the brutal plantation regime, Napoleon could no longer hope to restore the empire lost with France's defeat in the French and Indian

War (1754–1763). His vision of Louisiana and the Mississippi Valley as the source for food for Haiti, the most profitable sugar island in the world, had failed. The emperor therefore agreed to the sale in early 1803.

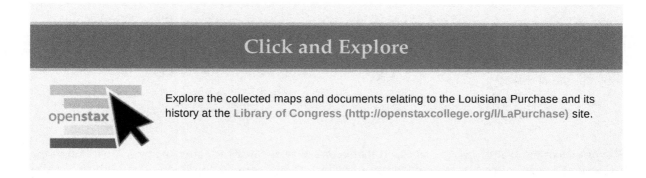

Click and Explore

Explore the collected maps and documents relating to the Louisiana Purchase and its history at the Library of Congress (http://openstaxcollege.org/l/LaPurchase) site.

The true extent of the United States' new territory remained unknown (Figure 8.14). Would it provide the long-sought quick access to Asian markets? Geographical knowledge was limited; indeed, no one knew precisely what lay to the west or how long it took to travel from the Mississippi to the Pacific. Jefferson selected two fellow Virginians, Meriwether Lewis and William Clark, to lead an expedition to the new western lands. Their purpose was to discover the commercial possibilities of the new land and, most importantly, potential trade routes. From 1804 to 1806, Lewis and Clark traversed the West.

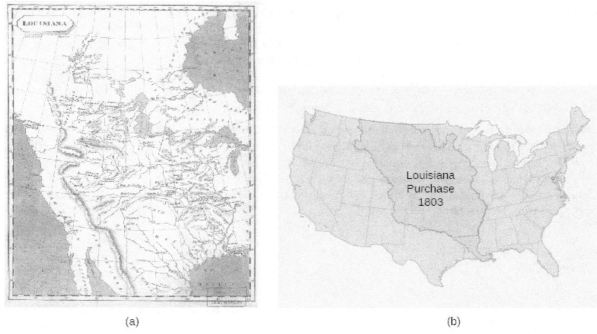

(a)   (b)

Figure 8.14 This 1804 map (a) shows the territory added to the United States in the Louisiana Purchase of 1803. Compare this depiction to the contemporary map (b). How does the 1804 version differ from what you know of the geography of the United States?

The Louisiana Purchase helped Jefferson win reelection in 1804 by a landslide. Of 176 electoral votes cast, all but 14 were in his favor. The great expansion of the United States did have its critics, however, especially northerners who feared the addition of more slave states and a corresponding lack of representation of their interests in the North. And under a strict interpretation of the Constitution, it remained unclear whether the president had the power to add territory in this fashion. But the vast majority of citizens cheered the increase in the size of the republic. For slaveholders, new western lands would be a boon; for slaves, the Louisiana Purchase threatened to entrench their suffering further.

8.4 The United States Goes Back to War

By the end of this section, you will be able to:
- Describe the causes and consequences of the War of 1812
- Identify the important events of the War of 1812 and explain their significance

The origins of the War of 1812, often called the Second War of American Independence, are found in the unresolved issues between the United States and Great Britain. One major cause was the British practice of impressment, whereby American sailors were taken at sea and forced to fight on British warships; this issue was left unresolved by Jay's Treaty in 1794. In addition, the British in Canada supported Indians in their fight against further U.S. expansion in the Great Lakes region. Though Jefferson wanted to avoid what he called "entangling alliances," staying neutral proved impossible.

THE EMBARGO OF 1807

France and England, engaged in the Napoleonic Wars, which raged between 1803 and 1815, both declared open season on American ships, which they seized on the high seas. England was the major offender, since the Royal Navy, following a time-honored practice, "impressed" American sailors by forcing them into its service. The issue came to a head in 1807 when the HMS *Leopard*, a British warship, fired on a U.S. naval ship, the *Chesapeake*, off the coast of Norfolk, Virginia. The British then boarded the ship and took four sailors. Jefferson chose what he thought was the best of his limited options and responded to the crisis through the economic means of a sweeping ban on trade, the Embargo Act of 1807. This law prohibited American ships from leaving their ports until Britain and France stopped seizing them on the high seas. As a result of the embargo, American commerce came to a near-total halt.

The logic behind the embargo was that cutting off all trade would so severely hurt Britain and France that the seizures at sea would end. However, while the embargo did have some effect on the British economy, it was American commerce that actually felt the brunt of the impact (Figure 8.15). The embargo hurt American farmers, who could no longer sell their goods overseas, and seaport cities experienced a huge increase in unemployment and an uptick in bankruptcies. All told, American business activity declined by 75 percent from 1808 to 1809.

Figure 8.15 In this political cartoon from 1807, a snapping turtle (holding a shipping license) grabs a smuggler in the act of sneaking a barrel of sugar to a British ship. The smuggler cries, "Oh, this cursed Ograbme!" ("Ograbme" is "embargo" spelled backwards.)

Enforcement of the embargo proved very difficult, especially in the states bordering British Canada. Smuggling was widespread; Smugglers' Notch in Vermont, for example, earned its name from illegal trade with British Canada. Jefferson attributed the problems with the embargo to lax enforcement.

At the very end of his second term, Jefferson signed the Non-Intercourse Act of 1808, lifting the unpopular embargoes on trade except with Britain and France. In the election of 1808, American voters elected another Democratic-Republican, James Madison. Madison inherited Jefferson's foreign policy issues involving Britain and France. Most people in the United States, especially those in the West, saw Great Britain as the major problem.

TECUMSEH AND THE WESTERN CONFEDERACY

Another underlying cause of the War of 1812 was British support for native resistance to U.S. western expansion. For many years, white settlers in the American western territories had besieged the Indians living there. Under Jefferson, two Indian policies existed: forcing Indians to adopt American ways of agricultural life, or aggressively driving Indians into debt in order to force them to sell their lands.

In 1809, Tecumseh, a Shawnee war chief, rejuvenated the Western Confederacy. His brother, Tenskwatawa, was a prophet among the Shawnee who urged a revival of native ways and rejection of Anglo-American culture, including alcohol. In 1811, William Henry Harrison, the governor of the Indiana Territory, attempted to eliminate the native presence by attacking Prophetstown, a Shawnee settlement named in honor of Tenskwatawa. In the ensuing Battle of Tippecanoe, U.S. forces led by Harrison destroyed the settlement (Figure 8.16). They also found ample evidence that the British had supplied the Western Confederacy with weapons, despite the stipulations of earlier treaties.

(a)   (b)

Figure 8.16 Portrait (a), painted by Charles Bird King in 1820, is a depiction of Shawnee prophet Tenskwatawa. Portrait (b) is Rembrandt Peele's 1813 depiction of William Henry Harrison. What are the significant similarities and differences between the portraits? What was each artist trying to convey?

THE WAR OF 1812

The seizure of American ships and sailors, combined with the British support of Indian resistance, led to strident calls for war against Great Britain. The loudest came from the "war hawks," led by Henry Clay from Kentucky and John C. Calhoun from South Carolina, who would not tolerate British insults to American honor. Opposition to the war came from Federalists, especially those in the Northeast, who knew war would disrupt the maritime trade on which they depended. In a narrow vote, Congress authorized the president to declare war against Britain in June 1812.

The war went very badly for the United States at first. In August 1812, the United States lost Detroit to the British and their Indian allies, including a force of one thousand men led by Tecumseh. By the end of the year, the British controlled half the Northwest. The following year, however, U.S. forces scored several victories. Captain Oliver Hazard Perry and his naval force defeated the British on Lake Erie. At the Battle of the Thames in Ontario, the United States defeated the British and their native allies, and Tecumseh was counted among the dead. Indian resistance began to ebb, opening the Indiana and Michigan territories for white settlement.

These victories could not turn the tide of the war, however. With the British gaining the upper hand during the Napoleonic Wars and Napoleon's French army on the run, Great Britain now could divert skilled combat troops from Europe to fight in the United States. In July 1814, forty-five hundred hardened British soldiers sailed up the Chesapeake Bay and burned Washington, DC, to the ground, forcing President Madison and his wife to run for their lives (Figure 8.17). According to one report, they left behind a dinner the British officers ate. That summer, the British shelled Baltimore, hoping for another victory. However, they failed to dislodge the U.S. forces, whose survival of the bombardment inspired Francis Scott Key to write "The Star-Spangled Banner."

Figure 8.17 George Munger painted *The President's House* shortly after the War of 1812, ca. 1814–1815. The painting shows the result of the British burning of Washington, DC.

AMERICANA

✦ *Francis Scott Key's "In Defense of Fort McHenry"*

After the British bombed Baltimore's Fort McHenry in 1814 but failed to overcome the U.S. forces there, Francis Scott Key was inspired by the sight of the American flag, which remained hanging proudly in the aftermath. He wrote the poem "In Defense of Fort McHenry," which was later set to the tune of a British song called "The Anacreontic Song" and eventually became the U.S. national anthem, "The Star-Spangled Banner."

Oh, say, can you see, by the dawn's early light,
What so proudly we hailed at the twilight's last gleaming?
Whose broad stripes and bright stars, thru the perilous fight,
O'er the ramparts we watched, were so gallantly streaming?
And the rockets' red glare, the bombs bursting in air,
Gave proof through the night that our flag was still there.
O say, does that star-spangled banner yet wave
O'er the land of the free and the home of the brave?

On the shore dimly seen through the mists of the deep,
Where the foe's haughty host in dread silence reposes,
What is that which the breeze, o'er the towering steep,
As it fitfully blows, half conceals, half discloses?
Now it catches the gleam of the morning's first beam,
In full glory reflected, now shines on the stream:
Tis the star-spangled banner: O, long may it wave
O'er the land of the free and the home of the brave!

And where is that band who so vauntingly swore
That the havoc of war and the battle's confusion
A home and a country should leave us no more?
Their blood has washed out their foul footsteps' pollution.
No refuge could save the hireling and slave
From the terror of flight or the gloom of the grave:
And the star-spangled banner in triumph doth wave
O'er the land of the free and the home of the brave.

O, thus be it ever when freemen shall stand,
Between their loved home and the war's desolation!
Blest with victory and peace, may the heav'n-rescued land
Praise the Power that hath made and preserved us a nation!
Then conquer we must, when our cause it is just,
And this be our motto: "In God is our trust"
And the star-spangled banner in triumph shall wave
O'er the land of the free and the home of the brave!
—Francis Scott Key, "In Defense of Fort McHenry," 1814

What images does Key use to describe the American spirit? Most people are familiar with only the first verse of the song; what do you think the last three verses add?

Click and Explore

Visit the **Smithsonian Institute (http://openstaxcollege.org/l/flag)** to explore an interactive feature on the flag that inspired "The Star-Spangled Banner," where clickable "hot spots" on the flag reveal elements of its history.

With the end of the war in Europe, Britain was eager to end the conflict in the Americas as well. In 1814, British and U.S. diplomats met in Flanders, in northern Belgium, to negotiate the Treaty of Ghent, signed in December. The boundaries between the United States and British Canada remained as they were before the war, an outcome welcome to those in the United States who feared a rupture in the country's otherwise steady expansion into the West.

The War of 1812 was very unpopular in New England because it inflicted further economic harm on a region dependent on maritime commerce. This unpopularity caused a resurgence of the Federalist Party in New England. Many Federalists deeply resented the power of the slaveholding Virginians (Jefferson and then Madison), who appeared indifferent to their region. The depth of the Federalists' discontent is illustrated by the proceedings of the December 1814 Hartford Convention, a meeting of twenty-six Federalists in Connecticut, where some attendees issued calls for New England to secede from the United States. These arguments for disunion during wartime, combined with the convention's condemnation of the government, made Federalists appear unpatriotic. The convention forever discredited the Federalist Party and led to its downfall.

EPILOGUE: THE BATTLE OF NEW ORLEANS

Due to slow communication, the last battle in the War of 1812 happened after the Treaty of Ghent had been signed ending the war. Andrew Jackson had distinguished himself in the war by defeating the Creek Indians in March 1814 before invading Florida in May of that year. After taking Pensacola, he moved his force of Tennessee fighters to New Orleans to defend the strategic port against British attack.

On January 8, 1815 (despite the official end of the war), a force of battle-tested British veterans of the Napoleonic Wars attempted to take the port. Jackson's forces devastated the British, killing over two thousand. New Orleans and the vast Mississippi River Valley had been successfully defended, ensuring the future of American settlement and commerce. The Battle of New Orleans immediately catapulted Jackson to national prominence as a war hero, and in the 1820s, he emerged as the head of the new Democratic Party.

Key Terms

Bill of Rights the first ten amendments to the United States Constitution, which guarantee individual rights

Citizen Genêt affair the controversy over the French representative who tried to involve the United States in France's war against Great Britain

Democratic-Republicans advocates of limited government who were troubled by the expansive domestic policies of Washington's administration and opposed the Federalists

impressment the practice of capturing sailors and forcing them into military service

letters of marque French warrants allowing ships and their crews to engage in piracy

Louisiana Purchase the U.S. purchase of the large territory of Louisiana from France in 1803

Marbury v. Madison the landmark 1803 case establishing the Supreme Court's powers of judicial review, specifically the power to review and possibly nullify actions of Congress and the president

Revolution of 1800 the peaceful transfer of power from the Federalists to the Democratic-Republicans with the election of 1800

the Terror a period during the French Revolution characterized by extreme violence and the execution of numerous enemies of the revolutionary government, from 1793 through 1794

XYZ affair the French attempt to extract a bribe from the United States during the Quasi-War of 1798–1800

Summary

8.1 Competing Visions: Federalists and Democratic-Republicans
While they did not yet constitute distinct political parties, Federalists and Anti-Federalists, shortly after the Revolution, found themselves at odds over the Constitution and the power that it concentrated in the federal government. While many of the Anti-Federalists' fears were assuaged by the adoption of the Bill of Rights in 1791, the early 1790s nevertheless witnessed the rise of two political parties: the Federalists and the Democratic-Republicans. These rival political factions began by defining themselves in relationship to Hamilton's financial program, a debate that exposed contrasting views of the proper role of the federal government. By championing Hamilton's bold financial program, Federalists, including President Washington, made clear their intent to use the federal government to stabilize the national economy and overcome the financial problems that had plagued it since the 1780s. Members of the Democratic-Republican opposition, however, deplored the expanded role of the new national government. They argued that the Constitution did not permit the treasury secretary's expansive program and worried that the new national government had assumed powers it did not rightfully possess. Only on the question of citizenship was there broad agreement: only free, white males who met taxpayer or property qualifications could cast ballots as full citizens of the republic.

8.2 The New American Republic
Federalists and Democratic-Republicans interpreted the execution of the French monarch and the violent establishment of a French republic in very different ways. Revolutionaries' excesses in France and the slaves' revolt in the French colony of Haiti raised fears among Federalists of similar radicalism and slave uprisings on American shores. They looked to better relationships with Great Britain through Jay's Treaty.

Pinckney's Treaty, which came about as a result of Jay's Treaty, improved U.S. relations with the Spanish and opened the Spanish port of New Orleans to American commerce. Democratic-Republicans took a more positive view of the French Revolution and grew suspicious of the Federalists when they brokered Jay's Treaty. Domestically, the partisan divide came to a dramatic head in western Pennsylvania when distillers of whiskey, many aligned with the Democratic-Republicans, took action against the federal tax on their product. Washington led a massive force to put down the uprising, demonstrating Federalist intolerance of mob action. Though divided on many issues, the majority of white citizens agreed on the necessity of eradicating the Indian presence on the frontier.

8.3 Partisan Politics

Partisan politics dominated the American political scene at the close of the eighteenth century. The Federalists' and Democratic-Republicans' views of the role of government were in direct opposition to each other, and the close elections of 1796 and 1801 show how the nation grappled with these opposing visions. The high tide of the Federalist Party came after the election of 1796, when the United States engaged in the Quasi-War with France. The issues arising from the Quasi-War gave Adams and the Federalists license to expand the powers of the federal government. However, the tide turned with the close election of 1800, when Jefferson began an administration based on Democratic-Republican ideals. A major success of Jefferson's administration was the Louisiana Purchase of 1803, which helped to fulfill his vision of the United States as an agrarian republic.

8.4 The United States Goes Back to War

The United States was drawn into its "Second War of Independence" against Great Britain when the British, engaged in the Napoleonic Wars against France, took liberties with the fledgling nation by impressing (capturing) its sailors on the high seas and arming its Indian enemies. The War of 1812 ended with the boundaries of the United Stated remaining as they were before the war. The Indians in the Western Confederacy suffered a significant defeat, losing both their leader Tecumseh and their fight for contested land in the Northwest. The War of 1812 proved to be of great importance because it generated a surge of national pride, with expressions of American identity such as the poem by Francis Scott Key. The United States was unequivocally separate from Britain and could now turn as never before to expansion in the West.

Review Questions

1. Which of the following is *not* one of the rights the Bill of Rights guarantees?
    A. the right to freedom of speech
    B. the right to an education
    C. the right to bear arms
    D. the right to a trial by jury

2. Which of Alexander Hamilton's financial policies and programs seemed to benefit speculators at the expense of poor soldiers?
    A. the creation of a national bank
    B. the public credit plan
    C. the tax on whiskey
    D. the "Report on Manufactures"

3. What were the fundamental differences between the Federalist and Democratic-Republican visions?

4. Which of the following was *not* true of Jay's Treaty of 1794?
    A. It gave the United States land rights in the West Indies.
    B. It gave American ships the right to trade in the West Indies.
    C. It hardened differences between the political parties of the United States.
    D. It stipulated that U.S. citizens would repay their debts from the Revolutionary War.

5. What was the primary complaint of the rebels in the Whiskey Rebellion?

   A. the ban on alcohol

   B. the lack of political representation for farmers

   C. the need to fight Indians for more land

   D. the tax on whiskey and rum

6. How did the French Revolution in the early 1790s influence the evolution of the American political system?

7. What was the primary issue of Adams's presidency?

   A. war with Spain

   B. relations with the native population

   C. infighting within the Federalist Party

   D. relations with France

8. Which of the following events is *not* an example of partisan acrimony?

   A. the jailing of Matthew Lyon

   B. the XYZ affair

   C. the *Marbury v. Madison* case

   D. the Hamilton-Burr duel

9. What was the importance of the Louisiana Purchase?

   A. It gave the United States control of the port of New Orleans for trade.

   B. It opened up the possibility of quick trade routes to Asia.

   C. It gave the United States political leverage against the Spanish.

   D. It provided Napoleon with an impetus to restore France's empire.

10. How did U.S. relations with France influence events at the end of the eighteenth century?

11. Why do historians refer to the election of Thomas Jefferson as the Revolution of 1800?

12. What prompted the Embargo of 1807?

   A. British soldiers burned the U.S. capitol.

   B. The British supplied arms to Indian insurgents.

   C. The British navy captured American ships on the high seas and impressed their sailors into service for the British.

   D. The British hadn't abandoned their posts in the Northwest Territory as required by Jay's Treaty.

13. What event inspired "The Star-Spangled Banner"?

   A. Betsy Ross sewing the first American flag raised during a time of war

   B. the British bombardment of Baltimore

   C. the British burning of Washington, DC

   D. the naval battle between the *Leopard* and the *Chesapeake*

Critical Thinking Questions

14. Describe Alexander Hamilton's plans to address the nation's financial woes. Which aspects proved most controversial, and why? What elements of the foundation Hamilton laid can still be found in the system today?

15. Describe the growth of the first party system in the United States. How did these parties come to develop? How did they define themselves, both independently and in opposition to one another? Where did they find themselves in agreement?

16. What led to the passage of the Alien and Sedition Acts? What made them so controversial?

17. What was the most significant impact of the War of 1812?

18. In what ways did the events of this era pose challenges to the U.S. Constitution? What constitutional issues were raised, and how were they addressed?

CHAPTER 9

Industrial Transformation in the North, 1800–1850

Figure 9.1 *Five Points* (1827), by George Catlin, depicts the infamous Five Points neighborhood of New York City, so called because it was centered at the intersection of five streets. Five Points was home to a polyglot mix of recent immigrants, freed slaves, and other members of the working class.

Chapter Outline

9.1 Early Industrialization in the Northeast
9.2 A Vibrant Capitalist Republic
9.3 On the Move: The Transportation Revolution
9.4 A New Social Order: Class Divisions

Introduction

By the 1830s, the United States had developed a thriving industrial and commercial sector in the Northeast. Farmers embraced regional and distant markets as the primary destination for their products. Artisans witnessed the methodical division of the labor process in factories. Wage labor became an increasingly common experience. These industrial and market revolutions, combined with advances in transportation, transformed the economic and social landscape. Americans could now quickly produce larger amounts of goods for a nationwide, and sometimes an international, market and rely less on foreign imports than in colonial times.

As American economic life shifted rapidly and modes of production changed, new class divisions emerged and solidified, resulting in previously unknown economic and social inequalities. This image of the Five Points district in New York City captures the turbulence of the time (Figure 9.1). Five Points began as a settlement for freed slaves, but it soon became a crowded urban world of American day laborers and low-wage workers who lived a precarious existence that the economic benefits of the new economy largely bypassed. An influx of immigrant workers swelled and diversified an already crowded urban population. By the 1830s, the area had become a slum, home to widespread poverty, crime, and disease. Advances in industrialization and the market revolution came at a human price.

9.1 Early Industrialization in the Northeast

By the end of this section, you will be able to:
- Explain the role of the putting-out system in the rise of industrialization
- Understand industrialization's impact on the nature of production and work
- Describe the effect of industrialization on consumption
- Identify the goals of workers' organizations like the Working Men's Party

Northern industrialization expanded rapidly following the War of 1812. Industrialized manufacturing began in New England, where wealthy merchants built water-powered textile mills (and mill towns to support them) along the rivers of the Northeast. These mills introduced new modes of production centralized within the confines of the mill itself. As never before, production relied on mechanized sources with water power, and later steam, to provide the force necessary to drive machines. In addition to the mechanization and centralization of work in the mills, specialized, repetitive tasks assigned to wage laborers replaced earlier modes of handicraft production done by artisans at home. The operations of these mills irrevocably changed the nature of work by deskilling tasks, breaking down the process of production to its most basic, elemental parts. In return for their labor, the workers, who at first were young women from rural New England farming families, received wages. From its origin in New England, manufacturing soon spread to other regions of the United States.

FROM ARTISANS TO WAGE WORKERS

During the seventeenth and eighteenth centuries, **artisans**—skilled, experienced craft workers—produced goods by hand. The production of shoes provides a good example. In colonial times, people bought their shoes from master shoemakers, who achieved their status by living and working as apprentices under the rule of an older master artisan. An apprenticeship would be followed by work as a journeyman (a skilled worker without his own shop). After sufficient time as a journeyman, a shoemaker could at last set up his own shop as a master artisan. People came to the shop, usually attached to the back of the master artisan's house, and there the shoemaker measured their feet in order to cut and stitch together an individualized product for each customer.

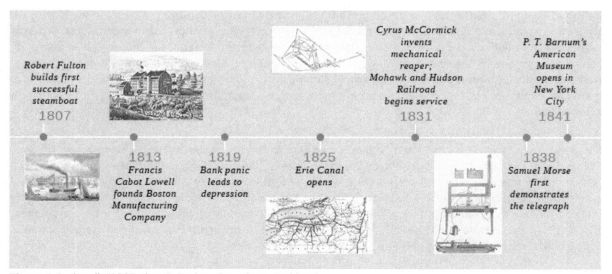

Figure 9.2 (credit "1807 photo": Project Gutenberg Archives)

In the late eighteenth and early nineteenth century, merchants in the Northeast and elsewhere turned their attention as never before to the benefits of using unskilled wage labor to make a greater profit by reducing labor costs. They used the **putting-out system**, which the British had employed at the beginning of their own Industrial Revolution, whereby they hired farming families to perform specific tasks in the production process for a set wage. In the case of shoes, for instance, American merchants hired one group of workers to cut soles into standardized sizes. A different group of families cut pieces of leather for the uppers, while still another was employed to stitch the standardized parts together.

This process proved attractive because it whittled production costs. The families who participated in the putting-out system were not skilled artisans. They had not spent years learning and perfecting their craft and did not have ambitious journeymen to pay. Therefore, they could not demand—and did not receive—high wages. Most of the year they tended fields and orchards, ate the food that they produced, and sold the surplus. Putting-out work proved a welcome source of extra income for New England farm families who saw their profits dwindle from new competition from midwestern farms with higher-yield lands.

Much of this part-time production was done under contract to merchants. Some farming families engaged in shoemaking (or shoe assemblage), as noted above. Many made brooms, plaited hats from straw or palm leaves (which merchants imported from Cuba and the West Indies), crafted furniture, made pottery, or wove baskets. Some, especially those who lived in Connecticut, made parts for clocks. The most common part-time occupation, however, was the manufacture of textiles. Farm women spun woolen thread and wove fabric. They also wove blankets, made rugs, and knit stockings. All this manufacturing took place on the farm, giving farmers and their wives control over the timing and pace of their labor. Their domestic productivity increased the quantity of goods available for sale in country towns and nearby cities.

THE RISE OF MANUFACTURING

In the late 1790s and early 1800s, Great Britain boasted the most advanced textile mills and machines in the world, and the United States continued to rely on Great Britain for finished goods. Great Britain hoped to maintain its economic advantage over its former colonies in North America. So, in an effort to prevent the knowledge of advanced manufacturing from leaving the Empire, the British banned the emigration of mechanics, skilled workers who knew how to build and repair the latest textile machines.

Some skilled British mechanics, including Samuel Slater, managed to travel to the United States in the hopes of profiting from their knowledge and experience with advanced textile manufacturing. Slater (Figure 9.3) understood the workings of the latest water-powered textile mills, which British industrialist Richard Arkwright had pioneered. In the 1790s in Pawtucket, Rhode Island, Slater convinced several American merchants, including the wealthy Providence industrialist Moses Brown, to finance and build a water-powered cotton mill based on the British models. Slater's knowledge of both technology and mill organization made him the founder of the first truly successful cotton mill in the United States.

(a)   (b)

Figure 9.3 Samuel Slater (a) was a British migrant who brought plans for English textile mills to the United States and built the nation's first successful water-powered mill in Pawtucket, Massachusetts (b).

The success of Slater and his partners Smith Brown and William Almy, relatives of Moses Brown, inspired others to build additional mills in Rhode Island and Massachusetts. By 1807, thirteen more mills had been established. President Jefferson's embargo on British manufactured goods from late 1807 to early 1809 (discussed in a previous chapter) spurred more New England merchants to invest in industrial enterprises. By 1812, seventy-eight new textile mills had been built in rural New England towns. More than half turned out woolen goods, while the rest produced cotton cloth.

Slater's mills and those built in imitation of his were fairly small, employing only seventy people on average. Workers were organized the way that they had been in English factories, in family units. Under the "Rhode Island system," families were hired. The father was placed in charge of the family unit, and he directed the labor of his wife and children. Instead of being paid in cash, the father was given "credit" equal to the extent of his family's labor that could be redeemed in the form of rent (of company-owned housing) or goods from the company-owned store.

The Embargo of 1807 and the War of 1812 played a pivotal role in spurring industrial development in the United States. Jefferson's embargo prevented American merchants from engaging in the Atlantic trade, severely cutting into their profits. The War of 1812 further compounded the financial woes of American merchants. The acute economic problems led some New England merchants, including Francis Cabot Lowell, to cast their gaze on manufacturing. Lowell had toured English mills during a stay in Great Britain. He returned to Massachusetts having memorized the designs for the advanced textile machines he had seen in his travels, especially the power loom, which replaced individual hand weavers. Lowell convinced other wealthy merchant families to invest in the creation of new mill towns. In 1813, Lowell and these wealthy investors, known as the Boston Associates, created the Boston Manufacturing Company. Together they raised $400,000 and, in 1814, established a textile mill in Waltham and a second one in the same town shortly thereafter (Figure 9.4).

Figure 9.4 The Boston Manufacturing Company, shown in this engraving made in 1813–1816, was headquartered in Waltham, Massachusetts. The company started the northeastern textile industry by building water-powered textile mills along suitable rivers and developing mill towns around them.

At Waltham, cotton was carded and drawn into coarse strands of cotton fibers called rovings. The rovings were then spun into yarn, and the yarn woven into cotton cloth. Yarn no longer had to be put out to farm families for further processing. All the work was now performed at a central location—the factory.

The work in Lowell's mills was both mechanized and specialized. Specialization meant the work was broken down into specific tasks, and workers repeatedly did the one task assigned to them in the course of a day. As machines took over labor from humans and people increasingly found themselves confined to the same repetitive step, the process of **deskilling** began.

The Boston Associates' mills, which each employed hundreds of workers, were located in company towns, where the factories and worker housing were owned by a single company. This gave the owners and their agents control over their workers. The most famous of these company towns was Lowell, Massachusetts. The new town was built on land the Boston Associates purchased in 1821 from the village of East Chelmsford at the falls of the Merrimack River, north of Boston. The mill buildings themselves were constructed of red brick with large windows to let in light. Company-owned boarding houses to shelter employees were constructed near the mills. The mill owners planted flowers and trees to maintain the appearance of a rural New England town and to forestall arguments, made by many, that factory work was unnatural and unwholesome.

In contrast to many smaller mills, the Boston Associates' enterprises avoided the Rhode Island system, preferring individual workers to families. These employees were not difficult to find. The competition New England farmers faced from farmers now settling in the West, and the growing scarcity of land in population-dense New England, had important implications for farmers' children. Realizing their chances of inheriting a large farm or receiving a substantial dowry were remote, these teenagers sought other employment opportunities, often at the urging of their parents. While young men could work at a variety of occupations, young women had more limited options. The textile mills provided suitable employment for the daughters of Yankee farm families.

Needing to reassure anxious parents that their daughters' virtue would be protected and hoping to avoid what they viewed as the problems of industrialization—filth and vice—the Boston Associates established strict rules governing the lives of these young workers. The women lived in company-owned boarding houses to which they paid a portion of their wages. They woke early at the sound of a bell and worked a twelve-hour day during which talking was forbidden. They could not swear or drink alcohol, and they were required to attend church on Sunday. Overseers at the mills and boarding-house keepers kept a close eye on the young women's behavior; workers who associated with people of questionable reputation or acted in ways that called their virtue into question lost their jobs and were evicted.

DEFINING "AMERICAN"

✪ *Michel Chevalier on Mill Worker Rules and Wages*

In the 1830s, the French government sent engineer and economist Michel Chevalier to study industrial and financial affairs in Mexico and the United States. In 1839, he published *Society, Manners, and Politics in the United States*, in which he recorded his impressions of the Lowell textile mills. In the excerpt below, Chevalier describes the rules and wages of the Lawrence Company in 1833.

> All persons employed by the Company must devote themselves assiduously to their duty during working-hours. They must be capable of doing the work which they undertake, or use all their efforts to this effect. They must on all occasions, both in their words and in their actions, show that they are penetrated by a laudable love of temperance and virtue, and animated by a sense of their moral and social obligations. The Agent of the Company shall endeavour to set to all a good example in this respect. Every individual who shall be notoriously dissolute, idle, dishonest, or intemperate, who shall be in the practice of absenting himself from divine service, or shall violate the Sabbath, or shall be addicted to gaming, shall be dismissed from the service of the Company. . . . All ardent spirits are banished from the Company's grounds, except when prescribed by a physician. All games of hazard and cards are prohibited within their limits and in the boarding-houses.
> Weekly wages were as follows:
> For picking and carding, $2.78 to $3.10
> For spinning, $3.00
> For weaving, $3.10 to $3.12
> For warping and sizing, $3.45 to $4.00
> For measuring and folding, $3.12

What kind of world were the factory owners trying to create with these rules? How do you think those who believed all white people were born free and equal would react to them?

Click and Explore

Visit the Textile Industry History (http://openstaxcollege.org/l/15textHistory) site to explore the mills of New England through its collection of history, images, and ephemera.

The mechanization of formerly handcrafted goods, and the removal of production from the home to the factory, dramatically increased output of goods. For example, in one nine-month period, the numerous Rhode Island women who spun yarn into cloth on hand looms in their homes produced a total of thirty-four thousand yards of fabrics of different types. In 1855, the women working in just one of Lowell's mechanized mills produced more than forty-three thousand yards.

The Boston Associates' cotton mills quickly gained a competitive edge over the smaller mills established by Samuel Slater and those who had imitated him. Their success prompted the Boston Associates to expand. In Massachusetts, in addition to Lowell, they built new mill towns in Chicopee, Lawrence, and Holyoke. In New Hampshire, they built them in Manchester, Dover, and Nashua. And in Maine, they built a large mill in Saco on the Saco River. Other entrepreneurs copied them. By the time of the Civil War, 878 textile factories had been built in New England. All together, these factories employed more than 100,000 people and produced more than 940 million yards of cloth.

Success in New England was repeated elsewhere. Small mills, more like those in Rhode Island than those in northern Massachusetts, New Hampshire, and Maine, were built in New York, Delaware, and Pennsylvania. By midcentury, three hundred textile mills were located in and near Philadelphia. Many produced specialty goods, such as silks and printed fabrics, and employed skilled workers, including people working in their own homes. Even in the South, the region that otherwise relied on slave labor to produce the very cotton that fed the northern factory movement, more than two hundred textile mills were built. Most textiles, however, continued to be produced in New England before the Civil War.

Alongside the production of cotton and woolen cloth, which formed the backbone of the Industrial Revolution in the United States as in Britain, other crafts increasingly became mechanized and centralized in factories in the first half of the nineteenth century. Shoe making, leather tanning, papermaking, hat making, clock making, and gun making had all become mechanized to one degree or another by the time of the Civil War. Flour milling, because of the inventions of Oliver Evans (Figure 9.5), had become almost completely automated and centralized by the early decades of the nineteenth century. So efficient were Evans-style mills that two employees were able to do work that had originally required five, and mills using Evans's system spread throughout the mid-Atlantic states.

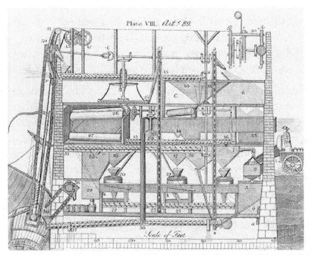

Figure 9.5 Oliver Evans was an American engineer and inventor, best known for developing ways to automate the flour milling process, which is illustrated here in a drawing from a 1785 instructional book called *The Young Mill-Wright & Miller's Guide*.

THE RISE OF CONSUMERISM

At the end of the eighteenth century, most American families lived in candlelit homes with bare floors and unadorned walls, cooked and warmed themselves over fireplaces, and owned few changes of clothing. All manufactured goods were made by hand and, as a result, were usually scarce and fairly expensive.

The automation of the manufacturing process changed that, making consumer goods that had once been thought of as luxury items widely available for the first time. Now all but the very poor could afford the necessities and some of the small luxuries of life. Rooms were lit by oil lamps, which gave brighter light than candles. Homes were heated by parlor stoves, which allowed for more privacy; people no longer needed to huddle together around the hearth. Iron cookstoves with multiple burners made it possible for housewives to prepare more elaborate meals. Many people could afford carpets and upholstered furniture, and even farmers could decorate their homes with curtains and wallpaper. Clocks, which had once been quite expensive, were now within the reach of most ordinary people.

THE WORK EXPERIENCE TRANSFORMED

As production became mechanized and relocated to factories, the experience of workers underwent significant changes. Farmers and artisans had controlled the pace of their labor and the order in which things were done. If an artisan wanted to take the afternoon off, he could. If a farmer wished to rebuild his fence on Thursday instead of on Wednesday, he could. They conversed and often drank during the workday. Indeed, journeymen were often promised alcohol as part of their wages. One member of the group might be asked to read a book or a newspaper aloud to the others. In the warm weather, doors and windows might be opened to the outside, and work stopped when it was too dark to see.

Work in factories proved to be quite different. Employees were expected to report at a certain time, usually early in the morning, and to work all day. They could not leave when they were tired or take breaks other than at designated times. Those who arrived late found their pay docked; five minutes' tardiness could result in several hours' worth of lost pay, and repeated tardiness could result in dismissal. The monotony of repetitive tasks made days particularly long. Hours varied according to the factory, but most factory employees toiled ten to twelve hours a day, six days a week. In the winter, when the sun set early, oil lamps were used to light the factory floor, and employees strained their eyes to see their work and coughed as the rooms filled with smoke from the lamps. In the spring, as the days began to grow longer, factories held "blowing-out" celebrations to mark the extinguishing of the oil lamps. These "blow-outs" often featured processions and dancing.

Freedom within factories was limited. Drinking was prohibited. Some factories did not allow employees to sit down. Doors and windows were kept closed, especially in textile factories where fibers could be easily disturbed by incoming breezes, and mills were often unbearably hot and humid in the summer. In the winter, workers often shivered in the cold. In such environments, workers' health suffered.

The workplace posed other dangers as well. The presence of cotton bales alongside the oil used to lubricate machines made fire a common problem in textile factories. Workplace injuries were also common. Workers' hands and fingers were maimed or severed when they were caught in machines; in some cases, their limbs or entire bodies were crushed. Workers who didn't die from such injuries almost certainly lost their jobs, and with them, their income. Corporal punishment of both children and adults was common in factories; where abuse was most extreme, children sometimes died as a result of injuries suffered at the hands of an overseer.

As the decades passed, working conditions deteriorated in many mills. Workers were assigned more machines to tend, and the owners increased the speed at which the machines operated. Wages were cut in many factories, and employees who had once labored for an hourly wage now found themselves reduced to piecework, paid for the amount they produced and not for the hours they toiled. Owners also reduced compensation for piecework. Low wages combined with regular periods of unemployment to make the lives of workers difficult, especially for those with families to support. In New York City in 1850, for example, the average male worker earned $300 a year; it cost approximately $600 a year to support a family of five.

WORKERS AND THE LABOR MOVEMENT

Many workers undoubtedly enjoyed some of the new wage opportunities factory work presented. For many of the young New England women who ran the machines in Waltham, Lowell, and elsewhere, the experience of being away from the family was exhilarating and provided a sense of solidarity among them. Though most sent a large portion of their wages home, having even a small amount of money of their own was a liberating experience, and many used their earnings to purchase clothes, ribbons, and other consumer goods for themselves.

The long hours, strict discipline, and low wages, however, soon led workers to organize to protest their working conditions and pay. In 1821, the young women employed by the Boston Manufacturing Company in Waltham went on strike for two days when their wages were cut. In 1824, workers in Pawtucket struck to protest reduced pay rates and longer hours, the latter of which had been achieved by cutting back the amount of time allowed for meals. Similar strikes occurred at Lowell and in other mill towns like Dover, New Hampshire, where the women employed by the Cocheco Manufacturing Company ceased working in December 1828 after their wages were reduced. In the 1830s, female mill operatives in Lowell formed the Lowell Factory Girls Association to organize strike activities in the face of wage cuts (Figure 9.6) and, later, established the Lowell Female Labor Reform Association to protest the twelve-hour workday. Even though strikes were rarely successful and workers usually were forced to accept reduced wages and increased hours, work stoppages as a form of labor protest represented the beginnings of the labor movement in the United States.

(a)   (b)

Figure 9.6 New England mill workers were often young women, as seen in this early tintype made ca. 1870 (a). When management proposed rent increases for those living in company boarding houses, female textile workers in Lowell responded by forming the Lowell Factory Girls Association—its constitution is shown in image (b)—in 1836 and organizing a "turn-out" or strike.

Critics of industrialization blamed it for the increased concentration of wealth in the hands of the few: the factory owners made vast profits while the workers received only a small fraction of the revenue from what they produced. Under the **labor theory of value**, said critics, the value of a product should accurately reflect the labor needed to produce it. Profits from the sale of goods produced by workers should be distributed so laborers recovered in the form of wages the value their effort had added to the finished product. While factory owners, who contributed the workspace, the machinery, and the raw materials needed to create a product, should receive a share of the profits, their share should not be greater than the value of their contribution. Workers should thus receive a much larger portion of the profits than they currently did, and factory owners should receive less.

In Philadelphia, New York, and Boston—all cities that experienced dizzying industrial growth during the nineteenth century—workers united to form political parties. Thomas Skidmore, from Connecticut, was the outspoken organizer of the **Working Men's Party**, which lodged a radical protest against the exploitation of workers that accompanied industrialization. Skidmore took his cue from Thomas Paine and the American Revolution to challenge the growing inequity in the United States. He argued that inequality originated in the unequal distribution of property through inheritance laws. In his 1829 treatise, *The Rights of Man to Property*, Skidmore called for the abolition of inheritance and the redistribution of property. The Working Men's Party also advocated the end of imprisonment for debt, a common practice whereby the debtor who could not pay was put in jail and his tools and property, if any, were confiscated. Skidmore's vision of radical equality extended to all; women and men, no matter their race, should be allowed to vote and receive property, he believed. Skidmore died in 1832 when a cholera epidemic swept New York City, but the state of New York did away with imprisonment for debt in the same year.

Worker activism became less common in the late 1840s and 1850s. As German and Irish immigrants poured into the United States in the decades preceding the Civil War, native-born laborers found themselves competing for jobs with new arrivals who were willing to work longer hours for less pay. In Lowell, Massachusetts, for example, the daughters of New England farmers encountered competition from the daughters of Irish farmers suffering the effects of the potato famine; these immigrant women were willing to work for far less and endure worse conditions than native-born women. Many of these native-born "daughters of freemen," as they referred to themselves, left the factories and returned to their families. Not all wage workers had this luxury, however. Widows with children to support and girls from destitute families had no choice but to stay and accept the faster pace and lower pay. Male German and Irish immigrants competed with native-born men. Germans, many of whom were skilled workers, took jobs in furniture making. The Irish provided a ready source of unskilled labor needed to lay railroad track and dig canals. American men with families to support grudgingly accepted low wages in order to keep their jobs. As work became increasingly deskilled, no worker was irreplaceable, and no one's job was safe.

9.2 A Vibrant Capitalist Republic

By the end of this section, you will be able to:
- Explain the process of selling western land
- Discuss the causes of the Panic of 1819
- Identify key American innovators and inventors

By the 1840s, the United States economy bore little resemblance to the import-and-export economy of colonial days. It was now a market economy, one in which the production of goods, and their prices, were unregulated by the government. Commercial centers, to which job seekers flocked, mushroomed. New York City's population skyrocketed. In 1790, it was 33,000; by 1820, it had reached 200,000; and by 1825, it had swelled to 270,000. New opportunities for wealth appeared to be available to anyone.

However, the expansion of the American economy made it prone to the boom-and-bust cycle. Market economies involve fluctuating prices for labor, raw materials, and consumer goods and depend on credit and financial instruments—any one of which can be the source of an imbalance and an economic downturn in which businesses and farmers default, wage workers lose their employment, and investors lose their assets. This happened for the first time in the United States in 1819, when waves of enthusiastic speculation (expectations of rapidly rising prices) in land and commodities gave way to drops in prices.

THE LAND OFFICE BUSINESS

In the early nineteenth century, people poured into the territories west of the long-settled eastern seaboard. Among them were speculators seeking to buy cheap parcels from the federal government in anticipation of a rise in prices. The Ohio Country in the Northwest Territory appeared to offer the best prospects for many in the East, especially New Englanders. The result was "Ohio fever," as thousands traveled there to reap the benefits of settling in this newly available territory (Figure 9.7).

Figure 9.7 Cartographer John Cary drew this map "exhibiting The Western Territory, Kentucky, Pennsylvania, Maryland, Virginia &c" for his 1808 atlas; it depicted the huge western territory that fascinated settlers in the early nineteenth century.

The federal government oversaw the orderly transfer of public land to citizens at public auctions. The Land Law of 1796 applied to the territory of Ohio after it had been wrested from Indians. Under this law, the United States would sell a minimum parcel of 640 acres for $2 an acre. The Land Law of 1800 further encouraged land sales in the Northwest Territory by reducing the minimum parcel size by half and enabling sales on credit, with the goal of stimulating settlement by ordinary farmers. The government created **land offices** to handle these sales and established them in the West within easy reach of prospective landowners. They could thus purchase land directly from the government, at the price the government had set. Buyers were given low interest rates, with payments that could be spread over four years. Surveyors marked off the parcels in straight lines, creating a landscape of checkerboard squares.

The future looked bright for those who turned their gaze on the land in the West. Surveying, settling, and farming, turning the wilderness into a profitable commodity, gave purchasers a sense of progress. A uniquely American story of settling the land developed: hardy individuals wielding an axe cleared it, built a log cabin, and turned the frontier into a farm that paved the way for mills and towns (Figure 9.8).

Figure 9.8 Thomas Cole, who painted *Home in the Woods* in 1847, was an American artist. Cole founded the Hudson River School, a style renowned for portrayals of landscapes and wilderness influenced by the emotional aesthetic known as romanticism. In what ways is this image realistic, and how is it idealized or romanticized?

MY STORY

⊙ *A New Englander Heads West*

A native of Vermont, Gershom Flagg was one of thousands of New Englanders who caught "Ohio fever." In this letter to his brother, Azariah Flagg, dated August 3, 1817, he describes the hustle and bustle of the emerging commercial town of Cincinnati.

> DEAR BROTHER,
>
> Cincinnati is an incorporated City. It contained in 1815, 1,100 buildings of different descriptions among which are above 20 of Stone 250 of brick & 800 of Wood. The population in 1815 was 6,500. There are about 60 Mercantile stores several of which are wholesale. Here are a great share of Mechanics of all kinds.
>
> Here is one Woolen Factory four Cotton factories but not now in operation. A most stupendously large building of Stone is likewise erected immediately on the bank of the River for a steam Mill. It is nine stories high at the Waters edge & is 87 by 62 feet. It drives four pair of Stones besides various other Machinery as Wool carding &c &c. There is also a valuable Steam Saw Mill driving four saws also an inclined Wheel ox Saw Mill with two saws, one Glass Factory. The town is Rapidly increasing in Wealth & population. Here is a Branch of the United States Bank and three other banks & two Printing offices. The country around is rich. . . .
>
> That you may all be prospered in the world is the anxious wish of your affectionate Brother
> GERSHOM FLAGG

What caught Flagg's attention? From your reading of this letter and study of the engraving below (Figure 9.9), what impression can you take away of Cincinnati in 1817?

Figure 9.9 This engraving from *A Topographical Description of the State of Ohio, Indiana Territory, and Louisiana* (1812), by Jervis Cutler, presents a view of Cincinnati as it may have looked to Gershom Flagg.

Click and Explore

Learn more about settlement of and immigration to the Northwest Territory by exploring the National Park Service's Historic Resource Study (http://openstaxcollege.org/l/15LincMemorial) related to the Lincoln Boyhood National Memorial. According to the guide's maps, what lands were available for purchase?

THE PANIC OF 1819

The first major economic crisis in the United States after the War of 1812 was due, in large measure, to factors in the larger Atlantic economy. It was made worse, however, by land speculation and poor banking practices at home. British textile mills voraciously consumed American cotton, and the devastation of the Napoleonic Wars made Europe reliant on other American agricultural commodities such as wheat. This drove up both the price of American agricultural products and the value of the land on which staples such as cotton, wheat, corn, and tobacco were grown.

Many Americans were struck with "land fever." Farmers strove to expand their acreage, and those who lived in areas where unoccupied land was scarce sought holdings in the West. They needed money to purchase this land, however. Small merchants and factory owners, hoping to take advantage of this boom time, also sought to borrow money to expand their businesses. When existing banks refused to lend money to small farmers and others without a credit history, state legislatures chartered new banks to meet the demand. In one legislative session, Kentucky chartered forty-six. As loans increased, paper money from new state banks flooded the country, creating inflation that drove the price of land and goods still higher. This, in turn, encouraged even more people to borrow money with which to purchase land or to expand or start their own businesses. Speculators took advantage of this boom in the sale of land by purchasing property not to live on, but to buy cheaply and resell at exorbitant prices.

During the War of 1812, the Bank of the United States had suspended payments in **specie**, "hard money" usually in the form of gold and silver coins. When the war ended, the bank continued to issue only paper banknotes and to redeem notes issued by state banks with paper only. The newly chartered banks also adopted this practice, issuing banknotes in excess of the amount of specie in their vaults. This shaky economic scheme worked only so long as people were content to conduct business with paper money and refrain from demanding that banks instead give them the gold and silver that was supposed to back it. If large numbers of people, or banks that had loaned money to other banks, began to demand specie payments, the banking system would collapse, because there was no longer enough specie to support the amount of paper money the banks had put into circulation. So terrified were bankers that customers would demand gold and silver that an irate bank employee in Ohio stabbed a customer who had the audacity to ask for specie in exchange for the banknotes he held.

In an effort to bring stability to the nation's banking system, Congress chartered the Second Bank of the United States (a revival of Alexander Hamilton's national bank) in 1816. But this new institution only compounded the problem by making risky loans, opening branches in the South and West where land fever was highest, and issuing a steady stream of Bank of the United States notes, a move that increased inflation and speculation.

The inflated economic bubble burst in 1819, resulting in a prolonged economic depression or severe downturn in the economy called the Panic of 1819. It was the first economic depression experienced by the American public, who panicked as they saw the prices of agricultural products fall and businesses fail. Prices had already begun falling in 1815, at the end of the Napoleonic Wars, when Britain began to "dump" its surplus manufactured goods, the result of wartime overproduction, in American ports, where they were sold for low prices and competed with American-manufactured goods. In 1818, to make the economic situation worse, prices for American agricultural products began to fall both in the United States and in Europe; the overproduction of staples such as wheat and cotton coincided with the recovery of European agriculture, which reduced demand for American crops. Crop prices tumbled by as much 75 percent.

This dramatic decrease in the value of agricultural goods left farmers unable to pay their debts. As they defaulted on their loans, banks seized their property. However, because the drastic fall in agricultural prices had greatly reduced the value of land, the banks were left with farms they were unable to sell. Land speculators lost the value of their investments. As the countryside suffered, hard-hit farmers ceased to purchase manufactured goods. Factories responded by cutting wages or firing employees.

In 1818, the Second Bank of the United States needed specie to pay foreign investors who had loaned money to the United States to enable the country to purchase Louisiana. The bank began to call in the loans it had made and required that state banks pay their debts in gold and silver. State banks that could not collect loan payments from hard-pressed farmers could not, in turn, meet their obligations to the Second Bank of the United States. Severe consequences followed as banks closed their doors and businesses failed. Three-quarters of the work force in Philadelphia was unemployed, and charities were swamped by thousands of newly destitute people needing assistance. In states with imprisonment for debt, the prison population swelled. As a result, many states drafted laws to provide relief for debtors. Even those at the top of the social ladder were affected by the Panic of 1819. Thomas Jefferson, who had cosigned a loan for a friend, nearly lost Monticello when his acquaintance defaulted, leaving Jefferson responsible for the debt.

In an effort to stimulate the economy in the midst of the economic depression, Congress passed several acts modifying land sales. The Land Law of 1820 lowered the price of land to $1.25 per acre and allowed small parcels of eighty acres to be sold. The Relief Act of 1821 allowed Ohioans to return land to the government if they could not afford to keep it. The money they received in return was credited toward their debt. The act also extended the credit period to eight years. States, too, attempted to aid those faced with economic hard times by passing laws to prevent mortgage foreclosures so buyers could keep their homes. Americans made the best of the opportunities presented in business, in farming, or on the frontier, and by 1823 the Panic of 1819 had ended. The recovery provided ample evidence of the vibrant and resilient nature of the American people.

ENTREPRENEURS AND INVENTORS

The volatility of the U.S. economy did nothing to dampen the creative energies of its citizens in the years before the Civil War. In the 1800s, a frenzy of entrepreneurship and invention yielded many new products and machines. The republic seemed to be a laboratory of innovation, and technological advances appeared unlimited.

One of the most influential advancements of the early nineteenth century was the cotton engine or gin, invented by Eli Whitney and patented in 1794. Whitney, who was born in Massachusetts, had spent time in the South and knew that a device to speed up the production of cotton was desperately needed so cotton farmers could meet the growing demand for their crop. He hoped the cotton gin would render slavery obsolete. Whitney's seemingly simple invention cleaned the seeds from the raw cotton far more quickly and efficiently than could slaves working by hand (Figure 9.10). The raw cotton with seeds was placed in the cotton gin, and with the use of a hand crank, the seeds were extracted through a carding device that aligned the cotton fibers in strands for spinning.

Figure 9.10 *The First Cotton-Gin*, an 1869 drawing by William L. Sheppard, shows the first use of a cotton gin "at the close of the last century." African American slaves handle the gin while white men conduct business in the background. What do you think the artist was trying to convey with this image? (credit: Library of Congress)

Whitney also worked on **machine tools**, devices that cut and shaped metal to make standardized, interchangeable parts for other mechanical devices like clocks and guns. Whitney's machine tools to manufacture parts for muskets enabled guns to be manufactured and repaired by people other than skilled gunsmiths. His creative genius served as a source of inspiration for many other American inventors.

Another influential new technology of the early 1800s was the steamship engine, invented by Robert Fulton in 1807. Fulton's first steamship, the *Clermont*, used paddle wheels to travel the 150 miles from New York City to Albany in a record time of only thirty-two hours (Figure 9.11). Soon, a fleet of steamboats was traversing the Hudson River and New York Harbor, later expanding to travel every major American river including the mighty Mississippi. By the 1830s there were over one thousand of these vessels, radically changing water transportation by ending its dependence on the wind. Steamboats could travel faster and more cheaply than sailing vessels or keelboats, which floated downriver and had to be poled or towed upriver on the return voyage. Steamboats also arrived with much greater dependability. The steamboat facilitated the rapid economic development of the massive Mississippi River Valley and the settlement of the West.

Figure 9.11 Fulton's steamboat the *Clermont* transformed the speed, cost, and dependability of water transportation in the United States. (credit: Project Gutenberg Archives)

Virginia-born Cyrus McCormick wanted to replace the laborious process of using a scythe to cut and gather wheat for harvest. In 1831, he and the slaves on his family's plantation tested a horse-drawn mechanical reaper, and over the next several decades, he made constant improvements to it (Figure 9.12). More farmers began using it in the 1840s, and greater demand for the McCormick reaper led McCormick and his brother to establish the McCormick Harvesting Machine Company in Chicago, where labor was more readily available. By the 1850s, McCormick's mechanical reaper had enabled farmers to vastly increase their output. McCormick—and also John Deere, who improved on the design of plows—opened the prairies to agriculture. McCormick's bigger machine could harvest grain faster, and Deere's plow could cut through the thick prairie sod. Agriculture north of the Ohio River became the pantry that would lower food prices and feed the major cities in the East. In short order, Ohio, Indiana, and Illinois all become major agricultural states.

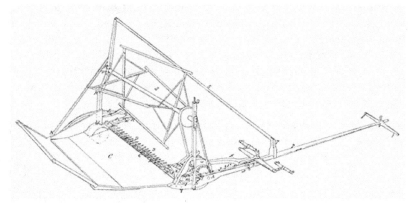

Figure 9.12 This sketch is from the 1845 patent for an improved grain reaper invented by Cyrus Hall McCormick. The reaper mechanized the labor-intensive use of scythes to harvest wheat.

Samuel Morse added the telegraph to the list of American innovations introduced in the years before the Civil War. Born in Massachusetts in 1791, Morse first gained renown as a painter before turning his attention to the development of a method of rapid communication in the 1830s. In 1838, he gave the first public demonstration of his method of conveying electric pulses over a wire, using the basis of what became known as Morse code. In 1843, Congress agreed to help fund the new technology by allocating

$30,000 for a telegraph line to connect Washington, DC, and Baltimore along the route of the Baltimore and Ohio Railroad. In 1844, Morse sent the first telegraph message on the new link. Improved communication systems fostered the development of business, economics, and politics by allowing for dissemination of news at a speed previously unknown.

9.3 On the Move: The Transportation Revolution

By the end of this section, you will be able to:
- Describe the development of improved methods of nineteenth-century domestic transportation
- Identify the ways in which roads, canals, and railroads impacted Americans' lives in the nineteenth century

Americans in the early 1800s were a people on the move, as thousands left the eastern coastal states for opportunities in the West. Unlike their predecessors, who traveled by foot or wagon train, these settlers had new transport options. Their trek was made possible by the construction of roads, canals, and railroads, projects that required the funding of the federal government and the states.

New technologies, like the steamship and railroad lines, had brought about what historians call the transportation revolution. States competed for the honor of having the most advanced transport systems. People celebrated the transformation of the wilderness into an orderly world of improvement demonstrating the steady march of progress and the greatness of the republic. In 1817, John C. Calhoun of South Carolina looked to a future of rapid internal improvements, declaring, "Let us . . . bind the Republic together with a perfect system of roads and canals." Americans agreed that internal transportation routes would promote progress. By the eve of the Civil War, the United States had moved beyond roads and canals to a well-established and extensive system of railroads.

ROADS AND CANALS

One key part of the transportation revolution was the widespread building of roads and turnpikes. In 1811, construction began on the **Cumberland Road**, a national highway that provided thousands with a route from Maryland to Illinois. The federal government funded this important artery to the West, beginning the creation of a transportation infrastructure for the benefit of settlers and farmers. Other entities built turnpikes, which (as today) charged fees for use. New York State, for instance, chartered turnpike companies that dramatically increased the miles of state roads from one thousand in 1810 to four thousand by 1820. New York led the way in building turnpikes.

Canal mania swept the United States in the first half of the nineteenth century. Promoters knew these artificial rivers could save travelers immense amounts of time and money. Even short waterways, such as the two-and-a-half-mile canal going around the rapids of the Ohio River near Louisville, Kentucky, proved a huge leap forward, in this case by opening a water route from Pittsburgh to New Orleans. The preeminent example was the **Erie Canal** (Figure 9.13), which linked the Hudson River, and thus New York City and the Atlantic seaboard, to the Great Lakes and the Mississippi River Valley.

With its central location, large harbor, and access to the hinterland via the Hudson River, New York City already commanded the lion's share of commerce. Still, the city's merchants worried about losing ground to their competitors in Philadelphia and Baltimore. Their search for commercial advantage led to the dream of creating a water highway connecting the city's Hudson River to Lake Erie and markets in the West. The result was the Erie Canal. Chartered in 1817 by the state of New York, the canal took seven years to complete. When it opened in 1825, it dramatically decreased the cost of shipping while reducing the time to travel to the West. Soon $15 million worth of goods (more than $200 million in today's money) was being transported on the 363-mile waterway every year.

Figure 9.13 Although the Erie Canal was primarily used for commerce and trade, in *Pittsford on the Erie Canal* (1837), George Harvey portrays it in a pastoral, natural setting. Why do you think the painter chose to portray the canal this way?

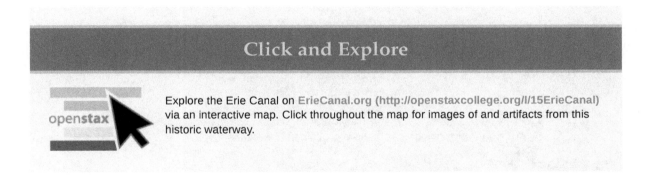

Click and Explore

Explore the Erie Canal on ErieCanal.org (http://openstaxcollege.org/l/15ErieCanal) via an interactive map. Click throughout the map for images of and artifacts from this historic waterway.

The success of the Erie Canal led to other, similar projects. The Wabash and Erie Canal, which opened in the early 1840s, stretched over 450 miles, making it the longest canal in North America (Figure 9.14). Canals added immensely to the country's sense of progress. Indeed, they appeared to be the logical next step in the process of transforming wilderness into civilization.

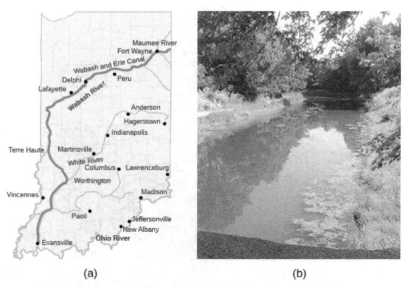

(a)   (b)

Figure 9.14 This map (a) shows the route taken by the Wabash and Erie Canal through the state of Indiana. The canal began operation in 1843 and boats operated on it until the 1870s. Sections have since been restored, as shown in this 2007 photo (b) from Delphi, Indiana.

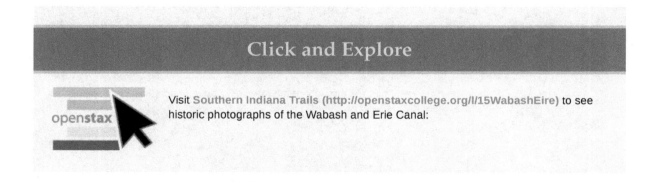

Click and Explore

Visit **Southern Indiana Trails (http://openstaxcollege.org/l/15WabashEire)** to see historic photographs of the Wabash and Erie Canal:

As with highway projects such as the Cumberland Road, many canals were federally sponsored, especially during the presidency of John Quincy Adams in the late 1820s. Adams, along with Secretary of State Henry Clay, championed what was known as the American System, part of which included plans for a broad range of internal transportation improvements. Adams endorsed the creation of roads and canals to facilitate commerce and develop markets for agriculture as well as to advance settlement in the West.

RAILROADS

Starting in the late 1820s, steam locomotives began to compete with horse-drawn locomotives. The railroads with steam locomotives offered a new mode of transportation that fascinated citizens, buoying their optimistic view of the possibilities of technological progress. The **Mohawk and Hudson Railroad** was the first to begin service with a steam locomotive. Its inaugural train ran in 1831 on a track outside Albany and covered twelve miles in twenty-five minutes. Soon it was traveling regularly between Albany and Schenectady.

Toward the middle of the century, railroad construction kicked into high gear, and eager investors quickly formed a number of railroad companies. As a railroad grid began to take shape, it stimulated a greater demand for coal, iron, and steel. Soon, both railroads and canals crisscrossed the states (**Figure**

9.15), providing a transportation infrastructure that fueled the growth of American commerce. Indeed, the transportation revolution led to development in the coal, iron, and steel industries, providing many Americans with new job opportunities.

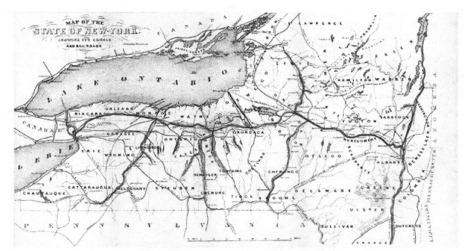

Figure 9.15 This 1853 map of the "Empire State" shows the extent of New York's canal and railroad networks. The entire country's transportation infrastructure grew dramatically during the first half of the nineteenth century.

AMERICANS ON THE MOVE

The expansion of roads, canals, and railroads changed people's lives. In 1786, it had taken a minimum of four days to travel from Boston, Massachusetts, to Providence, Rhode Island. By 1840, the trip took half a day on a train. In the twenty-first century, this may seem intolerably slow, but people at the time were amazed by the railroad's speed. Its average of twenty miles per hour was twice as fast as other available modes of transportation.

By 1840, more than three thousand miles of canals had been dug in the United States, and thirty thousand miles of railroad track had been laid by the beginning of the Civil War. Together with the hundreds of steamboats that plied American rivers, these advances in transportation made it easier and less expensive to ship agricultural products from the West to feed people in eastern cities, and to send manufactured goods from the East to people in the West. Without this ability to transport goods, the market revolution would not have been possible. Rural families also became less isolated as a result of the transportation revolution. Traveling circuses, menageries, peddlers, and itinerant painters could now more easily make their way into rural districts, and people in search of work found cities and mill towns within their reach.

9.4 A New Social Order: Class Divisions

By the end of this section, you will be able to:
- Identify the shared perceptions and ideals of each social class
- Assess different social classes' views of slavery

The profound economic changes sweeping the United States led to equally important social and cultural transformations. The formation of distinct classes, especially in the rapidly industrializing North, was one of the most striking developments. The unequal distribution of newly created wealth spurred new divisions along class lines. Each class had its own specific culture and views on the issue of slavery.

THE ECONOMIC ELITE

Economic elites gained further social and political ascendance in the United States due to a fast-growing economy that enhanced their wealth and allowed distinctive social and cultural characteristics to develop among different economic groups. In the major northern cities of Boston, New York, and Philadelphia, leading merchants formed an industrial capitalist elite. Many came from families that had been deeply engaged in colonial trade in tea, sugar, pepper, slaves, and other commodities and that were familiar with trade networks connecting the United States with Europe, the West Indies, and the Far East. These colonial merchants had passed their wealth to their children.

After the War of 1812, the new generation of merchants expanded their economic activities. They began to specialize in specific types of industry, spearheading the development of industrial capitalism based on factories they owned and on specific commercial services such as banking, insurance, and shipping. Junius Spencer Morgan (Figure 9.16), for example, rose to prominence as a banker. His success began in Boston, where he worked in the import business in the 1830s. He then formed a partnership with a London banker, George Peabody, and created Peabody, Morgan & Co. In 1864, he renamed the enterprise J. S. Morgan & Co. His son, J. P. Morgan, became a noted financier in the later nineteenth and early twentieth century.

Figure 9.16 Junius Spencer Morgan of Boston was one of the fathers of the American private banking system. (credit: Project Gutenberg Archives)

Click and Explore

Visit the Internet Archive (http://openstaxcollege.org/l/15Hunts) to see scanned pages from *Hunt's Merchant's Magazine and Commercial Review*. This monthly business review provided the business elite with important information about issues pertaining to trade and finance: commodity prices, new laws affecting business, statistics regarding imports and exports, and similar content. Choose three articles and decide how they might have been important to the northern business elite.

Members of the northern business elite forged close ties with each other to protect and expand their economic interests. Marriages between leading families formed a crucial strategy to advance economic advantage, and the homes of the northern elite became important venues for solidifying social bonds. Exclusive neighborhoods started to develop as the wealthy distanced themselves from the poorer urban residents, and cities soon became segregated by class.

Industrial elites created chambers of commerce to advance their interests; by 1858 there were ten in the United States. These networking organizations allowed top bankers and merchants to stay current on the economic activities of their peers and further strengthen the bonds among themselves. The elite also established social clubs to forge and maintain ties. The first of these, the Philadelphia Club, came into being in 1834. Similar clubs soon formed in other cities and hosted a range of social activities designed to further bind together the leading economic families. Many northern elites worked hard to ensure the transmission of their inherited wealth from one generation to the next. Politically, they exercised considerable power in local and state elections. Most also had ties to the cotton trade, so they were strong supporters of slavery.

The Industrial Revolution led some former artisans to reinvent themselves as manufacturers. These enterprising leaders of manufacturing differed from the established commercial elite in the North and South because they did not inherit wealth. Instead, many came from very humble working-class origins and embodied the dream of achieving upward social mobility through hard work and discipline. As the beneficiaries of the economic transformations sweeping the republic, these newly established manufacturers formed a new economic elite that thrived in the cities and cultivated its own distinct sensibilities. They created a culture that celebrated hard work, a position that put them at odds with southern planter elites who prized leisure and with other elite northerners who had largely inherited their wealth and status.

Peter Cooper provides one example of the new northern manufacturing class. Ever inventive, Cooper dabbled in many different moneymaking enterprises before gaining success in the glue business. He opened his Manhattan glue factory in the 1820s and was soon using his profits to expand into a host of other activities, including iron production. One of his innovations was the steam locomotive, which he invented in 1827 (Figure 9.17). Despite becoming one of the wealthiest men in New York City, Cooper lived simply. Rather than buying an ornate bed, for example, he built his own. He believed respectability came through hard work, not family pedigree.

Figure 9.17 Peter Cooper, who would go on to found the Cooper Union for the Advancement of Science and Art in New York City, designed and built the Tom Thumb, the first American-built steam locomotive, a replica of which is shown here.

Those who had inherited their wealth derided self-made men like Cooper, and he and others like him were excluded from the social clubs established by the merchant and financial elite of New York City. Self-made northern manufacturers, however, created their own organizations that aimed to promote upward mobility. The Providence Association of Mechanics and Manufacturers was formed in 1789 and promoted both industrial arts and education as a pathway to economic success. In 1859, Peter Cooper established the Cooper Union for the Advancement of Science and Art, a school in New York City dedicated to providing education in technology. Merit, not wealth, mattered most according to Cooper, and admission to the school was based solely on ability; race, sex, and family connections had no place. The best and brightest could attend Cooper Union tuition-free, a policy that remained in place until 2014.

THE MIDDLE CLASS

Not all enterprising artisans were so successful that they could rise to the level of the elite. However, many artisans and small merchants, who owned small factories and stores, did manage to achieve and maintain respectability in an emerging middle class. Lacking the protection of great wealth, members of the middle class agonized over the fear that they might slip into the ranks of wage laborers; thus they strove to maintain or improve their middle-class status and that of their children.

To this end, the middle class valued cleanliness, discipline, morality, hard work, education, and good manners. Hard work and education enabled them to rise in life. Middle-class children, therefore, did not work in factories. Instead they attended school and in their free time engaged in "self-improving" activities, such as reading or playing the piano, or they played with toys and games that would teach them the skills and values they needed to succeed in life. In the early nineteenth century, members of the middle class began to limit the number of children they had. Children no longer contributed economically to the household, and raising them "correctly" required money and attention. It therefore made sense to have fewer of them.

Middle-class women did not work for wages. Their job was to care for the children and to keep the house in a state of order and cleanliness, often with the help of a servant. They also performed the important tasks of cultivating good manners among their children and their husbands and of purchasing consumer goods; both activities proclaimed to neighbors and prospective business partners that their families were educated, cultured, and financially successful.

Northern business elites, many of whom owned or had invested in businesses like cotton mills that profited from slave labor, often viewed the institution of slavery with ambivalence. Most members of the middle class took a dim view of it, however, since it promoted a culture of leisure. Slavery stood as the antithesis of the middle-class view that dignity and respectability were achieved through work, and many members of this class became active in efforts to end it.

This class of upwardly mobile citizens promoted temperance, or abstinence from alcohol. They also gave their support to Protestant ministers like George Grandison Finney, who preached that all people possessed **free moral agency**, meaning they could change their lives and bring about their own salvation, a message that resonated with members of the middle class, who already believed their worldly efforts had led to their economic success.

THE WORKING CLASS

The Industrial Revolution in the United States created a new class of wage workers, and this working class also developed its own culture. They formed their own neighborhoods, living away from the oversight of bosses and managers. While industrialization and the market revolution brought some improvements to the lives of the working class, these sweeping changes did not benefit laborers as much as they did the middle class and the elites. The working class continued to live an often precarious existence. They suffered greatly during economic slumps, such as the Panic of 1819.

Although most working-class men sought to emulate the middle class by keeping their wives and children out of the work force, their economic situation often necessitated that others besides the male head of the family contribute to its support. Thus, working-class children might attend school for a few years or learn to read and write at Sunday school, but education was sacrificed when income was needed, and many working-class children went to work in factories. While the wives of wage laborers usually did not work for wages outside the home, many took in laundry or did piecework at home to supplement the family's income.

Although the urban working class could not afford the consumer goods that the middle class could, its members did exercise a great deal of influence over popular culture. Theirs was a festive public culture of release and escape from the drudgery of factory work, catered to by the likes of Phineas Taylor Barnum, the celebrated circus promoter and showman. Taverns also served an important function as places to forget the long hours and uncertain wages of the factories. Alcohol consumption was high among the working class, although many workers did take part in the temperance movement. It is little wonder that middle-class manufacturers attempted to abolish alcohol.

AMERICANA

⊛ *P. T. Barnum and the Feejee Mermaid*

The Connecticut native P. T. Barnum catered to the demand for escape and cheap amusements among the working class. His American Museum in New York City opened in 1841 and achieved great success. Millions flocked to see Barnum's exhibits, which included a number of fantastic human and animal oddities, almost all of which were hoaxes. One exhibit in the 1840s featured the "Feejee Mermaid," which Barnum presented as proof of the existence of the mythical mermaids of the deep (Figure 9.18). In truth, the mermaid was a half-monkey, half-fish stitched together.

(a)   (b)

Figure 9.18 Spurious though they were, attractions such as the Feejee mermaid (a) from P. T. Barnum's American Museum in New York City (b) drew throngs of working-class wage earners in the middle of the nineteenth century.

Click and Explore

Visit **The Lost Museum (http://openstaxcollege.org/l/15LostMuseum)** to take a virtual tour of P. T. Barnum's incredible museum.

Wage workers in the North were largely hostile to the abolition of slavery, fearing it would unleash more competition for jobs from free blacks. Many were also hostile to immigration. The pace of immigration to the United States accelerated in the 1840s and 1850s as Europeans were drawn to the promise of employment and land in the United States. Many new members of the working class came from the ranks of these immigrants, who brought new foods, customs, and religions. The Roman Catholic population of the United States, fairly small before this period, began to swell with the arrival of the Irish and the Germans.

Key Terms

artisan skilled, experienced worker who produces specialized goods by hand

Cumberland Road a national highway that provided thousands with a route from Maryland to Illinois

deskilling breaking an artisanal production process into smaller steps that unskilled workers can perform

Erie Canal a canal that connected the Hudson River to Lake Erie and markets in the West

free moral agency the freedom to change one's own life and bring about one's own salvation

labor theory of value an economic theory holding that profits from the sale of the goods produced by workers should be equitably distributed to those workers

land offices sites where prospective landowners could buy public land from the government

machine tools machines that cut and shape metal to produce standardized, interchangeable parts for mechanical devices such as clocks or guns

Mohawk and Hudson Railroad the first steam-powered locomotive railroad in the United States

putting-out system a labor system whereby a merchant hired different families to perform specific tasks in a production process

specie "hard" money, usually in the form of gold and silver coins

Working Men's Party a political group that radically opposed what they viewed as the exploitation of workers

Summary

9.1 Early Industrialization in the Northeast
Industrialization led to radical changes in American life. New industrial towns, like Waltham, Lowell, and countless others, dotted the landscape of the Northeast. The mills provided many young women an opportunity to experience a new and liberating life, and these workers relished their new freedom. Workers also gained a greater appreciation of the value of their work and, in some instances, began to question the basic fairness of the new industrial order. The world of work had been fundamentally reorganized.

9.2 A Vibrant Capitalist Republic
The selling of the public domain was one of the key features of the early nineteenth century in the United States. Thousands rushed west to take part in the bounty. In the wild frenzy of land purchases and speculation in land, state banks advanced risky loans and created unstable paper money not backed by gold or silver, ultimately leading to the Panic of 1819. The ensuing economic depression was the first in U.S. history. Recovery came in the 1820s, followed by a period of robust growth. In this age of entrepreneurship, in which those who invested their money wisely in land, business ventures, or technological improvements reaped vast profits, inventors produced new wonders that transformed American life.

9.3 On the Move: The Transportation Revolution

A transportation infrastructure rapidly took shape in the 1800s as American investors and the government began building roads, turnpikes, canals, and railroads. The time required to travel shrank vastly, and people marveled at their ability to conquer great distances, enhancing their sense of the steady advance of progress. The transportation revolution also made it possible to ship agricultural and manufactured goods throughout the country and enabled rural people to travel to towns and cities for employment opportunities.

9.4 A New Social Order: Class Divisions

The creation of distinctive classes in the North drove striking new cultural developments. Even among the wealthy elites, northern business families, who had mainly inherited their money, distanced themselves from the newly wealthy manufacturing leaders. Regardless of how they had earned their money, however, the elite lived and socialized apart from members of the growing middle class. The middle class valued work, consumption, and education and dedicated their energies to maintaining or advancing their social status. Wage workers formed their own society in industrial cities and mill villages, though lack of money and long working hours effectively prevented the working class from consuming the fruits of their labor, educating their children, or advancing up the economic ladder.

Review Questions

1. How were the New England textile mills planned and built?
  A. Experienced British builders traveled to the United States to advise American merchants.
  B. New England merchants paid French and German mechanics to design factories for them.
  C. New England merchants and British migrants memorized plans from British mills.
  D. Textile mills were a purely American creation, invented by Francis Cabot Lowell in 1813.

2. Which is the best characterization of textile mill workers in the early nineteenth century?
  A. male and female indentured servants from Great Britain who worked hard to win their freedom
  B. young men who found freedom in the rowdy lifestyle of mill work
  C. experienced artisans who shared their knowledge in exchange for part ownership in the company
  D. young farm women whose behavior was closely monitored

3. What effect did industrialization have on consumers?

4. Most people who migrated within the United States in the early nineteenth century went _____.
  A. north toward Canada
  B. west toward Ohio
  C. south toward Georgia
  D. east across the Mississippi River

5. Which of the following was *not* a cause of the Panic of 1819?
  A. The Second Bank of the United States made risky loans.
  B. States chartered too many banks.
  C. Prices for American commodities dropped.
  D. Banks hoarded gold and silver.

6. Robert Fulton is known for inventing _____.
  A. the cotton gin
  B. the mechanical reaper
  C. the steamship engine
  D. machine tools

7. What did federal and state governments do to help people who were hurt in the Panic of 1819?

8. Which of the following was *not* a factor in the transportation revolution?
  A. the steam-powered locomotive

B. the canal system

C. the combustion engine

D. the government-funded road system

9. What was the significance of the Cumberland Road?

A. It gave settlers a quicker way to move west.

B. It reduced the time it took to move goods from New York Harbor to Lake Erie.

C. It improved trade from the Port of New Orleans.

D. It was the first paved road.

10. What were the benefits of the transportation revolution?

11. Which of the following groups supported the abolition of slavery?

A. northern business elites

B. southern planter elites

C. wage workers

D. middle-class northerners

12. Which social class was most drawn to amusements like P. T. Barnum's museum?

A. wage workers

B. middle-class northerners

C. southern planter elites

D. northern business elites

13. What did Peter Cooper envision for the United States, and how did he work to bring his vision to life?

Critical Thinking Questions

14. Industrialization in the Northeast produced great benefits and also major problems. What were they? Who benefited and who suffered? Did the benefits outweigh the problems, or vice versa?

15. What factors led to the Panic of 1819? What government regulations might have prevented it?

16. Would the Industrial Revolution have been possible without the use of slave labor? Why or why not?

17. What might have been the advantages and disadvantages of railroads for the people who lived along the routes or near the stations?

18. What were the values of the middle class? How did they differ from the values of those above and below them on the socioeconomic ladder? In what ways are these values similar to or different from those held by the middle class today?

CHAPTER 10

Jacksonian Democracy, 1820–1840

Figure 10.1 In *President's Levee, or all Creation going to the White House, Washington* (1841), by Robert Cruikshank, the artist depicts Andrew Jackson's inauguration in 1829, with crowds surging into the White House to join the celebrations. Rowdy revelers destroyed many White House furnishings in their merriment. A new political era of democracy had begun, one characterized by the rule of the majority.

Chapter Outline

10.1 A New Political Style: From John Quincy Adams to Andrew Jackson

10.2 The Rise of American Democracy

10.3 The Nullification Crisis and the Bank War

10.4 Indian Removal

10.5 The Tyranny and Triumph of the Majority

Introduction

The most extraordinary political development in the years before the Civil War was the rise of American democracy. Whereas the founders envisioned the United States as a republic, not a democracy, and had placed safeguards such as the Electoral College in the 1787 Constitution to prevent simple majority rule, the early 1820s saw many Americans embracing majority rule and rejecting old forms of deference that were based on elite ideas of virtue, learning, and family lineage.

A new breed of politicians learned to harness the magic of the many by appealing to the resentments, fears, and passions of ordinary citizens to win elections. The charismatic Andrew Jackson gained a reputation as a fighter and defender of American expansion, emerging as the quintessential figure leading the rise of American democracy. In the image above (Figure 10.1), crowds flock to the White House to celebrate his inauguration as president. While earlier inaugurations had been reserved for Washington's political elite, Jackson's was an event for the people, so much so that the pushing throngs caused thousands of dollars of damage to White House property. Characteristics of modern American democracy, including the turbulent nature of majority rule, first appeared during the Age of Jackson.

10.1 A New Political Style: From John Quincy Adams to Andrew Jackson

By the end of this section, you will be able to:
- Explain and illustrate the new style of American politics in the 1820s
- Describe the policies of John Quincy Adams's presidency and explain the political divisions that resulted

In the 1820s, American political culture gave way to the democratic urges of the citizenry. Political leaders and parties rose to popularity by championing the will of the people, pushing the country toward a future in which a wider swath of citizens gained a political voice. However, this expansion of political power was limited to white men; women, free blacks, and Indians remained—or grew increasingly—disenfranchised by the American political system.

THE DECLINE OF FEDERALISM

The first party system in the United States shaped the political contest between the Federalists and the Democratic-Republicans. The Federalists, led by Washington, Hamilton, and Adams, dominated American politics in the 1790s. After the election of Thomas Jefferson—the Revolution of 1800—the Democratic-Republicans gained ascendance. The gradual decline of the Federalist Party is evident in its losses in the presidential contests that occurred between 1800 and 1820. After 1816, in which Democratic-Republican James Monroe defeated his Federalist rival Rufus King, the Federalists never ran another presidential candidate.

Before the 1820s, a **code of deference** had underwritten the republic's political order. Deference was the practice of showing respect for individuals who had distinguished themselves through military accomplishments, educational attainment, business success, or family pedigree. Such individuals were

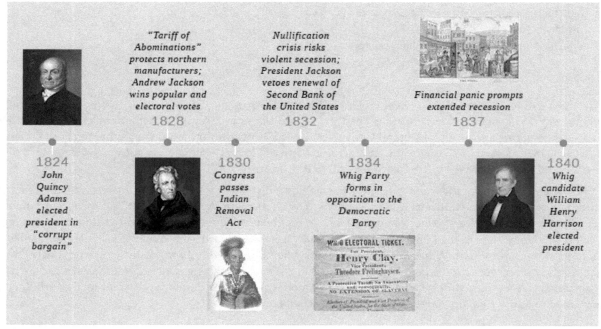

Figure 10.2

members of what many Americans in the early republic agreed was a natural aristocracy. Deference shown to them dovetailed with republicanism and its emphasis on virtue, the ideal of placing the common good above narrow self-interest. Republican statesmen in the 1780s and 1790s expected and routinely received deferential treatment from others, and ordinary Americans deferred to their "social betters" as a matter of course.

For the generation who lived through the American Revolution, for instance, George Washington epitomized republican virtue, entitling him to great deference from his countrymen. His judgment and decisions were considered beyond reproach. An Anglican minister named Mason Locke Weems wrote the classic tale of Washington's unimpeachable virtue in his 1800 book, *The Life of Washington*. Generations of nineteenth-century American children read its fictional story of a youthful Washington chopping down one of his father's cherry trees and, when confronted by his father, confessing: "I cannot tell a lie" (Figure 10.3). The story spoke to Washington's unflinching honesty and integrity, encouraging readers to remember the deference owed to such towering national figures.

Figure 10.3 *"Father, I Can Not Tell a Lie: I Cut the Tree"* (1867) by John McRae, after a painting by George Gorgas White, illustrates Mason Locke Weems's tale of Washington's honesty and integrity as revealed in the incident of the cherry tree. Although it was fiction, this story about Washington taught generations of children about the importance of virtue.

Washington and those who celebrated his role as president established a standard for elite, virtuous leadership that cast a long shadow over subsequent presidential administrations. The presidents who followed Washington shared the first president's pedigree. With the exception of John Adams, who was from Massachusetts, all the early presidents—Thomas Jefferson, James Madison, and James Monroe—were members of Virginia's elite slaveholder aristocracy.

DEMOCRATIC REFORMS

In the early 1820s, deference to pedigree began to wane in American society. A new type of deference—to the will of the majority and not to a ruling class—took hold. The spirit of democratic reform became most evident in the widespread belief that all white men, regardless of whether they owned property, had the right to participate in elections.

Before the 1820s, many state constitutions had imposed property qualifications for voting as a means to keep democratic tendencies in check. However, as Federalist ideals fell out of favor, ordinary men from the middle and lower classes increasingly questioned the idea that property ownership was an indication of virtue. They argued for **universal manhood suffrage**, or voting rights for all white male adults.

New states adopted constitutions that did not contain property qualifications for voting, a move designed to stimulate migration across their borders. Vermont and Kentucky, admitted to the Union in 1791 and

1792 respectively, granted the right to vote to all white men regardless of whether they owned property or paid taxes. Ohio's state constitution placed a minor taxpaying requirement on voters but otherwise allowed for expansive white male suffrage. Alabama, admitted to the Union in 1819, eliminated property qualifications for voting in its state constitution. Two other new states, Indiana (1816) and Illinois (1818), also extended the right to vote to white men regardless of property. Initially, the new state of Mississippi (1817) restricted voting to white male property holders, but in 1832 it eliminated this provision.

In Connecticut, Federalist power largely collapsed in 1818 when the state held a constitutional convention. The new constitution granted the right to vote to all white men who paid taxes or served in the militia. Similarly, New York amended its state constitution in 1821–1822 and removed the property qualifications for voting.

Expanded voting rights did not extend to women, Indians, or free blacks in the North. Indeed, race replaced property qualifications as the criterion for voting rights. American democracy had a decidedly racist orientation; a white majority limited the rights of black minorities. New Jersey explicitly restricted the right to vote to white men only. Connecticut passed a law in 1814 taking the right to vote away from free black men and restricting suffrage to white men only. By the 1820s, 80 percent of the white male population could vote in New York State elections. No other state had expanded suffrage so dramatically. At the same time, however, New York effectively disenfranchised free black men in 1822 (black men had had the right to vote under the 1777 constitution) by requiring that "men of color" must possess property over the value of $250.

PARTY POLITICS AND THE ELECTION OF 1824

In addition to expanding white men's right to vote, democratic currents also led to a new style of political party organization, most evident in New York State in the years after the War of 1812. Under the leadership of Martin Van Buren, New York's "Bucktail" Republican faction (so named because members wore a deer's tail on their hats, a symbol of membership in the Tammany Society) gained political power by cultivating loyalty to the will of the majority, not to an elite family or renowned figure. The Bucktails emphasized a pragmatic approach. For example, at first they opposed the Erie Canal project, but when the popularity of the massive transportation venture became clear, they supported it.

One of the Bucktails' greatest achievements in New York came in the form of revisions to the state constitution in the 1820s. Under the original constitution, a Council of Appointments selected local officials such as sheriffs and county clerks. The Bucktails replaced this process with a system of direct elections, which meant thousands of jobs immediately became available to candidates who had the support of the majority. In practice, Van Buren's party could nominate and support their own candidates based on their loyalty to the party. In this way, Van Buren helped create a political machine of disciplined party members who prized loyalty above all else, a harbinger of future patronage politics in the United States. This system of rewarding party loyalists is known as the **spoils system** (from the expression, "To the victor belong the spoils"). Van Buren's political machine helped radically transform New York politics.

Party politics also transformed the national political landscape, and the election of 1824 proved a turning point in American politics. With tens of thousands of new voters, the older system of having members of Congress form congressional caucuses to determine who would run no longer worked. The new voters had regional interests and voted on them. For the first time, the popular vote mattered in a presidential election. Electors were chosen by popular vote in eighteen states, while the six remaining states used the older system in which state legislatures chose electors.

With the caucus system defunct, the presidential election of 1824 featured five candidates, all of whom ran as Democratic-Republicans (the Federalists having ceased to be a national political force). The crowded field included John Quincy Adams, the son of the second president, John Adams. Candidate Adams had broken with the Federalists in the early 1800s and served on various diplomatic missions, including the mission to secure peace with Great Britain in 1814. He represented New England. A second candidate, John C. Calhoun from South Carolina, had served as secretary of war and represented the slaveholding

South. He dropped out of the presidential race to run for vice president. A third candidate, Henry Clay, the Speaker of the House of Representatives, hailed from Kentucky and represented the western states. He favored an active federal government committed to internal improvements, such as roads and canals, to bolster national economic development and settlement of the West. William H. Crawford, a slaveholder from Georgia, suffered a stroke in 1823 that left him largely incapacitated, but he ran nonetheless and had the backing of the New York machine headed by Van Buren. Andrew Jackson, the famed "hero of New Orleans," rounded out the field. Jackson had very little formal education, but he was popular for his military victories in the War of 1812 and in wars against the Creek and the Seminole. He had been elected to the Senate in 1823, and his popularity soared as pro-Jackson newspapers sang the praises of the courage and daring of the Tennessee slaveholder (Figure 10.4).

(a)   (b)

Figure 10.4 The two most popular presidential candidates in the election of 1824 were Andrew Jackson (a), who won the popular vote but failed to secure the requisite number of votes in the Electoral College, and John Quincy Adams (b), who emerged victorious after a contentious vote in the U.S. House of Representatives.

Results from the eighteen states where the popular vote determined the electoral vote gave Jackson the election, with 152,901 votes to Adams's 114,023, Clay's 47,217, and Crawford's 46,979. The Electoral College, however, was another matter. Of the 261 electoral votes, Jackson needed 131 or better to win but secured only 99. Adams won 84, Crawford 41, and Clay 37. Because Jackson did not receive a majority vote from the Electoral College, the election was decided following the terms of the Twelfth Amendment, which stipulated that when a candidate did not receive a majority of electoral votes, the election went to the House of Representatives, where each state would provide one vote. House Speaker Clay did not want to see his rival, Jackson, become president and therefore worked within the House to secure the presidency for Adams, convincing many to cast their vote for the New Englander. Clay's efforts paid off; despite not having won the popular vote, John Quincy Adams was certified by the House as the next president. Once in office, he elevated Henry Clay to the post of secretary of state.

Jackson and his supporters cried foul. To them, the election of Adams reeked of anti-democratic corruption. So too did the appointment of Clay as secretary of state. John C. Calhoun labeled the whole affair a "**corrupt bargain**" (Figure 10.5). Everywhere, Jackson supporters vowed revenge against the anti-majoritarian result of 1824.

(a)   (b)

Figure 10.5 John C. Calhoun (a) believed that the assistance Henry Clay (b) gave to John Quincy Adams in the U.S. House of Representatives' vote to decide the presidential election of 1824 indicated that a "corrupt bargain" had been made.

THE PRESIDENCY OF JOHN QUINCY ADAMS

Secretary of State Clay championed what was known as the **American System** of high tariffs, a national bank, and federally sponsored internal improvements of canals and roads. Once in office, President Adams embraced Clay's American System and proposed a national university and naval academy to train future leaders of the republic. The president's opponents smelled elitism in these proposals and pounced on what they viewed as the administration's catering to a small privileged class at the expense of ordinary citizens.

Clay also envisioned a broad range of internal transportation improvements. Using the proceeds from land sales in the West, Adams endorsed the creation of roads and canals to facilitate commerce and the advance of settlement in the West. Many in Congress vigorously opposed federal funding of internal improvements, citing among other reasons that the Constitution did not give the federal government the power to fund these projects. However, in the end, Adams succeeded in extending the Cumberland Road into Ohio (a federal highway project). He also broke ground for the Chesapeake and Ohio Canal on July 4, 1828.

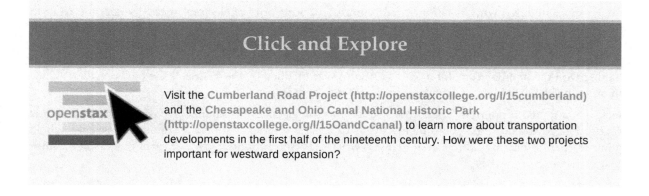

Click and Explore

Visit the Cumberland Road Project (http://openstaxcollege.org/l/15cumberland) and the Chesapeake and Ohio Canal National Historic Park (http://openstaxcollege.org/l/15OandCcanal) to learn more about transportation developments in the first half of the nineteenth century. How were these two projects important for westward expansion?

Tariffs, which both Clay and Adams promoted, were not a novel idea; since the birth of the republic they had been seen as a way to advance domestic manufacturing by making imports more expensive. Congress had approved a tariff in 1789, for instance, and Alexander Hamilton had proposed a protective tariff in

1790. Congress also passed tariffs in 1816 and 1824. Clay spearheaded the drive for the federal government to impose high tariffs to help bolster domestic manufacturing. If imported goods were more expensive than domestic goods, then people would buy American-made goods.

President Adams wished to promote manufacturing, especially in his home region of New England. To that end, in 1828 he proposed a high tariff on imported goods, amounting to 50 percent of their value. The tariff raised questions about how power should be distributed, causing a fiery debate between those who supported states' rights and those who supported the expanded power of the federal government (Figure 10.6). Those who championed states' rights denounced the 1828 measure as the **Tariff of Abominations**, clear evidence that the federal government favored one region, in this case the North, over another, the South. They made their case by pointing out that the North had an expanding manufacturing base while the South did not. Therefore, the South imported far more manufactured goods than the North, causing the tariff to fall most heavily on the southern states.

Figure 10.6 *The Monkey System or 'Every one for himself at the expense of his neighbor!!!!!!!!'* (1831) critiqued Henry Clay's proposed tariff and system of internal improvements. In this political cartoon by Edward Williams Clay, four caged monkeys labeled "Home," "Consumption," "Internal," and "Improv" (improvements)—different parts of the nation's economy—steal each other's food while Henry Clay, in the foreground, extols the virtues of his "grand original American System." (credit: Project Gutenberg Archives)

The 1828 tariff generated additional fears among southerners. In particular, it suggested to them that the federal government would unilaterally take steps that hurt the South. This line of reasoning led some southerners to fear that the very foundation of the South—slavery—could come under attack from a hostile northern majority in Congress. The spokesman for this southern view was President Adams's vice president, John C. Calhoun.

DEFINING "AMERICAN"

✣ John C. Calhoun on the Tariff of 1828

Vice President John C. Calhoun, angry about the passage of the Tariff of 1828, anonymously wrote a report titled "South Carolina Exposition and Protest" (later known as "Calhoun's Exposition") for the South Carolina legislature. As a native of South Carolina, Calhoun articulated the fear among many southerners that the federal government could exercise undue power over the states.

> If it be conceded, as it must be by every one who is the least conversant with our institutions, that the sovereign powers delegated are divided between the General and State Governments, and that the latter hold their portion by the same tenure as the former, it would seem impossible to deny to the States the right of deciding on the infractions of their powers, and the proper remedy to be applied for their correction. The right of judging, in such cases, is an essential attribute of sovereignty, of which the States cannot be divested without losing their sovereignty itself, and being reduced to a subordinate corporate condition. In fact, to divide power, and to give to one of the parties the exclusive right of judging of the portion allotted to each, is, in reality, not to divide it at all; and to reserve such exclusive right to the General Government (it matters not by what department) to be exercised, is to convert it, in fact, into a great consolidated government, with unlimited powers, and to divest the States, in reality, of all their rights, It is impossible to understand the force of terms, and to deny so plain a conclusion.
> —John C. Calhoun, "South Carolina Exposition and Protest," 1828

What is Calhoun's main point of protest? What does he say about the sovereignty of the states?

10.2 The Rise of American Democracy

By the end of this section, you will be able to:
- Describe the key points of the election of 1828
- Explain the scandals of Andrew Jackson's first term in office

A turning point in American political history occurred in 1828, which witnessed the election of Andrew Jackson over the incumbent John Quincy Adams. While democratic practices had been in ascendance since 1800, the year also saw the further unfolding of a democratic spirit in the United States. Supporters of Jackson called themselves Democrats or the Democracy, giving birth to the Democratic Party. Political authority appeared to rest with the majority as never before.

THE CAMPAIGN AND ELECTION OF 1828

During the 1800s, democratic reforms made steady progress with the abolition of property qualifications for voting and the birth of new forms of political party organization. The 1828 campaign pushed new democratic practices even further and highlighted the difference between the Jacksonian expanded electorate and the older, exclusive Adams style. A slogan of the day, "Adams who can write/Jackson who can fight," captured the contrast between Adams the aristocrat and Jackson the frontiersman.

The 1828 campaign differed significantly from earlier presidential contests because of the party organization that promoted Andrew Jackson. Jackson and his supporters reminded voters of the "corrupt bargain" of 1824. They framed it as the work of a small group of political elites deciding who would lead the nation, acting in a self-serving manner and ignoring the will of the majority (Figure 10.7). From Nashville, Tennessee, the Jackson campaign organized supporters around the nation through editorials in partisan newspapers and other publications. Pro-Jackson newspapers heralded the "hero of New Orleans" while denouncing Adams. Though he did not wage an election campaign filled with public appearances, Jackson did give one major campaign speech in New Orleans on January 8, the anniversary of the defeat of the British in 1815. He also engaged in rounds of discussion with politicians who came to his home, the Hermitage, in Nashville.

Figure 10.7 The bitter rivalry between Andrew Jackson and Henry Clay was exacerbated by the "corrupt bargain" of 1824, which Jackson made much of during his successful presidential campaign in 1828. This drawing, published in the 1830s during the debates over the future of the Second Bank of the United States, shows Clay sewing up Jackson's mouth while the "cure for calumny [slander]" protrudes from his pocket.

At the local level, Jackson's supporters worked to bring in as many new voters as possible. Rallies, parades, and other rituals further broadcast the message that Jackson stood for the common man against the corrupt elite backing Adams and Clay. Democratic organizations called Hickory Clubs, a tribute to Jackson's nickname, Old Hickory, also worked tirelessly to ensure his election.

In November 1828, Jackson won an overwhelming victory over Adams, capturing 56 percent of the popular vote and 68 percent of the electoral vote. As in 1800, when Jefferson had won over the Federalist incumbent John Adams, the presidency passed to a new political party, the Democrats. The election was the climax of several decades of expanding democracy in the United States and the end of the older politics of deference.

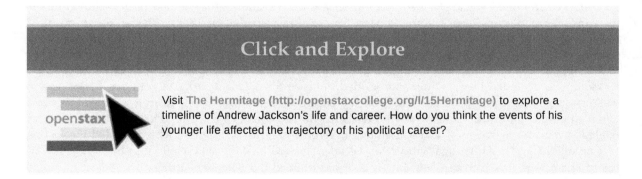

Click and Explore

Visit The Hermitage (http://openstaxcollege.org/l/15Hermitage) to explore a timeline of Andrew Jackson's life and career. How do you think the events of his younger life affected the trajectory of his political career?

SCANDAL IN THE PRESIDENCY

Amid revelations of widespread fraud, including the disclosure that some $300,000 was missing from the Treasury Department, Jackson removed almost 50 percent of appointed civil officers, which allowed him to handpick their replacements. This replacement of appointed federal officials is called **rotation in office**. Lucrative posts, such as postmaster and deputy postmaster, went to party loyalists, especially in places where Jackson's support had been weakest, such as New England. Some Democratic newspaper editors who had supported Jackson during the campaign also gained public jobs.

Jackson's opponents were angered and took to calling the practice the spoils system, after the policies of Van Buren's Bucktail Republican Party. The rewarding of party loyalists with government jobs resulted in spectacular instances of corruption. Perhaps the most notorious occurred in New York City, where a Jackson appointee made off with over $1 million. Such examples seemed proof positive that the Democrats were disregarding merit, education, and respectability in decisions about the governing of the nation.

In addition to dealing with rancor over rotation in office, the Jackson administration became embroiled in a personal scandal known as the Petticoat affair. This incident exacerbated the division between the president's team and the insider class in the nation's capital, who found the new arrivals from Tennessee lacking in decorum and propriety. At the center of the storm was Margaret ("Peggy") O'Neal, a well-known socialite in Washington, DC (Figure 10.8). O'Neal cut a striking figure and had connections to the republic's most powerful men. She married John Timberlake, a naval officer, and they had three children. Rumors abounded, however, about her involvement with John Eaton, a U.S. senator from Tennessee who had come to Washington in 1818.

Figure 10.8 Peggy O'Neal was so well known that advertisers used her image to sell products to the public. In this anonymous nineteenth-century cigar-box lid, her portrait is flanked by vignettes showing her scandalous past. On the left, President Andrew Jackson presents her with flowers. On the right, two men fight a duel for her.

Timberlake committed suicide in 1828, setting off a flurry of rumors that he had been distraught over his wife's reputed infidelities. Eaton and Mrs. Timberlake married soon after, with the full approval of President Jackson. The so-called Petticoat affair divided Washington society. Many Washington socialites snubbed the new Mrs. Eaton as a woman of low moral character. Among those who would have nothing to do with her was Vice President John C. Calhoun's wife, Floride. Calhoun fell out of favor with President Jackson, who defended Peggy Eaton and derided those who would not socialize with her, declaring she was "as chaste as a virgin." (Jackson had personal reasons for defending Eaton: he drew a parallel between Eaton's treatment and that of his late wife, Rachel, who had been subjected to attacks on her reputation related to her first marriage, which had ended in divorce.) Martin Van Buren, who defended the Eatons and organized social gatherings with them, became close to Jackson, who came to rely on a group of informal advisers that included Van Buren and was dubbed the **Kitchen Cabinet**. This select group of presidential supporters highlights the importance of party loyalty to Jackson and the Democratic Party.

10.3 The Nullification Crisis and the Bank War

By the end of this section, you will be able to:
- Explain the factors that contributed to the Nullification Crisis
- Discuss the origins and creation of the Whig Party

The crisis over the Tariff of 1828 continued into the 1830s and highlighted one of the currents of democracy in the Age of Jackson: namely, that many southerners believed a democratic majority could be harmful to their interests. These southerners saw themselves as an embattled minority and claimed the right of states to nullify federal laws that appeared to threaten state sovereignty. Another undercurrent was the resentment and anger of the majority against symbols of elite privilege, especially powerful financial institutions like the Second Bank of the United States.

THE NULLIFICATION CRISIS

The Tariff of 1828 had driven Vice President Calhoun to pen his "South Carolina Exposition and Protest," in which he argued that if a national majority acted against the interest of a regional minority, then individual states could void—or nullify—federal law. By the early 1830s, the battle over the tariff took on new urgency as the price of cotton continued to fall. In 1818, cotton had been thirty-one cents per pound. By 1831, it had sunk to eight cents per pound. While production of cotton had soared during this time and this increase contributed to the decline in prices, many southerners blamed their economic problems squarely on the tariff for raising the prices they had to pay for imported goods while their own income shrank.

Resentment of the tariff was linked directly to the issue of slavery, because the tariff demonstrated the use of federal power. Some southerners feared the federal government would next take additional action against the South, including the abolition of slavery. The theory of **nullification**, or the voiding of unwelcome federal laws, provided wealthy slaveholders, who were a minority in the United States, with an argument for resisting the national government if it acted contrary to their interests. James Hamilton, who served as governor of South Carolina in the early 1830s, denounced the "despotic majority that oppresses us." Nullification also raised the specter of secession; aggrieved states at the mercy of an aggressive majority would be forced to leave the Union.

On the issue of nullification, South Carolina stood alone. Other southern states backed away from what they saw as the extremism behind the idea. President Jackson did not make the repeal of the 1828 tariff a priority and denied the nullifiers' arguments. He and others, including former President Madison, argued that Article 1, Section 8 of the Constitution gave Congress the power to "lay and collect taxes, duties, imposts, and excises." Jackson pledged to protect the Union against those who would try to tear it apart over the tariff issue. "The union shall be preserved," he declared in 1830.

To deal with the crisis, Jackson advocated a reduction in tariff rates. The Tariff of 1832, passed in the summer, lowered the rates on imported goods, a move designed to calm southerners. It did not have the desired effect, however, and Calhoun's nullifiers still claimed their right to override federal law. In November, South Carolina passed the Ordinance of Nullification, declaring the 1828 and 1832 tariffs null and void in the Palmetto State. Jackson responded, however, by declaring in the December 1832 Nullification Proclamation that a state did not have the power to void a federal law.

With the states and the federal government at an impasse, civil war seemed a real possibility. The next governor of South Carolina, Robert Hayne, called for a force of ten thousand volunteers (Figure 10.9) to defend the state against any federal action. At the same time, South Carolinians who opposed the nullifiers told Jackson that eight thousand men stood ready to defend the Union. Congress passed the Force Bill of 1833, which gave the federal government the right to use federal troops to ensure compliance with

---

federal law. The crisis—or at least the prospect of armed conflict in South Carolina—was defused by the Compromise Tariff of 1833, which reduced tariff rates considerably. Nullifiers in South Carolina accepted it, but in a move that demonstrated their inflexibility, they nullified the Force Bill.

Figure 10.9 The governor of South Carolina, Robert Hayne, elected in 1832, was a strong proponent of states' rights and the theory of nullification.

The Nullification Crisis illustrated the growing tensions in American democracy: an aggrieved minority of elite, wealthy slaveholders taking a stand against the will of a democratic majority; an emerging sectional divide between South and North over slavery; and a clash between those who believed in free trade and those who believed in protective tariffs to encourage the nation's economic growth. These tensions would color the next three decades of politics in the United States.

THE BANK WAR

Congress established the Bank of the United States in 1791 as a key pillar of Alexander Hamilton's financial program, but its twenty-year charter expired in 1811. Congress, swayed by the majority's hostility to the bank as an institution catering to the wealthy elite, did not renew the charter at that time. In its place, Congress approved a new national bank—the Second Bank of the United States—in 1816. It too had a twenty-year charter, set to expire in 1836.

The Second Bank of the United States was created to stabilize the banking system. More than two hundred banks existed in the United States in 1816, and almost all of them issued paper money. In other words, citizens faced a bewildering welter of paper money with no standard value. In fact, the problem of paper money had contributed significantly to the Panic of 1819.

In the 1820s, the national bank moved into a magnificent new building in Philadelphia. However, despite Congress's approval of the Second Bank of the United States, a great many people continued to view it as tool of the wealthy, an anti-democratic force. President Jackson was among them; he had faced economic crises of his own during his days speculating in land, an experience that had made him uneasy about paper money. To Jackson, hard currency—that is, gold or silver—was the far better alternative. The president also personally disliked the bank's director, Nicholas Biddle.

A large part of the allure of mass democracy for politicians was the opportunity to capture the anger and resentment of ordinary Americans against what they saw as the privileges of a few. One of the leading opponents of the bank was Thomas Hart Benton, a senator from Missouri, who declared that the bank served "to make the rich richer, and the poor poorer." The self-important statements of Biddle, who claimed to have more power that President Jackson, helped fuel sentiments like Benton's.

In the reelection campaign of 1832, Jackson's opponents in Congress, including Henry Clay, hoped to use their support of the bank to their advantage. In January 1832, they pushed for legislation that would re-charter it, even though its charter was not scheduled to expire until 1836. When the bill for re-chartering passed and came to President Jackson, he used his executive authority to veto the measure.

The defeat of the Second Bank of the United States demonstrates Jackson's ability to focus on the specific issues that aroused the democratic majority. Jackson understood people's anger and distrust toward the bank, which stood as an emblem of special privilege and big government. He skillfully used that perception to his advantage, presenting the bank issue as a struggle of ordinary people against a rapacious elite class who cared nothing for the public and pursued only their own selfish ends. As Jackson portrayed it, his was a battle for small government and ordinary Americans. His stand against what bank opponents called the "**monster bank**" proved very popular, and the Democratic press lionized him for it (Figure 10.10). In the election of 1832, Jackson received nearly 53 percent of the popular vote against his opponent Henry Clay.

GENERAL JACKSON SLAYING THE MANY HEADED MONSTER.

Figure 10.10 In *General Jackson Slaying the Many Headed Monster* (1836), the artist, Henry R. Robinson, depicts President Jackson using a cane marked "Veto" to battle a many-headed snake representing state banks, which supported the national bank. Battling alongside Martin Van Buren and Jack Downing, Jackson addresses the largest head, that of Nicholas Biddle, the director of the national bank: "Biddle thou Monster Avaunt [go away]!! . . ."

Jackson's veto was only one part of the war on the "monster bank." In 1833, the president removed the deposits from the national bank and placed them in state banks. Biddle, the bank's director, retaliated by restricting loans to the state banks, resulting in a reduction of the money supply. The financial turmoil only increased when Jackson issued an executive order known as the Specie Circular, which required that western land sales be conducted using gold or silver only. Unfortunately, this policy proved a disaster when the Bank of England, the source of much of the hard currency borrowed by American businesses, dramatically cut back on loans to the United States. Without the flow of hard currency from England, American depositors drained the gold and silver from their own domestic banks, making hard currency scarce. Adding to the economic distress of the late 1830s, cotton prices plummeted, contributing to a financial crisis called the Panic of 1837. This economic panic would prove politically useful for Jackson's opponents in the coming years and Van Buren, elected president in 1836, would pay the price for Jackson's hard-currency preferences.

WHIGS

Jackson's veto of the bank and his Specie Circular helped galvanize opposition forces into a new political party, the **Whigs**, a faction that began to form in 1834. The name was significant; opponents of Jackson saw him as exercising tyrannical power, so they chose the name Whig after the eighteenth-century political party that resisted the monarchical power of King George III. One political cartoon dubbed the president "King Andrew the First" and displayed Jackson standing on the Constitution, which has been ripped to shreds (Figure 10.11).

(a)   (b)

Figure 10.11 This anonymous 1833 political caricature (a) represents President Andrew Jackson as a despotic ruler, holding a scepter in one hand and a veto in the other. Contrast the image of "King Andrew" with a political cartoon from 1831 (b) of Jackson overseeing a scene of uncontrollable chaos as he falls from a hickory chair "coming to pieces at last."

Whigs championed an active federal government committed to internal improvements, including a national bank. They made their first national appearance in the presidential election of 1836, a contest that pitted Jackson's handpicked successor, Martin Van Buren, against a field of several Whig candidates. Indeed, the large field of Whig candidates indicated the new party's lack of organization compared to the Democrats. This helped Van Buren, who carried the day in the Electoral College. As the effects of the Panic of 1837 continued to be felt for years afterward, the Whig press pinned the blame for the economic crisis on Van Buren and the Democrats.

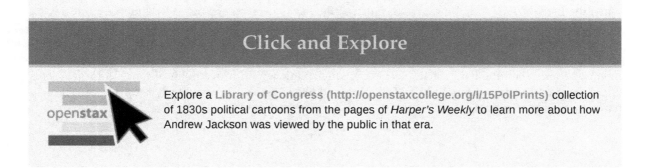

Click and Explore

Explore a Library of Congress (http://openstaxcollege.org/l/15PolPrints) collection of 1830s political cartoons from the pages of *Harper's Weekly* to learn more about how Andrew Jackson was viewed by the public in that era.

10.4 Indian Removal

By the end of this section, you will be able to:
- Explain the legal wrangling that surrounded the Indian Removal Act
- Describe how depictions of Indians in popular culture helped lead to Indian removal

Pro-Jackson newspapers touted the president as a champion of opening land for white settlement and moving native inhabitants beyond the boundaries of "American civilization." In this effort, Jackson reflected majority opinion: most Americans believed Indians had no place in the white republic. Jackson's animosity toward Indians ran deep. He had fought against the Creek in 1813 and against the Seminole in 1817, and his reputation and popularity rested in large measure on his firm commitment to remove Indians from states in the South. The 1830 Indian Removal Act and subsequent displacement of the Creek, Choctaw, Chickasaw, Seminole, and Cherokee tribes of the Southeast fulfilled the vision of a white nation and became one of the identifying characteristics of the Age of Jackson.

INDIANS IN POPULAR CULTURE

Popular culture in the first half of the nineteenth century reflected the aversion to Indians that was pervasive during the Age of Jackson. Jackson skillfully played upon this racial hatred to engage the United States in a policy of ethnic cleansing, eradicating the Indian presence from the land to make way for white civilization.

In an age of mass democracy, powerful anti-Indian sentiments found expression in mass culture, shaping popular perceptions. James Fenimore Cooper's very popular historical novel, *The Last of the Mohicans*, published in 1826 as part of his Leatherstocking series, told the tale of Nathaniel "Natty" Bumppo (aka Hawkeye), who lived among Indians but had been born to white parents. Cooper provides a romantic version of the French and Indian War in which Natty helps the British against the French and the feral, bloodthirsty Huron. Natty endures even as his Indian friends die, including the noble Uncas, the last Mohican, in a narrative that dovetailed with most people's approval of Indian removal.

Indians also made frequent appearances in art. George Catlin produced many paintings of native peoples, which he offered as true representations despite routinely emphasizing their supposed savage nature. *The Cutting Scene, Mandan O-kee-pa Ceremony* (Figure 10.12) is one example. Scholars have long questioned the accuracy of this portrayal of a rite of passage among the Mandan people. Accuracy aside, the painting captured the imaginations of white viewers, reinforcing their disgust at the savagery of Indians.

Figure 10.12 *The Cutting Scene, Mandan O-kee-pa Ceremony*, an 1832 painting by George Catlin, depicts a rite-of-passage ceremony that Catlin said he witnessed. It featured wooden splints inserted into the chest and back muscles of young men. Such paintings increased Indians' reputation as savages.

AMERICANA

✪ *The Paintings of George Catlin*

George Catlin seized upon the public fascination with the supposedly exotic and savage Indian, seeing an opportunity to make money by painting them in a way that conformed to popular white stereotypes (Figure 10.13). In the late 1830s, he toured major cities with his Indian Gallery, a collection of paintings of native peoples. Though he hoped his exhibition would be profitable, it did not bring him financial security.

(a)   (b)

Figure 10.13   In *Attacking the Grizzly Bear* (a), painted in 1844, Catlin focused on the Indians' own vanishing culture, while in *Wi-jún-jon, Pigeon's Egg Head (The Light) Going To and Returning From Washington* (b), painted in 1837–1839, he contrasted their ways with those of whites by showing an Assiniboine chief transformed by a visit to Washington, DC.

Catlin routinely painted Indians in a supposedly aboriginal state. In *Attacking the Grizzly Bear*, the hunters do not have rifles and instead rely on spears. Such a portrayal stretches credibility as native peoples had long been exposed to and adopted European weapons. Indeed, the painting's depiction of Indians riding horses, which were introduced by the Spanish, makes clear that, as much as Catlin and white viewers wanted to believe in the primitive and savage native, the reality was otherwise.

In *Wi-jún-jon, Pigeon's Egg Head (The Light) Going To and Returning From Washington*, the viewer is shown a before and after portrait of Wi-jún-jon, who tried to emulate white dress and manners after going to Washington, DC. What differences do you see between these two representations of Wi-jún-jon? Do you think his attempt to imitate whites was successful? Why or why not? What do you think Catlin was trying to convey with this depiction of Wi-jún-jon's assimilation?

THE INDIAN REMOVAL ACT

In his first message to Congress, Jackson had proclaimed that Indian groups living independently within states, as sovereign entities, presented a major problem for state sovereignty. This message referred directly to the situation in Georgia, Mississippi, and Alabama, where the Creek, Choctaw, Chickasaw, Seminole, and Cherokee peoples stood as obstacles to white settlement. These groups were known as the **Five Civilized Tribes**, because they had largely adopted Anglo-American culture, speaking English and practicing Christianity. Some held slaves like their white counterparts.

Whites especially resented the Cherokee in Georgia, coveting the tribe's rich agricultural lands in the northern part of the state. The impulse to remove the Cherokee only increased when gold was discovered on their lands. Ironically, while whites insisted the Cherokee and other native peoples could never be good citizens because of their savage ways, the Cherokee had arguably gone farther than any other indigenous group in adopting white culture. The *Cherokee Phoenix*, the newspaper of the Cherokee, began publication in 1828 (Figure 10.14) in English and the Cherokee language. Although the Cherokee followed the lead of their white neighbors by farming and owning property, as well as embracing Christianity and owning their own slaves, this proved of little consequence in an era when whites perceived all Indians as incapable of becoming full citizens of the republic.

Figure 10.14 This image depicts the front page of the *Cherokee Phoenix* newspaper from May 21, 1828. The paper was published in both English and the Cherokee language.

Jackson's anti-Indian stance struck a chord with a majority of white citizens, many of whom shared a hatred of nonwhites that spurred Congress to pass the 1830 Indian Removal Act. The act called for the removal of the Five Civilized Tribes from their home in the southeastern United States to land in the West, in present-day Oklahoma. Jackson declared in December 1830, "It gives me pleasure to announce to Congress that the benevolent policy of the Government, steadily pursued for nearly thirty years, in relation to the removal of the Indians beyond the white settlements is approaching to a happy consummation. Two important tribes have accepted the provision made for their removal at the last session of Congress, and it is believed that their example will induce the remaining tribes also to seek the same obvious advantages."

The Cherokee decided to fight the federal law, however, and took their case to the Supreme Court. Their legal fight had the support of anti-Jackson members of Congress, including Henry Clay and Daniel Webster, and they retained the legal services of former attorney general William Wirt. In *Cherokee Nation v. Georgia*, Wirt argued that the Cherokee constituted an independent foreign nation, and that an injunction (a stop) should be placed on Georgia laws aimed at eradicating them. In 1831, the Supreme Court found the Cherokee did not meet the criteria for being a foreign nation.

Another case involving the Cherokee also found its way to the highest court in the land. This legal struggle—*Worcester v. Georgia*—asserted the rights of non-natives to live on Indian lands. Samuel Worcester was a Christian missionary and federal postmaster of New Echota, the capital of the Cherokee nation. A Congregationalist, he had gone to live among the Cherokee in Georgia to further the spread of Christianity, and he strongly opposed Indian removal.

By living among the Cherokee, Worcester had violated a Georgia law forbidding whites, unless they were agents of the federal government, to live in Indian territory. Worcester was arrested, but because his federal job as postmaster gave him the right to live there, he was released. Jackson supporters then succeeded in taking away Worcester's job, and he was re-arrested. This time, a court sentenced him and nine others for violating the Georgia state law banning whites from living on Indian land. Worcester was sentenced to four years of hard labor. When the case of *Worcester v. Georgia* came before the Supreme Court in 1832, Chief Justice John Marshall ruled in favor of Worcester, finding that the Cherokee constituted "distinct political communities" with sovereign rights to their own territory.

DEFINING "AMERICAN"

⚙ *Chief Justice John Marshall's Ruling in Worcester v. Georgia*

In 1832, Chief Justice of the Supreme Court John Marshall ruled in favor of Samuel Worcester in *Worcester v. Georgia*. In doing so, he established the principle of tribal sovereignty. Although this judgment contradicted *Cherokee Nation v. Georgia*, it failed to halt the Indian Removal Act. In his opinion, Marshall wrote the following:

> From the commencement of our government Congress has passed acts to regulate trade and intercourse with the Indians; which treat them as nations, respect their rights, and manifest a firm purpose to afford that protection which treaties stipulate. All these acts, and especially that of 1802, which is still in force, manifestly consider the several Indian nations as distinct political communities, having territorial boundaries, within which their authority is exclusive, and having a right to all the lands within those boundaries, which is not only acknowledged, but guaranteed by the United States. . . .
>
> The Cherokee Nation, then, is a distinct community, occupying its own territory, with boundaries accurately described, in which the laws of Georgia can have no force, and which the citizens of Georgia have no right to enter but with the assent of the Cherokees themselves or in conformity with treaties and with the acts of Congress. The whole intercourse between the United States and this nation is, by our Constitution and laws, vested in the government of the United States.
>
> The act of the State of Georgia under which the plaintiff in error was prosecuted is consequently void, and the judgment a nullity. . . . The Acts of Georgia are repugnant to the Constitution, laws, and treaties of the United States.

How does this opinion differ from the outcome of *Cherokee Nation v. Georgia* just one year earlier? Why do you think the two outcomes were different?

The Supreme Court did not have the power to enforce its ruling in *Worcester v. Georgia*, however, and it became clear that the Cherokee would be compelled to move. Those who understood that the only option was removal traveled west, but the majority stayed on their land. In order to remove them, the president relied on the U.S. military. In a series of forced marches, some fifteen thousand Cherokee were finally relocated to Oklahoma. This forced migration, known as the **Trail of Tears**, caused the deaths of as many as four thousand Cherokee (Figure 10.15). The Creek, Choctaw, Chickasaw, and Seminole peoples were also compelled to go. The removal of the Five Civilized Tribes provides an example of the power of majority opinion in a democracy.

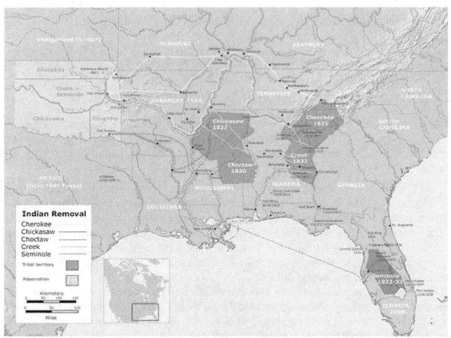

Figure 10.15 After the passage of the Indian Removal Act, the U.S. military forced the Cherokee, Creek, Choctaw, Chickasaw, and Seminole to relocate from the Southeast to an area in the western territory (now Oklahoma), marching them along the routes shown here.

Click and Explore

Explore the interactive Trail of Tears map (http://openstaxcollege.org/l/ 15NativeAm) at PBS.org to see the routes the Five Civilized Tribes traveled when they were expelled from their lands. Then listen to a collection of Cherokee oral histories (http://openstaxcollege.org/l/15NativeAm2) including verses of a Cherokee-language song about the Trail of Tears. What do you think is the importance of oral history in documenting the Cherokee experience?

BLACK HAWK'S WAR

The policy of removal led some Indians to actively resist. In 1832, the Fox and the Sauk, led by Sauk chief Black Hawk (Makataimeshekiakiah), moved back across the Mississippi River to reclaim their ancestral home in northern Illinois. A brief war in 1832, Black Hawk's War, ensued. White settlers panicked at the return of the native peoples, and militias and federal troops quickly mobilized. At the Battle of Bad Axe (also known as the Bad Axe Massacre), they killed over two hundred men, women, and children. Some seventy white settlers and soldiers also lost their lives in the conflict (Figure 10.16). The war, which lasted only a matter of weeks, illustrates how much whites on the frontier hated and feared Indians during the Age of Jackson.

Download for free at http://cnx.org/content/col11740/latest/

Figure 10.16 Charles Bird King's 1837 portrait *Sauk Chief Makataimeshekiakiah, or Black Hawk* (a), depicts the Sauk chief who led the Fox and Sauk peoples in an ill-fated effort to return to their native lands in northern Illinois. This engraving depicting the Battle of Bad Axe (b) shows U.S. soldiers on a steamer firing on Indians aboard a raft. (credit b: modification of work by Library of Congress)

10.5 The Tyranny and Triumph of the Majority

By the end of this section, you will be able to:
- Explain Alexis de Tocqueville's analysis of American democracy
- Describe the election of 1840 and its outcome

To some observers, the rise of democracy in the United States raised troubling questions about the new power of the majority to silence minority opinion. As the will of the majority became the rule of the day, everyone outside of mainstream, white American opinion, especially Indians and blacks, were vulnerable to the wrath of the majority. Some worried that the rights of those who opposed the will of the majority would never be safe. Mass democracy also shaped political campaigns as never before. The 1840 presidential election marked a significant turning point in the evolving style of American democratic politics.

ALEXIS DE TOCQUEVILLE

Perhaps the most insightful commentator on American democracy was the young French aristocrat Alexis de Tocqueville, whom the French government sent to the United States to report on American prison reforms (Figure 10.17). Tocqueville marveled at the spirit of democracy that pervaded American life. Given his place in French society, however, much of what he saw of American democracy caused him concern.

(a)   (b)

Figure 10.17 Alexis de Tocqueville is best known for his insightful commentary on American democracy found in *De la démocratie en Amérique*. The first volume of Tocqueville's two-volume work was immediately popular throughout Europe. The first English translation, by Henry Reeve and titled *Democracy in America* (a), was published in New York in 1838. Théodore Chassériau painted this portrait of Alexis de Tocqueville in 1850 (b).

Tocqueville's experience led him to believe that democracy was an unstoppable force that would one day overthrow monarchy around the world. He wrote and published his findings in 1835 and 1840 in a two-part work entitled *Democracy in America*. In analyzing the democratic revolution in the United States, he wrote that the major benefit of democracy came in the form of equality before the law. A great deal of the social revolution of democracy, however, carried negative consequences. Indeed, Tocqueville described a new type of tyranny, the **tyranny of the majority**, which overpowers the will of minorities and individuals and was, in his view, unleashed by democracy in the United States.

In this excerpt from *Democracy in America*, Alexis de Tocqueville warns of the dangers of democracy when the majority will can turn to tyranny:

> When an individual or a party is wronged in the United States, to whom can he apply for redress? If to public opinion, public opinion constitutes the majority; if to the legislature, it represents the majority, and implicitly obeys its injunctions; if to the executive power, it is appointed by the majority, and remains a passive tool in its hands; the public troops consist of the majority under arms; the jury is the majority invested with the right of hearing judicial cases; and in certain States even the judges are elected by the majority. However iniquitous or absurd the evil of which you complain may be, you must submit to it as well as you can.
>
> The authority of a king is purely physical, and it controls the actions of the subject without subduing his private will; but the majority possesses a power which is physical and moral at the same time; it acts upon the will as well as upon the actions of men, and it represses not only all contest, but all controversy. I know no country in which there is so little true independence of mind and freedom of discussion as in America.

Download for free at http://cnx.org/content/col11740/latest/

Click and Explore

Take the **Alexis de Tocqueville Tour (http://openstaxcollege.org/l/15Tocqueville)** to experience nineteenth-century America as Tocqueville did, by reading his journal entries about the states and territories he visited with fellow countryman Gustave de Beaumont. What regional differences can you draw from his descriptions?

THE 1840 ELECTION

The presidential election contest of 1840 marked the culmination of the democratic revolution that swept the United States. By this time, the **second party system** had taken hold, a system whereby the older Federalist and Democratic-Republican Parties had been replaced by the new Democratic and Whig Parties. Both Whigs and Democrats jockeyed for election victories and commanded the steady loyalty of political partisans. Large-scale presidential campaign rallies and emotional propaganda became the order of the day. Voter turnout increased dramatically under the second party system. Roughly 25 percent of eligible voters had cast ballots in 1828. In 1840, voter participation surged to nearly 80 percent.

The differences between the parties were largely about economic policies. Whigs advocated accelerated economic growth, often endorsing federal government projects to achieve that goal. Democrats did not view the federal government as an engine promoting economic growth and advocated a smaller role for the national government. The membership of the parties also differed: Whigs tended to be wealthier; they were prominent planters in the South and wealthy urban northerners—in other words, the beneficiaries of the market revolution. Democrats presented themselves as defenders of the common people against the elite.

In the 1840 presidential campaign, taking their cue from the Democrats who had lionized Jackson's military accomplishments, the Whigs promoted William Henry Harrison as a war hero based on his 1811 military service against the Shawnee chief Tecumseh at the Battle of Tippecanoe. John Tyler of Virginia ran as the vice presidential candidate, leading the Whigs to trumpet, "Tippecanoe and Tyler too!" as a campaign slogan.

The campaign thrust Harrison into the national spotlight. Democrats tried to discredit him by declaring, "Give him a barrel of hard [alcoholic] cider and settle a pension of two thousand a year on him, and take my word for it, he will sit the remainder of his days in his log cabin." The Whigs turned the slur to their advantage by presenting Harrison as a man of the people who had been born in a log cabin (in fact, he came from a privileged background in Virginia), and the contest became known as the **log cabin campaign** (Figure 10.18). At Whig political rallies, the faithful were treated to whiskey made by the E. C. Booz Company, leading to the introduction of the word "booze" into the American lexicon. Tippecanoe Clubs, where booze flowed freely, helped in the marketing of the Whig candidate.

(a)   (b)

Figure 10.18 The Whig campaign song "Tippecanoe and Tyler Too!" (a) and the anti-Whig flyers (b) that were circulated in response to the "log cabin campaign" illustrate the partisan fervor of the 1840 election.

The Whigs' efforts, combined with their strategy of blaming Democrats for the lingering economic collapse that began with the hard-currency Panic of 1837, succeeded in carrying the day. A mass campaign with political rallies and party mobilization had molded a candidate to fit an ideal palatable to a majority of American voters, and in 1840 Harrison won what many consider the first modern election.

Key Terms

American System the program of federally sponsored roads and canals, protective tariffs, and a national bank advocated by Henry Clay and enacted by President Adams

code of deference the practice of showing respect for individuals who had distinguished themselves through accomplishments or birth

corrupt bargain the term that Andrew Jackson's supporters applied to John Quincy Adams's 1824 election, which had occurred through the machinations of Henry Clay in the U.S. House of Representatives

Five Civilized Tribes the five tribes—Cherokee, Seminole, Creek, Choctaw, and Chickasaw—who had most thoroughly adopted Anglo-American culture; they also happened to be the tribes that were believed to stand in the way of western settlement in the South

Kitchen Cabinet a nickname for Andrew Jackson's informal group of loyal advisers

log cabin campaign the 1840 election, in which the Whigs painted William Henry Harrison as a man of the people

monster bank the term Democratic opponents used to denounce the Second Bank of the United States as an emblem of special privilege and big government

nullification the theory, advocated in response to the Tariff of 1828, that states could void federal law at their discretion

rotation in office originally, simply the system of having term limits on political appointments; in the Jackson era, this came to mean the replacement of officials with party loyalists

second party system the system in which the Democratic and Whig Parties were the two main political parties after the decline of the Federalist and Democratic-Republican Parties

spoils system the political system of rewarding friends and supporters with political appointments

Tariff of Abominations a federal tariff introduced in 1828 that placed a high duty on imported goods in order to help American manufacturers, which southerners viewed as unfair and harmful to their region

Trail of Tears the route of the forced removal of the Cherokee and other tribes from the southeastern United States to the territory that is now Oklahoma

tyranny of the majority Alexis de Tocqueville's phrase warning of the dangers of American democracy

universal manhood suffrage voting rights for all male adults

Whigs a political party that emerged in the early 1830s to oppose what members saw as President Andrew Jackson's abuses of power

Summary

10.1 A New Political Style: From John Quincy Adams to Andrew Jackson

The early 1800s saw an age of deference give way to universal manhood suffrage and a new type of political organization based on loyalty to the party. The election of 1824 was a fight among Democratic-Republicans that ended up pitting southerner Andrew Jackson against northerner John Quincy Adams. When Adams won through political negotiations in the House of Representatives, Jackson's supporters derided the election as a "corrupt bargain." The Tariff of 1828 further stirred southern sentiment, this time against a perceived bias in the federal government toward northeastern manufacturers. At the same time, the tariff stirred deeper fears that the federal government might take steps that could undermine the system of slavery.

10.2 The Rise of American Democracy

The Democratic-Republicans' "corrupt bargain" that brought John Quincy Adams and Henry Clay to office in 1824 also helped to push them out of office in 1828. Jackson used it to highlight the cronyism of Washington politics. Supporters presented him as a true man of the people fighting against the elitism of Clay and Adams. Jackson rode a wave of populist fervor all the way to the White House, ushering in the ascendency of a new political party: the Democrats. Although Jackson ran on a platform of clearing the corruption out of Washington, he rewarded his own loyal followers with plum government jobs, thus continuing and intensifying the cycle of favoritism and corruption.

10.3 The Nullification Crisis and the Bank War

Andrew Jackson's election in 1832 signaled the rise of the Democratic Party and a new style of American politics. Jackson understood the views of the majority, and he skillfully used the popular will to his advantage. He adroitly navigated through the Nullification Crisis and made headlines with what his supporters viewed as his righteous war against the bastion of money, power, and entrenched insider interests, the Second Bank of the United States. His actions, however, stimulated opponents to fashion an opposition party, the Whigs.

10.4 Indian Removal

Popular culture in the Age of Jackson emphasized the savagery of the native peoples and shaped domestic policy. Popular animosity found expression in the Indian Removal Act. Even the U.S. Supreme Court's ruling in favor of the Cherokee in Georgia offered no protection against the forced removal of the Five Civilized Tribes from the Southeast, mandated by the 1830 Indian Removal Act and carried out by the U.S. military.

10.5 The Tyranny and Triumph of the Majority

American culture of the 1830s reflected the rise of democracy. The majority exercised a new type of power that went well beyond politics, leading Alexis de Tocqueville to write about the "tyranny of the majority." Very quickly, politicians among the Whigs and Democrats learned to master the magic of the many by presenting candidates and policies that catered to the will of the majority. In the 1840 "log cabin campaign," both sides engaged in the new democratic electioneering. The uninhibited expression during the campaign inaugurated a new political style.

Review Questions

1. Which group saw an expansion of their voting rights in the early nineteenth century?
  A. free blacks
  B. non-property-owning men
  C. women
  D. Indians

2. What was the lasting impact of the Bucktail Republican Party in New York?
  A. They implemented universal suffrage.
  B. They pushed for the expansion of the canal system.
  C. They elevated Martin Van Buren to the national political stage.

D. They changed state election laws from an appointee system to a system of open elections.

3. Who won the popular vote in the election of 1824?
    A. Andrew Jackson
    B. Martin Van Buren
    C. Henry Clay
    D. John Quincy Adams

4. Why did Andrew Jackson and his supporters consider the election of John Quincy Adams to be a "corrupt bargain"?

5. Who stood to gain from the Tariff of Abominations, and who expected to lose by it?

6. What was the actual result of Jackson's policy of "rotation in office"?
    A. an end to corruption in Washington
    B. a replacement of Adams's political loyalists with Jackson's political loyalists
    C. the filling of government posts with officials the people chose themselves
    D. the creation of the Kitchen Cabinet

7. The election of 1828 brought in the first presidency of which political party?
    A. the Democrats
    B. the Democratic-Republicans
    C. the Republicans
    D. the Bucktails

8. What were the planks of Andrew Jackson's campaign platform in 1828?

9. What was the significance of the Petticoat affair?

10. South Carolina threatened to nullify which federal act?
    A. the abolition of slavery
    B. the expansion of the transportation infrastructure
    C. the protective tariff on imported goods
    D. the rotation in office that expelled several federal officers

11. How did President Jackson respond to Congress's re-chartering of the Second Bank of the United States?
    A. He vetoed it.
    B. He gave states the right to implement it or not.
    C. He signed it into law.
    D. He wrote a counterproposal.

12. Why did the Second Bank of the United States make such an inviting target for President Jackson?

13. What were the philosophies and policies of the new Whig Party?

14. How did most whites in the United States view Indians in the 1820s?
    A. as savages
    B. as being in touch with nature
    C. as slaves
    D. as shamans

15. The 1830 Indian Removal Act is best understood as _____.
    A. an example of President Jackson forcing Congress to pursue an unpopular policy
    B. an illustration of the widespread hatred of Indians during the Age of Jackson
    C. an example of laws designed to integrate Indians into American life
    D. an effort to deprive the Cherokee of their slave property

16. What was the Trail of Tears?

17. The winner of the 1840 election was _____.

    A. a Democrat
    B. a Democratic-Republican
    C. an Anti-Federalist
    D. a Whig

18. Which of the following did *not* characterize political changes in the 1830s?
    A. higher voter participation
    B. increasing political power of free black voters
    C. stronger partisan ties

D. political battles between Whigs and
    Democrats

19. How did Alexis de Tocqueville react to his
visit to the United States? What impressed and
what worried him?

Critical Thinking Questions

20. What were some of the social and cultural beliefs that became widespread during the Age of Jackson?
What lay behind these beliefs, and do you observe any of them in American culture today?

21. Were the political changes of the early nineteenth century positive or negative? Explain your opinion.

22. If you were defending the Cherokee and other native nations before the U.S. Supreme Court in the
1830s, what arguments would you make? If you were supporting Indian removal, what arguments would
you make?

23. How did depictions of Indians in popular culture help to sway popular opinion? Does modern
popular culture continue to wield this kind of power over us? Why or why not?

24. Does Alexis de Tocqueville's argument about the tyranny of the majority reflect American democracy
today? Provide examples to support your answer.

CHAPTER 11

A Nation on the Move: Westward Expansion, 1800–1860

Figure 11.1 In the first half of the nineteenth century, settlers began to move west of the Mississippi River in large numbers. In John Gast's *American Progress* (ca. 1872), the figure of Columbia, representing the United States and the spirit of democracy, makes her way westward, literally bringing light to the darkness as she advances.

Chapter Outline
11.1 Lewis and Clark
11.2 The Missouri Crisis
11.3 Independence for Texas
11.4 The Mexican-American War, 1846–1848
11.5 Free Soil or Slave? The Dilemma of the West

Introduction

After 1800, the United States militantly expanded westward across North America, confident of its right and duty to gain control of the continent and spread the benefits of its "superior" culture. In John Gast's *American Progress* (Figure 11.1), the white, blonde figure of Columbia—a historical personification of the United States—strides triumphantly westward with the Star of Empire on her head. She brings education, symbolized by the schoolbook, and modern technology, represented by the telegraph wire. White settlers follow her lead, driving the helpless natives away and bringing successive waves of technological progress in their wake. In the first half of the nineteenth century, the quest for control of the West led to the Louisiana Purchase, the annexation of Texas, and the Mexican-American War. Efforts to seize western territories from native peoples and expand the republic by warring with Mexico succeeded beyond expectations. Few nations ever expanded so quickly. Yet, this expansion led to debates about the fate of slavery in the West, creating tensions between North and South that ultimately led to the collapse of American democracy and a brutal civil war.

11.1 Lewis and Clark

By the end of this section, you will be able to:
- Explain the significance of the Louisiana Purchase
- Describe the terms of the Adams-Onís Treaty
- Describe the role played by the filibuster in American expansion

For centuries Europeans had mistakenly believed an all-water route across the North American continent existed. This **"Northwest Passage"** would afford the country that controlled it not only access to the interior of North America but also—more importantly—a relatively quick route to the Pacific Ocean and to trade with Asia. The Spanish, French, and British searched for years before American explorers took up the challenge of finding it. Indeed, shortly before Lewis and Clark set out on their expedition for the U.S. government, Alexander Mackenzie, an officer of the British North West Company, a fur trading outfit, had attempted to discover the route. Mackenzie made it to the Pacific and even believed (erroneously) he had discovered the headwaters of the Columbia River, but he could not find an easy water route with a minimum of difficult portages, that is, spots where boats must be carried overland.

Many Americans also dreamed of finding a Northwest Passage and opening the Pacific to American commerce and influence, including President Thomas Jefferson. In April 1803, Jefferson achieved his goal of purchasing the Louisiana Territory from France, effectively doubling the size of the United States. The purchase was made possible due to events outside the nation's control. With the success of the Haitian Revolution, an uprising of slaves against the French, France's Napoleon abandoned his quest to re-establish an extensive French Empire in America. As a result, he was amenable to selling off the vast Louisiana territory. President Jefferson quickly set out to learn precisely what he had bought and to assess its potential for commercial exploitation. Above all else, Jefferson wanted to exert U.S. control over the territory, an area already well known to French and British explorers. It was therefore vital for the United States to explore and map the land to pave the way for future white settlement.

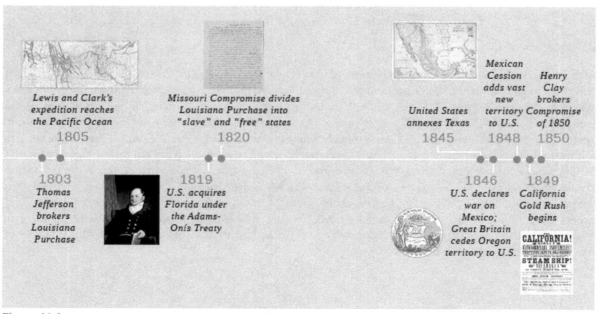

Figure 11.2

JEFFERSON'S CORPS OF DISCOVERY HEADS WEST

To head the expedition into the Louisiana territory, Jefferson appointed his friend and personal secretary, twenty-nine-year-old army captain Meriwether Lewis, who was instructed to form a **Corps of Discovery**. Lewis in turn selected William Clark, who had once been his commanding officer, to help him lead the group (Figure 11.3).

(a)   (b)

Figure 11.3 Charles Willson Peale, celebrated portraitist of the American Revolution, painted both William Clark (a) and Meriwether Lewis (b) in 1810 and 1807, respectively, after they returned from their expedition west.

Jefferson wanted to improve the ability of American merchants to access the ports of China. Establishing a river route from St. Louis to the Pacific Ocean was crucial to capturing a portion of the fur trade that had proven so profitable to Great Britain. He also wanted to legitimize American claims to the land against rivals, such as Great Britain and Spain. Lewis and Clark were thus instructed to map the territory through which they would pass and to explore all tributaries of the Missouri River. This part of the expedition struck fear into Spanish officials, who believed that Lewis and Clark would encroach on New Mexico, the northern part of New Spain. Spain dispatched four unsuccessful expeditions from Santa Fe to intercept the explorers. Lewis and Clark also had directives to establish friendly relationships with the western tribes, introducing them to American trade goods and encouraging warring groups to make peace. Establishing an overland route to the Pacific would bolster U.S. claims to the Pacific Northwest, first established in 1792 when Captain Robert Gray sailed his ship *Columbia* into the mouth of the river that now bears his vessel's name and forms the present-day border between Oregon and Washington. Finally, Jefferson, who had a keen interest in science and nature, ordered Lewis and Clark to take extensive notes on the geography, plant life, animals, and natural resources of the region into which they would journey.

After spending the winter of 1803–1804 encamped at the mouth of the Missouri River while the men prepared for their expedition, the corps set off in May 1804. Although the thirty-three frontiersmen, boatmen, and hunters took with them Alexander Mackenzie's account of his explorations and the best maps they could find, they did not have any real understanding of the difficulties they would face. Fierce storms left them drenched and freezing. Enormous clouds of gnats and mosquitos swarmed about their heads as they made their way up the Missouri River. Along the way they encountered (and killed) a variety of animals including elk, buffalo, and grizzly bears. One member of the expedition survived a rattlesnake bite. As the men collected minerals and specimens of plants and animals, the overly curious Lewis sampled minerals by tasting them and became seriously ill at one point. What they did not collect, they sketched and documented in the journals they kept. They also noted the customs of the Indian tribes who controlled the land and attempted to establish peaceful relationships with them in order to ensure that future white settlement would not be impeded.

The corps spent their first winter in the wilderness, 1804–1805, in a Mandan village in what is now North Dakota. There they encountered a reminder of France's former vast North American empire when they met a French fur trapper named Toussaint Charbonneau. When the corps left in the spring of 1805, Charbonneau accompanied them as a guide and interpreter, bringing his teenage Shoshone wife Sacagawea and their newborn son. Charbonneau knew the land better than the Americans, and Sacagawea proved invaluable in many ways, not least of which was that the presence of a young woman and her infant convinced many groups that the men were not a war party and meant no harm (Figure 11.4).

Figure 11.4   In this idealized image, Sacagawea leads Lewis and Clark through the Montana wilderness. In reality, she was still a teenager at the time and served as interpreter; she did not actually guide the party, although legend says she did. Kidnapped as a child, she would not likely have retained detailed memories about the place where she grew up.

The corps set about making friends with native tribes while simultaneously attempting to assert American power over the territory. Hoping to overawe the people of the land, Lewis would let out a blast of his air rifle, a relatively new piece of technology the Indians had never seen. The corps also followed native custom by distributing gifts, including shirts, ribbons, and kettles, as a sign of goodwill. The explorers presented native leaders with medallions, many of which bore Jefferson's image, and invited them to visit their new "ruler" in the East. These medallions or peace medals were meant to allow future explorers to identify friendly native groups. Not all efforts to assert U.S. control went peacefully; some Indians rejected the explorers' intrusion onto their land. An encounter with the Blackfoot turned hostile, for example, and members of the corps killed two Blackfoot men.

After spending eighteen long months on the trail and nearly starving to death in the Bitterroot Mountains of Montana, the Corps of Discovery finally reached the Pacific Ocean in 1805 and spent the winter of 1805–1806 in Oregon. They returned to St. Louis later in 1806 having lost only one man, who had died of appendicitis. Upon their return, Meriwether Lewis was named governor of the Louisiana Territory. Unfortunately, he died only three years later in circumstances that are still disputed, before he could write a complete account of what the expedition had discovered.

Although the Corps of Discovery failed to find an all-water route to the Pacific Ocean (for none existed), it nevertheless accomplished many of the goals Jefferson had set. The men traveled across the North American continent and established relationships with many Indian tribes, paving the way for fur traders like John Jacob Astor who later established trading posts solidifying U.S. claims to Oregon. Delegates of several tribes did go to Washington to meet the president. Hundreds of plant and animal specimens were collected, several of which were named for Lewis and Clark in recognition of their efforts. And the territory was now more accurately mapped and legally claimed by the United States. Nonetheless, most of the vast territory, home to a variety of native peoples, remained unknown to Americans (Figure 11.5).

Figure 11.5 This 1814 map of Lewis and Clark's path across North America from the Missouri River to the Pacific Ocean was based on maps and notes made by William Clark. Although most of the West still remained unknown, the expedition added greatly to knowledge of what lay west of the Mississippi. Most important, it allowed the United States to solidify its claim to the immense territory.

AMERICANA

✪ *A Selection of Hats for the Fashionable Gentleman*

Beaver hats (Figure 11.6) were popular apparel in the eighteenth and nineteenth centuries in both Europe and the United States because they were naturally waterproof and bore a glossy sheen. Demand for beaver pelts (and for the pelts of sea otters, foxes, and martens) by hat makers, dressmakers, and tailors led many fur trappers into the wilderness in pursuit of riches. Beaver hats fell out of fashion in the 1850s when silk hats became the rage and beaver became harder to find. In some parts of the West, the animals had been hunted nearly to extinction.

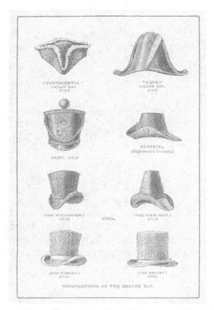

Figure 11.6 This illustration from *Castrologia, Or, The History and Traditions of the Canadian Beaver* shows a variety of beaver hat styles. Beaver pelts were also used to trim women's bonnets.

Are there any contemporary fashions or fads that likewise promise to alter the natural world?

SPANISH FLORIDA AND THE ADAMS-ONÍS TREATY

Despite the Lewis and Clark expedition, the boundaries of the Louisiana Purchase remained contested. Expansionists chose to believe the purchase included vast stretches of land, including all of Spanish Texas. The Spanish government disagreed, however. The first attempt to resolve this issue took place in February 1819 with the signing of the Adams-Onís Treaty, which was actually intended to settle the problem of Florida.

Spanish Florida had presented difficulties for its neighbors since the settlement of the original North American colonies, first for England and then for the United States. By 1819, American settlers no longer feared attack by Spanish troops garrisoned in Florida, but hostile tribes like the Creek and Seminole raided Georgia and then retreated to the relative safety of the Florida wilderness. These tribes also sheltered runaway slaves, often intermarrying with them and making them members of their tribes. Sparsely populated by Spanish colonists and far from both Mexico City and Madrid, the frontier in Florida proved next to impossible for the Spanish government to control.

In March 1818, General Andrew Jackson, frustrated by his inability to punish Creek and Seminole raiders, pursued them across the international border into Spanish Florida. Under Jackson's command, U.S. troops defeated the Creek and Seminole, occupied several Florida settlements, and executed two British citizens accused of acting against the United States. Outraged by the U.S. invasion of its territory, the Spanish government demanded that Jackson and his troops withdraw. In agreeing to the withdrawal, however, U.S. Secretary of State John Quincy Adams also offered to purchase the colony. Realizing that conflict between the United States and the Creeks and Seminoles would continue, Spain opted to cede the Spanish colony to its northern neighbor. The Adams-Onís Treaty, named for Adams and the Spanish ambassador, Luís de Onís, made the cession of Florida official while also setting the boundary between the United States and Mexico at the Sabine River (**Figure 11.7**). In exchange, Adams gave up U.S. claims to lands west of the Sabine and forgave Spain's $5 million debt to the United States.

The Adams-Onís Treaty

Figure 11.7 The red line indicates the border between U.S. and Spanish territory established by the Adams-Onís Treaty of 1819.

The Adams-Onís Treaty upset many American expansionists, who criticized Adams for not laying claim to all of Texas, which they believed had been included in the Louisiana Purchase. In the summer of 1819, James Long, a planter from Natchez, Mississippi, became a **filibuster**, or a private, unauthorized military adventurer, when he led three hundred men on an expedition across the Sabine River to take control of Texas. Long's men succeeded in capturing Nacogdoches, writing a Declaration of Independence (see below), and setting up a republican government. Spanish troops drove them out a month later. Returning in 1820 with a much smaller force, Long was arrested by the Spanish authorities, imprisoned, and killed. Long was but one of many nineteenth-century American filibusters who aimed at seizing territory in the Caribbean and Central America.

DEFINING "AMERICAN"

✹ *The Long Expedition's Declaration of Independence*

The Long Expedition's short-lived Republic of Texas was announced with the drafting of a Declaration of Independence in 1819. The declaration named settlers' grievances against the limits put on expansion by the Adams-Onís treaty and expressed their fears of Spain:

> The citizens of Texas have long indulged the hope, that in the adjustment of the boundaries of the Spanish possessions in America, and of the territories of the United States, that they should be included within the limits of the latter. The claims of the United States, long and strenuously urged, encouraged the hope. The recent [Adams-Onís] treaty between Spain and the United States of America has dissipated an illusion too long fondly cherished, and has roused the citizens of Texas . . . They have seen themselves . . . literally abandoned to the dominion of the crown of Spain and left a prey . . . to all those exactions which Spanish rapacity is fertile in devising. The citizens of Texas would have proved themselves unworthy of the age . . . unworthy of their ancestry, of the kindred of the republics of the American continent, could they have hesitated in this emergency . . . Spurning the fetters of colonial vassalage, disdaining to submit to the most atrocious despotism that ever disgraced the annals of Europe, they have resolved under the blessing of God to be free.

How did the filibusters view Spain? What do their actions say about the nature of American society and of U.S. expansion?

11.2 The Missouri Crisis

By the end of this section, you will be able to:
* Explain why the North and South differed over the admission of Missouri as a state
* Explain how the admission of new states to the Union threatened to upset the balance between free and slave states in Congress

Another stage of U.S. expansion took place when inhabitants of Missouri began petitioning for statehood beginning in 1817. The Missouri territory had been part of the Louisiana Purchase and was the first part of that vast acquisition to apply for statehood. By 1818, tens of thousands of settlers had flocked to Missouri, including slaveholders who brought with them some ten thousand slaves. When the status of the Missouri territory was taken up in earnest in the U.S. House of Representatives in early 1819, its admission to the Union proved to be no easy matter, since it brought to the surface a violent debate over whether slavery would be allowed in the new state.

Politicians had sought to avoid the issue of slavery ever since the 1787 Constitutional Convention arrived at an uneasy compromise in the form of the "three-fifths clause." This provision stated that the entirety of a state's free population and 60 percent of its enslaved population would be counted in establishing the number of that state's members in the House of Representatives and the size of its federal tax bill. Although slavery existed in several northern states at the time, the compromise had angered many northern politicians because, they argued, the "extra" population of slaves would give southern states more votes than they deserved in both the House and the Electoral College. Admitting Missouri as a slave state also threatened the tenuous balance between free and slave states in the Senate by giving slave states a two-vote advantage.

The debate about representation shifted to the morality of slavery itself when New York representative James Tallmadge, an opponent of slavery, attempted to amend the statehood bill in the House of Representatives. Tallmadge proposed that Missouri be admitted as a free state, that no more slaves be allowed to enter Missouri after it achieved statehood, and that all enslaved children born there after its admission be freed at age twenty-five. The amendment shifted the terms of debate by presenting slavery as an evil to be stopped.

Northern representatives supported the **Tallmadge Amendment**, denouncing slavery as immoral and opposed to the nation's founding principles of equality and liberty. Southerners in Congress rejected the amendment as an attempt to gradually abolish slavery—not just in Missouri but throughout the Union—by violating the property rights of slaveholders and their freedom to take their property wherever they wished. Slavery's apologists, who had long argued that slavery was a necessary evil, now began to perpetuate the idea that slavery was a positive good for the United States. They asserted that it generated wealth and left white men free to exercise their true talents instead of toiling in the soil, as the descendants of Africans were better suited to do. Slaves were cared for, supporters argued, and were better off exposed to the teachings of Christianity as slaves than living as free heathens in uncivilized Africa. Above all, the United States had a destiny, they argued, to create an empire of slavery throughout the Americas. These proslavery arguments were to be made repeatedly and forcefully as expansion to the West proceeded.

Most disturbing for the unity of the young nation, however, was that debaters divided along sectional lines, not party lines. With only a few exceptions, northerners supported the Tallmadge Amendment regardless of party affiliation, and southerners opposed it despite having party differences on other matters. It did not pass, and the crisis over Missouri led to strident calls of disunion and threats of civil war.

Congress finally came to an agreement, called the **Missouri Compromise**, in 1820. Missouri and Maine (which had been part of Massachusetts) would enter the Union at the same time, Maine as a free state, Missouri as a slave state. The Tallmadge Amendment was narrowly rejected, the balance between free and slave states was maintained in the Senate, and southerners did not have to fear that Missouri slaveholders would be deprived of their human property. To prevent similar conflicts each time a territory applied for statehood, a line coinciding with the southern border of Missouri (at latitude 36° 30') was drawn across the remainder of the Louisiana Territory (Figure 11.8). Slavery could exist south of this line but was forbidden north of it, with the obvious exception of Missouri.

Figure 11.8 The Missouri Compromise resulted in the District of Maine, which had originally been settled in 1607 by the Plymouth Company and was a part of Massachusetts, being admitted to the Union as a free state and Missouri being admitted as a slave state.

MY STORY

✸ *Thomas Jefferson on the Missouri Crisis*

On April 22, 1820, Thomas Jefferson wrote to John Holmes to express his reaction to the Missouri Crisis, especially the open threat of disunion and war:

> I thank you, Dear Sir, for the copy you have been so kind as to send me of the letter to your constituents on the Missouri question. it is a perfect justification to them. I had for a long time ceased to read the newspapers or pay any attention to public affairs, confident they were in good hands, and content to be a passenger in our bark to the shore from which I am not distant. but this momentous question [over slavery in Missouri], like a fire bell in the night, awakened and filled me with terror. I considered it at once as the knell of the Union. it is hushed indeed for the moment. but this is a reprieve only, not a final sentence. a geographical line, coinciding with a marked principle, moral and political, once concieved [sic] and held up to the angry passions of men, will never be obliterated; and every new irritation will mark it deeper and deeper. I can say with conscious truth that there is not a man on earth who would sacrifice more than I would, to relieve us from this heavy reproach, in any practicable way. . . .
>
> I regret that I am now to die in the belief that the useless sacrifice of themselves, by the generation of 76. to acquire self government and happiness to their country, is to be thrown away by the unwise and unworthy passions of their sons, and that my only consolation is to be that I live not to weep over it. if they would but dispassionately weigh the blessings they will throw away against an abstract principle more likely to be effected by union than by scission, they would pause before they would perpetuate this act of suicide themselves and of treason against the hopes of the world. to yourself as the faithful advocate of union I tender the offering of my high esteem and respect.
> Th. Jefferson

How would you characterize the former president's reaction? What do you think he means by writing that the Missouri Compromise line "is a reprieve only, not a final sentence"?

Click and Explore

Access a collection of primary documents relating to the Missouri Compromise, including Missouri's application for admission into the Union and Jefferson's correspondence on the Missouri question, at the Library of Congress (http://openstaxcollege.org/l/15MOComp) website.

11.3 Independence for Texas

By the end of this section, you will be able to:
- Explain why American settlers in Texas sought independence from Mexico
- Discuss early attempts to make Texas independent of Mexico
- Describe the relationship between Anglo-Americans and Tejanos in Texas before and after independence

As the incursions of the earlier filibusters into Texas demonstrated, American expansionists had desired this area of Spain's empire in America for many years. After the 1819 Adams-Onís treaty established the boundary between Mexico and the United States, more American expansionists began to move into the northern portion of Mexico's province of Coahuila y Texas. Following Mexico's independence from Spain in 1821, American settlers immigrated to Texas in even larger numbers, intent on taking the land from the new and vulnerable Mexican nation in order to create a new American slave state.

AMERICAN SETTLERS MOVE TO TEXAS

After the 1819 Adams-Onís Treaty defined the U.S.-Mexico boundary, Spain began actively encouraging Americans to settle their northern province. Texas was sparsely settled, and the few Mexican farmers and ranchers who lived there were under constant threat of attack by hostile Indian tribes, especially the Comanche, who supplemented their hunting with raids in pursuit of horses and cattle.

To increase the non-Indian population in Texas and provide a buffer zone between its hostile tribes and the rest of Mexico, Spain began to recruit *empresarios*. An **empresario** was someone who brought settlers to the region in exchange for generous grants of land. Moses Austin, a once-prosperous entrepreneur reduced to poverty by the Panic of 1819, requested permission to settle three hundred English-speaking American residents in Texas. Spain agreed on the condition that the resettled people convert to Roman Catholicism.

On his deathbed in 1821, Austin asked his son Stephen to carry out his plans, and Mexico, which had won independence from Spain the same year, allowed Stephen to take control of his father's grant. Like Spain, Mexico also wished to encourage settlement in the state of Coahuila y Texas and passed colonization laws to encourage immigration. Thousands of Americans, primarily from slave states, flocked to Texas and quickly came to outnumber the **Tejanos**, the Mexican residents of the region. The soil and climate offered good opportunities to expand slavery and the cotton kingdom. Land was plentiful and offered at generous terms. Unlike the U.S. government, Mexico allowed buyers to pay for their land in installments and did not require a minimum purchase. Furthermore, to many whites, it seemed not only their God-given right but also their patriotic duty to populate the lands beyond the Mississippi River, bringing with them American slavery, culture, laws, and political traditions (Figure 11.9).

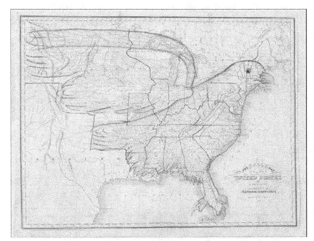

Figure 11.9 By the early 1830s, all the lands east of the Mississippi River had been settled and admitted to the Union as states. The land west of the river, though in this contemporary map united with the settled areas in the body of an eagle symbolizing the territorial ambitions of the United States, remained largely unsettled by white Americans. Texas (just southwest of the bird's tail feathers) remained outside the U.S. border.

THE TEXAS WAR FOR INDEPENDENCE

Many Americans who migrated to Texas at the invitation of the Mexican government did not completely shed their identity or loyalty to the United States. They brought American traditions and expectations with them (including, for many, the right to own slaves). For instance, the majority of these new settlers were Protestant, and though they were not required to attend the Catholic mass, Mexico's prohibition on the public practice of other religions upset them and they routinely ignored it.

Accustomed to representative democracy, jury trials, and the defendant's right to appear before a judge, the Anglo-American settlers in Texas also disliked the Mexican legal system, which provided for an initial hearing by an *alcalde*, an administrator who often combined the duties of mayor, judge, and law enforcement officer. The *alcalde* sent a written record of the proceeding to a judge in Saltillo, the state capital, who decided the outcome. Settlers also resented that at most two Texas representatives were allowed in the state legislature.

Their greatest source of discontent, though, was the Mexican government's 1829 abolition of slavery. Most American settlers were from southern states, and many had brought slaves with them. Mexico tried to accommodate them by maintaining the fiction that the slaves were indentured servants. But American slaveholders in Texas distrusted the Mexican government and wanted Texas to be a new U.S. slave state. The dislike of most for Roman Catholicism (the prevailing religion of Mexico) and a widely held belief in American racial superiority led them generally to regard Mexicans as dishonest, ignorant, and backward.

Belief in their own superiority inspired some Texans to try to undermine the power of the Mexican government. When *empresario* Haden Edwards attempted to evict people who had settled his land grant before he gained title to it, the Mexican government nullified its agreement with him. Outraged, Edwards and a small party of men took prisoner the *alcalde* of Nacogdoches. The Mexican army marched to the town, and Edwards and his troop then declared the formation of the Republic of Fredonia between the Sabine and Rio Grande Rivers. To demonstrate loyalty to their adopted country, a force led by Stephen Austin hastened to Nacogdoches to support the Mexican army. Edwards's revolt collapsed, and the revolutionaries fled Texas.

The growing presence of American settlers in Texas, their reluctance to abide by Mexican law, and their desire for independence caused the Mexican government to grow wary. In 1830, it forbade future U.S. immigration and increased its military presence in Texas. Settlers continued to stream illegally across the long border; by 1835, after immigration resumed, there were twenty thousand Anglo-Americans in Texas (Figure 11.10).

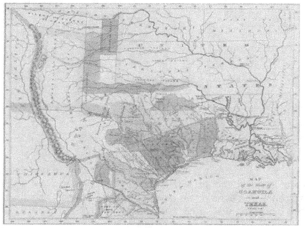

Figure 11.10 This 1833 map shows the extent of land grants made by Mexico to American settlers in Texas. Nearly all are in the eastern portion of the state, one factor that led to war with Mexico in 1846.

Fifty-five delegates from the Anglo-American settlements gathered in 1831 to demand the suspension of customs duties, the resumption of immigration from the United States, better protection from Indian tribes, the granting of promised land titles, and the creation of an independent state of Texas separate from Coahuila. Ordered to disband, the delegates reconvened in early April 1833 to write a constitution for an independent Texas. Surprisingly, General Antonio Lopez de Santa Anna, Mexico's new president, agreed to all demands, except the call for statehood (Figure 11.11). Coahuila y Texas made provisions for jury trials, increased Texas's representation in the state legislature, and removed restrictions on commerce.

Figure 11.11   This portrait of General Antonio Lopez de Santa Anna depicts the Mexican president and general in full military regalia.

Texans' hopes for independence were quashed in 1834, however, when Santa Anna dismissed the Mexican Congress and abolished all state governments, including that of Coahuila y Texas. In January 1835, reneging on earlier promises, he dispatched troops to the town of Anahuac to collect customs duties. Lawyer and soldier William B. Travis and a small force marched on Anahuac in June, and the fort surrendered. On October 2, Anglo-American forces met Mexican troops at the town of Gonzales; the Mexican troops fled and the Americans moved on to take San Antonio. Now more cautious, delegates to the Consultation of 1835 at San Felipe de Austin voted against declaring independence, instead drafting a statement, which became known as the Declaration of Causes, promising continued loyalty if Mexico returned to a constitutional form of government. They selected Henry Smith, leader of the Independence Party, as governor of Texas and placed Sam Houston, a former soldier who had been a congressman and governor of Tennessee, in charge of its small military force.

The Consultation delegates met again in March 1836. They declared their independence from Mexico and drafted a constitution calling for an American-style judicial system and an elected president and legislature. Significantly, they also established that slavery would not be prohibited in Texas. Many wealthy Tejanos supported the push for independence, hoping for liberal governmental reforms and economic benefits.

REMEMBER THE ALAMO!

Mexico had no intention of losing its northern province. Santa Anna and his army of four thousand had besieged San Antonio in February 1836. Hopelessly outnumbered, its two hundred defenders, under Travis, fought fiercely from their refuge in an old mission known as the Alamo (Figure 11.12). After ten days, however, the mission was taken and all but a few of the defenders were dead, including Travis and James Bowie, the famed frontiersman who was also a land speculator and slave trader. A few male survivors, possibly including the frontier legend and former Tennessee congressman Davy Crockett, were led outside the walls and executed. The few women and children inside the mission were allowed to leave with the only adult male survivor, a slave owned by Travis who was then freed by the Mexican Army. Terrified, they fled.

Figure 11.12 The *Fall of the Alamo*, painted by Theodore Gentilz fewer than ten years after this pivotal moment in the Texas Revolution, depicts the 1836 assault on the Alamo complex.

Although hungry for revenge, the Texas forces under Sam Houston nevertheless withdrew across Texas, gathering recruits as they went. Coming upon Santa Anna's encampment on the banks of San Jacinto River on April 21, 1836, they waited as the Mexican troops settled for an afternoon nap. Assured by Houston that "Victory is certain!" and told to "Trust in God and fear not!" the seven hundred men descended on a sleeping force nearly twice their number with cries of "Remember the Alamo!" Within fifteen minutes the Battle of San Jacinto was over. Approximately half the Mexican troops were killed, and the survivors, including Santa Anna, taken prisoner.

Santa Anna grudgingly signed a peace treaty and was sent to Washington, where he met with President Andrew Jackson and, under pressure, agreed to recognize an independent Texas with the Rio Grande River as its southwestern border. By the time the agreement had been signed, however, Santa Anna had been removed from power in Mexico. For that reason, the Mexican Congress refused to be bound by Santa Anna's promises and continued to insist that the renegade territory still belonged to Mexico.

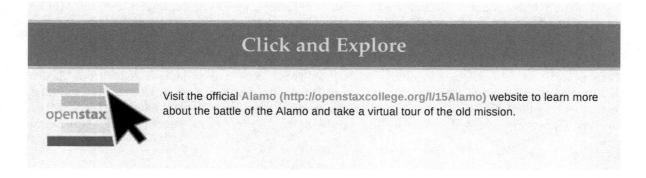

Click and Explore

Visit the official Alamo (http://openstaxcollege.org/l/15Alamo) website to learn more about the battle of the Alamo and take a virtual tour of the old mission.

THE LONE STAR REPUBLIC

In September 1836, military hero Sam Houston was elected president of Texas, and, following the relentless logic of U.S. expansion, Texans voted in favor of annexation to the United States. This had been the dream of many settlers in Texas all along. They wanted to expand the United States west and saw Texas as the next logical step. Slaveholders there, such as Sam Houston, William B. Travis and James Bowie (the latter two of whom died at the Alamo), believed too in the destiny of slavery. Mindful of the vicious debates over Missouri that had led to talk of disunion and war, American politicians were reluctant to annex Texas or, indeed, even to recognize it as a sovereign nation. Annexation would almost certainly mean war with Mexico, and the admission of a state with a large slave population, though permissible under the Missouri Compromise, would bring the issue of slavery once again to the fore. Texas had no choice but to organize itself as the independent Lone Star Republic. To protect itself from Mexican attempts to reclaim it, Texas sought and received recognition from France, Great Britain, Belgium, and the Netherlands. The United States did not officially recognize Texas as an independent nation until March 1837, nearly a year after the final victory over the Mexican army at San Jacinto.

Uncertainty about its future did not discourage Americans committed to expansion, especially slaveholders, from rushing to settle in the Lone Star Republic, however. Between 1836 and 1846, its population nearly tripled. By 1840, nearly twelve thousand enslaved Africans had been brought to Texas by American slaveholders. Many new settlers had suffered financial losses in the severe financial depression of 1837 and hoped for a new start in the new nation. According to folklore, across the United States, homes and farms were deserted overnight, and curious neighbors found notes reading only "GTT" ("Gone to Texas"). Many Europeans, especially Germans, also immigrated to Texas during this period.

In keeping with the program of ethnic cleansing and white racial domination, as illustrated by the image at the beginning of this chapter, Americans in Texas generally treated both Tejano and Indian residents with utter contempt, eager to displace and dispossess them. Anglo-American leaders failed to return the support their Tejano neighbors had extended during the rebellion and repaid them by seizing their lands. In 1839, the republic's militia attempted to drive out the Cherokee and Comanche.

The impulse to expand did not lay dormant, and Anglo-American settlers and leaders in the newly formed Texas republic soon cast their gaze on the Mexican province of New Mexico as well. Repeating the tactics of earlier filibusters, a Texas force set out in 1841 intent on taking Santa Fe. Its members encountered an army of New Mexicans and were taken prisoner and sent to Mexico City. On Christmas Day, 1842, Texans avenged a Mexican assault on San Antonio by attacking the Mexican town of Mier. In August, another Texas army was sent to attack Santa Fe, but Mexican troops forced them to retreat. Clearly, hostilities between Texas and Mexico had not ended simply because Texas had declared its independence.

11.4 The Mexican-American War, 1846–1848

By the end of this section, you will be able to:
- Identify the causes of the Mexican-American War
- Describe the outcomes of the war in 1848, especially the Mexican Cession
- Describe the effect of the California Gold Rush on westward expansion

Tensions between the United States and Mexico rapidly deteriorated in the 1840s as American expansionists eagerly eyed Mexican land to the west, including the lush northern Mexican province of California. Indeed, in 1842, a U.S. naval fleet, incorrectly believing war had broken out, seized Monterey, California, a part of Mexico. Monterey was returned the next day, but the episode only added to the uneasiness with which Mexico viewed its northern neighbor. The forces of expansion, however, could not be contained, and American voters elected James Polk in 1844 because he promised to deliver more lands. President Polk fulfilled his promise by gaining Oregon and, most spectacularly, provoking a war with Mexico that ultimately fulfilled the wildest fantasies of expansionists. By 1848, the United States encompassed much of North America, a republic that stretched from the Atlantic to the Pacific.

JAMES K. POLK AND THE TRIUMPH OF EXPANSION

A fervent belief in expansion gripped the United States in the 1840s. In 1845, a New York newspaper editor, John O'Sullivan, introduced the concept of "manifest destiny" to describe the very popular idea of the special role of the United States in overspreading the continent—the divine right and duty of white Americans to seize and settle the American West, thus spreading Protestant, democratic values. In this climate of opinion, voters in 1844 elected James K. Polk, a slaveholder from Tennessee, because he vowed to annex Texas as a new slave state and take Oregon.

Annexing Oregon was an important objective for U.S. foreign policy because it appeared to be an area rich in commercial possibilities. Northerners favored U.S. control of Oregon because ports in the Pacific Northwest would be gateways for trade with Asia. Southerners hoped that, in exchange for their support of expansion into the northwest, northerners would not oppose plans for expansion into the southwest.

President Polk—whose campaign slogan in 1844 had been "Fifty-four forty or fight!"—asserted the United States' right to gain full control of what was known as Oregon Country, from its southern border at 42° latitude (the current boundary with California) to its northern border at 54° 40' latitude. According to an 1818 agreement, Great Britain and the United States held joint ownership of this territory, but the 1827 Treaty of Joint Occupation opened the land to settlement by both countries. Realizing that the British were not willing to cede all claims to the territory, Polk proposed the land be divided at 49° latitude (the current border between Washington and Canada). The British, however, denied U.S. claims to land north of the Columbia River (Oregon's current northern border) (Figure 11.13). Indeed, the British foreign secretary refused even to relay Polk's proposal to London. However, reports of the difficulty Great Britain would face defending Oregon in the event of a U.S. attack, combined with concerns over affairs at home and elsewhere in its empire, quickly changed the minds of the British, and in June 1846, Queen Victoria's government agreed to a division at the forty-ninth parallel.

Figure 11.13 This map of the Oregon territory during the period of joint occupation by the United States and Great Britain shows the area whose ownership was contested by the two powers.

In contrast to the diplomatic solution with Great Britain over Oregon, when it came to Mexico, Polk and the American people proved willing to use force to wrest more land for the United States. In keeping with voters' expectations, President Polk set his sights on the Mexican state of California. After the mistaken capture of Monterey, negotiations about purchasing the port of San Francisco from Mexico broke off until September 1845. Then, following a revolt in California that left it divided in two, Polk attempted to purchase Upper California and New Mexico as well. These efforts went nowhere. The Mexican government, angered by U.S. actions, refused to recognize the independence of Texas.

Finally, after nearly a decade of public clamoring for the annexation of Texas, in December 1845 Polk officially agreed to the annexation of the former Mexican state, making the Lone Star Republic an additional slave state. Incensed that the United States had annexed Texas, however, the Mexican government refused to discuss the matter of selling land to the United States. Indeed, Mexico refused even to acknowledge Polk's emissary, John Slidell, who had been sent to Mexico City to negotiate. Not to be deterred, Polk encouraged Thomas O. Larkin, the U.S. consul in Monterey, to assist any American settlers and any **Californios**, the Mexican residents of the state, who wished to proclaim their independence from Mexico. By the end of 1845, having broken diplomatic ties with the United States over Texas and having grown alarmed by American actions in California, the Mexican government warily anticipated the next move. It did not have long to wait.

WAR WITH MEXICO, 1846–1848

Expansionistic fervor propelled the United States to war against Mexico in 1846. The United States had long argued that the Rio Grande was the border between Mexico and the United States, and at the end of the Texas war for independence Santa Anna had been pressured to agree. Mexico, however, refused to be bound by Santa Anna's promises and insisted the border lay farther north, at the Nueces River (Figure 11.14). To set it at the Rio Grande would, in effect, allow the United States to control land it had never occupied. In Mexico's eyes, therefore, President Polk violated its sovereign territory when he ordered U.S. troops into the disputed lands in 1846. From the Mexican perspective, it appeared the United States had invaded their nation.

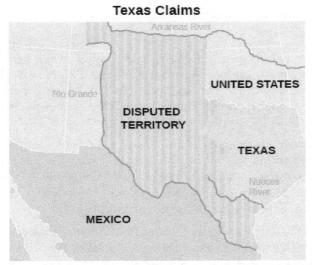

Figure 11.14 In 1845, when Texas joined the United States, Mexico insisted the United States had a right only to the territory northeast of the Nueces River. The United States argued in turn that it should have title to all land between the Nueces and the Rio Grande as well.

In January 1846, the U.S. force that was ordered to the banks of the Rio Grande to build a fort on the "American" side encountered a Mexican cavalry unit on patrol. Shots rang out, and sixteen U.S. soldiers were killed or wounded. Angrily declaring that Mexico "has invaded our territory and shed American blood upon American soil," President Polk demanded the United States declare war on Mexico. On May 12, Congress obliged.

The small but vocal antislavery faction decried the decision to go to war, arguing that Polk had deliberately provoked hostilities so the United States could annex more slave territory. Illinois representative Abraham Lincoln and other members of Congress issued the "Spot Resolutions" in which they demanded to know the precise spot on U.S. soil where American blood had been spilled. Many Whigs also denounced the war. Democrats, however, supported Polk's decision, and volunteers for the army came forward in droves from every part of the country except New England, the seat of abolitionist activity. Enthusiasm for the war was aided by the widely held belief that Mexico was a weak, impoverished country and that the Mexican people, perceived as ignorant, lazy, and controlled by a corrupt Roman Catholic clergy, would be easy to defeat. (**Figure 11.15**).

Figure 11.15   Anti-Catholic sentiment played an important role in the Mexican-American War. The American public widely regarded Roman Catholics as cowardly and vice-ridden, like the clergy in this ca. 1846 lithograph who are shown fleeing the Mexican town of Matamoros accompanied by pretty women and baskets full of alcohol. (credit: Library of Congress)

U.S. military strategy had three main objectives: 1) Take control of northern Mexico, including New Mexico; 2) seize California; and 3) capture Mexico City. General Zachary Taylor and his Army of the Center were assigned to accomplish the first goal, and with superior weapons they soon captured the Mexican city of Monterrey. Taylor quickly became a hero in the eyes of the American people, and Polk appointed him commander of all U.S. forces.

General Stephen Watts Kearny, commander of the Army of the West, accepted the surrender of Santa Fe, New Mexico, and moved on to take control of California, leaving Colonel Sterling Price in command. Despite Kearny's assurances that New Mexicans need not fear for their lives or their property, and in fact the region's residents rose in revolt in January 1847 in an effort to drive the Americans away. Although Price managed to put an end to the rebellion, tensions remained high.

Kearny, meanwhile, arrived in California to find it already in American hands through the joint efforts of California settlers, U.S. naval commander John D. Sloat, and John C. Fremont, a former army captain and son-in-law of Missouri senator Thomas Benton. Sloat, at anchor off the coast of Mazatlan, learned that war had begun and quickly set sail for California. He seized the town of Monterey in July 1846, less than a month after a group of American settlers led by William B. Ide had taken control of Sonoma and declared California a republic. A week after the fall of Monterey, the navy took San Francisco with no resistance. Although some Californios staged a short-lived rebellion in September 1846, many others submitted to the U.S. takeover. Thus Kearny had little to do other than take command of California as its governor.

Leading the Army of the South was General Winfield Scott. Both Taylor and Scott were potential competitors for the presidency, and believing—correctly—that whoever seized Mexico City would become a hero, Polk assigned Scott the campaign to avoid elevating the more popular Taylor, who was affectionately known as "Old Rough and Ready."

Scott captured Veracruz in March 1847, and moving in a northwesterly direction from there (much as Spanish conquistador Hernán Cortés had done in 1519), he slowly closed in on the capital. Every step of the way was a hard-fought victory, however, and Mexican soldiers and civilians both fought bravely to save their land from the American invaders. Mexico City's defenders, including young military cadets, fought to the end. According to legend, cadet Juan Escutia's last act was to save the Mexican flag, and he leapt from the city's walls with it wrapped around his body. On September 14, 1847, Scott entered Mexico City's central plaza; the city had fallen (Figure 11.16). While Polk and other expansionists called for "all Mexico," the Mexican government and the United States negotiated for peace in 1848, resulting in the Treaty of Guadalupe Hidalgo.

Figure 11.16 In *General Scott's Entrance into Mexico* (1851), Carl Nebel depicts General Winfield Scott on a white horse entering Mexico City's Plaza de la Constitución as anxious residents of the city watch. One woman peers furtively from behind the curtain of an upstairs window. On the left, a man bends down to pick up a paving stone to throw at the invaders.

The Treaty of Guadalupe Hidalgo, signed in February 1848, was a triumph for American expansionism under which Mexico ceded nearly half its land to the United States. The **Mexican Cession**, as the conquest of land west of the Rio Grande was called, included the current states of California, New Mexico, Arizona, Nevada, Utah, and portions of Colorado and Wyoming. Mexico also recognized the Rio Grande as the border with the United States. Mexican citizens in the ceded territory were promised U.S. citizenship in the future when the territories they were living in became states. In exchange, the United States agreed to assume $3.35 million worth of Mexican debts owed to U.S. citizens, paid Mexico $15 million for the loss of its land, and promised to guard the residents of the Mexican Cession from Indian raids.

As extensive as the Mexican Cession was, some argued the United States should not be satisfied until it had taken all of Mexico. Many who were opposed to this idea were southerners who, while desiring the annexation of more slave territory, did not want to make Mexico's large mestizo (people of mixed Indian and European ancestry) population part of the United States. Others did not want to absorb a large group of Roman Catholics. These expansionists could not accept the idea of new U.S. territory filled with mixed-race, Catholic populations.

Click and Explore

Explore the **U.S.-Mexican War (http://openstaxcollege.org/l/15MexAmWar)** at PBS to read about life in the Mexican and U.S. armies during the war and to learn more about the various battles.

CALIFORNIA AND THE GOLD RUSH

The United States had no way of knowing that part of the land about to be ceded by Mexico had just become far more valuable than anyone could have imagined. On January 24, 1848, James Marshall discovered gold in the millrace of the sawmill he had built with his partner John Sutter on the south fork of California's American River. Word quickly spread, and within a few weeks all of Sutter's employees had left to search for gold. When the news reached San Francisco, most of its inhabitants abandoned the town and headed for the American River. By the end of the year, thousands of California's residents had gone north to the gold fields with visions of wealth dancing in their heads, and in 1849 thousands of people from around the world followed them (Figure 11.17). The Gold Rush had begun.

Figure 11.17 Word about the discovery of gold in California in 1848 quickly spread and thousands soon made their way to the West Coast in search of quick riches.

The fantasy of instant wealth induced a mass exodus to California. Settlers in Oregon and Utah rushed to the American River. Easterners sailed around the southern tip of South America or to Panama's Atlantic coast, where they crossed the Isthmus of Panama to the Pacific and booked ship's passage for San Francisco. As California-bound vessels stopped in South American ports to take on food and fresh water, hundreds of Peruvians and Chileans streamed aboard. Easterners who could not afford to sail to California crossed the continent on foot, on horseback, or in wagons. Others journeyed from as far away as Hawaii and Europe. Chinese people came as well, adding to the polyglot population in the California boomtowns (Figure 11.18).

Figure 11.18 This Currier & Ives lithograph from 1849 imagines the extreme lengths that people might go to in order to be part of the California Gold Rush. In addition to the men with picks and shovels trying to reach the ship from the dock, airships and rocket are shown flying overhead. (credit: Library of Congress)

Once in California, gathered in camps with names like Drunkard's Bar, Angel's Camp, Gouge Eye, and Whiskeytown, the **"forty-niners"** did not find wealth so easy to come by as they had first imagined. Although some were able to find gold by panning for it or shoveling soil from river bottoms into sieve-like contraptions called rockers, most did not. The placer gold, the gold that had been washed down the mountains into streams and rivers, was quickly exhausted, and what remained was deep below ground. Independent miners were supplanted by companies that could afford not only to purchase hydraulic mining technology but also to hire laborers to work the hills. The frustration of many a miner was expressed in the words of Sullivan Osborne. In 1857, Osborne wrote that he had arrived in California "full of high hopes and bright anticipations of the future" only to find his dreams "have long since perished." Although $550 million worth of gold was found in California between 1849 and 1850, very little of it went to individuals.

Observers in the gold fields also reported abuse of Indians by miners. Some miners forced Indians to work their claims for them; others drove Indians off their lands, stole from them, and even murdered them. Foreigners were generally disliked, especially those from South America. The most despised, however, were the thousands of Chinese migrants. Eager to earn money to send to their families in Hong Kong and southern China, they quickly earned a reputation as frugal men and hard workers who routinely took over diggings others had abandoned as worthless and worked them until every scrap of gold had been found. Many American miners, often spendthrifts, resented their presence and discriminated against them, believing the Chinese, who represented about 8 percent of the nearly 300,000 who arrived, were depriving them of the opportunity to make a living.

Click and Explore

Visit **The Chinese in California (http://openstaxcollege.org/l/15ChinaCA)** to learn more about the experience of Chinese migrants who came to California in the Gold Rush era.

In 1850, California imposed a tax on foreign miners, and in 1858 it prohibited all immigration from China. Those Chinese who remained in the face of the growing hostility were often beaten and killed, and some Westerners made a sport of cutting off Chinese men's queues, the long braids of hair worn down their backs (**Figure 11.19**). In 1882, Congress took up the power to restrict immigration by banning the further immigration of Chinese.

Figure 11.19 "Pacific Chivalry: Encouragement to Chinese Immigration," which appeared in *Harper's Weekly* in 1869, depicts a white man attacking a Chinese man with a whip as he holds him by the queue. Americans sometimes forcefully cut off the queues of Chinese immigrants. This could have serious consequences for the victim. Until 1911, all Chinese men were required by their nation's law to wear the queue as a sign of loyalty. Miners returning to China without it could be put to death. (credit: Library of Congress)

As people flocked to California in 1849, the population of the new territory swelled from a few thousand to about 100,000. The new arrivals quickly organized themselves into communities, and the trappings of "civilized" life—stores, saloons, libraries, stage lines, and fraternal lodges—began to appear. Newspapers were established, and musicians, singers, and acting companies arrived to entertain the gold seekers. The epitome of these Gold Rush boomtowns was San Francisco, which counted only a few hundred residents in 1846 but by 1850 had reached a population of thirty-four thousand (**Figure 11.20**). So quickly did the territory grow that by 1850 California was ready to enter the Union as a state. When it sought admission, however, the issue of slavery expansion and sectional tensions emerged once again.

Figure 11.20 This daguerreotype shows the bustling port of San Francisco in January 1851, just a few months after San Francisco became part of the new U.S. state of California. (credit: Library of Congress)

11.5 Free Soil or Slave? The Dilemma of the West

By the end of this section, you will be able to:
- Describe the terms of the Wilmot Proviso
- Discuss why the Free-Soil Party objected to the westward expansion of slavery
- Explain why sectional and political divisions in the United States grew
- Describe the terms of the Compromise of 1850

The 1848 treaty with Mexico did not bring the United States domestic peace. Instead, the acquisition of new territory revived and intensified the debate over the future of slavery in the western territories, widening the growing division between North and South and leading to the creation of new single-issue parties. Increasingly, the South came to regard itself as under attack by radical northern abolitionists, and many northerners began to speak ominously of a southern drive to dominate American politics for the purpose of protecting slaveholders' human property. As tensions mounted and both sides hurled accusations, national unity frayed. Compromise became nearly impossible and antagonistic sectional rivalries replaced the idea of a unified, democratic republic.

THE LIBERTY PARTY, THE WILMOT PROVISO, AND THE ANTISLAVERY MOVEMENT

Committed to protecting white workers by keeping slavery out of the lands taken from Mexico, Pennsylvania congressman David Wilmot attached to an 1846 revenue bill an amendment that would prohibit slavery in the new territory. The **Wilmot Proviso** was not entirely new. Other congressmen had drafted similar legislation, and Wilmot's language was largely copied from the 1787 Northwest Ordinance that had banned slavery in that territory. His ideas were very controversial in the 1840s, however, because his proposals would prevent American slaveholders from bringing what they viewed as their lawful property, their slaves, into the western lands. The measure passed the House but was defeated in the Senate. When Polk tried again to raise revenue the following year (to pay for lands taken from Mexico), the Wilmot Proviso was reintroduced, this time calling for the prohibition of slavery not only in the Mexican Cession but in all U.S. territories. The revenue bill passed, but without the proviso.

That Wilmot, a loyal Democrat, should attempt to counter the actions of a Democratic president hinted at the party divisions that were to come. The 1840s were a particularly active time in the creation and reorganization of political parties and constituencies, mainly because of discontent with the positions of the mainstream Whig and Democratic Parties in regard to slavery and its extension into the territories. The first new party, the small and politically weak **Liberty Party** founded in 1840, was a single-issue party, as were many of those that followed it. Its members were abolitionists who fervently believed slavery was evil and should be ended, and that this was best accomplished by political means.

The Wilmot Proviso captured the "antislavery" sentiments during and after the Mexican War. Antislavery advocates differed from the abolitionists. While abolitionists called for the end of slavery everywhere, antislavery advocates, for various reasons, did not challenge the presence of slavery in the states where it already existed. Those who supported antislavery fervently opposed its expansion westward because, they argued, slavery would degrade white labor and reduce its value, cast a stigma upon hard-working whites, and deprive them of a chance to advance economically. The western lands, they argued, should be open to white men only—small farmers and urban workers for whom the West held the promise of economic advancement. Where slavery was entrenched, according to antislavery advocates, there was little land left for small farmers to purchase, and such men could not compete fairly with slaveholders who held large farms and gangs of slaves. Ordinary laborers suffered also; no one would pay a white man a decent wage when a slave worked for nothing. When labor was associated with loss of freedom, antislavery supporters argued, all white workers carried a stigma that marked them as little better than slaves.

Wilmot opposed the extension of slavery into the Mexican Cession not because of his concern for African Americans, but because of his belief that slavery hurt white workers, and that lands acquired by the government should be used to better the position of white small farmers and laborers. Work was not simply something that people did; it gave them dignity, but in a slave society, labor had no dignity. In response to these arguments, southerners maintained that laborers in northern factories were treated worse than slaves. Their work was tedious and low paid. Their meager income was spent on inadequate food, clothing, and shelter. There was no dignity in such a life. In contrast, they argued, southern slaves were provided with a home, the necessities of life, and the protection of their masters. Factory owners did not care for or protect their employees in the same way.

THE FREE-SOIL PARTY AND THE ELECTION OF 1848

The Wilmot Proviso was an issue of great importance to the Democrats. Would they pledge to support it? At the party's New York State convention in Buffalo, Martin Van Buren's antislavery supporters—called **Barnburners** because they were likened to farmers who were willing to burn down their own barn to get rid of a rat infestation—spoke in favor of the proviso. Their opponents, known as Hunkers, refused to support it. Angered, the Barnburners organized their own convention, where they chose antislavery, pro–Wilmot Proviso delegates to send to the Democrats' national convention in Baltimore. In this way, the controversy over the expansion of slavery divided the Democratic Party.

At the national convention, both sets of delegates were seated—the pro-proviso ones chosen by the Barnburners and the anti-proviso ones chosen by the Hunkers. When it came time to vote for the party's presidential nominee, the majority of votes were for Lewis Cass, an advocate of popular sovereignty. Popular sovereignty was the belief that citizens should be able to decide issues based on the principle of majority rule; in this case, residents of a territory should have the right to decide whether slavery would be allowed in it. Theoretically, this doctrine would allow slavery to become established in any U.S. territory, including those from which it had been banned by earlier laws.

Disgusted by the result, the Barnburners united with antislavery Whigs and former members of the Liberty Party to form a new political party—the **Free-Soil Party**, which took as its slogan "Free Soil, Free Speech, Free Labor, and Free Men." The party had one real goal—to oppose the extension of slavery into the territories (Figure 11.21). In the minds of its members and many other northerners of the time, southern slaveholders had marshaled their wealth and power to control national politics for the purpose of protecting the institution of slavery and extending it into the territories. Many in the Free-Soil Party believed in this far-reaching conspiracy of the slaveholding elite to control both foreign affairs and domestic policies for their own ends, a cabal that came to be known as the **Slave Power**.

SMOKING HIM OUT.

Figure 11.21 This political cartoon depicts Martin Van Buren and his son John, both Barnburners, forcing the slavery issue within the Democratic Party by "smoking out" fellow Democrat Lewis Cass on the roof. Their support of the Wilmot Proviso and the new Free-Soil Party is demonstrated by John's declaration, "That's you Dad! more 'Free-Soil.' We'll rat 'em out yet. Long life to Davy Wilmot." (credit: Library of Congress)

In the wake of the Mexican War, antislavery sentiment entered mainstream American politics when the new Free-Soil party promptly selected Martin Van Buren as its presidential candidate. For the first time, a national political party committed itself to the goal of stopping the expansion of slavery. The Democrats chose Lewis Cass, and the Whigs nominated General Zachary Taylor, as Polk had assumed they would. On Election Day, Democrats split their votes between Van Buren and Cass. With the strength of the Democratic vote diluted, Taylor won. His popularity with the American people served him well, and his status as a slaveholder helped him win the South.

Click and Explore

Visit the archives of the Gilder Lehrman Institute (http://openstaxcollege.org/l/15GerritSmith) to read an August 1848 letter from Gerrit Smith, a staunch abolitionist, regarding the Free-Soil candidate, Martin Van Buren. Smith played a major role in the Liberty Party and was their presidential candidate in 1848.

THE COMPROMISE OF 1850

The election of 1848 did nothing to quell the controversy over whether slavery would advance into the Mexican Cession. Some slaveholders, like President Taylor, considered the question a moot point because the lands acquired from Mexico were far too dry for growing cotton and therefore, they thought, no slaveholder would want to move there. Other southerners, however, argued that the question was not whether slaveholders *would* want to move to the lands of the Mexican Cession, but whether they *could* and still retain control of their slave property. Denying them the right to freely relocate with their lawful property was, they maintained, unfair and unconstitutional. Northerners argued, just as fervidly, that because Mexico had abolished slavery, no slaves currently lived in the Mexican Cession, and to introduce slavery there would extend it to a new territory, thus furthering the institution and giving the Slave Power more control over the United States. The strong current of antislavery sentiment—that is, the desire to protect white labor—only increased the opposition to the expansion of slavery into the West.

Most northerners, except members of the Free-Soil Party, favored popular sovereignty for California and the New Mexico territory. Many southerners opposed this position, however, for they feared residents of these regions might choose to outlaw slavery. Some southern politicians spoke ominously of secession from the United States. Free-Soilers rejected popular sovereignty and demanded that slavery be permanently excluded from the territories.

Beginning in January 1850, Congress worked for eight months on a compromise that might quiet the growing sectional conflict. Led by the aged Henry Clay, members finally agreed to the following:

1. California, which was ready to enter the Union, was admitted as a free state in accordance with its state constitution.
2. Popular sovereignty was to determine the status of slavery in New Mexico and Utah, even though Utah and part of New Mexico were north of the Missouri Compromise line.
3. The slave trade was banned in the nation's capital. Slavery, however, was allowed to remain.
4. Under a new fugitive slave law, those who helped runaway slaves or refused to assist in their return would be fined and possibly imprisoned.
5. The border between Texas and New Mexico was established.

The **Compromise of 1850** brought temporary relief. It resolved the issue of slavery in the territories for the moment and prevented secession. The peace would not last, however. Instead of relieving tensions between North and South, it had actually made them worse.

Download for free at http://cnx.org/content/col11740/latest/

Key Terms

alcalde a Mexican official who often served as combined civil administrator, judge, and law enforcement officer

Barnburners northern Democrats loyal to Martin Van Buren who opposed the extension of slavery into the territories and broke away from the main party when it nominated a pro-popular sovereignty candidate

Californios Mexican residents of California

Compromise of 1850 five separate laws passed by Congress in September 1850 to resolve issues stemming from the Mexican Cession and the sectional crisis

Corps of Discovery the group led by Meriwether Lewis and William Clark on the expedition to explore and map the territory acquired in the Louisiana Purchase

empresario a person who brought new settlers to Texas in exchange for a grant of land

filibuster a person who engages in an unofficial military operation intended to seize land from foreign countries or foment revolution there

forty-niners the nickname for those who traveled to California in 1849 in hopes of finding gold

Free-Soil Party a political party that sought to exclude slavery from the western territories, leaving these areas open for settlement by white farmers and ensuring that white laborers would not have to compete with slaves

Liberty Party a political party formed in 1840 by those who believed political measures were the best means by which abolition could be accomplished

Mexican Cession the lands west of the Rio Grande ceded to the United States by Mexico in 1848, including California, Arizona, New Mexico, Nevada, Utah, and parts of Wyoming and Colorado

Missouri Compromise an agreement reached in Congress in 1820 that allowed Missouri to enter the Union as a slave state, brought Maine into the Union as a free state, and prohibited slavery north of 36° 30' latitude

Northwest Passage the nonexistent all-water route across the North American continent sought by European and American explorers

Slave Power a term northerners used to describe the disproportionate influence that they felt elite southern slaveholders wielded in both domestic and international affairs

Tallmadge Amendment an amendment (which did not pass) proposed by representative James Tallmadge in 1819 that called for Missouri to be admitted as a free state and for all slaves there to be gradually emancipated

Tejanos Mexican residents of Texas

Wilmot Proviso an amendment to a revenue bill that would have barred slavery from all the territory acquired from Mexico

Summary

11.1 Lewis and Clark

In 1803, Thomas Jefferson appointed Meriwether Lewis to organize an expedition into the Louisiana Territory to explore and map the area but also to find an all-water route from the Missouri River to the Pacific Coast. The Louisiana Purchase and the journey of Lewis and Clark's Corps of Discovery captured the imagination of many, who dedicated themselves to the economic exploitation of the western lands and the expansion of American influence and power. In the South, the Adams-Onís treaty legally secured Florida for the United States, though it did nothing to end the resistance of the Seminoles against American expansionists. At the same time, the treaty frustrated those Americans who considered Texas a part of the Louisiana Purchase. Taking matters into their own hands, some American settlers tried to take Texas by force.

11.2 The Missouri Crisis

The Missouri Crisis created a division over slavery that profoundly and ominously shaped sectional identities and rivalries as never before. Conflict over the uneasy balance between slave and free states in Congress came to a head when Missouri petitioned to join the Union as a slave state in 1819, and the debate broadened from simple issues of representation to a critique of the morality of slavery. The debates also raised the specter of disunion and civil war, leading many, including Thomas Jefferson, to fear for the future of the republic. Under the Missouri Compromise, Missouri and Maine entered the Union at the same time, Maine as a free state, Missouri as a slave state, and a line was drawn across the remainder of the Louisiana territory north of which slavery was forbidden.

11.3 Independence for Texas

The establishment of the Lone Star Republic formed a new chapter in the history of U.S. westward expansion. In contrast to the addition of the Louisiana Territory through diplomacy with France, Americans in Texas employed violence against Mexico to achieve their goals. Orchestrated largely by slaveholders, the acquisition of Texas appeared the next logical step in creating an American empire that included slavery. Nonetheless, with the Missouri Crisis in mind, the United States refused the Texans' request to enter the United States as a slave state in 1836. Instead, Texas formed an independent republic where slavery was legal. But American settlers there continued to press for more land. The strained relationship between expansionists in Texas and Mexico in the early 1840s hinted of things to come.

11.4 The Mexican-American War, 1846–1848

President James K. Polk's administration was a period of intensive expansion for the United States. After overseeing the final details regarding the annexation of Texas from Mexico, Polk negotiated a peaceful settlement with Great Britain regarding ownership of the Oregon Country, which brought the United States what are now the states of Washington and Oregon. The acquisition of additional lands from Mexico, a country many in the United States perceived as weak and inferior, was not so bloodless. The Mexican Cession added nearly half of Mexico's territory to the United States, including New Mexico and California, and established the U.S.-Mexico border at the Rio Grande. The California Gold Rush rapidly expanded the population of the new territory, but also prompted concerns over immigration, especially from China.

11.5 Free Soil or Slave? The Dilemma of the West

The acquisition of lands from Mexico in 1848 reawakened debates regarding slavery. The suggestion that slavery be barred from the Mexican Cession caused rancorous debate between North and South and split the Democratic Party when many northern members left to create the Free-Soil Party. Although the

Download for free at http://cnx.org/content/col11740/latest/

Compromise of 1850 resolved the question of whether slavery would be allowed in the new territories, the solution pleased no one. The peace brought by the compromise was short-lived, and the debate over slavery continued.

Review Questions

1. As a result of the Adams-Onís Treaty, the United States gained which territory from Spain?
  A. Florida
  B. New Mexico
  C. California
  D. Nevada

2. The Long Expedition established a short-lived republic in Texas known as _____.
  A. the Lone Star Republic
  B. the Republic of Texas
  C. Columbiana
  D. the Republic of Fredonia

3. For what purposes did Thomas Jefferson send Lewis and Clark to explore the Louisiana Territory? What did he want them to accomplish?

4. A proposal to prohibit the importation of slaves to Missouri following its admission to the United States was made by _____.
  A. John C. Calhoun
  B. Henry Clay
  C. James Tallmadge
  D. John Quincy Adams

5. To balance votes in the Senate, _____ was admitted to the Union as a free state at the same time that Missouri was admitted as a slave state.
  A. Florida
  B. Maine
  C. New York
  D. Arkansas

6. Why did the Missouri Crisis trigger threats of disunion and war? Identify the positions of both southern slaveholders and northern opponents of the spread of slavery.

7. Texas won its independence from Mexico in _____.
  A. 1821
  B. 1830
  C. 1836

  D. 1845

8. Texans defeated the army of General Antonio Lopez de Santa Anna at the battle of _____.
  A. the Alamo
  B. San Jacinto
  C. Nacogdoches
  D. Austin

9. How did Texas settlers' view of Mexico and its people contribute to the history of Texas in the 1830s?

10. Which of the following was *not* a reason the United States was reluctant to annex Texas?
  A. The United States did not want to fight a war with Mexico.
  B. Annexing Texas would add more slave territory to the United States and anger abolitionists.
  C. Texans considered U.S. citizens inferior and did not want to be part of their country.
  D. Adding Texas would upset the balance between free and slave states in Congress.

11. According to treaties signed in 1818 and 1827, with which country did the United States jointly occupy Oregon?
  A. Great Britain
  B. Spain
  C. Mexico
  D. France

12. During the war between the United States and Mexico, revolts against U.S. control broke out in _____.
  A. Florida and Texas
  B. New Mexico and California
  C. California and Texas
  D. Florida and California

13. Why did whites in California dislike the Chinese so much?

14. The practice of allowing residents of territories to decide whether their land should be slave or free was called _____.

    A. the democratic process

    B. the Wilmot Proviso

    C. popular sovereignty

    D. the Free Soil solution

15. Which of the following was not a provision of the Compromise of 1850?

    A. California was admitted as a free state.

    B. Slavery was abolished in Washington, DC.

    C. A stronger fugitive slave law was passed.

    D. Residents of New Mexico and Utah were to decide for themselves whether their territories would be slave or free.

16. Describe the events leading up to the formation of the Free-Soil Party.

Critical Thinking Questions

17. Consider the role of filibusters in American expansion. What are some arguments in favor of filibustering? What are some arguments against it?

18. What are the economic and political issues raised by having an imbalance between free and slave states? Why did the balance of free and slave states matter?

19. How did Anglo-American settlers in Texas see themselves? Did they adopt a Mexican identity because they were living in Mexican territory? Why or why not?

20. Consider the annexation of Texas and the Mexican-American War from a Mexican perspective. What would you find objectionable about American actions, foreign policy, and attitudes in the 1840s?

21. Describe the place of Texas in the history of American westward expansion by comparing Texas's early history to the Missouri Crisis in 1819–1820. What are the similarities and what are the differences?

22. Consider the arguments over the expansion of slavery made by both northerners and southerners in the aftermath of the U.S. victory over Mexico. Who had the more compelling case? Or did each side make equally significant arguments?

CHAPTER 12

Cotton is King: The Antebellum South, 1800–1860

Figure 12.1 *Bateaux à Vapeur Géant, la Nouvelle-Orléans 1853* (*Giant Steamboats at New Orleans, 1853*), by Hippolyte Sebron, shows how New Orleans, at the mouth of the Mississippi River, was the primary trading hub for the cotton that fueled the growth of the southern economy.

Chapter Outline
12.1 The Economics of Cotton
12.2 African Americans in the Antebellum United States
12.3 Wealth and Culture in the South
12.4 The Filibuster and the Quest for New Slave States

Introduction

Nine new slave states entered the Union between 1789 and 1860, rapidly expanding and transforming the South into a region of economic growth built on slave labor. In the image above (Figure 12.1), innumerable slaves load cargo onto a steamship in the Port of New Orleans, the commercial center of the antebellum South, while two well-dressed white men stand by talking. Commercial activity extends as far as the eye can see.

By the mid-nineteenth century, southern commercial centers like New Orleans had become home to the greatest concentration of wealth in the United States. While most white southerners did not own slaves, they aspired to join the ranks of elite slaveholders, who played a key role in the politics of both the South and the nation. Meanwhile, slavery shaped the culture and society of the South, which rested on a racial ideology of white supremacy and a vision of the United States as a white man's republic. Slaves endured the traumas of slavery by creating their own culture and using the Christian message of redemption to find hope for a world of freedom without violence.

12.1 The Economics of Cotton

By the end of this section, you will be able to:
- Explain the labor-intensive processes of cotton production
- Describe the importance of cotton to the Atlantic and American antebellum economy

In the **antebellum** era—that is, in the years before the Civil War—American planters in the South continued to grow Chesapeake tobacco and Carolina rice as they had in the colonial era. Cotton, however, emerged as the antebellum South's major commercial crop, eclipsing tobacco, rice, and sugar in economic importance. By 1860, the region was producing two-thirds of the world's cotton. In 1793, Eli Whitney revolutionized the production of cotton when he invented the **cotton gin**, a device that separated the seeds from raw cotton. Suddenly, a process that was extraordinarily labor-intensive when done by hand could be completed quickly and easily. American plantation owners, who were searching for a successful staple crop to compete on the world market, found it in cotton.

As a commodity, cotton had the advantage of being easily stored and transported. A demand for it already existed in the industrial textile mills in Great Britain, and in time, a steady stream of slave-grown American cotton would also supply northern textile mills. Southern cotton, picked and processed by American slaves, helped fuel the nineteenth-century Industrial Revolution in both the United States and Great Britain.

KING COTTON

Almost no cotton was grown in the United States in 1787, the year the federal constitution was written. However, following the War of 1812, a huge increase in production resulted in the so-called **cotton boom**, and by midcentury, cotton became the key **cash crop** (a crop grown to sell rather than for the farmer's sole use) of the southern economy and the most important American commodity. By 1850, of the 3.2 million slaves in the country's fifteen slave states, 1.8 million were producing cotton; by 1860, slave labor was producing over two billion pounds of cotton per year. Indeed, American cotton soon made up two-thirds of the global supply, and production continued to soar. By the time of the Civil War, South Carolina

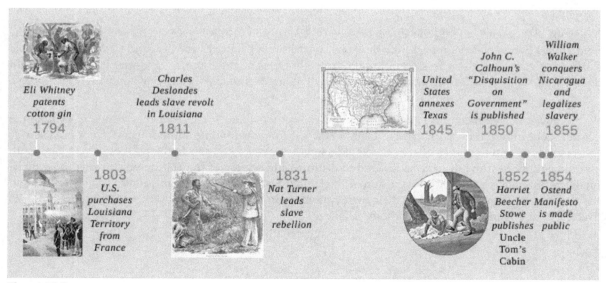

Figure 12.2

Download for free at http://cnx.org/content/col11740/latest/

politician James Hammond confidently proclaimed that the North could never threaten the South because "cotton is king."

The crop grown in the South was a hybrid: *Gossypium barbadense*, known as Petit Gulf cotton, a mix of Mexican, Georgia, and Siamese strains. Petit Gulf cotton grew extremely well in different soils and climates. It dominated cotton production in the Mississippi River Valley—home of the new slave states of Louisiana, Mississippi, Arkansas, Tennessee, Kentucky, and Missouri—as well as in other states like Texas. Whenever new slave states entered the Union, white slaveholders sent armies of slaves to clear the land in order to grow and pick the lucrative crop. The phrase "to be sold down the river," used by Harriet Beecher Stowe in her 1852 novel *Uncle Tom's Cabin*, refers to this forced migration from the upper southern states to the Deep South, lower on the Mississippi, to grow cotton.

The slaves who built this cotton kingdom with their labor started by clearing the land. Although the Jeffersonian vision of the settlement of new U.S. territories entailed white yeoman farmers single-handedly carving out small independent farms, the reality proved quite different. Entire old-growth forests and cypress swamps fell to the axe as slaves labored to strip the vegetation to make way for cotton. With the land cleared, slaves readied the earth by plowing and planting. To ambitious white planters, the extent of new land available for cotton production seemed almost limitless, and many planters simply leapfrogged from one area to the next, abandoning their fields every ten to fifteen years after the soil became exhausted. Theirs was a world of mobility and restlessness, a constant search for the next area to grow the valuable crop. Slaves composed the vanguard of this American expansion to the West.

Cotton planting took place in March and April, when slaves planted seeds in rows around three to five feet apart. Over the next several months, from April to August, they carefully tended the plants. Weeding the cotton rows took significant energy and time. In August, after the cotton plants had flowered and the flowers had begun to give way to cotton bolls (the seed-bearing capsule that contains the cotton fiber), all the plantation's slaves—men, women, and children—worked together to pick the crop (Figure 12.3). On each day of cotton picking, slaves went to the fields with sacks, which they would fill as many times as they could. The effort was laborious, and a white "driver" employed the lash to make slaves work as quickly as possible.

Figure 12.3 In the late nineteenth century, J. N. Wilson captured this image of harvest time at a southern plantation. While the workers in this photograph are not slave laborers, the process of cotton harvesting shown here had changed little from antebellum times.

Cotton planters projected the amount of cotton they could harvest based on the number of slaves under their control. In general, planters expected a good "hand," or slave, to work ten acres of land and pick two hundred pounds of cotton a day. An overseer or master measured each individual slave's daily yield.

Great pressure existed to meet the expected daily amount, and some masters whipped slaves who picked less than expected.

Cotton picking occurred as many as seven times a season as the plant grew and continued to produce bolls through the fall and early winter. During the picking season, slaves worked from sunrise to sunset with a ten-minute break at lunch; many slaveholders tended to give them little to eat, since spending on food would cut into their profits. Other slaveholders knew that feeding slaves could increase productivity and therefore provided what they thought would help ensure a profitable crop. The slaves' day didn't end after they picked the cotton; once they had brought it to the gin house to be weighed, they then had to care for the animals and perform other chores. Indeed, slaves often maintained their own gardens and livestock, which they tended after working the cotton fields, in order to supplement their supply of food.

Sometimes the cotton was dried before it was ginned (put through the process of separating the seeds from the cotton fiber). The cotton gin allowed a slave to remove the seeds from fifty pounds of cotton a day, compared to one pound if done by hand. After the seeds had been removed, the cotton was pressed into bales. These bales, weighing about four hundred to five hundred pounds, were wrapped in burlap cloth and sent down the Mississippi River.

Click and Explore

Visit the Internet Archive (http://openstaxcollege.org/l/15LoadCotton) to watch a 1937 WPA film showing cotton bales being loaded onto a steamboat.

As the cotton industry boomed in the South, the Mississippi River quickly became the essential water highway in the United States. Steamboats, a crucial part of the transportation revolution thanks to their enormous freight-carrying capacity and ability to navigate shallow waterways, became a defining component of the cotton kingdom. Steamboats also illustrated the class and social distinctions of the antebellum age. While the decks carried precious cargo, ornate rooms graced the interior. In these spaces, whites socialized in the ship's saloons and dining halls while black slaves served them (Figure 12.4).

Figure 12.4 As in this depiction of the saloon of the Mississippi River steamboat *Princess*, elegant and luxurious rooms often occupied the interiors of antebellum steamships, whose decks were filled with cargo.

Investors poured huge sums into steamships. In 1817, only seventeen plied the waters of western rivers, but by 1837, there were over seven hundred steamships in operation. Major new ports developed at St. Louis, Missouri; Memphis, Tennessee; and other locations. By 1860, some thirty-five hundred vessels were steaming in and out of New Orleans, carrying an annual cargo made up primarily of cotton that amounted to $220 million worth of goods (approximately $6.5 billion in 2014 dollars).

New Orleans had been part of the French empire before the United States purchased it, along with the rest of the Louisiana Territory, in 1803. In the first half of the nineteenth century, it rose in prominence and importance largely because of the cotton boom, steam-powered river traffic, and its strategic position near the mouth of the Mississippi River. Steamboats moved down the river transporting cotton grown on plantations along the river and throughout the South to the port at New Orleans. From there, the bulk of American cotton went to Liverpool, England, where it was sold to British manufacturers who ran the cotton mills in Manchester and elsewhere. This lucrative international trade brought new wealth and new residents to the city. By 1840, New Orleans alone had 12 percent of the nation's total banking capital, and visitors often commented on the great cultural diversity of the city. In 1835, Joseph Holt Ingraham wrote: "Truly does New-Orleans represent every other city and nation upon earth. I know of none where is congregated so great a variety of the human species." Slaves, cotton, and the steamship transformed the city from a relatively isolated corner of North America in the eighteenth century to a thriving metropolis that rivaled New York in importance (Figure 12.5).

Figure 12.5 This print of *The Levee - New Orleans* (1884) shows the bustling port of New Orleans with bales of cotton waiting to be shipped. The sheer volume of cotton indicates its economic importance throughout the century.

THE DOMESTIC SLAVE TRADE

The South's dependence on cotton was matched by its dependence on slaves to harvest the cotton. Despite the rhetoric of the Revolution that "all men are created equal," slavery not only endured in the American republic but formed the very foundation of the country's economic success. Cotton and slavery occupied a central—and intertwined—place in the nineteenth-century economy.

In 1807, the U.S. Congress abolished the foreign slave trade, a ban that went into effect on January 1, 1808. After this date, importing slaves from Africa became illegal in the United States. While smuggling continued to occur, the end of the international slave trade meant that domestic slaves were in very high demand. Fortunately for Americans whose wealth depended upon the exploitation of slave labor, a fall in the price of tobacco had caused landowners in the Upper South to reduce their production of this crop and use more of their land to grow wheat, which was far more profitable. While tobacco was a labor-intensive crop that required many people to cultivate it, wheat was not. Former tobacco farmers in the older states of Virginia and Maryland found themselves with "surplus" slaves whom they were obligated to feed, clothe, and shelter. Some slaveholders responded to this situation by freeing slaves; far more decided to sell their excess bondsmen. Virginia and Maryland therefore took the lead in the **domestic slave trade**, the trading of slaves within the borders of the United States.

The domestic slave trade offered many economic opportunities for white men. Those who sold their slaves could realize great profits, as could the slave brokers who served as middlemen between sellers and buyers. Other white men could benefit from the trade as owners of warehouses and pens in which slaves were held, or as suppliers of clothing and food for slaves on the move. Between 1790 and 1859, slaveholders in Virginia sold more than half a million slaves. In the early part of this period, many of these slaves were sold to people living in Kentucky, Tennessee, and North and South Carolina. By the 1820s, however, people in Kentucky and the Carolinas had begun to sell many of their slaves as well. Maryland slave dealers sold at least 185,000 slaves. Kentucky slaveholders sold some seventy-one thousand individuals. Most of the slave traders carried these slaves further south to Alabama, Louisiana, and Mississippi. New Orleans, the hub of commerce, boasted the largest slave market in the United States and grew to become the nation's fourth-largest city as a result. Natchez, Mississippi, had the second-largest market. In Virginia, Maryland, the Carolinas, and elsewhere in the South, slave auctions happened every day.

All told, the movement of slaves in the South made up one of the largest forced internal migrations in the United States. In each of the decades between 1820 and 1860, about 200,000 people were sold and relocated. The 1800 census recorded over one million African Americans, of which nearly 900,000 were slaves. By 1860, the total number of African Americans increased to 4.4 million, and of that number, 3.95 million were held in bondage. For many slaves, the domestic slave trade incited the terror of being sold away from family and friends.

Download for free at http://cnx.org/content/col11740/latest/

MY STORY

✪ *Solomon Northup Remembers the New Orleans Slave Market*

Solomon Northup was a free black man living in Saratoga, New York, when he was kidnapped and sold into slavery in 1841. He later escaped and wrote a book about his experiences: *Twelve Years a Slave. Narrative of Solomon Northup, a Citizen of New-York, Kidnapped in Washington City in 1841 and Rescued in 1853* (the basis of a 2013 Academy Award–winning film). This excerpt derives from Northup's description of being sold in New Orleans, along with fellow slave Eliza and her children Randall and Emily.

> One old gentleman, who said he wanted a coachman, appeared to take a fancy to me. . . .
> The same man also purchased Randall. The little fellow was made to jump, and run across
> the floor, and perform many other feats, exhibiting his activity and condition. All the time the
> trade was going on, Eliza was crying aloud, and wringing her hands. She besought the man
> not to buy him, unless he also bought her self and Emily. . . . Freeman turned round to her,
> savagely, with his whip in his uplifted hand, ordering her to stop her noise, or he would flog
> her. He would not have such work—such snivelling; and unless she ceased that minute, he
> would take her to the yard and give her a hundred lashes. . . . Eliza shrunk before him, and
> tried to wipe away her tears, but it was all in vain. She wanted to be with her children, she
> said, the little time she had to live. All the frowns and threats of Freeman, could not wholly
> silence the afflicted mother.

What does Northup's narrative tell you about the experience of being a slave? How does he characterize Freeman, the slave trader? How does he characterize Eliza?

THE SOUTH IN THE AMERICAN AND WORLD MARKETS

The first half of the nineteenth century saw a market revolution in the United States, one in which industrialization brought changes to both the production and the consumption of goods. Some southerners of the time believed that their region's reliance on a single cash crop and its use of slaves to produce it gave the South economic independence and made it immune from the effects of these changes, but this was far from the truth. Indeed, the production of cotton brought the South more firmly into the larger American and Atlantic markets. Northern mills depended on the South for supplies of raw cotton that was then converted into textiles. But this domestic cotton market paled in comparison to the Atlantic market. About 75 percent of the cotton produced in the United States was eventually exported abroad. Exporting at such high volumes made the United States the undisputed world leader in cotton production. Between the years 1820 and 1860, approximately 80 percent of the global cotton supply was produced in the United States. Nearly all the exported cotton was shipped to Great Britain, fueling its burgeoning textile industry and making the powerful British Empire increasingly dependent on American cotton and southern slavery.

The power of cotton on the world market may have brought wealth to the South, but it also increased its economic dependence on other countries and other parts of the United States. Much of the corn and pork that slaves consumed came from farms in the West. Some of the inexpensive clothing, called "slops," and shoes worn by slaves were manufactured in the North. The North also supplied the furnishings found in the homes of both wealthy planters and members of the middle class. Many of the trappings of domestic life, such as carpets, lamps, dinnerware, upholstered furniture, books, and musical instruments—all the accoutrements of comfortable living for southern whites—were made in either the North or Europe. Southern planters also borrowed money from banks in northern cities, and in the southern summers, took advantage of the developments in transportation to travel to resorts at Saratoga, New York; Litchfield, Connecticut; and Newport, Rhode Island.

12.2 African Americans in the Antebellum United States

By the end of this section, you will be able to:
- Discuss the similarities and differences in the lives of slaves and free blacks
- Describe the independent culture and customs that slaves developed

In addition to cotton, the great commodity of the antebellum South was human chattel. Slavery was the cornerstone of the southern economy. By 1850, about 3.2 million slaves labored in the United States, 1.8 million of whom worked in the cotton fields. Slaves faced arbitrary power abuses from whites; they coped by creating family and community networks. Storytelling, song, and Christianity also provided solace and allowed slaves to develop their own interpretations of their condition.

LIFE AS A SLAVE

Southern whites frequently relied upon the idea of **paternalism**—the premise that white slaveholders acted in the best interests of slaves, taking responsibility for their care, feeding, discipline, and even their Christian morality—to justify the existence of slavery. This grossly misrepresented the reality of slavery, which was, by any measure, a dehumanizing, traumatizing, and horrifying human disaster and crime against humanity. Nevertheless, slaves were hardly passive victims of their conditions; they sought and found myriad ways to resist their shackles and develop their own communities and cultures.

Slaves often used the notion of paternalism to their advantage, finding opportunities within this system to engage in acts of resistance and win a degree of freedom and autonomy. For example, some slaves played into their masters' racism by hiding their intelligence and feigning childishness and ignorance. The slaves could then slow down the workday and sabotage the system in small ways by "accidentally" breaking tools, for example; the master, seeing his slaves as unsophisticated and childlike, would believe these incidents were accidents rather than rebellions. Some slaves engaged in more dramatic forms of resistance, such as poisoning their masters slowly. Other slaves reported rebellious slaves to their masters, hoping to gain preferential treatment. Slaves who informed their masters about planned slave rebellions could often expect the slaveholder's gratitude and, perhaps, more lenient treatment. Such expectations were always tempered by the individual personality and caprice of the master.

Slaveholders used both psychological coercion and physical violence to prevent slaves from disobeying their wishes. Often, the most efficient way to discipline slaves was to threaten to sell them. The lash, while the most common form of punishment, was effective but not efficient; whippings sometimes left slaves incapacitated or even dead. Slave masters also used punishment gear like neck braces, balls and chains, leg irons, and paddles with holes to produce blood blisters. Slaves lived in constant terror of both physical violence and separation from family and friends (Figure 12.6).

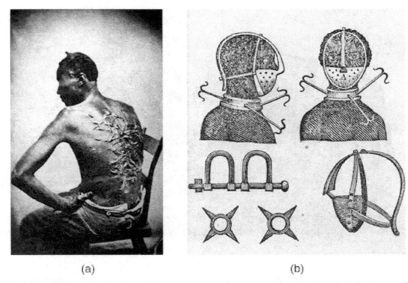

(a)   (b)

Figure 12.6   The original caption of this photograph of a slave's scarred back (a), taken in Baton Rouge, Louisiana, in 1863, reads as follows: *"Overseer Artayou Carrier whipped me. I was two months in bed sore from the whipping. My master come after I was whipped; he discharged the overseer. The very words of poor Peter, taken as he sat for his picture."* Images like this one helped bolster the northern abolitionist message of the inhumanity of slavery. The drawing of an iron mask, collar, leg shackles, and spurs (b) demonstrates the various cruel and painful instruments used to restrain slaves.

Under southern law, slaves could not marry. Nonetheless, some slaveholders allowed marriages to promote the birth of children and to foster harmony on plantations. Some masters even forced certain slaves to form unions, anticipating the birth of more children (and consequently greater profits) from them. Masters sometimes allowed slaves to choose their own partners, but they could also veto a match. Slave couples always faced the prospect of being sold away from each other, and, once they had children, the horrifying reality that their children could be sold and sent away at any time.

Slave parents had to show their children the best way to survive under slavery. This meant teaching them to be discreet, submissive, and guarded around whites. Parents also taught their children through the stories they told. Popular stories among slaves included tales of tricksters, sly slaves, or animals like Brer Rabbit, who outwitted their antagonists (Figure 12.7). Such stories provided comfort in humor and conveyed the slaves' sense of the wrongs of slavery. Slaves' work songs commented on the harshness of their life and often had double meanings—a literal meaning that whites would not find offensive and a deeper meaning for slaves.

Figure 12.7 Brer Rabbit, depicted here in an illustration from *Uncle Remus, His Songs and His Sayings: The Folk-Lore of the Old Plantation* (1881) by Joel Chandler Harris, was a trickster who outwitted his opponents.

African beliefs, including ideas about the spiritual world and the importance of African healers, survived in the South as well. Whites who became aware of non-Christian rituals among slaves labeled such practices as witchcraft. Among Africans, however, the rituals and use of various plants by respected slave healers created connections between the African past and the American South while also providing a sense of community and identity for slaves. Other African customs, including traditional naming patterns, the making of baskets, and the cultivation of certain native African plants that had been brought to the New World, also endured.

AMERICANA

✷ *African Americans and Christian Spirituals*

Many slaves embraced Christianity. Their masters emphasized a scriptural message of obedience to whites and a better day awaiting slaves in heaven, but slaves focused on the uplifting message of being freed from bondage.

The styles of worship in the Methodist and Baptist churches, which emphasized emotional responses to scripture, attracted slaves to those traditions and inspired some to become preachers. Spiritual songs that referenced the Exodus (the biblical account of the Hebrews' escape from slavery in Egypt), such as "Roll, Jordan, Roll," allowed slaves to freely express messages of hope, struggle, and overcoming adversity (Figure 12.8).

Figure 12.8 This version of "Roll, Jordan, Roll" was included in *Slave Songs of the United States*, the first published collection of African American music, which appeared in 1867.

What imagery might the Jordan River suggest to slaves working in the Deep South? What lyrics in this song suggest redemption and a better world ahead?

Click and Explore

Listen to a rendition of "Roll, Jordan, Roll" (http://openstaxcollege.org/l/15RollJordan) from the movie based on Solomon Northup's memoir and life.

THE FREE BLACK POPULATION

Complicating the picture of the antebellum South was the existence of a large free black population. In fact, more free blacks lived in the South than in the North; roughly 261,000 lived in slave states, while 226,000 lived in northern states without slavery. Most free blacks did not live in the Lower, or Deep South: the states of Alabama, Arkansas, Florida, Georgia, Louisiana, Mississippi, South Carolina, and Texas. Instead, the largest number lived in the upper southern states of Delaware, Maryland, Virginia, North Carolina, and later Kentucky, Missouri, Tennessee, and the District of Columbia.

Part of the reason for the large number of free blacks living in slave states were the many instances of manumission—the formal granting of freedom to slaves—that occurred as a result of the Revolution, when many slaveholders put into action the ideal that "all men are created equal" and freed their slaves. The transition in the Upper South to the staple crop of wheat, which did not require large numbers of slaves to produce, also spurred manumissions. Another large group of free blacks in the South had been free residents of Louisiana before the 1803 Louisiana Purchase, while still other free blacks came from Cuba and Haiti.

Most free blacks in the South lived in cities, and a majority of free blacks were lighter-skinned women, a reflection of the interracial unions that formed between white men and black women. Everywhere in the United States blackness had come to be associated with slavery, the station at the bottom of the social ladder. Both whites and those with African ancestry tended to delineate varying degrees of lightness in skin color in a social hierarchy. In the slaveholding South, different names described one's distance from blackness or whiteness: mulattos (those with one black and one white parent), quadroons (those with one black grandparent), and octoroons (those with one black great-grandparent) (Figure 12.9). Lighter-skinned blacks often looked down on their darker counterparts, an indication of the ways in which both whites and blacks internalized the racism of the age.

Figure 12.9   In this late eighteenth-century painting, a free woman of color stands with her quadroon daughter in New Orleans. Families with members that had widely varying ethnic characteristics were not uncommon at the time, especially in the larger cities.

Some free blacks in the South owned slaves of their own. Andrew Durnford, for example, was born in New Orleans in 1800, three years before the Louisiana Purchase. His father was white, and his mother was a free black. Durnford became an American citizen after the Louisiana Purchase, rising to prominence as a Louisiana sugar planter and slaveholder. William Ellison, another free black who amassed great wealth and power in the South, was born a slave in 1790 in South Carolina. After buying his freedom and that of his wife and daughter, he proceeded to purchase his own slaves, whom he then put to work manufacturing cotton gins. By the eve of the Civil War, Ellison had become one of the richest and largest slaveholders in the entire state.

The phenomenon of free blacks amassing large fortunes within a slave society predicated on racial difference, however, was exceedingly rare. Most free blacks in the South lived under the specter of slavery and faced many obstacles. Beginning in the early nineteenth century, southern states increasingly made manumission of slaves illegal. They also devised laws that divested free blacks of their rights, such as the right to testify against whites in court or the right to seek employment where they pleased. Interestingly, it was in the upper southern states that such laws were the harshest. In Virginia, for example, legislators made efforts to require free blacks to leave the state. In parts of the Deep South, free blacks were able to maintain their rights more easily. The difference in treatment between free blacks in the Deep South and those in the Upper South, historians have surmised, came down to economics. In the Deep South, slavery as an institution was strong and profitable. In the Upper South, the opposite was true. The anxiety of this economic uncertainty manifested in the form of harsh laws that targeted free blacks.

SLAVE REVOLTS

Slaves resisted their enslavement in small ways every day, but this resistance did not usually translate into mass uprisings. Slaves understood that the chances of ending slavery through rebellion were slim and would likely result in massive retaliation; many also feared the risk that participating in such actions would pose to themselves and their families. White slaveholders, however, constantly feared uprisings and took drastic steps, including torture and mutilation, whenever they believed that rebellions might be simmering. Gripped by the fear of insurrection, whites often imagined revolts to be in the works even when no uprising actually happened.

At least two major slave uprisings did occur in the antebellum South. In 1811, a major rebellion broke out in the sugar parishes of the booming territory of Louisiana. Inspired by the successful overthrow of the white planter class in Haiti, Louisiana slaves took up arms against planters. Perhaps as many five hundred slaves joined the rebellion, led by Charles Deslondes, a mixed-race slave driver on a sugar plantation owned by Manuel Andry.

The revolt began in January 1811 on Andry's plantation. Deslondes and other slaves attacked the Andry household, where they killed the slave master's son (although Andry himself escaped). The rebels then began traveling toward New Orleans, armed with weapons gathered at Andry's plantation. Whites mobilized to stop the rebellion, but not before Deslondes and the other rebelling slaves set fire to three plantations and killed numerous whites. A small white force led by Andry ultimately captured Deslondes, whose body was mutilated and burned following his execution. Other slave rebels were beheaded, and their heads placed on pikes along the Mississippi River.

The second rebellion, led by the slave Nat Turner, occurred in 1831 in Southampton County, Virginia. Turner had suffered not only from personal enslavement, but also from the additional trauma of having his wife sold away from him. Bolstered by Christianity, Turner became convinced that like Christ, he should lay down his life to end slavery. Mustering his relatives and friends, he began the rebellion August 22, killing scores of whites in the county. Whites mobilized quickly and within forty-eight hours had brought the rebellion to an end. Shocked by Nat Turner's Rebellion, Virginia's state legislature considered ending slavery in the state in order to provide greater security. In the end, legislators decided slavery would remain and that their state would continue to play a key role in the domestic slave trade.

SLAVE MARKETS

As discussed above, after centuries of slave trade with West Africa, Congress banned the further importation of slaves beginning in 1808. The domestic slave trade then expanded rapidly. As the cotton trade grew in size and importance, so did the domestic slave trade; the cultivation of cotton gave new life and importance to slavery, increasing the value of slaves. To meet the South's fierce demand for labor, American smugglers illegally transferred slaves through Florida and later through Texas. Many more slaves arrived illegally from Cuba; indeed, Cubans relied on the smuggling of slaves to prop up their finances. The largest number of slaves after 1808, however, came from the massive, legal internal slave market in which slave states in the Upper South sold enslaved men, women, and children to states in the Lower South. For slaves, the domestic trade presented the full horrors of slavery as children were ripped from their mothers and fathers and families destroyed, creating heartbreak and alienation.

Some slaveholders sought to increase the number of slave children by placing male slaves with fertile female slaves, and slave masters routinely raped their female slaves. The resulting births played an important role in slavery's expansion in the first half of the nineteenth century, as many slave children were born as a result of rape. One account written by a slave named William J. Anderson captures the horror of sexual exploitation in the antebellum South. Anderson wrote about how a Mississippi slaveholder

> divested a poor female slave of all wearing apparel, tied her down to stakes, and whipped her with a handsaw until he broke it over her naked body. In process of time he ravished [raped] her person, and became the father of a child by her. Besides, he always kept a colored Miss in the house with him. This is another curse of Slavery—concubinage and illegitimate connections—which is carried on to an alarming extent in the far South. A poor slave man who lives close by his wife, is permitted to visit her but very seldom, and other men, both white and colored, cohabit with her. It is undoubtedly the worst place of incest and bigamy in the world. A white man thinks nothing of putting a colored man out to carry the fore row [front row in field work], and carry on the same sport with the colored man's wife at the same time.

Anderson, a devout Christian, recognized and explains in his narrative that one of the evils of slavery is the way it undermines the family. Anderson was not the only critic of slavery to emphasize this point. Frederick Douglass, a Maryland slave who escaped to the North in 1838, elaborated on this dimension of slavery in his 1845 narrative. He recounted how slave masters had to sell their own children whom they had with slave women to appease the white wives who despised their offspring.

The selling of slaves was a major business enterprise in the antebellum South, representing a key part of the economy. White men invested substantial sums in slaves, carefully calculating the annual returns they could expect from a slave as well as the possibility of greater profits through natural increase. The domestic slave trade was highly visible, and like the infamous Middle Passage that brought captive Africans to the Americas, it constituted an equally disruptive and horrifying journey now called the **second middle passage**. Between 1820 and 1860, white American traders sold a million or more slaves in the domestic slave market. Groups of slaves were transported by ship from places like Virginia, a state that specialized in raising slaves for sale, to New Orleans, where they were sold to planters in the Mississippi Valley. Other slaves made the overland trek from older states like North Carolina to new and booming Deep South states like Alabama.

New Orleans had the largest slave market in the United States (Figure 12.10). Slaveholders brought their slaves there from the East (Virginia, Maryland, and the Carolinas) and the West (Tennessee and Kentucky) to be sold for work in the Mississippi Valley. The slave trade benefited whites in the Chesapeake and Carolinas, providing them with extra income: A healthy young male slave in the 1850s could be sold for $1,000 (approximately $30,000 in 2014 dollars), and a planter who could sell ten such slaves collected a windfall.

Figure 12.10 In *Sale of Estates, Pictures and Slaves in the Rotunda, New Orleans* (1853) by J. M. Starling, it is clear that slaves are considered property to be auctioned off, just like pictures or other items.

In fact, by the 1850s, the demand for slaves reached an all-time high, and prices therefore doubled. A slave who would have sold for $400 in the 1820s could command a price of $800 in the 1850s. The high price of slaves in the 1850s and the inability of natural increase to satisfy demands led some southerners to demand the reopening of the international slave trade, a movement that caused a rift between the Upper South and the Lower South. Whites in the Upper South who sold slaves to their counterparts in the Lower South worried that reopening the trade would lower prices and therefore hurt their profits.

MY STORY

⚙ *John Brown on Slave Life in Georgia*

A slave named John Brown lived in Virginia, North Carolina, and Georgia before he escaped and moved to England. While there, he dictated his autobiography to someone at the British and Foreign Anti-Slavery Society, who published it in 1855.

> I really thought my mother would have died of grief at being obliged to leave her two children, her mother, and her relations behind. But it was of no use lamenting, the few things we had were put together that night, and we completed our preparations for being parted for life by kissing one another over and over again, and saying good bye till some of us little ones fell asleep. . . . And here I may as well tell what kind of man our new master was. He was of small stature, and thin, but very strong. He had sandy hair, a very red face, and chewed tobacco. His countenance had a very cruel expression, and his disposition was a match for it. He was, indeed, a very bad man, and used to flog us dreadfully. He would make his slaves work on one meal a day, until quite night, and after supper, set them to burn brush or spin cotton. We worked from four in the morning till twelve before we broke our fast, and from that time till eleven or twelve at night . . . we labored eighteen hours a day.
> —John Brown, *Slave Life in Georgia: A Narrative of the Life, Sufferings, and Escape of John Brown, A Fugitive Slave, Now in England*, 1855

What features of the domestic slave trade does Brown's narrative illuminate? Why do you think he brought his story to an antislavery society? How do you think people responded to this narrative?

Click and Explore

Read through several narratives at "Born in Slavery," part of the American Memory (http://openstaxcollege.org/l/15BornSlavery) collection at the Library of Congress. Do these narratives have anything in common? What differences can you find between them?

12.3 Wealth and Culture in the South

By the end of this section, you will be able to:
- Assess the distribution of wealth in the antebellum South
- Describe the southern culture of honor
- Identify the main proslavery arguments in the years prior to the Civil War

During the antebellum years, wealthy southern planters formed an elite master class that wielded most of the economic and political power of the region. They created their own standards of gentility and honor, defining ideals of southern white manhood and womanhood and shaping the culture of the South. To defend the system of forced labor on which their economic survival and genteel lifestyles depended, elite southerners developed several proslavery arguments that they levied at those who would see the institution dismantled.

SLAVERY AND THE WHITE CLASS STRUCTURE

The South prospered, but its wealth was very unequally distributed. Upward social mobility did not exist for the millions of slaves who produced a good portion of the nation's wealth, while poor southern whites envisioned a day when they might rise enough in the world to own slaves of their own. Because of the cotton boom, there were more millionaires per capita in the Mississippi River Valley by 1860 than anywhere else in the United States. However, in that same year, only 3 percent of whites owned more than fifty slaves, and two-thirds of white households in the South did not own any slaves at all (Figure 12.11). Distribution of wealth in the South became less democratic over time; fewer whites owned slaves in 1860 than in 1840.

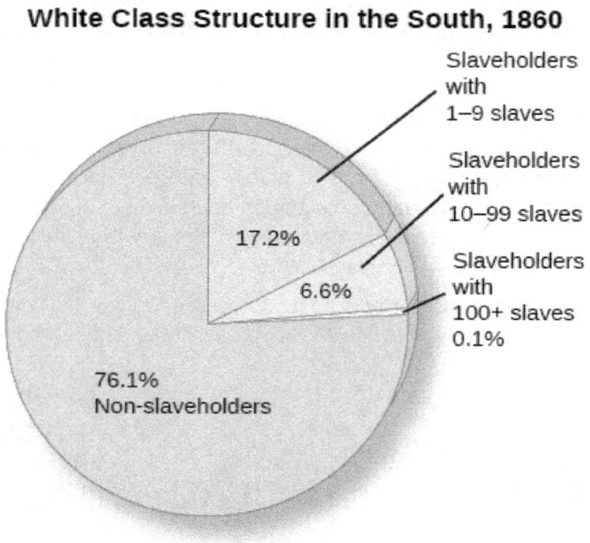

White Class Structure in the South, 1860

Figure 12.11 As the wealth of the antebellum South increased, it also became more unequally distributed, and an ever-smaller percentage of slaveholders held a substantial number of slaves.

At the top of southern white society stood the planter elite, which comprised two groups. In the Upper South, an aristocratic gentry, generation upon generation of whom had grown up with slavery, held a privileged place. In the Deep South, an elite group of slaveholders gained new wealth from cotton. Some members of this group hailed from established families in the eastern states (Virginia and the Carolinas), while others came from humbler backgrounds. South Carolinian Nathaniel Heyward, a wealthy rice planter and member of the aristocratic gentry, came from an established family and sat atop the pyramid of southern slaveholders. He amassed an enormous estate; in 1850, he owned more than eighteen hundred slaves. When he died in 1851, he left an estate worth more than $2 million (approximately $63 million in 2014 dollars).

As cotton production increased, new wealth flowed to the cotton planters. These planters became the staunchest defenders of slavery, and as their wealth grew, they gained considerable political power.

One member of the planter elite was Edward Lloyd V, who came from an established and wealthy family of Talbot County, Maryland. Lloyd had inherited his position rather than rising to it through his own labors. His hundreds of slaves formed a crucial part of his wealth. Like many of the planter elite, Lloyd's plantation was a masterpiece of elegant architecture and gardens (Figure 12.12).

Figure 12.12   The grand house of Edward Lloyd V advertised the status and wealth of its owner. In its heyday, the Lloyd family's plantation boasted holdings of forty-two thousand acres and one thousand slaves.

One of the slaves on Lloyd's plantation was Frederick Douglass, who escaped in 1838 and became an abolitionist leader, writer, statesman, and orator in the North. In his autobiography, Douglass described the plantation's elaborate gardens and racehorses, but also its underfed and brutalized slave population. Lloyd provided employment opportunities to other whites in Talbot County, many of whom served as slave traders and the "slave breakers" entrusted with beating and overworking unruly slaves into submission. Like other members of the planter elite, Lloyd himself served in a variety of local and national political offices. He was governor of Maryland from 1809 to 1811, a member of the House of Representatives from 1807 to 1809, and a senator from 1819 to 1826. As a representative and a senator, Lloyd defended slavery as the foundation of the American economy.

Wealthy plantation owners like Lloyd came close to forming an American ruling class in the years before the Civil War. They helped shape foreign and domestic policy with one goal in view: to expand the power and reach of the cotton kingdom of the South. Socially, they cultivated a refined manner and believed whites, especially members of their class, should not perform manual labor. Rather, they created an identity for themselves based on a world of leisure in which horse racing and entertainment mattered greatly, and where the enslavement of others was the bedrock of civilization.

Below the wealthy planters were the yeoman farmers, or small landowners (Figure 12.13). Below yeomen were poor, landless whites, who made up the majority of whites in the South. These landless white men dreamed of owning land and slaves and served as slave overseers, drivers, and traders in the southern economy. In fact, owning land and slaves provided one of the only opportunities for upward social and economic mobility. In the South, living the American dream meant possessing slaves, producing cotton, and owning land.

Figure 12.13 In this painting by Felix Octavius Carr Darley, a yeoman farmer carrying a scythe follows his livestock down the road.

Despite this unequal distribution of wealth, non-slaveholding whites shared with white planters a common set of values, most notably a belief in white supremacy. Whites, whether rich or poor, were bound together by racism. Slavery defused class tensions among them, because no matter how poor they were, white southerners had race in common with the mighty plantation owners. Non-slaveholders accepted the rule of the planters as defenders of their shared interest in maintaining a racial hierarchy. Significantly, all whites were also bound together by the constant, prevailing fear of slave uprisings.

MY STORY

✪ *D. R. Hundley on the Southern Yeoman*

D. R. Hundley was a well-educated planter, lawyer, and banker from Alabama. Something of an amateur sociologist, he argued against the common northern assumption that the South was made up exclusively of two tiers of white residents: the very wealthy planter class and the very poor landless whites. In his 1860 book, *Social Relations in Our Southern States*, Hundley describes what he calls the "Southern Yeomen," a social group he insists is roughly equivalent to the middle-class farmers of the North.

> *But you have no Yeomen in the South, my dear Sir?* Beg your pardon, our dear Sir, but we have—hosts of them. *I thought you had only poor White Trash?* Yes, we dare say as much—and that the moon is made of green cheese! . . . Know, then, that the Poor Whites of the South constitute a separate class to themselves; the Southern Yeomen are as distinct from them as the Southern Gentleman is from the Cotton Snob. Certainly the Southern Yeomen are nearly always poor, at least so far as this world's goods are to be taken into account. As a general thing they own no slaves; and even in case they do, the wealthiest of them rarely possess more than from ten to fifteen. . . . The Southern Yeoman much resembles in his speech, religious opinions, household arrangements, indoor sports, and family traditions, the middle class farmers of the Northern States. He is fully as intelligent as the latter, and is on the whole much better versed in the lore of politics and the provisions of our Federal and State Constitutions. . . . [A]lthough not as a class pecuniarily interested in slave property, the Southern Yeomanry are almost unanimously pro-slavery in sentiment. Nor do we see how any honest, thoughtful person can reasonably find fault with them on this account.
>
> —D. R. Hundley, *Social Relations in Our Southern States*, 1860

What elements of social relations in the South is Hundley attempting to emphasize for his readers? In what respects might his position as an educated and wealthy planter influence his understanding of social relations in the South?

Because race bound all whites together as members of the master race, non-slaveholding whites took part in civil duties. They served on juries and voted. They also engaged in the daily rounds of maintaining slavery by serving on neighborhood patrols to ensure that slaves did not escape and that rebellions did not occur. The practical consequence of such activities was that the institution of slavery, and its perpetuation, became a source of commonality among different economic and social tiers that otherwise were separated by a gulf of difference.

Southern planters exerted a powerful influence on the federal government. Seven of the first eleven presidents owned slaves, and more than half of the Supreme Court justices who served on the court from its inception to the Civil War came from slaveholding states. However, southern white yeoman farmers generally did not support an active federal government. They were suspicious of the state bank and supported President Jackson's dismantling of the Second Bank of the United States. They also did not support taxes to create internal improvements such as canals and railroads; to them, government involvement in the economic life of the nation disrupted what they perceived as the natural workings of the economy. They also feared a strong national government might tamper with slavery.

Planters operated within a larger capitalist society, but the labor system they used to produce goods—that is, slavery—was similar to systems that existed before capitalism, such as feudalism and serfdom. Under capitalism, free workers are paid for their labor (by owners of capital) to produce commodities; the money from the sale of the goods is used to pay for the work performed. As slaves did not reap any earnings from their forced labor, some economic historians consider the antebellum plantation system a "pre-capitalist" system.

HONOR IN THE SOUTH

A complicated code of honor among privileged white southerners, dictating the beliefs and behavior of "gentlemen" and "ladies," developed in the antebellum years. Maintaining appearances and reputation was supremely important. It can be argued that, as in many societies, the concept of honor in the antebellum South had much to do with control over dependents, whether slaves, wives, or relatives. Defending their honor and ensuring that they received proper respect became preoccupations of whites in the slaveholding South. To question another man's assertions was to call his honor and reputation into question. Insults in the form of words or behavior, such as calling someone a coward, could trigger a rupture that might well end on the dueling ground (Figure 12.14). Dueling had largely disappeared in the antebellum North by the early nineteenth century, but it remained an important part of the southern code of honor through the Civil War years. Southern white men, especially those of high social status, settled their differences with duels, before which antagonists usually attempted reconciliation, often through the exchange of letters addressing the alleged insult. If the challenger was not satisfied by the exchange, a duel would often result.

Figure 12.14 "The Modern Tribunal and Arbiter of Men's Differences," an illustration that appeared on the cover of *The Mascot*, a newspaper published in nineteenth-century New Orleans, reveals the importance of dueling in southern culture; it shows men bowing before an altar on which are laid a pistol and knife.

The dispute between South Carolina's James Hammond and his erstwhile friend (and brother-in-law) Wade Hampton II illustrates the southern culture of honor and the place of the duel in that culture. A strong friendship bound Hammond and Hampton together. Both stood at the top of South Carolina's society as successful, married plantation owners involved in state politics. Prior to his election as governor of the state in 1842, Hammond became sexually involved with each of Hampton's four teenage daughters, who were his nieces by marriage. "[A]ll of them rushing on every occasion into my arms," Hammond confided in his private diary, "covering me with kisses, lolling on my lap, pressing their bodies almost into mine . . . and permitting my hands to stray unchecked." Hampton found out about these dalliances, and in keeping with the code of honor, could have demanded a duel with Hammond. However, Hampton instead tried to use the liaisons to destroy his former friend politically. This effort proved disastrous for Hampton, because it represented a violation of the southern code of honor. "As matters now stand," Hammond wrote, "he [Hampton] is a convicted dastard who, not having nerve to redress his own wrongs, put forward bullies to do it for him. . . . To challenge me [to a duel] would be to throw himself upon my mercy for he knows I am not bound to meet him [for a duel]." Because Hampton's behavior marked him as a man who lacked honor, Hammond was no longer bound to meet Hampton in a duel even if Hampton were to demand one. Hammond's reputation, though tarnished, remained high in the esteem of South Carolinians, and the governor went on to serve as a U.S. senator from 1857 to 1860. As for the four Hampton daughters, they never married; their names were disgraced, not only by the whispered-about scandal but by their father's actions in response to it; and no man of honor in South Carolina would stoop so low as to marry them.

GENDER AND THE SOUTHERN HOUSEHOLD

The antebellum South was an especially male-dominated society. Far more than in the North, southern men, particularly wealthy planters, were patriarchs and sovereigns of their own household. Among the white members of the household, labor and daily ritual conformed to rigid gender delineations. Men represented their household in the larger world of politics, business, and war. Within the family, the patriarchal male was the ultimate authority. White women were relegated to the household and lived under the thumb and protection of the male patriarch. The ideal southern lady conformed to her prescribed gender role, a role that was largely domestic and subservient. While responsibilities and experiences varied across different social tiers, women's subordinate state in relation to the male patriarch remained the same.

Writers in the antebellum period were fond of celebrating the image of the ideal southern woman (Figure 12.15). One such writer, Thomas Roderick Dew, president of Virginia's College of William and Mary in the mid-nineteenth century, wrote approvingly of the virtue of southern women, a virtue he concluded derived from their natural weakness, piety, grace, and modesty. In his *Dissertation on the Characteristic Differences Between the Sexes*, he writes that southern women derive their power not by

> leading armies to combat, or of enabling her to bring into more formidable action the physical power which nature has conferred on her. No! It is but the better to perfect all those feminine graces, all those fascinating attributes, which render her the center of attraction, and which delight and charm all those who breathe the atmosphere in which she moves; and, in the language of Mr. Burke, would make ten thousand swords leap from their scabbards to avenge the insult that might be offered to her. By her very meekness and beauty does she subdue all around her.

Such popular idealizations of elite southern white women, however, are difficult to reconcile with their lived experience: in their own words, these women frequently described the trauma of childbirth, the loss of children, and the loneliness of the plantation.

Figure 12.15 This cover illustration from *Harper's Weekly* in 1861 shows the ideal of southern womanhood.

MY STORY

✿ *Louisa Cheves McCord's "Woman's Progress"*

Louisa Cheves McCord was born in Charleston, South Carolina, in 1810. A child of some privilege in the South, she received an excellent education and became a prolific writer. As the excerpt from her poem "Woman's Progress" indicates, some southern women also contributed to the idealization of southern white womanhood.

Sweet Sister! stoop not thou to be a man!
Man has his place as woman hers; and she
As made to comfort, minister and help;
Moulded for gentler duties, ill fulfils
His jarring destinies. Her mission is
To labour and to pray; to help, to heal,
To soothe, to bear; patient, with smiles, to suffer;
And with self-abnegation noble lose
Her private interest in the dearer weal
Of those she loves and lives for. Call not this—
(The all-fulfilling of her destiny;
She the world's soothing mother)—call it not,
With scorn and mocking sneer, a drudgery.
The ribald tongue profanes Heaven's holiest things,
But holy still they are. The lowliest tasks
Are sanctified in nobly acting them.
Christ washed the apostles' feet, not thus cast shame
Upon the God-like in him. Woman lives
Man's constant prophet. If her life be true
And based upon the instincts of her being,
She is a living sermon of that truth
Which ever through her gentle actions speaks,
That life is given to labour and to love.
—Louisa Susanna Cheves McCord, "Woman's Progress," 1853

What womanly virtues does Louisa Cheves McCord emphasize? How might her social status, as an educated southern woman of great privilege, influence her understanding of gender relations in the South?

For slaveholding whites, the male-dominated household operated to protect gendered divisions and prevalent gender norms; for slave women, however, the same system exposed them to brutality and frequent sexual domination. The demands on the labor of slave women made it impossible for them to perform the role of domestic caretaker that was so idealized by southern men. That slaveholders put them out into the fields, where they frequently performed work traditionally thought of as male, reflected little the ideal image of gentleness and delicacy reserved for white women. Nor did the slave woman's role as daughter, wife, or mother garner any patriarchal protection. Each of these roles and the relationships they defined was subject to the prerogative of a master, who could freely violate enslaved women's persons, sell off their children, or separate them from their families.

DEFENDING SLAVERY

With the rise of democracy during the Jacksonian era in the 1830s, slaveholders worried about the power of the majority. If political power went to a majority that was hostile to slavery, the South—and the honor of white southerners—would be imperiled. White southerners keen on preserving the institution of slavery bristled at what they perceived to be northern attempts to deprive them of their livelihood. Powerful southerners like South Carolinian John C. Calhoun (Figure 12.16) highlighted laws like the Tariff of

1828 as evidence of the North's desire to destroy the southern economy and, by extension, its culture. Such a tariff, he and others concluded, would disproportionately harm the South, which relied heavily on imports, and benefit the North, which would receive protections for its manufacturing centers. The tariff appeared to open the door for other federal initiatives, including the abolition of slavery. Because of this perceived threat to southern society, Calhoun argued that states could nullify federal laws. This belief illustrated the importance of the states' rights argument to the southern states. It also showed slaveholders' willingness to unite against the federal government when they believed it acted unjustly against their interests.

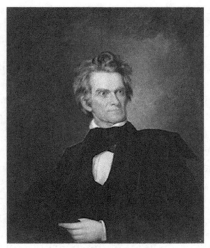

Figure 12.16 John C. Calhoun, shown here in a ca. 1845 portrait by George Alexander Healy, defended states' rights, especially the right of the southern states to protect slavery from a hostile northern majority.

As the nation expanded in the 1830s and 1840s, the writings of abolitionists—a small but vocal group of northerners committed to ending slavery—reached a larger national audience. White southerners responded by putting forth arguments in defense of slavery, their way of life, and their honor. Calhoun became a leading political theorist defending slavery and the rights of the South, which he saw as containing an increasingly embattled minority. He advanced the idea of a **concurrent majority**, a majority of a separate region (that would otherwise be in the minority of the nation) with the power to veto or disallow legislation put forward by a hostile majority.

Calhoun's idea of the concurrent majority found full expression in his 1850 essay "Disquisition on Government." In this treatise, he wrote about government as a necessary means to ensure the preservation of society, since society existed to "preserve and protect our race." If government grew hostile to society, then a concurrent majority had to take action, including forming a new government. "Disquisition on Government" advanced a profoundly anti-democratic argument. It illustrates southern leaders' intense suspicion of democratic majorities and their ability to effect legislation that would challenge southern interests.

Click and Explore

Go to the Internet Archive (http://openstaxcollege.org/l/15Disquisition) to read John C. Calhoun's "Disquisition on Government." Why do you think he proposed the creation of a concurrent majority?

White southerners reacted strongly to abolitionists' attacks on slavery. In making their defense of slavery, they critiqued wage labor in the North. They argued that the Industrial Revolution had brought about a new type of slavery—wage slavery—and that this form of "slavery" was far worse than the slave labor used on southern plantations. Defenders of the institution also lashed out directly at abolitionists such as William Lloyd Garrison for daring to call into question their way of life. Indeed, Virginians cited Garrison as the instigator of Nat Turner's 1831 rebellion.

The Virginian George Fitzhugh contributed to the defense of slavery with his book *Sociology for the South, or the Failure of Free Society* (1854). Fitzhugh argued that laissez-faire capitalism, as celebrated by Adam Smith, benefited only the quick-witted and intelligent, leaving the ignorant at a huge disadvantage. Slaveholders, he argued, took care of the ignorant—in Fitzhugh's argument, the slaves of the South. Southerners provided slaves with care from birth to death, he asserted; this offered a stark contrast to the wage slavery of the North, where workers were at the mercy of economic forces beyond their control. Fitzhugh's ideas exemplified southern notions of paternalism.

DEFINING "AMERICAN"

⚙ George Fitzhugh's Defense of Slavery

George Fitzhugh, a southern writer of social treatises, was a staunch supporter of slavery, not as a necessary evil but as what he argued was a necessary good, a way to take care of slaves and keep them from being a burden on society. He published *Sociology for the South, or the Failure of Free Society* in 1854, in which he laid out what he believed to be the benefits of slavery to both the slaves and society as a whole. According to Fitzhugh:

> [I]t is clear the Athenian democracy would not suit a negro nation, nor will the government of mere law suffice for the individual negro. He is but a grown up child and must be governed as a child . . . The master occupies towards him the place of parent or guardian. . . . The negro is improvident; will not lay up in summer for the wants of winter; will not accumulate in youth for the exigencies of age. He would become an insufferable burden to society. Society has the right to prevent this, and can only do so by subjecting him to domestic slavery.
> In the last place, the negro race is inferior to the white race, and living in their midst, they would be far outstripped or outwitted in the chase of free competition. . . . Our negroes are not only better off as to physical comfort than free laborers, but their moral condition is better.

What arguments does Fitzhugh use to promote slavery? What basic premise underlies his ideas? Can you think of a modern parallel to Fitzhugh's argument?

The North also produced defenders of slavery, including Louis Agassiz, a Harvard professor of zoology and geology. Agassiz helped to popularize **polygenism**, the idea that different human races came from separate origins. According to this formulation, no single human family origin existed, and blacks made up a race wholly separate from the white race. Agassiz's notion gained widespread popularity in the 1850s with the 1854 publication of George Gliddon and Josiah Nott's *Types of Mankind* and other books. The theory of polygenism codified racism, giving the notion of black inferiority the lofty mantle of science. One popular advocate of the idea posited that blacks occupied a place in evolution between the Greeks and chimpanzees (Figure 12.17).

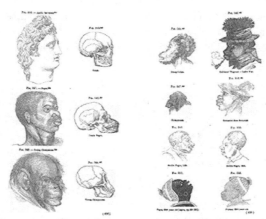

Figure 12.17   This 1857 illustration by an advocate of polygenism indicates that the "Negro" occupies a place between the Greeks and chimpanzees. What does this image reveal about the methods of those who advocated polygenism?

12.4 The Filibuster and the Quest for New Slave States

By the end of this section, you will be able to:
- Explain the expansionist goals of advocates of slavery
- Describe the filibuster expeditions undertaken during the antebellum era

Southern expansionists had spearheaded the drive to add more territory to the United States. They applauded the Louisiana Purchase and fervently supported Indian removal, the annexation of Texas, and the Mexican-American War. Drawing inspiration from the annexation of Texas, proslavery expansionists hoped to replicate that feat by bringing Cuba and other territories into the United States and thereby enlarging the American empire of slavery.

In the 1850s, the expansionist drive among white southerners intensified. Among southern imperialists, one way to push for the creation of an American empire of slavery was through the actions of filibusters—men who led unofficial military operations intended to seize land from foreign countries or foment revolution there. These unsanctioned military adventures were not part of the official foreign policy of the United States; American citizens simply formed themselves into private armies to forcefully annex new land without the government's approval.

An 1818 federal law made it a crime to undertake such adventures, which was an indication of both the reality of efforts at expansion through these illegal expeditions and the government's effort to create a U.S. foreign policy. Nonetheless, Americans continued to filibuster throughout the nineteenth century. In 1819, an expedition of two hundred Americans invaded Spanish Texas, intent on creating a republic modeled on the United States, only to be driven out by Spanish forces. Using force, taking action, and asserting white supremacy in these militaristic drives were seen by many as an ideal of American male vigor. President Jackson epitomized this military prowess as an officer in the Tennessee militia, where earlier in the century he had played a leading role in ending the Creek War and driving Indian peoples out of Alabama and Georgia. His reputation helped him to win the presidency in 1828 and again in 1832.

Filibustering plots picked up pace in the 1850s as the drive for expansion continued. Slaveholders looked south to the Caribbean, Mexico, and Central America, hoping to add new slave states. Spanish Cuba became the objective of many American slaveholders in the 1850s, as debate over the island dominated the national conversation. Many who urged its annexation believed Cuba had to be made part of the United States to prevent it from going the route of Haiti, with black slaves overthrowing their masters and creating another black republic, a prospect horrifying to many in the United States. Americans also feared that the British, who had an interest in the sugar island, would make the first move and snatch Cuba from the United States. Since Britain had outlawed slavery in its colonies in 1833, blacks on the island of Cuba would then be free.

Narisco López, a Cuban who wanted to end Spanish control of the island, gained American support. He tried five times to take the island, with his last effort occurring in the summer of 1851 when he led an armed group from New Orleans. Thousands came out to cheer his small force as they set off to wrest Cuba from the Spanish. Unfortunately for López and his supporters, however, the effort to take Cuba did not produce the hoped-for spontaneous uprising of the Cuban people. Spanish authorities in Cuba captured and executed López and the American filibusters.

Efforts to take Cuba continued under President Franklin Pierce, who had announced at his inauguration in 1853 his intention to pursue expansion. In 1854, American diplomats met in Ostend, Belgium, to find a way to gain Cuba. They wrote a secret memo, known as the **Ostend Manifesto** (thought to be penned by James Buchanan, who was elected president two years later), stating that if Spain refused to sell Cuba to the United States, the United States was justified in taking the island as a national security measure.

The contents of this memo were supposed to remain secret, but details were leaked to the public, leading the House of Representatives to demand a copy. Many in the North were outraged over what appeared to be a southern scheme, orchestrated by what they perceived as the Slave Power—a term they used to describe the disproportionate influence that elite slaveholders wielded—to expand slavery. European powers also reacted with anger. Southern annexationists, however, applauded the effort to take Cuba. The Louisiana legislature in 1854 asked the federal government to take decisive action, and John Quitman, a former Mississippi governor, raised money from slaveholders to fund efforts to take the island.

Click and Explore

Read an 1860 editorial titled Annexation of Cuba Made Easy (http://openstaxcollege.org/l/15AnnexCuba) from the online archives of *The New York Times*. Does the author support annexation? Why or why not?

Controversy around the Ostend Manifesto caused President Pierce to step back from the plan to take Cuba. After his election, President Buchanan, despite his earlier expansionist efforts, denounced filibustering as the action of pirates. Filibustering caused an even wider gulf between the North and the South (Figure 12.18).

Download for free at http://cnx.org/content/col11740/latest/

Figure 12.18 *The "Ostend Doctrine"* (1856), by artist Louis Maurer and lithographer Nathaniel Currier, mocks James Buchanan by depicting him being robbed, just as many northerners believed slaveholders were attempting to rob Spain. The thugs robbing Buchanan use specific phrases from the Ostend Manifesto as they relieve him of his belongings.

Cuba was not the only territory in slaveholders' expansionist sights: some focused on Mexico and Central America. In 1855, Tennessee-born William Walker, along with an army of no more than sixty mercenaries, gained control of the Central American nation of Nicaragua. Previously, Walker had launched a successful invasion of Mexico, dubbing his conquered land the Republic of Sonora. In a relatively short period of time, Walker was dislodged from Sonora by Mexican authorities and forced to retreat back to the United States. His conquest of Nicaragua garnered far more attention, catapulting him into national popularity as the heroic embodiment of white supremacy (Figure 12.19).

(a)   (b)

Figure 12.19 Famed Civil War photographer Mathew Brady took this photograph (a) of "General" William Walker circa 1855–1860. Walker led a filibuster expedition and briefly conquered Nicaragua, fulfilling a dream of many pro-expansionist southern slaveholders. Cornelius Vanderbilt (b), the shipping tycoon who controlled much of the traffic across Nicaragua between the Atlantic and the Pacific, clashed with Walker and ultimately supported Costa Rica in its war against him.

Why Nicaragua? Nicaragua presented a tempting target because it provided a quick route from the Caribbean to the Pacific: Only twelve miles of land stood between the Pacific Ocean, the inland Lake

Nicaragua, and the river that drained into the Atlantic. Shipping from the East Coast to the West Coast of the United States had to travel either by land across the continent, south around the entire continent of South America, or through Nicaragua. Previously, American tycoon Cornelius Vanderbilt (Figure 12.19) had recognized the strategic importance of Nicaragua and worked with the Nicaraguan government to control shipping there. The filibustering of William Walker may have excited expansionist-minded southerners, but it greatly upset Vanderbilt's business interests in the region.

Walker clung to the racist, expansionist philosophies of the proslavery South. In 1856, Walker made slavery legal in Nicaragua—it had been illegal there for thirty years—in a move to gain the support of the South. He also reopened the slave trade. In 1856, he was elected president of Nicaragua, but in 1857, he was chased from the country. When he returned to Central America in 1860, he was captured by the British and released to Honduran authorities, who executed him by firing squad.

Key Terms

antebellum a term meaning "before the war" and used to describe the decades before the American Civil War began in 1861

cash crop a crop grown to be sold for profit instead of consumption by the farmer's family

concurrent majority a majority of a separate region (that would otherwise be in the minority of the nation) with the power to veto or disallow legislation put forward by a hostile majority

cotton boom the upswing in American cotton production during the nineteenth century

cotton gin a device, patented by Eli Whitney in 1794, that separated the seeds from raw cotton quickly and easily

domestic slave trade the trading of slaves within the borders of the United States

Ostend Manifesto the secret diplomatic memo stating that if Spain refused to sell Cuba to the United States, the United States was justified in taking the island as a national security measure

paternalism the premise that southern white slaveholders acted in the best interests of their slaves

polygenism the idea that blacks and whites come from different origins

second middle passage the internal forced migration of slaves to the South and West in the United States

Summary

12.1 The Economics of Cotton
In the years before the Civil War, the South produced the bulk of the world's supply of cotton. The Mississippi River Valley slave states became the epicenter of cotton production, an area of frantic economic activity where the landscape changed dramatically as land was transformed from pinewoods and swamps into cotton fields. Cotton's profitability relied on the institution of slavery, which generated the product that fueled cotton mill profits in the North. When the international slave trade was outlawed in 1808, the domestic slave trade exploded, providing economic opportunities for whites involved in many aspects of the trade and increasing the possibility of slaves' dislocation and separation from kin and friends. Although the larger American and Atlantic markets relied on southern cotton in this era, the South depended on these other markets for food, manufactured goods, and loans. Thus, the market revolution transformed the South just as it had other regions.

12.2 African Americans in the Antebellum United States
Slave labor in the antebellum South generated great wealth for plantation owners. Slaves, in contrast, endured daily traumas as the human property of masters. Slaves resisted their condition in a variety of ways, and many found some solace in Christianity and the communities they created in the slave quarters. While some free blacks achieved economic prosperity and even became slaveholders themselves, the vast majority found themselves restricted by the same white-supremacist assumptions upon which the institution of slavery was based.

12.3 Wealth and Culture in the South
Although a small white elite owned the vast majority of slaves in the South, and most other whites could only aspire to slaveholders' wealth and status, slavery shaped the social life of all white southerners

in profound ways. Southern culture valued a behavioral code in which men's honor, based on the domination of others and the protection of southern white womanhood, stood as the highest good. Slavery also decreased class tensions, binding whites together on the basis of race despite their inequalities of wealth. Several defenses of slavery were prevalent in the antebellum era, including Calhoun's argument that the South's "concurrent majority" could overrule federal legislation deemed hostile to southern interests; the notion that slaveholders' care of their chattel made slaves better off than wage workers in the North; and the profoundly racist ideas underlying polygenism.

12.4 The Filibuster and the Quest for New Slave States

The decade of the 1850s witnessed various schemes to expand the American empire of slavery. The Ostend Manifesto articulated the right of the United States to forcefully seize Cuba if Spain would not sell it, while filibuster expeditions attempted to annex new slave states without the benefit of governmental approval. Those who pursued the goal of expanding American slavery believed they embodied the true spirit of white racial superiority.

Review Questions

1. Which of the following was *not* one of the effects of the cotton boom?
    A. U.S. trade increased with France and Spain.
    B. Northern manufacturing expanded.
    C. The need for slave labor grew.
    D. Port cities like New Orleans expanded.

2. The abolition of the foreign slave trade in 1807 led to _____.
    A. a dramatic decrease in the price and demand for slaves
    B. the rise of a thriving domestic slave trade
    C. a reform movement calling for the complete end to slavery in the United States
    D. the decline of cotton production

3. Why did some southerners believe their region was immune to the effects of the market revolution? Why was this thinking misguided?

4. Under the law in the antebellum South, slaves were _____.
    A. servants
    B. animals
    C. property
    D. indentures

5. How did both slaveholders and slaves use the concept of paternalism to their advantage?

6. The largest group of whites in the South _____.

    A. owned no slaves
    B. owned between one and nine slaves each
    C. owned between ten and ninety-nine slaves each
    D. owned over one hundred slaves each

7. John C. Calhoun argued for greater rights for southerners with which idea?
    A. polygenism
    B. nullification
    C. concurrent majority
    D. paternalism

8. How did defenders of slavery use the concept of paternalism to structure their ideas?

9. Why did southern expansionists conduct filibuster expeditions?
    A. to gain political advantage
    B. to annex new slave states
    C. to prove they could raise an army
    D. to map unknown territories

10. The controversy at the heart of the Ostend Manifesto centered on the fate of:
    A. Ostend, Belgium
    B. Nicaragua
    C. Cuba
    D. Louisiana

11. Why did expansionists set their sights on the annexation of Spanish Cuba?

Critical Thinking Questions

12. Compare and contrast the steamboats of the antebellum years with technologies today. In your estimation, what modern technology compares to steamboats in its transformative power?

13. Does the history of the cotton kingdom support or undermine the Jeffersonian vision of white farmers on self-sufficient farms? Explain your answer.

14. Based on your reading of William J. Anderson's and John Brown's accounts, what types of traumas did slaves experience? How were the experiences of black women and men similar and different?

15. What strategies did slaves employ to resist, revolt, and sustain their own independent communities and cultures? How did slaves use white southerners' own philosophies—paternalism and Christianity, for example—to their advantage in these efforts?

16. What are the major arguments put forward by proslavery advocates? How would you argue against their statements?

17. Consider filibustering from the point of view of the Cuban or Nicaraguan people. If you lived in Cuba or Nicaragua, would you support filibustering? Why or why not?

CHAPTER 13

Antebellum Idealism and Reform Impulses, 1820–1860

Figure 13.1 The masthead of *The Liberator*, by Hammatt Billings in 1850, highlights the religious aspect of antislavery crusades. *The Liberator* was an abolitionist newspaper published by William Lloyd Garrison, one of the leaders of the abolitionist movement in the United States.

Chapter Outline

Introduction

This masthead for the abolitionist newspaper *The Liberator* shows two Americas (Figure 13.1). On the left is the southern version where slaves are being sold; on the right, free blacks enjoy the blessing of liberty. Reflecting the role of evangelical Protestantism in reforms such as abolition, the image features Jesus as the central figure. The caption reads, "I come to break the bonds of the oppressor," and below the masthead, "Our country is the World, our Countrymen are all Mankind."

The reform efforts of the antebellum years, including abolitionism, aimed to perfect the national destiny and redeem the souls of individual Americans. A great deal of optimism, fueled by evangelical Protestantism revivalism, underwrote the moral crusades of the first half of the nineteenth century. Some reformers targeted what they perceived as the shallow, materialistic, and democratic market culture of the United States and advocated a stronger sense of individualism and self-reliance. Others dreamed of a more equal society and established their own idealistic communities. Still others, who viewed slavery as the most serious flaw in American life, labored to end the institution. Women's rights, temperance, health reforms, and a host of other efforts also came to the forefront during the heyday of reform in the 1830s and 1840s.

13.1 An Awakening of Religion and Individualism

By the end of this section, you will be able to:
- Explain the connection between evangelical Protestantism and the Second Great Awakening
- Describe the message of the transcendentalists

Protestantism shaped the views of the vast majority of Americans in the antebellum years. The influence of religion only intensified during the decades before the Civil War, as religious camp meetings spread the word that people could bring about their own salvation, a direct contradiction to the Calvinist doctrine of predestination. Alongside this religious fervor, transcendentalists advocated a more direct knowledge of the self and an emphasis on individualism. The writers and thinkers devoted to transcendentalism, as well as the reactions against it, created a trove of writings, an outpouring that has been termed the American Renaissance.

THE SECOND GREAT AWAKENING

The reform efforts of the antebellum era sprang from the Protestant revival fervor that found expression in what historians refer to as the **Second Great Awakening**. (The First Great Awakening of evangelical Protestantism had taken place in the 1730s and 1740s.) The Second Great Awakening emphasized an emotional religious style in which sinners grappled with their unworthy nature before concluding that they were born again, that is, turning away from their sinful past and devoting themselves to living a righteous, Christ-centered life. This emphasis on personal salvation, with its rejection of predestination (the Calvinist concept that God selected only a chosen few for salvation), was the religious embodiment of the Jacksonian celebration of the individual. Itinerant ministers preached the message of the awakening to hundreds of listeners at outdoors revival meetings (Figure 13.3).

Figure 13.2

Figure 13.3 This 1819 engraving by Jacques Gerard shows a Methodist camp meeting. Revivalist camp meetings held by itinerant Protestant ministers became a feature of nineteenth-century American life.

The burst of religious enthusiasm that began in Kentucky and Tennessee in the 1790s and early 1800s among Baptists, Methodists, and Presbyterians owed much to the uniqueness of the early decades of the republic. These years saw swift population growth, broad western expansion, and the rise of participatory democracy. These political and social changes made many people anxious, and the more egalitarian, emotional, and individualistic religious practices of the Second Great Awakening provided relief and comfort for Americans experiencing rapid change. The awakening soon spread to the East, where it had a profound impact on Congregationalists and Presbyterians. The thousands swept up in the movement believed in the possibility of creating a much better world. Many adopted **millennialism**, the fervent belief that the Kingdom of God would be established on earth and that God would reign on earth for a thousand years, characterized by harmony and Christian morality. Those drawn to the message of the Second Great Awakening yearned for stability, decency, and goodness in the new and turbulent American republic.

The Second Great Awakening also brought significant changes to American culture. Church membership doubled in the years between 1800 and 1835. Several new groups formed to promote and strengthen the message of religious revival. The American Bible Society, founded in 1816, distributed Bibles in an effort to ensure that every family had access to the sacred text, while the American Sunday School Union, established in 1824, focused on the religious education of children and published religious materials specifically for young readers. In 1825, the American Tract Society formed with the goal of disseminating the Protestant revival message in a flurry of publications.

Missionaries and circuit riders (ministers without a fixed congregation) brought the message of the awakening across the United States, including into the lives of slaves. The revival spurred many slaveholders to begin encouraging their slaves to become Christians. Previously, many slaveholders feared allowing their slaves to convert, due to a belief that Christians could not be enslaved and because of the fear that slaves might use Christian principles to oppose their enslavement. However, by the 1800s, Americans established a legal foundation for the enslavement of Christians. Also, by this time, slaveholders had come to believe that if slaves learned the "right" (that is, white) form of Christianity, then slaves would be more obedient and hardworking. Allowing slaves access to Christianity also served to ease the consciences of Christian slaveholders, who argued that slavery was divinely ordained, yet it was a faith that also required slaveholders to bring slaves to the "truth." Also important to this era was the creation of African American forms of worship as well as African American churches such as the African Methodist Episcopal Church, the first independent black Protestant church in the United States. Formed in the 1790s by Richard Allen, the African Methodist Episcopal Church advanced the African American effort to express their faith apart from white Methodists (Figure 13.4).

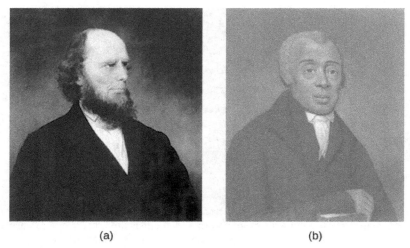

(a)   (b)

Figure 13.4 Charles Grandison Finney (a) was one of the best-known ministers of the Second Great Awakening. Richard Allen (b) created the first separate African American church, the African Methodist Episcopal Church, in the 1790s.

In the Northeast, Presbyterian minister Charles Grandison Finney rose to prominence as one of the most important evangelicals in the movement (Figure 13.4). Born in 1792 in western New York, Finney studied to be a lawyer until 1821, when he experienced a religious conversion and thereafter devoted himself to revivals. He led revival meetings in New York and Pennsylvania, but his greatest success occurred after he accepted a ministry in Rochester, New York, in 1830. At the time, Rochester was a boomtown because the Erie Canal had brought a lively shipping business.

The new middle class—an outgrowth of the Industrial Revolution—embraced Finney's message. It fit perfectly with their understanding of themselves as people shaping their own destiny. Workers also latched onto the message that they too could control their salvation, spiritually and perhaps financially as well. Western New York gained a reputation as the "burned over district," a reference to the intense flames of religious fervor that swept the area during the Second Great Awakening.

TRANSCENDENTALISM

Beginning in the 1820s, a new intellectual movement known as **transcendentalism** began to grow in the Northeast. In this context, to transcend means to go beyond the ordinary sensory world to grasp personal insights and gain appreciation of a deeper reality, and transcendentalists believed that all people could attain an understanding of the world that surpassed rational, sensory experience. Transcendentalists were critical of mainstream American culture. They reacted against the age of mass democracy in Jacksonian America—what Tocqueville called the "tyranny of majority"—by arguing for greater individualism against conformity. European romanticism, a movement in literature and art that stressed emotion over cold, calculating reason, also influenced transcendentalists in the United States, especially the transcendentalists' celebration of the uniqueness of individual feelings.

Ralph Waldo Emerson emerged as the leading figure of this movement (Figure 13.5). Born in Boston in 1803, Emerson came from a religious family. His father served as a Unitarian minister and, after graduating from Harvard Divinity School in the 1820s, Emerson followed in his father's footsteps. However, after his wife died in 1831, he left the clergy. On a trip to Europe in 1832, he met leading figures of romanticism who rejected the hyper-rationalism of the Enlightenment, emphasizing instead emotion and the sublime.

(a)   (b)

Figure 13.5 Ralph Waldo Emerson (a), shown here circa 1857, is considered the father of transcendentalism. This letter (b) from Emerson to Walt Whitman, another brilliant writer of the transcendentalist movement, demonstrates the closeness of a number of these writers.

When Emerson returned home the following year, he began giving lectures on his romanticism-influenced ideas. In 1836, he published "Nature," an essay arguing that humans can find their true spirituality in nature, not in the everyday bustling working world of Jacksonian democracy and industrial transformation. In 1841, Emerson published his essay "Self-Reliance," which urged readers to think for themselves and reject the mass conformity and mediocrity he believed had taken root in American life. In this essay, he wrote, "Whoso would be a man must be a nonconformist," demanding that his readers be true to themselves and not blindly follow a herd mentality. Emerson's ideas dovetailed with those of the French aristocrat, Alexis de Tocqueville, who wrote about the "tyranny of the majority" in his *Democracy in America*. Tocqueville, like Emerson, expressed concern that a powerful majority could overpower the will of individuals.

Click and Explore

Visit Emerson Central (http://openstaxcollege.org/l/15SelfReliance) to read the full text of "Self Reliance" by Ralph Waldo Emerson. How have Emerson's ideas influenced American society?

Emerson's ideas struck a chord with a class of literate adults who also were dissatisfied with mainstream American life and searching for greater spiritual meaning. Many writers were drawn to transcendentalism, and they started to express its ideas through new stories, poems, essays, and articles. The ideas of transcendentalism were able to permeate American thought and culture through a prolific print culture, which allowed magazines and journals to be widely disseminated.

Among those attracted to Emerson's ideas was his friend Henry David Thoreau, whom he encouraged to write about his own ideas. Thoreau placed a special emphasis on the role of nature as a gateway to the transcendentalist goal of greater individualism. In 1848, Thoreau gave a lecture in which he argued that individuals must stand up to governmental injustice, a topic he chose because of his disgust over the Mexican-American War and slavery. In 1849, he published his lecture "Civil Disobedience" and urged readers to refuse to support a government that was immoral. In 1854, he published *Walden; Or, Life in the Woods*, a book about the two years he spent in a small cabin on Walden Pond near Concord, Massachusetts (Figure 13.6). Thoreau had lived there as an experiment in living apart, but not too far apart, from his conformist neighbors.

(a)   (b)

Figure 13.6 Henry David Thoreau (a) argued that men had the right to resist authority if they deemed it unjust. "All men recognize the right of revolution; that is, the right to refuse allegiance to, and to resist, the government, when its tyranny or its inefficiency are great and unendurable." Thoreau's *Walden; or, Life in the Woods* (b) articulated his emphasis on the importance of nature as a gateway to greater individuality.

Margaret Fuller also came to prominence as a leading transcendentalist and advocate for women's equality. Fuller was a friend of Emerson and Thoreau, and other intellectuals of her day. Because she was a woman, she could not attend Harvard, as it was a male-only institution for undergraduate students until 1973. However, she was later granted the use of the library there because of her towering intellect. In 1840, she became the editor of *The Dial*, a transcendentalist journal, and she later found employment as a book reviewer for the *New York Tribune* newspaper. Tragically, in 1850, she died at the age of forty in a shipwreck off Fire Island, New York.

Walt Whitman also added to the transcendentalist movement, most notably with his 1855 publication of twelve poems, entitled *Leaves of Grass*, which celebrated the subjective experience of the individual. One of the poems, "Song of Myself," amplified the message of individualism, but by uniting the individual with all other people through a transcendent bond.

AMERICANA

☼ *Walt Whitman's "Song of Myself"*

Walt Whitman (Figure 13.7) was a poet associated with the transcendentalists. His 1855 poem, "Song of Myself," shocked many when it was first published, but it has been called one of the most influential poems in American literature.

Figure 13.7   This steel engraving of Walt Whitman by Samuel Hollyer is from a lost daguerreotype by Gabriel Harrison, taken in 1854.

> I CELEBRATE myself, and sing myself,
> And what I assume you shall assume,
> For every atom belonging to me as good belongs to you.
> I loafe and invite my soul,
> I lean and loafe at my ease observing a spear of summer grass.
> My tongue, every atom of my blood, form'd from this soil, this air,
> Born here of parents born here from parents the same, and their parents the same,
> I, now thirty-seven years old in perfect health begin,
> Hoping to cease not till death. . . .
> And I say to mankind, Be not curious about God,
> For I who am curious about each am not curious about God,
> (No array of terms can say how much I am at peace about God and about death.)
> I hear and behold God in every object, yet understand God not in the least,
> Nor do I understand who there can be more wonderful than myself. . . .
> I too am not a bit tamed, I too am untranslatable,
> I sound my barbaric yawp over the roofs of the world. . . .
> You will hardly know who I am or what I mean,
> But I shall be good health to you nevertheless,
> And filter and fibre your blood.
> Failing to fetch me at first keep encouraged,
> Missing me one place search another,
> I stop somewhere waiting for you.

What images does Whitman use to describe himself and the world around him? What might have been shocking about this poem in 1855? Why do you think it has endured?

Some critics took issue with transcendentalism's emphasis on rampant individualism by pointing out the destructive consequences of compulsive human behavior. Herman Melville's novel *Moby Dick, Or, The Whale* emphasized the perils of individual obsession by telling the tale of Captain Ahab's single-minded quest to kill a white whale, Moby Dick, which had destroyed Ahab's original ship and caused him to lose one of his legs. Edgar Allan Poe, a popular author, critic, and poet, decried "the so-called poetry of the so-called transcendentalists." These American writers who questioned transcendentalism illustrate the underlying tension between individualism and conformity in American life.

13.2 Antebellum Communal Experiments

By the end of this section, you will be able to:
- Identify similarities and differences among utopian groups of the antebellum era
- Explain how religious utopian communities differed from nonreligious ones

Prior to 1815, in the years before the market and Industrial Revolution, most Americans lived on farms where they produced much of the foods and goods they used. This largely pre-capitalist culture centered on large family units whose members all lived in the same towns, counties, and parishes.

Economic forces unleashed after 1815, however, forever altered that world. More and more people now bought their food and goods in the thriving market economy, a shift that opened the door to a new way of life. These economic transformations generated various reactions; some people were nostalgic for what they viewed as simpler, earlier times, whereas others were willing to try new ways of living and working. In the early nineteenth century, experimental communities sprang up, created by men and women who hoped not just to create a better way of life but to recast American civilization, so that greater equality and harmony would prevail. Indeed, some of these reformers envisioned the creation of alternative ways of living, where people could attain perfection in human relations. The exact number of these societies is unknown because many of them were so short-lived, but the movement reached its apex in the 1840s.

RELIGIOUS UTOPIAN SOCIETIES

Most of those attracted to utopian communities had been profoundly influenced by evangelical Protestantism, especially the Second Great Awakening. However, their experience of revivalism had left them wanting to further reform society. The communities they formed and joined adhered to various socialist ideas and were considered radical, because members wanted to create a new social order, not reform the old.

German Protestant migrants formed several **pietistic** societies: communities that stressed transformative individual religious experience or piety over religious rituals and formality. One of the earliest of these, the Ephrata Cloister in Pennsylvania, was founded by a charismatic leader named Conrad Beissel in the 1730s. By the antebellum era, it was the oldest communal experiment in the United States. Its members devoted themselves to spiritual contemplation and a disciplined work regime while they awaited the millennium. They wore homespun rather than buying cloth or premade clothing, and encouraged celibacy. Although the Ephrata Cloister remained small, it served as an early example of the type of community that antebellum reformers hoped to create.

In 1805, a second German religious society, led by George Rapp, took root in Pennsylvania with several hundred members called Rappites who encouraged celibacy and adhered to the socialist principle of holding all goods in common (as opposed to allowing individual ownership). They not only built the town of Harmony but also produced surplus goods to sell to the outside world. In 1815, the group sold its Pennsylvanian holdings and moved to Indiana, establishing New Harmony on a twenty-thousand-acre plot along the Wabash River. In 1825, members returned to Pennsylvania, and established themselves in the town called Economy.

The **Shakers** provide another example of a community established with a religious mission. The Shakers started in England as an outgrowth of the Quaker religion in the middle of the eighteenth century. Ann Lee, a leader of the group in England, emigrated to New York in the 1770s, having experienced a profound religious awakening that convinced her that she was "mother in Christ." She taught that God was both male and female; Jesus embodied the male side, while Mother Ann (as she came to be known by her followers) represented the female side. To Shakers in both England and the United States, Mother Ann represented the completion of divine revelation and the beginning of the millennium of heaven on earth.

In practice, men and women in Shaker communities were held as equals—a radical departure at the time—and women often outnumbered men. Equality extended to the possession of material goods as well; no one could hold private property. Shaker communities aimed for self-sufficiency, raising food and making all that was necessary, including furniture that emphasized excellent workmanship as a substitute for worldly pleasure.

The defining features of the Shakers were their spiritual mysticism and their prohibition of sexual intercourse, which they held as an example of a lesser spiritual life and a source of conflict between women and men. Rapturous Shaker dances, for which the group gained notoriety, allowed for emotional release (Figure 13.8). The high point of the Shaker movement came in the 1830s, when about six thousand members populated communities in New England, New York, Ohio, Indiana, and Kentucky.

Figure 13.8 In this image of a Shaker dance from 1840, note the raised arms, indicating emotional expression.

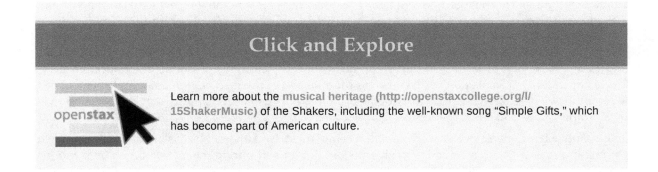

Click and Explore

Learn more about the musical heritage (http://openstaxcollege.org/l/15ShakerMusic) of the Shakers, including the well-known song "Simple Gifts," which has become part of American culture.

Another religious utopian experiment, the Oneida Community, began with the teachings of John Humphrey Noyes, a Vermonter who had graduated from Dartmouth, Andover Theological Seminary, and Yale. The Second Great Awakening exerted a powerful effect on him, and he came to believe in perfectionism, the idea that it is possible to be perfect and free of sin. Noyes claimed to have achieved this state of perfection in 1834.

Noyes applied his idea of perfection to relationships between men and women, earning notoriety for his unorthodox views on marriage and sexuality. Beginning in his home town of Putney, Vermont, he began to advocate what he called "complex marriage:" a form of communal marriage in which women and men who had achieved perfection could engage in sexual intercourse without sin. Noyes also promoted "male continence," whereby men would not ejaculate, thereby freeing women from pregnancy and the difficulty of determining paternity when they had many partners. Intercourse became fused with spiritual power among Noyes and his followers.

The concept of complex marriage scandalized the townspeople in Putney, so Noyes and his followers removed to Oneida, New York. Individuals who wanted to join the Oneida Community underwent a tough screening process to weed out those who had not reached a state of perfection, which Noyes believed promoted self-control, not out-of-control behavior. The goal was a balance between individuals in a community of love and respect. The perfectionist community Noyes envisioned ultimately dissolved in 1881, although the Oneida Community itself continues to this day (Figure 13.9).

Figure 13.9 The Oneida Community was a utopian experiment located in Oneida, New York, from 1848 to 1881.

The most successful religious utopian community to arise in the antebellum years was begun by Joseph Smith. Smith came from a large Vermont family that had not prospered in the new market economy and moved to the town of Palmyra, in the "burned over district" of western New York. In 1823, Smith claimed to have to been visited by the angel Moroni, who told him the location of a trove of golden plates or tablets. During the late 1820s, Smith translated the writing on the golden plates, and in 1830, he published his finding as *The Book of Mormon*. That same year, he organized the Church of Christ, the progenitor of the Church of Latter-Day Saints popularly known as **Mormons**. He presented himself as a prophet and aimed to recapture what he viewed as the purity of the primitive Christian church, purity that had been lost over the centuries. To Smith, this meant restoring male leadership.

Smith emphasized the importance of families being ruled by fathers. His vision of a reinvigorated patriarchy resonated with men and women who had not thrived during the market revolution, and his claims attracted those who hoped for a better future. Smith's new church placed great stress on work and discipline. He aimed to create a New Jerusalem where the church exercised oversight of its members.

Smith's claims of translating the golden plates antagonized his neighbors in New York. Difficulties with anti-Mormons led him and his followers to move to Kirtland, Ohio, in 1831. By 1838, as the United States experienced continued economic turbulence following the Panic of 1837, Smith and his followers were facing financial collapse after a series of efforts in banking and money-making ended in disaster. They moved to Missouri, but trouble soon developed there as well, as citizens reacted against the Mormons' beliefs. Actual fighting broke out in 1838, and the ten thousand or so Mormons removed to Nauvoo, Illinois, where they founded a new center of Mormonism.

By the 1840s, Nauvoo boasted a population of thirty thousand, making it the largest utopian community in the United States. Thanks to some important conversions to Mormonism among powerful citizens in Illinois, the Mormons had virtual autonomy in Nauvoo, which they used to create the largest armed force in the state. Smith also received further revelations there, including one that allowed male church leaders to practice polygamy. He also declared that all of North and South America would be the new Zion and announced that he would run for president in the 1844 election.

Smith and the Mormons' convictions and practices generated a great deal of opposition from neighbors in surrounding towns. Smith was arrested for treason (for destroying the printing press of a newspaper that criticized Mormonism), and while he was in prison, an anti-Mormon mob stormed into his cell and killed him. Brigham Young (Figure 13.10) then assumed leadership of the group, which he led to a permanent home in what is now Salt Lake City, Utah.

(a)   (b)

Figure 13.10 Carl Christian Anton Christensen depicts *The angel Moroni delivering the plates of the Book of Mormon to Joseph Smith*, circa 1886 (a). On the basis of these plates, Joseph Smith (b) founded the Church of Latter-Day Saints. Following Smith's death at the hands of a mob in Illinois, Brigham Young took control of the church and led them west to the Salt Lake Valley, which at that time was still part of Mexico.

SECULAR UTOPIAN SOCIETIES

Not all utopian communities were prompted by the religious fervor of the Second Great Awakening; some were outgrowths of the intellectual ideas of the time, such as romanticism with its emphasis on the importance of individualism over conformity. One of these, Brook Farm, took shape in West Roxbury, Massachusetts, in the 1840s. It was founded by George Ripley, a transcendentalist from Massachusetts. In the summer of 1841, this utopian community gained support from Boston-area thinkers and writers, an intellectual group that included many important transcendentalists. Brook Farm is best characterized as a community of intensely individualistic personalities who combined manual labor, such as the growing and harvesting food, with intellectual pursuits. They opened a school that specialized in the liberal arts rather than rote memorization and published a weekly journal called *The Harbinger*, which was "Devoted to Social and Political Progress" (Figure 13.11). Members of Brook Farm never totaled more than one hundred, but it won renown largely because of the luminaries, such as Emerson and Thoreau, whose names were attached to it. Nathaniel Hawthorne, a Massachusetts writer who took issue with some of the transcendentalists' claims, was a founding member of Brook Farm, and he fictionalized some of his experiences in his novel *The Blithedale Romance*. In 1846, a fire destroyed the main building of Brook Farm, and already hampered by financial problems, the Brook Farm experiment came to an end in 1847.

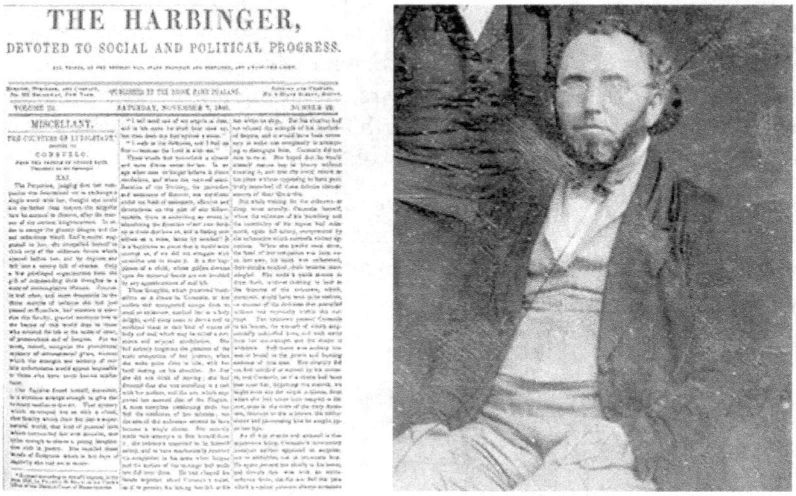
THE HARBINGER,
DEVOTED TO SOCIAL AND POLITICAL PROGRESS.

(a) (b)

Figure 13.11 Brook Farm printed *The Harbinger* (a) to share its ideals more widely. George Ripley (b), who founded the farm, was burdened with a huge debt several years later when the community collapsed.

Robert Owen, a British industrialist, helped inspire those who dreamed of a more equitable world in the face of the changes brought about by industrialization. Owen had risen to prominence before he turned thirty by running cotton mills in New Lanark, Scotland; these were considered the most successful cotton mills in Great Britain. Owen was very uneasy about the conditions of workers, and he devoted both his life and his fortune to trying to create cooperative societies where workers would lead meaningful, fulfilled lives. Unlike the founders of many utopian communities, he did not gain inspiration from religion; his vision derived instead from his faith in human reason to make the world better.

When the Rappite community in Harmony, Indiana, decided to sell its holdings and relocate to Pennsylvania, Owen seized the opportunity to put his ideas into action. In 1825, he bought the twenty-thousand-acre parcel in Indiana and renamed it New Harmony (Figure 13.12). After only a few years, however, a series of bad decisions by Owen and infighting over issues like the elimination of private property led to the dissolution of the community. But Owen's ideas of cooperation and support inspired other "Owenite" communities in the United States, Canada, and Great Britain.

Figure 13.12 This 1838 engraving of New Harmony shows the ideal collective community that Robert Owen hoped to build.

A French philosopher who advocated the creation of a new type of utopian community, Charles Fourier also inspired American readers, notably Arthur Brisbane, who popularized Fourier's ideas in the United States. Fourier emphasized collective effort by groups of people or "associations." Members of the association would be housed in large buildings or "phalanxes," a type of communal living arrangement. Converts to Fourier's ideas about a new science of living published and lectured vigorously. They believed labor was a type of capital, and the more unpleasant the job, the higher the wages should be. Fourierists in the United States created some twenty-eight communities between 1841 and 1858, but by the late 1850s, the movement had run its course in the United States.

13.3 Reforms to Human Health

By the end of this section, you will be able to:
- Explain the different reforms aimed at improving the health of the human body
- Describe the various factions and concerns within the temperance movement

Antebellum reform efforts aimed at perfecting the spiritual and social worlds of individuals, and as an outgrowth of those concerns, some reformers moved in the direction of ensuring the health of American citizens. Many Americans viewed drunkenness as a major national problem, and the battle against alcohol and the many problems associated with it led many to join the temperance movement. Other reformers offered plans to increase physical well-being, instituting plans designed to restore vigor. Still others celebrated new sciences that would unlock the mysteries of human behavior and, by doing so, advance American civilization.

TEMPERANCE

According to many antebellum reformers, intemperance (drunkenness) stood as the most troubling problem in the United States, one that eroded morality, Christianity, and played a starring role in corrupting American democracy. Americans consumed huge quantities of liquor in the early 1800s, including gin, whiskey, rum, and brandy. Indeed, scholars agree that the rate of consumption of these drinks during the first three decades of the 1800s reached levels that have never been equaled in American history.

A variety of reformers created organizations devoted to **temperance**, that is, moderation or self-restraint. Each of these organizations had its own distinct orientation and target audience. The earliest ones were formed in the 1810s in New England. The Massachusetts Society for the Suppression of Intemperance and the Connecticut Society for the Reformation of Morals were both formed in 1813. Protestant ministers led both organizations, which enjoyed support from New Englanders who clung to the ideals of the Federalist Party and later the Whigs. These early temperance societies called on individuals to lead pious lives and avoid sin, including the sin of overindulging in alcohol. They called not for the eradication of drinking but for a more restrained and genteel style of imbibing.

AMERICANA

✺ *The Drunkard's Progress*

This 1840 temperance illustration (Figure 13.13) charts the path of destruction for those who drink. The step-by-step progression reads:

Step 1. A glass with a friend.
Step 2. A glass to keep the cold out.
Step 3. A glass too much.
Step 4. Drunk and riotous.
Step 5. The summit attained. Jolly companions. A confirmed drunkard.
Step 6. Poverty and disease.
Step 7. Forsaken by Friends.
Step 8. Desperation and crime.
Step 9. Death by suicide.

Figure 13.13 This 1846 image, *The Drunkards Progress. From the First Glass to the Grave*, by Nathaniel Currier, shows the destruction that prohibitionists thought could result from drinking alcoholic beverages.

Who do you think was the intended audience for this engraving? How do you think different audiences (children, drinkers, nondrinkers) would react to the story it tells? Do you think it is an effective piece of propaganda? Why or why not?

In the 1820s, temperance gained ground largely through the work of Presbyterian minister Lyman Beecher. In 1825, Beecher delivered six sermons on temperance that were published the follow year as *Six Sermons on the Nature, Occasions, Signs, Evils, and Remedy of Intemperance*. He urged total abstinence from hard liquor and called for the formation of voluntary associations to bring forth a new day without spirits (whiskey, rum, gin, brandy). Lyman's work enjoyed a wide readership and support from leading Protestant ministers as well as the emerging middle class; temperance fit well with the middle-class ethic of encouraging hard work and a sober workforce.

In 1826, the American Temperance Society was formed, and by the early 1830s, thousands of similar societies had sprouted across the country. Members originally pledged to shun only hard liquor. By 1836, however, leaders of the temperance movement, including Beecher, called for a more comprehensive approach. Thereafter, most temperance societies advocated total abstinence; no longer would beer and wine be tolerated. Such total abstinence from alcohol is known as **teetotalism**.

Teetotalism led to disagreement within the movement and a loss of momentum for reform after 1836. However, temperance enjoyed a revival in the 1840s, as a new type of reformer took up the cause against alcohol. The engine driving the new burst of enthusiastic temperance reform was the Washington Temperance Society (named in deference to George Washington), which organized in 1840. The leaders of the Washingtonians came not from the ranks of Protestant ministers but from the working class. They aimed their efforts at confirmed alcoholics, unlike the early temperance advocates who mostly targeted the middle class.

Washingtonians welcomed the participation of women and children, as they cast alcohol as the destroyer of families, and those who joined the group took a public pledge of teetotalism. Americans flocked to the Washingtonians; as many as 600,000 had taken the pledge by 1844. The huge surge in membership had much to do with the style of this reform effort. The Washingtonians turned temperance into theater by dramatizing the plight of those who fell into the habit of drunkenness. Perhaps the most famous fictional drama put forward by the temperance movement was *Ten Nights in a Bar-Room* (1853), a novel that became the basis for popular theatrical productions. The Washingtonians also sponsored picnics and parades that drew whole families into the movement. The group's popularity quickly waned in the late 1840s and early 1850s, when questions arose about the effectiveness of merely taking a pledge. Many who had done so soon relapsed into alcoholism.

Still, by that time, temperance had risen to a major political issue. Reformers lobbied for laws limiting or prohibiting alcohol, and states began to pass the first temperance laws. The earliest, an 1838 law in Massachusetts, prohibited the sale of liquor in quantities less than fifteen gallons, a move designed to make it difficult for ordinary workmen of modest means to buy spirits. The law was repealed in 1840, but Massachusetts towns then took the initiative by passing local laws banning alcohol. In 1845, close to one hundred towns in the state went "dry."

An 1839 Mississippi law, similar to Massachusetts' original law, outlawed the sale of less than a gallon of liquor. Mississippi's law illustrates the national popularity of temperance; regional differences notwithstanding, citizens in northern and southern states agreed on the issue of alcohol. Nonetheless, northern states pushed hardest for outlawing alcohol. Maine enacted the first statewide prohibition law in 1851. New England, New York, and states in the Midwest passed local laws in the 1850s, prohibiting the sale and manufacture of intoxicating beverages.

REFORMS FOR THE BODY AND THE MIND

Beyond temperance, other reformers looked to ways to maintain and improve health in a rapidly changing world. Without professional medical organizations or standards, health reform went in many different directions; although the American Medical Association was formed in 1847, it did not have much power to oversee medical practices. Too often, quack doctors prescribed regimens and medicines that did far more harm that good.

Sylvester Graham stands out as a leading light among the health reformers in the antebellum years. A Presbyterian minister, Graham began his career as a reformer, lecturing against the evils of strong drink. He combined an interest in temperance with vegetarianism and sexuality into what he called a "Science of Human Life," calling for a regimented diet of more vegetables, fruits, and grain, and no alcohol, meat, or spices.

Graham advocated baths and cleanliness in general to preserve health; hydropathy, or water cures for various ailments, became popular in the United States in the 1840s and 1850s. He also viewed masturbation and excessive sex as a cause of disease and debility. His ideas led him to create what he believed to be a perfect food that would maintain health: the Graham cracker, which he invented in 1829. Followers of

Graham, known as Grahamites, established boardinghouses where lodgers followed the recommended strict diet and sexual regimen.

During the early nineteenth century, reformers also interested themselves in the workings of the mind in an effort to better understand the effects of a rapidly changing world awash with religious revivals and democratic movements. **Phrenology**—the mapping of the cranium to specific human attributes—stands as an early type of science, related to what would become psychology and devoted to understanding how the mind worked. Phrenologists believed that the mind contained thirty-seven "faculties," the strengths or weaknesses of which could be determined by a close examination of the size and shape of the cranium (**Figure 13.14**).

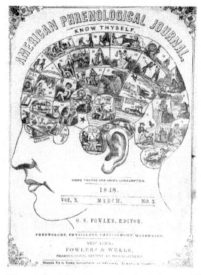

Figure 13.14 This March 1848 cover of the *American Phrenological Journal* illustrates the different faculties of the mind as envisioned by phrenologists.

Initially developed in Europe by Franz Joseph Gall, a German doctor, phrenology first came to the United States in the 1820s. In the 1830s and 1840s, it grew in popularity as lecturers crisscrossed the republic. It was sometimes used as an educational test, and like temperance, it also became a form of popular entertainment.

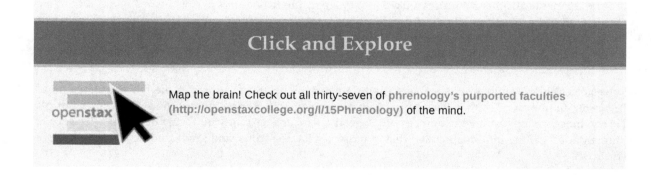

Click and Explore

Map the brain! Check out all thirty-seven of phrenology's purported faculties (http://openstaxcollege.org/l/15Phrenology) of the mind.

The popularity of phrenology offers us some insight into the emotional world of the antebellum United States. Its popularity speaks to the desire of those living in a rapidly changing society, where older ties to community and family were being challenged, to understand one another. It appeared to offer a way to quickly recognize an otherwise-unknown individual as a readily understood set of human faculties.

13.4 Addressing Slavery

By the end of this section, you will be able to:
- Identify the different approaches to reforming the institution of slavery
- Describe the abolitionist movement in the early to mid-nineteenth century

The issue of slavery proved especially combustible in the reform-minded antebellum United States. Those who hoped to end slavery had different ideas about how to do it. Some could not envision a biracial society and advocated sending blacks to Africa or the Caribbean. Others promoted the use of violence as the best method to bring American slavery to an end. Abolitionists, by contrast, worked to end slavery and to create a multiracial society of equals using moral arguments—moral suasion—to highlight the immorality of slavery. In keeping with the religious fervor of the era, abolitionists hoped to bring about a mass conversion in public opinion to end slavery.

"REFORMS" TO SLAVERY

An early and popular "reform" to slavery was **colonization**, or a movement advocating the displacement of African Americans out of the country, usually to Africa. In 1816, the Society for the Colonization of Free People of Color of America (also called the American Colonization Society or ACS) was founded with this goal. Leading statesmen including Thomas Jefferson endorsed the idea of colonization.

Members of the ACS did not believe that blacks and whites could live as equals, so they targeted the roughly 200,000 free blacks in the United States for relocation to Africa. For several years after the ACS's founding, they raised money and pushed Congress for funds. In 1819, they succeeded in getting $100,000 from the federal government to further the colonization project. The ACS played a major role in the creation of the colony of Liberia, on the west coast of Africa. The country's capital, Monrovia, was named in honor of President James Monroe. The ACS stands as an example of how white reformers, especially men of property and standing, addressed the issue of slavery. Their efforts stand in stark contrast with other reformers' efforts to deal with slavery in the United States.

Although rebellion stretches the definition of reform, another potential solution to slavery was its violent overthrow. Nat Turner's Rebellion, one of the largest slave uprisings in American history, took place in 1831, in Southampton County, Virginia. Like many slaves, Nat Turner was inspired by the evangelical Protestant fervor sweeping the republic. He preached to fellow slaves in Southampton County, gaining a reputation among them as a prophet. He organized them for rebellion, awaiting a sign to begin, until an eclipse in August signaled that the appointed time had come.

Turner and as many as seventy other slaves killed their masters and their masters' families, murdering a total of around sixty-five people (Figure 13.15). Turner eluded capture until late October, when he was tried, hanged, and then beheaded and quartered. Virginia put to death fifty-six other slaves whom they believed to have taken part in the rebellion. White vigilantes killed two hundred more as panic swept through Virginia and the rest of the South.

Figure 13.15 In *Horrid Massacre in Virginia*, circa 1831, the text on the bottom reads, "The Scenes which the above plate is designed to represent are Fig 1. a mother intreating for the lives of her children. -2. Mr. Travis, cruelly murdered by his own Slaves. -3. Mr. Barrow, who bravely defended himself until his wife escaped. -4. A comp. of mounted Dragoons in pursuit of the Blacks." From whose side do you think the illustrator is telling this story?

MY STORY

✪ *Nat Turner on His Battle against Slavery*

Thomas R. Gray was a lawyer in Southampton, Virginia, where he visited Nat Turner in jail. He published *The Confessions of Nat Turner, the leader of the late insurrection in Southampton, Va., as fully and voluntarily made to Thomas R. Gray* in November 1831, after Turner had been executed.

> For as the blood of Christ had been shed on this earth, and had ascended to heaven for the salvation of sinners, and was now returning to earth again in the form of dew . . . it was plain to me that the Saviour was about to lay down the yoke he had borne for the sins of men, and the great day of judgment was at hand. . . . And on the 12th of May, 1828, I heard a loud noise in the heavens, and the Spirit instantly appeared to me and said the Serpent was loosened, and Christ had laid down the yoke he had borne for the sins of men, and that I should take it on and fight against the Serpent, . . . *Ques.* Do you not find yourself mistaken now? *Ans.* Was not Christ crucified. And by signs in the heavens that it would make known to me when I should commence the great work—and on the appearance of the sign, (the eclipse of the sun last February) I should arise and prepare myself, and slay my enemies with their own weapons.

How did Turner interpret his fight against slavery? What did he mean by the "serpent?"

Nat Turner's Rebellion provoked a heated discussion in Virginia over slavery. The Virginia legislature was already in the process of revising the state constitution, and some delegates advocated for an easier manumission process. The rebellion, however, rendered that reform impossible. Virginia and other slave states recommitted themselves to the institution of slavery, and defenders of slavery in the South increasingly blamed northerners for provoking their slaves to rebel.

Literate, educated blacks, including David Walker, also favored rebellion. Walker was born a free black man in North Carolina in 1796. He moved to Boston in the 1820s, lectured on slavery, and promoted the first African American newspaper, *Freedom's Journal*. He called for blacks to actively resist slavery and to use violence if needed. He published *An Appeal to the Colored Citizens of the World* in 1829, denouncing the scheme of colonization and urging blacks to fight for equality in the United States, to take action against racism. Walker died months after the publication of his *Appeal*, and debate continues to this day over the cause of his death. Many believe he was murdered. Walker became a symbol of hope to free people in the North and a symbol of the terrors of literate, educated blacks to the slaveholders of the South.

ABOLITIONISM

Abolitionists took a far more radical approach to the issue of the slavery by using moral arguments to advocate its immediate elimination. They publicized the atrocities committed under slavery and aimed to create a society characterized by equality of blacks and whites. In a world of intense religious fervor, they hoped to bring about a mass awakening in the United States of the sin of slavery, confident that they could transform the national conscience against the South's peculiar institution.

William Lloyd Garrison and Antislavery Societies

William Lloyd Garrison of Massachusetts distinguished himself as the leader of the **abolitionist** movement. Although he had once been in favor of colonization, he came to believe that such a scheme only deepened racism and perpetuated the sinful practices of his fellow Americans. In 1831, he founded the abolitionist newspaper *The Liberator*, whose first edition declared:

> I am aware that many object to the severity of my language; but is there not cause for severity? I will be as harsh as truth, and as uncompromising as justice. On this subject, I do not wish to think, or speak, or write, with moderation. No! No! Tell a man whose house is on fire to give a moderate alarm; tell him to moderately rescue his wife from the hands of the ravisher; tell the mother to gradually extricate her babe from the fire into which it has fallen;—but urge me not to use moderation in a cause like the present. I am in earnest—I will not equivocate—I will not excuse—I will not retreat a single inch—AND I WILL BE HEARD.

White Virginians blamed Garrison for stirring up slaves and instigating slave rebellions like Nat Turner's.

Garrison founded the New England Anti-Slavery Society in 1831, and the American Anti-Slavery Society (AASS) in 1833. By 1838, the AASS had 250,000 members, sometimes called Garrisonians. They rejected colonization as a racist scheme and opposed the use of violence to end slavery. Influenced by evangelical Protestantism, Garrison and other abolitionists believed in **moral suasion**, a technique of appealing to the conscience of the public, especially slaveholders. Moral suasion relied on dramatic narratives, often from former slaves, about the horrors of slavery, arguing that slavery destroyed families, as children were sold and taken away from their mothers and fathers (Figure 13.16). Moral suasion resonated with many women, who condemned the sexual violence against slave women and the victimization of southern white women by adulterous husbands.

(a)　　　　　　　　　　　　　　　　　　　　(b)

Figure 13.16 These woodcuts of a chained and pleading slave, *Am I Not a Man and a Brother?* (a) and *Am I Not a Woman and a Sister?*, accompanied abolitionist John Greenleaf Whittier's antislavery poem, "Our Countrymen in Chains." Such images exemplified moral suasion: showing with pathos and humanity the moral wrongness of slavery.

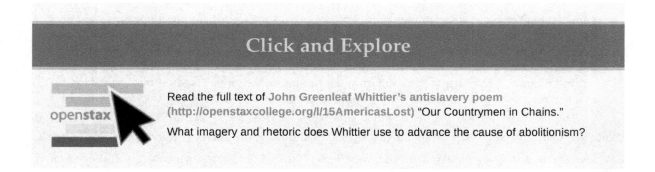

Click and Explore

Read the full text of John Greenleaf Whittier's antislavery poem (http://openstaxcollege.org/l/15AmericasLost) "Our Countrymen in Chains."

What imagery and rhetoric does Whittier use to advance the cause of abolitionism?

Garrison also preached **immediatism**: the moral demand to take immediate action to end slavery. He wrote of equal rights and demanded that blacks be treated as equal to whites. He appealed to women and men, black and white, to join the fight. The abolition press, which produced hundreds of tracts, helped to circulate moral suasion. Garrison and other abolitionists also used the power of petitions, sending hundreds of petitions to Congress in the early 1830s, demanding an end to slavery. Since most newspapers published congressional proceedings, the debate over abolition petitions reached readers throughout the nation.

Although Garrison rejected the U.S. political system as a tool of slaveholders, other abolitionists believed mainstream politics could bring about their goal, and they helped create the Liberty Party in 1840. Its first candidate was James G. Birney, who ran for president that year. Birney epitomized the ideal and goals of the abolitionist movement. Born in Kentucky in 1792, Birney owned slaves and, searching for a solution to what he eventually condemned as the immorality of slavery, initially endorsed colonization. In the 1830s, however, he rejected colonization, freed his slaves, and began to advocate the immediate end of slavery. The Liberty Party did not generate much support and remained a fringe third party. Many of its supporters turned to the Free-Soil Party in the aftermath of the Mexican Cession.

The vast majority of northerners rejected abolition entirely. Indeed, abolition generated a fierce backlash in the United States, especially during the Age of Jackson, when racism saturated American culture. Anti-abolitionists in the North saw Garrison and other abolitionists as the worst of the worst, a threat to the republic that might destroy all decency and order by upending time-honored distinctions between blacks and whites, and between women and men. Northern anti-abolitionists feared that if slavery ended, the North would be flooded with blacks who would take jobs from whites.

Opponents made clear their resistance to Garrison and others of his ilk; Garrison nearly lost his life in 1835, when a Boston anti-abolitionist mob dragged him through the city streets. Anti-abolitionists tried to pass federal laws that made the distribution of abolitionist literature a criminal offense, fearing that such literature, with its engravings and simple language, could spark rebellious blacks to action. Their sympathizers in Congress passed a "gag rule" that forbade the consideration of the many hundreds of petitions sent to Washington by abolitionists. A mob in Illinois killed an abolitionist named Elijah Lovejoy in 1837, and the following year, ten thousand protestors destroyed the abolitionists' newly built Pennsylvania Hall in Philadelphia, burning it to the ground.

Frederick Douglass

Many escaped slaves joined the abolitionist movement, including Frederick Douglass. Douglass was born in Maryland in 1818, escaping to New York in 1838. He later moved to New Bedford, Massachusetts, with his wife. Douglass's commanding presence and powerful speaking skills electrified his listeners when he began to provide public lectures on slavery. He came to the attention of Garrison and others, who encouraged him to publish his story. In 1845, Douglass published *Narrative of the Life of Frederick Douglass, An American Slave Written by Himself*, in which he told about his life of slavery in Maryland (**Figure 13.17**). He identified by name the whites who had brutalized him, and for that reason, along with the mere act of publishing his story, Douglass had to flee the United States to avoid being murdered.

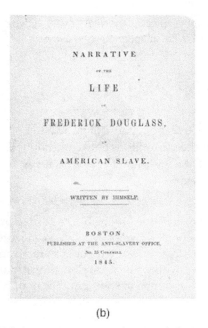

(a)   (b)

Figure 13.17 This 1856 ambrotype of Frederick Douglass (a) demonstrates an early type of photography developed on glass. Douglass was an escaped slave who was instrumental in the abolitionism movement. His slave narrative, told in *Narrative of the Life of Frederick Douglass, An American Slave Written by Himself* (b), followed a long line of similar narratives that demonstrated the brutality of slavery for northerners unfamiliar with the institution.

British abolitionist friends bought his freedom from his Maryland owner, and Douglass returned to the United States. He began to publish his own abolitionist newspaper, *North Star*, in Rochester, New York. During the 1840s and 1850s, Douglass labored to bring about the end of slavery by telling the story of his life and highlighting how slavery destroyed families, both black and white.

MY STORY

✣ *Frederick Douglass on Slavery*

Most white slaveholders frequently raped female slaves. In this excerpt, Douglass explains the consequences for the children fathered by white masters and slave women.

> Slaveholders have ordained, and by law established, that the children of slave women shall in all cases follow the condition of their mothers . . . this is done too obviously to administer to their own lusts, and make a gratification of their wicked desires profitable as well as pleasurable . . . the slaveholder, in cases not a few, sustains to his slaves the double relation of master and father. . . .
>
> Such slaves [born of white masters] invariably suffer greater hardships . . . They are . . . a constant offence to their mistress . . . she is never better pleased than when she sees them under the lash, . . . The master is frequently compelled to sell this class of his slaves, out of deference to the feelings of his white wife; and, cruel as the deed may strike any one to be, for a man to sell his own children to human flesh-mongers, . . . for, unless he does this, he must not only whip them himself, but must stand by and see one white son tie up his brother, of but few shades darker . . . and ply the gory lash to his naked back.
>
> —Frederick Douglass, *Narrative of the Life of Frederick Douglass, An American Slave Written by Himself* (1845)

What moral complications did slavery unleash upon white slaveholders in the South, according to Douglass? What imagery does he use?

13.5 Women's Rights

By the end of this section, you will be able to:
- Explain the connections between abolition, reform, and antebellum feminism
- Describe the ways antebellum women's movements were both traditional and revolutionary

Women took part in all the antebellum reforms, from transcendentalism to temperance to abolition. In many ways, traditional views of women as nurturers played a role in encouraging their participation. Women who joined the cause of temperance, for example, amplified their accepted role as moral guardians of the home. Some women advocated a much more expansive role for themselves and their peers by educating children and men in solid republican principles. But it was their work in antislavery efforts that served as a springboard for women to take action against gender inequality. Many, especially northern women, came to the conclusion that they, like slaves, were held in shackles in a society dominated by men.

Despite the radical nature of their effort to end slavery and create a biracial society, most abolitionist men clung to traditional notions of proper gender roles. White and black women, as well as free black men, were forbidden from occupying leadership positions in the AASS. Because women were not allowed to join the men in playing leading roles in the organization, they formed separate societies, such as the Boston Female Anti-Slavery Society, the Philadelphia Female Anti-Slavery Society, and similar groups.

THE GRIMKÉ SISTERS

Two leading abolitionist women, Sarah and Angelina Grimké, played major roles in combining the fight to end slavery with the struggle to achieve female equality. The sisters had been born into a prosperous slaveholding family in South Carolina. Both were caught up in the religious fervor of the Second Great Awakening, and they moved to the North and converted to Quakerism.

In the mid-1830s, the sisters joined the abolitionist movement, and in 1837, they embarked on a public lecture tour, speaking about immediate abolition to "promiscuous assemblies," that is, to audiences of women and men. This public action thoroughly scandalized respectable society, where it was unheard of for women to lecture to men. William Lloyd Garrison endorsed the Grimké sisters' public lectures, but other abolitionists did not. Their lecture tour served as a turning point; the reaction against them propelled the question of women's proper sphere in society to the forefront of public debate.

THE DECLARATION OF RIGHTS AND SENTIMENTS

Participation in the abolitionist movement led some women to embrace feminism, the advocacy of women's rights. Lydia Maria Child, an abolitionist and feminist, observed, "The comparison between women and the colored race is striking . . . both have been kept in subjection by physical force." Other women, including Elizabeth Cady Stanton, Lucy Stone, and Susan B. Anthony, agreed (Figure 13.18).

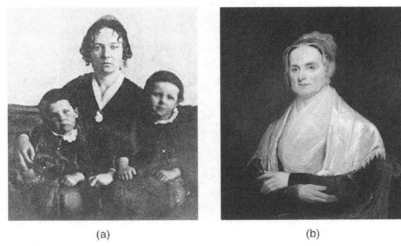

(a)   (b)

Figure 13.18   Elizabeth Cady Stanton (a) and Lucretia Mott (b) both emerged from the abolitionist movement as strong advocates of women's rights.

In 1848, about three hundred male and female feminists, many of them veterans of the abolition campaign, gathered at the **Seneca Falls** Convention in New York for a conference on women's rights that was organized by Lucretia Mott and Elizabeth Cady Stanton. It was the first of what became annual meetings that have continued to the present day. Attendees agreed to a "Declaration of Rights and Sentiments" based on the Declaration of Independence; it declared, "We hold these truths to be self-evident: that all men and women are created equal; that they are endowed by their Creator with certain inalienable rights; that among these are life, liberty, and the pursuit of happiness." "The history of mankind," the document continued, "is a history of repeated injuries and usurpations on the part of man toward woman, having in direct object the establishment of an absolute tyranny over her."

Click and Explore

Read the entire text of the Declaration of Rights and Sentiments (http://openstaxcollege.org/l/15SenecaFalls) in the Internet Modern History Sourcebook at Fordham University.

REPUBLICAN MOTHERHOOD IN THE ANTEBELLUM YEARS

Some northern female reformers saw new and vital roles for their sex in the realm of education. They believed in traditional gender roles, viewing women as inherently more moral and nurturing than men. Because of these attributes, the feminists argued, women were uniquely qualified to take up the roles of educators of children.

Catharine Beecher, the daughter of Lyman Beecher, pushed for women's roles as educators. In her 1845 book, *The Duty of American Women to Their Country*, she argued that the United States had lost its moral compass due to democratic excess. Both "intelligence and virtue" were imperiled in an age of riots and disorder. Women, she argued, could restore the moral center by instilling in children a sense of right and wrong. Beecher represented a northern, middle-class female sensibility. The home, especially the parlor, became the site of northern female authority.

Key Terms

abolitionist a believer in the complete elimination of slavery

colonization the strategy of moving African Americans out of the United States, usually to Africa

immediatism the moral demand to take immediate action against slavery to bring about its end

millennialism the belief that the Kingdom of God would be established on earth and that God would reign on earth for a thousand years characterized by harmony and Christian morality

moral suasion an abolitionist technique of appealing to the consciences of the public, especially slaveholders

Mormons an American denomination, also known as the Latter-Day Saints, that emphasized patriarchal leadership

phrenology the mapping of the mind to specific human attributes

pietistic the stressing of stressed transformative individual religious experience or piety over religious rituals and formality

Second Great Awakening a revival of evangelical Protestantism in the early nineteenth century

Seneca Falls the location of the first American conference on women's rights and the signing of the "Declaration of Rights and Sentiments" in 1848

Shakers a religious sect that emphasized communal living and celibacy

teetotalism complete abstinence from all alcohol

temperance a social movement encouraging moderation or self-restraint in the consumption of alcoholic beverages

transcendentalism the belief that all people can attain an understanding of the world that transcends rational, sensory experience

Summary

13.1 An Awakening of Religion and Individualism

Evangelical Protestantism pervaded American culture in the antebellum era and fueled a belief in the possibility of changing society for the better. Leaders of the Second Great Awakening like Charles G. Finney urged listeners to take charge of their own salvation. This religious message dovetailed with the new economic possibilities created by the market and Industrial Revolution, making the Protestantism of the Second Great Awakening, with its emphasis on individual spiritual success, a reflection of the individualistic, capitalist spirit of the age. Transcendentalists took a different approach, but like their religiously oriented brethren, they too looked to create a better existence. These authors, most notably Emerson, identified a major tension in American life between the effort to be part of the democratic majority and the need to remain true to oneself as an individual.

13.2 Antebellum Communal Experiments

Reformers who engaged in communal experiments aimed to recast economic and social relationships by introducing innovations designed to create a more stable and equitable society. Their ideas found many expressions, from early socialist experiments (such as by the Fourierists and the Owenites) to the dreams of the New England intellectual elite (such as Brook Farm). The Second Great Awakening also prompted many religious utopias, like those of the Rappites and Shakers. By any measure, the Mormons emerged as the most successful of these.

13.3 Reforms to Human Health

Reformers targeted vices that corrupted the human body and society: the individual and the national soul. For many, alcohol appeared to be the most destructive and widespread. Indeed, in the years before the Civil War, the United States appeared to be a republic of drunkenness to many. To combat this national substance abuse problem, reformers created a host of temperance organizations that first targeted the middle and upper classes, and then the working classes. Thanks to Sylvester Graham and other health reformers, exercise and fresh air, combined with a good diet, became fashionable. Phrenologists focused on revealing the secrets of the mind and personality. In a fast-paced world, phrenology offered the possibility of knowing different human characteristics.

13.4 Addressing Slavery

Contrasting proposals were put forth to deal with slavery. Reformers in the antebellum United States addressed the thorny issue of slavery through contrasting proposals that offered profoundly different solutions to the dilemma of the institution. Many leading American statesmen, including slaveholders, favored colonization, relocating American blacks to Africa, which abolitionists scorned. Slave rebellions sought the end of the institution through its violent overthrow, a tactic that horrified many in the North and the South. Abolitionists, especially those who followed William Lloyd Garrison, provoked equally strong reactions by envisioning a new United States without slavery, where blacks and whites stood on equal footing. Opponents saw abolition as the worst possible reform, a threat to all order and decency. Slaveholders, in particular, saw slavery as a positive aspect of American society, one that reformed the lives of slaves by exposing them to civilization and religion.

13.5 Women's Rights

The spirit of religious awakening and reform in the antebellum era impacted women lives by allowing them to think about their lives and their society in new and empowering ways. Of all the various antebellum reforms, however, abolition played a significant role in generating the early feminist movement in the United States. Although this early phase of American feminism did not lead to political rights for women, it began the long process of overcoming gender inequalities in the republic.

Review Questions

1. Which of the following is *not* a characteristic of the Second Great Awakening?
   A. greater emphasis on nature
   B. greater emphasis on religious education of children
   C. greater church attendance
   D. belief in the possibility of a better world

2. Transcendentalists were most concerned with _____.
   A. the afterlife
   B. predestination
   C. the individual
   D. democracy

3. What do the Second Great Awakening and transcendentalism have in common?

4. Which religious community focused on the power of patriarchy?
   A. Shakers
   B. Mormons
   C. Owenites
   D. Rappites

5. Which community or movement is associated with transcendentalism?
    A. the Oneida Community
    B. the Ephrata Cloister
    C. Brook Farm
    D. Fourierism

6. How were the reform communities of the antebellum era treated by the general population?

7. The first temperance laws were enacted by

_____.

    A. state governments
    B. local governments
    C. the federal government
    D. temperance organizations

8. Sylvester Graham's reformers targeted

_____.

    A. the human body
    B. nutrition
    C. sexuality
    D. all of the above

9. Whom did temperance reformers target?

10. In the context of the antebellum era, what does colonization refer to?
    A. Great Britain's colonization of North America

    B. the relocation of African Americans to Africa
    C. American colonization of the Caribbean
    D. American colonization of Africa

11. Which of the following did William Lloyd Garrison *not* employ in his abolitionist efforts?
    A. moral suasion
    B. immediatism
    C. political involvement
    D. pamphleteering

12. Why did William Lloyd Garrison's endorsement of the Grimké sisters divide the abolitionist movement?
    A. They advocated equal rights for women.
    B. They supported colonization.
    C. They attended the Seneca Falls Convention.
    D. They lectured to co-ed audiences.

13. Which female reformer focused on women's roles as the educators of children?
    A. Lydia Maria Child
    B. Sarah Grimké
    C. Catherine Beecher
    D. Susan B. Anthony

14. How did the abolitionist movement impact the women's movement?

Critical Thinking Questions

15. In what ways did the Second Great Awakening and transcendentalism reflect and react to the changes in antebellum American thought and culture?

16. What did the antebellum communal projects have in common? How did the ones most influenced by religion differ from those that had other influences?

17. In what ways do temperance, health reforms, and phrenology offer reflections on the changes in the United States before the Civil War? What needs did these reforms fill in the lives of antebellum Americans?

18. Of the various approaches to the problem of slavery, which one do you find to be the most effective and why?

19. In what ways were antebellum feminists radical? In what ways were they traditional?

CHAPTER 14

Troubled Times: the Tumultuous 1850s

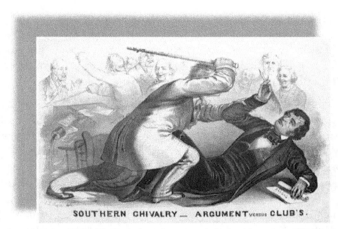

Figure 14.1 In *Southern Chivalry: Argument versus Club's* (1856), by John Magee, South Carolinian Preston Brooks attacks Massachusetts senator Charles Sumner after his speech denouncing "border ruffians" pouring into Kansas from Missouri. For southerners, defending slavery meant defending southern honor.

Chapter Outline

14.1 The Compromise of 1850
14.2 The Kansas-Nebraska Act and the Republican Party
14.3 The Dred Scott Decision and Sectional Strife
14.4 John Brown and the Election of 1860

Introduction

The heated sectional controversy between the North and the South reached new levels of intensity in the 1850s. Southerners and northerners grew ever more antagonistic as they debated the expansion of slavery in the West. The notorious confrontation between Representative Preston Brooks of South Carolina and Massachusetts senator Charles Sumner depicted in the image above (Figure 14.1), illustrates the contempt between extremists on both sides. The "Caning of Sumner" in May 1856 followed upon a speech given by Sumner two days earlier in which he condemned slavery in no uncertain terms, declaring: "[Admitting Kansas as a slave state] is the rape of a virgin territory, compelling it to the hateful embrace of slavery; and it may be clearly traced to a depraved longing for a new slave state, the hideous offspring of such a crime, in the hope of adding to the power of slavery in the national government." Sumner criticized proslavery legislators, particularly attacking a fellow senator and relative of Preston Brooks. Brooks responded by beating Sumner with a cane, a thrashing that southerners celebrated as a manly defense of gentlemanly honor and their way of life. The episode highlights the violent clash between pro- and antislavery factions in the 1850s, a conflict that would eventually lead to the traumatic unraveling of American democracy and civil war.

14.1 The Compromise of 1850

By the end of this section, you will be able to:
* Explain the contested issues that led to the Compromise of 1850
* Describe and analyze the reactions to the 1850 Fugitive Slave Act

At the end of the Mexican-American War, the United States gained a large expanse of western territory known as the Mexican Cession. The disposition of this new territory was in question; would the new states be slave states or free-soil states? In the long run, the Mexican-American War achieved what abolitionism alone had failed to do: it mobilized many in the North against slavery.

Antislavery northerners clung to the idea expressed in the 1846 Wilmot Proviso: slavery would not expand into the areas taken, and later bought, from Mexico. Though the proviso remained a proposal and never became a law, it defined the sectional division. The Free-Soil Party, which formed at the conclusion of the Mexican-American War in 1848 and included many members of the failed Liberty Party, made this position the centerpiece of all its political activities, ensuring that the issue of slavery and its expansion remained at the front and center of American political debate. Supporters of the Wilmot Proviso and members of the new Free-Soil Party did not want to abolish slavery in the states where it already existed; rather, Free-Soil advocates demanded that the western territories be kept free of slavery for the benefit of white laborers who might settle there. They wanted to protect white workers from having to compete with slave labor in the West. (Abolitionists, in contrast, looked to destroy slavery everywhere in the United States.) Southern extremists, especially wealthy slaveholders, reacted with outrage at this effort to limit slavery's expansion. They argued for the right to bring their slave property west, and they vowed to leave the Union if necessary to protect their way of life—meaning the right to own slaves—and ensure that the American empire of slavery would continue to grow.

BROKERING THE COMPROMISE

The issue of what to do with the western territories added to the republic by the Mexican Cession consumed Congress in 1850. Other controversial matters, which had been simmering over time,

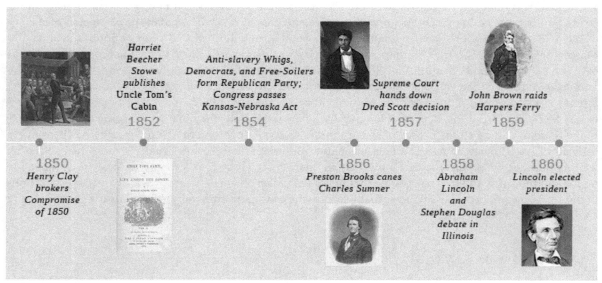

Figure 14.2

complicated the problem further. Chief among these issues were the slave trade in the District of Columbia, which antislavery advocates hoped to end, and the fugitive slave laws, which southerners wanted to strengthen. The border between Texas and New Mexico remained contested because many Texans hoped to enlarge their state further, and, finally, the issue of California had not been resolved. California was the crown jewel of the Mexican Cession, and following the discovery of gold, it was flush with thousands of emigrants. By most estimates, however, it would be a free state, since the former Mexican ban on slavery still remained in force and slavery had not taken root in California. The map below (Figure 14.3) shows the disposition of land before the 1850 compromise.

States and Territories of the United States of America March 3, 1849–September 9, 1850

Figure 14.3 This map shows the states and territories of the United States as they were in 1849–1850. (credit "User:Golbez"/Wikimedia Commons)

The presidential election of 1848 did little to solve the problems resulting from the Mexican Cession. Both the Whigs and the Democrats attempted to avoid addressing the issue of slavery publicly as much as possible. The Democrats nominated Lewis Cass of Michigan, a supporter of the idea of popular sovereignty, or letting the people in the territories decide the issue of whether or not to permit slavery based on majority rule. The Whigs nominated General Zachary Taylor, a slaveholder from Louisiana, who had achieved national prominence as a military hero in the Mexican-American War. Taylor did not take a personal stand on any issue and remained silent throughout the campaign. The fledgling Free-Soil Party put forward former president Martin Van Buren as their candidate. The Free-Soil Party attracted northern Democrats who supported the Wilmot Proviso, northern Whigs who rejected Taylor because he was a slaveholder, former members of the Liberty Party, and other abolitionists.

Both the Whigs and the Democrats ran different campaigns in the North and South. In the North, all three parties attempted to win voters with promises of keeping the territories free of slavery, while in the South, Whigs and Democrats promised to protect slavery in the territories. For southern voters, the slaveholder Taylor appeared the natural choice. In the North, the Free-Soil Party took votes away from Whigs and Democrats and helped to ensure Taylor's election in 1848.

As president, Taylor sought to defuse the sectional controversy as much as possible, and, above all else, to preserve the Union. Although Taylor was born in Virginia before relocating to Kentucky and owned more than one hundred slaves by the late 1840s, he did not push for slavery's expansion into the Mexican Cession. However, the California Gold Rush made California's statehood into an issue demanding immediate attention. In 1849, after California residents adopted a state constitution prohibiting slavery, President Taylor called on Congress to admit California and New Mexico as free states, a move that infuriated southern defenders of slavery who argued for the right to bring their slave property wherever they chose. Taylor, who did not believe slavery could flourish in the arid lands of the Mexican Cession because the climate prohibited plantation-style farming, proposed that the Wilmot Proviso be applied to the entire area.

In Congress, Kentucky senator Henry Clay, a veteran of congressional conflicts, offered a series of resolutions addressing the list of issues related to slavery and its expansion. Clay's resolutions called for the admission of California as a free state; no restrictions on slavery in the rest of the Mexican Cession (a rejection of the Wilmot Proviso and the Free-Soil Party's position); a boundary between New Mexico and Texas that did not expand Texas (an important matter, since Texas allowed slavery and a larger Texas meant more opportunities for the expansion of slavery); payment of outstanding Texas debts from the Lone Star Republic days; and the end of the slave trade (but not of slavery) in the nation's capital, coupled with a more robust federal fugitive slave law. Clay presented these proposals as an omnibus bill, that is, one that would be voted on its totality.

Clay's proposals ignited a spirited and angry debate that lasted for eight months. The resolution calling for California to be admitted as a free state aroused the wrath of the aged and deathly ill John C. Calhoun, the elder statesman for the proslavery position. Calhoun, too sick to deliver a speech, had his friend Virginia senator James Mason present his assessment of Clay's resolutions and the current state of sectional strife.

In Calhoun's eyes, blame for the stalemate fell squarely on the North, which stood in the way of southern and American prosperity by limiting the zones where slavery could flourish. Calhoun called for a vigorous federal law to ensure that runaway slaves were returned to their masters. He also proposed a constitutional amendment specifying a dual presidency—one office that would represent the South and another for the North—a suggestion that hinted at the possibility of disunion. Calhoun's argument portrayed an embattled South faced with continued northern aggression—a line of reasoning that only furthered the sectional divide.

Several days after Mason delivered Calhoun's speech, Massachusetts senator Daniel Webster countered Calhoun in his "Seventh of March" speech. Webster called for national unity, famously declaring that he spoke "not as a Massachusetts man, not as a Northern man, but as an American." Webster asked southerners to end threats of disunion and requested that the North stop antagonizing the South by harping on the Wilmot Proviso. Like Calhoun, Webster also called for a new federal law to ensure the return of runaway slaves.

Webster's efforts to compromise led many abolitionist sympathizers to roundly denounce him as a traitor. Whig senator William H. Seward, who aspired to be president, declared that slavery—which he characterized as incompatible with the assertion in the Declaration of Independence that "all men are created equal"—would one day be extinguished in the United States. Seward's speech, in which he invoked the idea of a higher moral law than the Constitution, secured his reputation in the Senate as an advocate of abolition.

The speeches made in Congress were published in the nation's newspapers, and the American public followed the debates with great interest, anxious to learn how the issues of the day, especially the potential advance of slavery, would be resolved. Colorful reports of wrangling in Congress further piqued public interest. Indeed, it was not uncommon for arguments to devolve into fistfights or worse. One of the most astonishing episodes of the debate occurred in April 1850, when a quarrel erupted between Missouri Democratic senator Thomas Hart Benton, who by the time of the debate had become a critic of slavery (despite owning slaves), and Mississippi Democratic senator Henry S. Foote. When the burly Benton appeared ready to assault Foote, the Mississippi senator drew his pistol (Figure 14.4).

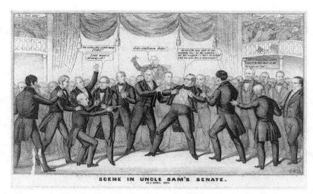

Figure 14.4 This 1850 print, *Scene in Uncle Sam's Senate*, depicts Mississippi senator Henry S. Foote taking aim at Missouri senator Thomas Hart Benton. In the print, Benton declares: "Get out of the way, and let the assassin fire! let the scoundrel use his weapon! I have no arm's! I did not come here to assassinate!" Foote responds, "I only meant to defend myself!" (credit: Library of Congress)

President Taylor and Henry Clay, whose resolutions had begun the verbal fireworks in the Senate, had no patience for each other. Clay had long harbored ambitions for the White House, and, for his part, Taylor resented Clay and disapproved of his resolutions. With neither side willing to budge, the government stalled on how to resolve the disposition of the Mexican Cession and the other issues of slavery. The drama only increased when on July 4, 1850, President Taylor became gravely ill, reportedly after eating an excessive amount of fruit washed down with milk. He died five days later, and Vice President Millard Fillmore became president. Unlike his predecessor, who many believed would be opposed to a compromise, Fillmore worked with Congress to achieve a solution to the crisis of 1850.

In the end, Clay stepped down as leader of the compromise effort in frustration, and Illinois senator Stephen Douglas pushed five separate bills through Congress, collectively composing the Compromise of 1850. First, as advocated by the South, Congress passed the Fugitive Slave Act, a law that provided federal money—or "bounties"—to slave-catchers. Second, to balance this concession to the South, Congress admitted California as a free state, a move that cheered antislavery advocates and abolitionists in the North. Third, Congress settled the contested boundary between New Mexico and Texas by favoring New Mexico and not allowing for an enlarged Texas, another outcome pleasing to the North. Fourth, antislavery advocates welcomed Congress's ban on the slave trade in Washington, DC, although slavery continued to thrive in the nation's capital. Finally, on the thorny issue of whether slavery would expand into the territories, Congress avoided making a direct decision and instead relied on the principle of popular sovereignty. This put the onus on residents of the territories to decide for themselves whether to allow slavery. Popular sovereignty followed the logic of American democracy; majorities in each territory would decide the territory's laws. The compromise, however, further exposed the sectional divide as votes on the bills divided along strict regional lines.

Most Americans breathed a sigh of relief over the deal brokered in 1850, choosing to believe it had saved the Union. Rather than resolving divisions between the North and the South, however, the compromise stood as a truce in an otherwise white-hot sectional conflict. Tensions in the nation remained extremely high; indeed, southerners held several conventions after the compromise to discuss ways to protect the South. At these meetings, extremists who called for secession found themselves in the minority, since most southerners committed themselves to staying in the Union—but only if slavery remained in the states where it already existed, and if no effort was made to block its expansion into areas where citizens wanted it, thereby applying the idea of popular sovereignty (Figure 14.5).

Figure 14.5 This map shows the states and territories of the United States as they were from 1850 to March 1853. (credit "User:Golbez"/Wikimedia Commons)

THE FUGITIVE SLAVE ACT AND ITS CONSEQUENCES

The hope that the Compromise of 1850 would resolve the sectional crisis proved short-lived when the Fugitive Slave Act turned into a major source of conflict. The federal law imposed heavy fines and prison sentences on northerners and midwesterners who aided runaway slaves or refused to join posses to catch fugitives. Many northerners felt the law forced them to act as slave-catchers against their will.

The law also established a new group of federal commissioners who would decide the fate of fugitives brought before them. In some instances, slave-catchers even brought in free northern blacks, prompting abolitionist societies to step up their efforts to prevent kidnappings (Figure 14.6). The commissioners had a financial incentive to send fugitives and free blacks to the slaveholding South, since they received ten dollars for every African American sent to the South and only five if they decided the person who came before them was actually free. The commissioners used no juries, and the alleged runaways could not testify in their own defense.

Figure 14.6 This 1851 poster, written by Boston abolitionist Theodore Parker, warned that any black person, free or slave, risked kidnapping by slave-catchers.

The operation of the law further alarmed northerners and confirmed for many the existence of a "Slave Power"—that is, a minority of elite slaveholders who wielded a disproportionate amount of power over the federal government, shaping domestic and foreign policies to suit their interests. Despite southerners' repeated insistence on states' rights, the Fugitive Slave Act showed that slaveholders were willing to use the power of the federal government to bend people in other states to their will. While rejecting the use of federal power to restrict the expansion of slavery, proslavery southerners turned to the federal government to protect and promote the institution of slavery.

The actual number of runaway slaves who were not captured within a year of escaping remained very low, perhaps no more than one thousand per year in the early 1850s. Most stayed in the South, hiding in plain sight among free blacks in urban areas. Nonetheless, southerners feared the influence of a vast **Underground Railroad**: the network of northern whites and free blacks who sympathized with runaway slaves and provided safe houses and safe passage from the South. Quakers, who had long been troubled by slavery, were especially active in this network. It is unclear how many slaves escaped through the Underground Railroad, but historians believe that between 50,000 and 100,000 slaves used the network in their bids for freedom. Meanwhile, the 1850 Fugitive Slave Act greatly increased the perils of being captured. For many thousands of fugitives, escaping the United States completely by going to southern Ontario, Canada, where slavery had been abolished, offered the best chance of a better life beyond the reach of slaveholders.

Harriet Tubman, one of the thousands of slaves who made their escape through the Underground Railroad, distinguished herself for her efforts in helping other enslaved men and women escape. Born a slave in Maryland around 1822, Tubman, who suffered greatly under slavery but found solace in Christianity, made her escape in the late 1840s. She returned to the South more than a dozen times to lead other slaves, including her family and friends, along the Underground Railroad to freedom.

DEFINING "AMERICAN"

✪ *Harriet Tubman: An American Moses?*

Harriet Tubman (Figure 14.7) was a legendary figure in her own time and beyond. An escaped slave herself, she returned to the South thirteen times to help over three hundred slaves through the Underground Railroad to liberty in the North. In 1869, printer William J. Moses published Sarah H. Bradford's *Scenes in the Life of Harriet Tubman*. Bradford was a writer and biographer who had known Tubman's family for years. The excerpt below is from the beginning of her book, which she updated in 1886 under the title *Harriet, the Moses of Her People*.

Figure 14.7   This full-length portrait of Harriet Tubman hangs in the National Portrait Gallery of the Smithsonian.

> It is proposed in this little book to give a plain and unvarnished account of some scenes and adventures in the life of a woman who, though one of earth's lowly ones, and of dark-hued skin, has shown an amount of heroism in her character rarely possessed by those of any station in life. Her name (we say it advisedly and without exaggeration) deserves to be handed down to posterity side by side with the names of Joan of Arc, Grace Darling, and Florence Nightingale; for not one of these women has shown more courage and power of endurance in facing danger and death to relieve human suffering, than has this woman in her heroic and successful endeavors to reach and save all whom she might of her oppressed and suffering race, and to pilot them from the land of Bondage to the promised land of Liberty. Well has she been called "Moses," for she has been a leader and deliverer unto hundreds of her people.
> —Sarah H. Bradford, *Scenes in the Life of Harriet Tubman*

How does Bradford characterize Tubman? What language does Bradford use to tie religion into the fight for freedom?

The Fugitive Slave Act provoked widespread reactions in the North. Some abolitionists, such as Frederick Douglass, believed that standing up against the law necessitated violence. In Boston and elsewhere, abolitionists tried to protect fugitives from federal authorities. One case involved Anthony Burns, who had escaped slavery in Virginia in 1853 and made his way to Boston (Figure 14.8). When federal officials arrested Burns in 1854, abolitionists staged a series of mass demonstrations and a confrontation at the courthouse. Despite their best efforts, however, Burns was returned to Virginia when President Franklin Pierce supported the Fugitive Slave Act with federal troops. Boston abolitionists eventually bought Burns's freedom. For many northerners, however, the Burns incident, combined with Pierce's response, only amplified their sense of a conspiracy of southern power.

Figure 14.8 *Anthony Burns*, drawn ca. 1855 by an artist identified only as "Barry," shows a portrait of the fugitive slave surrounded by scenes from his life, including his escape from Virginia, his arrest in Boston, and his address to the court.

The most consequential reaction against the Fugitive Slave Act came in the form of a novel, *Uncle Tom's Cabin*. In it, author Harriet Beecher Stowe, born in Connecticut, made use of slaves' stories she had heard firsthand after marrying and moving to Ohio, then on the country's western frontier. Her novel first appeared as a series of stories in a Free-Soil newspaper, the *National Era*, in 1851 and was published as a book the following year. Stowe told the tale of slaves who were sold by their Kentucky master. While Uncle Tom is indeed sold down the river, young Eliza escapes with her baby (Figure 14.9). The story highlighted the idea that slavery was a sin because it destroyed families, ripping children from their parents and husbands and wives from one another. Stowe also emphasized the ways in which slavery corrupted white citizens. The cruelty of some of the novel's white slaveholders (who genuinely believe that slaves don't feel things the way that white people do) and the brutality of the slave dealer Simon Legree, who beats slaves and sexually exploits a slave woman, demonstrate the dehumanizing effect of the institution even on those who benefit from it.

Figure 14.9 This drawing from *Uncle Tom's Cabin*, captioned "Eliza comes to tell Uncle Tom that he is sold, and that she is running away to save her child," illustrates the ways in which Harriet Beecher Stowe's antislavery novel bolstered abolitionists' arguments against slavery.

Stowe's novel proved a runaway bestseller and was the most-read novel of the nineteenth century, inspiring multiple theatrical productions and musical compositions. It was translated into sixty languages and remains in print to this day. Its message about the evils of slavery helped convince many northerners of the righteousness of the cause of abolition. The novel also demonstrated the power of women to shape public opinion. Stowe and other American women believed they had a moral obligation to mold the conscience of the United States, even though they could not vote (Figure 14.10).

Figure 14.10 This photograph shows Harriet Beecher Stowe, the author of *Uncle Tom's Cabin*, in 1852. Stowe's work was an inspiration not only to abolitionists, but also to those who believed that women could play a significant role in upholding the nation's morality and shaping public opinion.

Click and Explore

Visit the **Documenting the American South (http://openstaxcollege.org/l/15LeviCoffin)** collection on the University of North Carolina at Chapel Hill website to read the memoirs of Levi Coffin, a prominent Quaker abolitionist who was known as the "president" of the Underground Railroad for his active role in helping slaves to freedom. The memoirs include the story of Eliza Harris, which inspired Harriet Beecher Stowe's famous character.

The backlash against the Fugitive Slave Act, fueled by *Uncle Tom's Cabin* and well-publicized cases like that of Anthony Burns, also found expression in personal liberty laws passed by eight northern state legislatures. These laws emphasized that the state would provide legal protection to anyone arrested as a fugitive slave, including the right to trial by jury. The personal liberty laws stood as a clear-cut example of the North's use of states' rights in opposition to federal power while providing further evidence to southerners that northerners had no respect for the Fugitive Slave Act or slaveholders' property rights.

Click and Explore

Go to an archived page from the **Michigan Department of Natural Resources (http://openstaxcollege.org/l/15MIPFreedom)** site to read the original text of Michigan's 1855 personal liberty laws. How do these laws refute the provisions of the federal Fugitive Slave Act of 1850?

14.2 The Kansas-Nebraska Act and the Republican Party

By the end of this section, you will be able to:
- Explain the political ramifications of the Kansas-Nebraska Act
- Describe the founding of the Republican Party

In the early 1850s, the United States' sectional crisis had abated somewhat, cooled by the Compromise of 1850 and the nation's general prosperity. In 1852, voters went to the polls in a presidential contest between Whig candidate Winfield Scott and Democratic candidate Franklin Pierce. Both men endorsed the Compromise of 1850. Though it was considered unseemly to hit the campaign trail, Scott did so—much to the benefit of Pierce, as Scott's speeches focused on forty-year-old battles during the War of 1812 and the weather. In New York, Scott, known as "Old Fuss and Feathers," talked about a thunderstorm that did not occur and greatly confused the crowd. In Ohio, a cannon firing to herald Scott's arrival killed a spectator.

Pierce was a supporter of the "Young America" movement of the Democratic Party, which enthusiastically anticipated extending democracy around the world and annexing additional territory for the United

States. Pierce did not take a stance on the slavery issue. Helped by Scott's blunders and the fact that he had played no role in the bruising political battles of the past five years, Pierce won the election. The brief period of tranquility between the North and South did not last long, however; it came to an end in 1854 with the passage of the Kansas-Nebraska Act. This act led to the formation of a new political party, the Republican Party, that committed itself to ending the further expansion of slavery.

THE KANSAS-NEBRASKA ACT

The relative calm over the sectional issue was broken in 1854 over the issue of slavery in the territory of Kansas. Pressure had been building among northerners to organize the territory west of Missouri and Iowa, which had been admitted to the Union as a free state in 1846. This pressure came primarily from northern farmers, who wanted the federal government to survey the land and put it up for sale. Promoters of a transcontinental railroad were also pushing for this westward expansion.

Southerners, however, had long opposed the Wilmot Proviso's stipulation that slavery should not expand into the West. By the 1850s, many in the South were also growing resentful of the Missouri Compromise of 1820, which established the 36° 30' parallel as the geographical boundary of slavery on the north-south axis. Proslavery southerners now contended that popular sovereignty should apply to all territories, not just Utah and New Mexico. They argued for the right to bring their slave property wherever they chose.

Attitudes toward slavery in the 1850s were represented by a variety of regional factions. Throughout the South, slaveholders entrenched themselves in defense of their "way of life," which depended on the ownership of slaves. Since the 1830s, abolitionists, led by journalist and reformer William Lloyd Garrison, had cast slavery as a national sin and called for its immediate end. For three decades, the abolitionists remained a minority, but they had a significant effect on American society by bringing the evils of slavery into the public consciousness. By the 1850s, some abolitionists advocated the use of violence against those who owned slaves. In 1840, the Liberty Party, whose members came from the ranks of ministers, was founded; this group sought to work within the existing political system, a strategy Garrison and others rejected. Meanwhile, the Free-Soil Party committed itself to ensuring that white laborers would find work in newly acquired territories and not have to compete with unpaid slaves.

It is important to note that, even among those who opposed the expansion of slavery in the West, very different attitudes toward slavery existed. Some antislavery northerners wanted the West to be the best country for poor whites to go and seek opportunity. They did not want white workers to have to compete with slave labor, a contest that they believed demeaned white labor. Radical abolitionists, in contrast, envisioned the end of all slavery, and a society of equality between blacks and whites. Others opposed slavery in principle, but believed that the best approach was colonization; that is, settling freed slaves in a colony in Africa.

The growing political movement to address the issue of slavery stiffened the resolve of southern slaveholders to defend themselves and their society at all costs. Prohibiting slavery's expansion, they argued, ran counter to basic American property rights. As abolitionists fanned the flames of antislavery sentiment, southerners solidified their defense of their enormous investment in human chattel. Across the country, people of all political stripes worried that the nation's arguments would cause irreparable rifts in the country (Figure 14.11).

Figure 14.11 In this 1850 political cartoon, the artist takes aim at abolitionists, the Free-Soil Party, Southern states' rights activists, and others he believes risk the health of the Union.

As these different factions were agitating for the settlement of Kansas and Nebraska, leaders of the Democratic Party in 1853 and 1854 sought to bind their party together in the aftermath of intraparty fights over the distribution of patronage jobs. Illinois Democratic senator Stephen Douglas believed he had found a solution—the Kansas-Nebraska bill—that would promote party unity and also satisfy his colleagues from the South, who detested the Missouri Compromise line. In January 1854, Douglas introduced the bill (Figure 14.12). The act created two territories: Kansas, directly west of Missouri; and Nebraska, west of Iowa. The act also applied the principle of popular sovereignty, dictating that the people of these territories would decide for themselves whether to adopt slavery. In a concession crucial to many southerners, the proposed bill would also repeal the 36° 30' line from the Missouri Compromise. Douglas hoped his bill would increase his political capital and provide a step forward on his quest for the presidency. Douglas also wanted the territory organized in hopes of placing the eastern terminus of a transcontinental railroad in Chicago, rather than St. Louis or New Orleans.

Figure 14.12 This 1855 map shows the new territories of Kansas and Nebraska, complete with proposed routes of the transcontinental railroad.

After heated debates, Congress narrowly passed the Kansas-Nebraska Act. (In the House of Representatives, the bill passed by a mere three votes: 113 to 110.) This move had major political consequences. The Democrats divided along sectional lines as a result of the bill, and the Whig party, in decline in the early 1850s, found its political power slipping further. Most important, the Kansas-Nebraska Act gave rise to the **Republican Party**, a new political party that attracted northern Whigs, Democrats who shunned the Kansas-Nebraska Act, members of the Free-Soil Party, and assorted abolitionists. Indeed, with the formation of the Republican Party, the Free-Soil Party ceased to exist.

The new Republican Party pledged itself to preventing the spread of slavery into the territories and railed against the Slave Power, infuriating the South. As a result, the party became a solidly northern political organization. As never before, the U.S. political system was polarized along sectional fault lines.

BLEEDING KANSAS

In 1855 and 1856, pro- and antislavery activists flooded Kansas with the intention of influencing the popular-sovereignty rule of the territories. Proslavery Missourians who crossed the border to vote in Kansas became known as **border ruffians**; these gained the advantage by winning the territorial elections, most likely through voter fraud and illegal vote counting. (By some estimates, up to 60 percent of the votes cast in Kansas were fraudulent.) Once in power, the proslavery legislature, meeting at Lecompton, Kansas, drafted a proslavery constitution known as the Lecompton Constitution. It was supported by President Buchanan, but opposed by Democratic Senator Stephen A. Douglas of Illinois.

DEFINING "AMERICAN"

✷ *The Lecompton Constitution*

Kansas was home to no fewer than four state constitutions in its early years. Its first constitution, the Topeka Constitution, would have made Kansas a free-soil state. A proslavery legislature, however, created the 1857 Lecompton Constitution to enshrine the institution of slavery in the new Kansas-Nebraska territories. In January 1858, Kansas voters defeated the proposed Lecompton Constitution, excerpted below, with an overwhelming margin of 10,226 to 138.

> ARTICLE VII.—SLAVERY
> SECTION 1. The right of property is before and higher than any constitutional sanction, and the right of the owner of a slave to such slave and its increase is the same and as inviolable as the right of the owner of any property whatever.
> SEC. 2. The Legislature shall have no power to pass laws for the emancipation of slaves without the consent of the owners, or without paying the owners previous to their emancipation a full equivalent in money for the slaves so emancipated. They shall have no power to prevent immigrants to the State from bringing with them such persons as are deemed slaves by the laws of any one of the United States or Territories, so long as any person of the same age or description shall be continued in slavery by the laws of this State: Provided, That such person or slave be the bona fide property of such immigrants.

How are slaves defined in the 1857 Kansas constitution? How does this constitution safeguard the rights of slaveholders?

The majority in Kansas, however, were Free-Soilers who seethed at the border ruffians' co-opting of the democratic process (Figure 14.13). Many had come from New England to ensure a numerical advantage over the border ruffians. The New England Emigrant Aid Society, a northern antislavery group, helped fund these efforts to halt the expansion of slavery into Kansas and beyond.

Figure 14.13 This full-page editorial ran in the Free-Soiler *Kansas Tribune* on September 15, 1855, the day Kansas' Act to Punish Offences against Slave Property of 1855 went into effect. This law made it punishable by death to aid or abet a fugitive slave, and it called for punishment of no less than two years for anyone who might: "print, publish, write, circulate, or cause to be introduced into this Territory . . . [any materials] . . . containing any denial of the right of persons to hold slaves in this Territory."

Click and Explore

Go to the Kansas Historical Society's Kansapedia (http://openstaxcollege.org/l/ 15KSConst) to read the four different state constitutions that Kansas had during its early years as a United States Territory. What can you deduce about the authors of each constitution?

In 1856, clashes between antislavery Free-Soilers and border ruffians came to a head in Lawrence, Kansas. The town had been founded by the New England Emigrant Aid Society, which funded antislavery settlement in the territory and were determined that Kansas should be a free-soil state. Proslavery emigrants from Missouri were equally determined that no "abolitionist tyrants" or "negro thieves" would control the territory. In the spring of 1856, several of Lawrence's leading antislavery citizens were indicted for treason, and federal marshal Israel Donaldson called for a posse to help make arrests. He did not have trouble finding volunteers from Missouri. When the posse, which included Douglas County sheriff Samuel Jones, arrived outside Lawrence, the antislavery town's "committee of safety" agreed on a policy of nonresistance. Most of those who were indicted fled. Donaldson arrested two men without incident and dismissed the posse.

However, Jones, who had been shot during an earlier confrontation in the town, did not leave. On May 21, falsely claiming that he had a court order to do so, Jones took command of the posse and rode into town armed with rifles, revolvers, cutlasses and bowie knives. At the head of the procession, two flags flew: an American flag and a flag with a crouching tiger. Other banners followed, bearing the words "Southern rights" and "The Superiority of the White Race." In the rear were five artillery pieces, which were dragged to the center of town. The posse smashed the presses of the two newspapers, *Herald of Freedom* and the *Kansas Free State*, and burned down the deserted Free State Hotel (Figure 14.14). When the posse finally left, Lawrence residents found themselves unharmed but terrified.

The next morning, a man named John Brown and his sons, who were on their way to provide Lawrence with reinforcements, heard the news of the attack. Brown, a strict, God-fearing Calvinist and staunch abolitionist, once remarked that "God had raised him up on purpose to break the jaws of the wicked." Disappointed that the citizens of Lawrence did not resist the "slave hounds" of Missouri, Brown opted not to go to Lawrence, but to the homes of proslavery settlers near Pottawatomie Creek in Kansas. The group of seven, including Brown's four sons, arrived on May 24, 1856, and announced they were the "Northern Army" that had come to serve justice. They burst into the cabin of proslavery Tennessean James Doyle and marched him and two of his sons off, sparing the youngest at the desperate request of Doyle's wife, Mahala. One hundred yards down the road, Owen and Salmon Brown hacked their captives to death with broadswords and John Brown shot a bullet into Doyle's forehead. Before the night was done, the Browns visited two more cabins and brutally executed two other proslavery settlers. None of those executed owned any slaves or had had anything to do with the raid on Lawrence.

Brown's actions precipitated a new wave of violence. All told, the guerilla warfare between proslavery "border ruffians" and antislavery forces, which would continue and even escalate during the Civil War, resulted in over 150 deaths and significant property loss. The events in Kansas served as an extreme reply to Douglas's proposition of popular sovereignty. As the violent clashes increased, Kansas became known as "**Bleeding Kansas**." Antislavery advocates' use of force carved out a new direction for some who opposed slavery. Distancing themselves from William Lloyd Garrison and other pacifists, Brown and fellow abolitionists believed the time had come to fight slavery with violence.

Figure 14.14 This undated image shows the aftermath of the sacking of Lawrence, Kansas, by border ruffians. Shown are the ruins of the Free State Hotel.

The violent hostilities associated with Bleeding Kansas were not limited to Kansas itself. It was the controversy over Kansas that prompted the caning of Charles Sumner, introduced at the beginning of this chapter with the political cartoon *Southern Chivalry: Argument versus Club's* (Figure 14.1). Note the title of the cartoon; it lampoons the southern ideal of chivalry, the code of behavior that Preston Brooks believed he was following in his attack on Sumner. In Sumner's "Crime against Kansas" speech he went much further than politics, filling his verbal attack with allusions to sexuality by singling out fellow senator Andrew Butler from South Carolina, a zealous supporter of slavery and Brooks's uncle. Sumner insulted Butler by comparing slavery to prostitution, declaring, "Of course he [Butler] has chosen a mistress to whom he has made his vows, and who, though ugly to others, is always lovely to him; though polluted in the sight of the world, is chaste in his sight. I mean the harlot Slavery." Because Butler was aged, it was his nephew, Brooks, who sought satisfaction for Sumner's attack on his family and southern honor. Brooks did not challenge Sumner to a duel; by choosing to beat him with a cane instead, he made it clear that he did not consider Sumner a gentleman. Many in the South rejoiced over Brooks's defense of slavery, southern society, and family honor, sending him hundreds of canes to replace the one he had broken assaulting Sumner. The attack by Brooks left Sumner incapacitated physically and mentally for a long period of time. Despite his injuries, the people of Massachusetts reelected him.

THE PRESIDENTIAL ELECTION OF 1856

The electoral contest in 1856 took place in a transformed political landscape. A third political party appeared: the anti-immigrant **American Party**, a formerly secretive organization with the nickname "the Know-Nothing Party" because its members denied knowing anything about it. By 1856, the American or Know-Nothing Party had evolved into a national force committed to halting further immigration. Its members were especially opposed to the immigration of Irish Catholics, whose loyalty to the Pope, they believed, precluded their loyalty to the United States. On the West Coast, they opposed the entry of immigrant laborers from China, who were thought to be too foreign to ever assimilate into a white America.

The election also featured the new Republican Party, which offered John C. Fremont as its candidate. Republicans accused the Democrats of trying to nationalize slavery through the use of popular sovereignty in the West, a view captured in the 1856 political cartoon *Forcing Slavery Down the Throat of a Free Soiler* (Figure 14.15). The cartoon features the image of a Free-Soiler settler tied to the Democratic Party platform while Senator Douglas (author of the Kansas-Nebraska Act) and President Pierce force a slave down his throat. Note that the slave cries out "Murder!!! Help—neighbors help, O my poor Wife and Children," a reference to the abolitionists' argument that slavery destroyed families.

Figure 14.15 This 1856 political cartoon, *Forcing Slavery Down the Throat of a Free Soiler*, by John Magee, shows Republican resentment of the Democratic platform—here represented as an actual platform—of expanding slavery into new western territories.

The Democrats offered James Buchanan as their candidate. Buchanan did not take a stand on either side of the issue of slavery; rather, he attempted to please both sides. His qualification, in the minds of many, was that he was out of the country when the Kansas-Nebraska Act was passed. In the above political cartoon, Buchanan, along with Democratic senator Lewis Cass, holds down the Free-Soil advocate. Buchanan won the election, but Fremont garnered more than 33 percent of the popular vote, an impressive return for a new party. The Whigs had ceased to exist and had been replaced by the Republican Party. Know-Nothings also transferred their allegiance to the Republicans because the new party also took an anti-immigrant stance, a move that further boosted the new party's standing. (The Democrats courted the Catholic immigrant vote.) The Republican Party was a thoroughly northern party; no southern delegate voted for Fremont.

14.3 The Dred Scott Decision and Sectional Strife

By the end of this section, you will be able to:
* Explain the importance of the Supreme Court's Dred Scott ruling
* Discuss the principles of the Republican Party as expressed by Abraham Lincoln in 1858

As president, Buchanan confronted a difficult and volatile situation. The nation needed a strong personality to lead it, and Buchanan did not possess this trait. The violence in Kansas demonstrated that applying popular sovereignty—the democratic principle of majority rule—to the territory offered no solution to the national battle over slavery. A decision by the Supreme Court in 1857, which concerned the slave Dred Scott, only deepened the crisis.

DRED SCOTT

In 1857, several months after President Buchanan took the oath of office, the Supreme Court ruled in *Dred Scott v. Sandford*. Dred Scott (Figure 14.16), born a slave in Virginia in 1795, had been one of the thousands forced to relocate as a result of the massive internal slave trade and taken to Missouri, where slavery had been adopted as part of the Missouri Compromise. In 1820, Scott's owner took him first to Illinois and then to the Wisconsin territory. However, both of those regions were part of the Northwest Territory, where the 1787 Northwest Ordinance had prohibited slavery. When Scott returned to Missouri, he attempted to buy his freedom. After his owner refused, he sought relief in the state courts, arguing that by virtue of having lived in areas where slavery was banned, he should be free.

Figure 14.16 This 1888 portrait by Louis Schultze shows Dred Scott, who fought for his freedom through the American court system.

In a complicated set of legal decisions, a jury found that Scott, along with his wife and two children, were free. However, on appeal from Scott's owner, the state Superior Court reversed the decision, and the Scotts remained slaves. Scott then became the property of John Sanford (his name was misspelled as "Sandford" in later court documents), who lived in New York. He continued his legal battle, and because the issue involved Missouri and New York, the case fell under the jurisdiction of the federal court. In 1854, Scott lost in federal court and appealed to the United States Supreme Court.

In 1857, the Supreme Court—led by Chief Justice Roger Taney, a former slaveholder who had freed his slaves—handed down its decision. On the question of whether Scott was free, the Supreme Court decided he remained a slave. The court then went beyond the specific issue of Scott's freedom to make a sweeping and momentous judgment about the status of blacks, both free and slave. Per the court, blacks could never be citizens of the United States. Further, the court ruled that Congress had no authority to stop or limit the spread of slavery into American territories. This proslavery ruling explicitly made the Missouri Compromise unconstitutional; implicitly, it made Douglas's popular sovereignty unconstitutional.

DEFINING "AMERICAN"

✪ Roger Taney on Dred Scott v. Sandford

In 1857, the United States Supreme Court ended years of legal battles when it ruled that Dred Scott, a slave who had resided in several free states, should remain a slave. The decision, written by Chief Justice Roger Taney, also stated that blacks could not be citizens and that Congress had no power to limit the spread of slavery. The excerpt below is from Taney's decision.

> A free negro of the African race, whose ancestors were brought to this country and sold as slaves, is not a "citizen" within the meaning of the Constitution of the United States. . . .
> The only two clauses in the Constitution which point to this race treat them as persons whom it was morally lawfully to deal in as articles of property and to hold as slaves. . . .
> Every citizen has a right to take with him into the Territory any article of property which the Constitution of the United States recognises as property. . . .
> The Constitution of the United States recognises slaves as property, and pledges the Federal Government to protect it. And Congress cannot exercise any more authority over property of that description than it may constitutionally exercise over property of any other kind. . . .
> Prohibiting a citizen of the United States from taking with him his slaves when he removes to the Territory . . . is an exercise of authority over private property which is not warranted by the Constitution, and the removal of the plaintiff [Dred Scott] by his owner to that Territory gave him no title to freedom.

How did the Supreme Court define Dred Scott? How did the court interpret the Constitution on this score?

The Dred Scott decision infuriated Republicans by rendering their goal—to prevent slavery's spread into the territories—unconstitutional. To Republicans, the decision offered further proof of the reach of the South's Slave Power, which now apparently extended even to the Supreme Court. The decision also complicated life for northern Democrats, especially Stephen Douglas, who could no longer sell popular sovereignty as a symbolic concession to southerners from northern voters. Few northerners favored slavery's expansion westward.

THE LINCOLN-DOUGLAS DEBATES

The turmoil in Kansas, combined with the furor over the Dred Scott decision, provided the background for the 1858 senatorial contest in Illinois between Democratic senator Stephen Douglas and Republican hopeful Abraham Lincoln (Figure 14.17). Lincoln and Douglas engaged in seven debates before huge crowds that met to hear the two men argue the central issue of slavery and its expansion. Newspapers throughout the United States published their speeches. Whereas Douglas already enjoyed national recognition, Lincoln remained largely unknown before the debates. These appearances provided an opportunity for him to raise his profile with both northerners and southerners.

(a)   (b)

Figure 14.17 In 1858, Abraham Lincoln (a) debated Stephen Douglas (b) seven times in the Illinois race for the U.S. Senate. Although Douglas won the seat, the debates propelled Lincoln into the national political spotlight.

Douglas portrayed the Republican Party as an abolitionist effort—one that aimed to bring about **miscegenation**, or race-mixing through sexual relations or marriage. The "black Republicans," Douglas declared, posed a dangerous threat to the Constitution. Indeed, because Lincoln declared the nation could not survive if the slave state–free state division continued, Douglas claimed the Republicans aimed to destroy what the founders had created.

For his part, Lincoln said: "A house divided against itself cannot stand. I believe this government cannot endure permanently half Slave and half Free. I do not expect the Union to be dissolved—I do not expect the house to fall—but I do expect it will cease to be divided. It will become all one thing, or all the other. Either the opponents of slavery will arrest the further spread of it, and place it where the public mind shall rest in the belief that it is in the course of ultimate extinction: or its advocates will push it forward till it shall became alike lawful in all the States—old as well as new, North as well as South." Lincoln interpreted the Dred Scott decision and the Kansas-Nebraska Act as efforts to nationalize slavery: that is, to make it legal everywhere from New England to the Midwest and beyond.

DEFINING "AMERICAN"

✷ *The Lincoln-Douglas Debates*

On August 21, 1858, Abraham Lincoln and Stephen Douglas met in Ottawa, Illinois, for the first of seven debates. People streamed into Ottawa from neighboring counties and from as far away as Chicago. Reporting on the event was strictly partisan, with each of the candidates' supporters claiming victory for their candidate. In this excerpt, Lincoln addresses the issues of equality between blacks and whites.

> [A]nything that argues me into his idea of perfect social and political equality with the negro, is but a specious and fantastic arrangement of words, . . . I have no purpose, directly or indirectly, to interfere with the institution of slavery in the States where it exists. I believe I have no lawful right to do so, and I have no inclination to do so. I have no purpose to introduce political and social equality between the white and the black races. There is a physical difference between the two, which, in my judgment, will probably forever forbid their living together upon the footing of perfect equality, . . . I, as well as Judge Douglas, am in favor of the race to which I belong having the superior position. . . . [N]otwithstanding all this, there is no reason in the world why the negro is not entitled to all the natural rights enumerated in the Declaration of Independence, the right to life, liberty, and the pursuit of happiness. I hold that he is as much entitled to these as the white man. . . . [I]n the right to eat the bread, without the leave of anybody else, which his own hand earns, he is my equal and the equal of Judge Douglas, and the equal of every living man.
> —Lincoln's speech on August 21, 1858, in Ottawa, Illinois

How would you characterize Lincoln's position on equality between blacks and whites? What types of equality exist, according to Lincoln?

Click and Explore

Go to the Lincoln Home National Historic Site (http://openstaxcollege.org/l/15LincDoug) on the National Park Service's website to read excerpts from and full texts of the debates. Then, visit The Lincoln/Douglas Debates of 1858 (http://openstaxcollege.org/l/15LincDoug2) on the Northern Illinois University website to read different newspaper accounts of the debates. Do you see any major differences in the way the newspapers reported the debates? How does the commentary vary, and why?

During the debates, Lincoln demanded that Douglas explain whether or not he believed that the 1857 Supreme Court decision in the Dred Scott case trumped the right of a majority to prevent the expansion of slavery under the principle of popular sovereignty. Douglas responded to Lincoln during the second debate at Freeport, Illinois. In what became known as the **Freeport Doctrine**, Douglas adamantly upheld popular sovereignty, declaring: "It matters not what way the Supreme Court may hereafter decide as to the abstract question whether slavery may or may not go into a territory under the Constitution, the people have the lawful means to introduce it or exclude it as they please." The Freeport Doctrine antagonized southerners and caused a major rift in the Democratic Party. The doctrine did help Douglas in Illinois, however, where most voters opposed the further expansion of slavery. The Illinois legislature selected Douglas over Lincoln for the senate, but the debates had the effect of launching Lincoln into the national spotlight. Lincoln had argued that slavery was morally wrong, even as he accepted the racism inherent in slavery. He warned that Douglas and the Democrats would nationalize slavery through the policy of popular sovereignty. Though Douglas had survived the election challenge from Lincoln, his Freeport Doctrine undermined the Democratic Party as a national force.

14.4 John Brown and the Election of 1860

By the end of this section, you will be able to:
- Describe John Brown's raid on Harpers Ferry and its results
- Analyze the results of the election of 1860

Events in the late 1850s did nothing to quell the country's sectional unrest, and compromise on the issue of slavery appeared impossible. Lincoln's 1858 speeches during his debates with Douglas made the Republican Party's position well known; Republicans opposed the extension of slavery and believed a Slave Power conspiracy sought to nationalize the institution. They quickly gained political momentum and took control of the House of Representatives in 1858. Southern leaders were divided on how to respond to Republican success. Southern extremists, known as "**Fire-Eaters**," openly called for secession. Others, like Mississippi senator Jefferson Davis, put forward a more moderate approach by demanding constitutional protection of slavery.

JOHN BROWN

In October 1859, the radical abolitionist John Brown and eighteen armed men, both blacks and whites, attacked the federal arsenal in **Harpers Ferry**, Virginia. They hoped to capture the weapons there and distribute them among slaves to begin a massive uprising that would bring an end to slavery. Brown had already demonstrated during the 1856 Pottawatomie attack in Kansas that he had no patience for the nonviolent approach preached by pacifist abolitionists like William Lloyd Garrison. Born in Connecticut in 1800, Brown (**Figure 14.18**) spent much of his life in the North, moving from Ohio to Pennsylvania and then upstate New York as his various business ventures failed. To him, slavery appeared an unacceptable evil that must be purged from the land, and like his Puritan forebears, he believed in using the sword to defeat the ungodly.

Figure 14.18 John Brown, shown here in a photograph from 1859, was a radical abolitionist who advocated the violent overthrow of slavery.

Brown had gone to Kansas in the 1850s in an effort to stop slavery, and there, he had perpetrated the killings at Pottawatomie. He told other abolitionists of his plan to take Harpers Ferry Armory and initiate a massive slave uprising. Some abolitionists provided financial support, while others, including Frederick Douglass, found the plot suicidal and refused to join. On October 16, 1859, Brown's force easily took control of the federal armory, which was unguarded (Figure 14.19). However, his vision of a mass uprising failed completely. Very few slaves lived in the area to rally to Brown's side, and the group found themselves holed up in the armory's engine house with townspeople taking shots at them. Federal troops, commanded by Colonel Robert E. Lee, soon captured Brown and his followers. On December 2, Brown was hanged by the state of Virginia for treason.

Figure 14.19   John Brown's raid on Harpers Ferry represented the radical abolitionist's attempt to start a revolt that would ultimately end slavery. This 1859 illustration, captioned "Harper's Ferry insurrection—Interior of the Engine-House, just before the gate is broken down by the storming party—Col. Washington and his associates as captives, held by Brown as hostages," is from *Frank Leslie's Illustrated Magazine*. Do you think this image represents a southern or northern version of the raid? How are the characters in the scene depicted?

Click and Explore

Visit the Avalon Project (http://openstaxcollege.org/l/15JohnBrown) on Yale Law School's website to read the impassioned speech that Henry David Thoreau delivered on October 30, 1859, arguing against the execution of John Brown. How does Thoreau characterize Brown? What does he ask of his fellow citizens?

John Brown's raid on Harpers Ferry generated intense reactions in both the South and the North. Southerners grew especially apprehensive of the possibility of other violent plots. They viewed Brown as a terrorist bent on destroying their civilization, and support for secession grew. Their anxiety led several southern states to pass laws designed to prevent slave rebellions. It seemed that the worst fears of the South had come true: A hostile majority would stop at nothing to destroy slavery. Was it possible, one resident of Maryland asked, to "live under a government, a majority of whose subjects or citizens regard John Brown as a martyr and Christian hero?" Many antislavery northerners did in fact consider Brown a martyr to the cause, and those who viewed slavery as a sin saw easy comparisons between him and Jesus Christ.

Download for free at http://cnx.org/content/col11740/latest/

THE ELECTION OF 1860

The election of 1860 triggered the collapse of American democracy when the elevation of Abraham Lincoln to the presidency inspired secessionists in the South to withdraw their states from the Union.

Lincoln's election owed much to the disarray in the Democratic Party. The Dred Scott decision and the Freeport Doctrine had opened up huge sectional divisions among Democrats. Though Brown did not intend it, his raid had furthered the split between northern and southern Democrats. Fire-Eaters vowed to prevent a northern Democrat, especially Illinois's Stephen Douglas, from becoming their presidential candidate. These proslavery zealots insisted on a southern Democrat.

The Democratic nominating convention met in April 1860 in Charleston, South Carolina. However, it broke up after northern Democrats, who made up a majority of delegates, rejected Jefferson Davis's efforts to protect slavery in the territories. These northern Democratic delegates knew that supporting Davis on this issue would be very unpopular among the people in their states. A second conference, held in Baltimore, further illustrated the divide within the Democratic Party. Northern Democrats nominated Stephen Douglas, while southern Democrats, who met separately, put forward Vice President John Breckinridge from Kentucky. The Democratic Party had fractured into two competing sectional factions.

By offering two candidates for president, the Democrats gave the Republicans an enormous advantage. Also hoping to prevent a Republican victory, pro-Unionists from the border states organized the Constitutional Union Party and put up a fourth candidate, John Bell, for president, who pledged to end slavery agitation and preserve the Union but never fully explained how he'd accomplish this objective. In a pro-Lincoln political cartoon of the time (Figure 14.20), the presidential election is presented as a baseball game. Lincoln stands on home plate. A skunk raises its tail at the other candidates. Holding his nose, southern Democrat John Breckinridge holds a bat labeled "Slavery Extension" and declares "I guess I'd better leave for Kentucky, for I smell something strong around here, and begin to think, that we are completely skunk'd."

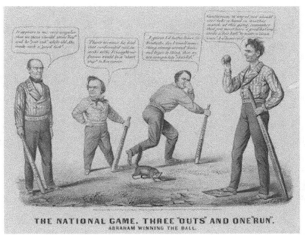

Figure 14.20 *The national game. Three "outs" and one "run"* (1860), by Currier and Ives, shows the two Democratic candidates and one Constitutional Union candidate who lost the 1860 election to Republican Lincoln, shown at right.

The Republicans nominated Lincoln, and in the November election, he garnered a mere 40 percent of the popular vote, though he won every northern state except New Jersey. (Lincoln's name was blocked from even appearing on many southern states' ballots by southern Democrats.) More importantly, Lincoln did gain a majority in the Electoral College (Figure 14.21). The Fire-Eaters, however, refused to accept the results. With South Carolina leading the way, Fire-Eaters in southern states began to withdraw formally from the United States in 1860. South Carolinian Mary Boykin Chesnut wrote in her diary about the reaction to the Lincoln's election. "Now that the black radical Republicans have the power," she wrote,

"I suppose they will Brown us all." Her statement revealed many southerners' fear that with Lincoln as President, the South could expect more mayhem like the John Brown raid.

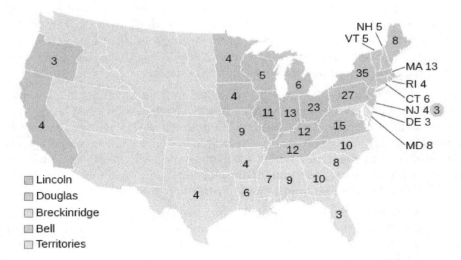

Figure 14.21 This map shows the disposition of electoral votes for the election of 1860. The votes were divided along almost perfect sectional lines.

Key Terms

American Party also called the Know-Nothing Party, a political party that emerged in 1856 with an anti-immigration platform

Bleeding Kansas a reference to the violent clashes in Kansas between Free-Soilers and slavery supporters

border ruffians proslavery Missourians who crossed the border into Kansas to influence the legislature

Compromise of 1850 five laws passed by Congress to resolve issues stemming from the Mexican Cession and the sectional crisis

Dred Scott v. Sandford an 1857 case in which the Supreme Court ruled that blacks could not be citizens and Congress had no jurisdiction to impede the expansion of slavery

Fire-Eaters radical southern secessionists

Free-Soil Party a political party committed to ensuring that white laborers would not have to compete with unpaid slaves in newly acquired territories

Freeport Doctrine a doctrine that emerged during the Lincoln-Douglas debates in which Douglas reaffirmed his commitment to popular sovereignty, including the right to halt the spread of slavery, despite the 1857 Dred Scott decision affirming slaveholders' right to bring their property wherever they wished

Harpers Ferry the site of a federal arsenal in Virginia, where radical abolitionist John Brown staged an ill-fated effort to end slavery by instigating a mass uprising among slaves

miscegenation race-mixing through sexual relations or marriage

popular sovereignty the principle of letting the people residing in a territory decide whether or not to permit slavery in that area based on majority rule

Republican Party an antislavery political party formed in 1854 in response to Stephen Douglas's Kansas-Nebraska Act

Underground Railroad a network of free blacks and northern whites who helped slaves escape bondage through a series of designated routes and safe houses

Summary

14.1 The Compromise of 1850

The difficult process of reaching a compromise on slavery in 1850 exposed the sectional fault lines in the United States. After several months of rancorous debate, Congress passed five laws—known collectively as the Compromise of 1850—that people on both sides of the divide hoped had solved the nation's problems. However, many northerners feared the impact of the Fugitive Slave Act, which made it a crime not only to help slaves escape, but also to fail to help capture them. Many Americans, both black and white, flouted the Fugitive Slave Act by participating in the Underground Railroad, providing safe houses for slaves on the run from the South. Eight northern states passed personal liberty laws to counteract the effects of the Fugitive Slave Act.

14.2 The Kansas-Nebraska Act and the Republican Party

The application of popular sovereignty to the organization of the Kansas and Nebraska territories ended the sectional truce that had prevailed since the Compromise of 1850. Senator Douglas's Kansas-Nebraska Act opened the door to chaos in Kansas as proslavery and Free-Soil forces waged war against each other, and radical abolitionists, notably John Brown, committed themselves to violence to end slavery. The act also upended the second party system of Whigs and Democrats by inspiring the formation of the new Republican Party, committed to arresting the further spread of slavery. Many voters approved its platform in the 1856 presidential election, though the Democrats won the race because they remained a national, rather than a sectional, political force.

14.3 The Dred Scott Decision and Sectional Strife

The Dred Scott decision of 1857 went well beyond the question of whether or not Dred Scott gained his freedom. Instead, the Supreme Court delivered a far-reaching pronouncement about African Americans in the United States, finding they could never be citizens and that Congress could not interfere with the expansion of slavery into the territories. Republicans erupted in anger at this decision, which rendered their party's central platform unconstitutional. Abraham Lincoln fully articulated the Republican position on the issue of slavery in his 1858 debates with Senator Stephen Douglas. By the end of that year, Lincoln had become a nationally known Republican icon. For the Democrats' part, unity within their party frayed over both the Dred Scott case and the Freeport Doctrine, undermining the Democrats' future ability to retain control of the presidency.

14.4 John Brown and the Election of 1860

A new level of animosity and distrust emerged in 1859 in the aftermath of John Brown's raid. The South exploded in rage at the northern celebration of Brown as a heroic freedom fighter. Fire-Eaters called openly for disunion. Poisoned relations split the Democrats into northern and southern factions, a boon to the Republican candidate Lincoln. His election triggered the downfall of the American experiment with democracy as southern states began to leave the Union.

Review Questions

1. What was President Zachary Taylor's top priority as president?
   A. preserving the Union
   B. ensuring the recapture of runaway slaves
   C. expanding slavery
   D. enlarging the state of Texas

2. Which of the following was *not* a component of the Compromise of 1850?
   A. the passage of the Fugitive Slave Act
   B. the admission of Kansas as a free state
   C. the admission of California as a free state
   D. a ban on the slave trade in Washington, DC

3. Why did many in the North resist the Fugitive Slave Act?

4. Which of the following was a focus of the new Republican Party?
   A. supporting Irish Catholic immigration
   B. encouraging the use of popular sovereignty to determine where slavery could exist
   C. promoting states' rights
   D. halting the spread of slavery

5. Border ruffians helped to _____.
   A. chase abolitionists out of Missouri
   B. elect a proslavery legislature in Kansas
   C. capture runaway slaves
   D. disseminate abolitionist literature in Kansas

6. How did the "Bleeding Kansas" incident change the face of antislavery advocacy?

7. On what grounds did Dred Scott sue for freedom?
  A. the inherent inhumanity of slavery
  B. the cruelty of his master
  C. the fact that he had lived in free states
  D. the fact that his family would be torn apart

8. Which of the following was *not* a result of the Lincoln-Douglas debates?
  A. Douglas was elected senator of Illinois.
  B. Lincoln's national profile was raised.
  C. Citizens in both the North and South followed the debates closely.
  D. Lincoln successfully defended the principle of popular sovereignty.

9. What are the main points of the Dred Scott decision?

10. Why did John Brown attack the armory at Harpers Ferry?

  A. to seize weapons to distribute to slaves for a massive uprising
  B. to hold as a military base against proslavery forces
  C. in revenge after the sacking of Lawrence
  D. to prevent southern states from seceding

11. Which of the following did *not* contribute to Lincoln's victory in the election of 1860?
  A. the split between northern and southern democrats
  B. the defeat of the Whig party
  C. Lincoln's improved national standing after his senatorial debates with Stephen Douglas
  D. the Constitutional Union party's further splintering the vote

12. What were southerners' and northerners' views of John Brown?

Critical Thinking Questions

13. Why would Americans view the Compromise of 1850 as a final solution to the sectional controversy that began with the Wilmot Proviso in 1846?

14. If you were a proslavery advocate, how would you feel about the platform of the newly formed Republican Party?

15. Based on the text of the Lincoln-Douglas debates, what was the position of the Republican Party in 1858? Was the Republican Party an abolitionist party? Why or why not?

16. John Brown is often described as a terrorist. Do you agree with this description? Why or why not? What attributes might make him fit this profile?

17. Was it possible to save American democracy in 1860? What steps might have been taken to maintain unity? Why do you think these steps were not taken?

CHAPTER 15

The Civil War, 1860–1865

Figure 15.1 This photograph by John Reekie, entitled, "A burial party on the battle-field of Cold Harbor," drives home the brutality and devastation wrought by the Civil War. Here, in April 1865, African Americans collect the bones of soldiers killed in Virginia during General Ulysses S. Grant's Wilderness Campaign of May–June 1864.

Chapter Outline

15.1 The Origins and Outbreak of the Civil War
15.2 Early Mobilization and War
15.3 1863: The Changing Nature of the War
15.4 The Union Triumphant

Introduction

In May 1864, General Ulysses S. Grant ordered the Union's Army of the Potomac to cross the Rapidan River in Virginia. Grant knew that Confederate general Robert E. Lee would defend the Confederate capital at Richmond at all costs, committing troops that might otherwise be sent to the Shenandoah or the Deep South to stop Union general William Tecumseh Sherman from capturing Atlanta, a key Confederate city. For two days, the Army of the Potomac fought Lee's troops in the Wilderness, a wooded area along the Rapidan River. Nearly ten thousand Confederate soldiers were killed or wounded, as were more than seventeen thousand Union troops. A few weeks later, the armies would meet again at the Battle of Cold Harbor, where another fifteen thousand men would be wounded or killed. As in many battles, the bodies of those who died were left on the field where they fell. A year later, African Americans, who were often called upon to perform menial labor for the Union army (Figure 15.1), collected the skeletal remains of the dead for a proper burial. The state of the graves of many Civil War soldiers partly inspired the creation of Memorial Day, a day set aside for visiting and decorating the graves of the dead.

15.1 The Origins and Outbreak of the Civil War

By the end of this section, you will be able to:
- Explain the major events that occurred during the Secession Crisis
- Describe the creation and founding principles of the Confederate States of America

The 1860 election of Abraham Lincoln was a turning point for the United States. Throughout the tumultuous 1850s, the Fire-Eaters of the southern states had been threatening to leave the Union. With Lincoln's election, they prepared to make good on their threats. Indeed, the Republican president-elect appeared to be their worst nightmare. The Republican Party committed itself to keeping slavery out of the territories as the country expanded westward, a position that shocked southern sensibilities. Meanwhile, southern leaders suspected that Republican abolitionists would employ the violent tactics of John Brown to deprive southerners of their slave property. The threat posed by the Republican victory in the election of 1860 spurred eleven southern states to leave the Union to form the Confederate States of America, a new republic dedicated to maintaining and expanding slavery. The Union, led by President Lincoln, was unwilling to accept the departure of these states and committed itself to restoring the country. Beginning in 1861 and continuing until 1865, the United States engaged in a brutal Civil War that claimed the lives of over 600,000 soldiers. By 1863, the conflict had become not only a war to save the Union, but also a war to end slavery in the United States. Only after four years of fighting did the North prevail. The Union was preserved, and the institution of slavery had been destroyed in the nation.

THE CAUSES OF THE CIVIL WAR

Lincoln's election sparked the southern secession fever into flame, but it did not cause the Civil War. For decades before Lincoln took office, the sectional divisions in the country had been widening. Both the Northern and southern states engaged in inflammatory rhetoric and agitation, and violent emotions ran strong on both sides. Several factors played into the ultimate split between the North and the South.

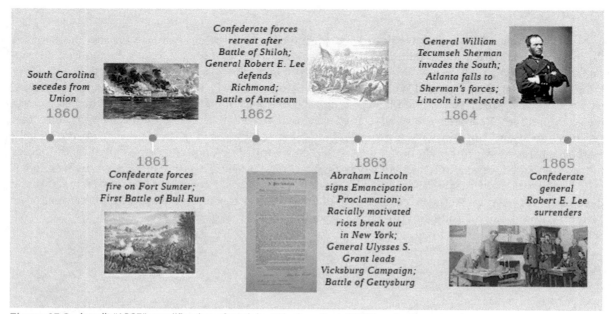

Figure 15.2 (credit "1865": modification of work by "Alaskan Dude"/Wikimedia Commons)

Download for free at http://cnx.org/content/col11740/latest/

One key irritant was the question of slavery's expansion westward. The debate over whether new states would be slave or free reached back to the controversy over statehood for Missouri beginning in 1819 and Texas in the 1830s and early 1840s. This question arose again after the Mexican-American War (1846–1848), when the government debated whether slavery would be permitted in the territories taken from Mexico. Efforts in Congress to reach a compromise in 1850 fell back on the principle of popular sovereignty—letting the people in the new territories south of the 1820 Missouri Compromise line decide whether to allow slavery. This same principle came to be applied to the Kansas-Nebraska territories in 1854, a move that added fuel to the fire of sectional conflict by destroying the Missouri Compromise boundary and leading to the birth of the Republican Party. In the end, popular sovereignty proved to be no solution at all. This was especially true in "Bleeding Kansas" in the mid-1850s, as pro- and antislavery forces battled each another in an effort to gain the upper hand.

The small but very vocal abolitionist movement further contributed to the escalating tensions between the North and the South. Since the 1830s, abolitionists, led by journalist and reformer William Lloyd Garrison, had cast slavery as a national sin and called for its immediate end. For three decades, the abolitionists—a minority even within the antislavery movement—had had a significant effect on American society by bringing the evils of slavery into the public consciousness. By the 1850s, some of the most radical abolitionists, such as John Brown, had resorted to violence in their efforts to destroy the institution of slavery.

The formation of the Liberty Party (1840), the Free-Soil Party (1848), and the Republican Party (1854), all of which strongly opposed the spread of slavery to the West, brought the question solidly into the political arena. Although not all those who opposed the westward expansion of slavery had a strong abolitionist bent, the attempt to limit slaveholders' control of their human property stiffened the resolve of southern leaders to defend their society at all costs. Prohibiting slavery's expansion, they argued, ran counter to fundamental American property rights. Across the country, people of all political stripes worried that the nation's arguments would cause irreparable rifts in the country.

Despite the ruptures and tensions, by the 1860s, some hope of healing the nation still existed. Before Lincoln took office, John Crittenden, a senator from Kentucky who had helped form the Constitutional Union Party during the 1860 presidential election, attempted to diffuse the explosive situation by offering six constitutional amendments and a series of resolutions, known as the **Crittenden Compromise**. Crittenden's goal was to keep the South from seceding, and his strategy was to transform the Constitution to explicitly protect slavery forever. Specifically, Crittenden proposed an amendment that would restore the 36°30′ line from the Missouri Compromise and extend it all the way to the Pacific Ocean, protecting and ensuring slavery south of the line while prohibiting it north of the line (Figure 15.3). He further proposed an amendment that would prohibit Congress from abolishing slavery anywhere it already existed or from interfering with the interstate slave trade.

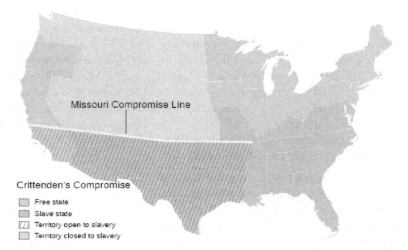

Figure 15.3 Crittenden's Compromise would protect slavery in all states where it already existed. More importantly, however, it proposed to allow the western expansion of slavery into states below the Missouri Compromise line.

Republicans, including President-elect Lincoln, rejected Crittenden's proposals because they ran counter to the party's goal of keeping slavery out of the territories. The southern states also rejected Crittenden's attempts at compromise, because it would prevent slaveholders from taking their human chattel north of the 36°30′ line. On December 20, 1860, only a few days after Crittenden's proposal was introduced in Congress, South Carolina began the march towards war when it seceded from the United States. Three more states of the Deep South—Mississippi, Florida, and Alabama—seceded before the U.S. Senate rejected Crittenden's proposal on January 16, 1861. Georgia, Louisiana, and Texas joined them in rapid succession on January 19, January 26, and February 1, respectively (Figure 15.4). In many cases, these secessions occurred after extremely divided conventions and popular votes. A lack of unanimity prevailed in much of the South.

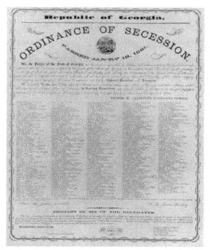

Figure 15.4 Georgia's Ordinance of Secession and those of the other Deep South states were all based on that of South Carolina, which was drafted just a month after Abraham Lincoln was elected.

Click and Explore

Explore the causes, battles, and aftermath of the Civil War at the interactive website (http://openstaxcollege.org/l/15Causes) offered by the National Parks Service.

THE CREATION OF THE CONFEDERATE STATES OF AMERICA

The seven Deep South states that seceded quickly formed a new government. In the opinion of many Southern politicians, the federal Constitution that united the states as one nation was a contract by which individual states had agreed to be bound. However, they maintained, the states had not sacrificed their autonomy and could withdraw their consent to be controlled by the federal government. In their eyes, their actions were in keeping with the nature of the Constitution and the social contract theory of government that had influenced the founders of the American Republic.

The new nation formed by these men would not be a federal union, but a confederation. In a confederation, individual member states agree to unite under a central government for some purposes, such as defense, but to retain autonomy in other areas of government. In this way, states could protect themselves, and slavery, from interference by what they perceived to be an overbearing central government. The constitution of the Confederate States of America (CSA), or the **Confederacy**, drafted at a convention in Montgomery, Alabama, in February 1861, closely followed the 1787 Constitution. The only real difference between the two documents centered on slavery. The Confederate Constitution declared that the new nation existed to defend and perpetuate racial slavery, and the leadership of the slaveholding class. Specifically, the constitution protected the interstate slave trade, guaranteed that slavery would exist in any new territory gained by the Confederacy, and, perhaps most importantly, in Article One, Section Nine, declared that "No . . . law impairing or denying the right of property in negro slaves shall be passed." Beyond its focus on slavery, the Confederate Constitution resembled the 1787 U.S. Constitution. It allowed for a Congress composed of two chambers, a judicial branch, and an executive branch with a president to serve for six years.

The convention delegates chose Jefferson Davis of Mississippi to lead the new provisional government as president and Alexander Stephens of Georgia to serve as vice president until elections could be held in the spring and fall of 1861. By that time, four new states—Virginia, Arkansas, Tennessee, and North Carolina—had joined the CSA. As 1861 progressed, the Confederacy claimed Missouri and Kentucky, even though no ordinance of secession had been approved in those states. Southern nationalism ran high, and the Confederacy, buoyed by its sense of purpose, hoped that their new nation would achieve eminence in the world.

By the time Lincoln reached Washington, DC, in February 1861, the CSA had already been established. The new president confronted an unprecedented crisis. A conference held that month with delegates from the Southern states failed to secure a promise of peace or to restore the Union. On inauguration day, March 4, 1861, the new president repeated his views on slavery: "I have no purpose, directly or indirectly, to interfere with the institution of slavery in the States where it exists. I believe I have no lawful right to do so, and I have no inclination to do so." His recognition of slavery in the South did nothing to mollify slaveholders, however, because Lincoln also pledged to keep slavery from expanding into the new western territories. Furthermore, in his inaugural address, Lincoln made clear his commitment to maintaining federal power against the secessionists working to destroy it. Lincoln declared that the Union could not be dissolved by individual state actions, and, therefore, secession was unconstitutional.

Click and Explore

Read **Lincoln's entire inaugural address (http://openstaxcollege.org/l/ 15LincAddress)** at the Yale Avalon project's website. How would Lincoln's audience have responded to this speech?

FORT SUMTER

President Lincoln made it clear to Southern secessionists that he would fight to maintain federal property and to keep the Union intact. Other politicians, however, still hoped to avoid the use of force to resolve the crisis. In February 1861, in an effort to entice the rebellious states to return to the Union without resorting to force, Thomas Corwin, a representative from Ohio, introduced a proposal to amend the Constitution in the House of Representatives. His was but one of several measures proposed in January and February 1861, to head off the impending conflict and save the United States. The proposed amendment would have made it impossible for Congress to pass any law abolishing slavery. The proposal passed the House on February 28, 1861, and the Senate passed the proposal on March 2, 1861. It was then sent to the states to be ratified. Once ratified by three-quarters of state legislatures, it would become law. In his inaugural address, Lincoln stated that he had no objection to the amendment, and his predecessor James Buchanan had supported it. By the time of Lincoln's inauguration, however, seven states had already left the Union. Of the remaining states, Ohio ratified the amendment in 1861, and Maryland and Illinois did so in 1862. Despite this effort at reconciliation, the Confederate states did not return to the Union.

Indeed, by the time of the Corwin amendment's passage through Congress, Confederate forces in the Deep South had already begun to take over federal forts. The loss of **Fort Sumter**, in the harbor of Charleston, South Carolina, proved to be the flashpoint in the contest between the new Confederacy and the federal government. A small Union garrison of fewer than one hundred soldiers and officers held the fort, making it a vulnerable target for the Confederacy. Fire-Eaters pressured Jefferson Davis to take Fort Sumter and thereby demonstrate the Confederate government's resolve. Some also hoped that the Confederacy would gain foreign recognition, especially from Great Britain, by taking the fort in the South's most important Atlantic port. The situation grew dire as local merchants refused to sell food to the fort's Union soldiers, and by mid-April, the garrison's supplies began to run out. President Lincoln let it be known to Confederate leaders that he planned to resupply the Union forces. His strategy was clear: The decision to start the war would rest squarely on the Confederates, not on the Union. On April 12, 1861, Confederate forces in Charleston began a bombardment of Fort Sumter (**Figure 15.5**). Two days later, the Union soldiers there surrendered.

Download for free at http://cnx.org/content/col11740/latest/

Figure 15.5 The Confederacy's attack on Fort Sumter, depicted here in an 1861 lithograph by Currier and Ives, stoked pro-war sentiment on both sides of the conflict.

The attack on Fort Sumter meant war had come, and on April 15, 1861, Lincoln called upon loyal states to supply armed forces to defeat the rebellion and regain Fort Sumter. Faced with the need to choose between the Confederacy and the Union, border states and those of the Upper South, which earlier had been reluctant to dissolve their ties with the United States, were inspired to take action. They quickly voted for secession. A convention in Virginia that had been assembled earlier to consider the question of secession voted to join the Confederacy on April 17, two days after Lincoln called for troops. Arkansas left the Union on May 6 along with Tennessee one day later. North Carolina followed on May 20.

Not all residents of the border states and the Upper South wished to join the Confederacy, however. Pro-Union feelings remained strong in Tennessee, especially in the eastern part of the state where slaves were few and consisted largely of house servants owned by the wealthy. The state of Virginia—home of revolutionary leaders and presidents such as George Washington, Thomas Jefferson, James Madison, and James Monroe—literally was split on the issue of secession. Residents in the north and west of the state, where few slaveholders resided, rejected secession. These counties subsequently united to form "West Virginia," which entered the Union as a free state in 1863. The rest of Virginia, including the historic lands along the Chesapeake Bay that were home to such early American settlements as Jamestown and Williamsburg, joined the Confederacy. The addition of this area gave the Confederacy even greater hope and brought General Robert E. Lee, arguably the best military commander of the day, to their side. In addition, the secession of Virginia brought Washington, DC, perilously close to the Confederacy, and fears that the border state of Maryland would also join the CSA, thus trapping the U.S. capital within Confederate territories, plagued Lincoln.

The Confederacy also gained the backing of the Five Civilized Tribes, as they were called, in the Indian Territory. The Five Civilized Tribes comprised the Choctaws, Chickasaws, Creeks, Seminoles, and Cherokees. The tribes supported slavery and many members owned slaves. These Indian slaveholders, who had been forced from their lands in Georgia and elsewhere in the Deep South during the presidency of Andrew Jackson, now found unprecedented common cause with white slaveholders. The CSA even allowed them to send delegates to the Confederate Congress.

While most slaveholding states joined the Confederacy, four crucial slave states remained in the Union (Figure 15.6). Delaware, which was technically a slave state despite its tiny slave population, never voted to secede. Maryland, despite deep divisions, remained in the Union as well. Missouri became the site of vicious fighting and the home of pro-Confederate guerillas but never joined the Confederacy. Kentucky declared itself neutral, although that did little to stop the fighting that occurred within the state. In all, these four states deprived the Confederacy of key resources and soldiers.

Figure 15.6 This map illustrates the southern states that seceded from the Union and formed the Confederacy in 1861, at the outset of the Civil War.

15.2 Early Mobilization and War

By the end of this section, you will be able to:
- Assess the strengths and weaknesses of the Confederacy and the Union
- Explain the strategic importance of the Battle of Bull Run and the Battle of Shiloh

In 1861, enthusiasm for war ran high on both sides. The North fought to restore the Union, which Lincoln declared could never be broken. The Confederacy, which by the summer of 1861 consisted of eleven states, fought for its independence from the United States. The continuation of slavery was a central issue in the war, of course, although abolitionism and western expansion also played roles, and Northerners and Southerners alike flocked eagerly to the conflict. Both sides thought it would be over quickly. Militarily, however, the North and South were more equally matched than Lincoln had realized, and it soon became clear that the war effort would be neither brief nor painless. In 1861, Americans in both the North and South romanticized war as noble and positive. Soon the carnage and slaughter would awaken them to the horrors of war.

THE FIRST BATTLE OF BULL RUN

After the fall of Fort Sumter on April 15, 1861, Lincoln called for seventy-five thousand volunteers from state militias to join federal forces. His goal was a ninety-day campaign to put down the Southern rebellion. The response from state militias was overwhelming, and the number of Northern troops exceeded the requisition. Also in April, Lincoln put in place a naval blockade of the South, a move that gave tacit recognition of the Confederacy while providing a legal excuse for the British and the French to trade with Southerners. The Confederacy responded to the blockade by declaring that a state of war existed with the United States. This official pronouncement confirmed the beginning of the Civil War. Men rushed to enlist, and the Confederacy turned away tens of thousands who hoped to defend the new nation.

Many believed that a single, heroic battle would decide the contest. Some questioned how committed Southerners really were to their cause. Northerners hoped that most Southerners would not actually fire on the American flag. Meanwhile, Lincoln and military leaders in the North hoped a quick blow to the South, especially if they could capture the Confederacy's new capital of Richmond, Virginia, would end the rebellion before it went any further. On July 21, 1861, the two armies met near Manassas, Virginia, along Bull Run Creek, only thirty miles from Washington, DC. So great was the belief that this would be a climactic Union victory that many Washington socialites and politicians brought picnic lunches to a nearby area, hoping to witness history unfolding before them. At the First Battle of Bull Run, also known as First Manassas, some sixty thousand troops assembled, most of whom had never seen combat, and each side sent eighteen thousand into the fray. The Union forces attacked first, only to be pushed back. The Confederate forces then carried the day, sending the Union soldiers and Washington, DC, onlookers scrambling back from Virginia and destroying Union hopes of a quick, decisive victory. Instead, the war would drag on for four long, deadly years (Figure 15.7).

Figure 15.7 The First Battle of Bull Run, which many Northerners thought would put a quick and decisive end to the South's rebellion, ended with a Confederate victory.

BALANCE SHEET: THE UNION AND THE CONFEDERACY

As it became clearer that the Union would not be dealing with an easily quashed rebellion, the two sides assessed their strengths and weaknesses. At the onset on the war, in 1861 and 1862, they stood as relatively equal combatants.

The Confederates had the advantage of being able to wage a defensive war, rather than an offensive one. They had to protect and preserve their new boundaries, but they did not have to be the aggressors against the Union. The war would be fought primarily in the South, which gave the Confederates the advantages of the knowledge of the terrain and the support of the civilian population. Further, the vast coastline from Texas to Virginia offered ample opportunities to evade the Union blockade. And with the addition of the Upper South states, especially Virginia, North Carolina, Tennessee, and Arkansas, the Confederacy gained a much larger share of natural resources and industrial might than the Deep South states could muster.

Still, the Confederacy had disadvantages. The South's economy depended heavily on the export of cotton, but with the naval blockade, the flow of cotton to England, the region's primary importer, came to an end. The blockade also made it difficult to import manufactured goods. Although the secession of the Upper South added some industrial assets to the Confederacy, overall, the South lacked substantive industry or an extensive railroad infrastructure to move men and supplies. To deal with the lack of commerce and the resulting lack of funds, the Confederate government began printing paper money, leading to runaway inflation (Figure 15.8). The advantage that came from fighting on home territory quickly turned to a disadvantage when Confederate armies were defeated and Union forces destroyed Southern farms and towns, and forced Southern civilians to take to the road as refugees. Finally, the population of the South stood at fewer than nine million people, of whom nearly four million were black slaves, compared to over twenty million residents in the North. These limited numbers became a major factor as the war dragged on and the death toll rose.

Figure 15.8 The Confederacy started printing paper money at an accelerated rate, causing runaway inflation and an economy in which formerly well-off people were unable to purchase food.

The Union side held many advantages as well. Its larger population, bolstered by continued immigration from Europe throughout the 1860s, gave it greater manpower reserves to draw upon. The North's greater industrial capabilities and extensive railroad grid made it far better able to mobilize men and supplies for the war effort. The Industrial Revolution and the transportation revolution, beginning in the 1820s and continuing over the next several decades, had transformed the North. Throughout the war, the North was able to produce more war materials and move goods more quickly than the South. Furthermore, the farms of New England, the Mid-Atlantic, the Old Northwest, and the prairie states supplied Northern civilians and Union troops with abundant food throughout the war. Food shortages and hungry civilians were common in the South, where the best land was devoted to raising cotton, but not in the North.

Unlike the South, however, which could hunker down to defend itself and needed to maintain relatively short supply lines, the North had to go forth and conquer. Union armies had to establish long supply lines, and Union soldiers had to fight on unfamiliar ground and contend with a hostile civilian population off the battlefield. Furthermore, to restore the Union—Lincoln's overriding goal, in 1861—the United States, after defeating the Southern forces, would then need to pacify a conquered Confederacy, an area of over half a million square miles with nearly nine million residents. In short, although it had better resources and a larger population, the Union faced a daunting task against the well-positioned Confederacy.

MILITARY STALEMATE

The military forces of the Confederacy and the Union battled in 1861 and early 1862 without either side gaining the upper hand. The majority of military leaders on both sides had received the same military education and often knew one another personally, either from their time as students at West Point or as commanding officers in the Mexican-American War. This familiarity allowed them to anticipate each other's strategies. Both sides believed in the use of concentrated armies charged with taking the capital city of the enemy. For the Union, this meant the capture of the Confederate capital in Richmond, Virginia, whereas Washington, DC, stood as the prize for Confederate forces. After hopes of a quick victory faded at Bull Run, the months dragged on without any major movement on either side (Figure 15.9).

Figure 15.9 As this cartoon indicates, the fighting strategy at the beginning of the war included watchful waiting by the leaders of the North and South.

General George B. McClellan, the **general in chief** of the army, responsible for overall control of Union land forces, proved especially reluctant to engage in battle with the Confederates. In direct command of the **Army of the Potomac**, the Union fighting force operating outside Washington, DC, McClellan believed, incorrectly, that Confederate forces were too strong to defeat and was reluctant to risk his troops in battle. His cautious nature made him popular with his men but not with the president or Congress. By 1862, however, both President Lincoln and the new Secretary of War Edwin Stanton had tired of waiting. The Union put forward a new effort to bolster troop strength, enlisting one million men to serve for three-year stints in the Army of the Potomac. In January 1862, Lincoln and Stanton ordered McClellan to invade the Confederacy with the goal of capturing Richmond.

To that end, General McClellan slowly moved 100,000 soldiers of the Army of the Potomac toward Richmond but stopped a few miles outside the city. As he did so, a Confederate force led by Thomas "Stonewall" Jackson moved north to take Washington, DC. To fend off Jackson's attack, somewhere between one-quarter and one-third of McClellan's soldiers, led by Major General Irvin McDowell, returned to defend the nation's capital, a move that Jackson hoped would leave the remaining troops near Richmond more vulnerable. Having succeeding in drawing off a sizable portion of the Union force, he joined General Lee to launch an attack on McClellan's remaining soldiers near Richmond. From June 25 to July 1, 1862, the two sides engaged in the brutal Seven Days Battles that killed or wounded almost twenty thousand Confederate and ten thousand Union soldiers. McClellan's army finally returned north, having failed to take Richmond.

General Lee, flush from his success at keeping McClellan out of Richmond, tried to capitalize on the Union's failure by taking the fighting northward. He moved his forces into northern Virginia, where, at the Second Battle of Bull Run, the Confederates again defeated the Union forces. Lee then pressed into Maryland, where his troops met the much larger Union forces near Sharpsburg, at Antietam Creek. The ensuing one-day battle on September 17, 1862, led to a tremendous loss of life. Although there are varying opinions about the total number of deaths, eight thousand soldiers were killed or wounded, more than on any other single day of combat. Once again, McClellan, mistakenly believing that the Confederate troops outnumbered his own, held back a significant portion of his forces. Lee withdrew from the field first, but McClellan, fearing he was outnumbered, refused to pursue him.

The Union army's inability to destroy Lee's army at Antietam made it clear to Lincoln that McClellan would never win the war, and the president was forced to seek a replacement. Lincoln wanted someone who could deliver a decisive Union victory. He also personally disliked McClellan, who referred to the president as a "baboon" and a "gorilla," and constantly criticized his decisions. Lincoln chose General Ambrose E. Burnside to replace McClellan as commander of the Army of the Potomac, but Burnside's efforts to push into Virginia failed in December 1862, as Confederates held their position at Fredericksburg and devastated Burnside's forces with heavy artillery fire. The Union's defeat at Fredericksburg harmed morale in the North but bolstered Confederate spirits. By the end of 1862, the Confederates were still holding their ground in Virginia. Burnside's failure led Lincoln to make another change in leadership, and Joseph "Fighting Joe" Hooker took over command of the Army of the Potomac in January 1863.

General Ulysses S. Grant's **Army of the West**, operating in Kentucky, Tennessee, and the Mississippi River Valley, had been more successful. In the western campaign, the goal of both the Union and the Confederacy was to gain control of the major rivers in the west, especially the Mississippi. If the Union could control the Mississippi, the Confederacy would be split in two. The fighting in this campaign initially centered in Tennessee, where Union forces commanded by Grant pushed Confederate troops back and gained control of the state. The major battle in the western theater took place at Pittsburgh Landing, Tennessee, on April 6 and 7, 1862. Grant's army was camped on the west side of the Tennessee River near a small log church called Shiloh, which gave the battle its name. On Sunday morning, April 6, Confederate forces under General Albert Sidney Johnston attacked Grant's encampment with the goal of separating them from their supply line on the Tennessee River and driving them into the swamps on the river's western side, where they could be destroyed. Union general William Tecumseh Sherman tried to rally the Union forces as Grant, who had been convalescing from an injured leg when the attack began and was unable to walk without crutches, called for reinforcements and tried to mount a defense. Many of Union troops fled in terror.

Unfortunately for the Confederates, Johnston was killed on the afternoon of the first day. Leadership of the Southern forces fell to General P. G. T. Beauregard, who ordered an assault at the end of that day. This assault was so desperate that one of the two attacking columns did not even have ammunition. Heavily reinforced Union forces counterattacked the next day, and the Confederate forces were routed. Grant had maintained the Union foothold in the western part of the Confederacy. The North could now concentrate on its efforts to gain control of the Mississippi River, splitting the Confederacy in two and depriving it of its most important water route.

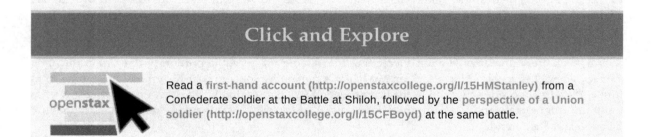

Read a **first-hand account** (http://openstaxcollege.org/l/15HMStanley) from a Confederate soldier at the Battle at Shiloh, followed by the **perspective of a Union soldier** (http://openstaxcollege.org/l/15CFBoyd) at the same battle.

In the spring and summer of 1862, the Union was successful in gaining control of part of the Mississippi River. In April 1862, the Union navy under Admiral David Farragut fought its way past the forts that guarded New Orleans and fired naval guns upon the below-sea-level city. When it became obvious that New Orleans could no longer be defended, Confederate major general Marshall Lovell sent his artillery upriver to Vicksburg, Mississippi. Armed civilians in New Orleans fought the Union forces that entered the city. They also destroyed ships and military supplies that might be used by the Union. Upriver, Union naval forces also bombarded Fort Pillow, forty miles from Memphis, Tennessee, a Southern industrial center and one of the largest cities in the Confederacy. On June 4, 1862, the Confederate defenders abandoned the fort. On June 6, Memphis fell to the Union after the ships defending it were destroyed.

15.3 1863: The Changing Nature of the War

By the end of this section, you will be able to:
- Explain what is meant by the term "total war" and provide examples
- Describe mobilization efforts in the North and the South
- Explain why 1863 was a pivotal year in the war

Wars have their own logic; they last far longer than anyone anticipates at the beginning of hostilities. As they drag on, the energy and zeal that marked the entry into warfare often wane, as losses increase and people on both sides suffer the tolls of war. The American Civil War is a case study of this characteristic of modern war.

Although Northerners and Southerners both anticipated that the battle between the Confederacy and the Union would be settled quickly, it soon became clear to all that there was no resolution in sight. The longer the war continued, the more it began to affect life in both the North and the South. Increased need for manpower, the issue of slavery, and the ongoing challenges of keeping the war effort going changed the way life on both sides as the conflict progressed.

MASS MOBILIZATION

By late 1862, the course of the war had changed to take on the characteristics of **total war**, in which armies attempt to demoralize the enemy by both striking military targets and disrupting their opponent's ability to wage war through destruction of their resources. In this type of war, armies often make no distinction between civilian and military targets. Both the Union and Confederate forces moved toward total war, although neither side ever entirely abolished the distinction between military and civilian. Total war also requires governments to mobilize all resources, extending their reach into their citizens' lives as never before. Another reality of war that became apparent in 1862 and beyond was the influence of combat on the size and scope of government. Both the Confederacy and the Union governments had to continue to grow in order to manage the logistics of recruiting men and maintaining, feeding, and equipping an army.

Confederate Mobilization

The Confederate government in Richmond, Virginia, exercised sweeping powers to ensure victory, in stark contradiction to the states' rights sentiments held by many Southern leaders. The initial emotional outburst of enthusiasm for war in the Confederacy waned, and the Confederate government instituted a military draft in April 1862. Under the terms of the draft, all men between the ages of eighteen and thirty-five would serve three years. The draft had a different effect on men of different socioeconomic classes. One loophole permitted men to hire substitutes instead of serving in the Confederate army. This provision favored the wealthy over the poor, and led to much resentment and resistance. Exercising its power over the states, the Confederate Congress denied state efforts to circumvent the draft.

In order to fund the war, the Confederate government also took over the South's economy. The government ran Southern industry and built substantial transportation and industrial infrastructure to make the weapons of war. Over the objections of slaveholders, it impressed slaves, seizing these workers from their owners and forcing them to work on fortifications and rail lines. Concerned about the resistance to and unhappiness with the government measures, in 1862, the Confederate Congress gave President Davis the power to suspend the writ of **habeas corpus**, the right of those arrested to be brought before a judge or court to determine whether there is cause to hold the prisoner. With a stated goal of bolstering national security in the fledgling republic, this change meant that the Confederacy could arrest and detain indefinitely any suspected enemy without giving a reason. This growth of the Confederate central government stood as a glaring contradiction to the earlier states' rights argument of pro-Confederate advocates.

The war efforts were costing the new nation dearly. Nevertheless, the Confederate Congress heeded the pleas of wealthy plantation owners and refused to place a tax on slaves or cotton, despite the Confederacy's desperate need for the revenue that such a tax would have raised. Instead, the Confederacy drafted a taxation plan that kept the Southern elite happy but in no way met the needs of the war. The government also resorted to printing immense amounts of paper money, which quickly led to runaway inflation. Food prices soared, and poor, white Southerners faced starvation. In April 1863, thousands of hungry people rioted in Richmond, Virginia (Figure 15.10). Many of the rioters were mothers who could not feed their children. The riot ended when President Davis threatened to have Confederate forces open fire on the crowds.

Figure 15.10 Rampant inflation in the 1860s made food too expensive for many Southerners, leading to widespread starvation.

One of the reasons that the Confederacy was so economically devastated was its ill-advised gamble that cotton sales would continue during the war. The government had high hopes that Great Britain and France, which both used cotton as the raw material in their textile mills, would ensure the South's economic strength—and therefore victory in the war—by continuing to buy. Furthermore, the Confederate government hoped that Great Britain and France would make loans to their new nation in order to ensure the continued flow of raw materials. These hopes were never realized. Great Britain in particular did not wish to risk war with the United States, which would have meant the invasion of Canada. The United States was also a major source of grain for Britain and an important purchaser of British goods. Furthermore, the blockade made Southern trade with Europe difficult. Instead, Great Britain, the major consumer of American cotton, found alternate sources in India and Egypt, leaving the South without the income or alliance it had anticipated.

Dissent within the Confederacy also affected the South's ability to fight the war. Confederate politicians disagreed over the amount of power that the central government should be allowed to exercise. Many states' rights advocates, who favored a weak central government and supported the sovereignty of individual states, resented President Davis's efforts to conscript troops, impose taxation to pay for the war, and requisition necessary resources. Governors in the Confederate states often proved reluctant to provide supplies or troops for the use of the Confederate government. Even Jefferson Davis's vice president Alexander Stephens opposed conscription, the seizure of slave property to work for the Confederacy, and suspension of habeas corpus. Class divisions also divided Confederates. Poor whites resented the ability of wealthy slaveholders to excuse themselves from military service. Racial tensions plagued the

South as well. On those occasions when free blacks volunteered to serve in the Confederate army, they were turned away, and enslaved African Americans were regarded with fear and suspicion, as whites whispered among themselves about the possibility of slave insurrections.

Union Mobilization

Mobilization for war proved to be easier in the North than it was in the South. During the war, the federal government in Washington, DC, like its Southern counterpart, undertook a wide range of efforts to ensure its victory over the Confederacy. To fund the war effort and finance the expansion of Union infrastructure, Republicans in Congress drastically expanded government activism, impacting citizens' everyday lives through measures such as new types of taxation. The government also contracted with major suppliers of food, weapons, and other needed materials. Virtually every sector of the Northern economy became linked to the war effort.

In keeping with their longstanding objective of keeping slavery out of the newly settled western territories, the Republicans in Congress (the dominant party) passed several measures in 1862. First, the Homestead Act provided generous inducements for Northerners to relocate and farm in the West. Settlers could lay claim to 160 acres of federal land by residing on the property for five years and improving it. The act not only motivated free-labor farmers to move west, but it also aimed to increase agricultural output for the war effort. The federal government also turned its attention to creating a transcontinental railroad to facilitate the movement of people and goods across the country. Congress chartered two companies, the Union Pacific and the Central Pacific, and provided generous funds for these two businesses to connect the country by rail.

The Republican emphasis on free labor, rather than slave labor, also influenced the 1862 Land Grant College Act, commonly known as the Morrill Act after its author, Vermont Republican senator Justin Smith Morrill. The measure provided for the creation of agricultural colleges, funded through federal grants, to teach the latest agricultural techniques. Each state in the Union would be granted thirty thousand acres of federal land for the use of these institutions of higher education.

Congress paid for the war using several strategies. They levied a tax on the income of the wealthy, as well as a tax on all inheritances. They also put high tariffs in place. Finally, they passed two National Bank Acts, one in 1863 and one in 1864, calling on the U.S. Treasury to issue war bonds and on Union banks to buy the bonds. A Union campaign to convince individuals to buy the bonds helped increase sales. The Republicans also passed the Legal Tender Act of 1862, calling for paper money—known as **greenbacks**—to be printed Figure 15.11). Some $150 million worth of greenbacks became legal tender, and the Northern economy boomed, although high inflation also resulted.

Figure 15.11 The Union began printing these paper "greenbacks" to use as legal tender as one of its strategies for funding the war effort.

Like the Confederacy, the Union turned to conscription to provide the troops needed for the war. In March 1863, Congress passed the Enrollment Act, requiring all unmarried men between the ages of twenty and twenty-five, and all married men between the ages of thirty-five and forty-five—including immigrants who had filed for citizenship—to register with the Union to fight in the Civil War. All who registered were subject to military service, and draftees were selected by a lottery system (Figure 15.12). As in the South, a loophole in the law allowed individuals to hire substitutes if they could afford it. Others could avoid enlistment by paying $300 to the federal government. In keeping with the Supreme Court decision in *Dred Scott v. Sandford*, African Americans were not citizens and were therefore exempt from the draft.

(a)   (b)

Figure 15.12 The Union tried to provide additional incentives for soldiers, in the form of bounties, to enlist without waiting for the draft, as shown in recruitment posters (a) and (b).

Like the Confederacy, the Union also took the step of suspending habeas corpus rights, so those suspected of pro-Confederate sympathies could be arrested and held without being given the reason. Lincoln had selectively suspended the writ of habeas corpus in the slave state of Maryland, home to many Confederate sympathizers, in 1861 and 1862, in an effort to ensure that the Union capital would be safe. In March 1863, he signed into law the Habeas Corpus Suspension Act, giving him the power to detain suspected Confederate operatives throughout the Union. The Lincoln administration also closed down three hundred newspapers as a national security measure during the war.

In both the North and the South, the Civil War dramatically increased the power of the belligerent governments. Breaking all past precedents in American history, both the Confederacy and the Union employed the power of their central governments to mobilize resources and citizens.

Women's Mobilization

As men on both sides mobilized for the war, so did women. In both the North and the South, women were forced to take over farms and businesses abandoned by their husbands as they left for war. Women organized themselves into ladies' aid societies to sew uniforms, knit socks, and raise money to purchase necessities for the troops. In the South, women took wounded soldiers into their homes to nurse. In the North, women volunteered for the United States Sanitary Commission, which formed in June 1861. They inspected military camps with the goal of improving cleanliness and reducing the number of soldiers who died from disease, the most common cause of death in the war. They also raised money to buy medical supplies and helped with the injured. Other women found jobs in the Union army as cooks and laundresses. Thousands volunteered to care for the sick and wounded in response to a call by reformer Dorothea Dix, who was placed in charge of the Union army's nurses. According to rumor, Dix sought respectable women over the age of thirty who were "plain almost to repulsion in dress" and thus could be trusted not to form romantic liaisons with soldiers. Women on both sides also acted as spies and, disguised as men, engaged in combat.

EMANCIPATION

Early in the war, President Lincoln approached the issue of slavery cautiously. While he disapproved of slavery personally, he did not believe that he had the authority to abolish it. Furthermore, he feared that making the abolition of slavery an objective of the war would cause the border slave states to join the Confederacy. His one objective in 1861 and 1862 was to restore the Union.

DEFINING "AMERICAN"

⚙ *Lincoln's Evolving Thoughts on Slavery*

President Lincoln wrote the following letter to newspaper editor Horace Greeley on August 22, 1862. In it, Lincoln states his position on slavery, which is notable for being a middle-of-the-road stance. Lincoln's later public speeches on the issue take the more strident antislavery tone for which he is remembered.

> I would save the Union. I would save it the shortest way under the Constitution. The sooner the national authority can be restored the nearer the Union will be "the Union as it was." If there be those who would not save the Union unless they could at the same time save Slavery, I do not agree with them. If there be those who would not save the Union unless they could at the same time destroy Slavery, I do not agree with them. My paramount object in this struggle is to save the Union, and is not either to save or destroy Slavery. If I could save the Union without freeing any slave, I would do it, and if I could save it by freeing all the slaves, I would do it, and if I could save it by freeing some and leaving others alone, I would also do that. What I do about Slavery and the colored race, I do because I believe it helps to save this Union, and what I forbear, I forbear because I do not believe it would help to save the Union. I shall do less whenever I shall believe what I am doing hurts the cause, and I shall do more whenever I shall believe doing more will help the cause. I shall try to correct errors when shown to be errors; and I shall adopt new views so fast as they shall appear to be true views. I have here stated my purpose according to my view of official duty, and I intend no modification of my oft-expressed personal wish that all men, everywhere, could be free. Yours, A. LINCOLN.

How would you characterize Lincoln's public position in August 1862? What was he prepared to do for slaves, and under what conditions?

Since the beginning of the war, thousands of slaves had fled to the safety of Union lines. In May 1861, Union general Benjamin Butler and others labeled these refugees from slavery **contrabands**. Butler reasoned that since Southern states had left the United States, he was not obliged to follow federal fugitive slave laws. Slaves who made it through the Union lines were shielded by the U.S. military and not returned to slavery. The intent was not only to assist slaves but also to deprive the South of a valuable source of manpower.

Congress began to define the status of these ex-slaves in 1861 and 1862. In August 1861, legislators approved the Confiscation Act of 1861, empowering the Union to seize property, including slaves, used by the Confederacy. The Republican-dominated Congress took additional steps, abolishing slavery in Washington, DC, in April 1862. Congress passed a second Confiscation Act in July 1862, which extended freedom to runaway slaves and those captured by Union armies. In that month, Congress also addressed the issue of slavery in the West, banning the practice in the territories. This federal law made the 1846 Wilmot Proviso and the dreams of the Free-Soil Party a reality. However, even as the Union government took steps to aid individual slaves and to limit the practice of slavery, it passed no measure to address the institution of slavery as a whole.

Lincoln moved slowly and cautiously on the issue of abolition. His primary concern was the cohesion of the Union and the bringing of the Southern states back into the fold. However, as the war dragged on and many thousands of contrabands made their way north, Republicans in Congress continued to call for the end of slavery. Throughout his political career, Lincoln's plans for former slaves had been to send them to

Liberia. As late as August 1862, he had hoped to interest African Americans in building a colony for former slaves in Central America, an idea that found favor neither with black leaders nor with abolitionists, and thus was abandoned by Lincoln. Responding to Congressional demands for an end to slavery, Lincoln presented an ultimatum to the Confederates on September 22, 1862, shortly after the Confederate retreat at Antietam. He gave the Confederate states until January 1, 1863, to rejoin the Union. If they did, slavery would continue in the slave states. If they refused to rejoin, however, the war would continue and all slaves would be freed at its conclusion. The Confederacy took no action. It had committed itself to maintaining its independence and had no interest in the president's ultimatum.

On January 1, 1863, Lincoln made good on his promise and signed the **Emancipation Proclamation**. It stated "That on the first day of January, in the year of our Lord one thousand eight hundred and sixty-three, all persons held as slaves within any State or designated part of a State, the people whereof shall then be in rebellion against the United States, shall be then, thenceforward, and forever free." The proclamation did not immediately free the slaves in the Confederate states. Although they were in rebellion against the United States, the lack of the Union army's presence in such areas meant that the president's directive could not be enforced. The proclamation also did not free slaves in the border states, because these states were not, by definition, in rebellion. Lincoln relied on his powers as commander-in-chief in issuing the Emancipation Proclamation. He knew the proclamation could be easily challenged in court, but by excluding the territories still outside his control, slaveholders and slave governments could not sue him. Moreover, slave states in the Union, such as Kentucky, could not sue because the proclamation did not apply to them. Slaveholders in Kentucky knew full well that if the institution were abolished throughout the South, it would not survive in a handful of border territories. Despite the limits of the proclamation, Lincoln dramatically shifted the objective of the war increasingly toward ending slavery. The Emancipation Proclamation became a monumental step forward on the road to changing the character of the United States.

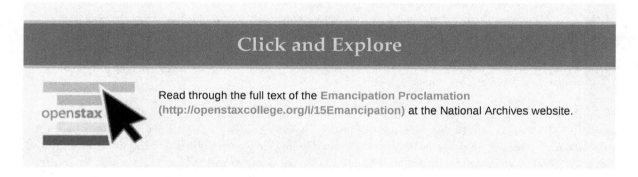

Click and Explore

Read through the full text of the Emancipation Proclamation (http://openstaxcollege.org/l/15Emancipation) at the National Archives website.

The proclamation generated quick and dramatic reactions. The news created euphoria among slaves, as it signaled the eventual end of their bondage. Predictably, Confederate leaders raged against the proclamation, reinforcing their commitment to fight to maintain slavery, the foundation of the Confederacy. In the North, opinions split widely on the issue. Abolitionists praised Lincoln's actions, which they saw as the fulfillment of their long campaign to strike down an immoral institution. But other Northerners, especially Irish, working-class, urban dwellers loyal to the Democratic Party and others with racist beliefs, hated the new goal of emancipation and found the idea of freed slaves repugnant. At its core, much of this racism had an economic foundation: Many Northerners feared competing with emancipated slaves for scarce jobs.

In New York City, the Emancipation Proclamation, combined with unhappiness over the Union draft, which began in March 1863, fanned the flames of white racism. Many New Yorkers supported the Confederacy for business reasons, and, in 1861, the city's mayor actually suggested that New York City leave the Union. On July 13, 1863, two days after the first draft lottery took place, this racial hatred erupted into violence. A volunteer fire company whose commander had been drafted initiated a riot, and the violence spread quickly across the city. The rioters chose targets associated either with the Union army or with African Americans. An armory was destroyed, as was a Brooks Brothers' store, which supplied uniforms to the army. White mobs attacked and killed black New Yorkers and destroyed an African American orphanage (Figure 15.13). On the fourth day of the riots, federal troops dispatched by Lincoln arrived in the city and ended the violence. Millions of dollars in property had been destroyed. More than one hundred people died, approximately one thousand were left injured, and about one-fifth of the city's African American population fled New York in fear.

Figure 15.13 The race riots in New York showed just how divided the North was on the issue of equality, even as the North went to war with the South over the issue of slavery.

UNION ADVANCES

The war in the west continued in favor of the North in 1863. At the start of the year, Union forces controlled much of the Mississippi River. In the spring and summer of 1862, they had captured New Orleans—the most important port in the Confederacy, through which cotton harvested from all the Southern states was exported—and Memphis. Grant had then attempted to capture Vicksburg, Mississippi, a commercial center on the bluffs above the Mississippi River. Once Vicksburg fell, the Union would have won complete control over the river. A military bombardment that summer failed to force a Confederate surrender. An assault by land forces also failed in December 1862.

In April 1863, the Union began a final attempt to capture Vicksburg. On July 3, after more than a month of a Union siege, during which Vicksburg's residents hid in caves to protect themselves from the bombardment and ate their pets to stay alive, Grant finally achieved his objective. The trapped Confederate forces surrendered. The Union had succeeded in capturing Vicksburg and splitting the Confederacy (Figure 15.14). This victory inflicted a serious blow to the Southern war effort.

Figure 15.14 In this illustration, Union gun boats fire on Vicksburg in the campaign that helped the Union take control of the Mississippi River.

As Grant and his forces pounded Vicksburg, Confederate strategists, at the urging of General Lee, who had defeated a larger Union army at Chancellorsville, Virginia, in May 1863, decided on a bold plan to invade the North. Leaders hoped this invasion would force the Union to send troops engaged in the Vicksburg campaign east, thus weakening their power over the Mississippi. Further, they hoped the aggressive action of pushing north would weaken the Union's resolve to fight. Lee also hoped that a significant Confederate victory in the North would convince Great Britain and France to extend support to Jefferson Davis's government and encourage the North to negotiate peace.

Beginning in June 1863, General Lee began to move the Army of Northern Virginia north through Maryland. The Union army—the Army of the Potomac—traveled east to end up alongside the Confederate forces. The two armies met at Gettysburg, Pennsylvania, where Confederate forces had gone to secure supplies. The resulting battle lasted three days, July 1–3 (Figure 15.15) and remains the biggest and costliest battle ever fought in North America. The climax of the Battle of Gettysburg occurred on the third day. In the morning, after a fight lasting several hours, Union forces fought back a Confederate attack on Culp's Hill, one of the Union's defensive positions. To regain a perceived advantage and secure victory, Lee ordered a frontal assault, known as Pickett's Charge (for Confederate general George Pickett), against the center of the Union lines on Cemetery Ridge. Approximately fifteen thousand Confederate soldiers took part, and more than half lost their lives, as they advanced nearly a mile across an open field to attack the entrenched Union forces. In all, more than a third of the Army of Northern Virginia had been lost, and on the evening of July 4, Lee and his men slipped away in the rain. General George Meade did not pursue them. Both sides suffered staggering losses. Total casualties numbered around twenty-three thousand for the Union and some twenty-eight thousand among the Confederates. With its defeats at Gettysburg and Vicksburg, both on the same day, the Confederacy lost its momentum. The tide had turned in favor of the Union in both the east and the west.

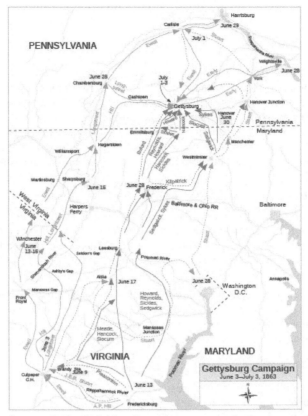

Figure 15.15 As this map indicates, the battlefield at Gettysburg was the farthest north that the Confederate army advanced. (credit: Hal Jesperson)

Following the Battle of Gettysburg, the bodies of those who had fallen were hastily buried. Attorney David Wills, a resident of Gettysburg, campaigned for the creation of a national cemetery on the site of the battlefield, and the governor of Pennsylvania tasked him with creating it. President Lincoln was invited to attend the cemetery's dedication. After the featured orator had delivered a two-hour speech, Lincoln addressed the crowd for several minutes. In his speech, known as the **Gettysburg Address**, which he had finished writing while a guest in David Wills' home the day before the dedication, Lincoln invoked the Founding Fathers and the spirit of the American Revolution. The Union soldiers who had died at Gettysburg, he proclaimed, had died not only to preserve the Union, but also to guarantee freedom and equality for all.

DEFINING "AMERICAN"

✺ Lincoln's Gettysburg Address

Several months after the battle at Gettysburg, Lincoln traveled to Pennsylvania and, speaking to an audience at the dedication of the new Soldiers' National Ceremony near the site of the battle, he delivered his now-famous Gettysburg Address to commemorate the turning point of the war and the soldiers whose sacrifices had made it possible. The two-minute speech was politely received at the time, although press reactions split along party lines. Upon receiving a letter of congratulations from Massachusetts politician and orator William Everett, whose speech at the ceremony had lasted for two hours, Lincoln said he was glad to know that his brief address, now virtually immortal, was not "a total failure."

> Four score and seven years ago our fathers brought forth on this continent, a new nation, conceived in Liberty, and dedicated to the proposition that all men are created equal.
>
> Now we are engaged in a great civil war, testing whether that nation, or any nation so conceived and so dedicated, can long endure. We are met on a great battle-field of that war. We have come to dedicate a portion of that field, as a final resting place for those who here gave their lives that that nation might live. It is altogether fitting and proper that we should do this.
>
> It is for us the living . . . to be here dedicated to the great task remaining before us—that from these honored dead we take increased devotion to that cause for which they gave the last full measure of devotion—that we here highly resolve that these dead shall not have died in vain—that this nation, under God, shall have a new birth of freedom—and that government of the people, by the people, for the people, shall not perish from the earth.
> —Abraham Lincoln, Gettysburg Address, November 19, 1863

What did Lincoln mean by "a new birth of freedom"? What did he mean when he said "a government of the people, by the people, for the people, shall not perish from the earth"?

Click and Explore

Acclaimed filmmaker Ken Burns has created a documentary (http://openstaxcollege.org/l/15Address) about a small boys' school in Vermont where students memorize the Gettysburg Address. It explores the value the address has in these boys' lives, and why the words still matter.

15.4 The Union Triumphant

By the end of this section, you will be able to:
- Describe the reasons why many Americans doubted that Abraham Lincoln would be reelected
- Explain how the Union forces overpowered the Confederacy

By the outset of 1864, after three years of war, the Union had mobilized its resources for the ongoing struggle on a massive scale. The government had overseen the construction of new railroad lines and for the first time used standardized rail tracks that allowed the North to move men and materials with greater ease. The North's economy had shifted to a wartime model. The Confederacy also mobilized, perhaps to a greater degree than the Union, its efforts to secure independence and maintain slavery. Yet the Confederacy experienced ever-greater hardships after years of war. Without the population of the North, it faced a shortage of manpower. The lack of industry, compared to the North, undercut the ability to sustain and wage war. Rampant inflation as well as food shortages in the South lowered morale.

THE RELATIONSHIP WITH EUROPE

From the beginning of the war, the Confederacy placed great hope in being recognized and supported by Great Britain and France. European intervention in the conflict remained a strong possibility, but when it did occur, it was not in a way anticipated by either the Confederacy or the Union.

Napoleon III of France believed the Civil War presented an opportunity for him to restore a French empire in the Americas. With the United States preoccupied, the time seemed ripe for action. Napoleon's target was Mexico, and in 1861, a large French fleet took Veracruz. The French then moved to capture Mexico City, but the advance came to an end when Mexican forces defeated the French in 1862. Despite this setback, France eventually did conquer Mexico, establishing a regime that lasted until 1867. Rather than coming to the aid of the Confederacy, France used the Civil War to provide a pretext for efforts to reestablish its former eighteenth-century colonial holdings.

Still, the Confederacy had great confidence that it would find an ally in Great Britain despite the antislavery sentiment there. Southerners hoped Britain's dependence on cotton for its textile mills would keep the country on their side. The fact that the British proved willing to build and sell ironclad ships intended to smash through the Union naval blockade further raised Southern hopes. The Confederacy purchased two of these armored blockade runners, the CSS *Florida* and the CSS *Alabama*. Both were destroyed during the war.

The Confederacy's staunch commitment to slavery eventually worked against British recognition and support, since Great Britain had abolished slavery in 1833. The 1863 Emancipation Proclamation ended any doubts the British had about the goals of the Union cause. In the aftermath of the proclamation, many in Great Britain cheered for a Union victory. Ultimately, Great Britain, like France, disappointed the Confederacy's hope of an alliance, leaving the outnumbered and out-resourced states that had left the Union to fend for themselves.

AFRICAN AMERICAN SOLDIERS

At the beginning of the war, in 1861 and 1862, Union forces had used contrabands, or escaped slaves, for manual labor. The Emancipation Proclamation, however, led to the enrollment of African American men as Union soldiers. Huge numbers, former slaves as well as free blacks from the North, enlisted, and by the end of the war in 1865, their numbers had swelled to over 190,000. Racism among whites in the Union army ran deep, however, fueling the belief that black soldiers could never be effective or trustworthy. The Union also feared for the fate of captured black soldiers. Although many black soldiers saw combat duty, these factors affected the types of tasks assigned to them. Many black regiments were limited to hauling supplies, serving as cooks, digging trenches, and doing other types of labor, rather than serving on the battlefield (Figure 15.16).

Figure 15.16 This 1865 daguerreotype illustrates three of the Union's distinct advantages: African American soldiers, a stream of cannons and supplies, and an extensive railroad grid. (credit: Library of Congress)

African American soldiers also received lower wages than their white counterparts: ten dollars per month, with three dollars deducted for clothing. White soldiers, in contrast, received thirteen dollars monthly, with no deductions. Abolitionists and their Republican supporters in Congress worked to correct this discriminatory practice, and in 1864, black soldiers began to receive the same pay as white soldiers plus retroactive pay to 1863 (**Figure 15.17**).

Figure 15.17 African American and white soldiers of the Union army pose together in this photograph, although in reality, black soldiers were often kept separate and given only menial jobs.

For their part, African American soldiers welcomed the opportunity to prove themselves. Some 85 percent were former slaves who were fighting for the liberation of all slaves and the end of slavery. When given the opportunity to serve, many black regiments did so heroically. One such regiment, the Fifty-Fourth Regiment of Massachusetts Volunteers, distinguished itself at Fort Wagner in South Carolina by fighting valiantly against an entrenched Confederate position. They willingly gave their lives for the cause.

The Confederacy, not surprisingly, showed no mercy to African American troops. In April 1864, Southern forces attempted to take Fort Pillow in Tennessee from the Union forces that had captured it in 1862.

Confederate troops under Major General Nathan Bedford Forrest, the future founder of the Ku Klux Klan, quickly overran the fort, and the Union defenders surrendered. Instead of taking the African American soldiers prisoner, as they did the white soldiers, the Confederates executed them. The massacre outraged the North, and the Union refused to engage in any future exchanges of prisoners with the Confederacy.

THE CAMPAIGNS OF 1864 AND 1865

In the final years of the war, the Union continued its efforts on both the eastern and western fronts while bringing the war into the Deep South. Union forces increasingly engaged in total war, not distinguishing between military and civilian targets. They destroyed everything that lay in their path, committed to breaking the will of the Confederacy and forcing an end to the war. General Grant, mastermind of the Vicksburg campaign, took charge of the war effort. He understood the advantage of having large numbers of soldiers at his disposal and recognized that Union soldiers could be replaced, whereas the Confederates, whose smaller population was feeling the strain of the years of war, could not. Grant thus pushed forward relentlessly, despite huge losses of men. In 1864, Grant committed his forces to destroying Lee's army in Virginia.

In the Virginia campaign, Grant hoped to use his larger army to his advantage. But at the Battle of the Wilderness, fought from May 5 to May 7, Confederate forces stopped Grant's advance. Rather than retreating, he pushed forward. At the Battle of Spotsylvania on May 8 through 12, Grant again faced determined Confederate resistance, and again his advance was halted. As before, he renewed the Union campaign. At the Battle of Cold Harbor in early June, Grant had between 100,000 and 110,000 soldiers, whereas the Confederates had slightly more than half that number. Again, the Union advance was halted, if only momentarily, as Grant awaited reinforcements. An attack on the Confederate position on June 3 resulted in heavy casualties for the Union, and nine days later, Grant led his army away from Cold Harbor to Petersburg, Virginia, a rail center that supplied Richmond. The immense losses that Grant's forces suffered severely hurt Union morale. The war seemed unending, and with the tremendous loss of life, many in the North began to question the war and desire peace. Undaunted by the changing opinion in the North and hoping to destroy the Confederate rail network in the Upper South, however, Grant laid siege to Petersburg for nine months. As the months wore on, both sides dug in, creating miles of trenches and gun emplacements.

The other major Union campaigns of 1864 were more successful and gave President Lincoln the advantage that he needed to win reelection in November. In August 1864, the Union navy captured Mobile Bay. General Sherman invaded the Deep South, advancing slowly from Tennessee into Georgia, confronted at every turn by the Confederates, who were commanded by Johnston. When President Davis replaced Johnston with General John B. Hood, the Confederates made a daring but ultimately costly direct attack on the Union army that failed to drive out the invaders. Atlanta fell to Union forces on September 2, 1864. The fall of Atlanta held tremendous significance for the war-weary Union and helped to reverse the North's sinking morale. In keeping with the logic of total war, Sherman's forces cut a swath of destruction to Savannah. On **Sherman's March to the Sea**, the Union army, seeking to demoralize the South, destroyed everything in its path, despite strict instructions regarding the preservation of civilian property. Although towns were left standing, houses and barns were burned. Homes were looted, food was stolen, crops were destroyed, orchards were burned, and livestock was killed or confiscated. Savannah fell on December 21, 1864—a Christmas gift for Lincoln, Sherman proclaimed. In 1865, Sherman's forces invaded South Carolina, capturing Charleston and Columbia. In Columbia, the state capital, the Union army burned slaveholders' homes and destroyed much of the city. From South Carolina, Sherman's force moved north in an effort to join Grant and destroy Lee's army.

MY STORY

✪ *Dolly Sumner Lunt on Sherman's March to the Sea*

The following account is by Dolly Sumner Lunt, a widow who ran her Georgia cotton plantation after the death of her husband. She describes General Sherman's march to Savannah, where he enacted the policy of total war by burning and plundering the landscape to inhibit the Confederates' ability to keep fighting.

> Alas! little did I think while trying to save my house from plunder and fire that they were forcing my boys [slaves] from home at the point of the bayonet. One, Newton, jumped into bed in his cabin, and declared himself sick. Another crawled under the floor,—a lame boy he was,—but they pulled him out, placed him on a horse, and drove him off. Mid, poor Mid! The last I saw of him, a man had him going around the garden, looking, as I thought, for my sheep, as he was my shepherd. Jack came crying to me, the big tears coursing down his cheeks, saying they were making him go. I said: 'Stay in my room.'

> But a man followed in, cursing him and threatening to shoot him if he did not go; so poor Jack had to yield. . . .

> Sherman himself and a greater portion of his army passed my house that day. All day, as the sad moments rolled on, were they passing not only in front of my house, but from behind; they tore down my garden palings, made a road through my back-yard and lot field, driving their stock and riding through, tearing down my fences and desolating my home—wantonly doing it when there was no necessity for it. . . .

> About ten o'clock they had all passed save one, who came in and wanted coffee made, which was done, and he, too, went on. A few minutes elapsed, and two couriers riding rapidly passed back. Then, presently, more soldiers came by, and this ended the passing of Sherman's army by my place, leaving me poorer by thirty thousand dollars than I was yesterday morning. And a much stronger Rebel!

According to this account, what was the reaction of slaves to the arrival of the Union forces? What did the Union forces do with the slaves? For Lunt, did the strategy of total war work as planned?

THE ELECTION OF 1864

Despite the military successes for the Union army in 1863, in 1864, Lincoln's status among many Northern voters plummeted. Citing the suspension of the writ of habeas corpus, many saw him as a dictator, bent on grabbing power while senselessly and uncaringly drafting more young men into combat. Arguably, his greatest liability, however, was the Emancipation Proclamation and the enlistment of African American soldiers. Many whites in the North found this deeply offensive, since they still believed in racial inequality. The 1863 New York City Draft Riots illustrated the depth of white anger.

Northern Democrats railed against Lincoln and the war. Republicans labeled these vocal opponents of the President **Copperheads**, a term that many antiwar Democrats accepted. As the anti-Lincoln poster below illustrates, his enemies tried to paint him as an untrustworthy and suspect leader (Figure 15.18). It seemed to most in the North that the Democratic candidate, General George B. McClellan, who did not support abolition and was replaced with another commander by Lincoln, would win the election.

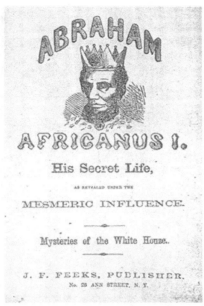

ABRAHAM

AFRICANUS I.

His Secret Life,

AS REVEALED UNDER THE

MESMERIC INFLUENCE.

Mysteries of the White House.

J. F. FEEKS, PUBLISHER,
No. 26 ANN STREET, N. Y.

Figure 15.18 Anti-Lincoln sentiment in the North ran high in 1864, and many believed he would not be reelected president that year.

The Republican Party also split over the issue of reelecting Lincoln. Those who found him timid and indecisive, and favored extending full rights to African Americans, as well as completely refashioning the South after its defeat, earned the name Radicals. A moderate faction of Republicans opposed the Radicals. For his part, Lincoln did not align himself with either group.

The tide of the election campaign turned in favor of Lincoln, however, in the fall of 1864. Above all else, Union victories, including the fall of Atlanta in September and General Philip Sheridan's successes in the Shenandoah Valley of Virginia, bolstered Lincoln's popularity and his reelection bid. In November 1864, despite earlier forecasts to the contrary, Lincoln was reelected. Lincoln won all but three states—New Jersey and the border states of Delaware and Kentucky. To the chagrin of his opponent, McClellan, even Union army troops voted overwhelmingly for the incumbent President.

THE WAR ENDS

By the spring of 1865, it had become clear to both sides that the Confederacy could not last much longer. Most of its major cities, ports, and industrial centers—Atlanta, Savannah, Charleston, Columbia, Mobile, New Orleans, and Memphis—had been captured. In April 1865, Lee had abandoned both Petersburg and Richmond. His goal in doing so was to unite his depleted army with Confederate forces commanded by General Johnston. Grant effectively cut him off. On April 9, 1865, Lee surrendered to Grant at Appomattox Court House in Virginia (Figure 15.19). By that time, he had fewer than 35,000 soldiers, while Grant had some 100,000. Meanwhile, Sherman's army proceeded to North Carolina, where General Johnston surrendered on April 19, 1865. The Civil War had come to an end. The war had cost the lives of more than 600,000 soldiers. Many more had been wounded. Thousands of women were left widowed. Children were left without fathers, and many parents were deprived of a source of support in their old age. In some areas, where local volunteer units had marched off to battle, never to return, an entire generation of young women was left without marriage partners. Millions of dollars' worth of property had been destroyed, and towns and cities were laid to waste. With the conflict finally over, the very difficult work of reconciling North and South and reestablishing the United States lay ahead.

Figure 15.19   Vastly outnumbered by the Union army, the Confederate general Robert E. Lee (seated at the left) surrendered to Ulysses S. Grant at Appomattox Courthouse. (credit: "Alaskan Dude"/Wikimedia Commons)

Key Terms

Army of the Potomac the Union fighting force operating outside Washington, DC

Army of the West the Union fighting force operating in Kentucky, Tennessee, and the Mississippi River Valley

Confederacy the new nation formed by the seceding southern states, also known as the Confederate States of America (CSA)

contrabands slaves who escaped to the Union army's lines

Copperheads Democrats who opposed Lincoln in the 1864 election

Crittenden Compromise a compromise, suggested by Kentucky senator John Crittenden, that would restore the 36°30′ line from the Missouri Compromise and extend it to the Pacific Ocean, allowing slavery to expand into the southwestern territories

Emancipation Proclamation signed on January 1, 1863, the document with which President Lincoln transformed the Civil War into a struggle to end slavery

Fort Sumter a fort in the harbor of Charleston, South Carolina, where the Union garrison came under siege by Confederate forces in an attack on April 12, 1861, beginning the Civil War

general in chief the commander of army land forces

Gettysburg Address a speech by Abraham Lincoln dedicating the military cemetery at Gettysburg on November 19, 1863

greenbacks paper money the United States began to issue during the Civil War

habeas corpus the right of those arrested to be brought before a judge or court to determine whether there is cause to hold the prisoner

Sherman's March to the Sea the scorched-earth campaign employed in Georgia by Union general William Tecumseh Sherman

total war a state of war in which the government makes no distinction between military and civilian targets, and mobilizes all resources, extending its reach into all areas of citizens' lives

Summary

15.1 The Origins and Outbreak of the Civil War
The election of Abraham Lincoln to the presidency in 1860 proved to be a watershed event. While it did not cause the Civil War, it was the culmination of increasing tensions between the proslavery South and the antislavery North. Before Lincoln had even taken office, seven Deep South states had seceded from the Union to form the CSA, dedicated to maintaining racial slavery and white supremacy. Last-minute efforts to reach a compromise, such as the proposal by Senator Crittenden and the Corwin amendment, went nowhere. The time for compromise had come to an end. With the Confederate attack on Fort Sumter, the Civil War began.

15.2 Early Mobilization and War

Many in both the North and the South believed that a short, decisive confrontation in 1861 would settle the question of the Confederacy. These expectations did not match reality, however, and the war dragged on into a second year. Both sides mobilized, with advantages and disadvantages on each side that led to a rough equilibrium. The losses of battles at Manassas and Fredericksburg, Virginia, kept the North from achieving the speedy victory its generals had hoped for, but the Union did make gains and continued to press forward. While they could not capture the Southern capital of Richmond, they were victorious in the Battle of Shiloh and captured New Orleans and Memphis. Thus, the Confederates lost major ground on the western front.

15.3 1863: The Changing Nature of the War

The year 1863 proved decisive in the Civil War for two major reasons. First, the Union transformed the purpose of the struggle from restoring the Union to ending slavery. While Lincoln's Emancipation Proclamation actually succeeded in freeing few slaves, it made freedom for African Americans a cause of the Union. Second, the tide increasingly turned against the Confederacy. The success of the Vicksburg Campaign had given the Union control of the Mississippi River, and Lee's defeat at Gettysburg had ended the attempted Confederate invasion of the North.

15.4 The Union Triumphant

Having failed to win the support it expected from either Great Britain or France, the Confederacy faced a long war with limited resources and no allies. Lincoln won reelection in 1864, and continued to pursue the Union campaign, not only in the east and west, but also with a drive into the South under the leadership of General Sherman, whose March to the Sea through Georgia destroyed everything in its path. Cut off and outnumbered, Confederate general Lee surrendered to Union general Grant on April 9 at Appomattox Court House in Virginia. Within days of Lee's surrender, Confederate troops had lay down their arms, and the devastating war came to a close.

Review Questions

1. Which of the following does *not* represent a goal of the Confederate States of America?
  A. to protect slavery from any effort to abolish it
  B. to protect the domestic slave trade
  C. to ensure that slavery would be allowed to spread into western territories
  D. to ensure that the international slave trade would be allowed to continue

2. Which was *not* a provision of the Crittenden Compromise?
  A. that the Five Civilized Tribes would be admitted into the Confederacy
  B. that the 36°30′ line from the Missouri Compromise would be restored and extended
  C. that Congress would be prohibited from abolishing slavery where it already existed

  D. that the interstate slave trade would be allowed to continue

3. Why did the states of the Deep South secede from the Union sooner than the states of the Upper South and the border states?

4. All the following were strengths of the Union except _____.
  A. a large population
  B. substantial industry
  C. an extensive railroad
  D. the ability to fight defensively, rather than offensively

5. All the following were strengths of the Confederacy except _____.
  A. the ability to wage a defensive war
  B. shorter supply lines

C. the resources of the Upper South states

D. a strong navy

6. What military successes and defeats did the Union experience in 1862?

7. Which of the following did the North *not* do to mobilize for war?

A. institute a military draft

B. form a military alliance with Great Britain

C. print paper money

D. pass the Homestead Act

8. Why is 1863 considered a turning point in the Civil War?

9. Which of the following is *not* a reason why many people opposed Lincoln's reelection in 1864?

A. He appeared to have overstepped his authority by suspending the writ of habeas corpus.

B. He issued the Emancipation Proclamation.

C. He had replaced General George B. McClellan.

D. He was seen as a power-hungry dictator.

10. What was General Sherman's objective on his March to the Sea?

A. to destroy military and civilian resources wherever possible

B. to free black prisoners of war

C. to join his army to that of General Grant

D. to capture General Robert E. Lee

Critical Thinking Questions

11. Could the differences between the North and South have been worked out in late 1860 and 1861? Could war have been avoided? Provide evidence to support your answer.

12. Why did the North prevail in the Civil War? What might have turned the tide of the war *against* the North?

13. If you were in charge of the Confederate war effort, what strategy or strategies would you have pursued? Conversely, if you had to devise the Union strategy, what would you propose? How does your answer depend on your knowledge of how the war actually played out?

14. What do you believe to be the enduring qualities of the Gettysburg Address? Why has this two-minute speech so endured?

15. What role did women and African Americans play in the war?

CHAPTER 16

The Era of Reconstruction, 1865–1877

Figure 16.1 In this political cartoon by Thomas Nast, which appeared in *Harper's Weekly* in October 1874, the "White League" shakes hands with the Ku Klux Klan over a shield that shows a couple weeping over a baby. In the background, a schoolhouse burns, and a lynched freedman is shown hanging from a tree. Above the shield, which is labeled "Worse than Slavery," the text reads, "The Union as It Was: This Is a White Man's Government."

Chapter Outline

Introduction

Few times in U.S. history have been as turbulent and transformative as the Civil War and the twelve years that followed. Between 1865 and 1877, one president was murdered and another impeached. The Constitution underwent major revision with the addition of three amendments. The effort to impose Union control and create equality in the defeated South ignited a fierce backlash as various terrorist and vigilante organizations, most notably the Ku Klux Klan, battled to maintain a pre–Civil War society in which whites held complete power. These groups unleashed a wave of violence, including lynching and arson, aimed at freed blacks and their white supporters. Historians refer to this era as Reconstruction, when an effort to remake the South faltered and ultimately failed.

The above political cartoon (Figure 16.1) expresses the anguish many Americans felt in the decade after the Civil War. The South, which had experienced catastrophic losses during the conflict, was reduced to political dependence and economic destitution. This humiliating condition led many southern whites to vigorously contest Union efforts to transform the South's racial, economic, and social landscape. Supporters of equality grew increasingly dismayed at Reconstruction's failure to undo the old system, which further compounded the staggering regional and racial inequalities in the United States.

16.1 Restoring the Union

By the end of this section, you will be able to:
- Describe Lincoln's plan to restore the Union at the end of the Civil War
- Discuss the tenets of Radical Republicanism
- Analyze the success or failure of the Thirteenth Amendment

The end of the Civil War saw the beginning of the **Reconstruction** era, when former rebel Southern states were integrated back into the Union. President Lincoln moved quickly to achieve the war's ultimate goal: reunification of the country. He proposed a generous and non-punitive plan to return the former Confederate states speedily to the United States, but some Republicans in Congress protested, considering the president's plan too lenient to the rebel states that had torn the country apart. The greatest flaw of Lincoln's plan, according to this view, was that it appeared to forgive traitors instead of guaranteeing civil rights to former slaves. President Lincoln oversaw the passage of the Thirteenth Amendment abolishing slavery, but he did not live to see its ratification.

THE PRESIDENT'S PLAN

From the outset of the rebellion in 1861, Lincoln's overriding goal had been to bring the Southern states quickly back into the fold in order to restore the Union (Figure 16.3). In early December 1863, the president began the process of reunification by unveiling a three-part proposal known as the **ten percent plan** that outlined how the states would return. The ten percent plan gave a general pardon to all Southerners except high-ranking Confederate government and military leaders; required 10 percent of the 1860 voting population in the former rebel states to take a binding oath of future allegiance to the United States and the emancipation of slaves; and declared that once those voters took those oaths, the restored Confederate states would draft new state constitutions.

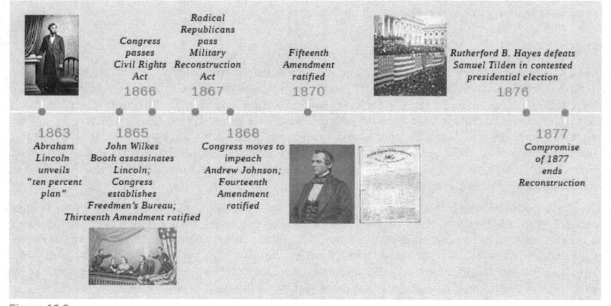

Figure 16.2

(a)   (b)

Figure 16.3   Thomas Le Mere took this albumen silver print (a) of Abraham Lincoln in April 1863. Le Mere thought a standing pose of Lincoln would be popular. In this political cartoon from 1865 (b), Lincoln and his vice president, Andrew Johnson, endeavor to sew together the torn pieces of the Union.

Lincoln hoped that the leniency of the plan—90 percent of the 1860 voters did not have to swear allegiance to the Union or to emancipation—would bring about a quick and long-anticipated resolution and make emancipation more acceptable everywhere. This approach appealed to some in the moderate wing of the Republican Party, which wanted to put the nation on a speedy course toward reconciliation. However, the proposal instantly drew fire from a larger faction of Republicans in Congress who did not want to deal moderately with the South. These members of Congress, known as **Radical Republicans**, wanted to remake the South and punish the rebels. Radical Republicans insisted on harsh terms for the defeated Confederacy and protection for former slaves, going far beyond what the president proposed.

In February 1864, two of the Radical Republicans, Ohio senator Benjamin Wade and Maryland representative Henry Winter Davis, answered Lincoln with a proposal of their own. Among other stipulations, the Wade-Davis Bill called for a majority of voters and government officials in Confederate states to take an oath, called the **Ironclad Oath**, swearing that they had never supported the Confederacy or made war against the United States. Those who could not or would not take the oath would be unable to take part in the future political life of the South. Congress assented to the Wade-Davis Bill, and it went to Lincoln for his signature. The president refused to sign, using the pocket veto (that is, taking no action) to kill the bill. Lincoln understood that no Southern state would have met the criteria of the Wade-Davis Bill, and its passage would simply have delayed the reconstruction of the South.

THE THIRTEENTH AMENDMENT

Despite the 1863 Emancipation Proclamation, the legal status of slaves and the institution of slavery remained unresolved. To deal with the remaining uncertainties, the Republican Party made the abolition of slavery a top priority by including the issue in its 1864 party platform. The platform read: "That as slavery was the cause, and now constitutes the strength of this Rebellion, and as it must be, always and everywhere, hostile to the principles of Republican Government, justice and the National safety demand its utter and complete extirpation from the soil of the Republic; and that, while we uphold and maintain the acts and proclamations by which the Government, in its own defense, has aimed a deathblow at this gigantic evil, we are in favor, furthermore, of such an amendment to the Constitution, to be made by the people in conformity with its provisions, as shall terminate and forever prohibit the existence of Slavery within the limits of the jurisdiction of the United States." The platform left no doubt about the intention to abolish slavery.

The president, along with the Radical Republicans, made good on this campaign promise in 1864 and 1865. A proposed constitutional amendment passed the Senate in April 1864, and the House of Representatives concurred in January 1865. The amendment then made its way to the states, where it swiftly gained the necessary support, including in the South. In December 1865, the Thirteenth Amendment was officially ratified and added to the Constitution. The first amendment added to the Constitution since 1804, it overturned a centuries-old practice by permanently abolishing slavery.

Click and Explore

Explore a comprehensive collection of documents, images, and ephemera related to Abraham Lincoln (http://openstaxcollege.org/l/15Lincoln) on the Library of Congress website.

President Lincoln never saw the final ratification of the Thirteenth Amendment. On April 14, 1865, the Confederate supporter and well-known actor John Wilkes Booth shot Lincoln while he was attending a play, *Our American Cousin*, at Ford's Theater in Washington. The president died the next day (Figure 16.4). Booth had steadfastly defended the Confederacy and white supremacy, and his act was part of a larger conspiracy to eliminate the heads of the Union government and keep the Confederate fight going. One of Booth's associates stabbed and wounded Secretary of State William Seward the night of the assassination. Another associate abandoned the planned assassination of Vice President Andrew Johnson at the last moment. Although Booth initially escaped capture, Union troops shot and killed him on April 26, 1865, in a Maryland barn. Eight other conspirators were convicted by a military tribunal for participating in the conspiracy, and four were hanged. Lincoln's death earned him immediate martyrdom, and hysteria spread throughout the North. To many Northerners, the assassination suggested an even greater conspiracy than what was revealed, masterminded by the unrepentant leaders of the defeated Confederacy. Militant Republicans would use and exploit this fear relentlessly in the ensuing months.

Figure 16.4 In *The Assassination of President Lincoln* (1865), by Currier and Ives, John Wilkes Booth shoots Lincoln in the back of the head as he sits in the theater box with his wife, Mary Todd Lincoln, and their guests, Major Henry R. Rathbone and Clara Harris.

ANDREW JOHNSON AND THE BATTLE OVER RECONSTRUCTION

Lincoln's assassination elevated Vice President Andrew Johnson, a Democrat, to the presidency. Johnson had come from very humble origins. Born into extreme poverty in North Carolina and having never attended school, Johnson was the picture of a self-made man. His wife had taught him how to read and he had worked as a tailor, a trade he had been apprenticed to as a child. In Tennessee, where he had moved as a young man, he gradually rose up the political ladder, earning a reputation for being a skillful stump speaker and a staunch defender of poor southerners. He was elected to serve in the House of Representatives in the 1840s, became governor of Tennessee the following decade, and then was elected a U.S. senator just a few years before the country descended into war. When Tennessee seceded, Johnson remained loyal to the Union and stayed in the Senate. As Union troops marched on his home state of North Carolina, Lincoln appointed him governor of the then-occupied state of Tennessee, where he served until being nominated by the Republicans to run for vice president on a Lincoln ticket. The nomination of Johnson, a Democrat and a slaveholding southerner, was a pragmatic decision made by concerned Republicans. It was important for them to show that the party supported all loyal men, regardless of their origin or political persuasion. Johnson appeared an ideal choice, because his nomination would bring with it the support of both pro-Southern elements and the War Democrats who rejected the conciliatory stance of the Copperheads, the northern Democrats who opposed the Civil War.

Unexpectedly elevated to the presidency in 1865, this formerly impoverished tailor's apprentice and unwavering antagonist of the wealthy southern planter class now found himself tasked with administering the restoration of a destroyed South. Lincoln's position as president had been that the secession of the Southern states was never legal; that is, they had not succeeded in leaving the Union, therefore they still had certain rights to self-government as states. In keeping with Lincoln's plan, Johnson desired to quickly reincorporate the South back into the Union on lenient terms and heal the wounds of the nation. This position angered many in his own party. The northern Radical Republican plan for Reconstruction looked to overturn southern society and specifically aimed at ending the plantation system. President Johnson quickly disappointed Radical Republicans when he rejected their idea that the federal government could provide voting rights for freed slaves. The initial disagreements between the president and the Radical Republicans over how best to deal with the defeated South set the stage for further conflict.

In fact, President Johnson's Proclamation of Amnesty and Reconstruction in May 1865 provided sweeping "amnesty and pardon" to rebellious Southerners. It returned to them their property, with the notable exception of their former slaves, and it asked only that they affirm their support for the Constitution of the United States. Those Southerners excepted from this amnesty included the Confederate political leadership, high-ranking military officers, and persons with taxable property worth more than $20,000. The inclusion of this last category was specifically designed to make it clear to the southern planter class that they had a unique responsibility for the outbreak of hostilities. But it also satisfied Johnson's desire to exact vengeance on a class of people he had fought politically for much of his life. For this class of wealthy Southerners to regain their rights, they would have to swallow their pride and request a personal pardon from Johnson himself.

For the Southern states, the requirements for readmission to the Union were also fairly straightforward. States were required to hold individual state conventions where they would repeal the ordinances of secession and ratify the Thirteenth Amendment. By the end of 1865, a number of former Confederate leaders were in the Union capital looking to claim their seats in Congress. Among them was Alexander Stephens, the vice president of the Confederacy, who had spent several months in a Boston jail after the war. Despite the outcries of Republicans in Congress, by early 1866 Johnson announced that all former Confederate states had satisfied the necessary requirements. According to him, nothing more needed to be done; the Union had been restored.

Understandably, Radical Republicans in Congress did not agree with Johnson's position. They, and their northern constituents, greatly resented his lenient treatment of the former Confederate states, and especially the return of former Confederate leaders like Alexander Stephens to Congress. They refused to acknowledge the southern state governments he allowed. As a result, they would not permit senators and representatives from the former Confederate states to take their places in Congress.

Instead, the Radical Republicans created a joint committee of representatives and senators to oversee Reconstruction. In the 1866 congressional elections, they gained control of the House, and in the ensuing years they pushed for the dismantling of the old southern order and the complete reconstruction of the South. This effort put them squarely at odds with President Johnson, who remained unwilling to compromise with Congress, setting the stage for a series of clashes.

16.2 Congress and the Remaking of the South, 1865–1866

By the end of this section, you will be able to:
- Describe the efforts made by Congress in 1865 and 1866 to bring to life its vision of Reconstruction
- Explain how the Fourteenth Amendment transformed the Constitution

President Johnson and Congress's views on Reconstruction grew even further apart as Johnson's presidency progressed. Congress repeatedly pushed for greater rights for freed people and a far more thorough reconstruction of the South, while Johnson pushed for leniency and a swifter reintegration. President Johnson lacked Lincoln's political skills and instead exhibited a stubbornness and confrontational approach that aggravated an already difficult situation.

THE FREEDMEN'S BUREAU

Freed people everywhere celebrated the end of slavery and immediately began to take steps to improve their own condition by seeking what had long been denied to them: land, financial security, education, and the ability to participate in the political process. They wanted to be reunited with family members, grasp the opportunity to make their own independent living, and exercise their right to have a say in their own government.

However, they faced the wrath of defeated but un-reconciled southerners who were determined to keep blacks an impoverished and despised underclass. Recognizing the widespread devastation in the

South and the dire situation of freed people, Congress created the Bureau of Refugees, Freedmen, and Abandoned Lands in March 1865, popularly known as the **Freedmen's Bureau**. Lincoln had approved of the bureau, giving it a charter for one year.

The Freedmen's Bureau engaged in many initiatives to ease the transition from slavery to freedom. It delivered food to blacks and whites alike in the South. It helped freed people gain labor contracts, a significant step in the creation of wage labor in place of slavery. It helped reunite families of freedmen, and it also devoted much energy to education, establishing scores of public schools where freed people and poor whites could receive both elementary and higher education. Respected institutions such as Fisk University, Hampton University, and Dillard University are part of the legacy of the Freedmen's Bureau.

In this endeavor, the Freedmen's Bureau received support from Christian organizations that had long advocated for abolition, such as the American Missionary Association (AMA). The AMA used the knowledge and skill it had acquired while working in missions in Africa and with American Indian groups to establish and run schools for freed slaves in the postwar South. While men and women, white and black, taught in these schools, the opportunity was crucially important for participating women (Figure 16.5). At the time, many opportunities, including admission to most institutes of higher learning, remained closed to women. Participating in these schools afforded these women the opportunities they otherwise may have been denied. Additionally, the fact they often risked life and limb to work in these schools in the South demonstrated to the nation that women could play a vital role in American civic life.

Figure 16.5 The Freedmen's Bureau, as shown in this 1866 illustration from *Frank Leslie's Illustrated Newspaper*, created many schools for black elementary school students. Many of the teachers who provided instruction in these southern schools, though by no means all, came from northern states.

The schools that the Freedmen's Bureau and the AMA established inspired great dismay and resentment among the white populations in the South and were sometimes targets of violence. Indeed, the Freedmen's Bureau's programs and its very existence were sources of controversy. Racists and others who resisted this type of federal government activism denounced it as both a waste of federal money and a foolish effort that encouraged laziness among blacks. Congress renewed the bureau's charter in 1866, but President Johnson, who steadfastly believed that the work of restoring the Union had been completed, vetoed the re-chartering. Radical Republicans continued to support the bureau, igniting a contest between Congress and the president that intensified during the next several years. Part of this dispute involved conflicting visions of the proper role of the federal government. Radical Republicans believed in the constructive power of the federal government to ensure a better day for freed people. Others, including Johnson, denied that the government had any such role to play.

AMERICANA

✦ *The Freedmen's Bureau*

The image below (Figure 16.6) shows a campaign poster for Hiester Clymer, who ran for governor of Pennsylvania in 1866 on a platform of white supremacy.

Figure 16.6   The caption of this image reads, "The Freedman's Bureau! An agency to keep the Negro in idleness at the expense of the white man. Twice vetoed by the President, and made a law by Congress. Support Congress & you support the Negro. Sustain the President & you protect the white man."

The image in the foreground shows an indolent black man wondering, "Whar is de use for me to work as long as dey make dese appropriations." White men toil in the background, chopping wood and plowing a field. The text above them reads, "In the sweat of thy face shall thou eat bread. . . . The white man must work to keep his children and pay his taxes." In the middle background, the Freedmen's Bureau looks like the Capitol, and the pillars are inscribed with racist assumptions of things blacks value, like "rum," "idleness," and "white women." On the right are estimates of the costs of the Freedmen's Bureau and the bounties (fees for enlistment) given to both white and black Union soldiers.

What does this poster indicate about the political climate of the Reconstruction era? How might different people have received this image?

BLACK CODES

In 1865 and 1866, as Johnson announced the end of Reconstruction, southern states began to pass a series of discriminatory state laws collectively known as **black codes**. While the laws varied in both content and severity from state to state, the goal of the laws remained largely consistent. In effect, these codes were designed to maintain the social and economic structure of racial slavery in the absence of slavery itself. The laws codified white supremacy by restricting the civic participation of freed slaves—depriving them of the right to vote, the right to serve on juries, the right to own or carry weapons, and, in some cases, even the right to rent or lease land.

A chief component of the black codes was designed to fulfill an important economic need in the postwar South. Slavery had been a pillar of economic stability in the region before the war. To maintain agricultural production, the South had relied on slaves to work the land. Now the region was faced with the daunting prospect of making the transition from a slave economy to one where labor was purchased on the open market. Not surprisingly, planters in the southern states were reluctant to make such a transition. Instead, they drafted black laws that would re-create the antebellum economic structure with the façade of a free-labor system.

Black codes used a variety of tactics to tie freed slaves to the land. To work, the freed slaves were forced to sign contracts with their employer. These contracts prevented blacks from working for more than one employer. This meant that, unlike in a free labor market, blacks could not positively influence wages and conditions by choosing to work for the employer who gave them the best terms. The predictable outcome was that freed slaves were forced to work for very low wages. With such low wages, and no ability to supplement income with additional work, workers were reduced to relying on loans from their employers. The debt that these workers incurred ensured that they could never escape from their condition. Those former slaves who attempt to violate these contracts could be fined or beaten. Those who refused to sign contracts at all could be arrested for vagrancy and then made to work for no wages, essentially being reduced to the very definition of a slave.

The black codes left no doubt that the former breakaway Confederate states intended to maintain white supremacy at all costs. These draconian state laws helped spur the congressional Joint Committee on Reconstruction into action. Its members felt that ending slavery with the Thirteenth Amendment did not go far enough. Congress extended the life of the Freedmen's Bureau to combat the black codes and in April 1866 passed the first Civil Rights Act, which established the citizenship of African Americans. This was a significant step that contradicted the Supreme Court's 1857 Dred Scott decision, which declared that blacks could never be citizens. The law also gave the federal government the right to intervene in state affairs to protect the rights of citizens, and thus, of African Americans. President Johnson, who continued to insist that restoration of the United States had already been accomplished, vetoed the 1866 Civil Rights Act. However, Congress mustered the necessary votes to override his veto. Despite the Civil Rights Act, the black codes endured, forming the foundation of the racially discriminatory Jim Crow segregation policies that impoverished generations of African Americans.

THE FOURTEENTH AMENDMENT

Questions swirled about the constitutionality of the Civil Rights Act of 1866. The Supreme Court, in its 1857 decision forbidding black citizenship, had interpreted the Constitution in a certain way; many argued that the 1866 statute, alone, could not alter that interpretation. Seeking to overcome all legal questions, Radical Republicans drafted another constitutional amendment with provisions that followed those of the 1866 Civil Rights Act. In July 1866, the Fourteenth Amendment went to state legislatures for ratification.

The Fourteenth Amendment stated, "All persons born or naturalized in the United States and subject to the jurisdiction thereof, are citizens of the United States and of the State wherein they reside." It gave citizens equal protection under both the state and federal law, overturning the Dred Scott decision. It eliminated the three-fifths compromise of the 1787 Constitution, whereby slaves had been counted as three-fifths of a free white person, and it reduced the number of House representatives and Electoral College electors for any state that denied suffrage to any adult male inhabitant, black or white. As Radical Republicans had proposed in the Wade-Davis bill, individuals who had "engaged in insurrection or rebellion [against] . . . or given aid or comfort to the enemies [of]" the United States were barred from holding political (state or federal) or military office unless pardoned by two-thirds of Congress.

The amendment also answered the question of debts arising from the Civil War by specifying that all debts incurred by fighting to defeat the Confederacy would be honored. Confederate debts, however, would not: "[N]either the United States nor any State shall assume or pay any debt or obligation incurred in aid of insurrection or rebellion against the United States, or any claim for the loss or emancipation of any slave; but all such debts, obligations and claims shall be held illegal and void." Thus, claims by former slaveholders requesting compensation for slave property had no standing. Any state that ratified the Fourteenth Amendment would automatically be readmitted. Yet, all former Confederate states refused to ratify the amendment in 1866.

President Johnson called openly for the rejection of the Fourteenth Amendment, a move that drove a further wedge between him and congressional Republicans. In late summer of 1866, he gave a series of speeches, known as the "swing around the circle," designed to gather support for his mild version of Reconstruction. Johnson felt that ending slavery went far enough; extending the rights and protections of citizenship to freed people, he believed, went much too far. He continued to believe that blacks were inferior to whites. The president's "swing around the circle" speeches to gain support for his program and derail the Radical Republicans proved to be a disaster, as hecklers provoked Johnson to make damaging statements. Radical Republicans charged that Johnson had been drunk when he made his speeches. As a result, Johnson's reputation plummeted.

Click and Explore

Read the text of the Fourteenth Amendment (http://openstaxcollege.org/l/ 15Fourteena) and then view the original document (http://openstaxcollege.org/l/ 15Fourteenb) at Our Documents.

16.3 Radical Reconstruction, 1867–1872

By the end of this section, you will be able to:
- Explain the purpose of the second phase of Reconstruction and some of the key legislation put forward by Congress
- Describe the impeachment of President Johnson
- Discuss the benefits and drawbacks of the Fifteenth Amendment

During the Congressional election in the fall of 1866, Republicans gained even greater victories. This was due in large measure to the northern voter opposition that had developed toward President Johnson because of the inflexible and overbearing attitude he had exhibited in the White House, as well as his missteps during his 1866 speaking tour. Leading Radical Republicans in Congress included Massachusetts senator Charles Sumner (the same senator whom proslavery South Carolina representative Preston Brooks had thrashed with his cane in 1856 during the Bleeding Kansas crisis) and Pennsylvania representative Thaddeus Stevens. These men and their supporters envisioned a much more expansive change in the South. Sumner advocated integrating schools and giving black men the right to vote while disenfranchising many southern voters. For his part, Stevens considered that the southern states had forfeited their rights as states when they seceded, and were no more than conquered territory that the federal government could organize as it wished. He envisioned the redistribution of plantation lands and U.S. military control over the former Confederacy.

Their goals included the transformation of the South from an area built on slave labor to a free-labor society. They also wanted to ensure that freed people were protected and given the opportunity for a better life. Violent race riots in Memphis, Tennessee, and New Orleans, Louisiana, in 1866 gave greater urgency to the second phase of Reconstruction, begun in 1867.

THE RECONSTRUCTION ACTS

The 1867 Military Reconstruction Act, which encompassed the vision of Radical Republicans, set a new direction for Reconstruction in the South. Republicans saw this law, and three supplementary laws passed by Congress that year, called the Reconstruction Acts, as a way to deal with the disorder in the South. The 1867 act divided the ten southern states that had yet to ratify the Fourteenth Amendment into five military districts (Tennessee had already been readmitted to the Union by this time and so was excluded from these acts). Martial law was imposed, and a Union general commanded each district. These generals and twenty thousand federal troops stationed in the districts were charged with protecting freed people. When a supplementary act extended the right to vote to all freed men of voting age (21 years old), the military in each district oversaw the elections and the registration of voters. Only after new state constitutions had been written and states had ratified the Fourteenth Amendment could these states rejoin the Union. Predictably, President Johnson vetoed the Reconstruction Acts, viewing them as both unnecessary and unconstitutional. Once again, Congress overrode Johnson's vetoes, and by the end of 1870, all the southern states under military rule had ratified the Fourteenth Amendment and been restored to the Union (**Figure 16.7**).

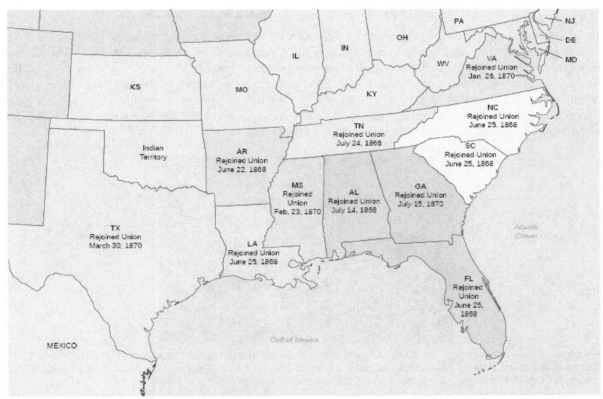

Figure 16.7 The map above shows the five military districts established by the 1867 Military Reconstruction Act and the date each state rejoined the Union. Tennessee was not included in the Reconstruction Acts as it had already been readmitted to the Union at the time of their passage.

THE IMPEACHMENT OF PRESIDENT JOHNSON

President Johnson's relentless vetoing of congressional measures created a deep rift in Washington, DC, and neither he nor Congress would back down. Johnson's prickly personality proved to be a liability, and many people found him grating. Moreover, he firmly believed in white supremacy, declaring in his 1868 State of the Union address, "The attempt to place the white population under the domination of persons of color in the South has impaired, if not destroyed, the kindly relations that had previously existed between them; and mutual distrust has engendered a feeling of animosity which leading in some instances to collision and bloodshed, has prevented that cooperation between the two races so essential to the success of industrial enterprise in the southern states." The president's racism put him even further at odds with those in Congress who wanted to create full equality between blacks and whites.

The Republican majority in Congress by now despised the president, and they wanted to prevent him from interfering in congressional Reconstruction. To that end, Radical Republicans passed two laws of dubious constitutionality. The Command of the Army Act prohibited the president from issuing military orders except through the commanding general of the army, who could not be relieved or reassigned without the consent of the Senate. The Tenure of Office Act, which Congress passed in 1867, required the president to gain the approval of the Senate whenever he appointed or removed officials. Congress had passed this act to ensure that Republicans who favored Radical Reconstruction would not be barred or stripped of their jobs. In August 1867, President Johnson removed Secretary of War Edwin M. Stanton, who had aligned himself with the Radical Republicans, without gaining Senate approval. He replaced Stanton with Ulysses S. Grant, but Grant resigned and sided with the Republicans against the president. Many Radical Republicans welcomed this blunder by the president as it allowed them to take action to remove Johnson from office, arguing that Johnson had openly violated the Tenure of Office Act. The House of Representatives quickly drafted a resolution to impeach him, a first in American history.

In impeachment proceedings, the House of Representatives serves as the prosecution and the Senate acts as judge, deciding whether the president should be removed from office (Figure 16.8). The House brought eleven counts against Johnson, all alleging his encroachment on the powers of Congress. In the Senate, Johnson barely survived. Seven Republicans joined the Democrats and independents to support acquittal; the final vote was 35 to 19, one vote short of the required two-thirds majority. The Radicals then dropped the impeachment effort, but the events had effectively silenced President Johnson, and Radical Republicans continued with their plan to reconstruct the South.

Figure 16.8 This illustration by Theodore R. Davis, which was captioned "The Senate as a court of impeachment for the trial of Andrew Johnson," appeared in *Harper's Weekly* in 1868. Here, the House of Representatives brings its grievances against Johnson to the Senate during impeachment hearings.

THE FIFTEENTH AMENDMENT

In November 1868, Ulysses S. Grant, the Union's war hero, easily won the presidency in a landslide victory. The Democratic nominee was Horatio Seymour, but the Democrats carried the stigma of disunion. The Republicans, in their campaign, blamed the devastating Civil War and the violence of its aftermath on the rival party, a strategy that southerners called "waving the bloody shirt."

Though Grant did not side with the Radical Republicans, his victory allowed the continuance of the Radical Reconstruction program. In the winter of 1869, Republicans introduced another constitutional amendment, the third of the Reconstruction era. When Republicans had passed the Fourteenth

Amendment, which addressed citizenship rights and equal protections, they were unable to explicitly ban states from withholding the franchise based on race. With the Fifteenth Amendment, they sought to correct this major weakness by finally extending to black men the right to vote. The amendment directed that "[t]he right of citizens of the United States to vote shall not be denied or abridged by the United States or by any State on account of race, color, or previous condition of servitude." Unfortunately, the new amendment had weaknesses of its own. As part of a compromise to ensure the passage of the amendment with the broadest possible support, drafters of the amendment specifically excluded language that addressed literacy tests and poll taxes, the most common ways blacks were traditionally disenfranchised in both the North and the South. Indeed, Radical Republican leader Charles Sumner of Massachusetts, himself an ardent supporter of legal equality without exception to race, refused to vote for the amendment precisely because it did not address these obvious loopholes.

Despite these weaknesses, the language of the amendment did provide for universal manhood suffrage—the right of all men to vote—and crucially identified black men, including those who had been slaves, as deserving the right to vote. This, the third and final of the Reconstruction amendments, was ratified in 1870 (Figure 16.9). With the ratification of the Fifteenth Amendment, many believed that the process of restoring the Union was safely coming to a close and that the rights of freed slaves were finally secure. African American communities expressed great hope as they celebrated what they understood to be a national confirmation of their unqualified citizenship.

Figure 16.9 *The Fifteenth Amendment. Celebrated May 19th, 1870*, a commemorative print by Thomas Kelly, celebrates the passage of the Fifteenth Amendment with a series of vignettes highlighting black rights and those who championed them. Portraits include Ulysses S. Grant, Abraham Lincoln, and John Brown, as well as black leaders Martin Delany, Frederick Douglass, and Hiram Revels. Vignettes include the celebratory parade for the amendment's passage, "The Ballot Box is open to us," and "Our representative Sits in the National Legislature."

Click and Explore

Visit the Library of Congress (http://openstaxcollege.org/l/15Fifteen) to take a closer look at *The Fifteenth Amendment* by Thomas Kelly. Examine each individual vignette and the accompanying text. Why do you think Kelly chose these to highlight?

WOMEN'S SUFFRAGE

While the Fifteenth Amendment may have been greeted with applause in many corners, leading women's rights activists, who had been campaigning for decades for the right to vote, saw it as a major disappointment. More dispiriting still was the fact that many women's rights activists, such as Susan B. Anthony and Elizabeth Cady Stanton, had played a large part in the abolitionist movement leading up to the Civil War. Following the war, women and men, white and black, formed the American Equal Rights Association (AERA) for the expressed purpose of securing "equal Rights to all American citizens, especially the right of suffrage, irrespective of race, color or sex." Two years later, with the adoption of the Fourteenth Amendment, section 2 of which specifically qualified the liberties it extended to "male citizens," it seemed as though the progress made in support of civil rights was not only passing women by but was purposely codifying their exclusion. As Congress debated the language of the Fifteenth Amendment, some held out hope that it would finally extend the franchise to women. Those hopes were dashed when Congress adopted the final language.

The consequence of these frustrated hopes was the effective split of a civil rights movement that had once been united in support of African Americans and women. Seeing this split occur, Frederick Douglass, a great admirer of Stanton, struggled to argue for a piecemeal approach that should prioritize the franchise for black men if that was the only option. He insisted that his support for women's right to vote was sincere, but that getting black men the right to vote was "of the most urgent necessity." "The government of this country loves women," he argued. "They are the sisters, mothers, wives and daughters of our rulers; but the negro is loathed. . . . The negro needs suffrage to protect his life and property, and to ensure him respect and education."

These appeals were largely accepted by women's rights leaders and AERA members like Lucy Stone and Henry Browne Blackwell, who believed that more time was needed to bring about female suffrage. Others demanded immediate action. Among those who pressed forward despite the setback were Stanton and Anthony. They felt greatly aggrieved at the fact that other abolitionists, with whom they had worked closely for years, did not demand that women be included in the language of the amendments. Stanton argued that the women's vote would be necessary to counter the influence of uneducated freedmen in the South and the waves of poor European immigrants arriving in the East.

In 1869, Stanton and Anthony helped organize the National Woman Suffrage Association (NWSA), an organization dedicated to ensuring that women gained the right to vote immediately, not at some future, undetermined date. Some women, including Virginia Minor, a member of the NWSA, took action by trying to register to vote; Minor attempted this in St. Louis, Missouri, in 1872. When election officials turned her away, Minor brought the issue to the Missouri state courts, arguing that the Fourteenth Amendment ensured that she was a citizen with the right to vote. This legal effort to bring about women's suffrage eventually made its way to the Supreme Court, which declared in 1874 that "the constitution of the United States does not confer the right of suffrage upon any one," effectively dismissing Minor's claim.

DEFINING "AMERICAN"

✸ *Constitution of the National Woman Suffrage Association*

Despite the Fifteenth Amendment's failure to guarantee female suffrage, women did gain the right to vote in western territories, with the Wyoming Territory leading the way in 1869. One reason for this was a belief that giving women the right to vote would provide a moral compass to the otherwise lawless western frontier. Extending the right to vote in western territories also provided an incentive for white women to emigrate to the West, where they were scarce. However, Susan B. Anthony, Elizabeth Cady Stanton, and others believed that immediate action on the national front was required, leading to the organization of the NWSA and its resulting constitution.

> ARTICLE 1.—This organization shall be called the National Woman Suffrage Association.

> ARTICLE 2.—The object of this Association shall be to secure STATE and NATIONAL protection for women citizens in the exercise of their right to vote.

> ARTICLE 3.—All citizens of the United States subscribing to this Constitution, and contributing not less than one dollar annually, shall be considered members of the Association, with the right to participate in its deliberations.

> ARTICLE 4.—The officers of this Association shall be a President, Vice-Presidents from each of the States and Territories, Corresponding and Recording Secretaries, a Treasurer, an Executive Committee of not less than five, and an Advisory Committee consisting of one or more persons from each State and Territory.

> ARTICLE 5.—All Woman Suffrage Societies throughout the country shall be welcomed as auxiliaries; and their accredited officers or duly appointed representatives shall be recognized as members of the National Association.
> OFFICERS OF THE NATIONAL WOMAN SUFFRAGE ASSOCIATION.

> PRESIDENT.
> SUSAN B. ANTHONY, Rochester, N. Y.

How was the NWSA organized? How would the fact that it operated at the national level, rather than at the state or local level, help it to achieve its goals?

BLACK POLITICAL ACHIEVEMENTS

Black voter registration in the late 1860s and the ratification of the Fifteenth Amendment finally brought what Lincoln had characterized as "a new birth of freedom." **Union Leagues**, fraternal groups founded in the North that promoted loyalty to the Union and the Republican Party during the Civil War, expanded into the South after the war and were transformed into political clubs that served both political and civic functions. As centers of the black communities in the South, the leagues became vehicles for the dissemination of information, acted as mediators between members of the black community and the white establishment, and served other practical functions like helping to build schools and churches for the community they served. As extensions of the Republican Party, these leagues worked to enroll newly enfranchised black voters, campaign for candidates, and generally help the party win elections (Figure 16.10).

Figure 16.10 *The First Vote*, by Alfred R. Waud, appeared in *Harper's Weekly* in 1867. The Fifteenth Amendment gave black men the right to vote for the first time.

The political activities of the leagues launched a great many African Americans and former slaves into politics throughout the South. For the first time, blacks began to hold political office, and several were elected to the U.S. Congress. In the 1870s, fifteen members of the House of Representatives and two senators were black. The two senators, Blanche K. Bruce and Hiram Revels, were both from Mississippi, the home state of former U.S. senator and later Confederate president Jefferson Davis. Hiram Revels (Figure 16.11), was a freeborn man from North Carolina who rose to prominence as a minister in the African Methodist Episcopal Church and then as a Mississippi state senator in 1869. The following year he was elected by the state legislature to fill one of Mississippi's two U.S. Senate seats, which had been vacant since the war. His arrival in Washington, DC, drew intense interest: as the *New York Times* noted, when "the colored Senator from Mississippi, was sworn in and admitted to his seat this afternoon . . . there was not an inch of standing or sitting room in the galleries, so densely were they packed. . . . When the Vice-President uttered the words, 'The Senator elect will now advance and take the oath,' a pin might have been heard drop."

Figure 16.11 Hiram Revels served as a preacher throughout the Midwest before settling in Mississippi in 1866. When he was elected by the Mississippi state legislature in 1870, he became the country's first African American senator.

DEFINING "AMERICAN"

✪ *Senator Revels on Segregated Schools in Washington, DC*

Hiram R. Revels became the first African American to serve in the U.S. Senate in 1870. In 1871, he gave the following speech about Washington's segregated schools before Congress.

> Will establishing such [desegregated] schools as I am now advocating in this District harm our white friends? . . . By some it is contended that if we establish mixed schools here a great insult will be given to the white citizens, and that the white schools will be seriously damaged. . . . When I was on a lecturing tour in the state of Ohio . . . [o]ne of the leading gentlemen connected with the schools in that town came to see me. . . . He asked me, "Have you been to New England, where they have mixed schools?" I replied, "I have sir." "Well," said he, "please tell me this: does not social equality result from mixed schools?" "No, sir; very far from it," I responded. "Why," said he, "how can it be otherwise?" I replied, "I will tell you how it can be otherwise, and how it is otherwise. Go to the schools and you see there white children and colored children seated side by side, studying their lessons, standing side by side and reciting their lessons, and perhaps in walking to school they may walk together; but that is the last of it. The white children go to their homes; the colored children go to theirs; and on the Lord's day you will see those colored children in colored churches, and the white family, you will see the white children there, and the colored children at entertainments given by persons of their color." I aver, sir, that mixed schools are very far from bringing about social equality."

According to Senator Revels's speech, what is "social equality" and why is it important to the issue of desegregated schools? Does Revels favor social equality or social segregation? Did social equality exist in the United States in 1871?

Though the fact of their presence was dramatic and important, as the *New York Times* description above demonstrates, the few African American representatives and senators who served in Congress during Reconstruction represented only a tiny fraction of the many hundreds, possibly thousands, of blacks who served in a great number of capacities at the local and state levels. The South during the early 1870s brimmed with freed slaves and freeborn blacks serving as school board commissioners, county commissioners, clerks of court, board of education and city council members, justices of the peace, constables, coroners, magistrates, sheriffs, auditors, and registrars. This wave of local African American political activity contributed to and was accompanied by a new concern for the poor and disadvantaged in the South. The southern Republican leadership did away with the hated black codes, undid the work of white supremacists, and worked to reduce obstacles confronting freed people.

Reconstruction governments invested in infrastructure, paying special attention to the rehabilitation of the southern railroads. They set up public education systems that enrolled both white and black students. They established or increased funding for hospitals, orphanages, and asylums for the insane. In some states, the state and local governments provided the poor with basic necessities like firewood and even bread. And to pay for these new services and subsidies, the governments levied taxes on land and property, an action that struck at the heart of the foundation of southern economic inequality. Indeed, the land tax compounded the existing problems of white landowners, who were often cash-poor, and contributed to resentment of what southerners viewed as another northern attack on their way of life.

White southerners reacted with outrage at the changes imposed upon them. The sight of once-enslaved blacks serving in positions of authority as sheriffs, congressmen, and city council members stimulated great resentment at the process of Reconstruction and its undermining of the traditional social and economic foundations of the South. Indignant southerners referred to this period of reform as a time of "negro misrule." They complained of profligate corruption on the part of vengeful freed slaves and greedy northerners looking to fill their pockets with the South's riches. Unfortunately for the great many honest reformers, southerners did have a handful of real examples of corruption they could point to, such as legislators using state revenues to buy hams and perfumes or giving themselves inflated salaries.

Such examples, however, were relatively few and largely comparable to nineteenth-century corruption across the country. Yet these powerful stories, combined with deep-seated racial animosity toward blacks in the South, led to Democratic campaigns to "redeem" state governments. Democrats across the South leveraged planters' economic power and wielded white vigilante violence to ultimately take back state political power from the Republicans. By the time President Grant's attentions were being directed away from the South and toward the Indian Wars in the West in 1876, power in the South had largely been returned to whites and Reconstruction was effectively abandoned. By the end of 1876, only South Carolina, Louisiana, and Florida still had Republican governments.

The sense that the South had been unfairly sacrificed to northern vice and black vengeance, despite a wealth of evidence to the contrary, persisted for many decades. So powerful and pervasive was this narrative that by the time D. W. Griffith released his 1915 motion picture, *The Birth of a Nation*, whites around the country were primed to accept the fallacy that white southerners were the frequent victims of violence and violation at the hands of unrestrained blacks. The reality is that the opposite was true. White southerners orchestrated a sometimes violent and generally successful counterrevolution against Reconstruction policies in the South beginning in the 1860s. Those who worked to change and modernize the South typically did so under the stern gaze of exasperated whites and threats of violence. Black Republican officials in the South were frequently terrorized, assaulted, and even murdered with impunity by organizations like the Ku Klux Klan. When not ignoring the Fourteenth and Fifteenth Amendments altogether, white leaders often used trickery and fraud at the polls to get the results they wanted. As Reconstruction came to a close, these methods came to define southern life for African Americans for nearly a century afterward.

16.4 The Collapse of Reconstruction

By the end of this section, you will be able to:
- Explain the reasons for the collapse of Reconstruction
- Describe the efforts of white southern "redeemers" to roll back the gains of Reconstruction

The effort to remake the South generated a brutal reaction among southern whites, who were committed to keeping blacks in a subservient position. To prevent blacks from gaining economic ground and to maintain cheap labor for the agricultural economy, an exploitative system of sharecropping spread throughout the South. Domestic terror organizations, most notably the Ku Klux Klan, employed various methods (arson, whipping, murder) to keep freed people from voting and achieving political, social, or economic equality with whites.

BUILDING BLACK COMMUNITIES

The degraded status of black men and women had placed them outside the limits of what antebellum southern whites considered appropriate gender roles and familial hierarchies. Slave marriages did not enjoy legal recognition. Enslaved men were humiliated and deprived of authority and of the ability to protect enslaved women, who were frequently exposed to the brutality and sexual domination of white masters and vigilantes alike. Slave parents could not protect their children, who could be bought, sold, put to work, brutally disciplined, and abused without their consent; parents, too, could be sold away from their children (Figure 16.12). Moreover, the division of labor idealized in white southern society, in which men worked the land and women performed the role of domestic caretaker, was null and void where slaves were concerned. Both slave men and women were made to perform hard labor in the fields.

Figure 16.12 After emancipation, many fathers who had been sold from their families as slaves—a circumstance illustrated in the engraving above, which shows a male slave forced to leave his wife and children—set out to find those lost families and rebuild their lives.

In the Reconstruction era, African Americans embraced the right to enjoy the family bonds and the expression of gender norms they had been systematically denied. Many thousands of freed black men who had been separated from their families as slaves took to the road to find their long-lost spouses and children and renew their bonds. In one instance, a journalist reported having interviewed a freed slave who traveled over six hundred miles on foot in search of the family that was taken from him while in bondage. Couples that had been spared separation quickly set out to legalize their marriages, often by way of the Freedmen's Bureau, now that this option was available. Those who had no families would sometimes relocate to southern towns and cities, so as to be part of the larger black community where churches and other mutual aid societies offered help and camaraderie.

SHARECROPPING

Most freed people stayed in the South on the lands where their families and loved ones had worked for generations as slaves. They hungered to own and farm their own lands instead of the lands of white plantation owners. In one case, former slaves on the Sea Islands off the coast of South Carolina initially had hopes of owning the land they had worked for many decades after General Sherman directed that freed people be granted title to plots of forty acres.

The Freedmen's Bureau provided additional cause for such hopes by directing that leases and titles to lands in the South be made available to former slaves. However, these efforts ran afoul of President Johnson. In 1865, he ordered the return of land to white landowners, a setback for those freed people, such as those on the South Carolina Sea Islands, who had begun to cultivate the land as their own. Ultimately, there was no redistribution of land in the South.

The end of slavery meant the transition to wage labor. However, this conversion did not entail a new era of economic independence for former slaves. While they no longer faced relentless toil under the lash, freed people emerged from slavery without any money and needed farm implements, food, and other basic necessities to start their new lives. Under the **crop-lien system**, store owners extended credit to farmers under the agreement that the debtors would pay with a portion of their future harvest. However, the creditors charged high interest rates, making it even harder for freed people to gain economic independence.

Throughout the South, **sharecropping** took root, a crop-lien system that worked to the advantage of landowners. Under the system, freed people rented the land they worked, often on the same plantations where they had been slaves. Some landless whites also became sharecroppers. Sharecroppers paid their landlords with the crops they grew, often as much as half their harvest. Sharecropping favored the landlords and ensured that freed people could not attain independent livelihoods. The year-to-year leases meant no incentive existed to substantially improve the land, and high interest payments siphoned additional money away from the farmers. Sharecroppers often became trapped in a never-ending cycle of debt, unable to buy their own land and unable to stop working for their creditor because of what they owed. The consequences of sharecropping affected the entire South for many generations, severely limiting economic development and ensuring that the South remained an agricultural backwater.

THE "INVISIBLE EMPIRE OF THE SOUTH"

Paramilitary white-supremacist terror organizations in the South helped bring about the collapse of Reconstruction, using violence as their primary weapon. The "Invisible Empire of the South," or **Ku Klux Klan**, stands as the most notorious. The Klan was founded in 1866 as an oath-bound fraternal order of Confederate veterans in Tennessee, with former Confederate General Nathan Bedford Forrest as its first leader. The organization—its name likely derived from *kuklos*, a Greek word meaning circle—devised elaborate rituals and grandiose names for its ranking members: Grand Wizard, Grand Dragon, Grand Titan, and Grand Cyclops. Soon, however, this fraternal organization evolved into a vigilante terrorist group that vented southern whites' collective frustration over the loss of the war and the course of Radical Reconstruction through acts of intimidation and violence.

The Klan terrorized newly freed blacks to deter them from exercising their citizenship rights and freedoms. Other anti-black vigilante groups around the South began to adopt the Klan name and perpetrate acts of unspeakable violence against anyone they considered a tool of Reconstruction. Indeed, as historians have noted, Klan units around the South operated autonomously and with a variety of motives. Some may have sincerely believed they were righting wrongs, others merely satisfying their lurid desires for violence. Nor was the Klan the only racist vigilante organization. Other groups, like the Red Shirts from Mississippi and the Knights of the White Camelia and the White League, both from Louisiana, also sprang up at this time. The Klan and similar organizations also worked as an extension of the Democratic Party to win elections.

Despite the great variety in Klan membership, on the whole, the group tended to direct its attention toward persecuting freed people and people they considered **carpetbaggers**, a term of abuse applied to northerners accused of having come to the South to acquire wealth through political power at the expense of southerners. The colorful term captured the disdain of southerners for these people, reflecting the common assumption that these men, sensing great opportunity, packed up all their worldly possessions in carpetbags, a then-popular type of luggage, and made their way to the South. Implied in this definition is the notion that these men came from little and were thus shiftless wanderers motivated only by the desire for quick money. In reality, these northerners tended to be young, idealistic, often well-educated men who responded to northern campaigns urging them to lead the modernization of the South. But the image of them as swindlers taking advantage of the South at its time of need resonated with a white southern population aggrieved by loss and economic decline. Southern whites who supported Reconstruction, known as **scalawags**, also generated great hostility as traitors to the South. They, too, became targets of the Klan and similar groups.

The Klan seized on the pervasive but largely fictional narrative of the northern carpetbagger as a powerful tool for restoring white supremacy and overturning Republican state governments in the South (Figure 16.13). To preserve a white-dominated society, Klan members punished blacks for attempting to improve their station in life or acting "uppity." To prevent freed people from attaining an education, the Klan burned public schools. In an effort to stop blacks from voting, the Klan murdered, whipped, and otherwise intimidated freed people and their white supporters. It wasn't uncommon for Klan members to intimidate Union League members and Freedmen's Bureau workers. The Klan even perpetrated acts of political assassination, killing a sitting U.S. congressman from Arkansas and three state congressmen from South Carolina.

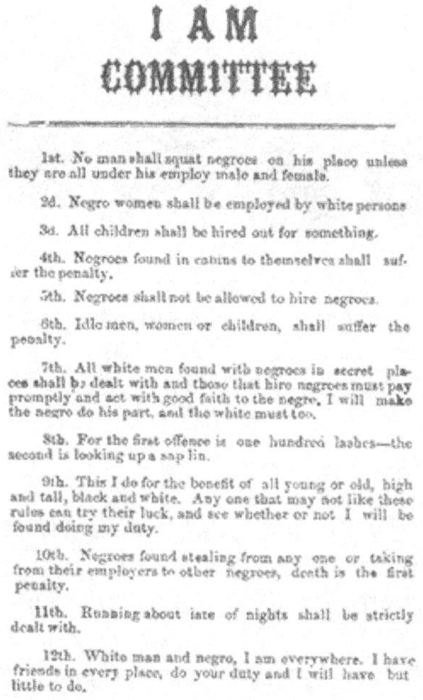

I AM COMMITTEE

1st. No man shall squat negroes on his place unless they are all under his employ male and female.

2d. Negro women shall be employed by white persons

3d. All children shall be hired out for something.

4th. Negroes found in cabins to themselves shall suffer the penalty.

5th. Negroes shall not be allowed to hire negroes.

8th. Idle men, women or children, shall suffer the penalty.

7th. All white men found with negroes in secret places shall be dealt with and those that hire negroes must pay promptly and act with good faith to the negro. I will make the negro do his part, and the white must too.

8th. For the first offence is one hundred lashes—the second is looking up a sap lin.

9th. This I do for the benefit of all young or old, high and tall, black and white. Any one that may not like these rules can try their luck, and see whether or not I will be found doing my duty.

10th. Negroes found stealing from any one or taking from their employers to other negroes, death is the first penalty.

11th. Running about late of nights shall be strictly dealt with.

12th. White man and negro, I am everywhere. I have friends in every place, do your duty and I will have but little to do.

Figure 16.13 The Ku Klux Klan posted circulars such as this 1867 West Virginia broadside to warn blacks and white sympathizers of the power and ubiquity of the Klan.

Klan tactics included riding out to victims' houses, masked and armed, and firing into the homes or burning them down (Figure 16.14). Other tactics relied more on the threat of violence, such as happened in Mississippi when fifty masked Klansmen rode out to a local schoolteacher's house to express their displeasure with the school tax and to suggest that she consider leaving. Still other tactics intimidated through imaginative trickery. One such method was to dress up as ghosts of slain Confederate soldiers and stage stunts designed to convince their victims of their supernatural abilities.

Figure 16.14 This illustration by Frank Bellew, captioned "Visit of the Ku-Klux," appeared in *Harper's Weekly* in 1872. A hooded Klansman surreptitiously points a rifle at an unaware black family in their home.

Regardless of the method, the general goal of reinstating white supremacy as a foundational principle and returning the South to a situation that largely resembled antebellum conditions remained a constant. The

Klan used its power to eliminate black economic independence, decimate blacks' political rights, reclaim white dominance over black women's bodies and black men's masculinity, tear apart black communities, and return blacks to earlier patterns of economic and political subservience and social deference. In this, they were largely successful.

Click and Explore

Visit **Freedmen's Bureau Online (http://openstaxcollege.org/l/15Freedmen)** to view digitized records of attacks on freed people that were reported in Albany, Georgia, between January 1 and October 31, 1868.

The president and Congress, however, were not indifferent to the violence, and they worked to bring it to an end. In 1870, at the insistence of the governor of North Carolina, President Grant told Congress to investigate the Klan. In response, Congress in 1871 created the Joint Select Committee to Inquire into the Condition of Affairs in the Late Insurrectionary States. The committee took testimony from freed people in the South, and in 1872, it published a thirteen-volume report on the tactics the Klan used to derail democracy in the South through the use of violence.

MY STORY

✪ Abram Colby on the Methods of the Ku Klux Klan

The following statements are from the October 27, 1871, testimony of fifty-two-year-old former slave Abram Colby, which the joint select committee investigating the Klan took in Atlanta, Georgia. Colby had been elected to the lower house of the Georgia State legislature in 1868.

> On the 29th of October, they came to my house and broke my door open, took me out of my bed and took me to the woods and whipped me three hours or more and left me in the woods for dead. They said to me, "Do you think you will ever vote another damned Radical ticket?" I said, "I will not tell you a lie." They said, "No; don't tell a lie." . . . I said, "If there was an election to-morrow, I would vote the Radical ticket." They set in and whipped me a thousand licks more, I suppose. . . .
>
> They said I had influence with the negroes of other counties, and had carried the negroes against them. About two days before they whipped me they offered me $5,000 to turn and go with them, and said they would pay me $2,500 cash if I would turn and let another man go to the legislature in my place. . . .
>
> I would have come before the court here last week, but I knew it was no use for me to try to get Ku-Klux condemned by Ku-Klux, and I did not come. Mr. Saunders, a member of the grand jury here last week, is the father of one of the very men I knew whipped me. . . .
>
> They broke something inside of me, and the doctor has been attending to me for more than a year. Sometimes I cannot get up and down off my bed, and my left hand is not of much use to me.
> —Abram Colby testimony, Joint Select Committee Report, 1872

Why did the Klan target Colby? What methods did they use?

Congress also passed a series of three laws designed to stamp out the Klan. Passed in 1870 and 1871, the Enforcement Acts or "Force Acts" were designed to outlaw intimidation at the polls and to give the federal government the power to prosecute crimes against freed people in federal rather than state courts. Congress believed that this last step, a provision in the third Enforcement Act, also called the Ku Klux Klan Act, was necessary in order to ensure that trials would not be decided by white juries in southern states friendly to the Klan. The act also allowed the president to impose martial law in areas controlled by the Klan and gave President Grant the power to suspend the writ of habeas corpus, a continuation of the wartime power granted to President Lincoln. The suspension meant individuals suspected of engaging in Klan activity could be jailed indefinitely.

President Grant made frequent use of the powers granted to him by Congress, especially in South Carolina, where federal troops imposed martial law in nine counties in an effort to derail Klan activities. However, the federal government faced entrenched local organizations and a white population firmly opposed to Radical Reconstruction. Changes came slowly or not at all, and disillusionment set in. After 1872, federal government efforts to put down paramilitary terror in the South waned.

"REDEEMERS" AND THE END OF RECONSTRUCTION

While the president and Congress may have seen the Klan and other clandestine white supremacist, terrorist organizations as a threat to stability and progress in the South, many southern whites saw them as an instrument of order in a world turned upside down. Many white southerners felt humiliated by the process of Radical Reconstruction and the way Republicans had upended southern society, placing blacks in positions of authority while taxing large landowners to pay for the education of former slaves. Those committed to rolling back the tide of Radical Reconstruction in the South called themselves **redeemers**, a label that expressed their desire to redeem their states from northern control and to restore the antebellum social order whereby blacks were kept safely under the boot heel of whites. They represented the Democratic Party in the South and worked tirelessly to end what they saw as an era of "negro misrule." By 1877, they had succeeded in bringing about the "redemption" of the South, effectively destroying the dream of Radical Reconstruction.

Although Ulysses S. Grant won a second term in the presidential election of 1872, the Republican grip on national political power began to slip in the early 1870s. Three major events undermined Republican control. First, in 1873, the United States experienced the start of a long economic downturn, the result of economic instability in Europe that spread to the United States. In the fall of 1873, the bank of Jay Cooke & Company failed to meet its financial obligations and went bankrupt, setting off a panic in American financial markets. An economic depression ensued, which Democrats blamed on Republicans and which lasted much of the decade.

Second, the Republican Party experienced internal squabbles and divided into two factions. Some Republicans began to question the expansive role of the federal government, arguing for limiting the size and scope of federal initiatives. These advocates, known as Liberal Republicans because they followed classical liberalism in championing small government, formed their own breakaway party. Their ideas changed the nature of the debate over Reconstruction by challenging reliance on federal government help to bring about change in the South. Now some Republicans argued for downsizing Reconstruction efforts.

Third, the Grant administration became mired in scandals, further tarnishing the Republicans while giving Democrats the upper hand. One scandal arose over the siphoning off of money from excise taxes on whiskey. The "Whiskey Ring," as it was called, involved people at the highest levels of the Grant administration, including the president's personal secretary, Orville Babcock. Another scandal entangled Crédit Mobilier of America, a construction company and part of the important French Crédit Mobilier banking company. The Union Pacific Railroad company, created by the federal government during the Civil War to construct a transcontinental railroad, paid Crédit Mobilier to build the railroad. However, Crédit Mobilier used the funds it received to buy Union Pacific Railroad bonds and resell them at a huge profit. Some members of Congress, as well as Vice President Schuyler Colfax, had accepted funds from

Crédit Mobilier in return for forestalling an inquiry. When the scam became known in 1872, Democratic opponents of Reconstruction pointed to Crédit Mobilier as an example of corruption in the Republican-dominated federal government and evidence that smaller government was better.

The Democratic Party in the South made significant advances in the 1870s in its efforts to wrest political control from the Republican-dominated state governments. The Ku Klux Klan, as well as other paramilitary groups in the South, often operated as military wings of the Democratic Party in former Confederate states. In one notorious episode following a contested 1872 gubernatorial election in Louisiana, as many as 150 freedmen loyal to the Republican Party were killed at the Colfax courthouse by armed members of the Democratic Party, even as many of them tried to surrender (Figure 16.15).

Figure 16.15 In this illustration by Charles Harvey Weigall, captioned "The Louisiana Murders—Gathering the Dead and Wounded" and published in *Harper's Weekly* in 1873, survivors of the Colfax Massacre tend to those involved in the conflict. The dead and wounded all appear to be black, and two white men on horses watch over them. Another man stands with a gun pointed at the survivors.

In other areas of the South, the Democratic Party gained control over state politics. Texas came under Democratic control by 1873, and in the following year Alabama and Arkansas followed suit. In national politics, too, the Democrats gained ground—especially during the 1874 elections, when they recaptured control of the House of Representatives for the first time since before the Civil War. Every other southern state, with the exception of Florida, South Carolina, and Louisiana—the states where federal troops remained a force—also fell to the Democratic Party and the restoration of white supremacy. Southerners everywhere celebrated their "redemption" from Radical Republican rule.

THE CONTESTED ELECTION OF 1876

By the time of the 1876 presidential election, Reconstruction had come to an end in most southern states. In Congress, the political power of the Radical Republicans had waned, although some continued their efforts to realize the dream of equality between blacks and whites. One of the last attempts to do so was the passage of the 1875 Civil Rights Act, which required equality in public places and on juries. This law was challenged in court, and in 1883 the Supreme Court ruled it unconstitutional, arguing that the Thirteenth and Fourteenth Amendments did not prohibit discrimination by private individuals. By the 1870s, the Supreme Court had also undercut the letter and the spirit of the Fourteenth Amendment by interpreting it as affording freed people only limited federal protection from the Klan and other terror groups.

The country remained bitterly divided, and this was reflected in the contested election of 1876. While Grant wanted to run for a third term, scandals and Democratic successes in the South dashed those hopes. Republicans instead selected Rutherford B. Hayes, the three-time governor of Ohio. Democrats nominated Samuel Tilden, the reform governor of New York, who was instrumental in ending the Tweed Ring and Tammany Hall corruption in New York City. The November election produced an apparent Democratic victory, as Tilden carried the South and large northern states with a 300,000-vote advantage in the popular vote. However, disputed returns from Louisiana, South Carolina, Florida, and Oregon, whose electoral votes totaled twenty, threw the election into doubt.

Hayes could still win if he gained those twenty electoral votes. As the Constitution did not provide a method to determine the validity of disputed votes, the decision fell to Congress, where Republicans controlled the Senate and Democrats controlled the House of Representatives. In late January 1877, Congress tried to break the deadlock by creating a special electoral commission composed of five senators, five representatives, and five justices of the Supreme Court. The congressional delegation represented both parties equally, with five Democrats and five Republicans. The court delegation had two Democrats, two Republicans, and one independent—David Davis, who resigned from the Supreme Court (and from the commission) when the Illinois legislature elected him to the Senate. After Davis's resignation, President Grant selected a Republican to take his place, tipping the scales in favor of Hayes. The commission then awarded the disputed electoral votes and the presidency to Hayes, voting on party lines, 8 to 7 (Figure 16.16). The Democrats called foul, threatening to hold up the commission's decision in the courts.

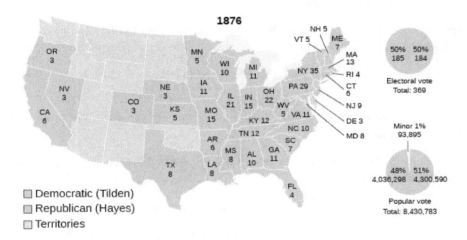

Figure 16.16 This map illustrates the results of the presidential election of 1876. Tilden, the Democratic candidate, swept the South, with the exception of the contested states of Florida, Louisiana, and South Carolina.

In what became known as the **Compromise of 1877**, Republican Senate leaders worked with the Democratic leadership so they would support Hayes and the commission's decision. The two sides agreed that one Southern Democrat would be appointed to Hayes's cabinet, Democrats would control federal patronage (the awarding of government jobs) in their areas in the South, and there would be a commitment to generous internal improvements, including federal aid for the Texas and Pacific Railway. Perhaps most important, all remaining federal troops would be withdrawn from the South, a move that effectively ended Reconstruction. Hayes believed that southern leaders would obey and enforce the Reconstruction-era constitutional amendments that protected the rights of freed people. His trust was soon proved to be misguided, much to his dismay, and he devoted a large part of his life to securing rights for freedmen. For their part, the Democrats took over the remaining southern states, creating what became known as the "Solid South"—a region that consistently voted in a bloc for the Democratic Party.

Key Terms

black codes laws some southern states designed to maintain white supremacy by keeping freed people impoverished and in debt

carpetbagger a term used for northerners working in the South during Reconstruction; it implied that these were opportunists who came south for economic or political gain

Compromise of 1877 the agreement between Republicans and Democrats, after the contested election of 1876, in which Rutherford B. Hayes was awarded the presidency in exchange for withdrawing the last of the federal troops from the South

crop-lien system a loan system in which store owners extended credit to farmers for the purchase of goods in exchange for a portion of their future crops

Freedmen's Bureau the Bureau of Refugees, Freedmen, and Abandoned Lands, which was created in 1865 to ease blacks' transition from slavery to freedom

Ironclad Oath an oath that the Wade-Davis Bill required a majority of voters and government officials in Confederate states to take; it involved swearing that they had never supported the Confederacy

Ku Klux Klan a white vigilante organization that engaged in terroristic violence with the aim of stopping Reconstruction

Radical Republicans northern Republicans who contested Lincoln's treatment of Confederate states and proposed harsher punishments

Reconstruction the twelve-year period after the Civil War in which the rebel Southern states were integrated back into the Union

redeemers a term used for southern whites committed to rolling back the gains of Reconstruction

scalawags a pejorative term used for southern whites who supported Reconstruction

sharecropping a crop-lien system in which people paid rent on land they farmed (but did not own) with the crops they grew

ten percent plan Lincoln's Reconstruction plan, which required only 10 percent of the 1860 voters in Confederate states to take an oath of allegiance to the Union

Union Leagues fraternal groups loyal to the Union and the Republican Party that became political and civic centers for blacks in former Confederate states

Summary

16.1 Restoring the Union

President Lincoln worked to reach his goal of reunifying the nation quickly and proposed a lenient plan to reintegrate the Confederate states. After his murder in 1865, Lincoln's vice president, Andrew Johnson, sought to reconstitute the Union quickly, pardoning Southerners en masse and providing Southern states with a clear path back to readmission. By 1866, Johnson announced the end of Reconstruction. Radical Republicans in Congress disagreed, however, and in the years ahead would put forth their own plan of Reconstruction.

16.2 Congress and the Remaking of the South, 1865–1866

The conflict between President Johnson and the Republican-controlled Congress over the proper steps to be taken with the defeated Confederacy grew in intensity in the years immediately following the Civil War. While the president concluded that all that needed to be done in the South had been done by early 1866, Congress forged ahead to stabilize the defeated Confederacy and extend to freed people citizenship and equality before the law. Congress prevailed over Johnson's vetoes as the friction between the president and the Republicans increased.

16.3 Radical Reconstruction, 1867–1872

Though President Johnson declared Reconstruction complete less than a year after the Confederate surrender, members of Congress disagreed. Republicans in Congress began to implement their own plan of bringing law and order to the South through the use of military force and martial law. Radical Republicans who advocated for a more equal society pushed their program forward as well, leading to the ratification of the Fifteenth Amendment, which finally gave blacks the right to vote. The new amendment empowered black voters, who made good use of the vote to elect black politicians. It disappointed female suffragists, however, who had labored for years to gain women's right to vote. By the end of 1870, all the southern states under Union military control had satisfied the requirements of Congress and been readmitted to the Union.

16.4 The Collapse of Reconstruction

The efforts launched by Radical Republicans in the late 1860s generated a massive backlash in the South in the 1870s as whites fought against what they considered "negro misrule." Paramilitary terrorist cells emerged, committing countless atrocities in their effort to "redeem" the South from black Republican rule. In many cases, these organizations operated as an extension of the Democratic Party. Scandals hobbled the Republican Party, as did a severe economic depression. By 1875, Reconstruction had largely come to an end. The contested presidential election the following year, which was decided in favor of the Republican candidate, and the removal of federal troops from the South only confirmed the obvious: Reconstruction had failed to achieve its primary objective of creating an interracial democracy that provided equal rights to all citizens.

Review Questions

1. What was Lincoln's primary goal immediately following the Civil War?
  A. punishing the rebel states
  B. improving the lives of former slaves
  C. reunifying the country
  D. paying off the debts of the war

2. In 1864 and 1865, Radical Republicans were most concerned with _____.
  A. securing civil rights for freed slaves
  B. barring ex-Confederates from political office
  C. seeking restitution from Confederate states
  D. preventing Andrew Johnson's ascent to the presidency

3. What was the purpose of the Thirteenth Amendment? How was it different from the Emancipation Proclamation?

4. Which of the following was *not* one of the functions of the Freedmen's Bureau?
  A. collecting taxes
  B. reuniting families
  C. establishing schools
  D. helping workers secure labor contracts

5. Which person or group was most responsible for the passage of the Fourteenth Amendment?
  A. President Johnson
  B. northern voters
  C. southern voters
  D. Radical Republicans in Congress

6. What was the goal of the black codes?

7. Under Radical Reconstruction, which of the following did former Confederate states *not* need to do in order to rejoin the Union?
  A. pass the Fourteenth Amendment
  B. pass the Fifteenth Amendment
  C. revise their state constitution
  D. allow all freed men over the age of 21 to vote

8. The House of Representatives impeached Andrew Johnson over _____.
  A. the Civil Rights Act
  B. the Fourteenth Amendment
  C. the Military Reconstruction Act
  D. the Tenure of Office Act

9. What were the benefits and drawbacks of the Fifteenth Amendment?

10. Which of the following is *not* one of the methods the Ku Klux Klan and other terrorist groups used to intimidate blacks and white sympathizers?
  A. burning public schools
  B. petitioning Congress
  C. murdering freedmen who tried to vote
  D. threatening, beating, and killing those who disagreed with them

11. Which of the following was the term southerners used for a white southerner who tried to overturn the changes of Reconstruction?
  A. scalawag
  B. carpetbagger
  C. redeemer
  D. white knight

12. Why was it difficult for southern free blacks to gain economic independence after the Civil War?

Critical Thinking Questions

13. How do you think would history have been different if Lincoln had not been assassinated? How might his leadership after the war have differed from that of Andrew Johnson?

14. Was the Thirteenth Amendment a success or a failure? Discuss the reasons for your answer.

15. Consider the differences between the Thirteenth and Fourteenth Amendments. What does the Fourteenth Amendment do that the Thirteenth does not?

16. Consider social, political, and economic equality. In what ways did Radical Reconstruction address and secure these forms of equality? Where did it fall short?

17. Consider the problem of terrorism during Radical Reconstruction. If you had been an adviser to President Grant, how would you propose to deal with the problem?

CHAPTER 17

Go West Young Man! Westward Expansion, 1840-1900

Figure 17.1 Widely held rhetoric of the nineteenth century suggested to Americans that it was their divine right and responsibility to settle the West with Protestant democratic values. Newspaper editor Horace Greely, who coined the phrase "Go west, young man," encouraged Americans to fulfill this dream. Artists of the day depicted this western expansion in idealized landscapes that bore little resemblance to the difficulties of life on the trail.

Chapter Outline

17.1 The Westward Spirit
17.2 Homesteading: Dreams and Realities
17.3 Making a Living in Gold and Cattle
17.4 The Loss of American Indian Life and Culture
17.5 The Impact of Expansion on Chinese Immigrants and Hispanic Citizens

Introduction

In the middle of the nineteenth century, farmers in the "Old West"—the land across the Allegheny Mountains in Pennsylvania—began to hear about the opportunities to be found in the "New West." They had long believed that the land west of the Mississippi was a great desert, unfit for human habitation. But now, the federal government was encouraging them to join the migratory stream westward to this unknown land. For a variety of reasons, Americans increasingly felt compelled to fulfill their "Manifest Destiny," a phrase that came to mean that they were expected to spread across the land given to them by God and, most importantly, spread predominantly American values to the frontier (Figure 17.1).

With great trepidation, hundreds, and then hundreds of thousands, of settlers packed their lives into wagons and set out, following the Oregon, California, and Santa Fe Trails, to seek a new life in the West. Some sought open lands and greater freedom to fulfill the democratic vision originally promoted by Thomas Jefferson and experienced by their ancestors. Others saw economic opportunity. Still others believed it was their job to spread the word of God to the "heathens" on the frontier. Whatever their motivation, the great migration was underway. The American pioneer spirit was born.

17.1 The Westward Spirit

By the end of this section, you will be able to:
- Explain the evolution of American views about westward migration in the mid-nineteenth century
- Analyze the ways in which the federal government facilitated Americans' westward migration in the mid-nineteenth century

While a small number of settlers had pushed westward before the mid-nineteenth century, the land west of the Mississippi was largely unexplored. Most Americans, if they thought of it at all, viewed this territory as an arid wasteland suitable only for Indians whom the federal government had displaced from eastern lands in previous generations. The reflections of early explorers who conducted scientific treks throughout the West tended to confirm this belief. Major Stephen Harriman Long, who commanded an expedition through Missouri and into the Yellowstone region in 1819–1820, frequently described the Great Plains as a arid and useless region, suitable as nothing more than a "great American desert." But, beginning in the 1840s, a combination of economic opportunity and ideological encouragement changed the way Americans thought of the West. The federal government offered a number of incentives, making it viable for Americans to take on the challenge of seizing these rough lands from others and subsequently taming them. Still, most Americans who went west needed some financial security at the outset of their journey; even with government aid, the truly poor could not make the trip. The cost of moving an entire family westward, combined with the risks as well as the questionable chances of success, made the move prohibitive for most. While the economic Panic of 1837 led many to question the promise of urban America, and thus turn their focus to the promise of commercial farming in the West, the Panic also resulted in many lacking the financial resources to make such a commitment. For most, the dream to "Go west, young man" remained unfulfilled.

While much of the basis for westward expansion was economic, there was also a more philosophical reason, which was bound up in the American belief that the country—and the "heathens" who populated it—was destined to come under the civilizing rule of Euro-American settlers and their superior technology,

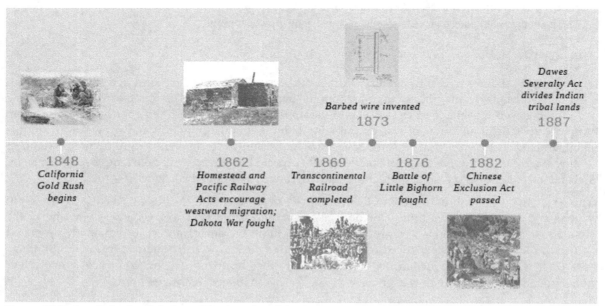

Figure 17.2 (credit "barbed wire": modification of work by the U.S. Department of Commerce)

most notably railroads and the telegraph. While the extent to which that belief was a heartfelt motivation held by most Americans, or simply a rationalization of the conquests that followed, remains debatable, the clashes—both physical and cultural—that followed this western migration left scars on the country that are still felt today.

MANIFEST DESTINY

The concept of **Manifest Destiny** found its roots in the long-standing traditions of territorial expansion upon which the nation itself was founded. This phrase, which implies divine encouragement for territorial expansion, was coined by magazine editor John O'Sullivan in 1845, when he wrote in the *United States Magazine and Democratic Review* that "it was our manifest destiny to overspread the continent allotted by Providence for the free development of our multiplying millions." Although the context of O'Sullivan's original article was to encourage expansion into the newly acquired Texas territory, the spirit it invoked would subsequently be used to encourage westward settlement throughout the rest of the nineteenth century. Land developers, railroad magnates, and other investors capitalized on the notion to encourage westward settlement for their own financial benefit. Soon thereafter, the federal government encouraged this inclination as a means to further develop the West during the Civil War, especially at its outset, when concerns over the possible expansion of slavery deeper into western territories was a legitimate fear.

The idea was simple: Americans were destined—and indeed divinely ordained—to expand democratic institutions throughout the continent. As they spread their culture, thoughts, and customs, they would, in the process, "improve" the lives of the native inhabitants who might otherwise resist Protestant institutions and, more importantly, economic development of the land. O'Sullivan may have coined the phrase, but the concept had preceded him: Throughout the 1800s, politicians and writers had stated the belief that the United States was destined to rule the continent. O'Sullivan's words, which resonated in the popular press, matched the economic and political goals of a federal government increasingly committed to expansion.

Manifest Destiny justified in Americans' minds their right and duty to govern any other groups they encountered during their expansion, as well as absolved them of any questionable tactics they employed in the process. While the commonly held view of the day was of a relatively empty frontier, waiting for the arrival of the settlers who could properly exploit the vast resources for economic gain, the reality was quite different. Hispanic communities in the Southwest, diverse Indian tribes throughout the western states, as well as other settlers from Asia and Western Europe already lived in many parts of the country. American expansion would necessitate a far more complex and involved exchange than simply filling empty space.

Still, in part as a result of the spark lit by O'Sullivan and others, waves of Americans and recently arrived immigrants began to move west in wagon trains. They travelled along several identifiable trails: first the Oregon Trail, then later the Santa Fe and California Trails, among others. The Oregon Trail is the most famous of these western routes. Two thousand miles long and barely passable on foot in the early nineteenth century, by the 1840s, wagon trains were a common sight. Between 1845 and 1870, considered to be the height of migration along the trail, over 400,000 settlers followed this path west from Missouri (Figure 17.3).

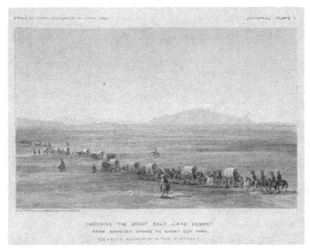

Figure 17.3 Hundreds of thousands of people travelled west on the Oregon, California, and Santa Fe Trails, but their numbers did not ensure their safety. Illness, starvation, and other dangers—both real and imagined— made survival hard. (credit: U.S. National Archives and Records Administration)

DEFINING "AMERICAN"

✪ *Who Will Set Limits to Our Onward March?*

America is destined for better deeds. It is our unparalleled glory that we have no reminiscences of battle fields, but in defense [sic] of humanity, of the oppressed of all nations, of the rights of conscience, the rights of personal enfranchisement. Our annals describe no scenes of horrid carnage, where men were led on by hundreds of thousands to slay one another, dupes and victims to emperors, kings, nobles, demons in the human form called heroes. We have had patriots to defend our homes, our liberties, but no aspirants to crowns or thrones; nor have the American people ever suffered themselves to be led on by wicked ambition to depopulate the land, to spread desolation far and wide, that a human being might be placed on a seat of supremacy. . . .

The expansive future is our arena, and for our history. We are entering on its untrodden space, with the truths of God in our minds, beneficent objects in our hearts, and with a clear conscience unsullied by the past. We are the nation of human progress, and who will, what can, set limits to our onward march? Providence is with us, and no earthly power can.

—John O'Sullivan, 1839

Think about how this quotation resonated with different groups of Americans at the time. When looked at through today's lens, the actions of the westward-moving settlers were fraught with brutality and racism. At the time, however, many settlers felt they were at the pinnacle of democracy, and that with no aristocracy or ancient history, America was a new world where anyone could succeed. Even then, consider how the phrase "anyone" was restricted by race, gender, and nationality.

Click and Explore

Visit **Across the Plains in '64 (http://openstaxcollege.org/l/iowaoregon)** to follow one family making their way westward from Iowa to Oregon. Click on a few of the entries and see how the author describes their journey, from the expected to the surprising.

FEDERAL GOVERNMENT ASSISTANCE

To assist the settlers in their move westward and transform the migration from a trickle into a steady flow, Congress passed two significant pieces of legislation in 1862: the Homestead Act and the Pacific Railway Act. Born largely out of President Abraham Lincoln's growing concern that a potential Union defeat in the early stages of the Civil War might result in the expansion of slavery westward, Lincoln hoped that such laws would encourage the expansion of a "free soil" mentality across the West.

The Homestead Act allowed any head of household, or individual over the age of twenty-one—including unmarried women—to receive a parcel of 160 acres for only a nominal filing fee. All that recipients were required to do in exchange was to "improve the land" within a period of five years of taking possession. The standards for improvement were minimal: Owners could clear a few acres, build small houses or barns, or maintain livestock. Under this act, the government transferred over 270 million acres of public domain land to private citizens.

The Pacific Railway Act was pivotal in helping settlers move west more quickly, as well as move their farm products, and later cattle and mining deposits, back east. The first of many railway initiatives, this act commissioned the Union Pacific Railroad to build new track west from Omaha, Nebraska, while the Central Pacific Railroad moved east from Sacramento, California. The law provided each company with ownership of all public lands within two hundred feet on either side of the track laid, as well as additional land grants and payment through load bonds, prorated on the difficulty of the terrain it crossed. Because of these provisions, both companies made a significant profit, whether they were crossing hundreds of miles of open plains, or working their way through the Sierra Nevada Mountains of California. As a result, the nation's first transcontinental railroad was completed when the two companies connected their tracks at Promontory Point, Utah, in the spring of 1869. Other tracks, including lines radiating from this original one, subsequently created a network that linked all corners of the nation (Figure 17.4).

Figure 17.4 The "Golden Spike" connecting the country by rail was driven into the ground in Promontory Point, Utah, in 1869. The completion of the first transcontinental railroad dramatically changed the tenor of travel in the country, as people were able to complete in a week a route that had previously taken months.

In addition to legislation designed to facilitate western settlement, the U.S. government assumed an active role on the ground, building numerous forts throughout the West to protect and assist settlers during their migration. Forts such as Fort Laramie in Wyoming (built in 1834) and Fort Apache in Arizona (1870) served as protection from nearby Indians as well as maintained peace between potential warring tribes. Others located throughout Colorado and Wyoming became important trading posts for miners and fur trappers. Those built in Kansas, Nebraska, and the Dakotas served primarily to provide relief for farmers during times of drought or related hardships. Forts constructed along the California coastline provided protection in the wake of the Mexican-American War as well as during the American Civil War. These locations subsequently serviced the U.S. Navy and provided important support for growing Pacific trade routes. Whether as army posts constructed for the protection of white settlers and to maintain peace among Indian tribes, or as trading posts to further facilitate the development of the region, such forts proved to be vital contributions to westward migration.

WHO WERE THE SETTLERS?

In the nineteenth century, as today, it took money to relocate and start a new life. Due to the initial cost of relocation, land, and supplies, as well as months of preparing the soil, planting, and subsequent harvesting before any produce was ready for market, the original wave of western settlers along the Oregon Trail in the 1840s and 1850s consisted of moderately prosperous, white, native-born farming families of the East. But the passage of the Homestead Act and completion of the first transcontinental railroad meant that, by 1870, the possibility of western migration was opened to Americans of more modest means. What started as a trickle became a steady flow of migration that would last until the end of the century.

Nearly 400,000 settlers had made the trek westward by the height of the movement in 1870. The vast majority were men, although families also migrated, despite incredible hardships for women with young children. More recent immigrants also migrated west, with the largest numbers coming from Northern Europe and Canada. Germans, Scandinavians, and Irish were among the most common. These ethnic groups tended to settle close together, creating strong rural communities that mirrored the way of life they had left behind. According to U.S. Census Bureau records, the number of Scandinavians living in the United States during the second half of the nineteenth century exploded, from barely 18,000 in 1850 to over 1.1 million in 1900. During that same time period, the German-born population in the United States grew from 584,000 to nearly 2.7 million and the Irish-born population grew from 961,000 to 1.6 million. As they moved westward, several thousand immigrants established homesteads in the Midwest, primarily in Minnesota and Wisconsin, where, as of 1900, over one-third of the population was foreign-born, and in North Dakota, whose immigrant population stood at 45 percent at the turn of the century. Compared to

European immigrants, those from China were much less numerous, but still significant. More than 200,000 Chinese arrived in California between 1876 and 1890, albeit for entirely different reasons related to the Gold Rush.

In addition to a significant European migration westward, several thousand African Americans migrated west following the Civil War, as much to escape the racism and violence of the Old South as to find new economic opportunities. They were known as **exodusters**, referencing the biblical flight from Egypt, because they fled the racism of the South, with most of them headed to Kansas from Kentucky, Tennessee, Louisiana, Mississippi, and Texas. Over twenty-five thousand exodusters arrived in Kansas in 1879–1880 alone. By 1890, over 500,000 blacks lived west of the Mississippi River. Although the majority of black migrants became farmers, approximately twelve thousand worked as cowboys during the Texas cattle drives. Some also became "Buffalo Soldiers" in the wars against Indians. "Buffalo Soldiers" were African Americans allegedly so-named by various Indian tribes who equated their black, curly hair with that of the buffalo. Many had served in the Union army in the Civil War and were now organized into six, all-black cavalry and infantry units whose primary duties were to protect settlers from Indian attacks during the westward migration, as well as to assist in building the infrastructure required to support western settlement (Figure 17.5).

Figure 17.5 "Buffalo Soldiers," the first peacetime all-black regiments in the U.S. Army, protected settlers from Indian attacks. These soldiers also served as some of the country's first national park rangers.

Click and Explore

The Oxford African American Studies Center (http://openstaxcollege.org/l/homesteads) features photographs and stories about black homesteaders. From exodusters to all-black settlements, the essay describes the largely hidden role that African Americans played in western expansion.

While white easterners, immigrants, and African Americans were moving west, several hundred thousand Hispanics had already settled in the American Southwest prior to the U.S. government seizing the land during its war with Mexico (1846–1848). The Treaty of Guadalupe Hidalgo, which ended the war in 1848, granted American citizenship to those who chose to stay in the United States, as the land switched from Mexican to U.S. ownership. Under the conditions of the treaty, Mexicans retained the right to their language, religion, and culture, as well as the property they held. As for citizenship, they could choose one of three options: 1) declare their intent to live in the United States but retain Mexican citizenship; 2) become U.S. citizens with all rights under the constitution; or 3) leave for Mexico. Despite such guarantees, within one generation, these new Hispanic American citizens found their culture under attack, and legal protection of their property all but non-existent.

17.2 Homesteading: Dreams and Realities

By the end of this section, you will be able to:
- Identify the challenges that farmers faced as they settled west of the Mississippi River
- Describe the unique experiences of women who participated in westward migration

As settlers and homesteaders moved westward to improve the land given to them through the Homestead Act, they faced a difficult and often insurmountable challenge. The land was difficult to farm, there were few building materials, and harsh weather, insects, and inexperience led to frequent setbacks. The prohibitive prices charged by the first railroad lines made it expensive to ship crops to market or have goods sent out. Although many farms failed, some survived and grew into large "bonanza" farms that hired additional labor and were able to benefit enough from economies of scale to grow profitable. Still, small family farms, and the settlers who worked them, were hard-pressed to do more than scrape out a living in an unforgiving environment that comprised arid land, violent weather shifts, and other challenges (Figure 17.6).

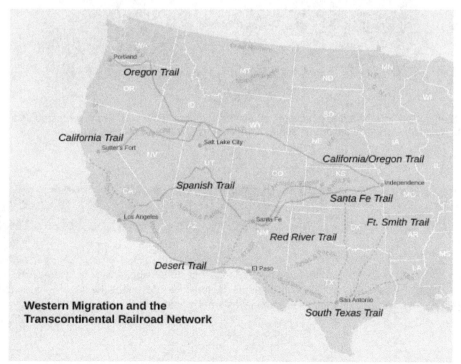

Figure 17.6   This map shows the trails (orange) used in westward migration and the development of railroad lines (blue) constructed after the completion of the first transcontinental railroad.

THE DIFFICULT LIFE OF THE PIONEER FARMER

Of the hundreds of thousands of settlers who moved west, the vast majority were homesteaders. These pioneers, like the Ingalls family of *Little House on the Prairie* book and television fame (see inset below), were seeking land and opportunity. Popularly known as "sodbusters," these men and women in the Midwest faced a difficult life on the frontier. They settled throughout the land that now makes up the Midwestern states of Wisconsin, Minnesota, Kansas, Nebraska, and the Dakotas. The weather and environment were bleak, and settlers struggled to eke out a living. A few unseasonably rainy years had led would-be settlers to believe that the "great desert" was no more, but the region's typically low rainfall and harsh temperatures made crop cultivation hard. Irrigation was a requirement, but finding water and building adequate systems proved too difficult and expensive for many farmers. It was not until 1902 and the passage of the Newlands Reclamation Act that a system finally existed to set aside funds from the sale of public lands to build dams for subsequent irrigation efforts. Prior to that, farmers across the Great Plains relied primarily on dry-farming techniques to grow corn, wheat, and sorghum, a practice that many continued in later years. A few also began to employ windmill technology to draw water, although both the drilling and construction of windmills became an added expense that few farmers could afford.

AMERICANA

⚙ The Enduring Appeal of Little House on the Prairie

The story of western migration and survival has remained a touchstone of American culture, even today. The television show *Frontier Life* on PBS is one example, as are countless other modern-day evocations of the settlers. Consider the enormous popularity of the *Little House* series. The books, originally published in the 1930s and 1940s, have been in print continuously. The television show, *Little House on the Prairie*, ran for over a decade and was hugely successful (and was said to be President Ronald Reagan's favorite show). The books, although fictional, were based on Laura Ingalls Wilder's own childhood, as she travelled west with her family via covered wagon, stopping in Kansas, Wisconsin, South Dakota, and beyond (Figure 17.7).

(a)

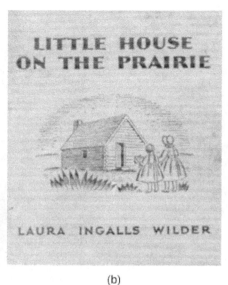

(b)

Figure 17.7 Laura Ingalls Wilder (a) is the celebrated author of the *Little House* series, which began in 1932 with the publication of *Little House in the Big Woods*. The third, and best known, book in the series, *Little House on the Prairie* (b), was published just three years later.

Wilder wrote of her stories, "As you read my stories of long ago I hope you will remember that the things that are truly worthwhile and that will give you happiness are the same now as they were then. Courage and kindness, loyalty, truth, and helpfulness are always the same and always needed." While Ingalls makes the point that her stories underscore traditional values that remain the same over time, this is not necessarily the only thing that made these books so popular. Perhaps part of their appeal is that they are adventure stories, with wild weather, wild animals, and wild Indians all playing a role. Does this explain their ongoing popularity? What other factors might make these stories appealing so long after they were originally written?

The first houses built by western settlers were typically made of mud and sod with thatch roofs, as there was little timber for building. Rain, when it arrived, presented constant problems for these **sod houses**, with mud falling into food, and vermin, most notably lice, scampering across bedding (Figure 17.8). Weather patterns not only left the fields dry, they also brought tornadoes, droughts, blizzards, and insect swarms. Tales of swarms of locusts were commonplace, and the crop-eating insects would at times cover the ground six to twelve inches deep. One frequently quoted Kansas newspaper reported a locust swarm in 1878 during which the insects devoured "everything green, stripping the foliage off the bark and from the tender twigs of the fruit trees, destroying every plant that is good for food or pleasant to the eye, that man has planted."

Figure 17.8 Sod houses were common in the Midwest as settlers moved west. There was no lumber to gather and no stones with which to build. These mud homes were vulnerable to weather and vermin, making life incredibly hard for the newly arrived homesteaders.

Farmers also faced the ever-present threat of debt and farm foreclosure by the banks. While land was essentially free under the Homestead Act, all other farm necessities cost money and were initially difficult to obtain in the newly settled parts of the country where market economies did not yet fully reach. Horses, livestock, wagons, wells, fencing, seed, and fertilizer were all critical to survival, but often hard to come by as the population initially remained sparsely settled across vast tracts of land. Railroads charged notoriously high rates for farm equipment and livestock, making it difficult to procure goods or make a profit on anything sent back east. Banks also charged high interest rates, and, in a cycle that replayed itself year after year, farmers would borrow from the bank with the intention of repaying their debt after the harvest. As the number of farmers moving westward increased, the market price of their produce steadily declined, even as the value of the actual land increased. Each year, hard-working farmers produced ever-larger crops, flooding the markets and subsequently driving prices down even further. Although some understood the economics of supply and demand, none could overtly control such forces.

Eventually, the arrival of a more extensive railroad network aided farmers, mostly by bringing much-needed supplies such as lumber for construction and new farm machinery. While John Deere sold a steel-faced plow as early as 1838, it was James Oliver's improvements to the device in the late 1860s that transformed life for homesteaders. His new, less expensive "chilled plow" was better equipped to cut through the shallow grass roots of the Midwestern terrain, as well as withstand damage from rocks just below the surface. Similar advancements in hay mowers, manure spreaders, and threshing machines greatly improved farm production for those who could afford them. Where capital expense became a significant factor, larger commercial farms—known as "**bonanza farms**"—began to develop. Farmers in Minnesota, North Dakota, and South Dakota hired migrant farmers to grow wheat on farms in excess of twenty thousand acres each. These large farms were succeeding by the end of the century, but small family farms continued to suffer. Although the land was nearly free, it cost close to $1000 for the necessary supplies to start up a farm, and many would-be landowners lured westward by the promise of cheap land became migrant farmers instead, working other peoples' land for a wage. The frustration of small farmers grew, ultimately leading to a revolt of sorts, discussed in a later chapter.

Click and Explore

Frontier House (http://openstaxcollege.org/l/homesteader) includes information on the logistics of moving across the country as a homesteader. Take a look at the list of supplies and gear. It is easy to understand why, even when the government gave the land away for free, it still took significant resources to make such a journey.

AN EVEN MORE CHALLENGING LIFE: A PIONEER WIFE

Although the West was numerically a male-dominated society, homesteading in particular encouraged the presence of women, families, and a domestic lifestyle, even if such a life was not an easy one. Women faced all the physical hardships that men encountered in terms of weather, illness, and danger, with the added complication of childbirth. Often, there was no doctor or midwife providing assistance, and many women died from treatable complications, as did their newborns. While some women could find employment in the newly settled towns as teachers, cooks, or seamstresses, they originally did not enjoy many rights. They could not sell property, sue for divorce, serve on juries, or vote. And for the vast majority of women, their work was not in towns for money, but on the farm. As late as 1900, a typical farm wife could expect to devote nine hours per day to chores such as cleaning, sewing, laundering, and preparing food. Two additional hours per day were spent cleaning the barn and chicken coop, milking the cows, caring for the chickens, and tending the family garden. One wife commented in 1879, "[We are] not much better than slaves. It is a weary, monotonous round of cooking and washing and mending and as a result the insane asylum is a third filled with wives of farmers."

Despite this grim image, the challenges of farm life eventually empowered women to break through some legal and social barriers. Many lived more equitably as partners with their husbands than did their eastern counterparts, helping each other through both hard times and good. If widowed, a wife typically took over responsibility for the farm, a level of management that was very rare back east, where the farm would fall to a son or other male relation. Pioneer women made important decisions and were considered by their husbands to be more equal partners in the success of the homestead, due to the necessity that all members had to work hard and contribute to the farming enterprise for it to succeed. Therefore, it is not surprising that the first states to grant women's rights, including the right to vote, were those in the Pacific Northwest and Upper Midwest, where women pioneers worked the land side by side with men. Some women seemed to be well suited to the challenges that frontier life presented them. Writing to her Aunt Martha from their homestead in Minnesota in 1873, Mary Carpenter refused to complain about the hardships of farm life: "I try to trust in God's promises, but we can't expect him to work miracles nowadays. Nevertheless, all that is expected of us is to do the best we can, and that we shall certainly endeavor to do. Even if we do freeze and starve in the way of duty, it will not be a dishonorable death."

17.3 Making a Living in Gold and Cattle

By the end of this section, you will be able to:
- Identify the major discoveries and developments in western gold, silver, and copper mining in the mid-nineteenth century
- Explain why the cattle industry was paramount to the development of the West and how it became the catalyst for violent range wars

Although homestead farming was the primary goal of most western settlers in the latter half of the nineteenth century, a small minority sought to make their fortunes quickly through other means. Specifically, gold (and, subsequently, silver and copper) prospecting attracted thousands of miners looking to "get rich quick" before returning east. In addition, ranchers capitalized on newly available railroad lines to move longhorn steers that populated southern and western Texas. This meat was highly sought after in eastern markets, and the demand created not only wealthy ranchers but an era of cowboys and cattle drives that in many ways defines how we think of the West today. Although neither miners nor ranchers intended to remain permanently in the West, many individuals from both groups ultimately stayed and settled there, sometimes due to the success of their gamble, and other times due to their abject failure.

THE CALIFORNIA GOLD RUSH AND BEYOND

The allure of gold has long sent people on wild chases; in the American West, the possibility of quick riches was no different. The search for gold represented an opportunity far different from the slow plod that homesteading farmers faced. The discovery of gold at Sutter's Mill in Coloma, California, set a pattern for such strikes that was repeated again and again for the next decade, in what collectively became known as the **California Gold Rush**. In what became typical, a sudden disorderly rush of prospectors descended upon a new discovery site, followed by the arrival of those who hoped to benefit from the strike by preying off the newly rich. This latter group of camp followers included saloonkeepers, prostitutes, store owners, and criminals, who all arrived in droves. If the strike was significant in size, a town of some magnitude might establish itself, and some semblance of law and order might replace the vigilante justice that typically grew in the small and short-lived mining outposts.

The original Forty-Niners were individual prospectors who sifted gold out of the dirt and gravel through "panning" or by diverting a stream through a sluice box (Figure 17.9). To varying degrees, the original California Gold Rush repeated itself throughout Colorado and Nevada for the next two decades. In 1859, Henry T. P. Comstock, a Canadian-born fur trapper, began gold mining in Nevada with other prospectors but then quickly found a blue-colored vein that proved to be the first significant silver discovery in the United States. Within twenty years, the **Comstock Lode**, as it was called, yielded more than $300 million in shafts that reached hundreds of feet into the mountain. Subsequent mining in Arizona and Montana yielded copper, and, while it lacked the glamour of gold, these deposits created huge wealth for those who exploited them, particularly with the advent of copper wiring for the delivery of electricity and telegraph communication.

(a)   (b)

Figure 17.9 The first gold prospectors in the 1850s and 1860s worked with easily portable tools that allowed anyone to follow their dream and strike it rich (a). It didn't take long for the most accessible minerals to be stripped, making way for large mining operations, including hydraulic mining, where high-pressure water jets removed sediment and rocks (b).

By the 1860s and 1870s, however, individual efforts to locate precious metals were less successful. The lowest-hanging fruit had been picked, and now it required investment capital and machinery to dig mine shafts that could reach remaining ore. With a much larger investment, miners needed a larger strike to be successful. This shift led to larger businesses underwriting mining operations, which eventually led to the development of greater urban stability and infrastructure. Denver, Colorado, was one of several cities that became permanent settlements, as businesses sought a stable environment to use as a base for their mining ventures.

For miners who had not yet struck it rich, this development was not a good one. They were now paid a daily or weekly wage to work underground in very dangerous conditions. They worked in shafts where the temperature could rise to above one hundred degrees Fahrenheit, and where poor ventilation might lead to long-term lung disease. They coped with shaft fires, dynamite explosions, and frequent cave-ins. By some historical accounts, close to eight thousand miners died on the frontier during this period, with over three times that number suffering crippling injuries. Some miners organized into unions and led strikes for better conditions, but these efforts were usually crushed by state militias.

Eventually, as the ore dried up, most mining towns turned into ghost towns. Even today, a visit through the American West shows old saloons and storefronts, abandoned as the residents moved on to their next shot at riches. The true lasting impact of the early mining efforts was the resulting desire of the U.S. government to bring law and order to the "Wild West" in order to more efficiently extract natural resources and encourage stable growth in the region. As more Americans moved to the region to seek permanent settlement, as opposed to brief speculative ventures, they also sought the safety and support that government order could bring. Nevada was admitted to the Union as a state in 1864, with Colorado following in 1876, then North Dakota, South Dakota, Montana, and Washington in 1889; and Idaho and Wyoming in 1890.

THE CATTLE KINGDOM

While the cattle industry lacked the romance of the Gold Rush, the role it played in western expansion should not be underestimated. For centuries, wild cattle roamed the Spanish borderlands. At the end of the Civil War, as many as five million longhorn steers could be found along the Texas frontier, yet few settlers had capitalized on the opportunity to claim them, due to the difficulty of transporting them to eastern markets. The completion of the first transcontinental railroad and subsequent railroad lines changed the game dramatically. Cattle ranchers and eastern businessmen realized that it was profitable to round up the wild steers and transport them by rail to be sold in the East for as much as thirty to fifty dollars per head.

These ranchers and businessmen began the rampant speculation in the cattle industry that made, and lost, many fortunes.

So began the impressive cattle drives of the 1860s and 1870s. The famous Chisholm Trail provided a quick path from Texas to railroad terminals in Abilene, Wichita, and Dodge City, Kansas, where cowboys would receive their pay. These "cowtowns," as they became known, quickly grew to accommodate the needs of cowboys and the cattle industry. Cattlemen like Joseph G. McCoy, born in Illinois, quickly realized that the railroad offered a perfect way to get highly sought beef from Texas to the East. McCoy chose Abilene as a locale that would offer cowboys a convenient place to drive the cattle, and went about building stockyards, hotels, banks, and more to support the business. He promoted his services and encouraged cowboys to bring their cattle through Abilene for good money; soon, the city had grown into a bustling western city, complete with ways for the cowboys to spend their hard-earned pay (Figure 17.10).

Figure 17.10 Cattle drives were an integral part of western expansion. Cowboys worked long hours in the saddle, driving hardy longhorns to railroad towns that could ship the meat back east.

Between 1865 and 1885, as many as forty thousand cowboys roamed the Great Plains, hoping to work for local ranchers. They were all men, typically in their twenties, and close to one-third of them were Hispanic or African American. It is worth noting that the stereotype of the American cowboy—and indeed the cowboys themselves—borrowed much from the Mexicans who had long ago settled those lands. The saddles, lassos, chaps, and lariats that define cowboy culture all arose from the Mexican ranchers who had used them to great effect before the cowboys arrived.

Life as a cowboy was dirty and decidedly unglamorous. The terrain was difficult; conflicts with Native Americans, especially in Indian Territory (now Oklahoma), were notoriously deadly. But the longhorn cattle were hardy stock, and could survive and thrive while grazing along the long trail, so cowboys braved the trip for the promise of steady employment and satisfying wages. Eventually, however, the era of the free range ended. Ranchers developed the land, limiting grazing opportunities along the trail, and in 1873, the new technology of barbed wire allowed ranchers to fence off their lands and cattle claims. With the end of the free range, the cattle industry, like the mining industry before it, grew increasingly dominated by eastern businessmen. Capital investors from the East expanded rail lines and invested in ranches, ending the reign of the cattle drives.

AMERICANA

✳ *Barbed Wire and a Way of Life Gone*

Called the "devil's rope" by Indians, barbed wire had a profound impact on the American West. Before its invention, settlers and ranchers alike were stymied by a lack of building materials to fence off land. Communal grazing and long cattle drives were the norm. But with the invention of barbed wire, large cattle ranchers and their investors were able to cheaply and easily parcel off the land they wanted—whether or not it was legally theirs to contain. As with many other inventions, several people "invented" barbed wire around the same time. In 1873, it was Joseph Glidden, however, who claimed the winning design and patented it. Not only did it spell the end of the free range for settlers and cowboys, it kept more land away from Indian tribes, who had never envisioned a culture that would claim to own land (Figure 17.11).

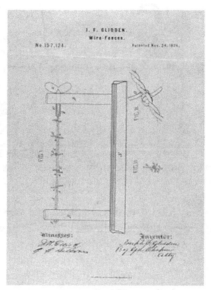

Figure 17.11 Joseph Glidden's invention of barbed wire in 1873 made him rich, changing the face of the American West forever. (credit: modification of work by the U.S. Department of Commerce)

In the early twentieth century, songwriter Cole Porter would take a poem by a Montana poet named Bob Fletcher and convert it into a cowboy song called, "Don't Fence Me In." As the lyrics below show, the song gave voice to the feeling that, as the fences multiplied, the ethos of the West was forever changed:

> Oh, give me land, lots of land, under starry skies above
> Don't fence me in
> Let me ride thru the wide-open country that I love
> Don't fence me in . . .
> Just turn me loose
> Let me straddle my old saddle underneath the western skies
> On my cayuse
> Let me wander over yonder till I see the mountains rise
> I want to ride to the ridge where the west commences
> Gaze at the moon until I lose my senses
> I can't look at hobbles and I can't stand fences
> Don't fence me in.

VIOLENCE IN THE WILD WEST: MYTH AND REALITY

The popular image of the Wild West portrayed in books, television, and film has been one of violence and mayhem. The lure of quick riches through mining or driving cattle meant that much of the West did indeed consist of rough men living a rough life, although the violence was exaggerated and even glorified in the dime store novels of the day. The exploits of Wyatt Earp, Doc Holiday, and others made for good stories, but the reality was that western violence was more isolated than the stories might suggest. These clashes often occurred as people struggled for the scarce resources that could make or break their chance at riches, or as they dealt with the sudden wealth or poverty that prospecting provided.

Where sporadic violence did erupt, it was concentrated largely in mining towns or during range wars among large and small cattle ranchers. Some mining towns were indeed as rough as the popular stereotype. Men, money, liquor, and disappointment were a recipe for violence. Fights were frequent, deaths were commonplace, and frontier justice reigned. The notorious mining town of Bodie, California, had twenty-nine murders between 1877 and 1883, which translated to a murder rate higher than any other city at that time, and only one person was ever convicted of a crime. The most prolific gunman of the day was John Wesley Hardin, who allegedly killed over twenty men in Texas in various gunfights, including one victim he killed in a hotel for snoring too loudly (Figure 17.12).

Figure 17.12 The towns that sprouted up around gold strikes existed first and foremost as places for the men who struck it rich to spend their money. Stores, saloons, and brothels were among the first businesses to arrive. The combination of lawlessness, vice, and money often made for a dangerous mix.

Ranching brought with it its own dangers and violence. In the Texas cattle lands, owners of large ranches took advantage of their wealth and the new invention of barbed wire to claim the prime grazing lands and few significant watering holes for their herds. Those seeking only to move their few head of cattle to market grew increasingly frustrated at their inability to find even a blade of grass for their meager herds. Eventually, frustration turned to violence, as several ranchers resorted to vandalizing the barbed wire fences to gain access to grass and water for their steers. Such vandalism quickly led to cattle rustling, as these cowboys were not averse to leading a few of the rancher's steers into their own herds as they left.

One example of the violence that bubbled up was the infamous **Fence Cutting War** in Clay County, Texas (1883–1884). There, cowboys began destroying fences that several ranchers erected along public lands: land they had no right to enclose. Confrontations between the cowboys and armed guards hired by the ranchers resulted in three deaths—hardly a "war," but enough of a problem to get the governor's attention. Eventually, a special session of the Texas legislature addressed the problem by passing laws to outlaw fence cutting, but also forced ranchers to remove fences illegally erected along public lands, as well as to place gates for passage where public areas adjoined private lands.

An even more violent confrontation occurred between large ranchers and small farmers in Johnson County, Wyoming, where cattle ranchers organized a "lynching bee" in 1891–1892 to make examples of cattle rustlers. Hiring twenty-two "invaders" from Texas to serve as hired guns, the ranch owners and their foremen hunted and subsequently killed the two rustlers best known for organizing the owners of the smaller Wyoming farms. Only the intervention of federal troops, who arrested and then later released the invaders, allowing them to return to Texas, prevented a greater massacre.

While there is much talk—both real and mythical—of the rough men who lived this life, relatively few women experienced it. While homesteaders were often families, gold speculators and cowboys tended to be single men in pursuit of fortune. The few women who went to these wild outposts were typically prostitutes, and even their numbers were limited. In 1860, in the Comstock Lode region of Nevada, for example, there were reportedly only thirty women total in a town of twenty-five hundred men. Some of the "painted ladies" who began as prostitutes eventually owned brothels and emerged as businesswomen in their own right; however, life for these young women remained a challenging one as western settlement progressed. A handful of women, numbering no more than six hundred, braved both the elements and male-dominated culture to become teachers in several of the more established cities in the West. Even fewer arrived to support husbands or operate stores in these mining towns.

As wealthy men brought their families west, the lawless landscape began to change slowly. Abilene, Kansas, is one example of a lawless town, replete with prostitutes, gambling, and other vices, transformed when middle-class women arrived in the 1880s with their cattle baron husbands. These women began to organize churches, school, civic clubs, and other community programs to promote family values. They fought to remove opportunities for prostitution and all the other vices that they felt threatened the values that they held dear. Protestant missionaries eventually joined the women in their efforts, and, while they were not widely successful, they did bring greater attention to the problems. As a response, the U.S. Congress passed both the Comstock Law (named after its chief proponent, anti-obscenity crusader Anthony Comstock) in 1873 to ban the spread of "lewd and lascivious literature" through the mail and the subsequent Page Act of 1875 to prohibit the transportation of women into the United States for employment as prostitutes. However, the "houses of ill repute" continued to operate and remained popular throughout the West despite the efforts of reformers.

Click and Explore

Take a look at the National Cowboy and Western Heritage Museum (http://openstaxcollege.org/l/natcowboy) to determine whether this site's portrayal of cowboy culture matches or contradicts the history shared in this chapter.

17.4 The Loss of American Indian Life and Culture

By the end of this section, you will be able to:
- Describe the methods that the U.S. government used to address the "Indian threat" during the settlement of the West
- Explain the process of "Americanization" as it applied to Indians in the nineteenth century

As American settlers pushed westward, they inevitably came into conflict with Indian tribes that had long been living on the land. Although the threat of Indian attacks was quite slim and nowhere proportionate to the number of U.S. Army actions directed against them, the occasional attack—often one of retaliation—was enough to fuel the popular fear of the "savage" Indians. The clashes, when they happened, were indeed brutal, although most of the brutality occurred at the hands of the settlers. Ultimately, the settlers, with the support of local militias and, later, with the federal government behind them, sought to eliminate the tribes from the lands they desired. The result was devastating for the Indian tribes, which lacked the weapons and group cohesion to fight back against such well-armed forces. The Manifest Destiny of the settlers spelled the end of the Indian way of life.

CLAIMING LAND, RELOCATING LANDOWNERS

Back east, the popular vision of the West was of a vast and empty land. But of course this was an exaggerated depiction. On the eve of westward expansion, as many as 250,000 Indians, representing a variety of tribes, populated the Great Plains. Previous wars against these tribes in the early nineteenth century, as well as the failure of earlier treaties, had led to a general policy of the forcible removal of many tribes in the eastern United States. The Indian Removal Act of 1830 resulted in the infamous "Trail of Tears," which saw nearly fifty thousand Seminole, Choctaw, Chickasaw, and Creek Indians relocated west of the Mississippi River to what is now Oklahoma between 1831 and 1838. Building upon such a history, the U.S. government was prepared, during the era of western settlement, to deal with tribes that settlers viewed as obstacles to expansion.

As settlers sought more land for farming, mining, and cattle ranching, the first strategy employed to deal with the perceived Indian threat was to negotiate settlements to move tribes out of the path of white settlers. In 1851, the chiefs of most of the Great Plains tribes agreed to the First Treaty of Fort Laramie. This agreement established distinct tribal borders, essentially codifying the reservation system. In return for annual payments of $50,000 to the tribes (originally guaranteed for fifty years, but later revised to last for only ten) as well as the hollow promise of noninterference from westward settlers, Indians agreed to stay clear of the path of settlement. Due to government corruption, many annuity payments never reached the tribes, and some reservations were left destitute and near starving. In addition, within a decade, as the pace and number of western settlers increased, even designated reservations became prime locations for farms and mining. Rather than negotiating new treaties, settlers—oftentimes backed by local or state militia units—simply attacked the tribes out of fear or to force them from the land. Some Indians resisted, only to then face massacres.

In 1862, frustrated and angered by the lack of annuity payments and the continuous encroachment on their reservation lands, Dakota Sioux Indians in Minnesota rebelled in what became known as the Dakota War, killing the white settlers who moved onto their tribal lands. Over one thousand white settlers were captured or killed in the attack, before an armed militia regained control. Of the four hundred Sioux captured by U.S. troops, 303 were sentenced to death, but President Lincoln intervened, releasing all but thirty-eight of the men. The thirty-eight who were found guilty were hanged in the largest mass execution in the country's history, and the rest of the tribe was banished. Settlers in other regions responded to news of this raid with fear and aggression. In Colorado, Arapahoe and Cheyenne tribes fought back against land encroachment; white militias then formed, decimating even some of the tribes that were willing to cooperate. One of the more vicious examples was near Sand Creek, Colorado, where Colonel John Chivington led a militia raid upon a camp in which the leader had already negotiated a peaceful settlement. The camp was flying both the American flag and the white flag of surrender when Chivington's troops murdered close to one hundred people, the majority of them women and children, in what became known as the **Sand Creek Massacre**. For the rest of his life, Chivington would proudly display his collection of nearly one hundred Indian scalps from that day. Subsequent investigations by the U.S. Army condemned Chivington's tactics and their results; however, the raid served as a model for some settlers who sought any means by which to eradicate the perceived Indian threat.

Hoping to forestall similar uprisings and all-out Indian wars, the U.S. Congress commissioned a committee to investigate the causes of such incidents. The subsequent report of their findings led to the passage of two additional treaties: the Second Treaty of Fort Laramie and the Treaty of Medicine Lodge Creek, both designed to move the remaining tribes to even more remote reservations. The Second Treaty of Fort Laramie moved the remaining Sioux to the Black Hills in the Dakota Territory and the Treaty of Medicine Lodge Creek moved the Cheyenne, Arapaho, Kiowa, and Comanche to "Indian Territory," later to become the State of Oklahoma.

The agreements were short-lived, however. With the subsequent discovery of gold in the Black Hills, settlers seeking their fortune began to move upon the newly granted Sioux lands with support from U.S. cavalry troops. By the middle of 1875, thousands of white prospectors were illegally digging and panning in the area. The Sioux protested the invasion of their territory and the violation of sacred ground. The government offered to lease the Black Hills or to pay $6 million if the Indians were willing to sell the land. When the tribes refused, the government imposed what it considered a fair price for the land, ordered the Indians to move, and in the spring of 1876, made ready to force them onto the reservation.

In the Battle of Little Bighorn, perhaps the most famous battle of the American West, a Sioux chieftain, Sitting Bull, urged Indians from all neighboring tribes to join his men in defense of their lands (Figure 17.13). At the Little Bighorn River, the U.S. Army's Seventh Cavalry, led by Colonel George Custer, sought a showdown. Driven by his own personal ambition, on June 25, 1876, Custer foolishly attacked what he thought was a minor Indian encampment. Instead, it turned out to be the main Sioux force. The Sioux warriors—nearly three thousand in strength—surrounded and killed Custer and 262 of his men and support units, in the single greatest loss of U.S. troops to an Indian attack in the era of westward expansion. Eyewitness reports of the attack indicated that the victorious Sioux bathed and wrapped Custer's body in the tradition of a chieftain burial; however, they dismembered many other soldiers' corpses in order for a few distant observers from Major Marcus Reno's wounded troops and Captain Frederick Benteen's company to report back to government officials about the ferocity of the Sioux enemy.

Figure 17.13 The iconic figure who led the battle at Little Bighorn River, Sitting Bull led Indians in what was their largest victory against American settlers. While the battle was a rout by the Sioux over Custer's troops, the ultimate outcome for his tribe and the men who had joined him was one of constant harassment, arrest, and death at the hands of federal troops.

AMERICAN INDIAN SUBMISSION

Despite their success at Little Bighorn, neither the Sioux nor any other Plains tribe followed this battle with any other armed encounter. Rather, they either returned to tribal life or fled out of fear of remaining troops, until the U.S. Army arrived in greater numbers and began to exterminate Indian encampments and force others to accept payment for forcible removal from their lands. Sitting Bull himself fled to Canada, although he later returned in 1881 and subsequently worked in Buffalo Bill's Wild West show. In Montana, the Blackfoot and Crow were forced to leave their tribal lands. In Colorado, the Utes gave up their lands after a brief period of resistance. In Idaho, most of the Nez Perce gave up their lands peacefully, although in an incredible episode, a band of some eight hundred Indians sought to evade U.S. troops and escape into Canada.

MY STORY

✦ *I Will Fight No More: Chief Joseph's Capitulation*

Chief Joseph, known to his people as "Thunder Traveling to the Loftier Mountain Heights," was the chief of the Nez Perce tribe, and he had realized that they could not win against the whites. In order to avoid a war that would undoubtedly lead to the extermination of his people, he hoped to lead his tribe to Canada, where they could live freely. He led a full retreat of his people over fifteen hundred miles of mountains and harsh terrain, only to be caught within fifty miles of the Canadian border in late 1877. His speech has remained a poignant and vivid reminder of what the tribe had lost.

> Tell General Howard I know his heart. What he told me before, I have it in my heart. I am tired of fighting. Our Chiefs are killed; Looking Glass is dead, Ta Hool Hool Shute is dead. The old men are all dead. It is the young men who say yes or no. He who led on the young men is dead. It is cold, and we have no blankets; the little children are freezing to death. My people, some of them, have run away to the hills, and have no blankets, no food. No one knows where they are—perhaps freezing to death. I want to have time to look for my children, and see how many of them I can find. Maybe I shall find them among the dead. Hear me, my Chiefs! I am tired; my heart is sick and sad. From where the sun now stands I will fight no more forever.

—Chief Joseph, 1877

The final episode in the so-called Indian Wars occurred in 1890, at the **Battle of Wounded Knee** in South Dakota. On their reservation, the Sioux had begun to perform the "Ghost Dance," which told of an Indian Messiah who would deliver the tribe from its hardship, with such frequency that white settlers began to worry that another uprising would occur. The militia prepared to round up the Sioux. The tribe, after the death of Sitting Bull, who had been arrested, shot, and killed in 1890, prepared to surrender at Wounded Knee, South Dakota, on December 29, 1890. Although the accounts are unclear, an apparent accidental rifle discharge by a young male Indian preparing to lay down his weapon led the U.S. soldiers to begin firing indiscriminately upon the Indians. What little resistance the Indians mounted with a handful of concealed rifles at the outset of the fight diminished quickly, with the troops eventually massacring between 150 and 300 men, women, and children. The U.S. troops suffered twenty-five fatalities, some of which were the result of their own crossfire. Captain Edward Godfrey of the Seventh Cavalry later commented, "I know the men did not aim deliberately and they were greatly excited. I don't believe they saw their sights. They fired rapidly but it seemed to me only a few seconds till there was not a living thing before us; warriors, squaws, children, ponies, and dogs . . . went down before that unaimed fire." With this last show of brutality, the Indian Wars came to a close. U.S. government officials had already begun the process of seeking an alternative to the meaningless treaties and costly battles. A more effective means with which to address the public perception of the "Indian threat" was needed. **Americanization** provided the answer.

AMERICANIZATION

Through the years of the Indian Wars of the 1870s and early 1880s, opinion back east was mixed. There were many who felt, as General Philip Sheridan (appointed in 1867 to pacify the Plains Indians) allegedly said, that the only good Indian was a dead Indian. But increasingly, several American reformers who would later form the backbone of the Progressive Era had begun to criticize the violence, arguing that the Indians should be helped through "Americanization" to become assimilated into American society. Individual land ownership, Christian worship, and education for children became the cornerstones of this new, and final, assault on Indian life and culture.

Beginning in the 1880s, clergymen, government officials, and social workers all worked to assimilate Indians into American life. The government permitted reformers to remove Indian children from their homes and place them in boarding schools, such as the Carlisle Indian School or the Hampton Institute, where they were taught to abandon their tribal traditions and embrace the tools of American productivity, modesty, and sanctity through total immersion. Such schools not only acculturated Indian boys and girls, but also provided vocational training for males and domestic science classes for females. Adults were also targeted by religious reformers, specifically evangelical Protestants as well as a number of Catholics, who sought to convince Indians to abandon their language, clothing, and social customs for a more Euro-American lifestyle (Figure 17.14).

Figure 17.14 The federal government's policy towards the Indians shifted in the late 1880s from relocating them to assimilating them into the American ideal. Indians were given land in exchange for renouncing their tribe, traditional clothing, and way of life.

A vital part of the assimilation effort was land reform. During earlier negotiations, the government had respected that the Indian tribes used their land communally. Most Indian belief structures did not allow for the concept of individual land ownership; rather, land was available for all to use, and required responsibility from all to protect it. As a part of their plan to Americanize the tribes, reformers sought legislation to replace this concept with the popular Euro-American notion of real estate ownership and self-reliance. One such law was the Dawes Severalty Act of 1887, named after a reformer and senator from Massachusetts, which struck a deadly blow to the Indian way of life. In what was essentially an Indian version of the original Homestead Act, the Dawes Act permitted the federal government to divide the lands of any tribe and grant 160 acres of farmland or 320 acres of grazing land to each head of family, with lesser amounts to others. In a nod towards the paternal relationship with which whites viewed Indians—similar to the justification of the previous treatment of African American slaves—the Dawes Act permitted the federal government to hold an individual Indian's newly acquired land in trust for twenty-five years. Only then would he obtain full title and be granted the citizenship rights that land ownership entailed. It would not be until 1924 that formal citizenship was granted to all Native Americans. Under the Dawes Act, Indians were given the most arid, useless land. Further, inefficiencies and corruption in the government meant that much of the land due to be allotted to Indians was simply deemed "surplus" and claimed by settlers. Once all allotments were determined, the remaining tribal lands—as much as eighty million acres—were sold to white American settlers.

The final element of "Americanization" was the symbolic "last arrow" pageant, which often coincided with the formal redistribution of tribal lands under the Dawes Act. At these events, Indians were forced to assemble in their tribal garb, carrying a bow and arrow. They would then symbolically fire their "last arrow" into the air, enter a tent where they would strip away their Indian clothing, dress in a white farmer's coveralls, and emerge to take a plow and an American flag to show that they had converted to a new way of life. It was a seismic shift for the Indians, and one that left them bereft of their culture and history.

Click and Explore

Take a look at the Carlisle Industrial Indian School (http://openstaxcollege.org/l/carlisleschool) where Indian students were "civilized" from 1879 to 1918. It is worth looking through the photographs and records of the school to see how this well-intended program obliterated Indian culture.

17.5 The Impact of Expansion on Chinese Immigrants and Hispanic Citizens

By the end of this section, you will be able to:
- Describe the treatment of Chinese immigrants and Hispanic citizens during the westward expansion of the nineteenth century

As white Americans pushed west, they not only collided with Indian tribes but also with Hispanic Americans and Chinese immigrants. Hispanics in the Southwest had the opportunity to become American citizens at the end of the Mexican-American war, but their status was markedly second-class. Chinese immigrants arrived en masse during the California Gold Rush and numbered in the hundreds of thousands by the late 1800s, with the majority living in California, working menial jobs. These distinct cultural and ethnic groups strove to maintain their rights and way of life in the face of persistent racism and entitlement. But the large number of white settlers and government-sanctioned land acquisitions left them at a profound disadvantage. Ultimately, both groups withdrew into homogenous communities in which their language and culture could survive.

CHINESE IMMIGRANTS IN THE AMERICAN WEST

The initial arrival of Chinese immigrants to the United States began as a slow trickle in the 1820s, with barely 650 living in the U.S. by the end of 1849. However, as gold rush fever swept the country, Chinese immigrants, too, were attracted to the notion of quick fortunes. By 1852, over 25,000 Chinese immigrants had arrived, and by 1880, over 300,000 Chinese lived in the United States, most in California. While they had dreams of finding gold, many instead found employment building the first transcontinental railroad (Figure 17.15). Some even traveled as far east as the former cotton plantations of the Old South, which they helped to farm after the Civil War. Several thousand of these immigrants booked their passage to the United States using a "credit-ticket," in which their passage was paid in advance by American businessmen to whom the immigrants were then indebted for a period of work. Most arrivals were men: Few wives or children ever traveled to the United States. As late as 1890, less than 5 percent of the Chinese population in the U.S. was female. Regardless of gender, few Chinese immigrants intended to stay permanently in the United States, although many were reluctantly forced to do so, as they lacked the financial resources to return home.

Figure 17.15 Building the railroads was dangerous and backbreaking work. On the western railroad line, Chinese migrants, along with other nonwhite workers, were often given the most difficult and dangerous jobs of all.

Prohibited by law since 1790 from obtaining U.S. citizenship through naturalization, Chinese immigrants faced harsh discrimination and violence from American settlers in the West. Despite hardships like the special tax that Chinese miners had to pay to take part in the Gold Rush, or their subsequent forced relocation into Chinese districts, these immigrants continued to arrive in the United States seeking a better life for the families they left behind. Only when the Chinese Exclusion Act of 1882 forbade further immigration from China for a ten-year period did the flow stop.

The Chinese community banded together in an effort to create social and cultural centers in cities such as San Francisco. In a haphazard fashion, they sought to provide services ranging from social aid to education, places of worship, health facilities, and more to their fellow Chinese immigrants. But only American Indians suffered greater discrimination and racial violence, legally sanctioned by the federal government, than did Chinese immigrants at this juncture in American history. As Chinese workers began competing with white Americans for jobs in California cities, the latter began a system of built-in discrimination. In the 1870s, white Americans formed "anti-coolie clubs" ("coolie" being a racial slur directed towards people of any Asian descent), through which they organized boycotts of Chinese-produced products and lobbied for anti-Chinese laws. Some protests turned violent, as in 1885 in Rock Springs, Wyoming, where tensions between white and Chinese immigrant miners erupted in a riot, resulting in over two dozen Chinese immigrants being murdered and many more injured.

Slowly, racism and discrimination became law. The new California constitution of 1879 denied naturalized Chinese citizens the right to vote or hold state employment. Additionally, in 1882, the U.S. Congress passed the Chinese Exclusion Act, which forbade further Chinese immigration into the United States for ten years. The ban was later extended on multiple occasions until its repeal in 1943. Eventually, some Chinese immigrants returned to China. Those who remained were stuck in the lowest-paying, most menial jobs. Several found assistance through the creation of benevolent associations designed to both support Chinese communities and defend them against political and legal discrimination; however, the history of Chinese immigrants to the United States remained largely one of deprivation and hardship well into the twentieth century.

Click and Explore

The **Central Pacific Railroad Photographic History Museum** (http://openstaxcollege.org/l/railroadchina) provides a context for the role of the Chinese who helped build the railroads. What does the site celebrate, and what, if anything, does it condemn?

DEFINING "AMERICAN"

☼ *The Backs that Built the Railroad*

Below is a description of the construction of the railroad in 1867. Note the way it describes the scene, the laborers, and the effort.

> The cars now (1867) run nearly to the summit of the Sierras. . . . four thousand laborers were at work—one-tenth Irish, the rest Chinese. They were a great army laying siege to Nature in her strongest citadel. The rugged mountains looked like stupendous ant-hills. They swarmed with Celestials, shoveling, wheeling, carting, drilling and blasting rocks and earth, while their dull, moony eyes stared out from under immense basket-hats, like umbrellas. At several dining camps we saw hundreds sitting on the ground, eating soft boiled rice with chopsticks as fast as terrestrials could with soup-ladles. Irish laborers received thirty dollars per month (gold) and board; Chinese, thirty-one dollars, boarding themselves. After a little experience the latter were quite as efficient and far less troublesome.

—Albert D. Richardson, *Beyond the Mississippi*

Several great American advancements of the nineteenth century were built with the hands of many other nations. It is interesting to ponder how much these immigrant communities felt they were building their own fortunes and futures, versus the fortunes of others. Is it likely that the Chinese laborers, many of whom died due to the harsh conditions, considered themselves part of "a great army"? Certainly, this account reveals the unwitting racism of the day, where workers were grouped together by their ethnicity, and each ethnic group was labeled monolithically as "good workers" or "troublesome," with no regard for individual differences among the hundreds of Chinese or Irish workers.

HISPANIC AMERICANS IN THE AMERICAN WEST

The Treaty of Guadalupe Hidalgo, which ended the Mexican-American War in 1848, promised U.S. citizenship to the nearly seventy-five thousand Hispanics now living in the American Southwest; approximately 90 percent accepted the offer and chose to stay in the United States despite their immediate relegation to second-class citizenship status. Relative to the rest of Mexico, these lands were sparsely populated and had been so ever since the country achieved its freedom from Spain in 1821. In fact, New Mexico—not Texas or California—was the center of settlement in the region in the years immediately preceding the war with the United States, containing nearly fifty thousand Mexicans. However, those who did settle the area were proud of their heritage and ability to develop *rancheros* of great size and success. Despite promises made in the treaty, these Californios—as they came to be known—quickly lost their land to white settlers who simply displaced the rightful landowners, by force if necessary. Repeated efforts at legal redress mostly fell upon deaf ears. In some instances, judges and lawyers would permit the legal cases to proceed through an expensive legal process only to the point where Hispanic landowners who insisted on holding their ground were rendered penniless for their efforts.

Much like Chinese immigrants, Hispanic citizens were relegated to the worst-paying jobs under the most terrible working conditions. They worked as *peóns* (manual laborers similar to slaves), *vaqueros* (cattle herders), and cartmen (transporting food and supplies) on the cattle ranches that white landowners possessed, or undertook the most hazardous mining tasks (Figure 17.16).

Figure 17.16   Mexican ranchers had worked the land in the American Southwest long before American "cowboys" arrived. In what ways might the Mexican *vaquero* pictured above have influenced the American cowboy?

In a few instances, frustrated Hispanic citizens fought back against the white settlers who dispossessed them of their belongings. In 1889–1890 in New Mexico, several hundred Mexican Americans formed *las Gorras Blancas* (the White Caps) to try and reclaim their land and intimidate white Americans, preventing further land seizures. White Caps conducted raids of white farms, burning homes, barns, and crops to express their growing anger and frustration. However, their actions never resulted in any fundamental changes. Several White Caps were captured, beaten, and imprisoned, whereas others eventually gave up, fearing harsh reprisals against their families. Some White Caps adopted a more political strategy, gaining election to local offices throughout New Mexico in the early 1890s, but growing concerns over the potential impact upon the territory's quest for statehood led several citizens to heighten their repression of the movement. Other laws passed in the United States intended to deprive Mexican Americans of their heritage as much as their lands. "Sunday Laws" prohibited "noisy amusements" such as bullfights, cockfights, and other cultural gatherings common to Hispanic communities at the time. "Greaser Laws" permitted the imprisonment of any unemployed Mexican American on charges of vagrancy. Although Hispanic Americans held tightly to their cultural heritage as their remaining form of self-identity, such laws did take a toll.

In California and throughout the Southwest, the massive influx of Anglo-American settlers simply overran the Hispanic populations that had been living and thriving there, sometimes for generations. Despite being U.S. citizens with full rights, Hispanics quickly found themselves outnumbered, outvoted, and, ultimately, outcast. Corrupt state and local governments favored whites in land disputes, and mining companies and cattle barons discriminated against them, as with the Chinese workers, in terms of pay and working conditions. In growing urban areas such as Los Angeles, *barrios*, or clusters of working-class homes, grew more isolated from the white American centers. Hispanic Americans, like the Native Americans and Chinese, suffered the fallout of the white settlers' relentless push west.

Key Terms

Americanization the process by which an Indian was "redeemed" and assimilated into the American way of life by changing his clothing to western clothing and renouncing his tribal customs in exchange for a parcel of land

Battle of Wounded Knee an attempt to disarm a group of Lakota Sioux Indians near Wounded Knee, South Dakota, which resulted in members of the Seventh Cavalry of the U.S. Army opening fire and killing over 150 Indians

bonanza farms large farms owned by speculators who hired laborers to work the land; these large farms allowed their owners to benefit from economies of scale and prosper, but they did nothing to help small family farms, which continued to struggle

California Gold Rush the period between 1848 and 1849 when prospectors found large strikes of gold in California, leading others to rush in and follow suit; this period led to a cycle of boom and bust through the area, as gold was discovered, mined, and stripped

Comstock Lode the first significant silver find in the country, discovered by Henry T. P. Comstock in 1859 in Nevada

exodusters a term used to describe African Americans who moved to Kansas from the Old South to escape the racism there

Fence Cutting War this armed conflict between cowboys moving cattle along the trail and ranchers who wished to keep the best grazing lands for themselves occurred in Clay County, Texas, between 1883 and 1884

las Gorras Blancas the Spanish name for White Caps, the rebel group of Hispanic Americans who fought back against the appropriation of Hispanic land by whites; for a period in 1889–1890, they burned farms, homes, and crops to express their growing anger at the injustice of the situation

Manifest Destiny the phrase, coined by journalist John O'Sullivan, which came to stand for the idea that white Americans had a calling and a duty to seize and settle the American West with Protestant democratic values

Sand Creek Massacre a militia raid led by Colonel Chivington on an Indian camp in Colorado, flying both the American flag and the white flag of surrender; over one hundred men, women, and children were killed

sod house a frontier home constructed of dirt held together by thick-rooted prairie grass that was prevalent in the Midwest; sod, cut into large rectangles, was stacked to make the walls of the structure, providing an inexpensive, yet damp, house for western settlers

Summary

17.1 The Westward Spirit

While a few bold settlers had moved westward before the middle of the nineteenth century, they were the exception, not the rule. The "great American desert," as it was called, was considered a vast and empty place, unfit for civilized people. In the 1840s, however, this idea started to change, as potential settlers began to learn more from promoters and land developers of the economic opportunities that awaited them in the West, and Americans extolled the belief that it was their Manifest Destiny—their divine right—to explore and settle the western territories in the name of the United States.

Most settlers in this first wave were white Americans of means. Whether they sought riches in gold, cattle, or farming, or believed it their duty to spread Protestant ideals to native inhabitants, they headed west in wagon trains along paths such as the Oregon Trail. European immigrants, particularly those from Northern Europe, also made the trip, settling in close-knit ethnic enclaves out of comfort, necessity, and familiarity. African Americans escaping the racism of the South also went west. In all, the newly settled areas were neither a fast track to riches nor a simple expansion into an empty land, but rather a clash of cultures, races, and traditions that defined the emerging new America.

17.2 Homesteading: Dreams and Realities

The concept of Manifest Destiny and the strong incentives to relocate sent hundreds of thousands of people west across the Mississippi. The rigors of this new way of life presented many challenges and difficulties to homesteaders. The land was dry and barren, and homesteaders lost crops to hail, droughts, insect swarms, and more. There were few materials with which to build, and early homes were made of mud, which did not stand up to the elements. Money was a constant concern, as the cost of railroad freight was exorbitant, and banks were unforgiving of bad harvests. For women, life was difficult in the extreme. Farm wives worked at least eleven hours per day on chores and had limited access to doctors or midwives. Still, they were more independent than their eastern counterparts and worked in partnership with their husbands.

As the railroad expanded and better farm equipment became available, by the 1870s, large farms began to succeed through economies of scale. Small farms still struggled to stay afloat, however, leading to a rising discontent among the farmers, who worked so hard for so little success.

17.3 Making a Living in Gold and Cattle

While homesteading was the backbone of western expansion, mining and cattle also played significant roles in shaping the West. Much rougher in character and riskier in outcomes than farming, these two opportunities brought forward a different breed of settler than the homesteaders. Many of the long-trail cattle riders were Mexican American or African American, and most of the men involved in both pursuits were individuals willing to risk what little they had in order to strike it rich.

In both the mining and cattle industries, however, individual opportunities slowly died out, as resources—both land for grazing and easily accessed precious metals—disappeared. In their place came big business, with the infrastructure and investments to make a profit. These businesses built up small towns into thriving cities, and the influx of middle-class families sought to drive out some of the violence and vice that characterized the western towns. Slowly but inexorably, the "American" way of life, as envisioned by the eastern establishment who initiated and promoted the concept of Manifest Destiny, was spreading west.

17.4 The Loss of American Indian Life and Culture

The interaction of the American Indians with white settlers during the western expansion movement was a painful and difficult one. For settlers raised on the notion of Manifest Destiny and empty lands, the Indians added a terrifying element to what was already a difficult and dangerous new world. For the Indians, the arrival of the settlers meant nothing less than the end of their way of life. Rather than cultural exchange, contact led to the virtual destruction of Indian life and culture. While violent acts broke out on both sides, the greatest atrocities were perpetrated by whites, who had superior weapons and often superior numbers, as well as the support of the U.S. government.

The death of the Indian way of life happened as much at the hands of well-intentioned reformers as those who wished to see the Indians exterminated. Individual land ownership, boarding schools, and pleas to renounce Indian gods and culture were all elements of the reformers' efforts. With so much of their life stripped away, it was ever more difficult for the Indians to maintain their tribal integrity.

17.5 The Impact of Expansion on Chinese Immigrants and Hispanic Citizens

In the nineteenth century, the Hispanic, Chinese, and white populations of the country collided. Whites moved further west in search of land and riches, bolstered by government subsidies and an inherent and unshakable belief that the land and its benefits existed for their use. In some ways, it was a race to the prize: White Americans believed that they deserved the best lands and economic opportunities the country afforded, and did not consider prior claims to be valid.

Neither Chinese immigrants nor Hispanic Americans could withstand the assault on their rights by the tide of white settlers. Sheer numbers, matched with political backing, gave the whites the power they needed to overcome any resistance. Ultimately, both ethnic groups retreated into urban enclaves, where their language and traditions could survive.

Review Questions

1. Which of the following does *not* represent a group that participated significantly in westward migration after 1870?
  A. African American "exodusters" escaping racism and seeking economic opportunities
  B. former Southern slaveholders seeking land and new financial opportunities
  C. recent immigrants from Northern Europe and Canada
  D. recent Chinese immigrants seeking gold in California

2. Which of the following represents an action that the U.S. government took to help Americans fulfill the goal of western expansion?
  A. the passage of the Homestead Act
  B. the official creation of the philosophy of Manifest Destiny
  C. the development of stricter immigration policies
  D. the introduction of new irrigation techniques

3. Why and how did the U.S. government promote western migration in the midst of fighting the Civil War?

4. What specific types of hardships did an average American farmer *not* face as he built his homestead in the Midwest?
  A. droughts
  B. insect swarms
  C. hostile Indian attacks
  D. limited building supplies

5. What accounts for the success of large, commercial "bonanza farms?" What benefits did they enjoy over their smaller family-run counterparts?

6. How did everyday life in the American West hasten equality for women who settled the land?

7. Which of the following groups was *not* impacted by the invention of barbed wire?
  A. ranchers
  B. cowboys
  C. farmers
  D. illegal prostitutes

8. The American cowboy owes much of its model to what other culture?
  A. Mexicans
  B. Indians
  C. Northern European immigrants
  D. Chinese immigrants

9. How did mining and cattle ranching transform individual "get rich quick" efforts into "big business" efforts when the nineteenth century came to a close?

10. Which of the following was *not* a primary method by which the American government dealt with American Indians during the period of western settlement?

A. relocation
B. appeasement
C. extermination
D. assimilation

11. What did the Last Arrow pageant symbolize?
A. the continuing fight of the Indians
B. the total extermination of the Indians from the West
C. the final step in the Americanization process
D. the rebellion at Little Bighorn

12. What brought the majority of Chinese immigrants to the U.S.?
A. gold

B. work opportunities on the railroads
C. the Homestead Act
D. Chinese benevolent associations

13. How were Hispanic citizens deprived of their wealth and land in the course of western settlement?
A. Indian raids
B. land seizures
C. prisoner of war status
D. infighting

14. Compare and contrast the treatment of Chinese immigrants and Hispanic citizens to that of Indians during the period of western settlement.

Critical Thinking Questions

15. Describe the philosophy of Manifest Destiny. What effect did it have on Americans' westward migration? How might the different groups that migrated have sought to apply this philosophy to their individual circumstances?

16. Compare the myth of the "Wild West" with its reality. What elements of truth would these stories have contained, and what was fabricated or left out? What was life actually like for cowboys, ranchers, and the few women present in mining towns or along the cattle range?

17. What were the primary methods that the U.S. government, as well as individual reformers, used to deal with the perceived Indian threat to westward settlement? In what ways were these methods successful and unsuccessful? What were their short-term and long-term effects on Native Americans?

18. Describe the ways in which the U.S. government, local governments, and/or individuals attempted to interfere with the specific cultural traditions and customs of Indians, Hispanics, and Chinese immigrants. What did these efforts have in common? How did each group respond?

19. In what ways did westward expansion provide new opportunities for women and African Americans? In what ways did it limit these opportunities?

CHAPTER 18

Industrialization and the Rise of Big Business, 1870-1900

Figure 18.1 The Electrical Building, constructed in 1892 for the World's Columbian Exposition, included displays from General Electric and Westinghouse, and introduced the American public to alternating current and neon lights. The Chicago World's Fair, as the universal exposition was more commonly known, featured architecture, inventions, and design, serving as both a showcase for and an influence on the country's optimism about the Industrial Age.

Chapter Outline

18.1 Inventors of the Age
18.2 From Invention to Industrial Growth
18.3 Building Industrial America on the Backs of Labor
18.4 A New American Consumer Culture

Introduction

"The electric age was ushered into being in this last decade of the nineteenth century today when President Cleveland, by pressing a button, started the mighty machinery, rushing waters and revolving wheels in the World's Columbian exhibition." With this announcement about the official start of the Chicago World's Fair in 1893 (Figure 18.1), the *Salt Lake City Herald* captured the excitement and optimism of the machine age. "In the previous expositions," the editorial continued, "the possibilities of electricity had been limited to the mere starting of the engines in the machinery hall, but in this it made thousands of servants do its bidding . . . the magic of electricity did the duty of the hour."

The fair, which commemorated the four hundredth anniversary of Columbus's journey to America, was a potent symbol of the myriad inventions that changed American life and contributed to the significant economic growth of the era, as well as the new wave of industrialization that swept the country. While businessmen capitalized upon such technological innovations, the new industrial working class faced enormous challenges. Ironically, as the World's Fair welcomed its first visitors, the nation was spiraling downward into the worst depression of the century. Subsequent frustrations among working-class Americans laid the groundwork for the country's first significant labor movement.

18.1 Inventors of the Age

By the end of this section, you will be able to:
- Explain how the ideas and products of late nineteenth-century inventors contributed to the rise of big business
- Explain how the inventions of the late nineteenth century changed everyday American life

The late nineteenth century was an energetic era of inventions and entrepreneurial spirit. Building upon the mid-century Industrial Revolution in Great Britain, as well as answering the increasing call from Americans for efficiency and comfort, the country found itself in the grip of invention fever, with more people working on their big ideas than ever before. In retrospect, harnessing the power of steam and then electricity in the nineteenth century vastly increased the power of man and machine, thus making other advances possible as the century progressed.

Facing an increasingly complex everyday life, Americans sought the means by which to cope with it. Inventions often provided the answers, even as the inventors themselves remained largely unaware of the life-changing nature of their ideas. To understand the scope of this zeal for creation, consider the U.S. Patent Office, which, in 1790—its first decade of existence—recorded only 276 inventions. By 1860, the office had issued a total of 60,000 patents. But between 1860 and 1890, that number exploded to nearly 450,000, with another 235,000 in the last decade of the century. While many of these patents came to naught, some inventions became lynchpins in the rise of big business and the country's move towards an industrial-based economy, in which the desire for efficiency, comfort, and abundance could be more fully realized by most Americans.

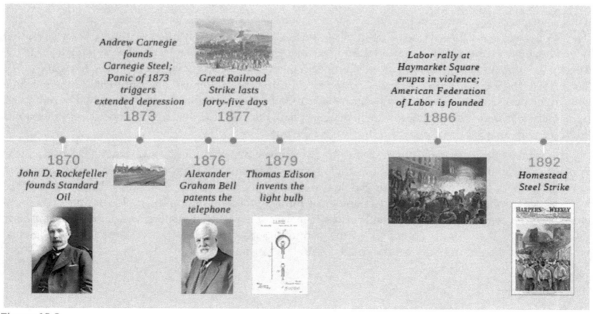

Figure 18.2

Download for free at http://cnx.org/content/col11740/latest/

AN EXPLOSION OF INVENTIVE ENERGY

From corrugated rollers that could crack hard, homestead-grown wheat into flour to refrigerated train cars and garment-sewing machines (Figure 18.3), new inventions fueled industrial growth around the country. As late as 1880, fully one-half of all Americans still lived and worked on farms, whereas fewer than one in seven—mostly men, except for long-established textile factories in which female employees tended to dominate—were employed in factories. However, the development of commercial electricity by the close of the century, to complement the steam engines that already existed in many larger factories, permitted more industries to concentrate in cities, away from the previously essential water power. In turn, newly arrived immigrants sought employment in new urban factories. Immigration, urbanization, and industrialization coincided to transform the face of American society from primarily rural to significantly urban. From 1880 to 1920, the number of industrial workers in the nation quadrupled from 2.5 million to over 10 million, while over the same period urban populations doubled, to reach one-half of the country's total population.

Figure 18.3 Advertisements of the late nineteenth century promoted the higher quality and lower prices that people could expect from new inventions. Here, a knitting factory promotes the fact that its machines make seamless hose, while still acknowledging the traditional role of women in the garment industry, from grandmothers who used to sew by hand to young women who now used machines.

In offices, worker productivity benefited from the typewriter, invented in 1867, the cash register, invented in 1879, and the adding machine, invented in 1885. These tools made it easier than ever to keep up with the rapid pace of business growth. Inventions also slowly transformed home life. The vacuum cleaner arrived during this era, as well as the flush toilet. These indoor "water closets" improved public health through the reduction in contamination associated with outhouses and their proximity to water supplies and homes. Tin cans and, later, Clarence Birdseye's experiments with frozen food, eventually changed how women shopped for, and prepared, food for their families, despite initial health concerns over preserved foods. With the advent of more easily prepared food, women gained valuable time in their daily schedules, a step that partially laid the groundwork for the modern women's movement. Women who had the means to purchase such items could use their time to seek other employment outside of the home, as well as broaden their knowledge through education and reading. Such a transformation did not occur overnight, as these inventions also increased expectations for women to remain tied to the home and their domestic chores; slowly, the culture of domesticity changed.

Perhaps the most important industrial advancement of the era came in the production of steel. Manufacturers and builders preferred steel to iron, due to its increased strength and durability. After the Civil War, two new processes allowed for the creation of furnaces large enough and hot enough to melt the wrought iron needed to produce large quantities of steel at increasingly cheaper prices. The Bessemer process, named for English inventor Henry Bessemer, and the open-hearth process, changed the way the United States produced steel and, in doing so, led the country into a new industrialized age. As the new material became more available, builders eagerly sought it out, a demand that steel mill owners were happy to supply.

In 1860, the country produced thirteen thousand tons of steel. By 1879, American furnaces were producing over one million tons per year; by 1900, this figure had risen to ten million. Just ten years later, the United States was the top steel producer in the world, at over twenty-four million tons annually. As production increased to match the overwhelming demand, the price of steel dropped by over 80 percent. When quality steel became cheaper and more readily available, other industries relied upon it more heavily as a key to their growth and development, including construction and, later, the automotive industry. As a result, the steel industry rapidly became the cornerstone of the American economy, remaining the primary indicator of industrial growth and stability through the end of World War II.

ALEXANDER GRAHAM BELL AND THE TELEPHONE

Advancements in communications matched the pace of growth seen in industry and home life. Communication technologies were changing quickly, and they brought with them new ways for information to travel. In 1858, British and American crews laid the first transatlantic cable lines, enabling messages to pass between the United States and Europe in a matter of hours, rather than waiting the few weeks it could take for a letter to arrive by steamship. Although these initial cables worked for barely a month, they generated great interest in developing a more efficient telecommunications industry. Within twenty years, over 100,000 miles of cable crisscrossed the ocean floors, connecting all the continents. Domestically, Western Union, which controlled 80 percent of the country's telegraph lines, operated nearly 200,000 miles of telegraph routes from coast to coast. In short, people were connected like never before, able to relay messages in minutes and hours rather than days and weeks.

One of the greatest advancements was the telephone, which Alexander Graham Bell patented in 1876 (Figure 18.4). While he was not the first to invent the concept, Bell was the first one to capitalize on it; after securing the patent, he worked with financiers and businessmen to create the National Bell Telephone Company. Western Union, which had originally turned down Bell's machine, went on to commission Thomas Edison to invent an improved version of the telephone. It is actually Edison's version that is most like the modern telephone used today. However, Western Union, fearing a costly legal battle they were likely to lose due to Bell's patent, ultimately sold Edison's idea to the Bell Company. With the communications industry now largely in their control, along with an agreement from the federal government to permit such control, the Bell Company was transformed into the American Telephone and Telegraph Company, which still exists today as AT&T. By 1880, fifty thousand telephones were in use in the United States, including one at the White House. By 1900, that number had increased to 1.35 million, and hundreds of American cities had obtained local service for their citizens. Quickly and inexorably, technology was bringing the country into closer contact, changing forever the rural isolation that had defined America since its beginnings.

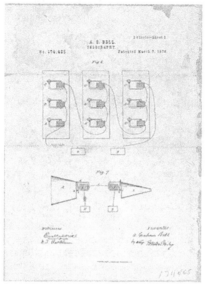

Figure 18.4 Alexander Graham Bell's patent of the telephone was one of almost 700,000 U.S. patents issued between 1850 and 1900. Although the patent itself was only six pages long, including two pages of illustrations, it proved to be one of the most contested and profitable of the nineteenth century. (credit: U.S. National Archives and Records Administration)

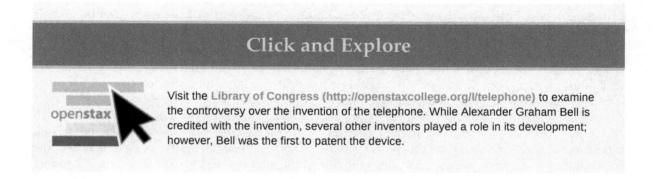

Click and Explore

Visit the **Library of Congress (http://openstaxcollege.org/l/telephone)** to examine the controversy over the invention of the telephone. While Alexander Graham Bell is credited with the invention, several other inventors played a role in its development; however, Bell was the first to patent the device.

THOMAS EDISON AND ELECTRIC LIGHTING

Although Thomas Alva Edison (Figure 18.5) is best known for his contributions to the electrical industry, his experimentation went far beyond the light bulb. Edison was quite possibly the greatest inventor of the turn of the century, saying famously that he "hoped to have a minor invention every ten days and a big thing every month or so." He registered 1,093 patents over his lifetime and ran a world-famous laboratory, Menlo Park, which housed a rotating group of up to twenty-five scientists from around the globe.

Edison became interested in the telegraph industry as a boy, when he worked aboard trains selling candy and newspapers. He soon began tinkering with telegraph technology and, by 1876, had devoted himself full time to lab work as an inventor. He then proceeded to invent a string of items that are still used today: the phonograph, the mimeograph machine, the motion picture projector, the dictaphone, and the storage battery, all using a factory-oriented assembly line process that made the rapid production of inventions possible.

Figure 18.5 Thomas Alva Edison was the quintessential inventor of the era, with a passion for new ideas and over one thousand patents to his name. Seen here with his incandescent light bulb, which he invented in 1879, Edison produced many inventions that subsequently transformed the country and the world.

In 1879, Edison invented the item that has led to his greatest fame: the incandescent light bulb. He allegedly explored over six thousand different materials for the filament, before stumbling upon tungsten as the ideal substance. By 1882, with financial backing largely from financier J. P. Morgan, he had created the Edison Electric Illuminating Company, which began supplying electrical current to a small number of customers in New York City. Morgan guided subsequent mergers of Edison's other enterprises, including a machine works firm and a lamp company, resulting in the creation of the Edison General Electric Company in 1889.

The next stage of invention in electric power came about with the contribution of George Westinghouse. Westinghouse was responsible for making electric lighting possible on a national scale. While Edison used "direct current" or DC power, which could only extend two miles from the power source, in 1886, Westinghouse invented "alternating current" or AC power, which allowed for delivery over greater distances due to its wavelike patterns. The Westinghouse Electric Company delivered AC power, which meant that factories, homes, and farms—in short, anything that needed power—could be served, regardless of their proximity to the power source. A public relations battle ensued between the Westinghouse and Edison camps, coinciding with the invention of the electric chair as a form of prisoner execution. Edison publicly proclaimed AC power to be best adapted for use in the chair, in the hope that such a smear campaign would result in homeowners becoming reluctant to use AC power in their houses. Although Edison originally fought the use of AC power in other devices, he reluctantly adapted to it as its popularity increased.

Click and Explore

openstax

Not all of Edison's ventures were successful. Read about Edison's Folly (http://openstaxcollege.org/l/edisonfail) to learn the story behind his greatest failure. Was there some benefit to his efforts? Or was it wasted time and money?

18.2 From Invention to Industrial Growth

By the end of this section, you will be able to:
- Explain how the inventions of the late nineteenth century contributed directly to industrial growth in America
- Identify the contributions of Andrew Carnegie, John Rockefeller, and J. P. Morgan to the new industrial order emerging in the late nineteenth century
- Describe the visions, philosophies, and business methods of the leaders of the new industrial order

As discussed previously, new processes in steel refining, along with inventions in the fields of communications and electricity, transformed the business landscape of the nineteenth century. The exploitation of these new technologies provided opportunities for tremendous growth, and business entrepreneurs with financial backing and the right mix of business acumen and ambition could make their fortunes. Some of these new millionaires were known in their day as **robber barons**, a negative term that connoted the belief that they exploited workers and bent laws to succeed. Regardless of how they were perceived, these businessmen and the companies they created revolutionized American industry.

RAILROADS AND ROBBER BARONS

Earlier in the nineteenth century, the first transcontinental railroad and subsequent spur lines paved the way for rapid and explosive railway growth, as well as stimulated growth in the iron, wood, coal, and other related industries. The railroad industry quickly became the nation's first "big business." A powerful, inexpensive, and consistent form of transportation, railroads accelerated the development of virtually every other industry in the country. By 1890, railroad lines covered nearly every corner of the United States, bringing raw materials to industrial factories and finished goods to consumer markets. The amount of track grew from 35,000 miles at the end of the Civil War to over 200,000 miles by the close of the century. Inventions such as car couplers, air brakes, and Pullman passenger cars allowed the volume of both freight and people to increase steadily. From 1877 to 1890, both the amount of goods and the number of passengers traveling the rails tripled.

Financing for all of this growth came through a combination of private capital and government loans and grants. Federal and state loans of cash and land grants totaled $150 million and 185 million acres of public land, respectively. Railroads also listed their stocks and bonds on the New York Stock Exchange to attract investors from both within the United States and Europe. Individual investors consolidated their power as railroads merged and companies grew in size and power. These individuals became some of the wealthiest Americans the country had ever known. Midwest farmers, angry at large railroad owners for their exploitative business practices, came to refer to them as "robber barons," as their business dealings were frequently shady and exploitative. Among their highly questionable tactics was the practice of differential shipping rates, in which larger business enterprises received discounted rates to transport their goods, as opposed to local producers and farmers whose higher rates essentially subsidized the discounts.

Jay Gould was perhaps the first prominent railroad magnate to be tarred with the "robber baron" brush. He bought older, smaller, rundown railroads, offered minimal improvements, and then capitalized on factory owners' desires to ship their goods on this increasingly popular and more cost-efficient form of transportation. His work with the Erie Railroad was notorious among other investors, as he drove the company to near ruin in a failed attempt to attract foreign investors during a takeover attempt. His model worked better in the American West, where the railroads were still widely scattered across the country, forcing farmers and businesses to pay whatever prices Gould demanded in order to use his trains. In addition to owning the Union Pacific Railroad that helped to construct the original transcontinental railroad line, Gould came to control over ten thousand miles of track across the United States, accounting for 15 percent of all railroad transportation. When he died in 1892, Gould had a personal worth of over $100 million, although he was a deeply unpopular figure.

In contrast to Gould's exploitative business model, which focused on financial profit more than on tangible industrial contributions, Commodore Cornelius Vanderbilt was a "robber baron" who truly cared about the success of his railroad enterprise and its positive impact on the American economy. Vanderbilt consolidated several smaller railroad lines, called trunk lines, to create the powerful New York Central Railroad Company, one of the largest corporations in the United States at the time (Figure 18.6). He later purchased stock in the major rail lines that would connect his company to Chicago, thus expanding his reach and power while simultaneously creating a railroad network to connect Chicago to New York City. This consolidation provided more efficient connections from Midwestern suppliers to eastern markets. It was through such consolidation that, by 1900, seven major railroad tycoons controlled over 70 percent of all operating lines. Vanderbilt's personal wealth at his death (over $100 million in 1877), placed him among the top three wealthiest individuals in American history.

Figure 18.6   "The Great Race for the Western Stakes," a Currier & Ives lithograph from 1870, depicts one of Cornelius Vanderbilt's rare failed attempts at further consolidating his railroad empire, when he lost his 1866–1868 battle with James Fisk, Jay Gould, and Daniel Drew for control of the Erie Railway Company.

GIANTS OF WEALTH: CARNEGIE, ROCKEFELLER, AND MORGAN

The post-Civil War inventors generated ideas that transformed the economy, but they were not big businessmen. The evolution from technical innovation to massive industry took place at the hands of the entrepreneurs whose business gambles paid off, making them some of the richest Americans of their day. Steel magnate Andrew Carnegie, oil tycoon John D. Rockefeller, and business financier J. P. Morgan were all businessmen who grew their respective businesses to a scale and scope that were unprecedented. Their companies changed how Americans lived and worked, and they themselves greatly influenced the growth of the country.

Andrew Carnegie and *The Gospel of Wealth*

Andrew Carnegie, steel magnate, has the prototypical rags-to-riches story. Although such stories resembled more myth than reality, they served to encourage many Americans to seek similar paths to fame and fortune. In Carnegie, the story was one of few derived from fact. Born in Scotland, Carnegie immigrated with his family to Pennsylvania in 1848. Following a brief stint as a "bobbin boy," changing spools of thread at a Pittsburgh clothing manufacturer at age thirteen, he subsequently became a telegram messenger boy. As a messenger, he spent much of his time around the Pennsylvania Railroad office and developed parallel interests in railroads, bridge building, and, eventually, the steel industry.

Ingratiating himself to his supervisor and future president of the Pennsylvania Railroad, Tom Scott, Carnegie worked his way into a position of management for the company and subsequently began to invest some of his earnings, with Scott's guidance. One particular investment, in the booming oil fields of northwest Pennsylvania in 1864, resulted in Carnegie earning over $1 million in cash dividends, thus providing him with the capital necessary to pursue his ambition to modernize the iron and steel industries, transforming the United States in the process. Having seen firsthand during the Civil War, when he served as Superintendent of Military Railways and telegraph coordinator for the Union forces, the importance of industry, particularly steel, to the future growth of the country, Carnegie was convinced of his strategy. His first company was the J. Edgar Thompson Steel Works, and, a decade later, he bought out the newly built Homestead Steel Works from the Pittsburgh Bessemer Steel Company. By the end of the century, his enterprise was running an annual profit in excess of $40 million (Figure 18.7).

Figure 18.7 Andrew Carnegie made his fortune in steel at such factories as the Carnegie Steel Works located in Youngstown, Ohio, where new technologies allowed the strong metal to be used in far more applications than ever before. Carnegie's empire grew to include iron ore mines, furnaces, mills, and steel works companies.

Although not a scientific expert in steel, Carnegie was an excellent promoter and salesman, able to locate financial backing for his enterprise. He was also shrewd in his calculations on consolidation and expansion, and was able to capitalize on smart business decisions. Always thrifty with the profits he earned, a trait owed to his upbringing, Carnegie saved his profits during prosperous times and used them to buy out other steel companies at low prices during the economic recessions of the 1870s and 1890s. He insisted on up-to-date machinery and equipment, and urged the men who worked at and managed his steel mills to constantly think of innovative ways to increase production and reduce cost.

Carnegie, more than any other businessman of the era, championed the idea that America's leading tycoons owed a debt to society. He believed that, given the circumstances of their successes, they should serve as benefactors to the less fortunate public. For Carnegie, poverty was not an abstract concept, as his family had been a part of the struggling masses. He desired to set an example of philanthropy for all other prominent industrialists of the era to follow. Carnegie's famous essay, *The Gospel of Wealth*, featured below, expounded on his beliefs. In it, he borrowed from Herbert Spencer's theory of **social Darwinism**, which held that society developed much like plant or animal life through a process of evolution in which the most fit and capable enjoyed the greatest material and social success.

MY STORY

✿ *Andrew Carnegie on Wealth*

Carnegie applauded American capitalism for creating a society where, through hard work, ingenuity, and a bit of luck, someone like himself could amass a fortune. In return for that opportunity, Carnegie wrote that the wealthy should find proper uses for their wealth by funding hospitals, libraries, colleges, the arts, and more. *The Gospel of Wealth* spelled out that responsibility.

> Poor and restricted are our opportunities in this life; narrow our horizon; our best work most imperfect; but rich men should be thankful for one inestimable boon. They have it in their power during their lives to busy themselves in organizing benefactions from which the masses of their fellows will derive lasting advantage, and thus dignify their own lives. . . .
>
> This, then, is held to be the duty of the man of Wealth: First, to set an example of modest, unostentatious living, shunning display or extravagance; to provide moderately for the legitimate wants of those dependent upon him; and after doing so to consider all surplus revenues which come to him simply as trust funds, which he is called upon to administer, and strictly bound as a matter of duty to administer in the manner which, in his judgment, is best calculated to produce the most beneficial results for the community—the man of wealth thus becoming the mere agent and trustee for his poorer brethren, bringing to their service his superior wisdom, experience and ability to administer, doing for them better than they would or could do for themselves. . . .
>
> In bestowing charity, the main consideration should be to help those who will help themselves; to provide part of the means by which those who desire to improve may do so; to give those who desire to use the aids by which they may rise; to assist, but rarely or never to do all. Neither the individual nor the race is improved by alms-giving. Those worthy of assistance, except in rare cases, seldom require assistance. The really valuable men of the race never do, except in cases of accident or sudden change. Every one has, of course, cases of individuals brought to his own knowledge where temporary assistance can do genuine good, and these he will not overlook. But the amount which can be wisely given by the individual for individuals is necessarily limited by his lack of knowledge of the circumstances connected with each. He is the only true reformer who is as careful and as anxious not to aid the unworthy as he is to aid the worthy, and, perhaps, even more so, for in alms-giving more injury is probably done by rewarding vice than by relieving virtue.
>
> —Andrew Carnegie, *The Gospel of Wealth*

Social Darwinism added a layer of pseudoscience to the idea of the self-made man, a desirable thought for all who sought to follow Carnegie's example. The myth of the rags-to-riches businessman was a potent one. Author Horatio Alger made his own fortune writing stories about young enterprising boys who beat poverty and succeeded in business through a combination of "luck and pluck." His stories were immensely popular, even leading to a board game (Figure 18.8) where players could hope to win in the same way that his heroes did.

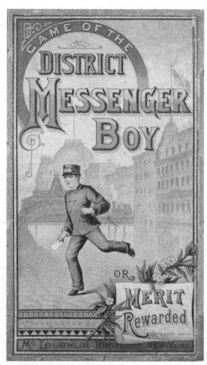

Figure 18.8 Based on a book by Horatio Alger, District Messenger Boy was a board game where players could achieve the ultimate goal of material success. Alger wrote hundreds of books on a common theme: A poor but hardworking boy can get ahead and make his fortune through a combination of "luck and pluck."

John D. Rockefeller and Business Integration Models

Like Carnegie, John D. Rockefeller was born in 1839 of modest means, with a frequently absent traveling salesman of a father who sold medicinal elixirs and other wares. Young Rockefeller helped his mother with various chores and earned extra money for the family through the sale of family farm products. When the family moved to a suburb of Cleveland in 1853, he had an opportunity to take accounting and bookkeeping courses while in high school and developed a career interest in business. While living in Cleveland in 1859, he learned of Colonel Edwin Drake who had struck "black gold," or oil, near Titusville, Pennsylvania, setting off a boom even greater than the California Gold Rush of the previous decade. Many sought to find a fortune through risky and chaotic "wildcatting," or drilling exploratory oil wells, hoping to strike it rich. But Rockefeller chose a more certain investment: refining crude oil into kerosene, which could be used for both heating and lamps. As a more efficient source of energy, as well as less dangerous to produce, kerosene quickly replaced whale oil in many businesses and homes. Rockefeller worked initially with family and friends in the refining business located in the Cleveland area, but by 1870, Rockefeller ventured out on his own, consolidating his resources and creating the Standard Oil Company of Ohio, initially valued at $1 million.

Rockefeller was ruthless in his pursuit of total control of the oil refining business. As other entrepreneurs flooded the area seeking a quick fortune, Rockefeller developed a plan to crush his competitors and create a true **monopoly** in the refining industry. Beginning in 1872, he forged agreements with several large railroad companies to obtain discounted freight rates for shipping his product. He also used the railroad companies to gather information on his competitors. As he could now deliver his kerosene at lower prices, he drove his competition out of business, often offering to buy them out for pennies on the dollar. He hounded those who refused to sell out to him, until they were driven out of business. Through his method of growth via mergers and acquisitions of similar companies—known as **horizontal**

integration —Standard Oil grew to include almost all refineries in the area. By 1879, the Standard Oil Company controlled nearly 95 percent of all oil refining businesses in the country, as well as 90 percent of all the refining businesses in the world. Editors of the *New York World* lamented of Standard Oil in 1880 that, "When the nineteenth century shall have passed into history, the impartial eyes of the reviewers will be amazed to find that the U.S. . . . tolerated the presence of the most gigantic, the most cruel, impudent, pitiless and grasping monopoly that ever fastened itself upon a country."

Seeking still more control, Rockefeller recognized the advantages of controlling the transportation of his product. He next began to grow his company through **vertical integration**, wherein a company handles all aspects of a product's lifecycle, from the creation of raw materials through the production process to the delivery of the final product. In Rockefeller's case, this model required investment and acquisition of companies involved in everything from barrel-making to pipelines, tanker cars to railroads. He came to own almost every type of business and used his vast power to drive competitors from the market through intense price wars. Although vilified by competitors who suffered from his takeovers and considered him to be no better than a robber baron, several observers lauded Rockefeller for his ingenuity in integrating the oil refining industry and, as a result, lowering kerosene prices by as much as 80 percent by the end of the century. Other industrialists quickly followed suit, including Gustavus Swift, who used vertical integration to dominate the U.S. meatpacking industry in the late nineteenth century.

In order to control the variety of interests he now maintained in industry, Rockefeller created a new legal entity, known as a **trust**. In this arrangement, a small group of trustees possess legal ownership of a business that they operate for the benefit of other investors. In 1882, all thirty-seven stockholders in the various Standard Oil enterprises gave their stock to nine trustees who were to control and direct all of the company's business ventures. State and federal challenges arose, due to the obvious appearance of a monopoly, which implied sole ownership of all enterprises composing an entire industry. When the Ohio Supreme Court ruled that the Standard Oil Company must dissolve, as its monopoly control over all refining operations in the U.S. was in violation of state and federal statutes, Rockefeller shifted to yet another legal entity, called a **holding company** model. The holding company model created a central corporate entity that controlled the operations of multiple companies by holding the majority of stock for each enterprise. While not technically a "trust" and therefore not vulnerable to anti-monopoly laws, this consolidation of power and wealth into one entity was on par with a monopoly; thus, progressive reformers of the late nineteenth century considered holding companies to epitomize the dangers inherent in capitalistic big business, as can be seen in the political cartoon below (Figure 18.9). Impervious to reformers' misgivings, other businessmen followed Rockefeller's example. By 1905, over three hundred business mergers had occurred in the United States, affecting more than 80 percent of all industries. By that time, despite passage of federal legislation such as the Sherman Anti-Trust Act in 1890, 1 percent of the country's businesses controlled over 40 percent of the nation's economy.

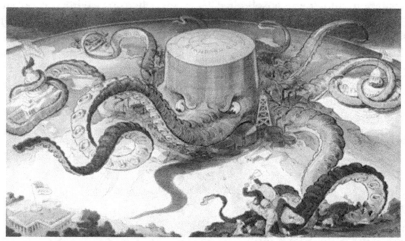

Figure 18.9 John D. Rockefeller, like Carnegie, grew from modest means to a vast fortune. Unlike Carnegie, however, his business practices were often predatory and aggressive. This cartoon from the era shows how his conglomerate, Standard Oil, was perceived by progressive reformers and other critics.

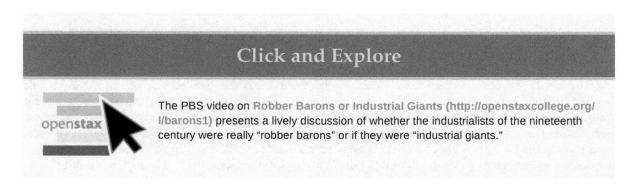

Click and Explore

The PBS video on **Robber Barons or Industrial Giants (http://openstaxcollege.org/l/barons1)** presents a lively discussion of whether the industrialists of the nineteenth century were really "robber barons" or if they were "industrial giants."

J. Pierpont Morgan

Unlike Carnegie and Rockefeller, J. P. Morgan was no rags-to-riches hero. He was born to wealth and became much wealthier as an investment banker, making wise financial decisions in support of the hard-working entrepreneurs building their fortunes. Morgan's father was a London banker, and Morgan the son moved to New York in 1857 to look after the family's business interests there. Once in America, he separated from the London bank and created the J. Pierpont Morgan and Company financial firm. The firm bought and sold stock in growing companies, investing the family's wealth in those that showed great promise, turning an enormous profit as a result. Investments from firms such as his were the key to the success stories of up-and-coming businessmen like Carnegie and Rockefeller. In return for his investment, Morgan and other investment bankers demanded seats on the companies' boards, which gave them even greater control over policies and decisions than just investment alone. There were many critics of Morgan and these other bankers, particularly among members of a U.S. congressional subcommittee who investigated the control that financiers maintained over key industries in the country. The subcommittee referred to Morgan's enterprise as a form of "money trust" that was even more powerful than the trusts operated by Rockefeller and others. Morgan argued that his firm, and others like it, brought stability and organization to a hypercompetitive capitalist economy, and likened his role to a kind of public service.

Ultimately, Morgan's most notable investment, and greatest consolidation, was in the steel industry, when he bought out Andrew Carnegie in 1901. Initially, Carnegie was reluctant to sell, but after repeated badgering by Morgan, Carnegie named his price: an outrageously inflated sum of $500 million. Morgan agreed without hesitation, and then consolidated Carnegie's holdings with several smaller steel firms to create the U.S. Steel Corporation. U.S. Steel was subsequently capitalized at $1.4 billion. It was the country's first billion-dollar firm. Lauded by admirers for the efficiency and modernization he brought to investment banking practices, as well as for his philanthropy and support of the arts, Morgan was also criticized by reformers who subsequently blamed his (and other bankers') efforts for contributing to the artificial bubble of prosperity that eventually burst in the Great Depression of the 1930s. What none could doubt was that Morgan's financial aptitude and savvy business dealings kept him in good stead. A subsequent U.S. congressional committee, in 1912, reported that his firm held 341 directorships in 112 corporations that controlled over $22 billion in assets. In comparison, that amount of wealth was greater than the assessed value of all the land in the United States west of the Mississippi River.

18.3 Building Industrial America on the Backs of Labor

By the end of this section, you will be able to:
- Explain the qualities of industrial working-class life in the late nineteenth century
- Analyze both workers' desire for labor unions and the reasons for unions' inability to achieve their goals

The growth of the American economy in the last half of the nineteenth century presented a paradox. The standard of living for many American workers increased. As Carnegie said in *The Gospel of Wealth*, "the poor enjoy what the rich could not before afford. What were the luxuries have become the necessaries of life. The laborer has now more comforts than the landlord had a few generations ago." In many ways, Carnegie was correct. The decline in prices and the cost of living meant that the industrial era offered many Americans relatively better lives in 1900 than they had only decades before. For some Americans, there were also increased opportunities for upward mobility. For the multitudes in the working class, however, conditions in the factories and at home remained deplorable. The difficulties they faced led many workers to question an industrial order in which a handful of wealthy Americans built their fortunes on the backs of workers.

WORKING-CLASS LIFE

Between the end of the Civil War and the turn of the century, the American workforce underwent a transformative shift. In 1865, nearly 60 percent of Americans still lived and worked on farms; by the early 1900s, that number had reversed itself, and only 40 percent still lived in rural areas, with the remainder living and working in urban and early suburban areas. A significant number of these urban and suburban dwellers earned their wages in factories. Advances in farm machinery allowed for greater production with less manual labor, thus leading many Americans to seek job opportunities in the burgeoning factories in the cities. Not surprisingly, there was a concurrent trend of a decrease in American workers being self-employed and an increase of those working for others and being dependent on a factory wage system for their living.

Yet factory wages were, for the most part, very low. In 1900, the average factory wage was approximately twenty cents per hour, for an annual salary of barely six hundred dollars. According to some historical estimates, that wage left approximately 20 percent of the population in industrialized cities at, or below, the poverty level. An average factory work week was sixty hours, ten hours per day, six days per week, although in steel mills, the workers put in twelve hours per day, seven days a week. Factory owners had little concern for workers' safety. According to one of the few available accurate measures, as late as 1913, nearly 25,000 Americans lost their lives on the job, while another 700,000 workers suffered from injuries that resulted in at least one missed month of work. Another element of hardship for workers was the increasingly dehumanizing nature of their work. Factory workers executed repetitive tasks throughout the long hours of their shifts, seldom interacting with coworkers or supervisors. This solitary and repetitive work style was a difficult adjustment for those used to more collaborative and skill-based work, whether on farms or in crafts shops. Managers embraced Fredrick Taylor's principles of **scientific management**, also called "stop-watch management," where he used stop-watch studies to divide manufacturing tasks into short, repetitive segments. A mechanical engineer by training, Taylor encouraged factory owners to seek efficiency and profitability over any benefits of personal interaction. Owners adopted this model, effectively making workers cogs in a well-oiled machine.

One result of the new breakdown of work processes was that factory owners were able to hire women and children to perform many of the tasks. From 1870 through 1900, the number of women working outside the home tripled. By the end of this period, five million American women were wage earners, with one-quarter of them working factory jobs. Most were young, under twenty-five, and either immigrants themselves or the daughters of immigrants. Their foray into the working world was not seen as a step towards empowerment or equality, but rather a hardship born of financial necessity. Women's factory work tended to be in clothing or textile factories, where their appearance was less offensive to men who felt that heavy industry was their purview. Other women in the workforce worked in clerical positions as bookkeepers and secretaries, and as salesclerks. Not surprisingly, women were paid less than men, under the pretense that they should be under the care of a man and did not require a living wage.

Factory owners used the same rationale for the exceedingly low wages they paid to children. Children were small enough to fit easily among the machines and could be hired for simple work for a fraction of an adult man's pay. The image below (**Figure 18.10**) shows children working the night shift in a glass factory. From 1870 through 1900, child labor in factories tripled. Growing concerns among progressive reformers over the safety of women and children in the workplace would eventually result in the development of political lobby groups. Several states passed legislative efforts to ensure a safe workplace, and the lobby groups pressured Congress to pass protective legislation. However, such legislation would not be forthcoming until well into the twentieth century. In the meantime, many working-class immigrants still desired the additional wages that child and women labor produced, regardless of the harsh working conditions.

Figure 18.10 A photographer took this image of children working in a New York glass factory at midnight. There, as in countless other factories around the country, children worked around the clock in difficult and dangerous conditions.

WORKER PROTESTS AND VIOLENCE

Workers were well aware of the vast discrepancy between their lives and the wealth of the factory owners. Lacking the assets and legal protection needed to organize, and deeply frustrated, some working communities erupted in spontaneous violence. The coal mines of eastern Pennsylvania and the railroad yards of western Pennsylvania, central to both respective industries and home to large, immigrant, working enclaves, saw the brunt of these outbursts. The combination of violence, along with several other factors, blunted any significant efforts to organize workers until well into the twentieth century.

Business owners viewed organization efforts with great mistrust, capitalizing upon widespread anti-union sentiment among the general public to crush unions through open shops, the use of strikebreakers, yellow-dog contracts (in which the employee agrees to not join a union as a pre-condition of employment), and other means. Workers also faced obstacles to organization associated with race and ethnicity, as questions arose on how to address the increasing number of low-paid African American workers, in addition to the language and cultural barriers introduced by the large wave of southeastern European immigration to the United States. But in large part, the greatest obstacle to effective unionization was the general public's continued belief in a strong work ethic and that an individual work ethic—not organizing into radical collectives—would reap its own rewards. As violence erupted, such events seemed only to confirm widespread popular sentiment that radical, un-American elements were behind all union efforts.

In the 1870s, Irish coal miners in eastern Pennsylvania formed a secret organization known as the **Molly Maguires**, named for the famous Irish patriot. Through a series of scare tactics that included kidnappings, beatings, and even murder, the Molly Maguires sought to bring attention to the miners' plight, as well as to cause enough damage and concern to the mine owners that the owners would pay attention to their concerns. Owners paid attention, but not in the way that the protesters had hoped. They hired detectives to pose as miners and mingle among the workers to obtain the names of the Molly Maguires. By 1875, they had acquired the names of twenty-four suspected Maguires, who were subsequently convicted of murder and violence against property. All were convicted and ten were hanged in 1876, at a public "Day of the Rope." This harsh reprisal quickly crushed the remaining Molly Maguires movement. The only substantial gain the workers had from this episode was the knowledge that, lacking labor organization, sporadic violent protest would be met by escalated violence.

Public opinion was not sympathetic towards labor's violent methods as displayed by the Molly Maguires. But the public was further shocked by some of the harsh practices employed by government agents to crush the labor movement, as seen the following year in the Great Railroad Strike of 1877. After incurring a significant pay cut earlier that year, railroad workers in West Virginia spontaneously went on strike and blocked the tracks (Figure 18.11). As word spread of the event, railroad workers across the country joined in sympathy, leaving their jobs and committing acts of vandalism to show their frustration with the ownership. Local citizens, who in many instances were relatives and friends, were largely sympathetic to the railroad workers' demands.

Figure 18.11 This engraving of the "Blockade of Engines at Martinsburg, West Virginia" appeared on the front cover of *Harper's Weekly* on August 11, 1877, while the Great Railroad Strike was still underway.

The most significant violent outbreak of the railroad strike occurred in Pittsburgh, beginning on July 19. The governor ordered militiamen from Philadelphia to the Pittsburgh roundhouse to protect railroad property. The militia opened fire to disperse the angry crowd and killed twenty individuals while wounding another twenty-nine. A riot erupted, resulting in twenty-four hours of looting, violence, fire, and mayhem, and did not die down until the rioters wore out in the hot summer weather. In a subsequent skirmish with strikers while trying to escape the roundhouse, militiamen killed another twenty individuals. Violence erupted in Maryland and Illinois as well, and President Hayes eventually sent federal troops into major cities to restore order. This move, along with the impending return of cooler weather that brought with it the need for food and fuel, resulted in striking workers nationwide returning to the railroad. The strike had lasted for forty-five days, and they had gained nothing but a reputation for violence and aggression that left the public less sympathetic than ever. Dissatisfied laborers began to realize that there would be no substantial improvement in their quality of life until they found a way to better organize themselves.

WORKER ORGANIZATION AND THE STRUGGLES OF UNIONS

Prior to the Civil War, there were limited efforts to create an organized labor movement on any large scale. With the majority of workers in the country working independently in rural settings, the idea of organized labor was not largely understood. But, as economic conditions changed, people became more aware of the inequities facing factory wage workers. By the early 1880s, even farmers began to fully recognize the strength of unity behind a common cause.

Models of Organizing: The Knights of Labor and American Federation of Labor

In 1866, seventy-seven delegates representing a variety of different occupations met in Baltimore to form the National Labor Union (NLU). The NLU had ambitious ideas about equal rights for African Americans and women, currency reform, and a legally mandated eight-hour workday. The organization was successful in convincing Congress to adopt the eight-hour workday for federal employees, but their reach did not progress much further. The Panic of 1873 and the economic recession that followed as a result of overspeculation on railroads and the subsequent closing of several banks—during which workers actively sought any employment regardless of the conditions or wages—as well as the death of the NLU's founder, led to a decline in their efforts.

A combination of factors contributed to the debilitating Panic of 1873, which triggered what the public referred to at the time as the "Great Depression" of the 1870s. Most notably, the railroad boom that had occurred from 1840 to 1870 was rapidly coming to a close. Overinvestment in the industry had extended many investors' capital resources in the form of railroad bonds. However, when several economic developments in Europe affected the value of silver in America, which in turn led to a de facto gold standard that shrunk the U.S. monetary supply, the amount of cash capital available for railroad investments rapidly declined. Several large business enterprises were left holding their wealth in all but worthless railroad bonds. When Jay Cooke & Company, a leader in the American banking industry, declared bankruptcy on the eve of their plans to finance the construction of a new transcontinental railroad, the panic truly began. A chain reaction of bank failures culminated with the New York Stock Exchange suspending all trading for ten days at the end of September 1873. Within a year, over one hundred railroad enterprises had failed; within two years, nearly twenty thousand businesses had failed. The loss of jobs and wages sent workers throughout the United States seeking solutions and clamoring for scapegoats.

Although the NLU proved to be the wrong effort at the wrong time, in the wake of the Panic of 1873 and the subsequent frustration exhibited in the failed Molly Maguires uprising and the national railroad strike, another, more significant, labor organization emerged. The Knights of Labor (KOL) was more able to attract a sympathetic following than the Molly Maguires and others by widening its base and appealing to more members. Philadelphia tailor Uriah Stephens grew the KOL from a small presence during the Panic of 1873 to an organization of national importance by 1878. That was the year the KOL held their first general assembly, where they adopted a broad reform platform, including a renewed call for an eight-hour workday, equal pay regardless of gender, the elimination of convict labor, and the creation of greater cooperative enterprises with worker ownership of businesses. Much of the KOL's strength came from its concept of "One Big Union"—the idea that it welcomed all wage workers, regardless of occupation, with the exception of doctors, lawyers, and bankers. It welcomed women, African Americans, Native Americans, and immigrants, of all trades and skill levels. This was a notable break from the earlier tradition of craft unions, which were highly specialized and limited to a particular group. In 1879, a new leader, Terence V. Powderly, joined the organization, and he gained even more followers due to his marketing and promotional efforts. Although largely opposed to strikes as effective tactics, through their sheer size, the Knights claimed victories in several railroad strikes in 1884–1885, including one against notorious "robber baron" Jay Gould, and their popularity consequently rose among workers. By 1886, the KOL had a membership in excess of 700,000.

In one night, however, the KOL's popularity—and indeed the momentum of the labor movement as a whole—plummeted due to an event known as the **Haymarket affair**, which occurred on May 4, 1886, in Chicago's Haymarket Square (Figure 18.12). There, an anarchist group had gathered in response to a death at an earlier nationwide demonstration for the eight-hour workday. At the earlier demonstration, clashes between police and strikers at the International Harvester Company of Chicago led to the death of a striking worker. The anarchist group decided to hold a protest the following night in Haymarket Square, and, although the protest was quiet, the police arrived armed for conflict. Someone in the crowd threw a bomb at the police, killing one officer and injuring another. The seven anarchists speaking at the protest were arrested and charged with murder. They were sentenced to death, though two were later pardoned and one committed suicide in prison before his execution.

Figure 18.12 The Haymarket affair, as it was known, began as a rally for the eight-hour workday. But when police broke it up, someone threw a bomb into the crowd, causing mayhem. The organizers of the rally, although not responsible, were sentenced to death. The affair and subsequent hangings struck a harsh blow against organized labor.

The press immediately blamed the KOL as well as Powderly for the Haymarket affair, despite the fact that neither the organization nor Powderly had anything to do with the demonstration. Combined with the American public's lukewarm reception to organized labor as a whole, the damage was done. The KOL saw its membership decline to barely 100,000 by the end of 1886. Nonetheless, during its brief success, the Knights illustrated the potential for success with their model of "industrial unionism," which welcomed workers from all trades.

AMERICANA

⚙ *The Haymarket Rally*

On May 1, 1886, recognized internationally as a day for labor celebration, labor organizations around the country engaged in a national rally for the eight-hour workday. While the number of striking workers varied around the country, estimates are that between 300,000 and 500,000 workers protested in New York, Detroit, Chicago, and beyond. In Chicago, clashes between police and protesters led the police to fire into the crowd, resulting in fatalities. Afterward, angry at the deaths of the striking workers, organizers quickly organized a "mass meeting," per the poster below (Figure 18.13).

Figure 18.13 This poster invited workers to a meeting denouncing the violence at the labor rally earlier in the week. Note that the invitation is written in both English and German, evidence of the large role that the immigrant population played in the labor movement.

While the meeting was intended to be peaceful, a large police presence made itself known, prompting one of the event organizers to state in his speech, "There seems to prevail the opinion in some quarters that this meeting has been called for the purpose of inaugurating a riot, hence these warlike preparations on the part of so-called 'law and order.' However, let me tell you at the beginning that this meeting has not been called for any such purpose. The object of this meeting is to explain the general situation of the eight-hour movement and to throw light upon various incidents in connection with it." The mayor of Chicago later corroborated accounts of the meeting, noted that it was a peaceful rally, but as it was winding down, the police marched into the crowd, demanding they disperse. Someone in the crowd threw a bomb, killing one policeman immediately and wounding many others, some of whom died later. Despite the aggressive actions of the police, public opinion was strongly against the striking laborers. The *New York Times*, after the events played out, reported on it with the headline "Rioting and Bloodshed in the Streets of Chicago: Police Mowed Down with Dynamite." Other papers echoed the tone and often exaggerated the chaos, undermining organized labor's efforts and leading to the ultimate conviction and hanging of the rally organizers. Labor activists considered those hanged after the Haymarket affair to be martyrs for the cause and created an informal memorial at their gravesides in Park Forest, Illinois.

Click and Explore

This article about the "Rioting and Bloodshed in the Streets of Chicago" (http://openstaxcollege.org/l/haymarket) reveals how the *New York Times* reported on the Haymarket affair. Assess whether the article gives evidence of the information it lays out. Consider how it portrays the events, and how different, more sympathetic coverage might have changed the response of the general public towards immigrant workers and labor unions.

During the effort to establish industrial unionism in the form of the KOL, craft unions had continued to operate. In 1886, twenty different craft unions met to organize a national federation of autonomous craft unions. This group became the American Federation of Labor (AFL), led by Samuel Gompers from its inception until his death in 1924. More so than any of its predecessors, the AFL focused almost all of its efforts on economic gains for its members, seldom straying into political issues other than those that had a direct impact upon working conditions. The AFL also kept a strict policy of not interfering in each union's individual business. Rather, Gompers often settled disputes between unions, using the AFL to represent all unions of matters of federal legislation that could affect all workers, such as the eight-hour workday.

By 1900, the AFL had 500,000 members; by 1914, its numbers had risen to one million, and by 1920 they claimed four million working members. Still, as a federation of craft unions, it excluded many factory workers and thus, even at its height, represented only 15 percent of the nonfarm workers in the country. As a result, even as the country moved towards an increasingly industrial age, the majority of American workers still lacked support, protection from ownership, and access to upward mobility.

The Decline of Labor: The Homestead and Pullman Strikes

While workers struggled to find the right organizational structure to support a union movement in a society that was highly critical of such worker organization, there came two final violent events at the close of the nineteenth century. These events, the Homestead Steel Strike of 1892 and the Pullman Strike of 1894, all but crushed the labor movement for the next forty years, leaving public opinion of labor strikes lower than ever and workers unprotected.

At the Homestead factory of the Carnegie Steel Company, workers represented by the Amalgamated Association of Iron and Steel Workers enjoyed relatively good relations with management until Henry C. Frick became the factory manager in 1889. When the union contract was up for renewal in 1892, Carnegie—long a champion of living wages for his employees—had left for Scotland and trusted Frick—noted for his strong anti-union stance—to manage the negotiations. When no settlement was reached by June 29, Frick ordered a lockout of the workers and hired three hundred Pinkerton detectives to protect company property. On July 6, as the Pinkertons arrived on barges on the river, union workers along the shore engaged them in a gunfight that resulted in the deaths of three Pinkertons and six workers. One week later, the Pennsylvania militia arrived to escort strike-breakers into the factory to resume production. Although the lockout continued until November, it ended with the union defeated and individual workers asking for their jobs back. A subsequent failed assassination attempt by anarchist Alexander Berkman on Frick further strengthened public animosity towards the union.

Two years later, in 1894, the Pullman Strike was another disaster for unionized labor. The crisis began in the company town of Pullman, Illinois, where Pullman "sleeper" cars were manufactured for America's railroads. When the depression of 1893 unfolded in the wake of the failure of several northeastern railroad companies, mostly due to overconstruction and poor financing, company owner George Pullman fired three thousand of the factory's six thousand employees, cut the remaining workers' wages by an average of 25 percent, and then continued to charge the same high rents and prices in the company homes and store where workers were required to live and shop. Workers began the strike on May 11, when Eugene V. Debs, the president of the American Railway Union, ordered rail workers throughout the country to stop handling any trains that had Pullman cars on them. In practicality, almost all of the trains fell into this category, and, therefore, the strike created a nationwide train stoppage, right on the heels of the depression of 1893. Seeking justification for sending in federal troops, President Grover Cleveland turned to his attorney general, who came up with a solution: Attach a mail car to every train and then send in troops to ensure the delivery of the mail. The government also ordered the strike to end; when Debs refused, he was arrested and imprisoned for his interference with the delivery of U.S. mail. The image below (Figure 18.14) shows the standoff between federal troops and the workers. The troops protected the hiring of new workers, thus rendering the strike tactic largely ineffective. The strike ended abruptly on July 13, with no labor gains and much lost in the way of public opinion.

Figure 18.14 In this photo of the Pullman Strike of 1894, the Illinois National Guard and striking workers face off in front of a railroad building.

MY STORY

☼ *George Estes on the Order of Railroad Telegraphers*

The following excerpt is a reflection from George Estes, an organizer and member of the Order of Railroad Telegraphers, a labor organization at the end of the nineteenth century. His perspective on the ways that labor and management related to each other illustrates the difficulties at the heart of their negotiations. He notes that, in this era, the two groups saw each other as enemies and that any gain by one was automatically a loss by the other.

> I have always noticed that things usually have to get pretty bad before they get any better. When inequities pile up so high that the burden is more than the underdog can bear, he gets his dander up and things begin to happen. It was that way with the telegraphers' problem. These exploited individuals were determined to get for themselves better working conditions—higher pay, shorter hours, less work which might not properly be classed as telegraphy, and the high and mighty Mr. Fillmore [railroad company president] was not going to stop them. It was a bitter fight. At the outset, Mr. Fillmore let it be known, by his actions and comments, that he held the telegraphers in the utmost contempt.
>
> With the papers crammed each day with news of labor strife—and with two great labor factions at each other's throats, I am reminded of a parallel in my own early and more active career. Shortly before the turn of the century, in 1898 and 1899 to be more specific, I occupied a position with regard to a certain class of skilled labor, comparable to that held by the Lewises and Greens of today. I refer, of course, to the telegraphers and station agents. These hard-working gentlemen—servants of the public—had no regular hours, performed a multiplicity of duties, and, considering the service they rendered, were sorely and inadequately paid. A telegrapher's day included a considerable number of chores that present-day telegraphers probably never did or will do in the course of a day's work. He used to clean and fill lanterns, block lights, etc. Used to do the janitor work around the small town depot, stoke the pot-bellied stove of the waiting-room, sweep the floors, picking up papers and waiting-room litter. . . .
>
> Today, capital and labor seem to understand each other better than they did a generation or so ago. Capital is out to make money. So is labor—and each is willing to grant the other a certain amount of tolerant leeway, just so he doesn't go too far. In the old days there was a breach as wide as the Pacific separating capital and labor. It wasn't money altogether in those days, it was a matter of principle. Capital and labor couldn't see eye to eye on a single point. Every gain that either made was at the expense of the other, and was fought tooth and nail. No difference seemed ever possible of amicable settlement. Strikes were riots. Murder and mayhem was common. Railroad labor troubles were frequent. The railroads, in the nineties, were the country's largest employers. They were so big, so powerful, so perfectly organized themselves—I mean so in accord among themselves as to what treatment they felt like offering the man who worked for them—that it was extremely difficult for labor to gain a single advantage in the struggle for better conditions.
>
> —George Estes, interview with Andrew Sherbert, 1938

18.4 A New American Consumer Culture

By the end of this section, you will be able to:
* Describe the characteristics of the new consumer culture that emerged at the end of the nineteenth century

Despite the challenges workers faced in their new roles as wage earners, the rise of industry in the United States allowed people to access and consume goods as never before. The rise of big business had turned

America into a culture of consumers desperate for time-saving and leisure commodities, where people could expect to find everything they wanted in shops or by mail order. Gone were the days where the small general store was the only option for shoppers; at the end of the nineteenth century, people could take a train to the city and shop in large department stores like Macy's in New York, Gimbel's in Philadelphia, and Marshall Fields in Chicago. Chain stores, like A&P and Woolworth's, both of which opened in the 1870s, offered options to those who lived farther from major urban areas and clearly catered to classes other than the wealthy elite. Industrial advancements contributed to this proliferation, as new construction techniques permitted the building of stores with higher ceilings for larger displays, and the production of larger sheets of plate glass lent themselves to the development of larger store windows, glass countertops, and display cases where shoppers could observe a variety of goods at a glance. L. Frank Baum, of *Wizard of Oz* fame, later founded the National Association of Window Trimmers in 1898, and began publishing *The Store Window* journal to advise businesses on space usage and promotion.

Even families in rural America had new opportunities to purchase a greater variety of products than ever before, at ever decreasing prices. Those far from chain stores could benefit from the newly developed business of mail-order catalogs, placing orders by telephone. Aaron Montgomery Ward established the first significant mail-order business in 1872, with Sears, Roebuck & Company following in 1886. Sears distributed over 300,000 catalogs annually by 1897, and later broke the one million annual mark in 1907. Sears in particular understood that farmers and rural Americans sought alternatives to the higher prices and credit purchases they were forced to endure at small-town country stores. By clearly stating the prices in his catalog, Richard Sears steadily increased his company's image of their catalog serving as "the consumer's bible." In the process, Sears, Roebuck & Company supplied much of America's hinterland with products ranging from farm supplies to bicycles, toilet paper to automobiles, as seen below in a page from the catalog (Figure 18.15).

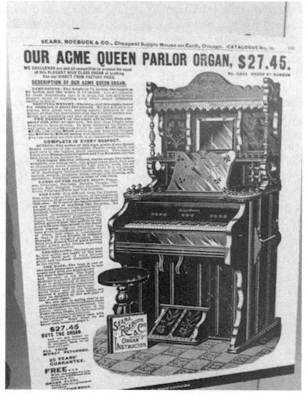

Figure 18.15   This page from the Sears, Roebuck & Co. catalog illustrates how luxuries that would only belong to wealthy city dwellers were now available by mail order to those all around the country.

The tremendous variety of goods available for sale required businesses to compete for customers in ways they had never before imagined. Suddenly, instead of a single option for clothing or shoes, customers were faced with dozens, whether ordered by mail, found at the local chain store, or lined up in massive rows at department stores. This new level of competition made advertising a vital component of all businesses. By 1900, American businesses were spending almost $100 million annually on advertising. Competitors offered "new and improved" models as frequently as possible in order to generate interest. From toothpaste and mouthwash to books on entertaining guests, new goods were constantly offered. Newspapers accommodated the demand for advertising by shifting their production to include full-page advertisements, as opposed to the traditional column width, agate-type advertisements that dominated mid-nineteenth century newspapers (similar to classified advertisements in today's publications). Likewise, professional advertising agencies began to emerge in the 1880s, with experts in consumer demand bidding for accounts with major firms.

It may seem strange that, at a time when wages were so low, people began buying readily; however, the slow emergence of a middle class by the end of the century, combined with the growing practice of buying on credit, presented more opportunities to take part in the new consumer culture. Stores allowed people to open accounts and purchase on credit, thus securing business and allowing consumers to buy without ready cash. Then, as today, the risks of buying on credit led many into debt. As advertising expert Roland Marchand described in his *Parable on the Democracy of Goods*, in an era when access to products became more important than access to the means of production, Americans quickly accepted the notion that they could live a better lifestyle by purchasing the right clothes, the best hair cream, and the shiniest shoes, regardless of their class. For better or worse, American consumerism had begun.

AMERICANA

✪ Advertising in the Industrial Age: Credit, Luxury, and the Advent of "New and Improved"

Before the industrial revolution, most household goods were either made at home or purchased locally, with limited choices. By the end of the nineteenth century, factors such as the population's move towards urban centers and the expansion of the railroad changed how Americans shopped for, and perceived, consumer goods. As mentioned above, advertising took off, as businesses competed for customers.

Many of the elements used widely in nineteenth-century advertisements are familiar. Companies sought to sell luxury, safety, and, as the ad for the typewriter below shows (Figure 18.16), the allure of the new-and-improved model. One advertising tactic that truly took off in this era was the option to purchase on credit. For the first time, mail order and mass production meant that the aspiring middle class could purchase items that could only be owned previously by the wealthy. While there was a societal stigma for buying everyday goods on credit, certain items, such as fine furniture or pianos, were considered an investment in the move toward entry into the middle class.

Figure 18.16 This typewriter advertisement, like others of the era, tried to lure customers by offering a new model.

Additionally, farmers and housewives purchased farm equipment and sewing machines on credit, considering these items investments rather than luxuries. For women, the purchase of a sewing machine meant that a shirt could be made in one hour, instead of fourteen. The Singer Sewing Machine Company was one of the most aggressive at pushing purchase on credit. They advertised widely, and their "Dollar Down, Dollar a Week" campaign made them one of the fastest-growing companies in the country.

For workers earning lower wages, these easy credit terms meant that the middle-class lifestyle was within their reach. Of course, it also meant they were in debt, and changes in wages, illness, or other unexpected expenses could wreak havoc on a household's tenuous finances. Still, the opportunity to own new and luxurious products was one that many Americans, aspiring to improve their place in society, could not resist.

Key Terms

Haymarket affair the rally and subsequent riot in which several policemen were killed when a bomb was thrown at a peaceful workers rights rally in Chicago in 1866

holding company a central corporate entity that controls the operations of multiple companies by holding the majority of stock for each enterprise

horizontal integration method of growth wherein a company grows through mergers and acquisitions of similar companies

Molly Maguires a secret organization made up of Pennsylvania coal miners, named for the famous Irish patriot, which worked through a series of scare tactics to bring the plight of the miners to public attention

monopoly the ownership or control of all enterprises comprising an entire industry

robber baron a negative term for the big businessmen who made their fortunes in the massive railroad boom of the late nineteenth century

scientific management mechanical engineer Fredrick Taylor's management style, also called "stop-watch management," which divided manufacturing tasks into short, repetitive segments and encouraged factory owners to seek efficiency and profitability over any benefits of personal interaction

social Darwinism Herbert Spencer's theory, based upon Charles Darwin's scientific theory, which held that society developed much like plant or animal life through a process of evolution in which the most fit and capable enjoyed the greatest material and social success

trust a legal arrangement where a small group of trustees have legal ownership of a business that they operate for the benefit of other investors

vertical integration a method of growth where a company acquires other companies that include all aspects of a product's lifecycle from the creation of the raw materials through the production process to the delivery of the final product

Summary

18.1 Inventors of the Age

Inventors in the late nineteenth century flooded the market with new technological advances. Encouraged by Great Britain's Industrial Revolution, and eager for economic development in the wake of the Civil War, business investors sought the latest ideas upon which they could capitalize, both to transform the nation as well as to make a personal profit. These inventions were a key piece of the massive shift towards industrialization that followed. For both families and businesses, these inventions eventually represented a fundamental change in their way of life. Although the technology spread slowly, it did spread across the country. Whether it was a company that could now produce ten times more products with new factories, or a household that could communicate with distant relations, the old way of doing things was disappearing.

Communication technologies, electric power production, and steel production were perhaps the three most significant developments of the time. While the first two affected both personal lives and business development, the latter influenced business growth first and foremost, as the ability to produce large steel elements efficiently and cost-effectively led to permanently changes in the direction of industrial growth.

18.2 From Invention to Industrial Growth

As the three tycoons profiled in this section illustrate, the end of the nineteenth century was a period in history that offered tremendous financial rewards to those who had the right combination of skill, ambition, and luck. Whether self-made millionaires like Carnegie or Rockefeller, or born to wealth like Morgan, these men were the lynchpins that turned inventors' ideas into industrial growth. Steel production, in particular, but also oil refining techniques and countless other inventions, changed how industries in the country could operate, allowing them to grow in scale and scope like never before.

It is also critical to note how these different men managed their businesses and ambition. Where Carnegie felt strongly that it was the job of the wealthy to give back in their lifetime to the greater community, his fellow tycoons did not necessarily agree. Although he contributed to many philanthropic efforts, Rockefeller's financial success was built on the backs of ruined and bankrupt companies, and he came to be condemned by progressive reformers who questioned the impact on the working class as well as the dangers of consolidating too much power and wealth into one individual's hands. Morgan sought wealth strictly through the investment in, and subsequent purchase of, others' hard work. Along the way, the models of management they adopted—horizontal and vertical integration, trusts, holding companies, and investment brokerages—became commonplace in American businesses. Very quickly, large business enterprises fell under the control of fewer and fewer individuals and trusts. In sum, their ruthlessness, their ambition, their generosity, and their management made up the workings of America's industrial age.

18.3 Building Industrial America on the Backs of Labor

After the Civil War, as more and more people crowded into urban areas and joined the ranks of wage earners, the landscape of American labor changed. For the first time, the majority of workers were employed by others in factories and offices in the cities. Factory workers, in particular, suffered from the inequity of their positions. Owners had no legal restrictions on exploiting employees with long hours in dehumanizing and poorly paid work. Women and children were hired for the lowest possible wages, but even men's wages were barely enough upon which to live.

Poor working conditions, combined with few substantial options for relief, led workers to frustration and sporadic acts of protest and violence, acts that rarely, if ever, gained them any lasting, positive effects. Workers realized that change would require organization, and thus began early labor unions that sought to win rights for all workers through political advocacy and owner engagement. Groups like the National Labor Union and Knights of Labor both opened their membership to any and all wage earners, male or female, black or white, regardless of skill. Their approach was a departure from the craft unions of the very early nineteenth century, which were unique to their individual industries. While these organizations gained members for a time, they both ultimately failed when public reaction to violent labor strikes turned opinion against them. The American Federation of Labor, a loose affiliation of different unions, grew in the wake of these universal organizations, although negative publicity impeded their work as well. In all, the century ended with the vast majority of American laborers unrepresented by any collective or union, leaving them vulnerable to the power wielded by factory ownership.

18.4 A New American Consumer Culture

While tensions between owners and workers continued to grow, and wage earners struggled with the challenges of industrial work, the culture of American consumerism was changing. Greater choice, easier access, and improved goods at lower prices meant that even lower-income Americans, whether rural and shopping via mail order, or urban and shopping in large department stores, had more options. These increased options led to a rise in advertising, as businesses competed for customers. Furthermore, the opportunity to buy on credit meant that Americans could have their goods, even without ready cash. The result was a population that had a better standard of living than ever before, even as they went into debt or worked long factory hours to pay for it.

Review Questions

1. Which of these was *not* a successful invention of the era?

    A. high-powered sewing machines

    B. movies with sound

    C. frozen foods

    D. typewriters

2. What was the major advantage of Westinghouse's "alternating current" power invention?

    A. It was less prone to fire.

    B. It cost less to produce.

    C. It allowed machines to be farther from the power source.

    D. It was not under Edison's control.

3. How did the burst of new inventions during this era fuel the process of urbanization?

4. Which of the following "robber barons" was notable for the exploitative way he made his fortune in railroads?

    A. Jay Gould

    B. Cornelius Vanderbilt

    C. Andrew Carnegie

    D. J. Pierpont Morgan

5. Which of the following does *not* represent one of the management strategies that John D. Rockefeller used in building his empire?

    A. horizontal integration

    B. vertical integration

    C. social Darwinism

    D. the holding company model

6. Why was Rockefeller's use of horizontal integration such an effective business tool at this time? Were his choices legal? Why or why not?

7. What differentiated a "robber baron" from other "captains of industry" in late nineteenth-century America?

8. What was one of the key goals for which striking workers fought in the late nineteenth century?

    A. health insurance

    B. disability pay

    C. an eight-hour workday

    D. women's right to hold factory jobs

9. Which of the following was *not* a key goal of the Knights of Labor?

    A. an end to convict labor

    B. a graduated income tax on personal wealth

    C. equal pay regardless of gender

    D. the creation of cooperative business enterprises

10. What were the core differences in the methods and agendas of the Knights of Labor and the American Federation of Labor?

11. Which of the following did *not* contribute to the growth of a consumer culture in the United States at the close of the nineteenth century?

    A. personal credit

    B. advertising

    C. greater disposable income

    D. mail-order catalogs

12. Briefly explain Roland Marchand's argument in the *Parable of the Democracy of Goods*.

Critical Thinking Questions

13. Consider the fact that the light bulb and the telephone were invented only three years apart. Although it took many more years for such devices to find their way into common household use, they eventually wrought major changes in a relatively brief period of time. What effects did these inventions have on the lives of those who used them? Are there contemporary analogies in your lifetime of significant changes due to inventions or technological innovations?

14. Industrialization, immigration, and urbanization all took place on an unprecedented scale during this era. What were the relationships of these processes to one another? How did each process serve to catalyze and fuel the others?

15.   Describe the various attempts at labor organization in this era, from the Molly Maguires to the Knights of Labor and American Federation of Labor. How were the goals, philosophies, and tactics of these groups similar and different? How did their agendas represent the concerns and grievances of their members and of workers more generally?

16.   Describe the various violent clashes between labor and management that occurred during this era. What do these events reveal about how each group had come to view the other?

17.   How did the new industrial order represent both new opportunities and new limitations for rural and working-class urban Americans?

18.   How did the emergent consumer culture change what it meant to be "American" at the turn of the century?

CHAPTER 19

The Growing Pains of Urbanization, 1870-1900

Figure 19.1 For the millions of immigrants arriving by ship in New York City's harbor, the sight of the Statue of Liberty, as in *Unveiling the Statue of Liberty* (1886) by Edward Moran, stood as a physical representation of the new freedoms and economic opportunities they hoped to find.

Chapter Outline

19.1 Urbanization and Its Challenges
19.2 The African American "Great Migration" and New European Immigration
19.3 Relief from the Chaos of Urban Life
19.4 Change Reflected in Thought and Writing

Introduction

"We saw the big woman with spikes on her head." So begins Sadie Frowne's first memory of arriving in the United States. Many Americans experienced in their new home what the thirteen-year-old Polish girl had seen in the silhouette of the Statue of Liberty (Figure 19.1): a wondrous world of new opportunities fraught with dangers. Sadie and her mother, for instance, had left Poland after her father's death. Her mother died shortly thereafter, and Sadie had to find her own way in New York, working in factories and slowly assimilating to life in a vast multinational metropolis. Her story is similar to millions of others, as people came to the United States seeking a better future than the one they had at home.

The future they found, however, was often grim. While many believed in the land of opportunity, the reality of urban life in the United States was more chaotic and difficult than people expected. In addition to the challenges of language, class, race, and ethnicity, these new arrivals dealt with low wages, overcrowded buildings, poor sanitation, and widespread disease. The land of opportunity, it seemed, did not always deliver on its promises.

19.1 Urbanization and Its Challenges

By the end of this section, you will be able to:
- Explain the growth of American cities in the late nineteenth century
- Identify the key challenges that Americans faced due to urbanization, as well as some of the possible solutions to those challenges

Urbanization occurred rapidly in the second half of the nineteenth century in the United States for a number of reasons. The new technologies of the time led to a massive leap in industrialization, requiring large numbers of workers. New electric lights and powerful machinery allowed factories to run twenty-four hours a day, seven days a week. Workers were forced into grueling twelve-hour shifts, requiring them to live close to the factories.

While the work was dangerous and difficult, many Americans were willing to leave behind the declining prospects of preindustrial agriculture in the hope of better wages in industrial labor. Furthermore, problems ranging from famine to religious persecution led a new wave of immigrants to arrive from central, eastern, and southern Europe, many of whom settled and found work near the cities where they first arrived. Immigrants sought solace and comfort among others who shared the same language and customs, and the nation's cities became an invaluable economic and cultural resource.

Although cities such as Philadelphia, Boston, and New York sprang up from the initial days of colonial settlement, the explosion in urban population growth did not occur until the mid-nineteenth century (Figure 19.3). At this time, the attractions of city life, and in particular, employment opportunities, grew exponentially due to rapid changes in industrialization. Before the mid-1800s, factories, such as the early textile mills, had to be located near rivers and seaports, both for the transport of goods and the necessary water power. Production became dependent upon seasonal water flow, with cold, icy winters all but stopping river transportation entirely. The development of the steam engine transformed this need, allowing businesses to locate their factories near urban centers. These factories encouraged more and more

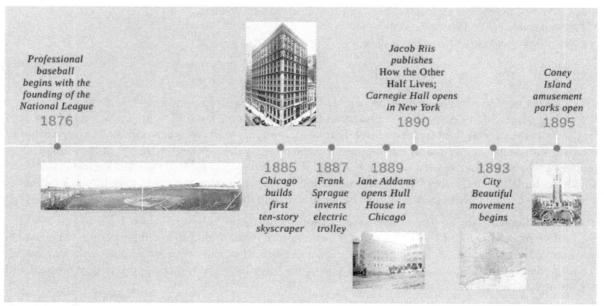

Figure 19.2

people to move to urban areas where jobs were plentiful, but hourly wages were often low and the work was routine and grindingly monotonous.

Rural and Urban Populations in the United States, 1860–1920		
Year	Rural	Urban
1860	25,226,803	6,216,518
1870	28,656,010	9,902,361
1880	36,059,474	14,129,735
1890	40,873,501	22,106,265
1900	45,997,336	30,214,832
1910	50,164,495	42,064,001
1920	51,768,255	54,253,282
Source: Bureau of the Census		

(a)

Populations of Major Cities in the United States, 1860–1900			
City	1860	1880	1900
New York	1,174,800	1,912,000	3,437,000
Philadelphia	565,500	847,000	1,294,000
Boston	177,800	363,000	561,000
Baltimore	212,400	332,000	509,000
Cincinnati	161,000	255,000	326,000
St. Louis	160,800	350,000	575,000
Chicago	109,300	503,000	1,698,000

(b)

Figure 19.3 As these panels illustrate, the population of the United States grew rapidly in the late 1800s (a). Much of this new growth took place in urban areas (defined by the census as twenty-five hundred people or more), and this urban population, particularly that of major cities (b), dealt with challenges and opportunities that were unknown in previous generations.

Eventually, cities developed their own unique characters based on the core industry that spurred their growth. In Pittsburgh, it was steel; in Chicago, it was meat packing; in New York, the garment and financial industries dominated; and Detroit, by the mid-twentieth century, was defined by the automobiles it built. But all cities at this time, regardless of their industry, suffered from the universal problems that rapid expansion brought with it, including concerns over housing and living conditions, transportation, and communication. These issues were almost always rooted in deep class inequalities, shaped by racial divisions, religious differences, and ethnic strife, and distorted by corrupt local politics.

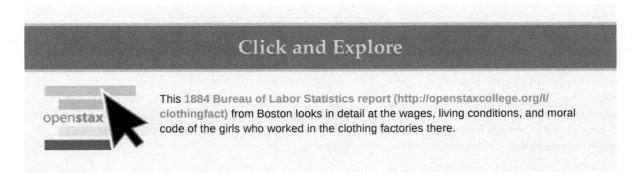

Click and Explore

This 1884 Bureau of Labor Statistics report (http://openstaxcollege.org/l/clothingfact) from Boston looks in detail at the wages, living conditions, and moral code of the girls who worked in the clothing factories there.

THE KEYS TO SUCCESSFUL URBANIZATION

As the country grew, certain elements led some towns to morph into large urban centers, while others did not. The following four innovations proved critical in shaping urbanization at the turn of the century: electric lighting, communication improvements, intracity transportation, and the rise of skyscrapers. As people migrated for the new jobs, they often struggled with the absence of basic urban infrastructures, such as better transportation, adequate housing, means of communication, and efficient sources of light and energy. Even the basic necessities, such as fresh water and proper sanitation—often taken for granted in the countryside—presented a greater challenge in urban life.

Electric Lighting

Thomas Edison patented the incandescent light bulb in 1879. This development quickly became common in homes as well as factories, transforming how even lower- and middle-class Americans lived. Although slow to arrive in rural areas of the country, electric power became readily available in cities when the first commercial power plants began to open in 1882. When Nikola Tesla subsequently developed the AC (alternating current) system for the Westinghouse Electric & Manufacturing Company, power supplies for lights and other factory equipment could extend for miles from the power source. AC power transformed the use of electricity, allowing urban centers to physically cover greater areas. In the factories, electric lights permitted operations to run twenty-four hours a day, seven days a week. This increase in production required additional workers, and this demand brought more people to cities.

Gradually, cities began to illuminate the streets with electric lamps to allow the city to remain alight throughout the night. No longer did the pace of life and economic activity slow substantially at sunset, the way it had in smaller towns. The cities, following the factories that drew people there, stayed open all the time.

Communications Improvements

The telephone, patented in 1876, greatly transformed communication both regionally and nationally. The telephone rapidly supplanted the telegraph as the preferred form of communication; by 1900, over 1.5 million telephones were in use around the nation, whether as private lines in the homes of some middle- and upper-class Americans, or jointly used "party lines" in many rural areas. By allowing instant communication over larger distances at any given time, growing telephone networks made urban sprawl possible.

In the same way that electric lights spurred greater factory production and economic growth, the telephone increased business through the more rapid pace of demand. Now, orders could come constantly via telephone, rather than via mail-order. More orders generated greater production, which in turn required still more workers. This demand for additional labor played a key role in urban growth, as expanding companies sought workers to handle the increasing consumer demand for their products.

Intracity Transportation

As cities grew and sprawled outward, a major challenge was efficient travel within the city—from home to factories or shops, and then back again. Most transportation infrastructure was used to connect cities to each other, typically by rail or canal. Prior to the 1880s, the most common form of transportation within cities was the omnibus. This was a large, horse-drawn carriage, often placed on iron or steel tracks to provide a smoother ride. While omnibuses worked adequately in smaller, less congested cities, they were not equipped to handle the larger crowds that developed at the close of the century. The horses had to stop and rest, and horse manure became an ongoing problem.

In 1887, Frank Sprague invented the electric trolley, which worked along the same concept as the omnibus, with a large wagon on tracks, but was powered by electricity rather than horses. The electric trolley could run throughout the day and night, like the factories and the workers who fueled them. But it also modernized less important industrial centers, such as the southern city of Richmond, Virginia. As early as 1873, San Francisco engineers adopted pulley technology from the mining industry to introduce cable cars and turn the city's steep hills into elegant middle-class communities. However, as crowds continued to grow in the largest cities, such as Chicago and New York, trolleys were unable to move efficiently through the crowds of pedestrians (Figure 19.4). To avoid this challenge, city planners elevated the trolley lines above the streets, creating elevated trains, or L-trains, as early as 1868 in New York City, and quickly spreading to Boston in 1887 and Chicago in 1892. Finally, as skyscrapers began to dominate the air, transportation evolved one step further to move underground as subways. Boston's subway system began operating in 1897, and was quickly followed by New York and other cities.

(a)   (b)

Figure 19.4 Although trolleys were far more efficient than horse-drawn carriages, populous cities such as New York experienced frequent accidents, as depicted in this 1895 illustration from *Leslie's Weekly* (a). To avoid overcrowded streets, trolleys soon went underground, as at the Public Gardens Portal in Boston (b), where three different lines met to enter the Tremont Street Subway, the oldest subway tunnel in the United States, opening on September 1, 1897.

The Rise of Skyscrapers

The last limitation that large cities had to overcome was the ever-increasing need for space. Eastern cities, unlike their midwestern counterparts, could not continue to grow outward, as the land surrounding them was already settled. Geographic limitations such as rivers or the coast also hampered sprawl. And in all cities, citizens needed to be close enough to urban centers to conveniently access work, shops, and other core institutions of urban life. The increasing cost of real estate made upward growth attractive, and so did the prestige that towering buildings carried for the businesses that occupied them. Workers completed the first skyscraper in Chicago, the ten-story Home Insurance Building, in 1885 (Figure 19.5). Although engineers had the capability to go higher, thanks to new steel construction techniques, they required another vital invention in order to make taller buildings viable: the elevator. In 1889, the Otis Elevator Company, led by inventor James Otis, installed the first electric elevator. This began the skyscraper craze, allowing developers in eastern cities to build and market prestigious real estate in the hearts of crowded eastern metropoles.

Figure 19.5 While the technology existed to engineer tall buildings, it was not until the invention of the electric elevator in 1889 that skyscrapers began to take over the urban landscape. Shown here is the Home Insurance Building in Chicago, considered the first modern skyscraper.

DEFINING "AMERICAN"

❂ *Jacob Riis and the Window into "How the Other Half Lives"*

Jacob Riis was a Danish immigrant who moved to New York in the late nineteenth century and, after experiencing poverty and joblessness first-hand, ultimately built a career as a police reporter. In the course of his work, he spent much of his time in the slums and tenements of New York's working poor. Appalled by what he found there, Riis began documenting these scenes of squalor and sharing them through lectures and ultimately through the publication of his book, *How the Other Half Lives*, in 1890 (Figure 19.6).

Figure 19.6 In photographs such as *Bandit's Roost* (1888), taken on Mulberry Street in the infamous Five Points neighborhood of Manhattan's Lower East Side, Jacob Riis documented the plight of New York City slums in the late nineteenth century.

By most contemporary accounts, Riis was an effective storyteller, using drama and racial stereotypes to tell his stories of the ethnic slums he encountered. But while his racial thinking was very much a product of his time, he was also a reformer; he felt strongly that upper and middle-class Americans could and should care about the living conditions of the poor. In his book and lectures, he argued against the immoral landlords and useless laws that allowed dangerous living conditions and high rents. He also suggested remodeling existing tenements or building new ones. He was not alone in his concern for the plight of the poor; other reporters and activists had already brought the issue into the public eye, and Riis's photographs added a new element to the story.

To tell his stories, Riis used a series of deeply compelling photographs. Riis and his group of amateur photographers moved through the various slums of New York, laboriously setting up their tripods and explosive chemicals to create enough light to take the photographs. His photos and writings shocked the public, made Riis a well-known figure both in his day and beyond, and eventually led to new state legislation curbing abuses in tenements.

THE IMMEDIATE CHALLENGES OF URBAN LIFE

Congestion, pollution, crime, and disease were prevalent problems in all urban centers; city planners and inhabitants alike sought new solutions to the problems caused by rapid urban growth. Living conditions for most working-class urban dwellers were atrocious. They lived in crowded tenement houses and cramped apartments with terrible ventilation and substandard plumbing and sanitation. As a result, disease ran rampant, with typhoid and cholera common. Memphis, Tennessee, experienced waves of cholera (1873) followed by yellow fever (1878 and 1879) that resulted in the loss of over ten thousand lives. By the late 1880s, New York City, Baltimore, Chicago, and New Orleans had all introduced sewage pumping systems to provide efficient waste management. Many cities were also serious fire hazards. An average working-class family of six, with two adults and four children, had at best a two-bedroom tenement. By one 1900 estimate, in the New York City borough of Manhattan alone, there were nearly fifty thousand tenement houses. The photographs of these tenement houses are seen in Jacob Riis's book, *How the Other Half Lives*, discussed in the feature above. Citing a study by the New York State Assembly at this time, Riis found New York to be the most densely populated city in the world, with as many as eight hundred residents per square acre in the Lower East Side working-class slums, comprising the Eleventh and Thirteenth Wards.

Click and Explore

Visit New York City, Tenement Life (http://openstaxcollege.org/l/tenement) to get an impression of the everyday life of tenement dwellers on Manhattan's Lower East Side.

Churches and civic organizations provided some relief to the challenges of working-class city life. Churches were moved to intervene through their belief in the concept of the **social gospel**. This philosophy stated that all Christians, whether they were church leaders or social reformers, should be as concerned about the conditions of life in the secular world as the afterlife, and the Reverend Washington Gladden was a major advocate. Rather than preaching sermons on heaven and hell, Gladden talked about social changes of the time, urging other preachers to follow his lead. He advocated for improvements in daily life and encouraged Americans of all classes to work together for the betterment of society. His sermons included the message to "love thy neighbor" and held that all Americans had to work together to help the masses. As a result of his influence, churches began to include gymnasiums and libraries as well as offer evening classes on hygiene and health care. Other religious organizations like the Salvation Army and the Young Men's Christian Association (YMCA) expanded their reach in American cities at this time as well. Beginning in the 1870s, these organizations began providing community services and other benefits to the urban poor.

In the secular sphere, the **settlement house movement** of the 1890s provided additional relief. Pioneering women such as Jane Addams in Chicago and Lillian Wald in New York led this early progressive reform movement in the United States, building upon ideas originally fashioned by social reformers in England. With no particular religious bent, they worked to create settlement houses in urban centers where they could help the working class, and in particular, working-class women, find aid. Their help included child daycare, evening classes, libraries, gym facilities, and free health care. Addams opened her now-famous Hull House (Figure 19.7) in Chicago in 1889, and Wald's Henry Street Settlement opened in New York six years later. The movement spread quickly to other cities, where they not only provided relief to working-class women but also offered employment opportunities for women graduating college in the growing field of social work. Oftentimes, living in the settlement houses among the women they helped, these college graduates experienced the equivalent of living social classrooms in which to practice their skills, which also frequently caused friction with immigrant women who had their own ideas of reform and self-improvement.

Figure 19.7   Jane Addams opened Hull House in Chicago in 1889, offering services and support to the city's working poor.

The success of the settlement house movement later became the basis of a political agenda that included pressure for housing laws, child labor laws, and worker's compensation laws, among others. Florence Kelley, who originally worked with Addams in Chicago, later joined Wald's efforts in New York; together, they created the National Child Labor Committee and advocated for the subsequent creation of the Children's Bureau in the U.S. Department of Labor in 1912. Julia Lathrop—herself a former resident of Hull House—became the first woman to head a federal government agency, when President William Howard Taft appointed her to run the bureau. Settlement house workers also became influential leaders in the women's suffrage movement as well as the antiwar movement during World War I.

MY STORY

❃ *Jane Addams Reflects on the Settlement House Movement*

Jane Addams was a social activist whose work took many forms. She is perhaps best known as the founder of Hull House in Chicago, which later became a model for settlement houses throughout the country. Here, she reflects on the role that the settlement played.

> Life in the Settlement discovers above all what has been called 'the extraordinary pliability of human nature,' and it seems impossible to set any bounds to the moral capabilities which might unfold under ideal civic and educational conditions. But in order to obtain these conditions, the Settlement recognizes the need of cooperation, both with the radical and the conservative, and from the very nature of the case the Settlement cannot limit its friends to any one political party or economic school.
>
> The Settlement casts side none of those things which cultivated men have come to consider reasonable and goodly, but it insists that those belong as well to that great body of people who, because of toilsome and underpaid labor, are unable to procure them for themselves. Added to this is a profound conviction that the common stock of intellectual enjoyment should not be difficult of access because of the economic position of him who would approach it, that those 'best results of civilization' upon which depend the finer and freer aspects of living must be incorporated into our common life and have free mobility through all elements of society if we would have our democracy endure.
>
> The educational activities of a Settlement, as well its philanthropic, civic, and social undertakings, are but differing manifestations of the attempt to socialize democracy, as is the very existence of the Settlement itself.

In addition to her pioneering work in the settlement house movement, Addams also was active in the women's suffrage movement as well as an outspoken proponent for international peace efforts. She was instrumental in the relief effort after World War I, a commitment that led to her winning the Nobel Peace Prize in 1931.

19.2 The African American "Great Migration" and New European Immigration

By the end of this section, you will be able to:
- Identify the factors that prompted African American and European immigration to American cities in the late nineteenth century
- Explain the discrimination and anti-immigration legislation that immigrants faced in the late nineteenth century

New cities were populated with diverse waves of new arrivals, who came to the cities to seek work in the businesses and factories there. While a small percentage of these newcomers were white Americans seeking jobs, most were made up of two groups that had not previously been factors in the urbanization movement: African Americans fleeing the racism of the farms and former plantations in the South, and southern and eastern European immigrants. These new immigrants supplanted the previous waves of northern and western European immigrants, who had tended to move west to purchase land. Unlike their predecessors, the newer immigrants lacked the funds to strike out to the western lands and instead remained in the urban centers where they arrived, seeking any work that would keep them alive.

THE AFRICAN AMERICAN "GREAT MIGRATION"

Between the end of the Civil War and the beginning of the Great Depression, nearly two million African Americans fled the rural South to seek new opportunities elsewhere. While some moved west, the vast majority of this **Great Migration**, as the large exodus of African Americans leaving the South in the early twentieth century was called, traveled to the Northeast and Upper Midwest. The following cities were the primary destinations for these African Americans: New York, Chicago, Philadelphia, St. Louis, Detroit, Pittsburgh, Cleveland, and Indianapolis. These eight cities accounted for over two-thirds of the total population of the African American migration.

A combination of both "push" and "pull" factors played a role in this movement. Despite the end of the Civil War and the passage of the Thirteenth, Fourteenth, and Fifteenth Amendments to the U.S. Constitution (ensuring freedom, the right to vote regardless of race, and equal protection under the law, respectively), African Americans were still subjected to intense racial hatred. The rise of the Ku Klux Klan in the immediate aftermath of the Civil War led to increased death threats, violence, and a wave of lynchings. Even after the formal dismantling of the Klan in the late 1870s, racially motivated violence continued. According to researchers at the Tuskegee Institute, there were thirty-five hundred racially motivated lynchings and other murders committed in the South between 1865 and 1900. For African Americans fleeing this culture of violence, northern and midwestern cities offered an opportunity to escape the dangers of the South.

In addition to this "push" out of the South, African Americans were also "pulled" to the cities by factors that attracted them, including job opportunities, where they could earn a wage rather than be tied to a landlord, and the chance to vote (for men, at least), supposedly free from the threat of violence. Although many lacked the funds to move themselves north, factory owners and other businesses that sought cheap labor assisted the migration. Often, the men moved first then sent for their families once they were ensconced in their new city life. Racism and a lack of formal education relegated these African American workers to many of the lower-paying unskilled or semi-skilled occupations. More than 80 percent of African American men worked menial jobs in steel mills, mines, construction, and meat packing. In the railroad industry, they were often employed as porters or servants (Figure 19.8). In other businesses, they worked as janitors, waiters, or cooks. African American women, who faced discrimination due to both their race and gender, found a few job opportunities in the garment industry or laundries, but were more often employed as maids and domestic servants. Regardless of the status of their jobs, however, African Americans earned higher wages in the North than they did for the same occupations in the South, and typically found housing to be more available.

(a)   (b)

Figure 19.8 African American men who moved north as part of the Great Migration were often consigned to menial employment, such as working in construction or as porters on the railways (a), such as in the celebrated Pullman dining and sleeping cars (b).

However, such economic gains were offset by the higher cost of living in the North, especially in terms of rent, food costs, and other essentials. As a result, African Americans often found themselves living in overcrowded, unsanitary conditions, much like the tenement slums in which European immigrants lived in the cities. For newly arrived African Americans, even those who sought out the cities for the opportunities they provided, life in these urban centers was exceedingly difficult. They quickly learned that racial discrimination did not end at the Mason-Dixon Line, but continued to flourish in the North as well as the South. European immigrants, also seeking a better life in the cities of the United States, resented the arrival of the African Americans, whom they feared would compete for the same jobs or offer to work at lower wages. Landlords frequently discriminated against them; their rapid influx into the cities created severe housing shortages and even more overcrowded tenements. Homeowners in traditionally white neighborhoods later entered into covenants in which they agreed not to sell to African American buyers; they also often fled neighborhoods into which African Americans had gained successful entry. In addition, some bankers practiced mortgage discrimination, later known as "redlining," in order to deny home loans to qualified buyers. Such pervasive discrimination led to a concentration of African Americans in some of the worst slum areas of most major metropolitan cities, a problem that remained ongoing throughout most of the twentieth century.

So why move to the North, given that the economic challenges they faced were similar to those that African Americans encountered in the South? The answer lies in noneconomic gains. Greater educational opportunities and more expansive personal freedoms mattered greatly to the African Americans who made the trek northward during the Great Migration. State legislatures and local school districts allocated more funds for the education of both blacks and whites in the North, and also enforced compulsory school attendance laws more rigorously. Similarly, unlike the South where a simple gesture (or lack of a deferential one) could result in physical harm to the African American who committed it, life in larger, crowded northern urban centers permitted a degree of anonymity—and with it, personal freedom—that enabled African Americans to move, work, and speak without deferring to every white person with whom they crossed paths. Psychologically, these gains more than offset the continued economic challenges that black migrants faced.

THE CHANGING NATURE OF EUROPEAN IMMIGRATION

Immigrants also shifted the demographics of the rapidly growing cities. Although immigration had always been a force of change in the United States, it took on a new character in the late nineteenth century. Beginning in the 1880s, the arrival of immigrants from mostly southern and eastern European countries rapidly increased while the flow from northern and western Europe remained relatively constant (Table 19.1).

Table 19.1 Cumulative Total of the Foreign-Born Population in the United States, 1870–1910 (by major country of birth and European region)

Region Country	1870	1880	1890	1900	1910
Northern and Western Europe	4,845,679	5,499,889	7,288,917	7,204,649	7,306,325
Germany	1,690,533	1,966,742	2,784,894	2,663,418	2,311,237
Ireland	1,855,827	1,854,571	1,871,509	1,615,459	1,352,251
England	550,924	662,676	908,141	840,513	877,719
Sweden	97,332	194,337	478,041	582,014	665,207
Austria	30,508	38,663	123,271	275,907	626,341
Norway	114,246	181,729	322,665	336,388	403,877
Scotland	140,835	170,136	242,231	233,524	261,076
Southern and Eastern Europe	93,824	248,620	728,851	1,674,648	4,500,932
Italy	17,157	44,230	182,580	484,027	1,343,125
Russia	4,644	35,722	182,644	423,726	1,184,412
Poland	14,436	48,557	147,440	383,407	937,884
Hungary	3,737	11,526	62,435	145,714	495,609
Czechoslovakia	40,289	85,361	118,106	156,891	219,214

The previous waves of immigrants from northern and western Europe, particularly Germany, Great Britain, and the Nordic countries, were relatively well off, arriving in the country with some funds and often moving to the newly settled western territories. In contrast, the newer immigrants from southern and eastern European countries, including Italy, Greece, and several Slavic countries including Russia, came over due to "push" and "pull" factors similar to those that influenced the African Americans arriving from the South. Many were "pushed" from their countries by a series of ongoing famines, by the need to escape religious, political, or racial persecution, or by the desire to avoid compulsory military service. They were also "pulled" by the promise of consistent, wage-earning work.

Whatever the reason, these immigrants arrived without the education and finances of the earlier waves of immigrants, and settled more readily in the port towns where they arrived, rather than setting out to seek their fortunes in the West. By 1890, over 80 percent of the population of New York would be either foreign-born or children of foreign-born parentage. Other cities saw huge spikes in foreign populations as well, though not to the same degree, due in large part to Ellis Island in New York City being the primary port of entry for most European immigrants arriving in the United States.

The number of immigrants peaked between 1900 and 1910, when over nine million people arrived in the United States. To assist in the processing and management of this massive wave of immigrants, the Bureau of Immigration in New York City, which had become the official port of entry, opened Ellis Island in 1892. Today, nearly half of all Americans have ancestors who, at some point in time, entered the country through the portal at Ellis Island. Doctors or nurses inspected the immigrants upon arrival, looking for any signs of infectious diseases (Figure 19.9). Most immigrants were admitted to the country with only a cursory glance at any other paperwork. Roughly 2 percent of the arriving immigrants were denied entry due to a medical condition or criminal history. The rest would enter the country by way of the streets of New York, many unable to speak English and totally reliant on finding those who spoke their native tongue.

Figure 19.9 This photo shows newly arrived immigrants at Ellis Island in New York. Inspectors are examining them for contagious health problems, which could require them to be sent back. (credit: NIAID)

Seeking comfort in a strange land, as well as a common language, many immigrants sought out relatives, friends, former neighbors, townspeople, and countrymen who had already settled in American cities. This led to a rise in ethnic enclaves within the larger city. Little Italy, Chinatown, and many other communities developed in which immigrant groups could find everything to remind them of home, from local language newspapers to ethnic food stores. While these enclaves provided a sense of community to their members, they added to the problems of urban congestion, particularly in the poorest slums where immigrants could afford housing.

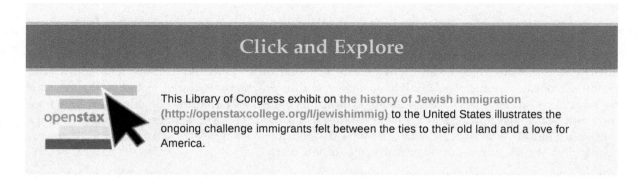

Click and Explore

This Library of Congress exhibit on the history of Jewish immigration (http://openstaxcollege.org/l/jewishimmig) to the United States illustrates the ongoing challenge immigrants felt between the ties to their old land and a love for America.

The demographic shift at the turn of the century was later confirmed by the Dillingham Commission, created by Congress in 1907 to report on the nature of immigration in America; the commission reinforced this ethnic identification of immigrants and their simultaneous discrimination. The report put it simply: These newer immigrants looked and acted differently. They had darker skin tone, spoke languages with which most Americans were unfamiliar, and practiced unfamiliar religions, specifically Judaism and Catholicism. Even the foods they sought out at butchers and grocery stores set immigrants apart. Because of these easily identifiable differences, new immigrants became easy targets for hatred and discrimination. If jobs were hard to find, or if housing was overcrowded, it became easy to blame the immigrants. Like African Americans, immigrants in cities were blamed for the problems of the day.

Growing numbers of Americans resented the waves of new immigrants, resulting in a backlash. The Reverend Josiah Strong fueled the hatred and discrimination in his bestselling book, *Our Country: Its Possible Future and Its Present Crisis*, published in 1885. In a revised edition that reflected the 1890 census records, he clearly identified undesirable immigrants—those from southern and eastern European countries—as a key threat to the moral fiber of the country, and urged all good Americans to face the challenge. Several thousand Americans answered his call by forming the American Protective Association, the chief political activist group to promote legislation curbing immigration into the United States. The group successfully lobbied Congress to adopt both an English language literacy test for immigrants, which eventually passed in 1917, and the Chinese Exclusion Act (discussed in a previous chapter). The group's political lobbying also laid the groundwork for the subsequent Emergency Quota Act of 1921 and the Immigration Act of 1924, as well as the National Origins Act.

Click and Explore

The **global timeline of immigration (http://openstaxcollege.org/l/immig1)** at the Library of Congress offers a summary of immigration policies and the groups affected by it, as well as a compelling overview of different ethnic groups' immigration stories. Browse through to see how different ethnic groups made their way in the United States.

19.3 Relief from the Chaos of Urban Life

By the end of this section, you will be able to:
- Identify how each class of Americans—working class, middle class, and upper class—responded to the challenges associated with urban life
- Explain the process of machine politics and how it brought relief to working-class Americans

Settlement houses and religious and civic organizations attempted to provide some support to working-class city dwellers through free health care, education, and leisure opportunities. Still, for urban citizens, life in the city was chaotic and challenging. But how that chaos manifested and how relief was sought differed greatly, depending on where people were in the social caste—the working class, the upper class, or the newly emerging professional middle class—in addition to the aforementioned issues of race and ethnicity. While many communities found life in the largest American cities disorganized and overwhelming, the ways they answered these challenges were as diverse as the people who lived there. Broad solutions emerged that were typically class specific: The rise of machine politics and popular culture provided relief to the working class, higher education opportunities and suburbanization benefitted the professional middle class, and reminders of their elite status gave comfort to the upper class. And everyone, no matter where they fell in the class system, benefited from the efforts to improve the physical landscapes of the fast-growing urban environment.

THE LIFE AND STRUGGLES OF THE URBAN WORKING CLASS

For the working-class residents of America's cities, one practical way of coping with the challenges of urban life was to take advantage of the system of machine politics, while another was to seek relief in the variety of popular culture and entertainment found in and around cities. Although neither of these forms of relief was restricted to the working class, they were the ones who relied most heavily on them.

Machine Politics

The primary form of relief for working-class urban Americans, and particularly immigrants, came in the form of **machine politics**. This phrase referred to the process by which every citizen of the city, no matter their ethnicity or race, was a ward resident with an alderman who spoke on their behalf at city hall. When everyday challenges arose, whether sanitation problems or the need for a sidewalk along a muddy road, citizens would approach their alderman to find a solution. The aldermen knew that, rather than work through the long bureaucratic process associated with city hall, they could work within the "machine" of local politics to find a speedy, mutually beneficial solution. In machine politics, favors were exchanged for votes, votes were given in exchange for fast solutions, and the price of the solutions included a kickback to the boss. In the short term, everyone got what they needed, but the process was neither transparent nor democratic, and it was an inefficient way of conducting the city's business.

One example of a machine political system was the Democratic political machine **Tammany Hall** in New York, run by machine boss William Tweed with assistance from George Washington Plunkitt (Figure 19.10). There, citizens knew their immediate problems would be addressed in return for their promise of political support in future elections. In this way, machines provided timely solutions for citizens and votes for the politicians. For example, if in Little Italy there was a desperate need for sidewalks in order to improve traffic to the stores on a particular street, the request would likely get bogged down in the bureaucratic red tape at city hall. Instead, store owners would approach the machine. A district captain would approach the "boss" and make him aware of the problem. The boss would contact city politicians and strongly urge them to appropriate the needed funds for the sidewalk in exchange for the promise that the boss would direct votes in their favor in the upcoming election. The boss then used the funds to pay one of his friends for the sidewalk construction, typically at an exorbitant cost, with a financial kickback to the boss, which was known as **graft**. The sidewalk was built more quickly than anyone hoped, in exchange for the citizens' promises to vote for machine-supported candidates in the next elections. Despite its corrupt nature, Tammany Hall essentially ran New York politics from the 1850s until the 1930s. Other large cities, including Boston, Philadelphia, Cleveland, St. Louis, and Kansas City, made use of political machines as well.

Download for free at http://cnx.org/content/col11740/latest/

"THAT'S WHAT'S THE MATTER."

Boss Tweed. " As long as I count the Votes, what are you going to do about it? say?"

Figure 19.10   This political cartoon depicts the control of Boss Tweed, of Tammany Hall, over the election process in New York. Why were people willing to accept the corruption involved in machine politics?

Popular Culture and Entertainment

Working-class residents also found relief in the diverse and omnipresent offerings of popular culture and entertainment in and around cities. These offerings provided an immediate escape from the squalor and difficulties of everyday life. As improved means of internal transportation developed, working-class residents could escape the city and experience one of the popular new forms of entertainment—the amusement park. For example, Coney Island on the Brooklyn shoreline consisted of several different amusement parks, the first of which opened in 1895 (Figure 19.11). At these parks, New Yorkers enjoyed wild rides, animal attractions, and large stage productions designed to help them forget the struggles of their working-day lives. Freak "side" shows fed the public's curiosity about physical deviance. For a mere ten cents, spectators could watch a high-diving horse, take a ride to the moon to watch moon maidens eat green cheese, or witness the electrocution of an elephant, a spectacle that fascinated the public both with technological marvels and exotic wildlife. The treatment of animals in many acts at Coney Island and other public amusement parks drew the attention of middle-class reformers such as the American Society for the Prevention of Cruelty to Animals. Despite questions regarding the propriety of many of the acts, other cities quickly followed New York's lead with similar, if smaller, versions of Coney Island's attractions.

Figure 19.11   The Dreamland Amusement Park tower was just one of Coney Island's amusements.

Click and Explore

openstax   The **American Experience Timeline of Coney Island (http://openstaxcollege.org/l/coney)** shows a timeline, photo gallery, and other elements of Coney Island. Look to see what elements of American culture, from the hot dog to the roller coaster, debuted there.

Another common form of popular entertainment was vaudeville—large stage variety shows that included everything from singing, dancing, and comedy acts to live animals and magic. The vaudeville circuit gave rise to several prominent performers, including magician Harry Houdini, who began his career in these variety shows before his fame propelled him to solo acts. In addition to live theater shows, it was primarily working-class citizens who enjoyed the advent of the nickelodeon, a forerunner to the movie theater. The first nickelodeon opened in Pittsburgh in 1905, where nearly one hundred visitors packed into a storefront theater to see a traditional vaudeville show interspersed with one-minute film clips. Several theaters initially used the films as "chasers" to indicate the end of the show to the live audience so they would clear the auditorium. However, a vaudeville performers' strike generated even greater interest in the films, eventually resulting in the rise of modern movie theaters by 1910.

One other major form of entertainment for the working class was professional baseball (Figure 19.12). Club teams transformed into professional baseball teams with the Cincinnati Red Stockings, now the Cincinnati Reds, in 1869. Soon, professional teams sprang up in several major American cities. Baseball games provided an inexpensive form of entertainment, where for less than a dollar, a person could enjoy a double-header, two hot dogs, and a beer. But more importantly, the teams became a way for newly relocated Americans and immigrants of diverse backgrounds to develop a unified civic identity, all cheering for one team. By 1876, the National League had formed, and soon after, cathedral-style ballparks began to spring up in many cities. Fenway Park in Boston (1912), Forbes Field in Pittsburgh (1909), and the Polo Grounds in New York (1890) all became touch points where working-class Americans came together to support a common cause.

Figure 19.12 Boston's Fenway Park opened in 1912 and was a popular site for working-class Bostonians to spend their leisure time. The "Green Monster," the iconic, left field wall, makes it one of the most recognizable stadiums in baseball today.

Other popular sports included prize-fighting, which attracted a predominantly male, working- and middle-class audience who lived vicariously through the triumphs of the boxers during a time where opportunities for individual success were rapidly shrinking, and college football, which paralleled a modern corporation in its team hierarchy, divisions of duties, and emphasis on time management.

THE UPPER CLASS IN THE CITIES

The American financial elite did not need to crowd into cities to find work, like their working-class counterparts. But as urban centers were vital business cores, where multi-million-dollar financial deals were made daily, those who worked in that world wished to remain close to the action. The rich chose to be in the midst of the chaos of the cities, but they were also able to provide significant measures of comfort, convenience, and luxury for themselves.

Wealthy citizens seldom attended what they considered the crass entertainment of the working class. Instead of amusement parks and baseball games, urban elites sought out more refined pastimes that underscored their knowledge of art and culture, preferring classical music concerts, fine art collections, and social gatherings with their peers. In New York, Andrew Carnegie built Carnegie Hall in 1891, which quickly became the center of classical music performances in the country. Nearby, the Metropolitan Museum of Art opened its doors in 1872 and still remains one of the largest collections of fine art in the world. Other cities followed suit, and these cultural pursuits became a way for the upper class to remind themselves of their elevated place amid urban squalor.

As new opportunities for the middle class threatened the austerity of upper-class citizens, including the newer forms of transportation that allowed middle-class Americans to travel with greater ease, wealthier Americans sought unique ways to further set themselves apart in society. These included more expensive excursions, such as vacations in Newport, Rhode Island, winter relocation to sunny Florida, and frequent trips aboard steamships to Europe. For those who were not of the highly respected "old money," but only recently obtained their riches through business ventures, the relief they sought came in the form of one book—the annual *Social Register*. First published in 1886 by Louis Keller in New York City, the register became a directory of the wealthy socialites who populated the city. Keller updated it annually, and people would watch with varying degrees of anxiety or complacency to see their names appear in print. Also called the *Blue Book*, the register was instrumental in the planning of society dinners, balls, and other social events. For those of newer wealth, there was relief found simply in the notion that they and others witnessed their wealth through the publication of their names in the register.

A NEW MIDDLE CLASS

While the working class were confined to tenement houses in the cities by their need to be close to their work and the lack of funds to find anyplace better, and the wealthy class chose to remain in the cities to stay close to the action of big business transactions, the emerging middle class responded to urban challenges with their own solutions. This group included the managers, salesmen, engineers, doctors, accountants, and other salaried professionals who still worked for a living, but were significantly better educated and compensated than the working-class poor. For this new middle class, relief from the trials of the cities came through education and suburbanization.

In large part, the middle class responded to the challenges of the city by physically escaping it. As transportation improved and outlying communities connected to urban centers, the middle class embraced a new type of community—the suburbs. It became possible for those with adequate means to work in the city and escape each evening, by way of a train or trolley, to a house in the suburbs. As the number of people moving to the suburbs grew, there also grew a perception among the middle class that the farther one lived from the city and the more amenities one had, the more affluence one had achieved.

Although a few suburbs existed in the United States prior to the 1880s (such as Llewellyn Park, New Jersey), the introduction of the electric railway generated greater interest and growth during the last decade of the century. The ability to travel from home to work on a relatively quick and cheap mode of transportation encouraged more Americans of modest means to consider living away from the chaos of the city. Eventually, Henry Ford's popularization of the automobile, specifically in terms of a lower price, permitted more families to own cars and thus consider suburban life. Later in the twentieth century, both the advent of the interstate highway system, along with federal legislation designed to allow families to construct homes with low-interest loans, further sparked the suburban phenomenon.

New Roles for Middle-Class Women

Social norms of the day encouraged middle-class women to take great pride in creating a positive home environment for their working husbands and school-age children, which reinforced the business and educational principles that they practiced on the job or in school. It was at this time that the magazines *Ladies Home Journal* and *Good Housekeeping* began distribution, to tremendous popularity (Figure 19.13).

Figure 19.13 The middle-class family of the late nineteenth century largely embraced a separation of gendered spheres that had first emerged during the market revolution of the antebellum years. Whereas the husband earned money for the family outside the home, the wife oversaw domestic chores, raised the children, and tended to the family's spiritual, social, and cultural needs. The magazine *Good Housekeeping*, launched in 1885, capitalized on the middle-class woman's focus on maintaining a pride-worthy home.

While the vast majority of middle-class women took on the expected role of housewife and homemaker, some women were finding paths to college. A small number of men's colleges began to open their doors to women in the mid-1800s, and co-education became an option. Some of the most elite universities created affiliated women's colleges, such as Radcliffe College with Harvard, and Pembroke College with Brown University. But more importantly, the first women's colleges opened at this time. Mount Holyoke, Vassar, Smith, and Wellesley Colleges, still some of the best known women's schools, opened their doors between 1865 and 1880, and, although enrollment was low (initial class sizes ranged from sixty-one students at Vassar to seventy at Wellesley, seventy-one at Smith, and up to eighty-eight at Mount Holyoke), the opportunity for a higher education, and even a career, began to emerge for young women. These schools offered a unique, all-women environment in which professors and a community of education-seeking young women came together. While most college-educated young women still married, their education offered them new opportunities to work outside the home, most frequently as teachers, professors, or in the aforementioned settlement house environments created by Jane Addams and others.

Education and the Middle Class

Since the children of the professional class did not have to leave school and find work to support their families, they had opportunities for education and advancement that would solidify their position in the middle class. They also benefited from the presence of stay-at-home mothers, unlike working-class children, whose mothers typically worked the same long hours as their fathers. Public school enrollment exploded at this time, with the number of students attending public school tripling from seven million in 1870 to twenty-one million in 1920. Unlike the old-fashioned one-room schoolhouses, larger schools slowly began the practice of employing different teachers for each grade, and some even began hiring discipline-specific instructors. High schools also grew at this time, from one hundred high schools nationally in 1860 to over six thousand by 1900.

The federal government supported the growth of higher education with the Morrill Acts of 1862 and 1890. These laws set aside public land and federal funds to create land-grant colleges that were affordable to middle-class families, offering courses and degrees useful in the professions, but also in trade, commerce, industry, and agriculture (Figure 19.14). Land-grant colleges stood in contrast to the expensive, private Ivy League universities such as Harvard and Yale, which still catered to the elite. Iowa became the first state to accept the provisions of the original Morrill Act, creating what later became Iowa State University. Other states soon followed suit, and the availability of an affordable college education encouraged a boost in enrollment, from 50,000 students nationwide in 1870 to over 600,000 students by 1920.

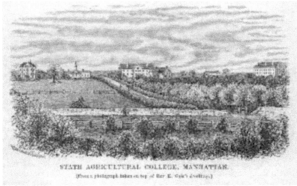

STATE AGRICULTURAL COLLEGE, MANHATTAN.
(From a photograph taken on top of Rev. E. Gale's dwelling.)

Figure 19.14 This rendering of Kansas State University in 1878 shows an early land-grant college, created by the Morrill Act. These newly created schools allowed many more students to attend college than the elite Ivy League system, and focused more on preparing them for professional careers in business, medicine, and law, as well as business, agriculture, and other trades.

College curricula also changed at this time. Students grew less likely to take traditional liberal arts classes in rhetoric, philosophy, and foreign language, and instead focused on preparing for the modern work world. Professional schools for the study of medicine, law, and business also developed. In short, education for the children of middle-class parents catered to class-specific interests and helped ensure that parents could establish their children comfortably in the middle class as well.

"CITY BEAUTIFUL"

While the working poor lived in the worst of it and the wealthy elite sought to avoid it, all city dwellers at the time had to deal with the harsh realities of urban sprawl. Skyscrapers rose and filled the air, streets were crowded with pedestrians of all sorts, and, as developers worked to meet the always-increasing demand for space, the few remaining green spaces in the city quickly disappeared. As the U.S. population became increasingly centered in urban areas while the century drew to a close, questions about the quality of city life—particularly with regard to issues of aesthetics, crime, and poverty—quickly consumed many reformers' minds. Those middle-class and wealthier urbanites who enjoyed the costlier amenities presented by city life—including theaters, restaurants, and shopping—were free to escape to the suburbs, leaving behind the poorer working classes living in squalor and unsanitary conditions. Through the **City Beautiful** movement, leaders such as Frederick Law Olmsted and Daniel Burnham sought to champion middle- and upper-class progressive reforms. They improved the quality of life for city dwellers, but also cultivated middle-class-dominated urban spaces in which Americans of different ethnicities, racial origins, and classes worked and lived.

Olmsted, one of the earliest and most influential designers of urban green space, and the original designer of Central Park in New York, worked with Burnham to introduce the idea of the City Beautiful movement at the Columbian Exposition in 1893. There, they helped to design and construct the "White City"—so named for the plaster of Paris construction of several buildings that were subsequently painted a bright white—an example of landscaping and architecture that shone as an example of perfect city planning. From wide-open green spaces to brightly painted white buildings, connected with modern transportation services and appropriate sanitation, the "White City" set the stage for American urban city planning for the next generation, beginning in 1901 with the modernization of Washington, DC. This model encouraged city planners to consider three principal tenets: First, create larger park areas inside cities; second, build wider boulevards to decrease traffic congestion and allow for lines of trees and other greenery between lanes; and third, add more suburbs in order to mitigate congested living in the city itself (Figure 19.15). As each city adapted these principles in various ways, the City Beautiful movement became a cornerstone of urban development well into the twentieth century.

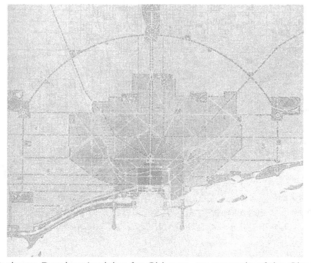

Figure 19.15 This blueprint shows Burnham's vision for Chicago, an example of the City Beautiful movement. His goal was to preserve much of the green space along the city's lakefront, and to ensure that all city dwellers had access to green space.

Download for free at http://cnx.org/content/col11740/latest/

19.4 Change Reflected in Thought and Writing

By the end of this section, you will be able to:
- Explain how American writers, both fiction and nonfiction, helped Americans to better understand the changes they faced in the late nineteenth and early twentieth centuries
- Identify some of the influential women and African American writers of the era

In the late nineteenth century, Americans were living in a world characterized by rapid change. Western expansion, dramatic new technologies, and the rise of big business drastically influenced society in a matter of a few decades. For those living in the fast-growing urban areas, the pace of change was even faster and harder to ignore. One result of this time of transformation was the emergence of a series of notable authors, who, whether writing fiction or nonfiction, offered a lens through which to better understand the shifts in American society.

UNDERSTANDING SOCIAL PROGRESS

One key idea of the nineteenth century that moved from the realm of science to the murkier ground of social and economic success was Charles Darwin's theory of evolution. Darwin was a British naturalist who, in his 1859 work *On the Origin of Species*, made the case that species develop and evolve through natural selection, not through divine intervention. The idea quickly drew fire from the Anglican Church (although a liberal branch of Anglicans embraced the notion of natural selection being part of God's plan) and later from many others, both in England and abroad, who felt that the theory directly contradicted the role of God in the earth's creation. Although biologists, botanists, and most of the scientific establishment widely accepted the theory of evolution at the time of Darwin's publication, which they felt synthesized much of the previous work in the field, the theory remained controversial in the public realm for decades.

Political philosopher Herbert Spencer took Darwin's theory of evolution further, coining the actual phrase "survival of the fittest," and later helping to popularize the phrase social Darwinism to posit that society evolved much like a natural organism, wherein some individuals will succeed due to racially and ethnically inherent traits, and their ability to adapt. This model allowed that a collection of traits and skills, which could include intelligence, inherited wealth, and so on, mixed with the ability to adapt, would let all Americans rise or fall of their own accord, so long as the road to success was accessible to all. William Graham Sumner, a sociologist at Yale, became the most vocal proponent of social Darwinism. Not surprisingly, this ideology, which Darwin himself would have rejected as a gross misreading of his scientific discoveries, drew great praise from those who made their wealth at this time. They saw their success as proof of biological fitness, although critics of this theory were quick to point out that those who did not succeed often did not have the same opportunities or equal playing field that the ideology of social Darwinism purported. Eventually, the concept fell into disrepute in the 1930s and 1940s, as eugenicists began to utilize it in conjunction with their racial theories of genetic superiority.

Other thinkers of the day took Charles Darwin's theories in a more nuanced direction, focusing on different theories of **realism** that sought to understand the truth underlying the changes in the United States. These thinkers believed that ideas and social constructs must be proven to work before they could be accepted. Philosopher William James was one of the key proponents of the closely related concept of **pragmatism**, which held that Americans needed to experiment with different ideas and perspectives to find the truth about American society, rather than assuming that there was truth in old, previously accepted models. Only by tying ideas, thoughts, and statements to actual objects and occurrences could one begin to identify a coherent truth, according to James. His work strongly influenced the subsequent avant-garde and modernist movements in literature and art, especially in understanding the role of the observer, artist, or writer in shaping the society they attempted to observe. John Dewey built on the idea of pragmatism to create a theory of **instrumentalism**, which advocated the use of education in the search for truth. Dewey believed that education, specifically observation and change through the scientific method, was the best tool by which to reform and improve American society as it continued to grow ever more complex. To that end, Dewey strongly encouraged educational reforms designed to create an informed American citizenry that could then form the basis for other, much-needed progressive reforms in society.

In addition to the new medium of photography, popularized by Riis, novelists and other artists also embraced realism in their work. They sought to portray vignettes from real life in their stories, partly in response to the more sentimental works of their predecessors. Visual artists such as George Bellows, Edward Hopper, and Robert Henri, among others, formed the Ashcan School of Art, which was interested primarily in depicting the urban lifestyle that was quickly gripping the United States at the turn of the century. Their works typically focused on working-class city life, including the slums and tenement houses, as well as working-class forms of leisure and entertainment (Figure 19.16).

Figure 19.16 Like most examples of works by Ashcan artists, *The Cliff Dwellers*, by George Wesley Bellows, depicts the crowd of urban life realistically. (credit: Los Angeles County Museum of Art)

Novelists and journalists also popularized realism in literary works. Authors such as Stephen Crane, who wrote stark stories about life in the slums or during the Civil War, and Rebecca Harding Davis, who in 1861 published *Life in the Iron Mills*, embodied this popular style. Mark Twain also sought realism in his books, whether it was the reality of the pioneer spirit, seen in *The Adventures of Huckleberry Finn*, published in 1884, or the issue of corruption in *The Gilded Age*, co-authored with Charles Dudley Warner in 1873. The narratives and visual arts of these realists could nonetheless be highly stylized, crafted, and even fabricated, since their goal was the effective portrayal of social realities they thought required reform. Some authors, such as Jack London, who wrote *Call of the Wild*, embraced a school of thought called **naturalism**, which concluded that the laws of nature and the natural world were the only truly relevant laws governing humanity (Figure 19.17).

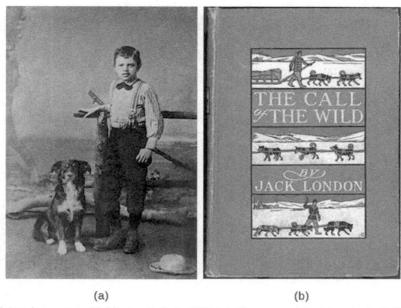

(a)   (b)

Figure 19.17 Jack London poses with his dog Rollo in 1885 (a). The cover of Jack London's *Call of the Wild* (b) shows the dogs in the brutal environment of the Klondike. The book tells the story of Buck, a dog living happily in California until he is sold to be a sled dog in Canada. There, he must survive harsh conditions and brutal behavior, but his innate animal nature takes over and he prevails. The story clarifies the struggle between humanity's nature versus the nurturing forces of society.

Kate Chopin, widely regarded as the foremost woman short story writer and novelist of her day, sought to portray a realistic view of women's lives in late nineteenth-century America, thus paving the way for more explicit feminist literature in generations to come. Although Chopin never described herself as a feminist per se, her reflective works on her experiences as a southern woman introduced a form of creative nonfiction that captured the struggles of women in the United States through their own individual experiences. She also was among the first authors to openly address the race issue of miscegenation. In her work *Desiree's Baby*, Chopin specifically explores the Creole community of her native Louisiana in depths that exposed the reality of racism in a manner seldom seen in literature of the time.

African American poet, playwright, and novelist of the realist period, Paul Laurence Dunbar dealt with issues of race at a time when most reform-minded Americans preferred to focus on other issues. Through his combination of writing in both standard English and black dialect, Dunbar delighted readers with his rich portrayals of the successes and struggles associated with African American life. Although he initially struggled to find the patronage and financial support required to develop a full-time literary career, Dunbar's subsequent professional relationship with literary critic and *Atlantic Monthly* editor William Dean Howells helped to firmly cement his literary credentials as the foremost African American writer of his generation. As with Chopin and Harding, Dunbar's writing highlighted parts of the American experience that were not well understood by the dominant demographic of the country. In their work, these authors provided readers with insights into a world that was not necessarily familiar to them and also gave hidden communities—be it iron mill workers, southern women, or African American men—a sense of voice.

Click and Explore

Mark Twain's lampoon of author Horatio Alger (http://openstaxcollege.org/l/twain1) demonstrates Twain's commitment to realism by mocking the myth set out by Alger, whose stories followed a common theme in which a poor but honest boy goes from rags to riches through a combination of "luck and pluck." See how Twain twists Alger's hugely popular storyline in this piece of satire.

DEFINING "AMERICAN"

✪ *Kate Chopin: An Awakening in an Unpopular Time*

Author Kate Chopin grew up in the American South and later moved to St. Louis, where she began writing stories to make a living after the death of her husband. She published her works throughout the late 1890s, with stories appearing in literary magazines and local papers. It was her second novel, *The Awakening*, which gained her notoriety and criticism in her lifetime, and ongoing literary fame after her death (Figure 19.18).

(a)   (b)

Figure 19.18 Critics railed against Kate Chopin, the author of the 1899 novel *The Awakening*, criticizing its stark portrayal of a woman struggling with societal confines and her own desires. In the twentieth century, scholars rediscovered Chopin's work and *The Awakening* is now considered part of the canon of American literature.

The Awakening, set in the New Orleans society that Chopin knew well, tells the story of a woman struggling with the constraints of marriage who ultimately seeks her own fulfillment over the needs of her family. The book deals far more openly than most novels of the day with questions of women's sexual desires. It also flouted nineteenth-century conventions by looking at the protagonist's struggles with the traditional role expected of women.

While a few contemporary reviewers saw merit in the book, most criticized it as immoral and unseemly. It was censored, called "pure poison," and critics railed against Chopin herself. While Chopin wrote squarely in the tradition of realism that was popular at this time, her work covered ground that was considered "too real" for comfort. After the negative reception of the novel, Chopin retreated from public life and discontinued writing. She died five years after its publication. After her death, Chopin's work was largely ignored, until scholars rediscovered it in the late twentieth century, and her books and stories came back into print. *The Awakening* in particular has been recognized as vital to the earliest edges of the modern feminist movement.

Click and Explore

Excerpts from interviews (http://openstaxcollege.org/l/katechopin) with David Chopin, Kate Chopin's grandson, and a scholar who studies her work provide interesting perspectives on the author and her views.

CRITICS OF MODERN AMERICA

While many Americans at this time, both everyday working people and theorists, felt the changes of the era would lead to improvements and opportunities, there were critics of the emerging social shifts as well. Although less popular than Twain and London, authors such as Edward Bellamy, Henry George, and Thorstein Veblen were also influential in spreading critiques of the industrial age. While their critiques were quite distinct from each other, all three believed that the industrial age was a step in the wrong direction for the country.

In the 1888 novel *Looking Backward, 2000-1887*, Edward Bellamy portrays a utopian America in the year 2000, with the country living in peace and harmony after abandoning the capitalist model and moving to a socialist state. In the book, Bellamy predicts the future advent of credit cards, cable entertainment, and "super-store" cooperatives that resemble a modern day Wal-Mart. *Looking Backward* proved to be a popular bestseller (third only to *Uncle Tom's Cabin* and *Ben Hur* among late nineteenth-century publications) and appealed to those who felt the industrial age of big business was sending the country in the wrong direction. Eugene Debs, who led the national Pullman Railroad Strike in 1894, later commented on how Bellamy's work influenced him to adopt socialism as the answer to the exploitative industrial capitalist model. In addition, Bellamy's work spurred the publication of no fewer than thirty-six additional books or articles by other writers, either supporting Bellamy's outlook or directly criticizing it. In 1897, Bellamy felt compelled to publish a sequel, entitled *Equality*, in which he further explained ideas he had previously introduced concerning educational reform and women's equality, as well as a world of vegetarians who speak a universal language.

Another author whose work illustrated the criticisms of the day was nonfiction writer Henry George, an economist best known for his 1879 work *Progress and Poverty*, which criticized the inequality found in an industrial economy. He suggested that, while people should own that which they create, all land and natural resources should belong to all equally, and should be taxed through a "single land tax" in order to disincentivize private land ownership. His thoughts influenced many economic progressive reformers, as well as led directly to the creation of the now-popular board game, Monopoly.

Another critique of late nineteenth-century American capitalism was Thorstein Veblen, who lamented in *The Theory of the Leisure Class* (1899) that capitalism created a middle class more preoccupied with its own comfort and consumption than with maximizing production. In coining the phrase "conspicuous consumption," Veblen identified the means by which one class of nonproducers exploited the working class that produced the goods for their consumption. Such practices, including the creation of business trusts, served only to create a greater divide between the haves and have-nots in American society, and resulted in economic inefficiencies that required correction or reform.

Key Terms

City Beautiful a movement begun by Daniel Burnham and Fredrick Law Olmsted, who believed that cities should be built with three core tenets in mind: the inclusion of parks within city limits, the creation of wide boulevards, and the expansion of more suburbs

graft the financial kickback provided to city bosses in exchange for political favors

Great Migration the name for the large wave of African Americans who left the South after the Civil War, mostly moving to cities in the Northeast and Upper Midwest

instrumentalism a theory promoted by John Dewey, who believed that education was key to the search for the truth about ideals and institutions

machine politics the process by which citizens of a city used their local ward alderman to work the "machine" of local politics to meet local needs within a neighborhood

naturalism a theory of realism that states that the laws of nature and the natural world were the only relevant laws governing humanity

pragmatism a doctrine supported by philosopher William James, which held that Americans needed to experiment and find the truth behind underlying institutions, religions, and ideas in American life, rather than accepting them on faith

realism a collection of theories and ideas that sought to understand the underlying changes in the United States during the late nineteenth century

settlement house movement an early progressive reform movement, largely spearheaded by women, which sought to offer services such as childcare and free healthcare to help the working poor

social gospel the belief that the church should be as concerned about the conditions of people in the secular world as it was with their afterlife

Social Register a de facto directory of the wealthy socialites in each city, first published by Louis Keller in 1886

Tammany Hall a political machine in New York, run by machine boss William Tweed with assistance from George Washington Plunkitt

Summary

19.1 Urbanization and Its Challenges

Urbanization spread rapidly in the mid-nineteenth century due to a confluence of factors. New technologies, such as electricity and steam engines, transformed factory work, allowing factories to move closer to urban centers and away from the rivers that had previously been vital sources of both water power and transportation. The growth of factories—as well as innovations such as electric lighting, which allowed them to run at all hours of the day and night—created a massive need for workers, who poured in from both rural areas of the United States and from eastern and southern Europe. As cities grew, they were unable to cope with this rapid influx of workers, and the living conditions for the working class were terrible. Tight living quarters, with inadequate plumbing and sanitation, led to widespread illness. Churches, civic organizations, and the secular settlement house movement all sought to provide some relief to the urban working class, but conditions remained brutal for many new city dwellers.

19.2 The African American "Great Migration" and New European Immigration

For both African Americans migrating from the postwar South and immigrants arriving from southeastern Europe, a combination of "push" and "pull" factors influenced their migration to America's urban centers. African Americans moved away from the racial violence and limited opportunities that existed in the rural South, seeking wages and steady work, as well as the opportunity to vote safely as free men; however, they quickly learned that racial discrimination and violence were not limited to the South. For European immigrants, famine and persecution led them to seek a new life in the United States, where, the stories said, the streets were paved in gold. Of course, in northeastern and midwestern cities, both groups found a more challenging welcome than they had anticipated. City residents blamed recent arrivals for the ills of the cities, from overcrowding to a rise in crime. Activist groups pushed for anti-immigration legislation, seeking to limit the waves of immigrants that sought a better future in the United States.

19.3 Relief from the Chaos of Urban Life

The burgeoning cities brought together both rich and poor, working class and upper class; however, the realities of urban dwellers' lives varied dramatically based on where they fell in the social chain. Entertainment and leisure-time activities were heavily dependent on one's status and wealth. For the working poor, amusement parks and baseball games offered inexpensive entertainment and a brief break from the squalor of the tenements. For the emerging middle class of salaried professionals, an escape to the suburbs kept them removed from the city's chaos outside of working hours. And for the wealthy, immersion in arts and culture, as well as inclusion in the *Social Register*, allowed them to socialize exclusively with those they felt were of the same social status. The City Beautiful movement benefitted all city dwellers, with its emphasis on public green spaces, and more beautiful and practical city boulevards. In all, these different opportunities for leisure and pleasure made city life manageable for the citizens who lived there.

19.4 Change Reflected in Thought and Writing

Americans were overwhelmed by the rapid pace and scale of change at the close of the nineteenth century. Authors and thinkers tried to assess the meaning of the country's seismic shifts in culture and society through their work. Fiction writers often used realism in an attempt to paint an accurate portrait of how people were living at the time. Proponents of economic developments and cultural changes cited social Darwinism as an acceptable model to explain why some people succeeded and others failed, whereas other philosophers looked more closely at Darwin's work and sought to apply a model of proof and pragmatism to all ideas and institutions. Other sociologists and philosophers criticized the changes of the era, citing the inequities found in the new industrial economy and its negative effects on workers.

Review Questions

1. Which of the following four elements was *not* essential for creating massive urban growth in late nineteenth-century America?
    A. electric lighting
    B. communication improvements
    C. skyscrapers
    D. settlement houses

2. Which of the following did the settlement house movement offer as a means of relief for working-class women?
    A. childcare

    B. job opportunities
    C. political advocacy
    D. relocation services

3. What technological and economic factors combined to lead to the explosive growth of American cities at this time?

4. Why did African Americans consider moving from the rural South to the urban North following the Civil War?
    A. to be able to buy land

B. to avoid slavery
C. to find wage-earning work
D. to further their education

5. Which of the following is true of late nineteenth-century southern and eastern European immigrants, as opposed to their western and northern European predecessors?
   A. Southern and eastern European immigrants tended to be wealthier.
   B. Southern and eastern European immigrants were, on the whole, more skilled and able to find better paying employment.
   C. Many southern and eastern European immigrants acquired land in the West, while western and northern European immigrants tended to remain in urban centers.
   D. Ellis Island was the first destination for most southern and eastern Europeans.

6. What made recent European immigrants the ready targets of more established city dwellers? What was the result of this discrimination?

7. Which of the following was a popular pastime for working-class urban dwellers?
   A. football games
   B. opera
   C. museums
   D. amusement parks

8. Which of the following was a disadvantage of machine politics?
   A. Immigrants did not have a voice.

B. Taxpayers ultimately paid higher city taxes due to graft.
C. Only wealthy parts of the city received timely responses.
D. Citizens who voiced complaints were at risk for their safety.

9. In what way did education play a crucial role in the emergence of the middle class?

10. Which of the following statements accurately represents Thorstein Veblen's argument in *The Theory of the Leisure Class*?
    A. All citizens of an industrial society would rise or fall based on their own innate merits.
    B. The tenets of naturalism were the only laws through which society should be governed.
    C. The middle class was overly focused on its own comfort and consumption.
    D. Land and natural resources should belong equally to all citizens.

11. Which of the following was *not* an element of realism?
    A. social Darwinism
    B. instrumentalism
    C. naturalism
    D. pragmatism

12. In what ways did writers, photographers, and visual artists begin to embrace more realistic subjects in their work? How were these responses to the advent of the industrial age and the rise of cities?

Critical Thinking Questions

13. What triumphs did the late nineteenth century witness in the realms of industrial growth, urbanization, and technological innovation? What challenges did these developments pose for urban dwellers, workers, and recent immigrants? How did city officials and everyday citizens respond to these challenges?

14. What were the effects of urbanization on the working, middle, and elite classes of American society? Conversely, how did the different social classes and their activities change the scope, character, and use of urban spaces?

15. How do you think that different classes of city dwellers would have viewed the City Beautiful movement? What potential benefits and drawbacks of this new direction in urban planning might members of each class have cited?

16. How was Darwin's work on the evolution of species exploited by proponents of the industrial age? Why might they have latched on to this idea in particular?

17. Historians often mine the arts for clues to the social, cultural, political, and intellectual shifts that characterized a given era. How do the many works of visual art, literature, and social philosophy that emerged from this period reflect the massive changes that were taking place? How were Americans—both those who created these works and those who read or viewed them—struggling to understand the new reality through art, literature, and scholarship?

CHAPTER 20

Politics in the Gilded Age, 1870-1900

Figure 20.1 L. Frank Baum's story of a Kansas girl and the magical land of Oz has become a classic of both film and screen, but it may have originated in part as an allegory of late nineteenth-century politics and the rise of the Populist movement.

Chapter Outline

20.1 Political Corruption in Postbellum America

20.2 The Key Political Issues: Patronage, Tariffs, and Gold

20.3 Farmers Revolt in the Populist Era

20.4 Social and Labor Unrest in the 1890s

Introduction

L. Frank Baum was a journalist who rose to prominence at the end of the nineteenth century. Baum's most famous story, *The Wizard of Oz* (**Figure 20.1**), was published in 1900, but "Oz" first came into being years earlier, when he told a story to a group of schoolchildren visiting his newspaper office in South Dakota. He made up a tale of a wonderful land, and, searching for a name, he allegedly glanced down at his file cabinet, where the bottom drawer was labeled "O-Z." Thus was born the world of Oz, where a girl from struggling Kansas hoped to get help from a "wonderful wizard" who proved to be a fraud. Since then, many have speculated that the story reflected Baum's political sympathies for the Populist Party, which galvanized midwestern and southern farmers' demands for federal reform. Whether he intended the story to act as an allegory for the plight of farmers and workers in late nineteenth-century America, or whether he simply wanted to write an "American fairy tale" set in the heartland, Populists looked for answers much like Dorothy did. And the government in Washington proved to be meek rather than magical.

20.1 Political Corruption in Postbellum America

By the end of this section, you will be able to:
- Discuss the national political scene during the Gilded Age
- Analyze why many critics considered the Gilded Age a period of ineffective national leadership

The challenges Americans faced in the post-Civil War era extended far beyond the issue of Reconstruction and the challenge of an economy without slavery. Political and social repair of the nation was paramount, as was the correlative question of race relations in the wake of slavery. In addition, farmers faced the task of cultivating arid western soils and selling crops in an increasingly global commodities market, while workers in urban industries suffered long hours and hazardous conditions at stagnant wages.

Farmers, who still composed the largest percentage of the U.S. population, faced mounting debts as agricultural prices spiraled downward. These lower prices were due in large part to the cultivation of more acreage using more productive farming tools and machinery, global market competition, as well as price manipulation by commodity traders, exorbitant railroad freight rates, and costly loans upon which farmers depended. For many, their hard work resulted merely in a continuing decline in prices and even greater debt. These farmers, and others who sought leaders to heal the wounds left from the Civil War, organized in different states, and eventually into a national third-party challenge, only to find that, with the end of Reconstruction, federal political power was stuck in a permanent partisan stalemate, and corruption was widespread at both the state and federal levels.

As the **Gilded Age** unfolded, presidents had very little power, due in large part to highly contested elections in which relative popular majorities were razor-thin. Two presidents won the Electoral College without a popular majority. Further undermining their efficacy was a Congress comprising mostly politicians operating on the principle of political patronage. Eventually, frustrated by the lack of leadership in Washington, some Americans began to develop their own solutions, including the establishment of new political parties and organizations to directly address the problems they faced. Out of the frustration

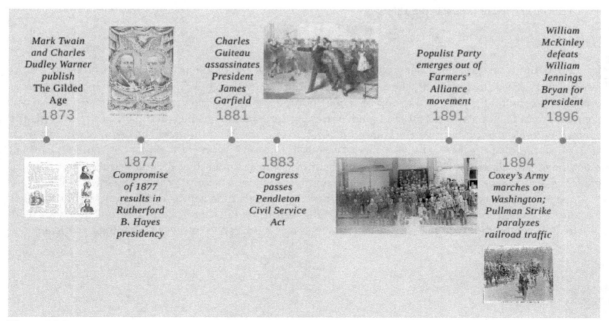

Figure 20.2

wrought by war and presidential political impotence, as well as an overwhelming pace of industrial change, farmers and workers formed a new grassroots reform movement that, at the end of the century, was eclipsed by an even larger, mostly middle-class, Progressive movement. These reform efforts did bring about change—but not without a fight.

THE GILDED AGE

Mark Twain coined the phrase "Gilded Age" in a book he co-authored with Charles Dudley Warner in 1873, *The Gilded Age: A Tale of Today*. The book satirized the corruption of post-Civil War society and politics. Indeed, popular excitement over national growth and industrialization only thinly glossed over the stark economic inequalities and various degrees of corruption of the era (Figure 20.3). Politicians of the time largely catered to business interests in exchange for political support and wealth. Many participated in graft and bribery, often justifying their actions with the excuse that corruption was too widespread for a successful politician to resist. The machine politics of the cities, specifically Tammany Hall in New York, illustrate the kind of corrupt, but effective, local and national politics that dominated the era.

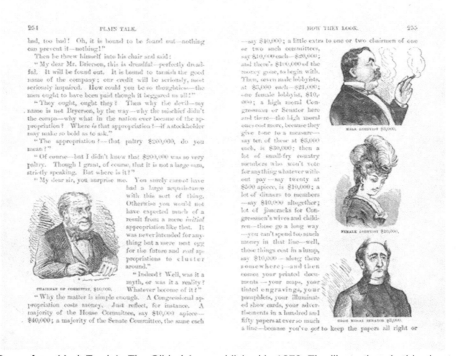

Figure 20.3 Pages from Mark Twain's *The Gilded Age*, published in 1873. The illustrations in this chapter reveal the cost of doing business in Washington in this new age of materialism and corruption, with the cost of obtaining a female lobbyist's support set at $10,000, while that of a male lobbyist or a "high moral" senator can be had for $3,000.

Nationally, between 1872 and 1896, the lack of clear popular mandates made presidents reluctant to venture beyond the interests of their traditional supporters. As a result, for nearly a quarter of a century, presidents had a weak hold on power, and legislators were reluctant to tie their political agendas to such weak leaders. On the contrary, weakened presidents were more susceptible to support various legislators' and lobbyists' agendas, as they owed tremendous favors to their political parties, as well as to key financial contributors, who helped them garner just enough votes to squeak into office through the Electoral College. As a result of this relationship, the rare pieces of legislation passed were largely responses to the desires of businessmen and industrialists whose support helped build politicians' careers.

What was the result of this political malaise? Not surprisingly, almost nothing was accomplished on the federal level. However, problems associated with the tremendous economic growth during this time continued to mount. More Americans were moving to urban centers, which were unable to accommodate the massive numbers of working poor. Tenement houses with inadequate sanitation led to widespread illness. In rural parts of the country, people fared no better. Farmers were unable to cope with the challenges of low prices for their crops and exorbitant costs for everyday goods. All around the country, Americans in need of solutions turned further away from the federal government for help, leading to the rise of fractured and corrupt political groups.

DEFINING "AMERICAN"

⊕ *Mark Twain and the Gilded Age*

Mark Twain (Figure 20.4) wrote *The Gilded Age: A Tale of Today* with his neighbor, Charles Dudley Warner, as a satire about the corrupt politics and lust for power that he felt characterized American society at the time. The book, the only novel Twain ever co-authored, tells of the characters' desire to sell their land to the federal government and become rich. It takes aim at both the government in Washington and those Americans, in the South and elsewhere, whose lust for money and status among the newly rich in the nation's capital leads them to corrupt and foolish choices.

Figure 20.4 Mark Twain was a noted humorist, recognized by most Americans as the greatest writer of his day. He co-wrote the novel *The Gilded Age: A Tale of Today* with Charles Dudley Warner in 1873.

In the following conversation from Chapter Fifty-One of the book, Colonel Sellers instructs young Washington Hawkins on the routine practices of Congress:

> "Now let's figure up a little on, the preliminaries. I think Congress always tries to do as near right as it can, according to its lights. A man can't ask any fairer than that. The first preliminary it always starts out on, is to clean itself, so to speak. It will arraign two or three dozen of its members, or maybe four or five dozen, for taking bribes to vote for this and that and the other bill last winter."
>
> "It goes up into the dozens, does it?"
>
> "Well, yes; in a free country likes ours, where any man can run for Congress and anybody can vote for him, you can't expect immortal purity all the time—it ain't in nature. Sixty or eighty or a hundred and fifty people are bound to get in who are not angels in disguise, as young Hicks the correspondent says; but still it is a very good average; very good indeed. . . . Well, after they have finished the bribery cases, they will take up cases of members who have bought their seats with money. That will take another four weeks."
>
> "Very good; go on. You have accounted for two-thirds of the session."
>
> "Next they will try each other for various smaller irregularities, like the sale of appointments to West Point cadetships, and that sort of thing— . . . "
>
> "How long does it take to disinfect itself of these minor impurities?"
>
> "Well, about two weeks, generally."
>
> "So Congress always lies helpless in quarantine ten weeks of a session. That's encouraging."

The book was a success, in part because it amused people even as it excoriated the politics of the day. For this humor, as well as its astute analysis, Twain and Warner's book still offers entertainment and insight today.

Click and Explore

Visit the **PBS Scrap Book (http://openstaxcollege.org/l/gage)** for information on Mark Twain's life and marriage at the time he wrote *The Gilded Age: A Tale of Today.*

THE ELECTION OF 1876 SETS THE TONE

In many ways, the presidential election of 1876 foreshadowed the politics of the era, in that it resulted in one of the most controversial results in all of presidential history. The country was in the middle of the economic downturn caused by the Panic of 1873, a downturn that would ultimately last until 1879, all but assuring that Republican incumbent Ulysses S. Grant would not be reelected. Instead, the Republican Party nominated a three-time governor from Ohio, Rutherford B. Hayes. Hayes was a popular candidate who advocated for both "hard money"—an economy based upon gold currency transactions—to protect against inflationary pressures and **civil service** reform, that is, recruitment based upon merit and qualifications, which was to replace the practice of handing out government jobs as "spoils." Most importantly, he had no significant political scandals in his past, unlike his predecessor Grant, who suffered through the Crédit Mobilier of America scandal. In this most notorious example of Gilded Age corruption, several congressmen accepted cash and stock bribes in return for appropriating inflated federal funds for the construction of the transcontinental railroad.

The Democrats likewise sought a candidate who could champion reform against growing political corruption. They found their man in Samuel J. Tilden, governor of New York and a self-made millionaire, who had made a successful political career fighting corruption in New York City, including spearheading the prosecution against Tammany Hall Boss William Tweed, who was later jailed. Both parties tapped into the popular mood of the day, each claiming to champion reform and promising an end to the corruption that had become rampant in Washington (Figure 20.5). Likewise, both parties promised an end to post-Civil War Reconstruction.

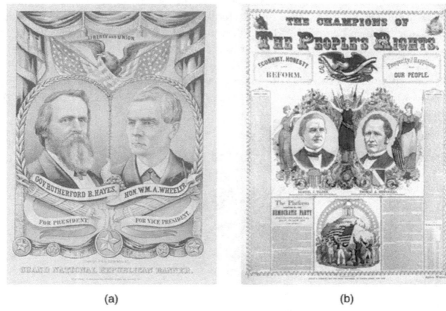

(a)   (b)

Figure 20.5 These campaign posters for Rutherford B. Hayes (a) and Samuel Tilden (b) underscore the tactics of each party, which remained largely unchanged, regardless of the candidates. The Republican placard highlights the party's role in preserving "liberty and union" in the wake of the Civil War, hoping to tap into the northern voters' pride in victory over secession. The Democratic poster addresses the economic turmoil and corruption of the day, specifically that of the Grant administration, promising "honesty, reform, and prosperity" for all.

The campaign was a typical one for the era: Democrats shone a spotlight on earlier Republican scandals, such as the Crédit Mobilier affair, and Republicans relied upon the **bloody shirt campaign**, reminding the nation of the terrible human toll of the war against southern confederates who now reappeared in national politics under the mantle of the Democratic Party. President Grant previously had great success with the "bloody shirt" strategy in the 1868 election, when Republican supporters attacked Democratic candidate Horatio Seymour for his sympathy with New York City draft rioters during the war. In 1876, true to the campaign style of the day, neither Tilden nor Hayes actively campaigned for office, instead relying upon supporters and other groups to promote their causes.

Fearing a significant African American and white Republican voter turnout in the South, particularly in the wake of the Civil Rights Act of 1875, which further empowered African Americans with protection in terms of public accommodations, Democrats relied upon white supremacist terror organizations to intimidate blacks and Republicans, including physically assaulting many while they attempted to vote. The Redshirts, based in Mississippi and the Carolinas, and the White League in Louisiana, relied upon intimidation tactics similar to the Ku Klux Klan but operated in a more open and organized fashion with the sole goal of restoring Democrats to political predominance in the South. In several instances, Redshirts would attack freedmen who attempted to vote, whipping them openly in the streets while simultaneously hosting barbecues to attract Democratic voters to the polls. Women throughout South Carolina began to sew red flannel shirts for the men to wear as a sign of their political views; women themselves began wearing red ribbons in their hair and bows about their waists.

The result of the presidential election, ultimately, was close. Tilden won the popular vote by nearly 300,000 votes; however, he had only 184 electoral votes, with 185 needed to proclaim formal victory. Three states, Florida, Louisiana, and South Carolina, were in dispute due to widespread charges of voter fraud and miscounting. Questions regarding the validity of one of the three electors in Oregon cast further doubt on the final vote; however, that state subsequently presented evidence to Congress confirming all three electoral votes for Hayes.

As a result of the disputed election, the House of Representatives established a special electoral commission to determine which candidate won the challenged electoral votes of these three states. In what later became known as the Compromise of 1877, Republican Party leaders offered southern Democrats an enticing deal. The offer was that if the commission found in favor of a Hayes victory, Hayes would order the withdrawal of the remaining U.S. troops from those three southern states, thus allowing the collapse of the radical Reconstruction governments of the immediate post-Civil War era. This move would permit southern Democrats to end federal intervention and control their own states' fates in the wake of the end of slavery (Figure 20.6).

Figure 20.6   Titled "A Truce not a Compromise," this cartoon suggests the lack of consensus after the election of 1876 could have ended in another civil war.

After weeks of deliberation, the electoral commission voted eight to seven along straight party lines, declaring Hayes the victor in each of the three disputed states. As a result, Hayes defeated Tilden in the electoral vote by a count of 185–184 and became the next president. By April of that year, radical Reconstruction ended as promised, with the removal of federal troops from the final two Reconstruction states, South Carolina and Louisiana. Within a year, Redeemers—largely Southern Democrats—had regained control of the political and social fabric of the South.

Although unpopular among the voting electorate, especially among African Americans who referred to it as "The Great Betrayal," the compromise exposed the willingness of the two major political parties to avoid a "stand-off" via a southern Democrat filibuster, which would have greatly prolonged the final decision regarding the election. Democrats were largely satisfied to end Reconstruction and maintain "home rule" in the South in exchange for control over the White House. Likewise, most realized that Hayes would likely be a one-term president at best and prove to be as ineffectual as his pre-Civil War predecessors.

Perhaps most surprising was the lack of even greater public outrage over such a transparent compromise, indicative of the little that Americans expected of their national government. In an era where voter turnout remained relatively high, the two major political parties remained largely indistinguishable in their agendas as well as their propensity for questionable tactics and backroom deals. Likewise, a growing belief in laissez-faire principles as opposed to reforms and government intervention (which many Americans believed contributed to the outbreak of the Civil War) led even more Americans to accept the nature of an inactive federal government (Figure 20.7).

Download for free at http://cnx.org/content/col11740/latest/

Figure 20.7 Powerful Republican Party leader Roscoe Conkling is shown here as the devil. Hayes walks off with the prize of the 1876 election, the South, personified as a woman. The cartoon, drawn by Joseph Keppler, has a caption that quotes Goethe: "Unto that Power he doth belong Which only doeth Right while ever willing Wrong."

20.2 The Key Political Issues: Patronage, Tariffs, and Gold

By the end of this section, you will be able to:
- Explain the difference between the spoils system and civil service, and discuss the importance of this issue in the period from 1872 to 1896
- Recognize the ways in which the issue of tariffs impacted different sectors of the economy in late nineteenth-century America
- Explain why Americans were split on the issue of a national gold standard versus free coinage of silver
- Explain why political patronage was a key issue for political parties in the late nineteenth century

Although Hayes' questionable ascendancy to the presidency did not create political corruption in the nation's capital, it did set the stage for politically motivated agendas and widespread inefficiency in the White House for the next twenty-four years. Weak president after weak president took office, and, as mentioned above, not one incumbent was reelected. The populace, it seemed, preferred the devil they *didn't* know to the one they did. Once elected, presidents had barely enough power to repay the political favors they owed to the individuals who ensured their narrow victories in cities and regions around the country. Their four years in office were spent repaying favors and managing the powerful relationships that put them in the White House. Everyday Americans were largely left on their own. Among the few political issues that presidents routinely addressed during this era were ones of patronage, tariffs, and the nation's monetary system.

PATRONAGE: THE SPOILS SYSTEM VS CIVIL SERVICE

At the heart of each president's administration was the protection of the spoils system, that is, the power of the president to practice widespread political patronage. Patronage, in this case, took the form of the president naming his friends and supporters to various political posts. Given the close calls in presidential elections during the era, the maintenance of political machinery and repaying favors with patronage was important to all presidents, regardless of party affiliation. This had been the case since the advent of a two-party political system and universal male suffrage in the Jacksonian era. For example, upon assuming office in March 1829, President Jackson immediately swept employees from over nine hundred political offices, amounting to 10 percent of all federal appointments. Among the hardest-hit was the U.S. Postal Service, which saw Jackson appoint his supporters and closest friends to over four hundred positions in the service (Figure 20.8).

Figure 20.8 This political cartoon shows Andrew Jackson riding a pig, which is walking over "fraud," "bribery," and "spoils," and feeding on "plunder."

As can be seen in the table below (Table 20.1), every single president elected from 1876 through 1892 won despite receiving less than 50 percent of the popular vote. This established a repetitive cycle of relatively weak presidents who owed many political favors, which could be repaid through one prerogative power: patronage. As a result, the spoils system allowed those with political influence to ascend to powerful positions within the government, regardless of their level of experience or skill, thus compounding both the inefficiency of government as well as enhancing the opportunities for corruption.

Table 20.1 U.S. Presidential Election Results (1876–1896)

Year	Candidates	Popular Vote	Percentage	Electoral Vote
1876	Rutherford B. Hayes	4,034,132	47.9%	185
	Samuel Tilden	4,286,808	50.9%	184
	Others	97,709	1.2%	0
1880	James Garfield	4,453,337	48.3%	214

Table 20.1 U.S. Presidential Election Results (1876–1896)

Year	Candidates	Popular Vote	Percentage	Electoral Vote
	Winfield Hancock	4,444,267	48.2%	155
	Others	319,806	3.5%	0
1884	Grover Cleveland	4,914,482	48.8%	219
	James Blaine	4,856,903	48.3%	182
	Others	288,660	2.9%	0
1888	Benjamin Harrison	5,443,663	47.8%	233
	Grover Cleveland	5,538,163	48.6%	168
	Others	407,050	3.6%	0
1892	Grover Cleveland	5,553,898	46.0%	277
	Benjamin Harrison	5,190,799	43.0%	145
	Others	1,323,330	11.0%	22
1896	William McKinley	7,112,138	51.0%	271
	William Jennings Bryan	6,510,807	46.7%	176
	Others	315,729	2.3%	0

At the same time, a movement emerged in support of reforming the practice of political appointments. As early as 1872, civil service reformers gathered to create the Liberal Republican Party in an effort to unseat incumbent President Grant. Led by several midwestern Republican leaders and newspaper editors, this party provided the impetus for other reform-minded Republicans to break free from the party and actually join the Democratic Party ranks. With newspaper editor Horace Greeley as their candidate, the party called for a "thorough reform of the civil service as one the most pressing necessities" facing the nation. Although easily defeated in the election that followed, the work of the Liberal Republican Party set the stage for an even stronger push for patronage reform.

Clearly owing favors to his Republican handlers for his surprise compromise victory by the slimmest of margins in 1876, President Hayes was ill-prepared to heed those cries for reform, despite his own stated preference for a new civil service system. In fact, he accomplished little during his four years in office other than granting favors, as dictated by Republic Party handlers. Two powerful Republican leaders attempted to control the president. The first was Roscoe Conkling, Republican senator from New York and leader of the **Stalwarts**, a group that strongly supported continuation of the current spoils system (Figure 20.9). Long supporting former President Grant, Conkling had no sympathy for some of Hayes' early appeals for civil service reform. The other was James G. Blaine, Republican senator from Maine and leader of the **Half-Breeds**. The Half-Breeds, who received their derogatory nickname from Stalwart supporters who considered Blaine's group to be only "half-Republican," advocated for some measure of civil service reform.

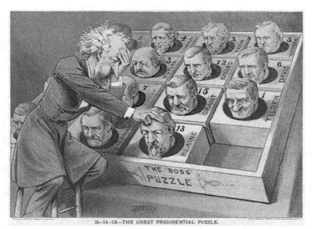

15—14—13—THE GREAT PRESIDENTIAL PUZZLE.

Figure 20.9 This cartoon shows Roscoe Conkling playing a popular puzzle game of the day with the heads of potential Republican presidential candidates, illustrating his control over the picks of the party.

With his efforts towards ensuring African American civil rights stymied by a Democratic Congress, and his decision to halt the coinage of silver merely adding to the pressures of the economic Panic of 1873, Hayes failed to achieve any significant legislation during his presidency. However, he did make a few overtures towards civil service reform. First, he adopted a new patronage rule, which held that a person appointed to an office could be dismissed only in the interest of efficient government operation but not for overtly political reasons. Second, he declared that party leaders could have no official say in political appointments, although Conkling sought to continue his influence. Finally, he decided that government appointees were ineligible to manage campaign elections. Although not sweeping reforms, these were steps in a civil service direction.

Hayes' first target in his meager reform effort was to remove Chester A. Arthur, a strong Conkling man, from his post as head of the New York City Customs House. Arthur had been notorious for using his post as customs collector to gain political favors for Conkling. When Hayes forcibly removed him from the position, even Half-Breeds questioned the wisdom of the move and began to distance themselves from Hayes. The loss of his meager public support due to the Compromise of 1877 and the declining Congressional faction together sealed Hayes fate and made his reelection impossible.

AN ASSASSIN'S BULLET SETS THE STAGE FOR CIVIL SERVICE REFORM

In the wake of President Hayes' failure, Republicans began to battle over a successor for the 1880 presidential election. Initially, Stalwarts favored Grant's return to the White House, while Half-Breeds promoted their leader, James Blaine. Following an expected convention deadlock, both factions agreed to a compromise presidential candidate, Senator James A. Garfield of Ohio, with Chester Arthur as his vice-presidential running mate. The Democratic Party turned to Winfield Scott Hancock, a former Union commander who was a hero of the Battle of Gettysburg, as their candidate.

Garfield won a narrow victory over Hancock by forty thousand votes, although he still did not win a majority of the popular vote. But less than four months into his presidency, events pushed civil service reform on the fast track. On July 2, 1881, Charles Guiteau shot and killed Garfield (Figure 20.10), allegedly uttering at the time, "I am a Stalwart of Stalwarts!" Guiteau himself had wanted to be rewarded for his political support—he had written a speech for the Garfield campaign—with an ambassadorship to France. His actions at the time were largely blamed on the spoils system, prompting more urgent cries for change.

Figure 20.10 Garfield's shooting and the subsequent capture of the assassin, Charles Guiteau, are depicted in this illustration for a newspaper of the day. The president clung to life for another two months after the assassination.

DEFINING "AMERICAN"

❂ *The Assassination of a President*

> I executed
> the Divine command.
> And Garfield did remove,
> To save my party,
> and my country
> From the bitter fate of War.
> —Charles Guiteau

Charles Guiteau was a lawyer and supporter of the Republican Party, although not particularly well known in either area. But he gave a few speeches, to modest crowds, in support of the Republican nominee James Garfield, and ultimately deluded himself that his speeches influenced the country enough to cause Garfield's victory. After the election, Guiteau immediately began pressuring the new president, requesting a post as ambassador. When his queries went unanswered, Guiteau, out of money and angry that his supposed help had been ignored, planned to kill the president.

He spent significant time planning his attack and considered weapons as diverse as dynamite and a stiletto before deciding on a gun, stating, "I wanted it done in an American manner." He followed the president around the Capitol and let several opportunities pass, unwilling to kill Garfield in front of his wife or son. Frustrated with himself, Guiteau recommitted to the plan and wrote a letter to the White House, explaining how this act would "unite the Republican Party and save the Republic."

Guiteau shot the president from behind and continued to shoot until police grabbed him and hauled him away. He went to jail, and, the following November after Garfield had died, he stood trial for murder. His poor mental health, which had been evident for some time, led to eccentric courtroom behavior that the newspapers eagerly reported and the public loved. He defended his case with a poem that used religious imagery and suggested that God had ordered him to commit the murder. He defended himself in court by saying, "The doctors killed Garfield, I just shot him." While this in fact was true, it did not save him. Guiteau was convicted and hanged in the summer of 1882.

Click and Explore

Take a look at **America's Story (http://openstaxcollege.org/l/guiteau)** from the Library of Congress, which highlights the fact that Guiteau in fact did not kill the president, but rather infection from his medical treatment did.

Surprising both his party and the Democrats when he assumed the office of president, Chester Arthur immediately distanced himself from the Stalwarts. Although previously a loyal party man, Arthur understood that he owed his current position to no particular faction or favor. He was in the unique position to usher in a wave a civil service reform unlike any other political candidate, and he chose to do just that. In 1883, he signed into law the Pendleton Civil Service Act, the first significant piece of antipatronage legislation. This law created the Civil Service Commission, which listed all government patronage jobs and then set aside 15 percent of the list as appointments to be determined through a competitive civil service examination process. Furthermore, to prevent future presidents from undoing this reform, the law declared that future presidents could enlarge the list but could never shrink it by moving a civil service job back into the patronage column.

TARIFFS IN THE GILDED AGE

In addition to civil service, President Arthur also carried the reformist spirit into the realm of tariffs, or taxes on international imports to the United States. Tariffs had long been a controversial topic in the United States, especially as the nineteenth century came to a close. Legislators appeared to be bending to the will of big businessmen who desired higher tariffs in order to force Americans to buy their domestically produced goods rather than higher-priced imports. Lower tariffs, on the other hand, would reduce prices and lower the average American's cost of living, and were therefore favored by many working-class families and farmers, to the extent that any of them fully understood such economic forces beyond the prices they paid at stores. Out of growing concern for the latter group, Arthur created the U.S. Tariff Commission in 1882 to investigate the propriety of increasingly high tariffs. Despite his concern, along with the commission's recommendation for a 25 percent rollback in most tariffs, the most Arthur could accomplish was the "Mongrel Tariff" of 1883, which lowered tariff rates by barely 5 percent.

Such bold attempts at reform further convinced Republican Party leaders, as the 1884 election approached, that Arthur was not their best option to continue in the White House. Arthur quickly found himself a man without a party. As the 1884 election neared, the Republican Party again searched their ranks for a candidate who could restore some semblance of the spoils system while maintaining a reformist image. Unable to find such a man, the predominant Half-Breeds again turned to their own leader, Senator Blaine. However, when news of his many personal corrupt bargains began to surface, a significant portion of the party chose to break from the traditional Stalwarts-versus-Half-Breeds debate and form their own faction, the **Mugwumps**, a name taken from the Algonquin phrase for "great chief."

Anxious to capitalize on the disarray within the Republican Party, as well as to return to the White House for the first time in nearly thirty years, the Democratic Party chose to court the Mugwump vote by nominating Grover Cleveland, the reform governor from New York who had built a reputation by attacking machine politics in New York City. Despite several personal charges against him for having fathered a child out of wedlock, Cleveland managed to hold on for a close victory with a margin of less than thirty thousand votes.

Cleveland's record on civil service reform added little to the initial blows struck by President Arthur. After electing the first Democratic president since 1856, the Democrats could actually make great use of the spoils system. Cleveland was, however, a notable reform president in terms of business regulation and tariffs. When the U.S. Supreme Court ruled in 1886 that individual states could not regulate interstate transportation, Cleveland urged Congress to pass the Interstate Commerce Act of 1887. Among several other powers, this law created the Interstate Commerce Commission (ICC) to oversee railroad prices and ensure that they remained reasonable to all customers. This was an important shift. In the past, railroads had granted special rebates to big businesses, such as John D. Rockefeller's Standard Oil, while charging small farmers with little economic muscle exorbitant rates. Although the act eventually provided for real regulation of the railroad industry, initial progress was slow due to the lack of enforcement power held by the ICC. Despite its early efforts to regulate railroad rates, the U.S. Supreme Court undermined the commission in *Interstate Commerce Commission v. Cincinnati, New Orleans, and Texas Pacific Railway Cos.* in 1897. Rate regulations were limits on profits that, in the opinion of a majority of the justices, violated the Fourteenth Amendment protection against depriving persons of their property without due process of the law.

As for tariff reform, Cleveland agreed with Arthur's position that tariffs remained far too high and were clearly designed to protect big domestic industries at the expense of average consumers who could benefit from international competition. While the general public applauded Cleveland's efforts at both civil service and tariff reform, influential businessmen and industrialists remained adamant that the next president must restore the protective tariffs at all costs.

To counter the Democrats' re-nomination of Cleveland, the Republican Party turned to Benjamin Harrison, grandson of former president William Henry Harrison. Although Cleveland narrowly won the overall popular vote, Harrison rode the influential coattails of several businessmen and party bosses to win the key electoral states of New York and New Jersey, where party officials stressed Harrison's support for a higher tariff, and thus secure the White House. Not surprisingly, after Harrison's victory, the United States witnessed a brief return to higher tariffs and a strengthening of the spoils system. In fact, the McKinley Tariff raised some rates as much as 50 percent, which was the highest tariff in American history to date.

Some of Harrison's policies were intended to offer relief to average Americans struggling with high costs and low wages, but remained largely ineffective. First, the Sherman Anti-Trust Act of 1890 sought to prohibit business monopolies as "conspiracies in restraint of trade," but it was seldom enforced during the first decade of its existence. Second, the Sherman Silver Purchase Act of the same year required the U.S. Treasury to mint over four million ounces of silver into coins each month to circulate more cash into the economy, raise prices for farm goods, and help farmers pay their way out of debt. But the measure could not undo the previous "hard money" policies that had deflated prices and pulled farmers into well-entrenched cycles of debt. Other measures proposed by Harrison intended to support African Americans, including a Force Bill to protect voters in the South, as well as an Education Bill designed to support public education and improve literacy rates among African Americans, also met with defeat.

MONETARY POLICIES AND THE ISSUE OF GOLD VS SILVER

Although political corruption, the spoils system, and the question of tariff rates were popular discussions of the day, none were more relevant to working-class Americans and farmers than the issue of the nation's monetary policy and the ongoing debate of gold versus silver (**Figure 20.11**). There had been frequent attempts to establish a bimetallic standard, which in turn would have created inflationary pressures and placed more money into circulation that could have subsequently benefitted farmers. But the government remained committed to the gold standard, including the official demonetizing of silver altogether in 1873. Such a stance greatly benefitted prominent businessmen engaged in foreign trade while forcing more farmers and working-class Americans into greater debt.

Figure 20.11 This cartoon illustrates the potential benefits of a bimetal system, but the benefits did not actually extend to big business, which preferred the gold standard and worked to keep it.

As farmers and working-class Americans sought the means by which to pay their bills and other living expenses, especially in the wake of increased tariffs as the century came to a close, many saw adherence to a strict gold standard as their most pressing problem. With limited gold reserves, the money supply remained constrained. At a minimum, a return to a bimetallic policy that would include the production of silver dollars would provide some relief. However, the aforementioned Sherman Silver Purchase Act was largely ineffective to combat the growing debts that many Americans faced. Under the law, the federal government purchased 4.5 million ounces of silver on a monthly basis in order to mint silver dollars. However, many investors exchanged the bank notes with which the government purchased the silver for gold, thus severely depleting the nation's gold reserve. Fearing the latter, President Grover Cleveland signed the act's repeal in 1893. This lack of meaningful monetary measures from the federal government would lead one group in particular who required such assistance—American farmers—to attempt to take control over the political process itself.

20.3 Farmers Revolt in the Populist Era

By the end of this section, you will be able to:
- Understand how the economic and political climate of the day promoted the formation of the farmers' protest movement in the latter half of the nineteenth century
- Explain how the farmers' revolt moved from protest to politics

The challenges that many American farmers faced in the last quarter of the nineteenth century were significant. They contended with economic hardships born out of rapidly declining farm prices, prohibitively high tariffs on items they needed to purchase, and foreign competition. One of the largest challenges they faced was overproduction, where the glut of their products in the marketplace drove the price lower and lower.

Overproduction of crops occurred in part due to the westward expansion of homestead farms and in part because industrialization led to new farm tools that dramatically increased crop yields. As farmers fell deeper into debt, whether it be to the local stores where they bought supplies or to the railroads that shipped their produce, their response was to increase crop production each year in the hope of earning more money with which to pay back their debt. The more they produced, the lower prices dropped. To a hard-working farmer, the notion that their own overproduction was the greatest contributing factor to their debt was a completely foreign concept (Figure 20.12).

Figure 20.12 This North Dakota sod hut, built by a homesteading farmer for his family, was photographed in 1898, two years after it was built. While the country was quickly industrializing, many farmers still lived in rough, rural conditions.

In addition to the cycle of overproduction, tariffs were a serious problem for farmers. Rising tariffs on industrial products made purchased items more expensive, yet tariffs were *not* being used to keep farm prices artificially high as well. Therefore, farmers were paying inflated prices but not receiving them. Finally, the issue of gold versus silver as the basis of U.S. currency was a very real problem to many farmers. Farmers needed more money in circulation, whether it was paper or silver, in order to create inflationary pressure. Inflationary pressure would allow farm prices to increase, thus allowing them to earn more money that they could then spend on the higher-priced goods in stores. However, in 1878, federal law set the amount of paper money in circulation, and, as mentioned above, Harrison's Sherman Silver Act, intended to increase the amount of silver coinage, was too modest to do any real good, especially in light of the unintended consequence of depleting the nation's gold reserve. In short, farmers had a big stack of bills and wanted a big stack of money—be it paper or silver—to pay them. Neither was forthcoming from a government that cared more about issues of patronage and how to stay in the White House for more than four years at a time.

FARMERS BEGIN TO ORGANIZE

The initial response by increasingly frustrated and angry farmers was to organize into groups that were similar to early labor unions. Taking note of how the industrial labor movement had unfolded in the last quarter of the century, farmers began to understand that a collective voice could create significant pressure among political leaders and produce substantive change. While farmers had their own challenges, including that of geography and diverse needs among different types of famers, they believed this model to be useful to their cause.

One of the first efforts to organize farmers came in 1867 with Oliver Hudson Kelly's creation of the Patrons of Husbandry, more popularly known as the **Grange**. In the wake of the Civil War, the Grangers quickly grew to over 1.5 million members in less than a decade (Figure 20.13). Kelly believed that farmers could best help themselves by creating farmers' cooperatives in which they could pool resources and obtain better shipping rates, as well as prices on seeds, fertilizer, machinery, and other necessary inputs. These cooperatives, he believed, would let them self-regulate production as well as collectively obtain better rates from railroad companies and other businesses.

Figure 20.13 This print from the early 1870s, with scenes of farm life, was a promotional poster for the Grangers, one of the earliest farmer reform groups.

At the state level, specifically in Wisconsin, Minnesota, Illinois, and Iowa, the Patrons of Husbandry did briefly succeed in urging the passage of Granger Laws, which regulated some railroad rates along with the prices charged by grain elevator operators. The movement also created a political party—the Greenback Party, so named for its support of print currency (or "greenbacks") not based upon a gold standard—which saw brief success with the election of fifteen congressmen. However, such successes were short-lived and had little impact on the lives of everyday farmers. In the Wabash case of 1886, brought by the Wabash, St. Louis, and Pacific Railroad Company, the U.S. Supreme Court ruled against the State of Illinois for passing Granger Laws controlling railroad rates; the court found such laws to be unconstitutional. Their argument held that states did not have the authority to control interstate commerce. As for the Greenback Party, when only seven delegates appeared at an 1888 national convention of the group, the party faded from existence.

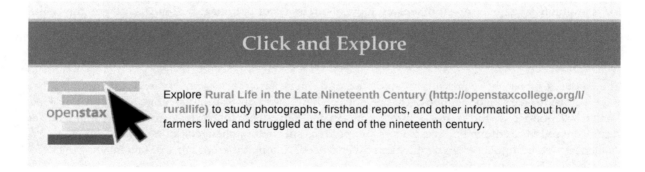

Click and Explore

Explore Rural Life in the Late Nineteenth Century (http://openstaxcollege.org/l/rurallife) to study photographs, firsthand reports, and other information about how farmers lived and struggled at the end of the nineteenth century.

The **Farmers' Alliance**, a conglomeration of three regional alliances formed in the mid-1880s, took root in the wake of the Grange movement. In 1890, Dr. Charles Macune, who led the Southern Alliance, which was based in Texas and had over 100,000 members by 1886, urged the creation of a national alliance between his organization, the Northwest Alliance, and the Colored Alliance, the largest African American organization in the United States. Led by Tom Watson, the Colored Alliance, which was founded in Texas but quickly spread throughout the Old South, counted over one million members. Although they originally advocated for self-help, African Americans in the group soon understood the benefits of political organization and a unified voice to improve their plight, regardless of race. While racism kept the alliance splintered among the three component branches, they still managed to craft a national agenda that appealed to their large membership. All told, the Farmers' Alliance brought together over 2.5 million members, 1.5 million white and 1 million black (Figure 20.14).

Figure 20.14 The Farmers' Alliance flag displays the motto: "The most good for the most PEOPLE," clearly a sentiment they hoped that others would believe.

The alliance movement, and the subsequent political party that emerged from it, also featured prominent roles for women. Nearly 250,000 women joined the movement due to their shared interest in the farmers' worsening situation as well as the promise of being a full partner with political rights within the group, which they saw as an important step towards advocacy for women's suffrage on a national level. The ability to vote and stand for office within the organization encouraged many women who sought similar rights on the larger American political scene. Prominent alliance spokeswoman, Mary Elizabeth Lease of Kansas, often spoke of membership in the Farmers' Alliance as an opportunity to "raise less corn and more hell!"

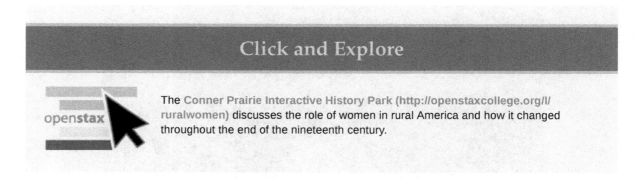

Click and Explore

The Conner Prairie Interactive History Park (http://openstaxcollege.org/l/ruralwomen) discusses the role of women in rural America and how it changed throughout the end of the nineteenth century.

The alliance movement had several goals similar to those of the original Grange, including greater regulation of railroad prices and the creation of an inflationary national monetary policy. However, most creative among the solutions promoted by the Farmers' Alliance was the call for a subtreasury plan. Under this plan, the federal government would store farmers' crops in government warehouses for a brief period of time, during which the government would provide loans to farmers worth 80 percent of the current crop prices. Thus, farmers would have immediate cash on hand with which to settle debts and purchase goods, while their crops sat in warehouses and farm prices increased due to this control over supply at the market. When market prices rose sufficiently high enough, the farmer could withdraw his crops, sell at the higher price, repay the government loan, and still have profit remaining.

Economists of the day thought the plan had some merit; in fact, a greatly altered version would subsequently be adopted during the Great Depression of the 1930s, in the form of the Agricultural Adjustment Act. However, the federal government never seriously considered the plan, as congressmen questioned the propriety of the government serving as a rural creditor making loans to farmers with no assurance that production controls would result in higher commodity prices. The government's refusal to act on the proposal left many farmers wondering what it would take to find solutions to their growing indebtedness.

FROM ORGANIZATION TO POLITICAL PARTY

Angry at the federal government's continued unwillingness to substantively address the plight of the average farmer, Charles Macune and the Farmers' Alliance chose to create a political party whose representatives—if elected—could enact real change. Put simply, if the government would not address the problem, then it was time to change those elected to power.

In 1891, the alliance formed the **Populist Party**, or People's Party, as it was more widely known. Beginning with nonpresidential-year elections, the Populist Party had modest success, particularly in Kansas, Nebraska, and the Dakotas, where they succeeded in electing several state legislators, one governor, and a handful of congressmen. As the 1892 presidential election approached, the Populists chose to model themselves after the Democratic and Republican Parties in the hope that they could shock the country with a "third-party" victory.

At their national convention that summer in Omaha, Nebraska, they wrote the Omaha Platform to more fully explain to all Americans the goals of the new party (Figure 20.15). Written by Ignatius Donnelly, the platform statement vilified railroad owners, bankers, and big businessmen as all being part of a widespread conspiracy to control farmers. As for policy changes, the platform called for adoption of the subtreasury plan, government control over railroads, an end to the national bank system, the creation of a federal income tax, the direct election of U.S. senators, and several other measures, all of which aimed at a more proactive federal government that would support the economic and social welfare of all Americans. At the close of the convention, the party nominated James B. Weaver as its presidential candidate.

Figure 20.15 The People's Party gathered for its nominating convention in Nebraska, where they wrote the Omaha Platform to state their concerns and goals.

In a rematch of the 1888 election, the Democrats again nominated Grover Cleveland, while Republicans went with Benjamin Harrison. Despite the presence of a third-party challenger, Cleveland won another close popular vote to become the first U.S. president to be elected to nonconsecutive terms. Although he finished a distant third, Populist candidate Weaver polled a respectable one million votes. Rather than being disappointed, several Populists applauded their showing—especially for a third party with barely two years of national political experience under its belt. They anxiously awaited the 1896 election, believing that if the rest of the country, in particular industrial workers, experienced hardships similar to those that farmers already faced, a powerful alliance among the two groups could carry the Populists to victory.

20.4 Social and Labor Unrest in the 1890s

By the end of this section, you will be able to:
- Explain how the Depression of 1893 helped the Populist Party to grow in popularity in the 1890s
- Understand the forces that contributed to the Populist Party's decline following the 1896 presidential election

Insofar as farmers wanted the rest of the country to share their plight, they got their wish. Soon after Cleveland's election, the nation catapulted into the worst economic depression in its history to date. As the government continued to fail in its efforts to address the growing problems, more and more Americans sought relief outside of the traditional two-party system. To many industrial workers, the Populist Party began to seem like a viable solution.

FROM FARMERS' HARDSHIPS TO A NATIONAL DEPRESSION

The late 1880s and early 1890s saw the American economy slide precipitously. As mentioned above, farmers were already struggling with economic woes, and the rest of the country followed quickly. Following a brief rebound from the speculation-induced Panic of 1873, in which bank investments in railroad bonds spread the nation's financial resources too thin—a rebound due in large part to the protective tariffs of the 1880s—a greater economic catastrophe hit the nation, as the decade of the 1890s began to unfold.

The causes of the Depression of 1893 were manifold, but one major element was the speculation in railroads over the previous decades. The rapid proliferation of railroad lines created a false impression of growth for the economy as a whole. Banks and investors fed the growth of the railroads with fast-paced investment in industry and related businesses, not realizing that the growth they were following was built on a bubble. When the railroads began to fail due to expenses outpacing returns on their construction, the supporting businesses, from banks to steel mills, failed also.

Beginning with the closure of the Philadelphia & Reading Railroad Company in 1893, several railroads ceased their operations as a result of investors cashing in their bonds, thus creating a ripple effect throughout the economy. In a single year, from 1893 to 1894, unemployment estimates increased from 3 percent to nearly 19 percent of all working-class Americans. In some states, the unemployment rate soared even higher: over 35 percent in New York State and 43 percent in Michigan. At the height of this depression, over three million American workers were unemployed. By 1895, Americans living in cities grew accustomed to seeing the homeless on the streets or lining up at soup kitchens.

Immediately following the economic downturn, people sought relief through their elected federal government. Just as quickly, they learned what farmers had been taught in the preceding decades: A weak, inefficient government interested solely in patronage and the spoils system in order to maintain its power was in no position to help the American people face this challenge. The federal government had little in place to support those looking for work or to provide direct aid to those in need. Of course, to be fair, the government had seldom faced these questions before. Americans had to look elsewhere.

A notable example of the government's failure to act was the story of **Coxey's Army**. In the spring of 1894, businessman Jacob Coxey led a march of unemployed Ohioans from Cincinnati to Washington, DC, where leaders of the group urged Congress to pass public works legislation for the federal government to hire unemployed workers to build roads and other public projects. From the original one hundred protesters, the march grew five hundred strong as others joined along the route to the nation's capital. Upon their arrival, not only were their cries for federal relief ignored, but Coxey and several other marchers were arrested for trespassing on the grass outside the U.S. Capitol. Frustration over the event led many angry works to consider supporting the Populist Party in subsequent elections.

AMERICANA

✪ *L. Frank Baum: Did Coxey's Army inspire Dorothy and the Wizard of Oz?*

Scholars, historians, and economists have long argued inconclusively that L. Frank Baum intended the story of *The Wizard of Oz* as an allegory for the politics of the day. Whether that actually was Baum's intention is up for debate, but certainly the story could be read as support for the Populist Party's crusade on behalf of American farmers. In 1894, Baum witnessed Coxey's Army's march firsthand, and some feel it may have influenced the story (Figure 20.16).

THE COMMONWEAL ARMY LEAVING BRIGHTWOOD CAMP.

Figure 20.16 This image of Coxey's Army marching on Washington to ask for jobs may have helped inspire L. Frank Baum's story of Dorothy and her friends seeking help from the Wizard of Oz.

According to this theory, the Scarecrow represents the American farmer, the Tin Woodman is the industrial worker, and the Cowardly Lion is William Jennings Bryan, a prominent "Silverite" (strong supporters of the Populist Party who advocated for the free coinage of silver) who, in 1900 when the book was published, was largely criticized by the Republicans as being cowardly and indecisive. In the story, the characters march towards Oz, much as Coxey's Army marched to Washington. Like Dorothy and her companions, Coxey's Army gets in trouble, before being turned away with no help.

Following this reading, the seemingly powerful but ultimately impotent Wizard of Oz is a representation of the president, and Dorothy only finds happiness by wearing the silver slippers—they only became ruby slippers in the later movie version—along the Yellow Brick Road, a reference to the need for the country to move from the gold standard to a two-metal silver and gold plan. While no literary theorists or historians have proven this connection to be true, it is possible that Coxey's Army inspired Baum to create Dorothy's journey on the yellow brick road.

Several strikes also punctuated the growing depression, including a number of violent uprisings in the coal regions of Ohio and Pennsylvania. But the infamous Pullman Strike of 1894 was most notable for its nationwide impact, as it all but shut down the nation's railroad system in the middle of the depression. The strike began immediately on the heels of the Coxey's Army march when, in the summer of 1894, company owner George Pullman fired over two thousand employees at Pullman Co.—which made railroad cars, such as Pullman sleeper cars—and reduced the wages of the remaining three thousand workers. Since the factory operated in the company town of Pullman, Illinois, where workers rented homes from George Pullman and shopped at the company store owned by him as well, unemployment also meant eviction. Facing such harsh treatment, all of the Pullman workers went on strike to protest the decisions. Eugene V. Debs, head of the American Railway Union, led the strike.

In order to bring the plight of Pullman, Illinois, to Americans all around the country, Debs adopted the strike strategy of ordering all American Railroad Union members to refuse to handle any train that had Pullman cars on it. Since virtually every train in the United States operated with Pullman cars, the strike truly brought the transportation industry to its knees. Fearful of his ability to end the economic depression with such a vital piece of the economy at a standstill, President Cleveland turned to his attorney general for the answer. The attorney general proposed a solution: use federal troops to operate the trains under the pretense of protecting the delivery of the U.S. mail that was typically found on all trains. When Debs and the American Railway Union refused to obey the court injunction prohibiting interference with the mail, the troops began operating the trains, and the strike quickly ended. Debs himself was arrested, tried, convicted, and sentenced to six months in prison for disobeying the court injunction. The American Railway Union was destroyed, leaving workers even less empowered than before, and Debs was in prison, contemplating alternatives to a capitalist-based national economy. The Depression of 1893 left the country limping towards the next presidential election with few solutions in sight.

THE ELECTION OF 1896

As the final presidential election of the nineteenth century unfolded, all signs pointed to a possible Populist victory. Not only had the ongoing economic depression convinced many Americans—farmers and factory workers alike—of the inability of either major political party to address the situation, but also the Populist Party, since the last election, benefited from four more years of experience and numerous local victories. As they prepared for their convention in St. Louis that summer, the Populists watched with keen interest as the Republicans and Democrats hosted their own conventions.

The Republicans remained steadfast in their defense of a gold-based standard for the American economy, as well as high protective tariffs. They turned to William McKinley, former congressman and current governor of Ohio, as their candidate. At their convention, the Democrats turned to William Jennings Bryan—a congressman from Nebraska. Bryan defended the importance of a silver-based monetary system and urged the government to coin more silver. Furthermore, being from farm country, he was very familiar with the farmers' plight and saw some merit in the subtreasury system proposal. In short, Bryan could have been the ideal Populist candidate, but the Democrats got to him first. The Populist Party subsequently endorsed Bryan as well, with their party's nomination three weeks later (Figure 20.17).

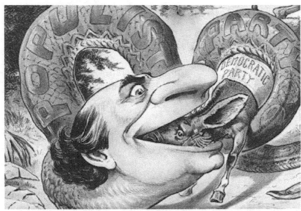

Figure 20.17 Republicans portrayed presidential candidate Bryan as a grasping politician whose Populist leanings could swallow the Democratic Party. Bryan was in fact not a Populist at all, but a Democrat whose views aligned with the Populists on some issues. He was formally nominated by the Democratic Party, the Populist Party, and the Silver Republican Party for the 1896 presidential election.

Click and Explore

Browse through the cartoons and commentary at 1896 (http://openstaxcollege.org/l/ 1896election) at Vassar College, a site that contains a wealth of information about the major players and themes of the presidential election of 1896.

As the Populist convention unfolded, the delegates had an important decision to make: either locate another candidate, even though Bryan would have been an excellent choice, or join the Democrats and support Bryan as the best candidate but risk losing their identity as a third political party as a result. The Populist Party chose the latter and endorsed Bryan's candidacy. However, they also nominated their own vice-presidential candidate, Georgia Senator Tom Watson, as opposed to the Democratic nominee, Arthur Sewall, presumably in an attempt to maintain some semblance of a separate identity.

The race was a heated one, with McKinley running a typical nineteenth-century style "front porch" campaign, during which he espoused the long-held Republican Party principles to visitors who would call on him at his Ohio home. Bryan, to the contrary, delivered speeches all throughout the country, bringing his message to the people that Republicans "shall not crucify mankind on a cross of gold."

DEFINING "AMERICAN"

⚙ William Jennings Bryan and the "Cross of Gold"

William Jennings Bryan was a politician and speechmaker in the late nineteenth century, and he was particularly well known for his impassioned argument that the country move to a bimetal or silver standard. He received the Democratic presidential nomination in 1896, and, at the nominating convention, he gave his most famous speech. He sought to argue against Republicans who stated that the gold standard was the only way to ensure stability and prosperity for American businesses. In the speech he said:

> We say to you that you have made the definition of a business man too limited in its application. The man who is employed for wages is as much a business man as his employer; the attorney in a country town is as much a business man as the corporation counsel in a great metropolis; the merchant at the cross-roads store is as much a business man as the merchant of New York; the farmer who goes forth in the morning and toils all day, who begins in spring and toils all summer, and who by the application of brain and muscle to the natural resources of the country creates wealth, is as much a business man as the man who goes upon the Board of Trade and bets upon the price of grain; . . . We come to speak of this broader class of business men.

This defense of working Americans as critical to the prosperity of the country resonated with his listeners, as did his passionate ending when he stated, "Having behind us the producing masses of this nation and the world, supported by the commercial interests, the laboring interests, and the toilers everywhere, we will answer their demand for a gold standard by saying to them: 'You shall not press down upon the brow of labor this crown of thorns; you shall not crucify mankind upon a cross of gold.'"

The speech was an enormous success and played a role in convincing the Populist Party that he was the candidate for them.

The result was a close election that finally saw a U.S. president win a majority of the popular vote for the first time in twenty-four years. McKinley defeated Bryan by a popular vote of 7.1 million to 6.5 million. Bryan's showing was impressive by any standard, as his popular vote total exceeded that of any other presidential candidate in American history to that date—winner or loser. He polled nearly one million more votes than did the previous Democratic victor, Grover Cleveland; however, his campaign also served to split the Democratic vote, as some party members remained convinced of the propriety of the gold standard and supported McKinley in the election.

Amid a growing national depression where Americans truly recognized the importance of a strong leader with sound economic policies, McKinley garnered nearly two million more votes than his Republican predecessor Benjamin Harrison. Put simply, the American electorate was energized to elect a strong candidate who could adequately address the country's economic woes. Voter turnout was the largest in American history to that date; while both candidates benefitted, McKinley did more so than Bryan (Figure 20.18).

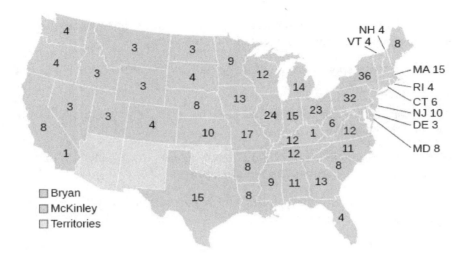

Figure 20.18 The electoral vote map of the 1896 election illustrates the stark divide in the country between the industry-rich coasts and the rural middle.

In the aftermath, it is easy to say that it was Bryan's defeat that all but ended the rise of the Populist Party. Populists had thrown their support to the Democrats who shared similar ideas for the economic rebound of the country and lost. In choosing principle over distinct party identity, the Populists aligned themselves to the growing two-party American political system and would have difficulty maintaining party autonomy afterwards. Future efforts to establish a separate party identity would be met with ridicule by critics who would say that Populists were merely "Democrats in sheep's clothing."

But other factors also contributed to the decline of Populism at the close of the century. First, the discovery of vast gold deposits in Alaska during the Klondike Gold Rush of 1896–1899 (also known as the "Yukon Gold Rush") shored up the nation's weakening economy and made it possible to thrive on a gold standard. Second, the impending Spanish-American War, which began in 1898, further fueled the economy and increased demand for American farm products. Still, the Populist spirit remained, although it lost some momentum at the close of the nineteenth century. As will be seen in a subsequent chapter, the reformist zeal took on new forms as the twentieth century unfolded.

Key Terms

bloody shirt campaign the strategy of Republican candidates to stress the sacrifices that the nation had to endure in its Civil War against Democratic southern secessionists

civil service the contrast to the spoils system, where political appointments were based on merit, not favoritism

Coxey's Army an 1894 protest, led by businessman Jacob Coxey, to advocate for public works jobs for the unemployed by marching on Washington, DC

Farmers' Alliance a national conglomeration of different regional farmers' alliances that joined together in 1890 with the goal of furthering farmers' concerns in politics

Gilded Age the period in American history during which materialism, a quest for personal gain, and corruption dominated both politics and society

Grange a farmers' organization, launched in 1867, which grew to over 1.5 million members in less than a decade

Half-Breeds the group of Republicans led by James G. Blaine, named because they supported some measure of civil service reform and were thus considered to be only "half Republican"

Mugwumps a portion of the Republican Party that broke away from the Stalwart-versus-Half-Breed debate due to disgust with their candidate's corruption

Populist Party a political party formed in 1890 that sought to represent the rights of primarily farmers but eventually all workers in regional and federal elections

Stalwarts the group of Republicans led by Roscoe Conkling who strongly supported the continuation of the patronage system

subtreasury plan a plan that called for storing crops in government warehouses for a brief period of time, during which the federal government would provide loans to farmers worth 80 percent of the current crop prices, releasing the crops for sale when prices rose

Summary

20.1 Political Corruption in Postbellum America

In the years following the Civil War, American politics were disjointed, corrupt, and, at the federal level, largely ineffective in terms of addressing the challenges that Americans faced. Local and regional politics, and the bosses who ran the political machines, dominated through systematic graft and bribery. Americans around the country recognized that solutions to the mounting problems they faced would not come from Washington, DC, but from their local political leaders. Thus, the cycle of federal ineffectiveness and machine politics continued through the remainder of the century relatively unabated.

Meanwhile, in the Compromise of 1877, an electoral commission declared Rutherford B. Hayes the winner of the contested presidential election in exchange for the withdrawal of federal troops from South Carolina, Louisiana, and Florida. As a result, Southern Democrats were able to reestablish control over their home governments, which would have a tremendous impact on the direction of southern politics and society in the decades to come.

20.2 The Key Political Issues: Patronage, Tariffs, and Gold

All told, from 1872 through 1892, Gilded Age politics were little more than political showmanship. The political issues of the day, including the spoils system versus civil service reform, high tariffs versus low, and business regulation, all influenced politicians more than the country at large. Very few measures offered direct assistance to Americans who continued to struggle with the transformation into an industrial society; the inefficiency of a patronage-driven federal government, combined with a growing laissez-faire attitude among the American public, made the passage of effective legislation difficult. Some of Harrison's policies, such as the Sherman Anti-Trust Act and the Sherman Silver Purchase Act, aimed to provide relief but remained largely ineffective.

20.3 Farmers Revolt in the Populist Era

Factors such as overproduction and high tariffs left the country's farmers in increasingly desperate straits, and the federal government's inability to address their concerns left them disillusioned and worried. Uneven responses from state governments had many farmers seeking an alternative solution to their problems. Taking note of the labor movements growing in industrial cities around the country, farmers began to organize into alliances similar to workers' unions; these were models of cooperation where larger numbers could offer more bargaining power with major players such as railroads. Ultimately, the alliances were unable to initiate widespread change for their benefit. Still, drawing from the cohesion of purpose, farmers sought to create change from the inside: through politics. They hoped the creation of the Populist Party in 1891 would lead to a president who put the people—and in particular the farmers—first.

20.4 Social and Labor Unrest in the 1890s

As the economy worsened, more Americans suffered; as the federal government continued to offer few solutions, the Populist movement began to grow. Populist groups approached the 1896 election anticipating that the mass of struggling Americans would support their movement for change. When Democrats chose William Jennings Bryan for their candidate, however, they chose a politician who largely fit the mold of the Populist platform—from his birthplace of Nebraska to his advocacy of the silver standard that most farmers desired. Throwing their support behind Bryan as well, Populists hoped to see a candidate in the White House who would embody the Populist goals, if not the party name. When Bryan lost to Republican William McKinley, the Populist Party lost much of its momentum. As the country climbed out of the depression, the interest in a third party faded away, although the reformist movement remained intact.

Review Questions

1. Mark Twain's *Gilded Age* is a reference to _____.

    A. conditions in the South in the pre-Civil War era

    B. the corrupt politics of the post-Civil War era

    C. the populist movement

    D. the Republican Party

2. How did the Great Compromise of 1877 influence the election?

    A. It allowed a bilateral government agreement.

    B. It gave new power to northern Republicans.

    C. It encouraged southern states to support Hayes.

    D. It gave the federal government new powers.

3. What accounted for the relative weakness of the federal government during this era?

4. A Mugwump is _____.

    A. a supporter of the spoils system

    B. a liberal Democrat

    C. a former member of the Republican Party

    D. a moderate Stalwart

5. Which president made significant steps towards civil service reform?

   A. Chester A. Arthur

   B. Benjamin Harrison

   C. Grover Cleveland

   D. Roscoe Conkling

6. Why were U.S. presidents (with few exceptions) so adamant about protecting the spoils system of patronage during the late nineteenth century?

7. Which of the following was *not* a vehicle for the farmers' protest?

   A. the Mugwumps

   B. the Grange

   C. the Farmers' Alliance

   D. the People's Party

8. Which of the following contributed directly to the plight of farmers?

   A. machine politics

   B. labor unions

   C. overproduction

   D. inadequate supply

9. What were women's roles within the Farmer's Alliance?

10. How were members of Coxey's Army received when they arrived in Washington?

   A. They were given an audience with the president.

   B. They were given an audience with members of Congress.

   C. They were ignored.

   D. They were arrested.

11. Which of the following does *not* represent one of the ways in which William Jennings Bryan appealed to Populists?

   A. He came from farm country.

   B. He supported free silver.

   C. He supported the subtreasury system.

   D. He advocated for higher tariffs.

Critical Thinking Questions

12. How does the term "Gilded Age" characterize American society in the late nineteenth century? In what ways is this characterization accurate or inaccurate?

13. With farmers still representing a significant segment of American society, why did government officials—Democrats and Republicans alike—prove unwilling to help find solutions to farmers' problems?

14. Upon reflection, did the Populist Party make a wise decision in choosing to support the Democratic Party's candidate in the 1896 presidential election? Why or why not?

15. Despite its relative weakness during this period, the federal government made several efforts to provide a measure of relief for struggling Americans. What were these initiatives? In what ways were they more or less successful?

CHAPTER 21

Leading the Way: The Progressive Movement, 1890-1920

Figure 21.1 The western states were the first to allow women the right to vote, a freedom that grew out of the less deeply entrenched gendered spheres in the region. This illustration, from 1915, shows a suffragist holding a torch over the western states and inviting the beckoning women from the rest of the country to join her.

Chapter Outline

21.1 The Origins of the Progressive Spirit in America
21.2 Progressivism at the Grassroots Level
21.3 New Voices for Women and African Americans
21.4 Progressivism in the White House

Introduction

Women's suffrage was one of many causes that emerged in the Progressive Era, as Americans confronted the numerous challenges of the late nineteenth century. Starting in the late 1800s, women increasingly were working outside the home—a task almost always done for money, not empowerment—as well as pursuing higher education, both at universities that were beginning to allow women to enroll and at female-only schools. Often, it was educated middle-class women with more time and resources that took up causes such as child labor and family health. As more women led new organizations or institutions, such as the settlement houses, they grew to have a greater voice on issues of social change. By the turn of the century, a strong movement had formed to advocate for a woman's right to vote. For three decades, suffragist groups pushed for legislation to give women the right to vote in every state. As the illustration above shows (Figure 21.1), the western states were the first to grant women the right to vote; it would not be until 1920 that the nation would extend that right to all women.

21.1 The Origins of the Progressive Spirit in America

By the end of this section, you will be able to:
* Describe the role that muckrakers played in catalyzing the Progressive Era
* Explain the main features of Progressivism

The Progressive Era was a time of wide-ranging causes and varied movements, where activists and reformers from diverse backgrounds and with very different agendas pursued their goals of a better America. These reformers were reacting to the challenges that faced the country at the end of the nineteenth century: rapid urban sprawl, immigration, corruption, industrial working conditions, the growth of large corporations, women's rights, and surging anti-black violence and white supremacy in the South. Investigative journalists of the day uncovered social inequality and encouraged Americans to take action. The campaigns of the Progressives were often grassroots in their origin. While different causes shared some underlying elements, each movement largely focused on its own goals, be it the right of women to vote, the removal of alcohol from communities, or the desire for a more democratic voting process.

THE MUCKRAKERS

A group of journalists and writers collectively known as **muckrakers** provided an important spark that ignited the Progressive movement. Unlike the "yellow journalists" who were interested only in sensationalized articles designed to sell newspapers, muckrakers exposed problems in American society and urged the public to identify solutions. Whether those problems were associated with corrupt machine politics, poor working conditions in factories, or the questionable living conditions of the working class (among others), muckrakers shined a light on the problem and provoked outraged responses from Americans. President Theodore Roosevelt knew many of these investigative journalists well and considered himself a Progressive. Yet, unhappy with the way they forced agendas into national politics,

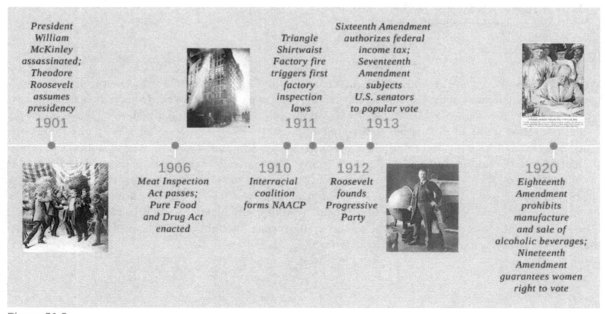

Figure 21.2

he was the one who first gave them the disparaging nickname "muckrakers," invoking an ill-spirited character obsessed with filth from *The Pilgrim's Progress*, a 1678 Christian allegory written by John Bunyan.

Beginning in the second half of the nineteenth century, these Progressive journalists sought to expose critical social problems and exhort the public to take action. In his book, *How the Other Half Lives* (1890), journalist and photographer Jacob Riis used photojournalism to capture the dismal and dangerous living conditions in working-class tenements in New York City (Figure 21.3). Ida Tarbell, perhaps the most well-known female muckraker, wrote a series of articles on the dangers of John D. Rockefeller's powerful monopoly, Standard Oil. Her articles followed Henry Demarest Lloyd's book, *Wealth Against Commonwealth*, published in 1894, which examined the excesses of Standard Oil. Other writers, like Lincoln Steffens, explored corruption in city politics, or, like Ray Standard Baker, researched unsafe working conditions and low pay in the coal mines.

Figure 21.3   Jacob Riis's images of New York City slums in the late nineteenth century, such as this 1890 photograph of children sleeping in Mulberry Street, exposed Americans all over the country to the living conditions of the urban poor.

The work of the muckrakers not only revealed serious problems in American society, but also agitated, often successfully, for change. Their articles, in magazines such as *McClure's*, as well as books garnered attention for issues such as child labor, anti-trust, big business break-ups, and health and safety. Progressive activists took up these causes and lobbied for legislation to address some of the ills troubling industrial America.

Click and Explore

To learn more about one of the most influential muckrakers of the late nineteenth century, peruse the photographs, writings, and more at the Ida M. Tarbell archives (http://openstaxcollege.org/l/tarbell) that are housed at Tarbell's alma mater, Allegheny College, where she matriculated in 1876 as the only woman in her class.

THE FEATURES OF PROGRESSIVISM

Muckrakers drew public attention to some of the most glaring inequities and scandals that grew out of the social ills of the Gilded Age and the hands-off approach of the federal government since the end of Reconstruction. These writers by and large addressed a white, middle-class and elite, native-born audience, even though Progressive movements and organizations involved a diverse range of Americans. What united these Progressives beyond their different backgrounds and causes was a set of uniting principles, however. Most strove for a perfection of democracy, which required the expansion of suffrage to worthy citizens and the restriction of political participation for those considered "unfit" on account of health, education, or race. Progressives also agreed that democracy had to be balanced with an emphasis on efficiency, a reliance on science and technology, and deference to the expertise of professionals. They repudiated party politics but looked to government to regulate the modern market economy. And they saw themselves as the agents of social justice and reform, as well as the stewards and guides of workers and the urban poor. Often, reformers' convictions and faith in their own expertise led them to dismiss the voices of the very people they sought to help.

The expressions of these Progressive principles developed at the grassroots level. It was not until Theodore Roosevelt unexpectedly became president in 1901 that the federal government would engage in Progressive reforms. Before then, **Progressivism** was work done by the people, for the people. What knit Progressives together was the feeling that the country was moving at a dangerous pace in a dangerous direction and required the efforts of everyday Americans to help put it back on track.

21.2 Progressivism at the Grassroots Level

By the end of this section, you will be able to:
- Identify specific examples of grassroots Progressivism relating to the spread of democracy, efficiency in government, and social justice
- Describe the more radical movements associated with the Progressive Era

A wide variety of causes fell under the Progressive label. For example, Wisconsin's Robert M. ("Fighting Bob") La Follette, one of the most Progressive politicians of his day, fought hard to curb the power of special interests in politics and reform the democratic process at state and local levels. Others sought out safer working conditions for factory workers. Different groups prioritized banning the sale of alcohol, which, they believed, was the root of much of the trouble for the working poor. No matter what the cause, Progressive campaigns often started with issues brought to the public's attention by muckraking journalists.

EXPANDING DEMOCRACY

One of the key ideals that Progressives considered vital to the growth and health of the country was the concept of a perfected democracy. They felt, quite simply, that Americans needed to exert more control over their government. This shift, they believed, would ultimately lead to a system of government that was better able to address the needs of its citizens. Grassroots Progressives pushed forward their agenda of direct democracy through the passage of three state-level reforms.

The first law involved the creation of the **direct primary**. Prior to this time, the only people who had a hand in selecting candidates for elections were delegates at conventions. Direct primaries allowed party members to vote directly for a candidate, with the nomination going to the one with the most votes. This was the beginning of the current system of holding a primary election before a general election. South Carolina adopted this system for statewide elections in 1896; in 1901, Florida became the first state to use

Download for free at http://cnx.org/content/col11740/latest/

the direct primary in nominations for the presidency. It is the method currently used in three-quarters of U.S. states.

Another series of reforms pushed forward by Progressives that sought to sidestep the power of special interests in state legislatures and restore the democratic political process were three election innovations—the **initiative, referendum**, and **recall**. The first permitted voters to enact legislation by petitioning to place an idea, or initiative, on the ballot. In 1898, South Dakota became the first state to allow initiatives to appear on a ballot. By 1920, twenty states had adopted the procedure. The second innovation allowed voters to counteract legislation by holding a referendum—that is, putting an existing law on the ballot for voters to either affirm or reject. Currently twenty-four states allow some form of initiative and referendum. The third element of this direct democracy agenda was the recall. The recall permitted citizens to remove a public official from office through a process of petition and vote, similar to the initiative and referendum. While this measure was not as widely adopted as the others, Oregon, in 1910, became the first state to allow recalls. By 1920, twelve states had adopted this tool. It has only been used successfully a handful of times on the statewide level, for example, to remove the governor of North Dakota in 1921, and, more recently, the governor of California in 2003.

Progressives also pushed for democratic reform that affected the federal government. In an effort to achieve a fairer representation of state constituencies in the U.S. Congress, they lobbied for approval of the Seventeenth Amendment to the U.S. Constitution, which mandated the direct election of U.S. senators. The Seventeenth Amendment replaced the previous system of having state legislatures choose senators. William Jennings Bryan, the 1896 Democratic presidential candidate who received significant support from the Populist Party, was among the leading Progressives who championed this cause.

EXPERTISE AND EFFICIENCY

In addition to making government more directly accountable to the voters, Progressives also fought to rid politics of inefficiency, waste, and corruption. Progressives in large cities were particularly frustrated with the corruption and favoritism of machine politics, which wasted enormous sums of taxpayer money and ultimately stalled the progress of cities for the sake of entrenched politicians, like the notorious Democratic Party Boss William Tweed in New York's Tammany Hall. Progressives sought to change this corrupt system and had success in places like Galveston, Texas, where, in 1901, they pushed the city to adopt a commission system. A hurricane the previous year (Figure 21.4) had led to the collapse of the old city government, which had proved incapable of leading the city through the natural disaster. The storm claimed over eight thousand lives—the highest death toll from a natural disaster in the history of the country—and afterwards, the community had no faith that the existing government could rebuild. The commission system involved the election of a number of commissioners, each responsible for one specific operation of the city, with titles like water commissioner, fire commissioner, police commissioner, and so on. With no single political "boss" in charge, the prevalence of graft and corruption greatly decreased. The commissioner system is widely used in modern cities throughout the United States.

Figure 21.4 The 1900 hurricane in Galveston, Texas, claimed more lives than any other natural disaster in American history. In its wake, fearing that the existing corrupt and inefficient government was not up to the job of rebuilding, the remaining residents of the town adopted the commission system of local government.

Another model of municipal government reform took shape in Staunton, Virginia, in 1908, where the citizens switched to the city manager form of government. Designed to avoid the corruption inherent in political machines, the city manager system separated the daily operations of the city from both the electoral process and political parties. In this system, citizens elected city councilors who would pass laws and handle all legislative issues. However, their first job was to hire a city manager to deal with the daily management operation of the city. This person, unlike the politicians, was an engineer or businessman who understood the practical elements of city operations and oversaw city workers. Currently, over thirty-seven hundred cities have adopted the city manager system, including some of the largest cities in the country, such as Austin, Dallas, and Phoenix.

At the state level, perhaps the greatest advocate of Progressive government was Robert La Follette (**Figure 21.5**). During his time as governor, from 1901 through 1906, La Follette introduced the **Wisconsin Idea**, wherein he hired experts to research and advise him in drafting legislation to improve conditions in his state. "Fighting Bob" supported numerous Progressive ideas while governor: He signed into law the first workman's compensation system, approved a minimum wage law, developed a progressive tax law, adopted the direct election of U.S. senators before the subsequent constitutional amendment made it mandatory, and advocated for women's suffrage. La Follette subsequently served as a popular U.S. senator from Wisconsin from 1906 through 1925, and ran for president on the Progressive Party ticket in 1924.

Figure 21.5 An energetic speaker and tireless Progressive, Governor Robert "Fighting Bob" La Follette turned the state of Wisconsin into a flagship for democratic reform.

Click and Explore

Read how Robert La Follette's legacy (http://openstaxcollege.org/l/follette) still inspires progressives in Wisconsin.

Many Progressive reformers were also committed to the principle of efficiency in business as well as in government. The growth of large corporations at the time fostered the emergence of a class of professional managers. Fredrick Winslow Taylor, arguably the first American management consultant, laid out his argument of increased industrial efficiency through improvements in human productivity in his book *The Principles of Scientific Management* (1911). Through time-motion studies and the principles of standardization, Taylor sought to place workers in the most efficient positions of the industrial process. Management, he argued, should determine the work routine, leaving workers to simply execute the task at hand. The image below (Figure 21.6) shows a machinist in a factory where Taylor had consulted; he is alone and focused solely on his job. Progressive in its emphasis on efficiency, the use of science, and the reliance on experts, **Taylorism**, as scientific management became known, was not widely popular among workers who resented managerial authority and the loss of autonomy over their work. Many workers went on strikes in response, although some favored Taylor's methods, since their pay was directly linked to the productivity increases that his methods achieved and since increased efficiency allowed companies to charge consumers lower prices.

Figure 21.6 This machinist works alone in a factory that adopted Taylorism, the scientific time management principle that sought to bring ultimate efficiency to factories. Many workers found the focus on repetitive tasks to be dehumanizing and unpleasant.

SOCIAL JUSTICE

The Progressives' work towards social justice took many forms. In some cases, it was focused on those who suffered due to pervasive inequality, such as African Americans, other ethnic groups, and women. In others, the goal was to help those who were in desperate need due to circumstance, such as poor immigrants from southern and eastern Europe who often suffered severe discrimination, the working poor, and those with ill health. Women were in the vanguard of social justice reform. Jane Addams, Lillian Wald, and Ellen Gates Starr, for example, led the settlement house movement of the 1880s (discussed in a previous chapter). Their work to provide social services, education, and health care to working-class women and their children was among the earliest Progressive grassroots efforts in the country.

Building on the successes of the settlement houses, social justice reformers took on other, related challenges. The National Child Labor Committee (NCLC), formed in 1904, urged the passage of labor legislation to ban child labor in the industrial sector. In 1900, U.S. census records indicated that one out of every six children between the ages of five and ten were working, a 50-percent increase over the previous decade. If the sheer numbers alone were not enough to spur action, the fact that managers paid child workers noticeably less for their labor gave additional fuel to the NCLC's efforts to radically curtail child labor. The committee employed photographer Lewis Hine to engage in a decade-long pictorial campaign to educate Americans on the plight of children working in factories (Figure 21.7).

(a)   (b)

Figure 21.7 As part of the National Child Labor Committee's campaign to raise awareness about the plight of child laborers, Lewis Hine photographed dozens of children in factories around the country, including Addie Card (a), a twelve-year-old spinner working in a mill in Vermont in 1910, and these young boys working at Bibb Mill No. 1 in Macon, Georgia in 1909 (b). Working ten- to twelve-hour shifts, children often worked large machines where they could reach into gaps and remove lint and other debris, a practice that caused plenty of injuries. (credit a/b: modification of work by Library of Congress)

Although low-wage industries fiercely opposed any federal restriction on child labor, the NCLC did succeed in 1912, urging President William Howard Taft to sign into law the creation of the U.S. Children's Bureau. As a branch of the Department of Labor, the bureau worked closely with the NCLC to bring greater awareness to the issue of child labor. In 1916, the pressure from the NCLC and the general public resulted in the passage of the Keating-Owen Act, which prohibited the interstate trade of any goods produced with child labor. Although the U.S. Supreme Court later declared the law unconstitutional, Keating-Owen reflected a significant shift in the public perception of child labor. Finally, in 1938, the passage of the Fair Labor Standards Act signaled the victory of supporters of Keating-Owen. This new law outlawed the interstate trade of any products produced by children under the age of sixteen.

Florence Kelley, a Progressive supporter of the NCLC, championed other social justice causes as well. As the first general secretary of the National Consumers League, which was founded in 1899 by Jane Addams and others, Kelley led one of the original battles to try and secure safety in factory working conditions. She particularly opposed sweatshop labor and urged the passage of an eight-hour-workday law in order to specifically protect women in the workplace. Kelley's efforts were initially met with strong resistance from factory owners who exploited women's labor and were unwilling to give up the long hours and low wages they paid in order to offer the cheapest possible product to consumers. But in 1911, a tragedy turned the tide of public opinion in favor of Kelley's cause. On March 25 of that year, a fire broke out at the Triangle Shirtwaist Company on the eighth floor of the Asch building in New York City, resulting in the deaths of 146 garment workers, most of them young, immigrant women (Figure 21.8). Management had previously blockaded doors and fire escapes in an effort to control workers and keep out union organizers; in the blaze, many died due to the crush of bodies trying to evacuate the building. Others died when they fell off the flimsy fire escape or jumped to their deaths to escape the flames. This tragedy provided the National Consumers League with the moral argument to convince politicians of the need to pass workplace safety laws and codes.

Figure 21.8 On March 25, 1911, a fire broke out at the Triangle Shirtwaist Factory in New York City. Despite the efforts of firefighters, 146 workers died in the fire, mostly because the owners had trapped them on the sweatshop floors.

MY STORY

✪ *William Shepherd on the Triangle Shirtwaist Factory Fire*

The tragedy of the Triangle Shirtwaist Factory fire was a painful wake-up call to a country that was largely ignoring issues of poor working conditions and worker health and safety. While this fire was far from the only instance of worker death, the sheer number of people killed—almost one hundred fifty—and the fact they were all young women, made a strong impression. Furthering the power of this tragedy was the first-hand account shared by William Shepherd, a United Press reporter who was on the scene, giving his eyewitness account over a telephone. His account appeared, just two days later, in the *Milwaukee Journal*, and word of the tragedy spread from there. Public outrage over their deaths was enough to give the National Consumers League the power it needed to push politicians to get involved.

> I saw every feature of the tragedy visible from outside the building. I learned a new sound—a more horrible sound than description can picture. It was the thud of a speeding, living body on a stone sidewalk.
>
> Thud-dead, thud-dead, thud-dead, thud-dead.Sixty-two thud-deads. I call them that, because the sound and the thought of death came to me each time, at the same instant. There was plenty of chance to watch them as they came down. The height was eighty feet.
>
> The first ten thud-deads shocked me. I looked up—saw that there were scores of girls at the windows. The flames from the floor below were beating in their faces. Somehow I knew that they, too, must come down. . . .
>
> A policeman later went about with tags, which he fastened with wires to the wrists of the dead girls, numbering each with a lead pencil, and I saw him fasten tag no. 54 to the wrist of a girl who wore an engagement ring. A fireman who came downstairs from the building told me that there were at least fifty bodies in the big room on the seventh floor. Another fireman told me that more girls had jumped down an air shaft in the rear of the building. I went back there, into the narrow court, and saw a heap of dead girls. . . .
>
> The floods of water from the firemen's hose that ran into the gutter were actually stained red with blood. I looked upon the heap of dead bodies and I remembered these girls were the shirtwaist makers. I remembered their great strike of last year in which these same girls had demanded more sanitary conditions and more safety precautions in the shops. These dead bodies were the answer.

What do you think about William Shepherd's description? What effect do you think it had on newspaper readers in the Midwest?

Another cause that garnered support from a key group of Progressives was the prohibition of liquor. This crusade, which gained followers through the Women's Christian Temperance Union (WCTU) and the Anti-Saloon League, directly linked Progressivism with morality and Christian reform initiatives, and saw in alcohol both a moral vice and a practical concern, as workingmen spent their wages on liquor and saloons, often turning violent towards each other or their families at home. The WCTU and Anti-Saloon League moved the efforts to eliminate the sale of alcohol from a bar-to-bar public opinion campaign to one of city-to-city and state-by-state votes (Figure 21.9). Through local option votes and subsequent statewide initiatives and referendums, the Anti-Saloon League succeeded in urging 40 percent of the nation's counties to "go dry" by 1906, and a full dozen states to do the same by 1909. Their political pressure culminated in the passage of the Eighteenth Amendment to the U.S. Constitution, ratified in 1919, which prohibited the manufacture, sale, and transportation of alcoholic beverages nationwide.

Figure 21.9 This John R. Chapin illustration shows the women of the temperance movement holding an open-air prayer meeting outside an Ohio saloon. (credit: Library of Congress)

RADICAL PROGRESSIVES

The Progressive Era also witnessed a wave of radicalism, with leaders who believed that America was beyond reform and that only a complete revolution of sorts would bring about the necessary changes. The radicals had early roots in the labor and political movements of the mid-nineteenth century but soon grew to feel that the more moderate Progressive ideals were inadequate. Conversely, one reason mainstream why Progressives felt the need to succeed on issues of social inequity was because radicals offered remedies that middle-class Americans considered far more dangerous. The two most prominent radical movements to emerge at the beginning of the century were the Socialist Party of America (SPA), founded in 1901, and the Industrial Workers of the World (IWW), founded in 1905, whose emphasis on worker empowerment deviated from the more paternalistic approach of Progressive reformers.

Labor leader Eugene Debs, disenchanted with the failures of the labor movement, was a founding member and prominent leader of the SPA (Figure 21.10). Advocating for change via the ballot box, the SPA sought to elect Socialists to positions at the local, state, and federal levels in order to initiate change from within. Between 1901 and 1918, the SPA enjoyed tremendous success, electing over seventy Socialist mayors, over thirty state legislators, and two U.S. congressmen, Victor Berger from Wisconsin and Meyer London from New York. Debs himself ran for president as the SPA candidate in five elections between 1900 and 1920, twice earning nearly one million votes.

Figure 21.10 This image of Eugene Debs speaking to a crowd in Canton, Ohio, in 1918, illustrates the passion and intensity that made him such a compelling figure to the more radical Progressives.

As had been true for the Populist and Progressive movements, the radical movement suffered numerous fissures. Although Debs established a tenuous relationship with Samuel Gompers and the American Federation of Labor, some within the Socialist Party favored a more radical political stance than Debs's craft union structure. As a result, William "Big Bill" Haywood formed the more radical IWW, or **Wobblies**, in 1905. Although he remained an active member of the Socialist Party until 1919, Haywood appreciated the outcry of the more radical arm of the party that desired an industrial union approach to labor organization. The IWW advocated for direct action and, in particular, the general strike, as the most effective revolutionary method to overthrow the capitalist system. By 1912, the Wobblies had played a significant role in a number of major strikes, including the Paterson Silk Strike, the Lawrence Textile Strike, and the Mesabi Range Iron Strike. The government viewed the Wobblies as a significant threat, and in a response far greater than their actions warranted, targeted them with arrests, tar-and-featherings, shootings, and lynchings.

Both the Socialist Party and the IWW reflected elements of the Progressive desire for democracy and social justice. The difference was simply that for this small but vocal minority in the United States, the corruption of government at all levels meant that the desire for a better life required a different approach. What they sought mirrored the work of all grassroots Progressives, differing only in degree and strategy.

21.3 New Voices for Women and African Americans

By the end of this section, you will be able to:
- Understand the origins and growth of the women's rights movement
- Identify the different strands of the early African American civil rights movement

The Progressive drive for a more perfect democracy and social justice also fostered the growth of two new movements that attacked the oldest and most long-standing betrayals of the American promise of equal opportunity and citizenship—the disfranchisement of women and civil rights for African Americans. African Americans across the nation identified an agenda for civil rights and economic opportunity during the Progressive Era, but they disagreed strongly on how to meet these goals in the face of universal discrimination and disfranchisement, segregation, and racial violence in the South. And beginning in the late nineteenth century, the women's movement cultivated a cadre of new leaders, national organizations, and competing rationales for women's rights—especially the right to vote.

LEADERS EMERGE IN THE WOMEN'S MOVEMENT

Women like Jane Addams and Florence Kelley were instrumental in the early Progressive settlement house movement, and female leaders dominated organizations such as the WCTU and the Anti-Saloon League. From these earlier efforts came new leaders who, in their turn, focused their efforts on the key goal of the Progressive Era as it pertained to women: the right to vote.

Women had first formulated their demand for the right to vote in the Declaration of Sentiments at a convention in Seneca Falls, New York, in 1848, and saw their first opportunity of securing suffrage during Reconstruction when legislators—driven by racial animosity—sought to enfranchise women to counter the votes of black men following the ratification of the Fifteenth Amendment. By 1900, the western frontier states of Colorado, Idaho, Utah, and Wyoming had already responded to women's movements with the right to vote in state and local elections, regardless of gender. They conceded to the suffragists' demands, partly in order to attract more women to these male-dominated regions. But women's lives in the West also rarely fit with the nineteenth-century ideology of "separate spheres" that had legitimized the exclusion of women from the rough-and-tumble party competitions of public politics. In 1890, the National American Women's Suffrage Association (NAWSA) organized several hundred state and local chapters to urge the passage of a federal amendment to guarantee a woman's right to vote. Its leaders, Elizabeth Cady Stanton and Susan B. Anthony, were veterans of the women's suffrage movement and had formulated the first demand for the right to vote at Seneca Falls in 1848 (Figure 21.11). Under the subsequent leadership of Carrie Chapman Catt, beginning in 1900, the group decided to make suffrage its first priority. Soon, its membership began to grow. Using modern marketing efforts like celebrity endorsements to attract a younger audience, the NAWSA became a significant political pressure group for the passage of an amendment to the U.S. Constitution.

Figure 21.11 Women suffragists in Ohio sought to educate and convince men that they should support a woman's rights to vote. As the feature below on the backlash against suffragists illustrates, it was a far from simple task.

For some in the NAWSA, however, the pace of change was too slow. Frustrated with the lack of response by state and national legislators, Alice Paul, who joined the organization in 1912, sought to expand the scope of the organization as well as to adopt more direct protest tactics to draw greater media attention. When others in the group were unwilling to move in her direction, Paul split from the NAWSA to create the Congressional Union for Woman Suffrage, later renamed the National Woman's Party, in 1913. Known as the **Silent Sentinels** (Figure 21.12), Paul and her group picketed outside the White House for nearly two years, starting in 1917. In the latter stages of their protests, many women, including Paul, were arrested and thrown in jail, where they staged a hunger strike as self-proclaimed political prisoners. Prison guards ultimately force-fed Paul to keep her alive. At a time—during World War I—when women volunteered as army nurses, worked in vital defense industries, and supported Wilson's campaign to "make the world safe for democracy," the scandalous mistreatment of Paul embarrassed President Woodrow Wilson. Enlightened to the injustice toward all American women, he changed his position in support of a woman's constitutional right to vote.

Figure 21.12 Alice Paul and her Silent Sentinels picketed outside the White House for almost two years, and, when arrested, went on hunger strike until they were force-fed in order to save their lives.

While Catt and Paul used different strategies, their combined efforts brought enough pressure to bear for Congress to pass the Nineteenth Amendment, which prohibited voter discrimination on the basis of sex, during a special session in the summer of 1919. Subsequently, the required thirty-six states approved its adoption, with Tennessee doing so in August of 1920, in time for that year's presidential election.

DEFINING "AMERICAN"

✪ *The Anti-Suffragist Movement*

The early suffragists may have believed that the right to vote was a universal one, but they faced waves of discrimination and ridicule from both men and women. The image below (Figure 21.13) shows one of the organizations pushing back against the suffragist movement, but much of the anti-suffrage campaign was carried out through ridiculing postcards and signs that showed suffragists as sexually wanton, grasping, irresponsible, or impossibly ugly. Men in anti-suffragist posters were depicted as henpecked, crouching to clean the floor, while their suffragist wives marched out the door to campaign for the vote. They also showed cartoons of women gambling, drinking, and smoking cigars, that is, taking on men's vices, once they gained voting rights.

Figure 21.13 The anti-suffrage group used ridicule and embarrassment to try and sway the public away from supporting a woman's right to vote.

Other anti-suffragists believed that women could better influence the country from outside the realm of party politics, through their clubs, petitions, and churches. Many women also opposed women's suffrage because they thought the dirty world of politics was a morass to which ladies should not be exposed. The National Association Opposed to Woman Suffrage formed in 1911; around the country, state representatives used the organization's speakers, funds, and literature to promote the anti-suffragist cause. As the link below illustrates, the suffragists endured much prejudice and backlash in their push for equal rights.

Click and Explore

Browse this collection of anti-suffragist cartoons (http://openstaxcollege.org/l/postcard) to see examples of the stereotypes and fear-mongering that the anti-suffragist campaign promoted.

LEADERS EMERGE IN THE EARLY CIVIL RIGHTS MOVEMENT

Racial mob violence against African Americans permeated much of the "New South"—and, to a lesser extent, the West, where Mexican Americans and other immigrant groups also suffered severe discrimination and violence—by the late nineteenth century. The Ku Klux Klan and a system of Jim Crow laws governed much of the South (discussed in a previous chapter). White middle-class reformers were appalled at the violence of race relations in the nation but typically shared the belief in racial characteristics and the superiority of Anglo-Saxon whites over African Americans, Asians, "ethnic" Europeans, Indians, and Latin American populations. Southern reformers considered segregation a Progressive solution to racial violence; across the nation, educated middle-class Americans enthusiastically followed the work of eugenicists who identified virtually all human behavior as inheritable traits and issued awards at county fairs to families and individuals for their "racial fitness." It was against this tide that African American leaders developed their own voice in the Progressive Era, working along diverse paths to improve the lives and conditions of African Americans throughout the country.

Born into slavery in Virginia in 1856, Booker T. Washington became an influential African American leader at the outset of the Progressive Era. In 1881, he became the first principal for the Tuskegee Normal and Industrial Institute in Alabama, a position he held until he died in 1915. Tuskegee was an all-black "normal school"—an old term for a teachers' college—teaching African Americans a curriculum geared towards practical skills such as cooking, farming, and housekeeping. Graduates would often then travel through the South, teaching new farming and industrial techniques to rural communities. Washington extolled the school's graduates to focus on the black community's self-improvement and prove that they were productive members of society even in freedom—something white Americans throughout the nation had always doubted.

In a speech delivered at the Cotton States and International Exposition in Atlanta in 1895, which was meant to promote the economy of a "New South," Washington proposed what came to be known as the **Atlanta Compromise** (Figure 21.14). Speaking to a racially mixed audience, Washington called upon African Americans to work diligently for their own uplift and prosperity rather than preoccupy themselves with political and civil rights. Their success and hard work, he implied, would eventually convince southern whites to grant these rights. Not surprisingly, most whites liked Washington's model of race relations, since it placed the burden of change on blacks and required nothing of them. Wealthy industrialists such as Andrew Carnegie and John D. Rockefeller provided funding for many of Washington's self-help programs, as did Sears, Roebuck & Co. co-founder Julius Rosenwald, and Washington was the first African American invited to the White House by President Roosevelt in 1901. At the same time, his message also appealed to many in the black community, and some attribute this widespread popularity to his consistent message that social and economic growth, even within a segregated society, would do more for African Americans than an all-out agitation for equal rights on all fronts.

Figure 21.14 In Booker T. Washington's speech at the Cotton States and International Exposition in Atlanta, he urged his audience to "cast down your bucket where you are" and make friends with the people around them.

Click and Explore

Visit George Mason University's History Matters website for the text and audio of Booker T. Washington's famous Atlanta Compromise (http://openstaxcollege.org/l/booker) speech.

Yet, many African Americans disagreed with Washington's approach. Much in the same manner that Alice Paul felt the pace of the struggle for women's rights was moving too slowly under the NAWSA, some within the African American community felt that immediate agitation for the rights guaranteed under the Thirteenth, Fourteenth, and Fifteenth Amendments, established during the immediate aftermath of the Civil War, was necessary. In 1905, a group of prominent civil rights leaders, led by W. E. B. Du Bois, met in a small hotel on the Canadian side of Niagara Falls—where segregation laws did not bar them from hotel accommodations—to discuss what immediate steps were needed for equal rights (Figure 21.15). Du Bois, a professor at the all-black Atlanta University and the first African American with a doctorate from Harvard, emerged as the prominent spokesperson for what would later be dubbed the **Niagara Movement**. By 1905, he had grown wary of Booker T. Washington's calls for African Americans to accommodate white racism and focus solely on self-improvement. Du Bois, and others alongside him, wished to carve a more direct path towards equality that drew on the political leadership and litigation skills of the black, educated elite, which he termed the "talented tenth."

Figure 21.15 This photo of the Niagara Movement shows W. E. B. Du Bois seated in the second row, center, in the white hat. The proud and self-confident postures of this group stood in marked contrast to the humility that Booker T. Washington urged of blacks.

At the meeting, Du Bois led the others in drafting the "Declaration of Principles," which called for immediate political, economic, and social equality for African Americans. These rights included universal suffrage, compulsory education, and the elimination of the convict lease system in which tens of thousands of blacks had endured slavery-like conditions in southern road construction, mines, prisons, and penal farms since the end of Reconstruction. Within a year, Niagara chapters had sprung up in twenty-one states across the country. By 1908, internal fights over the role of women in the fight for African American equal rights lessened the interest in the Niagara Movement. But the movement laid the groundwork for the creation of the National Association for the Advancement of Colored People (**NAACP**), founded in 1909. Du Bois served as the influential director of publications for the NAACP from its inception until 1933. As the editor of the journal *The Crisis*, Du Bois had a platform to express his views on a variety of issues facing African Americans in the later Progressive Era, as well as during World War I and its aftermath.

In both Washington and Du Bois, African Americans found leaders to push forward the fight for their place in the new century, each with a very different strategy. Both men cultivated ground for a new generation of African American spokespeople and leaders who would then pave the road to the modern civil rights movement after World War II.

21.4 Progressivism in the White House

By the end of this section, you will be able to:
- Explain the key features of Theodore Roosevelt's "Square Deal"
- Explain the key features of William Howard Taft's Progressive agenda
- Identify the main pieces of legislation that Woodrow Wilson's "New Freedom" agenda comprised

Progressive groups made tremendous strides on issues involving democracy, efficiency, and social justice. But they found that their grassroots approach was ill-equipped to push back against the most powerful beneficiaries of growing inequality, economic concentration, and corruption—big business. In their fight against the trusts, Progressives needed the leadership of the federal government, and they found it in Theodore Roosevelt in 1901, through an accident of history.

In 1900, a sound economic recovery, a unifying victory in the Spanish-American War, and the annexation of the Philippines had helped President William McKinley secure his reelection with the first solid popular majority since 1872. His new vice president was former New York Governor and Assistant Secretary of the Navy, Theodore Roosevelt. But when an assassin shot and killed President McKinley in 1901 (Figure 21.16) at the Pan-American Exposition in Buffalo, New York, Theodore Roosevelt unexpectedly became the youngest president in the nation's history. More importantly, it ushered in a new era of progressive national politics and changed the role of the presidency for the twentieth century.

(a)   (b)

Figure 21.16   President William McKinley's assassination (a) at the hands of an anarchist made Theodore Roosevelt (b) the country's youngest president.

BUSTING THE TRUSTS

Roosevelt's early career showed him to be a dynamic leader with a Progressive agenda. Many Republican Party leaders disliked Roosevelt's Progressive ideas and popular appeal and hoped to end his career with a nomination to the vice presidency—long considered a dead end in politics. When an assassin's bullet toppled this scheme, Mark Hanna, a prominent Republican senator and party leader, lamented, "Now look! That damned cowboy is now president!"

As the new president, however, Roosevelt moved cautiously with his agenda while he finished out McKinley's term. Roosevelt kept much of McKinley's cabinet intact, and his initial message to Congress gave only one overriding Progressive goal for his presidency: to eliminate business trusts. In the three years prior to Roosevelt's presidency, the nation had witnessed a wave of mergers and the creation of mega-corporations. To counter this trend, Roosevelt created the Department of Commerce and Labor in 1903, which included the Bureau of Corporations, whose job it was to investigate trusts. He also asked the Department of Justice to resume prosecutions under the Sherman Antitrust Act of 1890. Intended to empower federal prosecutors to ban monopolies as conspiracies against interstate trade, the law had run afoul of a conservative Supreme Court.

In 1902, Roosevelt launched his administration's first antitrust suit against the Northern Securities Trust Company, which included powerful businessmen, like John D. Rockefeller and J. P. Morgan, and controlled many of the large midwestern railroads. The suit wound through the judicial system, all the way to the U.S. Supreme Court. In 1904, the highest court in the land ultimately affirmed the ruling to break up the trust in a narrow five-to-four vote. For Roosevelt, that was enough of a mandate;

he immediately moved against other corporations as well, including the American Tobacco Company and—most significantly—Rockefeller's Standard Oil Company.

Although Roosevelt enjoyed the nickname "the Trustbuster," he did not consider all trusts dangerous to the public welfare. The "good trusts," Roosevelt reasoned, used their power in the marketplace and economies of scale to deliver goods and services to customers more cheaply. For example, he allowed Morgan's U.S. Steel Corporation to continue its operations and let it take over smaller steel companies. At the same time, Roosevelt used the presidency as a "bully pulpit" to publicly denounce "bad trusts"—those corporations that exploited their market positions for short-term gains—before he ordered prosecutions by the Justice Department. In total, Roosevelt initiated over two dozen successful anti-trust suits, more than any president before him.

Roosevelt also showed in other contexts that he dared to face the power of corporations. When an anthracite coal strike gripped the nation for much of the year in 1902, Roosevelt directly intervened in the dispute and invited both sides to the White House to negotiate a deal that included minor wage increases and a slight improvement in working hours. For Roosevelt, his intervention in the matter symbolized his belief that the federal government should adopt a more proactive role and serve as a steward of all Americans (Figure 21.17). This stood in contrast to his predecessors, who had time and again bolstered industrialists in their fight against workers' rights with the deployment of federal troops.

THE WASHINGTON SCHOOLMASTER
From the *Chronicle* (Chicago)

Figure 21.17 This cartoon shows President Roosevelt disciplining coal barons like J. P. Morgan, threatening to beat them with a stick labeled "Federal Authority." It illustrates Roosevelt's new approach to business.

THE SQUARE DEAL

Roosevelt won his second term in 1904 with an overwhelming 57 percent of the popular vote. After the election, he moved quickly to enact his own brand of Progressivism, which he called a **Square Deal** for the American people. Early in his second term, Roosevelt read muckraker Upton Sinclair's 1905 novel and exposé on the meatpacking industry, *The Jungle*. Although Roosevelt initially questioned the book due to Sinclair's professed Socialist leanings, a subsequent presidential commission investigated the industry and corroborated the deplorable conditions under which Chicago's meatpackers processed meats for American consumers. Alarmed by the results and under pressure from an outraged public disgusted with the revelations, Roosevelt moved quickly to protect public health. He urged the passage of two laws to do so. The first, the Meat Inspection Act of 1906, established a system of government inspection for meat products, including grading the meat based on its quality. This standard was also used for imported meats. The second was the Pure Food and Drug Act of 1906, which required labels on all food and drug products that clearly stated the materials in the product. The law also prohibited any "adulterated" products, a measure aimed at some specific, unhealthy food preservatives. For Sinclair, this outcome was a disappointment nonetheless, since he had sought to draw attention to the plight of workers in the slaughterhouses, not the poor quality of the meat products. "I aimed at the public's heart, and by accident I hit it in the stomach," he concluded with frustration.

Another key element of Roosevelt's Progressivism was the protection of public land (Figure 21.18). Roosevelt was a longtime outdoorsman, with an interest that went back to his childhood and college days, as well as his time cattle ranching in the West, and he chose to appoint his good friend Gifford Pinchot as the country's first chief of the newly created U.S. Forestry Service. Under Pinchot's supervision, the department carved out several nature habitats on federal land in order to preserve the nation's environmental beauty and protect it from development or commercial use. Apart from national parks like Oregon's Crater Lake or Colorado's Mesa Verde, and monuments designed for preservation, Roosevelt conserved public land for regulated use for future generations. To this day, the 150 national forests created under Roosevelt's stewardship carry the slogan "land of many uses." In all, Roosevelt established eighteen national monuments, fifty-one federal bird preserves, five national parks, and over one hundred fifty national forests, which amounted to about 230 million acres of public land.

Figure 21.18 Theodore Roosevelt's interest in the protection of public lands was encouraged by conservationists such as John Muir, founder of the Sierra Club, with whom he toured Yosemite National Park in California, ca. 1906.

In his second term in office, Roosevelt signed legislation on Progressive issues such as factory inspections, child labor, and business regulation. He urged the passage of the Elkins Act of 1903 and the Hepburn Act of 1906, both of which strengthened the position of the Interstate Commerce Commission to regulate railroad prices. These laws also extended the Commission's authority to regulate interstate transportation on bridges, ferries, and even oil pipelines.

As the 1908 election approached, Roosevelt was at the height of popularity among the American public, if not among the big businesses and conservative leaders of his own Republican Party. Nonetheless, he promised on the night of his reelection in 1904 that he would not seek a third term. Roosevelt stepped aside as the election approached, but he did hand-pick a successor—Secretary of War and former Governor General of the Philippines William Howard Taft of Ohio—a personal friend who, he assured the American public, would continue the path of the "Square Deal" (Figure 21.19). With such a ringing endorsement, Taft easily won the 1908 presidential election, defeating three-time Democratic presidential nominee William Jennings Bryan, whose ideas on taxes and corporate regulations reminded voters of the more far-reaching Populist platforms of Bryan's past candidacies.

(a)   (b)

Figure 21.19 This photograph (a) of Theodore Roosevelt (left) and his hand-picked successor William Howard Taft (right) just before Taft's inauguration in 1909, was echoed in a Puck magazine cartoon (b) where "cowboy" Roosevelt hands off his "Policies" baby to "nurse-maid" Taft. Taft was seen, initially at least, as being a president who would continue Roosevelt's same policies.

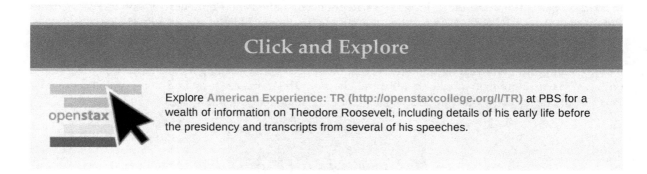

Explore American Experience: TR (http://openstaxcollege.org/l/TR) at PBS for a wealth of information on Theodore Roosevelt, including details of his early life before the presidency and transcripts from several of his speeches.

THE TAFT PRESIDENCY

Although six feet tall and nearly 340 pounds, as Roosevelt's successor, Taft had big shoes to fill. The public expected much from Roosevelt's hand-picked replacement, as did Roosevelt himself, who kept a watchful eye over Taft's presidency.

The new president's background suggested he would be a strong administrator. He had previously served as the governor of the Philippines following the Spanish-American War, had a distinguished judicial career, and served as Roosevelt's Secretary of War from 1904 to 1908. Republican leaders, however, were anxious to reestablish tighter control over the party after Roosevelt's departure, and they left Taft little room to maneuver. He stayed the course of his predecessor by signing the Mann-Elkins Act of 1910, which extended the authority of the Interstate Commerce Commission over telephones and telegraphs. Additionally, during his tenure, Congress proposed constitutional amendments to authorize a federal income tax and mandate the direct election of U.S. senators. But even though Taft initiated twice as many antitrust suits against big business as Roosevelt, he lacked the political negotiating skills and focus on the public good of his predecessor, who felt betrayed when Taft took J.P. Morgan's U.S. Steel Corporation to court over an acquisition that Roosevelt had promised Morgan would not result in a prosecution.

Political infighting within his own party exposed the limitations of Taft's presidential authority, especially on the issue of protective tariffs. When House Republicans passed a measure to significantly reduce tariffs on several imported goods, Taft endorsed the Senate version, later known as the Payne-Aldrich Act of 1909, which raised tariff rates on over eight hundred products in the original bill. Taft also angered Progressives in his own party when he created the U.S. Chamber of Commerce in 1912, viewed by many as an attempt to offset the growing influence of the labor union movement at the time. The rift between Taft and his party's Progressives widened when the president supported conservative party candidates for the 1910 House and Senate elections.

Taft's biggest political blunder came in the area of land conservation. In 1909, Taft's Secretary of the Interior, Richard Ballinger, approved the sale of millions of acres of federal land to a company for which he had previously worked over Gifford Pinchot's objections. Pinchot publicly criticized the secretary for violating the principle of conservation and for his conflict of interest—a charge that in the public debate also reflected on the president. Taft fired Pinchot, a move that widened the gap between him and the former president. Upon his return from Africa, Roosevelt appeared primed to attack. He referred to the sitting president as a "fathead" and a "puzzlewit," and announced his intention to "throw my hat in the ring for the 1912 presidential election."

THE 1912 PRESIDENTIAL ELECTION

Although not as flamboyant or outwardly progressive as Roosevelt, Taft's organizational skills and generally solid performance as president aligned with the party leadership's concerns over another Roosevelt presidency and secured for him the Republican Party's nomination. Angry over this snub, in 1912, Roosevelt and the other Progressive Republicans bolted the Republican Party and formed the **Progressive Party**. His popularity had him hoping to win the presidential race as a third-party candidate. When he survived an assassination attempt in Milwaukee, Wisconsin, in October 1912—the assassin's bullet hit his eyeglass case and only injured him superficially—he turned the near-death experience into a political opportunity. Insisting upon delivering the speech before seeking medical attention, he told the crowd, "It takes more than a bullet to kill a bull moose!" The moniker stuck, and Roosevelt's Progressive Party would be known as the Bull Moose Party for the remainder of the campaign (Figure 21.20).

Figure 21.20 Theodore Roosevelt, now running as the Progressive Party, or Bull Moose Party, candidate, created an unprecedented moment in the country's history, where a former president was running against both an incumbent president and a future president.

The Democrats realized that a split Republican Party gave them a good chance of regaining the White House for the first time since 1896. They found their candidate in the Progressive governor of New

Jersey, Woodrow Wilson. A former history professor and president at Princeton University, Wilson had an academic demeanor that appealed to many Progressive reformers. Many Democrats also viewed Wilson as a Washington outsider who had made far fewer political enemies than Roosevelt and Taft.

Taft never truly campaigned for the post, did not deliver a single speech, and did not seem like a serious contender. In their campaigns, Roosevelt and Wilson formulated competing Progressive platforms. Wilson described his more moderate approach as one of **New Freedom**, which stood for a smaller federal government to protect public interests from the evils associated with big businesses and banks. Roosevelt campaigned on the promise of **New Nationalism**, a charge that he said required a vigorous and powerful federal government to protect public interests. He sought to capitalize on the stewardship approach that he had made famous during his previous administration.

Wilson won the 1912 election with over six million votes, with four million votes going to Roosevelt and three and one-half million for Taft. The internal split among Republicans not only cost them the White House but control of the Senate as well—and Democrats had already won a House majority in 1910. Wilson won the presidency with just 42 percent of the popular vote, which meant that he would have to sway a large number of voters should he have any aspirations for a second term.

DEFINING "AMERICAN"

✲ *The Unprecedented Election of 1912*

In his 2002 article on the 1912 election, historian Sidney M. Milkis writes,

> The Progressive Party's "compromise" with public opinion in the United States points to its legacy for American politics and government. Arguably, the failure of the 1912 experiment and the Progressive Party's demise underscore the incoherence of the Progressive movement. Nevertheless, it was neither the Democrats, nor the Republicans, nor the Socialists who set the tone of the 1912 campaign. It was the Progressives. Beyond the 1912 election, their program of political and social reform has been an enduring feature of American political discourse and electoral struggle. The Progressive Party forged a path of reform that left both social democracy and conservatism—Taft's constitutional sobriety—behind. Similarly, T.R.'s celebrity, and the popularity of the Progressive doctrine of the people's right to rule, tended to subordinate the more populist to the more plebiscitary schemes in the platform, such as the initiative, the referendum, and the direct primary, which exalted not the "grass roots" but mass opinion. Indeed, in the wake of the excitement aroused by the Progressive Party, Wilson, whose New Freedom campaign was far more sympathetic to the decentralized state of courts and parties than T.R.'s, felt compelled, as president, to govern as a New Nationalist Progressive.

It is interesting to think of how this most unusual election—one with three major candidates that pitted a former president against an incumbent and a major party contender—related to the larger Progressive movement. The cartoon below is only one of many cartoons of that era that sought to point out the differences between the candidates (Figure 21.21). While Roosevelt and the Progressive Party ultimately lost the election, they required the dialogue of the campaign to remain on the goals of Progressivism, particularly around more direct democracy and business regulation. The American public responded with fervor to Roosevelt's campaign, partly because of his immense popularity, but partly also because he espoused a kind of direct democracy that gave people a voice in federal politics. Although Wilson and his New Freedom platform won the election, his presidency undertook a more activist role than his campaign suggested. The American public had made clear that, no matter who sat in the White House, they were seeking a more progressive America.

Figure 21.21 This cartoon, from the 1912 election, parodies how the voters might perceive the three major candidates. As can be seen, Taft was never a serious contender.

WILSON'S NEW FREEDOM

When Wilson took office in March 1913, he immediately met with Congress to outline his New Freedom agenda for how progressive interests could be best preserved. His plan was simple: regulate the banks and big businesses, and lower tariff rates to increase international trade, increasing competition in the interest of consumers. Wilson took the unusual step of calling a special session of Congress in April 1913 to tackle the tariff question, which resulted in the Revenue Act of 1913, also known as the Underwood Tariff Act. This legislation lowered tariff rates across the board by approximately 15 percent and completely eliminated tariffs on several imports, including steel, iron ore, woolen products, and farm tools. To offset the potential loss of federal revenue, this new law reinstituted the federal income tax, which followed the ratification of the Sixteenth Amendment. This first income tax required married couples who earned $4000 or more, and single people who earned $3000 or more, to pay a 1-percent, graduated income tax, with the tax rate getting progressively higher for those who earned more.

Late in 1913, Wilson signed the Federal Reserve Act to regulate the banking industry and establish a federal banking system (Figure 21.22). Designed to remove power over interest rates from the hands of private bankers, the new system created twelve privately owned regional reserve banks regulated by a presidentially appointed Federal Reserve Board. The Board, known informally as the Fed, regulated the interest rate at which reserve banks loaned or distributed money to other banks around the country. Thus, when economic times were challenging, such as during a recession, the Fed could lower this "discount rate" and encourage more borrowing, which put more currency in circulation for people to spend or invest. Conversely, the Fed could curb inflationary trends with interest hikes that discouraged borrowing. This system is still the basis for the country's modern banking model.

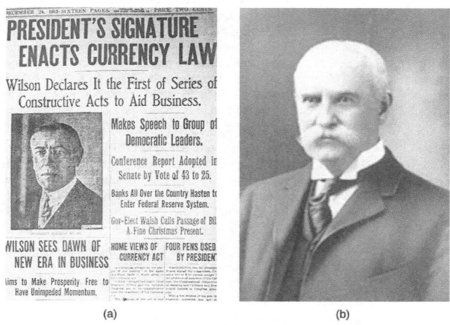

(a)   (b)

Figure 21.22 With the creation of the Federal Reserve Board, President Wilson set the stage for the modern banking system (a). This restructuring of the American financial system, which included the authorization of a federal income tax, was supported in large part by an influential Republican senator from Rhode Island, Nelson Aldrich (b), co-author of the Payne-Aldrich Act of 1909.

Click and Explore

The history of the Federal Reserve Act (http://openstaxcollege.org/l/Fedreserve) is explored in *The Washington Post*, reflecting back on the act one hundred years later.

In early 1914, Wilson completed his New Freedom agenda with the passage of the Clayton Antitrust Act. This law expanded the power of the original Sherman Antitrust Act in order to allow the investigation and dismantling of more monopolies. The new act also took on the "interlocking directorates"—competing companies that still operated together in a form of oligopoly or conspiracy to restrain trade. His New Freedom agenda complete, Wilson turned his attention to foreign affairs, as war was quickly encompassing Europe.

THE FINAL VESTIGES OF PROGRESSIVISM

As the 1916 election approached, Wilson's focus on foreign affairs, as well as the natural effect of his small government agenda, left the 60 percent of the American public who had not voted for him the first time disinclined to change their minds and keep him in office. Realizing this, Wilson began a flurry of new Progressive reforms that impressed the voting public and ultimately proved to be the last wave of the Progressive Era. Some of the important measures that Wilson undertook to pass included the Federal Farm Act, which provided oversight of low-interest loans to millions of farmers in need of debt relief; the Keating-Owen Child Labor Act, which, although later deemed unconstitutional by the U.S. Supreme Court, prohibited the interstate distribution of products by child workers under the age of fourteen; and the Adamson Act, which put in place the first federally mandated eight-hour workday for railroad workers.

Wilson also gained significant support from Jewish voters with his 1916 appointment of the first Jewish U.S. Supreme Court justice, Louis D. Brandeis. Popular among social justice Progressives, Brandeis went on to become one of the most renowned justices on the court for his defense of freedom of speech and right to privacy issues. Finally, Wilson gained the support of many working-class voters with his defense of labor and union rights during a violent coal strike in Ludlow, Colorado, as well as his actions to forestall a potential railroad strike with the passage of the aforementioned Adamson Act.

Wilson's actions in 1916 proved enough, but barely. In a close presidential election, he secured a second term by defeating former New York governor Charles Evans Hughes by a scant twenty-three electoral votes, and less than 600,000 popular votes. Influential states like Minnesota and New Hampshire were decided by less than four hundred votes.

Despite the fact that he ran for reelection with the slogan, "He Kept Us Out of the War," Wilson could not avoid the reach of World War I much longer. For Wilson and the American public, the Progressive Era was rapidly winding down. Although a few Progressive achievements were still to come in the areas of women's suffrage and prohibition, the country would soon be gripped by the war that Wilson had tried to avoid during his first term in office. When he took the oath for his second term, on March 4, 1917, Wilson was barely five weeks away from leading the United States in declaring war on Germany, a move that would put an end to the Progressive Era.

Key Terms

Atlanta Compromise Booker T. Washington's speech, given at the Atlanta Exposition in 1895, where he urged African Americans to work hard and get along with others in their white communities, so as to earn the goodwill of the country

direct primary a political reform that allowed for the nomination of candidates through a direct vote by party members, rather than by the choice of delegates at conventions; in the South, this strengthened all-white solidarity within the Democratic Party

initiative a proposed law, or initiative, placed on the ballot by public petition

muckrakers investigative journalists and authors who wrote about social ills, from child labor to the corrupt business practices of big businesses, and urged the public to take action

NAACP the National Association for the Advancement of Colored People, a civil rights organization formed in 1909 by an interracial coalition including W. E. B. Du Bois and Florence Kelley

New Freedom Woodrow Wilson's campaign platform for the 1912 election that called for a small federal government to protect public interests from the evils associated with bad businesses

New Nationalism Theodore Roosevelt's 1912 campaign platform, which called for a powerful federal government to protect the American public

Niagara Movement a campaign led by W. E. B. Du Bois and other prominent African American reformers that departed from Booker T. Washington's model of accommodation and advocated for a "Declaration of Principles" that called for immediate political, social, and economic equality for African Americans

Progressive Party a political party started by Roosevelt and other Progressive Republicans who were unhappy with Taft and wanted Roosevelt to run for a nonconsecutive third term in 1912

Progressivism a broad movement between 1896 and 1916 led by white, middle-class professionals for legal, scientific, managerial, and institutional solutions to the ills of urbanization, industrialization, and corruption

recall to remove a public official from office by virtue of a petition and vote process

referendum a process that allows voters to counteract legislation by putting an existing law on the ballot for voters to either affirm or reject

Silent Sentinels women protesters who picketed the White House for years to protest for women's right to vote; they went on a hunger strike after their arrest, and their force-feeding became a national scandal

Square Deal Theodore Roosevelt's name for the kind of involved, hands-on government he felt the country needed

Taylorism a system named for Fredrick Winslow Taylor, aimed at improving factory efficiency rates through the principle of standardization; Taylor's model limited workers to repetitive tasks, reducing human contact and opportunities to think or collaborate

Wisconsin Idea a political system created by Robert La Follette, governor of Wisconsin, that embodied many progressive ideals; La Follette hired experts to advise him on improving conditions in his state

Wobblies a nickname for the Industrial Workers of the World, a radical Progressive group that grew out of the earlier labor movement and desired an industrial union model of labor organization

Summary

21.1 The Origins of the Progressive Spirit in America

In its first decade, the Progressive Era was a grassroots effort that ushered in reforms at state and local levels. At the beginning of the twentieth century, however, Progressive endeavors captured the attention of the federal government. The challenges of the late nineteenth century were manifold: fast-growing cities that were ill-equipped to house the working poor, hands-off politicians shackled into impotence by their system of political favors, and rural Americans struggling to keep their farms afloat. The muckraking journalists of the era published books and articles highlighting the social inequities of the day and extolling everyday Americans to help find solutions. Educated, middle-class, Anglo-Saxon Protestants dominated the movement, but Progressives were not a homogenous group: The movement counted African Americans, both women and men, and urban as well as rural dwellers among its ranks. Progressive causes ranged from anti-liquor campaigns to fair pay. Together, Progressives sought to advance the spread of democracy, improve efficiency in government and industry, and promote social justice.

21.2 Progressivism at the Grassroots Level

Progressive campaigns stretched from the hurricane-ruined townships of Texas to the slums of New York, from the factory floor to the saloon door. But what tied together these disparate causes and groups was the belief that the country was in dire need of reform, and that answers were to be found within the activism and expertise of predominantly middle-class Americans on behalf of troubled communities. Some efforts, such as the National Child Labor Committee, pushed for federal legislation; however, most Progressive initiatives took place at the state and local levels, as Progressives sought to harness public support to place pressure on politicians.

At the beginning of the twentieth century, a more radical, revolutionary breed of Progressivism began to evolve. While these radical Progressives generally shared the goals of their more mainstream counterparts, their strategies differed significantly. Mainstream Progressives and many middle-class Americans feared groups such as the Socialist Party of America and the Industrial Workers of the World, which emphasized workers' empowerment and direct action.

21.3 New Voices for Women and African Americans

The Progressive commitment to promoting democracy and social justice created an environment within which the movements for women's and African American rights grew and flourished. Emergent leaders such as Elizabeth Cady Stanton, Susan B. Anthony, Carrie Chapman Catt, and Alice Paul spread the cause of woman suffrage, drawing in other activists and making the case for a constitutional amendment ensuring a woman's right to vote. African Americans—guided by leaders such as Booker T. Washington and W. E. B. Du Bois—strove for civil rights and economic opportunity, although their philosophies and strategies differed significantly. In the women's and civil rights movements alike, activists both advanced their own causes and paved the way for later efforts aimed at expanding equal opportunity and citizenship.

21.4 Progressivism in the White House

Theodore Roosevelt became president only by historical accident, but his activism in the executive branch spoke to the Progressive spirit in the nation and transformed the president's office for the twentieth century. The courage he displayed in his confrontation of big business and willingness to side with workers in capital-labor disputes, as well as his commitment to the preservation of federal lands, set an agenda his successors had to match. Like Roosevelt, William Howard Taft pushed antitrust rulings and expanded federal oversight of interstate commerce. But estrangement from his predecessor and mentor left Taft in a difficult position for reelection. Roosevelt's third-party challenge as a Progressive split the Republican vote and handed Woodrow Wilson the presidency in 1912.

A Progressive like his predecessors, Wilson was also a political creature who understood the need to do more in order to ensure his reelection. He, too, sought to limit the power of big businesses and stabilize the economy, and he ushered in a wave of Progressive legislation that grassroots Progressives had long called for. The nation's entanglement in World War I, however, soon shunted the Progressive goals of democracy, efficiency, regulation, and social justice to the back burner. The nation's new priorities included national security and making the world "safe for democracy."

Review Questions

1. Ida Tarbell wrote publicly about
  A. the need for better housing in rural America
  B. the sinister business practices of Standard Oil
  C. the need for a national temperance movement
  D. the women's suffrage cause in the American West

2. Which of the following was *not* a key area of focus for the Progressives?
  A. land reform
  B. democracy
  C. business regulation
  D. social justice

3. How did muckrakers help initiate the Progressive Era?

4. What system did the direct primary replace?
  A. candidate selection by secret ballots
  B. candidate selection by machine bosses
  C. candidate selection by convention delegates
  D. an indirect primary

5. Which of the following is *not* an example of social justice Progressivism?
  A. anti-liquor campaigns
  B. referendums
  C. workplace safety initiatives
  D. improvements in education

6. Which of the following was *not* a feature of Booker T. Washington's strategy to improve the lives of African Americans?
  A. self-help
  B. accommodating/tolerating white racism
  C. immediate protests for equal rights
  D. learning new trades/skills

7. Who were the "Silent Sentinels"?
  A. a group of progressive African Americans who drafted the Declaration of Principles
  B. anti-suffrage women
  C. an offshoot of the Industrial Workers of the World
  D. suffragists who protested outside the White House

8. Describe the philosophy and strategies of the Niagara Movement. How did it differ from Washington's way of thinking?

9. How did Roosevelt intercede in the Anthracite Coal Strike of 1902?
  A. He invited strikers and workers to the White House.
  B. He urged the owners to negotiate a deal.
  C. He threatened to send in the army to work the mines.
  D. He ordered the National Guard to protect the strikers.

10. Which of the following was a key Progressive item passed by Taft?
  A. the Pure Food and Drug Act
  B. the U.S. Forestry Service

C. the Mann-Elkins Act

D. the Payne-Aldrich Act

D. It established a federal banking system to oversee tariffs.

11. Which of the following was *not* an outcome of the Underwood Tariff Act?

A. It reduced tariffs 15 percent across all imports.

B. It eliminated tariffs for steel.

C. It eliminated tariffs for iron ore.

12. Explain the fundamental differences between Roosevelt's "New Nationalism" and Wilson's "New Freedom."

13. Why did Wilson's "New Freedom" agenda come in two distinct phases (1913 and 1916)?

Critical Thinking Questions

14. Which of the primary features of grassroots Progressivism was the most essential to the continued growth and success of the reformist movement? Why?

15. Describe the multiple groups and leaders that emerged in the fight for the Progressive agenda, including women's rights, African American rights, and workers' rights. How were the philosophies, agendas, strategies, and approaches of these leaders and organizations similar and different? What made it difficult for all Progressive activists to present a united front?

16. How did President Theodore Roosevelt's "Square Deal" epitomize the notion that the federal government should serve as a steward protecting the public's interests?

17. How did the goals and reform agenda of the Progressive Era manifest themselves during the presidential administrations of Roosevelt, Taft, and Wilson?

18. What vestiges of Progressivism can we see in our modern lives—politically, economically, and socially? Which of our present-day political processes, laws, institutions, and attitudes have roots in this era? Why have they had such staying power?

CHAPTER 22

Age of Empire: American Foreign Policy, 1890-1914

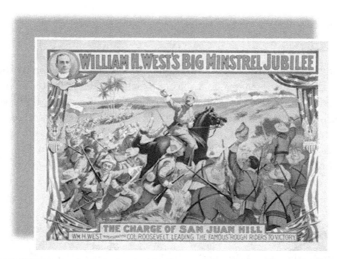

Figure 22.1 This poster advertises a minstrel show wherein an actor playing Theodore Roosevelt reenacts his leadership of the Rough Riders in the Spanish-American War and illustrates the American public's zeal for tales of American expansionist glory.

Chapter Outline

22.1 Turner, Mahan, and the Roots of Empire
22.2 The Spanish-American War and Overseas Empire
22.3 Economic Imperialism in East Asia
22.4 Roosevelt's "Big Stick" Foreign Policy
22.5 Taft's "Dollar Diplomacy"

Introduction

As he approached the rostrum to speak before historians gathered in Chicago in 1893, Frederick Jackson Turner appeared nervous. He was presenting a conclusion that would alarm all who believed that westward expansion had fostered the nation's principles of democracy. His conclusion: The frontier—the encounter between European traditions and the native wilderness—had played a fundamental role in shaping American character, but the American frontier no longer existed. Turner's statement raised questions. How would Americans maintain their unique political culture and innovative spirit in the absence of the frontier? How would the nation expand its economy if it could no longer expand its territory?

Later historians would see Turner's Frontier Thesis as deeply flawed, a gross mischaracterization of the West. But the young historian's work greatly influenced politicians and thinkers of the day. Like a muckraker, Turner exposed the problem; others found a solution by seeking out new frontiers in the creation of an American empire. The above advertisement for a theater reenactment of the Spanish-American War (Figure 22.1) shows the American appetite for expansion. Many Americans felt that it was time for their nation to offer its own brand of international leadership and dominance as an alternative to the land-grabbing empires of Europe.

22.1 Turner, Mahan, and the Roots of Empire

By the end of this section, you will be able to:

- Explain the evolution of American interest in foreign affairs from the end of the Civil War through the early 1890s
- Identify the contributions of Frederick Jackson Turner and Alfred Thayer Mahan to the conscious creation of an American empire

During the time of Reconstruction, the U.S. government showed no significant initiative in foreign affairs. Western expansion and the goal of Manifest Destiny still held the country's attention, and American missionaries proselytized as far abroad as China, India, the Korean Peninsula, and Africa, but reconstruction efforts took up most of the nation's resources. As the century came to a close, however, a variety of factors, from the closing of the American frontier to the country's increased industrial production, led the United States to look beyond its borders. Countries in Europe were building their empires through global power and trade, and the United States did not want to be left behind.

AMERICA'S LIMITED BUT AGGRESSIVE PUSH OUTWARD

On the eve of the Civil War, the country lacked the means to establish a strong position in international diplomacy. As of 1865, the U.S. State Department had barely sixty employees and no ambassadors representing American interests abroad. Instead, only two dozen American foreign ministers were located in key countries, and those often gained their positions not through diplomatic skills or expertise in foreign affairs but through bribes. Further limiting American potential for foreign impact was the fact that a strong international presence required a strong military—specifically a navy—which the United States, after the Civil War, was in no position to maintain. Additionally, as late as 1890, with the U.S. Navy significantly reduced in size, a majority of vessels were classified as "Old Navy," meaning a mixture of iron hulled and wholly wooden ships. While the navy had introduced the first all-steel, triple-hulled steam engine vessels seven years earlier, they had only thirteen of them in operation by 1890.

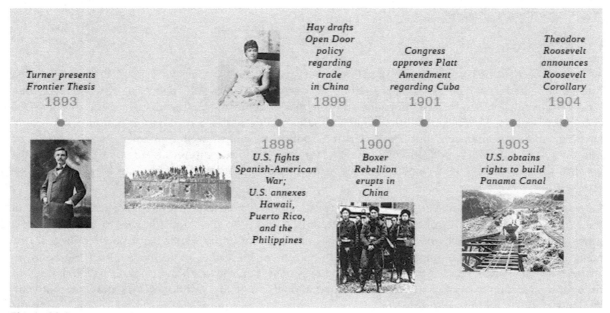

Figure 22.2

Despite such widespread isolationist impulses and the sheer inability to maintain a strong international position, the United States moved ahead sporadically with a modest foreign policy agenda in the three decades following the Civil War. Secretary of State William Seward, who held that position from 1861 through 1869, sought to extend American political and commercial influence in both Asia and Latin America. He pursued these goals through a variety of actions. A treaty with Nicaragua set the early course for the future construction of a canal across Central America. He also pushed through the annexation of the Midway Islands in the Pacific Ocean, which subsequently opened a more stable route to Asian markets. In frequent conversations with President Lincoln, among others, Seward openly spoke of his desire to obtain British Columbia, the Hawaiian Islands, portions of the Dominican Republic, Cuba, and other territories. He explained his motives to a Boston audience in 1867, when he professed his intention to give the United States "control of the world."

Most notably, in 1867, Seward obtained the Alaskan Territory from Russia for a purchase price of $7.2 million. Fearing future loss of the territory through military conflict, as well as desiring to create challenges for Great Britain (which they had fought in the Crimean War), Russia had happily accepted the American purchase offer. In the United States, several newspaper editors openly questioned the purchase and labeled it **"Seward's Folly"** (Figure 22.3). They highlighted the lack of Americans to populate the vast region and lamented the challenges in attempting to govern the native peoples in that territory. Only if gold were to be found, the editors decried, would the secretive purchase be justified. That is exactly what happened. Seward's purchase added an enormous territory to the country—nearly 600,000 square miles—and also gave the United States access to the rich mineral resources of the region, including the gold that trigged the Klondike Gold Rush at the close of the century. As was the case elsewhere in the American borderlands, Alaska's industrial development wreaked havoc on the region's indigenous and Russian cultures.

Figure 22.3 Although mocked in the press at the time as "Seward's Folly," Secretary of State William Seward's acquisition of Alaska from Russia was a strategic boon to the United States.

Seward's successor as Secretary of State, Hamilton Fish, held the position from 1869 through 1877. Fish spent much of his time settling international disputes involving American interests, including claims that British assistance to the Confederates prolonged the Civil War for about two years. In these so-called Alabama claims, a U.S. senator charged that the Confederacy won a number of crucial battles with the help of one British cruiser and demanded $2 billion in British reparations. Alternatively, the United States would settle for the rights to Canada. A joint commission representing both countries eventually settled on a British payment of $15 million to the United States. In the negotiations, Fish also suggested adding the Dominican Republic as a territorial possession with a path towards statehood, as well as discussing the construction of a transoceanic canal with Columbia. Although neither negotiation ended in the desired result, they both expressed Fish's intent to cautiously build an American empire without creating any unnecessary military entanglements in the wake of the Civil War.

BUSINESS, RELIGIOUS, AND SOCIAL INTERESTS SET THE STAGE FOR EMPIRE

While the United States slowly pushed outward and sought to absorb the borderlands (and the indigenous cultures that lived there), the country was also changing how it functioned. As a new industrial United States began to emerge in the 1870s, economic interests began to lead the country toward a more expansionist foreign policy. By forging new and stronger ties overseas, the United States would gain access to international markets for export, as well as better deals on the raw materials needed domestically. The concerns raised by the economic depression of the early 1890s further convinced business owners that they needed to tap into new markets, even at the risk of foreign entanglements.

As a result of these growing economic pressures, American exports to other nations skyrocketed in the years following the Civil War, from $234 million in 1865 to $605 million in 1875. By 1898, on the eve of the Spanish-American War, American exports had reached a height of $1.3 billion annually. Imports over the same period also increased substantially, from $238 million in 1865 to $616 million in 1898. Such an increased investment in overseas markets in turn strengthened Americans' interest in foreign affairs.

Businesses were not the only ones seeking to expand. Religious leaders and Progressive reformers joined businesses in their growing interest in American expansion, as both sought to increase the democratic and Christian influences of the United States abroad. Imperialism and Progressivism were compatible in the minds of many reformers who thought the Progressive impulses for democracy at home translated overseas as well. Editors of such magazines as *Century*, *Outlook*, and *Harper's* supported an imperialistic stance as the democratic responsibility of the United States. Several Protestant faiths formed missionary societies in the years after the Civil War, seeking to expand their reach, particularly in Asia. Influenced by such works as Reverend Josiah Strong's *Our Country: Its Possible Future and Its Present Crisis* (1885), missionaries sought to spread the gospel throughout the country and abroad. Led by the American Board of Commissioners for Foreign Missions, among several other organizations, missionaries conflated Christian ethics with American virtues, and began to spread both gospels with zeal. This was particularly true among women missionaries, who composed over 60 percent of the overall missionary force. By 1870, missionaries abroad spent as much time advocating for the American version of a modern civilization as they did teaching the Bible.

Social reformers of the early Progressive Era also performed work abroad that mirrored the missionaries. Many were influenced by recent scholarship on race-based intelligence and embraced the implications of social Darwinist theory that alleged inferior races were destined to poverty on account of their lower evolutionary status. While certainly not all reformers espoused a racist view of intelligence and civilization, many of these reformers believed that the Anglo-Saxon race was mentally superior to others and owed the presumed less evolved populations their stewardship and social uplift—a service the British writer Rudyard Kipling termed "the white man's burden."

By trying to help people in less industrialized countries achieve a higher standard of living and a better understanding of the principles of democracy, reformers hoped to contribute to a noble cause, but their approach suffered from the same paternalism that hampered Progressive reforms at home. Whether reformers and missionaries worked with native communities in the borderlands such as New Mexico; in the inner cities, like the Salvation Army; or overseas, their approaches had much in common. Their good intentions and willingness to work in difficult conditions shone through in the letters and articles they wrote from the field. Often in their writing, it was clear that they felt divinely empowered to change the lives of other, less fortunate, and presumably, less enlightened, people. Whether oversees or in the urban slums, they benefitted from the same passions but expressed the same paternalism.

MY STORY

✣ *Lottie Moon, Missionary*

Lottie Moon was a Southern Baptist missionary who spent more than forty years living and working in China. She began in 1873 when she joined her sister in China as a missionary, teaching in a school for Chinese women. Her true passion, however, was to evangelize and minister, and she undertook a campaign to urge the Southern Baptist missionaries to allow women to work beyond the classroom. Her letter campaign back to the head of the Mission Board provided a vivid picture of life in China and exhorted the Southern Baptist women to give more generously of their money and their time. Her letters appeared frequently in religious publications, and it was her suggestion—that the week before Christmas be established as a time to donate to foreign missions—that led to the annual Christmas giving tradition. Lottie's rhetoric caught on, and still today, the annual Christmas offering is done in her name.

> We had the best possible voyage over the water—good weather, no headwinds, scarcely any rolling or pitching—in short, all that reasonable people could ask. . . . I spent a week here last fall and of course feel very natural to be here again. I do so love the East and eastern life! Japan fascinated my heart and fancy four years ago, but now I honestly believe I love China the best, and actually, which is stranger still, like the Chinese best.
> —Charlotte "Lottie" Moon, 1877

Lottie remained in China through famines, the Boxer Rebellion, and other hardships. She fought against foot binding, a cultural tradition where girls' feet were tightly bound to keep them from growing, and shared her personal food and money when those around her were suffering. But her primary goal was to evangelize her Christian beliefs to the people in China. She won the right to minister and personally converted hundreds of Chinese to Christianity. Lottie's combination of moral certainty and selfless service was emblematic of the missionary zeal of the early American empire.

TURNER, MAHAN, AND THE PLAN FOR EMPIRE

The initial work of businesses, missionaries, and reformers set the stage by the early 1890s for advocates of an expanded foreign policy and a vision of an American empire. Following decades of an official stance of isolationism combined with relatively weak presidents who lacked the popular mandate or congressional support to undertake substantial overseas commitments, a new cadre of American leaders—many of whom were too young to fully comprehend the damage inflicted by the Civil War—assumed leadership roles. Eager to be tested in international conflict, these new leaders hoped to prove America's might on a global stage. The Assistant Secretary of the Navy, Theodore Roosevelt, was one of these leaders who sought to expand American influence globally, and he advocated for the expansion of the U.S. Navy, which at the turn of the century was the only weapons system suitable for securing overseas expansion.

Turner (Figure 22.4) and naval strategist Alfred Thayer Mahan were instrumental in the country's move toward foreign expansion, and writer Brooks Adams further dramatized the consequences of the nation's loss of its frontier in his *The Law of Civilization and Decay* in 1895. As mentioned in the chapter opening, Turner announced his **Frontier Thesis**—that American democracy was largely formed by the American frontier—at the Chicago World's Colombian Exposition. He noted that "for nearly three centuries the dominant fact in American life has been expansion." He continued: "American energy will continually demand a wider field for its exercise."

Figure 22.4 Historian Fredrick Jackson Turner's Frontier Thesis stated explicitly that the existence of the western frontier forged the very basis of the American identity.

Although there was no more room for these forces to proceed domestically, they would continue to find an outlet on the international stage. Turner concluded that "the demands for a vigorous foreign policy, for an interoceanic canal, for a revival of our power upon our seas, and for the extension of American influence to outlying islands and adjoining countries are indications that the forces [of expansion] will continue." Such policies would permit Americans to find new markets. Also mindful of the mitigating influence of a frontier—in terms of easing pressure from increased immigration and population expansion in the eastern and midwestern United States—he encouraged new outlets for further population growth, whether as lands for further American settlement or to accommodate more immigrants. Turner's thesis was enormously influential at the time but has subsequently been widely criticized by historians. Specifically, the thesis underscores the pervasive racism and disregard for the indigenous communities, cultures, and individuals in the American borderlands and beyond.

Click and Explore

Explore the controversy associated with Turner's Frontier Thesis (http://openstaxcollege.org/l/conquest) at U.S. History Scene.

While Turner provided the idea for an empire, Mahan provided the more practical guide. In his 1890 work, *The Influence of Seapower upon History*, he suggested three strategies that would assist the United States in both constructing and maintaining an empire. First, noting the sad state of the U.S. Navy, he called for the government to build a stronger, more powerful version. Second, he suggested establishing a network of naval bases to fuel this expanding fleet. Seward's previous acquisition of the Midway Islands served this purpose by providing an essential naval coaling station, which was vital, as the limited reach of steamships and their dependence on coal made naval coaling stations imperative for increasing the navy's geographic reach. Future acquisitions in the Pacific and Caribbean increased this naval supply network (Figure 22.5). Finally, Mahan urged the future construction of a canal across the isthmus of Central America, which would decrease by two-thirds the time and power required to move the new navy from the Pacific to the Atlantic oceans. Heeding Mahan's advice, the government moved quickly, passing the Naval Act of 1890, which set production levels for a new, modern fleet. By 1898, the government had succeeded in increasing the size of the U.S. Navy to an active fleet of 160 vessels, of which 114 were newly built of steel. In addition, the fleet now included six battleships, compared to zero in the previous decade. As a naval power, the country catapulted to the third strongest in world rankings by military experts, trailing only Spain and Great Britain.

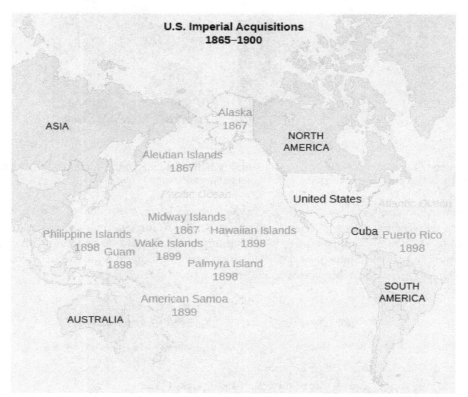

Figure 22.5 American imperial acquisitions as of the end of the Spanish-American War in 1898. Note how the spread of island acquisitions across the Pacific Ocean fulfills Alfred Mahan's call for more naval bases in order to support a larger and more effective U.S. Navy rather than mere territorial expansion.

The United States also began to expand its influence to other Pacific Islands, most notably Samoa and Hawaii. With regard to the latter, American businessmen were most interested in the lucrative sugar industry that lay at the heart of the Hawaiian Islands' economy. By 1890, through a series of reciprocal trade agreements, Hawaiians exported nearly all of their sugar production to the United States, tariff-free. When Queen Liliuokalani tapped into a strong anti-American resentment among native Hawaiians over the economic and political power of exploitative American sugar companies between 1891 and 1893, worried businessmen worked with the American minister to Hawaii, John Stevens, to stage a quick, armed revolt to counter her efforts and seize the islands as an American protectorate (Figure 22.6). Following five more years of political wrangling, the United States annexed Hawaii in 1898, during the Spanish-American War.

(a)   (b)

Figure 22.6 Queen Liliuokalani of Hawaii (a) was unhappy with the one-sided trade agreement Hawaii held with the United States (b), but protests were squashed by an American-armed revolt.

The United States had similar strategic interests in the Samoan Islands of the South Pacific, most notably, access to the naval refueling station at Pago Pago where American merchant vessels as well as naval ships could take on food, fuel, and supplies. In 1899, in an effort to mitigate other foreign interests and still protect their own, the United States joined Great Britain and Germany in a three-party protectorate over the islands, which assured American access to the strategic ports located there.

22.2 The Spanish-American War and Overseas Empire

By the end of this section, you will be able to:
- Explain the origins and events of the Spanish-American War
- Analyze the different American opinions on empire at the conclusion of the Spanish-American War
- Describe how the Spanish-American War intersected with other American expansions to solidify the nation's new position as an empire

The Spanish-American War was the first significant international military conflict for the United States since its war against Mexico in 1846; it came to represent a critical milestone in the country's development as an empire. Ostensibly about the rights of Cuban rebels to fight for freedom from Spain, the war had, for the United States at least, a far greater importance in the country's desire to expand its global reach.

The Spanish-American War was notable not only because the United States succeeded in seizing territory from another empire, but also because it caused the global community to recognize that the United States was a formidable military power. In what Secretary of State John Hay called "a splendid little war," the United States significantly altered the balance of world power, just as the twentieth century began to unfold (Figure 22.7).

LA FATLÉRA DEL ONCLE SAM (por M. MOLINÉ).

Guardarse l' Isla porque no 's perdi.

Figure 22.7 Whereas Americans thought of the Spanish colonial regime in Cuba as a typical example of European imperialism, this 1896 Spanish cartoon depicts the United States as a land-grabbing empire. The caption, written in Catalan, states "Keep the island so it won't get lost."

THE CHALLENGE OF DECLARING WAR

Despite its name, the Spanish-American War had less to do with the foreign affairs between the United States and Spain than Spanish control over Cuba and its possessions in the Far East. Spain had dominated Central and South America since the late fifteenth century. But, by 1890, the only Spanish colonies that had not yet acquired their independence were Cuba and Puerto Rico. On several occasions prior to the war, Cuban independence fighters in the Cuba Libre movement had attempted unsuccessfully to end Spanish control of their lands. In 1895, a similar revolt for independence erupted in Cuba; again, Spanish forces under the command of General Valeriano Weyler repressed the insurrection. Particularly notorious was their policy of re-concentration in which Spanish troops forced rebels from the countryside into military-controlled camps in the cities, where many died from harsh conditions.

As with previous uprisings, Americans were largely sympathetic to the Cuban rebels' cause, especially as the Spanish response was notably brutal. Evoking the same rhetoric of independence with which they fought the British during the American Revolution, several people quickly rallied to the Cuban fight for freedom. Shippers and other businessmen, particularly in the sugar industry, supported American intervention to safeguard their own interests in the region. Likewise, the "Cuba Libre" movement founded by José Martí, who quickly established offices in New York and Florida, further stirred American interest in the liberation cause. The difference in this uprising, however, was that supporters saw in the renewed U.S. Navy a force that could be a strong ally for Cuba. Additionally, the late 1890s saw the height of **yellow journalism**, in which newspapers such as the *New York Journal*, led by William Randolph Hearst, and the *New York World*, published by Joseph Pulitzer, competed for readership with sensationalistic stories. These publishers, and many others who printed news stories for maximum drama and effect, knew that war would provide sensational copy.

However, even as sensationalist news stories fanned the public's desire to try out their new navy while supporting freedom, one key figure remained unmoved. President William McKinley, despite commanding a new, powerful navy, also recognized that the new fleet—and soldiers—were untested. Preparing for a reelection bid in 1900, McKinley did not see a potential war with Spain, acknowledged to be the most powerful naval force in the world, as a good bet. McKinley did publicly admonish Spain for its actions against the rebels, and urged Spain to find a peaceful solution in Cuba, but he remained resistant to public pressure for American military intervention.

McKinley's reticence to involve the United States changed in February 1898. He had ordered one of the newest navy battleships, the USS *Maine*, to drop anchor off the coast of Cuba in order to observe the situation, and to prepare to evacuate American citizens from Cuba if necessary. Just days after it arrived, on February 15, an explosion destroyed the *Maine*, killing over 250 American sailors (Figure 22.8). Immediately, yellow journalists jumped on the headline that the explosion was the result of a Spanish attack, and that all Americans should rally to war. The newspaper battle cry quickly emerged, "Remember the Maine!" Recent examinations of the evidence of that time have led many historians to conclude that the explosion was likely an accident due to the storage of gun powder close to the very hot boilers. But in 1898, without ready evidence, the newspapers called for a war that would sell papers, and the American public rallied behind the cry.

Figure 22.8 Although later reports would suggest the explosion was due to loose gunpowder onboard the ship, the press treated the explosion of the USS *Maine* as high drama. Note the lower headline citing that the ship was destroyed by a mine, despite the lack of evidence.

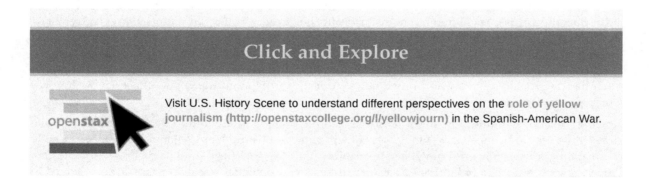

Click and Explore

Visit U.S. History Scene to understand different perspectives on the role of yellow journalism (http://openstaxcollege.org/l/yellowjourn) in the Spanish-American War.

McKinley made one final effort to avoid war, when late in March, he called on Spain to end its policy of concentrating the native population in military camps in Cuba, and to formally declare Cuba's independence. Spain refused, leaving McKinley little choice but to request a declaration of war from

Congress. Congress received McKinley's war message, and on April 19, 1898, they officially recognized Cuba's independence and authorized McKinley to use military force to remove Spain from the island. Equally important, Congress passed the Teller Amendment to the resolution, which stated that the United States would not annex Cuba following the war.

WAR: BRIEF AND DECISIVE

The Spanish-American War lasted approximately ten weeks, and the outcome was clear: The United States triumphed in its goal of helping liberate Cuba from Spanish control. Despite the positive result, the conflict did present significant challenges to the United States military. Although the new navy was powerful, the ships were, as McKinley feared, largely untested. Similarly untested were the American soldiers. The country had fewer than thirty thousand soldiers and sailors, many of whom were unprepared to do battle with a formidable opponent. But volunteers sought to make up the difference. Over one million American men—many lacking a uniform and coming equipped with their own guns—quickly answered McKinley's call for able-bodied men. Nearly ten thousand African American men also volunteered for service, despite the segregated conditions and additional hardships they faced, including violent uprisings at a few American bases before they departed for Cuba. The government, although grateful for the volunteer effort, was still unprepared to feed and supply such a force, and many suffered malnutrition and malaria for their sacrifice.

To the surprise of the Spanish forces who saw the conflict as a clear war over Cuba, American military strategists prepared for it as a war for empire. More so than simply the liberation of Cuba and the protection of American interests in the Caribbean, military strategists sought to further Mahan's vision of additional naval bases in the Pacific Ocean, reaching as far as mainland Asia. Such a strategy would also benefit American industrialists who sought to expand their markets into China. Just before leaving his post for volunteer service as a lieutenant colonel in the U.S. cavalry, Assistant Secretary of the Navy Theodore Roosevelt ordered navy ships to attack the Spanish fleet in the Philippines, another island chain under Spanish control. As a result, the first significant military confrontation took place not in Cuba but halfway around the world in the Philippines. Commodore George Dewey led the U.S. Navy in a decisive victory, sinking all of the Spanish ships while taking almost no American losses. Within a month, the U.S. Army landed a force to take the islands from Spain, which it succeeded in doing by mid-August 1899.

The victory in Cuba took a little longer. In June, seventeen thousand American troops landed in Cuba. Although they initially met with little Spanish resistance, by early July, fierce battles ensued near the Spanish stronghold in Santiago. Most famously, Theodore Roosevelt led his **Rough Riders**, an all-volunteer cavalry unit made up of adventure-seeking college graduates, and veterans and cowboys from the Southwest, in a charge up Kettle Hill, next to San Juan Hill, which resulted in American forces surrounding Santiago. The victories of the Rough Riders are the best known part of the battles, but in fact, several African American regiments, made up of veteran soldiers, were instrumental to their success. The Spanish fleet made a last-ditch effort to escape to the sea but ran into an American naval blockade that resulted in total destruction, with every Spanish vessel sunk. Lacking any naval support, Spain quickly lost control of Puerto Rico as well, offering virtually no resistance to advancing American forces. By the end of July, the fighting had ended and the war was over. Despite its short duration and limited number of casualties—fewer than 350 soldiers died in combat, about 1,600 were wounded, while almost 3,000 men died from disease—the war carried enormous significance for Americans who celebrated the victory as a reconciliation between North and South.

DEFINING "AMERICAN"

⊛ *"Smoked Yankees": Black Soldiers in the Spanish-American War*

The most popular image of the Spanish-American War is of Theodore Roosevelt and his Rough Riders, charging up San Juan Hill. But less well known is that the Rough Riders struggled mightily in several battles and would have sustained far more serious casualties, if not for the experienced black veterans—over twenty-five hundred of them—who joined them in battle (Figure 22.9). These soldiers, who had been fighting the Indian wars on the American frontier for many years, were instrumental in the U.S. victory in Cuba.

Figure 22.9   The decision to fight or not was debated in the black community, as some felt they owed little to a country that still granted them citizenship in name only, while others believed that proving their patriotism would enhance their opportunities. (credit: Library of Congress)

The choice to serve in the Spanish-American War was not a simple one. Within the black community, many spoke out both for and against involvement in the war. Many black Americans felt that because they were not offered the true rights of citizenship it was not their burden to volunteer for war. Others, in contrast, argued that participation in the war offered an opportunity for black Americans to prove themselves to the rest of the country. While their presence was welcomed by the military which desperately needed experienced soldiers, the black regiments suffered racism and harsh treatment while training in the southern states before shipping off to battle.

Once in Cuba, however, the "Smoked Yankees," as the Cubans called the black American soldiers, fought side-by-side with Roosevelt's Rough Riders, providing crucial tactical support to some of the most important battles of the war. After the Battle of San Juan, five black soldiers received the Medal of Honor and twenty-five others were awarded a certificate of merit. One reporter wrote that "if it had not been for the Negro cavalry, the Rough Riders would have been exterminated." He went on to state that, having grown up in the South, he had never been fond of black people before witnessing the battle. For some of the soldiers, their recognition made the sacrifice worthwhile. Others, however, struggled with American oppression of Cubans and Puerto Ricans, feeling kinship with the black residents of these countries now under American rule.

ESTABLISHING PEACE AND CREATING AN EMPIRE

As the war closed, Spanish and American diplomats made arrangements for a peace conference in Paris. They met in October 1898, with the Spanish government committed to regaining control of the Philippines, which they felt were unjustly taken in a war that was solely about Cuban independence. While the Teller Amendment ensured freedom for Cuba, President McKinley was reluctant to relinquish the strategically useful prize of the Philippines. He certainly did not want to give the islands back to Spain, nor did he want another European power to step in to seize them. Neither the Spanish nor the Americans considered giving the islands their independence, since, with the pervasive racism and cultural stereotyping of the day, they believed the Filipino people were not capable of governing themselves. William Howard Taft, the first American governor-general to oversee the administration of the new U.S. possession, accurately captured American sentiments with his frequent reference to Filipinos as "our little brown brothers."

As the peace negotiations unfolded, Spain agreed to recognize Cuba's independence, as well as recognize American control of Puerto Rico and Guam. McKinley insisted that the United States maintain control over the Philippines as an annexation, in return for a $20 million payment to Spain. Although Spain was reluctant, they were in no position militarily to deny the American demand. The two sides finalized the Treaty of Paris on December 10, 1898. With it came the international recognition that there was a new American empire that included the Philippines, Puerto Rico, and Guam. The American press quickly glorified the nation's new reach, as expressed in the cartoon below, depicting the glory of the American eagle reaching from the Philippines to the Caribbean (Figure 22.10).

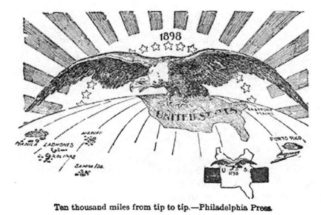

Ten thousand miles from tip to tip.—Philadelphia Press.

Figure 22.10 This cartoon from the *Philadelphia Press*, showed the reach of the new American empire, from Puerto Rico to the Philippines.

Domestically, the country was neither unified in their support of the treaty nor in the idea of the United States building an empire at all. Many prominent Americans, including Jane Addams, former President Grover Cleveland, Andrew Carnegie, Mark Twain, and Samuel Gompers, felt strongly that the country should not be pursuing an empire, and, in 1898, they formed the **Anti-Imperialist League** to oppose this expansionism. The reasons for their opposition were varied: Some felt that empire building went against the principles of democracy and freedom upon which the country was founded, some worried about competition from foreign workers, and some held the xenophobic viewpoint that the assimilation of other races would hurt the country. Regardless of their reasons, the group, taken together, presented a formidable challenge. As foreign treaties require a two-thirds majority in the U.S. Senate to pass, the Anti-Imperialist League's pressure led them to a clear split, with the possibility of defeat of the treaty seeming imminent. Less than a week before the scheduled vote, however, news of a Filipino uprising against American forces reached the United States. Undecided senators were convinced of the need to maintain an American presence in the region and preempt the intervention of another European power, and the Senate formally ratified the treaty on February 6, 1899.

The newly formed American empire was not immediately secure, as Filipino rebels, led by Emilio Aguinaldo (Figure 22.11), fought back against American forces stationed there. The Filipinos' war for independence lasted three years, with over four thousand American and twenty thousand Filipino combatant deaths; the civilian death toll is estimated as high as 250,000. Finally, in 1901, President McKinley appointed William Howard Taft as the civil governor of the Philippines in an effort to disengage the American military from direct confrontations with the Filipino people. Under Taft's leadership, Americans built a new transportation infrastructure, hospitals, and schools, hoping to win over the local population. The rebels quickly lost influence, and Aguinaldo was captured by American forces and forced to swear allegiance to the United States. The Taft Commission, as it became known, continued to introduce reforms to modernize and improve daily life for the country despite pockets of resistance that continued to fight through the spring of 1902. Much of the commission's rule centered on legislative reforms to local government structure and national agencies, with the commission offering appointments to resistance leaders in exchange for their support. The Philippines continued under American rule until they became self-governing in 1946.

Figure 22.11 Philippine president Emilio Aguinaldo was captured after three years of fighting with U.S. troops. He is seen here boarding the USS *Vicksburg* after taking an oath of loyalty to the United States in 1901.

After the conclusion of the Spanish-American War and the successful passage of the peace treaty with Spain, the United States continued to acquire other territories. Seeking an expanded international presence, as well as control of maritime routes and naval stations, the United States grew to include Hawaii, which was granted territorial status in 1900, and Alaska, which, although purchased from Russia decades earlier, only became a recognized territory in 1912. In both cases, their status as territories granted U.S. citizenship to their residents. The Foraker Act of 1900 established Puerto Rico as an American territory with its own civil government. It was not until 1917 that Puerto Ricans were granted American citizenship. Guam and Samoa, which had been taken as part of the war, remained under the control of the U.S. Navy. Cuba, which after the war was technically a free country, adopted a constitution based on the U.S. Constitution. While the Teller Amendment had prohibited the United States from annexing the country, a subsequent amendment, the Platt Amendment, secured the right of the United States to interfere in Cuban affairs if threats to a stable government emerged. The Platt Amendment also guaranteed the United States its own naval and coaling station on the island's southern Guantanamo Bay and prohibited Cuba from making treaties with other countries that might eventually threaten their independence. While Cuba remained an independent nation on paper, in all practicality the United States governed Cuba's foreign policy and economic agreements.

Click and Explore

Explore the resources at U.S. History Scene to better understand the long and involved history of Hawaii (http://openstaxcollege.org/l/createHawaii) with respect to its intersection with the United States.

22.3 Economic Imperialism in East Asia

By the end of this section, you will be able to:
- Explain how economic power helped to expand America's empire in China
- Describe how the foreign partitioning of China in the last decade of the nineteenth century influenced American policy

While American forays into empire building began with military action, the country concurrently grew its scope and influence through other methods as well. In particular, the United States used its economic and industrial capacity to add to its empire, as can be seen in a study of the China market and the "Open Door notes" discussed below.

WHY CHINA?

Since the days of Christopher Columbus's westward journey to seek a new route to the East Indies (essentially India and China, but loosely defined as all of Southeast Asia), many westerners have dreamt of the elusive "China Market." With the defeat of the Spanish navy in the Atlantic and Pacific, and specifically with the addition of the Philippines as a base for American ports and coaling stations, the United States was ready to try and make the myth a reality. Although China originally accounted for only a small percentage of American foreign trade, captains of American industry dreamed of a vast market of Asian customers desperate for manufactured goods they could not yet produce in large quantities for themselves.

American businesses were not alone in seeing the opportunities. Other countries—including Japan, Russia, Great Britain, France, and Germany—also hoped to make inroads in China. Previous treaties between Great Britain and China in 1842 and 1844 during the Opium Wars, when the British Empire militarily coerced the Chinese empire to accept the import of Indian opium in exchange for its tea, had forced an "open door" policy on China, in which all foreign nations had free and equal access to Chinese ports. This was at a time when Great Britain maintained the strongest economic relationship with China; however, other western nations used the new arrangement to send Christian missionaries, who began to work across inland China. Following the Sino-Japanese War of 1894–1895 over China's claims to Korea, western countries hoped to exercise even greater influence in the region. By 1897, Germany had obtained exclusive mining rights in northern coastal China as reparations for the murder of two German missionaries. In 1898, Russia obtained permission to build a railroad across northeastern Manchuria. One by one, each country carved out their own **sphere of influence**, where they could control markets through tariffs and transportation, and thus ensure their share of the Chinese market.

Alarmed by the pace at which foreign powers further divided China into pseudo-territories, and worried that they had no significant piece for themselves, the United States government intervened. In contrast to

European nations, however, American businesses wanted the whole market, not just a share of it. They wanted to do business in China with no artificially constructed spheres or boundaries to limit the extent of their trade, but without the territorial entanglements or legislative responsibilities that anti-imperialists opposed. With the blessing and assistance of Secretary of State John Hay, several American businessmen created the American Asiatic Association in 1896 to pursue greater trade opportunities in China.

THE OPEN DOOR NOTES

In 1899, Secretary of State Hay made a bold move to acquire China's vast markets for American access by introducing **Open Door notes**, a series of circular notes that Hay himself drafted as an expression of U.S. interests in the region and sent to the other competing powers (Figure 22.12). These notes, if agreed to by the other five nations maintaining spheres of influences in China, would erase all spheres and essentially open all doors to free trade, with no special tariffs or transportation controls that would give unfair advantages to one country over another. Specifically, the notes required that all countries agree to maintain free access to all treaty ports in China, to pay railroad charges and harbor fees (with no special access), and that only China would be permitted to collect any taxes on trade within its borders. While on paper, the Open Door notes would offer equal access to all, the reality was that it greatly favored the United States. Free trade in China would give American businesses the ultimate advantage, as American companies were producing higher-quality goods than other countries, and were doing so more efficiently and less expensively. The "open doors" would flood the Chinese market with American goods, virtually squeezing other countries out of the market.

Figure 22.12 This political cartoon shows Uncle Sam standing on a map of China, while Europe's imperialist nations (from left to right: Germany, Spain, Great Britain, Russia, and France) try to cut out their "sphere of influence."

Although the foreign ministers of the other five nations sent half-hearted replies on behalf of their respective governments, with some outright denying the viability of the notes, Hay proclaimed them the new official policy on China, and American goods were unleashed throughout the nation. China was quite welcoming of the notes, as they also stressed the U.S. commitment to preserving the Chinese government and territorial integrity.

The notes were invoked barely a year later, when a group of Chinese insurgents, the Righteous and Harmonious Fists—also known as the Boxer Rebellion—fought to expel all western nations and their influences from China (Figure 22.13). The United States, along with Great Britain and Germany, sent over two thousand troops to withstand the rebellion. The troops signified American commitment to the territorial integrity of China, albeit one flooded with American products. Despite subsequent efforts, by Japan in particular, to undermine Chinese authority in 1915 and again during the Manchurian crisis of 1931, the United States remained resolute in defense of the open door principles through World War II. Only when China turned to communism in 1949 following an intense civil war did the principle become relatively meaningless. However, for nearly half a century, U.S. military involvement and a continued relationship with the Chinese government cemented their roles as preferred trading partners, illustrating how the country used economic power, as well as military might, to grow its empire.

Figure 22.13 The Boxer Rebellion in China sought to expel all western influences, including Christian missionaries and trade partners. The Chinese government appreciated the American, British, and German troops that helped suppress the rebellion.

Click and Explore

Browse the U.S. State Department's Milestones: 1899—1913 (http://openstaxcollege.org/l/haychina) to learn more about Secretary of State John Hay and the strategy and thinking behind the Open Door notes.

22.4 Roosevelt's "Big Stick" Foreign Policy

By the end of this section, you will be able to:
- Explain the meaning of "big stick" foreign policy
- Describe Theodore Roosevelt's use of the "big stick" to construct the Panama Canal
- Explain the role of the United States in ending the Russo-Japanese War

While President McKinley ushered in the era of the American empire through military strength and economic coercion, his successor, Theodore Roosevelt, established a new foreign policy approach, allegedly based on a favorite African proverb, "speak softly, and carry a big stick, and you will go far" (Figure 22.14). At the crux of his foreign policy was a thinly veiled threat. Roosevelt believed that in light of the country's recent military successes, it was unnecessary to *use* force to achieve foreign policy goals, so long as the military could *threaten* force. This rationale also rested on the young president's philosophy, which he termed the "strenuous life," and that prized challenges overseas as opportunities to instill American men with the resolve and vigor they allegedly had once acquired in the Trans-Mississippi West.

THE BIG STICK IN THE CARIBBEAN SEA

Figure 22.14 Roosevelt was often depicted in cartoons wielding his "big stick" and pushing the U.S. foreign agenda, often through the power of the U.S. Navy.

Roosevelt believed that while the coercive power wielded by the United States could be harmful in the wrong hands, the Western Hemisphere's best interests were also the best interests of the United States. He felt, in short, that the United States had the right and the obligation to be the policeman of the hemisphere. This belief, and his strategy of "speaking softly and carrying a big stick," shaped much of Roosevelt's foreign policy.

THE CONSTRUCTION OF THE PANAMA CANAL

As early as the mid-sixteenth century, interest in a canal across the Central American isthmus began to take root, primarily out of trade interests. The subsequent discovery of gold in California in 1848 further spurred interest in connecting the Atlantic and Pacific Oceans, and led to the construction of the Panama Railway, which began operations in 1855. Several attempts by France to construct a canal between 1881 and 1894 failed due to a combination of financial crises and health hazards, including malaria and yellow fever, which led to the deaths of thousands of French workers.

Upon becoming president in 1901, Roosevelt was determined to succeed where others had failed. Following the advice that Mahan set forth in his book *The Influence of Seapower upon History*, he sought to achieve the construction of a canal across Central America, primarily for military reasons associated with empire, but also for international trade considerations. The most strategic point for the construction was across the fifty-mile isthmus of Panama, which, at the turn of the century, was part of the nation of Colombia. Roosevelt negotiated with the government of Colombia, sometimes threatening to take the project away and build through Nicaragua, until Colombia agreed to a treaty that would grant the United States a lease on the land across Panama in exchange for a payment of $10 million and an additional $250,000 annual rental fee. The matter was far from settled, however. The Colombian people were outraged over the loss of their land to the United States, and saw the payment as far too low. Influenced by the public outcry, the Colombian Senate rejected the treaty and informed Roosevelt there would be no canal.

Undaunted, Roosevelt chose to now wield the "big stick." In comments to journalists, he made it clear that the United States would strongly support the Panamanian people should they choose to revolt against Colombia and form their own nation. In November 1903, he even sent American battleships to the coast of Colombia, ostensibly for practice maneuvers, as the Panamanian revolution unfolded. The warships effectively blocked Colombia from moving additional troops into the region to quell the growing Panamanian uprising. Within a week, Roosevelt immediately recognized the new country of Panama, welcoming them to the world community and offering them the same terms—$10 million plus the annual $250,000 rental fee—he had previously offered Colombia. Following the successful revolution, Panama became an American protectorate, and remained so until 1939.

Once the Panamanian victory was secured, with American support, construction on the canal began in May 1904. For the first year of operations, the United States worked primarily to build adequate housing, cafeterias, warehouses, machine shops, and other elements of infrastructure that previous French efforts had failed to consider. Most importantly, the introduction of fumigation systems and mosquito nets following Dr. Walter Reed's discovery of the role of mosquitoes in the spread of malaria and yellow fever reduced the death rate and restored the fledgling morale among workers and American-born supervisors. At the same time, a new wave of American engineers planned for the construction of the canal. Even though they decided to build a lock-system rather than a sea-level canal, workers still had to excavate over 170 million cubic yards of earth with the use of over one hundred new rail-mounted steam shovels (**Figure 22.15**). Excited by the work, Roosevelt became the first sitting U.S. president to leave the country while in office. He traveled to Panama where he visited the construction site, taking a turn at the steam shovel and removing dirt. The canal opened in 1914, permanently changing world trade and military defense patterns.

Figure 22.15 Recurring landslides made the excavation of the Culebra Cut one of the most technically challenging elements in the construction of the Panama Canal.

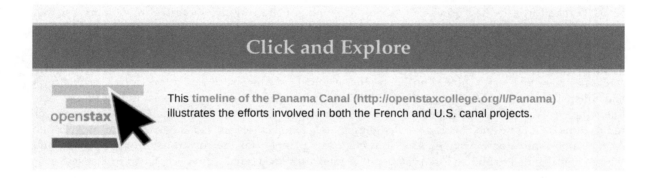

Click and Explore

This timeline of the Panama Canal (http://openstaxcollege.org/l/Panama) illustrates the efforts involved in both the French and U.S. canal projects.

THE ROOSEVELT COROLLARY

With the construction of the canal now underway, Roosevelt next wanted to send a clear message to the rest of the world—and in particular to his European counterparts—that the colonization of the Western Hemisphere had now ended, and their interference in the countries there would no longer be tolerated. At the same time, he sent a message to his counterparts in Central and South America, should the United States see problems erupt in the region, that it would intervene in order to maintain peace and stability throughout the hemisphere.

Roosevelt articulated this seeming double standard in a 1904 address before Congress, in a speech that became known as the **Roosevelt Corollary**. The Roosevelt Corollary was based on the original Monroe Doctrine of the early nineteenth century, which warned European nations of the consequences of their interference in the Caribbean. In this addition, Roosevelt states that the United States would use military force "as an international police power" to correct any "chronic wrongdoing" by any Latin American nation that might threaten stability in the region. Unlike the Monroe Doctrine, which proclaimed an American policy of noninterference with its neighbors' affairs, the Roosevelt Corollary loudly proclaimed the right and obligation of the United States to involve itself whenever necessary.

Roosevelt immediately began to put the new corollary to work. He used it to establish protectorates over Cuba and Panama, as well as to direct the United States to manage the Dominican Republic's custom service revenues. Despite growing resentment from neighboring countries over American intervention in their internal affairs, as well as European concerns from afar, knowledge of Roosevelt's previous actions in Colombia concerning acquisition of land upon which to build the Panama Canal left many fearful of American reprisals should they resist. Eventually, Presidents Herbert Hoover and Franklin Roosevelt softened American rhetoric regarding U.S. domination of the Western Hemisphere, with the latter proclaiming a new "Good Neighbor Policy" that renounced American intervention in other nations' affairs. However, subsequent presidents would continue to reference aspects of the Roosevelt Corollary to justify American involvement in Haiti, Nicaragua, and other nations throughout the twentieth century. The map below (Figure 22.16) shows the widespread effects of Roosevelt's policies throughout Latin America.

Figure 22.16   From underwriting a revolution in Panama with the goal of building a canal to putting troops in Cuba, Roosevelt vastly increased the U.S. impact in Latin America.

DEFINING "AMERICAN"

✪ *The Roosevelt Corollary and Its Impact*

In 1904, Roosevelt put the United States in the role of the "police power" of the Western Hemisphere and set a course for the U.S. relationship with Central and Latin America that played out over the next several decades. He did so with the Roosevelt Corollary, in which he stated:

> It is not true that the United States feels any land hunger or entertains any projects as regards the other nations of the Western Hemisphere save as such are for their welfare. All that this country desires is to see the neighboring countries stable, orderly, and prosperous. Any country whose people conduct themselves well can count upon our hearty friendship. . . . Chronic wrongdoing, or an impotence which results in a general loosening of the ties of civilized society, may in America, as elsewhere, require intervention by some civilized nation, and in the Western Hemisphere the adherence of the United States to the Monroe Doctrine may force the United States, however, reluctantly, in flagrant cases of such wrongdoing or impotence, to the exercise of an international police power."

In the twenty years after he made this statement, the United States would use military force in Latin America over a dozen times. The Roosevelt Corollary was used as a rationale for American involvement in the Dominican Republic, Nicaragua, Haiti, and other Latin American countries, straining relations between Central America and its dominant neighbor to the north throughout the twentieth century.

AMERICAN INTERVENTION IN THE RUSSO-JAPANESE WAR

Although he supported the Open Door notes as an excellent economic policy in China, Roosevelt lamented the fact that the United States had no strong military presence in the region to enforce it. Clearly, without a military presence there, he could not as easily use his "big stick" threat credibly to achieve his foreign policy goals. As a result, when conflicts did arise on the other side of the Pacific, Roosevelt adopted a policy of maintaining a balance of power among the nations there. This was particularly evident when the Russo-Japanese War erupted in 1904.

In 1904, angered by the massing of Russian troops along the Manchurian border, and the threat it represented to the region, Japan launched a surprise naval attack upon the Russian fleet. Initially, Roosevelt supported the Japanese position. However, when the Japanese fleet quickly achieved victory after victory, Roosevelt grew concerned over the growth of Japanese influence in the region and the continued threat that it represented to China and American access to those markets (Figure 22.17). Wishing to maintain the aforementioned balance of power, in 1905, Roosevelt arranged for diplomats from both nations to attend a secret peace conference in Portsmouth, New Hampshire. The resultant negotiations secured peace in the region, with Japan gaining control over Korea, several former Russian bases in Manchuria, and the southern half of Sakhalin Island. These negotiations also garnered the Nobel Peace Prize for Roosevelt, the first American to receive the award.

Figure 22.17 Japan's defense against Russia was supported by President Roosevelt, but when Japan's ongoing victories put the United States' own Asian interests at risk, he stepped in.

When Japan later exercised its authority over its gains by forcing American business interests out of Manchuria in 1906–1907, Roosevelt felt he needed to invoke his "big stick" foreign policy, even though the distance was great. He did so by sending the U.S. Great White Fleet on maneuvers in the western Pacific Ocean as a show of force from December 1907 through February 1909. Publicly described as a goodwill tour, the message to the Japanese government regarding American interests was equally clear. Subsequent negotiations reinforced the Open Door policy throughout China and the rest of Asia. Roosevelt had, by both the judicious use of the "big stick" and his strategy of maintaining a balance of power, kept U.S. interests in Asia well protected.

Click and Explore

Browse the Smithsonian National Portrait Gallery (http://openstaxcollege.org/l/RooseveltIcon) to follow Theodore Roosevelt from Rough Rider to president and beyond.

22.5 Taft's "Dollar Diplomacy"

By the end of this section, you will be able to:
- Explain how William Howard Taft used American economic power to protect the nation's interests in its new empire

When William Howard Taft became president in 1909, he chose to adapt Roosevelt's foreign policy philosophy to one that reflected American economic power at the time. In what became known as "**dollar diplomacy**," Taft announced his decision to "substitute dollars for bullets" in an effort to use foreign policy to secure markets and opportunities for American businessmen (Figure 22.18). Not unlike Roosevelt's threat of force, Taft used the threat of American economic clout to coerce countries into agreements to benefit the United States.

Figure 22.18 Although William Howard Taft was Theodore Roosevelt's hand-picked successor to the presidency, he was less inclined to use Roosevelt's "big stick," choosing instead to use the economic might of the United States to influence foreign affairs.

Of key interest to Taft was the debt that several Central American nations still owed to various countries in Europe. Fearing that the debt holders might use the monies owed as leverage to use military intervention in the Western Hemisphere, Taft moved quickly to pay off these debts with U.S. dollars. Of course, this move made the Central American countries indebted to the United States, a situation that not all nations wanted. When a Central American nation resisted this arrangement, however, Taft responded with military force to achieve the objective. This occurred in Nicaragua when the country refused to accept American loans to pay off its debt to Great Britain. Taft sent a warship with marines to the region to pressure the government to agree. Similarly, when Mexico considered the idea of allowing a Japanese corporation to gain significant land and economic advantages in its country, Taft urged Congress to pass the Lodge Corollary, an addendum to the Roosevelt Corollary, stating that no foreign corporation—other than American ones—could obtain strategic lands in the Western Hemisphere.

In Asia, Taft's policies also followed those of Theodore Roosevelt. He attempted to bolster China's ability to withstand Japanese interference and thereby maintain a balance of power in the region. Initially, he experienced tremendous success in working with the Chinese government to further develop the railroad industry in that country through arranging international financing. However, efforts to expand the Open Door policy deeper into Manchuria met with resistance from Russia and Japan, exposing the limits of the American government's influence and knowledge about the intricacies of diplomacy. As a result, he reorganized the U.S. State Department to create geographical divisions (such as the Far East Division, the Latin American Division, etc.) in order to develop greater foreign policy expertise in each area.

Taft's policies, although not as based on military aggression as his predecessors, did create difficulties for the United States, both at the time and in the future. Central America's indebtedness would create economic concerns for decades to come, as well as foster nationalist movements in countries resentful of American's interference. In Asia, Taft's efforts to mediate between China and Japan served only to heighten tensions between Japan and the United States. Furthermore, it did not succeed in creating a balance of power, as Japan's reaction was to further consolidate its power and reach throughout the region.

As Taft's presidency came to a close in early 1913, the United States was firmly entrenched on its path towards empire. The world perceived the United States as the predominant power of the Western Hemisphere—a perception that few nations would challenge until the Soviet Union during the Cold War era. Likewise, the United States had clearly marked its interests in Asia, although it was still searching for an adequate approach to guard and foster them. The development of an American empire had introduced with it several new approaches to American foreign policy, from military intervention to economic coercion to the mere threat of force.

The playing field would change one year later in 1914 when the United States witnessed the unfolding of World War I, or "the Great War." A new president would attempt to adopt a new approach to diplomacy—one that was well-intentioned but at times impractical. Despite Woodrow Wilson's best efforts to the contrary, the United States would be drawn into the conflict and subsequently attempt to reshape the world order as a result.

Click and Explore

Read this brief biography of President Taft (http://openstaxcollege.org/l/Taft) to understand his foreign policy in the context of his presidency.

Key Terms

Anti-Imperialist League a group of diverse and prominent Americans who banded together in 1898 to protest the idea of American empire building

dollar diplomacy Taft's foreign policy, which involved using American economic power to push for favorable foreign policies

Frontier Thesis an idea proposed by Fredrick Jackson Turner, which stated that the encounter of European traditions and a native wilderness was integral to the development of American democracy, individualism, and innovative character

Open Door notes the circular notes sent by Secretary of State Hay claiming that there should be "open doors" in China, allowing all countries equal and total access to all markets, ports, and railroads without any special considerations from the Chinese authorities; while ostensibly leveling the playing field, this strategy greatly benefited the United States

Roosevelt Corollary a statement by Theodore Roosevelt that the United States would use military force to act as an international police power and correct any chronic wrongdoing by any Latin American nation threatening the stability of the region

Rough Riders Theodore Roosevelt's cavalry unit, which fought in Cuba during the Spanish-American War

Seward's Folly the pejorative name given by the press to Secretary of State Seward's acquisition of Alaska in 1867

sphere of influence the goal of foreign countries such as Japan, Russia, France, and Germany to carve out an area of the Chinese market that they could exploit through tariff and transportation agreements

yellow journalism sensationalist newspapers who sought to manufacture news stories in order to sell more papers

Summary

22.1 Turner, Mahan, and the Roots of Empire

In the last decades of the nineteenth century, after the Civil War, the United States pivoted from a profoundly isolationist approach to a distinct zeal for American expansion. The nation's earlier isolationism originated from the deep scars left by the Civil War and its need to recover both economically and mentally from that event. But as the industrial revolution changed the way the country worked and the American West reached its farthest point, American attitudes toward foreign expansion shifted. Businesses sought new markets to export their factory-built goods, oil, and tobacco products, as well as generous trade agreements to secure access to raw materials. Early social reformers saw opportunities to spread Christian gospel and the benefits of American life to those in less developed nations. With the rhetoric of Fredrick J. Turner and the strategies of Alfred Mahan underpinning the desire for expansion abroad, the country moved quickly to ready itself for the creation of an American empire.

22.2 The Spanish-American War and Overseas Empire

In the wake of the Civil War, American economic growth combined with the efforts of Evangelist missionaries to push for greater international influence and overseas presence. By confronting Spain over its imperial rule in Cuba, the United States took control of valuable territories in Central America and the Pacific. For the United States, the first step toward becoming an empire was a decisive military one. By engaging with Spain, the United States was able to gain valuable territories in Latin America and Asia, as well as send a message to other global powers. The untested U.S. Navy proved superior to the Spanish fleet, and the military strategists who planned the war in the broader context of empire caught the Spanish by surprise. The annexation of the former Spanish colonies of Guam, Puerto Rico, and the Philippines, combined with the acquisition of Hawaii, Samoa, and Wake Island, positioned the United States as the predominant world power in the South Pacific and the Caribbean. While some prominent figures in the United States vehemently disagreed with the idea of American empire building, their concerns were overruled by an American public—and a government—that understood American power overseas as a form of prestige, prosperity, and progress.

22.3 Economic Imperialism in East Asia

The United States shifted from isolationism to empire building with its involvement—and victory—in the Spanish-American War. But at the same time, the country sought to expand its reach through another powerful tool: its economic clout. The Industrial Revolution gave American businesses an edge in delivering high-quality products at lowered costs, and the pursuit of an "open door" policy with China opened new markets to American goods. This trade agreement allowed the United States to continue to build power through economic advantage.

22.4 Roosevelt's "Big Stick" Foreign Policy

When Roosevelt succeeded McKinley as president, he implemented a key strategy for building an American empire: the threat, rather than the outright use, of military force. McKinley had engaged the U.S. military in several successful skirmishes and then used the country's superior industrial power to negotiate beneficial foreign trade agreements. Roosevelt, with his "big stick" policy, was able to keep the United States out of military conflicts by employing the legitimate threat of force. Nonetheless, as negotiations with Japan illustrated, the maintenance of an empire was fraught with complexity. Changing alliances, shifting economic needs, and power politics all meant that the United States would need to tread carefully to maintain its status as a world power.

22.5 Taft's "Dollar Diplomacy"

All around the globe, Taft sought to use U.S. economic might as a lever in foreign policy. He relied less on military action, or the threat of such action, than McKinley or Roosevelt before him; however, he both threatened and used military force when economic coercion proved unsuccessful, as it did in his bid to pay off Central America's debts with U.S. dollars. In Asia, Taft tried to continue to support the balance of power, but his efforts backfired and alienated Japan. Increasing tensions between the United States and Japan would finally explode nearly thirty years later, with the outbreak of World War II.

Review Questions

1. Why did the United States express limited interest in overseas expansion in the 1860s and 1870s?

   A. fear of attacks on their borders
   B. post-Civil War reconstruction
   C. the Anti-Imperialist League
   D. Manifest Destiny

2. Which of the following did Mahan *not* believe was needed to build an American empire?

   A. a navy
   B. military bases around the world
   C. the reopening of the American frontier
   D. a canal through Central America

3. Why were the Midway Islands important to American expansion?

4. Which is *not* one of the reasons the Anti-Imperial League gave for opposing the creation of an American empire?
    A. fear of competition from foreign workers
    B. fear that the United States would suffer a foreign invasion
    C. concerns about the integration of other races
    D. concerns that empire building ran counter to American democratic principles

5. What was the role of the Taft Commission?

6. What challenges did the U.S. military have to overcome in the Spanish-American War? What accounted for the nation's eventual victory?

7. How did Hay's suggestion of an open door policy in China benefit the United States over other nations?
    A. The United States produced goods of better quality and lower cost than other countries.
    B. The United States enjoyed a historically stronger relationship with the Chinese government.
    C. The United States was the only nation granted permission to collect taxes on the goods it traded within China's borders.
    D. The United States controlled more foreign ports than other countries.

8. How did the Boxer Rebellion strengthen American ties with China?
    A. The United States supported the rebels and gained their support.
    B. The United States provided troops to fight the rebels.
    C. The United States sent arms and financial support to the Chinese government.
    D. The United States thwarted attempts by Great Britain and Germany to fortify the rebels.

9. How does the "Open Door notes" episode represent a new, nonmilitary tactic in the expansion of the American empire?

10. How did Colombia react to the United States' proposal to construct a canal through Central America?

    A. They preferred to build such a canal themselves.
    B. They preferred that no canal be built at all.
    C. They agreed to sell land to the United States to build the canal, but in a less advantageous location than the Panamanians.
    D. They felt that Roosevelt's deal offered too little money.

11. With the Roosevelt Corollary, Roosevelt sought to establish _____.
    A. the consequences for any European nation that involved itself in Latin American affairs
    B. the right of the United States to involve itself in Latin American affairs whenever necessary
    C. the idea that Latin America was free and independent from foreign intervention
    D. the need for further colonization efforts in the Western Hemisphere

12. Compare Roosevelt's foreign policy in Latin America and Asia. Why did he employ these different methods?

13. Why did some Central American nations object to Taft's paying off their debt to Europe with U.S. dollars?
    A. because American currency wasn't worth as much as local currencies
    B. because they felt it gave the United States too much leverage
    C. because they were forced to give land grants to the United States in return
    D. because they wanted Asian countries to pay off their debts instead

14. What two countries were engaged in a negotiation that the Lodge Corollary disallowed?
    A. Mexico and Japan
    B. Nicaragua and France
    C. Colombia and Japan
    D. Mexico and Spain

15. What problems did Taft's foreign policy create for the United States?

Critical Thinking Questions

16. Describe the United States' movement from isolationism to expansion-mindedness in the final decades of the nineteenth century. What ideas and philosophies underpinned this transformation?

17. What specific forces or interests transformed the relationship between the United States and the rest of the world between 1865 and 1890?

18. How did Taft's "dollar diplomacy" differ from Roosevelt's "big stick" policy? Was one approach more or less successful than the other? How so?

19. What economic and political conditions had to exist for Taft's "dollar diplomacy" to be effective?

20. What factors conspired to propel the United States to emerge as a military and economic powerhouse prior to World War II?

CHAPTER 23

Americans and the Great War, 1914-1919

Figure 23.1 *Return of the Useless* (1918), by George Bellows, is an example of a kind of artistic imagery used to galvanize reluctant Americans into joining World War I. The scene shows German soldiers unloading and mistreating imprisoned civilians after their return home to Belgium from German forced-labor camps.

Chapter Outline

23.1 American Isolationism and the European Origins of War
23.2 The United States Prepares for War
23.3 A New Home Front
23.4 From War to Peace
23.5 Demobilization and Its Difficult Aftermath

Introduction

On the eve of World War I, the U.S. government under President Woodrow Wilson opposed any entanglement in international military conflicts. But as the war engulfed Europe and the belligerents' total war strategies targeted commerce and travel across the Atlantic, it became clear that the United States would not be able to maintain its position of neutrality. Still, the American public was of mixed opinion; many resisted the idea of American intervention and American lives lost, no matter how bad the circumstances.

In 1918, artist George Bellows created a series of paintings intended to strengthen public support for the war effort. His paintings depicted German war atrocities in explicit and expertly captured detail, from children run through with bayonets to torturers happily resting while their victims suffered. The image above, entitled *Return of the Useless* (Figure 23.1), shows Germans unloading sick or disabled labor camp prisoners from a boxcar. These paintings, while not regarded as Bellows' most important artistic work, were typical for anti-German propaganda at the time. The U.S. government sponsored much of this propaganda out of concern that many American immigrants sympathized with the Central powers and would not support the U.S. war effort.

23.1 American Isolationism and the European Origins of War

By the end of this section, you will be able to:
- Explain Woodrow Wilson's foreign policy and the difficulties of maintaining American neutrality at the outset of World War I
- Identify the key factors that led to the U.S. declaration of war on Germany in April 1917

Unlike his immediate predecessors, President Woodrow Wilson had planned to shrink the role of the United States in foreign affairs. He believed that the nation needed to intervene in international events only when there was a moral imperative to do so. But as Europe's political situation grew dire, it became increasingly difficult for Wilson to insist that the conflict growing overseas was not America's responsibility. Germany's war tactics struck most observers as morally reprehensible, while also putting American free trade with the Entente at risk. Despite campaign promises and diplomatic efforts, Wilson could only postpone American involvement in the war.

WOODROW WILSON'S NEW FREEDOM

When Woodrow Wilson took over the White House in March 1913, he promised a less expansionist approach to American foreign policy than Theodore Roosevelt and William Howard Taft had pursued. Wilson did share the commonly held view that American values were superior to those of the rest of the world, that democracy was the best system to promote peace and stability, and that the United States should continue to actively pursue economic markets abroad. But he proposed an idealistic foreign policy based on morality, rather than American self-interest, and felt that American interference in another nation's affairs should occur only when the circumstances rose to the level of a moral imperative.

Wilson appointed former presidential candidate William Jennings Bryan, a noted anti-imperialist and proponent of world peace, as his Secretary of State. Bryan undertook his new assignment with great vigor, encouraging nations around the world to sign "cooling off treaties," under which they agreed to resolve international disputes through talks, not war, and to submit any grievances to an international commission. Bryan also negotiated friendly relations with Colombia, including a $25 million apology for

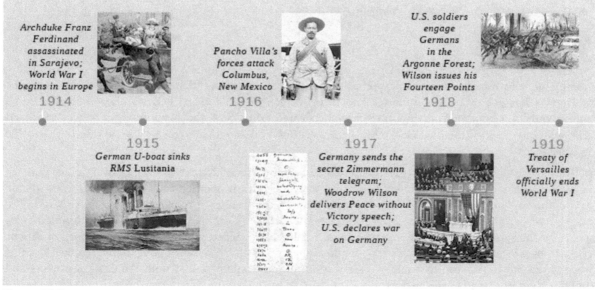

Figure 23.2

Roosevelt's actions during the Panamanian Revolution, and worked to establish effective self-government in the Philippines in preparation for the eventual American withdrawal. Even with Bryan's support, however, Wilson found that it was much harder than he anticipated to keep the United States out of world affairs (Figure 23.3). In reality, the United States was interventionist in areas where its interests—direct or indirect—were threatened.

THE BRONCHO-BUSTER.

Figure 23.3 While Wilson strove to be less of an interventionist, he found that to be more difficult in practice than in theory. Here, a political cartoon depicts him as a rather hapless cowboy, unclear on how to harness a foreign challenge, in this case, Mexico.

Wilson's greatest break from his predecessors occurred in Asia, where he abandoned Taft's "dollar diplomacy," a foreign policy that essentially used the power of U.S. economic dominance as a threat to gain favorable terms. Instead, Wilson revived diplomatic efforts to keep Japanese interference there at a minimum. But as World War I, also known as the Great War, began to unfold, and European nations largely abandoned their imperialistic interests in order to marshal their forces for self-defense, Japan demanded that China succumb to a Japanese protectorate over their entire nation. In 1917, William Jennings Bryan's successor as Secretary of State, Robert Lansing, signed the Lansing-Ishii Agreement, which recognized Japanese control over the Manchurian region of China in exchange for Japan's promise not to exploit the war to gain a greater foothold in the rest of the country.

Furthering his goal of reducing overseas interventions, Wilson had promised not to rely on the Roosevelt Corollary, Theodore Roosevelt's explicit policy that the United States could involve itself in Latin American politics whenever it felt that the countries in the Western Hemisphere needed policing. Once president, however, Wilson again found that it was more difficult to avoid American interventionism in practice than in rhetoric. Indeed, Wilson intervened more in Western Hemisphere affairs than either Taft or Roosevelt. In 1915, when a revolution in Haiti resulted in the murder of the Haitian president and threatened the safety of New York banking interests in the country, Wilson sent over three hundred U.S. Marines to establish order. Subsequently, the United States assumed control over the island's foreign policy as well as its financial administration. One year later, in 1916, Wilson again sent marines to Hispaniola, this time to the Dominican Republic, to ensure prompt payment of a debt that nation owed. In 1917, Wilson sent troops to Cuba to protect American-owned sugar plantations from attacks by Cuban rebels; this time, the troops remained for four years.

Wilson's most noted foreign policy foray prior to World War I focused on Mexico, where rebel general Victoriano Huerta had seized control from a previous rebel government just weeks before Wilson's inauguration. Wilson refused to recognize Huerta's government, instead choosing to make an example of Mexico by demanding that they hold democratic elections and establish laws based on the moral principles he espoused. Officially, Wilson supported Venustiano Carranza, who opposed Huerta's military control of the country. When American intelligence learned of a German ship allegedly preparing to deliver weapons to Huerta's forces, Wilson ordered the U.S. Navy to land forces at Veracruz to stop the shipment.

On April 22, 1914, a fight erupted between the U.S. Navy and Mexican troops, resulting in nearly 150 deaths, nineteen of them American. Although Carranza's faction managed to overthrow Huerta in the summer of 1914, most Mexicans—including Carranza—had come to resent American intervention in their affairs. Carranza refused to work with Wilson and the U.S. government, and instead threatened to defend Mexico's mineral rights against all American oil companies established there. Wilson then turned to support rebel forces who opposed Carranza, most notably Pancho Villa (Figure 23.4). However, Villa lacked the strength in number or weapons to overtake Carranza; in 1915, Wilson reluctantly authorized official U.S. recognition of Carranza's government.

Figure 23.4 Pancho Villa, a Mexican rebel who Wilson supported, then ultimately turned from, attempted an attack on the United States in retaliation. Wilson's actions in Mexico were emblematic of how difficult it was to truly set the United States on a course of moral leadership.

As a postscript, an irate Pancho Villa turned against Wilson, and on March 9, 1916, led a fifteen-hundred-man force across the border into New Mexico, where they attacked and burned the town of Columbus. Over one hundred people died in the attack, seventeen of them American. Wilson responded by sending General John Pershing into Mexico to capture Villa and return him to the United States for trial. With over eleven thousand troops at his disposal, Pershing marched three hundred miles into Mexico before an angry Carranza ordered U.S. troops to withdraw from the nation. Although reelected in 1916, Wilson reluctantly ordered the withdrawal of U.S. troops from Mexico in 1917, avoiding war with Mexico and enabling preparations for American intervention in Europe. Again, as in China, Wilson's attempt to impose a moral foreign policy had failed in light of economic and political realities.

WAR ERUPTS IN EUROPE

When a Serbian nationalist murdered the Archduke Franz Ferdinand of the Austro-Hungarian Empire on June 29, 1914, the underlying forces that led to World War I had already long been in motion and seemed, at first, to have little to do with the United States. At the time, the events that pushed Europe from ongoing tensions into war seemed very far away from U.S. interests. For nearly a century, nations had negotiated a series of mutual defense alliance treaties to secure themselves against their imperialistic rivals. Among the largest European powers, the Triple Entente included an alliance of France, Great Britain, and Russia. Opposite them, the Central powers, also known as the Triple Alliance, included Germany, Austria-Hungary, the Ottoman Empire, and initially Italy. A series of "side treaties" likewise entangled the larger European powers to protect several smaller ones should war break out.

At the same time that European nations committed each other to defense pacts, they jockeyed for power over empires overseas and invested heavily in large, modern militaries. Dreams of empire and military

Download for free at http://cnx.org/content/col11740/latest/

supremacy fueled an era of nationalism that was particularly pronounced in the newer nations of Germany and Italy, but also provoked separatist movements among Europeans. The Irish rose up in rebellion against British rule, for example. And in Bosnia's capital of Sarajevo, Gavrilo Princip and his accomplices assassinated the Austro-Hungarian archduke in their fight for a pan-Slavic nation. Thus, when Serbia failed to accede to Austro-Hungarian demands in the wake of the archduke's murder, Austria-Hungary declared war on Serbia with the confidence that it had the backing of Germany. This action, in turn, brought Russia into the conflict, due to a treaty in which they had agreed to defend Serbia. Germany followed suit by declaring war on Russia, fearing that Russia and France would seize this opportunity to move on Germany if it did not take the offensive. The eventual German invasion of Belgium drew Great Britain into the war, followed by the attack of the Ottoman Empire on Russia. By the end of August 1914, it seemed as if Europe had dragged the entire world into war.

The Great War was unlike any war that came before it. Whereas in previous European conflicts, troops typically faced each other on open battlefields, World War I saw new military technologies that turned war into a conflict of prolonged trench warfare. Both sides used new artillery, tanks, airplanes, machine guns, barbed wire, and, eventually, poison gas: weapons that strengthened defenses and turned each military offense into barbarous sacrifices of thousands of lives with minimal territorial advances in return. By the end of the war, the total military death toll was ten million, as well as another million civilian deaths attributed to military action, and another six million civilian deaths caused by famine, disease, or other related factors.

One terrifying new piece of technological warfare was the German *unterseeboot*—an "undersea boat" or U-boat. By early 1915, in an effort to break the British naval blockade of Germany and turn the tide of the war, the Germans dispatched a fleet of these submarines around Great Britain to attack both merchant and military ships. The U-boats acted in direct violation of international law, attacking without warning from beneath the water instead of surfacing and permitting the surrender of civilians or crew. By 1918, German U-boats had sunk nearly five thousand vessels. Of greatest historical note was the attack on the British passenger ship, RMS *Lusitania*, on its way from New York to Liverpool on May 7, 1915. The German Embassy in the United States had announced that this ship would be subject to attack for its cargo of ammunition: an allegation that later proved accurate. Nonetheless, almost 1,200 civilians died in the attack, including 128 Americans. The attack horrified the world, galvanizing support in England and beyond for the war (Figure 23.5). This attack, more than any other event, would test President Wilson's desire to stay out of what had been a largely European conflict.

(a)   (b)

Figure 23.5 The torpedoing and sinking of the *Lusitania*, depicted in the English drawing above (a), resulted in the death over twelve hundred civilians and was an international incident that shifted American sentiment as to their potential role in the war, as illustrated in a British recruiting poster (b).

THE CHALLENGE OF NEUTRALITY

Despite the loss of American lives on the *Lusitania*, President Wilson stuck to his path of **neutrality** in Europe's escalating war: in part out of moral principle, in part as a matter of practical necessity, and in part for political reasons. Few Americans wished to participate in the devastating battles that ravaged Europe, and Wilson did not want to risk losing his reelection by ordering an unpopular military intervention. Wilson's "neutrality" did not mean isolation from all warring factions, but rather open markets for the United States and continued commercial ties with all belligerents. For Wilson, the conflict did not reach the threshold of a moral imperative for U.S. involvement; it was largely a European affair involving numerous countries with whom the United States wished to maintain working relations. In his message to Congress in 1914, the president noted that "Every man who really loves America will act and speak in the true spirit of neutrality, which is the spirit of impartiality and fairness and friendliness to all concerned."

Wilson understood that he was already looking at a difficult reelection bid. He had only won the 1912 election with 42 percent of the popular vote, and likely would not have been elected at all had Roosevelt not come back as a third-party candidate to run against his former protégée Taft. Wilson felt pressure from all different political constituents to take a position on the war, yet he knew that elections were seldom won with a campaign promise of "If elected, I will send your sons to war!" Facing pressure from some businessmen and other government officials who felt that the protection of America's best interests required a stronger position in defense of the Allied forces, Wilson agreed to a "preparedness campaign" in the year prior to the election. This campaign included the passage of the National Defense Act of 1916, which more than doubled the size of the army to nearly 225,000, and the Naval Appropriations Act of 1916, which called for the expansion of the U.S. fleet, including battleships, destroyers, submarines, and other ships.

As the 1916 election approached, the Republican Party hoped to capitalize on the fact that Wilson was making promises that he would not be able to keep. They nominated Charles Evans Hughes, a former governor of New York and sitting U.S. Supreme Court justice at the time of his nomination. Hughes focused his campaign on what he considered Wilson's foreign policy failures, but even as he did so, he himself tried to walk a fine line between neutrality and belligerence, depending on his audience. In contrast, Wilson and the Democrats capitalized on neutrality and campaigned under the slogan "Wilson—he kept us out of war." The election itself remained too close to call on election night. Only when a tight race in California was decided two days later could Wilson claim victory in his reelection bid, again with less than 50 percent of the popular vote. Despite his victory based upon a policy of neutrality, Wilson would find true neutrality a difficult challenge. Several different factors pushed Wilson, however reluctantly, toward the inevitability of American involvement.

A key factor driving U.S. engagement was economics. Great Britain was the country's most important trading partner, and the Allies as a whole relied heavily on American imports from the earliest days of the war forward. Specifically, the value of all exports to the Allies quadrupled from $750 million to $3 billion in the first two years of the war. At the same time, the British naval blockade meant that exports to Germany all but ended, dropping from $350 million to $30 million. Likewise, numerous private banks in the United States made extensive loans—in excess of $500 million—to England. J. P. Morgan's banking interests were among the largest lenders, due to his family's connection to the country.

Another key factor in the decision to go to war were the deep ethnic divisions between native-born Americans and more recent immigrants. For those of Anglo-Saxon descent, the nation's historic and ongoing relationship with Great Britain was paramount, but many Irish-Americans resented British rule over their place of birth and opposed support for the world's most expansive empire. Millions of Jewish immigrants had fled anti-Semitic pogroms in Tsarist Russia and would have supported any nation fighting that authoritarian state. German Americans saw their nation of origin as a victim of British and Russian aggression and a French desire to settle old scores, whereas emigrants from Austria-Hungary and the Ottoman Empire were mixed in their sympathies for the old monarchies or ethnic communities that these empires suppressed. For interventionists, this lack of support for Great Britain and its allies among recent immigrants only strengthened their conviction.

Germany's use of submarine warfare also played a role in challenging U.S. neutrality. After the sinking of the *Lusitania*, and the subsequent August 30 sinking of another British liner, the *Arabic*, Germany had promised to restrict their use of submarine warfare. Specifically, they promised to surface and visually identify any ship before they fired, as well as permit civilians to evacuate targeted ships. Instead, in February 1917, Germany intensified their use of submarines in an effort to end the war quickly before Great Britain's naval blockade starved them out of food and supplies.

The German high command wanted to continue unrestricted warfare on all Atlantic traffic, including unarmed American freighters, in order to cripple the British economy and secure a quick and decisive victory. Their goal: to bring an end to the war before the United States could intervene and tip the balance in this grueling war of attrition. In February 1917, a German U-boat sank the American merchant ship, the *Laconia*, killing two passengers, and, in late March, quickly sunk four more American ships. These attacks increased pressure on Wilson from all sides, as government officials, the general public, and both Democrats and Republicans urged him to declare war.

The final element that led to American involvement in World War I was the so-called **Zimmermann telegram**. British intelligence intercepted and decoded a top-secret telegram from German foreign minister Arthur Zimmermann to the German ambassador to Mexico, instructing the latter to invite Mexico to join the war effort on the German side, should the United States declare war on Germany. It further went on to encourage Mexico to invade the United States if such a declaration came to pass, as Mexico's invasion would create a diversion and permit Germany a clear path to victory. In exchange, Zimmermann offered to return to Mexico land that was previously lost to the United States in the Mexican-American War, including Arizona, New Mexico, and Texas (Figure 23.6).

Figure 23.6   "The Temptation," which appeared in the *Dallas Morning News* on March 2, 1917, shows Germany as the Devil, tempting Mexico to join their war effort against the United States in exchange for the return of land formerly belonging to Mexico. The prospect of such a move made it all but impossible for Wilson to avoid war. (credit: Library of Congress)

The likelihood that Mexico, weakened and torn by its own revolution and civil war, could wage war against the United States and recover territory lost in the Mexican-American war with Germany's help was remote at best. But combined with Germany's unrestricted use of submarine warfare and the sinking of American ships, the Zimmermann telegram made a powerful argument for a declaration of war. The outbreak of the Russian Revolution in February and abdication of Tsar Nicholas II in March raised the prospect of democracy in the Eurasian empire and removed an important moral objection to entering the war on the side of the Allies. On April 2, 1917, Wilson asked Congress to declare war on Germany. Congress debated for four days, and several senators and congressmen expressed their concerns that the war was being fought over U.S. economic interests more than strategic need or democratic ideals. When Congress voted on April 6, fifty-six voted against the resolution, including the first woman ever elected to Congress, Representative Jeannette Rankin. This was the largest "no" vote against a war resolution in American history.

DEFINING "AMERICAN"

✪ *Wilson's Peace without Victory Speech*

Wilson's last-ditch effort to avoid bringing the United States into World War I is captured in a speech he gave before the U.S. Senate on January 22, 1917. This speech, known as the "Peace without Victory" speech, extolled the country to be patient, as the countries involved in the war were nearing a peace. Wilson stated:

> It must be a peace without victory. It is not pleasant to say this. I beg that I may be permitted to put my own interpretation upon it and that it may be understood that no other interpretation was in my thought. I am seeking only to face realities and to face them without soft concealments. Victory would mean peace forced upon the loser, a victor's terms imposed upon the vanquished. It would be accepted in humiliation, under duress, at an intolerable sacrifice, and would leave a sting, a resentment, a bitter memory upon which terms of peace would rest, not permanently, but only as upon quicksand. Only a peace between equals can last, only a peace the very principle of which is equality and a common participation in a common benefit.

Not surprisingly, this speech was not well received by either side fighting the war. England resisted being put on the same moral ground as Germany, and France, whose country had been battered by years of warfare, had no desire to end the war without victory and its spoils. Still, the speech as a whole illustrates Wilson's idealistic, if failed, attempt to create a more benign and high-minded foreign policy role for the United States. Unfortunately, the Zimmermann telegram and the sinking of the American merchant ships proved too provocative for Wilson to remain neutral. Little more than two months after this speech, he asked Congress to declare war on Germany.

Click and Explore

Read the full transcript of the Peace without Victory speech (http://openstaxcollege.org/l/15WWilson) that clearly shows Wilson's desire to remain out of the war, even when it seemed inevitable.

23.2 The United States Prepares for War

By the end of this section, you will be able to:
- Identify the steps taken by the U.S. government to secure enough men, money, food, and supplies to prosecute World War I
- Explain how the U.S. government attempted to sway popular opinion in favor of the war effort

Wilson knew that the key to America's success in war lay largely in its preparation. With both the Allied and enemy forces entrenched in battles of attrition, and supplies running low on both sides, the United States needed, first and foremost, to secure enough men, money, food, and supplies to be successful. The country needed to first supply the basic requirements to fight a war, and then work to ensure military leadership, public support, and strategic planning.

THE INGREDIENTS OF WAR

The First World War was, in many ways, a war of attrition, and the United States needed a large army to help the Allies. In 1917, when the United States declared war on Germany, the U.S. Army ranked seventh in the world in terms of size, with an estimated 200,000 enlisted men. In contrast, at the outset of the war in 1914, the German force included 4.5 million men, and the country ultimately mobilized over eleven million soldiers over the course of the entire war.

To compose a fighting force, Congress passed the Selective Service Act in 1917, which initially required all men aged twenty-one through thirty to register for the draft (Figure 23.7). In 1918, the act was expanded to include all men between eighteen and forty-five. Through a campaign of patriotic appeals, as well as an administrative system that allowed men to register at their local draft boards rather than directly with the federal government, over ten million men registered for the draft on the very first day. By the war's end, twenty-two million men had registered for the U.S. Army draft. Five million of these men were actually drafted, another 1.5 million volunteered, and over 500,000 additional men signed up for the navy or marines. In all, two million men participated in combat operations overseas. Among the volunteers were also twenty thousand women, a quarter of whom went to France to serve as nurses or in clerical positions.

But the draft also provoked opposition, and almost 350,000 eligible Americans refused to register for military service. About 65,000 of these defied the conscription law as conscientious objectors, mostly on the grounds of their deeply held religious beliefs. Such opposition was not without risks, and whereas most objectors were never prosecuted, those who were found guilty at military hearings received stiff punishments: Courts handed down over two hundred prison sentences of twenty years or more, and seventeen death sentences.

Figure 23.7 While many young men were eager to join the war effort, there were a sizable number who did not want to join, either due to a moral objection or simply because they did not want to fight in a war that seemed far from American interests. (credit: Library of Congress)

With the size of the army growing, the U.S. government next needed to ensure that there were adequate supplies—in particular food and fuel—for both the soldiers and the home front. Concerns over shortages led to the passage of the Lever Food and Fuel Control Act, which empowered the president to control the production, distribution, and price of all food products during the war effort. Using this law, Wilson created both a Fuel Administration and a Food Administration. The Fuel Administration, run by Harry Garfield, created the concept of "fuel holidays," encouraging civilian Americans to do their part for the war effort by rationing fuel on certain days. Garfield also implemented "daylight saving time" for the first time in American history, shifting the clocks to allow more productive daylight hours. Herbert Hoover coordinated the Food Administration, and he too encouraged volunteer rationing by invoking patriotism. With the slogan "food will win the war," Hoover encouraged "Meatless Mondays," "Wheatless Wednesdays," and other similar reductions, with the hope of rationing food for military use (Figure 23.8).

Figure 23.8 With massive propaganda campaigns linking rationing and frugality to patriotism, the government sought to ensure adequate supplies to fight the war.

Wilson also created the War Industries Board, run by Bernard Baruch, to ensure adequate military supplies. The War Industries Board had the power to direct shipments of raw materials, as well as to control government contracts with private producers. Baruch used lucrative contracts with guaranteed profits to encourage several private firms to shift their production over to wartime materials. For those firms that refused to cooperate, Baruch's government control over raw materials provided him with the necessary leverage to convince them to join the war effort, willingly or not.

As a way to move all the personnel and supplies around the country efficiently, Congress created the U.S. Railroad Administration. Logistical problems had led trains bound for the East Coast to get stranded as far away as Chicago. To prevent these problems, Wilson appointed William McAdoo, the Secretary of the Treasury, to lead this agency, which had extraordinary war powers to control the entire railroad industry, including traffic, terminals, rates, and wages.

Almost all the practical steps were in place for the United States to fight a successful war. The only step remaining was to figure out how to pay for it. The war effort was costly—with an eventual price tag in excess of $32 billion by 1920—and the government needed to finance it. The Liberty Loan Act allowed the federal government to sell **liberty bonds** to the American public, extolling citizens to "do their part" to help the war effort and bring the troops home. The government ultimately raised $23 billion through liberty bonds. Additional monies came from the government's use of federal income tax revenue, which was made possible by the passage of the Sixteenth Amendment to the U.S. Constitution in 1913. With the financing, transportation, equipment, food, and men in place, the United States was ready to enter the war. The next piece the country needed was public support.

CONTROLLING DISSENT

Although all the physical pieces required to fight a war fell quickly into place, the question of national unity was another concern. The American public was strongly divided on the subject of entering the war.

Download for free at http://cnx.org/content/col11740/latest/

While many felt it was the only choice, others protested strongly, feeling it was not America's war to fight. Wilson needed to ensure that a nation of diverse immigrants, with ties to both sides of the conflict, thought of themselves as American first, and their home country's nationality second. To do this, he initiated a propaganda campaign, pushing the "America First" message, which sought to convince Americans that they should do everything in their power to ensure an American victory, even if that meant silencing their own criticisms.

AMERICANA

☼ *American First, American Above All*

At the outset of the war, one of the greatest challenges for Wilson was the lack of national unity. The country, after all, was made up of immigrants, some recently arrived and some well established, but all with ties to their home countries. These home countries included Germany and Russia, as well as Great Britain and France. In an effort to ensure that Americans eventually supported the war, the government pro-war propaganda campaign focused on driving home that message. The posters below, shown in both English and Yiddish, prompted immigrants to remember what they owed to America (Figure 23.9).

(a)   (b)

Figure 23.9 These posters clearly illustrate the pressure exerted on immigrants to quell any dissent they might feel about the United States at war.

Regardless of how patriotic immigrants might feel and act, however, an anti-German xenophobia overtook the country. German Americans were persecuted and their businesses shunned, whether or not they voiced any objection to the war. Some cities changed the names of the streets and buildings if they were German. Libraries withdrew German-language books from the shelves, and German Americans began to avoid speaking German for fear of reprisal. For some immigrants, the war was fought on two fronts: on the battlefields of France and again at home.

The Wilson administration created the Committee of Public Information under director George Creel, a former journalist, just days after the United States declared war on Germany. Creel employed artists, speakers, writers, and filmmakers to develop a propaganda machine. The goal was to encourage all Americans to make sacrifices during the war and, equally importantly, to hate all things German (Figure 23.10). Through efforts such as the establishment of "loyalty leagues" in ethnic immigrant communities,

Creel largely succeeded in molding an anti-German sentiment around the country. The result? Some schools banned the teaching of the German language and some restaurants refused to serve frankfurters, sauerkraut, or hamburgers, instead serving "liberty dogs with liberty cabbage" and "liberty sandwiches." Symphonies refused to perform music written by German composers. The hatred of Germans grew so widespread that, at one point, at a circus, audience members cheered when, in an act gone horribly wrong, a Russian bear mauled a German animal trainer (whose ethnicity was more a part of the act than reality).

Figure 23.10 Creel's propaganda campaign embodied a strongly anti-German message. The depiction of Germans as brutal apes, stepping on the nation's shores with their crude weapon of "Kultur" (culture), stood in marked contrast to the idealized rendition of the nation's virtue as a fair beauty whose clothes had been ripped off her.

In addition to its propaganda campaign, the U.S. government also tried to secure broad support for the war effort with repressive legislation. The Trading with the Enemy Act of 1917 prohibited individual trade with an enemy nation and banned the use of the postal service for disseminating any literature deemed treasonous by the postmaster general. That same year, the Espionage Act prohibited giving aid to the enemy by spying, or espionage, as well as any public comments that opposed the American war effort. Under this act, the government could impose fines and imprisonment of up to twenty years. The Sedition Act, passed in 1918, prohibited any criticism or disloyal language against the federal government and its policies, the U.S. Constitution, the military uniform, or the American flag. More than two thousand persons were charged with violating these laws, and many received prison sentences of up to twenty years. Immigrants faced deportation as punishment for their dissent. Not since the Alien and Sedition Acts of 1798 had the federal government so infringed on the freedom of speech of loyal American citizens.

Click and Explore

For a sense of the response and pushback that antiwar sentiments incited, read this newspaper article (http://openstaxcollege.org/l/15antiDraft) from 1917, discussing the dissemination of 100,000 antidraft flyers by the No Conscription League.

In the months and years after these laws came into being, over one thousand people were convicted for their violation, primarily under the Espionage and Sedition Acts. More importantly, many more war critics were frightened into silence. One notable prosecution was that of Socialist Party leader Eugene Debs, who received a ten-year prison sentence for encouraging draft resistance, which, under the Espionage Act, was considered "giving aid to the enemy." Prominent Socialist Victor Berger was also prosecuted under the Espionage Act and subsequently twice denied his seat in Congress, to which he had been properly elected by the citizens of Milwaukee, Wisconsin. One of the more outrageous prosecutions was that of a film producer who released a film about the American Revolution: Prosecutors found the film seditious, and a court convicted the producer to ten years in prison for portraying the British, who were now American allies, as the obedient soldiers of a monarchical empire.

State and local officials, as well as private citizens, aided the government's efforts to investigate, identify, and crush subversion. Over 180,000 communities created local "councils of defense," which encouraged members to report any antiwar comments to local authorities. This mandate encouraged spying on neighbors, teachers, local newspapers, and other individuals. In addition, a larger national organization—the American Protective League—received support from the Department of Justice to spy on prominent dissenters, as well as open their mail and physically assault draft evaders.

Understandably, opposition to such repression began mounting. In 1917, Roger Baldwin formed the National Civil Liberties Bureau—a forerunner to the American Civil Liberties Union, which was founded in 1920—to challenge the government's policies against wartime dissent and conscientious objection. In 1919, the case of *Schenck v. United States* went to the U.S. Supreme Court to challenge the constitutionality of the Espionage and Sedition Acts. The case concerned Charles Schenck, a leader in the Socialist Party of Philadelphia, who had distributed fifteen thousand leaflets, encouraging young men to avoid conscription. The court ruled that during a time of war, the federal government was justified in passing such laws to quiet dissenters. The decision was unanimous, and in the court's opinion, Justice Oliver Wendell Holmes wrote that such dissent presented a **"clear and present danger"** to the safety of the United States and the military, and was therefore justified. He further explained how the First Amendment right of free speech did not protect such dissent, in the same manner that a citizen could not be freely permitted to yell "fire!" in a crowded theater, due to the danger it presented. Congress ultimately repealed most of the Espionage and Sedition Acts in 1921, and several who were imprisoned for violation of those acts were then quickly released. But the Supreme Court's deference to the federal government's restrictions on civil liberties remained a volatile topic in future wars.

23.3 A New Home Front

By the end of this section, you will be able to:
- Explain how the status of organized labor changed during the First World War
- Describe how the lives of women and African Americans changed as a result of American participation in World War I
- Explain how America's participation in World War I allowed for the passage of prohibition and women's suffrage

The lives of all Americans, whether they went abroad to fight or stayed on the home front, changed dramatically during the war. Restrictive laws censored dissent at home, and the armed forces demanded unconditional loyalty from millions of volunteers and conscripted soldiers. For organized labor, women, and African Americans in particular, the war brought changes to the prewar status quo. Some white women worked outside of the home for the first time, whereas others, like African American men, found that they were eligible for jobs that had previously been reserved for white men. African American women, too, were able to seek employment beyond the domestic servant jobs that had been their primary opportunity. These new options and freedoms were not easily erased after the war ended.

NEW OPPORTUNITIES BORN FROM WAR

After decades of limited involvement in the challenges between management and organized labor, the need for peaceful and productive industrial relations prompted the federal government during wartime to invite organized labor to the negotiating table. Samuel Gompers, head of the American Federation of Labor (AFL), sought to capitalize on these circumstances to better organize workers and secure for them better wages and working conditions. His efforts also solidified his own base of power. The increase in production that the war required exposed severe labor shortages in many states, a condition that was further exacerbated by the draft, which pulled millions of young men from the active labor force.

Wilson only briefly investigated the longstanding animosity between labor and management before ordering the creation of the National Labor War Board in April 1918. Quick negotiations with Gompers and the AFL resulted in a promise: Organized labor would make a "no-strike pledge" for the duration of the war, in exchange for the U.S. government's protection of workers' rights to organize and bargain collectively. The federal government kept its promise and promoted the adoption of an eight-hour workday (which had first been adopted by government employees in 1868), a living wage for all workers, and union membership. As a result, union membership skyrocketed during the war, from 2.6 million members in 1916 to 4.1 million in 1919. In short, American workers received better working conditions and wages, as a result of the country's participation in the war. However, their economic gains were limited. While prosperity overall went up during the war, it was enjoyed more by business owners and corporations than by the workers themselves. Even though wages increased, inflation offset most of the gains. Prices in the United States increased an average of 15–20 percent annually between 1917 and 1920. Individual purchasing power actually declined during the war due to the substantially higher cost of living. Business profits, in contrast, increased by nearly a third during the war.

Women in Wartime

For women, the economic situation was complicated by the war, with the departure of wage-earning men and the higher cost of living pushing many toward less comfortable lives. At the same time, however, wartime presented new opportunities for women in the workplace. More than one million women entered the workforce for the first time as a result of the war, while more than eight million working women found higher paying jobs, often in industry. Many women also found employment in what were typically considered male occupations, such as on the railroads (Figure 23.11), where the number of women tripled, and on assembly lines. After the war ended and men returned home and searched for work, women were fired from their jobs, and expected to return home and care for their families. Furthermore, even when they were doing men's jobs, women were typically paid lower wages than male workers, and unions were ambivalent at best—and hostile at worst—to women workers. Even under these circumstances, wartime employment familiarized women with an alternative to a life in domesticity and dependency, making a life of employment, even a career, plausible for women. When, a generation later, World War II arrived, this trend would increase dramatically.

(a)   (b)

Figure 23.11   The war brought new opportunities to women, such as the training offered to those who joined the Land Army (a) or the opening up of traditionally male occupations. In 1918, Eva Abbott (b) was one of many new women workers on the Erie Railroad. However, once the war ended and veterans returned home, these opportunities largely disappeared. (credit b: modification of work by U.S. Department of Labor)

One notable group of women who exploited these new opportunities was the Women's Land Army of America. First during World War I, then again in World War II, these women stepped up to run farms and other agricultural enterprises, as men left for the armed forces (Figure 23.11). Known as Farmerettes, some twenty thousand women—mostly college educated and from larger urban areas—served in this capacity. Their reasons for joining were manifold. For some, it was a way to serve their country during a time of war. Others hoped to capitalize on the efforts to further the fight for women's suffrage.

Also of special note were the approximately thirty thousand American women who served in the military, as well as a variety of humanitarian organizations, such as the Red Cross and YMCA, during the war. In addition to serving as military nurses (without rank), American women also served as telephone operators in France. Of this latter group, 230 of them, known as "Hello Girls," were bilingual and stationed in combat areas. Over eighteen thousand American women served as Red Cross nurses, providing much of the medical support available to American troops in France. Close to three hundred nurses died during service. Many of those who returned home continued to work in hospitals and home healthcare, helping wounded veterans heal both emotionally and physically from the scars of war.

African Americans in the Crusade for Democracy

African Americans also found that the war brought upheaval and opportunity. Blacks composed 13 percent of the enlisted military, with 350,000 men serving. Colonel Charles Young of the Tenth Cavalry division served as the highest-ranking African American officer. Blacks served in segregated units and suffered from widespread racism in the military hierarchy, often serving in menial or support roles. Some troops saw combat, however, and were commended for serving with valor. The 369th Infantry, for example, known as the **Harlem Hellfighters**, served on the frontline of France for six months, longer than any other American unit. One hundred seventy-one men from that regiment received the Legion of Merit for meritorious service in combat. The regiment marched in a homecoming parade in New York City, was remembered in paintings (Figure 23.12), and was celebrated for bravery and leadership. The accolades given to them, however, in no way extended to the bulk of African Americans fighting in the war.

Figure 23.12 African American soldiers suffered under segregation and second-class treatment in the military. Still, the 369th Infantry earned recognition and reward for its valor in service both in France and the United States.

On the home front, African Americans, like American women, saw economic opportunities increase during the war. During the so-called Great Migration (discussed in a previous chapter), nearly 350,000 African Americans had fled the post-Civil War South for opportunities in northern urban areas. From 1910–1920, they moved north and found work in the steel, mining, shipbuilding, and automotive industries, among others. African American women also sought better employment opportunities beyond their traditional roles as domestic servants. By 1920, over 100,000 women had found work in diverse manufacturing industries, up from 70,000 in 1910. Despite such opportunities, racism continued to be a major force in both the North and South. Worried about the large influx of black Americans into their cities, several municipalities passed residential codes designed to prohibit African Americans from settling in certain neighborhoods. Race riots also increased in frequency: In 1917 alone, there were race riots in twenty-five cities, including East Saint Louis, where thirty-nine blacks were killed. In the South, white business and plantation owners feared that their cheap workforce was fleeing the region, and used violence to intimidate blacks into staying. According to NAACP statistics, recorded incidences of lynching increased from thirty-eight in 1917 to eighty-three in 1919. These numbers did not start to decrease until 1923, when the number of annual lynchings dropped below thirty-five for the first time since the Civil War.

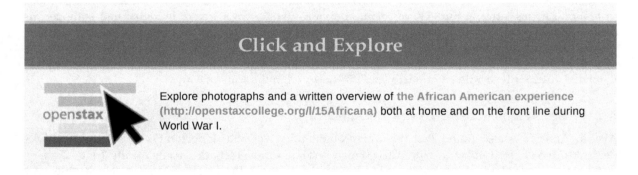

Explore photographs and a written overview of the African American experience (http://openstaxcollege.org/l/15Africana) both at home and on the front line during World War I.

THE LAST VESTIGES OF PROGRESSIVISM

Across the United States, the war intersected with the last lingering efforts of the Progressives who sought to use the war as motivation for their final push for change. It was in large part due to the war's influence that Progressives were able to lobby for the passage of the Eighteenth and Nineteenth Amendments to the U.S. Constitution. The Eighteenth Amendment, prohibiting alcohol, and the Nineteenth Amendment, giving women the right to vote, received their final impetus due to the war effort.

Prohibition, as the anti-alcohol movement became known, had been a goal of many Progressives for decades. Organizations such as the Women's Christian Temperance Union and the Anti-Saloon League linked alcohol consumption with any number of societal problems, and they had worked tirelessly with municipalities and counties to limit or prohibit alcohol on a local scale. But with the war, prohibitionists saw an opportunity for federal action. One factor that helped their cause was the strong anti-German sentiment that gripped the country, which turned sympathy away from the largely German-descended immigrants who ran the breweries. Furthermore, the public cry to ration food and grain—the latter being a key ingredient in both beer and hard alcohol—made prohibition even more patriotic. Congress ratified the Eighteenth Amendment in January 1919, with provisions to take effect one year later. Specifically, the amendment prohibited the manufacture, sale, and transportation of intoxicating liquors. It did not prohibit the drinking of alcohol, as there was a widespread feeling that such language would be viewed as too intrusive on personal rights. However, by eliminating the manufacture, sale, and transport of such beverages, drinking was effectively outlawed. Shortly thereafter, Congress passed the Volstead Act, translating the Eighteenth Amendment into an enforceable ban on the consumption of alcoholic beverages, and regulating the scientific and industrial uses of alcohol. The act also specifically excluded from prohibition the use of alcohol for religious rituals (Figure 23.13).

Figure 23.13   Surrounded by prominent "dry workers," Governor James P. Goodrich of Indiana signs a statewide bill to prohibit alcohol.

Unfortunately for proponents of the amendment, the ban on alcohol did not take effect until one full year following the end of the war. Almost immediately following the war, the general public began to oppose—and clearly violate—the law, making it very difficult to enforce. Doctors and druggists, who could prescribe whisky for medicinal purposes, found themselves inundated with requests. In the 1920s, organized crime and gangsters like Al Capone would capitalize on the persistent demand for liquor, making fortunes in the illegal trade. A lack of enforcement, compounded by an overwhelming desire by the public to obtain alcohol at all costs, eventually resulted in the repeal of the law in 1933.

The First World War also provided the impetus for another longstanding goal of some reformers: universal suffrage. Supporters of equal rights for women pointed to Wilson's rallying cry of a war "to make the world safe for democracy," as hypocritical, saying he was sending American boys to die for such principles while simultaneously denying American women their democratic right to vote (Figure 23.14). Carrie Chapman Catt, president of the National American Women Suffrage Movement, capitalized on the growing patriotic fervor to point out that every woman who gained the vote could exercise that right in a show of loyalty to the nation, thus offsetting the dangers of draft-dodgers or naturalized Germans who already had the right to vote.

Alice Paul, of the National Women's Party, organized more radical tactics, bringing national attention to the issue of women's suffrage by organizing protests outside the White House and, later, hunger strikes among arrested protesters. By the end of the war, the abusive treatment of suffragist hunger-strikers in prison, women's important contribution to the war effort, and the arguments of his suffragist daughter Jessie Woodrow Wilson Sayre moved President Wilson to understand women's right to vote as an ethical mandate for a true democracy. He began urging congressmen and senators to adopt the legislation. The amendment finally passed in June 1919, and the states ratified it by August 1920. Specifically, the Nineteenth Amendment prohibited all efforts to deny the right to vote on the basis of sex. It took effect in time for American women to vote in the presidential election of 1920.

Figure 23.14 Suffragists picketed the White House in 1917, leveraging the war and America's stance on democracy to urge Woodrow Wilson to support an amendment giving women the right to vote.

23.4 From War to Peace

By the end of this section, you will be able to:
* Identify the role that the United States played at the end of World War I
* Describe Woodrow Wilson's vision for the postwar world
* Explain why the United States never formally approved the Treaty of Versailles nor joined the League of Nations

The American role in World War I was brief but decisive. While millions of soldiers went overseas, and many thousands paid with their lives, the country's involvement was limited to the very end of the war. In fact, the peace process, with the international conference and subsequent ratification process, took longer than the time U.S. soldiers were "in country" in France. For the Allies, American reinforcements came at a decisive moment in their defense of the western front, where a final offensive had exhausted German forces. For the United States, and for Wilson's vision of a peaceful future, the fighting was faster and more successful than what was to follow.

WINNING THE WAR

When the United States declared war on Germany in April 1917, the Allied forces were close to exhaustion. Great Britain and France had already indebted themselves heavily in the procurement of vital American military supplies. Now, facing near-certain defeat, a British delegation to Washington, DC, requested immediate troop reinforcements to boost Allied spirits and help crush German fighting morale, which was already weakened by short supplies on the frontlines and hunger on the home front. Wilson agreed and immediately sent 200,000 American troops in June 1917. These soldiers were placed in "quiet zones" while they trained and prepared for combat.

By March 1918, the Germans had won the war on the eastern front. The Russian Revolution of the previous year had not only toppled the hated regime of Tsar Nicholas II but also ushered in a civil war from which the Bolshevik faction of Communist revolutionaries under the leadership of Vladimir Lenin emerged victorious. Weakened by war and internal strife, and eager to build a new Soviet Union, Russian delegates agreed to a generous peace treaty with Germany. Thus emboldened, Germany quickly moved upon the Allied lines, causing both the French and British to ask Wilson to forestall extensive training to U.S. troops and instead commit them to the front immediately. Although wary of the move, Wilson complied, ordering the commander of the American Expeditionary Force, General John "Blackjack" Pershing, to offer U.S. troops as replacements for the Allied units in need of relief. By May 1918, Americans were fully engaged in the war (Figure 23.15).

Figure 23.15   U.S. soldiers run past fallen Germans on their way to a bunker. In World War I, for the first time, photographs of the battles brought the war vividly to life for those at home.

In a series of battles along the front that took place from May 28 through August 6, 1918, including the battles of Cantigny, Chateau Thierry, Belleau Wood, and the Second Battle of the Marne, American forces alongside the British and French armies succeeded in repelling the German offensive. The Battle of Cantigny, on May 28, was the first American offensive in the war: In less than two hours that morning, American troops overran the German headquarters in the village, thus convincing the French commanders of their ability to fight against the German line advancing towards Paris. The subsequent battles of Chateau Thierry and Belleau Wood proved to be the bloodiest of the war for American troops. At the latter, faced with a German onslaught of mustard gas, artillery fire, and mortar fire, U.S. Marines attacked German units in the woods on six occasions—at times meeting them in hand-to-hand and bayonet combat—before finally repelling the advance. The U.S. forces suffered 10,000 casualties in the three-week battle, with almost 2,000 killed in total and 1,087 on a single day. Brutal as they were, they amounted to small losses compared to the casualties suffered by France and Great Britain. Still, these summer battles turned the tide of the war, with the Germans in full retreat by the end of July 1918 (Figure 23.16).

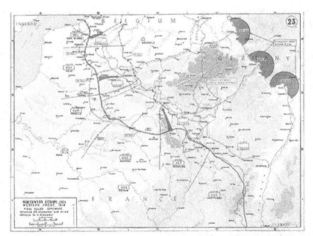

Figure 23.16   This map shows the western front at the end of the war, as the Allied Forces decisively break the German line.

Download for free at http://cnx.org/content/col11740/latest/

MY STORY

✣ *Sgt. Charles Leon Boucher: Life and Death in the Trenches of France*

Wounded in his shoulder by enemy forces, George, a machine gunner posted on the right end of the American platoon, was taken prisoner at the Battle of Seicheprey in 1918. However, as darkness set in that evening, another American soldier, Charlie, heard a noise from a gully beside the trench in which he had hunkered down. "I figured it must be the enemy mop-up patrol," Charlie later said.

> I only had a couple of bullets left in the chamber of my forty-five. The noise stopped and a head popped into sight. When I was about to fire, I gave another look and a white and distorted face proved to be that of George, so I grabbed his shoulders and pulled him down into our trench beside me. He must have had about twenty bullet holes in him but not one of them was well placed enough to kill him. He made an effort to speak so I told him to keep quiet and conserve his energy. I had a few malted milk tablets left and, I forced them into his mouth. I also poured the last of the water I had left in my canteen into his mouth.

Following a harrowing night, they began to crawl along the road back to their platoon. As they crawled, George explained how he survived being captured. Charlie later told how George "was taken to an enemy First Aid Station where his wounds were dressed. Then the doctor motioned to have him taken to the rear of their lines. But, the Sergeant Major pushed him towards our side and 'No Mans Land,' pulled out his Luger Automatic and shot him down. Then, he began to crawl towards our lines little by little, being shot at consistently by the enemy snipers till, finally, he arrived in our position."

The story of Charlie and George, related later in life by Sgt. Charles Leon Boucher to his grandson, was one replayed many times over in various forms during the American Expeditionary Force's involvement in World War I. The industrial scale of death and destruction was as new to American soldiers as to their European counterparts, and the survivors brought home physical and psychological scars that influenced the United States long after the war was won (Figure 23.17).

Figure 23.17 This photograph of U.S. soldiers in a trench hardly begins to capture the brutal conditions of trench warfare, where disease, rats, mud, and hunger plagued the men.

By the end of September 1918, over one million U.S. soldiers staged a full offensive into the Argonne Forest. By November—after nearly forty days of intense fighting—the German lines were broken, and their military command reported to German Emperor Kaiser Wilhelm II of the desperate need to end the war and enter into peace negotiations. Facing civil unrest from the German people in Berlin, as well as the loss of support from his military high command, Kaiser Wilhelm abdicated his throne on November 9, 1918, and immediately fled by train to the Netherlands. Two days later, on November 11, 1918, Germany and the Allies declared an immediate armistice, thus bring the fighting to a stop and signaling the beginning of the peace process.

When the armistice was declared, a total of 117,000 American soldiers had been killed and 206,000 wounded. The Allies as a whole suffered over 5.7 million military deaths, primarily Russian, British, and French men. The Central powers suffered four million military deaths, with half of them German soldiers. The total cost of the war to the United States alone was in excess of $32 billion, with interest expenses and veterans' benefits eventually bringing the cost to well over $100 billion. Economically, emotionally, and geopolitically, the war had taken an enormous toll.

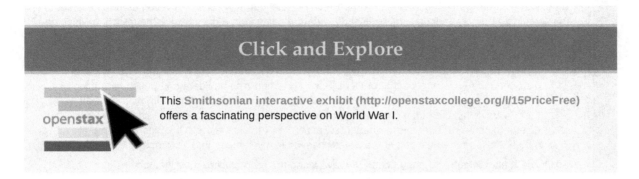

THE BATTLE FOR PEACE

While Wilson had been loath to involve the United States in the war, he saw the country's eventual participation as justification for America's involvement in developing a moral foreign policy for the entire world. The "new world order" he wished to create from the outset of his presidency was now within his grasp. The United States emerged from the war as the predominant world power. Wilson sought to capitalize on that influence and impose his moral foreign policy on all the nations of the world.

The Paris Peace Conference

As early as January 1918—a full five months before U.S. military forces fired their first shot in the war, and eleven months before the actual armistice—Wilson announced his postwar peace plan before a joint session of Congress. Referring to what became known as the **Fourteen Points**, Wilson called for openness in all matters of diplomacy and trade, specifically, free trade, freedom of the seas, an end to secret treaties and negotiations, promotion of self-determination of all nations, and more. In addition, he called for the creation of a **League of Nations** to promote the new world order and preserve territorial integrity through open discussions in place of intimidation and war.

As the war concluded, Wilson announced, to the surprise of many, that he would attend the Paris Peace Conference himself, rather than ceding to the tradition of sending professional diplomats to represent the country (Figure 23.18). His decision influenced other nations to follow suit, and the Paris conference became the largest meeting of world leaders to date in history. For six months, beginning in December 1918, Wilson remained in Paris to personally conduct peace negotiations. Although the French public greeted Wilson with overwhelming enthusiasm, other delegates at the conference had deep misgivings about the American president's plans for a "peace without victory." Specifically, Great Britain, France, and Italy sought to obtain some measure of revenge against Germany for drawing them into the war, to secure themselves against possible future aggressions from that nation, and also to maintain or even strengthen their own colonial possessions. Great Britain and France in particular sought substantial monetary reparations, as well as territorial gains, at Germany's expense. Japan also desired concessions in Asia, whereas Italy sought new territory in Europe. Finally, the threat posed by a Bolshevik Russia under Vladimir Lenin, and more importantly, the danger of revolutions elsewhere, further spurred on these allies to use the treaty negotiations to expand their territories and secure their strategic interests, rather than strive towards world peace.

Download for free at http://cnx.org/content/col11740/latest/

Figure 23.18 The Paris Peace Conference held the largest number of world leaders in one place to date. The photograph shows (from left to right) Prime Minister David Lloyd George of Great Britain; Vittorio Emanuele Orlando, prime minister of Italy; Georges Clemenceau, prime minister of France; and President Woodrow Wilson discussing the terms of the peace.

In the end, the Treaty of Versailles that officially concluded World War I resembled little of Wilson's original Fourteen Points. The Japanese, French, and British succeeded in carving up many of Germany's colonial holdings in Africa and Asia. The dissolution of the Ottoman Empire created new nations under the quasi-colonial rule of France and Great Britain, such as Iraq and Palestine. France gained much of the disputed territory along their border with Germany, as well as passage of a "war guilt clause" that demanded Germany take public responsibility for starting and prosecuting the war that led to so much death and destruction. Great Britain led the charge that resulted in Germany agreeing to pay reparations in excess of $33 billion to the Allies. As for Bolshevik Russia, Wilson had agreed to send American troops to their northern region to protect Allied supplies and holdings there, while also participating in an economic blockade designed to undermine Lenin's power. This move would ultimately have the opposite effect of galvanizing popular support for the Bolsheviks.

The sole piece of the original Fourteen Points that Wilson successfully fought to keep intact was the creation of a League of Nations. At a covenant agreed to at the conference, all member nations in the League would agree to defend all other member nations against military threats. Known as Article X, this agreement would basically render each nation equal in terms of power, as no member nation would be able to use its military might against a weaker member nation. Ironically, this article would prove to be the undoing of Wilson's dream of a new world order.

Ratification of the Treaty of Versailles

Although the other nations agreed to the final terms of the Treaty of Versailles, Wilson's greatest battle lay in the ratification debate that awaited him upon his return. As with all treaties, this one would require two-thirds approval by the U.S. Senate for final ratification, something Wilson knew would be difficult to achieve. Even before Wilson's return to Washington, Senator Henry Cabot Lodge, chairman of the Senate Foreign Relations Committee that oversaw ratification proceedings, issued a list of fourteen reservations he had regarding the treaty, most of which centered on the creation of a League of Nations. An isolationist in foreign policy issues, Cabot feared that Article X would require extensive American intervention, as more countries would seek her protection in all controversial affairs. But on the other side of the political spectrum, interventionists argued that Article X would impede the United States from using her rightfully attained military power to secure and protect America's international interests.

Wilson's greatest fight was with the Senate, where most Republicans opposed the treaty due to the clauses surrounding the creation of the League of Nations. Some Republicans, known as **Irreconcilables**, opposed the treaty on all grounds, whereas others, called **Reservationists**, would support the treaty if sufficient amendments were introduced that could eliminate Article X. In an effort to turn public support into a weapon against those in opposition, Wilson embarked on a cross-country railway speaking tour. He began travelling in September 1919, and the grueling pace, after the stress of the six months in Paris, proved too much. Wilson fainted following a public event on September 25, 1919, and immediately returned to Washington. There he suffered a debilitating stroke, leaving his second wife Edith Wilson in charge as de facto president for a period of about six months.

Frustrated that his dream of a new world order was slipping away—a frustration that was compounded by the fact that, now an invalid, he was unable to speak his own thoughts coherently—Wilson urged Democrats in the Senate to reject any effort to compromise on the treaty. As a result, Congress voted on, and defeated, the originally worded treaty in November. When the treaty was introduced with "reservations," or amendments, in March 1920, it again fell short of the necessary margin for ratification. As a result, the United States never became an official signatory of the Treaty of Versailles. Nor did the country join the League of Nations, which shattered the international authority and significance of the organization. Although Wilson received the Nobel Peace Prize in October 1919 for his efforts to create a model of world peace, he remained personally embarrassed and angry at his country's refusal to be a part of that model. As a result of its rejection of the treaty, the United States technically remained at war with Germany until July 21, 1921, when it formally came to a close with Congress's quiet passage of the Knox-Porter Resolution.

Click and Explore

Read about the Treaty of Versailles (http://openstaxcollege.org/l/15Versailles) here, particularly how it sowed the seeds for Hitler's rise to power and World War II.

23.5 Demobilization and Its Difficult Aftermath

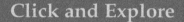

By the end of this section, you will be able to:
- Identify the challenges that the United States faced following the conclusion of World War I
- Explain Warren G. Harding's landslide victory in the 1920 presidential election

As world leaders debated the terms of the peace, the American public faced its own challenges at the conclusion of the First World War. Several unrelated factors intersected to create a chaotic and difficult time, just as massive numbers of troops rapidly demobilized and came home. Racial tensions, a terrifying flu epidemic, anticommunist hysteria, and economic uncertainty all combined to leave many Americans wondering what, exactly, they had won in the war. Adding to these problems was the absence of President Wilson, who remained in Paris for six months, leaving the country leaderless. The result of these factors was that, rather than a celebratory transition from wartime to peace and prosperity, and ultimately the Jazz Age of the 1920s, 1919 was a tumultuous year that threatened to tear the country apart.

DISORDER AND FEAR IN AMERICA

After the war ended, U.S. troops were demobilized and rapidly sent home. One unanticipated and unwanted effect of their return was the emergence of a new strain of influenza that medical professionals had never before encountered. Within months of the war's end, over twenty million Americans fell ill from the flu (Figure 23.19). Eventually, 675,000 Americans died before the disease mysteriously ran its course in the spring of 1919. Worldwide, recent estimates suggest that 500 million people suffered from this flu strain, with as many as fifty million people dying. Throughout the United States, from the fall of 1918 to the spring of 1919, fear of the flu gripped the country. Americans avoided public gatherings, children wore surgical masks to school, and undertakers ran out of coffins and burial plots in cemeteries. Hysteria grew as well, and instead of welcoming soldiers home with a postwar celebration, people hunkered down and hoped to avoid contagion.

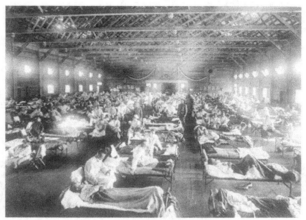

Figure 23.19 The flu pandemic that came home with the returning troops swept through the United States, as evidenced by this overcrowded flu ward at Camp Funstun, Kansas, adding another trauma onto the recovering postwar psyche.

Another element that greatly influenced the challenges of immediate postwar life was economic upheaval. As discussed above, wartime production had led to steady inflation; the rising cost of living meant that few Americans could comfortably afford to live off their wages. When the government's wartime control over the economy ended, businesses slowly recalibrated from the wartime production of guns and ships to the peacetime production of toasters and cars. Public demand quickly outpaced the slow production, leading to notable shortages of domestic goods. As a result, inflation skyrocketed in 1919. By the end of the year, the cost of living in the United States was nearly double what it had been in 1916. Workers, facing a shortage in wages to buy more expensive goods, and no longer bound by the no-strike pledge they made for the National War Labor Board, initiated a series of strikes for better hours and wages. In 1919 alone, more than four million workers participated in a total of nearly three thousand strikes: both records within all of American history.

In addition to labor clashes, race riots shattered the peace at the home front. The sporadic race riots that had begun during the Great Migration only grew in postwar America. White soldiers returned home to find black workers in their former jobs and neighborhoods, and were committed to restoring their position of white supremacy. Black soldiers returned home with a renewed sense of justice and strength, and were determined to assert their rights as men and as citizens. Meanwhile, southern lynchings continued to escalate, with white mobs burning African Americans at the stake. During the "**Red Summer**" of 1919, northern cities recorded twenty-five bloody race riots that killed over 250 people. Among these was the Chicago Race Riot of 1919, where a white mob stoned a young black boy to death because he swam too close to the "white beach" on Lake Michigan. Police at the scene did not arrest the perpetrator who threw the rock. This crime prompted a week-long riot that left twenty-three blacks and fifteen whites dead, as well as millions of dollars' worth of damage to the city (Figure 23.20). Riots in Tulsa, Oklahoma, in

1921, turned out even more deadly, with estimates of black fatalities ranging from fifty to three hundred. Americans thus entered the new decade with a profound sense of disillusionment over the prospects of peaceful race relations.

(a)   (b)

Figure 23.20 Riots broke out in Chicago in the wake of the stoning of a black boy. After two weeks, thirty-eight more people had died, some were stoned (a), and many had to abandon their vandalized homes (b).

Click and Explore

Read a Chicago newspaper report (http://historymatters.gmu.edu/d/4976) of the race riot, as well as a commentary on how the different newspapers—those written for the black community as well as those written by the mainstream press—sought to sensationalize the story.

While illness, economic hardship, and racial tensions all came from within, another destabilizing factor arrived from overseas. As revolutionary rhetoric emanating from Bolshevik Russia intensified in 1918 and 1919, a **Red Scare** erupted in the United States over fear that Communist infiltrators sought to overthrow the American government as part of an international revolution (Figure 23.21). When investigators uncovered a collection of thirty-six letter bombs at a New York City post office, with recipients that included several federal, state, and local public officials, as well as industrial leaders such as John D. Rockefeller, fears grew significantly. And when eight additional bombs actually exploded simultaneously on June 2, 1919, including one that destroyed the entrance to U.S. attorney general A. Mitchell Palmer's house in Washington, the country was convinced that all radicals, no matter what ilk, were to blame. Socialists, Communists, members of the Industrial Workers of the World (Wobblies), and anarchists: They were all threats to be taken down.

Download for free at http://cnx.org/content/col11740/latest/

Figure 23.21 Some Americans feared that labor strikes were the first step on a path that led ultimately to Bolshevik revolutions and chaos. This political cartoon depicts that fear.

Private citizens who considered themselves upstanding and loyal Americans, joined by discharged soldiers and sailors, raided radical meeting houses in many major cities, attacking any alleged radicals they found inside. By November 1919, Palmer's new assistant in charge of the Bureau of Investigation, J. Edgar Hoover, organized nationwide raids on radical headquarters in twelve cities around the country. Subsequent "Palmer raids" resulted in the arrests of four thousand alleged American radicals who were detained for weeks in overcrowded cells. Almost 250 of those arrested were subsequently deported on board a ship dubbed "the Soviet Ark" (Figure 23.22).

Figure 23.22 This cartoon advocates for a restrictive immigration policy, recommending the United States "close the gate" on undesirable (and presumably dangerous) immigrants.

A RETURN TO NORMALCY

By 1920, Americans had failed their great expectations to make the world safer and more democratic. The flu epidemic had demonstrated the limits of science and technology in making Americans less vulnerable. The Red Scare signified Americans' fear of revolutionary politics and the persistence of violent capital-labor conflicts. And race riots made it clear that the nation was no closer to peaceful race relations either. After a long era of Progressive initiatives and new government agencies, followed by a costly war that did not end in a better world, most of the public sought to focus on economic progress and success in their private lives instead. As the presidential election of 1920 unfolded, the extent of just how tired Americans were of an interventionist government—whether in terms of Progressive reform or international involvement—became exceedingly clear. Republicans, anxious to return to the White House after eight years of Wilson idealism, capitalized on this growing American sentiment to find the candidate who would promise a return to normalcy.

The Republicans found their man in Senator Warren G. Harding from Ohio. Although not the most energetic candidate for the White House, Harding offered what party handlers desired—a candidate around whom they could mold their policies of low taxes, immigration restriction, and noninterference in world affairs. He also provided Americans with what they desired: a candidate who could look and act presidential, and yet leave them alone to live their lives as they wished.

Click and Explore

Learn more about **President Harding's campaign promise of a return to normalcy (http://openstaxcollege.org/l/15Readjustment)** by listening to an audio recording or reading the text of his promise.

Democratic leaders realized they had little chance at victory. Wilson remained adamant that the election be a referendum over his League of Nations, yet after his stroke, he was in no physical condition to run for a third term. Political in-fighting among his cabinet, most notably between A. Mitchell Palmer and William McAdoo, threatened to split the party convention until a compromise candidate could be found in Ohio governor James Cox. Cox chose, for his vice presidential running mate, the young Assistant Secretary of the Navy, Franklin Delano Roosevelt.

At a time when Americans wanted prosperity and normalcy, rather than continued interference in their lives, Harding won in an overwhelming landslide, with 404 votes to 127 in the Electoral College, and 60 percent of the popular vote. With the war, the flu epidemic, the Red Scare, and other issues behind them, American looked forward to Harding's inauguration in 1921, and to an era of personal freedoms and hedonism that would come to be known as the Jazz Age.

Key Terms

clear and present danger the expression used by Supreme Court Justice Oliver Wendell Holmes in the case of *Schenck v. United States* to characterize public dissent during wartime, akin to shouting "fire!" in a crowded theater

Fourteen Points Woodrow Wilson's postwar peace plan, which called for openness in all matters of diplomacy, including free trade, freedom of the seas, and an end to secret treaties and negotiations, among others

Harlem Hellfighters a nickname for the decorated, all-black 369th Infantry, which served on the frontlines of France for six months, longer than any other American unit

Irreconcilables Republicans who opposed the Treaty of Versailles on all grounds

League of Nations Woodrow Wilson's idea for a group of countries that would promote a new world order and territorial integrity through open discussions, rather than intimidation and war

liberty bonds the name for the war bonds that the U.S. government sold, and strongly encouraged Americans to buy, as a way of raising money for the war effort

neutrality Woodrow Wilson's policy of maintaining commercial ties with all belligerents and insisting on open markets throughout Europe during World War I

prohibition the campaign for a ban on the sale and manufacturing of alcoholic beverages, which came to fruition during the war, bolstered by anti-German sentiment and a call to preserve resources for the war effort

Red Scare the term used to describe the fear that Americans felt about the possibility of a Bolshevik revolution in the United States; fear over Communist infiltrators led Americans to restrict and discriminate against any forms of radical dissent, whether Communist or not

Red Summer the summer of 1919, when numerous northern cities experienced bloody race riots that killed over 250 persons, including the Chicago race riot of 1919

Reservationists Republicans who would support the Treaty of Versailles if sufficient amendments were introduced that could eliminate Article X

Zimmermann telegram the telegram sent from German foreign minister Arthur Zimmermann to the German ambassador in Mexico, which invited Mexico to fight alongside Germany should the United States enter World War I on the side of the Allies

Summary

23.1 American Isolationism and the European Origins of War

President Wilson had no desire to embroil the United States in the bloody and lengthy war that was devastating Europe. His foreign policy, through his first term and his campaign for reelection, focused on keeping the United States out of the war and involving the country in international affairs only when there was a moral imperative to do so. After his 1916 reelection, however, the free trade associated with neutrality proved impossible to secure against the total war strategies of the belligerents, particularly Germany's submarine warfare. Ethnic ties to Europe meant that much of the general public was more than happy to remain neutral. Wilson's reluctance to go to war was mirrored in Congress, where fifty-six voted against the war resolution. The measure still passed, however, and the United States went to war against the wishes of many of its citizens.

23.2 The United States Prepares for War

Wilson might have entered the war unwillingly, but once it became inevitable, he quickly moved to use federal legislation and government oversight to put into place the conditions for the nation's success. First, he sought to ensure that all logistical needs—from fighting men to raw materials for wartime production—were in place and within government reach. From legislating rail service to encouraging Americans to buy liberty loans and "bring the boys home sooner," the government worked to make sure that the conditions for success were in place. Then came the more nuanced challenge of ensuring that a country of immigrants from both sides of the conflict fell in line as Americans, first and foremost. Aggressive propaganda campaigns, combined with a series of restrictive laws to silence dissenters, ensured that Americans would either support the war or at least stay silent. While some conscientious objectors and others spoke out, the government efforts were largely successful in silencing those who had favored neutrality.

23.3 A New Home Front

The First World War remade the world for all Americans, whether they served abroad or stayed at home. For some groups, such as women and blacks, the war provided opportunities for advancement. As soldiers went to war, women and African Americans took on jobs that had previously been reserved for white men. In return for a no-strike pledge, workers gained the right to organize. Many of these shifts were temporary, however, and the end of the war came with a cultural expectation that the old social order would be reinstated.

Some reform efforts also proved short-lived. President Wilson's wartime agencies managed the wartime economy effectively but closed immediately with the end of the war (although they reappeared a short while later with the New Deal). While patriotic fervor allowed Progressives to pass prohibition, the strong demand for alcohol made the law unsustainable. Women's suffrage, however, was a Progressive movement that came to fruition in part because of the circumstances of the war, and unlike prohibition, it remained.

23.4 From War to Peace

American involvement in World War I came late. Compared to the incredible carnage endured by Europe, the United States' battles were brief and successful, although the appalling fighting conditions and significant casualties made it feel otherwise to Americans, both at war and at home. For Wilson, victory in the fields of France was not followed by triumphs in Versailles or Washington, DC, where his vision of a new world order was summarily rejected by his allied counterparts and then by the U.S. Congress. Wilson had hoped that America's political influence could steer the world to a place of more open and tempered international negotiations. His influence did lead to the creation of the League of Nations, but concerns at home impeded the process so completely that the United States never signed the treaty that Wilson worked so hard to create.

23.5 Demobilization and Its Difficult Aftermath

The end of a successful war did not bring the kind of celebration the country craved or anticipated. The flu pandemic, economic troubles, and racial and ideological tensions combined to make the immediate postwar experience in the United States one of anxiety and discontent. As the 1920 presidential election neared, Americans made it clear that they were seeking a break from the harsh realities that the country had been forced to face through the previous years of Progressive mandates and war. By voting in President Warren G. Harding in a landslide election, Americans indicated their desire for a government that would leave them alone, keep taxes low, and limit social Progressivism and international intervention.

Review Questions

1. In order to pursue his goal of using American influence overseas only when it was a moral imperative, Wilson put which man in the position of Secretary of State?

    A. Charles Hughes

    B. Theodore Roosevelt

    C. William Jennings Bryan

    D. John Pershing

2. Why was the German use of the *unterseeboot* considered to defy international law?

    A. because other countries did not have similar technology

    B. because they refused to warn their targets before firing

    C. because they constituted cruel and unusual methods

    D. because no international consensus existed to employ submarine technology

3. To what extent were Woodrow Wilson's actual foreign policy decisions consistent with his foreign policy philosophy or vision?

4. Which of the following was *not* enacted in order to secure men and materials for the war effort?

    A. the Food Administration

    B. the Selective Service Act

    C. the War Industries Board

    D. the Sedition Act

5. What of the following was *not* used to control American dissent against the war effort?

    A. propaganda campaigns

    B. repressive legislation

    C. National Civil Liberties Bureau

    D. loyalty leagues

6. How did the government work to ensure unity on the home front, and why did Wilson feel that this was so important?

7. Why did the war not increase overall prosperity?

    A. because inflation made the cost of living higher

    B. because wages were lowered due to the war effort

    C. because workers had no bargaining power due to the "no-strike pledge"

    D. because women and African American men were paid less for the same work

8. Which of the following did *not* influence the eventual passage of the Nineteenth Amendment?

    A. women's contributions to the war effort

    B. the dramatic tactics and harsh treatment of radical suffragists

    C. the passage of the Volstead Act

    D. the arguments of President Wilson's daughter

9. Why was prohibition's success short-lived?

10. What was Article X in the Treaty of Versailles?

    A. the "war guilt clause" that France required

    B. the agreement that all nations in the League of Nations would be rendered equal

    C. the Allies' division of Germany's holdings in Asia

    D. the refusal to allow Bolshevik Russia membership in the League of Nations

11. Which of the following was *not* included in the Treaty of Versailles?

    A. extensive German reparations to be paid to the Allies

    B. a curtailment of German immigration to Allied nations

    C. France's acquisition of disputed territory along the French-German border

    D. a mandate for Germany to accept responsibility for the war publicly

12. What barriers did Wilson face in his efforts to ratify the Treaty of Versailles? What objections did those opposed to the treaty voice?

13. Which of the following was *not* a destabilizing factor immediately following the end of the war?

    A. a flu pandemic

    B. a women's liberation movement

    C. high inflation and economic uncertainty

    D. political paranoia

14. What was the inciting event that led to the
Chicago Race Riot of 1919?
  A. a strike at a local factory
  B. a protest march of black activists
  C. the murder of a black boy who swam too
     close to a white beach

  D. the assault of a white man on a streetcar by
     black youths

15. How did postwar conditions explain Warren
Harding's landslide victory in the 1920
presidential election?

Critical Thinking Questions

16. Why was preparation crucial to ensuring U.S. victory in World War I?

17. Why was the peace process at the war's end so lengthy? What complications did Wilson encounter in
his attempts to promote the process and realize his postwar vision?

18. What changes did the war bring to the everyday lives of Americans? How lasting were these changes?

19. What role did propaganda play in World War I? How might the absence of propaganda have changed
the circumstances or the outcome of the war?

20. What new opportunities did the war present for women and African Americans? What limitations did
these groups continue to face in spite of these opportunities?

CHAPTER 24

The Jazz Age: Redefining the Nation, 1919-1929

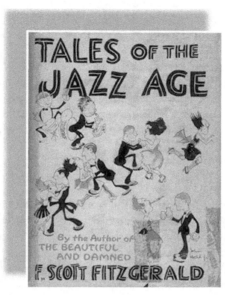

Figure 24.1 The illustrations for F. Scott Fitzgerald's *Tales of the Jazz Age*, drawn by John Held, Jr., epitomized the carefree flapper era of the 1920s.

Chapter Outline

24.1 Prosperity and the Production of Popular Entertainment
24.2 Transformation and Backlash
24.3 A New Generation
24.4 Republican Ascendancy: Politics in the 1920s

Introduction

Following the hardships of the immediate postwar era, the United States embarked upon one of the most prosperous decades in history. Mass production, especially of the automobile, increased mobility and fostered new industries. Unemployment plummeted as businesses grew to meet this increased demand. Cities continued to grow and, according to the 1920 census, a majority of the population lived in urban areas of twenty-five hundred or more residents.

Jazz music, movies, speakeasies, and new dances dominated the urban evening scene. Recent immigrants from southern and eastern Europe, many of them Catholic, now participated in the political system. This challenged rural Protestant fundamentalism, even as quota laws sought to limit new immigration patterns. The Ku Klux Klan rose to greater power, as they protested not only the changing role of African Americans but also the growing population of immigrant, Catholic, and Jewish Americans.

This mixture of social, political, economic, and cultural change and conflict gave the decade the nickname the "Roaring Twenties" or the "Jazz Age." The above illustration (Figure 24.1), which graced the cover of F. Scott Fitzgerald's *Tales of the Jazz Age*, embodies the popular view of the 1920s as a nonstop party, replete with dancing, music, flappers, and illegal drinking.

24.1 Prosperity and the Production of Popular Entertainment

By the end of this section, you will be able to:
- Discuss the role of movies in the evolution of American culture
- Explain the rise of sports as a dominant social force
- Analyze the ways in which the automobile, especially the Model T, transformed American life

In the 1920s, prosperity manifested itself in many forms, most notably in advancements in entertainment and technology that led to new patterns of leisure and consumption. Movies and sports became increasingly popular and buying on credit or "carrying" the debt allowed for the sale of more consumer goods and put automobiles within reach of average Americans. Advertising became a central institution in this new consumer economy, and commercial radio and magazines turned athletes and actors into national icons.

MOVIES

The increased prosperity of the 1920s gave many Americans more disposable income to spend on entertainment. As the popularity of "moving pictures" grew in the early part of the decade, "movie palaces," capable of seating thousands, sprang up in major cities. A ticket for a double feature and a live show cost twenty-five cents; for a quarter, Americans could escape from their problems and lose themselves in another era or world. People of all ages attended the movies with far more regularity than today, often going more than once per week. By the end of the decade, weekly movie attendance swelled to ninety million people.

The silent movies of the early 1920s gave rise to the first generation of movie stars. Rudolph Valentino, the lothario with the bedroom eyes, and Clara Bow, the "It Girl" with sex appeal, filled the imagination of millions of American moviegoers. However, no star captured the attention of the American viewing public

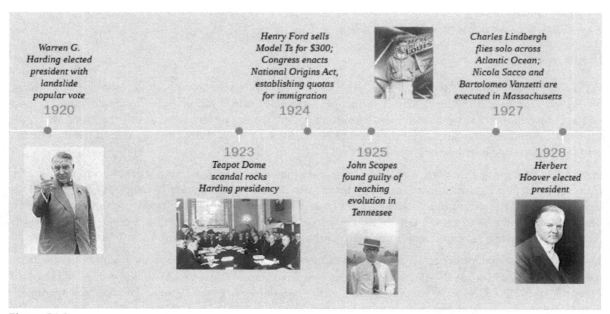

Figure 24.2

more than Charlie Chaplin. This sad-eyed tramp with a moustache, baggy pants, and a cane was the top box office attraction of his time (Figure 24.3).

Figure 24.3 Charlie Chaplin's nickname "The Tramp" came from the recurring character he played in many of his silent films, such as 1921's *The Kid*, which starred Jackie Coogan in the title role.

In 1927, the world of the silent movie began to wane with the New York release of the first "talkie": *The Jazz Singer*. The plot of this film, which starred Al Jolson, told a distinctively American story of the 1920s. It follows the life of a Jewish man from his boyhood days of being groomed to be the cantor at the local synagogue to his life as a famous and "Americanized" jazz singer. Both the story and the new sound technology used to present it were popular with audiences around the country. It quickly became a huge hit for Warner Brothers, one of the "big five" motion picture studios in Hollywood along with Twentieth Century Fox, RKO Pictures, Paramount Pictures, and Metro-Goldwyn-Mayer.

Southern California in the 1920s, however, had only recently become the center of the American film industry. Film production was originally based in and around New York, where Thomas Edison first debuted the kinetoscope in 1893. But in the 1910s, as major filmmakers like D. W. Griffith looked to escape the cost of Edison's patents on camera equipment, this began to change. When Griffith filmed *In Old California* (1910), the first movie ever shot in **Hollywood**, California, the small town north of Los Angeles was little more than a village. As moviemakers flocked to southern California, not least because of its favorable climate and predictable sunshine, Hollywood swelled with moviemaking activity. By the 1920s, the once-sleepy village was home to a majorly profitable innovative industry in the United States.

AUTOMOBILES AND AIRPLANES: AMERICANS ON THE MOVE

Cinema was not the only major industry to make great technological strides in this decade. The 1920s opened up new possibilities of mobility for a large percentage of the U.S. population, as automobile manufacturers began to mass produce what had once been a luxury item, and daring aviators both demonstrated and drove advancements in aircraft technology. The most significant innovation of this era was Henry Ford's **Model T** Ford, which made car ownership available to the average American.

Ford did not invent the automobile—the Duryea brothers in Massachusetts as well as Gottlieb W. Daimler and Karl Friedrich Benz in Germany were early pioneers. By the early twentieth century, hundreds of car manufacturers existed. However, they all made products that were too expensive for most Americans. Ford's innovation lay in his focus on using mass production to manufacture automobiles; he revolutionized industrial work by perfecting the assembly line, which enabled him to lower the Model T's price from $850 in 1908 to $300 in 1924, making car ownership a real possibility for a large share of the population (Figure 24.4). As prices dropped, more and more people could afford to own a car. Soon, people could buy used Model Ts for as little as five dollars, allowing students and others with low incomes to enjoy the freedom and mobility of car ownership. By 1929, there were over twenty-three million automobiles on American roads.

Figure 24.4 This advertisement for Ford's Model T ran in the New Orleans *Times Picayune* in 1911. Note that the prices have not yet dropped far from their initial high of $850.

The assembly line helped Ford reduce labor costs within the production process by moving the product from one team of workers to the next, each of them completing a step so simple they had to be, in Ford's words, "no smarter than an ox" (Figure 24.5). Ford's reliance on the **moving assembly line**, scientific management, and time-motion studies added to his emphasis on efficiency over craftsmanship.

Figure 24.5 In this image from a 1928 *Literary Digest* interview with Henry Ford, workers on an assembly line produce new models of Ford automobiles.

Ford's emphasis on cheap mass production brought both benefits and disadvantages to its workers. Ford would not allow his workers to unionize, and the boring, repetitive nature of the assembly line work generated a high turnover rate. However, he doubled workers' pay to five dollars a day and standardized the workday to eight hours (a reduction from the norm). Ford's assembly line also offered greater equality than most opportunities of the time, as he paid white and black workers equally. Seeking these wages, many African Americans from the South moved to Detroit and other large northern cities to work in factories.

Ford even bought a plot of land in the Amazonian jungle twice the size of Delaware to build a factory town he called Fordlandia. Workers there rejected his midwestern Puritanism even more than his factory discipline, and the project ended in an epic failure. In the United States, however, Ford shaped the nation's mode of industrialism—one that relied on paying decent wages so that workers could afford to be the consumers of their own products.

The automobile changed the face of America, both economically and socially. Industries like glass, steel, and rubber processing expanded to keep up with auto production. The oil industry in California, Oklahoma, and Texas expanded, as Americans' reliance on oil increased and the nation transitioned from a coal-based economy to one driven by petroleum. The need for public roadways required local and state governments to fund a dramatic expansion of infrastructure, which permitted motels and restaurants to spring up and offer new services to millions of newly mobile Americans with cash to spend. With this new infrastructure, new shopping and living patterns emerged, and streetcar suburbs gave way to automobile suburbs as private automobile traffic on public roads began to replace mass transit on trains and trolleys.

The 1920s not only witnessed a transformation in ground transportation but also major changes in air travel. By the mid-1920s, men—as well as some pioneering women like the African American stunt pilot Bessie Coleman (Figure 24.6)—had been flying for two decades. But there remained doubts about the suitability of airplanes for long-distance travel. Orville Wright, one of the pioneers of airplane technology in the United States, once famously declared, "No flying machine will ever fly from New York to Paris [because] no known motor can run at the requisite speed for four days without stopping." However, in 1927, this skepticism was finally put to rest when Charles Lindbergh became the first person to fly solo across the Atlantic Ocean, flying from New York to Paris in thirty-three hours (Figure 24.6).

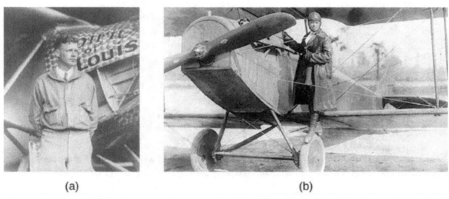

(a)   (b)

Figure 24.6 Aviator Charles Lindbergh stands in front of the *Spirit of St Louis* (a), the plane in which he flew from New York to Paris, France, in 1927. Because American flight schools barred black students, stunt pilot Bessie Coleman (b), the daughter of Texas sharecroppers, taught herself French to earn her pilot's license overseas.

Lindbergh's flight made him an international hero: the best-known American in the world. On his return, Americans greeted him with a ticker-tape parade—a celebration in which shredded paper thrown from surrounding buildings creates a festive, flurry effect. His flight, which he completed in the monoplane *Spirit of St. Louis*, seemed like a triumph of individualism in modern mass society and exemplified Americans' ability to conquer the air with new technology. Following his success, the small airline industry began to blossom, fully coming into its own in the 1930s, as companies like Boeing and Ford developed airplanes designed specifically for passenger air transport. As technologies in engine and passenger compartment design improved, air travel became more popular. In 1934, the number of U.S. domestic air passengers was just over 450,000 annually. By the end of the decade, that number had increased to nearly two million.

Technological innovation influenced more than just transportation. As access to electricity became more common and the electric motor was made more efficient, inventors began to churn out new and more complex household appliances. Newly developed innovations like radios, phonographs, vacuum cleaners, washing machines, and refrigerators emerged on the market during this period. While expensive, new consumer-purchasing innovations like store credit and installment plans made them available to a larger segment of the population. Many of these devices promised to give women—who continued to have primary responsibility for housework—more opportunities to step out of the home and expand their horizons. Ironically, however, these labor-saving devices tended to increase the workload for women by raising the standards of domestic work. With the aid of these tools, women ended up cleaning more frequently, washing more often, and cooking more elaborate meals rather than gaining spare time.

Despite the fact that the promise of more leisure time went largely unfulfilled, the lure of technology as the gateway to a more relaxed lifestyle endured. This enduring dream was a testament to the influence of another growing industry: advertising. The mass consumption of cars, household appliances, ready-to-wear clothing, and processed foods depended heavily on the work of advertisers. Magazines like *Ladies' Home Journal* and *The Saturday Evening Post* became vehicles to connect advertisers with middle-class consumers. Colorful and occasionally provocative print advertisements decorated the pages of these publications and became a staple in American popular culture (Figure 24.7).

Figure 24.7 This advertisement for Palmolive soap, which appeared in *Ladies' Home Journal* in 1922, claimed that the soap's "moderate price is due to popularity, to the enormous demand which keeps Palmolive factories working day and night" and so "the old-time luxury of the few may now be enjoyed the world over."

The form of the advertisements, however, was not new. These colorful print ads were merely the modern incarnations of an advertising strategy that went back to the nineteenth century. The new medium for advertisers in the 1920s, the one that would reach out to consumers in radically new and innovative ways, was radio.

THE POWER OF RADIO AND THE WORLD OF SPORTS

After being introduced during World War I, radios became a common feature in American homes of the 1920s. Hundreds of radio stations popped up over the decade. These stations developed and broadcasted news, serial stories, and political speeches. Much like print media, advertising space was interspersed with entertainment. Yet, unlike magazines and newspapers, advertisers did not have to depend on the active participation of consumers: Advertisers could reach out to anyone within listening distance of the radio. On the other hand, their broader audience meant that they had to be more conservative and careful not to offend anyone.

Click and Explore

Listen to a recording of a broadcast (http://openstaxcollege.org/l/15Showboat) of the "WLS Showboat: "The Floating Palace of Wonder," a variety show from WLS Chicago, a radio station run by Sears Roebuck and Co. What does the clip tell you about the entertainment of the 1920s?

The power of radio further sped up the processes of nationalization and homogenization that were previously begun with the wide distribution of newspapers made possible by railroads and telegraphs. Far more effectively than these print media, however, radio created and pumped out American culture onto the airwaves and into the homes of families around the country. Syndicated radio programs like *Amos 'n' Andy*, which began in the late 1920s, entertained listeners around the country—in the case of the popular *Amos 'n' Andy*, it did so with racial stereotypes about African Americans familiar from minstrel shows of the previous century. No longer were small corners of the country separated by their access to information. With the radio, Americans from coast to coast could listen to exactly the same programming. This had the effect of smoothing out regional differences in dialect, language, music, and even consumer taste.

Radio also transformed how Americans enjoyed sports. The introduction of play-by-play descriptions of sporting events broadcast over the radio brought sports entertainment right into the homes of millions. Radio also helped to popularize sports figures and their accomplishments. Jim Thorpe, who grew up in the Sac and Fox Nation in Oklahoma, was known as one of the best athletes in the world: He medaled in the 1912 Olympic Games, played Major League Baseball, and was one of the founding members of the National Football League. Other sports superstars were soon household names. In 1926, Gertrude Ederle became the first woman to swim the English Channel. Helen Wills dominated women's tennis, winning Wimbledon eight times in the late 1920s (Figure 24.8), whereas "Big Bill" Tilden won the national singles title every year from 1920 to 1925. In football, Harold "Red" Grange played for the University of Illinois, averaging over ten yards per carry during his college career. The biggest star of all was the "Sultan of Swat," Babe Ruth, who became America's first baseball hero (Figure 24.8). He changed the game of baseball from a low-scoring one dominated by pitchers to one where his hitting became famous. By 1923, most pitchers intentionally walked him. In 1924, he hit sixty homeruns.

(a)   (b)

Figure 24.8 Babe Ruth (a) led the New York Yankees to four World Series championships. In this 1921 photograph, he stands outside of the New York Yankees dugout. Helen Wills (b) won a total of thirty-one Grand Slam titles in her career, including eight singles titles at Wimbledon from 1927 to 1938. (credit a: modification of work by Library of Congress)

24.2 Transformation and Backlash

By the end of this section, you will be able to:
- Define nativism and analyze the ways in which it affected the politics and society of the 1920s
- Describe the conflict between urban Americans and rural fundamentalists
- Explain the issues in question in the Scopes trial

While prosperous, middle-class Americans found much to celebrate about the new era of leisure and consumption, many Americans—often those in rural areas—disagreed on the meaning of a "good life" and how to achieve it. They reacted to the rapid social changes of modern urban society with a vigorous defense of religious values and a fearful rejection of cultural diversity and equality.

NATIVISM

Beginning at the end of the nineteenth century, immigration into the United States rocketed to never-before-seen heights. Many of these new immigrants were coming from eastern and southern Europe and, for many English-speaking, native-born Americans of northern European descent, the growing diversity of new languages, customs, and religions triggered anxiety and racial animosity. In reaction, some embraced **nativism**, prizing white Americans with older family trees over more recent immigrants, and rejecting outside influences in favor of their own local customs. Nativists also stoked a sense of fear over the perceived foreign threat, pointing to the anarchist assassinations of the Spanish prime minister in 1897, the Italian king in 1900, and even President William McKinley in 1901 as proof. Following the Bolshevik Revolution in Russia in November 1917, the sense of an inevitable foreign or communist threat only grew among those already predisposed to distrust immigrants.

The sense of fear and anxiety over the rising tide of immigration came to a head with the trial of Nicola Sacco and Bartolomeo Vanzetti (Figure 24.9). Sacco and Vanzetti were Italian immigrants who were accused of being part of a robbery and murder in Braintree, Massachusetts, in 1920. There was no direct evidence linking them to the crime, but (in addition to being immigrants) both men were anarchists who favored the destruction of the American market-based, capitalistic society through violence. At their trial, the district attorney emphasized Sacco and Vanzetti's radical views, and the jury found them guilty on July 14, 1921. Despite subsequent motions and appeals based on ballistics testing, recanted testimony, and an ex-convict's confession, both men were executed on August 23, 1927.

(a)   (b)

Figure 24.9 Bartolomeo Vanzetti and Nicola Sacco (a) sit in handcuffs at Dedham Superior Court in Massachusetts in 1923. After the verdict in 1921, protesters demonstrated (b) in London, England, hoping to save Sacco and Vanzetti from execution.

Opinions on the trial and judgment tended to divide along nativist-immigrant lines, with immigrants supporting the innocence of the condemned pair. The verdict sparked protests from Italian and other immigrant groups, as well as from noted intellectuals such as writer John Dos Passos, satirist Dorothy Parker, and famed physicist Albert Einstein. Muckraker Upton Sinclair based his indictment of the American justice system, the "documentary novel" *Boston*, on Sacco and Vanzetti's trial, which he considered a gross miscarriage of justice. As the execution neared, the radical labor union Industrial Workers of the World called for a three-day nationwide walkout, leading to the Great Colorado Coal Strike of 1927. Protests occurred worldwide from Tokyo to Buenos Aires to London (Figure 24.9).

One of the most articulate critics of the trial was then-Harvard Law School professor Felix Frankfurter, who would go on to be appointed to the U.S. Supreme Court by Franklin D. Roosevelt in 1939. In 1927, six years after the trial, he wrote in *The Atlantic*, "By systematic exploitation of the defendants' alien blood, their imperfect knowledge of English, their unpopular social views, and their opposition to the war, the District Attorney invoked against them a riot of political passion and patriotic sentiment; and the trial judge connived at—one had almost written, cooperated in—the process."

To "preserve the ideal of American homogeneity," the Emergency Immigration Act of 1921 introduced numerical limits on European immigration for the first time in U.S. history. These limits were based on a quota system that restricted annual immigration from any given country to 3 percent of the residents from that same country as counted in the 1910 census. The National Origins Act of 1924 went even further, lowering the level to 2 percent of the 1890 census, significantly reducing the share of eligible southern and eastern Europeans, since they had only begun to arrive in the United States in large numbers in the 1890s. Although New York congressmen Fiorello LaGuardia and Emanuel Celler spoke out against the act, there was minimal opposition in Congress, and both labor unions and the Ku Klux Klan supported the bill. When President Coolidge signed it into law, he declared, "America must be kept American."

Click and Explore

The Library of Congress's immigration collection (http://openstaxcollege.org/l/15Immigration) contains information on different immigrant groups, the timelines of their immigration, maps of their settlement routes, and the reasons they came. Click the images on the left navigation bar to learn about each group.

THE KU KLUX KLAN

The concern that a white, Protestant, Anglo-Saxon United States was under siege by throngs of undesirables was not exclusively directed at foreigners. The sense that the country was also facing a threat from within its borders and its own citizenry was also prevalent. This sense was clearly reflected in the popularity of the 1915 motion picture, D. W. Griffith's *The Birth of a Nation* (Figure 24.10). Based on *The Clansman*, a 1915 novel by Thomas Dixon, the film offers a racist, white-centric view of the Reconstruction Era. The film depicts noble white southerners made helpless by northern carpetbaggers who empower freed slaves to abuse white men and violate women. The heroes of the film were the Ku Klux Klan, who saved the whites, the South, and the nation. While the film was reviled by many African Americans and the NAACP for its historical inaccuracies and its maligning of freed slaves, it was celebrated by many whites who accepted the historical revisionism as an accurate portrayal of Reconstruction Era oppression. After viewing the film, President Wilson reportedly remarked, "It is like writing history with lightning, and my only regret is that it is all so terribly true."

Figure 24.10   A theatrical release poster for *The Birth of a Nation*, in 1915. The film glorified the role of the Ku Klux Klan in quelling the threat of black power during Reconstruction.

DEFINING "AMERICAN"

✪ *Artistic License and the Censor*

In a letter dated April 17, 1915, Mary Childs Nerney, a secretary of the NAACP, wrote to a local censor to request that certain scenes be cut from *The Birth of a Nation*.

> My dear Mr. Packard:
> I am utterly disgusted with the situation in regard to "The Birth of a Nation." As you will read in the next number of the Crisis, we have fought it at every possible point. In spite of the promise of the Mayor [of Chicago] to cut out the two objectionable scenes in the second part, which show a white girl committing suicide to escape from a Negro pursuer, and a mulatto politician trying to force marriage upon the daughter of his white benefactor, these two scenes still form the motif of the really unimportant incidents, of which I enclose a list. I have seen the thing four times and am positive that nothing more will be done about it. Jane Addams saw it when it was in its worst form in New York. I know of no one else from Chicago who saw it. I enclose Miss Addam's opinion.
> When we took the thing before the Police Magistrate he told us that he could do nothing about it unless it [led] to a breach of the peace. Some kind of demonstration began in the Liberty Theatre Wednesday night but the colored people took absolutely no part in it, and the only man arrested was a white man. This, of course, is exactly what Littleton, counsel for the producer, Griffith, held in the Magistrates' Court when we have our hearing and claimed that it might lead to a breach of the peace.
> Frankly, I do not think you can do one single thing. It has been to me a most liberal education and I purposely am through. The harm it is doing the colored people cannot be estimated. I hear echoes of it wherever I go and have no doubt that this was in the mind of the people who are producing it. Their profits here are something like $14,000 a day and their expenses about $400. I have ceased to worry about it, and if I seem disinterested, kindly remember that we have put six weeks of constant effort of this thing and have gotten nowhere.
> Sincerely yours,
> —Mary Childs Nerney, Secretary, NAACP

On what grounds does Nerney request censorship? What efforts to get the movie shut down did she describe?

The Ku Klux Klan, which had been dormant since the end of Reconstruction in 1877, experienced a resurgence of attention following the popularity of the film. Just months after the film's release, a second incarnation of the Klan was established at Stone Mountain, Georgia, under the leadership of William Simmons. This new Klan now publicly eschewed violence and received mainstream support. Its embrace of Protestantism, anti-Catholicism, and anti-Semitism, and its appeals for stricter immigration policies, gained the group a level of acceptance by nativists with similar prejudices. The group was not merely a male organization: The ranks of the Klan also included many women, with chapters of its women's auxiliary in locations across the country. These women's groups were active in a number of reform-minded activities, such as advocating for prohibition and the distribution of Bibles at public schools. But they also participated in more expressly Klan activities like burning crosses and the public denunciation of Catholics and Jews (**Figure 24.11**). By 1924, this **Second Ku Klux Klan** had six million members in the South, West, and, particularly, the Midwest—more Americans than there were in the nation's labor unions at the time. While the organization publicly abstained from violence, its member continued to employ intimidation, violence, and terrorism against its victims, particularly in the South.

Figure 24.11 In this 1921 image from the *Denver News*, three Ku Klux Klan members (two women and one man) stand in front of a burning cross.

The Klan's newfound popularity proved to be fairly short-lived. Several states effectively combatted the power and influence of the Klan through anti-masking legislation, that is, laws that barred the wearing of masks publicly. As the organization faced a series of public scandals, such as when the Grand Dragon of Indiana was convicted of murdering a white schoolteacher, prominent citizens became less likely to openly express their support for the group without a shield of anonymity. More importantly, influential people and citizen groups explicitly condemned the Klan. Reinhold Niebuhr, a popular Protestant minister and conservative intellectual in Detroit, admonished the group for its ostensibly Protestant zealotry and anti-Catholicism. Jewish organizations, especially the Anti-Defamation League, which had been founded just a couple of years before the reemergence of the Klan, amplified Jewish discontent at being the focus of Klan attention. And the NAACP, which had actively sought to ban the film *The Birth of a Nation*, worked to lobby congress and educate the public on lynchings. Ultimately, however, it was the Great Depression that put an end to the Klan. As dues-paying members dwindled, the Klan lost its organizational power and sunk into irrelevance until the 1950s.

FAITH, FUNDAMENTALISM, AND SCIENCE

The sense of degeneration that the Klan and anxiety over mass immigration prompted in the minds of many Americans was in part a response to the process of postwar urbanization. Cities were swiftly becoming centers of opportunity, but the growth of cities, especially the growth of immigrant populations in those cities, sharpened rural discontent over the perception of rapid cultural change. As more of the population flocked to cities for jobs and quality of life, many left behind in rural areas felt that their way of life was being threatened. To rural Americans, the ways of the city seemed sinful and profligate. Urbanites, for their part, viewed rural Americans as hayseeds who were hopelessly behind the times.

In this urban/rural conflict, Tennessee lawmakers drew a battle line over the issue of evolution and its contradiction of the accepted, biblical explanation of history. Charles Darwin had first published his theory of natural selection in 1859, and by the 1920s, many standard textbooks contained information about Darwin's theory of evolution. Fundamentalist Protestants targeted evolution as representative of all that was wrong with urban society. Tennessee's Butler Act made it illegal "to teach any theory that denies the story of the Divine Creation of man as taught in the Bible, and to teach instead that man has descended from a lower order of animals."

The American Civil Liberties Union (ACLU) hoped to challenge the Butler Act as an infringement of the freedom of speech. As a defendant, the ACLU enlisted teacher and coach John Scopes, who suggested that he may have taught evolution while substituting for an ill biology teacher. Town leaders in Dayton,

Tennessee, for their part, sensed an opportunity to promote their town, which had lost more than one-third of its population, and welcomed the ACLU to stage a test case against the Butler Act. The ACLU and the town got their wish as the **Scopes Monkey Trial**, as the newspapers publicized it, quickly turned into a carnival that captured the attention of the country and epitomized the nation's urban/rural divide (Figure 24.12).

Figure 24.12 During the Scopes Monkey Trial, supporters of the Butler Act read literature at the headquarters of the Anti-Evolution League in Dayton, Tennessee.

Fundamentalist champion William Jennings Bryan argued the case for the prosecution. Bryan was a three-time presidential candidate and Woodrow Wilson's Secretary of State until 1915, at which point he began preaching across the country about the spread of secularism and the declining role of religion in education. He was known for offering $100 to anyone who would admit to being descended from an ape. Clarence Darrow, a prominent lawyer and outspoken agnostic, led the defense team. His statement that, "Scopes isn't on trial, civilization is on trial. No man's belief will be safe if they win," struck a chord in society.

The outcome of the trial, in which Scopes was found guilty and fined $100, was never really in question, as Scopes himself had confessed to violating the law. Nevertheless, the trial itself proved to be high drama. The drama only escalated when Darrow made the unusual choice of calling Bryan as an expert witness on the Bible. Knowing of Bryan's convictions of a literal interpretation of the Bible, Darrow peppered him with a series of questions designed to ridicule such a belief. The result was that those who approved of the teaching of evolution saw Bryan as foolish, whereas many rural Americans considered the cross-examination an attack on the Bible and their faith.

DEFINING "AMERICAN"

✪ *H. L. Mencken on the Scopes Trial*

H. L. Mencken covered the trial for Baltimore's The Evening Sun. One of most popular writers of social satire of his age, Mencken was very critical of the South, the trial, and especially Bryan. He coined the terms "monkey trial "and "Bible belt." In the excerpt below, Mencken reflects on the trial's outcome and its overall importance for the United States.

> The Scopes trial, from the start, has been carried on in a manner exactly fitted to the anti-evolution law and the simian imbecility under it. There hasn't been the slightest pretense to decorum. The rustic judge, a candidate for re-election, has postured the yokels like a clown in a ten-cent side show, and almost every word he has uttered has been an undisguised appeal to their prejudices and superstitions. The chief prosecuting attorney, beginning like a competent lawyer and a man of self-respect, ended like a convert at a Billy Sunday revival. It fell to him, finally, to make a clear and astounding statement of theory of justice prevailing under fundamentalism. What he said, in brief, was that a man accused of infidelity had no rights whatever under Tennessee law. . . .
>
> Darrow has lost this case. It was lost long before he came to Dayton. But it seems to me that he has nevertheless performed a great public service by fighting it to a finish and in a perfectly serious way. Let no one mistake it for comedy, farcical though it may be in all its details. It serves notice on the country that Neanderthal man is organizing in these forlorn backwaters of the land, led by a fanatic, rid of sense and devoid of conscience. Tennessee, challenging him too timorously and too late, now sees its courts converted into camp meetings and its Bill of Rights made a mock of by its sworn officers of the law. There are other States that had better look to their arsenals before the Hun is at their gates.
>
> —H. L. Mencken, *The Evening Sun*, July 18, 1925

How does Mencken characterize Judge Raulston? About what threat is Mencken warning America?

Indicative of the revival of Protestant fundamentalism and the rejection of evolution among rural and white Americans was the rise of Billy Sunday. As a young man, Sunday had gained fame as a baseball player with exceptional skill and speed. Later, he found even more celebrity as the nation's most revered evangelist, drawing huge crowds at camp meetings around the country. He was one of the most influential evangelists of the time and had access to some of the wealthiest and most powerful families in the country (Figure 24.13). Sunday rallied many Americans around "old-time" fundamentalist religion and garnered support for prohibition. Recognizing Sunday's popular appeal, Bryan attempted to bring him to Dayton for the Scopes trial, although Sunday politely refused.

(a)   (b)

Figure 24.13   Billy Sunday, one of the most influential evangelists of his day, leaves the White House on February 20, 1922 (a). Aimee Semple McPherson, shown here preaching at the Angelus Temple in 1923 (b), founded the Foursquare Church. (credit a: modification of work by Library of Congress)

Even more spectacular than the rise of Billy Sunday was the popularity of Aimee Semple McPherson, a Canadian Pentecostal preacher whose Foursquare Church in Los Angeles catered to the large community of midwestern transplants and newcomers to California (Figure 24.13). Although her message promoted the fundamental truths of the Bible, her style was anything but old fashioned. Dressed in tight-fitting clothes and wearing makeup, she held radio-broadcast services in large venues that resembled concert halls and staged spectacular faith-healing performances. Blending Hollywood style and modern technology with a message of fundamentalist Christianity, McPherson exemplified the contradictions of the decade well before public revelations about her scandalous love affair cost her much of her status and following.

24.3 A New Generation

By the end of this section, you will be able to:
- Explain the factors that shaped the new morality and the changing role of women in the United States during the 1920s
- Describe the "new Negro" and the influence of the Harlem Renaissance
- Analyze the effects of prohibition on American society and culture
- Describe the character and main authors of the Lost Generation

The 1920s was a time of dramatic change in the United States. Many young people, especially those living in big cities, embraced a new morality that was much more permissive than that of previous generations. They listened to jazz music, especially in the nightclubs of Harlem. Although prohibition outlawed alcohol, criminal bootlegging and importing businesses thrived. The decade was not a pleasure cruise for everyone, however; in the wake of the Great War, many were left awaiting the promise of a new generation.

A NEW MORALITY

Many Americans were disillusioned in the post-World War I era, and their reactions took many forms. Rebellious American youth, in particular, adjusted to the changes by embracing a **new morality** that was far more permissive than the social mores of their parents. Many young women of the era shed their mother's morality and adopted the dress and mannerisms of a **flapper**, the Jazz Age female stereotype, seeking the endless party. Flappers wore shorter skirts, shorter hair, and more makeup, and they drank and smoked with the boys (Figure 24.14). Flappers' dresses emphasized straight lines from the shoulders to the knees, minimizing breasts and curves while highlighting legs and ankles. The male equivalent of a flapper was a "sheik," although that term has not remained as strong in the American vernacular. At the time, however, many of these fads became a type of conformity, especially among college-aged youths, with the signature bob haircut of the flapper becoming almost universal—in both the United States and overseas.

Figure 24.14 The flapper look, seen here in "Flapper" by Ellen Pyle for the cover of *The Saturday Evening Post* in February 1922, was a national craze in American cities during the 1920s.

As men and women pushed social and cultural boundaries in the Jazz Age, sexual mores changed and social customs grew more permissive. "Petting parties" or "necking parties" became the rage on college campuses. Psychologist Sigmund Freud and British "sexologist" Havelock Ellis emphasized that sex was a natural and pleasurable part of the human experience. Margaret Sanger, the founder of Planned Parenthood, launched an information campaign on birth control to give women a choice in the realm in which suffrage had changed little—the family. The popularization of contraception and the private space that the automobile offered to teenagers and unwed couples also contributed to changes in sexual behavior.

Flappers and sheiks also took their cues from the high-flying romances they saw on movie screens and confessions in movie magazines of immorality on movie sets. Movie posters promised: "Brilliant men, beautiful jazz babies, champagne baths, midnight revels, petting parties in the purple dawn, all ending in one terrific smashing climax that makes you gasp." And "neckers, petters, white kisses, red kisses, pleasure-mad daughters, sensation-craving mothers . . . the truth: bold, naked, sensational."

Click and Explore

Could you go "on a toot" with flappers and sheiks? Improve your chances with this collection (http://openstaxcollege.org/l/15JazzSlang) of Jazz Age slang.

New dances and new music—especially jazz—also characterized the Jazz Age. Born out of the African American community, jazz was a uniquely American music. The innovative sound emerged from a number of different communities and from a number of different musical traditions such as blues and ragtime. By the 1920s, jazz had spread from African American clubs in New Orleans and Chicago to reach greater popularity in New York and abroad. One New York jazz establishment, the Cotton Club, became particularly famous and attracted large audiences of hip, young, and white flappers and sheiks to see black entertainers play jazz (Figure 24.15).

Figure 24.15 Black jazz bands such as the King and Carter Jazzing Orchestra, photographed in 1921 by Robert Runyon, were immensely popular among white urbanites in the 1920s.

THE "NEW WOMAN"

The Jazz Age and the proliferation of the flapper lifestyle of the 1920s should not be seen merely as the product of postwar disillusionment and newfound prosperity. Rather, the search for new styles of dress and new forms of entertainment like jazz was part of a larger women's rights movement. The early 1920s, especially with the ratification of the Nineteenth Amendment guaranteeing full voting rights to women, was a period that witnessed the expansion of women's political power. The public flaunting of social and sexual norms by flappers represented an attempt to match gains in political equality with gains in the social sphere. Women were increasingly leaving the Victorian era norms of the previous generation behind, as they broadened the concept of women's liberation to include new forms of social expression such as dance, fashion, women's clubs, and forays into college and the professions.

Nor did the struggle for women's rights through the promotion and passage of legislation cease in the 1920s. In 1921, Congress passed the Promotion of the Welfare and Hygiene of Maternity and Infancy Act, also known as the Sheppard-Towner Act, which earmarked $1.25 million for well-baby clinics and educational programs, as well as nursing. This funding dramatically reduced the rate of infant mortality.

Two years later, in 1923, Alice Paul drafted and promoted an Equal Rights Amendment (ERA) that promised to end all sex discrimination by guaranteeing that "Men and women shall have equal rights throughout the United States and every place subject to its jurisdiction."

Yet, ironically, at precisely the time when the Progressive movement was achieving its long-sought-after goals, the movement itself was losing steam and the Progressive Era was coming to a close. As the heat of Progressive politics grew less intense, voter participation from both sexes declined over the course of the 1920s. After the passage of the Nineteenth Amendment, many women believed that they had accomplished their goals and dropped out of the movement. As a result, the proposed ERA stalled (the ERA eventually passed Congress almost fifty years later in 1972, but then failed to win ratification by a sufficient number of states), and, by the end of the 1920s, Congress even allowed funding for the Sheppard-Towner Act to lapse.

The growing lethargy toward women's rights was happening at a time when an increasing number of women were working for wages in the U.S. economy—not only in domestic service, but in retail, healthcare and education, offices, and manufacturing. Beginning in the 1920s, women's participation in the labor force increased steadily. However, most were paid less than men for the same type of work based on the rationale that they did not have to support a family. While the employment of single and unmarried women had largely won social acceptance, married women often suffered the stigma that they were working for pin money—frivolous additional discretionary income.

THE HARLEM RENAISSANCE AND THE NEW NEGRO

It wasn't only women who found new forms of expression in the 1920s. African Americans were also expanding their horizons and embracing the concept of the "new Negro." The decade witnessed the continued Great Migration of African Americans to the North, with over half a million fleeing the strict Jim Crow laws of the South. Life in the northern states, as many African Americans discovered, was hardly free of discrimination and segregation. Even without Jim Crow, businesses, property owners, employers, and private citizens typically practiced *de facto* segregation, which could be quite stifling and oppressive. Nonetheless, many southern blacks continued to move north into segregated neighborhoods that were already bursting at the seams, because the North, at the very least, offered two tickets toward black progress: schools and the vote. The black population of New York City doubled during the decade. As a result, Harlem, a neighborhood at the northern end of Manhattan, became a center for Afro-centric art, music, poetry, and politics. Political expression in the Harlem of the 1920s ran the gamut, as some leaders advocated a return to Africa, while others fought for inclusion and integration.

Revived by the wartime migration and fired up by the white violence of the postwar riots, urban blacks developed a strong cultural expression in the 1920s that came to be known as the Harlem Renaissance. In this rediscovery of black culture, African American artists and writers formulated an independent black culture and encouraged racial pride, rejecting any emulation of white American culture. Claude McKay's poem "If We Must Die" called on African Americans to start fighting back in the wake of the Red Summer riots of 1919 (discussed in a previous chapter, Figure 24.16). Langston Hughes, often nicknamed the "poet laureate" of the movement, invoked sacrifice and the just cause of civil rights in "The Colored Soldier," while another author of the movement, Zora Neale Hurston, celebrated the life and dialect of rural blacks in a fictional, all-black town in Florida. Hurston's *Their Eyes Were Watching God* was only published posthumously in 1937.

Figure 24.16 The Jamaican-born poet and novelist Claude McKay articulated the new sense of self and urban community of African Americans during the Harlem Renaissance. Although centered in the Harlem neighborhood of Manhattan, this cultural movement emerged in urban centers throughout the Northeast and Midwest.

The new Negro found political expression in a political ideology that celebrated African Americans distinct national identity. This **Negro nationalism**, as some referred to it, proposed that African Americans had a distinct and separate national heritage that should inspire pride and a sense of community. An early proponent of such nationalism was W. E. B. Du Bois. One of the founders of the NAACP, a brilliant writer and scholar, and the first African American to earn a Ph.D. from Harvard, Du Bois openly rejected assumptions of white supremacy. His conception of Negro nationalism encouraged Africans to work together in support of their own interests, promoted the elevation of black literature and cultural expression, and, most famously, embraced the African continent as the true homeland of all ethnic Africans—a concept known as Pan-Africanism.

Taking Negro nationalism to a new level was Marcus Garvey. Like many black Americans, the Jamaican immigrant had become utterly disillusioned with the prospect of overcoming white racism in the United States in the wake of the postwar riots and promoted a "Back to Africa" movement. To return African Americans to a presumably more welcoming home in Africa, Garvey founded the Black Star Steamship Line. He also started the United Negro Improvement Association (UNIA), which attracted thousands of primarily lower-income working people. UNIA members wore colorful uniforms and promoted the doctrine of a "negritude" that reversed the color hierarchy of white supremacy, prizing blackness and identifying light skin as a mark of inferiority. Intellectual leaders like Du Bois, whose lighter skin put him low on Garvey's social order, considered the UNIA leader a charlatan. Garvey was eventually imprisoned for mail fraud and then deported, but his legacy set the stage for Malcolm X and the Black Power movement of the 1960s.

PROHIBITION

At precisely the same time that African Americans and women were experimenting with new forms of social expression, the country as a whole was undergoing a process of austere and dramatic social reform in the form of alcohol prohibition. After decades of organizing to reduce or end the consumption of alcohol in the United States, temperance groups and the Anti-Saloon League finally succeeded in pushing through the Eighteenth Amendment in 1919, which banned the manufacture, sale, and transportation of intoxicating liquors (Figure 24.17). The law proved difficult to enforce, as illegal alcohol soon poured in from Canada and the Caribbean, and rural Americans resorted to home-brewed "moonshine." The result was an eroding of respect for law and order, as many people continued to drink illegal liquor. Rather than bringing about an age of sobriety, as Progressive reformers had hoped, it gave rise to a new subculture that included illegal importers, interstate smuggling (or **bootlegging**), clandestine saloons referred to as "speakeasies," hipflasks, cocktail parties, and the organized crime of trafficking liquor.

(a)   (b)

Figure 24.17 While forces of law and order confiscated and discarded alcohol when they found it (a), consumers found ingenious ways of hiding liquor during prohibition, such as this cane that served as a flask (b).

Prohibition also revealed deep political divisions in the nation. The Democratic Party found itself deeply divided between urban, northern "wets" who hated the idea of abstinence, and rural, southern "dries" who favored the amendment. This divided the party and opened the door for the Republican Party to gain ascendancy in the 1920s. All politicians, including Woodrow Wilson, Herbert Hoover, Robert La Follette, and Franklin D. Roosevelt, equivocated in their support for the law. Publicly, they catered to the Anti-Saloon League; however, they failed to provide funding for enforcement.

Prohibition sparked a rise in organized crime. "Scarface" Al Capone (Figure 24.18) ran an extensive bootlegging and criminal operation known as the Chicago Outfit or Chicago mafia. By 1927, Capone's organization included a number of illegal activities including bootlegging, prostitution, gambling, loan sharking, and even murder. His operation was earning him more than $100 million annually, and many local police were on his payroll. Although he did not have a monopoly on crime, his organizational structure was better than many other criminals of his era. His liquor trafficking business and his Chicago soup kitchens during the Great Depression led some Americans to liken Capone to a modern-day Robin Hood. Still, Capone was eventually imprisoned for eleven years for tax evasion, including a stint in California's notorious Alcatraz prison.

Figure 24.18 Al Capone, pictured here in his U.S. Department of Justice mug shot, was convicted of tax fraud and sent to prison in 1931.

THE LOST GENERATION

As the country struggled with the effects and side-effects of prohibition, many young intellectuals endeavored to come to grips with a lingering sense of disillusionment. World War I, fundamentalism, and the Red Scare—a pervasive American fear of Communist infiltrators prompted by the success of the Bolshevik Revolution—all left their mark on these intellectuals. Known as the **Lost Generation**, writers like F. Scott Fitzgerald, Ernest Hemingway, Sinclair Lewis, Edith Wharton, and John Dos Passos expressed their hopelessness and despair by skewering the middle class in their work. They felt alienated from society, so they tried to escape (some literally) to criticize it. Many lived an **expatriate** life in Paris for the decade, although others went to Rome or Berlin.

The Lost Generation writer that best exemplifies the mood of the 1920s was F. Scott Fitzgerald, now considered one of the most influential writers of the twentieth century. His debut novel, *This Side of Paradise*, describes a generation of youth "grown up to find all gods dead, all wars fought, all faith in man shaken." *The Great Gatsby*, published in 1925, exposed the doom that always follows the fun, fast-lived life. Fitzgerald depicted the modern millionaire Jay Gatsby living a profligate life: unscrupulous, coarse, and in love with another man's wife. Both Fitzgerald and his wife Zelda lived this life as well, squandering the money he made from his writing.

MY STORY

✸ *F. Scott Fitzgerald on the 1920s*

In the 1920s, Fitzgerald was one of the most celebrated authors of his day, publishing *This Side of Paradise*, *The Beautiful and Damned*, and *The Great Gatsby* in quick succession. However, his profligate lifestyle with his wife Zelda sapped their funds, and Fitzgerald had to struggle to maintain their lavish lifestyle. Below is an excerpt from "The Crack-Up," a personal essay by Fitzgerald originally published in *Esquire* in which he describes his "good life" during the 1920s.

> It seemed a romantic business to be a successful literary man—you were not ever going to be as famous as a movie star but what note you had was probably longer-lived; you were never going to have the power of a man of strong political or religious convictions but you were certainly more independent. Of course within the practice of your trade you were forever unsatisfied—but I, for one, would not have chosen any other.
>
> As the Twenties passed, with my own twenties marching a little ahead of them, my two juvenile regrets—at not being big enough (or good enough) to play football in college, and at not getting overseas during the war—resolved themselves into childish waking dreams of imaginary heroism that were good enough to go to sleep on in restless nights. The big problems of life seemed to solve themselves, and if the business of fixing them was difficult, it made one too tired to think of more general problems.
>
> —F. Scott Fitzgerald, "The Crack-Up," 1936

How does Fitzgerald describe his life in the 1920s? How did his interpretation reflect the reality of the decade?

Equally idiosyncratic and disillusioned was writer Ernest Hemingway (Figure 24.19). He lived a peripatetic and adventurous lifestyle in Europe, Cuba, and Africa, working as an ambulance driver in Italy during World War I and traveling to Spain in the 1930s to cover the civil war there. His experiences of war and tragedy stuck with him, emerging in colorful scenes in his novels *The Sun Also Rises* (1926), *A Farewell to Arms* (1929), and *For Whom the Bell Tolls* (1940). In 1952, his novella, *The Old Man and the Sea*, won the Pulitzer Prize. Two years later, he won the Nobel Prize in Literature for this book and his overall influence on contemporary style.

Figure 24.19 Ernest Hemingway was one of the most prominent members of the Lost Generation who went to live as expatriates in Europe during the 1920s.

Click and Explore

Listen to an audio (http://openstaxcollege.org/l/15Hemingway) of Hemingway's Nobel Prize acceptance speech.

Not all Lost Generation writers were like Fitzgerald or Hemingway. The writing of Sinclair Lewis, rather than expressing a defined disillusionment, was more influenced by the Progressivism of the previous generation. In *Babbitt* (1922), he examined the "sheep following the herd" mentality that conformity promoted. He satirized American middle-class life as pleasure seeking and mindless. Similarly, writer Edith Wharton celebrated life in old New York, a vanished society, in *The Age of Innocence*, in 1920. Wharton came from a very wealthy, socialite family in New York, where she was educated by tutors and never attended college. She lived for many years in Europe; during the Great War, she worked in Paris helping women establish businesses.

24.4 Republican Ascendancy: Politics in the 1920s

By the end of this section, you will be able to:
- Discuss Warren G. Harding's strengths and weaknesses as president
- Explain how Calvin Coolidge was able to defeat the Democratic Party
- Explain what Calvin Coolidge meant by "the business of America is business"

The election of 1920 saw the weakening of the Democratic Party. The death of Theodore Roosevelt and Woodrow Wilson's ill health meant the passing of a generation of Progressive leaders. The waning of the Red Scare took with it the last vestiges of Progressive zeal, and Wilson's support of the League of Nations turned Irish and German immigrants against the Democrats. Americans were tired of reform, tired of witch hunts, and were more than ready for a return to "normalcy."

Above all, the 1920s signaled a return to a pro-business government—almost a return to the laissez-faire politics of the Gilded Age of the late nineteenth century. Calvin Coolidge's statement that "the chief business of the American people is business," often rendered as "the business of America is business," became the dominant attitude.

WARREN HARDING AND THE RETURN TO NORMALCY

In the election of 1920, professional Republicans were eager to nominate a man whom they could manage and control. Warren G. Harding, a senator from Ohio, represented just such a man (Figure 24.20). Before his nomination, Harding stated, "America's present need is not heroics but healing; not nostrums but normalcy; not revolution but restoration." Harding was genial and affable, but not everyone appreciated his speeches; Democratic presidential-hopeful William Gibbs McAdoo described Harding's speeches as "an army of pompous phrases moving across the landscape in search of an idea." H. L. Mencken, the great social critic of the 1920s, wrote of Harding's speaking, "It drags itself out of the dark abysm of pish, and crawls insanely up to the top-most pinnacle of posh. It is rumble and bumble. It is flap and doodle. It is balder and dash."

Harding was known for enjoying golf, alcohol, and poker (not necessarily in that order). Although his critics depicted him as weak, lazy, or incompetent, he was actually quite shrewd and politically astute. Together with his running mate, Calvin Coolidge, the governor of Massachusetts, they attracted the votes of many Americans who sought Harding's promised **return to normalcy**. In the election, Harding defeated Governor James Cox of Ohio by the greatest majority in the history of two-party politics: 61 percent of the popular vote.

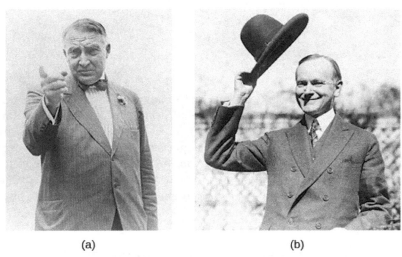

(a)   (b)

Figure 24.20 Warren Harding (a) poses on the campaign trail in 1920. His running mate, Calvin Coolidge (b), would go on to become president in 1923, when Harding died suddenly while touring the United States.

Harding's cabinet reflected his pro-business agenda. Herbert Hoover, a millionaire mechanical engineer and miner, became his Secretary of Commerce. Hoover had served as head of the relief effort for Belgium during World War I and helped to feed those in Russia and Germany after the war ended. He was a very effective administrator, seeking to limit inefficiency in the government and promoting partnerships between government and businesses. Harding's Secretary of the Treasury, Andrew Mellon, was also a pro-business multimillionaire with a fortune built in banking and aluminum. Even more so than Hoover, Mellon entered public service with a strong sense that government should run as efficiently as any business, famously writing that "the Government is just a business, and can and should be run on business principles."

Consistent with his principles of running government with business-like efficiency, Harding proposed and signed into law tax rate cuts as well as the country's first formal budgeting process, which created a presidential budget director and required that the president submit an annual budget to Congress. These policies helped to reduce the debt that the United States had incurred during World War I. However, as Europe began to recover, U.S. exports to the continent dwindled. In an effort to protect U.S. agriculture and other businesses threatened by lower-priced imports, Harding pushed through the Emergency Tariff of 1921. This defensive tariff had the effect of increasing American purchasing power, although it also inflated the prices of many goods.

In the area of foreign policy, Harding worked to preserve the peace through international cooperation and the reduction of armaments around the world. Despite the refusal of the U.S. Senate to ratify the Treaty of Versailles, Harding was able to work with Germany and Austria to secure a formal peace. He convened a conference in Washington that brought world leaders together to agree on reducing the threat of future wars by reducing armaments. Out of these negotiations came a number of treaties designed to foster cooperation in the Far East, reduce the size of navies around the world, and establish guidelines for submarine usage. These agreements ultimately fell apart in the 1930s, as the world descended into war again. But, at the time, they were seen as a promising path to maintaining the peace.

Despite these developments, the Harding administration has gone down in history as one that was especially ridden with scandal. While Harding was personally honest, he surrounded himself with politicians who weren't. Harding made the mistake of often turning to unscrupulous advisors or even his "Ohio Gang" of drinking and poker buddies for advice and guidance. And, as he himself recognized, this group tended to cause him grief. "I have no trouble with my enemies," he once commented. "I can take care of my enemies in a fight. But my friends, my goddamned friends, they're the ones who keep me walking the floor at nights!"

The scandals mounted quickly. From 1920 to 1923, Secretary of the Interior Albert B. Fall was involved in a scam that became known as the **Teapot Dome scandal**. Fall had leased navy reserves in Teapot Dome, Wyoming, and two other sites in California to private oil companies without opening the bidding to other companies. In exchange, the companies gave him $300,000 in cash and bonds, as well as a herd of cattle for his ranch. Fall was convicted of accepting bribes from the oil companies; he was fined $100,000 and sentenced to a year in prison. It was the first time that a cabinet official had received such a sentence.

In 1923, Harding also learned that the head of the Veterans' Bureau, Colonel Charles Forbes, had absconded with most of the $250 million set aside for extravagant bureau functions. Harding allowed Forbes to resign and leave the country; however, after the president died, Forbes returned and was tried, convicted, and sentenced to two years in Leavenworth prison.

Although the Harding presidency had a number of large successes and variety of dark scandals, it ended before the first term was up. In July 1923, while traveling in Seattle, the president suffered a heart attack. On August 2, in his weakened condition, he suffered a stroke and died in San Francisco, leaving the presidency to his vice president, Calvin Coolidge. As for Harding, few presidents were so deeply mourned by the populace. His kindly nature and ability to poke fun at himself endeared him to the public.

Click and Explore

Listen to some of Harding's speeches (http://openstaxcollege.org/l/15Harding) at The University of Virginia's Miller Center's website.

A MAN OF FEW WORDS

Coolidge ended the scandals, but did little beyond that. Walter Lippman wrote in 1926 that "Mr. Coolidge's genius for inactivity is developed to a very high point. It is a grim, determined, alert inactivity, which keeps Mr. Coolidge occupied constantly."

Coolidge had a strong belief in the Puritan work ethic: Work hard, save your money, keep your mouth shut and listen, and good things will happen to you. Known as "Silent Cal," his clean image seemed capable of cleaning up scandals left by Harding. Republicans—and the nation—now had a president who combined a preference for normalcy with the respectability and honesty that was absent from the Harding administration.

Coolidge's first term was devoted to eliminating the taint of scandal that Harding had brought to the White House. Domestically, Coolidge adhered to the creed: "The business of America is business." He stood in awe of Andrew Mellon and followed his fiscal policies, which made him the only president to turn a legitimate profit in the White House. Coolidge believed the rich were worthy of their property and that poverty was the wage of sin. Most importantly, Coolidge believed that since only the rich best understood their own interests, the government should let businessmen handle their own affairs with as little federal intervention as possible. Coolidge was quoted as saying, "The man who builds a factory builds a temple. The man who works there worships there."

Thus, silence and inactivity became the dominant characteristics of the Coolidge presidency. Coolidge's legendary reserve was famous in Washington society. Contemporaries told a possibly apocryphal story of how, at a dinner party at the White House, a woman bet her friends that she could get Coolidge to say more than three words. He looked at her and said, "you lose."

The 1924 election saw Coolidge win easily over the divided Democrats, who fought over their nomination. Southerners wanted to nominate pro-prohibition, pro-Klan, anti-immigrant candidate William G. McAdoo. The eastern establishment wanted Alfred E. Smith, a Catholic, urban, and anti-prohibition candidate. After many battles, they compromised on corporation lawyer John W. Davis. Midwesterner Robert M. La Follette, promoted by farmers, socialists, and labor unions, attempted to resurrect the Progressive Party. Coolidge easily beat both candidates.

THE ELECTION OF 1928

This cultural battle between the forces of reaction and rebellion appeared to culminate with the election of 1928, the height of Republican ascendancy. On August 2, 1927, Coolidge announced that he would not be participating in the 1928 election; "I choose not to run," was his comment (Figure 24.21). Republicans promoted the heir apparent, Secretary of Commerce Herbert Hoover. The Democrats nominated Governor Alfred E. Smith of New York. Smith represented everything that small-town, rural America hated: He was Irish, Catholic, anti-prohibition, and a big-city politician. He was very flamboyant and outspoken, which also did not go over well with many Americans.

Figure 24.21 In this cartoon, Clifford Berryman lampoons Coolidge's laid-back attitude as he chooses "not to run" in 1928.

Republican prosperity carried the day once again, and Hoover won easily with twenty-one million votes over Al Smith's fifteen million. The stock market continued to rise, and prosperity was the watchword of the day. Many Americans who had not done so before invested in the market, believing that the prosperous times would continue.

As Hoover came into office, Americans had every reason to believe that prosperity would continue forever. In less than a year, however, the bubble would burst, and a harsh reality would take its place.

Key Terms

bootlegging a nineteenth-century term for the illegal transport of alcoholic beverages that became popular during prohibition

expatriate someone who lives outside of their home country

flapper a young, modern woman who embraced the new morality and fashions of the Jazz Age

Hollywood a small town north of Los Angeles, California, whose reliable sunshine and cheaper production costs attracted filmmakers and producers starting in the 1910s; by the 1920s, Hollywood was the center of American movie production with five movie studios dominating the industry

Lost Generation a group of writers who came of age during World War I and expressed their disillusionment with the era

Model T the first car produced by the Ford Motor Company that took advantage of the economies of scale provided by assembly-line production and was therefore affordable to a large segment of the population

moving assembly line a manufacturing process that allowed workers to stay in one place as the work came to them

nativism the rejection of outside influences in favor of local or native customs

Negro nationalism the notion that African Americans had a distinct and separate national heritage that should inspire pride and a sense of community

new morality the more permissive mores adopted my many young people in the 1920s

return to normalcy the campaign promise made by Warren Harding in the presidential election of 1920

Scopes Monkey Trial the 1925 trial of John Scopes for teaching evolution in a public school; the trial highlighted the conflict between rural traditionalists and modern urbanites

Second Ku Klux Klan unlike the secret terror group of the Reconstruction Era, the Second Ku Klux Klan was a nationwide movement that expressed racism, nativism, anti-Semitism, and anti-Catholicism

Teapot Dome scandal the bribery scandal involving Secretary of the Interior Albert B. Fall in 1923

Summary

24.1 Prosperity and the Production of Popular Entertainment

For many middle-class Americans, the 1920s was a decade of unprecedented prosperity. Rising earnings generated more disposable income for the consumption of entertainment, leisure, and consumer goods. This new wealth coincided with and fueled technological innovations, resulting in the booming popularity of entertainments like movies, sports, and radio programs. Henry Ford's advances in assembly-line efficiency created a truly affordable automobile, making car ownership a possibility for many Americans. Advertising became as big an industry as the manufactured goods that advertisers represented, and many families relied on new forms of credit to increase their consumption levels and strive for a new American standard of living.

24.2 Transformation and Backlash

The old and the new came into sharp conflict in the 1920s. In many cases, this divide was geographic as well as philosophical; city dwellers tended to embrace the cultural changes of the era, whereas those who lived in rural towns clung to traditional norms. The Sacco and Vanzetti trial in Massachusetts, as well as the Scopes trial in Tennessee, revealed many Americans' fears and suspicions about immigrants, radical politics, and the ways in which new scientific theories might challenge traditional Christian beliefs. Some reacted more zealously than others, leading to the inception of nativist and fundamentalist philosophies, and the rise of terror groups such as the Second Ku Klux Klan.

24.3 A New Generation

Different groups reacted to the upheavals of the 1920s in different ways. Some people, especially young urbanites, embraced the new amusements and social venues of the decade. Women found new opportunities for professional and political advancement, as well as new models of sexual liberation; however, the women's rights movement began to wane with the passage of the Nineteenth Amendment. For black artists of the Harlem Renaissance, the decade was marked less by leisure and consumption than by creativity and purpose. African American leaders like Marcus Garvey and W. E. B. Du Bois responded to the retrenched racism of the time with different campaigns for civil rights and black empowerment. Others, like the writers of the Lost Generation, reveled in exposing the hypocrisies and shallowness of mainstream middle-class culture. Meanwhile, the passage of prohibition served to increase the illegal production of alcohol and led to a rise in organized crime.

24.4 Republican Ascendancy: Politics in the 1920s

After World War I, Americans were ready for "a return to normalcy," and Republican Warren Harding offered them just that. Under the guidance of his big-business backers, Harding's policies supported businesses at home and isolation from foreign affairs. His administration was wracked by scandals, and after he died in 1923, Calvin Coolidge continued his policy legacy in much the same vein. Herbert Hoover, elected as Coolidge's heir apparent, planned for more of the same until the stock market crash ended a decade of Republican ascendancy.

Review Questions

1. Which of the following films released in 1927 was the first successful talking motion picture?

    A. *The Clansman*

    B. *The Great Gatsby*

    C. *The Jazz Singer*

    D. *The Birth of a Nation*

2. The popularization of _____ expanded the communications and sports industries.

    A. radios

    B. talkies

    C. the Model T

    D. airplanes

3. Who was the first person to fly solo across the Atlantic Ocean?

    A. Orville Wright

    B. Jim Thorpe

    C. Charlie Chaplin

    D. Charles Lindbergh

4. How did Henry Ford transform the automobile industry?

5. The Scopes Monkey Trial revolved around a law that banned teaching about _____ in public schools.

    A. the Bible

    B. Darwinism

    C. primates

    D. Protestantism

6. Which man was both a professional baseball player and an influential evangelist during the 1920s?

A. Babe Ruth
B. H. L. Mencken
C. Jim Thorpe
D. Billy Sunday

7. What was the platform of the Second Ku Klux Klan, and in what activities did they engage to promote it?

8. The popularization of which psychologist's ideas encouraged the new morality of the 1920s?
 A. Sigmund Freud
 B. Alice Paul
 C. W. E. B. Du Bois
 D. Margaret Sanger

9. Which amendment did Alice Paul promote to end gender discrimination?
 A. Prohibition Amendment
 B. Equal Rights Amendment
 C. Sheppard-Towner Amendment
 D. Free Exercise Amendment

10. Which novel of the era satirized the conformity of the American middle class?
 A. *This Side of Paradise*
 B. *The Sun Also Rises*
 C. *A Farewell to Arms*
 D. *Babbitt*

11. Why did the prohibition amendment fail after its adoption in 1919?

12. What was the Harlem Renaissance, and who were some of the most famous participants?

13. Who was the Republican presidential nominee for the 1920 election?
 A. Calvin Coolidge
 B. Woodrow Wilson
 C. Warren Harding
 D. James Cox

14. In 1929, Albert Fall was convicted of bribery while holding the position of _____.
 A. Secretary of the Interior
 B. head of the Veterans' Bureau
 C. Secretary of the Treasury
 D. Secretary of Commerce

15. Coolidge's presidency was characterized by _____.
 A. scandal and dishonesty
 B. silence and inactivity
 C. flamboyancy and extravagance
 D. ambition and greed

16. What was the economic outlook of the average American when Herbert Hoover took office in 1929?

Critical Thinking Questions

17. Explain how the 1920s was a decade of contradictions. What does the relationship between mass immigration and the rise of the Second Ku Klux Klan tell us about American attitudes? How might we reconcile the decade as the period of both the flapper and prohibition?

18. What new opportunities did the 1920s provide for women and African Americans? What new limitations did this era impose?

19. Discuss what the concept of "modernity" meant in the 1920s. How did art and innovation in the decade reflect the new mood of the postwar era?

20. Explain how technology took American culture in new and different directions. What role did motion pictures and radio play in shaping cultural attitudes in the United States?

21. Discuss how politics of the 1920s reflected the new postwar mood of the country. What did the Harding administration's policies attempt to achieve, and how?

CHAPTER 25

Brother, Can You Spare a Dime? The Great Depression, 1929-1932

Figure 25.1 In 1935, American photographer Berenice Abbott photographed these shanties, which the unemployed in Lower Manhattan built during the depths of the Great Depression. (credit: modification of work by Works Progress Administration)

Chapter Outline

25.1 The Stock Market Crash of 1929
25.2 President Hoover's Response
25.3 The Depths of the Great Depression
25.4 Assessing the Hoover Years on the Eve of the New Deal

Introduction

On March 4, 1929, at his presidential inauguration, Herbert Hoover stated, "I have no fears for the future of our country. It is bright with hope." Most Americans shared his optimism. They believed that the prosperity of the 1920s would continue, and that the country was moving closer to a land of abundance for all. Little could Hoover imagine that barely a year into his presidency, shantytowns known as "Hoovervilles" would emerge on the fringes of most major cities (Figure 25.1), newspapers covering the homeless would be called "Hoover blankets," and pants pockets, turned inside-out to show their emptiness, would become "Hoover flags."

The stock market crash of October 1929 set the Great Depression into motion, but other factors were at the root of the problem, propelled onward by a series of both human-made and natural catastrophes. Anticipating a short downturn and living under an ethos of free enterprise and individualism, Americans suffered mightily in the first years of the Depression. As conditions worsened and the government failed to act, they grew increasingly desperate for change. While Hoover could not be blamed for the Great Depression, his failure to address the nation's hardships would remain his legacy.

25.1 The Stock Market Crash of 1929

By the end of this section, you will be able to:
- Identify the causes of the stock market crash of 1929
- Assess the underlying weaknesses in the economy that resulted in America's spiraling from prosperity to depression so quickly
- Explain how a stock market crash might contribute to a nationwide economic disaster

Herbert Hoover became president at a time of ongoing prosperity in the country. Americans hoped he would continue to lead the country through still more economic growth, and neither he nor the country was ready for the unraveling that followed. But Hoover's moderate policies, based upon a strongly held belief in the spirit of American individualism, were not enough to stem the ever-growing problems, and the economy slipped further and further into the Great Depression.

While it is misleading to view the stock market crash of 1929 as the sole cause of the Great Depression, the dramatic events of that October did play a role in the downward spiral of the American economy. The crash, which took place less than a year after Hoover was inaugurated, was the most extreme sign of the economy's weakness. Multiple factors contributed to the crash, which in turn caused a consumer panic that drove the economy even further downhill, in ways that neither Hoover nor the financial industry was able to restrain. Hoover, like many others at the time, thought and hoped that the country would right itself with limited government intervention. This was not the case, however, and millions of Americans sank into grinding poverty.

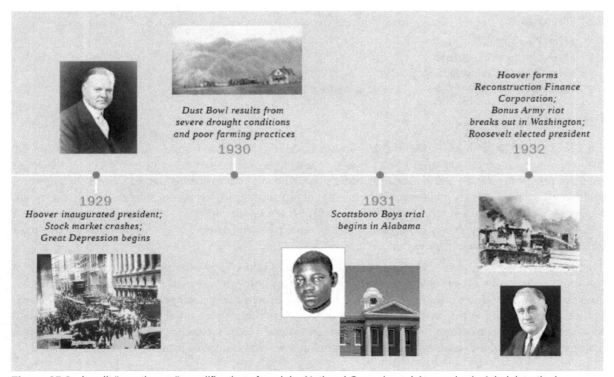

Figure 25.2 (credit "courthouse": modification of work by National Oceanic and Atmospheric Administration)

Download for free at http://cnx.org/content/col11740/latest/

THE EARLY DAYS OF HOOVER'S PRESIDENCY

Upon his inauguration, President Hoover set forth an agenda that he hoped would continue the "Coolidge prosperity" of the previous administration. While accepting the Republican Party's presidential nomination in 1928, Hoover commented, "Given the chance to go forward with the policies of the last eight years, we shall soon with the help of God be in sight of the day when poverty will be banished from this nation forever." In the spirit of normalcy that defined the Republican ascendancy of the 1920s, Hoover planned to immediately overhaul federal regulations with the intention of allowing the nation's economy to grow unfettered by any controls. The role of the government, he contended, should be to create a partnership with the American people, in which the latter would rise (or fall) on their own merits and abilities. He felt the less government intervention in their lives, the better.

Yet, to listen to Hoover's later reflections on Franklin Roosevelt's first term in office, one could easily mistake his vision for America for the one held by his successor. Speaking in 1936 before an audience in Denver, Colorado, he acknowledged that it was always his intent as president to ensure "a nation built of home owners and farm owners. We want to see more and more of them insured against death and accident, unemployment and old age," he declared. "We want them all secure." [1] Such humanitarianism was not uncommon to Hoover. Throughout his early career in public service, he was committed to relief for people around the world. In 1900, he coordinated relief efforts for foreign nationals trapped in China during the Boxer Rebellion. At the outset of World War I, he led the food relief effort in Europe, specifically helping millions of Belgians who faced German forces. President Woodrow Wilson subsequently appointed him head of the U.S. Food Administration to coordinate rationing efforts in America as well as to secure essential food items for the Allied forces and citizens in Europe.

Hoover's first months in office hinted at the reformist, humanitarian spirit that he had displayed throughout his career. He continued the civil service reform of the early twentieth century by expanding opportunities for employment throughout the federal government. In response to the Teapot Dome Affair, which had occurred during the Harding administration, he invalidated several private oil leases on public lands. He directed the Department of Justice, through its Bureau of Investigation, to crack down on organized crime, resulting in the arrest and imprisonment of Al Capone. By the summer of 1929, he had signed into law the creation of a Federal Farm Board to help farmers with government price supports, expanded tax cuts across all income classes, and set aside federal funds to clean up slums in major American cities. To directly assist several overlooked populations, he created the Veterans Administration and expanded veterans' hospitals, established the Federal Bureau of Prisons to oversee incarceration conditions nationwide, and reorganized the Bureau of Indian Affairs to further protect Native Americans. Just prior to the stock market crash, he even proposed the creation of an old-age pension program, promising fifty dollars monthly to all Americans over the age of sixty-five—a proposal remarkably similar to the social security benefit that would become a hallmark of Roosevelt's subsequent New Deal programs. As the summer of 1929 came to a close, Hoover remained a popular successor to Calvin "Silent Cal" Coolidge, and all signs pointed to a highly successful administration.

THE GREAT CRASH

The promise of the Hoover administration was cut short when the stock market lost almost one-half its value in the fall of 1929, plunging many Americans into financial ruin. However, as a singular event, the stock market crash itself did not cause the Great Depression that followed. In fact, only approximately 10 percent of American households held stock investments and speculated in the market; yet nearly a third would lose their lifelong savings and jobs in the ensuing depression. The connection between the crash and the subsequent decade of hardship was complex, involving underlying weaknesses in the economy that many policymakers had long ignored.

---

1. Herbert Hoover, address delivered in Denver, Colorado, 30 October 1936, compiled in Hoover, *Addresses Upon the American Road, 1933-1938* (New York, 1938), p. 216. This particular quotation is frequently misidentified as part of Hoover's inaugural address in 1932.

What Was the Crash?

To understand the crash, it is useful to address the decade that preceded it. The prosperous 1920s ushered in a feeling of euphoria among middle-class and wealthy Americans, and people began to speculate on wilder investments. The government was a willing partner in this endeavor: The Federal Reserve followed a brief postwar recession in 1920–1921 with a policy of setting interest rates artificially low, as well as easing the reserve requirements on the nation's largest banks. As a result, the money supply in the U.S. increased by nearly 60 percent, which convinced even more Americans of the safety of investing in questionable schemes. They felt that prosperity was boundless and that extreme risks were likely tickets to wealth. Named for Charles Ponzi, the original "Ponzi schemes" emerged early in the 1920s to encourage novice investors to divert funds to unfounded ventures, which in reality simply used new investors' funds to pay off older investors as the schemes grew in size. **Speculation**, where investors purchased into high-risk schemes that they hoped would pay off quickly, became the norm. Several banks, including deposit institutions that originally avoided investment loans, began to offer easy credit, allowing people to invest, even when they lacked the money to do so. An example of this mindset was the Florida land boom of the 1920s: Real estate developers touted Florida as a tropical paradise and investors went all in, buying land they had never seen with money they didn't have and selling it for even higher prices.

AMERICANA

✪ Selling Optimism and Risk

Advertising offers a useful window into the popular perceptions and beliefs of an era. By seeing how businesses were presenting their goods to consumers, it is possible to sense the hopes and aspirations of people at that moment in history. Maybe companies are selling patriotism or pride in technological advances. Maybe they are pushing idealized views of parenthood or safety. In the 1920s, advertisers were selling opportunity and euphoria, further feeding the notions of many Americans that prosperity would never end.

In the decade before the Great Depression, the optimism of the American public was seemingly boundless. Advertisements from that era show large new cars, timesaving labor devices, and, of course, land. This advertisement for California real estate illustrates how realtors in the West, much like the ongoing Florida land boom, used a combination of the hard sell and easy credit (Figure 25.3). "Buy now!!" the ad shouts. "You are sure to make money on these." In great numbers, people did. With easy access to credit and hard-pushing advertisements like this one, many felt that they could not afford to miss out on such an opportunity. Unfortunately, overspeculation in California and hurricanes along the Gulf Coast and in Florida conspired to burst this land bubble, and would-be millionaires were left with nothing but the ads that once pulled them in.

Figure 25.3 This real estate advertisement from Los Angeles illustrates the hard-sell techniques and easy credit offered to those who wished to buy in. Unfortunately, the opportunities being promoted with these techniques were of little value, and many lost their investments. (credit: "army.arch"/Flickr)

The Florida land boom went bust in 1925–1926. A combination of negative press about the speculative nature of the boom, IRS investigations into the questionable financial practices of several land brokers, and a railroad embargo that limited the delivery of construction supplies into the region significantly hampered investor interest. The subsequent Great Miami Hurricane of 1926 drove most land developers into outright bankruptcy. However, speculation continued throughout the decade, this time in the stock market. Buyers purchased stock "on margin"—buying for a small down payment with borrowed money, with the intention of quickly selling at a much higher price before the remaining payment came due—which worked well as long as prices continued to rise. Speculators were aided by retail stock brokerage firms, which catered to average investors anxious to play the market but lacking direct ties to investment banking houses or larger brokerage firms. When prices began to fluctuate in the summer of 1929, investors sought excuses to continue their speculation. When fluctuations turned to outright and steady losses, everyone started to sell. As September began to unfold, the Dow Jones Industrial Average peaked at a value of 381 points, or roughly ten times the stock market's value, at the start of the 1920s.

Several warning signs portended the impending crash but went unheeded by Americans still giddy over the potential fortunes that speculation might promise. A brief downturn in the market on September 18, 1929, raised questions among more-seasoned investment bankers, leading some to predict an end to high stock values, but did little to stem the tide of investment. Even the collapse of the London Stock Exchange on September 20 failed to fully curtail the optimism of American investors. However, when the New York Stock Exchange lost 11 percent of its value on October 24—often referred to as "Black Thursday"—key American investors sat up and took notice. In an effort to forestall a much-feared panic, leading banks, including Chase National, National City, J.P. Morgan, and others, conspired to purchase large amounts of blue chip stocks (including U.S. Steel) in order to keep the prices artificially high. Even that effort failed in the growing wave of stock sales. Nevertheless, Hoover delivered a radio address on Friday in which he assured the American people, "The fundamental business of the country . . . is on a sound and prosperous basis."

As newspapers across the country began to cover the story in earnest, investors anxiously awaited the start of the following week. When the Dow Jones Industrial Average lost another 13 percent of its value on Monday morning, many knew the end of stock market speculation was near. The evening before the infamous crash was ominous. Jonathan Leonard, a newspaper reporter who regularly covered the stock market beat, wrote of how Wall Street "lit up like a Christmas tree." Brokers and businessmen who feared the worst the next day crowded into restaurants and speakeasies (a place where alcoholic beverages were illegally sold). After a night of heavy drinking, they retreated to nearby hotels or flop-houses (cheap boarding houses), all of which were overbooked, and awaited sunrise. Children from nearby slums and tenement districts played stickball in the streets of the financial district, using wads of ticker tape for balls. Although they all awoke to newspapers filled with predictions of a financial turnaround, as well as technical reasons why the decline might be short-lived, the crash on Tuesday morning, October 29, caught few by surprise.

No one even heard the opening bell on Wall Street that day, as shouts of "Sell! Sell!" drowned it out. In the first three minutes alone, nearly three million shares of stock, accounting for $2 million of wealth, changed hands. The volume of Western Union telegrams tripled, and telephone lines could not meet the demand, as investors sought any means available to dump their stock immediately. Rumors spread of investors jumping from their office windows. Fistfights broke out on the trading floor, where one broker fainted from physical exhaustion. Stock trades happened at such a furious pace that runners had nowhere to store the trade slips, and so they resorted to stuffing them into trash cans. Although the stock exchange's board of governors briefly considered closing the exchange early, they subsequently chose to let the market run its course, lest the American public panic even further at the thought of closure. When the final bell rang, errand boys spent hours sweeping up tons of paper, tickertape, and sales slips. Among the more curious finds in the rubbish were torn suit coats, crumpled eyeglasses, and one broker's artificial leg. Outside a nearby brokerage house, a policeman allegedly found a discarded birdcage with a live parrot squawking, "More margin! More margin!"

On **Black Tuesday**, October 29, stock holders traded over sixteen million shares and lost over $14 billion in wealth in a single day. To put this in context, a trading day of three million shares was considered a busy day on the stock market. People unloaded their stock as quickly as they could, never minding the loss. Banks, facing debt and seeking to protect their own assets, demanded payment for the loans they had provided to individual investors. Those individuals who could not afford to pay found their stocks sold immediately and their life savings wiped out in minutes, yet their debt to the bank still remained (Figure 25.4).

Figure 25.4 October 29, 1929, or Black Tuesday, witnessed thousands of people racing to Wall Street discount brokerages and markets to sell their stocks. Prices plummeted throughout the day, eventually leading to a complete stock market crash.

The financial outcome of the crash was devastating. Between September 1 and November 30, 1929, the stock market lost over one-half its value, dropping from $64 billion to approximately $30 billion. Any effort to stem the tide was, as one historian noted, tantamount to bailing Niagara Falls with a bucket. The crash affected many more than the relatively few Americans who invested in the stock market. While only 10 percent of households had investments, over 90 percent of all banks had invested in the stock market. Many banks failed due to their dwindling cash reserves. This was in part due to the Federal Reserve lowering the limits of cash reserves that banks were traditionally required to hold in their vaults, as well as the fact that many banks invested in the stock market themselves. Eventually, thousands of banks closed their doors after losing all of their assets, leaving their customers penniless. While a few savvy investors got out at the right time and eventually made fortunes buying up discarded stock, those success stories were rare. Housewives who speculated with grocery money, bookkeepers who embezzled company funds hoping to strike it rich and pay the funds back before getting caught, and bankers who used customer deposits to follow speculative trends all lost. While the stock market crash was the trigger, the lack of appropriate economic and banking safeguards, along with a public psyche that pursued wealth and prosperity at all costs, allowed this event to spiral downward into a depression.

Click and Explore

The **National Humanities Center (http://openstaxcollege.org/l/crash)** has brought together a selection of newspaper commentary from the 1920s, from before the crash to its aftermath. Read through to see what journalists and financial analysts thought of the situation at the time.

Causes of the Crash

The crash of 1929 did not occur in a vacuum, nor did it cause the Great Depression. Rather, it was a tipping point where the underlying weaknesses in the economy, specifically in the nation's banking system, came to the fore. It also represented both the end of an era characterized by blind faith in American exceptionalism and the beginning of one in which citizens began increasingly to question some long-held American values. A number of factors played a role in bringing the stock market to this point and contributed to the downward trend in the market, which continued well into the 1930s. In addition to the Federal Reserve's questionable policies and misguided banking practices, three primary reasons for the collapse of the stock market were international economic woes, poor income distribution, and the psychology of public confidence.

After World War I, both America's allies and the defeated nations of Germany and Austria contended with disastrous economies. The Allies owed large amounts of money to U.S. banks, which had advanced them money during the war effort. Unable to repay these debts, the Allies looked to reparations from Germany and Austria to help. The economies of those countries, however, were struggling badly, and they could not pay their reparations, despite the loans that the U.S. provided to assist with their payments. The U.S. government refused to forgive these loans, and American banks were in the position of extending additional private loans to foreign governments, who used them to repay their debts to the U.S. government, essentially shifting their obligations to private banks. When other countries began to default on this second wave of private bank loans, still more strain was placed on U.S. banks, which soon sought to liquidate these loans at the first sign of a stock market crisis.

Poor income distribution among Americans compounded the problem. A strong stock market relies on today's buyers becoming tomorrow's sellers, and therefore it must always have an influx of new buyers. In the 1920s, this was not the case. Eighty percent of American families had virtually no savings, and only one-half to 1 percent of Americans controlled over a third of the wealth. This scenario meant that there were no new buyers coming into the marketplace, and nowhere for sellers to unload their stock as the speculation came to a close. In addition, the vast majority of Americans with limited savings lost their accounts as local banks closed, and likewise lost their jobs as investment in business and industry came to a screeching halt.

Finally, one of the most important factors in the crash was the contagion effect of panic. For much of the 1920s, the public felt confident that prosperity would continue forever, and therefore, in a self-fulfilling cycle, the market continued to grow. But once the panic began, it spread quickly and with the same cyclical results; people were worried that the market was going down, they sold their stock, and the market continued to drop. This was partly due to Americans' inability to weather market volatility, given the limited cash surpluses they had on hand, as well as their psychological concern that economic recovery might never happen.

IN THE AFTERMATH OF THE CRASH

After the crash, Hoover announced that the economy was "fundamentally sound." On the last day of trading in 1929, the New York Stock Exchange held its annual wild and lavish party, complete with confetti, musicians, and illegal alcohol. The U.S. Department of Labor predicted that 1930 would be "a splendid employment year." These sentiments were not as baseless as it may seem in hindsight. Historically, markets cycled up and down, and periods of growth were often followed by downturns that corrected themselves. But this time, there was no market correction; rather, the abrupt shock of the crash was followed by an even more devastating depression. Investors, along with the general public, withdrew their money from banks by the thousands, fearing the banks would go under. The more people pulled out their money in **bank runs**, the closer the banks came to insolvency (Figure 25.5).

Figure 25.5 As the financial markets collapsed, hurting the banks that had gambled with their holdings, people began to fear that the money they had in the bank would be lost. This began bank runs across the country, a period of still more panic, where people pulled their money out of banks to keep it hidden at home.

The contagion effect of the crash grew quickly. With investors losing billions of dollars, they invested very little in new or expanded businesses. At this time, two industries had the greatest impact on the country's economic future in terms of investment, potential growth, and employment: automotive and construction. After the crash, both were hit hard. In November 1929, fewer cars were built than in any other month since November 1919. Even before the crash, widespread saturation of the market meant that few Americans bought them, leading to a slowdown. Afterward, very few could afford them. By 1933, Stutz, Locomobile, Durant, Franklin, Deusenberg, and Pierce-Arrow automobiles, all luxury models, were largely unavailable; production had ground to a halt. They would not be made again until 1949. In construction, the drop-off was even more dramatic. It would be another thirty years before a new hotel or theater was built in New York City. The Empire State Building itself stood half empty for years after being completed in 1931.

The damage to major industries led to, and reflected, limited purchasing by both consumers and businesses. Even those Americans who continued to make a modest income during the Great Depression lost the drive for conspicuous consumption that they exhibited in the 1920s. People with less money to buy goods could not help businesses grow; in turn, businesses with no market for their products could not hire workers or purchase raw materials. Employers began to lay off workers. The country's gross national product declined by over 25 percent within a year, and wages and salaries declined by $4 billion. Unemployment tripled, from 1.5 million at the end of 1929 to 4.5 million by the end of 1930. By mid-1930, the slide into economic chaos had begun but was nowhere near complete.

THE NEW REALITY FOR AMERICANS

For most Americans, the crash affected daily life in myriad ways. In the immediate aftermath, there was a run on the banks, where citizens took their money out, if they could get it, and hid their savings under mattresses, in bookshelves, or anywhere else they felt was safe. Some went so far as to exchange their dollars for gold and ship it out of the country. A number of banks failed outright, and others, in their attempts to stay solvent, called in loans that people could not afford to repay. Working-class Americans saw their wages drop: Even Henry Ford, the champion of a high minimum wage, began lowering wages by as much as a dollar a day. Southern cotton planters paid workers only twenty cents for every one hundred pounds of cotton picked, meaning that the *strongest* picker might earn sixty cents for a fourteen-hour day of work. Cities struggled to collect property taxes and subsequently laid off teachers and police.

The new hardships that people faced were not always immediately apparent; many communities felt the changes but could not necessarily look out their windows and see anything different. Men who lost their jobs didn't stand on street corners begging; they disappeared. They might be found keeping warm by a trashcan bonfire or picking through garbage at dawn, but mostly, they stayed out of public view. As the effects of the crash continued, however, the results became more evident. Those living in cities grew accustomed to seeing long breadlines of unemployed men waiting for a meal (Figure 25.6). Companies fired workers and tore down employee housing to avoid paying property taxes. The landscape of the country had changed.

Figure 25.6 As the Great Depression set in, thousands of unemployed men lined up in cities around the country, waiting for a free meal or a hot cup of coffee.

The hardships of the Great Depression threw family life into disarray. Both marriage and birth rates declined in the decade after the crash. The most vulnerable members of society—children, women, minorities, and the working class—struggled the most. Parents often sent children out to beg for food at restaurants and stores to save themselves from the disgrace of begging. Many children dropped out of school, and even fewer went to college. Childhood, as it had existed in the prosperous twenties, was over. And yet, for many children living in rural areas where the affluence of the previous decade was not fully developed, the Depression was not viewed as a great challenge. School continued. Play was simple and enjoyed. Families adapted by growing more in gardens, canning, and preserving, wasting little food if any. Home-sewn clothing became the norm as the decade progressed, as did creative methods of shoe repair with cardboard soles. Yet, one always knew of stories of the "other" families who suffered more, including those living in cardboard boxes or caves. By one estimate, as many as 200,000 children moved about the country as vagrants due to familial disintegration.

Women's lives, too, were profoundly affected. Some wives and mothers sought employment to make ends meet, an undertaking that was often met with strong resistance from husbands and potential employers. Many men derided and criticized women who worked, feeling that jobs should go to unemployed men. Some campaigned to keep companies from hiring married women, and an increasing number of school districts expanded the long-held practice of banning the hiring of married female teachers. Despite the pushback, women entered the workforce in increasing numbers, from ten million at the start of the Depression to nearly thirteen million by the end of the 1930s. This increase took place in spite of the twenty-six states that passed a variety of laws to prohibit the employment of married women. Several women found employment in the emerging pink collar occupations, viewed as traditional women's work, including jobs as telephone operators, social workers, and secretaries. Others took jobs as maids and housecleaners, working for those fortunate few who had maintained their wealth.

White women's forays into domestic service came at the expense of minority women, who had even fewer employment options. Unsurprisingly, African American men and women experienced unemployment, and the grinding poverty that followed, at double and triple the rates of their white counterparts. By 1932, unemployment among African Americans reached near 50 percent. In rural areas, where large numbers of African Americans continued to live despite the Great Migration of 1910–1930, depression-era life represented an intensified version of the poverty that they traditionally experienced. Subsistence farming allowed many African Americans who lost either their land or jobs working for white landholders to survive, but their hardships increased. Life for African Americans in urban settings was equally trying, with blacks and working-class whites living in close proximity and competing for scarce jobs and resources.

Life for all rural Americans was difficult. Farmers largely did not experience the widespread prosperity of the 1920s. Although continued advancements in farming techniques and agricultural machinery led to increased agricultural production, decreasing demand (particularly in the previous markets created by World War I) steadily drove down commodity prices. As a result, farmers could barely pay the debt they owed on machinery and land mortgages, and even then could do so only as a result of generous lines of credit from banks. While factory workers may have lost their jobs and savings in the crash, many farmers also lost their homes, due to the thousands of farm foreclosures sought by desperate bankers. Between 1930 and 1935, nearly 750,000 family farms disappeared through foreclosure or bankruptcy. Even for those who managed to keep their farms, there was little market for their crops. Unemployed workers had less money to spend on food, and when they did purchase goods, the market excess had driven prices so low that farmers could barely piece together a living. A now-famous example of the farmer's plight is that, when the price of coal began to exceed that of corn, farmers would simply burn corn to stay warm in the winter.

As the effects of the Great Depression worsened, wealthier Americans had particular concern for "the deserving poor"—those who had lost all of their money due to no fault of their own. This concept gained greater attention beginning in the Progressive Era of the late nineteenth and early twentieth centuries, when early social reformers sought to improve the quality of life for all Americans by addressing the poverty that was becoming more prevalent, particularly in emerging urban areas. By the time of the Great Depression, social reformers and humanitarian agencies had determined that the "deserving poor" belonged to a different category from those who had speculated and lost. However, the sheer volume of Americans who fell into this group meant that charitable assistance could not begin to reach them all. Some fifteen million "deserving poor," or a full one-third of the labor force, were struggling by 1932. The country had no mechanism or system in place to help so many; however, Hoover remained adamant that such relief should rest in the hands of private agencies, not with the federal government (Figure 25.7).

Figure 25.7 In the early 1930s, without significant government relief programs, many people in urban centers relied on private agencies for assistance. In New York City, St. Peter's Mission distributed bread, soup, and canned goods to large numbers of the unemployed and others in need.

Unable to receive aid from the government, Americans thus turned to private charities; churches, synagogues, and other religious organizations; and state aid. But these organizations were not prepared to deal with the scope of the problem. Private aid organizations showed declining assets as well during the Depression, with fewer Americans possessing the ability to donate to such charities. Likewise, state governments were particularly ill-equipped. Governor Franklin D. Roosevelt was the first to institute a Department of Welfare in New York in 1929. City governments had equally little to offer. In New York City in 1932, family allowances were $2.39 per week, and only one-half of the families who qualified actually received them. In Detroit, allowances fell to fifteen cents a day per person, and eventually ran out completely. In most cases, relief was only in the form of food and fuel; organizations provided nothing in the way of rent, shelter, medical care, clothing, or other necessities. There was no infrastructure to support the elderly, who were the most vulnerable, and this population largely depended on their adult children to support them, adding to families' burdens (Figure 25.8).

Figure 25.8 Because there was no infrastructure to support them should they become unemployed or destitute, the elderly were extremely vulnerable during the Great Depression. As the depression continued, the results of this tenuous situation became more evident, as shown in this photo of a vacant storefront in San Francisco, captured by Dorothea Lange in 1935.

During this time, local community groups, such as police and teachers, worked to help the neediest. New York City police, for example, began contributing 1 percent of their salaries to start a food fund that was geared to help those found starving on the streets. In 1932, New York City schoolteachers also joined forces to try to help; they contributed as much as $250,000 per month from their own salaries to help needy children. Chicago teachers did the same, feeding some eleven thousand students out of their own pockets in 1931, despite the fact that many of them had not been paid a salary in months. These noble efforts, however, failed to fully address the level of desperation that the American public was facing.

25.2 President Hoover's Response

By the end of this section, you will be able to:
- Explain Herbert Hoover's responses to the Great Depression and how they reflected his political philosophy
- Identify the local, city, and state efforts to combat the Great Depression
- Analyze the frustration and anger that a majority of Americans directed at Herbert Hoover

President Hoover was unprepared for the scope of the depression crisis, and his limited response did not begin to help the millions of Americans in need. The steps he took were very much in keeping with his philosophy of limited government, a philosophy that many had shared with him until the upheavals of the Great Depression made it clear that a more direct government response was required. But Hoover was stubborn in his refusal to give "handouts," as he saw direct government aid. He called for a spirit of volunteerism among America's businesses, asking them to keep workers employed, and he exhorted the American people to tighten their belts and make do in the spirit of "rugged individualism." While Hoover's philosophy and his appeal to the country were very much in keeping with his character, it was not enough to keep the economy from plummeting further into economic chaos.

The steps Hoover did ultimately take were too little, too late. He created programs for putting people back to work and helping beleaguered local and state charities with aid. But the programs were small in scale and highly specific as to who could benefit, and they only touched a small percentage of those in need. As the situation worsened, the public grew increasingly unhappy with Hoover. He left office with one of the lowest approval ratings of any president in history.

THE INITIAL REACTION

In the immediate aftermath of Black Tuesday, Hoover sought to reassure Americans that all was well. Reading his words after the fact, it is easy to find fault. In 1929 he said, "Any lack of confidence in the economic future or the strength of business in the United States is foolish." In 1930, he stated, "The worst is behind us." In 1931, he pledged federal aid should he ever witness starvation in the country; but as of that date, he had yet to see such need in America, despite the very real evidence that children and the elderly were starving to death. Yet Hoover was neither intentionally blind nor unsympathetic. He simply held fast to a belief system that did not change as the realities of the Great Depression set in.

Hoover believed strongly in the ethos of **American individualism**: that hard work brought its own rewards. His life story testified to that belief. Hoover was born into poverty, made his way through college at Stanford University, and eventually made his fortune as an engineer. This experience, as well as his extensive travels in China and throughout Europe, shaped his fundamental conviction that the very existence of American civilization depended upon the moral fiber of its citizens, as evidenced by their ability to overcome all hardships through individual effort and resolve. The idea of government handouts to Americans was repellant to him. Whereas Europeans might need assistance, such as his hunger relief work in Belgium during and after World War I, he believed the American character to be different. In a 1931 radio address, he said, "The spread of government destroys initiative and thus destroys character."

Likewise, Hoover was not completely unaware of the potential harm that wild stock speculation might create if left unchecked. As secretary of commerce, Hoover often warned President Coolidge of the dangers that such speculation engendered. In the weeks before his inauguration, he offered many interviews to newspapers and magazines, urging Americans to curtail their rampant stock investments, and even encouraged the Federal Reserve to raise the discount rate to make it more costly for local banks to lend money to potential speculators. However, fearful of creating a panic, Hoover never issued a stern warning to discourage Americans from such investments. Neither Hoover, nor any other politician of that day, ever gave serious thought to outright government regulation of the stock market. This was even true in his personal choices, as Hoover often lamented poor stock advice he had once offered to a friend. When the stock nose-dived, Hoover bought the shares from his friend to assuage his guilt, vowing never again to advise anyone on matters of investment.

In keeping with these principles, Hoover's response to the crash focused on two very common American traditions: He asked individuals to tighten their belts and work harder, and he asked the business community to voluntarily help sustain the economy by retaining workers and continuing production. He immediately summoned a conference of leading industrialists to meet in Washington, DC, urging them to maintain their current wages while America rode out this brief economic panic. The crash, he assured business leaders, was not part of a greater downturn; they had nothing to worry about. Similar meetings with utility companies and railroad executives elicited promises for billions of dollars in new construction projects, while labor leaders agreed to withhold demands for wage increases and workers continued to labor. Hoover also persuaded Congress to pass a $160 million tax cut to bolster American incomes, leading many to conclude that the president was doing all he could to stem the tide of the panic. In April 1930, the *New York Times* editorial board concluded that "No one in his place could have done more."

However, these modest steps were not enough. By late 1931, when it became clear that the economy would not improve on its own, Hoover recognized the need for some government intervention. He created the President's Emergency Committee for Employment (PECE), later renamed the President's Organization of Unemployment Relief (POUR). In keeping with Hoover's distaste of what he viewed as handouts,

Download for free at http://cnx.org/content/col11740/latest/

this organization did *not* provide direct federal relief to people in need. Instead, it assisted state and private relief agencies, such as the Red Cross, Salvation Army, YMCA, and Community Chest. Hoover also strongly urged people of means to donate funds to help the poor, and he himself gave significant private donations to worthy causes. But these private efforts could not alleviate the widespread effects of poverty.

Congress pushed for a more direct government response to the hardship. In 1930–1931, it attempted to pass a $60 million bill to provide relief to drought victims by allowing them access to food, fertilizer, and animal feed. Hoover stood fast in his refusal to provide food, resisting any element of direct relief. The final bill of $47 million provided for everything *except* food but did not come close to adequately addressing the crisis. Again in 1931, Congress proposed the Federal Emergency Relief Bill, which would have provided $375 million to states to help provide food, clothing, and shelter to the homeless. But Hoover opposed the bill, stating that it ruined the balance of power between states and the federal government, and in February 1932, it was defeated by fourteen votes.

However, the president's adamant opposition to direct-relief federal government programs should not be viewed as one of indifference or uncaring toward the suffering American people. His personal sympathy for those in need was boundless. Hoover was one of only two presidents to reject his salary for the office he held. Throughout the Great Depression, he donated an average of $25,000 annually to various relief organizations to assist in their efforts. Furthermore, he helped to raise $500,000 in private funds to support the White House Conference on Child Health and Welfare in 1930. Rather than indifference or heartlessness, Hoover's steadfast adherence to a philosophy of individualism as the path toward long-term American recovery explained many of his policy decisions. "A voluntary deed," he repeatedly commented, "is infinitely more precious to our national ideal and spirit than a thousand-fold poured from the Treasury."

As conditions worsened, however, Hoover eventually relaxed his opposition to federal relief and formed the Reconstruction Finance Corporation (RFC) in 1932, in part because it was an election year and Hoover hoped to keep his office. Although not a form of direct relief to the American people in greatest need, the RFC was much larger in scope than any preceding effort, setting aside $2 billion in taxpayer money to rescue banks, credit unions, and insurance companies. The goal was to boost confidence in the nation's financial institutions by ensuring that they were on solid footing. This model was flawed on a number of levels. First, the program only lent money to banks with sufficient collateral, which meant that most of the aid went to large banks. In fact, of the first $61 million loaned, $41 million went to just three banks. Small town and rural banks got almost nothing. Furthermore, at this time, confidence in financial institutions was not the primary concern of most Americans. They needed food and jobs. Many had no money to put into the banks, no matter how confident they were that the banks were safe.

Hoover's other attempt at federal assistance also occurred in 1932, when he endorsed a bill by Senator Robert Wagner of New York. This was the Emergency Relief and Construction Act. This act authorized the RFC to expand beyond loans to financial institutions and allotted $1.5 billion to states to fund local public works projects. This program failed to deliver the kind of help needed, however, as Hoover severely limited the types of projects it could fund to those that were ultimately self-paying (such as toll bridges and public housing) and those that required skilled workers. While well intended, these programs maintained the status quo, and there was still no direct federal relief to the individuals who so desperately needed it.

PUBLIC REACTION TO HOOVER

Hoover's steadfast resistance to government aid cost him the reelection and has placed him squarely at the forefront of the most unpopular presidents, according to public opinion, in modern American history. His name became synonymous with the poverty of the era: "Hoovervilles" became the common name for homeless shantytowns (Figure 25.9) and "Hoover blankets" for the newspapers that the homeless used to keep warm. A "Hoover flag" was a pants pocket—empty of all money—turned inside out. By the 1932 election, hitchhikers held up signs reading: "If you don't give me a ride, I'll vote for Hoover." Americans did not necessarily believe that Hoover caused the Great Depression. Their anger stemmed instead from what appeared to be a willful refusal to help regular citizens with direct aid that might allow them to recover from the crisis.

(a)   (b)

Figure 25.9 Hoover became one of the least popular presidents in history. "Hoovervilles," or shantytowns, were a negative reminder of his role in the nation's financial crisis. This family (a) lived in a "Hooverville" in Elm Grove, Oklahoma. This shanty (b) was one of many making up a "Hooverville" in the Portland, Oregon area. (credit: modification of work by United States Farm Security Administration)

FRUSTRATION AND PROTEST: A BAD SITUATION GROWS WORSE FOR HOOVER

Desperation and frustration often create emotional responses, and the Great Depression was no exception. Throughout 1931–1932, companies trying to stay afloat sharply cut worker wages, and, in response, workers protested in increasingly bitter strikes. As the Depression unfolded, over 80 percent of automotive workers lost their jobs. Even the typically prosperous Ford Motor Company laid off two-thirds of its workforce.

In 1932, a major strike at the Ford Motor Company factory near Detroit resulted in over sixty injuries and four deaths. Often referred to as the Ford Hunger March, the event unfolded as a planned demonstration among unemployed Ford workers who, to protest their desperate situation, marched nine miles from Detroit to the company's River Rouge plant in Dearborn. At the Dearborn city limits, local police launched tear gas at the roughly three thousand protestors, who responded by throwing stones and clods of dirt. When they finally reached the gates of the plant, protestors faced more police and firemen, as well as private security guards. As the firemen turned hoses onto the protestors, the police and security guards opened fire. In addition to those killed and injured, police arrested fifty protestors. One week later, sixty thousand mourners attended the public funerals of the four victims of what many protesters labeled police brutality. The event set the tone for worsening labor relations in the U.S.

Farmers also organized and protested, often violently. The most notable example was the Farm Holiday Association. Led by Milo Reno, this organization held significant sway among farmers in Iowa, Nebraska, Wisconsin, Minnesota, and the Dakotas. Although they never comprised a majority of farmers in any of these states, their public actions drew press attention nationwide. Among their demands, the association sought a federal government plan to set agricultural prices artificially high enough to cover the farmers' costs, as well as a government commitment to sell any farm surpluses on the world market. To achieve their goals, the group called for farm holidays, during which farmers would neither sell their produce

Chapter 25 | Brother, Can You Spare a Dime? The Great Depression, 1929-1932

741

nor purchase any other goods until the government met their demands. However, the greatest strength of the association came from the unexpected and seldom-planned actions of its members, which included barricading roads into markets, attacking nonmember farmers, and destroying their produce. Some members even raided small town stores, destroying produce on the shelves. Members also engaged in "penny auctions," bidding pennies on foreclosed farm land and threatening any potential buyers with bodily harm if they competed in the sale. Once they won the auction, the association returned the land to the original owner. In Iowa, farmers threatened to hang a local judge if he signed any more farm foreclosures. At least one death occurred as a direct result of these protests before they waned following the election of Franklin Roosevelt.

One of the most notable protest movements occurred toward the end of Hoover's presidency and centered on the Bonus Expeditionary Force, or **Bonus Army**, in the spring of 1932. In this protest, approximately fifteen thousand World War I veterans marched on Washington to demand early payment of their veteran bonuses, which were not due to be paid until 1945. The group camped out in vacant federal buildings and set up camps in Anacostia Flats near the Capitol building (Figure 25.10).

Figure 25.10 In the spring of 1932, World War I veterans marched on Washington and set up camps in Anacostia Flats, remaining there for weeks. (credit: Library of Congress)

Many veterans remained in the city in protest for nearly two months, although the U.S. Senate officially rejected their request in July. By the middle of that month, Hoover wanted them gone. He ordered the police to empty the buildings and clear out the camps, and in the exchange that followed, police fired into the crowd, killing two veterans. Fearing an armed uprising, Hoover then ordered General Douglas MacArthur, along with his aides, Dwight Eisenhower and George Patton, to forcibly remove the veterans from Anacostia Flats. The ensuing raid proved catastrophic, as the military burned down the shantytown and injured dozens of people, including a twelve-week-old infant who was killed when accidentally struck by a tear gas canister (Figure 25.11).

Figure 25.11 When the U.S. Senate denied early payment of their veteran bonuses, and Hoover ordered their makeshift camps cleared, the Bonus Army protest turned violent, cementing Hoover's demise as a president. (credit: U.S. Department of Defense)

As Americans bore witness to photographs and newsreels of the U.S. Army forcibly removing veterans, Hoover's popularity plummeted even further. By the summer of 1932, he was largely a defeated man. His pessimism and failure mirrored that of the nation's citizens. America was a country in desperate need: in need of a charismatic leader to restore public confidence as well as provide concrete solutions to pull the economy out of the Great Depression.

Click and Explore

Whether he truly believed it or simply thought the American people wanted to hear it, Hoover continued to state publicly that the country was getting back on track. Listen as he speaks about the "Success of Recovery" (http://openstaxcollege.org/l/recovery) at a campaign stop in Detroit, Michigan on October 22, 1932.

25.3 The Depths of the Great Depression

By the end of this section, you will be able to:
- Identify the challenges that everyday Americans faced as a result of the Great Depression and analyze the government's initial unwillingness to provide assistance
- Explain the particular challenges that African Americans faced during the crisis
- Identify the unique challenges that farmers in the Great Plains faced during this period

From industrial strongholds to the rural Great Plains, from factory workers to farmers, the Great Depression affected millions. In cities, as industry slowed, then sometimes stopped altogether, workers lost jobs and joined breadlines, or sought out other charitable efforts. With limited government relief efforts, private charities tried to help, but they were unable to match the pace of demand. In rural areas, farmers suffered still more. In some parts of the country, prices for crops dropped so precipitously that farmers could not earn enough to pay their mortgages, losing their farms to foreclosure. In the Great Plains, one of the worst droughts in history left the land barren and unfit for growing even minimal food to live on.

The country's most vulnerable populations, such as children, the elderly, and those subject to discrimination, like African Americans, were the hardest hit. Most white Americans felt entitled to what few jobs were available, leaving African Americans unable to find work, even in the jobs once considered their domain. In all, the economic misery was unprecedented in the country's history.

STARVING TO DEATH

By the end of 1932, the Great Depression had affected some sixty million people, most of whom wealthier Americans perceived as the "deserving poor." Yet, at the time, federal efforts to help those in need were extremely limited, and national charities had neither the capacity nor the will to elicit the large-scale response required to address the problem. The American Red Cross did exist, but Chairman John Barton Payne contended that unemployment was not an "Act of God" but rather an "Act of Man," and therefore refused to get involved in widespread direct relief efforts. Clubs like the Elks tried to provide food, as did small groups of individually organized college students. Religious organizations remained on the front lines, offering food and shelter. In larger cities, breadlines and soup lines became a common sight. At one count in 1932, there were as many as eighty-two breadlines in New York City.

Despite these efforts, however, people were destitute and ultimately starving. Families would first run through any savings, if they were lucky enough to have any. Then, the few who had insurance would cash out their policies. Cash surrender payments of individual insurance policies tripled in the first three years of the Great Depression, with insurance companies issuing total payments in excess of $1.2 billion in 1932 alone. When those funds were depleted, people would borrow from family and friends, and when they could get no more, they would simply stop paying rent or mortgage payments. When evicted, they would move in with relatives, whose own situation was likely only a step or two behind. The added burden of additional people would speed along that family's demise, and the cycle would continue. This situation spiraled downward, and did so quickly. Even as late as 1939, over 60 percent of rural households, and 82 percent of farm families, were classified as "impoverished." In larger urban areas, unemployment levels exceeded the national average, with over half a million unemployed workers in Chicago, and nearly a million in New York City. Breadlines and soup kitchens were packed, serving as many as eighty-five thousand meals daily in New York City alone. Over fifty thousand New York citizens were homeless by the end of 1932.

Children, in particular, felt the brunt of poverty. Many in coastal cities would roam the docks in search of spoiled vegetables to bring home. Elsewhere, children begged at the doors of more well-off neighbors, hoping for stale bread, table scraps, or raw potato peelings. Said one childhood survivor of the Great Depression, "You get used to hunger. After the first few days it doesn't even hurt; you just get weak." In 1931 alone, there were at least twenty documented cases of starvation; in 1934, that number grew to 110. In rural areas where such documentation was lacking, the number was likely far higher. And while the middle class did not suffer from starvation, they experienced hunger as well.

By the time Hoover left office in 1933, the poor survived not on relief efforts, but because they had learned to be poor. A family with little food would stay in bed to save fuel and avoid burning calories. People began eating parts of animals that had normally been considered waste. They scavenged for scrap wood to burn in the furnace, and when electricity was turned off, it was not uncommon to try and tap into a neighbor's wire. Family members swapped clothes; sisters might take turns going to church in the one dress they owned. As one girl in a mountain town told her teacher, who had said to go home and get food, "I can't. It's my sister's turn to eat."

Click and Explore

For his book on the Great Depression, *Hard Times*, author Studs Terkel interviewed hundreds of Americans from across the country. He subsequently selected over seventy interviews to air on a radio show that was based in Chicago. Visit Studs Terkel: Conversations with America (http://openstaxcollege.org/l/hardtimes) to listen to those interviews, during which participants reflect on their personal hardships as well as on national events during the Great Depression.

BLACK AND POOR: AFRICAN AMERICANS AND THE GREAT DEPRESSION

Most African Americans did not participate in the land boom and stock market speculation that preceded the crash, but that did not stop the effects of the Great Depression from hitting them particularly hard. Subject to continuing racial discrimination, blacks nationwide fared even worse than their hard-hit white counterparts. As the prices for cotton and other agricultural products plummeted, farm owners paid workers less or simply laid them off. Landlords evicted sharecroppers, and even those who owned their land outright had to abandon it when there was no way to earn any income.

In cities, African Americans fared no better. Unemployment was rampant, and many whites felt that any available jobs belonged to whites first. In some Northern cities, whites would conspire to have African American workers fired to allow white workers access to their jobs. Even jobs traditionally held by black workers, such as household servants or janitors, were now going to whites. By 1932, approximately one-half of all black Americans were unemployed. Racial violence also began to rise. In the South, lynching became more common again, with twenty-eight documented lynchings in 1933, compared to eight in 1932. Since communities were preoccupied with their own hardships, and organizing civil rights efforts was a long, difficult process, many resigned themselves to, or even ignored, this culture of racism and violence. Occasionally, however, an incident was notorious enough to gain national attention.

One such incident was the case of the **Scottsboro Boys** (Figure 25.12). In 1931, nine black boys, who had been riding the rails, were arrested for vagrancy and disorderly conduct after an altercation with some white travelers on the train. Two young white women, who had been dressed as boys and traveling with a group of white boys, came forward and said that the black boys had raped them. The case, which was tried in Scottsboro, Alabama, reignited decades of racial hatred and illustrated the injustice of the court system. Despite significant evidence that the women had not been raped at all, along with one of the women subsequently recanting her testimony, the all-white jury quickly convicted the boys and sentenced all but one of them to death. The verdict broke through the veil of indifference toward the plight of African Americans, and protests erupted among newspaper editors, academics, and social reformers in the North. The Communist Party of the United States offered to handle the case and sought retrial; the NAACP later joined in this effort. In all, the case was tried three separate times. The series of trials and retrials, appeals, and overturned convictions shone a spotlight on a system that provided poor legal counsel and relied on all-white juries. In October 1932, the U.S. Supreme Court agreed with the Communist Party's defense attorneys that the defendants had been denied adequate legal representation at the original trial, and that due process as provided by the Fourteenth Amendment had been denied as a result of the exclusion of any potential black jurors. Eventually, most of the accused received lengthy prison terms and subsequent parole, but avoided the death penalty. The Scottsboro case ultimately laid some of the early groundwork for the modern American civil rights movement. Alabama granted posthumous pardons to all defendants in 2013.

The Scottsboro Boys

Left to right: Clarence Norris, Charlie Weems, Haywood Patterson, Ozie Powell, Willie Roberson, Eugene Williams, Olen Montgomery, Andy Wright, Roy Wright

Figure 25.12 The trial and conviction of nine African American boys in Scottsboro, Alabama, illustrated the numerous injustices of the American court system. Despite being falsely accused, the boys received lengthy prison terms and were not officially pardoned by the State of Alabama until 2013.

Click and Explore

Read Voices from Scottsboro (http://openstaxcollege.org/l/scottsboro) for the perspectives of both participants and spectators in the Scottsboro case, from the initial trial to the moment, in 1976, when one of the women sued for slander.

ENVIRONMENTAL CATASTROPHE MEETS ECONOMIC HARDSHIP: THE DUST BOWL

Despite the widely held belief that rural Americans suffered less in the Great Depression due to their ability to at least grow their own food, this was not the case. Farmers, ranchers, and their families suffered more than any group other than African Americans during the Depression.

From the turn of the century through much of World War I, farmers in the Great Plains experienced prosperity due to unusually good growing conditions, high commodity prices, and generous government farming policies that led to a rush for land. As the federal government continued to purchase all excess produce for the war effort, farmers and ranchers fell into several bad practices, including mortgaging their farms and borrowing money against future production in order to expand. However, after the war, prosperity rapidly dwindled, particularly during the recession of 1921. Seeking to recoup their losses through economies of scale in which they would expand their production even further to take full advantage of their available land and machinery, farmers plowed under native grasses to plant acre after acre of wheat, with little regard for the long-term repercussions to the soil. Regardless of these misguided efforts, commodity prices continued to drop, finally plummeting in 1929, when the price of wheat dropped from two dollars to forty cents per bushel.

Exacerbating the problem was a massive drought that began in 1931 and lasted for eight terrible years. Dust storms roiled through the Great Plains, creating huge, choking clouds that piled up in doorways and filtered into homes through closed windows. Even more quickly than it had boomed, the land of agricultural opportunity went bust, due to widespread overproduction and overuse of the land, as well as to the harsh weather conditions that followed, resulting in the creation of the **Dust Bowl** (Figure 25.13).

Figure 25.13 The dust storms that blew through the Great Plains were epic in scale. Drifts of dirt piled up against doors and windows. People wore goggles and tied rags over their mouths to keep the dust out. (credit: U.S. National Oceanic and Atmospheric Administration)

Livestock died, or had to be sold, as there was no money for feed. Crops intended to feed the family withered and died in the drought. Terrifying dust storms became more and more frequent, as "black blizzards" of dirt blew across the landscape and created a new illness known as "dust pneumonia." In 1935 alone, over 850 million tons of topsoil blew away. To put this number in perspective, geologists estimate that it takes the earth five hundred years to naturally regenerate one inch of topsoil; yet, just one significant dust storm could destroy a similar amount. In their desperation to get more from the land, farmers had stripped it of the delicate balance that kept it healthy. Unaware of the consequences, they had moved away from such traditional practices as crop rotation and allowing land to regain its strength by permitting it to lie fallow between plantings, working the land to death.

For farmers, the results were catastrophic. Unlike most factory workers in the cities, in most cases, farmers lost their homes when they lost their livelihood. Most farms and ranches were originally mortgaged to small country banks that understood the dynamics of farming, but as these banks failed, they often sold rural mortgages to larger eastern banks that were less concerned with the specifics of farm life. With the effects of the drought and low commodity prices, farmers could not pay their local banks, which in turn lacked funds to pay the large urban banks. Ultimately, the large banks foreclosed on the farms, often swallowing up the small country banks in the process. It is worth noting that of the five thousand banks that closed between 1930 and 1932, over 75 percent were country banks in locations with populations under 2,500. Given this dynamic, it is easy to see why farmers in the Great Plains remained wary of big city bankers.

For farmers who survived the initial crash, the situation worsened, particularly in the Great Plains where years of overproduction and rapidly declining commodity prices took their toll. Prices continued to decline, and as farmers tried to stay afloat, they produced still more crops, which drove prices even lower. Farms failed at an astounding rate, and farmers sold out at rock-bottom prices. One farm in Shelby, Nebraska was mortgaged at $4,100 and sold for $49.50. One-fourth of the entire state of Mississippi was auctioned off *in a single day* at a foreclosure auction in April 1932.

Not all farmers tried to keep their land. Many, especially those who had arrived only recently, in an attempt to capitalize on the earlier prosperity, simply walked away (**Figure 25.14**). In hard-hit Oklahoma, thousands of farmers packed up what they could and walked or drove away from the land they thought would be their future. They, along with other displaced farmers from throughout the Great Plains, became known as Okies. Okies were an emblem of the failure of the American breadbasket to deliver on its promise, and their story was made famous in John Steinbeck's novel, *The Grapes of Wrath*.

Figure 25.14 As the Dust Bowl continued in the Great Plains, many had to abandon their land and equipment, as captured in this image from 1936, taken in Dallas, South Dakota. (credit: United States Department of Agriculture)

Click and Explore

Experience the Interactive Dust Bowl (http://openstaxcollege.org/l/dustbowl1) to see how decisions compounded to create peoples' destiny. Click through to see what choices you would make and where that would take you.

MY STORY

✪ *Caroline Henderson on the Dust Bowl*

> Now we are facing a fourth year of failure. There can be no wheat for us in 1935 in spite of all our careful and expensive work in preparing ground, sowing and re-sowing our allocated acreage. Native grass pastures are permanently damaged, in many cases hopelessly ruined, smothered under by drifted sand. Fences are buried under banks of thistles and hard packed earth or undermined by the eroding action of the wind and lying flat on the ground. Less traveled roads are impassable, covered deep under by sand or the finer silt-like loam. Orchards, groves and hedge-rows cultivated for many years with patient care are dead or dying . . . Impossible it seems not to grieve that the work of hands should prove so perishable.
> —Caroline Henderson, Shelton, Oklahoma, 1935

Much like other farm families whose livelihoods were destroyed by the Dust Bowl, Caroline Henderson describes a level of hardship that many Americans living in Depression-ravaged cities could never understand. Despite their hard work, millions of Americans were losing both their produce and their homes, sometimes in as little as forty-eight hours, to environmental catastrophes. Lacking any other explanation, many began to question what they had done to incur God's wrath. Note in particular Henderson's references to "dead," "dying," and "perishable," and contrast those terms with her depiction of the "careful and expensive work" undertaken by their own hands. Many simply could not understand how such a catastrophe could have occurred.

CHANGING VALUES, CHANGING CULTURE

In the decades before the Great Depression, and particularly in the 1920s, American culture largely reflected the values of individualism, self-reliance, and material success through competition. Novels like F. Scott Fitzgerald's *The Great Gatsby* and Sinclair Lewis's *Babbit* portrayed wealth and the self-made man in America, albeit in a critical fashion. In film, many silent movies, such as Charlie Chaplin's *The Gold Rush*, depicted the rags-to-riches fable that Americans so loved. With the shift in U.S. fortunes, however, came a shift in values, and with it, a new cultural reflection. The arts revealed a new emphasis on the welfare of the whole and the importance of community in preserving family life. While box office sales briefly declined at the beginning of the Depression, they quickly rebounded. Movies offered a way for Americans to think of better times, and people were willing to pay twenty-five cents for a chance to escape, at least for a few hours.

Even more than escapism, other films at the close of the decade reflected on the sense of community and family values that Americans struggled to maintain throughout the entire Depression. John Ford's screen version of Steinbeck's *The Grapes of Wrath* came out in 1940, portraying the haunting story of the Joad family's exodus from their Oklahoma farm to California in search of a better life. Their journey leads them to realize that they need to join a larger social movement—communism—dedicated to bettering the lives of all people. Tom Joad says, "Well, maybe it's like Casy says, a fella ain't got a soul of his own, but on'y a piece of a soul—the one big soul that belongs to ever'body." The greater lesson learned was one of the strength of community in the face of individual adversity.

Another trope was that of the hard-working everyman against greedy banks and corporations. This was perhaps best portrayed in the movies of Frank Capra, whose *Mr. Smith Goes to Washington* was emblematic of his work. In this 1939 film, Jimmy Stewart plays a legislator sent to Washington to finish out the term of a deceased senator. While there, he fights corruption to ensure the construction of a boy's camp in his hometown rather than a dam project that would only serve to line the pockets of a few. He ultimately engages in a two-day filibuster, standing up to the power players to do what's right. The Depression era was a favorite of Capra's to depict in his films, including *It's a Wonderful Life*, released in 1946. In this film, Jimmy Stewart runs a family-owned savings and loan, which at one point faces a bank run similar to those seen in 1929–1930. In the end, community support helps Stewart retain his business and home against the unscrupulous actions of a wealthy banker who sought to bring ruin to his family.

AMERICANA

⬡ *"Brother, Can You Spare a Dime?"*

They used to tell me I was building a dream, and so I followed the mob
When there was earth to plow or guns to bear, I was always there, right on the job
They used to tell me I was building a dream, with peace and glory ahead
Why should I be standing in line, just waiting for bread?
Once I built a railroad, I made it run, made it race against time
Once I built a railroad, now it's done, Brother, can you spare a dime?
Once I built a tower up to the sun, brick and rivet and lime
Once I built a tower, now it's done, Brother, can you spare a dime?
—Jay Gorney and "Yip" Harburg

"Brother, Can You Spare a Dime?" first appeared in 1932, written for the Broadway musical *New Americana* by Jay Gorney, a composer who based the song's music on a Russian lullaby, and Edgar Yipsel "Yip" Harburg, a lyricist who would go on to win an Academy Award for the song "Over the Rainbow" from *The Wizard of Oz* (1939).

With its lyrics speaking to the plight of the common man during the Great Depression and the refrain appealing to the same sense of community later found in the films of Frank Capra, "Brother, Can You Spare a Dime?" quickly became the *de facto* anthem of the Great Depression. Recordings by Bing Crosby, Al Jolson, and Rudy Vallee all enjoyed tremendous popularity in the 1930s.

Click and Explore

For more on "Brother Can You Spare a Dime?" and the Great Depression, visit **ArtsEdge (http://openstaxcollege.org/l/sparedime)** to explore the Kennedy Center's digital resources and learn the "Story Behind the Song."

Finally, there was a great deal of pure escapism in the popular culture of the Depression. Even the songs found in films reminded many viewers of the bygone days of prosperity and happiness, from Al Dubin and Henry Warren's hit "We're in the Money" to the popular "Happy Days are Here Again." The latter eventually became the theme song of Franklin Roosevelt's 1932 presidential campaign. People wanted to forget their worries and enjoy the madcap antics of the Marx Brothers, the youthful charm of Shirley Temple, the dazzling dances of Fred Astaire and Ginger Rogers (Figure 25.15), or the comforting morals of the *Andy Hardy* series. The Hardy series—nine films in all, produced by MGM from 1936 to 1940—starred Judy Garland and Mickey Rooney, and all followed the adventures of a small-town judge and his son. No matter what the challenge, it was never so big that it could not be solved with a musical production put on by the neighborhood kids, bringing together friends and family members in a warm display of community values.

Figure 25.15 *Flying Down to Rio* (1933) was the first motion picture to feature the immensely popular dance duo of Fred Astaire and Ginger Rogers. The pair would go on to star in nine more Hollywood musicals throughout the 1930s and 1940s.

All of these movies reinforced traditional American values, which suffered during these hard times, in part due to declining marriage and birth rates, and increased domestic violence. At the same time, however, they reflected an increased interest in sex and sexuality. While the birth rate was dropping, surveys in *Fortune* magazine in 1936–1937 found that two-thirds of college students favored birth control, and that 50 percent of men and 25 percent of women admitted to premarital sex, continuing a trend among younger Americans that had begun to emerge in the 1920s. Contraceptive sales soared during the decade, and again, culture reflected this shift. Blonde bombshell Mae West was famous for her sexual innuendoes, and her flirtatious persona was hugely popular, although it got her banned on radio broadcasts throughout the Midwest. Whether West or Garland, Chaplin or Stewart, American film continued to be a barometer of American values, and their challenges, through the decade.

25.4 Assessing the Hoover Years on the Eve of the New Deal

By the end of this section, you will be able to:
- Identify the successes and failures of Herbert Hoover's presidency
- Determine the fairness and accuracy of assessments of Hoover's presidency

As so much of the Hoover presidency is circumscribed by the onset of the Great Depression, one must be careful in assessing his successes and failures, so as not to attribute all blame to Hoover. Given the suffering that many Americans endured between the fall of 1929 and Franklin Roosevelt's inauguration in the spring of 1933, it is easy to lay much of the blame at Hoover's doorstep (Figure 25.16). However, the extent to which Hoover was constrained by the economic circumstances unfolding well before he assumed office offers a few mitigating factors. Put simply, Hoover did not cause the stock market crash. However, his stubborn adherence to a questionable belief in "American individualism," despite mounting evidence that people were starving, requires that some blame be attributed to his policies (or lack thereof) for the depth and length of the Depression. Yet, Hoover's presidency was much more than simply combating the Depression. To assess the extent of his inability to provide meaningful national leadership through the darkest months of the Depression, his other policies require consideration.

Figure 25.16 Herbert Hoover (left) had the misfortune to be a president elected in prosperity and subsequently tasked with leading the country through the Great Depression. His unwillingness to face the harsh realities of widespread unemployment, farm foreclosures, business failures, and bank closings made him a deeply unpopular president, and he lost the 1932 election in a landslide to Franklin D. Roosevelt (right). (credit: Architect of the Capitol)

HOOVER'S FOREIGN POLICY

Although it was a relatively quiet period for U.S. diplomacy, Hoover did help to usher in a period of positive relations, specifically with several Latin American neighbors. This would establish the basis for Franklin Roosevelt's "Good Neighbor" policy. Following a goodwill tour of Central American countries immediately following his election in 1928, Hoover shaped the subsequent **Clark Memorandum**—released in 1930—which largely repudiated the previous Roosevelt Corollary, establishing a basis for unlimited American military intervention throughout Latin America. To the contrary, through the memorandum, Hoover asserted that greater emphasis should be placed upon the older Monroe Doctrine, in which the U.S. pledged assistance to her Latin American neighbors should any European powers interfere in Western Hemisphere affairs. Hoover further strengthened relations to the south by withdrawing American troops from Haiti and Nicaragua. Additionally, he outlined with Secretary of State Henry Stimson the Hoover-Stimson Doctrine, which announced that the United States would never recognize claims to territories seized by force (a direct response to the recent Japanese invasion of Manchuria).

Other diplomatic overtures met with less success for Hoover. Most notably, in an effort to support the American economy during the early stages of the Depression, the president signed into law the **Smoot-Hawley Tariff** in 1930. The law, which raised tariffs on thousands of imports, was intended to increase sales of American-made goods, but predictably angered foreign trade partners who in turn raised their tariffs on American imports, thus shrinking international trade and closing additional markets to desperate American manufacturers. As a result, the global depression worsened further. A similar attempt to spur the world economy, known as the Hoover Moratorium, likewise met with great opposition and little economic benefit. Issued in 1931, the moratorium called for a halt to World War I reparations to be paid by Germany to France, as well as forgiveness of Allied war debts to the U.S.

HOOVER AND CIVIL RIGHTS

Holding true to his belief in individualism, Hoover saw little need for significant civil rights legislation during his presidency, including any overtures from the NAACP to endorse federal anti-lynching legislation. He felt African Americans would benefit more from education and assimilation than from federal legislation or programs; yet he failed to recognize that, at this time in history, federal legislation and programs were required to ensure equal opportunities.

Hoover did give special attention to the improvement of Native American conditions, beginning with his selection of Charles Curtis as his vice-presidential running mate in the 1928 election. Curtis, of the Kaw Tribe, became the country's first Native American to hold so high an elected office. Hoover subsequently appointed Charles Rhoads as the new commissioner of the Bureau of Indian Affairs and advocated, with Rhoads' assistance, for Native American self-sufficiency and full assimilation as Americans under the Indian Citizenship Act of 1924. During Hoover's presidency, federal expenditures for Native American schools and health care doubled.

Click and Explore

Cartoons, especially political cartoons, provide a window into the frustrations and worries of an age. Browse the political cartoons at The Changing Face of Herbert Hoover (http://openstaxcollege.org/l/hoover) to better understand the historical context of Herbert Hoover's presidency.

A FINAL ASSESSMENT

Herbert Hoover's presidency, embarked upon with much promise following his election in November 1928, produced a legacy of mixed reactions. Some Americans blamed him for all of the economic and social woes from which they suffered for the next decade; all blamed him for simply not responding to their needs. As contemporary commentator and actor Will Rogers said at the time, "If an American was lucky enough to find an apple to eat in the Depression and bit into it only to find a worm, they would blame Hoover for the worm." Likewise, subsequent public opinion polls of presidential popularity, as well as polls of professional historians, routinely rate Hoover in the bottom seven of all U.S. presidents in terms of overall success.

However, Hoover the president was a product of his time. Americans sought a president in 1928 who would continue the policies of normalcy with which many associated the prosperity they enjoyed. They wanted a president who would forego government interference and allow industrial capitalism to grow unfettered. Hoover, from his days as the secretary of commerce, was the ideal candidate. In fact, he was *too* ideal when the Great Depression actually hit. Holding steadfast to his philosophy of "American individualism," Hoover proved largely incapable of shifting into economic crisis mode when Americans came to realize that prosperity could not last forever. Desperate to help, but unwilling to compromise on his philosophy, Hoover could not manage a comprehensive solution to the worldwide depression that few foresaw. Only when reelection was less than a year away did a reluctant Hoover initiate significant policies, but even then, they did not provide direct relief. By the start of 1932, unemployment hovered near 25 percent, and thousands of banks and factories were closing their doors. Combined with Hoover's ill-timed response to the Bonus Army crisis, his political fate was sealed. Americans would look to the next president for a solution. "Democracy is a harsh employer," Hoover concluded, as he awaited all but certain defeat in the November election of 1932 (Figure 25.17).

Download for free at http://cnx.org/content/col11740/latest/

Figure 25.17 By the election of 1932, Hoover (left) knew that he was beaten. In photos from this time, he tends to appear grim-faced and downtrodden.

Key Terms

American individualism the belief, strongly held by Herbert Hoover and others, that hard work and individual effort, absent government interference, comprised the formula for success in the U.S.

bank run the withdrawal by a large number of individuals or investors of money from a bank due to fears of the bank's instability, with the ironic effect of increasing the bank's vulnerability to failure

Black Tuesday October 29, 1929, when a mass panic caused a crash in the stock market and stockholders divested over sixteen million shares, causing the overall value of the stock market to drop precipitously

Bonus Army a group of World War I veterans and affiliated groups who marched to Washington in 1932 to demand their war bonuses early, only to be refused and forcibly removed by the U.S. Army

Clark Memorandum Hoover's repudiation of the Roosevelt Corollary that justified American military intervention in Latin American affairs; this memorandum improved relations with America's neighbors by reasserting that intervention would occur only in the event of European interference in the Western Hemisphere

Dust Bowl the area in the middle of the country that had been badly overfarmed in the 1920s and suffered from a terrible drought that coincided with the Great Depression; the name came from the "black blizzard" of topsoil and dust that blew through the area

Scottsboro Boys a reference to the infamous trial in Scottsboro, Alabama in 1931, where nine African American boys were falsely accused of raping two white women and sentenced to death; the extreme injustice of the trial, particularly given the age of the boys and the inadequacy of the testimony against them, garnered national and international attention

Smoot-Hawley Tariff the tariff approved by Hoover to raise the tax on thousands of imported goods in the hope that it would encourage people to buy American-made products; the unintended result was that other nations raised their tariffs, further hurting American exports and exacerbating the global financial crisis

speculation the practice of investing in risky financial opportunities in the hopes of a fast payout due to market fluctuations

Summary

25.1 The Stock Market Crash of 1929

The prosperous decade leading up to the stock market crash of 1929, with easy access to credit and a culture that encouraged speculation and risk-taking, put into place the conditions for the country's fall. The stock market, which had been growing for years, began to decline in the summer and early fall of 1929, precipitating a panic that led to a massive stock sell-off in late October. In one month, the market lost close to 40 percent of its value. Although only a small percentage of Americans had invested in the stock market, the crash affected everyone. Banks lost millions and, in response, foreclosed on business and personal loans, which in turn pressured customers to pay back their loans, whether or not they had the cash. As the pressure mounted on individuals, the effects of the crash continued to spread. The state of the international economy, the inequitable income distribution in the United States, and, perhaps most importantly, the contagion effect of panic all played roles in the continued downward spiral of the economy.

In the immediate aftermath of the crash, the government was confident that the economy would rebound. But several factors led it to worsen instead. One significant issue was the integral role of automobiles and construction in American industry. With the crash, there was no money for either auto purchases or major construction projects; these industries therefore suffered, laying off workers, cutting wages, and reducing benefits. Affluent Americans considered the deserving poor—those who lost their money due to no fault of their own—to be especially in need of help. But at the outset of the Great Depression, there were few social safety nets in place to provide them with the necessary relief. While some families retained their wealth and middle-class lifestyle, many more were plunged quite suddenly into poverty and often homelessness. Children dropped out of school, mothers and wives went into domestic service, and the fabric of American society changed inexorably.

25.2 President Hoover's Response

President Hoover's deeply held philosophy of American individualism, which he maintained despite extraordinary economic circumstances, made him particularly unsuited to deal with the crisis of the Great Depression. He greatly resisted government intervention, considering it a path to the downfall of American greatness. His initial response of asking Americans to find their own paths to recovery and seeking voluntary business measures to stimulate the economy could not stem the tide of the Depression. Ultimately, Hoover did create some federal relief programs, such as the Reconstruction Finance Corporation (RFC), which sought to boost public confidence in financial institutions by ensuring that they were on solid footing. When this measure did little to help impoverished individuals, he signed the Emergency Relief Act, which allowed the RFC to invest in local public works projects. But even this was too little, too late. The severe limits on the types of projects funded and type of workers used meant that most Americans saw no benefit.

The American public ultimately responded with anger and protest to Hoover's apparent inability to create solutions. Protests ranged from factory strikes to farm riots, culminating in the notorious Bonus Army protest in the spring of 1932. Veterans from World War I lobbied to receive their bonuses immediately, rather than waiting until 1945. The government denied them, and in the ensuing chaos, Hoover called in the military to disrupt the protest. The violence of this act was the final blow for Hoover, whose popularity was already at an all-time low.

25.3 The Depths of the Great Depression

The Great Depression affected huge segments of the American population—sixty million people by one estimate. But certain groups were hit harder than the rest. African Americans faced discrimination in finding employment, as white workers sought even low-wage jobs like housecleaning. Southern blacks moved away from their farms as crop prices failed, migrating en masse to Northern cities, which had little to offer them. Rural Americans were also badly hit. The eight-year drought that began shortly after the stock market crash exacerbated farmers' and ranchers' problems. The cultivation of greater amounts of acreage in the preceding decades meant that land was badly overworked, and the drought led to massive and terrible dust storms, creating the region's nickname, the Dust Bowl. Some farmers tried to remain and buy up more land as neighbors went broke; others simply fled their failed farms and moved away, often to the large-scale migrant farms found in California, to search for a better life that few ever found. Maltreated by Californians who wished to avoid the unwanted competition for jobs that these "Okies" represented, many of the Dust Bowl farmers were left wandering as a result.

There was very little in the way of public assistance to help the poor. While private charities did what they could, the scale of the problem was too large for them to have any lasting effects. People learned to survive as best they could by sending their children out to beg, sharing clothing, and scrounging wood to feed the furnace. Those who could afford it turned to motion pictures for escape. Movies and books during the Great Depression reflected the shift in American cultural norms, away from rugged individualism toward a more community-based lifestyle.

25.4 Assessing the Hoover Years on the Eve of the New Deal

In Hoover, Americans got the president they had wanted, at least at first. He was third in a line of free-market Republican presidents, elected to continue the policies that had served the economy so well. But when the stock market crashed in 1929, and the underlying weaknesses in the economy came to the fore, Hoover did not act with clear intentionality and speed. His record as a president will likely always bear the taint of his unwillingness to push through substantial government aid, but, despite that failing, his record is not without minor accomplishments. Hoover's international policies, particularly in regard to Latin America, served the country well. And while his attitude toward civil rights mirrored his conviction that government intervention was a negative force, he did play a key role changing living conditions for Native Americans. In all, it was his—and the country's—bad luck that his presidency ultimately required a very different philosophy than the one that had gotten him elected.

Review Questions

1. Which of the following is a cause of the stock market crash of 1929?

A. too many people invested in the market

B. investors made risky investments with borrowed money

C. the federal government invested heavily in business stock

D. World War I created optimal conditions for an eventual crash

2. Which of the following groups would not be considered "the deserving poor" by social welfare groups and humanitarians in the 1930s?

A. vagrant children

B. unemployed workers

C. stock speculators

D. single mothers

3. What were Hoover's plans when he first entered office, and how were these reflective of the years that preceded the Great Depression?

4. Which of the following protests was directly related to federal policies, and thus had the greatest impact in creating a negative public perception of the Hoover presidency?

A. the Farm Holiday Association

B. the Ford Motor Company labor strikes

C. the Bonus Expeditionary Force

D. the widespread appearance of "Hooverville" shantytowns

5. Which of the following groups or bodies did *not* offer direct relief to needy people?

A. the federal government

B. local police and schoolteachers

C. churches and synagogues

D. wealthy individuals

6. What attempts did Hoover make to offer federal relief? How would you evaluate the success or failure of these programs?

7. Which of the following hardships did African Americans *not* typically face during the Great Depression?

A. lower farm wages in the South

B. the belief that white workers needed jobs more than their black counterparts

C. white workers taking historically "black" jobs, such as maids and janitors

D. widespread race riots in large urban centers

8. Which of the following was *not* a key factor in the conditions that led to the Dust Bowl?

A. previous overcultivation of farmland

B. decreasing American demand for farm produce

C. unfavorable weather conditions

D. poor farming techniques regarding proper irrigation and acreage rotation

9. What did the popular movies of the Depression reveal about American values at that time? How did these values contrast with the values Americans held before the Depression?

10. Which assessment of Herbert Hoover's presidency is most accurate?

A. Hoover's policies caused the stock market crash and subsequent depression.

B. Although he did not cause the stock market crash, Hoover deserves criticism for his inadequate response to it.

C. Hoover pledged a great deal of direct federal aid to unemployed Americans, overtaxing the federal budget and worsening the financial crisis.

D. Hoover disapproved of American capitalism and therefore attempted to forestall any concrete solutions to the Depression.

11. Which of the following phrases best characterizes Herbert Hoover's foreign policy agenda?

A. interventionist, in terms of unwanted interference in other nations' affairs

B. militaristic, in terms of strengthening American armed forces

C. isolationist, in terms of preventing America's interaction with other nations

D. mutual respect, in terms of being available to support others when called upon, but not interfering unnecessarily in their affairs

Critical Thinking Questions

12. What were the possible causes of the Great Depression? To what extent could a stock market crash of the intensity of 1929 occur again in America?

13. Why did people feel so confident before the stock market crash of 1929? What were some factors that led to irrational investing?

14. Why was Herbert Hoover's response to the initial months of the Great Depression so limited in scope?

15. How did the cultural products of the Great Depression serve to reflect, shape, and assuage Americans' fears and concerns during this volatile period? How do our cultural products—such as books, movies, and music—reflect and reinforce our values in our own times?

16. To what extent did the Great Depression catalyze important changes in Americans' perceptions of themselves, their national identity, and the role of their government? What evidence of these shifts can you find in the politics and values of our own times?

17. Why is Herbert Hoover so often blamed for the Great Depression? To what extent is such an assessment fair or accurate?

CHAPTER 26

Franklin Roosevelt and the New Deal, 1932-1941

Figure 26.1 President Roosevelt's Federal One Project allowed thousands of artists to create public art. This initiative was a response to the Great Depression as part of the Works Project Administration, and much of the public art in cities today date from this era. *New Deal* by Charles Wells can be found in the Clarkson S. Fisher Federal Building and U.S. Courthouse in Trenton, New Jersey. (credit: modification of work by Library of Congress)

Chapter Outline

26.1 The Rise of Franklin Roosevelt
26.2 The First New Deal
26.3 The Second New Deal

Introduction

The election of President Franklin Delano Roosevelt signaled both immediate relief for the American public as well as a permanent shift in the role of the federal government in guiding the economy and providing direct assistance to the people, albeit through expensive programs that made extensive budget deficits commonplace. For many, the immediate relief was, at a minimum, psychological: Herbert Hoover was gone, and the situation could not grow worse under Roosevelt. But as his New Deal unfolded, Americans learned more about the fundamental changes their new president brought with him to the Oval Office. In the span of little more than one hundred days, the country witnessed a wave of legislation never seen before or since.

Roosevelt understood the need to "save the patient," to borrow a medical phrase he often employed, as well as to "cure the ill." This meant both creating jobs, through such programs as the Works Progress Administration, which provided employment to over eight million Americans (Figure 26.1), as well as reconfiguring the structure of the American economy. In pursuit of these two goals, Americans re-elected Roosevelt for three additional terms in the White House and became full partners in the reshaping of their country.

26.1 The Rise of Franklin Roosevelt

By the end of this section, you should be able to:
- Describe the events of the 1932 presidential election and identify the characteristics that made Franklin Roosevelt a desirable candidate
- Explain why Congress amended the U.S. Constitution to reduce the period of time between presidential elections and inaugurations

Franklin Roosevelt was part of the political establishment and the wealthy elite, but in the 1932 presidential campaign, he did not want to be perceived that way. Roosevelt felt that the country needed sweeping change, and he ran a campaign intended to convince the American people that he could deliver that change. It was not the specifics of his campaign promises that were different; in fact, he gave very few details and likely did not yet have a clear idea of how he would raise the country out of the Great Depression. But he campaigned tirelessly, talking to thousands of people, appearing at his party's national convention, and striving to show the public that he was a different breed of politician. As Hoover grew more morose and physically unwell in the face of the campaign, Roosevelt thrived. He was elected in a landslide by a country ready for the change he had promised.

THE ELECTION OF FRANKLIN ROOSEVELT

By the 1932 presidential election, Hoover's popularity was at an all-time low. Despite his efforts to address the hardships that many Americans faced, his ineffectual response to the Great Depression left Americans angry and ready for change. Franklin Roosevelt, though born to wealth and educated at the best schools, offered the change people sought. His experience in politics had previously included a seat in the New York State legislature, a vice-presidential nomination, and a stint as governor of New York. During the latter, he introduced many state-level reforms that later formed the basis of his New Deal as well as worked with several advisors who later formed the **Brains Trust** that advised his federal agenda.

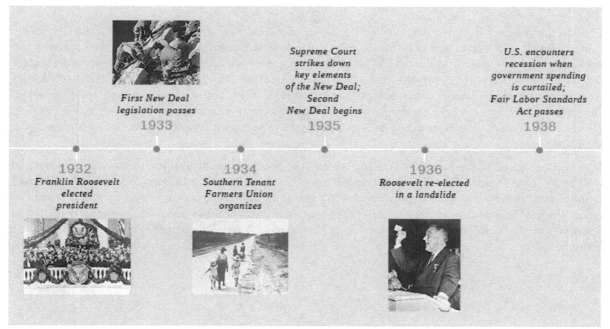

Figure 26.2

Roosevelt exuded confidence, which the American public desperately wished to see in their leader (Figure 26.3). And, despite his affluence, Americans felt that he could relate to their suffering due to his own physical hardships; he had been struck with polio a decade earlier and was essentially paralyzed from the waist down for the remainder of his life. Roosevelt understood that the public sympathized with his ailment; he likewise developed a genuine empathy for public suffering as a result of his illness. However, he never wanted to be photographed in his wheelchair or appear infirm in any way, for fear that the public's sympathy would transform into concern over his physical ability to discharge the duties of the Oval Office.

Figure 26.3 Franklin Roosevelt brought a new feeling of optimism and possibility to a country that was beaten down by hardship. His enthusiasm was in counterpoint to Herbert Hoover's discouraging last year in office.

Roosevelt also recognized the need to convey to the voting public that he was not simply another member of the political aristocracy. At a time when the country not only faced its most severe economic challenges to date, but Americans began to question some of the fundamental principles of capitalism and democracy, Roosevelt sought to show that he was different—that he could defy expectations—and through his actions could find creative solutions to address the nation's problems while restoring public confidence in fundamental American values. As a result, he not only was the first presidential candidate to appear in person at a national political convention to accept his party's nomination but also flew there through terrible weather from New York to Chicago in order to do so—a risky venture in what was still the early stages of flight as public transportation. At the Democratic National Convention in 1932, he coined the famous phrase: "I pledge myself to a new deal for the American people." The New Deal did not yet exist, but to the American people, any positive and optimistic response to the Great Depression was a welcome one.

Hoover assumed at first that Roosevelt would be easy to defeat, confident that he could never carry the eastern states and the business vote. He was sorely mistaken. Everywhere he went, Hoover was met with antagonism; anti-Hoover signs and protests were the norm. Hoover's public persona declined rapidly. Many news accounts reported that he seemed physically unwell, with an ashen face and shaking hands. Often, he seemed as though he would faint, and an aide constantly remained nearby with a chair in case he fell. In contrast, Roosevelt thrived on the campaign. He commented, "I have looked into the faces of thousands of Americans, and they have the frightened look of lost children."

The election results that November were never really in question: With three million more people voting than in 1928, Roosevelt won by a popular count of twenty-three million to fifteen million. He carried all but six states while winning over 57 percent of the popular vote. Whether they voted due to animosity towards Hoover for his relative inactivity, or out of hope for what Roosevelt would accomplish, the American public committed themselves to a new vision. Historians identify this election as the beginning of a new Democratic coalition, bringing together African Americans, other ethnic minorities, and organized labor as a voting bloc upon whom the party would rely for many of its electoral victories over the next fifty years. Unlike some European nations where similar challenges caused democratic constitutions to crumble and give way to radical ideologies and authoritarian governments, the Roosevelt administration changed the nation's economic fortunes with reforms, preserved the constitution, and expanded rather than limited the reach of democratic principles into the market economy. As a result, radical alternatives, such as the Fascist movement or Communist Party, remained on the margins of the nation's political culture.

THE INTERREGNUM

After the landslide election, the country—and Hoover—had to endure the **interregnum**, the difficult four months between the election and President Roosevelt's inauguration in March 1933. Congress did not pass a single significant piece of legislation during this period, although Hoover spent much of the time trying to get Roosevelt to commit publicly to a legislative agenda of Hoover's choosing. Roosevelt remained gracious but refused to begin his administration as the incumbent's advisor without any legal authority necessary to change policy. Unwilling to tie himself to Hoover's legacy of failed policies, Roosevelt kept quiet when Hoover supported the passage of a national sales tax. Meanwhile, the country suffered from Hoover's inability to further drive a legislative agenda through Congress. It was the worst winter since the beginning of the Great Depression, and the banking sector once again suffered another round of panics. While Roosevelt kept his distance from the final tremors of the Hoover administration, the country continued to suffer in wait. In part as a response to the challenges of this time, the U.S. Constitution was subsequently amended to reduce the period from election to inauguration to the now-commonplace two months.

Any ideas that Roosevelt held almost did not come to fruition, thanks to a would-be assassin's bullet. On February 15, 1933, after delivering a speech from his open car in Miami's Bayfront Park, local Italian bricklayer Giuseppe Zangara emerged from a crowd of well-wishers to fire six shots from his revolver. Although Roosevelt emerged from the assassination attempt unscathed, Zangara wounded five individuals that day, including Chicago Mayor Tony Cermak, who attended the speech in the hopes of resolving any long-standing differences with the president-elect. Roosevelt and his driver immediately rushed Cermak to the hospital where he died three days later. Roosevelt's calm and collected response to the event reassured many Americans of his ability to lead the nation through the challenges they faced. All that awaited was Roosevelt's inauguration before his ideas would unfold to the expectant public.

So what was Roosevelt's plan? Before he took office, it seems likely that he was not entirely sure. Certain elements were known: He believed in positive government action to solve the Depression; he believed in federal relief, public works, social security, and unemployment insurance; he wanted to restore public confidence in banks; he wanted stronger government regulation of the economy; and he wanted to directly help farmers. But how to take action on these beliefs was more in question. A month before his inauguration, he said to his advisors, "Let's concentrate upon one thing: Save the people and the nation, and if we have to change our minds twice every day to accomplish that end, we should do it."

Unlike Hoover, who professed an ideology of "American individualism," an adherence that rendered him largely incapable of widespread action, Roosevelt remained pragmatic and open-minded to possible solutions. To assist in formulating a variety of relief and recovery programs, Roosevelt turned to a group of men who had previously orchestrated his election campaign and victory. Collectively known as the "Brains Trust" (a phrase coined by a *New York Times* reporter to describe the multiple "brains" on Roosevelt's advisory team), the group most notably included Rexford Tugwell, Raymond Moley, and Adolph Berle. Moley, credited with bringing the group into existence, was a government professor who advocated for a new national tax policy to help the nation recover from its economic woes. Tugwell, who eventually focused his energy on the country's agricultural problems, saw an increased role for the federal government in setting wages and prices across the economy. Berle was a mediating influence, who often advised against a centrally controlled economy, but did see the role that the federal government could play in mediating the stark cycles of prosperity and depression that, if left unchecked, could result in the very situation in which the country presently found itself. Together, these men, along with others, advised

Roosevelt through the earliest days of the New Deal and helped to craft significant legislative programs for congressional review and approval.

INAUGURATION DAY: A NEW BEGINNING

March 4, 1933, dawned gray and rainy. Roosevelt rode in an open car along with outgoing president Hoover, facing the public, as he made his way to the U.S. Capitol. Hoover's mood was somber, still personally angry over his defeat in the general election the previous November; he refused to crack a smile at all during the ride among the crowd, despite Roosevelt's urging to the contrary. At the ceremony, Roosevelt rose with the aid of leg braces equipped under his specially tailored trousers and placed his hand on a Dutch family Bible as he took his solemn oath. At that very moment, the rain stopped and the sun began to shine directly on the platform, and those present would later claim that it was as though God himself was shining down on Roosevelt and the American people in that moment (Figure 26.4).

Figure 26.4 Roosevelt's inauguration was truly a day of new beginnings for the country. The sun breaking through the clouds as he was being sworn in became a metaphor for the hope that people felt at his presidency.

Bathed in the sunlight, Roosevelt delivered one of the most famous and oft-quoted inaugural addresses in history. He encouraged Americans to work with him to find solutions to the nation's problems and not to be paralyzed by fear into inaction. Borrowing a wartime analogy provided by Moley, who served as his speechwriter at the time, Roosevelt called upon all Americans to assemble and fight an essential battle against the forces of economic depression. He famously stated, "The only thing we have to fear is fear itself." Upon hearing his inaugural address, one observer in the crowd later commented, "Any man who can talk like that in times like these is worth every ounce of support a true American has." To borrow the popular song title of the day, "happy days were here again." Foregoing the traditional inaugural parties, the new president immediately returned to the White House to begin his work to save the nation.

Click and Explore

Visit the American Presidency Project (http://openstaxcollege.org/l/fdraug) to listen to Roosevelt's first inaugural speech and identify ways he conveyed optimism and a spirit of community to his listeners.

26.2 The First New Deal

By the end of this section, you should be able to:
- Identify the key pieces of legislation included in Roosevelt's "First New Deal"
- Assess the strengths, weaknesses, and general effectiveness of the First New Deal
- Explain Roosevelt's overall vision for addressing the structural problems in the U.S. economy

Much like a surgeon assessing the condition of an emergency room patient, Roosevelt began his administration with a broad, if not specific, strategy in mind: a combination of relief and recovery programs designed to first save the patient (in this case, the American people), and then to find a long-term cure (reform through federal regulation of the economy). What later became known as the "First New Deal" ushered in a wave of legislative activity seldom before seen in the history of the country. By the close of 1933, in an effort to stem the crisis, Congress had passed over fifteen significant pieces of legislation—many of the circulated bills allegedly still wet with ink from the printing presses as members voted upon them. Most bills could be grouped around issues of relief, recovery, and reform. At the outset of the First New Deal, specific goals included 1) bank reform; 2) job creation; 3) economic regulation; and 4) regional planning.

REFORM: THE BANKING CRISIS

When Roosevelt took office, he faced one of the worst moments in the country's banking history. States were in disarray. New York and Illinois had ordered the closure of their banks in the hopes of avoiding further "bank runs," which occurred when hundreds (if not thousands) of individuals ran to their banks to withdraw all of their savings. In all, over five thousand banks had been shuttered. Within forty-eight hours of his inauguration, Roosevelt proclaimed an official bank holiday and called Congress into a special session to address the crisis. The resulting Emergency Banking Act of 1933 was signed into law on March 9, 1933, a scant eight hours after Congress first saw it. The law officially took the country off the gold standard, a restrictive practice that, although conservative and traditionally viewed as safe, severely limited the circulation of paper money. Those who held gold were told to sell it to the U.S. Treasury for a discounted rate of a little over twenty dollars per ounce. Furthermore, dollar bills were no longer redeemable in gold. The law also gave the comptroller of currency the power to reorganize all national banks faced with insolvency, a level of federal oversight seldom seen prior to the Great Depression. Between March 11 and March 14, auditors from the Reconstruction Finance Corporation, the Treasury Department, and other federal agencies swept through the country, examining each bank. By March 15, 70 percent of the banks were declared solvent and allowed to reopen.

On March 12, the day before the banks were set to reopen, Roosevelt held his first "fireside chat" (Figure 26.5). In this initial radio address to the American people, he explained what the bank examiners had been doing over the previous week. He assured people that any bank open the next day had the federal government's stamp of approval. The combination of his reassuring manner and the promise that the government was addressing the problems worked wonders in changing the popular mindset. Just as the culture of panic had contributed to the country's downward spiral after the crash, so did this confidence-inducing move help to build it back up. Consumer confidence returned, and within weeks, close to $1 billion in cash and gold had been brought out from under mattresses and hidden bookshelves, and re-deposited in the nation's banks. The immediate crisis had been quelled, and the public was ready to believe in their new president.

Figure 26.5 Roosevelt's "fireside chats" provided an opportunity for him to speak directly to the American people, and the people were happy to listen. These radio addresses, commemorated at the Franklin D. Roosevelt Memorial in Washington, DC, with this bronze sculpture by George Segal, contributed to Roosevelt's tremendous popularity. (credit: Koshy Koshy)

DEFINING "AMERICAN"

✵ *The Power of Hearth and Home*

Fireside chats—Roosevelt's weekly radio addresses—underscored Roosevelt's savvy in understanding how best to reach people. Using simple terms and a reassuring tone, he invoked a family patriarch sitting by the fire, explaining to those who trusted him how he was working to help them. It is worth noting how he explained complex financial concepts quite simply, but at the same time, complimented the American people on their "intelligent support." One of his fireside chats is provided below:

> I recognize that the many proclamations from State capitols and from Washington, the legislation, the Treasury regulations, etc., couched for the most part in banking and legal terms, should be explained for the benefit of the average citizen. I owe this in particular because of the fortitude and good temper with which everybody has accepted the inconvenience and hardships of the banking holiday. I know that when you understand what we in Washington have been about I shall continue to have your cooperation as fully as I have had your sympathy and help during the past week. . . .
>
> The success of our whole great national program depends, of course, upon the cooperation of the public—on its intelligent support and use of a reliable system. . . . After all, there is an element in the readjustment of our financial system more important than currency, more important than gold, and that is the confidence of the people. Confidence and courage are the essentials of success in carrying out our plan. You people must have faith; you must not be stampeded by rumors or guesses. Let us unite in banishing fear. We have provided the machinery to restore our financial system; it is up to you to support and make it work. It is your problem no less than it is mine. Together we cannot fail.
>
> —Franklin D. Roosevelt, March 12, 1933

A huge part of Roosevelt's success in turning around the country can be seen in his addresses like these: He built support and galvanized the public. Ironically, Roosevelt, the man who famously said we have nothing to fear but fear itself, had a significant fear: fire. Being paralyzed with polio, he was very afraid of being left near a fireplace. But he knew the power of the hearth and home, and drew on this mental image to help the public view him the way that he hoped to be seen.

Click and Explore

Visit the American Presidency Project (http://openstaxcollege.org/l/fireside) to listen to one of Roosevelt's fireside chats. What kind of feeling does his language and demeanor evoke?

In June 1933, Roosevelt replaced the Emergency Banking Act with the more permanent Glass-Steagall Banking Act. This law prohibited commercial banks from engaging in investment banking, therefore stopping the practice of banks speculating in the stock market with deposits. This law also created the Federal Deposit Insurance Corporation, or FDIC, which insured personal bank deposits up to $2,500. Other measures designed to boost confidence in the overall economy beyond the banking system included passage of the Economy Act, which fulfilled Roosevelt's campaign pledge to reduce government spending by reducing salaries, including his own and those of the Congress. He also signed into law the Securities Act, which required full disclosure to the federal government from all corporations and investment banks that wanted to market stocks and bonds. Roosevelt also sought new revenue through the Beer Tax. As the Twenty-First Amendment, which would repeal the Eighteenth Amendment establishing Prohibition, moved towards ratification, this law authorized the manufacture of 3.2 percent beer and levied a tax on it.

THE FIRST HUNDRED DAYS

In his first hundred days in office, the new president pushed forward an unprecedented number of new bills, all geared towards stabilizing the economy, providing relief to individuals, creating jobs, and helping businesses. A sympathetic Democrat-controlled Congress helped propel his agenda forward.

Relief: Employment for the Masses

Even as he worked to rebuild the economy, Roosevelt recognized that the unemployed millions required jobs more quickly than the economy could provide. In a push to create new jobs, Roosevelt signed the Wagner-Peyser Act, creating the United States Employment Service, which promised states matching funds if they created local employment opportunities. He also authorized $500 million in direct grants through the Federal Emergency Relief Act (FERA). This money went directly to states to infuse relief agencies with the much-needed resources to help the nearly fifteen million unemployed. These two bills illustrate Roosevelt's dual purposes of providing short-term emergency help and building employment opportunities that would strengthen the economy in the long term.

Roosevelt was aware of the need for immediate help, but he mostly wanted to create more jobs. FERA overseer Harry Hopkins, who later was in charge of the Civil Works Administration (CWA), shared this sentiment. With Hopkins at its helm, the CWA, founded in early 1933, went on to put millions of men and women to work. At its peak, there were some four million Americans repairing bridges, building roads and airports, and undertaking other public projects. Another work program was the **Civilian Conservation Corps** Relief Act (CCC). The CCC provided government jobs for young men aged fourteen to twenty-four who came from relief families. They would earn thirty dollars per month planting trees, fighting forest fires, and refurbishing historic sites and parks, building an infrastructure that families would continue to enjoy for generations to come. Within the first two months, the CCC employed its first 250,000 men and eventually established about twenty-five hundred camps (Figure 26.6).

Figure 26.6 The CCC put hundreds of thousands of men to work on environmental projects around the country. Some call it the beginning of the modern environmentalist movement in the United States.

The various programs that made up the First New Deal are listed in the table below (Table 26.1).

Table 26.1 Key Programs from the First New Deal

New Deal Legislation	Years Enacted	Brief Description
Agricultural Adjustment Administration	1933–1935	Farm program designed to raise process by curtailing production
Civil Works Administration	1933–1934	Temporary job relief program
Civilian Conservation Corps	1933–1942	Employed young men to work in rural areas
Farm Credit Administration	1933-today	Low interest mortgages for farm owners
Federal Deposit Insurance Corporation	1933–today	Insure private bank deposits
Federal Emergency Relief Act	1933	Direct monetary relief to poor unemployed Americans
Glass-Steagall Act	1933	Regulate investment banking
Homeowners Loan Corporation	1933–1951	Government mortgages that allowed people to keep their homes
Indian Reorganization Act	1933	Abandoned federal policy of assimilation
National Recovery Administration	1933–1935	Industries agree to codes of fair practice to set price, wage, production levels
Public Works Administration	1933–1938	Large public works projects
Resettlement Administration	1933–1935	Resettles poor tenant farmers
Securities Act of 1933	1933–today	Created SEC; regulates stock transactions
Tennessee Valley Authority	1933–today	Regional development program; brought electrification to the valley

The final element of Roosevelt's efforts to provide relief to those in desperate straits was the Home Owners' Refinancing Act. Created by the Home Owners' Loan Corporation (HOLC), the program rescued homeowners from foreclosure by refinancing their mortgages. Not only did this save the homes of countless homeowners, but it also saved many of the small banks who owned the original mortgages by relieving them of that responsibility. Later New Deal legislation created the Federal Housing Authority, which eventually standardized the thirty-year mortgage and promoted the housing boom of the post-World War II era. A similar program, created through the Emergency Farm Mortgage Act and Farm Credit Act, provided the same service for farm mortgages.

Click and Explore

In this *American Experience (http://openstaxcollege.org/l/Maher)* interview, Neil Maher, author of *Nature's New Deal: The Civilian Conservation Corps and Roots of the Modern Environmental Movement*, provides a comprehensive look into what the CCC offered the country—and the president—on issues as diverse as economics, race, and recreation.

Rescuing Farms and Factories

While much of the legislation of the first hundred days focused on immediate relief and job creation through federal programs, Roosevelt was committed to addressing the underlying problems inherent in the American economy. In his efforts to do so, he created two of the most significant pieces of New Deal legislation: the Agricultural Adjustment Act (AAA) and the National Industry Recovery Act (NIRA).

Farms around the country were suffering, but from different causes. In the Great Plains, drought conditions meant that little was growing at all, while in the South, bumper crops and low prices meant that farmers could not sell their goods at prices that could sustain them. The AAA offered some direct relief: Farmers received $4.5 million through relief payments. But the larger part of the program paid southern farmers to reduce their production: Wheat, cotton, corn, hogs, tobacco, rice, and milk farmers were all eligible. Passed into law on May 12, 1933, it was designed to boost prices to a level that would alleviate rural poverty and restore profitability to American agriculture. These price increases would be achieved by encouraging farmers to limit production in order to increase demand while receiving cash payments in return. Corn producers would receive thirty cents per bushel for corn they did not grow. Hog farmers would get five dollars per head for hogs not raised. The program would be financed by a tax on processing plants, passed on to consumers in the form of higher prices.

This was a bold attempt to help farmers address the systemic problems of overproduction and lower commodity prices. Despite previous efforts to regulate farming through subsidies, never before had the federal government intervened on this scale; the notion of paying farmers *not* to produce crops was unheard of. One significant problem, however, was that, in some cases, there was already an excess of crops, in particular, cotton and hogs, which clogged the marketplace. A bumper crop in 1933, combined with the slow implementation of the AAA, led the government to order the plowing under of ten million acres of cotton, and the butchering of six million baby pigs and 200,000 sows. Although it worked to some degree—the price of cotton increased from six to twelve cents per pound—this move was deeply problematic. Critics saw it as the ultimate example of corrupt capitalism: a government destroying food, while its citizens were starving, in order to drive up prices.

Another problem plaguing this relief effort was the disparity between large commercial farms, which received the largest payments and set the quotas, and the small family farms that felt no relief. Large farms often cut production by laying off sharecroppers or evicting tenant farmers, making the program even worse for them than for small farm owners. Their frustration led to the creation of the Southern Tenant Farmers Union (STFU), an interracial organization that sought to gain government relief for these most disenfranchised of farmers. The STFU organized, protested, and won its members some wage increases through the mid-1930s, but the overall plight of these workers remained dismal. As a result, many of them followed the thousands of Dust Bowl refugees to California (Figure 26.7).

Figure 26.7 Sharecroppers and tenant farmers suffered enormously during the Great Depression. The STFU was created to help alleviate this suffering, but many farmers ending up taking to the road, along with other Dust Bowl refugees, on their way to California.

AMERICANA

⚙ *Labor Songs and the Southern Tenant Farmers Union*

> And if the growers get in the way, we're gonna roll right over them
> We're gonna roll right over them, we're gonna roll right over them
> And if the growers get in the way, we're gonna roll right over them
> We're gonna roll this union on
> —John Handcox, "Roll the Union On"

"Mean Things Happening in This Land," "Roll the Union On," and "Strike in Arkansas" are just a few of the folk songs written by John Handcox. A union organizer and STFU member, Handcox became the voice of the worker's struggle, writing dozens of songs that have continued to be sung by labor activists and folk singers over the years. Handcox joined the STFU in 1935, and used his songs to rally others, stating, "I found out singing was more inspiring than talking . . . to get the attention of the people."

Racially integrated and with active women members, the STFU was ahead of its time. Although criticized by other union leaders for its relationship with the Communist Party in creating the "Popular Front" for labor activism in 1934, the STFU succeeded in organizing strikes and bringing national attention to the issues that tenant farmers faced. While the programs Roosevelt put in place did not do enough to help these farmers, the STFU—and Handcox's music—remains a relevant part of the country's labor movement.

The AAA did succeed on some fronts. By the spring of 1934, farmers had formed over four thousand local committees, with more than three million farmers agreeing to participate. They signed individual contracts agreeing to take land out of production in return for government payments, and checks began to arrive by the end of 1934. For some farmers, especially those with large farms, the program spelled relief.

While Roosevelt hoped the AAA would help farms and farmers, he also sought aid for the beleaguered manufacturing sector. The Emergency Railroad Transportation Act created a national railroad office to encourage cooperation among different railroad companies, hoping to shore up an industry essential to the stability of the manufacturing sector, but one that had been devastated by mismanagement. More importantly, the NIRA suspended antitrust laws and allowed businesses and industries to work together in order to establish codes of fair competition, including issues of price setting and minimum wages. New Deal officials believed that allowing these collaborations would help industries stabilize prices and production levels in the face of competitive overproduction and declining profits; however, at the same time, many felt it important to protect workers from potentially unfair agreements.

A new government agency, the National Recovery Administration (NRA), was central to this plan, and mandated that businesses accept a code that included minimum wages and maximum work hours. In order to protect workers from potentially unfair agreements among factory owners, every industry had its own "code of fair practice" that included workers' rights to organize and use collective bargaining to ensure that wages rose with prices (Figure 26.8). Headed by General Hugh S. Johnson, the NRA worked to create over five hundred different codes for different industries. The administration of such a complex plan naturally created its own problems. While codes for key industries such as automotive and steel made sense, Johnson pushed to create similar codes for dog food manufacturers, those who made shoulder pads for women's clothing, and even burlesque shows (regulating the number of strippers in any one show).

(a)   (b)

Figure 26.8 Consumers were encouraged to buy from companies displaying the Blue Eagle (a), the logo signifying compliance with the new NRA regulations. With talons gripping a gear, representing industry, and lightning bolts, representing power, the eagle (b) was intended to be a symbol of economic recovery.

The NIRA also created the Public Works Administration (PWA). The PWA set aside $3.3 billion to build public projects such as highways, federal buildings, and military bases. Although this program suffered from political squabbles over appropriations for projects in various congressional districts, as well as significant underfunding of public housing projects, it ultimately offered some of the most lasting benefits of the NIRA. Secretary of the Interior Harold Ickes ran the program, which completed over thirty-four thousand projects, including the Golden Gate Bridge in San Francisco and the Queens-Midtown Tunnel in New York. Between 1933 and 1939, the PWA accounted for the construction of over one-third of all new hospitals and 70 percent of all new public schools in the country.

Another challenge faced by the NRA was that the provision granting workers the right to organize appeared to others as a mandate to do so. In previously unorganized industries, such as oil and gas, rubber, and service occupations, workers now sought groups that would assist in their organization, bolstered by the encouragement they now felt from the government. The Communist Party took advantage of the opportunity to assist in the hope of creating widespread protests against the American industrial structure. The number of strikes nationwide doubled between 1932 and 1934, with over 1.5 million workers going on strike in 1934 alone, often in protests that culminated in bloodshed. A strike at the Auto-Lite plant in Toledo, Ohio, that summer resulted in ten thousand workers from other factories joining in sympathy with their fellow workers to attack potential strike-breakers with stones and bricks. Simultaneously in

Minneapolis, a teamsters strike resulted in frequent, bloody confrontations between workers and police, leading the governor to contemplate declaring martial law before the companies agreed to negotiate better wages and conditions for the workers. Finally, a San Francisco strike among 14,000 longshoremen closed the city's waterfront and eventually led to a city-wide general strike of over 130,000 workers, essentially paralyzing the city. Clashes between workers, and police and National Guardsmen left many strikers bloodied, and at least two dead.

Although Roosevelt's relief efforts provided jobs to many and benefitted communities with the construction of several essential building projects, the violence that erupted amid clashes between organized labor and factories backed by police and the authorities exposed a fundamental flaw in the president's approach. Immediate relief did not address long-existing, inherent class inequities that left workers exposed to poor working conditions, low wages, long hours, and little protection. For many workers, life on the job was not much better than life as an unemployed American. Employment programs may have put men back to work and provided much needed relief, but the fundamental flaws in the system required additional attention—attention that Roosevelt was unable to pay in the early days of the New Deal. Critics were plentiful, and the president would be forced to address them in the years ahead.

Regional Planning

Regionally, Roosevelt's work was most famously seen in the **Tennessee Valley Authority** (TVA) (Figure 26.9), a federal agency tasked with the job of planning and developing the area through flood control, reforestation, and hydroelectric power. Employing several thousand Americans on a project that Roosevelt envisioned as a template for future regional redevelopment, the TVA revitalized a river valley that landowners had badly over-farmed, leaving behind eroded soil that lacked essential nutrients for future farming. Under the direction of David Lilienthal, beginning in 1933, the TVA workers erected a series of dams to harness the Tennessee River in the creation of much-needed hydroelectric power. The arrival of both electric lighting and machinery to the region eased the lives of the people who lived there, as well as encouraged industrial growth. The TVA also included an educational component, teaching farmers important lessons about crop rotation, soil replenishment, fertilizing, and reforestation.

Figure 26.9 The TVA helped a struggling part of the country through the creation of jobs, and flood control and reforestation programs. The Wilson Dam, shown here, is one of nine TVA dams on the Tennessee River. (credit: United States Geological Survey)

The TVA was not without its critics, however, most notably among the fifteen thousand families who were displaced due to the massive construction projects. Although eventually the project benefited farmers with the introduction of new farming and fertilizing techniques, as well as the added benefit of electric power, many local citizens were initially mistrustful of the TVA and the federal government's agenda. Likewise, as with several other New Deal programs, women did not directly benefit from these employment

Download for free at http://cnx.org/content/col11740/latest/

opportunities, as they were explicitly excluded for the benefit of men who most Americans still considered the family's primary breadwinner. However, with the arrival of electricity came new industrial ventures, including several textile mills up and down the valley, several of which offered employment to women. Throughout his presidency, Roosevelt frequently pointed to the TVA as one of the glowing accomplishments of the New Deal and its ability to bring together the machinery of the federal government along with private interests to revitalize a regional economy. Just months before his death in 1945, he continued to speak of the possibility of creating other regional authorities throughout the country.

ASSESSING THE FIRST NEW DEAL

While many were pleased with the president's bold plans, there were numerous critics of the New Deal, discussed in the following section. The New Deal was far from perfect, but Roosevelt's quickly implemented policies reversed the economy's long slide. It put new capital into ailing banks. It rescued homeowners and farmers from foreclosure and helped people keep their homes. It offered some direct relief to the unemployed poor. It gave new incentives to farmers and industry alike, and put people back to work in an effort to both create jobs and boost consumer spending. The total number of working Americans rose from twenty-four to twenty-seven million between 1933 and 1935, in contrast to the seven-million-worker decline during the Hoover administration. Perhaps most importantly, the First New Deal changed the pervasive pessimism that had held the country in its grip since the end of 1929. For the first time in years, people had hope.

It was the hard work of Roosevelt's advisors—the "Brains Trust" of scholars and thinkers from leading universities—as well as Congress and the American public who helped the New Deal succeed as well as it did. Ironically, it was the American people's volunteer spirit, so extolled by Hoover, that Roosevelt was able to harness. The first hundred days of his administration was not a master plan that Roosevelt dreamed up and executed on his own. In fact, it was not a master plan at all, but rather a series of, at times, disjointed efforts made from different assumptions. But after taking office and analyzing the crisis, Roosevelt and his advisors did feel that they had a larger sense of what had caused the Great Depression and thus attempted a variety of solutions to fix it. They believed that it was caused by abuses on the part of a small group of bankers and businessmen, aided by Republican policies that built wealth for a few at the expense of many. The answer, they felt, was to root out these abuses through banking reform, as well as adjust production and consumption of both farm and industrial goods. This adjustment would come about by increasing the purchasing power of everyday people, as well as through regulatory policies like the NRA and AAA. While it may seem counterintuitive to raise crop prices and set prices on industrial goods, Roosevelt's advisors sought to halt the deflationary spiral and economic uncertainty that had prevented businesses from committing to investments and consumers from parting with their money.

26.3 The Second New Deal

By the end of this section, you should be able to:
- Identify key pieces of legislation from the Second New Deal
- Assess the entire New Deal, especially in terms of its impact on women, African Americans, and Native Americans

Roosevelt won his second term in a landslide, but that did not mean he was immune to criticism. His critics came from both the left and the right, with conservatives deeply concerned over his expansion of government spending and power, and liberals angered that he had not done more to help those still struggling. Adding to Roosevelt's challenges, the Supreme Court struck down several key elements of the First New Deal, angering Roosevelt and spurring him to try and stack the courts in his second term.

Still, he entered his new term with the unequivocal support of the voting public, and he wasted no time beginning the second phase of his economic plan. While the First New Deal focused largely on stemming the immediate suffering of the American people, the Second New Deal put in place legislation that changed America's social safety net for good.

CHALLENGES FROM CRITICS ON ALL SIDES

While many people supported Roosevelt, especially in the first few years of his presidency, the New Deal did receive significant criticism, both from conservatives who felt that it was a radical agenda to ruin the country's model of free enterprise, and from liberals who felt that it did not provide enough help to those who needed it most (Figure 26.10).

Figure 26.10 Roosevelt used previously unheard of levels of government power in his attempt to push the country out of the Great Depression, as artist Joseph Parrish depicts here in this 1937 *Chicago Tribune* cartoon. While critics on the left felt that he had not done enough, critics on the right felt that his use of power was frighteningly close to fascism and socialism.

Industrialists and wealthy Americans led the conservative criticism against the president. Whether attacking his character or simply stating that he was moving away from American values toward fascism and socialism, they sought to undermine his power and popularity. Most notably, the American Liberty League—comprised largely of conservative Democrats who lamented the excesses of several of Roosevelt's New Deal programs—labeled the AAA as fascist and proclaimed later New Deal programs to be key threats to the very nature of democracy. Additional criticism came from the National Association of Manufacturers, which urged businessmen to outright ignore portions of the NRA that promoted collective bargaining, as well as subsequent labor protection legislation. In 1935, the U.S. Supreme Court dealt the most crushing blow to Roosevelt's vision, striking down several key pieces of the New Deal as unconstitutional. They found that both the AAA and the NIRA overreached federal authority. The negation of some of his most ambitious economic recovery efforts frustrated Roosevelt greatly, but he was powerless to stop it at this juncture.

Meanwhile, others felt that Roosevelt had not done enough. Dr. Francis E. Townsend of California was one who felt that Roosevelt had failed to adequately address the country's tremendous problems. Townsend, who was a retired dentist, proposed an expansive pension plan for the elderly. The Townsend Plan, as it was known, gained a great deal of popularity: It recommended paying every citizen over sixty who retired from work the sum of $200 per month, provided they spend it in thirty days. Another figure who gained national attention was Father Charles Coughlin. He was a "radio priest" from Michigan who, although he initially supported the New Deal, subsequently argued that Roosevelt stopped far too short in his defense of labor, monetary reform, and the nationalization of key industries. The president's plan, he proclaimed, was inadequate. He created the National Union for Social Justice and used his weekly radio show to gain followers.

A more direct political threat to Roosevelt came from muckraker Upton Sinclair, who pursued the California governorship in 1934 through a campaign based upon criticism of the New Deal's shortcomings. In his "End Poverty in California" program, Sinclair called for a progressive income tax, a pension program for the elderly, and state seizure of factories and farms where property taxes remained unpaid. The state would then offer jobs to the unemployed to work those farms and factories in a cooperative mode. Although Sinclair lost the election to his Republican opponent, he did draw local and national attention to several of his ideas.

The biggest threat to the president, however, came from corrupt but beloved Louisiana senator Huey "Kingfish" Long (Figure 26.11). His disapproval of Roosevelt came in part from his own ambitions for higher office; Long stated that the president was not doing enough to help people and proposed his own Share Our Wealth program. Under this plan, Long recommended the liquidation of all large personal fortunes in order to fund direct payments to less fortunate Americans. He foresaw giving $5,000 to every family, $2,500 to every worker, as well as a series of elderly pensions and education funds. Despite his questionable math, which numerous economists quickly pointed out rendered his program unworkable, by 1935, Long had a significant following of over four million people. If he had not been assassinated by the son-in-law of a local political rival, he may well have been a contender against Roosevelt for the 1936 presidential nomination.

Figure 26.11 Huey P. Long was a charismatic populist and governor of Louisiana from 1928 to 1932. In 1932, he became a member of the U.S. Senate and would have been a serious rival for Roosevelt in the 1936 presidential election if his life had not been cut short by an assassin's bullet.

ANSWERING THE CHALLENGE

Roosevelt recognized that some of the criticisms of the New Deal were valid. Although he was still reeling from the Supreme Court's invalidation of key statutes, he decided to face his re-election bid in 1936 by unveiling another wave of legislation that he dubbed the Second New Deal. In the first week of June

1935, Roosevelt called congressional leaders into the White House and gave them a list of "must-pass" legislation that he wanted before they adjourned for the summer. Whereas the policies of the first hundred days may have shored up public confidence and stopped the most drastic of the problems, the second hundred days changed the face of America for the next sixty years.

The Banking Act of 1935 was the most far-reaching revision of banking laws since the creation of the Federal Reserve System in 1914. Previously, regional reserve banks, particularly the New York Reserve Bank—controlled by the powerful Morgan and Rockefeller families—had dominated policy-making at the Federal Reserve. Under the new system, there would be a seven-member board of governors to oversee regional banks. They would have control over reserve requirements, discount rates, board member selection, and more. Not surprisingly, this new board kept initial interest rates quite low, allowing the federal government to borrow billions of dollars of additional cash to fund major relief and recovery programs.

In 1935, Congress also passed the Emergency Relief Appropriation Act, which authorized the single largest expenditure at that time in the country's history: $4.8 billion. Almost one-third of those funds were invested in a new relief agency, the **Works Progress Administration** (WPA). Harry Hopkins, formerly head of the CWA, took on the WPA and ran it until 1943. In that time, the program provided employment relief to over eight million Americans, or approximately 20 percent of the country's workforce. The WPA funded the construction of more than 2,500 hospitals, 5,900 schools, 570,000 miles of road, and more. The WPA also created the Federal One Project, which employed approximately forty thousand artists in theater, art, music, and writing. They produced state murals, guidebooks, concerts, and drama performances all around the country (Figure 26.12). Additionally, the project funded the collection of oral histories, including those of former slaves, which provided a valuable addition to the nation's understanding of slave life. Finally, the WPA also included the National Youth Administration (NYA), which provided work-study jobs to over 500,000 college students and four million high school students.

Figure 26.12 Painted by artists funded by the Federal One Project, this section of *Ohio*, a mural located in the Bellevue, Ohio post office, illustrates a busy industrial scene. Artists painted the communities where they lived, thus creating visions of farms, factories, urban life, harvest celebrations, and more that still reflect the life and work of that era. (credit: Works Progress Administration)

Click and Explore

Browse the *Born in Slavery* collection (http://openstaxcollege.org/l/slavery) to examine personal accounts of former slaves, recorded between 1936 and 1938, as part of the Federal Writers' Project of the WPA.

With the implementation of the Second New Deal, Roosevelt also created the country's present-day social safety net. The **Social Security** Act established programs intended to help the most vulnerable: the elderly, the unemployed, the disabled, and the young. It included a pension fund for all retired people—except domestic workers and farmers, which therefore left many women and African Americans beyond the scope of its benefits—over the age of sixty-five, to be paid through a payroll tax on both employee and employer. Related to this act, Congress also passed a law on unemployment insurance, to be funded by a tax on employers, and programs for unwed mothers, as well as for those who were blind, deaf, or disabled. It is worth noting that some elements of these reforms were pulled from Roosevelt detractors Coughlin and Townsend; the popularity of their movements gave the president more leverage to push forward this type of legislation.

To the benefit of industrial workers, Roosevelt signed into law the Wagner Act, also known as the National Labor Relations Act. The protections previously afforded to workers under the NIRA were inadvertently lost when the Supreme Court struck down the original law due to larger regulatory concerns, leaving workers vulnerable. Roosevelt sought to salvage this important piece of labor legislation, doing so with the Wagner Act. The act created the National Labor Relations Board (NLRB) to once again protect American workers' right to unionize and bargain collectively, as well as to provide a federal vehicle for labor grievances to be heard. Although roundly criticized by the Republican Party and factory owners, the Wagner Act withstood several challenges and eventually received constitutional sanction by the U.S. Supreme Court in 1937. The law received the strong support of John L. Lewis and the Congress of Industrial Organizations who had long sought government protection of industrial unionism, from the time they split from the American Federation of Labor in 1935 over disputes on whether to organize workers along craft or industrial lines. Following passage of the law, Lewis began a widespread publicity campaign urging industrial workers to join "the president's union." The relationship was mutually beneficial to Roosevelt, who subsequently received the endorsement of Lewis's United Mine Workers union in the 1936 presidential election, along with a sizeable $500,000 campaign contribution. The Wagner Act permanently established government-secured workers' rights and protections from their employers, and it marked the beginning of labor's political support for the Democratic Party.

The various programs that made up the Second New Deal are listed in the table below (Table 26.2).

Table 26.2 Key Programs from the Second New Deal

New Deal Legislation	Years Enacted	Brief Description
Fair Labor Standards Act	1938–today	Established minimum wage and forty-hour workweek
Farm Security Administration	1935–today	Provides poor farmers with education and economic support programs

Table 26.2 Key Programs from the Second New Deal

New Deal Legislation	Years Enacted	Brief Description
Federal Crop Insurance Corporation	1938–today	Insures crops and livestock against loss of revenue
National Labor Relations Act	1935–today	Recognized right of workers to unionize & collectively bargain
National Youth Administration	1935–1939 (part of WPA)	Part-time employment for college and high school students
Rural Electrification Administration	1935–today	Provides public utilities to rural areas
Social Security Act	1935–today	Aid to retirees, unemployed, disabled
Surplus Commodities Program	1936–today	Provides food to the poor (still exists in Food Stamps program)
Works Progress Administration	1935–1943	Jobs program (including artists and youth)

THE FINAL PIECES

Roosevelt entered the 1936 presidential election on a wave of popularity, and he beat Republican opponent Alf Landon by a nearly unanimous Electoral College vote of 523 to 8. Believing it to be his moment of strongest public support, Roosevelt chose to exact a measure of revenge against the U.S. Supreme Court for challenging his programs and to pressure them against challenging his more recent Second New Deal provisions. To this end, Roosevelt created the informally named "**Supreme Court Packing Plan**" and tried to pack the court in his favor by expanding the number of justices and adding new ones who supported his views. His plan was to add one justice for every current justice over the age of seventy who refused to step down. This would have allowed him to add six more justices, expanding the bench from nine to fifteen. Opposition was quick and thorough from both the Supreme Court and Congress, as well as from his own party. The subsequent retirement of Justice Van Devanter from the court, as well as the sudden death of Senator Joe T. Robinson, who championed Roosevelt's plan before the Senate, all but signaled Roosevelt's defeat. However, although he never received the support to make these changes, Roosevelt appeared to succeed in politically intimidating the current justices into supporting his newer programs, and they upheld both the Wagner Act and the Social Security Act. Never again during his presidency would the Supreme Court strike down any significant elements of his New Deal.

Roosevelt was not as successful in addressing the nation's growing deficit. When he entered the presidency in 1933, Roosevelt did so with traditionally held fiscal beliefs, including the importance of a balanced budget in order to maintain public confidence in federal government operations. However, the severe economic conditions of the depression quickly convinced the president of the importance of government spending to create jobs and relief for the American people. As he commented to a crowd in Pittsburgh in 1936, "To balance our budget in 1933 or 1934 or 1935 would have been a crime against the American people. To do so . . . we should have had to set our face against human suffering with callous indifference. When Americans suffered, we refused to pass by on the other side. Humanity came first." However, after his successful re-election, Roosevelt anticipated that the economy would recover enough by late 1936 that he could curtail spending by 1937. This reduction in spending, he hoped, would curb the deficit. As the early months of 1937 unfolded, Roosevelt's hopes seemed supported by the most recent economic snapshot of the country. Production, wages, and profits had all returned to pre-1929 levels, while unemployment was at its lowest rate in the decade, down from 25 percent to 14 percent. But no sooner did Roosevelt cut spending when a recession hit. Two million Americans were newly out of work as unemployment quickly rose by 5 percent and industrial production declined by a third. Breadlines began to build again, while banks prepared to close.

Historians continue to debate the causes of this recession within a depression. Some believe the fear of increased taxes forced factory owners to curtail planned expansion; others blame the Federal Reserve for tightening the nation's money supply. Roosevelt, however, blamed the downturn on his decision to significantly curtail federal government spending in job relief programs such as the WPA. Several of his closest advisors, including Harry Hopkins, Henry Wallace, and others, urged him to adopt the new economic theory espoused by British economic John Maynard Keynes, who argued that deficit spending was necessary in advanced capitalist economies in order to maintain employment and stimulate consumer spending. Convinced of the necessity of such an approach, Roosevelt asked Congress in the spring of 1938 for additional emergency relief spending. Congress immediately authorized $33 billion for PWA and WPA work projects. Although World War II would provide the final impetus for lasting economic recovery, Roosevelt's willingness to adapt in 1938 avoided another disaster.

Roosevelt signed the last substantial piece of New Deal legislation in the summer of 1938. The Fair Labor Standards Act established a federal minimum wage—at the time, forty cents per hour—a maximum workweek of forty hours (with an opportunity for four additional hours of work at overtime wages), and prohibited child labor for those under age sixteen. Roosevelt was unaware that the war would soon dominate his legacy, but this proved to be his last major piece of economic legislation in a presidency that changed the fabric of the country forever.

IN THE FINAL ANALYSIS

The legacy of the New Deal is in part seen in the vast increase in national power: The federal government accepted responsibility for the nation's economic stability and prosperity. In retrospect, the majority of historians and economists judge it to have been a tremendous success. The New Deal not only established minimum standards for wages, working conditions, and overall welfare, it also allowed millions of Americans to hold onto their homes, farms, and savings. It laid the groundwork for an agenda of expanded federal government influence over the economy that continued through President Harry Truman's "Fair Deal" in the 1950s and President Lyndon Johnson's call for a "Great Society" in the 1960s. The New Deal state that embraced its responsibility for the citizens' welfare and proved willing to use its power and resources to spread the nation's prosperity lasted well into the 1980s, and many of its tenets persist today. Many would also agree that the postwar economic stability of the 1950s found its roots in the stabilizing influences introduced by social security, the job stability that union contracts provided, and federal housing mortgage programs introduced in the New Deal. The environment of the American West in particular, benefited from New Deal projects such as the Soil Conservation program.

Still, Roosevelt's programs also had their critics. Following the conservative rise initiated by presidential candidate Barry Goldwater in 1964, and most often associated with the Ronald Reagan era of the 1980s, critics of the welfare state pointed to Roosevelt's presidency as the start of a slippery slope towards entitlement and the destruction of the individualist spirit upon which the United States had presumably developed in the nineteenth and early twentieth centuries. Although the growth of the GDP between 1934 and 1940 approached an average of 7.5 percent—higher than in any other peacetime period in U.S. history, critics of the New Deal point out that unemployment still hovered around 15 percent in 1940. While the New Deal resulted in some environmental improvements, it also inaugurated a number of massive infrastructural projects, such as the Grand Coulee Dam on the Columbia River, that came with grave environmental consequences. And other shortcomings of the New Deal were obvious and deliberate at the time.

African Americans under the New Deal

Critics point out that not all Americans benefited from the New Deal. African Americans in particular were left out, with overt discrimination in hiring practices within the federal job programs, such as the CCC, CWA, and WPA. The NRA was oftentimes criticized as the "Negro Run Around" or "Negroes Ruined Again" program. As well, the AAA left tenant farmers and sharecroppers, many of whom were black, with no support. Even Social Security originally excluded domestic workers, a primary source of employment for African American women. Facing such criticism early in his administration, Roosevelt undertook some efforts to ensure a measure of equality in hiring practices for the relief agencies, and opportunities began to present themselves by 1935. The WPA eventually employed 350,000 African Americans annually, accounting for nearly 15 percent of its workforce. By the close of the CCC in 1938, this program had employed over 300,000 African Americans, increasing the black percentage of its workforce from 3 percent at the outset to nearly 11 percent at its close. Likewise, in 1934, the PWA began to require that all government projects under its purview hire African Americans using a quota that reflected their percentage of the local population being served. Additionally, among several important WPA projects, the Federal One Project included a literacy program that eventually reached over one million African American children, helping them learn how to read and write.

On the issue of race relations themselves, Roosevelt has a mixed legacy. Within his White House, Roosevelt had a number of African American appointees, although most were in minor positions. Unofficially, Roosevelt relied upon advice from the Federal Council on Negro Affairs, also known as his "Black Cabinet." This group included a young Harvard economist, Dr. Robert Weaver, who subsequently became the nation's first black cabinet secretary in 1966, as President Lyndon Johnson's Secretary of Housing and Urban Development. Aubrey Williams, the director of the NYA, hired more black administrators than any other federal agency, and appointed them to oversee projects throughout the country. One key figure in the NYA was Mary McLeod Bethune (Figure 26.13), a prominent African American educator tapped by Roosevelt to act as the director of the NYA's Division of Negro Affairs. Bethune had been a spokesperson and an educator for years; with this role, she became one of the president's foremost African American advisors. During his presidency, Roosevelt became the first to appoint a black federal judge, as well as the first commander-in-chief to promote an African American to brigadier general. Most notably, he became the first president to publicly speak against lynching as a "vile form of collective murder."

Figure 26.13 This photo of Eleanor Roosevelt and Mary McLeod Bethune (second from left) was taken at the opening of Midway Hall, a federal building to house female African American government workers. Bethune was sometimes criticized for working with those in power, but her willingness to build alliances contributed to success in raising money and support for her causes.

Download for free at http://cnx.org/content/col11740/latest/

MY STORY

✦ *Mary McLeod Bethune on Racial Justice*

Democracy is for me, and for twelve million black Americans, a goal towards which our nation is marching. It is a dream and an ideal in whose ultimate realization we have a deep and abiding faith. For me, it is based on Christianity, in which we confidently entrust our destiny as a people. Under God's guidance in this great democracy, we are rising out of the darkness of slavery into the light of freedom. Here my race has been afforded [the] opportunity to advance from a people 80 percent illiterate to a people 80 percent literate; from abject poverty to the ownership and operation of a million farms and 750,000 homes; from total disfranchisement to participation in government; from the status of chattels to recognized contributors to the American culture.

When Mary McLeod Bethune spoke these words, she spoke on behalf of a race of American citizens for whom the Great Depression was much more than economic hardship. For African Americans, the Depression once again exposed the racism and inequality that gripped the nation economically, socially, and politically. Her work as a member of President Franklin Roosevelt's unofficial "Black Cabinet" as well as the Director of the Division of Negro Affairs for the NYA, presented her an opportunity to advance African American causes on all fronts—but especially in the area of black literacy. As part of the larger WPA, she also influenced employment programs in the arts and public work sectors, and routinely had the president's ear on matters related to racial justice.

Click and Explore

Listen to this audio clip (http://openstaxcollege.org/l/bethune) of Eleanor Roosevelt interviewing Mary McLeod Bethune. By listening to her talking to Bethune and offering up her support, it becomes clear how compelling the immensely popular first lady was when speaking about programs of close personal interest to her. How do you think this would have been received by Roosevelt's supporters?

However, despite these efforts, Roosevelt also understood the precariousness of his political position. In order to maintain a coalition of Democrats to support his larger relief and recovery efforts, Roosevelt could not afford to alienate Southern Democrats who might easily bolt should he openly advocate for civil rights. While he spoke about the importance of anti-lynching legislation, he never formally pushed Congress to propose such a law. He did publicly support the abolition of the poll tax, which Congress eventually accomplished in 1941. Likewise, although agency directors adopted changes to ensure job opportunities for African Americans at the federal level, at the local level, few advancements were made, and African Americans remained at the back of the employment lines. Despite such failures, however, Roosevelt deserves credit for acknowledging the importance of race relations and civil rights. At the federal level, more than any of his predecessors since the Civil War, Roosevelt remained aware of the role that the federal government can play in initiating important discussions about civil rights, as well as encouraging the development of a new cadre of civil rights leaders.

Although unable to bring about sweeping civil rights reforms for African Americans in the early stages of his administration, Roosevelt was able to work with Congress to significantly improve the lives of Indians. In 1934, he signed into law the Indian Reorganization Act (sometimes referred to as the "Indian New Deal"). This law formally abandoned the assimilationist policies set forth in the Dawes Severalty Act of

1887. Rather than forcing Indians to adapt to American culture, the new program encouraged them to develop forms of local self-government, as well as to preserve their artifacts and heritage. John Collier, the Commissioner on Indian Bureau Affairs from 1933 to 1945, championed this legislation and saw it as an opportunity to correct past injustices that land allotment and assimilation had wrought upon Indians. Although the re-establishment of communal tribal lands would prove to be difficult, Collier used this law to convince federal officials to return nearly two million acres of government-held land to various tribes in order to move the process along. Although subsequent legislation later circumscribed the degree to which tribes were allowed to self-govern on reservations, Collier's work is still viewed as a significant step in improving race relations with Indians and preserving their heritage.

Women and the New Deal

For women, Roosevelt's policies and practices had a similarly mixed effect. Wage discrimination in federal jobs programs was rampant, and relief policies encouraged women to remain home and leave jobs open for men. This belief was well in line with the gender norms of the day. Several federal relief programs specifically forbade husbands and wives' both drawing jobs or relief from the same agency. The WPA became the first specific New Deal agency to openly hire women—specifically widows, single women, and the wives of disabled husbands. While they did not take part in construction projects, these women did undertake sewing projects to provide blankets and clothing to hospitals and relief agencies. Likewise, several women took part in the various Federal One art projects. Despite the obvious gender limitations, many women strongly supported Roosevelt's New Deal, as much for its direct relief handouts for women as for its employment opportunities for men. One such woman was Mary (Molly) Dewson. A longtime activist in the women's suffrage movement, Dewson worked for women's rights and ultimately rose to be the Director of the Women's Division of the Democratic Party. Dewson and Mary McLeod Bethune, the national champion of African American education and literacy who rose to the level of Director of the Division of Negro Affairs for the NYA, understood the limitations of the New Deal, but also the opportunities for advancement it presented during very trying times. Rather than lamenting what Roosevelt could not or would not do, they felt, and perhaps rightly so, that Roosevelt would do more than most to help women and African Americans achieve a piece of the new America he was building.

Among the few, but notable, women who directly impacted Roosevelt's policies was Frances Perkins, who as Secretary of Labor was the first female member of any presidential cabinet, and First Lady Eleanor Roosevelt, who was a strong and public advocate for social causes. Perkins, one of only two original Cabinet members to stay with Roosevelt for his entire presidency, was directly involved in the administration of the CCC, PWA, NRA, and the Social Security Act. Among several important measures, she took greatest pleasure in championing minimum wage statutes as well as the penultimate piece of New Deal legislation, the Fair Labor Standards Act. Roosevelt came to trust Perkins' advice with few questions or concerns, and steadfastly supported her work through the end of his life (Figure 26_03_Perkins).

(a)   (b)

Figure 26.14   After leaving her post as head of the Women's Division of the Democratic Party, Molly Dewson (a) later accepted an appointment to the Social Security Board, working with fellow board members Arthur J. Altmeyer and George E. Bigge, shown here in 1937. Another influential advisor to President Franklin Roosevelt was Frances Perkins (b), who, as U.S. Secretary of Labor, graced the cover of *Time* magazine on August 14, 1933.

DEFINING "AMERICAN"

✪ *Molly Dewson and Women Democrats*

In her effort to get President Roosevelt re-elected in 1936, Dewson commented, "We don't make the old-fashioned plea to the women that our nominee is charming, and all that. We appeal to the intelligence of the country's women. Ours were economic issues and we found the women ready to listen."

As head of the Women's Division of the Democratic National Committee (DNC) in 1932, Molly Dewson proved to be an influential supporter of President Franklin Roosevelt and one of his key advisors regarding issues pertaining to women's rights. Agreeing with First Lady Eleanor Roosevelt that "Women must learn to play the games as men do," Dewson worked diligently in her position with the DNC to ensure that women could serve as delegates and alternates to the national conventions. Her approach, and her realization that women were intelligent enough to make rational choices, greatly appealed to Roosevelt. Her methods were perhaps not too different from his own, as he spoke to the public through his fireside chats. Dewson's impressive organizational skills on behalf of the party earned her the nickname "the little general" from President Roosevelt.

However, Eleanor Roosevelt, more so than any other individual, came to represent the strongest influence upon the president; and she used her unique position to champion several causes for women, African Americans, and the rural poor (Figure 26.15). She married Franklin Roosevelt, who was her fifth cousin, in 1905 and subsequently had six children, one of whom died at only seven months old. A strong supporter of her husband's political ambitions, Eleanor campaigned by his side through the failed vice-presidential bid in 1920 and on his behalf after he was diagnosed with polio in 1921. When she discovered letters of her husband's affair with her social secretary, Lucy Mercer, the marriage became less one of romance and more one of a political partnership that would continue—strained at times—until the president's death in 1945.

Figure 26.15 Eleanor Roosevelt travelled the country to promote New Deal programs. Here she visits a WPA nursery school in Des Moines, Iowa, on June 8, 1936. (credit: FDR Presidential Library & Museum)

Historians agree that the first lady used her presence in the White House, in addition to the leverage of her failed marriage and knowledge of her husband's infidelities, to her advantage. She promoted several causes that the president himself would have had difficulty championing at the time. From newspaper and magazine articles she authored, to a busy travel schedule that saw her regularly cross the country, the first lady sought to remind Americans that their plight was foremost on the minds of all working in the White House. Eleanor was so active in her public appearances that, by 1940, she began holding regular press conferences to answer reporters' questions. Among her first substantial projects was the creation of Arthurdale—a resettlement community for displaced coal miners in West Virginia. Although the planned community became less of an administration priority as the years progressed (eventually folding in 1940), for seven years, Eleanor remained committed to its success as a model of assistance for the rural poor.

Exposed to issues of racial segregation in the Arthurdale experiment, Eleanor subsequently supported many civil rights causes through the remainder of the Roosevelt presidency. When it further became clear that racial discrimination was rampant in the administration of virtually all New Deal job programs—especially in the southern states—she continued to pressure her husband for remedies. In 1934, she openly lobbied for passage of the federal anti-lynching bill that the president privately supported but could not politically endorse. Despite the subsequent failure of the Senate to pass such legislation, Eleanor succeeded in arranging a meeting between her husband and then-NAACP president Walter White to discuss anti-lynching and other pertinent calls for civil rights legislation.

White was only one of Eleanor's African American guests to the White House. Breaking with precedent, and much to the disdain of many White House officials, the first lady routinely invited prominent African Americans to dine with her and the president. Most notably, when the Daughters of the American Revolution (DAR) refused to permit internationally renowned black opera contralto Marian Anderson to sing in Constitution Hall, Eleanor resigned her membership in the DAR and arranged for Anderson to sing at a public concert on the steps of the Lincoln Memorial, followed by her appearance at a state dinner at the White House in honor of the king and queen of England. With regard to race relations in particular, Eleanor Roosevelt was able to accomplish what her husband—for delicate political reasons—could not: become the administration's face for civil rights.

Key Terms

Brains Trust an unofficial advisory cabinet to President Franklin Roosevelt, originally gathered while he was governor of New York, to present possible solutions to the nations' problems; among its prominent members were Rexford Tugwell, Raymond Moley, and Adolph Berle

Civilian Conservation Corps a public program for unemployed young men from relief families who were put to work on conservation and land management projects around the country

interregnum the period between the election and the inauguration of a new president; when economic conditions worsened significantly during the four-month lag between Roosevelt's win and his move into the Oval Office, Congress amended the Constitution to limit this period to two months

Social Security a series of programs designed to help the population's most vulnerable—the unemployed, those over age sixty-five, unwed mothers, and the disabled—through various pension, insurance, and aid programs

Supreme Court Packing Plan Roosevelt's plan, after being reelected, to pack the Supreme Court with an additional six justices, one for every justice over seventy who refused to step down

Tennessee Valley Authority a federal agency tasked with the job of planning and developing the area through flood control, reforestation, and hydroelectric power projects

Works Progress Administration a program run by Harry Hopkins that provided jobs for over eight million Americans from its inception to its closure in 1943

Summary

26.1 The Rise of Franklin Roosevelt

Franklin Roosevelt was a wealthy, well-educated, and popular politician whose history of polio made him a more sympathetic figure to the public. He did not share any specifics of his plan to bring the country out of the Great Depression, but his attitude of optimism and possibility contrasted strongly with Hoover's defeated misery. The 1932 election was never really in question, and Roosevelt won in a landslide. During the four-month interregnum, however, Americans continued to endure President Hoover's failed policies, which led the winter of 1932–1933 to be the worst of the Depression, with unemployment rising to record levels.

When Roosevelt took office in March 1933, he infused the country with a sense of optimism. He still did not have a formal plan but rather invited the American people to join him in the spirit of experimentation. Roosevelt did bring certain beliefs to office: the belief in an active government that would take direct action on federal relief, public works, social services, and direct aid to farmers. But as much as his policies, Roosevelt's own personality and engaging manner helped the country feel that they were going to get back on track.

26.2 The First New Deal

After assuming the presidency, Roosevelt lost no time in taking bold steps to fight back against the poverty and unemployment plaguing the country. He immediately created a bank holiday and used the time to bring before Congress legislation known as the Emergency Banking Act, which allowed federal agencies to examine all banks before they reopened, thus restoring consumer confidence. He then went on, in his historic first hundred days, to sign numerous other significant pieces of legislation that were geared towards creating jobs, shoring up industry and agriculture, and providing relief to individuals through both refinancing options and direct handouts. Not all of his programs were effective, and many generated significant criticism. Overall, however, these programs helped to stabilize the economy, restore confidence, and change the pessimistic mindset that had overrun the country.

26.3 The Second New Deal

Despite his popularity, Roosevelt had significant critics at the end of the First New Deal. Some on the right felt that he had moved the country in a dangerous direction towards socialism and fascism, whereas others on the left felt that he had not gone far enough to help the still-struggling American people. Reeling after the Supreme Court struck down two key pieces of New Deal legislation, the AAA and NIRA, Roosevelt pushed Congress to pass a new wave of bills to provide jobs, banking reforms, and a social safety net. The laws that emerged—the Banking Act, the Emergency Relief Appropriation Act, and the Social Security Act—still define our country today.

Roosevelt won his second term in a landslide and continued to push for legislation that would help the economy. The jobs programs employed over eight million people and, while systematic discrimination hurt both women and African American workers, these programs were still successful in getting people back to work. The last major piece of New Deal legislation that Roosevelt passed was the Fair Labor Standards Act, which set a minimum wage, established a maximum-hour workweek, and forbade child labor. This law, as well as Social Security, still provides much of the social safety net in the United States today.

While critics and historians continue to debate whether the New Deal ushered in a permanent change to the political culture of the country, from one of individualism to the creation of a welfare state, none deny the fact that Roosevelt's presidency expanded the role of the federal government in all people's lives, generally for the better. Even if the most conservative of presidential successors would question this commitment, the notion of some level of government involvement in economic regulation and social welfare had largely been settled by 1941. Future debates would be about the extent and degree of that involvement.

Review Questions

1. Which of the following best describes Roosevelt's attempts to push his political agenda in the last months of Hoover's presidency?
- A. Roosevelt spoke publicly on the issue of direct relief.
- B. Roosevelt met privately with Hoover to convince him to institute certain policy shifts before his presidency ended.
- C. Roosevelt awaited his inauguration before introducing any plans.
- D. Roosevelt met secretly with members of Congress to attempt to win their favor.

2. Which of the following policies did Roosevelt *not* include among his early ideas for a New Deal?
- A. public works
- B. government regulation of the economy
- C. elimination of the gold standard
- D. aid to farmers

3. What was the purpose of Roosevelt's "Brains Trust?"

4. Which of the following was *not* a policy undertaken by the NIRA?
- A. agreement among industries to set prices
- B. agreement among industries to reinvest profits into their firms
- C. agreement among industries to set production levels
- D. recognition of the right of workers to form unions

5. What type of help did the CWA provide?
- A. direct relief
- B. farm refinancing
- C. bank reform
- D. employment opportunities

6. In what ways did the New Deal both provide direct relief and create new jobs? Which programs served each of these goals?

7. How did the NRA seek to protect workers? What difficulties did this agency face?

8. Which of the following statements accurately describes Mary McLeod Bethune?
- A. She was a prominent supporter of the Townsend Plan.
- B. She was a key figure in the NYA.
- C. She was Eleanor Roosevelt's personal secretary.
- D. She was a labor organizer.

9. The Social Security Act borrowed some ideas from which of the following?
- A. the Townsend Plan
- B. the Division of Negro Affairs
- C. the Education Trust
- D. the NIRA

10. What was the first New Deal agency to hire women openly?
- A. the NRA
- B. the WPA
- C. the AAA
- D. the TVA

11. What were the major goals and accomplishments of the Indian New Deal?

Critical Thinking Questions

12. To what extent was Franklin Roosevelt's overwhelming victory in the 1932 presidential election a reflection of his own ideas for change? To what extent did it represent public discontent with Herbert Hoover's lack of answers?

13. Whom did the New Deal help the least? What hardships did these individuals continue to suffer? Why were Roosevelt's programs unsuccessful in the alleviation of their adversities?

14. Was Franklin Roosevelt successful at combatting the Great Depression? How did the New Deal affect future generations of Americans?

15. What were the key differences between the First New Deal and the Second New Deal? On the whole, what did each New Deal set out to accomplish?

16. What challenges did Roosevelt face in his work on behalf of African Americans? What impact did the New Deal have ultimately on race relations?

CHAPTER 27

Fighting the Good Fight in World War II, 1941-1945

Figure 27.1 During World War II, American propaganda was used to drum up patriotism and support for the war effort. This poster shows the grit and determination of infantrymen in the face of enemy fire.

Chapter Outline

27.1 The Origins of War: Europe, Asia, and the United States
27.2 The Home Front
27.3 Victory in the European Theater
27.4 The Pacific Theater and the Atomic Bomb

Introduction

World War II awakened the sleeping giant of the United States from the lingering effects of the Great Depression. Although the country had not entirely disengaged itself from foreign affairs following World War I, it had remained largely divorced from events occurring in Europe until the late 1930s. World War II forced the United States to involve itself once again in European affairs. It also helped to relieve the unemployment of the 1930s and stir industrial growth. The propaganda poster above (Figure 27.1) was part of a concerted effort to get Americans to see themselves as citizens of a strong, unified country, dedicated to the protection of freedom and democracy. However, the war that unified many Americans also brought to the fore many of the nation's racial and ethnic divisions, both on the frontlines—where military units, such as the one depicted in this poster, were segregated by race—and on the home front. Yet, the war also created new opportunities for ethnic minorities and women, which, in postwar America, would contribute to their demand for greater rights.

27.1 The Origins of War: Europe, Asia, and the United States

By the end of this section, you will be able to:
- Explain the factors in Europe that gave rise to Fascism and Nazism
- Discuss the events in Europe and Asia that led to the start of the war
- Identify the early steps taken by President Franklin D. Roosevelt to increase American aid to nations fighting totalitarianism while maintaining neutrality

The years between the First and Second World Wars were politically and economically tumultuous for the United States and especially for the world. The Russian Revolution of 1917, Germany's defeat in World War I, and the subsequent Treaty of Versailles had broken up the Austro-Hungarian, German, and Russian empires and significantly redrew the map of Europe. President Woodrow Wilson had wished to make World War I the "war to end all wars" and hoped that his new paradigm of "collective security" in international relations, as actualized through the League of Nations, would limit power struggles among the nations of the world. However, during the next two decades, America's attention turned away from global politics and toward its own needs. At the same time, much of the world was dealing with economic and political crises, and different types of totalitarian regimes began to take hold in Europe. In Asia, an ascendant Japan began to expand its borders. Although the United States remained focused on the economic challenges of the Great Depression as World War II approached, ultimately it became clear that American involvement in the fight against Nazi Germany and Japan was in the nation's interest.

ISOLATION

While during the 1920s and 1930s there were Americans who favored active engagement in Europe, most Americans, including many prominent politicians, were leery of getting too involved in European affairs or accepting commitments to other nations that might restrict America's ability to act independently, keeping with the isolationist tradition. Although the United States continued to intervene in the affairs

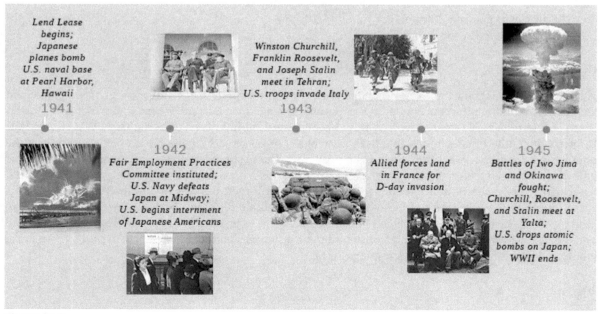

Figure 27.2

of countries in the Western Hemisphere during this period, the general mood in America was to avoid becoming involved in any crises that might lead the nation into another global conflict.

Despite its largely noninterventionist foreign policy, the United States did nevertheless take steps to try to lessen the chances of war and cut its defense spending at the same time. President Warren G. Harding's administration participated in the Washington Naval Conference of 1921–1922, which reduced the size of the navies of the nine signatory nations. In addition, the Four Power Treaty, signed by the United States, Great Britain, France, and Japan in 1921, committed the signatories to eschewing any territorial expansion in Asia. In 1928, the United States and fourteen other nations signed the Kellogg-Briand Pact, declaring war an international crime. Despite hopes that such agreements would lead to a more peaceful world—far more nations signed on to the agreement in later years—they failed because none of them committed any of the nations to take action in the event of treaty violations.

THE MARCH TOWARD WAR

While the United States focused on domestic issues, economic depression and political instability were growing in Europe. During the 1920s, the international financial system was propped up largely by American loans to foreign countries. The crash of 1929, when the U.S. stock market plummeted and American capital dried up, set in motion a series of financial chain reactions that contributed significantly to a global downward economic spiral. Around the world, industrialized economies faced significant problems of economic depression and worker unemployment.

Totalitarianism in Europe

Many European countries had been suffering even before the Great Depression began. A postwar recession and the continuation of wartime inflation had hurt many economies, as did a decrease in agricultural prices, which made it harder for farmers to buy manufactured goods or pay off loans to banks. In such an unstable environment, Benito Mussolini capitalized on the frustrations of the Italian people who felt betrayed by the Versailles Treaty. In 1919, Mussolini created the *Fasci Italiani di Combattimento* (Italian Combat Squadron). The organization's main tenets of **Fascism** called for a totalitarian form of government and a heightened focus on national unity, militarism, social Darwinism, and loyalty to the state. With the support of major Italian industrialists and the king, who saw Fascism as a bulwark against growing Socialist and Communist movements, Mussolini became prime minister in 1922. Between 1925 and 1927, Mussolini transformed the nation into a single party state and removed all restraints on his power.

In Germany, a similar pattern led to the rise of the totalitarian National Socialist Party. Political fragmentation through the 1920s accentuated the severe economic problems facing the country. As a result, the German Communist Party began to grow in strength, frightening many wealthy and middle-class Germans. In addition, the terms of the Treaty of Versailles had given rise to a deep-seated resentment of the victorious Allies. It was in such an environment that Adolf Hitler's anti-Communist National Socialist Party—the Nazis—was born.

The Nazis gained numerous followers during the Great Depression, which hurt Germany tremendously, plunging it further into economic crisis. By 1932, nearly 30 percent of the German labor force was unemployed. Not surprisingly, the political mood was angry and sullen. Hitler, a World War I veteran, promised to return Germany to greatness. By the beginning of 1933, the Nazis had become the largest party in the German legislature. Germany's president, Paul von Hindenburg, at the urging of large industrialists who feared a Communist uprising, appointed Hitler to the position of chancellor in January 1933. In the elections that took place in early March 1933, the Nazis gained the political power to pass the Enabling Act later that same month, which gave Hitler the power to make all laws for the next four years. Hitler thus effectively became the dictator of Germany and remained so long after the four-year term passed. Like Italy, Germany had become a one-party totalitarian state (Figure 27.3). Nazi Germany was an anti-Semitic nation, and in 1935, the Nuremberg Laws deprived Jews, whom Hitler blamed for Germany's downfall, of German citizenship and the rights thereof.

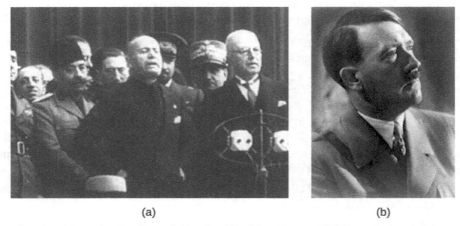

(a)   (b)

Figure 27.3 Italian Fascists under the dictatorial leadership of Benito Mussolini (a, center) and German National Socialist Party leader and dictator Adolf Hitler (b) systematically dismantled democratic institutions and pushed military buildups, racial supremacy, and an aggressive nationalism in the 1920s and early 1930s.

Once in power, Hitler began to rebuild German military might. He commenced his program by withdrawing Germany from the League of Nations in October 1933. In 1936, in accordance with his promise to restore German greatness, Hitler dispatched military units into the Rhineland, on the border with France, which was an act contrary to the provisions of the Versailles Treaty. In March 1938, claiming that he sought only to reunite ethnic Germans within the borders of one country, Hitler invaded Austria. At a conference in Munich later that year, Great Britain's prime minister, Neville Chamberlain, and France's prime minister, Édouard Daladier, agreed to the partial dismemberment of Czechoslovakia and the occupation of the Sudetenland (a region with a sizable German population) by German troops (**Figure 27.4**). This Munich Pact offered a policy of **appeasement**, in the hope that German expansionist appetites could be satisfied without war. But not long after the agreement, Germany occupied the rest of Czechoslovakia as well.

Figure 27.4 Prime Minister Neville Chamberlain arrives home in England bearing the Munich Pact agreement. The jubilant Chamberlain proclaimed that the agreement meant "peace in our time."

In the Soviet Union, Premier Joseph Stalin, observing Hitler's actions and listening to his public pronouncements, realized that Poland, part of which had once belonged to Germany and was home to people of German ancestry, was most likely next. Although fiercely opposed to Hitler, Stalin, sobered by the French and British betrayal of Czechoslovakia and unprepared for a major war, decided the best way to protect the Soviet Union, and gain additional territory, was to come to some accommodation with the German dictator. In August 1939, Germany and the Soviet Union essentially agreed to divide Poland between them and not make war upon one another.

Japan

Militaristic politicians also took control of Japan in the 1930s. The Japanese had worked assiduously for decades to modernize, build their strength, and become a prosperous, respected nation. The sentiment in Japan was decidedly pro-capitalist, and the Japanese militarists were fiercely supportive of a capitalist economy. They viewed with great concern the rise of Communism in the Soviet Union and in particular China, where the issue was fueling a civil war, and feared that the Soviet Union would make inroads in Asia by assisting China's Communists. The Japanese militarists thus found a common ideological enemy with Fascism and National Socialism, which had based their rise to power on anti-Communist sentiments. In 1936, Japan and Germany signed the Anti-Comintern Pact, pledging mutual assistance in defending themselves against the Comintern, the international agency created by the Soviet Union to promote worldwide Communist revolution. In 1937, Italy joined the pact, essentially creating the foundation of what became the military alliance of the Axis powers.

Like its European allies, Japan was intent upon creating an empire for itself. In 1931, it created a new nation, a puppet state called Manchukuo, which had been cobbled together from the three northernmost provinces of China. Although the League of Nations formally protested Japan's seizure of Chinese territory in 1931 and 1932, it did nothing else. In 1937, a clash between Japanese and Chinese troops, known as the Marco Polo Bridge Incident, led to a full-scale invasion of China by the Japanese. By the end of the year, the Chinese had suffered some serious defeats. In Nanjing, then called Nanking by Westerners, Japanese soldiers systematically raped Chinese women and massacred hundreds of thousands of civilians, leading to international outcry. Public sentiment against Japan in the United States reached new heights. Members of Protestant churches that were involved in missionary work in China were particularly outraged, as were Chinese Americans. A troop of Chinese American Boy Scouts in New York City's Chinatown defied Boy Scout policy and marched in protest against Japanese aggression.

FROM NEUTRALITY TO ENGAGEMENT

President Franklin Roosevelt was aware of the challenges facing the targets of Nazi aggression in Europe and Japanese aggression in Asia. Although he hoped to offer U.S. support, Congress's commitment to nonintervention was difficult to overcome. Such a policy in regards to Europe was strongly encouraged by Senator Gerald P. Nye of North Dakota. Nye claimed that the United States had been tricked into participating in World War I by a group of industrialists and bankers who sought to gain from the country's participation in the war. The United States, Nye urged, should not be drawn again into an international dispute over matters that did not concern it. His sentiments were shared by other noninterventionists in Congress (Figure 27.5).

Figure 27.5 This protest sign shows the unwillingness of many Americans to become involved in a foreign war. A reluctance to intervene in events outside of the Western Hemisphere had characterized American foreign policy since the administration of George Washington. World War I had been an exception that many American politicians regretted making.

Roosevelt's willingness to accede to the demands of the noninterventionists led him even to refuse assistance to those fleeing Nazi Germany. Although Roosevelt was aware of Nazi persecution of the Jews, he did little to aid them. In a symbolic act of support, he withdrew the American ambassador to Germany in 1938. He did not press for a relaxation of immigration quotas that would have allowed more refugees to enter the country, however. In 1939, he refused to support a bill that would have admitted twenty thousand Jewish refugee children to the United States. Again in 1939, when German refugees aboard the SS *St. Louis*, most of them Jews, were refused permission to land in Cuba and turned to the United States for help, the U.S. State Department informed them that immigration quotas for Germany had already been filled. Once again, Roosevelt did not intervene, because he feared that nativists in Congress might smear him as a friend of Jews.

To ensure that the United States did not get drawn into another war, Congress passed a series of Neutrality Acts in the second half of the 1930s. The Neutrality Act of 1935 banned the sale of armaments to warring nations. The following year, another Neutrality Act prohibited loaning money to belligerent countries. The last piece of legislation, the Neutrality Act of 1937, forbade the transportation of weapons or passengers to belligerent nations on board American ships and also prohibited American citizens from traveling on board the ships of nations at war.

Once all-out war began between Japan and China in 1937, Roosevelt sought ways to help the Chinese that did not violate U.S. law. Since Japan did not formally declare war on China, a state of belligerency did not technically exist. Therefore, under the terms of the Neutrality Acts, America was not prevented from transporting goods to China. In 1940, the president of China, Chiang Kai-shek, was able to prevail upon Roosevelt to ship to China one hundred P-40 fighter planes and to allow American volunteers, who technically became members of the Chinese Air Force, to fly them.

War Begins in Europe

In 1938, the agreement reached at the Munich Conference failed to satisfy Hitler—in fact, the refusal of Britain and France to go to war over the issue infuriated the German dictator. In May of the next year, Germany and Italy formalized their military alliance with the "Pact of Steel." On September 1, 1939, Hitler unleashed his Blitzkrieg, or "lightning war," against Poland, using swift, surprise attacks combining infantry, tanks, and aircraft to quickly overwhelm the enemy. Britain and France had already learned from Munich that Hitler could not be trusted and that his territorial demands were insatiable. On September 3, 1939, they declared war on Germany, and the European phase of World War II began. Responding to the German invasion of Poland, Roosevelt worked with Congress to alter the Neutrality Laws to permit a policy of "Cash and Carry" in munitions for Britain and France. The legislation, passed and signed by

Roosevelt in November 1939, permitted belligerents to purchase war **materiel** if they could pay cash for it and arrange for its transportation on board their own ships.

When the Germans commenced their spring offensive in 1940, they defeated France in six weeks with a highly mobile and quick invasion of France, Belgium, Luxembourg, and the Netherlands. In the Far East, Japan took advantage of France's surrender to Germany to occupy French Indochina. In response, beginning with the Export Control Act in July 1940, the United States began to embargo the shipment of various materials to Japan, starting first with aviation gasoline and machine tools, and proceeding to scrap iron and steel.

The Atlantic Charter

Following the surrender of France, the Battle of Britain began, as Germany proceeded to try to bomb England into submission. As the battle raged in the skies over Great Britain throughout the summer and autumn of 1940 (Figure 27.6), Roosevelt became increasingly concerned over England's ability to hold out against the German juggernaut. In June 1941, Hitler broke the nonaggression pact with the Soviet Union that had given him the backing to ravage Poland and marched his armies deep into Soviet territory, where they would kill Red Army regulars and civilians by the millions until their advances were stalled and ultimately reversed by the devastating battle of Stalingrad, which took place from August 23, 1942 until February 2, 1943 when, surrounded and out of ammunition, the German 6th army surrendered.

Click and Explore

Listen to the BBC's archived reports (http://openstaxcollege.org/l/15BattleBrit) of the Battle of Britain, including Winston Churchill's "Finest Hour" speech.

In August 1941, Roosevelt met with the British prime minister, Winston Churchill, off the coast of Newfoundland, Canada. At this meeting, the two leaders drafted the Atlantic Charter, the blueprint of Anglo-American cooperation during World War II. The charter stated that the United States and Britain sought no territory from the conflict. It proclaimed that citizens of all countries should be given the right of self-determination, self-government should be restored in places where it had been eliminated, and trade barriers should be lowered. Further, the charter mandated freedom of the seas, renounced the use of force to settle international disputes, and called for postwar disarmament.

Figure 27.6 London and other major British cities suffered extensive damaged from the bombing raids of the Battle of Britain. Over one million London houses were destroyed or damaged during "The Blitz" and almost twenty thousand Londoners were killed.

In March 1941, concerns over Britain's ability to defend itself also influenced Congress to authorize a policy of Lend Lease, a practice by which the United States could sell, lease, or transfer armaments to any nation deemed important to the defense of the United States. Lend Lease effectively ended the policy of nonintervention and dissolved America's pretense of being a neutral nation. The program ran from 1941 to 1945, and distributed some $45 billion worth of weaponry and supplies to Britain, the Soviet Union, China, and other allies.

A Date Which Will Live in Infamy

By the second half of 1941, Japan was feeling the pressure of the American embargo. As it could no longer buy strategic material from the United States, the Japanese were determined to obtain a sufficient supply of oil by taking control of the Dutch East Indies. However, they realized that such an action might increase the possibility of American intervention, since the Philippines, a U.S. territory, lay on the direct route that oil tankers would have to take to reach Japan from Indonesia. Japanese leaders thus attempted to secure a diplomatic solution by negotiating with the United States while also authorizing the navy to plan for war. The Japanese government also decided that if no peaceful resolution could be reached by the end of November 1941, then the nation would have to go to war against the United States.

The American final counterproposal to various offers by Japan was for the Japanese to completely withdraw, without any conditions, from China and enter into nonaggression pacts with all the Pacific powers. Japan found that proposal unacceptable but delayed its rejection for as long as possible. Then, at 7:48 a.m. on Sunday, December 7, the Japanese attacked the U.S. Pacific fleet at anchor in Pearl Harbor, Hawaii (Figure 27.7). They launched two waves of attacks from six aircraft carriers that had snuck into the central Pacific without being detected. The attacks brought some 353 fighters, bombers, and torpedo bombers down on the unprepared fleet. The Japanese hit all eight battleships in the harbor and sank four of them. They also damaged several cruisers and destroyers. On the ground, nearly two hundred aircraft were destroyed, and twenty-four hundred servicemen were killed. Another eleven hundred were wounded. Japanese losses were minimal. The strike was part of a more concerted campaign by the Japanese to gain territory. They subsequently attacked Hong Kong, Malaysia, Singapore, Guam, Wake Island, and the Philippines.

Figure 27.7 This famous shot captured the explosion of the USS *Shaw* after the Japanese bombed Pearl Harbor. While American losses were significant, the Japanese lost only twenty-nine planes and five miniature submarines.

Whatever reluctance to engage in conflict the American people had had before December 7, 1941, quickly evaporated. Americans' incredulity that Japan would take such a radical step quickly turned to a fiery anger, especially as the attack took place while Japanese diplomats in Washington were still negotiating a possible settlement. President Roosevelt, referring to the day of the attack as "a date which will live in infamy," asked Congress for a declaration of war, which it delivered to Japan on December 8. On December 11, Germany and Italy declared war on the United States in accordance with their alliance with Japan. Against its wishes, the United States had become part of the European conflict.

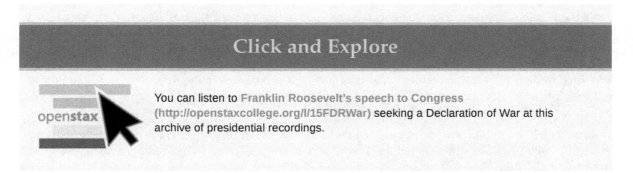

Click and Explore

You can listen to Franklin Roosevelt's speech to Congress (http://openstaxcollege.org/l/15FDRWar) seeking a Declaration of War at this archive of presidential recordings.

27.2 The Home Front

By the end of this section, you will be able to:
- Describe the steps taken by the United States to prepare for war
- Describe how the war changed employment patterns in the United States
- Discuss the contributions of civilians on the home front, especially women, to the war effort
- Analyze how the war affected race relations in the United States

The impact of the war on the United States was nowhere near as devastating as it was in Europe and the Pacific, where the battles were waged, but it still profoundly changed everyday life for all Americans.

On the positive side, the war effort finally and definitively ended the economic depression that had been plaguing the country since 1929. It also called upon Americans to unite behind the war effort and give of their money, their time, and their effort, as they sacrificed at home to assure success abroad. The upheaval caused by white men leaving for war meant that for many disenfranchised groups, such as women and African Americans, there were new opportunities in employment and wage earning. Still, fear and racism drove cracks in the nation's unified facade.

MOBILIZING A NATION

Although the United States had sought to avoid armed conflict, the country was not entirely unprepared for war. Production of armaments had increased since 1939, when, as a result of Congress's authorization of the Cash and Carry policy, contracts for weapons had begun to trickle into American factories. War production increased further following the passage of Lend Lease in 1941. However, when the United States entered the war, the majority of American factories were still engaged in civilian production, and many doubted that American businesses would be sufficiently motivated to convert their factories to wartime production.

Just a few years earlier, Roosevelt had been frustrated and impatient with business leaders when they failed to fully support the New Deal, but enlisting industrialists in the nation's crusade was necessary if the United States was to produce enough armaments to win the war. To encourage cooperation, the government agreed to assume all costs of development and production, and also guarantee a profit on the sale of what was produced. This arrangement resulted in 233 to 350 percent increases in profits over what the same businesses had been able to achieve from 1937 to 1940. In terms of dollars earned, corporate profits rose from $6.4 billion in 1940 to nearly $11 billion in 1944. As the country switched to wartime production, the top one hundred U.S. corporations received approximately 70 percent of government contracts; big businesses prospered.

In addition to gearing up industry to fight the war, the country also needed to build an army. A peacetime draft, the first in American history, had been established in September 1940, but the initial draftees were to serve for only one year, a length of time that was later extended. Furthermore, Congress had specified that no more than 900,000 men could receive military training at any one time. By December 1941, the United States had only one division completely ready to be deployed. Military planners estimated that it might take nine million men to secure victory. A massive draft program was required to expand the nation's military forces. Over the course of the war, approximately fifty million men registered for the draft; ten million were subsequently inducted into the service.

Approximately 2.5 million African Americans registered for the draft, and 1 million of them subsequently served. Initially, African American soldiers, who served in segregated units, had been used as support troops and not been sent into combat. By the end of the war, however, manpower needs resulted in African American recruits serving in the infantry and flying planes. The Tuskegee Institute in Alabama had instituted a civilian pilot training program for aspiring African American pilots. When the war began, the Department of War absorbed the program and adapted it to train combat pilots. First Lady Eleanor Roosevelt demonstrated both her commitment to African Americans and the war effort by visiting Tuskegee in 1941, shortly after the unit had been organized. To encourage the military to give the airmen a chance to serve in actual combat, she insisted on taking a ride in a plane flown by an African American pilot to demonstrate the Tuskegee Airmen's skill (Figure 27.8). When the Tuskegee Airmen did get their opportunity to serve in combat, they did so with distinction.

Figure 27.8 First Lady Eleanor Roosevelt insisted on flying with an African American pilot to help fight racism in the military. The First Lady was famous for her support of civil rights.

In addition, forty-four thousand Native Americans served in all theaters of the war. In some of the Pacific campaigns, Native Americans made distinct and unique contributions to Allied victories. Navajo marines served in communications units, exchanging information over radios using codes based on their native language, which the Japanese were unable to comprehend or to crack. They became known as code talkers and participated in the battles of Guadalcanal, Iwo Jima, Peleliu, and Tarawa. A smaller number of Comanche code talkers performed a similar function in the European theater.

While millions of Americans heeded the rallying cry for patriotism and service, there were those who, for various reasons, did not accept the call. Before the war began, American Peace Mobilization had campaigned against American involvement in the European conflict as had the noninterventionist America First organization. Both groups ended their opposition, however, at the time of the German invasion of the Soviet Union and the Japanese attack on Pearl Harbor, respectively. Nevertheless, during the war, some seventy-two thousand men registered as **conscientious objectors** (COs), and fifty-two thousand were granted that status. Of that fifty-two thousand, some accepted noncombat roles in the military, whereas others accepted unpaid work in civilian work camps. Many belonged to pacifist religious sects such as the Quakers or Mennonites. They were willing to serve their country, but they refused to kill. COs suffered public condemnation for disloyalty, and family members often turned against them. Strangers assaulted them. A portion of the town of Plymouth, NH, was destroyed by fire because the residents did not want to call upon the services of the COs trained as firemen at a nearby camp. Only a very small number of men evaded the draft completely.

Most Americans, however, were willing to serve, and they required a competent officer corps. The very same day that Germany invaded Poland in 1939, President Roosevelt promoted George C. Marshall, a veteran of World War I and an expert at training officers, from a one-star general to a four-star general, and gave him the responsibility of serving as Army Chief of Staff. The desire to create a command staff that could win the army's confidence no doubt contributed to the rather meteoric rise of Dwight D. Eisenhower (Figure 27.9). During World War I, Eisenhower had been assigned to organize America's new tank corps, and, although he never saw combat during the war, he demonstrated excellent organizational skills. When the United States entered World War II, Eisenhower was appointed commander of the General European Theater of Operations in June 1942.

Figure 27.9 Dwight D. Eisenhower rose quickly through the ranks to become commander of the European Theater of Operations by June 1942.

MY STORY

✪ *General Eisenhower on Winning a War*

Promoted to the level of one-star general just before the attack on Pearl Harbor, Dwight D. Eisenhower had never held an active command position above the level of a battalion and was not considered a potential commander of major military operations. However, after he was assigned to the General Staff in Washington, DC, he quickly rose through the ranks and, by late 1942, was appointed commander of the North African campaign.

Excerpts from General Eisenhower's diary reveal his dedication to the war effort. He continued to work despite suffering a great personal loss.

> March 9, 1942
> General McNaughton (commanding Canadians in Britain) came to see me. He believes in attacking in Europe (thank God). He's over here in an effort to speed up landing craft production and cargo ships. Has some d___ good ideas. Sent him to see Somervell and Admiral Land. How I hope he can do something on landing craft.
> March 10, 1942
> Father dies this morning. Nothing I can do but send a wire.
> One thing that might help win this war is to get someone to shoot [Admiral] King. He's the antithesis of cooperation, a deliberately rude person, which means he's a mental bully. He became Commander in Chief of the fleet some time ago. Today he takes over, also Stark's job as chief of naval operations. It's a good thing to get rid of the double head in the navy, and of course Stark was just a nice old lady, but this fellow is going to cause a blow-up sooner or later, I'll bet a cookie.
> Gradually some of the people with whom I have to deal are coming to agree with me that there are just three "musts" for the Allies this year: hold open the line to England and support her as necessary, keep Russia in the war as an active participant; hold the India-Middle East buttress between Japs and Germans. All this assumes the safety from major attack of North America, Hawaii, and Caribbean area.
> We lost eight cargo ships yesterday. That we must stop, because any effort we make depends upon sea communication.
> March 11, 1942
> I have felt terribly. I should like so much to be with my Mother these few days. But we're at war. And war is not soft, it has no time to indulge even the deepest and most sacred emotions. I loved my Dad. I think my Mother the finest person I've ever known. She has been the inspiration for Dad's life and a true helpmeet in every sense of the word.
> I'm quitting work now, 7:30 p.m. I haven't the heart to go on tonight.
> —Dwight D. Eisenhower, *The Eisenhower Diaries*

What does Eisenhower identify as the most important steps to take to win the war?

EMPLOYMENT AND MIGRATION PATTERNS IN THE UNITED STATES

Even before the official beginning of the war, the country started to prepare. In August 1940, Congress created the Defense Plant Corporation, which had built 344 plants in the West by 1945, and had funneled over $1.8 billion into the economies of western states. After Pearl Harbor, as American military strategists began to plan counterattacks and campaigns against the Axis powers, California became a training ground. Troops trained there for tank warfare and amphibious assaults as well as desert campaigns—since the first assault against the Axis powers was planned for North Africa.

As thousands of Americans swarmed to the West Coast to take jobs in defense plants and shipyards, cities like Richmond, California, and nearby Oakland, expanded quickly. Richmond grew from a city of 20,000 people to 100,000 in only three years. Almost overnight, the population of California skyrocketed. African Americans moved out of the rural South into northern or West Coast cities to provide the muscle and skill to build the machines of war. Building on earlier waves of African American migration after the Civil

War and during World War I, the demographics of the nation changed with the growing urbanization of the African American population. Women also relocated to either follow their husbands to military bases or take jobs in the defense industry, as the total mobilization of the national economy began to tap into previously underemployed populations.

Roosevelt and his administration already had experience in establishing government controls and taking the initiative in economic matters during the Depression. In April 1941, Roosevelt created the Office of Price Administration (OPA), and, once the United States entered the war, the OPA regulated prices and attempted to combat inflation. The OPA ultimately had the power to set ceiling prices for all goods, except agricultural commodities, and to ration a long list of items. During the war, major labor unions pledged not to strike in order to prevent disruptions in production; in return, the government encouraged businesses to recognize unions and promised to help workers bargain for better wages.

As in World War I, the government turned to bond drives to finance the war. Millions of Americans purchased more than $185 billion worth of war bonds. Children purchased Victory Stamps and exchanged full stamp booklets for bonds. The federal government also instituted the current tax-withholding system to ensure collection of taxes. Finally, the government once again urged Americans to plant victory gardens, using marketing campaigns and celebrities to promote the idea (Figure 27.10). Americans responded eagerly, planting gardens in their backyards and vacant lots.

(a)

(b)

Figure 27.10 Wartime rationing meant that Americans had to do without many everyday items and learn to grow their own produce in order to allow the country's food supply to go to the troops.

The federal government also instituted rationing to ensure that America's fighting men were well fed. Civilians were issued ration booklets, books of coupons that enabled them to buy limited amounts of meat, coffee, butter, sugar, and other foods. Wartime cookbooks were produced, such as the Betty Crocker cookbook *Your Share*, telling housewives how to prepare tasty meals without scarce food items. Other items were rationed as well, including shoes, liquor, cigarettes, and gasoline. With a few exceptions, such as doctors, Americans were allowed to drive their automobiles only on certain days of the week. Most Americans complied with these regulations, but some illegally bought and sold rationed goods on the black market.

Click and Explore

View an excerpt from a **PBS documentary on rationing** **(http://openstaxcollege.org/l/15Rationing)** during World War II.

Civilians on the home front also recycled, conserved, and participated in scrap drives to collect items needed for the production of war materiel. Housewives saved cooking fats, needed to produce explosives. Children collected scrap metal, paper, rubber, silk, nylon, and old rags. Some children sacrificed beloved metal toys in order to "win the war." Civilian volunteers, trained to recognize enemy aircraft, watched the skies along the coasts and on the borders.

WOMEN IN THE WAR: ROSIE THE RIVETER AND BEYOND

As in the previous war, the gap in the labor force created by departing soldiers meant opportunities for women. In particular, World War II led many to take jobs in defense plants and factories around the country. For many women, these jobs provided unprecedented opportunities to move into occupations previously thought of as exclusive to men, especially the aircraft industry, where a majority of workers were composed of women by 1943. Most women in the labor force did not work in the defense industry, however. The majority took over other factory jobs that had been held by men. Many took positions in offices as well. As white women, many of whom had been in the workforce before the war, moved into these more highly paid positions, African American women, most of whom had previously been limited to domestic service, took over white women's lower-paying positions in factories; some were also hired by defense plants, however. Although women often earned more money than ever before, it was still far less than men received for doing the same jobs. Nevertheless, many achieved a degree of financial self-reliance that was enticing. By 1944, as many as 33 percent of the women working in the defense industries were mothers and worked "double-day" shifts—one at the plant and one at home.

Still, there was some resistance to women going to work in such a male-dominated environment. In order to recruit women for factory jobs, the government created a propaganda campaign centered on a now-iconic figure known as **Rosie the Riveter** (Figure 27.11). Rosie, who was a composite based on several real women, was most famously depicted by American illustrator Norman Rockwell. Rosie was tough yet feminine. To reassure men that the demands of war would not make women too masculine, some factories gave female employees lessons in how to apply makeup, and cosmetics were never rationed during the war. Elizabeth Arden even created a special red lipstick for use by women reservists in the Marine Corps.

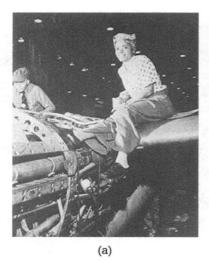

(a)   (b)

Figure 27.11 "Rosie the Riveter" became a generic term for all women working in the defense industry. Although the Rosie depicted on posters was white, many of the real Rosies were African American, such as this woman who poses atop an airplane at the Lockheed Aircraft Corporation in Burbank, California (a), and Anna Bland, a worker at the Richmond Shipyards (b).

Although many saw the entry of women into the workforce as a positive thing, they also acknowledged that working women, especially mothers, faced great challenges. To try to address the dual role of women as workers and mothers, Eleanor Roosevelt urged her husband to approve the first U.S. government childcare facilities under the Community Facilities Act of 1942. Eventually, seven centers, servicing 105,000 children, were built. The First Lady also urged industry leaders like Henry Kaiser to build model childcare facilities for their workers. Still, these efforts did not meet the full need for childcare for working mothers.

The lack of childcare facilities meant that many children had to fend for themselves after school, and some had to assume responsibility for housework and the care of younger siblings. Some mothers took younger children to work with them and left them locked in their cars during the workday. Police and social workers also reported an increase in juvenile delinquency during the war. New York City saw its average number of juvenile cases balloon from 9,500 in the prewar years to 11,200 during the war. In San Diego, delinquency rates for girls, including sexual misbehavior, shot up by 355 percent. It is unclear whether more juveniles were actually engaging in delinquent behavior; the police may simply have become more vigilant during wartime and arrested youngsters for activities that would have gone overlooked before the war. In any event, law enforcement and juvenile courts attributed the perceived increase to a lack of supervision by working mothers.

Tens of thousands of women served in the war effort more directly. Approximately 350,000 joined the military. They worked as nurses, drove trucks, repaired airplanes, and performed clerical work to free up men for combat. Those who joined the Women's Airforce Service Pilots (WASPs) flew planes from the factories to military bases. Some of these women were killed in combat and captured as prisoners of war. Over sixteen hundred of the women nurses received various decorations for courage under fire. Many women also flocked to work in a variety of civil service jobs. Others worked as chemists and engineers, developing weapons for the war. This included thousands of women who were recruited to work on the Manhattan Project, developing the atomic bomb.

THE CULTURE OF WAR: ENTERTAINERS AND THE WAR EFFORT

During the Great Depression, movies had served as a welcome diversion from the difficulties of everyday life, and during the war, this held still truer. By 1941, there were more movie theaters than banks in the United States. In the 1930s, newsreels, which were shown in movie theaters before feature films, had informed the American public of what was happening elsewhere in the world. This interest grew once American armies began to engage the enemy. Many informational documentaries about the war were also shown in movie theaters. The most famous were those in the *Why We Fight* series, filmed by Hollywood director Frank Capra. During the war, Americans flocked to the movies not only to learn what was happening to the troops overseas but also to be distracted from the fears and hardships of wartime by cartoons, dramas, and comedies. By 1945, movie attendance had reached an all-time high.

Click and Explore

This link shows newsreel footage of a raid (http://openstaxcollege.org/l/15Tarawa) on Tarawa Island. This footage was shown in movie theaters around the country.

Many feature films were patriotic stories that showed the day's biggest stars as soldiers fighting the nefarious German and Japanese enemy. During the war years, there was a consistent supply of patriotic movies, with actors glorifying and inspiring America's fighting men. John Wayne, who had become a star in the 1930s, appeared in many war-themed movies, including *The Fighting Seabees* and *Back to Bataan*.

Besides appearing in patriotic movies, many male entertainers temporarily gave up their careers to serve in the armed forces (Figure 27.12). Jimmy Stewart served in the Army Air Force and appeared in a short film entitled *Winning Your Wings* that encouraged young men to enlist. Tyrone Power joined the U.S. Marines. Female entertainers did their part as well. Rita Hayworth and Marlene Dietrich entertained the troops. African American singer and dancer Josephine Baker entertained Allied troops in North Africa and also carried secret messages for the French Resistance. Actress Carole Lombard was killed in a plane crash while returning home from a rally where she had sold war bonds.

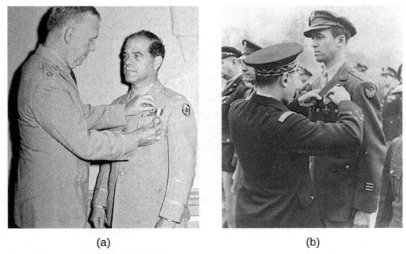

(a)   (b)

Figure 27.12   General George Marshall awards Frank Capra the Distinguished Service Cross in 1945 (a), in recognition of the important contribution that Capra's films made to the war effort. Jimmy Stewart was awarded numerous commendations for his military service, including the French Croix de Guerre (b).

DEFINING "AMERICAN"

⚙ *The Meaning of Democracy*

E. B. White was one of the most famous writers of the twentieth century. During the 1940s, he was known for the articles that he contributed to *The New Yorker* and the column that he wrote for *Harper's Magazine*. Today, he is remembered for his children's books *Stuart Little* and *Charlotte's Web*, and for his collaboration with William Strunk, Jr., *The Elements of Style*, a guide to writing. In 1943, he wrote a definition of democracy as an example of what Americans hoped that they were fighting for.

> We received a letter from the Writer's War Board the other day asking for a statement on 'The Meaning of Democracy.' It presumably is our duty to comply with such a request, and it is certainly our pleasure. Surely the Board knows what democracy is. It is the line that forms on the right. It is the 'don't' in don't shove. It is the hole in the stuffed shirt through which the sawdust slowly trickles; it is the dent in the high hat. Democracy is the recurrent suspicion that more than half of the people are right more than half of the time. It is the feeling of privacy in the voting booths, the feeling of communion in the libraries, the feeling of vitality everywhere. Democracy is a letter to the editor. Democracy is the score at the beginning of the ninth. It is an idea that hasn't been disproved yet, a song the words of which have not gone bad. It is the mustard on the hot dog and the cream in the rationed coffee. Democracy is a request from a War Board, in the middle of the morning in the middle of a war, wanting to know what democracy is.

Do you agree with this definition of democracy? Would you change anything to make it more contemporary?

SOCIAL TENSIONS ON THE HOME FRONT

The need for Americans to come together, whether in Hollywood, the defense industries, or the military, to support the war effort encouraged feelings of unity among the American population. However, the desire for unity did not always mean that Americans of color were treated as equals or even tolerated, despite their proclamations of patriotism and their willingness to join in the effort to defeat America's enemies in Europe and Asia. For African Americans, Mexican Americans, and especially for Japanese Americans, feelings of patriotism and willingness to serve one's country both at home and abroad was not enough to guarantee equal treatment by white Americans or to prevent the U.S. government from regarding them as the enemy.

African Americans and Double V

The African American community had, at the outset of the war, forged some promising relationships with the Roosevelt administration through civil rights activist Mary McLeod Bethune and Roosevelt's "Black Cabinet" of African American advisors. Through the intervention of Eleanor Roosevelt, Bethune was appointed to the advisory council set up by the War Department Women's Interest Section. In this position, Bethune was able to organize the first officer candidate school for women and enable African American women to become officers in the Women's Auxiliary Corps.

As the U.S. economy revived as a result of government defense contracts, African Americans wanted to ensure that their service to the country earned them better opportunities and more equal treatment. Accordingly, in 1942, after African American labor leader A. Philip Randolph pressured Roosevelt with a threatened "March on Washington," the president created, by Executive Order 8802, the Fair Employment Practices Committee. The purpose of this committee was to see that there was no discrimination in the defense industries. While they were effective in forcing defense contractors, such as the DuPont Corporation, to hire African Americans, they were not able to force corporations to place African Americans in well-paid positions. For example, at DuPont's plutonium production plant in Hanford,

Washington, African Americans were hired as low-paid construction workers but not as laboratory technicians.

During the war, the Congress of Racial Equality (CORE), founded by James Farmer in 1942, used peaceful civil disobedience in the form of sit-ins to desegregate certain public spaces in Washington, DC, and elsewhere, as its contribution to the war effort. Members of CORE sought support for their movement by stating that one of their goals was to deprive the enemy of the ability to generate anti-American propaganda by accusing the United States of racism. After all, they argued, if the United States were going to denounce Germany and Japan for abusing human rights, the country should itself be as exemplary as possible. Indeed, CORE's actions were in keeping with the goals of the **Double V campaign** that was begun in 1942 by the *Pittsburgh Courier*, the largest African American newspaper at the time (Figure 27.13). The campaign called upon African Americans to accomplish the two "Vs": victory over America's foreign enemies and victory over racism in the United States.

Figure 27.13 During World War II, African Americans volunteered for government work just as white Americans did. These Washington, DC, residents have become civil defense workers as part of the Double V campaign that called for victory at home and abroad.

Despite the willingness of African Americans to fight for the United States, racial tensions often erupted in violence, as the geographic relocation necessitated by the war brought African Americans into closer contact with whites. There were race riots in Detroit, Harlem, and Beaumont, Texas, in which white residents responded with sometimes deadly violence to their new black coworkers or neighbors. There were also racial incidents at or near several military bases in the South. Incidents of African American soldiers being harassed or assaulted occurred at Fort Benning, Georgia; Fort Jackson, South Carolina; Alexandria, Louisiana; Fayetteville, Arkansas; and Tampa, Florida. African American leaders such as James Farmer and Walter White, the executive secretary of the NAACP since 1931, were asked by General Eisenhower to investigate complaints of the mistreatment of African American servicemen while on active duty. They prepared a fourteen-point memorandum on how to improve conditions for African Americans in the service, sowing some of the seeds of the postwar civil rights movement during the war years.

The Zoot Suit Riots

Mexican Americans also encountered racial prejudice. The Mexican American population in Southern California grew during World War II due to the increased use of Mexican agricultural workers in the fields to replace the white workers who had left for better paying jobs in the defense industries. The United States and Mexican governments instituted the "bracero" program on August 4, 1942, which sought to address the needs of California growers for manual labor to increase food production during wartime. The result was the immigration of thousands of impoverished Mexicans into the United States to work as *braceros*, or manual laborers.

Forced by racial discrimination to live in the barrios of East Los Angeles, many Mexican American youths sought to create their own identity and began to adopt a distinctive style of dress known as **zoot suits**, which were also popular among many young African American men. The zoot suits, which required large amounts of cloth to produce, violated wartime regulations that restricted the amount of cloth that could be used in civilian garments. Among the charges leveled at young Mexican Americans was that they were un-American and unpatriotic; wearing zoot suits was seen as evidence of this. Many native-born Americans also denounced Mexican American men for being unwilling to serve in the military, even though some 350,000 Mexican Americans either volunteered to serve or were drafted into the armed services. In the summer of 1943, "zoot-suit riots" occurred in Los Angeles when carloads of white sailors, encouraged by other white civilians, stripped and beat a group of young men wearing the distinctive form of dress. In retaliation, young Mexican American men attacked and beat up sailors. The response was swift and severe, as sailors and civilians went on a spree attacking young Mexican Americans on the streets, in bars, and in movie theaters. More than one hundred people were injured.

Internment

Japanese Americans also suffered from discrimination. The Japanese attack on Pearl Harbor unleashed a cascade of racist assumptions about Japanese immigrants and Japanese Americans in the United States that culminated in the relocation and **internment** of 120,000 people of Japanese ancestry, 66 percent of whom had been born in the United States. **Executive Order 9066**, signed by Roosevelt on February 19, 1942, gave the army power to remove people from "military areas" to prevent sabotage or espionage. The army then used this authority to relocate people of Japanese ancestry living along the Pacific coast of Washington, Oregon, and California, as well as in parts of Arizona, to internment camps in the American interior. Although a study commissioned earlier by Roosevelt indicated that there was little danger of disloyalty on the part of West Coast Japanese, fears of sabotage, perhaps spurred by the attempted rescue of a Japanese airman shot down at Pearl Harbor by Japanese living in Hawaii, and racist sentiments led Roosevelt to act. Ironically, Japanese in Hawaii were not interned. Although characterized afterwards as America's worst wartime mistake by Eugene V. Rostow in the September 1945 edition of *Harper's Magazine*, the government's actions were in keeping with decades of anti-Asian sentiment on the West Coast.

After the order went into effect, Lt. General John L. DeWitt, in charge of the Western Defense command, ordered approximately 127,000 Japanese and Japanese Americans—roughly 90 percent of those of Japanese ethnicity living in the United States—to assembly centers where they were transferred to hastily prepared camps in the interior of California, Arizona, Colorado, Utah, Idaho, Wyoming, and Arkansas (Figure 27.14). Those who were sent to the camps reported that the experience was deeply traumatic. Families were sometimes separated. People could only bring a few of their belongings and had to abandon the rest of their possessions. The camps themselves were dismal and overcrowded. Despite the hardships, the Japanese attempted to build communities in the camps and resume "normal" life. Adults participated in camp government and worked at a variety of jobs. Children attended school, played basketball against local teams, and organized Boy Scout units. Nevertheless, they were imprisoned, and minor infractions, such as wandering too near the camp gate or barbed wire fences while on an evening stroll, could meet with severe consequences. Some sixteen thousand Germans, including some from Latin America, and German Americans were also placed in internment camps, as were 2,373 persons of Italian ancestry. However, unlike the case with Japanese Americans, they represented only a tiny percentage of the members of these ethnic groups living in the country. Most of these people were innocent of any wrongdoing, but some Germans were members of the Nazi party. No interned Japanese Americans were found guilty of sabotage or espionage.

Figure 27.14 Japanese Americans standing in line in front of a poster detailing internment orders in California.

Despite being singled out for special treatment, many Japanese Americans sought to enlist, but draft boards commonly classified them as 4-C: undesirable aliens. However, as the war ground on, some were reclassified as eligible for service. In total, nearly thirty-three thousand Japanese Americans served in the military during the war. Of particular note was the 442nd Regimental Combat Team, nicknamed the "Go For Broke," which finished the war as the most decorated unit in U.S. military history given its size and length of service. While their successes, and the successes of the African American pilots, were lauded, the country and the military still struggled to contend with its own racial tensions, even as the soldiers in Europe faced the brutality of Nazi Germany.

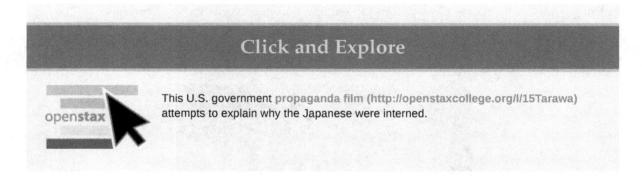

Click and Explore

This U.S. government propaganda film (http://openstaxcollege.org/l/15Tarawa) attempts to explain why the Japanese were interned.

27.3 Victory in the European Theater

By the end of this section, you will be able to:
- Identify the major battles of the European theater
- Analyze the goals and results of the major wartime summit meetings

Despite the fact that a Japanese attack in the Pacific was the tripwire for America's entrance into the war, Roosevelt had been concerned about Great Britain since the beginning of the Battle of Britain. Roosevelt viewed Germany as the greater threat to freedom. Hence, he leaned towards a "Europe First" strategy, even before the United States became an active belligerent. That meant that the United States would concentrate the majority of its resources and energies in achieving a victory over Germany first and then focus on defeating Japan. Within Europe, Churchill and Roosevelt were committed to saving Britain and acted with this goal in mind, often ignoring the needs of the Soviet Union. As Roosevelt imagined an "empire-free" postwar world, in keeping with the goals of the Atlantic Charter, he could also envision the United States becoming the preeminent world power economically, politically, and militarily.

WARTIME DIPLOMACY

Franklin Roosevelt entered World War II with an eye toward a new postwar world, one where the United States would succeed Britain as the leader of Western capitalist democracies, replacing the old British imperial system with one based on free trade and decolonization. The goals of the Atlantic Charter had explicitly included self-determination, self-government, and free trade. In 1941, although Roosevelt had yet to meet Soviet premier Joseph Stalin, he had confidence that he could forge a positive relationship with him, a confidence that Churchill believed was born of naiveté. These allied leaders, known as the **Big Three**, thrown together by the necessity to defeat common enemies, took steps towards working in concert despite their differences.

Through a series of wartime conferences, Roosevelt and the other global leaders sought to come up with a strategy to both defeat the Germans and bolster relationships among allies. In January 1943, at Casablanca, Morocco, Churchill convinced Roosevelt to delay an invasion of France in favor of an invasion of Sicily (Figure 27.15). It was also at this conference that Roosevelt enunciated the doctrine of "unconditional surrender." Roosevelt agreed to demand an unconditional surrender from Germany and Japan to assure the Soviet Union that the United States would not negotiate a separate peace and prepare the former belligerents for a thorough and permanent transformation after the war. Roosevelt thought that announcing this as a specific war aim would discourage any nation or leader from seeking any negotiated armistice that would hinder efforts to reform and transform the defeated nations. Stalin, who was not at the conference, affirmed the concept of unconditional surrender when asked to do so. However, he was dismayed over the delay in establishing a "second front" along which the Americans and British would directly engage German forces in western Europe. A western front, brought about through an invasion across the English Channel, which Stalin had been demanding since 1941, offered the best means of drawing Germany away from the east. At a meeting in Tehran, Iran, also in November 1943, Churchill, Roosevelt, and Stalin met to finalize plans for a cross-channel invasion.

Figure 27.15 Prime Minister Winston Churchill and President Roosevelt met together multiple times during the war. One such conference was located in Casablanca, Morocco, in January 1943.

THE INVASION OF EUROPE

Preparing to engage the Nazis in Europe, the United States landed in North Africa in 1942. The Axis campaigns in North Africa had begun when Italy declared war on England in June 1940, and British forces had invaded the Italian colony of Libya. The Italians had responded with a counteroffensive that penetrated into Egypt, only to be defeated by the British again. In response, Hitler dispatched the Afrika Korps under General Erwin Rommel, and the outcome of the situation was in doubt until shortly before American forces joined the British.

Although the Allied campaign secured control of the southern Mediterranean and preserved Egypt and the Suez Canal for the British, Stalin and the Soviets were still engaging hundreds of German divisions in bitter struggles at Stalingrad and Leningrad. The invasion of North Africa did nothing to draw German troops away from the Soviet Union. An invasion of Europe by way of Italy, which is what the British and American campaign in North Africa laid the ground for, pulled a few German divisions away from their Russian targets. But while Stalin urged his allies to invade France, British and American troops pursued the defeat of Mussolini's Italy. This choice greatly frustrated Stalin, who felt that British interests were taking precedence over the agony that the Soviet Union was enduring at the hands of the invading German army. However, Churchill saw Italy as the vulnerable underbelly of Europe and believed that Italian support for Mussolini was waning, suggesting that victory there might be relatively easy. Moreover, Churchill pointed out that if Italy were taken out of the war, then the Allies would control the Mediterranean, offering the Allies easier shipping access to both the Soviet Union and the British Far Eastern colonies.

D-Day

A direct assault on Nazi Germany's "Fortress Europe" was still necessary for final victory. On June 6, 1944, the second front became a reality when Allied forces stormed the beaches of northern France on **D-day**. Beginning at 6:30 a.m., some twenty-four thousand British, Canadian, and American troops waded ashore along a fifty-mile piece of the Normandy coast (**Figure 27.16**). Well over a million troops would follow their lead. German forces on the hills and cliffs above shot at them, and once they reached the beach, they encountered barbed wire and land mines. More than ten thousand Allied soldiers were wounded or killed during the assault. Following the establishment of beachheads at Normandy, it took months of difficult fighting before Paris was liberated on August 20, 1944. The invasion did succeed in diverting German forces from the eastern front to the western front, relieving some of the pressure on Stalin's troops. By that time, however, Russian forces had already defeated the German army at Stalingrad, an event that many consider the turning point of the war in Europe, and begun to push the Germans out of the Soviet Union.

Figure 27.16 U.S. troops in a military landing craft approach the beach code-named "Omaha" on June 6, 1944. More than ten thousand soldiers were killed or wounded during the D-day assault along the coast of Normandy, France.

Nazi Germany was not ready to surrender, however. On December 16, in a surprise move, the Germans threw nearly a quarter-million men at the Western Allies in an attempt to divide their armies and encircle major elements of the American forces. The struggle, known as the Battle of the Bulge, raged until the end of January. Some ninety thousand Americans were killed, wounded, or lost in action. Nevertheless, the Germans were turned back, and Hitler's forces were so spent that they could never again mount offensive operations.

Confronting the Holocaust

The Holocaust, Hitler's plan to kill the Jews of Europe, had begun as early as 1933, with the construction of Dachau, the first of more than forty thousand camps for incarcerating Jews, submitting them to forced labor, or exterminating them. Eventually, six extermination camps were established between 1941 and 1945 in Polish territory. Jewish men, women, and children from throughout Europe were transported to these camps in Germany and other areas under Nazi control. Although the majority of the people in the camps were Jews, the Nazis sent Roma (gypsies), gays and lesbians, Jehovah's Witnesses, and political opponents to the camps as well. Some prisoners were put to work at hard labor; many of them subsequently died of disease or starvation. Most of those sent to the extermination camps were killed upon arrival with poisoned gas. Ultimately, some eleven million people died in the camps. As Soviet troops began to advance from the east and U.S. forces from the west, camp guards attempted to hide the evidence of their crimes by destroying records and camp buildings, and marching surviving prisoners away from the sites (Figure 27.17).

Figure 27.17   A U.S. senator, and member of a congressional committee investigating Nazi atrocities, views the evidence first hand at Buchenwald concentration camp near Weimar, Germany, in the summer of 1945.

MY STORY

✦ *Felix L. Sparks on the Liberation of Dachau*

The horrors of the concentration camps remained with the soldiers who liberated them long after the war had ended. Below is an excerpt of the recollection of one soldier.

> Our first experience with the camp came as a traumatic shock. The first evidence of the horrors to come was a string of forty railway cars on a railway spur leading into the camp. Each car was filled with emaciated human corpses, both men and women. A hasty search by the stunned infantry soldiers revealed no signs of life among the hundreds of still bodies, over two thousand in all.
>
> It was in this atmosphere of human depravity, degradation and death that the soldiers of my battalion then entered the camp itself. Almost all of the SS command guarding the camp had fled before our arrival, leaving behind about two hundred lower ranking members of the command. There was some sporadic firing of weapons. As we approached the confinement area, the scene numbed my senses. Dante's Inferno seemed pale compared to the real hell of Dachau. A row of small cement structures near the prison entrance contained a coal-fired crematorium, a gas chamber, and rooms piled high with naked and emaciated corpses. As I turned to look over the prison yard with un-believing eyes, I saw a large number of dead inmates lying where they has fallen in the last few hours or days before our arrival. Since all of the bodies were in various stages of decomposition, the stench of death was overpowering. The men of the 45th Infantry Division were hardened combat veterans. We had been in combat almost two years at that point. While we were accustomed to death, we were not able to comprehend the type of death that we encountered at Dachau.
>
> —Felix L. Sparks, remarks at the U.S. Holocaust Museum, May 8, 1995

Click and Explore

Listen to the accounts of Holocaust survivors (http://openstaxcollege.org/l/15Holocaust) by clicking on "Listen Now" below the name of the person whose story you wish to hear.

YALTA AND PREPARING FOR VICTORY

The last time the Big Three met was in early February 1945 at Yalta in the Soviet Union. Roosevelt was sick, and Stalin's armies were pushing the German army back towards Berlin from the east. Churchill and Roosevelt thus had to accept a number of compromises that strengthened Stalin's position in eastern Europe. In particular, they agreed to allow the Communist government installed by the Soviet Union in Poland to remain in power until free elections took place. For his part, Stalin reaffirmed his commitment, first voiced at Tehran, to enter the war against Japan following the surrender of Germany (Figure 27.18). He also agreed that the Soviet Union would participate in the United Nations, a new peacekeeping body intended to replace the League of Nations. The Big Three left Yalta with many details remaining unclear, planning to finalize plans for the treatment of Germany and the shape of postwar Europe at a later conference. However, Roosevelt did not live to attend the next meeting. He died on April 12, 1945, and Harry S. Truman became president.

Figure 27.18 Prime Minister Winston Churchill, President Franklin Roosevelt, and Premier Joseph Stalin made final plans for the defeat of Nazi Germany at Yalta in February 1945.

By April 1945, Soviet forces had reached Berlin, and both the U.S. and British Allies were pushing up against Germany's last defenses in the western part of the nation. Hitler committed suicide on April 30, 1945. On May 8, 1945, Germany surrendered. The war in Europe was over, and the Allies and liberated regions celebrated the end of the long ordeal. Germany was thoroughly defeated; its industries and cities were badly damaged.

The victorious Allies set about determining what to do to rebuild Europe at the Potsdam Summit Conference in July 1945. Attending the conference were Stalin, Truman, and Churchill, now the outgoing prime minister, as well as the new British prime minister, Clement Atlee. Plans to divide Germany and Austria, and their capital cities, into four zones—to be occupied by the British, French, Americans, and Soviets—a subject discussed at Yalta, were finalized. In addition, the Allies agreed to dismantle Germany's heavy industry in order to make it impossible for the country to produce more armaments.

27.4 The Pacific Theater and the Atomic Bomb

By the end of this section, you will be able to:
- Discuss the strategy employed against the Japanese and some of the significant battles of the Pacific campaign
- Describe the effects of the atomic bombs on Hiroshima and Nagasaki
- Analyze the decision to drop atomic bombs on Japan

Japanese forces won a series of early victories against Allied forces from December 1941 to May 1942. They seized Guam and Wake Island from the United States, and streamed through Malaysia and Thailand into the Philippines and through the Dutch East Indies. By February 1942, they were threatening Australia. The Allies turned the tide in May and June 1942, at the Battle of Coral Sea and the Battle of Midway. The Battle of Midway witnessed the first Japanese naval defeat since the nineteenth century. Shortly after the American victory, U.S. forces invaded Guadalcanal and New Guinea. Slowly, throughout 1943, the United States engaged in a campaign of "island hopping," gradually moving across the Pacific to Japan. In 1944, the United States, seized Saipan and won the Battle of the Philippine Sea. Progressively, American forces drew closer to the strategically important targets of Iwo Jima and Okinawa.

THE PACIFIC CAMPAIGN

During the 1930s, Americans had caught glimpses of Japanese armies in action and grew increasingly sympathetic towards war-torn China. Stories of Japanese atrocities bordering on genocide and the shock of the attack on Pearl Harbor intensified racial animosity toward the Japanese. Wartime propaganda portrayed Japanese soldiers as uncivilized and barbaric, sometimes even inhuman (Figure 27.19), unlike America's German foes. Admiral William Halsey spoke for many Americans when he urged them to "Kill Japs! Kill Japs! Kill more Japs!" Stories of the dispiriting defeats at Bataan and the Japanese capture of the Philippines at Corregidor in 1942 revealed the Japanese cruelty and mistreatment of Americans. The "Bataan Death March," during which as many as 650 American and 10,000 Filipino prisoners of war died, intensified anti-Japanese feelings. Kamikaze attacks that took place towards the end of the war were regarded as proof of the irrationality of Japanese martial values and mindless loyalty to Emperor Hirohito.

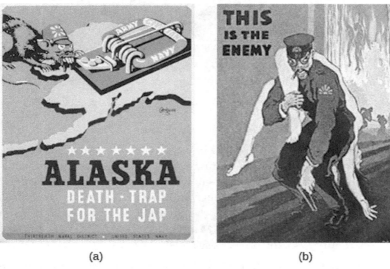

(a)   (b)

Figure 27.19 Anti-Japanese propaganda often portrayed the Japanese as inhuman (a). In addition to emphasizing the supposed apish features of the Japanese (b), this poster depicts the victim as a white woman, undoubtedly to increase American horror even more.

Despite the Allies' Europe First strategy, American forces took the resources that they could assemble and swung into action as quickly as they could to blunt the Japanese advance. Infuriated by stories of defeat at the hands of the allegedly racially inferior Japanese, many high-ranking American military leaders demanded that greater attention be paid to the Pacific campaign. Rather than simply wait for the invasion of France to begin, naval and army officers such as General Douglas MacArthur argued that American resources should be deployed in the Pacific to reclaim territory seized by Japan.

In the Pacific, MacArthur and the Allied forces pursued an island hopping strategy that bypassed certain island strongholds held by the Japanese that were of little or no strategic value. By seizing locations from which Japanese communications and transportation routes could be disrupted or destroyed, the Allies advanced towards Japan without engaging the thousands of Japanese stationed on garrisoned islands. The goal was to advance American air strength close enough to Japan proper to achieve air superiority over the home islands; the nation could then be bombed into submission or at least weakened in preparation for an amphibious assault. By February 1945, American forces had reached the island of Iwo Jima (Figure 27.20). Iwo Jima was originally meant to serve as a forward air base for fighter planes, providing cover for long-distance bombing raids on Japan. Two months later, an even larger engagement, the hardest fought and bloodiest battle of the Pacific theater, took place as American forces invaded Okinawa. The battle raged from April 1945 well into July 1945; the island was finally secured at the cost of seventeen thousand American soldiers killed and thirty-six thousand wounded. Japanese forces lost over 100,000 troops. Perhaps as many as 150,000 civilians perished as well.

Figure 27.20 American forces come ashore on Iwo Jima. Their vehicles had difficulty moving on the beach's volcanic sands. Troops endured shelling by Japanese troops on Mount Suribachi, the mountain in the background.

DROPPING THE ATOMIC BOMB

All belligerents in World War II sought to develop powerful and devastating weaponry. As early as 1939, German scientists had discovered how to split uranium atoms, the technology that would ultimately allow for the creation of the atomic bomb. Albert Einstein, who had emigrated to the United States in 1933 to escape the Nazis, urged President Roosevelt to launch an American atomic research project, and Roosevelt agreed to do so, with reservations. In late 1941, the program received its code name: the **Manhattan Project**. Located at Los Alamos, New Mexico, the Manhattan Project ultimately employed 150,000 people and cost some $2 billion. In July 1945, the project's scientists successfully tested the first atomic bomb.

In the spring of 1945, the military began to prepare for the possible use of an atomic bomb by choosing appropriate targets. Suspecting that the immediate bomb blast would extend over one mile and secondary effects would include fire damage, a compact city of significant military value with densely built frame buildings seemed to be the best target. Eventually, the city of Hiroshima, the headquarters of the Japanese Second Army, and the communications and supply hub for all of southern Japan, was chosen. The city of Kokura was chosen as the primary target of the second bomb, and Nagasaki, an industrial center producing war materiel and the largest seaport in southern Japan, was selected as a secondary target.

The *Enola Gay*, a B-29 bomber named after its pilot's mother, dropped an atomic bomb known as "Little Boy" on Hiroshima at 8:15 a.m. Monday morning, August 6, 1945. A huge mushroom cloud rose above the city. Survivors sitting down for breakfast or preparing to go to school recalled seeing a bright light and then being blown across the room. The immense heat of the blast melted stone and metal, and ignited fires throughout the city. One man later recalled watching his mother and brother burn to death as fire consumed their home. A female survivor, a child at the time of the attack, remembered finding the body of her mother, which had been reduced to ashes and fell apart as she touched it. Two-thirds of the buildings in Hiroshima were destroyed. Within an hour after the bombing, radioactive "black rain" began to fall. Approximately seventy thousand people died in the original blast. The same number would later die of radiation poisoning. When Japan refused to surrender, a second atomic bomb, named Fat Man, was dropped on Nagasaki on August 9, 1945. At least sixty thousand people were killed at Nagasaki. Kokura, the primary target, had been shrouded in clouds on that morning and thus had escaped destruction. It is impossible to say with certainty how many died in the two attacks; the heat of the bomb blasts incinerated or vaporized many of the victims (Figure 27.21).

(a)   (b)

Figure 27.21 According to estimates, the atomic bombs dropped on Hiroshima and Nagasaki (a) together killed anywhere from 125,000 to over 250,000 people. The so-called Genbaku (A-Bomb) Dome, now the Hiroshima Peace Memorial, was the only building left standing near the Hiroshima bomb's hypocenter (b).

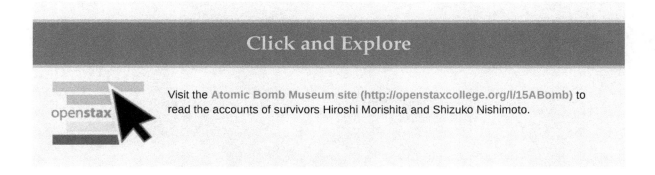

Click and Explore

Visit the **Atomic Bomb Museum site (http://openstaxcollege.org/l/15ABomb)** to read the accounts of survivors Hiroshi Morishita and Shizuko Nishimoto.

The decision to use nuclear weapons is widely debated. Why exactly did the United States deploy an atomic bomb? The fierce resistance that the Japanese forces mounted during their early campaigns led American planners to believe that any invasion of the Japanese home islands would be exceedingly bloody. According to some estimates, as many as 250,000 Americans might die in securing a final victory. Such considerations undoubtedly influenced President Truman's decision. Truman, who had not known about the Manhattan Project until Roosevelt's death, also may not have realized how truly destructive it was. Indeed, some of the scientists who had built the bomb were surprised by its power. One question that has not been fully answered is why the United States dropped the second bomb on Nagasaki. As some scholars have noted, if Truman's intention was to eliminate the need for a home island invasion, he could have given Japan more time to respond after bombing Hiroshima. He did not, however. The second bombing may have been intended to send a message to Stalin, who was becoming intransigent regarding postwar Europe. If it is indeed true that Truman had political motivations for using the bombs, then the destruction of Nagasaki might have been the first salvo of the Cold War with the Soviet Union. And yet, other historians have pointed out that the war had unleashed such massive atrocities against civilians by all belligerents—the United States included—that by the summer of 1945, the president no longer needed any particular reason to use his entire nuclear arsenal.

THE WAR ENDS

Whatever the true reasons for their use, the bombs had the desired effect of getting Japan to surrender. Even before the atomic attacks, the conventional bombings of Japan, the defeat of its forces in the field, and the entry of the Soviet Union into the war had convinced the Imperial Council that they had to end the war. They had hoped to negotiate the terms of the peace, but Emperor Hirohito intervened after the destruction of Nagasaki and accepted unconditional surrender. Although many Japanese shuddered at the humiliation of defeat, most were relieved that the war was over. Japan's industries and cities had been thoroughly destroyed, and the immediate future looked bleak as they awaited their fate at the hands of the American occupation forces.

The victors had yet another nation to rebuild and reform, but the war was finally over. Following the surrender, the Japanese colony of Korea was divided along the thirty-eighth parallel; the Soviet Union was given control of the northern half and the United States was given control of the southern portion. In Europe, as had been agreed upon at a meeting of the Allies in Potsdam in the summer of 1945, Germany was divided into four occupation zones that would be controlled by Britain, France, the Soviet Union, and the United States, respectively. The city of Berlin was similarly split into four. Plans were made to prosecute war criminals in both Japan and Germany. In October 1945, the United Nations was created. People around the world celebrated the end of the conflict, but America's use of atomic bombs and disagreements between the United States and the Soviet Union at Yalta and Potsdam would contribute to ongoing instability in the postwar world.

Key Terms

Big Three the nickname given to the leaders of the three major Allied nations: Winston Churchill, Franklin Roosevelt, and Joseph Stalin

conscientious objectors those who, for religious or philosophical reasons, refuse to serve in the armed forces

D-day June 6, 1944, the date of the invasion of Normandy, France, by British, Canadian, and American forces, which opened a second front in Europe

Double Vcampaign a campaign by African Americans to win victory over the enemy overseas and victory over racism at home

Enola Gay the plane that dropped the atomic bomb on Hiroshima

Executive Order 9066 the order given by President Roosevelt to relocate and detain people of Japanese ancestry, including those who were American citizens

Fascism a political ideology that places a heightened focus on national unity, through dictatorial rule, and militarism

internment the forced collection of the West Coast Japanese and Japanese American population into ten relocation centers for the greater part of World War II

Manhattan Project the code name given to the research project that developed the atomic bomb

materiel equipment and supplies used by the military

Rosie the Riveter a symbol of female workers in the defense industries

zoot suit a flamboyant outfit favored by young African American and Mexican American men

Summary

27.1 The Origins of War: Europe, Asia, and the United States

America sought, at the end of the First World War, to create new international relationships that would make such wars impossible in the future. But as the Great Depression hit Europe, several new leaders rose to power under the new political ideologies of Fascism and Nazism. Mussolini in Italy and Hitler in Germany were both proponents of Fascism, using dictatorial rule to achieve national unity. Still, the United States remained focused on the economic challenges of its own Great Depression. Hence, there was little interest in getting involved in Europe's problems or even the China-Japan conflict.

It soon became clear, however, that Germany and Italy's alliance was putting democratic countries at risk. Roosevelt first sought to support Great Britain and China by providing economic support without intervening directly. However, when Japan, an ally of Germany and Italy, attacked Pearl Harbor, catching the military base unaware and claiming thousands of lives, America's feelings toward war shifted, and the country was quickly pulled into the global conflict.

27.2 The Home Front

The brunt of the war's damage occurred far from United States soil, but Americans at home were still greatly affected by the war. Women struggled to care for children with scarce resources at their disposal and sometimes while working full time. Economically, the country surged forward, but strict rationing for the war effort meant that Americans still went without. New employment opportunities opened up for women and ethnic minorities, as white men enlisted or were drafted. These new opportunities were positive for those who benefited from them, but they also created new anxieties among white men about racial and gender equality. Race riots took place across the country, and Americans of Japanese ancestry were relocated to internment camps. Still, there was an overwhelming sense of patriotism in the country, which was reflected in the culture of the day.

27.3 Victory in the European Theater

Upon entering the war, President Roosevelt believed that the greatest threat to the long-term survival of democracy and freedom would be a German victory. Hence, he entered into an alliance with British prime minister Winston Churchill and Soviet premier Joseph Stalin to defeat the common enemy while also seeking to lay the foundation for a peaceful postwar world in which the United States would play a major and permanent role. Appeasement and nonintervention had been proven to be shortsighted and tragic policies that failed to provide security and peace either for the United States or for the world.

With the aid of the British, the United States invaded North Africa and from there invaded Europe by way of Italy. However, the cross-channel invasion of Europe through France that Stalin had long called for did not come until 1944, by which time the Soviets had turned the tide of battle in eastern Europe. The liberation of Hitler's concentration camps forced Allied nations to confront the grisly horrors that had been taking place as the war unfolded. The Big Three met for one last time in February 1945, at Yalta, where Churchill and Roosevelt agreed to several conditions that strengthened Stalin's position. They planned to finalize their plans at a later conference, but Roosevelt died two months later.

27.4 The Pacific Theater and the Atomic Bomb

The way in which the United States fought the war in the Pacific was fueled by fear of Japanese imperialistic aggression, as well as anger over Japan's attack on Pearl Harbor and its mistreatment of its enemies. It was also influenced by a long history of American racism towards Asians that dated back to the nineteenth century. From hostile anti-Japanese propaganda to the use of two atomic bombs on Japanese cities, America's actions during the Pacific campaign were far more aggressive than they were in the European theater. Using the strategy of island hopping, the United States was able to get within striking distance of Japan. Only once they adopted this strategy were the Allied troops able to turn the tide against what had been a series of challenging Japanese victories. The war ended with Japan's surrender.

The combined Allied forces had successfully waged a crusade against Nazi Germany, Italy, and Japan. The United States, forced to abandon a policy of nonintervention outside the Western Hemisphere, had been able to mobilize itself and produce the weapons and the warriors necessary to defeat its enemies. Following World War II, America would never again retreat from the global stage, and its early mastery of nuclear weapons would make it the dominant force in the postwar world.

Review Questions

1. The United States Senator who led the noninterventionists in Congress and called for neutrality legislation in the 1930s was _____.
   A. Gerald P. Nye
   B. Robert Wagner
   C. George C. Marshall
   D. Neville Chamberlain

2. Describe Franklin Roosevelt's efforts on behalf of German Jews in the 1930s. How was he able to help, and in what ways did his actions come up short?

3. During World War II, unionized workers agreed _____.
   A. to work without pay
   B. to go without vacations or days off

C. to live near the factories to save time commuting

D. to keep production going by not striking

4. The program to recruit Mexican agricultural workers during World War II was the _____.

A. bracero program
B. maquiladora program
C. brazzos program
D. campesino program

5. What were American women's contributions to the war effort?

6. Which of the following demands did the Soviet Union make of Britain and the United States?

A. the right to try all Nazi war criminals in the Soviet Union
B. the invasion of North Africa to help the Soviet Union's ally Iraq
C. the invasion of western Europe to draw German forces away from the Soviet Union
D. the right to place Communist Party leaders in charge of the German government

7. What did Roosevelt mean to achieve with his demand for Germany and Japan's unconditional surrender?

8. What were the phases of the Holocaust?

9. Which of the following islands had to be captured in order to provide a staging area for U.S. bombing raids against Japan?

A. Sakhalin
B. Iwo Jima
C. Molokai
D. Reunion

10. What purpose did the Allied strategy of island hopping serve?

11. Why might President Truman have made the decision to drop the second atomic bomb on Nagasaki?

Critical Thinking Questions

12. Given that the Japanese war against China began in 1937 and German aggression began in Europe in 1936, why was it not until 1941 that the United States joined the war against the Axis powers? Was the decision to stay out of the war until 1941 a wise one on the part of the United States?

13. Should the United States have done more to help European Jews during the 1930s? What could it have done?

14. In what ways did World War II improve the status of women and African Americans in the United States?

15. Should the U.S. government have ordered the internment of Japanese Americans? Does the fear of espionage or sabotage justify depriving American citizens of their rights?

16. Did the United States make the right decision to drop atomic bombs on Japan?

CHAPTER 28

Post-War Prosperity and Cold War Fears, 1945-1960

Figure 28.1 *Is This Tomorrow?* warned Americans about the potential horrors of living under a Communist dictatorship. Postwar propaganda such as this comic book, the cover of which showed invading Russians attacking Americans and the U.S. flag in flames, served to drum up fear during the Cold War.

Chapter Outline

28.1 The Challenges of Peacetime
28.2 The Cold War
28.3 The American Dream
28.4 Popular Culture and Mass Media
28.5 The African American Struggle for Civil Rights

Introduction

Is This Tomorrow? (Figure 28.1), a 1947 comic book, highlights one way that the federal government and some Americans revived popular sentiment in opposition to Communism. The United States and the Soviet Union, allies during World War II, had different visions for the postwar world. As Joseph Stalin, premier of the Soviet Union, tightened his grip on the countries of Eastern Europe, Americans began to fear that it was his goal to spread the Communist revolution throughout the world and make newly independent nations puppets of the Soviet Union. To enlist as many Americans as possible in the fight against Soviet domination, the U.S. government and purveyors of popular culture churned out propaganda intended to convince average citizens of the dangers posed by the Soviet Union. Artwork such as the cover of *Is This Tomorrow?*, which depicts Russians attacking Americans, including a struggling woman and an African American veteran still wearing his uniform, played upon postwar fears of Communism and of a future war with the Soviet Union. These fears dominated American life and affected foreign policy, military strategy, urban planning, popular culture, and the civil rights movement.

28.1 The Challenges of Peacetime

By the end of this section, you will be able to:
- Identify the issues that the nation faced during demobilization
- Explain the goals and objectives of the Truman administration
- Evaluate the actions taken by the U.S. government to address the concerns of returning veterans

The decade and a half immediately following the end of World War II was one in which middle- and working-class Americans hoped for a better life than the one they lived before the war. These hopes were tainted by fears of economic hardship, as many who experienced the Great Depression feared a return to economic decline. Others clamored for the opportunity to spend the savings they had accumulated through long hours on the job during the war when consumer goods were rarely available.

African Americans who had served in the armed forces and worked in the defense industry did not wish to return to "normal." Instead, they wanted the same rights and opportunities that other Americans had. Still other citizens were less concerned with the economy or civil rights; instead, they looked with suspicion at the Soviet presence in Eastern Europe. What would happen now that the United States and the Soviet Union were no longer allies, and the other nations that had long helped maintain a balance of power were left seriously damaged by the war? Harry Truman, president for less than a year when the war ended, was charged with addressing all of these concerns and giving the American people a "fair deal."

DEMOBILIZATION AND THE RETURN TO CIVILIAN LIFE

The most immediate task to be completed after World War II was demobilizing the military and reintegrating the veterans into civilian life. In response to popular pressure and concerns over the budget, the United States sought to demobilize its armed forces as quickly as possible. Many servicemen, labeled the "Ohio boys" (Over the Hill in October), threatened to vote Republican if they were not home by

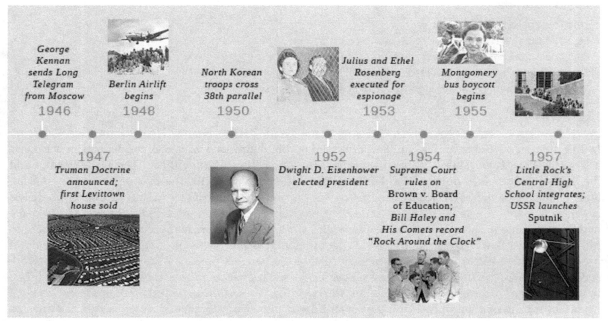

Figure 28.2   (credit: "1953": modification of work by Library of Congress)

Christmas 1946. Understandably, this placed a great deal of pressure on the still-inexperienced president to shrink the size of the U.S. military.

Not everyone wanted the government to reduce America's military might, however. Secretary of the Navy James Forrestal and Secretary of War Robert P. Patterson warned Truman in October 1945 that an overly rapid demobilization jeopardized the nation's strategic position in the world. While Truman agreed with their assessment, he felt powerless to put a halt to demobilization. In response to mounting political pressure, the government reduced the size of the U.S. military from a high of 12 million in June 1945 to 1.5 million in June 1947—still more troops than the nation ever had in arms during peacetime. Soldiers and sailors were not the only ones dismissed from service. As the war drew to a close, millions of women working the jobs of men who had gone off to fight were dismissed by their employers, often because the demand for war materiel had declined and because government propaganda encouraged them to go home to make way for the returning troops. While most women workers surveyed at the end of the war wished to keep their jobs (75–90 percent, depending on the study), many did in fact leave them. Nevertheless, throughout the late 1940s and the 1950s, women continued to make up approximately one-third of the U.S. labor force.

Readjustment to postwar life was difficult for the returning troops. The U.S. Army estimated that as many of 20 percent of its casualties were psychological. Although many eagerly awaited their return to civilian status, others feared that they would not be able to resume a humdrum existence after the experience of fighting on the front lines. Veterans also worried that they wouldn't find work and that civilian defense workers were better positioned to take advantage of the new jobs opening up in the peacetime economy. Some felt that their wives and children would not welcome their presence, and some children did indeed resent the return of fathers who threatened to disrupt the mother-child household. Those on the home front worried as well. Doctors warned fiancées, wives, and mothers that soldiers might return with psychological problems that would make them difficult to live with.

The GI Bill of Rights

Well before the end of the war, Congress had passed one of the most significant and far-reaching pieces of legislation to ease veterans' transition into civilian life: the Servicemen's Readjustment Act, also known as the **GI Bill** (Figure 28.3). Every honorably discharged veteran who had seen active duty, but not necessarily combat, was eligible to receive a year's worth of unemployment compensation. This provision not only calmed veterans' fears regarding their ability to support themselves, but it also prevented large numbers of men—as well as some women—from suddenly entering a job market that did not have enough positions for them. Another way that the GI Bill averted a glut in the labor market was by giving returning veterans the opportunity to pursue an education; it paid for tuition at a college or vocational school, and gave them a stipend to live on while they completed their studies.

Figure 28.3 President Franklin D. Roosevelt signed the Servicemen's Readjustment Act, or GI Bill, on June 22, 1944, just weeks after the Allied invasion of Normandy, France, and more than a year before the end of the war.

The result was a dramatic increase in the number of students—especially male ones—enrolled in American colleges and universities. In 1940, only 5.5 percent of American men had a college degree. By 1950, that percentage had increased to 7.3 percent, as more than two million servicemen took advantage of the benefits offered by the GI Bill to complete college. The numbers continued to grow throughout the 1950s. Upon graduation, these men were prepared for skilled blue-collar or white-collar jobs that paved the way for many to enter the middle class. The creation of a well-educated, skilled labor force helped the U.S. economy as well. Other benefits offered by the GI Bill included low-interest loans to purchase homes or start small businesses.

However, not all veterans were able to take advantage of the GI Bill. African American veterans could use their educational benefits only to attend schools that accepted black students. The approximately nine thousand servicemen and women who were dishonorably discharged because they were gay or lesbian were ineligible for GI Bill benefits. Benefits for some Mexican American veterans, mainly in Texas, were also denied or delayed.

The Return of the Japanese

While most veterans received assistance to help in their adjustment to postwar life, others returned home to an uncertain future without the promise of government aid to help them resume their prewar lives. Japanese Americans from the West Coast who had been interned during the war also confronted the task of rebuilding their lives. In December 1944, Franklin Roosevelt had declared an end to the forced relocation of Japanese Americans, and as of January 1945, they were free to return to their homes. In many areas, however, neighbors clung to their prejudices and denounced those of Japanese descent as disloyal and dangerous. These feelings had been worsened by wartime propaganda, which often featured horrific accounts of Japanese mistreatment of prisoners, and by the statements of military officers to the effect that the Japanese were inherently savage. Facing such animosity, many Japanese American families chose to move elsewhere. Those who did return often found that in their absence, "friends" and neighbors had sold possessions that had been left with them for safekeeping. Many homes had been vandalized and farms destroyed. When Japanese Americans reopened their businesses, former customers sometimes boycotted them.

Click and Explore

For more on the experiences of Japanese Americans (http://openstaxcollege.org/l/15JapaneseOR) after internment, read about their return to communities in Oregon after World War II.

THE FAIR DEAL

Early in his presidency, Truman sought to build on the promises of Roosevelt's New Deal. Besides demobilizing the armed forces and preparing for the homecoming of servicemen and women, he also had to guide the nation through the process of returning to a peacetime economy. To this end, he proposed an ambitious program of social legislation that included establishing a federal minimum wage, expanding Social Security and public housing, and prohibiting child labor. Wartime price controls were retained for some items but removed from others, like meat. In his 1949 inaugural address, Truman referred to his programs as the "**Fair Deal**," a nod to his predecessor's New Deal. He wanted the Fair Deal to include Americans of color and became the first president to address the National Association for the Advancement of Colored People (NAACP). He also took decisive steps towards extending civil rights to African Americans by establishing, by executive order in December 1946, a Presidential Committee on Civil Rights to investigate racial discrimination in the United States. Truman also desegregated the armed forces, again by executive order, in July 1948, overriding many objections that the military was no place for social experimentation.

Congress, however, which was dominated by Republicans and southern conservative Democrats, refused to pass more "radical" pieces of legislation, such as a bill providing for national healthcare. The American Medical Association spent some $1.5 million to defeat Truman's healthcare proposal, which it sought to discredit as socialized medicine in order to appeal to Americans' fear of Communism. The same Congress also refused to make lynching a federal crime or outlaw the poll tax that reduced the access of poor Americans to the ballot box. Congress also rejected a bill that would have made Roosevelt's Fair Employment Practices Committee, which prohibited racial discrimination by companies doing business with the federal government, permanent. At the same time, they passed many conservative pieces of legislation. For example, the Taft-Hartley Act, which limited the power of unions, became law despite Truman's veto.

28.2 The Cold War

By the end of this section, you will be able to:
* Explain how and why the Cold War emerged in the wake of World War II
* Describe the steps taken by the U.S. government to oppose Communist expansion in Europe and Asia
* Discuss the government's efforts to root out Communist influences in the United States

As World War II drew to a close, the alliance that had made the United States and the Soviet Union partners in their defeat of the Axis powers—Germany, Italy, and Japan—began to fall apart. Both sides realized that their visions for the future of Europe and the world were incompatible. Joseph Stalin, the premier of the Soviet Union, wished to retain hold of Eastern Europe and establish Communist, pro-Soviet governments there, in an effort to both expand Soviet influence and protect the Soviet Union from future invasions. He also sought to bring Communist revolution to Asia and to developing nations elsewhere in the world. The United States wanted to expand its influence as well by protecting or installing democratic governments throughout the world. It sought to combat the influence of the Soviet Union by forming alliances with Asian, African, and Latin American nations, and by helping these countries to establish or expand prosperous, free-market economies. The end of the war left the industrialized nations of Europe and Asia physically devastated and economically exhausted by years of invasion, battle, and bombardment. With Great Britain, France, Germany, Italy, Japan, and China reduced to shadows of their former selves, the United States and the Soviet Union emerged as the last two superpowers and quickly found themselves locked in a contest for military, economic, social, technological, and ideological supremacy.

FROM ISOLATIONISM TO ENGAGEMENT

The United States had a long history of avoiding foreign alliances that might require the commitment of its troops abroad. However, in accepting the realities of the post-World War II world, in which traditional powers like Great Britain or France were no longer strong enough to police the globe, the United States realized that it would have to make a permanent change in its foreign policy, shifting from relative isolation to active engagement.

On assuming the office of president upon the death of Franklin Roosevelt, Harry Truman was already troubled by Soviet actions in Europe. He disliked the concessions made by Roosevelt at Yalta, which had allowed the Soviet Union to install a Communist government in Poland. At the Potsdam conference, held from July 17 to August 2, 1945, Truman also opposed Stalin's plans to demand large reparations from Germany. He feared the burden that this would impose on Germany might lead to another cycle of German rearmament and aggression—a fear based on that nation's development after World War I (Figure 28.4).

Figure 28.4 At the postwar conference in Potsdam, Germany, Harry Truman stands between Joseph Stalin (right) and Clement Atlee (left). Atlee became prime minister of Great Britain, replacing Winston Churchill, while the conference was taking place.

Although the United States and the Soviet Union did finally reach an agreement at Potsdam, this was the final occasion on which they cooperated for quite some time. Each remained convinced that its own economic and political systems were superior to the other's, and the two superpowers quickly found themselves drawn into conflict. The decades-long struggle between them for technological and ideological supremacy became known as the **Cold War**. So called because it did not include direct military confrontation between Soviet and U.S. troops, the Cold War was fought with a variety of other weapons: espionage and surveillance, political assassinations, propaganda, and the formation of alliances with other nations. It also became an arms race, as both countries competed to build the greatest stockpile of nuclear weapons, and also competed for influence in poorer nations, supporting opposite sides in wars in some of those nations, such as Korea and Vietnam.

CONTAINMENT ABROAD

In February 1946, George Kennan, a State Department official stationed at the U.S. embassy in Moscow, sent an eight-thousand-word message to Washington, DC. In what became known as the "Long Telegram," Kennan maintained that Soviet leaders believed that the only way to protect the Soviet Union was to destroy "rival" nations and their influence over weaker nations. According to Kennan, the Soviet Union was not so much a revolutionary regime as a totalitarian bureaucracy that was unable to accept the prospect of a peaceful coexistence of the United States and itself. He advised that the best way to thwart Soviet plans for the world was to contain Soviet influence—primarily through economic policy—to those places where it already existed and prevent its political expansion into new areas. This strategy, which came to be known as the policy of **containment**, formed the basis for U.S. foreign policy and military decision making for more than thirty years.

As Communist governments came to power elsewhere in the world, American policymakers extended their strategy of containment to what became known as the **domino theory** under the Eisenhower administration: Neighbors to Communist nations, so was the assumption, were likely to succumb to the same allegedly dangerous and infectious ideology. Like dominos toppling one another, entire regions would eventually be controlled by the Soviets. The demand for anti-Communist containment appeared as early as March 1946 in a speech by Winston Churchill, in which he referred to an **Iron Curtain** that divided Europe into the "free" West and the Communist East controlled by the Soviet Union.

The commitment to containing Soviet expansion made necessary the ability to mount a strong military offense and defense. In pursuit of this goal, the U.S. military was reorganized under the National Security Act of 1947. This act streamlined the government in matters of security by creating the National Security Council and establishing the Central Intelligence Agency (CIA) to conduct surveillance and espionage in foreign nations. It also created the Department of the Air Force, which was combined with the Departments of the Army and Navy in 1949 to form one Department of Defense.

The Truman Doctrine

In Europe, the end of World War II witnessed the rise of a number of internal struggles for control of countries that had been occupied by Nazi Germany. Great Britain occupied Greece as the Nazi regime there collapsed. The British aided the authoritarian government of Greece in its battles against Greek Communists. In March 1947, Great Britain announced that it could no longer afford the cost of supporting government military activities and withdrew from participation in the Greek civil war. Stepping into this power vacuum, the United States announced the Truman Doctrine, which offered support to Greece and Turkey in the form of financial assistance, weaponry, and troops to help train their militaries and bolster their governments against Communism. Eventually, the program was expanded to include any state trying to withstand a Communist takeover. The Truman Doctrine thus became a hallmark of U.S. Cold War policy.

DEFINING "AMERICAN"

✷ *The Truman Doctrine*

In 1947, Great Britain, which had assumed responsibility for the disarming of German troops in Greece at the end of World War II, could no longer afford to provide financial support for the authoritarian Greek government, which was attempting to win a civil war against Greek leftist rebels. President Truman, unwilling to allow a Communist government to come to power there, requested Congress to provide funds for the government of Greece to continue its fight against the rebels. Truman also requested aid for the government of Turkey to fight the forces of Communism in that country. He said:

> At the present moment in world history nearly every nation must choose between alternative ways of life. The choice is too often not a free one.
> Should we fail to aid Greece and Turkey in this fateful hour, the effect will be far reaching to the West as well as to the East.
> The seeds of totalitarian regimes are nurtured by misery and want. They spread and grow in the evil soil of poverty and strife. They reach their full growth when the hope of a people for a better life has died. We must keep that hope alive.
> The free peoples of the world look to us for support in maintaining their freedoms.
> If we falter in our leadership, we may endanger the peace of the world—and we shall surely endanger the welfare of our own nation.
> Great responsibilities have been placed upon us by the swift movement of events.
> I am confident that the Congress will face these responsibilities squarely.

What role is Truman suggesting that the United States assume in the postwar world? Does the United States still assume this role?

The Marshall Plan

By 1946, the American economy was growing significantly. At the same time, the economic situation in Europe was disastrous. The war had turned much of Western Europe into a battlefield, and the rebuilding of factories, public transportation systems, and power stations progressed exceedingly slowly. Starvation loomed as a real possibility for many. As a result of these conditions, Communism was making significant inroads in both Italy and France. These concerns led Truman, along with Secretary of State George C. Marshall, to propose to Congress the European Recovery Program, popularly known as the **Marshall Plan**. Between its implantation in April 1948 and its termination in 1951, this program gave $13 billion in economic aid to European nations.

Truman's motivation was economic and political, as well as humanitarian. The plan stipulated that the European nations had to work together in order to receive aid, thus enforcing unity through enticement, while seeking to undercut the political popularity of French and Italian Communists and dissuading moderates from forming coalition governments with them. Likewise, much of the money had to be spent on American goods, boosting the postwar economy of the United States as well as the American cultural presence in Europe. Stalin regarded the program as a form of bribery. The Soviet Union refused to accept aid from the Marshall Plan, even though it could have done so, and forbade the Communist states of Eastern Europe to accept U.S. funds as well. Those states that did accept aid began to experience an economic recovery.

MY STORY

✪ *George C. Marshall and the Nobel Peace Prize*

The youngest child of a Pennsylvania businessman and Democrat, George C. Marshall (Figure 28.5) chose a military career. He attended the Virginia Military Institute, was a veteran of World War I, and spent the rest of his life either in the military or otherwise in the service of his country, including as President Truman's Secretary of State. He was awarded the Nobel Peace Prize in 1953, the only soldier to ever receive that honor. Below is an excerpt of his remarks as he accepted the award.

Figure 28.5 During World War II, George C. Marshall was responsible for expanding the 189,000-member U.S. Army into a modern, fighting force of eight million by 1942. As Secretary of State under Truman, he proposed the European Recovery Program to aid European economies struggling after the war.

> There has been considerable comment over the awarding of the Nobel Peace Prize to a soldier. I am afraid this does not seem as remarkable to me as it quite evidently appears to others. I know a great deal of the horrors and tragedies of war. Today, as chairman of the American Battle Monuments Commission, it is my duty to supervise the construction and maintenance of military cemeteries in many countries overseas, particularly in Western Europe. The cost of war in human lives is constantly spread before me, written neatly in many ledgers whose columns are gravestones. I am deeply moved to find some means or method of avoiding another calamity of war. Almost daily I hear from the wives, or mothers, or families of the fallen. The tragedy of the aftermath is almost constantly before me.
>
> I share with you an active concern for some practical method for avoiding war. . . . A very strong military posture is vitally necessary today. How long it must continue I am not prepared to estimate, but I am sure that it is too narrow a basis on which to build a dependable, long-enduring peace. The guarantee for a long continued peace will depend on other factors in addition to a moderated military strength, and no less important. Perhaps the most important single factor will be a spiritual regeneration to develop goodwill, faith, and understanding among nations. Economic factors will undoubtedly play an important part. Agreements to secure a balance of power, however disagreeable they may seem, must likewise be considered. And with all these there must be wisdom and the will to act on that wisdom.

What steps did Marshall recommend be taken to maintain a lasting peace? To what extent have today's nations heeded his advice?

Showdown in Europe

The lack of consensus with the Soviets on the future of Germany led the United States, Great Britain, and France to support joining their respective occupation zones into a single, independent state. In December 1946, they took steps to do so, but the Soviet Union did not wish the western zones of the country to unify under a democratic, pro-capitalist government. The Soviet Union also feared the possibility of a unified West Berlin, located entirely within the Soviet sector. Three days after the western allies authorized the introduction of a new currency in Western Germany—the Deutsche Mark—Stalin ordered all land and water routes to the western zones of the city Berlin to be cut off in June 1948. Hoping to starve the western parts of the city into submission, the Berlin blockade was also a test of the emerging U.S. policy of containment.

Unwilling to abandon Berlin, the United States, Great Britain, and France began to deliver all needed supplies to West Berlin by air (Figure 28.6). In April 1949, the three countries joined Canada and eight Western European nations to form the North Atlantic Treaty Organization (NATO), an alliance pledging its members to mutual defense in the event of attack. On May 12, 1949, a year and approximately two million tons of supplies later, the Soviets admitted defeat and ended the blockade of Berlin. On May 23, the Federal Republic of Germany (FRG), consisting of the unified western zones and commonly referred to as West Germany, was formed. The Soviets responded by creating the German Democratic Republic, or East Germany, in October 1949.

(a)   (b)

Figure 28.6   American C-47 transport planes (a) are loaded with staged supplies at a French airport before taking off for Berlin. Residents of Berlin wait for a U.S. plane (b) carrying needed supplies to land at Templehof Airport in the American sector of the city.

CONTAINMENT AT HOME

In 1949, two incidents severely disrupted American confidence in the ability of the United States to contain the spread of Communism and limit Soviet power in the world. First, on August 29, 1949, the Soviet Union exploded its first atomic bomb—no longer did the United States have a monopoly on nuclear power. A few months later, on October 1, 1949, Chinese Communist Party leader Mao Zedong announced the triumph of the Chinese Communists over their Nationalist foes in a civil war that had been raging since 1927. The Nationalist forces, under their leader Chiang Kai-shek, departed for Taiwan in December 1949.

Immediately, there were suspicions that spies had passed bomb-making secrets to the Soviets and that Communist sympathizers in the U.S. State Department had hidden information that might have enabled the United States to ward off the Communist victory in China. Indeed, in February 1950, Wisconsin senator Joseph McCarthy, a Republican, charged in a speech that the State Department was filled with Communists. Also in 1950, the imprisonment in Great Britain of Klaus Fuchs, a German-born physicist who had worked on the Manhattan Project and was then convicted of passing nuclear secrets to the Soviets, increased American fears. Information given by Fuchs to the British implicated a number of

American citizens as well. The most infamous trial of suspected American spies was that of Julius and Ethel Rosenberg, who were executed in June 1953 despite a lack of evidence against them. Several decades later, evidence was found that Julius, but not Ethel, had in fact given information to the Soviet Union.

Fears that Communists within the United States were jeopardizing the country's security had existed even before the victory of Mao Zedong and the arrest and conviction of the atomic spies. Roosevelt's New Deal and Truman's Fair Deal were often criticized as "socialist," which many mistakenly associated with Communism, and Democrats were often branded Communists by Republicans. In response, on March 21, 1947, Truman signed Executive Order 9835, which provided the Federal Bureau of Investigation with broad powers to investigate federal employees and identify potential security risks. State and municipal governments instituted their own loyalty boards to find and dismiss potentially disloyal workers.

In addition to loyalty review boards, the House Committee on Un-American Activities (HUAC), established in 1938 to investigate suspected Nazi sympathizers, after World War II also sought to root out suspected Communists in business, academia, and the media. HUAC was particularly interested in Hollywood because it feared that Communist sympathizers might use motion pictures as pro-Soviet propaganda. Witnesses were subpoenaed and required to testify before the committee; refusal could result in imprisonment. Those who invoked Fifth Amendment protections, or were otherwise suspected of Communist sympathies, often lost their jobs or found themselves on a **blacklist**, which prevented them from securing employment. Notable artists who were blacklisted in the 1940s and 1950s include composer Leonard Bernstein, novelist Dashiell Hammett, playwright and screenwriter Lillian Hellman, actor and singer Paul Robeson, and musician Artie Shaw.

TO THE TRENCHES AGAIN

Just as the U.S. government feared the possibility of Communist infiltration of the United States, so too was it alert for signs that Communist forces were on the move elsewhere. The Soviet Union had been granted control of the northern half of the Korean peninsula at the end of World War II, and the United States had control of the southern portion. The Soviets displayed little interest in extending its power into South Korea, and Stalin did not wish to risk confrontation with the United States over Korea. North Korea's leaders, however, wished to reunify the peninsula under Communist rule. In April 1950, Stalin finally gave permission to North Korea's leader Kim Il Sung to invade South Korea and provided the North Koreans with weapons and military advisors.

On June 25, 1950, troops of the North Korean People's Democratic Army crossed the thirty-eighth parallel, the border between North and South Korea. The first major test of the U.S. policy of containment in Asia had begun, for the domino theory held that a victory by North Korea might lead to further Communist expansion in Asia, in the virtual backyard of the United States' chief new ally in East Asia—Japan. The United Nations (UN), which had been established in 1945, was quick to react. On June 27, the UN Security Council denounced North Korea's actions and called upon UN members to help South Korea defeat the invading forces. As a permanent member of the Security Council, the Soviet Union could have vetoed the action, but it had boycotted UN meetings following the awarding of China's seat on the Security Council to Taiwan instead of to Mao Zedong's People's Republic of China.

On June 27, Truman ordered U.S. military forces into South Korea. They established a defensive line on the far southern part of the Korean peninsula near the town of Pusan. A U.S.-led invasion at Inchon on September 15 halted the North Korean advance and turned it into a retreat (Figure 28.7). As North Korean forces moved back across the thirty-eighth parallel, UN forces under the command of U.S. General Douglas MacArthur followed. MacArthur's goal was not only to drive the North Korean army out of South Korea but to destroy Communist North Korea as well. At this stage, he had the support of President Truman; however, as UN forces approached the Yalu River, the border between China and North Korea, MacArthur's and Truman's objectives diverged. Chinese premier Zhou Enlai, who had provided supplies and military advisors for North Korea before the conflict began, sent troops into battle to support North Korea and caught U.S. troops by surprise. Following a costly retreat from North Korea's Chosin Reservoir, a swift advance of Chinese and North Korean forces and another invasion of Seoul, MacArthur urged Truman to deploy nuclear weapons against China. Truman, however, did not wish to risk a broader war in Asia. MacArthur criticized Truman's decision and voiced his disagreement in a letter to a Republican congressman, who subsequently allowed the letter to become public. In April 1951, Truman accused MacArthur of insubordination and relieved him of his command. The Joint Chiefs of Staff agreed, calling the escalation MacArthur had called for "the wrong war, at the wrong place, at the wrong time, and with the wrong enemy." Nonetheless, the public gave MacArthur a hero's welcome in New York with the largest ticker tape parade in the nation's history.

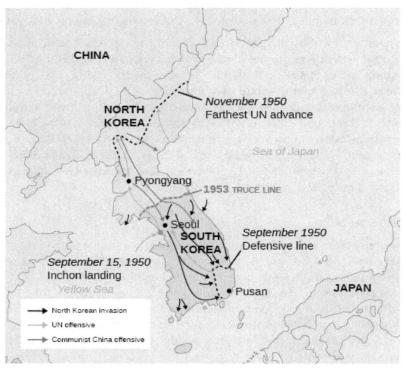

Figure 28.7   After the initial invasion of South Korea by the North Korean People's Democratic Army, the United Nations established a defensive line in the southern part of the country. The landing at Inchon in September reversed the tide of the war and allowed UN forces under General Douglas MacArthur to retake the city of Seoul, which had fallen to North Korean troops in the early days of the war.

By July 1951, the UN forces had recovered from the setbacks earlier in the year and pushed North Korean and Chinese forces back across the thirty-eighth parallel, and peace talks began. However, combat raged on for more than two additional years. The primary source of contention was the fate of prisoners of war. The Chinese and North Koreans insisted that their prisoners be returned to them, but many of these men did not wish to be repatriated. Finally, an armistice agreement was signed on July 27, 1953. A border between North and South Korea, one quite close to the original thirty-eighth parallel line, was agreed upon. A demilitarized zone between the two nations was established, and both sides agreed that prisoners of war would be allowed to choose whether to be returned to their homelands. Five million people died in the three-year conflict. Of these, around 36,500 were U.S. soldiers; a majority were Korean civilians.

Download for free at http://cnx.org/content/col11740/latest/

Click and Explore

Read **firsthand accounts (http://openstaxcollege.org/l/15KOWar)** of U.S. soldiers who served in Korea, including prisoners of war.

As the war in Korea came to an end, so did one of the most frightening anti-Communist campaigns in the United States. After charging the U.S. State Department with harboring Communists, Senator Joseph McCarthy had continued to make similar accusations against other government agencies. Prominent Republicans like Senator Robert Taft and Congressman Richard Nixon regarded McCarthy as an asset who targeted Democratic politicians, and they supported his actions. In 1953, as chair of the Senate Committee on Government Operations, McCarthy investigated the Voice of America, which broadcast news and pro-U.S. propaganda to foreign countries, and the State Department's overseas libraries. After an aborted effort to investigate Protestant clergy, McCarthy turned his attention to the U.S. Army. This proved to be the end of the senator's political career. From April to June 1954, the Army-McCarthy Hearings were televised, and the American public, able to witness his use of intimidation and innuendo firsthand, rejected McCarthy's approach to rooting out Communism in the United States (**Figure 28.8**). In December 1954, the U.S. Senate officially condemned his actions with a censure, ending his prospects for political leadership.

Figure 28.8 Senator Joseph McCarthy (left) consults with Roy Cohn (right) during the Army-McCarthy hearings. Cohn, a lawyer who worked for McCarthy, was responsible for investigating State Department libraries overseas for "subversive" books.

One particularly heinous aspect of the hunt for Communists in the United States, likened by playwright Arthur Miller to the witch hunts of old, was its effort to root out gay men and lesbians employed by the government. Many anti-Communists, including McCarthy, believed that gay men, referred to by Senator Everett Dirksen as "lavender lads," were morally weak and thus were particularly likely to betray their country. Many also believed that lesbians and gay men were prone to being blackmailed by Soviet agents because of their sexual orientation, which at the time was regarded by psychiatrists as a form of mental illness.

28.3 The American Dream

By the end of this section, you will be able to:
- Describe President Dwight D. Eisenhower's domestic and foreign policies
- Discuss gender roles in the 1950s
- Discuss the growth of the suburbs and the effect of suburbanization on American society

Against the backdrop of the Cold War, Americans dedicated themselves to building a peaceful and prosperous society after the deprivation and instability of the Great Depression and World War II. Dwight D. Eisenhower, the general who led the United States to victory in Europe in 1945, proved to be the perfect president for the new era. Lacking strong conservative positions, he steered a middle path between conservatism and liberalism, and presided over a peacetime decade of economic growth and social conformity. In foreign affairs, Eisenhower's New Look policy simultaneously expanded the nation's nuclear arsenal and prevented the expansion of the defense budget for conventional forces.

WE LIKE IKE

After Harry Truman declined to run again for the presidency, the election of 1952 emerged as a contest between the Democratic nominee, Illinois governor Adlai Stevenson, and Republican Dwight D. Eisenhower, who had directed American forces in Europe during World War II (Figure 28.9). Eisenhower campaigned largely on a promise to end the war in Korea, a conflict the public had grown weary of fighting. He also vowed to fight Communism both at home and abroad, a commitment he demonstrated by choosing as his running mate Richard M. Nixon, a congressman who had made a name for himself by pursuing Communists, notably former State Department employee and suspected Soviet agent Alger Hiss.

Figure 28.9   Dwight D. Eisenhower was the perfect presidential candidate in 1952. He had never before run for office or even cast a vote, and thus had no political record to be challenged or criticized.

In 1952, Eisenhower supporters enthusiastically proclaimed "We Like Ike," and Eisenhower defeated Stevenson by winning 54 percent of the popular vote and 87 percent of the electoral vote (Figure 28.10). When he assumed office in 1953, Eisenhower employed a leadership style he had developed during his years of military service. He was calm and willing to delegate authority regarding domestic affairs to his cabinet members, allowing him to focus his own efforts on foreign policy. Unlike many earlier presidents, such as Harry Truman, Eisenhower was largely nonpartisan and consistently sought a middle ground between liberalism and conservatism. He strove to balance the federal budget, which appealed to conservative Republicans, but retained much of the New Deal and even expanded Social Security. He maintained high levels of defense spending but, in his farewell speech in 1961, warned about the growth of the **military-industrial complex**, the matrix of relationships between officials in the Department of Defense and executives in the defense industry who all benefited from increases in defense spending. He disliked the tactics of Joseph McCarthy but did not oppose him directly, preferring to remain above the fray. He saw himself as a leader called upon to do his best for his country, not as a politician engaged in a contest for advantage over rivals.

Figure 28.10 The above map shows the resounding victory of Dwight D. Eisenhower over Adlai Stevenson in the 1952 election. Stevenson carried only the South, where whites had voted for Democratic Party candidates since the time of the Civil War.

In keeping with his goal of a balanced budget, Eisenhower switched the emphasis in defense from larger conventional forces to greater stockpiles of nuclear weapons. His New Look strategy embraced nuclear **"massive retaliation,"** a plan for nuclear response to a first Soviet strike so devastating that the attackers would not be able to respond. Some labeled this approach "Mutually Assured Destruction" or MAD.

Part of preparing for a possible war with the Soviet Union was informing the American public what to do in the event of a nuclear attack. The government provided instructions for building and equipping bomb shelters in the basement or backyard, and some cities constructed municipal shelters. Schools purchased dog tags to help identify students in the aftermath of an attack and showed children instructional films telling them what to do if atomic bombs were dropped on the city where they lived.

AMERICANA

✪ *"A Guide for Surviving Nuclear War"*

To prepare its citizens for the possibility of nuclear war, in 1950, the U.S. government published and distributed informative pamphlets such as "A Guide for Surviving Nuclear War" excerpted here.

> Just like fire bombs and ordinary high explosives, atomic weapons cause most of their death and damage by blast and heat. So first let's look at a few things you can do to escape these two dangers.
>
> Even if you have only a second's warning, there is one important thing you can do to lessen your chances of injury by blast: Fall flat on your face.
>
> More than half of all wounds are the result of being bodily tossed about or being struck by falling and flying objects. If you lie down flat, you are least likely to be thrown about. If you have time to pick a good spot, there is less chance of your being struck by flying glass and other things.
>
> If you are inside a building, the best place to flatten out is close against the cellar wall. If you haven't time to get down there, lie down along an inside wall, or duck under a bed or table. . . .
>
> If caught out-of-doors, either drop down alongside the base of a good substantial building—avoid flimsy, wooden ones likely to be blown over on top of you—or else jump in any handy ditch or gutter.
>
> When you fall flat to protect yourself from a bombing, don't look up to see what is coming. Even during the daylight hours, the flash from a bursting A-bomb can cause several moments of blindness, if you're facing that way. To prevent it, bury your face in your arms and hold it there for 10 to 12 seconds after the explosion. . . .
>
> If you work in the open, always wear full-length, loose-fitting, light-colored clothes in time of emergency. Never go around with your sleeves rolled up. Always wear a hat—the brim could save you a serious face burn.

What do you think was the purpose of these directions? Do you think they could actually help people survive an atomic bomb blast? If not, why publish such booklets?

Click and Explore

View this short instructional film (http://openstaxcollege.org/l/15DuckCover) made in 1951 that teaches elementary school children what to do in the event an atomic bomb is dropped. Why do you think officials tried to convey the message that a nuclear attack was survivable?

Government and industry allocated enormous amounts of money to the research and development of more powerful weapons. This investment generated rapid strides in missile technology as well as increasingly sensitive radar. Computers that could react more quickly than humans and thereby shoot down speeding missiles were also investigated. Many scientists on both sides of the Cold War, including captured Germans such as rocket engineer Werner von Braun, worked on these devices. An early success for the West came in 1950, when Alan Turing, a British mathematician who had broken Germany's Enigma code during World War II, created a machine that mimicked human thought. His discoveries led scientists to consider the possibility of developing true artificial intelligence.

However, the United States often feared that the Soviets were making greater strides in developing technology with potential military applications. This was especially true following the Soviet Union's launch of *Sputnik* (Figure 28.11), the first manmade satellite, in October 1957. In September 1958, Congress passed the National Defense Education Act, which pumped over $775 million into educational programs over four years, especially those programs that focused on math and science. Congressional appropriations to the National Science Foundation also increased by $100 million in a single year, from $34 million in 1958 to $134 million in 1959. One consequence of this increased funding was the growth of science and engineering programs at American universities.

Figure 28.11 The launch of the Soviet satellite *Sputnik* frightened many in the United States, who feared that Soviet technology had surpassed their own. To calm these fears, Americans domesticated *Sputnik*, creating children's games based on it and using its shape as a decorative motif.

In the diplomatic sphere, Eisenhower pushed Secretary of State John Foster Dulles to take a firmer stance against the Soviets to reassure European allies of continued American support. At the same time, keenly sensing that the stalemate in Korea had cost Truman his popularity, Eisenhower worked to avoid being drawn into foreign wars. Thus, when the French found themselves fighting Vietnamese Communists for control of France's former colony of Indochina, Eisenhower provided money but not troops. Likewise, the United States took no steps when Hungary attempted to break away from Soviet domination in 1956. The United States also refused to be drawn in when Great Britain, France, and Israel invaded the Suez Canal Zone following Egypt's nationalization of the canal in 1956. Indeed, Eisenhower, wishing to avoid conflict with the Soviet Union, threatened to impose economic sanctions on the invading countries if they did not withdraw.

SUBURBANIZATION

Although the Eisenhower years were marked by fear of the Soviet Union and its military might, they were also a time of peace and prosperity. Even as many Americans remained mired in poverty, many others with limited economic opportunities, like African Americans or union workers, were better off financially in the 1950s and rose into the ranks of the middle class. Wishing to build the secure life that the Great Depression had deprived their parents of, young men and women married in record numbers and purchased homes where they could start families of their own. In 1940, the rate of homeownership in the United States was 43.6 percent. By 1960, it was almost 62 percent. Many of these newly purchased homes had been built in the new suburban areas that began to encircle American cities after the war. Although middle-class families had begun to move to the suburbs beginning in the nineteenth century, suburban growth accelerated rapidly after World War II.

Several factors contributed to this development. During World War II, the United States had suffered from a housing shortage, especially in cities with shipyards or large defense plants. Now that the war was over, real estate developers and contractors rushed to alleviate the scarcity. Unused land on the fringes of American cities provided the perfect place for new housing, which attracted not only the middle class, which had long sought homes outside the crowded cities, but also blue-collar workers who took advantage of the low-interest mortgages offered by the GI Bill.

An additional factor was the use of prefabricated construction techniques pioneered during World War II, which allowed houses complete with plumbing, electrical wiring, and appliances to be built and painted in a day. Employing these methods, developers built acres of inexpensive tract housing throughout the country. One of the first developers to take advantage of this method was William Levitt, who purchased farmland in Nassau County, Long Island, in 1947 and built thousands of prefabricated houses. The new community was named **Levittown**.

Levitt's houses cost only $8,000 and could be bought with little or no down payment. The first day they were offered for sale, more than one thousand were purchased. Levitt went on to build similar developments, also called Levittown, in New Jersey and Pennsylvania (Figure 28.12). As developers around the country rushed to emulate him, the name Levittown became synonymous with suburban tract housing, in which entire neighborhoods were built to either a single plan or a mere handful of designs. The houses were so similar that workers told of coming home late at night and walking into the wrong one. Levittown homes were similar in other ways as well; most were owned by white families. Levitt used restrictive language in his agreements with potential homeowners to ensure that only whites would live in his communities.

Figure 28.12 This aerial view of Levittown, Pennsylvania, reveals acres of standardized homes. The roads were curved to prevent cars from speeding through the residential community that was home to many young families.

In the decade between 1950 and 1960, the suburbs grew by 46 percent. The transition from urban to suburban life exerted profound effects on both the economy and society. For example, fifteen of the largest U.S. cities saw their tax bases shrink significantly in the postwar period, and the apportionment of seats in the House of Representatives shifted to the suburbs and away from urban areas.

The development of the suburbs also increased reliance on the automobile for transportation. Suburban men drove to work in nearby cities or, when possible, were driven to commuter rail stations by their wives. In the early years of suburban development, before schools, parks, and supermarkets were built, access to an automobile was crucial, and the pressure on families to purchase a second one was strong. As families rushed to purchase them, the annual production of passenger cars leaped from 2.2 million to 8 million between 1946 and 1955, and by 1960, about 20 percent of suburban families owned two cars. The growing number of cars on the road changed consumption patterns, and drive-in and drive-through convenience stores, restaurants, and movie theaters began to dot the landscape. The first McDonalds opened in San Bernardino, California, in 1954 to cater to drivers in a hurry.

As drivers jammed highways and small streets in record numbers, cities and states rushed to build additional roadways and ease congestion. To help finance these massive construction efforts, states began taxing gasoline, and the federal government provided hundreds of thousands of dollars for the construction of the interstate highway system (Figure 28.13). The resulting construction projects, designed to make it easier for suburbanites to commute to and from cities, often destroyed urban working-class neighborhoods. Increased funding for highway construction also left less money for public transportation, making it impossible for those who could not afford automobiles to live in the suburbs.

Figure 28.13 In the late 1940s, a network of newly constructed highways connected suburban Long Island with Manhattan. The nation's new road network also served a military purpose; interstate highways made it easier to deploy troops in the event of a national emergency.

THE ORGANIZATION MAN

As the government poured money into the defense industry and into universities that conducted research for the government, the economy boomed. The construction and automobile industries employed thousands, as did the industries they relied upon: steel, oil and gasoline refining, rubber, and lumber. As people moved into new homes, their purchases of appliances, carpeting, furniture, and home decorations spurred growth in other industries. The building of miles of roads also employed thousands. Unemployment was low, and wages for members of both the working and middle classes were high.

Following World War II, the majority of white Americans were members of the middle class, based on such criteria as education, income, and home ownership. Even most blue-collar families could afford such elements of a middle-class lifestyle as new cars, suburban homes, and regular vacations. Most African Americans, however, were not members of the middle class. In 1950, the median income for white families was $20,656, whereas for black families it was $11,203. By 1960, when the average white family earned $28,485 a year, blacks still lagged behind at $15,786; nevertheless, this represented a more than 40 percent increase in African American income in the space of a decade.

While working-class men found jobs in factories and on construction crews, those in the middle class often worked for corporations that, as a result of government spending, had grown substantially during World War II and were still getting larger. Such corporations, far too large to allow managers to form personal relationships with all of their subordinates, valued conformity to company rules and standards above all else. In his best-selling book *The Organization Man*, however, William H. Whyte criticized the notion that conformity was the best path to success and self-fulfillment.

Conformity was still the watchword of suburban life: Many neighborhoods had rules mandating what types of clotheslines could be used and prohibited residents from parking their cars on the street. Above all, conforming to societal norms meant marrying young and having children. In the post-World War II period, marriage rates rose; the average age at first marriage dropped to twenty-three for men and twenty for women. Between 1946 and 1964, married couples also gave birth to the largest generation in U.S. history to date; this **baby boom** resulted in the cohort known as the baby boomers. Conformity also required that the wives of both working- and middle-class men stay home and raise children instead of working for wages outside the home. Most conformed to this norm, at least while their children were young. Nevertheless, 40 percent of women with young children and half of women with older children sought at least part-time employment. They did so partly out of necessity and partly to pay for the new elements of "the good life"—second cars, vacations, and college education for their children.

The children born during the baby boom were members of a more privileged generation than their parents had been. Entire industries sprang up to cater to their need for clothing, toys, games, books, and breakfast cereals. For the first time in U.S. history, attending high school was an experience shared by the majority, regardless of race or region. As the baby boomers grew into adolescence, marketers realized that they not only controlled large amounts of disposable income earned at part-time jobs, but they exerted a great deal of influence over their parents' purchases as well. Madison Avenue began to appeal to teenage interests. Boys yearned for cars, and girls of all ethnicities wanted boyfriends who had them. New fashion magazines for adolescent girls, such as *Seventeen*, advertised the latest clothing and cosmetics, and teen romance magazines, like *Copper Romance*, a publication for young African American women, filled drugstore racks. The music and movie industries also altered their products to appeal to affluent adolescents who were growing tired of parental constraints.

28.4 Popular Culture and Mass Media

By the end of this section, you will be able to:
- Describe Americans' different responses to rock and roll music
- Discuss the way contemporary movies and television reflected postwar American society

With a greater generational consciousness than previous generations, the baby boomers sought to define and redefine their identities in numerous ways. Music, especially rock and roll, reflected their desire to rebel against adult authority. Other forms of popular culture, such as movies and television, sought to entertain, while reinforcing values such as religious faith, patriotism, and conformity to societal norms.

ROCKING AROUND THE CLOCK

In the late 1940s, some white country musicians began to experiment with the rhythms of the blues, a decades-old musical genre of rural southern blacks. This experimentation led to the creation of a new musical form known as rockabilly, and by the 1950s, rockabilly had developed into **rock and roll**. Rock and roll music celebrated themes such as young love and freedom from the oppression of middle-class society. It quickly grew in favor among American teens, thanks largely to the efforts of disc jockey Alan Freed, who named and popularized the music by playing it on the radio in Cleveland, where he also organized the first rock and roll concert, and later in New York.

The theme of rebellion against authority, present in many rock and roll songs, appealed to teens. In 1954, Bill Haley and His Comets provided youth with an anthem for their rebellion—"Rock Around the Clock" (Figure 28.14). The song, used in the 1955 movie *Blackboard Jungle* about a white teacher at a troubled inner-city high school, seemed to be calling for teens to declare their independence from adult control.

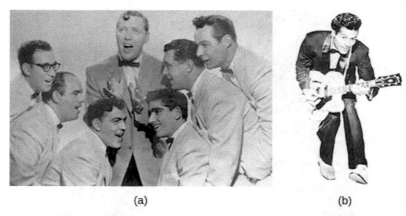

Figure 28.14 The band Bill Haley and His Comets (a) was among the first to launch the new genre of rock and roll. Their hit song "Rock Around the Clock" supposedly caused some teens to break into violent behavior when they heard it. Chuck Berry (b) was a performer who combined rhythm and blues and rock and roll. He dazzled crowds with guitar solos and electrifying performances.

Haley illustrated how white artists could take musical motifs from the African American community and achieve mainstream success. Teen heartthrob Elvis Presley rose to stardom doing the same. Thus, besides encouraging a feeling of youthful rebellion, rock and roll also began to tear down color barriers, as white youths sought out African American musicians such as Chuck Berry and Little Richard (Figure 28.14).

While youth had found an outlet for their feelings and concerns, parents were much less enthused about rock and roll and the values it seemed to promote. Many regarded the music as a threat to American values. When Elvis Presley appeared on *The Ed Sullivan Show*, a popular television variety program, the camera deliberately focused on his torso and did not show his swiveling hips or legs shaking in time to the music. Despite adults' dislike of the genre, or perhaps because of it, more than 68 percent of the music played on the radio in 1956 was rock and roll.

HOLLYWOOD ON THE DEFENSIVE

At first, Hollywood encountered difficulties in adjusting to the post-World War II environment. Although domestic audiences reached a record high in 1946 and the war's end meant expanding international markets too, the groundwork for the eventual dismantling of the traditional studio system was laid in 1948, with a landmark decision by the U.S. Supreme Court. Previously, film studios had owned their own movie theater chains in which they exhibited the films they produced; however, in *United States v. Paramount Pictures, Inc.*, this vertical integration of the industry—the complete control by one firm of the production, distribution, and exhibition of motion pictures—was deemed a violation of antitrust laws.

The HUAC hearings also targeted Hollywood. When Senator McCarthy called eleven "unfriendly witnesses" to testify before Congress about Communism in the film industry in October 1947, only playwright Bertolt Brecht answered questions. The other ten, who refused to testify, were cited for contempt of Congress on November 24. The next day, film executives declared that the so-called "Hollywood Ten" would no longer be employed in the industry until they had sworn they were not Communists (Figure 28.15). Eventually, more than three hundred actors, screenwriters, directors, musicians, and other entertainment professionals were placed on the industry blacklist. Some never worked in Hollywood again; others directed films or wrote screenplays under assumed names.

Figure 28.15 One of the original Hollywood Ten, director Edward Dmytryk publicly announced he had once been a Communist and, in April 1951, answered questions and "named names" before the House Committee on Un-American Activities.

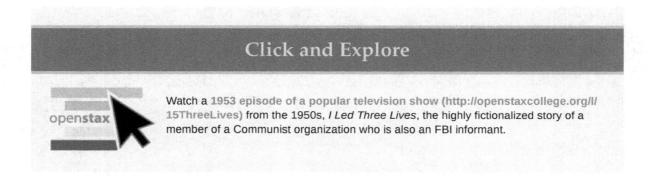

Click and Explore

Watch a **1953 episode of a popular television show (http://openstaxcollege.org/l/ 15ThreeLives)** from the 1950s, *I Led Three Lives*, the highly fictionalized story of a member of a Communist organization who is also an FBI informant.

Hollywood reacted aggressively to these various challenges. Filmmakers tried new techniques, like CinemaScope and Cinerama, which allowed movies to be shown on large screens and in 3-D. Audiences were drawn to movies not because of gimmicks, however, but because of the stories they told. Dramas and romantic comedies continued to be popular fare for adults, and, to appeal to teens, studios produced large numbers of horror films and movies starring music idols such as Elvis. Many films took espionage, a timely topic, as their subject matter, and science fiction hits such as *Invasion of the Body Snatchers*, about a small town whose inhabitants fall prey to space aliens, played on audience fears of both Communist invasion and nuclear technology.

THE TRIUMPH OF TELEVISION

By far the greatest challenge to Hollywood, however, came from the relatively new medium of television. Although the technology had been developed in the late 1920s, through much of the 1940s, only a fairly small audience of the wealthy had access to it. As a result, programming was limited. With the post-World War II economic boom, all this changed. Where there had been only 178,000 televisions in homes in 1948, by 1955, over three-quarters of a million U.S. households, about half of all homes, had television (Figure 28.16).

Figure 28.16 An American family relaxes in front of their television set in 1958. Many gathered not only to watch the programming but also to eat dinner. The marketing of small folding tray tables and frozen "TV dinners" encouraged such behavior.

Various types of programs were broadcast on the handful of major networks: situation comedies, variety programs, game shows, soap operas, talk shows, medical dramas, adventure series, cartoons, and police procedurals. Many comedies presented an idealized image of white suburban family life: Happy housewife mothers, wise fathers, and mischievous but not dangerously rebellious children were constants on shows like *Leave It to Beaver* and *Father Knows Best* in the late 1950s. These shows also reinforced certain perspectives on the values of individualism and family—values that came to be redefined as "American" in opposition to alleged Communist collectivism. Westerns, which stressed unity in the face of danger and the ability to survive in hostile environments, were popular too. Programming designed specifically for children began to emerge with shows such as *Captain Kangaroo, Romper Room*, and *The Mickey Mouse Club* designed to appeal to members of the baby boom.

28.5 The African American Struggle for Civil Rights

By the end of this section, you will be able to:
- Explain how Presidents Truman and Eisenhower addressed civil rights issues
- Discuss efforts by African Americans to end discrimination and segregation
- Describe southern whites' response to the civil rights movement

In the aftermath of World War II, African Americans began to mount organized resistance to racially discriminatory policies in force throughout much of the United States. In the South, they used a combination of legal challenges and grassroots activism to begin dismantling the racial segregation that had stood for nearly a century following the end of Reconstruction. Community activists and civil rights leaders targeted racially discriminatory housing practices, segregated transportation, and legal requirements that African Americans and whites be educated separately. While many of these challenges were successful, life did not necessarily improve for African Americans. Hostile whites fought these changes in any way they could, including by resorting to violence.

EARLY VICTORIES

During World War II, many African Americans had supported the "Double-V Campaign," which called on them to defeat foreign enemies while simultaneously fighting against segregation and discrimination at home. After World War II ended, many returned home to discover that, despite their sacrifices, the United States was not willing to extend them any greater rights than they had enjoyed before the war. Particularly rankling was the fact that although African American veterans were legally entitled to draw benefits under the GI Bill, discriminatory practices prevented them from doing so. For example, many banks would not give them mortgages if they wished to buy homes in predominantly African American neighborhoods, which banks often considered too risky an investment. However, African Americans who attempted to purchase homes in white neighborhoods often found themselves unable to do so because of real estate covenants that prevented owners from selling their property to blacks. Indeed, when a black family purchased a Levittown house in 1957, they were subjected to harassment and threats of violence.

Click and Explore

For a look at the experiences of an African American family (http://openstaxcollege.org/l/15Levittown) that tried to move to a white suburban community, view the 1957 documentary *Crisis in Levittown*.

The postwar era, however, saw African Americans make greater use of the courts to defend their rights. In 1944, an African American woman, Irene Morgan, was arrested in Virginia for refusing to give up her seat on an interstate bus and sued to have her conviction overturned. In *Morgan v. the Commonwealth of Virginia* in 1946, the U.S. Supreme Court ruled that the conviction should be overturned because it violated the interstate commerce clause of the Constitution. This victory emboldened some civil rights activists to launch the Journey of Reconciliation, a bus trip taken by eight African American men and eight white men through the states of the Upper South to test the South's enforcement of the *Morgan* decision.

Other victories followed. In 1948, in *Shelley v. Kraemer*, the U.S. Supreme Court held that courts could not enforce real estate covenants that restricted the purchase or sale of property based on race. In 1950, the NAACP brought a case before the U.S. Supreme Court that they hoped would help to undermine the concept of "separate but equal" as espoused in the 1896 decision in *Plessy v. Ferguson*, which gave legal sanction to segregated school systems. *Sweatt v. Painter* was a case brought by Herman Marion Sweatt, who sued the University of Texas for denying him admission to its law school because state law prohibited integrated education. Texas attempted to form a separate law school for African Americans only, but in its decision on the case, the U.S. Supreme Court rejected this solution, holding that the separate school provided neither equal facilities nor "intangibles," such as the ability to form relationships with other future lawyers, that a professional school should provide.

Not all efforts to enact desegregation required the use of the courts, however. On April 15, 1947, Jackie Robinson started for the Brooklyn Dodgers, playing first base. He was the first African American to play baseball in the National League, breaking the color barrier. Although African Americans had their own baseball teams in the Negro Leagues, Robinson opened the gates for them to play in direct competition with white players in the major leagues. Other African American athletes also began to challenge the segregation of American sports. At the 1948 Summer Olympics, Alice Coachman, an African American, was the only American woman to take a gold medal in the games (Figure 28.17). These changes, while symbolically significant, were mere cracks in the wall of segregation.

(a)   (b)

Figure 28.17 Baseball legend Jackie Robinson (a) was active in the civil rights movement. He served on the NAACP's board of directors and helped to found an African American-owned bank. Alice Coachman (b), who competed in track and field at Tuskegee University, was the first black woman to win an Olympic gold medal.

DESEGREGATION AND INTEGRATION

Until 1954, racial segregation in education was not only legal but was required in seventeen states and permissible in several others (Figure 28.18). Utilizing evidence provided in sociological studies conducted by Kenneth Clark and Gunnar Myrdal, however, Thurgood Marshall, then chief counsel for the NAACP, successfully argued the landmark case *Brown v. Board of Education of Topeka, Kansas* before the U.S. Supreme Court led by Chief Justice Earl Warren. Marshall showed that the practice of segregation in public schools made African American students feel inferior. Even if the facilities provided were equal in nature, the Court noted in its decision, the very fact that some students were separated from others on the basis of their race made segregation unconstitutional.

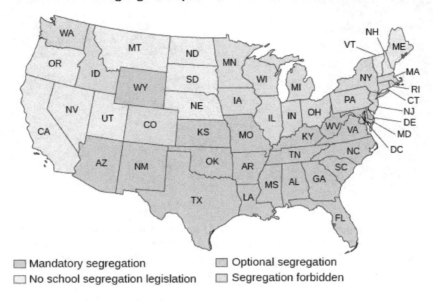

Figure 28.18 This map shows those states in which racial segregation in public education was required by law before the 1954 *Brown v. Board of Education* decision. In 1960, four years later, fewer than 10 percent of southern African American students attended the same schools as white students.

DEFINING "AMERICAN"

✪ *Thurgood Marshall on Fighting Racism*

As a law student in 1933, Thurgood Marshall (Figure 28.19) was recruited by his mentor Charles Hamilton Houston to assist in gathering information for the defense of a black man in Virginia accused of killing two white women. His continued close association with Houston led Marshall to aggressively defend blacks in the court system and to use the courts as the weapon by which equal rights might be extracted from the U.S. Constitution and a white racist system. Houston also suggested that it would be important to establish legal precedents regarding the *Plessy v. Ferguson* ruling of separate but equal.

Figure 28.19 In 1956, NAACP leaders (from left to right) Henry L. Moon, Roy Wilkins, Herbert Hill, and Thurgood Marshall present a new poster in the campaign against southern white racism. Marshall successfully argued the landmark case *Brown v. Board of Education* (1954) before the U.S. Supreme Court and later became the court's first African American justice.

By 1938, Marshall had become "Mr. Civil Rights" and formally organized the NAACP's Legal Defense and Education Fund in 1940 to garner the resources to take on cases to break the racist justice system of America. A direct result of Marshall's energies and commitment was his 1940 victory in a Supreme Court case, *Chambers v. Florida*, which held that confessions obtained by violence and torture were inadmissible in a court of law. His most well-known case was *Brown v. Board of Education* in 1954, which held that state laws establishing separate public schools for black and white students were unconstitutional.

Later in life, Marshall reflected on his career fighting racism in a speech at Howard Law School in 1978:

> Be aware of that myth, that everything is going to be all right. Don't give in. I add that, because it seems to me, that what we need to do today is to refocus. Back in the 30s and 40s, we could go no place but to court. We knew then, the court was not the final solution. Many of us knew the final solution would have to be politics, if for no other reason, politics is cheaper than lawsuits. So now we have both. We have our legal arm, and we have our political arm. Let's use them both. And don't listen to this myth that it can be solved by either or that it has already been solved. Take it from me, it has not been solved.

When Marshall says that the problems of racism have not been solved, to what was he referring?

Plessy v. Fergusson had been overturned. The challenge now was to integrate schools. A year later, the U.S. Supreme Court ordered southern school systems to begin **desegregation** "with all deliberate speed." Some school districts voluntarily integrated their schools. For many other districts, however, "deliberate speed" was very, very slow.

It soon became clear that enforcing *Brown v. the Board of Education* would require presidential intervention. Eisenhower did not agree with the U.S. Supreme Court's decision and did not wish to force southern states to integrate their schools. However, as president, he was responsible for doing so. In 1957, Central High School in Little Rock, Arkansas, was forced to accept its first nine African American students, who became known as the **Little Rock Nine**. In response, Arkansas governor Orval Faubus called out the state National Guard to prevent the students from attending classes, removing the troops only after Eisenhower told him to do so. A subsequent attempt by the nine students to attend school resulted in mob violence. Eisenhower then placed the Arkansas National Guard under federal control and sent the U.S. Army's 101st airborne unit to escort the students to and from school as well as from class to class (Figure 28.20). This was the first time since the end of Reconstruction that federal troops once more protected the rights of African Americans in the South.

Figure 28.20 In 1957, U.S. soldiers from the 101st Airborne were called in to escort the Little Rock Nine into and around formerly all-white Central High School in Little Rock, Arkansas.

Throughout the course of the school year, the Little Rock Nine were insulted, harassed, and physically assaulted; nevertheless, they returned to school each day. At the end of the school year, the first African American student graduated from Central High. At the beginning of the 1958–1959 school year, Orval Faubus ordered all Little Rock's public schools closed. In the opinion of white segregationists, keeping all students out of school was preferable to having them attend integrated schools. In 1959, the U.S. Supreme Court ruled that the school had to be reopened and that the process of desegregation had to proceed.

WHITE RESPONSES

Efforts to desegregate public schools led to a backlash among most southern whites. Many greeted the *Brown* decision with horror; some World War II veterans questioned how the government they had fought for could betray them in such a fashion. Some white parents promptly withdrew their children from public schools and enrolled them in all-white private academies, many newly created for the sole purpose of keeping white children from attending integrated schools. Often, these "academies" held classes in neighbors' basements or living rooms.

Other white southerners turned to state legislatures or courts to solve the problem of school integration. Orders to integrate school districts were routinely challenged in court. When the lawsuits proved unsuccessful, many southern school districts responded by closing all public schools, as Orval Faubus had done after Central High School was integrated. One county in Virginia closed its public schools for five years rather than see them integrated. Besides suing school districts, many southern segregationists filed lawsuits against the NAACP, trying to bankrupt the organization. Many national politicians supported the segregationist efforts. In 1956, ninety-six members of Congress signed "The Southern Manifesto," in which they accused the U.S. Supreme Court of misusing its power and violating the principle of **states' rights**, which maintained that states had rights equal to those of the federal government.

Unfortunately, many white southern racists, frightened by challenges to the social order, responded with violence. When Little Rock's Central High School desegregated, an irate Ku Klux Klansman from a neighboring community sent a letter to the members of the city's school board in which he denounced them as Communists and threatened to kill them. White rage sometimes erupted into murder. In August 1955, both white and black Americans were shocked by the brutality of the murder of Emmett Till. Till, a fourteen-year-old boy from Chicago, had been vacationing with relatives in Mississippi. While visiting a white-owned store, he had made a remark to the white woman behind the counter. A few days later, the husband and brother-in-law of the woman came to the home of Till's relatives in the middle of the night and abducted the boy. Till's beaten and mutilated body was found in a nearby river three days later. Till's mother insisted on an open-casket funeral; she wished to use her son's body to reveal the brutality of southern racism. The murder of a child who had been guilty of no more than a casual remark captured the nation's attention, as did the acquittal of the two men who admitted killing him.

THE MONTGOMERY BUS BOYCOTT

One of those inspired by Till's death was Rosa Parks, an NAACP member from Montgomery, Alabama, who became the face of the 1955–1956 Montgomery Bus Boycott. City ordinances in Montgomery segregated the city's buses, forcing African American passengers to ride in the back section. They had to enter through the rear of the bus, could not share seats with white passengers, and, if the front of the bus was full and a white passenger requested an African American's seat, had to relinquish their place to the white rider. The bus company also refused to hire African American drivers even though most of the people who rode the buses were black.

On December 1, 1955, Rosa Parks refused to give her seat to a white man, and the Montgomery police arrested her. After being bailed out of jail, she decided to fight the laws requiring segregation in court. To support her, the Women's Political Council, a group of African American female activists, organized a boycott of Montgomery's buses. News of the boycott spread through newspaper notices and by word of mouth; ministers rallied their congregations to support the Women's Political Council. Their efforts were successful, and forty thousand African American riders did not take the bus on December 5, the first day of the boycott.

Other African American leaders within the city embraced the boycott and maintained it beyond December 5, Rosa Parks' court date. Among them was a young minister named Martin Luther King, Jr. For the next year, black Montgomery residents avoided the city's buses. Some organized carpools. Others paid for rides in African American-owned taxis, whose drivers reduced their fees. Most walked to and from school, work, and church for 381 days, the duration of the boycott. In June 1956, an Alabama federal court found the segregation ordinance unconstitutional. The city appealed, but the U.S. Supreme Court upheld the decision. The city's buses were desegregated.

Key Terms

baby boom a marked increase in the U.S. birthrate during 1946–1964

blacklist a list of people suspected of having Communist sympathies who were denied work as a result

Cold War the prolonged period of tension between the United States and the Soviet Union, based on ideological conflicts and competition for military, economic, social, and technological superiority, and marked by surveillance and espionage, political assassinations, an arms race, attempts to secure alliances with developing nations, and proxy wars

containment the U.S. policy that sought to limit the expansion of Communism abroad

desegregation the removal of laws and policies requiring the separation of different racial or ethnic groups

domino theory the theory that if Communism made inroads in one nation, surrounding nations would also succumb one by one, like a chain of dominos toppling one another

Fair Deal President Harry Truman's program of economic and social reform

GI Bill a program that gave substantial benefits to those who served in World War II

Iron Curtain a term coined by Winston Churchill to refer to portions of Eastern Europe that the Soviet Union had incorporated into its sphere of influence and that no longer were free to manage their own affairs

Levittowns suburban housing developments consisting of acres of mass-produced homes

Little Rock Nine the nickname for the nine African American high school students who first integrated Little Rock's Central High School

Marshall Plan a program giving billions of dollars of U.S. aid to European countries to prevent them from turning to Communism

massive retaliation a defense strategy, sometimes called "mutually assured destruction" or MAD, adopted by Eisenhower that called for launching a large-scale nuclear attack on the Soviet Union in response to a first Soviet strike at the United States

military-industrial complex the matrix of relationships between officials in the Defense Department and executives in the defense industry who all benefited from increases in defense spending

rock and roll a musical form popular among the baby boomers that encompassed styles ranging from county to blues, and embraced themes such as youthful rebellion and love

Sputnik the first manmade orbital satellite, launched by the Soviet Union in October 1957

states' rights the political belief that states possess authority beyond federal law, which is usually seen as the supreme law of the land, and thus can act in opposition to federal law

Summary

28.1 The Challenges of Peacetime

At the end of World War II, U.S. servicemen and women returned to civilian life, and all hoped the prosperity of the war years would continue. The GI Bill eased many veterans' return by providing them with unemployment compensation, low-interest loans, and money to further their education; however, African American, Mexican American, and gay veterans were often unable to take advantage of these benefits fully or at all. Meanwhile, Japanese Americans faced an uphill struggle in their attempts to return to normalcy, and many women who had made significant professional gains in wartime found themselves dismissed from their positions. President Harry Truman attempted to extend Roosevelt's New Deal with his own Fair Deal, which had the goal of improving wages, housing, and healthcare, and protecting the rights of African Americans. Confronted by a Congress dominated by Republicans and southern Democrats, however, Truman was able to achieve only some of his goals.

28.2 The Cold War

Joy at the ending of World War II was quickly replaced by fears of conflict with the Soviet Union. The Cold War heated up as both the United States and Soviet Union struggled for world dominance. Fearing Soviet expansion, the United States committed itself to assisting countries whose governments faced overthrow by Communist forces and gave billions of dollars to war-torn Europe to help it rebuild. While the United States achieved victory in its thwarting of Soviet attempts to cut Berlin off from the West, the nation was less successful in its attempts to prevent Communist expansion in Korea. The development of atomic weapons by the Soviet Union and the arrest of Soviet spies in the United States and Britain roused fears in the United States that Communist agents were seeking to destroy the nation from within. Loyalty board investigations and hearings before House and Senate committees attempted to root out Soviet sympathizers in the federal government and in other sectors of American society, including Hollywood and the military.

28.3 The American Dream

In 1953, Dwight D. Eisenhower became president of the United States. Fiscally conservative but ideologically moderate, he sought to balance the budget while building a strong system of national defense. This defense policy led to a greater emphasis on the possible use of nuclear weapons in any confrontation with the Soviet Union. Committed to maintaining peace, however, Eisenhower avoided engaging the United States in foreign conflicts; during his presidency, the economy boomed. Young Americans married in record numbers, moved to the growing suburbs, and gave birth to the largest generation to date in U.S. history. As middle-class adults, they conformed to the requirements of corporate jobs and suburban life, while their privileged children enjoyed a consumer culture tailored to their desires.

28.4 Popular Culture and Mass Media

Young Americans in the postwar period had more disposable income and enjoyed greater material comfort than their forebears. These factors allowed them to devote more time and money to leisure activities and the consumption of popular culture. Rock and roll, which drew from African American roots in the blues, embraced themes popular among teenagers, such as young love and rebellion against authority. At the same time, traditional forms of entertainment, such as motion pictures, came under increasing competition from a relatively new technology, television.

28.5 The African American Struggle for Civil Rights

After World War II, African American efforts to secure greater civil rights increased across the United States. African American lawyers such as Thurgood Marshall championed cases intended to destroy the Jim Crow system of segregation that had dominated the American South since Reconstruction. The landmark Supreme Court case *Brown v. Board of Education* prohibited segregation in public schools, but not all school districts integrated willingly, and President Eisenhower had to use the military to desegregate

Little Rock's Central High School. The courts and the federal government did not assist African Americans in asserting their rights in other cases. In Montgomery, Alabama, it was the grassroots efforts of African American citizens who boycotted the city's bus system that brought about change. Throughout the region, many white southerners made their opposition to these efforts known. Too often, this opposition manifested itself in violence and tragedy, as in the murder of Emmett Till.

Review Questions

1. Truman referred to his program of economic and social reform as the _____.
A. New Deal
B. Square Deal
C. Fair Deal
D. Straight Deal

2. Which of the following pieces of Truman's domestic agenda was rejected by Congress?
A. the Taft-Hartley Act
B. national healthcare
C. the creation of a civil rights commission
D. funding for schools

3. How did the GI Bill help veterans return to civilian life? What were its limitations?

4. What was the policy of trying to limit the expansion of Soviet influence abroad?
A. restraint
B. containment
C. isolationism
D. quarantine

5. The Truman administration tried to help Europe recover from the devastation of World War II with the _____.
A. Economic Development Bank
B. Atlantic Free Trade Zone
C. Byrnes Budget
D. Marshall Plan

6. What was agreed to at the armistice talks between North and South Korea?

7. The name of the first manmade satellite, launched by the Soviet Union in 1957, was _____.
A. *Triton*
B. *Cosmolskaya*
C. *Pravda*
D. *Sputnik*

8. The first Levittown was built _____.
A. in Bucks County, Pennsylvania
B. in Nassau County, New York
C. near Newark, New Jersey
D. near Pittsburgh, Pennsylvania

9. How did suburbanization help the economy?

10. The disc jockey who popularized rock and roll was _____.
A. Bill Haley
B. Elvis Presley
C. Alan Freed
D. Ed Sullivan

11. What challenges did Hollywood face in the 1950s?

12. The NAACP lawyer who became known as "Mr. Civil Rights" was _____.
A. Earl Warren
B. Jackie Robinson
C. OrvalFaubus
D. Thurgood Marshall

13. The Arkansas governor who tried to prevent the integration of Little Rock High School was _____.
A. Charles Hamilton Houston
B. Kenneth Clark
C. OrvalFaubus
D. Clark Clifford

14. What was the significance of *Shelley v. Kraemer*?

Critical Thinking Questions

15. How did some Americans turn their wartime experiences into lasting personal gains (i.e. better employment, a new home, or an education) after the war was over? Why did others miss out on these opportunities?

16. What was the reason for the breakdown in friendly relations between the United States and the Soviet Union after World War II? What were the results of this conflict?

17. How did fear of the Soviet Union and Communism affect American culture and society?

18. What social changes took place in the United States after World War II? What role did the war play in those changes?

19. How did the wartime experiences of African Americans contribute to the drive for greater civil rights after the war?

CHAPTER 29

Contesting Futures: America in the 1960s

Figure 29.1 In Aaron Shikler's official portrait of *John Fitzgerald Kennedy* (1970), the president stands with arms folded, apparently deep in thought. The portrait was painted seven years after Kennedy's death, at the request of his widow, Jacqueline Kennedy Onassis. It depicts the president with his head down, because Shikler did not wish to paint the dead man's eyes.

Chapter Outline

29.1 The Kennedy Promise
29.2 Lyndon Johnson and the Great Society
29.3 The Civil Rights Movement Marches On
29.4 Challenging the Status Quo

Introduction

The 1960s was a decade of hope, change, and war that witnessed an important shift in American culture. Citizens from all walks of life sought to expand the meaning of the American promise. Their efforts helped unravel the national consensus and laid bare a far more fragmented society. As a result, men and women from all ethnic groups attempted to reform American society to make it more equitable. The United States also began to take unprecedented steps to exert what it believed to be a positive influence on the world. At the same time, the country's role in Vietnam revealed the limits of military power and the contradictions of U.S. foreign policy. The posthumous portrait of John F. Kennedy (Figure 29.1) captures this mix of the era's promise and defeat. His election encouraged many to work for a better future, for both the middle class *and* the marginalized. Kennedy's running mate, Lyndon B. Johnson, also envisioned a country characterized by the social and economic freedoms established during the New Deal years. Kennedy's assassination in 1963, and the assassinations five years later of Martin Luther King, Jr. and

Robert F. Kennedy, made it dramatically clear that not all Americans shared this vision of a more inclusive democracy.

29.1 The Kennedy Promise

By the end of this section, you will be able to:
*   Assess Kennedy's Cold War strategy
*   Describe Kennedy's contribution to the civil rights movement

In the 1950s, President Dwight D. Eisenhower presided over a United States that prized conformity over change. Although change naturally occurred, as it does in every era, it was slow and greeted warily. By the 1960s, however, the pace of change had quickened and its scope broadened, as restive and energetic waves of World War II veterans and baby boomers of both sexes and all ethnicities began to make their influence felt politically, economically, and culturally. No one symbolized the hopes and energies of the new decade more than John Fitzgerald Kennedy, the nation's new, young, and seemingly healthful, president. Kennedy had emphasized the country's aspirations and challenges as a "new frontier" when accepting his party's nomination at the Democratic National Convention in Los Angeles, California.

THE NEW FRONTIER

The son of Joseph P. Kennedy, a wealthy Boston business owner and former ambassador to Great Britain, John F. Kennedy graduated from Harvard University and went on to serve in the U.S. House of Representatives in 1946. Even though he was young and inexperienced, his reputation as a war hero who had saved the crew of his PT boat after it was destroyed by the Japanese helped him to win election over more seasoned candidates, as did his father's fortune. In 1952, he was elected to the U.S. Senate for the first of two terms. For many, including Arthur M. Schlesinger, Jr., a historian and member of Kennedy's

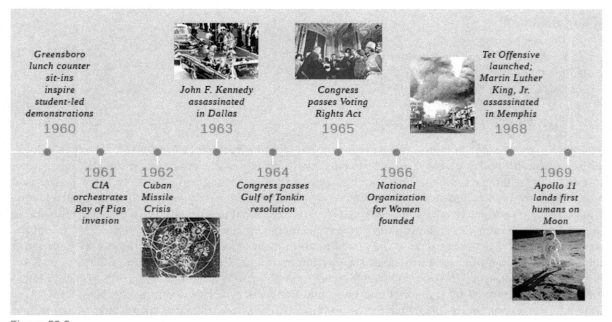

Figure 29.2

administration, Kennedy represented a bright, shining future in which the United States would lead the way in solving the most daunting problems facing the world.

Kennedy's popular reputation as a great politician undoubtedly owes much to the style and attitude he personified. He and his wife Jacqueline conveyed a sense of optimism and youthfulness. "Jackie" was an elegant first lady who wore designer dresses, served French food in the White House, and invited classical musicians to entertain at state functions. "Jack" Kennedy, or JFK, went sailing off the coast of his family's Cape Cod estate and socialized with celebrities (Figure 29.3). Few knew that behind Kennedy's healthful and sporty image was a gravely ill man whose wartime injuries caused him daily agony.

(a)   (b)

Figure 29.3   John F. Kennedy and first lady Jacqueline, shown here in the White House in 1962 (a) and watching the America's Cup race that same year (b), brought youth, glamour, and optimism to Washington, DC, and the nation.

Nowhere was Kennedy's style more evident than in the first televised presidential debate held on September 23, 1960, between him and his Republican opponent Vice President Richard M. Nixon. Seventy million viewers watched the debate on television; millions more heard it on the radio. Radio listeners judged Nixon the winner, whereas those who watched the debate on television believed the more telegenic Kennedy made the better showing.

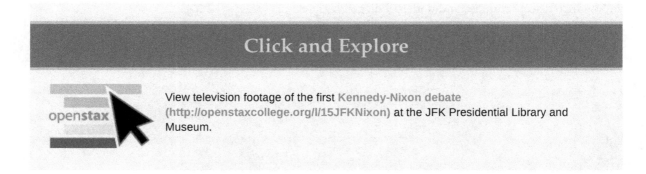

Click and Explore

View television footage of the first Kennedy-Nixon debate (http://openstaxcollege.org/l/15JFKNixon) at the JFK Presidential Library and Museum.

Kennedy did not appeal to all voters, however. Many feared that because he was Roman Catholic, his decisions would be influenced by the Pope. Even traditional Democratic supporters, like the head of the United Auto Workers, Walter Reuther, feared that a Catholic candidate would lose the support of Protestants. Many southern Democrats also disliked Kennedy because of his liberal position on civil rights. To shore up support for Kennedy in the South, Lyndon B. Johnson, the Protestant Texan who was Senate majority leader, was added to the Democratic ticket as the vice presidential candidate. In the end, Kennedy won the election by the closest margin since 1888, defeating Nixon with only 0.01 percent more of the record sixty-seven million votes cast. His victory in the Electoral College was greater: 303 electoral votes to Nixon's 219. Kennedy's win made him both the youngest man elected to the presidency and the first U.S. president born in the twentieth century.

Kennedy dedicated his inaugural address to the theme of a new future for the United States. "Ask not what your country can do for you; ask what you can do for your country," he challenged his fellow Americans. His lofty goals ranged from fighting poverty to winning the space race against the Soviet Union with a moon landing. He assembled an administration of energetic people assured of their ability to shape the future. Dean Rusk was named secretary of state. Robert McNamara, the former president of Ford Motor Company, became secretary of defense. Kennedy appointed his younger brother Robert as attorney general, much to the chagrin of many who viewed the appointment as a blatant example of nepotism.

Kennedy's domestic reform plans remained hampered, however, by his narrow victory and lack of support from members of his own party, especially southern Democrats. As a result, he remained hesitant to propose new civil rights legislation. His achievements came primarily in poverty relief and care for the disabled. Unemployment benefits were expanded, the food stamps program was piloted, and the school lunch program was extended to more students. In October 1963, the passage of the Mental Retardation Facilities and Community Mental Health Centers Construction Act increased support for public mental health services.

KENNEDY THE COLD WARRIOR

Kennedy focused most of his energies on foreign policy, an arena in which he had been interested since his college years and in which, like all presidents, he was less constrained by the dictates of Congress. Kennedy, who had promised in his inaugural address to protect the interests of the "free world," engaged in Cold War politics on a variety of fronts. For example, in response to the lead that the Soviets had taken in the space race when Yuri Gagarin became the first human to successfully orbit the earth, Kennedy urged Congress to not only put a man into space (Figure 29.4) but also land an American on the moon, a goal finally accomplished in 1969. This investment advanced a variety of military technologies, especially the nation's long-range missile capability, resulting in numerous profitable spin-offs for the aviation and communication industries. It also funded a growing middle class of government workers, engineers, and defense contractors in states ranging from California to Texas to Florida—a region that would come to be known as the Sun Belt—becoming a symbol of American technological superiority. At the same time, however, the use of massive federal resources for space technologies did not change the economic outlook for low-income communities and underprivileged regions.

Figure 29.4 On May 5, 1961, Alan Shepard became the first American to travel into space, as millions across the country watched the television coverage of his Apollo 11 mission, including Vice President Johnson, President Kennedy, and Jacqueline Kennedy in the White House. (credit: National Archives and Records Administration)

To counter Soviet influence in the developing world, Kennedy supported a variety of measures. One of these was the Alliance for Progress, which collaborated with the governments of Latin American countries to promote economic growth and social stability in nations whose populations might find themselves drawn to communism. Kennedy also established the Agency for International Development to oversee the distribution of foreign aid, and he founded the Peace Corps, which recruited idealistic young people to undertake humanitarian projects in Asia, Africa, and Latin America. He hoped that by augmenting the food supply and improving healthcare and education, the U.S. government could encourage developing nations to align themselves with the United States and reject Soviet or Chinese overtures. The first group of Peace Corps volunteers departed for the four corners of the globe in 1961, serving as an instrument of "soft power" in the Cold War.

Kennedy's various aid projects, like the Peace Corps, fit closely with his administration's **flexible response**, which Robert McNamara advocated as a better alternative to the all-or-nothing defensive strategy of mutually assured destruction favored during Eisenhower's presidency. The plan was to develop different strategies, tactics, and even military capabilities to respond more appropriately to small or medium-sized insurgencies, and political or diplomatic crises. One component of flexible response was the Green Berets, a U.S. Army Special Forces unit trained in **counterinsurgency**—the military suppression of rebel and nationalist groups in foreign nations. Much of the Kennedy administration's new approach to defense, however, remained focused on the ability and willingness of the United States to wage both conventional and nuclear warfare, and Kennedy continued to call for increases in the American nuclear arsenal.

Cuba

Kennedy's multifaceted approach to national defense is exemplified by his careful handling of the Communist government of Fidel Castro in Cuba. In January 1959, following the overthrow of the corrupt and dictatorial regime of Fulgencio Batista, Castro assumed leadership of the new Cuban government. The progressive reforms he began indicated that he favored Communism, and his pro-Soviet foreign policy frightened the Eisenhower administration, which asked the Central Intelligence Agency (CIA) to find a way to remove him from power. Rather than have the U.S. military invade the small island nation, less than one hundred miles from Florida, and risk the world's criticism, the CIA instead trained a small force of Cuban exiles for the job. After landing at the Bay of Pigs on the Cuban coast, these insurgents, the CIA believed, would inspire their countrymen to rise up and topple Castro's regime. The United States also promised air support for the invasion.

Kennedy agreed to support the previous administration's plans, and on April 17, 1961, approximately fourteen hundred Cuban exiles stormed ashore at the designated spot. However, Kennedy feared domestic criticism and worried about Soviet retaliation elsewhere in the world, such as Berlin. He cancelled the anticipated air support, which enabled the Cuban army to easily defeat the insurgents. The hoped-for uprising of the Cuban people also failed to occur. The surviving members of the exile army were taken into custody.

The Bay of Pigs invasion was a major foreign policy disaster for President Kennedy and highlighted Cuba's military vulnerability to the Castro administration. The following year, the Soviet Union sent troops and technicians to Cuba to strengthen its new ally against further U.S. military plots. Then, on October 14, U.S. spy planes took aerial photographs that confirmed the presence of long-range ballistic missile sites in Cuba. The United States was now within easy reach of Soviet nuclear warheads (Figure 29.5).

(a)   (b)

Figure 29.5   This low-level U.S. Navy photograph of San Cristobal, Cuba, clearly shows one of the sites built to launch intermediate-range missiles at the United States (a). As the date indicates, it was taken on the last day of the Cuban Missile Crisis. Following the crisis, Kennedy met with the reconnaissance pilots who flew the Cuban missions (b). credit a: modification of work by National Archives and Records Administration; credit b: modification of work by Central Intelligence Agency)

On October 22, Kennedy demanded that Soviet premier Nikita Khrushchev remove the missiles. He also ordered a **naval quarantine** placed around Cuba to prevent Soviet ships from approaching. Despite his use of the word "quarantine" instead of "blockade," for a blockade was considered an act of war, a potential war with the Soviet Union was nevertheless on the president's mind. As U.S. ships headed for Cuba, the army was told to prepare for war, and Kennedy appeared on national television to declare his intention to defend the Western Hemisphere from Soviet aggression.

The world held its breath awaiting the Soviet reply. Realizing how serious the United States was, Khrushchev sought a peaceful solution to the crisis, overruling those in his government who urged a harder stance. Behind the scenes, Robert Kennedy and Soviet ambassador Anatoly Dobrynin worked toward a compromise that would allow both superpowers to back down without either side's seeming intimidated by the other. On October 26, Khrushchev agreed to remove the Russian missiles in exchange for Kennedy's promise not to invade Cuba. On October 27, Kennedy's agreement was made public, and the crisis ended. Not made public, but nevertheless part of the agreement, was Kennedy's promise to remove U.S. warheads from Turkey, as close to Soviet targets as the Cuban missiles had been to American ones.

The showdown between the United States and the Soviet Union over Cuba's missiles had put the world on the brink of a nuclear war. Both sides already had long-range bombers with nuclear weapons airborne or ready for launch, and were only hours away from the first strike. In the long run, this nearly catastrophic example of nuclear brinksmanship ended up making the world safer. A telephone "hot line" was installed, linking Washington and Moscow to avert future crises, and in 1963, Kennedy and Khrushchev signed the Limited Test Ban Treaty, prohibiting tests of nuclear weapons in Earth's atmosphere.

Vietnam

Cuba was not the only arena in which the United States sought to contain the advance of Communism. In Indochina, nationalist independence movements, most notably Vietnam's Viet Minh under the leadership of Ho Chi Minh, had strong Communist sympathies. President Harry S. Truman had no love for France's colonial regime in Southeast Asia but did not want to risk the loyalty of its Western European ally against the Soviet Union. In 1950, the Truman administration sent a small military advisory group to Vietnam and provided financial aid to help France defeat the Viet Minh.

In 1954, Vietnamese forces finally defeated the French, and the country was temporarily divided at the seventeenth parallel. Ho Chi Minh and the Viet Minh controlled the North. In the South, the last Vietnamese emperor and ally to France, Bao Dai, named the French-educated, anti-Communist Ngo Dinh Diem as his prime minister. But Diem refused to abide by the Geneva Accords, the treaty ending the conflict that called for countrywide national elections in 1956, with the victor to rule a reunified nation. After a fraudulent election in the South in 1955, he ousted Bao Dai and proclaimed himself president of the Republic of Vietnam. He cancelled the 1956 elections in the South and began to round up Communists and supporters of Ho Chi Minh.

Realizing that Diem would never agree to the reunification of the country under Ho Chi Minh's leadership, the North Vietnamese began efforts to overthrow the government of the South by encouraging insurgents to attack South Vietnamese officials. By 1960, North Vietnam had also created the National Liberation Front (NLF) to resist Diem and carry out an insurgency in the South. The United States, fearing the spread of Communism under Ho Chi Minh, supported Diem, assuming he would create a democratic, pro-Western government in South Vietnam. However, Diem's oppressive and corrupt government made him a very unpopular ruler, particularly with farmers, students, and Buddhists, and many in the South actively assisted the NLF and North Vietnam in trying to overthrow his government.

When Kennedy took office, Diem's government was faltering. Continuing the policies of the Eisenhower administration, Kennedy supplied Diem with money and military advisors to prop up his government (Figure 29.6). By November 1963, there were sixteen thousand U.S. troops in Vietnam, training members of that country's special forces and flying air missions that dumped defoliant chemicals on the countryside to expose North Vietnamese and NLF forces and supply routes. A few weeks before Kennedy's own death, Diem and his brother Nhu were assassinated by South Vietnamese military officers after U.S. officials had indicated their support for a new regime.

Figure 29.6 Following the French retreat from Indochina, the United States stepped in to prevent what it believed was a building Communist threat in the region. Under President Kennedy's leadership, the United States sent thousands of military advisors to Vietnam. (credit: Abbie Rowe)

TENTATIVE STEPS TOWARD CIVIL RIGHTS

Cold War concerns, which guided U.S. policy in Cuba and Vietnam, also motivated the Kennedy administration's steps toward racial equality. Realizing that legal segregation and widespread discrimination hurt the country's chances of gaining allies in Africa, Asia, and Latin America, the federal government increased efforts to secure the civil rights of African Americans in the 1960s. During his presidential campaign, Kennedy had intimated his support for civil rights, and his efforts to secure the release of civil rights leader Martin Luther King, Jr., who was arrested following a demonstration, won him the African American vote. Lacking widespread backing in Congress, however, and anxious not to offend white southerners, Kennedy was cautious in assisting African Americans in their fight for full citizenship rights.

His strongest focus was on securing the voting rights of African Americans. Kennedy feared the loss of support from southern white Democrats and the impact a struggle over civil rights could have on his foreign policy agenda as well as on his reelection in 1964. But he thought voter registration drives far preferable to the boycotts, sit-ins, and integration marches that had generated such intense global media coverage in previous years. Encouraged by Congress's passage of the Civil Rights Act of 1960, which permitted federal courts to appoint referees to guarantee that qualified persons would be registered to vote, Kennedy focused on the passage of a constitutional amendment outlawing poll taxes, a tactic that southern states used to disenfranchise African American voters. Originally proposed by President Truman's Committee on Civil Rights, the idea had been largely forgotten during Eisenhower's time in office. Kennedy, however, revived it and convinced Spessard Holland, a conservative Florida senator, to introduce the proposed amendment in Congress. It passed both houses of Congress and was sent to the states for ratification in September 1962.

Kennedy also reacted to the demands of the civil rights movement for equality in education. For example, when African American student James Meredith, encouraged by Kennedy's speeches, attempted to enroll at the segregated University of Mississippi in 1962, riots broke out on campus (Figure 29.7). The president responded by sending the U.S. Army and National Guard to Oxford, Mississippi, to support the U.S. Marshals that his brother Robert, the attorney general, had dispatched.

Figure 29.7 Escorted by a U.S. marshal and the assistant attorney general for civil rights, James Meredith (center) enters the University of Mississippi over the riotous protests of white southerners. Meredith later attempted a "March against Fear" in 1966 to protest the inability of southern African Americans to vote. His walk ended when a passing motorist shot and wounded him. (credit: Library of Congress)

Following similar violence at the University of Alabama when two African American students, Vivian Malone and James Hood, attempted to enroll in 1963, Kennedy responded with a bill that would give the federal government greater power to enforce school desegregation, prohibit segregation in public accommodations, and outlaw discrimination in employment. Kennedy would not live to see his bill enacted; it would become law during Lyndon Johnson's administration as the 1964 Civil Rights Act.

TRAGEDY IN DALLAS

Although his stance on civil rights had won him support in the African American community and his steely performance during the Cuban Missile Crisis had led his overall popularity to surge, Kennedy understood that he had to solidify his base in the South to secure his reelection. On November 21, 1963, he accompanied Lyndon Johnson to Texas to rally his supporters. The next day, shots rang out as Kennedy's motorcade made its way through the streets of Dallas. Seriously injured, Kennedy was rushed to Parkland Hospital and pronounced dead.

The gunfire that killed Kennedy appeared to come from the upper stories of the Texas School Book Depository building; later that day, Lee Harvey Oswald, an employee at the depository and a trained sniper, was arrested (Figure 29.8). Two days later, while being transferred from Dallas police headquarters to the county jail, Oswald was shot and killed by Jack Ruby, a local nightclub owner who claimed he acted to avenge the president.

Figure 29.8 Lee Harvey Oswald (center) was arrested at the Texas Theatre in Dallas a few hours after shooting President Kennedy.

Almost immediately, rumors began to circulate regarding the Kennedy assassination, and conspiracy theorists, pointing to the unlikely coincidence of Oswald's murder a few days after Kennedy's, began to propose alternate theories about the events. To quiet the rumors and allay fears that the government was hiding evidence, Lyndon Johnson, Kennedy's successor, appointed a fact-finding commission headed by Earl Warren, chief justice of the U.S. Supreme Court, to examine all the evidence and render a verdict. The Warren Commission concluded that Lee Harvey Oswald had acted alone and there had been no conspiracy. The commission's ruling failed to satisfy many, and multiple theories have sprung up over time. No credible evidence has ever been uncovered, however, to prove either that someone other than Oswald murdered Kennedy or that Oswald acted with co-conspirators.

29.2 Lyndon Johnson and the Great Society

By the end of this section, you will be able to:
- Describe the major accomplishments of Lyndon Johnson's Great Society
- Identify the legal advances made in the area of civil rights
- Explain how Lyndon Johnson deepened the American commitment in Vietnam

On November 27, 1963, a few days after taking the oath of office, President Johnson addressed a joint session of Congress and vowed to accomplish the goals that John F. Kennedy had set and to expand the role of the federal government in securing economic opportunity and civil rights for all. Johnson brought to his presidency a vision of a **Great Society** in which everyone could share in the opportunities for a better life that the United States offered, and in which the words "liberty and justice for all" would have real meaning.

THE GREAT SOCIETY

In May 1964, in a speech at the University of Michigan, Lyndon Johnson described in detail his vision of the Great Society he planned to create (Figure 29.9). When the Eighty-Ninth Congress convened the following January, he and his supporters began their effort to turn the promise into reality. By combatting racial discrimination and attempting to eliminate poverty, the reforms of the Johnson administration changed the nation.

(a)   (b)

Figure 29.9 In a speech at the University of Michigan in Ann Arbor on May 22, 1964 (a), President Johnson announced some of his goals for the Great Society. These included rebuilding cities, preserving the natural environment, and improving education. Johnson signed the Elementary and Secondary Education Act in his hometown of Johnson City, Texas, alongside his childhood schoolteacher, Kate Deadrich Loney (b). (credit a: modification of work by Cecil Stoughton)

One of the chief pieces of legislation that Congress passed in 1965 was the Elementary and Secondary Education Act (Figure 29.9). Johnson, a former teacher, realized that a lack of education was the primary cause of poverty and other social problems. Educational reform was thus an important pillar of the society he hoped to build. This act provided increased federal funding to both elementary and secondary schools, allocating more than $1 billion for the purchase of books and library materials, and the creation of educational programs for disadvantaged children. The Higher Education Act, signed into law the same year, provided scholarships and low-interest loans for the poor, increased federal funding for colleges and universities, and created a corps of teachers to serve schools in impoverished areas.

Education was not the only area toward which Johnson directed his attention. Consumer protection laws were also passed that improved the safety of meat and poultry, placed warning labels on cigarette packages, required "truth in lending" by creditors, and set safety standards for motor vehicles. Funds were provided to improve public transportation and to fund high-speed mass transit. To protect the environment, the Johnson administration created laws protecting air and water quality, regulating the disposal of solid waste, preserving wilderness areas, and protecting endangered species. All of these laws fit within Johnson's plan to make the United States a better place to live. Perhaps influenced by Kennedy's commitment to the arts, Johnson also signed legislation creating the National Endowment for the Arts and the National Endowment for the Humanities, which provided funding for artists and scholars. The Public Broadcasting Act of 1967 authorized the creation of the private, not-for-profit Corporation for Public Broadcasting, which helped launch the Public Broadcasting Service (PBS) and National Public Radio (NPR) in 1970.

In 1965, the Johnson administration also encouraged Congress to pass the Immigration and Nationality Act, which essentially overturned legislation from the 1920s that had favored immigrants from western and northern Europe over those from eastern and southern Europe. The law lifted severe restrictions on immigration from Asia and gave preference to immigrants with family ties in the United States and immigrants with desirable skills. Although the measure seemed less significant than many of the other legislative victories of the Johnson administration at the time, it opened the door for a new era in immigration and made possible the formation of Asian and Latin American immigrant communities in the following decades.

While these laws touched on important aspects of the Great Society, the centerpiece of Johnson's plan was the eradication of poverty in the United States. The **war on poverty**, as he termed it, was fought on many fronts. The 1965 Housing and Urban Development Act offered grants to improve city housing and subsidized rents for the poor. The Model Cities program likewise provided money for urban development projects and the building of public housing.

The Economic Opportunity Act (EOA) of 1964 established and funded a variety of programs to assist the poor in finding jobs. The Office of Economic Opportunity (OEO), first administered by President Kennedy's brother-in-law Sargent Shriver, coordinated programs such as the Jobs Corps and the Neighborhood Youth Corps, which provided job training programs and work experience for the disadvantaged. Volunteers in Service to America recruited people to offer educational programs and other community services in poor areas, just as the Peace Corps did abroad. The Community Action Program, also under the OEO, funded local Community Action Agencies, organizations created and managed by residents of disadvantaged communities to improve their own lives and those of their neighbors. The Head Start program, intended to prepare low-income children for elementary school, was also under the OEO until it was transferred to Department of Health, Education, and Welfare in 1969.

The EOA fought rural poverty by providing low-interest loans to those wishing to improve their farms or start businesses (Figure 29.10). EOA funds were also used to provide housing and education for migrant farm workers. Other legislation created jobs in Appalachia, one of the poorest regions in the United States, and brought programs to Indian reservations. One of EOA's successes was the Rough Rock Demonstration School on the Navajo Reservation that, while respecting Navajo traditions and culture, also trained people for careers and jobs outside the reservation.

Figure 29.10 President Johnson visits a poor family in Appalachia in 1964. Government initiatives designed to combat poverty helped rural communities like this one by providing low-interest loans and housing. (credit: Cecil Stoughton)

The Johnson administration, realizing the nation's elderly were among its poorest and most disadvantaged citizens, passed the Social Security Act of 1965. The most profound change made by this act was the creation of Medicare, a program to pay the medical expenses of those over sixty-five. Although opposed by the American Medical Association, which feared the creation of a national healthcare system, the new program was supported by most citizens because it would benefit all social classes, not just the poor. The act and subsequent amendments to it also provided coverage for self-employed people in certain occupations and expanded the number of disabled who qualified for benefits. The following year, the Medicaid program allotted federal funds to pay for medical care for the poor.

JOHNSON'S COMMITMENT TO CIVIL RIGHTS

The eradication of poverty was matched in importance by the Great Society's advancement of civil rights. Indeed, the condition of the poor could not be alleviated if racial discrimination limited their access to jobs, education, and housing. Realizing this, Johnson drove the long-awaited civil rights act, proposed by Kennedy in June 1963 in the wake of riots at the University of Alabama, through Congress. Under

Kennedy's leadership, the bill had passed the House of Representatives but was stalled in the Senate by a filibuster. Johnson, a master politician, marshaled his considerable personal influence and memories of his fallen predecessor to break the filibuster. The Civil Rights Act of 1964, the most far-reaching civil rights act yet passed by Congress, banned discrimination in public accommodations, sought to aid schools in efforts to desegregate, and prohibited federal funding of programs that permitted racial segregation. Further, it barred discrimination in employment on the basis of race, color, national origin, religion, or gender, and established an Equal Employment Opportunity Commission.

Protecting African Americans' right to vote was as important as ending racial inequality in the United States. In January 1964, the Twenty-Fourth Amendment, prohibiting the imposition of poll taxes on voters, was finally ratified. Poverty would no longer serve as an obstacle to voting. Other impediments remained, however. Attempts to register southern African American voters encountered white resistance, and protests against this interference often met with violence. On March 7, 1965, a planned protest march from Selma, Alabama, to the state capitol in Montgomery, turned into "Bloody Sunday" when marchers crossing the Edmund Pettus Bridge encountered a cordon of state police, wielding batons and tear gas (Figure 29.11). Images of white brutality appeared on television screens throughout the nation and in newspapers around the world.

Figure 29.11 African American marchers in Selma, Alabama, were attacked by state police officers in 1965, and the resulting "Bloody Sunday" helped create support for the civil rights movement among northern whites. (credit: Library of Congress)

Deeply disturbed by the violence in Alabama and the refusal of Governor George Wallace to address it, Johnson introduced a bill in Congress that would remove obstacles for African American voters and lend federal support to their cause. His proposal, the Voting Rights Act of 1965, prohibited states and local governments from passing laws that discriminated against voters on the basis of race (Figure 29.12). Literacy tests and other barriers to voting that had kept ethnic minorities from the polls were thus outlawed. Following the passage of the act, a quarter of a million African Americans registered to vote, and by 1967, the majority of African Americans had done so. Johnson's final piece of civil rights legislation was the Civil Rights Act of 1968, which prohibited discrimination in housing on the basis of race, color, national origin, or religion.

(a)   (b)

Figure 29.12 The Voting Rights Act (a) was signed into law on August 6, 1965, in the presence of major figures of the civil rights movement, including Rosa Parks and Martin Luther King, Jr. (b).

INCREASED COMMITMENT IN VIETNAM

Building the Great Society had been Lyndon Johnson's biggest priority, and he effectively used his decades of experience in building legislative majorities in a style that ranged from diplomacy to quid pro quo deals to bullying. In the summer of 1964, he deployed these political skills to secure congressional approval for a new strategy in Vietnam—with fateful consequences.

President Johnson had never been the cold warrior Kennedy was, but believed that the credibility of the nation and his office depended on maintaining a foreign policy of containment. When, on August 2, the U.S. destroyer USS *Maddox* conducted an arguably provocative intelligence-gathering mission in the gulf of Tonkin, it reported an attack by North Vietnamese torpedo boats. Two days later, the *Maddox* was supposedly struck again, and a second ship, the USS *Turner Joy*, reported that it also had been fired upon. The North Vietnamese denied the second attack, and Johnson himself doubted the reliability of the crews' report. The National Security Agency has since revealed that the August 4 attacks did not occur. Relying on information available at the time, however, Secretary of Defense Robert McNamara reported to Congress that U.S. ships had been fired upon in international waters while conducting routine operations. On August 7, with only two dissenting votes, Congress passed the Gulf of Tonkin Resolution, and on August 10, the president signed the resolution into law. The resolution gave President Johnson the authority to use military force in Vietnam without asking Congress for a declaration of war. It dramatically increased the power of the U.S. president and transformed the American role in Vietnam from advisor to combatant.

In 1965, large-scale U.S. bombing of North Vietnam began. The intent of the campaign, which lasted three years under various names, was to force the North to end its support for the insurgency in the South. More than 200,000 U.S. military personnel, including combat troops, were sent to South Vietnam. At first, most of the American public supported the president's actions in Vietnam. Support began to ebb, however, as more troops were deployed. Frustrated by losses suffered by the South's Army of the Republic of Vietnam (ARVN), General William Westmoreland called for the United States to take more responsibility for fighting the war. By April 1966, more Americans were being killed in battle than ARVN troops. Johnson, however, maintained that the war could be won if the United States stayed the course, and in November 1967, Westmoreland proclaimed the end was in sight.

Click and Explore

To hear one soldier's story about his time in Vietnam, listen to **Sergeant Charles G. Richardson's recollections (http://openstaxcollege.org/l/15VietnamVet)** of his experience on the ground and his reflections on his military service.

Westmoreland's predictions were called into question, however, when in January 1968, the North Vietnamese launched their most aggressive assault on the South, deploying close to eighty-five thousand troops. During the Tet Offensive, as these attacks were known, nearly one hundred cities in the South were attacked, including the capital of Saigon (Figure 29.13). In heavy fighting, U.S. and South Vietnamese forces recaptured all the points taken by the enemy.

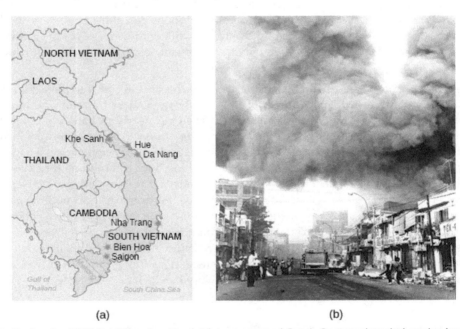

Figure 29.13 During the 1968 Tet Offensive, North Vietnamese and South Communist rebel armies known as Viet Cong attacked South Vietnamese and U.S. targets throughout Vietnam (a), with Saigon as the focus (b). Tet, the lunar New Year, was an important holiday in Vietnam and temporary ceasefires usually took place at this time. (credit a: modification of work by Central Intelligence Agency)

Although North Vietnamese forces suffered far more casualties than the roughly forty-one hundred U.S. soldiers killed, public opinion in the United States, fueled by graphic images provided in unprecedented media coverage, turned against the war. Disastrous surprise attacks like the Tet Offensive persuaded many that the war would not be over soon and raised doubts about whether Johnson's administration was telling the truth about the real state of affairs. In May 1968, with over 400,000 U.S. soldiers in Vietnam, Johnson began peace talks with the North.

It was too late to save Johnson himself, however. Many of the most outspoken critics of the war were Democratic politicians whose opposition began to erode unity within the party. Minnesota senator Eugene McCarthy, who had called for an end to the war and the withdrawal of troops from Vietnam, received nearly as many votes in the New Hampshire presidential primary as Johnson did, even though he had been expected to fare very poorly. McCarthy's success in New Hampshire encouraged Robert Kennedy to announce his candidacy as well. Johnson, suffering health problems and realizing his actions in Vietnam had hurt his public standing, announced that he would not seek reelection and withdrew from the 1968 presidential race.

THE END OF THE GREAT SOCIETY

Perhaps the greatest casualty of the nation's war in Vietnam was the Great Society. As the war escalated, the money spent to fund it also increased, leaving less to pay for the many social programs Johnson had created to lift Americans out of poverty. Johnson knew he could not achieve his Great Society while spending money to wage the war. He was unwilling to withdraw from Vietnam, however, for fear that the world would perceive this action as evidence of American failure and doubt the ability of the United States to carry out its responsibilities as a superpower.

Vietnam doomed the Great Society in other ways as well. Dreams of racial harmony suffered, as many African Americans, angered by the failure of Johnson's programs to alleviate severe poverty in the inner cities, rioted in frustration. Their anger was heightened by the fact that a disproportionate number of African Americans were fighting and dying in Vietnam. Nearly two-thirds of eligible African Americans were drafted, whereas draft deferments for college, exemptions for skilled workers in the military industrial complex, and officer training programs allowed white middle-class youth to either avoid the draft or volunteer for a military branch of their choice. As a result, less than one-third of white men were drafted.

Although the Great Society failed to eliminate suffering or increase civil rights to the extent that Johnson wished, it made a significant difference in people's lives. By the end of Johnson's administration, the percentage of people living below the poverty line had been cut nearly in half. While more people of color than whites continued to live in poverty, the percentage of poor African Americans had decreased dramatically. The creation of Medicare and Medicaid as well as the expansion of Social Security benefits and welfare payments improved the lives of many, while increased federal funding for education enabled more people to attend college than ever before. Conservative critics argued that, by expanding the responsibilities of the federal government to care for the poor, Johnson had hurt both taxpayers and the poor themselves. Aid to the poor, many maintained, would not only fail to solve the problem of poverty but would also encourage people to become dependent on government "handouts" and lose their desire and ability to care for themselves—an argument that many found intuitively compelling but which lacked conclusive evidence. These same critics also accused Johnson of saddling the United States with a large debt as a result of the deficit spending (funded by borrowing) in which he had engaged.

29.3 The Civil Rights Movement Marches On

By the end of this section, you will be able to:
- Explain the strategies of the African American civil rights movement in the 1960s
- Discuss the rise and philosophy of Black Power
- Identify achievements of the Mexican American civil rights movement in the 1960s

During the 1960s, the federal government, encouraged by both genuine concern for the dispossessed and the realities of the Cold War, had increased its efforts to protect civil rights and ensure equal economic and educational opportunities for all. However, most of the credit for progress toward racial equality in the Unites States lies with grassroots activists. Indeed, it was campaigns and demonstrations by ordinary people that spurred the federal government to action. Although the African American civil rights movement was the most prominent of the crusades for racial justice, other ethnic minorities also worked to seize their piece of the American dream during the promising years of the 1960s. Many were influenced by the African American cause and often used similar tactics.

CHANGE FROM THE BOTTOM UP

For many people inspired by the victories of *Brown v. Board of Education* and the Montgomery Bus Boycott, the glacial pace of progress in the segregated South was frustrating if not intolerable. In some places, such as Greensboro, North Carolina, local NAACP chapters had been influenced by whites who provided financing for the organization. This aid, together with the belief that more forceful efforts at reform would only increase white resistance, had persuaded some African American organizations to pursue a "politics of moderation" instead of attempting to radically alter the status quo. Martin Luther King Jr.'s inspirational appeal for peaceful change in the city of Greensboro in 1958, however, planted the seed for a more assertive civil rights movement.

On February 1, 1960, four sophomores at the North Carolina Agricultural & Technical College in Greensboro—Ezell Blair, Jr., Joseph McNeil, David Richmond, and Franklin McCain—entered the local Woolworth's and sat at the lunch counter. The lunch counter was segregated, and they were refused service as they knew they would be. They had specifically chosen Woolworth's, because it was a national chain and was thus believed to be especially vulnerable to negative publicity. Over the next few days, more protesters joined the four sophomores. Hostile whites responded with threats and taunted the students by pouring sugar and ketchup on their heads. The successful six-month-long Greensboro sit-in initiated the student phase of the African American civil rights movement and, within two months, the sit-in movement had spread to fifty-four cities in nine states (Figure 29.14).

Figure 29.14 Businesses such as this one were among those that became targets of activists protesting segregation. Segregated businesses could be found throughout the United States; this one was located in Ohio. (credit: Library of Congress)

In the words of grassroots civil rights activist Ella Baker, the students at Woolworth's wanted more than a hamburger; the movement they helped launch was about empowerment. Baker pushed for a "participatory Democracy" that built on the grassroots campaigns of active citizens instead of deferring to the leadership of educated elites and experts. As a result of her actions, in April 1960, the Student Nonviolent Coordinating Committee (SNCC) formed to carry the battle forward. Within a year, more than one hundred cities had desegregated at least some public accommodations in response to student-led demonstrations. The sit-ins inspired other forms of nonviolent protest intended to desegregate public spaces. "Sleep-ins" occupied motel lobbies, "read-ins" filled public libraries, and churches became the sites of "pray-ins."

Students also took part in the 1961 "freedom rides" sponsored by the Congress of Racial Equality (CORE) and SNCC. The intent of the African American and white volunteers who undertook these bus rides south was to test enforcement of a U.S. Supreme Court decision prohibiting segregation on interstate transportation and to protest segregated waiting rooms in southern terminals. Departing Washington, DC, on May 4, the volunteers headed south on buses that challenged the seating order of Jim Crow segregation. Whites would ride in the back, African-Americans would sit in the front, and on other occasions, riders of different races would share the same bench seat. The freedom riders encountered little difficulty until they reached Rock Hill, South Carolina, where a mob severely beat John Lewis, a freedom rider who later became chairman of SNCC (Figure 29.15). The danger increased as the riders continued through Georgia into Alabama, where one of the two buses was firebombed outside the town of Anniston. The second group continued to Birmingham, where the riders were attacked by the Ku Klux Klan as they attempted to disembark at the city bus station. The remaining volunteers continued to Mississippi, where they were arrested when they attempted to desegregate the waiting rooms in the Jackson bus terminal.

Figure 29.15 Civil rights activists Bayard Rustin, Andrew Young, Rep. William Fitts Ryan, James Farmer, and John Lewis (l to r) in a newspaper photograph from 1965.

FREE BY '63 (OR '64 OR '65)

The grassroots efforts of people like the Freedom Riders to change discriminatory laws and longstanding racist traditions grew more widely known in the mid-1960s. The approaching centennial of Abraham Lincoln's Emancipation Proclamation spawned the slogan "Free by '63" among civil rights activists. As African Americans increased their calls for full rights for all Americans, many civil rights groups changed their tactics to reflect this new urgency.

Perhaps the most famous of the civil rights-era demonstrations was the March on Washington for Jobs and Freedom, held in August 1963, on the one hundredth anniversary of Abraham Lincoln's Emancipation Proclamation. Its purpose was to pressure President Kennedy to act on his promises regarding civil rights. The date was the eighth anniversary of the brutal racist murder of fourteen-year-old Emmett Till in Money, Mississippi. As the crowd gathered outside the Lincoln Memorial and spilled across the National Mall (Figure 29.16), Martin Luther King, Jr. delivered his most famous speech. In "I Have a Dream," King called for an end to racial injustice in the United States and envisioned a harmonious, integrated society. The speech marked the high point of the civil rights movement and established the legitimacy of its goals. However, it did not prevent white terrorism in the South, nor did it permanently sustain the tactics of nonviolent civil disobedience.

(a)   (b)

Figure 29.16 During the March on Washington for Jobs and Freedom (a), a huge crowd gathered on the National Mall (b) to hear the speakers. Although thousands attended, many of the march's organizers had hoped that enough people would come to Washington to shut down the city.

Other gatherings of civil rights activists ended tragically, and some demonstrations were intended to provoke a hostile response from whites and thus reveal the inhumanity of the Jim Crow laws and their supporters. In 1963, the Southern Christian Leadership Conference (SCLC) led by Martin Luther King, Jr. mounted protests in some 186 cities throughout the South. The campaign in Birmingham that began in April and extended into the fall of 1963 attracted the most notice, however, when a peaceful protest was met with violence by police, who attacked demonstrators, including children, with fire hoses and dogs. The world looked on in horror as innocent people were assaulted and thousands arrested. King himself was jailed on Easter Sunday, 1963, and, in response to the pleas of white clergymen for peace and patience, he penned one of the most significant documents of the struggle—"Letter from a Birmingham Jail." In the letter, King argued that African Americans had waited patiently for more than three hundred years to be given the rights that all human beings deserved; the time for waiting was over.

DEFINING "AMERICAN"

✪ Letter from a Birmingham Jail

By 1963, Martin Luther King, Jr. had become one of the most prominent leaders of the civil rights movement, and he continued to espouse nonviolent civil disobedience as a way of registering African American resistance against unfair, discriminatory, and racist laws and behaviors. While the campaign in Birmingham began with an African American boycott of white businesses to end discrimination in employment practices and public segregation, it became a fight over free speech when King was arrested for violating a local injunction against demonstrations. King wrote his "Letter from a Birmingham Jail" in response to an op-ed by eight white Alabama clergymen who complained about the SCLC's fiery tactics and argued that social change needed to be pursued gradually. The letter criticizes those who did not support the cause of civil rights:

> In spite of my shattered dreams of the past, I came to Birmingham with the hope that the white religious leadership in the community would see the justice of our cause and, with deep moral concern, serve as the channel through which our just grievances could get to the power structure. I had hoped that each of you would understand. But again I have been disappointed. I have heard numerous religious leaders of the South call upon their worshippers to comply with a desegregation decision because it is the law, but I have longed to hear white ministers say follow this decree because integration is morally right and the Negro is your brother. In the midst of blatant injustices inflicted upon the Negro, I have watched white churches stand on the sideline and merely mouth pious irrelevancies and sanctimonious trivialities. In the midst of a mighty struggle to rid our nation of racial and economic injustice, I have heard so many ministers say, "Those are social issues with which the Gospel has no real concern," and I have watched so many churches commit themselves to a completely other-worldly religion which made a strange distinction between body and soul, the sacred and the secular.

Since its publication, the "Letter" has become one of the most cogent, impassioned, and succinct statements of the aspirations of the civil rights movement and the frustration over the glacial pace of progress in achieving justice and equality for all Americans.

What civil rights tactics raised the objections of the white clergymen King addressed in his letter? Why?

Some of the greatest violence during this era was aimed at those who attempted to register African Americans to vote. In 1964, SNCC, working with other civil rights groups, initiated its Mississippi Summer Project, also known as Freedom Summer. The purpose was to register African American voters in one of the most racist states in the nation. Volunteers also built "freedom schools" and community centers. SNCC invited hundreds of white middle-class students, mostly from the North, to help in the task. Many volunteers were harassed, beaten, and arrested, and African American homes and churches were burned. Three civil rights workers, James Chaney, Michael Schwerner, and Andrew Goodman, were killed by the Ku Klux Klan. That summer, civil rights activists Fannie Lou Hamer, Ella Baker, and Robert Parris Moses formally organized the Mississippi Freedom Democratic Party (MFDP) as an alternative to the all-white Mississippi Democratic Party. The Democratic National Convention's organizers, however, would allow only two MFDP delegates to be seated, and they were confined to the roles of nonvoting observers.

The vision of whites and African Americans working together peacefully to end racial injustice suffered a severe blow with the death of Martin Luther King, Jr. in Memphis, Tennessee, in April 1968. King had gone there to support sanitation workers trying to unionize. In the city, he found a divided civil rights movement; older activists who supported his policy of nonviolence were being challenged by younger African Americans who advocated a more militant approach. On April 4, King was shot and killed while standing on the balcony of his motel. Within hours, the nation's cities exploded with violence as angry African Americans, shocked by his murder, burned and looted inner-city neighborhoods across the country (Figure 29.17). While whites recoiled from news about the riots in fear and dismay, they also criticized African Americans for destroying their own neighborhoods; they did not realize that most of the violence was directed against businesses that were not owned by blacks and that treated African American customers with suspicion and hostility.

Figure 29.17 Many businesses, such as those in this neighborhood at the intersection of 7th and N Streets in NW, Washington, DC, were destroyed in riots that followed the assassination of Martin Luther King, Jr.

BLACK FRUSTRATION, BLACK POWER

The episodes of violence that accompanied Martin Luther King Jr.'s murder were but the latest in a string of urban riots that had shaken the United States since the mid-1960s. Between 1964 and 1968, there were 329 riots in 257 cities across the nation. In 1964, riots broke out in Harlem and other African American neighborhoods. In 1965, a traffic stop set in motion a chain of events that culminated in riots in Watts, an African American neighborhood in Los Angeles. Thousands of businesses were destroyed, and, by the time the violence ended, thirty-four people were dead, most of them African Americans killed by the Los Angeles police and the National Guard. More riots took place in 1966 and 1967.

Frustration and anger lay at the heart of these disruptions. Despite the programs of the Great Society, good healthcare, job opportunities, and safe housing were abysmally lacking in urban African American neighborhoods in cities throughout the country, including in the North and West, where discrimination was less overt but just as crippling. In the eyes of many rioters, the federal government either could not or would not end their suffering, and most existing civil rights groups and their leaders had been unable to achieve significant results toward racial justice and equality. Disillusioned, many African Americans turned to those with more radical ideas about how best to obtain equality and justice.

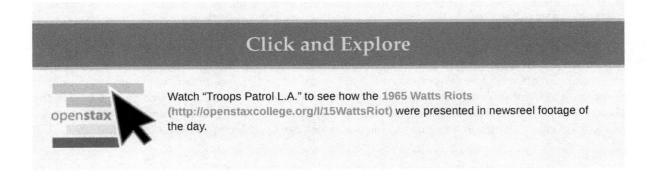

Click and Explore

Watch "Troops Patrol L.A." to see how the 1965 Watts Riots (http://openstaxcollege.org/l/15WattsRiot) were presented in newsreel footage of the day.

Within the chorus of voices calling for integration and legal equality were many that more stridently demanded empowerment and thus supported **Black Power**. Black Power meant a variety of things. One of the most famous users of the term was Stokely Carmichael, the chairman of SNCC, who later changed his name to Kwame Ture. For Carmichael, Black Power was the power of African Americans to unite as a political force and create their own institutions apart from white-dominated ones, an idea first suggested in the 1920s by political leader and orator Marcus Garvey. Like Garvey, Carmichael became an advocate of **black separatism**, arguing that African Americans should live apart from whites and solve their problems for themselves. In keeping with this philosophy, Carmichael expelled SNCC's white members. He left SNCC in 1967 and later joined the Black Panthers (see below).

Long before Carmichael began to call for separatism, the Nation of Islam, founded in 1930, had advocated the same thing. In the 1960s, its most famous member was Malcolm X, born Malcolm Little (Figure 29.18). The Nation of Islam advocated the separation of white Americans and African Americans because of a belief that African Americans could not thrive in an atmosphere of white racism. Indeed, in a 1963 interview, Malcolm X, discussing the teachings of the head of the Nation of Islam in America, Elijah Muhammad, referred to white people as "devils" more than a dozen times. Rejecting the nonviolent strategy of other civil rights activists, he maintained that violence in the face of violence was appropriate.

(a)   (b)

Figure 29.18 Stokely Carmichael (a), one of the most famous and outspoken advocates of Black Power, is surrounded by members of the media after speaking at Michigan State University in 1967. Malcolm X (b) was raised in a family influenced by Marcus Garvey and persecuted for its outspoken support of civil rights. While serving a stint in prison for armed robbery, he was introduced to and committed himself to the Nation of Islam. (credit b: modification of work by Library of Congress)

In 1964, after a trip to Africa, Malcolm X left the Nation of Islam to found the Organization of Afro-American Unity with the goal of achieving freedom, justice, and equality "by any means necessary." His views regarding black-white relations changed somewhat thereafter, but he remained fiercely committed to the cause of African American empowerment. On February 21, 1965, he was killed by members of the Nation of Islam. Stokely Carmichael later recalled that Malcolm X had provided an intellectual basis for Black Nationalism and given legitimacy to the use of violence in achieving the goals of Black Power.

DEFINING "AMERICAN"

⚙ *The New Negro*

In a roundtable conversation in October 1961, Malcolm X suggested that a "New Negro" was coming to the fore. The term and concept of a "New Negro" arose during the Harlem Renaissance of the 1920s and was revived during the civil rights movements of the 1960s.

> "I think there is a new so-called Negro. We don't recognize the term 'Negro' but I really believe that there's a new so-called Negro here in America. He not only is impatient. Not only is he dissatisfied, not only is he disillusioned, but he's getting very angry. And whereas the so-called Negro in the past was willing to sit around and wait for someone else to change his condition or correct his condition, there's a growing tendency on the part of a vast number of so-called Negroes today to take action themselves, not to sit and wait for someone else to correct the situation. This, in my opinion, is primarily what has produced this new Negro. He is not willing to wait. He thinks that what he wants is right, what he wants is just, and since these things are just and right, it's wrong to sit around and wait for someone else to correct a nasty condition when they get ready."

In what ways were Martin Luther King, Jr. and the members of SNCC "New Negroes?"

Unlike Stokely Carmichael and the Nation of Islam, most Black Power advocates did not believe African Americans needed to separate themselves from white society. The Black Panther Party, founded in 1966 in Oakland, California, by Bobby Seale and Huey Newton, believed African Americans were as much the victims of capitalism as of white racism. Accordingly, the group espoused Marxist teachings, and called for jobs, housing, and education, as well as protection from police brutality and exemption from military service in their Ten Point Program. The Black Panthers also patrolled the streets of African American neighborhoods to protect residents from police brutality, yet sometimes beat and murdered those who did not agree with their cause and tactics. Their militant attitude and advocacy of armed self-defense attracted many young men but also led to many encounters with the police, which sometimes included arrests and even shootouts, such as those that took place in Los Angeles, Chicago and Carbondale, Illinois.

The self-empowerment philosophy of Black Power influenced mainstream civil rights groups such as the National Economic Growth Reconstruction Organization (NEGRO), which sold bonds and operated a clothing factory and construction company in New York, and the Opportunities Industrialization Center in Philadelphia, which provided job training and placement—by 1969, it had branches in seventy cities. Black Power was also part of a much larger process of cultural change. The 1960s composed a decade not only of Black Power but also of **Black Pride**. African American abolitionist John S. Rock had coined the phrase "Black Is Beautiful" in 1858, but in the 1960s, it became an important part of efforts within the African American community to raise self-esteem and encourage pride in African ancestry. Black Pride urged African Americans to reclaim their African heritage and, to promote group solidarity, to substitute African and African-inspired cultural practices, such as handshakes, hairstyles, and dress, for white practices. One of the many cultural products of this movement was the popular television music program *Soul Train*, created by Don Cornelius in 1969, which celebrated black culture and aesthetics (Figure 29.19).

Figure 29.19 When the Jackson Five appeared on *Soul Train*, each of the five brothers sported a large afro, a symbol of Black Pride in the 1960s and 70s.

THE MEXICAN AMERICAN FIGHT FOR CIVIL RIGHTS

The African American bid for full citizenship was surely the most visible of the battles for civil rights taking place in the United States. However, other minority groups that had been legally discriminated against or otherwise denied access to economic and educational opportunities began to increase efforts to secure their rights in the 1960s. Like the African American movement, the Mexican American civil rights movement won its earliest victories in the federal courts. In 1947, in *Mendez v. Westminster*, the U.S. Court of Appeals for the Ninth Circuit ruled that segregating children of Hispanic descent was unconstitutional. In 1954, the same year as *Brown v. Board of Education*, Mexican Americans prevailed in *Hernandez v. Texas*, when the U.S. Supreme Court extended the protections of the Fourteenth Amendment to all ethnic groups in the United States.

The highest-profile struggle of the Mexican American civil rights movement was the fight that Caesar Chavez (Figure 29.20) and Dolores Huerta waged in the fields of California to organize migrant farm workers. In 1962, Chavez and Huerta founded the National Farm Workers Association (NFWA). In 1965, when Filipino grape pickers led by Filipino American Larry Itliong went on strike to call attention to their plight, Chavez lent his support. Workers organized by the NFWA also went on strike, and the two organizations merged to form the United Farm Workers. When Chavez asked American consumers to boycott grapes, politically conscious people around the country heeded his call, and many unionized longshoremen refused to unload grape shipments. In 1966, Chavez led striking workers to the state capitol in Sacramento, further publicizing the cause. Martin Luther King, Jr. telegraphed words of encouragement to Chavez, whom he called a "brother." The strike ended in 1970 when California farmers recognized the right of farm workers to unionize. However, the farm workers did not gain all they sought, and the larger struggle did not end.

Figure 29.20 Cesar Chavez was influenced by the nonviolent philosophy of Indian nationalist Mahatma Gandhi. In 1968, he emulated Gandhi by engaging in a hunger strike.

Download for free at http://cnx.org/content/col11740/latest/

The equivalent of the Black Power movement among Mexican Americans was the Chicano Movement. Proudly adopting a derogatory term for Mexican Americans, Chicano activists demanded increased political power for Mexican Americans, education that recognized their cultural heritage, and the restoration of lands taken from them at the end of the Mexican-American War in 1848. One of the founding members, Rodolfo "Corky" Gonzales, launched the Crusade for Justice in Denver in 1965, to provide jobs, legal services, and healthcare for Mexican Americans. From this movement arose La Raza Unida, a political party that attracted many Mexican American college students. Elsewhere, Reies López Tijerina fought for years to reclaim lost and illegally expropriated ancestral lands in New Mexico; he was one of the co-sponsors of the Poor People's March on Washington in 1967.

29.4 Challenging the Status Quo

By the end of this section, you will be able to:
- Describe the goals and activities of SDS, the Free Speech Movement, and the antiwar movement
- Explain the rise, goals, and activities of the women's movement

By the 1960s, a generation of white Americans raised in prosperity and steeped in the culture of conformity of the 1950s had come of age. However, many of these baby boomers (those born between 1946 and 1964) rejected the conformity and luxuries that their parents had provided. These young, middle-class Americans, especially those fortunate enough to attend college when many of their working-class and African American contemporaries were being sent to Vietnam, began to organize to fight for their own rights and end the war that was claiming the lives of so many.

THE NEW LEFT

By 1960, about one-third of the U.S. population was living in the suburbs; during the 1960s, the average family income rose by 33 percent. Material culture blossomed, and at the end of the decade, 70 percent of American families owned washing machines, 83 percent had refrigerators or freezers, and almost 80 percent had at least one car. Entertainment occupied a larger part of both working- and middle-class leisure hours. By 1960, American consumers were spending $85 billion a year on entertainment, double the spending of the preceding decade; by 1969, about 79 percent of American households had black-and-white televisions, and 31 percent could afford color sets. Movies and sports were regular aspects of the weekly routine, and the family vacation became an annual custom for both the middle and working class.

Meanwhile, baby boomers, many raised in this environment of affluence, streamed into universities across the nation in unprecedented numbers looking to "find" themselves. Instead, they found traditional systems that forced them to take required courses, confined them to rigid programs of study, and surrounded them with rules limiting what they could do in their free time. These young people were only too willing to take up Kennedy's call to action, and many did so by joining the civil rights movement. To them, it seemed only right for the children of the "greatest generation" to help those less privileged to fight battles for justice and equality. The more radical aligned themselves with the New Left, activists of the 1960s who rejected the staid liberalism of the Democratic Party. New Left organizations sought reform in areas such as civil rights and women's rights, campaigned for free speech and more liberal policies toward drug use, and condemned the war in Vietnam.

One of the most prominent New Left groups was Students for a Democratic Society (SDS). Organized in 1960, SDS held its first meeting at the University of Michigan, Ann Arbor. Its philosophy was expressed in its manifesto, the **Port Huron Statement**, written by Tom Hayden and adopted in 1962, affirming the group's dedication to fighting economic inequality and discrimination. It called for greater participation in the democratic process by ordinary people, advocated civil disobedience, and rejected the anti-Communist position held by most other groups committed to social reform in the United States.

Click and Explore

Read the full text of the Port Huron Statement (http://openstaxcollege.org/l/ 15PHStatement) by Tom Hayden.

SDS members demanded that universities allow more student participation in university governance and shed their entanglements with the military-industrial complex. They sought to rouse the poor to political action to defeat poverty and racism. In the summer of 1964, a small group of SDS members moved into the uptown district of Chicago and tried to take on racism and poverty through community organization. Under the umbrella of their Economic Research and Action Project, they created JOIN (Jobs or Income Now) to address problems of urban poverty and resisted plans to displace the poor under the guise of urban renewal. They also called for police review boards to end police brutality, organized free breakfast programs, and started social and recreational clubs for neighborhood youth. Eventually, the movement fissured over whether to remain a campus-based student organization or a community-based development organization.

During the same time that SDS became active in Chicago, another student movement emerged on the West Coast, when actions by student activists at the University of California, Berkeley, led to the formation of Berkeley's Free Speech Movement in 1964. University rules prohibited the solicitation of funds for political causes by anyone other than members of the student Democratic and Republican organizations, and restricted advocacy of political causes on campus. In October 1964, when a student handing out literature for CORE refused to show campus police officers his student ID card, he was promptly arrested. Instantly, the campus police car was surrounded by angry students, who refused to let the vehicle move for thirty-two hours until the student was released. In December, students organized a massive sit-in to resolve the issue of political activities on campus. While unsuccessful in the short term, the movement inspired student activism on campuses throughout the country.

A target of many student groups was the war in Vietnam (Figure 29.21). In April 1965, SDS organized a march on Washington for peace; about twenty thousand people attended. That same week, the faculty at the University of Michigan suspended classes and conducted a 24-hour "teach-in" on the war. The idea quickly spread, and on May 15, the first national "teach-in" was held at 122 colleges and universities across the nation. Originally designed to be a debate on the pros and cons of the war, at Berkeley, the teach-ins became massive antiwar rallies. By the end of that year, there had been antiwar rallies in some sixty cities.

Figure 29.21 Students at the University of Wisconsin-Madison protested the war in Vietnam in 1965. Their actions were typical of many on college campuses across the country during the 1960s. (credit: "Yarnalgo"/Flickr)

AMERICANA

⊛ *Blue Jeans: The Uniform of Nonconformist Radicalism*

Overwhelmingly, young cultural warriors and social activists of the 1960s, trying to escape the shackles of what they perceived to be limits on their freedoms, adopted blue jeans as the uniform of their generation. Originally worn by manual laborers because of their near-indestructibility, blue jeans were commonly associated with cowboys, the quintessential icon of American independence. During the 1930s, jeans were adopted by a broader customer base as a result of the popularity of cowboy movies and dude ranch vacations. After World War II, Levi Strauss, their original manufacturer, began to market them east of the Mississippi, and competitors such as Wrangler and Lee fought for a share of the market. In the 1950s, youths testing the limits of middle-class conformity adopted them in imitation of movie stars like James Dean. By the 1960s, jeans became even more closely associated with youthful rebellion against tradition, a symbol available to everyone, rich and poor, black and white, men and women.

What other styles and behaviors of the 1960s expressed nonconformity, and how?

WOMEN'S RIGHTS

On the national scene, the civil rights movement was creating a climate of protest and claiming rights and new roles in society for people of color. Women played significant roles in organizations fighting for civil rights like SNCC and SDS. However, they often found that those organizations, enlightened as they might be about racial issues or the war in Vietnam, could still be influenced by patriarchal ideas of male superiority. Two members of SNCC, Casey Hayden and Mary King, presented some of their concerns about their organization's treatment of women in a document entitled "On the Position of Women in SNCC." Stokely Carmichael responded that the appropriate position for women in SNCC was "prone."

Just as the abolitionist movement made nineteenth-century women more aware of their lack of power and encouraged them to form the first women's rights movement, the protest movements of the 1960s inspired many white and middle-class women to create their own organized movement for greater rights. Not all were young women engaged in social protest. Many were older, married women who found the traditional roles of housewife and mother unfulfilling. In 1963, writer and feminist Betty Friedan published *The Feminine Mystique* in which she contested the post-World War II belief that it was women's destiny to marry and bear children. Friedan's book was a best-seller and began to raise the consciousness of many women who agreed that homemaking in the suburbs sapped them of their individualism and left them unsatisfied.

The Civil Rights Act of 1964, which prohibited discrimination in employment on the basis of race, color, national origin, and religion, also prohibited, in **Title VII**, discrimination on the basis of sex. Ironically, protection for women had been included at the suggestion of a Virginia congressman in an attempt to *prevent* the act's passage; his reasoning seemed to be that, while a white man might accept that African Americans needed and deserved protection from discrimination, the idea that women deserved equality with men would be far too radical for any of his male colleagues to contemplate. Nevertheless, the act passed, although the struggle to achieve equal pay for equal work continues today.

Medical science also contributed a tool to assist women in their liberation. In 1960, the U.S. Food and Drug Administration approved the birth control pill, freeing women from the restrictions of pregnancy and childbearing. Women who were able to limit, delay, and prevent reproduction were freer to work, attend college, and delay marriage. Within five years of the pill's approval, some six million women were using it.

The pill was the first medicine ever intended to be taken by people who were not sick. Even conservatives saw it as a possible means of making marriages stronger by removing the fear of an unwanted pregnancy and improving the health of women. Its opponents, however, argued that it would promote sexual promiscuity, undermine the institutions of marriage and the family, and destroy the moral code of the nation. By the early 1960s, thirty states had made it a criminal offense to sell contraceptive devices.

In 1966, the National Organization for Women (NOW) formed and proceeded to set an agenda for the feminist movement (Figure 29.22). Framed by a statement of purpose written by Friedan, the agenda began by proclaiming NOW's goal to make possible women's participation in all aspects of American life and to gain for them all the rights enjoyed by men. Among the specific goals was the passage of the Equal Rights Amendment (yet to be adopted).

Figure 29.22 Early members of NOW discuss the problems faced by American women. Betty Friedan is second from the left. (credit: Smithsonian Institution Archives)

More radical feminists, like their colleagues in other movements, were dissatisfied with merely redressing economic issues and devised their own brand of consciousness-raising events and symbolic attacks on women's oppression. The most famous of these was an event staged in September 1968 by New York Radical Women. Protesting stereotypical notions of femininity and rejecting traditional gender expectations, the group demonstrated at the Miss America Pageant in Atlantic City, New Jersey, to bring attention to the contest's—and society's—exploitation of women. The protestors crowned a sheep Miss America and then tossed instruments of women's oppression, including high-heeled shoes, curlers, girdles, and bras, into a "freedom trash can." News accounts famously, and incorrectly, described the protest as a "bra burning."

Key Terms

Black Power a political ideology encouraging African Americans to create their own institutions and develop their own economic resources independent of whites

Black Pride a cultural movement among African Americans to encourage pride in their African heritage and to substitute African and African American art forms, behaviors, and cultural products for those of whites

black separatism an ideology that called upon African Americans to reject integration with the white community and, in some cases, to physically separate themselves from whites in order to create and preserve their self-determination

counterinsurgency a new military strategy under the Kennedy administration to suppress nationalist independence movements and rebel groups in the developing world

flexible response a military strategy that allows for the possibility of responding to threats in a variety of ways, including counterinsurgency, conventional war, and nuclear strikes

Great Society Lyndon Johnson's plan to eliminate poverty and racial injustice in the United States and to improve the lives of all Americans

naval quarantine Kennedy's use of ships to prevent Soviet access to Cuba during the Cuban Missile Crisis

Port Huron Statement the political manifesto of Students for a Democratic Society that called for social reform, nonviolent protest, and greater participation in the democratic process by ordinary Americans

Title VII the section of the Civil Rights Act of 1964 that prohibited discrimination in employment on the basis of gender

war on poverty Lyndon Johnson's plan to end poverty in the Unites States through the extension of federal benefits, job training programs, and funding for community development

Summary

29.1 The Kennedy Promise

The arrival of the Kennedys in the White House seemed to signal a new age of youth, optimism, and confidence. Kennedy spoke of a "new frontier" and promoted the expansion of programs to aid the poor, protect African Americans' right to vote, and improve African Americans' employment and education opportunities. For the most part, however, Kennedy focused on foreign policy and countering the threat of Communism—especially in Cuba, where he successfully defused the Cuban Missile Crisis, and in Vietnam, to which he sent advisors and troops to support the South Vietnamese government. The tragedy of Kennedy's assassination in Dallas brought an early end to the era, leaving Americans to wonder whether his vice president and successor, Lyndon Johnson, would bring Kennedy's vision for the nation to fruition.

29.2 Lyndon Johnson and the Great Society

Lyndon Johnson began his administration with dreams of fulfilling his fallen predecessor's civil rights initiative and accomplishing his own plans to improve lives by eradicating poverty in the United States. His social programs, investments in education, support for the arts, and commitment to civil rights changed the lives of countless people and transformed society in many ways. However, Johnson's insistence on maintaining American commitments in Vietnam, a policy begun by his predecessors, hurt both his ability to realize his vision of the Great Society and his support among the American people.

29.3 The Civil Rights Movement Marches On

The African American civil rights movement made significant progress in the 1960s. While Congress played a role by passing the Civil Rights Act of 1964, the Voting Rights Act of 1965, and the Civil Rights Act of 1968, the actions of civil rights groups such as CORE, the SCLC, and SNCC were instrumental in forging new paths, pioneering new techniques and strategies, and achieving breakthrough successes. Civil rights activists engaged in sit-ins, freedom rides, and protest marches, and registered African American voters. Despite the movement's many achievements, however, many grew frustrated with the slow pace of change, the failure of the Great Society to alleviate poverty, and the persistence of violence against African Americans, particularly the tragic 1968 assassination of Martin Luther King, Jr. Many African Americans in the mid- to late 1960s adopted the ideology of Black Power, which promoted their work within their own communities to redress problems without the aid of whites. The Mexican American civil rights movement, led largely by Cesar Chavez, also made significant progress at this time. The emergence of the Chicano Movement signaled Mexican Americans' determination to seize their political power, celebrate their cultural heritage, and demand their citizenship rights.

29.4 Challenging the Status Quo

During the 1960s, many people rejected traditional roles and expectations. Influenced and inspired by the civil rights movement, college students of the baby boomer generation and women of all ages began to fight to secure a stronger role in American society. As members of groups like SDS and NOW asserted their rights and strove for equality for themselves and others, they upended many accepted norms and set groundbreaking social and legal changes in motion. Many of their successes continue to be felt today, while other goals remain unfulfilled.

Review Questions

1. The term Kennedy chose to describe his sealing off of Cuba to prevent Soviet shipments of weapons or supplies was _____.

   A. interdiction
   B. quarantine
   C. isolation
   D. blockade

2. Kennedy proposed a constitutional amendment that would _____.

   A. provide healthcare for all Americans
   B. outlaw poll taxes
   C. make English the official language of the United States
   D. require all American men to register for the draft

3. What steps did Kennedy take to combat Communism?

4. _____ was Johnson's program to provide federal funding for healthcare for the poor.

   A. Medicare
   B. Social Security
   C. Medicaid
   D. AFDC

5. Many Americans began to doubt that the war in Vietnam could be won following _____.

   A. Khe Sanh
   B. Dien Bien Phu
   C. the Tonkin Gulf incident
   D. the Tet Offensive

6. How did the actions of the Johnson administration improve the lives of African Americans?

7. The new protest tactic against segregation used by students in Greensboro, North Carolina, in 1960 was the _____.
   A. boycott
   B. guerilla theater
   C. teach-in
   D. sit-in

8. The African American group that advocated the use of violence and espoused a Marxist ideology was called _____.
   A. the Black Panthers
   B. the Nation of Islam
   C. SNCC
   D. CORE

9. Who founded the Crusade for Justice in Denver, Colorado in 1965?
   A. Reies Lopez Tijerina
   B. Dolores Huerta
   C. Larry Itliong
   D. Rodolfo Gonzales

10. How did the message of Black Power advocates differ from that of more mainstream civil rights activists such as Martin Luther King, Jr.?

11. What was one of the major student organizations engaged in organizing protests and demonstrations against the Vietnam War?
   A. Committee for American Democracy
   B. Freedom Now Party
   C. Students for a Democratic Society
   D. Young Americans for Peace

12. Which of the following was *not* a founding goal of NOW?
   A. to gain for women all the rights enjoyed by men
   B. to ensure passage of the Equal Rights Amendment
   C. to de-criminalize the use of birth control
   D. to allow women to participate in all aspects of American life

13. In what ways did the birth control pill help to liberate women?

Critical Thinking Questions

14. Describe the changing role of the federal government in the 1960s. What new roles and responsibilities did the government assume? In your opinion, can the government effect permanent social change? Why or why not?

15. Discuss how and why various groups of people within American society began to challenge and criticize the nation's way of life in the 1960s. Were their criticisms valid? What were some of the goals of these groups, and how did they go about achieving them?

16. In your opinion, what is the most effective method for changing society—voting, challenges in the courts, nonviolent civil disobedience, or violence? What evidence can you provide from actual events in the 1960s to support your argument?

17. Were groups that advocated the use of violence in the 1960s justified in doing so? Why or why not?

18. Discuss how the United States became engaged in the Vietnam War. What were some of the results of that engagement?

CHAPTER 30

Political Storms at Home and Abroad, 1968-1980

Figure 30.1 Pop artist Peter Max designed this postage stamp to commemorate Expo '74, a world's fair held in Spokane, Washington. The fair's theme was the natural environment. Unfortunately, and ironically, gasoline shortages prevented many from attending the exposition.

Chapter Outline
   30.1 Identity Politics in a Fractured Society
   30.2 Coming Apart, Coming Together
   30.3 Vietnam: The Downward Spiral
   30.4 Watergate: Nixon's Domestic Nightmare
   30.5 Jimmy Carter in the Aftermath of the Storm

Introduction

From May 4 to November 4, 1974, a universal exposition was held in the city of Spokane, Washington. This world's fair, Expo '74, and the postage stamp issued to commemorate it, reflected many of the issues and interests of the 1970s (Figure 30.1). The stamp features psychedelic colors, and the character of the Cosmic Runner in the center wears bellbottoms, a popular fashion at the time. The theme of the fair was the environment, a subject beginning to be of great concern to people in the United States, especially the younger generation and those in the hippie counterculture. In the 1970s, the environment, social justice, distrust of the government, and a desire to end the war in Vietnam—the concerns and attitudes of younger people, women, gays and lesbians, and people of color—began to draw the attention of the mainstream as well.

30.1 Identity Politics in a Fractured Society

By the end of this section, you will be able to:
- Describe the counterculture of the 1960s
- Explain the origins of the American Indian Movement and its major activities
- Assess the significance of the gay rights and women's liberation movements

The political divisions that plagued the United States in the 1960s were reflected in the rise of **identity politics** in the 1970s. As people lost hope of reuniting as a society with common interests and goals, many focused on issues of significance to the subgroups to which they belonged, based on culture, ethnicity, sexual orientation, gender, and religion.

HIPPIES AND THE COUNTERCULTURE

In the late 1960s and early 1970s, many young people came to embrace a new wave of cultural dissent. The **counterculture** offered an alternative to the bland homogeneity of American middle-class life, patriarchal family structures, self-discipline, unquestioning patriotism, and the acquisition of property. In fact, there were many alternative cultures.

"Hippies" rejected the conventions of traditional society. Men sported beards and grew their hair long; both men and women wore clothing from non-Western cultures, defied their parents, rejected social etiquettes and manners, and turned to music as an expression of their sense of self. Casual sex between unmarried men and women was acceptable. Drug use, especially of marijuana and psychedelic drugs like LSD and peyote, was common. Most hippies were also deeply attracted to the ideas of peace and freedom. They protested the war in Vietnam and preached a doctrine of personal freedom to be and act as one wished.

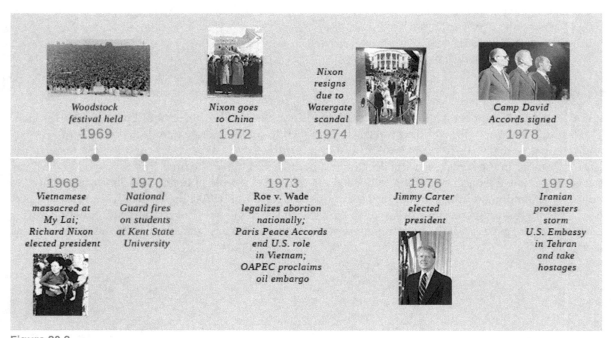

Figure 30.2

Some hippies dropped out of mainstream society altogether and expressed their disillusionment with the cultural and spiritual limitations of American freedom. They joined communes, usually in rural areas, to share a desire to live closer to nature, respect for the earth, a dislike of modern life, and a disdain for wealth and material goods. Many communes grew their own organic food. Others abolished the concept of private property, and all members shared willingly with one another. Some sought to abolish traditional ideas regarding love and marriage, and free love was practiced openly. One of the most famous communes was The Farm, established in Tennessee in 1971. Residents adopted a blend of Christian and Asian beliefs. They shared housing, owned no private property except tools and clothing, advocated nonviolence, and tried to live as one with nature, becoming vegetarians and avoiding the use of animal products. They smoked marijuana in an effort to reach a higher state of consciousness and to achieve a feeling of oneness and harmony.

Music, especially rock and folk music, occupied an important place in the counterculture. Concerts provided the opportunity to form seemingly impromptu communities to celebrate youth, rebellion, and individuality. In mid-August 1969, nearly 400,000 people attended a music festival in rural Bethel, New York, many for free (Figure 30.3). They jammed roads throughout the state, and thousands had to be turned around and sent home. Thirty-two acts performed for a crowd that partook freely of marijuana, LSD, and alcohol during the rainy three-day event that became known as Woodstock (after the nearby town) and became the cultural touchstone of a generation. No other event better symbolized the cultural independence and freedom of Americans coming of age in the 1960s.

Figure 30.3 The crowd at Woodstock greatly exceeded the fifty thousand expected. Mark Goff covered Woodstock as a young freelance reporter for *Kaleidoscope*, a Milwaukee-based alternative newspaper, and captured this image of Swami Satchidananda, who declared music "'the celestial sound that controls the whole universe" at the opening ceremony.

MY STORY

✪ Glenn Weiser on Attending Woodstock

On the way to Woodstock, Glenn Weiser remembers that the crowds were so large they essentially turned it into a free concert:

> As we got closer to the site [on Thursday, August 14, 1969] we heard that so many people had already arrived that the crowd had torn down the fences enclosing the festival grounds (in fact they were never put up to begin with). Everyone was being allowed in for free. . . .

> Early on Friday afternoon about a dozen of us got together and spread out some blankets on the grass at a spot about a third of the way up the hill on stage right and then dropped LSD. I took Orange Sunshine, a strong, clean dose in an orange tab that was perhaps the best street acid ever. Underground chemists in southern California had made millions of doses, and the nation was flooded with it that summer. We smoked some tasty black hashish to amuse ourselves while waiting for the acid to hit, and sat back to groove along with Richie Havens.

> In two hours we were all soaring, and everything was just fine. In fact, it couldn't have been better—there I was with my beautiful hometown friends, higher than a church steeple and listening to wonderful music in the cool summer weather of the Catskills. After all, the dirty little secret of the late '60s was that psychedelic drugs taken in a pleasant setting could be completely exhilarating.
> —Glenn Weiser, "Woodstock 1969 Remembered"

In this account, Glenn Weiser describes both the music and his drug use. What social trends did Woodstock reflect? How might the festival have influenced American culture and society, both aesthetically and behaviorally?

AMERICAN INDIAN PROTEST

As the young, primarily white men and women who became hippies strove to create new identities for themselves, they borrowed liberally from other cultures, including that of Native Americans. At the same time, many Indians were themselves seeking to maintain their culture or retrieve elements that had been lost. In 1968, a group of Indian activists, including Dennis Banks, George Mitchell, and Clyde Bellecourt, convened a gathering of two hundred people in Minneapolis, Minnesota, and formed the American Indian Movement (AIM) (Figure 30.4). The organizers were urban dwellers frustrated by decades of poverty and discrimination. In 1970, the average life expectancy of Indians was forty-six years compared to the national average of sixty-nine. The suicide rate was twice that of the general population, and the infant mortality rate was the highest in the country. Half of all Indians lived on reservations, where unemployment reached 50 percent. Among those in cities, 20 percent lived below the poverty line.

Figure 30.4 This teepee was erected on the National Mall near the Washington Monument as part of an AIM demonstration (a). Note that the AIM flag (b) combines an Indian silhouette with the peace sign, the ubiquitous symbol of the 1960s and '70s.

On November 20, 1969, a small group of Indian activists landed on Alcatraz Island (the former site of a notorious federal prison) in San Francisco Bay. They announced plans to build an American Indian cultural center, including a history museum, an ecology center, and a spiritual sanctuary. People on the mainland provided supplies by boat, and celebrities visited Alcatraz to publicize the cause. More people joined the occupiers until, at one point, they numbered about four hundred. From the beginning, the federal government negotiated with them to persuade them to leave. They were reluctant to accede, but over time, the occupiers began to drift away of their own accord. Government forces removed the final holdouts on June 11, 1971, nineteen months after the occupation began.

DEFINING "AMERICAN"

✷ *Proclamation to the Great White Father and All His People*

In occupying Alcatraz Island, Indian activists sought to call attention to their grievances and expectations about what America should mean. At the beginning of the nineteen-month occupation, Mohawk Richard Oakes delivered the following proclamation:

> We, the native Americans, re-claim the land known as Alcatraz Island in the name of all American Indians by right of discovery.
>
> We wish to be fair and honorable in our dealings with the Caucasian inhabitants of this land, and hereby offer the following treaty:
>
> We will purchase said Alcatraz Island for twenty-four dollars ($24) in glass beads and red cloth, a precedent set by the white man's purchase of a similar island about 300 years ago. . . .
>
> We feel that this so-called Alcatraz Island is more than suitable for an Indian Reservation, as determined by the white man's own standards. By this we mean that this place resembles most Indian reservations in that:
>
> 1. It is isolated from modern facilities, and without adequate means of transportation.
>
> 2. It has no fresh running water.
>
> 3. It has inadequate sanitation facilities.
>
> 4. There are no oil or mineral rights.
>
> 5. There is no industry and so unemployment is very great.
>
> 6. There are no health care facilities.
>
> 7. The soil is rocky and non-productive; and the land does not support game.
>
> 8. There are no educational facilities.
>
> 9. The population has always exceeded the land base.
>
> 10. The population has always been held as prisoners and kept dependent upon others.
>
> Further, it would be fitting and symbolic that ships from all over the world, entering the Golden Gate, would first see Indian land, and thus be reminded of the true history of this nation. This tiny island would be a symbol of the great lands once ruled by free and noble Indians.

What does the Alcatraz Proclamation reveal about the Indian view of U.S. history?

Click and Explore

Listen to Richard Oakes, one of the leaders of the Alcatraz Island occupation, as he reads the Alcatraz Proclamation (http://openstaxcollege.org/l/15PHStatement1) aloud.

The next major demonstration came in 1972 when AIM members and others marched on Washington, DC—a journey they called the "Trail of Broken Treaties"—and occupied the offices of the Bureau of Indian Affairs (BIA). The group presented a list of demands, which included improved housing, education, and economic opportunities in Indian communities; the drafting of new treaties; the return of Indian lands; and protections for native religions and culture.

The most dramatic event staged by AIM was the occupation of the Indian community of Wounded Knee, South Dakota, in February 1973. Wounded Knee, on the Pine Ridge Indian Reservation, had historical significance: It was the site of an 1890 massacre of members of the Lakota tribe by the U.S. Army. AIM went to the reservation following the failure of a group of Oglala to impeach the tribal president Dick Wilson, whom they accused of corruption and the use of strong-arm tactics to silence critics. AIM used the occasion to criticize the U.S. government for failing to live up to its treaties with native peoples.

The federal government surrounded the area with U.S. marshals, FBI agents, and other law enforcement forces. A siege ensued that lasted seventy-one days, with frequent gunfire from both sides, wounding a U.S. marshal as well as an FBI agent, and killing two Indians. The government did very little to meet the protesters' demands. Two AIM leaders, Dennis Banks and Russell Means, were arrested, but charges were later dismissed. The Nixon administration had already halted the federal policy of termination and restored millions of acres to tribes. Increased funding for Indian education, healthcare, legal services, housing, and economic development followed, along with the hiring of more Indian employees in the BIA.

GAY RIGHTS

Combined with the sexual revolution and the feminist movement of the 1960s, the counterculture helped establish a climate that fostered the struggle for gay and lesbian rights. Many gay rights groups were founded in Los Angeles and San Francisco, cities that were administrative centers in the network of U.S. military installations and the places where many gay men suffered dishonorable discharges. The first postwar organization for homosexual civil rights, the Mattachine Society, was launched in Los Angeles in 1950. The first national organization for lesbians, the Daughters of Bilitis, was founded in San Francisco five years later. In 1966, the city became home to the world's first organization for transsexual people, the National Transsexual Counseling Unit, and in 1967, the Sexual Freedom League of San Francisco was born.

Through these organizations and others, gay and lesbian activists fought against the criminalization and discrimination of their sexual identities on a number of occasions throughout the 1960s, employing strategies of both protests and litigation. However, the most famous event in the gay rights movement took place not in San Francisco but in New York City. Early in the morning of June 28, 1969, police raided a Greenwich Village gay bar called the Stonewall Inn. Although such raids were common, the response of the Stonewall patrons was anything but. As the police prepared to arrest many of the customers, especially transsexuals and cross-dressers, who were particular targets for police harassment, a crowd began to gather. Angered by the brutal treatment of the prisoners, the crowd attacked. Beer bottles and bricks were thrown. The police barricaded themselves inside the bar and waited for reinforcements. The riot continued for several hours and resumed the following night. Shortly thereafter, the Gay Liberation Front and Gay Activists' Alliance were formed, and began to protest discrimination, homophobia, and violence against gay people, promoting gay liberation and gay pride.

With a call for gay men and women to "come out"—a consciousness-raising campaign that shared many principles with the counterculture, gay and lesbian communities moved from the urban underground into the political sphere. Gay rights activists protested strongly against the official position of the American Psychiatric Association (APA), which categorized homosexuality as a mental illness and often resulted in job loss, loss of custody, and other serious personal consequences. By 1974, the APA had ceased to classify homosexuality as a form of mental illness but continued to consider it a "sexual orientation disturbance." Nevertheless, in 1974, Kathy Kozachenko became the first openly lesbian woman voted into office in Ann Arbor, Michigan. In 1977, Harvey Milk became California's first openly gay man elected to public office, although his service on San Francisco's board of supervisors, along with that of San Francisco mayor George Moscone, was cut short by the bullet of disgruntled former city supervisor Dan White.

MAYBE NOT NOW

The feminist push for greater rights continued through the 1970s (Figure 30.5). The media often ridiculed feminists as "women's libbers" and focused on more radical organizations like W.I.T.C.H. (Women's International Terrorist Conspiracy from Hell), a loose association of activist groups. Many reporters stressed the most unusual goals of the most radical women—calls for the abolition of marriage and demands that manholes be renamed "personholes."

Figure 30.5   In 1970, supporters of equal rights for women marched in Washington, DC.

The majority of feminists, however, sought meaningful accomplishments. In the 1970s, they opened battered women's shelters and successfully fought for protection from employment discrimination for pregnant women, reform of rape laws (such as the abolition of laws requiring a witness to corroborate a woman's report of rape), criminalization of domestic violence, and funding for schools that sought to counter sexist stereotypes of women. In 1973, the U.S. Supreme Court in *Roe v. Wade* affirmed a number of state laws under which abortions obtained during the first three months of pregnancy were legal. This made a nontherapeutic abortion a legal medical procedure nationwide.

Many advances in women's rights were the result of women's greater engagement in politics. For example, Patsy Mink, the first Asian American woman elected to Congress, was the co-author of the Education Amendments Act of 1972, Title IX of which prohibits sex discrimination in education. Mink had been interested in fighting discrimination in education since her youth, when she opposed racial segregation in campus housing while a student at the University of Nebraska. She went to law school after being denied admission to medical school because of her gender. Like Mink, many other women sought and won political office, many with the help of the National Women's Political Caucus (NWPC). In 1971, the NWPC was formed by Bella Abzug, Gloria Steinem, Shirley Chisholm, and other leading feminists to encourage women's participation in political parties, elect women to office, and raise money for their campaigns (Figure 30.6).

(a)   (b)

Figure 30.6 Patsy Mink (a), a Japanese American from Hawaii, was the first Asian American woman elected to the House of Representatives. In her successful 1970 congressional campaign, Bella Abzug (b) declared, "This woman's place is in the House... the House of Representatives!"

The ultimate political goal of the National Organization for Women (NOW) was the passage of an Equal Rights Amendment (ERA). The amendment passed Congress in March 1972, and was sent to the states for ratification with a deadline of seven years for passage; if the amendment was not ratified by thirty-eight states by 1979, it would die. Twenty-two states ratified the ERA in 1972, and eight more in 1973. In the next two years, only four states voted for the amendment. In 1979, still four votes short, the amendment received a brief reprieve when Congress agreed to a three-year extension, but it never passed, as the result of the well-organized opposition of Christian and other socially conservative, grassroots organizations.

30.2 Coming Apart, Coming Together

By the end of this section, you will be able to:
- Explain the factors responsible for Richard Nixon's election in 1968
- Describe the splintering of the Democratic Party in 1968
- Discuss Richard Nixon's economic policies
- Discuss the major successes of Richard Nixon's foreign policy

The presidential election of 1968 revealed a rupture of the New Deal coalition that had come together under Franklin Roosevelt in the 1930s. The Democrats were divided by internal dissension over the Vietnam War, the civil rights movement, and the challenges of the New Left. Meanwhile, the Republican candidate, Richard Nixon, won voters in the South, Southwest, and northern suburbs by appealing to their anxieties about civil rights, women's rights, antiwar protests, and the counterculture taking place around them. Nixon spent his first term in office pushing measures that slowed the progress of civil rights and sought to restore economic stability. His greatest triumphs were in foreign policy. But his largest priority throughout his first term was his reelection in 1972.

THE "NEW NIXON"

The Republicans held their 1968 national convention from August 5–8 in Miami, Florida. Richard Nixon quickly emerged as the frontrunner for the nomination, ahead of Nelson Rockefeller and Ronald Reagan. This success was not accidental: From 1962, when he lost his bid for the governorship of California, to 1968, Nixon had been collecting political credits by branding himself as a candidate who could appeal to mainstream voters and by tirelessly working for other Republican candidates. In 1964, for example, he vigorously supported Barry Goldwater's presidential bid and thus built good relationships with the new conservative movement in the Republican Party.

Although Goldwater lost the 1964 election, his vigorous rejection of New Deal state and social legislation, along with his support of states' rights, proved popular in the Deep South, which had resisted federal efforts at racial integration. Taking a lesson from Goldwater's experience, Nixon also employed a **southern strategy** in 1968. Denouncing segregation and the denial of the vote to African Americans, he nevertheless maintained that southern states be allowed to pursue racial equality at their own pace and criticized forced integration. Nixon thus garnered the support of South Carolina's senior senator and avid segregationist Strom Thurmond, which helped him win the Republican nomination on the first ballot.

Nixon also courted northern, blue-collar workers, whom he later called the **silent majority**, to acknowledge their belief that their voices were seldom heard. These voters feared the social changes taking place in the country: Antiwar protests challenged their own sense of patriotism and civic duty, whereas the recreational use of new drugs threatened their cherished principles of self-discipline, and urban riots invoked the specter of a racial reckoning. Government action on behalf of the marginalized raised the question of whether its traditional constituency—the white middle class—would lose its privileged place in American politics. Some felt left behind as the government turned to the problems of African Americans. Nixon's promises of stability and his emphasis on law and order appealed to them. He portrayed himself as a fervent patriot who would take a strong stand against racial unrest and antiwar protests. Nixon harshly critiqued Lyndon Johnson's Great Society, and he promised a secret plan to end the war in Vietnam honorably and bring home the troops. He also promised to reform the Supreme Court, which he contended had gone too far in "coddling criminals." Under Chief Justice Earl Warren, the court had used the due process and equal protection clauses of the Fourteenth Amendment to grant those accused under state law the ability to defend themselves and secure protections against unlawful search and seizure, cruel and unusual punishment, and self-incrimination.

Nixon had found the political capital that would ensure his victory in the suburbs, which produced more votes than either urban or rural areas. He championed "middle America," which was fed up with social convulsions, and called upon the country to come together. His running mate, Spiro T. Agnew, a former governor of Maryland, blasted the Democratic ticket as fiscally irresponsible and "soft on communism." Nixon and Agnew's message thus appealed to northern middle-class and blue-collar whites as well as southern whites who had fled to the suburbs in the wake of the Supreme Court's pro-integration decision in *Brown v. Board of Education* (Figure 30.7).

Download for free at http://cnx.org/content/col11740/latest/

(a)   (b)

Figure 30.7   On the 1968 campaign trail, Richard Nixon flashes his famous "V for Victory" gesture (a). Nixon's strategy was to appeal to working- and middle-class suburbanites. This image of him in the White House bowling alley seems calculated to appeal to his core constituency (b).

DEMOCRATS IN DISARRAY

By contrast, in early 1968, the political constituency that Lyndon Johnson had cobbled together to win the presidency in 1964 seemed to be falling apart. When Eugene McCarthy, the Democratic senator from Minnesota, announced that he would challenge Johnson in the primaries in an explicitly antiwar campaign, Johnson was overwhelmingly favored by Democratic voters. But then the Tet Offensive in Vietnam exploded on American television screens on January 31, playing out on the nightly news for weeks. On February 27, Walter Cronkite, a highly respected television journalist, offered his opinion that the war in Vietnam was unwinnable. When the votes were counted in New Hampshire on March 12, McCarthy had won twenty of the state's twenty-four delegates.

McCarthy's popularity encouraged Robert (Bobby) Kennedy to also enter the race. Realizing that his war policies could unleash a divisive fight within his own party for the nomination, Johnson announced his withdrawal on March 31, fracturing the Democratic Party. One faction consisted of the traditional party leaders who appealed to unionized, blue-collar constituents and white ethnics (Americans with recent European immigrant backgrounds). This group fell in behind Johnson's vice president, Hubert H. Humphrey, who took up the mainstream party's torch almost immediately after Johnson's announcement. The second group consisted of idealistic young activists who had slogged through the snows of New Hampshire to give McCarthy a boost and saw themselves as the future of the Democratic Party. The third group, composed of Catholics, African Americans and other minorities, and some of the young, antiwar element, galvanized around Robert Kennedy (Figure 30.8). Finally, there were the southern Democrats, the **Dixiecrats**, who opposed the advances made by the civil rights movement. Some found themselves attracted to the Republican candidate Richard Nixon. Many others, however, supported the third-party candidacy of segregationist George C. Wallace, the former governor of Alabama. Wallace won close to ten million votes, which was 13.5 percent of all votes cast. He was particularly popular in the South, where he carried five states and received forty-six Electoral College votes.

Figure 30.8 In his brother's (John F. Kennedy's) administration, Robert (Bobby) Kennedy had served as attorney general and had spoken out about racial equality.

Kennedy and McCarthy fiercely contested the remaining primaries of the 1968 season. There were only fifteen at that time. McCarthy beat Kennedy handily in Wisconsin, Pennsylvania, and Massachusetts. Kennedy took Indiana and Nebraska before losing Oregon to McCarthy. Kennedy's only hope was that a strong enough showing in the California primary on June 4 might swing uncommitted delegates his way. He did manage to beat McCarthy, winning 46 percent of the vote to McCarthy's 42 percent, but it was a fruitless victory. As he attempted to exit the Ambassador Hotel in Los Angeles after his victory speech, Kennedy was shot; he died twenty-six hours later. His killer, Sirhan B. Sirhan, a Jordanian immigrant, had allegedly targeted him for advocating military support for Israel in its conflict with neighboring Arab states.

Going into the nominating convention in Chicago in 1968, Humphrey, who promised to pursue the "Politics of Joy," seemed clearly in command of the regular party apparatus. But the national debates over civil rights, student protests, and the Vietnam War had made 1968 a particularly anguished year, and many people felt anything but joyful. Some party factions hoped to make their voices heard; others wished to disrupt the convention altogether. Among them were antiwar protestors, hippies, and **Yippies**—members of the leftist, anarchistic Youth International Party organized by Jerry Rubin and Abbie Hoffman—who called for the establishment of a new nation consisting of cooperative institutions to replace those currently in existence. To demonstrate their contempt for "the establishment" and the proceedings inside the hall, the Yippies nominated a pig named Pigasus for president.

A chaotic scene developed inside the convention hall and outside at Grant Park, where the protesters camped. Chicago's mayor, Richard J. Daley, was anxious to demonstrate that he could maintain law and order, especially because several days of destructive rioting had followed the murder of Martin Luther King, Jr. earlier that year. He thus let loose a force of twelve thousand police officers, six thousand members of the Illinois National Guard, and six thousand U.S. Army soldiers. Television cameras caught what later became known as a "police riot": Armed officers made their way into crowds of law-abiding protesters, clubbing anyone they encountered and setting off tear gas canisters. The protesters fought back. Inside the convention hall, a Democratic senator from Connecticut called for adjournment, whereas other delegates insisted on proceeding. Ironically, Hubert Humphrey received the nomination and gave an acceptance speech in which he spoke in support of "law and order." When the convention ended, Rubin,

Hoffman, and five other protesters (called the "Chicago Seven") were placed on trial for inciting a riot (Figure 30.9).

(a)   (b)

Figure 30.9 Despite facing charges following events at the Democratic National Convention in Chicago, Abbie Hoffman continued to protest the war on campuses across the country, as here (a) at the University of Oklahoma. Jerry Rubin (b) visited the campus of the University of Buffalo in March 1970, just one month after his conviction in the Chicago Seven trial. (credit a: modification of work by Richard O. Barry)

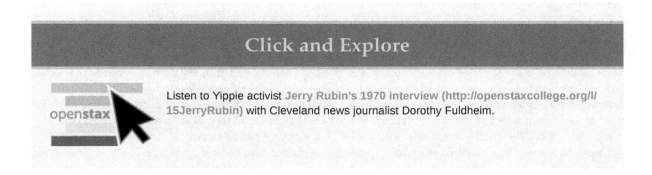

Click and Explore

Listen to Yippie activist Jerry Rubin's 1970 interview (http://openstaxcollege.org/l/15JerryRubin) with Cleveland news journalist Dorothy Fuldheim.

THE DOMESTIC NIXON

The images of violence and the impression of things spinning out of control seriously damaged Humphrey's chances for victory. Many liberals and young antiwar activists, disappointed by his selection over McCarthy and still shocked by the death of Robert Kennedy, did not vote for Humphrey. Others turned against him because of his failure to chastise the Chicago police for their violence. Some resented the fact that Humphrey had received 1,759 delegates on the first ballot at the convention, nearly three times the number won by McCarthy, even though in the primaries, he had received only 2 percent of the popular vote. Many loyal Democratic voters at home, shocked by the violence they saw on television, turned away from their party, which seemed to have attracted dangerous "radicals," and began to consider Nixon's promises of law and order.

As the Democratic Party collapsed, Nixon successfully campaigned for the votes of both working- and middle-class white Americans, winning the 1968 election. Although Humphrey received nearly the same percentage of the popular vote, Nixon easily won the Electoral College, gaining 301 votes to Humphrey's 191 and Wallace's 46.

Once elected, Nixon began to pursue a policy of deliberate neglect of the civil rights movement and the needs of ethnic minorities. For example, in 1969, for the first time in fifteen years, federal lawyers sided with the state of Mississippi when it sought to slow the pace of school desegregation. Similarly, Nixon consistently showed his opposition to busing to achieve racial desegregation. He saw that restricting African American activity was a way of undercutting a source of votes for the Democratic Party and sought to overhaul the provisions of the Voting Rights Act of 1965. In March 1970, he commented that he did not believe an "open" America had to be homogeneous or fully integrated, maintaining that it was "natural" for members of ethnic groups to live together in their own enclaves. In other policy areas, especially economic ones, Nixon was either moderate or supportive of the progress of African Americans; for example, he expanded affirmative action, a program begun during the Johnson administration to improve employment and educational opportunities for racial minorities.

Although Nixon always kept his eye on the political environment, the economy required attention. The nation had enjoyed seven years of expansion since 1961, but inflation (a general rise in prices) was threatening to constrict the purchasing power of the American consumer and therefore curtail economic expansion. Nixon tried to appeal to fiscal conservatives in the Republican Party, reach out to disaffected Democrats, and, at the same time, work with a Democratic Party-controlled Congress. As a result, Nixon's approach to the economy seemed erratic. Despite the heavy criticisms he had leveled against the Great Society, he embraced and expanded many of its features. In 1969, he signed a tax bill that eliminated the investment tax credit and moved some two million of the poorest people off the tax rolls altogether. He federalized the food stamp program and established national eligibility requirements, and signed into law the automatic adjustments for inflation of Social Security payments. On the other hand, he won the praise of conservatives with his "New Federalism"—drastically expanding the use of federal "block grants" to states to spend as they wished without strings attached.

By mid-1970, a recession was beginning and unemployment was 6.2 percent, twice the level under Johnson. After earlier efforts at controlling inflation with controlled federal spending—economists assumed that reduced federal spending and borrowing would curb the amount of money in circulation and stabilize prices—Nixon proposed a budget with an $11 billion deficit in 1971. The hope was that more federal funds in the economy would stimulate investment and job creation. When the unemployment rate refused to budge the following year, he proposed a budget with a $25 billion deficit. At the same time, he tried to fight continuing inflation by freezing wages and prices for ninety days, which proved to be only a temporary fix. The combination of unemployment and rising prices posed an unfamiliar challenge to economists whose fiscal policies of either expanding or contracting federal spending could only address one side of the problem at the cost of the other. This phenomenon of "**stagflation**"—a term that combined the economic conditions of stagnation and inflation—outlived the Nixon administration, enduring into the early 1980s.

The origins of the nation's new economic troubles were not just a matter of policy. Postwar industrial development in Asia and Western Europe—especially in Germany and Japan—had created serious competition to American businesses. By 1971, American appetites for imports left foreign central banks with billions of U.S. currency, which had been fixed to gold in the international monetary and trade agreement of Bretton Woods back in 1944. When foreign dollar holdings exceeded U.S. gold reserves in 1971, President Nixon allowed the dollar to flow freely against the price of gold. This caused an immediate 8 percent devaluation of the dollar, made American goods cheaper abroad, and stimulated exports. Nixon's move also marked the beginning of the end of the dollar's dominance in international trade.

The situation was made worse in October 1973, when Syria and Egypt jointly attacked Israel to recover territory that had been lost in 1967, starting the Yom Kippur War. The Soviet Union significantly aided its allies, Egypt and Syria, and the United States supported Israel, earning the enmity of Arab nations. In retaliation, the Organization of Arab Petroleum Exporting Countries (OAPEC) imposed an embargo on oil shipments to the United States from October 1973 to March 1974. The ensuing shortage of oil pushed its price from three dollars a barrel to twelve dollars a barrel. The average price of gasoline in the United States shot from thirty-eight cents a gallon before the embargo to fifty-five cents a gallon in June 1974, and the prices of other goods whose manufacture and transportation relied on oil or gas also rose and did not come down. The oil embargo had a lasting impact on the economy and underscored the nation's interdependency with international political and economic developments.

Faced with high fuel prices, American consumers panicked. Gas stations limited the amount customers could purchase and closed on Sundays as supplies ran low (Figure 30.10). To conserve oil, Congress reduced the speed limit on interstate highways to fifty-five miles per hour. People were asked to turn down their thermostats, and automobile manufacturers in Detroit explored the possibility of building more fuel-efficient cars. Even after the embargo ended, prices continued to rise, and by the end of the Nixon years in 1974, inflation had soared to 12.2 percent.

(a)   (b)

Figure 30.10   The oil shortage triggered a rush to purchase gasoline, and gas stations around the country were choked with cars waiting to fill up. Eventually, fuel shortages caused gas stations to develop various ways to ration gasoline to their customers (a), such as the "flag policy" used by gas dealers in Oregon (b).

Although Nixon's economic and civil rights policies differed from those of his predecessors, in other areas, he followed their lead. President Kennedy had committed the nation to putting a man on the moon before the end of the decade. Nixon, like Johnson before him, supported significant budget allocations to the National Aeronautics and Space Administration (NASA) to achieve this goal. On July 20, 1969, hundreds of millions of people around the world watched as astronauts Neil Armstrong and Edwin "Buzz" Aldrin walked on the surface of the moon and planted the U.S. flag. Watching from the White House, President Nixon spoke to the astronauts via satellite phone. The entire project cost the American taxpayer some $25 billion, approximately 4 percent of the nation's gross national product, and was such a source of pride for the nation that the Soviet Union and China refused to televise it. Coming amid all the struggles and crises that the country was enduring, the moon landing gave citizens a sense of accomplishment that stood in stark contrast to the foreign policy failures, growing economic challenges, and escalating divisions at home.

NIXON THE DIPLOMAT

Despite the many domestic issues on Nixon's agenda, he prioritized foreign policy and clearly preferred bold and dramatic actions in that arena. Realizing that five major economic powers—the United States, Western Europe, the Soviet Union, China, and Japan—dominated world affairs, he sought opportunities for the United States to pit the others against each other. In 1969, he announced a new Cold War principle known as the Nixon Doctrine, a policy whereby the United States would continue to assist its allies but would not assume the responsibility of defending the entire non-Communist world. Other nations, like Japan, needed to assume more of the burden of defending themselves.

Playing what was later referred to as "the China card," Nixon abruptly reversed two decades of U.S. diplomatic sanctions and hostility to the Communist regime in the People's Republic of China, when he announced, in August 1971, that he would personally travel to Beijing and meet with China's leader, Chairman Mao Zedong, in February 1972 (Figure 30.11). Nixon hoped that opening up to the Chinese government would prompt its bitter rival, the Soviet Union, to compete for global influence and seek a more productive relationship with the United States. He also hoped that establishing a friendly relationship with China would isolate North Vietnam and ease a peace settlement, allowing the United States to extract its troops from the war honorably. Concurring that the Soviet Union should be restrained from making advances in Asia, Nixon and Chinese premier Zhou Enlai agreed to disagree on several issues and ended up signing a friendship treaty. They promised to work towards establishing trade between the two nations and to eventually establishing full diplomatic relations with each other.

Figure 30.11 President Nixon and First Lady Patricia Nixon visited the Great Wall on their 1972 trip to China. The Chinese showed them the sights and hosted a banquet for them in the Great Hall of the People. Nixon was the first U.S. president to visit China following the Communist victory in the civil war in 1949.

Continuing his strategy of pitting one Communist nation against another, in May 1972, Nixon made another newsworthy trip, traveling to Moscow to meet with the Soviet leader Leonid Brezhnev. The two discussed a policy of **détente**, a relaxation of tensions between their nations, and signed the Strategic Arms Limitation Treaty (SALT), which limited each side to deploying only two antiballistic missile systems. It also limited the number of nuclear missiles maintained by each country. In 1974, a protocol was signed that reduced antiballistic missile sites to one per country, since neither country had yet begun to build its second system. Moreover, the two sides signed agreements to allow scientific and technological exchanges, and promised to work towards a joint space mission.

30.3 Vietnam: The Downward Spiral

By the end of this section, you will be able to:
- Describe the events that fueled antiwar sentiment in the Vietnam era
- Explain Nixon's steps to withdraw the United States from the conflict in South Vietnam

As early as 1967, critics of the war in Vietnam had begun to call for the repeal of the Gulf of Tonkin Resolution, which gave President Johnson the authority to conduct military operations in Vietnam in defense of an ally, South Vietnam. Nixon initially opposed the repeal efforts, claiming that doing so might have consequences that reached far beyond Vietnam. Nevertheless, by 1969, he was beginning troop withdrawals from Vietnam while simultaneously looking for a "knockout blow" against the North Vietnamese. In sum, the Nixon administration was in need of an exit strategy.

The escalation of the war, however, made an easy withdrawal increasingly difficult. Officially, the United States was the ally and partner of the South Vietnamese, whose "hearts and minds" it was trying to win through a combination of military assistance and economic development. In reality, however, U.S. soldiers, who found themselves fighting in an inhospitable environment thousands of miles from home to protect people who often resented their presence and aided their enemies, came to regard the Vietnamese as backward, cowardly people and the government of South Vietnam as hopelessly inefficient and corrupt. Instead of winning "hearts and minds," U.S. warfare in Vietnam cost the lives and limbs of U.S. troops and millions of Vietnamese combatants and civilians (Figure 30.12).

Figure 30.12 U.S. soldiers in Hue in 1968 at during the Tet Offensive. The frustrating experience of fighting the seemingly unwinnable war left many soldiers, and the public in general, disillusioned with the government.

For their part, the North Vietnamese forces and the National Liberation Front in South Vietnam also used brutal tactics to terrorize and kill their opponents or effectively control their territory. Political assassinations and forced indoctrination were common. Captured U.S. soldiers frequently endured torture and imprisonment.

MY LAI

Racism on the part of some U.S. soldiers and a desire to retaliate against those they perceived to be responsible for harming U.S. troops affected the conduct of the war. A war correspondent who served in Vietnam noted, "In motivating the GI to fight by appealing to his racist feelings, the United States military discovered that it had liberated an emotion over which it was to lose control." It was not unusual for U.S. soldiers to evacuate and burn villages suspected of shielding Viet Cong fighters, both to deprive the enemy of potential support and to enact revenge for enemy brutality. Troops shot at farmers' water buffalo for target practice. American and South Vietnamese use of napalm, a jellied gasoline that sticks to the objects it burns, was common. Originally developed to burn down structures during World War II, in Vietnam, it was directed against human beings as well, as had occurred during the Korean War.

DEFINING "AMERICAN"

✷ *Vietnam Veterans against the War Statement*

Many U.S. soldiers disapproved of the actions of their fellow troops. Indeed, a group of Vietnam veterans formed the organization Vietnam Veterans Against the War (VVAW). Small at first, it grew to perhaps as many as twenty thousand members. In April 1971, John Kerry, a former lieutenant in the U.S. Navy and a member of VVAW, testified before the U.S. Senate Committee on Foreign Relations about conditions in Vietnam based on his personal observations:

> I would like to talk on behalf of all those veterans and say that several months ago in Detroit we had an investigation at which over 150 honorably discharged, and many very highly decorated, veterans testified to war crimes committed in Southeast Asia. These were not isolated incidents but crimes committed on a day-to-day basis with the full awareness of officers at all levels of command. . . . They relived the absolute horror of what this country, in a sense, made them do.

> They told stories that at times they had personally raped, cut off ears, cut off heads . . . randomly shot at civilians, razed villages . . . and generally ravaged the countryside of South Vietnam in addition to the normal ravage of war and the normal and very particular ravaging which is done by the applied bombing power of this country. . . .

> We could come back to this country, we could be quiet, we could hold our silence, we could not tell what went on in Vietnam, but we feel because of what threatens this country, not the reds [Communists], but the crimes which we are committing that threaten it, that we have to speak out.
> —John Kerry, April 23, 1971

In what way did the actions of U.S. soldiers in Vietnam threaten the United States?

On March 16, 1968, men from the U.S. Army's Twenty-Third Infantry Division committed one of the most notorious atrocities of the war. About one hundred soldiers commanded by Captain Ernest Medina were sent to destroy the village of My Lai, which was suspected of hiding Viet Cong fighters. Although there was later disagreement regarding the captain's exact words, the platoon leaders believed the order to destroy the enemy included killing women and children. Having suffered twenty-eight casualties in the past three months, the men of Charlie Company were under severe stress and extremely apprehensive as they approached the village. Two platoons entered it, shooting randomly. A group of seventy to eighty unarmed people, including children and infants, were forced into an irrigation ditch by members of the First Platoon under the command of Lt. William L. Calley, Jr. Despite their proclamations of innocence, the villagers were shot (Figure 30.13). Houses were set on fire, and as the inhabitants tried to flee, they were killed with rifles, machine guns, and grenades. The U.S. troops were never fired upon, and one soldier later testified that he did not see any man who looked like a Viet Cong fighter.

Figure 30.13 Vietnamese civilians in My Lai await their fate. They were shot a few minutes after this 1968 photograph was taken.

The precise number of civilians killed that day is unclear: The numbers range from 347 to 504. None were armed. Although not all the soldiers in My Lai took part in the killings, no one attempted to stop the massacre before the arrival by helicopter of Warrant Officer Hugh Thompson, who, along with his crew, attempted to evacuate women and children. Upon returning to his base, Thompson immediately reported the events taking place at My Lai. Shortly thereafter, Medina ordered Charlie Company to cease fire. Although Thompson's crewmembers confirmed his account, none of the men from Charlie Company gave a report, and a cover-up began almost immediately. The army first claimed that 150 people, the majority of them Viet Cong, had been killed during a firefight with Charlie Company.

Hearing details from friends in Charlie Company, a helicopter gunner by the name of Ron Ridenhour began to conduct his own investigation and, in April 1969, wrote to thirty members of Congress, demanding an investigation. By September 1969, the army charged Lt. Calley with premeditated murder. Many Americans were horrified at the graphic footage of the massacre; the incident confirmed their belief that the war was unjust and not being fought on behalf of the Vietnamese people. However, nearly half of the respondents to a Minnesota poll did not believe that the incident at My Lai had actually happened. U.S. soldiers could not possibly do such horrible things, they felt; they were certain that American goals in Vietnam were honorable and speculated that the antiwar movement had concocted the story to generate sympathy for the enemy.

Calley was found guilty in March 1971, and sentenced to life in prison. Nationwide, hundreds of thousands of Americans joined a "Free Calley" campaign. Two days later, President Nixon released him from custody and placed him under him house arrest at Fort Benning, Georgia. In August of that same year, Calley's sentence was reduced to twenty years, and in September 1974, he was paroled. The only soldier convicted in the massacre, he spent a total of three-and-a-half years under house arrest for his crimes.

BATTLES AT HOME

As the conflict wore on and reports of brutalities increased, the antiwar movement grew in strength. To take the political pressure off himself and his administration, and find a way to exit Vietnam "with honor," Nixon began the process of **Vietnamization**, turning more responsibility for the war over to South Vietnamese forces by training them and providing American weaponry, while withdrawing U.S. troops from the field. At the same time, however, Nixon authorized the bombing of neighboring Cambodia, which had declared its neutrality, in an effort to destroy North Vietnamese and Viet Cong bases within that country and cut off supply routes between North and South Vietnam. The bombing was kept secret from both Congress and the American public. In April 1970, Nixon decided to follow up with an invasion of Cambodia.

The invasion could not be kept secret, and when Nixon announced it on television on April 30, 1970, protests sprang up across the country. The most tragic and politically damaging occurred on May 1, 1970, at Kent State University in Ohio. Violence erupted in the town of Kent after an initial student demonstration on campus, and the next day, the mayor asked Ohio's governor to send in the National Guard. Troops were sent to the university's campus, where students had set fire to the ROTC building and were fighting off firemen and policemen trying to extinguish it. The National Guard used teargas to break up the demonstration, and several students were arrested (Figure 30.14).

(a)   (b)

Figure 30.14 On April 30, 1970, Richard Nixon announces plans for the Cambodia Campaign (a), provoking protests on college campuses across the country. Within days, the governor of Ohio had called in the National Guard in response to student demonstrations at Kent State University. Bill Whitbeck, who was a student majoring in photo illustration at Kent State University in May 1970, captured this image (b) on campus on May 3, one day before the shootings that would result in four student deaths. (credit b: modification of work by Bill Whitbeck)

Tensions came to a head on May 4. Although campus officials had called off a planned demonstration, some fifteen hundred to two thousand students assembled, throwing rocks at a security officer who ordered them to leave. Seventy-seven members of the National Guard, with bayonets attached to their rifles, approached the students. After forcing most of them to retreat, the troops seemed to depart. Then, for reasons that are still unknown, they halted and turned; many began to fire at the students. Nine students were wounded; four were killed. Two of the dead had simply been crossing campus on their way to class. Peace was finally restored when a faculty member pleaded with the remaining students to leave.

Click and Explore

Read the *New York Times* account of the shootings at Kent State University (http://openstaxcollege.org/l/15KentState) and view (under the headline) one of the most iconic photographs in American history.

News of the Kent State shootings shocked students around the country. Millions refused to attend class, as strikes were held at hundreds of colleges and high schools across the United States. On May 8, an antiwar protest took place in New York City, and the next day, 100,000 protesters assembled in Washington,

DC. Not everyone sympathized with the slain students, however. Nixon had earlier referred to student demonstrators as "bums," and construction workers attacked the New York City protestors. A Gallup poll revealed that most Americans blamed the students for the tragic events at Kent State.

On May 15, a similar tragedy took place at Jackson State College, an African American college in Jackson, Mississippi. Once again, students gathered on campus to protest the invasion of Cambodia, setting fires and throwing rocks. The police arrived to disperse the protesters, who had gathered outside a women's dormitory. Shortly after midnight, the police opened fire with shotguns. The dormitory windows shattered, showering people with broken glass. Twelve were wounded, and two young men, one a student at the college and the other a local high school student, were killed.

PULLING OUT OF THE QUAGMIRE

Ongoing protests, campus violence, and the expansion of the war into Cambodia deeply disillusioned Americans about their role in Vietnam. Understanding the nation's mood, Nixon dropped his opposition to a repeal of the Gulf of Tonkin Resolution of 1964. In January 1971, he signed Congress's revocation of the notorious blanket military authorization. Gallup polls taken in May of that year revealed that only 28 percent of the respondents supported the war; many felt it was not only a mistake but also immoral.

Just as influential as antiwar protests and campus violence in turning people against the war was the publication of documents the media dubbed the **Pentagon Papers** in June 1971. These were excerpts from a study prepared during the Johnson administration that revealed the true nature of the conflict in Vietnam. The public learned for the first time that the United States had been planning to oust Ngo Dinh Diem from the South Vietnamese government, that Johnson meant to expand the U.S. role in Vietnam and bomb North Vietnam even as he stated publicly that he had no intentions of doing so, and that his administration had sought to deliberately provoke North Vietnamese attacks in order to justify escalating American involvement. Copies of the study had been given to the *New York Times* and other newspapers by Daniel Ellsberg, one of the military analysts who had contributed to it. To avoid setting a precedent by allowing the press to publish confidential documents, Nixon's attorney general, John Mitchell, sought an injunction against the *New York Times* to prevent its publication of future articles based on the Pentagon Papers. The newspaper appealed. On June 30, 1971, the U.S. Supreme Court held that the government could not prevent the publication of the articles.

Realizing that he must end the war but reluctant to make it look as though the United States was admitting its failure to subdue a small Asian nation, Nixon began maneuvering to secure favorable peace terms from the North Vietnamese. Thanks to his diplomatic efforts in China and the Soviet Union, those two nations cautioned North Vietnam to use restraint. The loss of strong support by their patrons, together with intensive bombing of Hanoi and the mining of crucial North Vietnamese harbors by U.S. forces, made the North Vietnamese more willing to negotiate.

Nixon's actions had also won him popular support at home. By the 1972 election, voters again favored his Vietnam policy by a ratio of two to one. On January 27, 1973, Secretary of State Henry Kissinger signed an accord with Le Duc Tho, the chief negotiator for the North Vietnamese, ending American participation in the war. The United States was given sixty days to withdraw its troops, and North Vietnam was allowed to keep its forces in places it currently occupied. This meant that over 100,000 northern soldiers would remain in the South—ideally situated to continue the war with South Vietnam. The United States left behind a small number of military advisors as well as equipment, and Congress continued to approve funds for South Vietnam, but considerably less than in earlier years. So the war continued, but it was clear the South could not hope to defeat the North.

As the end was nearing, the United States conducted several operations to evacuate children from the South. On the morning of April 29, 1975, as North Vietnamese and Viet Cong forces moved through the outskirts of Saigon, orders were given to evacuate Americans and South Vietnamese who had supported the United States. Unable to use the airport, helicopters ferried Americans and Vietnamese refugees who had fled to the American embassy to ships off the coast. North Vietnamese forces entered Saigon the next day, and the South surrendered.

The war had cost the lives of more than 1.5 million Vietnamese combatants and civilians, as well as over 58,000 U.S. troops. But the war had caused another, more intangible casualty: the loss of consensus, confidence, and a sense of moral high ground in the American political culture.

30.4 Watergate: Nixon's Domestic Nightmare

By the end of this section, you will be able to:
- Describe the actions that Nixon and his confederates took to ensure his reelection in 1972
- Explain the significance of the Watergate crisis
- Describe Gerald Ford's domestic policies and achievements in foreign affairs

Feeling the pressure of domestic antiwar sentiment and desiring a decisive victory, Nixon went into the 1972 reelection season having attempted to fashion a "new majority" of moderate southerners and northern, working-class whites. The Democrats, responding to the chaos and failings of the Chicago convention, had instituted new rules on how delegates were chosen, which they hoped would broaden participation and the appeal of the party. Nixon proved unbeatable, however. Even evidence that his administration had broken the law failed to keep him from winning the White House.

THE ELECTION OF 1972

Following the 1968 nominating convention in Chicago, the process of selecting delegates for the Democratic National Convention was redesigned. The new rules, set by a commission led by George McGovern, awarded delegates based on candidates' performance in state primaries (Figure 30.15). As a result, a candidate who won no primaries could not receive the party's nomination, as Hubert Humphrey had done in Chicago. This system gave a greater voice to people who voted in the primaries and reduced the influence of party leaders and power brokers.

(a)   (b)

Figure 30.15 In November 1968, Shirley Chisholm (a) became the first African American woman to be elected to the House of Representatives. In January 1972, she announced her intention to run for the Democratic presidential nomination. The nomination eventually went to George McGovern (b), an outspoken opponent of the war in Vietnam.

It also led to a more inclusive political environment in which Shirley Chisholm received 156 votes for the Democratic nomination on the first ballot (Figure 30.15). Eventually, the nomination went to George McGovern, a strong opponent of the Vietnam War. Many Democrats refused to support his campaign, however. Working- and middle-class voters turned against him too after allegations that he supported women's right to an abortion and the decriminalization of drug use. McGovern's initial support of vice presidential candidate Thomas Eagleton in the face of revelations that Eagleton had undergone electroshock treatment for depression, followed by his withdrawal of that support and acceptance of Eagleton's resignation, also made McGovern look indecisive and unorganized.

Nixon and the Republicans led from the start. To increase their advantage, they attempted to paint McGovern as a radical leftist who favored amnesty for draft dodgers. In the Electoral College, McGovern carried only Massachusetts and Washington, DC. Nixon won a decisive victory of 520 electoral votes to McGovern's 17. One Democrat described his role in McGovern's campaign as "recreation director on the Titanic."

HIGH CRIMES AND MISDEMEANORS

Nixon's victory over a Democratic party in disarray was the most remarkable landslide since Franklin D. Roosevelt's reelection in 1936. But Nixon's victory was short-lived, however, for it was soon discovered that he and members of his administration had routinely engaged in unethical and illegal behavior during his first term. Following the publication of the Pentagon Papers, for instance, the "**plumbers**," a group of men used by the White House to spy on the president's opponents and stop leaks to the press, broke into the office of Daniel Ellsberg's psychiatrist to steal Ellsberg's file and learn information that might damage his reputation.

During the presidential campaign, the Committee to Re-Elect the President (CREEP) decided to play "dirty tricks" on Nixon's opponents. Before the New Hampshire Democratic primary, a forged letter supposedly written by Democratic-hopeful Edmund Muskie in which he insulted French Canadians, one of the state's largest ethnic groups, was leaked to the press. Men were assigned to spy on both McGovern and Senator Edward Kennedy. One of them managed to masquerade as a reporter on board McGovern's press plane. Men pretending to work for the campaigns of Nixon's Democratic opponents contacted vendors in various states to rent or purchase materials for rallies; the rallies were never held, of course, and Democratic politicians were accused of failing to pay the bills they owed.

CREEP's most notorious operation, however, was its break-in at the offices of the Democratic National Committee (DNC) in the Watergate office complex in Washington, DC, as well as its subsequent cover-up. On the evening of June 17, 1972, the police arrested five men inside DNC headquarters (Figure 30.16). According to a plan originally proposed by CREEP's general counsel and White House plumber G. Gordon Liddy, the men were to wiretap DNC telephones. The FBI quickly discovered that two of the men had E. Howard Hunt's name in their address books. Hunt was a former CIA officer and also one of the plumbers. In the following weeks, yet more connections were found between the burglars and CREEP, and in October 1972, the FBI revealed evidence of illegal intelligence gathering by CREEP for the purpose of sabotaging the Democratic Party. Nixon won his reelection handily in November. Had the president and his reelection team not pursued a strategy of dirty tricks, Richard Nixon would have governed his second term with one of the largest political leads in the twentieth century.

Figure 30.16 The Watergate hotel and office complex, located on the Potomac River next to the John F. Kennedy Center for the Performing Arts, was the scene of the 1972 burglary and attempted wiretapping that eventually brought down the presidency of Richard Nixon.

In the weeks following the Watergate break-in, Bob Woodward and Carl Bernstein, reporters for *The Washington Post*, received information from several anonymous sources, including one known to them only as "**Deep Throat**," that led them to realize the White House was deeply implicated in the break-in. As the press focused on other events, Woodward and Bernstein continued to dig and publish their findings, keeping the public's attention on the unfolding scandal. Years later, Deep Throat was revealed to be Mark Felt, then the FBI's associate director.

THE WATERGATE CRISIS

Initially, Nixon was able to hide his connection to the break-in and the other wrongdoings alleged against members of CREEP. However, by early 1973, the situation quickly began to unravel. In January, the Watergate burglars were convicted, along with Hunt and Liddy. Trial judge John Sirica was not convinced that all the guilty had been discovered. In February, confronted with evidence that people close to the president were connected to the burglary, the Senate appointed the Watergate Committee to investigate. Ten days later, in his testimony before the Senate Judiciary Committee, L. Patrick Gray, acting director of the FBI, admitted destroying evidence taken from Hunt's safe by John Dean, the White House counsel, after the burglars were caught.

On March 23, 1973, Judge Sirica publicly read a letter from one of the Watergate burglars, alleging that perjury had been committed during the trial. Less than two weeks later, Jeb Magruder, a deputy director of CREEP, admitted lying under oath and indicated that Dean and John Mitchell, who had resigned as attorney general to become the director of CREEP, were also involved in the break-in and its cover-up. Dean confessed, and on April 30, Nixon fired him and requested the resignation of his aides John

Ehrlichman and H. R. Haldeman, also implicated. To defuse criticism and avoid suspicion that he was participating in a cover-up, Nixon also announced the resignation of the current attorney general, Richard Kleindienst, a close friend, and appointed Elliott Richardson to the position. In May 1973, Richardson named Archibald Cox special prosecutor to investigate the Watergate affair.

Throughout the spring and the long, hot summer of 1973, Americans sat glued to their television screens, as the major networks took turns broadcasting the Senate hearings. One by one, disgraced former members of the administration confessed, or denied, their role in the Watergate scandal. Dean testified that Nixon was involved in the conspiracy, allegations the president denied. In March 1974, Haldeman, Ehrlichman, and Mitchell were indicted and charged with conspiracy.

Without evidence clearly implicating the president, the investigation might have ended if not for the testimony of Alexander Butterfield, a low-ranking member of the administration, that a voice-activated recording system had been installed in the Oval Office. The President's most intimate conversations had been caught on tape. Cox and the Senate subpoenaed them.

Click and Explore

Listen to excerpts (http://openstaxcollege.org/l/15NixonTapes) from Nixon's White House tapes. Some of the recordings are a bit difficult to hear because of static. Transcripts are also available at this site.

Nixon, however, refused to hand the tapes over and cited **executive privilege**, the right of the president to refuse certain subpoenas. When he offered to supply summaries of the conversations, Cox refused. On October 20, 1973, in an event that became known as the Saturday Night Massacre, Nixon ordered Attorney General Richardson to fire Cox. Richardson refused and resigned, as did Deputy Attorney General William Ruckelshaus when confronted with the same order. Control of the Justice Department then fell to Solicitor General Robert Bork, who complied with Nixon's order. In December, the House Judiciary Committee began its own investigation to determine whether there was enough evidence of wrongdoing to impeach the president.

The public was enraged by Nixon's actions. It seemed as though the president had placed himself above the law. Telegrams flooded the White House. The House of Representatives began to discuss impeachment. In April 1974, when Nixon agreed to release transcripts of the tapes, it was too little, too late (Figure 30.17). Yet, while revealing nothing about Nixon's knowledge of Watergate, the transcripts showed him to be coarse, dishonest, and cruel.

Figure 30.17 In April 1974, President Richard Nixon prepares to address the nation to clarify his position on releasing the White House tapes.

At the end of its hearings, in July 1974, the House Judiciary Committee voted to impeach. However, before the full House could vote, the U.S. Supreme Court ordered Nixon to release the actual tapes of his conversations, not just transcripts or summaries. One of the tapes revealed that he had in fact been told about White House involvement in the Watergate break-in shortly after it occurred. In a speech on August 5, 1974, Nixon, pleading a poor memory, accepted blame for the Watergate scandal. Warned by other Republicans that he would be found guilty by the Senate and removed from office, he resigned the presidency on August 8.

Nixon's resignation, which took effect the next day, did not make the Watergate scandal vanish. Instead, it fed a growing suspicion of government felt by many. The events of Vietnam had already showed that the government could not be trusted to protect the interests of the people or tell them the truth. For many, Watergate confirmed these beliefs, and the suffix "-gate" attached to a word has since come to mean a political scandal.

FORD NOT A LINCOLN

When Gerald R. Ford took the oath of office on August 9, 1974, he understood that his most pressing task was to help the country move beyond the Watergate scandal. His declaration that "Our long national nightmare is over. . . . [O]ur great Republic is a government of laws and not of men" was met with almost universal applause.

It was indeed an unprecedented time. Ford was the first vice president chosen under the terms of the Twenty-Fifth Amendment, which provides for the appointment of a vice president in the event the incumbent dies or resigns; Nixon had appointed Ford, a longtime House representative from Michigan known for his honesty, following the resignation of embattled vice president Spiro T. Agnew over a charge of failing to report income—a lenient charge since this income stemmed from bribes he had received as the governor of Maryland. Ford was also the first vice president to take office after a sitting president's resignation, and the only chief executive never elected either president or vice president. One of his first actions as president was to grant Richard Nixon a full pardon (Figure 30.18). Ford thus prevented Nixon's indictment for any crimes he may have committed in office and ended criminal investigations into his actions. The public reacted with suspicion and outrage. Many were convinced that the extent of Nixon's wrongdoings would now never been known and he would never be called to account for them. When Ford chose to run for the presidency in 1976, the pardon returned to haunt him.

Download for free at http://cnx.org/content/col11740/latest/

Figure 30.18 In one of his first actions as president, Gerald R. Ford announced a full pardon for Richard Nixon on September 8, 1974. Nixon had appointed Ford vice president after the resignation of Spiro Agnew.

As president, Ford confronted monumental issues, such as inflation, a depressed economy, and chronic energy shortages. He established his policies during his first year in office, despite opposition from a heavily Democratic Congress. In October 1974, he labeled inflation the country's most dangerous public enemy and sought a grassroots campaign to curtail it by encouraging people to be disciplined in their consuming habits and increase their savings. The campaign was titled "Whip Inflation Now" and was advertised on brightly colored "Win" buttons volunteers were to wear. When recession became the nation's most serious domestic problem, Ford shifted to measures aimed at stimulating the economy. Still fearing inflation, however, he vetoed a number of nonmilitary appropriations bills that would have increased the already-large budget deficit.

Ford's economic policies ultimately proved unsuccessful. Because of opposition from a Democratic Congress, his foreign policy accomplishments were also limited. When he requested money to assist the South Vietnamese government in its effort to repel North Vietnamese forces, Congress refused. Ford was more successful in other parts of the world. He continued Nixon's policy of détente with the Soviet Union, and he and Secretary of State Kissinger achieved further progress in the second round of SALT talks. In August 1975, Ford went to Finland and signed the Helsinki Accords with Soviet premier Leonid Brezhnev. This agreement essentially accepted the territorial boundaries that had been established at the end of World War II in 1945. It also exacted a pledge from the signatory nations that they would protect human rights within their countries. Many immigrants to the United States protested Ford's actions, because it seemed as though he had accepted the status quo and left their homelands under Soviet domination. Others considered it a belated American acceptance of the world as it really was.

30.5 Jimmy Carter in the Aftermath of the Storm

By the end of this section, you will be able to:

- Explain why Gerald Ford lost the election of 1976
- Describe Jimmy Carter's domestic and foreign policy achievements
- Discuss how the Iranian hostage crisis affected the Carter presidency

At his inauguration in January 1977, President Jimmy Carter began his speech by thanking outgoing president Gerald Ford for all he had done to "heal" the scars left by Watergate. American gratitude had not been great enough to return Ford to the Oval Office, but enthusiasm for the new president was not much greater in the new atmosphere of disillusionment with political leaders. Indeed, Carter won his party's nomination and the presidency largely because the Democratic leadership had been decimated by assassination and the taint of Vietnam, and he had carefully positioned himself as an outsider who could not be blamed for current policies. Ultimately, Carter's presidency proved a lackluster one that was marked by economic stagnation at home and humiliation overseas.

THE ELECTION OF 1976

President Ford won the Republican nomination for the presidency in 1976, narrowly defeating former California governor Ronald Reagan, but he lost the election to his Democratic opponent Jimmy Carter. Carter ran on an "anti-Washington" ticket, making a virtue of his lack of experience in what was increasingly seen as the corrupt politics of the nation's capital. Accepting his party's nomination, the former governor of Georgia pledged to combat racism and sexism as well as overhaul the tax structure. He openly proclaimed his faith as a born-again Christian and promised to change the welfare system and provide comprehensive healthcare coverage for neglected citizens who deserved compassion. Most importantly, Jimmy Carter promised that he would "never lie."

Ford's pardon of Richard Nixon had alienated many Republicans. That, combined with the stagnant economy, cost him votes, and Jimmy Carter, an engineer and former naval officer who portrayed himself as a humble peanut farmer, prevailed, carrying all the southern states, except Virginia and Oklahoma (Figure 30.19). Ford did well in the West, but Carter received 50 percent of the popular vote to Ford's 48 percent, and 297 electoral votes to Ford's 240.

Figure 30.19 President Gerald Ford (right) and Democratic challenger Jimmy Carter dueled in Philadelphia in 1976, during the first televised presidential debate since that between Richard Nixon and John F. Kennedy in 1960.

Click and Explore

openstax   In the mid-1970s, the United States celebrated the two-hundredth anniversary of its independence from Great Britain. Peruse the collection of patriotic bicentennial memorabilia (http://openstaxcollege.org/l/15Bicent) at the Gerald R. Ford Presidential Library.

ON THE INSIDE

Making a virtue of his lack of political experience, especially in Washington, Jimmy Carter took office with less practical experience in executive leadership and the workings of the national government than any president since Calvin Coolidge. His first executive act was to fulfill a campaign pledge to grant unconditional amnesty to young men who had evaded the draft during the Vietnam War. Despite the early promise of his rhetoric, within a couple of years of his taking office, liberal Democrats claimed Carter was the most conservative Democratic president since Grover Cleveland.

In trying to manage the relatively high unemployment rate of 7.5 percent and inflation that had risen into the double digits by 1978, Carter was only marginally effective. His tax reform measure of 1977 was weak and failed to close the grossest of loopholes. His deregulation of major industries, such as aviation and trucking, was intended to force large companies to become more competitive. Consumers benefited in some ways: For example, airlines offered cheaper fares to beat their competitors. However, some companies, like Pan American World Airways, instead went out of business. Carter also expanded various social programs, improved housing for the elderly, and took steps to improve workplace safety.

Because the high cost of fuel continued to hinder economic expansion, the creation of an energy program became a central focus of his administration. Carter stressed energy conservation, encouraging people to insulate their houses and rewarding them with tax credits if they did so, and pushing for the use of coal, nuclear power, and alternative energy sources such as solar power to replace oil and natural gas. To this end, Carter created the Department of Energy.

CARTER AND A NEW DIRECTION IN FOREIGN AFFAIRS

Carter believed that U.S. foreign policy should be founded upon deeply held moral principles and national values. The mission in Vietnam had failed, he argued, because American actions there were contrary to moral values. His dedication to peace and human rights significantly changed the way that the United States conducted its foreign affairs. He improved relations with China, ended military support to Nicaraguan dictator Anastasio Somoza, and helped arrange for the Panama Canal to be returned to Panamanian control in 1999. He agreed to a new round of talks with the Soviet Union (SALT II) and brought Israeli prime minister Menachem Begin and Egyptian president Anwar Sadat to the United States to discuss peace between their countries. Their meetings at Camp David, the presidential retreat in Maryland, led to the signing of the Camp David Accords in September 1978 (Figure 30.20). This in turn resulted in the drafting of a historic peace treaty between Egypt and Israel in 1979.

Figure 30.20 President Jimmy Carter meets with Egypt's Anwar Sadat (left) and Israel's Menachem Begin (right) at Camp David in 1978. Sadat was assassinated in 1981, partly because of his willingness to make peace with Israel.

Despite achieving many successes in the area of foreign policy, Carter made a more controversial decision in response to the Soviet Union's 1979 invasion of Afghanistan. In January 1980, he declared that if the USSR did not withdraw its forces, the United States would boycott the 1980 Summer Olympic Games in Moscow. The Soviets did not retreat, and the United States did not send a team to Moscow. Only about half of the American public supported this decision, and despite Carter's call for other countries to join the boycott, very few did so.

HOSTAGES TO HISTORY

Carter's biggest foreign policy problem was the Iranian hostage crisis, whose roots lay in the 1950s. In 1953, the United States had assisted Great Britain in the overthrow of Prime Minister Mohammad Mossadegh, a rival of Mohammad Reza Pahlavi, the shah of Iran. Mossadegh had sought greater Iranian control over the nation's oil wealth, which was claimed by British companies. Following the coup, the shah assumed complete control of Iran's government. He then disposed of political enemies and eliminated dissent through the use of SAVAK, a secret police force trained by the United States. The United States also supplied the shah's government with billions of dollars in aid. As Iran's oil revenue grew, especially after the 1973 oil embargo against the United States, the pace of its economic development and the size of its educated middle class also increased, and the country became less dependent on U.S. aid. Its population increasingly blamed the United States for the death of Iranian democracy and faulted it for its consistent support of Israel.

Despite the shah's unpopularity among his own people, the result of both his brutal policies and his desire to Westernize Iran, the United States supported his regime. In February 1979, the shah was overthrown when revolution broke out, and a few months later, he departed for the United States for medical treatment. The long history of U.S. support for him and its offer of refuge greatly angered Iranian revolutionaries. On November 4, 1979, a group of Iranian students and activists, including Islamic fundamentalists who wished to end the Westernization and secularization of Iran, invaded the American embassy in Tehran and seized sixty-six embassy employees. The women and African Americans were soon released, leaving fifty-three men as hostages. Negotiations failed to free them, and in April 1980, a rescue attempt fell through when the aircraft sent to transport them crashed. Another hostage was released when he developed serious medical problems. President Carter's inability to free the other captives hurt his performance in the 1980 elections. The fifty-two men still held in Iran were finally freed on January 20, 1981, the day Ronald Reagan took office as president (Figure 30.21).

Figure 30.21 The fifty-two American hostages return from Iran in January 1981. They had been held for 444 days.

Carter's handling of the crisis appeared even less effective in the way the media portrayed it publicly. This contributed to a growing sense of malaise, a feeling that the United States' best days were behind it and the country had entered a period of decline. This belief was compounded by continuing economic problems, and the oil shortage and subsequent rise in prices that followed the Iranian Revolution. The president's decision to import less oil to the United States and remove price controls on oil and gasoline did not help matters. In 1979, Carter sought to reassure the nation and the rest of the world, especially the Soviet Union, that the United States was still able to defend its interests. To dissuade the Soviets from making additional inroads in southwest Asia, he proposed the **Carter Doctrine**, which stated that the United States would regard any attempt to interfere with its interests in the Middle East as an act of aggression to be met with force if necessary.

Carter had failed to solve the nation's problems. Some blamed these problems on dishonest politicians; others blamed the problems on the Cold War obsession with fighting Communism, even in small nations like Vietnam that had little influence on American national interests. Still others faulted American materialism. In 1980, a small but growing group called the Moral Majority faulted Carter for betraying his southern roots and began to seek a return to traditional values.

Key Terms

Carter Doctrine Jimmy Carter's declaration that efforts to interfere with American interests in the Middle East would be considered a act of aggression and be met with force if necessary

counterculture a culture that develops in opposition to the dominant culture of a society

Deep Throat the anonymous source, later revealed to be associate director of the FBI Mark Felt, who supplied reporters Bob Woodward and Carl Bernstein with information about White House involvement in the Watergate break-in

Dixiecrats conservative southern Democrats who opposed integration and the other goals of the African American civil rights movement

détente the relaxation of tensions between the United States and the Soviet Union

executive privilege the right of the U.S. president to refuse subpoenas requiring him to disclose private communications on the grounds that this might interfere with the functioning of the executive branch

identity politics political movements or actions intended to further the interests of a particular group membership, based on culture, race, ethnicity, religion, sex, gender, or sexual orientation

Pentagon Papers government documents leaked to the *New York Times* that revealed the true nature of the conflict in Vietnam and turned many definitively against the war

plumbers men used by the White House to spy on and sabotage President Nixon's opponents and stop leaks to the press

silent majority a majority whose political will is usually not heard—in this case, northern, white, blue-collar voters

southern strategy a political strategy that called for appealing to southern whites by resisting calls for greater advancements in civil rights

stagflation high inflation combined with high unemployment and slow economic growth

Vietnamization the Nixon administration's policy of turning over responsibility for the defense of South Vietnam to Vietnamese forces

Yippies the Youth International Party, a political party formed in 1967, which called for the establishment of a New Nation consisting of cooperative institutions that would replace those currently in existence

Summary

30.1 Identity Politics in a Fractured Society

In the late 1960s and 1970s, Indians, gays and lesbians, and women organized to change discriminatory laws and pursue government support for their interests, a strategy known as identity politics. Others, disenchanted with the status quo, distanced themselves from white, middle-class America by forming their own countercultures centered on a desire for peace, the rejection of material goods and traditional morality, concern for the environment, and drug use in pursuit of spiritual revelations. These groups, whose aims and tactics posed a challenge to the existing state of affairs, often met with hostility from individuals, local officials, and the U.S. government alike. Still, they persisted, determined to further their goals and secure for themselves the rights and privileges to which they were entitled as American citizens.

30.2 Coming Apart, Coming Together

When a new Republican constituency of moderate southerners and northern, blue-collar workers voted Richard Nixon into the White House in 1968, many were hopeful. In the wake of antiwar and civil rights protests, and the chaos of the 1968 Democratic National Convention, many Americans welcomed Nixon's promise to uphold law and order. During his first term, Nixon strode a moderate, middle path in domestic affairs, attempting with little success to solve the problems of inflation and unemployment through a combination of austerity and deficit spending. He made substantial progress in foreign policy, however, establishing diplomatic relations with China for the first time since the Communist Revolution and entering into a policy of détente with the Soviet Union.

30.3 Vietnam: The Downward Spiral

As the war in Vietnam raged on, Americans were horrified to hear of atrocities committed by U.S. soldiers, such as the 1968 massacre of villagers at My Lai. To try to end the conflict, Nixon escalated it by bombing Hanoi and invading Cambodia; his actions provoked massive antiwar demonstrations in the United States that often ended in violence, such as the tragic shooting of unarmed student protestors at Kent State University in 1970. The 1971 release of the Pentagon Papers revealed the true nature of the war to an increasingly disapproving and disenchanted public. Secretary of State Henry Kissinger eventually drafted a peace treaty with North Vietnam, and, after handing over responsibility for the war to South Vietnam, the United States withdrew its troops in 1973. South Vietnam surrendered to the North two years later.

30.4 Watergate: Nixon's Domestic Nightmare

In 1972, President Nixon faced an easy reelection against a Democratic Party in disarray. But even before his landslide victory, evidence had surfaced that the White House was involved in the break-in at the DNC's headquarters at the Watergate office complex. As the investigation unfolded, the depths to which Nixon and his advisers had sunk became clear. Some twenty-five of Nixon's aides were indicted for criminal activity, and he became the first president impeached since Andrew Johnson and the first to resign from office. His successor, Gerald Ford, was unable to solve the pressing problems the United States faced or erase the stain of Watergate.

30.5 Jimmy Carter in the Aftermath of the Storm

Jimmy Carter's administration began with great promise, but his efforts to improve the economy through deregulation largely failed. Carter's attempt at a foreign policy built on the principle of human rights also prompted much criticism, as did his decision to boycott the Summer Olympics in Moscow. On the other hand, he successfully brokered the beginnings of a historic peace treaty between Egypt and Israel. Remaining public faith in Carter was dealt a serious blow, however, when he proved unable to free the American hostages in Tehran.

Review Questions

1. One of the original founders of AIM was
   _____.

   A. Patsy Mink
   B. Dennis Banks
   C. Jerry Rubin
   D. Glenn Weiser

2. The Supreme Court's 1973 decision in *Roe v. Wade* established that _____.

A. abortions obtained during the first three months of pregnancy were legal
B. witnesses were not required to corroborate a charge of rape
C. marriage could not be abolished
D. homosexuality was a mental illness

3. What kinds of values did hippies adopt?

4. President Nixon took a bold diplomatic step in early 1972 when he _____.

    A. went to Vienna

    B. declared the Vietnam War over

    C. met with Chinese leaders in Beijing

    D. signed the Glasgow Accords

5. The blue-collar workers who Nixon called "the silent majority" _____.

    A. fled to the suburbs to avoid integration

    B. wanted to replace existing social institutions with cooperatives

    C. opposed the war in Vietnam

    D. believed their opinions were overlooked in the political process

6. What caused the rifts in the Democratic Party in the 1968 election?

7. The demonstrations at Kent State University in May 1970 were held to protest what event?

    A. the My Lai massacre

    B. the North Vietnamese invasion of Saigon

    C. the invasion of Cambodia by U.S. forces

    D. the signing of a peace agreement with North Vietnam

8. Recognizing that ongoing protests and campus violence reflected a sea change in public opinion about the war, in 1971 Nixon _____.

    A. repealed the Gulf of Tonkin Resolution

    B. postponed the invasion of Cambodia

    C. released the Pentagon Papers

    D. covered up the My Lai massacre

9. According to John Kerry, how did many U.S. soldiers treat Vietnamese civilians?

10. The agreement Gerald Ford signed with the leader of the Soviet Union that ended the territorial issues remaining from World War II was _____.

    A. the Moscow Communiqué

    B. the Beijing Treaty

    C. the Iceland Protocol

    D. the Helsinki Accords

11. Of these figures, who was *not* indicted following the Watergate break-in and cover-up?

    A. John Mitchell

    B. Bob Woodward

    C. John Ehrlichman

    D. H.R. Haldeman

12. In what types of unethical and illegal activities did the White House plumbers and the "dirty tricks" squad engage?

13. During the 1976 election campaign, Jimmy Carter famously promised _____.

    A. that he would never start a war

    B. that he would never be unfaithful to his wife

    C. that he had never smoked marijuana

    D. that he would never lie

14. Carter deregulated several major American industries in an effort to ensure that _____.

    A. companies would become more competitive

    B. airlines would merge

    C. oil prices would rise

    D. consumers would start conserving energy

15. What were President Carter's successes in the area of foreign policy?

Critical Thinking Questions

16. What common goals did American Indians, gay and lesbian citizens, and women share in their quests for equal rights? How did their agendas differ? What were the differences and similarities in the tactics they used to achieve their aims?

17. In what ways were the policies of Richard Nixon different from those of his Democratic predecessors John Kennedy and Lyndon Johnson? How were Jimmy Carter's policies different from those of Nixon?

18. To what degree did foreign policy issues affect politics and the economy in the United States in the late 1960s and 1970s?

19. What events caused voters to lose faith in the political system and the nation's leaders in the late 1960s and 1970s?

20. In what ways did the goals of the civil rights movement of the 1950s and 1960s manifest themselves in the identity politics of the 1970s?

CHAPTER 31

From Cold War to Culture Wars, 1980-2000

Figure 31.1 This striking piece of graffiti from the Berlin Wall, now housed in the Newseum in Washington, DC, contains the name of the AIDS Coalition to Unleash Power (ACT UP), a group formed in 1987 in New York City to combat the spread of AIDS and the perception that AIDS was the product of immoral behavior.

Chapter Outline

Introduction

"Act up!" might be called the unofficial slogan of the 1980s. Numerous groups were concerned by what they considered disturbing social, cultural, and political trends in the United States and lobbied for their vision of what the nation should be. Conservative politicians cut taxes for the wealthy and shrank programs for the poor, while conservative Christians blamed the legalization of abortion and the increased visibility of gays and lesbians for weakening the American family. When the U.S. Centers for Disease Control first recognized the Acquired Immune Deficiency Syndrome (AIDS) in 1981, the Religious Right regarded it as a plague sent by God to punish homosexual men for their "unnatural" behavior. Politicians, many of whom relied on religious conservatives for their votes, largely ignored the AIDS epidemic. In response, gay men and women formed organizations such as ACT UP to draw attention to their cause (Figure 31.1).

Toward the end of the decade in 1989, protesters from both East and West Berlin began "acting up" and tearing down large chunks of the Berlin Wall, essentially dismantling the Iron Curtain. This symbolic act was the culmination of earlier demonstrations that had swept across Eastern Europe, resulting in the collapse of Communist governments in both Central and Eastern Europe, and marking the beginning of the end of the Cold War.

31.1 The Reagan Revolution

By the end of this section, you will be able to:
- Explain Ronald Reagan's attitude towards government
- Discuss the Reagan administration's economic policies and their effects on the nation

Ronald Reagan entered the White House in 1981 with strongly conservative values but experience in moderate politics. He appealed to moderates and conservatives anxious about social change and the seeming loss of American power and influence on the world stage. Leading the so-called Reagan Revolution, he appealed to voters with the promise that the principles of conservatism could halt and revert the social and economic changes of the last generation. Reagan won the White House by citing big government and attempts at social reform as the problem, not the solution. He was able to capture the political capital of an unsettled national mood and, in the process, helped set an agenda and policies that would affect his successors and the political landscape of the nation.

REAGAN'S EARLY CAREER

Although many of his movie roles and the persona he created for himself seemed to represent traditional values, Reagan's rise to the presidency was an unusual transition from pop cultural significance to political success. Born and raised in the Midwest, he moved to California in 1937 to become a Hollywood actor. He also became a reserve officer in the U.S. Army that same year, but when the country entered World War II, he was excluded from active duty overseas because of poor eyesight and spent the war in the army's First Motion Picture Unit. After the war, he resumed his film career; rose to leadership in the Screen Actors Guild, a Hollywood union; and became a spokesman for General Electric and the host of a television series that the company sponsored. As a young man, he identified politically as a liberal Democrat, but his distaste for communism, along with the influence of the social conservative values of his second wife, actress Nancy Davis, edged him closer to conservative Republicanism (Figure 31.3). By 1962, he had

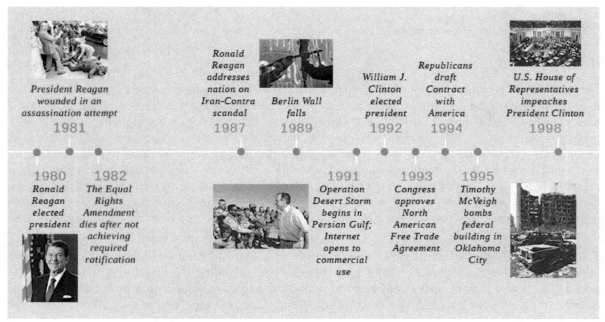

Figure 31.2

formally switched political parties, and in 1964, he actively campaigned for the Republican presidential nominee Barry Goldwater.

Figure 31.3 In 1961, when Congress began to explore nationwide health insurance for the elderly under Social Security, Reagan made a recording for the American Medical Association in which he denounced the idea—which was later adopted as Medicare—as "socialized medicine." Such a program, Reagan warned his listeners, was the first step to the nation's demise as a free society.

Reagan launched his own political career in 1966 when he successfully ran for governor of California. His opponent was the incumbent Pat Brown, a liberal Democrat who had already served two terms. Reagan, quite undeservedly, blamed Brown for race riots in California and student protests at the University of California at Berkeley. He criticized the Democratic incumbent's increases in taxes and state government, and denounced "big government" and the inequities of taxation in favor of free enterprise. As governor, however, he quickly learned that federal and state laws prohibited the elimination of certain programs and that many programs benefited his constituents. He ended up approving the largest budget in the state's history and approved tax increases on a number of occasions. The contrast between Reagan's rhetoric and practice made up his political skill: capturing the public mood and catering to it, but compromising when necessary.

REPUBLICANS BACK IN THE WHITE HOUSE

After two unsuccessful Republican primary bids in 1968 and 1976, Reagan won the presidency in 1980. His victory was the result of a combination of dissatisfaction with the presidential leadership of Gerald Ford and Jimmy Carter in the 1970s and the growth of the **New Right**. This group of conservative Americans included many very wealthy financial supporters and emerged in the wake of the social reforms and cultural changes of the 1960s and 1970s. Many were evangelical Christians, like those who joined Jerry Falwell's Moral Majority, and opposed the legalization of abortion, the feminist movement, and sex education in public schools. Reagan also attracted people, often dubbed neoconservatives, who would not previously have voted for the same candidate as conservative Protestants did. Many were middle- and working-class people who resented the growth of federal and state governments, especially benefit programs, and the subsequent increase in taxes during the late 1960s and 1970s. They favored the tax revolts that swept the nation in the late 1970s under the leadership of predominantly older, white, middle-class Americans, which had succeeded in imposing radical reductions in local property and state income taxes.

Voter turnout reflected this new conservative swing, which not only swept Reagan into the White House but created a Republican majority in the Senate. Only 52 percent of eligible voters went to the polls in 1980, the lowest turnout for a presidential election since 1948. Those who did cast a ballot were older, whiter, and wealthier than those who did not vote (Figure 31.4). Strong support among white voters, those over forty-five years of age, and those with incomes over $50,000 proved crucial for Reagan's victory.

Figure 31.4 Ronald Reagan campaigns for the presidency with his wife Nancy in South Carolina in 1980. Reagan won in all the Deep South states except Georgia, although he did not come from the South and his opponent Jimmy Carter did.

REAGANOMICS

Reagan's primary goal upon taking office was to stimulate the sagging economy while simultaneously cutting both government programs and taxes. His economic policies, called **Reaganomics** by the press, were based on a theory called supply-side economics, about which many economists were skeptical. Influenced by economist Arthur Laffer of the University of Southern California, Reagan cut income taxes for those at the top of the economic ladder, which was supposed to motivate the rich to invest in businesses, factories, and the stock market in anticipation of high returns. According to Laffer's argument, this would eventually translate into more jobs further down the socioeconomic ladder. Economic growth would also increase the total tax revenue—even at a lower tax rate. In other words, proponents of "trickle-down economics" promised to cut taxes and balance the budget at the same time. Reaganomics also included the deregulation of industry and higher interest rates to control inflation, but these initiatives preceded Reagan and were conceived in the Carter administration.

Many politicians, including Republicans, were wary of Reagan's economic program; even his eventual vice president, George H. W. Bush, had referred to it as "voodoo economics" when competing with him for the Republican presidential nomination. When Reagan proposed a 30 percent cut in taxes to be phased in over his first term in office, Congress balked. Opponents argued that the tax cuts would benefit the rich and not the poor, who needed help the most. In response, Reagan presented his plan directly to the people (Figure 31.5).

Figure 31.5 Ronald Reagan outlines his plan for tax reduction legislation in July 1981. Data suggest that the supply-side policies of the 1980s actually produced less investment, slightly slower growth, and a greater decline in wages than the non–supply side policies of the 1990s.

Reagan was an articulate spokesman for his political perspectives and was able to garner support for his policies. Often called "The Great Communicator," he was noted for his ability, honed through years as an actor and spokesperson, to convey a mixture of folksy wisdom, empathy, and concern while taking humorous digs at his opponents. Indeed, listening to Reagan speak often felt like hearing a favorite uncle recall stories about the "good old days" before big government, expensive social programs, and greedy politicians destroyed the country (Figure 31.6). Americans found this rhetorical style extremely compelling. Public support for the plan, combined with a surge in the president's popularity after he survived an assassination attempt in March 1981, swayed Congress, including many Democrats. On July 29, 1981, Congress passed the Economic Recovery Tax Act, which phased in a 25 percent overall reduction in taxes over a period of three years.

Figure 31.6 President Ronald Reagan signs economic reform legislation at his ranch in California. Note the blue jeans, denim jacket, and cowboy boots he wears.

MY STORY

⚙ Richard V. Allen on the Assassination Attempt on Ronald Reagan

On March 30, 1981, just months into the Reagan presidency, John Hinckley, Jr. attempted to assassinate the president as he left a speaking engagement at the Washington Hilton Hotel. Hinckley wounded Reagan and three others in the attempt. Here, National Security Adviser Richard V. Allen recalls what happened the day President Reagan was shot:

> By 2:52 PM I arrived at the White House and went to [Chief of Staff James] Baker's office . . . and we placed a call to Vice President George H. W. Bush. . . .
>
> [W]e sent a message with the few facts we knew: the bullets had been fired and press secretary Jim Brady had been hit, as had a Secret Service agent and a DC policeman. At first, the President was thought to be unscathed.
>
> Jerry Parr, the Secret Service Detail Chief, shoved the President into the limousine, codenamed "Stagecoach," and slammed the doors shut. The driver sped off. Headed back to the safety of the White House, Parr noticed that the red blood at the President's mouth was frothy, indicating an internal injury, and suddenly switched the route to the hospital. . . . Parr saved the President's life. He had lost a serious quantity of blood internally and reached [the emergency room] just in time. . . .
>
> Though the President never lost his sense of humor throughout, and had actually walked into the hospital under his own power before his knees buckled, his condition became grave.

Why do you think Allen mentions the president's sense of humor and his ability to walk into the hospital on his own? Why might the assassination attempt have helped Reagan achieve some of his political goals, such as getting his tax cuts through Congress?

Click and Explore

The largest of the presidential libraries, the Ronald Reagan Presidential Library (http://openstaxcollege.org/l/15ReaganLib) contains Reagan's most important speeches and pictures of Ronald and Nancy Reagan.

Reagan was successful at cutting taxes, but he failed to reduce government spending. Although he had long warned about the dangers of big government, he created a new cabinet-level agency, the Department of Veterans Affairs, and the number of federal employees increased during his time in office. He allocated a smaller share of the federal budget to antipoverty programs like Aid to Families with Dependent Children (AFDC), food stamps, rent subsidies, job training programs, and Medicaid, but Social Security and Medicare entitlements, from which his supporters benefited, were left largely untouched except for an increase in payroll taxes to pay for them. Indeed, in 1983, Reagan agreed to a compromise with the Democrats in Congress on a $165 billion injection of funds to save Social Security, which included this payroll tax increase.

But Reagan seemed less flexible when it came to deregulating industry and weakening the power of labor unions. Banks and savings and loan associations were deregulated. Pollution control was enforced less strictly by the Environmental Protection Agency, and restrictions on logging and drilling for oil on public lands were relaxed. Believing the free market was self-regulating, the Reagan administration had little use for labor unions, and in 1981, the president fired twelve thousand federal air traffic controllers who had gone on strike to secure better working conditions (which would also have improved the public's safety). His action effectively destroyed the Professional Air Traffic Controllers Organization (PATCO) and ushered in a new era of labor relations in which, following his example, employers simply replaced striking workers. The weakening of unions contributed to the leveling off of real wages for the average American family during the 1980s.

Reagan's economic policymakers succeeded in breaking the cycle of stagflation that had been plaguing the nation, but at significant cost. In its effort to curb high inflation with dramatically increased interest rates, the Federal Reserve also triggered a deep recession. Inflation did drop, but borrowing became expensive and consumers spent less. In Reagan's first years in office, bankruptcies increased and unemployment reached about 10 percent, its highest level since the Great Depression. Homelessness became a significant problem in cities, a fact the president made light of by suggesting that the press exaggerated the problem and that many homeless people chose to live on the streets. Economic growth resumed in 1983 and gross domestic product grew at an average of 4.5 percent during the rest of his presidency. By the end of Reagan's second term in office, unemployment had dropped to about 5.3 percent, but the nation was nearly $3 trillion in debt. An increase in defense spending coupled with $3.6 billion in tax relief for the 162,000 American families with incomes of $200,000 or more made a balanced budget, one of the president's campaign promises in 1980, impossible to achieve.

The Reagan years were a complicated era of social, economic, and political change, with many trends operating simultaneously and sometimes at cross-purposes. While many suffered, others prospered. The 1970s had been the era of the hippie, and *Newsweek* magazine declared 1984 to be the "year of the Yuppie." Yuppies, whose name derived from "(y)oung, (u)rban (p)rofessionals," were akin to hippies in being young people whose interests, values, and lifestyle influenced American culture, economy, and politics, just as the hippies' credo had done in the late 1960s and 1970s. Unlike hippies, however, yuppies were materialistic and obsessed with image, comfort, and economic prosperity. Although liberal on some social issues, economically they were conservative. Ironically, some yuppies were former hippies or yippies, like Jerry Rubin, who gave up his crusade against "the establishment" to become a businessman.

Click and Explore

Read more about yuppie culture (http://openstaxcollege.org/l/15YuppieCult) and then use the table of contents to access other information about the culture of the 1980s.

31.2 Political and Cultural Fusions

By the end of this section, you will be able to:
- Discuss the culture wars and political conflicts of the Reagan era
- Describe the Religious Right's response to the issues of the Reagan era

Ronald Reagan's victory in 1980 suggested to conservatives that the days of liberalism were over and the liberal establishment might be dismantled. Many looked forward to the discontinuation of policies like affirmative action. Conservative Christians sought to outlaw abortion and stop the movement for gay and lesbian rights. Republicans, and some moderate Democrats, demanded a return to "traditional" family values, a rhetorical ploy to suggest that male authority over women and children constituted a natural order that women's rights and the New Left had subverted since the 1960s. As the conservative message regarding the evils of government permeated society, distrust of the federal government grew, inspiring some to form organizations and communities that sought complete freedom from government control.

CREATING CONSERVATIVE POLICY

Ronald Reagan's popularity and effectiveness as a leader drew from his reputation as a man who fought for what he believed in. He was a very articulate spokesperson for a variety of political ideas based on conservative principles and perspectives. Much of the intellectual meat of the Reagan Revolution came from conservative think tanks (policy or advocacy groups) that specifically sought to shape American political and social dialogues. The **Heritage Foundation**, one such group, soon became the intellectual arm of the conservative movement.

Launched in 1973 with a $250,000 contribution from Joseph Coors (of Coors Brewing Company) and support from a variety of corporations and conservative foundations, the Heritage Foundation sought to counteract what conservatives believed to be Richard Nixon's acceptance of a liberal consensus on too many issues. In producing its policy position papers and political recommendations to conservative candidates and politicians, it helped contribute to a sanitization of U.S. history and a nostalgic glorification of what it deemed to be traditional values, seemingly threatened by the expansion of political and personal freedoms. The foundation had lent considerable support and encouragement to the conservative dialogues that helped carry Ronald Reagan into office in 1980. Just a year later, it produced a document entitled *Mandate for Leadership* that catalogued some two thousand specific recommendations on how to shrink the size and reach of the federal government and implement a more consistent conservative agenda. The newly elected Reagan administration looked favorably on the recommendations and recruited several of the paper's authors to serve in the White House.

CONSERVATIVE CHRISTIANS AND FAMILY VALUES

Among the strongest supporters of Ronald Reagan's campaign for president were members of the Religious Right, including Christian groups like the Moral Majority, 61 percent of whom voted for him. By 1980, evangelical Christians had become an important political and social force in the United States (Figure 31.7). Some thirteen hundred radio stations in the country were owned and operated by evangelicals. Christian television programs, such as Pat Robertson's *The 700 Club* and Jim Bakker's *The PTL* (Praise the Lord) *Club*, proved enormously popular and raised millions of dollars from viewer contributions. For some, evangelism was a business, but most conservative Christians were true believers who were convinced that premarital and extramarital sex, abortion, drug use, homosexuality, and "irreligious" forms of popular and high culture were responsible for a perceived decline in traditional family values that threatened American society.

Figure 31.7 This fundraising card was used by Anita Bryant, singer and beauty pageant winner, to gather support for Save Our Children Inc., a political coalition she formed in the late 1970s to overturn a Florida ordinance banning discrimination based on sexual orientation. Many of the group's strategies were soon embraced by the Moral Majority.

Despite the support he received from Christian conservative and family values voters, Reagan was hardly an ideologue when it came to policy. Indeed, he was often quite careful in using hot button, family-value issues to his greatest political advantage. For example, as governor of California, one of the states that ratified the Equal Rights Amendment (ERA) in its first year, he positioned himself as a supporter of the amendment. When he launched his bid for the Republican nomination in 1976, however, he withdrew his support to gain the backing of more conservative members of his party. This move demonstrated both political savvy and foresight. At the time he withdrew his support, the Republican National Convention was still officially backing the amendment. However, in 1980, the party began to qualify its stance, which dovetailed with Reagan's candidacy for the White House.

Reagan believed the Fourteenth Amendment to the Constitution was sufficient protection for women against discrimination. Once in office, he took a mostly neutral position, neither supporting nor working against the ERA. Nor did this middle position appear to hurt him at the polls; he attracted a significant number of votes from women in 1980, and in 1984, he polled 56 percent of the women's vote compared to 44 percent for the Democratic ticket of Walter Mondale and Geraldine Ferraro, the first female candidate for vice president from a major party.

DEFINING "AMERICAN"

⚙ *Phyllis Schlafly and the STOP ERA Movement*

In 1972, after a large number of states jumped to ratify the Equal Rights Amendment, most observers believed its ultimate ratification by all the necessary states was all but certain. But, a decade later, the amendment died without ever getting the necessary votes. There are many reasons it went down in defeat, but a major one was Phyllis Schlafly.

On the surface, Schlafly's life might suggest that she would naturally support the ERA. After all, she was a well-educated, professional woman who sought advancement in her field and even aspired to high political office. Yet she is a fascinating historical character, precisely because her life and goals don't conform to expected norms.

Schlafly's attack on the ERA was ingenious in its method and effectiveness. Rather than attacking the amendment directly as a gateway to unrestrained and immoral behavior as some had, she couched her opposition in language that was sensitive to both privilege and class. Her instrument was the STOP ERA movement, with the acronym STOP, standing for "Stop Taking our Privileges." Schlafly argued that women enjoyed special privileges such as gender-specific restrooms and exemption from the military draft. These, she claimed, would be lost should the ERA be ratified. But she also claimed to stand up for the dignity of being a homemaker and lambasted the feminist movement as elitist. In this, she was keenly aware of the power of class interests. Her organization suggested that privileged women could afford to support the ERA. Working women and poor housewives, however, would ultimately bear the brunt of the loss of protection it would bring. In the end, her tactics were successful in achieving exactly what the movement's name suggested; she stopped the ERA.

Reagan's political calculations notwithstanding, his belief that traditional values were threatened by a modern wave of immoral popular culture was genuine. He recognized that nostalgia was a powerful force in politics, and he drew a picture for his audiences of the traditional good old days under attack by immorality and decline. "Those of us who are over thirty-five or so years of age grew up in a different America," he explained in his farewell address. "We were taught, very directly, what it means to be an American. And we absorbed, almost in the air, a love of country and an appreciation of its institutions. . . . The movies celebrated democratic values and implicitly reinforced the idea that America was special." But this America, he insisted, was being washed away. "I'm warning of an eradication of the American memory that could result, ultimately, in an erosion of the American spirit."

Concern over a decline in the country's moral values welled up on both sides of the political aisle. In 1985, anxiety over the messages of the music industry led to the founding of the Parents Music Resource Center (PMRC), a bipartisan group formed by the wives of prominent Washington politicians including Susan Baker, the wife of Reagan's treasury secretary, James Baker, and Tipper Gore, the wife of then-senator Al Gore, who later became vice president under Bill Clinton. The goal of the PMRC was to limit the ability of children to listen to music with sexual or violent content. Its strategy was to get the recording industry to adopt a voluntary rating system for music and recordings, similar to the Motion Picture Association of America's system for movies.

The organization also produced a list of particularly offensive recordings known as the "filthy fifteen." By August 1985, nearly twenty record companies had agreed to put labels on their recordings indicating "explicit lyrics," but the Senate began hearings on the issue in September (Figure 31.8). While many parents and a number of witnesses advocated the labels, many in the music industry rejected them as censorship. *Twisted Sister*'s Dee Snider and folk musician John Denver both advised Congress against the restrictions. In the end, the recording industry suggested a voluntary generic label. Its effect on children's exposure to raw language is uncertain, but musicians roundly mocked the effort.

Figure 31.8 Tipper Gore, wife of then-senator (and later vice president) Al Gore, at the 1985 Senate hearings into rating labels proposed by the PMRC, of which she was a cofounder.

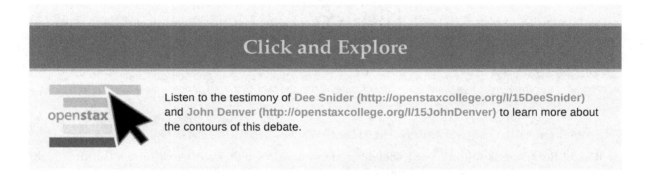

Listen to the testimony of Dee Snider (http://openstaxcollege.org/l/15DeeSnider) and John Denver (http://openstaxcollege.org/l/15JohnDenver) to learn more about the contours of this debate.

THE AIDS CRISIS

In the early 1980s, doctors noticed a disturbing trend: Young gay men in large cities, especially San Francisco and New York, were being diagnosed with, and eventually dying from, a rare cancer called Kaposi's sarcoma. Because the disease was seen almost exclusively in male homosexuals, it was quickly dubbed "gay cancer." Doctors soon realized it often coincided with other symptoms, including a rare form of pneumonia, and they renamed it "Gay Related Immune Deficiency" (GRID), although people other than gay men, primarily intravenous drug users, were dying from the disease as well. The connection between gay men and GRID—later renamed human immunodeficiency virus/autoimmune deficiency syndrome, or **HIV/AIDS**—led heterosexuals largely to ignore the growing health crisis in the gay community, wrongly assuming they were safe from its effects. The federal government also overlooked the disease, and calls for more money to research and find the cure were ignored.

Even after it became apparent that heterosexuals could contract the disease through blood transfusions and heterosexual intercourse, HIV/AIDS continued to be associated primarily with the gay community, especially by political and religious conservatives. Indeed, the Religious Right regarded it as a form of divine retribution meant to punish gay men for their "immoral" lifestyle. President Reagan, always politically careful, was reluctant to speak openly about the developing crisis even as thousands faced certain death from the disease.

With little help coming from the government, the gay community quickly began to organize its own response. In 1982, New York City men formed the Gay Men's Health Crisis (GMHC), a volunteer organization that operated an information hotline, provided counseling and legal assistance, and raised money for people with HIV/AIDS. Larry Kramer, one of the original members, left in 1983 and formed his own organization, the AIDS Coalition to Unleash Power (ACT UP), in 1987. ACT UP took a more militant approach, holding demonstrations on Wall Street, outside the U.S. Food and Drug Administration (FDA), and inside the New York Stock Exchange to call attention and shame the government into action. One of the images adopted by the group, a pink triangle paired with the phrase "Silence = Death," captured media attention and quickly became the symbol of the AIDS crisis (Figure 31.9).

Figure 31.9 The pink triangle was originally used in Nazi concentration camps to identify those there for acts of homosexuality. Reclaimed by gay activists in New York as a symbol of resistance and solidarity during the 1970s, it was further transformed as a symbol of governmental inaction in the face of the AIDS epidemic during the 1980s.

THE WAR ON DRUGS AND THE ROAD TO MASS INCARCERATION

As Ronald Reagan took office in 1981, violent crime in the United States was reaching an all-time high. While there were different reasons for the spike, the most important one was demographics: The primary category of offenders, males between the ages of sixteen and thirty-six, reached an all-time peak as the baby-boomer generation came of age. But the phenomenon that most politicians honed in on as a cause for violent crime was the abuse of a new, cheap drug dealt illegally on city streets. Crack cocaine, a smokable type of cocaine popular with poorer addicts, was hitting the streets in the 1980s, frightening middle-class Americans. Reagan and other conservatives led a campaign to "get tough on crime" and promised the nation a "**war on drugs**." Initiatives like the "Just Say No" campaign led by First Lady Nancy Reagan implied that drug addiction and drug-related crime reflected personal morality.

Nixon had first used the term in 1971, but in the 1980s the "war on drugs" took on an ominous dimension, as politicians scrambled over each other to enact harsher sentences for drug offenses so they could market themselves as tough on crime. State after state switched from variable to mandatory minimum sentences that were exceedingly long and particularly harsh for street drug crimes. The federal government supported the trend with federal sentencing guidelines and additional funds for local law enforcement agencies. This law-and-order movement peaked in the 1990s, when California introduced a "three strikes" law that mandated life imprisonment without parole for any third felony conviction—even nonviolent ones. As a result, prisons became crowded, and states went deep into debt to build more. By the end of the century, the war began to die down as the public lost interest in the problem, the costs of the punishment binge became politically burdensome, and scholars and politicians began to advocate the decriminalization of drug use. By this time, however, hundreds of thousands of people had been incarcerated for drug offenses and the total number of prisoners in the nation had grown four-fold in the last quarter of the century. Particularly glaring were the racial inequities of the new age of mass incarceration, with African Americans being seven times more likely to be in prison (Figure 31.10).

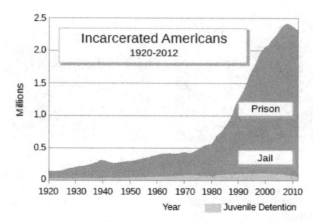

Figure 31.10 This graph of the number of people in jail, prison, and juvenile detention by decade in the United States shows the huge increase in incarceration during the war on drugs that began in the 1980s, during the Reagan administration. (Prisons are long-term state or federal facilities; jails are local, short-term facilities.)

31.3 A New World Order

By the end of this section, you will be able to:
- Describe the successes and failures of Ronald Reagan's foreign policy
- Compare the policies of Ronald Reagan with those of George H. W. Bush
- Explain the causes and results of the Persian Gulf War
- Discuss the events that constituted the end of the Cold War

In addition to reviving the economy and reducing the size of the federal government, Ronald Reagan also wished to restore American stature in the world. He entered the White House a "cold warrior" and referred to the Soviet Union in a 1983 speech as an "evil empire." Dedicated to upholding even authoritarian governments in foreign countries to keep them safe from Soviet influence, he was also desperate to put to rest **Vietnam Syndrome**, the reluctance to use military force in foreign countries for fear of embarrassing defeat, which had influenced U.S. foreign policy since the mid-1970s.

THE MIDDLE EAST AND CENTRAL AMERICA

Reagan's desire to demonstrate U.S. readiness to use military force abroad sometimes had tragic consequences. In 1983, he sent soldiers to Lebanon as part of a multinational force trying to restore order following an Israeli invasion the year before. On October 23, more than two hundred troops were killed in a barracks bombing in Beirut carried out by Iranian-trained militants known as Hezbollah (Figure 31.11). In February 1984, Reagan announced that, given intensified fighting, U.S. troops were being withdrawn.

(a)   (b)

Figure 31.11 The suicide bombing of the U.S. Embassy in Beirut (a) on April 18, 1983, marked the first of a number of attacks on U.S. targets in the region. Less than six months later, a truck bomb leveled the U.S. Marine barracks at the Beirut airport (b), part of a coordinated attack that killed 299 U.S and French members of the multinational peacekeeping force in Lebanon.

Two days after the bombing in Beirut, Reagan and Secretary of State George P. Shultz authorized the invasion of Grenada, a small Caribbean island nation, in an attempt to oust a Communist military junta that had overthrown a moderate regime. Communist Cuba already had troops and technical aid workers stationed on the island and were willing to defend the new regime, but the United States swiftly took command of the situation, and the Cuban soldiers surrendered after two days.

Reagan's intervention in Grenada was intended to send a message to Marxists in Central America. Meanwhile, however, decades of political repression and economic corruption by certain Latin American governments, sometimes generously supported by U.S. foreign aid, had sown deep seeds of revolutionary discontent. In El Salvador, a 1979 civil-military coup had put a military junta in power that was engaged in a civil war against left-leaning guerillas when Reagan took office. His administration supported the right-wing government, which used death squads to silence dissent.

Neighboring Nicaragua was also governed by a largely Marxist-inspired group, the Sandinistas. This organization, led by Daniel Ortega, had overthrown the brutal, right-wing dictatorship of Anastasio Somoza in 1979. Reagan, however, overlooked the legitimate complaints of the Sandinistas and believed that their rule opened the region to Cuban and Soviet influence. A year into his presidency, convinced it was folly to allow the expansion of Soviet and Communist influence in Latin America, he authorized the Central Intelligence Agency (CIA) to equip and train a group of anti-Sandinista Nicaraguans known as the Contras (*contrarevolucionários* or "counter-revolutionaries") to oust Ortega.

Reagan's desire to aid the Contras even after Congress ended its support led him, surprisingly, to Iran. In September 1980, Iraq had invaded neighboring Iran and, by 1982, had begun to gain the upper hand. The Iraqis needed weapons, and the Reagan administration, wishing to assist the enemy of its enemy, had agreed to provide Iraqi president Saddam Hussein with money, arms, and military intelligence. In 1983, however, the capture of Americans by Hezbollah forces in Lebanon changed the president's plans. In 1985, he authorized the sale of anti-tank and anti-aircraft missiles to Iran in exchange for help retrieving three of the American hostages.

A year later, Reagan's National Security Council aide, Lieutenant Colonel Oliver North, found a way to sell weapons to Iran and secretly use the proceeds to support the Nicaraguan Contras—in direct violation of a congressional ban on military aid to the anti-Communist guerillas in that Central American nation. Eventually the Senate became aware, and North and others were indicted on various charges, which were all dismissed, overturned on appeal, or granted presidential pardon. Reagan, known for delegating much authority to subordinates and unable to "remember" crucial facts and meetings, escaped the scandal with nothing more than criticism for his lax oversight. The nation was divided over the extent to which the president could go to "protect national interests," and the limits of Congress's constitutional authority to oversee the activities of the executive branch have yet to be resolved.

Click and Explore

Visit the Brown University site (http://openstaxcollege.org/l/15IranContra) to learn more about the Iran-Contra congressional hearings. Read transcripts of the testimony and watch the video of President Reagan's address to the nation regarding the operation.

THE COLD WAR WAXES AND WANES

While trying to shrink the federal budget and the size of government sphere at home, Reagan led an unprecedented military buildup in which money flowed to the Pentagon to pay for expensive new forms of weaponry. The press drew attention to the inefficiency of the nation's military industrial complex, offering as examples expense bills that included $640 toilet seats and $7,400 coffee machines. One of the most controversial aspects of Reagan's plan was the Strategic Defense Initiative (SDI), which he proposed in 1983. SDI, or "Star Wars," called for the development of a defensive shield to protect the United States from a Soviet missile strike. Scientists argued that much of the needed technology had not yet been developed and might never be. Others contended that the plan would violate existing treaties with the Soviet Union and worried about the Soviet response. The system was never built, and the plan, estimated to have cost some $7.5 billion, was finally abandoned.

Anticipating his reelection campaign in 1984, Reagan began to moderate his position toward the Soviet Union, largely at the initiative of his new counterpart, Mikhail Gorbachev. The new and comparatively young Soviet premier did not want to commit additional funds for another arms race, especially since the war in Afghanistan against mujahedeen—Islamic guerilla fighters—had depleted the Soviet Union's resources severely since its invasion of the central Asian nation in 1979. Gorbachev recognized that economic despair at home could easily result in larger political upheavals like those in neighboring Poland, where the Solidarity movement had taken hold. He withdrew troops from Afghanistan, introduced political reforms and new civil liberties at home—known as *perestroika* and *glasnost*—and proposed arms reduction talks with the United States. In 1985, Gorbachev and Reagan met in Geneva to reduce armaments and shrink their respective military budgets. The following year, meeting in Reykjavík, Iceland, they surprised the world by announcing that they would try to eliminate nuclear weapons by 1996. In 1987, they agreed to eliminate a whole category of nuclear weapons when they signed the Intermediate-Range Nuclear Forces (INF) Treaty at the White House (Figure 31.12). This laid the foundation for future agreements limiting nuclear weapons.

Figure 31.12   In the East Room of the White House, President Reagan and Soviet general secretary Mikhail Gorbachev sign the 1987 INF Treaty, eliminating one category of nuclear weapons.

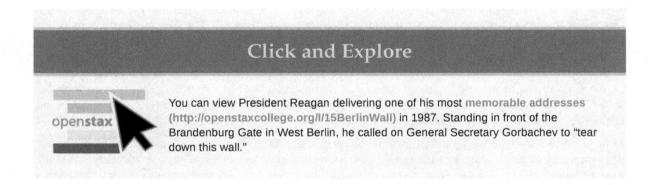

Click and Explore

You can view President Reagan delivering one of his most memorable addresses (http://openstaxcollege.org/l/15BerlinWall) in 1987. Standing in front of the Brandenburg Gate in West Berlin, he called on General Secretary Gorbachev to "tear down this wall."

"NO NEW TAXES"

Confident they could win back the White House, Democrats mounted a campaign focused on more effective and competent government under the leadership of Massachusetts governor Michael Dukakis. When George H. W. Bush, Reagan's vice president and Republican nominee, found himself down in the polls, political advisor Lee Atwater launched an aggressively negative media campaign, accusing Dukakis of being soft on crime and connecting his liberal policies to a brutal murder in Massachusetts. More importantly, Bush adopted a largely Reaganesque style on matters of economic policy, promising to shrink government and keep taxes low. These tactics were successful, and the Republican Party retained the White House.

Although he promised to carry on Reagan's economic legacy, the problems Bush inherited made it difficult to do so. Reagan's policies of cutting taxes and increasing defense spending had exploded the federal budget deficit, making it three times larger in 1989 than when Reagan took office in 1980. Bush was further constrained by the emphatic pledge he had made at the 1988 Republican Convention—"read my lips: no new taxes"—and found himself in the difficult position of trying to balance the budget and reduce the deficit without breaking his promise. However, he also faced a Congress controlled by the Democrats, who wanted to raise taxes on the rich, while Republicans thought the government should drastically cut domestic spending. In October, after a brief government shutdown when Bush vetoed the budget Congress delivered, he and Congress reached a compromise with the Omnibus Budget Reconciliation Act of 1990. The budget included measures to reduce the deficit by both cutting government expenditures and raising taxes, effectively reneging on the "no new taxes" pledge. These economic constraints are one reason why Bush supported a limited domestic agenda of education reform and antidrug efforts, relying on private volunteers and community organizations, which he referred to as "a thousand points of light," to address most social problems.

When it came to foreign affairs, Bush's attitude towards the Soviet Union differed little from Reagan's. Bush sought to ease tensions with America's rival superpower and stressed the need for peace and cooperation. The desire to avoid angering the Soviets led him to adopt a hands-off approach when, at the beginning of his term, a series of pro-democracy demonstrations broke out across the Communist Eastern Bloc.

In November 1989, the world—including foreign policy experts and espionage agencies from both sides of the Iron Curtain—watched in surprise as peaceful protesters in East Germany marched through checkpoints at the Berlin Wall. Within hours, people from both East and West Berlin flooded the checkpoints and began tearing down large chunks of the wall. Months of earlier demonstrations in East Germany had called on the government to allow citizens to leave the country. These demonstrations were one manifestation of a larger movement sweeping across East Germany, Poland, Hungary, Czechoslovakia, Bulgaria, and Romania, which swiftly led to revolutions, most of them peaceful, resulting in the collapse of Communist governments in Central and Eastern Europe.

In Budapest in 1956 and in Prague in 1968, the Soviet Union had restored order through a large show of force. That this didn't happen in 1989 was an indication to all that the Soviet Union was itself collapsing. Bush's refusal to gloat or declare victory helped him maintain the relationship with Gorbachev that Reagan had established. In July 1991, Gorbachev and Bush signed the Strategic Arms Reduction Treaty, or **START**, which committed their countries to reducing their nuclear arsenals by 25 percent. A month later, attempting to stop the changes begun by Gorbachev's reforms, Communist Party hardliners tried to remove him from power. Protests arose throughout the Soviet Union, and by December 1991, the nation had collapsed. In January 1992, twelve former Soviet republics formed the Commonwealth of Independent States to coordinate trade and security measures. The Cold War was over.

AMERICAN GLOBAL POWER IN THE WAKE OF THE COLD WAR

The dust had barely settled on the crumbling Berlin Wall when the Bush administration announced a bold military intervention in Panama in December 1989. Claiming to act on behalf of human rights, U.S. troops deposed the unpopular dictator and drug smuggler Manuel Noriega swiftly, but former CIA connections between President Bush and Noriega, as well as U.S. interests in maintaining control of the Canal Zone, prompted the United Nations and world public opinion to denounce the invasion as a power grab.

As the Soviet Union was ceasing to be a threat, the Middle East became a source of increased concern. In the wake of its eight-year war with Iran from 1980 to 1988, Iraq had accumulated a significant amount of foreign debt. At the same time, other Arab states had increased their oil production, forcing oil prices down and further hurting Iraq's economy. Iraq's leader, Saddam Hussein, approached these oil-producing states for assistance, particularly Saudi Arabia and neighboring Kuwait, which Iraq felt directly benefited from its war with Iran. When talks with these countries broke down, and Iraq found itself politically and economically isolated, Hussein ordered the invasion of oil-rich Kuwait in August 1990. Bush faced his first full-scale international crisis.

In response to the invasion, Bush and his foreign policy team forged an unprecedented international coalition of thirty-four countries, including many members of NATO (North Atlantic Treaty Organization) and the Middle Eastern countries of Saudi Arabia, Syria, and Egypt, to oppose Iraqi aggression. Bush hoped that this coalition would herald the beginning of a "new world order" in which the nations of the world would work together to deter belligerence. A deadline was set for Iraq to withdraw from Kuwait by January 15, or face serious consequences. Wary of not having sufficient domestic support for combat, Bush first deployed troops to the area to build up forces in the region and defend Saudi Arabia via Operation Desert Shield (Figure 31.13). On January 14, Bush succeeded in getting resolutions from Congress authorizing the use of military force against Iraq, and the U.S. then orchestrated an effective air campaign, followed by **Operation Desert Storm**, a one-hundred-hour land war involving over 500,000

U.S. troops and another 200,000 from twenty-seven other countries, which expelled Iraqi forces from Kuwait by the end of February.

Figure 31.13   George H. W. Bush greets U.S. troops stationed in Saudi Arabia on Thanksgiving Day in 1990. The first troops were deployed there in August 1990, as part of Operation Desert Shield, which was intended to build U.S. military strength in the area in preparation for an eventual military operation.

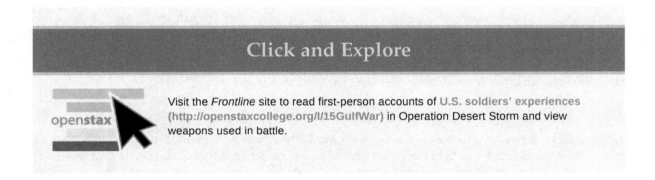

Click and Explore

Visit the *Frontline* site to read first-person accounts of U.S. soldiers' experiences (http://openstaxcollege.org/l/15GulfWar) in Operation Desert Storm and view weapons used in battle.

Some controversy arose among Bush's advisors regarding whether to end the war without removing Saddam Hussein from power, but General Colin Powell, the head of the Joint Chiefs of Staff, argued that to continue to attack a defeated army would be "un-American." Bush agreed and troops began moving out of the area in March 1991. Although Hussein was not removed from power, the war nevertheless suggested that the United States no longer suffered from "Vietnam Syndrome" and would deploy massive military resources if and when it thought necessary. In April 1991, United Nations (UN) Resolution 687 set the terms of the peace, with long-term implications. Its concluding paragraph authorizing the UN to take such steps as necessary to maintain the peace was later taken as the legal justification for the further use of force, as in 1996 and 1998, when Iraq was again bombed. It was also referenced in the lead-up to the second invasion of Iraq in 2003, when it appeared that Iraq was refusing to comply with other UN resolutions.

A CHANGING DOMESTIC LANDSCAPE

By nearly every measure, Operation Desert Storm was a resounding success. Through deft diplomatic efforts on the international stage, Bush had ensured that many around the world saw the action as legitimate. By making the goals of the military action both clear and limited, he also reassured an American public still skeptical of foreign entanglements. With the Soviet Union vanishing from the world stage, and the United States demonstrating the extent of its diplomatic influence and military potency with President Bush at the helm, his reelection seemed all but inevitable. Indeed, in March 1991, the president had an approval rating of 89 percent.

Despite Bush's successes internationally, the domestic situation at home was far more complicated. Unlike Reagan, Bush was not a natural culture warrior. Rather, he was a moderate, Connecticut-born Episcopalian, a pragmatic politician, and a life-long civil servant. He was not adept at catering to post-Reagan conservatives as his predecessor had been. By the same token, he appeared incapable of capitalizing on his history of moderation and pragmatism regarding women's rights and access to abortion. Together with a Democratic Senate, Bush broke new ground in civil rights with his support of the Americans with Disabilities Act, a far-reaching law that prohibited discrimination based on disability in public accommodations and by employers.

President Bush's weaknesses as a culture warrior were on full display during the controversy that erupted following his nomination of a new Supreme Court judge. In 1991, Justice Thurgood Marshall, the first African American ever to sit on the Supreme Court, opted to retire, thus opening a position on the court. Thinking he was doing the prudent thing by appealing to multiple interests, Bush nominated Clarence Thomas, another African American but also a strong social conservative. The decision to nominate Thomas, however, proved to be anything but prudent. During Thomas' confirmation hearings before the Senate Judiciary Committee, Anita Hill, a lawyer who had worked for Thomas when he was chairman of the Equal Employment Opportunity Commission (EEOC), came forward with allegations that he had sexually harassed her when he was her supervisor. Thomas denied the accusations and referred to the televised hearings as a "high tech lynching." He survived the controversy and was appointed to the Supreme Court by a narrow Senate vote of fifty-two to forty-eight. Hill, also African American, noted later in frustration: "I had a gender, he had a race." In the aftermath, however, sexual harassment of women in the workplace gained public attention, and harassment complaints made to the EEOC increased 50 percent by the fall of 1992. The controversy also reflected poorly on President Bush and may have hurt him with female voters in 1992.

31.4 Bill Clinton and the New Economy

By the end of this section, you will be able to:
- Explain political partisanship, antigovernment movements, and economic developments during the Clinton administration
- Discuss President Clinton's foreign policy
- Explain how George W. Bush won the election of 2000

By 1992, many had come to doubt that President George H. W. Bush could solve America's problems. He had alienated conservative Republicans by breaking his pledge not to raise taxes, and some faulted him for failing to remove Saddam Hussein from power during Operation Desert Storm. Furthermore, despite living much of his adult life in Texas, he could not overcome the stereotypes associated with his privileged New England and Ivy League background, which hurt him among working-class Reagan Democrats.

THE ROAD TO THE WHITE HOUSE

The contrast between George H. W. Bush and William Jefferson Clinton could not have been greater. Bill Clinton was a baby boomer born in 1946 in Hope, Arkansas. His biological father died in a car wreck three months before he was born. When he was a boy, his mother married Roger Clinton, an alcoholic who abused his family. However, despite a troubled home life, Clinton was an excellent student. He took an interest in politics from an early age. On a high school trip to Washington, DC, he met his political idol, President John F. Kennedy. As a student at Georgetown University, he supported both the civil rights and antiwar movements and ran for student council president (Figure 31.14).

Figure 31.14 During his 1967 campaign for student council president at Georgetown University, Bill Clinton told those who voted for him that he would invite them to the White House when he became president of the United States. He kept his promise.

In 1968, Clinton received a prestigious Rhodes scholarship to Oxford University. From Oxford he moved on to Yale, where he earned his law degree in 1973. He returned to Arkansas and became a professor at the University of Arkansas's law school. The following year, he tried his hand at state politics, running for Congress, and was narrowly defeated. In 1977, he became attorney general of Arkansas and was elected governor in 1978. Losing the office to his Republican opponent in 1980, he retook the governor's mansion in 1982 and remained governor of Arkansas until 1992, when he announced his candidacy for president.

During his campaign, Bill Clinton described himself as a New Democrat, a member of a faction of the Democratic Party that, like the Republicans, favored free trade and deregulation. He tried to appeal to the middle class by promising higher taxes on the rich and reform of the welfare system. Although Clinton garnered only 43 percent of the popular vote, he easily won in the Electoral College with 370 votes to President Bush's 188. Texas billionaire H. Ross Perot won 19 percent of the popular vote, the best showing by any third-party candidate since 1912. The Democrats took control of both houses of Congress.

"IT'S THE ECONOMY, STUPID"

Clinton took office towards the end of a recession. His administration's plans for fixing the economy included limiting spending and cutting the budget to reduce the nation's $60 billion deficit, keeping interest rates low to encourage private investment, and eliminating protectionist tariffs. Clinton also hoped to improve employment opportunities by allocating more money for education. In his first term, he expanded the Earned Income Tax Credit, which lowered the tax obligations of working families who were just above the poverty line. Addressing the budget deficit, the Democrats in Congress passed the Omnibus Budget Reconciliation Act of 1993 without a single Republican vote. The act raised taxes for the top 1.2 percent of the American people, lowered them for fifteen million low-income families, and offered tax breaks to 90 percent of small businesses.

Clinton also strongly supported ratification of the North American Free Trade Agreement (NAFTA), a treaty that eliminated tariffs and trade restrictions among the United States, Canada, and Mexico. The treaty had been negotiated by the Bush administration, and the leaders of all three nations had signed it in December 1992. However, because of strong opposition from American labor unions and some in Congress who feared the loss of jobs to Mexico, the treaty had not been ratified by the time Clinton took office. To allay the concerns of unions, he added an agreement to protect workers and also one to protect the environment. Congress ratified NAFTA late in 1993. The result was the creation of the world's largest common market in terms of population, including some 425 million people.

During Clinton's administration, the nation began to experience the longest period of economic expansion in its history, almost ten consecutive years. Year after year, job growth increased and the deficit shrank. Increased tax revenue and budget cuts turned the annual national budget deficit from close to $290 billion in 1992 to a record budget surplus of over $230 billion in 2000. Reduced government borrowing freed up capital for private-sector use, and lower interest rates in turn fueled more growth. During the Clinton years, more people owned homes than ever before in the country's history (67.7 percent). Inflation dipped to 2.3 percent and the unemployment rate declined, reaching a thirty-year low of 3.9 percent in 2000.

Much of the prosperity of the 1990s was related to technological change and the advent of new information systems. In 1994, the Clinton administration became the first to launch an official White House website and join the revolution of the electronically mediated world. By the 1990s, a new world of instantaneous global exposure was at the fingertips of billions worldwide.

AMERICANA

✿ *Hope and Anxiety in the Information Age*

While the roots of innovations like personal computers and the Internet go back to the 1960s and massive Department of Defense spending, it was in the 1980s and 90s that these technologies became part of everyday life. Like most technology-driven periods of transformation, the information age was greeted with a mixture of hope and anxiety upon its arrival.

In the late 1970s and early 1980s, computer manufacturers like Apple, Commodore, and Tandy began offering fully assembled personal computers. (Previously, personal computing had been accessible only to those adventurous enough to buy expensive kits that had to be assembled and programmed.) In short order, computers became a fairly common sight in businesses and upper-middle-class homes (Figure 31.15). Soon, computer owners, even young kids, were launching their own electronic bulletin board systems, small-scale networks that used modems and phone lines, and sharing information in ways not dreamed of just decades before. Computers, it seemed, held out the promise of a bright, new future for those who knew how to use them.

Figure 31.15   This ad for the Apple II appeared in *Byte* magazine in 1977.

Casting shadows over the bright dreams of a better tomorrow were fears that the development of computer technology would create a dystopian future in which technology became the instrument of society's undoing. Film audiences watched a teenaged Matthew Broderick hacking into a government computer and starting a nuclear war in *War Games*, Angelina Jolie being chased by a computer genius bent on world domination in *Hackers*, and Sandra Bullock watching helplessly as her life is turned inside out by conspirators who manipulate her virtual identity in *The Net*. Clearly, the idea of digital network connections as the root of our demise resonated in this period of rapid technological change.

DOMESTIC ISSUES

In addition to shifting the Democratic Party to the moderate center on economic issues, Clinton tried to break new ground on a number of domestic issues and make good on traditional Democratic commitments to the disadvantaged, minority groups, and women. At the same time, he faced the challenge of domestic terrorism when a federal building in Oklahoma City was bombed, killing 168 people and injuring hundreds more.

Healthcare Reform

An important and popular part of Clinton's domestic agenda was healthcare reform that would make universal healthcare a reality. When the plan was announced in September of the president's first year in office, pollsters and commentators both assumed it would sail through. Many were unhappy with the way the system worked in the United States, where the cost of health insurance seemed increasingly unaffordable for the middle class. Clinton appointed his wife, Hillary Clinton, a Yale Law School graduate and accomplished attorney, to head his Task Force on National Health Care Reform in 1993. The 1,342-page Health Security Act presented to Congress that year sought to offer universal coverage (Figure 31.16). All Americans were to be covered by a healthcare plan that could not reject them based on pre-existing medical conditions. Employers would be required to provide healthcare for their employees. Limits would be placed on the amount that people would have to pay for services; the poor would not have to pay at all.

Figure 31.16 C. Everett Koop, who had served as surgeon general under Ronald Reagan and was a strong advocate of healthcare reform, helped First Lady Hillary Clinton promote the Health Security Act in the fall of 1993.

The outlook for the plan looked good in 1993; it had the support of a number of institutions like the American Medical Association and the Health Insurance Association of America. But in relatively short order, the political winds changed. As budget battles distracted the administration and the midterm elections of 1994 approached, Republicans began to recognize the strategic benefits of opposing reform. Soon they were mounting fierce opposition to the bill. Moderate conservatives dubbed the reform proposals "Hillarycare" and argued that the bill was an unwarranted expansion of the powers of the federal government that would interfere with people's ability to choose the healthcare provider they wanted. Those further to the right argued that healthcare reform was part of a larger and nefarious plot to control the public.

To rally Republican opposition to Clinton and the Democrats, Newt Gingrich and Richard "Dick" Armey, two of the leaders of the Republican minority in the House of Representatives, prepared a document entitled **Contract with America**, signed by all but two of the Republican representatives. It listed eight specific legislative reforms or initiatives the Republicans would enact if they gained a majority in Congress in the 1994 midterm elections.

Click and Explore

View the **Contract with America (http://openstaxcollege.org/l/15ContractAm)** that the Republican Party drafted to continue the conservative shift begun by Ronald Reagan, which promised to cut waste and spend taxpayer money responsibly.

Lacking support on both sides, the healthcare bill was never passed and died in Congress. The reform effort finally ended in September 1994. Dislike of the proposed healthcare plan on the part of conservatives and the bold strategy laid out in the Contract with America enabled the Republican Party to win seven Senate seats and fifty-two House seats in the November elections. The Republicans then used their power to push for conservative reforms. One such piece of legislation was the Personal Responsibility and Work Opportunity Reconciliation Act, signed into law in August 1996. The act set time limits on welfare benefits and required most recipients to begin working within two years of receiving assistance.

Don't Ask, Don't Tell

Although Clinton had campaigned as an economically conservative New Democrat, he was thought to be socially liberal and, just days after his victory in the 1992 election, he promised to end the fifty-year ban on gays and lesbians serving in the military. However, in January 1993, after taking the oath of office, Clinton amended his promise in order to appease conservatives. Instead of lifting the longstanding ban, the armed forces would adopt a policy of "don't ask, don't tell." Those on active duty would not be asked their sexual orientation and, if they were gay, they were not to discuss their sexuality openly or they would be dismissed from military service. This compromise satisfied neither conservatives seeking the exclusion of gays nor the gay community, which argued that homosexuals, like heterosexuals, should be able to live without fear of retribution because of their sexuality.

Clinton again proved himself willing to appease political conservatives when he signed into law the Defense of Marriage Act (DOMA) in September 1996, after both houses of Congress had passed it with such wide margins that a presidential veto could easily be overridden. DOMA defined marriage as a heterosexual union and denied federal benefits to same-sex couples. It also allowed states to refuse to recognize same-sex marriages granted by other states. When Clinton signed the bill, he was personally opposed to same-sex marriage. Nevertheless, he disliked DOMA and later called for its repeal. He also later changed his position on same-sex marriage. On other social issues, however, Clinton was more liberal. He appointed openly gay and lesbian men and women to important positions in government and denounced discrimination against people with AIDS. He supported the idea of the ERA and believed that women should receive pay equal to that of men doing the same work. He opposed the use of racial quotas in employment, but he declared affirmative action programs to be necessary.

As a result of his economic successes and his moderate social policies, Clinton defeated Senator Robert Dole in the 1996 presidential election. With 49 percent of the popular vote and 379 electoral votes, he became the first Democrat to win reelection to the presidency since Franklin Roosevelt. Clinton's victory was partly due to a significant **gender gap** between the parties, with women tending to favor Democratic candidates. In 1992, Clinton won 45 percent of women's votes compared to Bush's 38 percent, and in 1996, he received 54 percent of women's votes while Dole won 38 percent.

Domestic Terrorism

The fears of those who saw government as little more than a necessary evil appeared to be confirmed in the spring of 1993, when federal and state law enforcement authorities laid siege to the compound of a religious sect called the Branch Davidians near Waco, Texas. The group, which believed the end of world was approaching, was suspected of weapons violations and resisted search-and-arrest warrants with deadly force. A standoff developed that lasted nearly two months and was captured on television each day. A final assault on the compound was made on April 19, and seventy-six men, women, and children died in a fire probably set by members of the sect. Many others committed suicide or were killed by fellow sect members.

During the siege, many antigovernment and militia types came to satisfy their curiosity or show support for those inside. One was Timothy McVeigh, a former U.S. Army infantry soldier. McVeigh had served in Operation Desert Storm in Iraq, earning a bronze star, but he became disillusioned with the military and the government when he was deemed psychologically unfit for the Army Special Forces. He was convinced that the Branch Davidians were victims of government terrorism, and he and his coconspirator, Terry Nichols, determined to avenge them.

Two years later, on the anniversary of the day that the Waco compound burned to the ground, McVeigh parked a rented truck full of explosives in front of the Alfred P. Murrah Federal Building in Oklahoma City and blew it up (Figure 31.17). More than 600 people were injured in the attack and 168 died, including nineteen children at the daycare center inside. McVeigh hoped that his actions would spark a revolution against government control. He and Nichols were both arrested and tried, and McVeigh was executed on June 11, 2001, for the worst act of terrorism committed on American soil. Just a few months later, the terrorist attacks of September 11, 2001 broke that dark record.

(a)   (b)

Figure 31.17 The remains of automobiles stand in front of the bombed federal building in Oklahoma City in 1995 (a). More than three hundred nearby buildings were damaged by the blast, an attack perpetrated at least partly to avenge the Waco siege (b) exactly two years earlier.

CLINTON AND AMERICAN HEGEMONY

For decades, the contours of the Cold War had largely determined U.S. action abroad. Strategists saw each coup, revolution, and civil war as part of the larger struggle between the United States and the Soviet Union. But with the Soviet Union vanquished, the United States was suddenly free of this paradigm, and President Clinton could see international crises in the Middle East, the Balkans, and Africa on their own terms and deal with them accordingly. He envisioned a post-Cold War role in which the United States used its overwhelming military superiority and influence as global policing tools to preserve the peace. This foreign policy strategy had both success and failure.

One notable success was a level of peace in the Middle East. In September 1993, at the White House, Yitzhak Rabin, prime minister of Israel, and Yasser Arafat, chairman of the Palestine Liberation Organization, signed the Oslo Accords, granting some self-rule to Palestinians living in the Israeli-occupied territories of the Gaza Strip and the West Bank (Figure 31.18). A year later, the Clinton administration helped facilitate the second settlement and normalization of relations between Israel and Jordan.

Figure 31.18 Yitzhak Rabin (left) and Yasser Arafat (right), shown with Bill Clinton, signed the Oslo Accords at the White House on September 13, 1993. Rabin was killed two years later by an Israeli who opposed the treaty.

As a small measure of stability was brought to the Middle East, violence erupted in the Balkans. The Communist country of Yugoslavia consisted of six provinces: Serbia, Croatia, Bosnia and Herzegovina, Slovenia, Montenegro, and Macedonia. Each was occupied by a number of ethnic groups, some of which shared a history of hostile relations. In May 1980, the leader of Yugoslavia, Josip Broz Tito, died. Without him to hold the country together, ethnic tensions increased, and this, along with the breakdown of Communism elsewhere in Europe, led to the breakup of Yugoslavia. In 1991, Croatia, Slovenia, and Macedonia declared their independence. In 1992, Bosnia and Herzegovina did as well. Only Serbia and Montenegro remained united as the Serbian-dominated Federal Republic of Yugoslavia.

Almost immediately, ethnic tensions within Bosnia and Herzegovina escalated into war when Yugoslavian Serbs aided Bosnian Serbs who did not wish to live in an independent Bosnia and Herzegovina. These Bosnian Serbs proclaimed the existence of autonomous Serbian regions within the country and attacked Bosnian Muslims and Croats. During the conflict, the Serbs engaged in genocide, described by some as "ethnic cleansing." The brutal conflict also gave rise to the systematic rape of "enemy" women—generally Muslim women exploited by Serbian military or paramilitary forces. The International Criminal Tribunal of Yugoslavia estimated that between twelve thousand and fifty thousand women were raped during the war.

NATO eventually intervened in 1995, and Clinton agreed to U.S. participation in airstrikes against Bosnian Serbs. That year, the Dayton Accords peace settlement was signed in Dayton, Ohio. Four years later, the United States, acting with other NATO members, launched an air campaign against Serbian-dominated Yugoslavia to stop it from attacking ethnic Albanians in Kosovo. Although these attacks were not sanctioned by the UN and were criticized by Russia and China, Yugoslavia withdrew its forces from Kosovo in June 1999.

The use of force did not always bring positive results. For example, back in December 1992, George H. W. Bush had sent a contingent of U.S. soldiers to Somalia, initially to protect and distribute relief supplies to civilians as part of a UN mission. Without an effective Somali government, however, the warlords who controlled different regions often stole food, and their forces endangered the lives of UN workers. In 1993, the Clinton administration sent soldiers to capture one of the warlords, Mohammed Farah Aidid, in the city of Mogadishu. The resulting battle proved disastrous. A Black Hawk helicopter was shot down, and

U.S. Army Rangers and members of Delta Force spent hours battling their way through the streets; eighty-four soldiers were wounded and nineteen died. The United States withdrew, leaving Somalia to struggle with its own anarchy.

The sting of the Somalia failure probably contributed to Clinton's reluctance to send U.S. forces to end the 1994 genocide in Rwanda. In the days of brutal colonial rule, Belgian administrators had given control to Tutsi tribal chiefs, although Hutus constituted a majority of the population. Resentment over ethnic privileges, and the discrimination that began then and continued after independence in 1962, erupted into civil war in 1980. The Hutu majority began to slaughter the Tutsi minority and their Hutu supporters. In 1998, while visiting Rwanda, Clinton apologized for having done nothing to save the lives of the 800,000 massacred in one hundred days of genocidal slaughter.

IMPEACHMENT

Public attention was diverted from Clinton's foreign policing actions by a series of scandals that marked the last few years of his presidency. From the moment he entered national politics, his opponents had attempted to tie Clinton and his First Lady to a number of loosely defined improprieties, even accusing him of murdering his childhood friend and Deputy White House Counsel Vince Foster. One accusation the Clintons could not shake was of possible improper involvement in a failed real estate venture associated with the Whitewater Development Corporation in Arkansas in the 1970s and 1980s. Kenneth Starr, a former federal appeals court judge, was appointed to investigate the matter in August 1994.

While Starr was never able to prove any wrongdoing, he soon turned up other allegations and his investigative authority was expanded. In May 1994, Paula Jones, a former Arkansas state employee, filed a sexual harassment lawsuit against Bill Clinton. Starr's office began to investigate this case as well. When a federal court dismissed Jones's suit in 1998, her lawyers promptly appealed the decision and submitted a list of other alleged victims of Clinton's harassment. That list included the name of Monica Lewinsky, a young White House intern. Both Lewinsky and Clinton denied under oath that they had had a sexual relationship. The evidence, however, indicated otherwise, and Starr began to investigate the possibility that Clinton had committed perjury. Again, Clinton denied any relationship and even went on national television to assure the American people that he had never had sexual relations with Lewinsky.

However, after receiving a promise of immunity, Lewinsky turned over to Starr evidence of her affair with Clinton, and the president admitted he had indeed had inappropriate relations with her. He nevertheless denied that he had lied under oath. In September, Starr reported to the House of Representatives that he believed Clinton had committed perjury. Voting along partisan lines, the Republican-dominated House of Representatives sent articles of impeachment to the Senate, charging Clinton with lying under oath and obstructing justice. In February 1998, the Senate voted forty-five to fifty-five on the perjury charge and fifty-fifty on obstruction of justice (Figure 31.19). Although acquitted, Clinton did become the first president to be found in contempt of court. Nevertheless, although he lost his law license, he remained a popular president and left office at the end of his second term with an approval rating of 66 percent, the highest of any U.S. president.

Figure 31.19 Floor proceedings in the U.S. Senate during the 1998 impeachment trial of Bill Clinton, who was narrowly acquitted of both charges.

THE ELECTION OF 2000

Despite Clinton's high approval rating, his vice president and the 2000 Democratic nominee for president, Al Gore, was eager to distance himself from scandal. Unfortunately, he also alienated Clinton loyalists and lost some of the benefit of Clinton's genuine popularity. Gore's desire to emphasize his concern for morality led him to select Connecticut senator Joseph I. Lieberman as his running mate. Lieberman had been quick to denounce Clinton's relationship with Monica Lewinsky. Consumer advocate Ralph Nader ran as the candidate of the **Green Party**, a party devoted to environmental issues and grassroots activism, and Democrats feared that he would attract votes that Gore might otherwise win.

On the Republican side, where strategists promised to "restore honor and dignity" to the White House, voters were divided between George W. Bush, governor of Texas and eldest son of former president Bush, and John McCain, an Arizona senator and Vietnam War veteran. Bush had the robust support of both the Christian Right and the Republican leadership. His campaign amassed large donations that it used to defeat McCain, himself an outspoken critic of the influence of money in politics. The nomination secured, Bush selected Dick Cheney, part of the Nixon and Ford administrations and secretary of defense under George H. W. Bush, as his running mate.

One hundred million votes were cast in the 2000 election, and Gore topped Bush in the popular vote by 540,000 ballots, or 0.5 percent. The race was so close that news reports declared each candidate the winner at various times during the evening. It all came down to Florida, where early returns called the election in Bush's favor by a mere 527 of 5,825,000 votes. Whoever won Florida would get the state's twenty-five electoral votes and secure the presidency (Figure 31.20).

Download for free at http://cnx.org/content/col11740/latest/

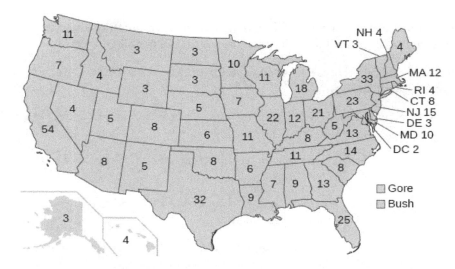

Figure 31.20 The map shows the results of the 2000 U.S. presidential election. While Bush won in the majority of states, Gore dominated in the more populous ones, winning the popular vote overall.

Because there seemed to be irregularities in four counties traditionally dominated by Democrats, especially in largely African American precincts, Gore called for a recount of the ballots by hand. Florida's secretary of state, Katherine Harris, set a deadline for the new vote tallies to be submitted, a deadline the counties could not meet. When the Democrats requested an extension, the Florida Supreme Court granted it, but Harris refused to accept the new tallies unless the counties could explain why they had not met the original deadline. When the explanations were submitted, they were rejected. Gore then asked the Florida Supreme Court for an injunction that would prevent Harris from declaring a winner until the recount was finished. On November 26, Harris declared Bush the winner in Florida. Gore protested that not all votes had been recounted by hand. When the Florida Supreme Court ordered the recount to continue, the Republicans appealed to the U.S. Supreme Court, which decided 5–4 to stop the recount. Bush received Florida's electoral votes and, with a total of 271 votes in the Electoral College to Gore's 266, became the forty-third president of the United States.

Key Terms

Contract with America a list of eight specific legislative reforms or initiatives that Republicans representatives promised to enact if they gained a majority in Congress in the 1994 midterm elections

gender gap the statistical differences between the voting preferences of women and men, with women favoring Democratic candidates

Green Party a political party founded in 1984 that advocates environmentalism and grassroots democracy

Heritage Foundation a professional organization conducting research and political advocacy on behalf of its values and perspectives

HIV/AIDS a deadly immune deficiency disorder discovered in 1981, and at first largely ignored by politicians because of its prevalence among gay men

New Right a loose coalition of American conservatives, consisting primarily of wealthy businesspeople and evangelical Christians, which developed in response to social changes of the 1960s and 1970s

Operation Desert Storm the U.S. name of the war waged from January to April 1991, by coalition forces against Iraq in reaction to Iraq's invasion of Kuwait in August 1990

Reaganomics Ronald Reagan's economic policy, which suggested that lowering taxes on the upper income brackets would stimulate investment and economic growth

START a treaty between the United States and the Soviet Union that limited the number of nuclear warheads, ballistic missiles, and strategic bombers held by both sides

Vietnam Syndrome reluctance on the part of American politicians to actively engage U.S. forces in a foreign war for fear of suffering a humiliating defeat

war on drugs a nationwide political campaign to implement harsh sentences for drug crimes, which produced an explosive growth of the prison population

Summary

31.1 The Reagan Revolution

After decades of liberalism and social reform, Ronald Reagan changed the face of American politics by riding a groundswell of conservatism into the White House. Reagan's superior rhetorical skills enabled him to gain widespread support for his plans for the nation. Implementing a series of economic policies dubbed "Reaganomics," the president sought to stimulate the economy while shrinking the size of the federal government and providing relief for the nation's wealthiest taxpayers. During his two terms in office, he cut spending on social programs, while increasing spending on defense. While Reagan was able to break the cycle of stagflation, his policies also triggered a recession, plunged the nation into a brief period of significant unemployment, and made a balanced budget impossible. In the end, Reagan's policies diminished many Americans' quality of life while enabling more affluent Americans—the "Yuppies" of the 1980s—to prosper.

31.2 Political and Cultural Fusions

The political conservatism of the 1980s and 1990s was matched by the social conservatism of the period. Conservative politicians wished to limit the size and curb the power of the federal government.

Download for free at http://cnx.org/content/col11740/latest/

Conservative think tanks flourished, the Christian Right defeated the ERA, and bipartisan efforts to add warning labels to explicit music lyrics were the subject of Congressional hearings. HIV/AIDS, which became chiefly and inaccurately associated with the gay community, grew to crisis proportions, as heterosexuals and the federal government failed to act. In response, gay men organized advocacy groups to fight for research on HIV/AIDS. Meanwhile, the so-called war on drugs began a get-tough trend in law enforcement that mandated lengthy sentences for drug-related offenses and hugely increased the American prison population.

31.3 A New World Order

While Ronald Reagan worked to restrict the influence of the federal government in people's lives, he simultaneously pursued interventionist policies abroad as part of a global Cold War strategy. Eager to cure the United States of "Vietnam Syndrome," he increased the American stockpile of weapons and aided anti-Communist groups in the Caribbean and Central America. The Reagan administration's secret sales of arms to Iran proved disastrous, however, and resulted in indictments for administration officials. With the end of the Cold War, attention shifted to escalating tensions in the Middle East, where an international coalition assembled by George H. W. Bush drove invading Iraqi forces from Kuwait. As Bush discovered in the last years of his presidency, even this almost-flawless exercise in international diplomatic and military power was not enough to calm a changing cultural and political climate at home.

31.4 Bill Clinton and the New Economy

Bill Clinton's presidency and efforts at remaking the Democratic Party reflect the long-term effects of the Reagan Revolution that preceded him. Reagan benefited from a resurgent conservatism that moved the American political spectrum several degrees to the right. Clinton managed to remake the Democratic Party in ways that effectively institutionalized some of the major tenets of the so-called Reagan Revolution. A "New Democrat," he moved the party significantly to the moderate center and supported the Republican call for law and order, and welfare reform—all while maintaining traditional Democratic commitments to minorities, women, and the disadvantaged, and using the government to stimulate economic growth. Nevertheless, Clinton's legacy was undermined by the shift in the control of Congress to the Republican Party and the loss by his vice president Al Gore in the 2000 presidential election.

Review Questions

1. Before becoming a conservative Republican, Ronald Reagan was _____.
- A.   a liberal Democrat
- B.   a Socialist
- C.   politically apathetic
- D.   a Herbert Hoover Republican

2. The belief that cutting taxes for the rich will eventually result in economic benefits for the poor is commonly referred to as _____.
- A.   socialism
- B.   pork barrel politics
- C.   Keynesian economics
- D.   trickle-down economics

3. What were the elements of Ronald Reagan's plan for economic reform?

4. Which statement best describes Reagan's political style?
- A.   folksy and likeable
- B.   conservative and inflexible
- C.   liberal and pragmatic
- D.   intelligent and elitist

5. What rationale did Phyllis Schlafly and her STOP ERA movement cite when opposing the ratification of the Equal Rights Amendment?
- A.   the ERA would ultimately lead to the legalization of abortion
- B.   the ERA provided insufficient civil rights protections for women
- C.   mothers could not be feminists
- D.   the ERA would end gender-specific privileges women enjoyed

6. What were some of the primary values of the Moral Majority?

7. The group the Reagan administration encouraged and supported in its fight against the Sandinista government in Nicaragua was known as the _____.
  A. anti-Somozas
  B. Shining Path
  C. Contras
  D. Red Faction

8. The country that Iraq invaded to trigger the crisis that resulted in the Persian Gulf War was

_____.
  A. Jordan
  B. Kuwait
  C. Saudi Arabia
  D. Iran

9. What was the Iran-Contra affair about?

10. Bill Clinton helped create a large free market among Canada, the United States, and Mexico with ratification of the _____ treaty.
  A. NAFTA
  B. NATO
  C. Organization of American States
  D. Alliance for Progress

11. The key state in the 2000 election where the U.S. Supreme Court stopped a recount of votes was _____.
  A. Florida
  B. Texas
  C. Georgia
  D. Virginia

12. What were some of the foreign policy successes of the Clinton administration?

Critical Thinking Questions

13. What were some of the long-term effects of the Reagan Revolution and the rise of conservatives?

14. What events led to the end of the Cold War? What impact did the end of the Cold War have on American politics and foreign policy concerns?

15. Which issues divided Americans most significantly during the culture wars of the 1980s and 1990s?

16. In what ways was Bill Clinton a traditional Democrat in the style of Kennedy and Johnson? In what ways was he a conservative, like Ronald Reagan and George H. W. Bush?

17. Describe American involvement in global affairs during this period. How did American foreign policy change and evolve between 1980 and 2000, in both its focus and its approach?

CHAPTER 32

The Challenges of the Twenty-First Century

Figure 32.1 In 2001, almost three thousand people died as a result of the September 11 attacks, when members of the terrorist group al-Qaeda hijacked four planes as part of a coordinated attack on sites in New York City and Washington, DC.

Chapter Outline

32.1 The War on Terror
32.2 The Domestic Mission
32.3 New Century, Old Disputes
32.4 Hope and Change

Introduction

On the morning of September 11, 2001, hopes that the new century would leave behind the conflicts of the previous one were dashed when two hijacked airliners crashed into the twin towers of New York's World Trade Center. When the first plane struck the north tower, many assumed that the crash was a horrific accident. But then a second plane hit the south tower less than thirty minutes later. People on the street watched in horror, as some of those trapped in the burning buildings jumped to their deaths and the enormous towers collapsed into dust. In the photo above, the Statue of Liberty appears to look on helplessly, as thick plumes of smoke obscure the Lower Manhattan skyline (Figure 32.1). The events set in motion by the September 11 attacks would raise fundamental questions about the United States' role in the world, the extent to which privacy should be protected at the cost of security, the definition of exactly who is an American, and the cost of liberty.

32.1 The War on Terror

By the end of this section, you will be able to:
- Discuss how the United States responded to the terrorist attacks of September 11, 2001
- Explain why the United States went to war against Afghanistan and Iraq
- Describe the treatment of suspected terrorists by U.S. law enforcement agencies and the U.S. military

As a result of the narrow decision of the U.S. Supreme Court in *Bush v. Gore*, Republican George W. Bush was the declared the winner of the 2000 presidential election with a majority in the Electoral College of 271 votes to 266, although he received approximately 540,000 fewer popular votes nationally than his Democratic opponent, Bill Clinton's vice president, Al Gore. Bush had campaigned with a promise of "compassionate conservatism" at home and nonintervention abroad. These platform planks were designed to appeal to those who felt that the Clinton administration's initiatives in the Balkans and Africa had unnecessarily entangled the United States in the conflicts of foreign nations. Bush's 2001 education reform act, dubbed No Child Left Behind, had strong bipartisan support and reflected his domestic interests. But before the president could sign the bill into law, the world changed when terrorists hijacked four American airliners to use them in the deadliest attack on the United States since the Japanese bombing of Pearl Harbor in December 1941. Bush's domestic agenda quickly took a backseat, as the president swiftly changed course from nonintervention in foreign affairs to a "war on terror."

9/11

Shortly after takeoff on the morning of September 11, 2001, teams of hijackers from the Islamist terrorist group **al-Qaeda** seized control of four American airliners. Two of the airplanes were flown into the twin towers of the World Trade Center in Lower Manhattan. Morning news programs that were filming the

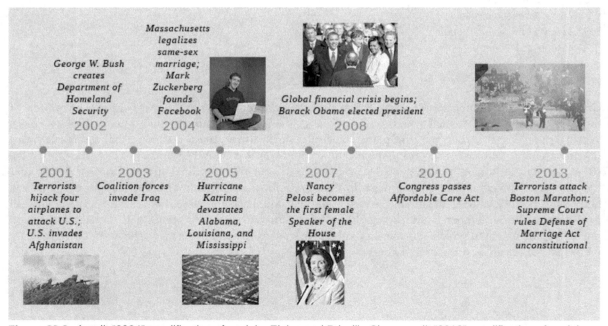

George W. Bush creates Department of Homeland Security
2002

Massachusetts legalizes same-sex marriage; Mark Zuckerberg founds Facebook
2004

Global financial crisis begins; Barack Obama elected president
2008

2001
Terrorists hijack four airplanes to attack U.S.; U.S. invades Afghanistan

2003
Coalition forces invade Iraq

2005
Hurricane Katrina devastates Alabama, Louisiana, and Mississippi

2007
Nancy Pelosi becomes the first female Speaker of the House

2010
Congress passes Affordable Care Act

2013
Terrorists attack Boston Marathon; Supreme Court rules Defense of Marriage Act unconstitutional

Figure 32.2 (credit "2004": modification of work by Elaine and Priscilla Chan; credit "2013": modification of work by Aaron Tang; credit "2001": modification of work by "DVIDSHUB"/Flickr)

moments after the first impact, then assumed to be an accident, captured and aired live footage of the second plane, as it barreled into the other tower in a flash of fire and smoke. Less than two hours later, the heat from the crash and the explosion of jet fuel caused the upper floors of both buildings to collapse onto the lower floors, reducing both towers to smoldering rubble. The passengers and crew on both planes, as well as 2,606 people in the two buildings, all died, including 343 New York City firefighters who rushed in to save victims shortly before the towers collapsed.

The third hijacked plane was flown into the Pentagon building in northern Virginia, just outside Washington, DC, killing everyone on board and 125 people on the ground. The fourth plane, also heading towards Washington, crashed in a field near Shanksville, Pennsylvania, when passengers, aware of the other attacks, attempted to storm the cockpit and disarm the hijackers. Everyone on board was killed (Figure 32.3).

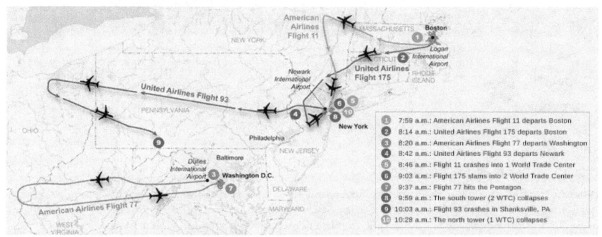

Figure 32.3   Three of the four airliners hijacked on September 11, 2001, reached their targets. United 93, presumably on its way to destroy either the Capitol or the White House, was brought down in a field after a struggle between the passengers and the hijackers.

That evening, President Bush promised the nation that those responsible for the attacks would be brought to justice. Three days later, Congress issued a joint resolution authorizing the president to use all means necessary against the individuals, organizations, or nations involved in the attacks. On September 20, in an address to a joint session of Congress, Bush declared war on terrorism, blamed al-Qaeda leader Osama bin Laden for the attacks, and demanded that the radical Islamic fundamentalists who ruled Afghanistan, the **Taliban**, turn bin Laden over or face attack by the United States. This speech encapsulated what became known as the **Bush Doctrine**, the belief that the United States has the right to protect itself from terrorist acts by engaging in pre-emptive wars or ousting hostile governments in favor of friendly, preferably democratic, regimes.

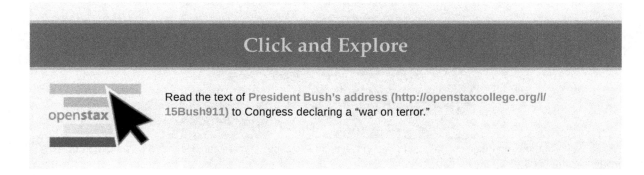

Click and Explore

Read the text of President Bush's address (http://openstaxcollege.org/l/15Bush911) to Congress declaring a "war on terror."

World leaders and millions of their citizens expressed support for the United States and condemned the deadly attacks. Russian president Vladimir Putin characterized them as a bold challenge to humanity itself. German chancellor Gerhard Schroder said the events of that day were "not only attacks on the people in the United States, our friends in America, but also against the entire civilized world, against our own freedom, against our own values, values which we share with the American people." Yasser Arafat, chairman of the Palestinian Liberation Organization and a veteran of several bloody struggles against Israel, was dumbfounded by the news and announced to reporters in Gaza, "We completely condemn this very dangerous attack, and I convey my condolences to the American people, to the American president and to the American administration."

Click and Explore

In May 2014, a Museum dedicated to the memory of the victims was completed. Watch this video (http://openstaxcollege.org/l/15CBSstory) and learn more about the victims and how the country seeks to remember them.

GOING TO WAR IN AFGHANISTAN

When it became clear that the mastermind behind the attack was Osama bin Laden, a wealthy Saudi Arabian national who ran his terror network from Afghanistan, the full attention of the United States turned towards Central Asia and the Taliban. Bin Laden had deep roots in Afghanistan. Like many others from around the Islamic world, he had come to the country to oust the Soviet army, which invaded Afghanistan in 1979. Ironically, both bin Laden and the Taliban received material support from the United States at that time. By the late 1980s, the Soviets and the Americans had both left, although bin Laden, by that time the leader of his own terrorist organization, al-Qaeda, remained.

The Taliban refused to turn bin Laden over, and the United States began a bombing campaign in October, allying with the Afghan Northern Alliance, a coalition of tribal leaders opposed to the Taliban. U.S. air support was soon augmented by ground troops (Figure 32.4). By November 2001, the Taliban had been ousted from power in Afghanistan's capital of Kabul, but bin Laden and his followers had already escaped across the Afghan border to mountain sanctuaries in northern Pakistan.

Figure 32.4 Marines fight against Taliban forces in Helmand Province, Afghanistan. Helmand was a center of Taliban strength. (credit: "DVIDSHUB"/Flickr)

Download for free at http://cnx.org/content/col11740/latest/

IRAQ

At the same time that the U.S. military was taking control of Afghanistan, the Bush administration was looking to a new and larger war with the country of Iraq. Relations between the United States and Iraq had been strained ever since the Gulf War a decade earlier. Economic sanctions imposed on Iraq by the United Nations, and American attempts to foster internal revolts against President Saddam Hussein's government, had further tainted the relationship. A faction within the Bush administration, sometimes labeled neoconservatives, believed Iraq's recalcitrance in the face of overwhelming U.S. military superiority represented a dangerous symbol to terrorist groups around the world, recently emboldened by the dramatic success of the al-Qaeda attacks in the United States. Powerful members of this faction, including Vice President Dick Cheney and Secretary of Defense Donald Rumsfeld, believed the time to strike Iraq and solve this festering problem was right then, in the wake of 9/11. Others, like Secretary of State Colin Powell, a highly respected veteran of the Vietnam War and former chair of the Joint Chiefs of Staff, were more cautious about initiating combat.

The more militant side won, and the argument for war was gradually laid out for the American people. The immediate impetus to the invasion, it argued, was the fear that Hussein was stockpiling weapons of mass destruction (**WMDs**): nuclear, chemical, or biological weapons capable of wreaking great havoc. Hussein had in fact used WMDs against Iranian forces during his war with Iran in the 1980s, and against the Kurds in northern Iraq in 1988—a time when the United States actively supported the Iraqi dictator. Following the Gulf War, inspectors from the United Nations Special Commission and International Atomic Energy Agency had in fact located and destroyed stockpiles of Iraqi weapons. Those arguing for a new Iraqi invasion insisted, however, that weapons still existed. President Bush himself told the nation in October 2002 that the United States was "facing clear evidence of peril, we cannot wait for the final proof—the smoking gun—that could come in the form of a mushroom cloud." The head of the United Nations Monitoring, Verification and Inspection Commission, Hanx Blix, dismissed these claims. Blix argued that while Saddam Hussein was not being entirely forthright, he did not appear to be in possession of WMDs. Despite Blix's findings and his own earlier misgivings, Powell argued in 2003 before the United Nations General Assembly that Hussein had violated UN resolutions. Much of his evidence relied on secret information provided by an informant that was later proven to be false. On March 17, 2003, the United States cut off all relations with Iraq. Two days later, in a coalition with Great Britain, Australia, and Poland, the United States began "Operation Iraqi Freedom" with an invasion of Iraq.

Other arguments supporting the invasion noted the ease with which the operation could be accomplished. In February 2002, some in the Department of Defense were suggesting the war would be "a cakewalk." In November, referencing the short and successful Gulf War of 1990–1991, Secretary of Defense Rumsfeld told the American people it was absurd, as some were claiming, that the conflict would degenerate into a long, drawn-out quagmire. "Five days or five weeks or five months, but it certainly isn't going to last any longer than that," he insisted. "It won't be a World War III." And, just days before the start of combat operations in 2003, Vice President Cheney announced that U.S. forces would likely "be greeted as liberators," and the war would be over in "weeks rather than months."

Early in the conflict, these predictions seemed to be coming true. The march into Bagdad went fairly smoothly. Soon Americans back home were watching on television as U.S. soldiers and the Iraqi people worked together to topple statues of the deposed leader Hussein around the capital. The reality, however, was far more complex. While American deaths had been few, thousands of Iraqis had died, and the seeds of internal strife and resentment against the United States had been sown. The United States was not prepared for a long period of occupation; it was also not prepared for the inevitable problems of law and order, or for the violent sectarian conflicts that emerged. Thus, even though Bush proclaimed a U.S. victory in May 2003, on the deck of the USS *Abraham Lincoln* with the banner "Mission Accomplished" prominently displayed behind him, the celebration proved premature by more than seven years (Figure 32.5).

Figure 32.5 President Bush gives the victory symbol on the aircraft carrier USS *Abraham Lincoln* in May 2003, after American troops had completed the capture of Iraq's capitol Baghdad. Yet, by the time the United States finally withdrew its forces from Iraq in 2011, nearly five thousand U.S. soldiers had died.

MY STORY

⚙ *Lt. General James Conway on the Invasion of Baghdad*

Lt. General James Conway, who commanded the First Marine Expeditionary Force in Iraq, answers a reporter's questions about civilian casualties during the 2003 invasion of Baghdad.

> "As a civilian in those early days, one definitely had the sense that the high command had expected something to happen which didn't. Was that a correct perception?"
> —We were told by our intelligence folks that the enemy is carrying civilian clothes in their packs because, as soon as the shooting starts, they're going put on their civilian clothes and they're going go home. Well, they put on their civilian clothes, but not to go home. They put on civilian clothes to blend with the civilians and shoot back at us. . . .
> "There's been some criticism of the behavior of the Marines at the Diyala bridge [across the Tigris River into Baghdad] in terms of civilian casualties."
> —Well, after the Third Battalion, Fourth Marines crossed, the resistance was not all gone. . . . They had just fought to take a bridge. They were being counterattacked by enemy forces. Some of the civilian vehicles that wound up with the bullet holes in them contained enemy fighters in uniform with weapons, some of them did not. Again, we're terribly sorry about the loss of any civilian life where civilians are killed in a battlefield setting. I will guarantee you, it was not the intent of those Marines to kill civilians. [The civilian casualties happened because the Marines] felt threatened, [and] they were having a tough time distinguishing from an enemy that [is violating] the laws of land warfare by going to civilian clothes, putting his own people at risk. All of those things, I think, [had an] impact [on the behavior of the Marines], and in the end it's very unfortunate that civilians died.

Who in your opinion bears primary responsibility for the deaths of Iraqi civilians?

DOMESTIC SECURITY

The attacks of September 11 awakened many to the reality that the end of the Cold War did not mean an end to foreign violent threats. Some Americans grew wary of alleged possible enemies in their midst and hate crimes against Muslim Americans—and those thought to be Muslims—surged in the aftermath.

Fearing that terrorists might strike within the nation's borders again, and aware of the chronic lack of cooperation among different federal law enforcement agencies, Bush created the Office of Homeland Security in October 2001. The next year, Congress passed the Homeland Security Act, creating the Department of Homeland Security, which centralized control over a number of different government functions in order to better control threats at home (Figure 32.6). The Bush administration also pushed the USA Patriot Act through Congress, which enabled law enforcement agencies to monitor citizens' e-mails and phone conversations without a warrant.

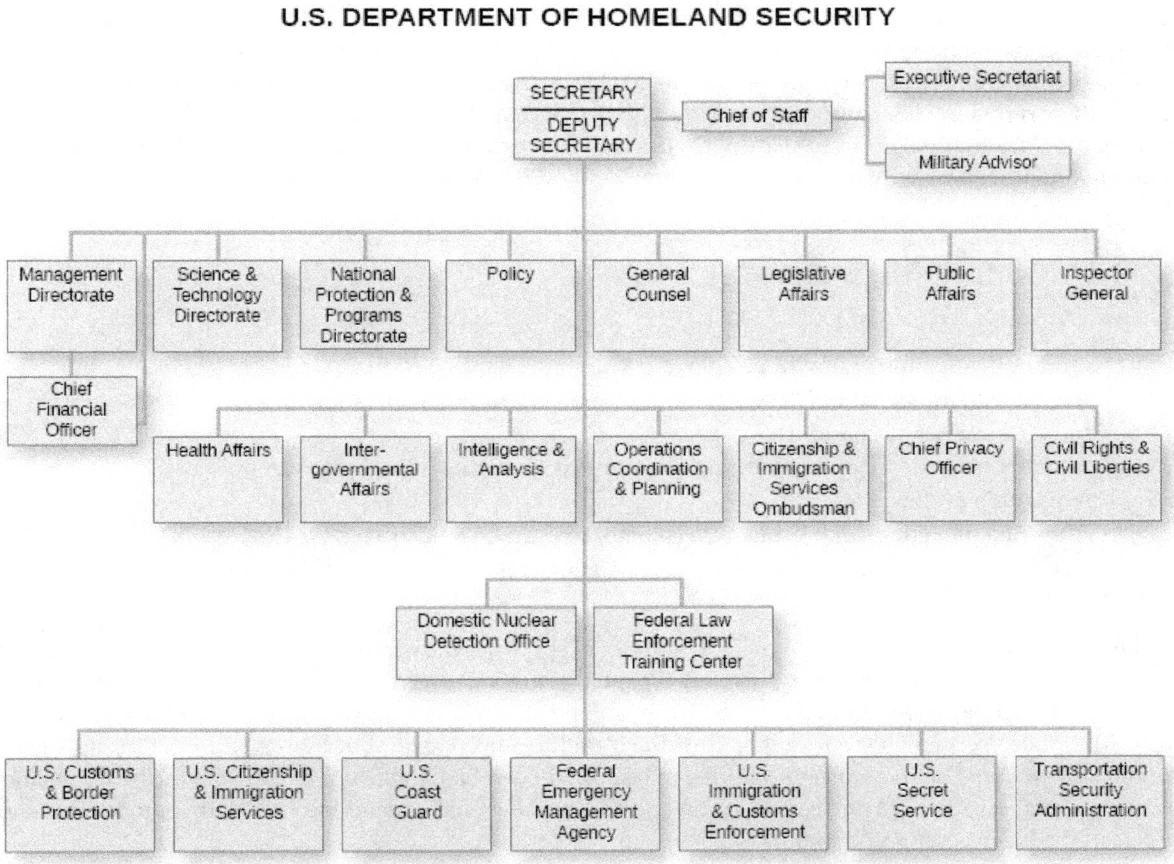

U.S. DEPARTMENT OF HOMELAND SECURITY

Figure 32.6 The Department of Homeland Security has many duties, including guarding U.S. borders and, as this organizational chart shows, wielding control over the Coast Guard, the Secret Service, U.S. Customs, and a multitude of other law enforcement agencies.

The Bush administration was fiercely committed to rooting out threats to the United States wherever they originated, and in the weeks after September 11, the Central Intelligence Agency (CIA) scoured the globe, sweeping up thousands of young Muslim men. Because U.S. law prohibits the use of torture, the CIA transferred some of these prisoners to other nations—a practice known as rendition or extraordinary rendition—where the local authorities can use methods of interrogation not allowed in the United States.

While the CIA operates overseas, the Federal Bureau of Investigation (FBI) is the chief federal law enforcement agency within U.S. national borders. Its activities are limited by, among other things, the Fourth Amendment, which protects citizens against unreasonable searches and seizures. Beginning in 2002, however, the Bush administration implemented a wide-ranging program of warrantless domestic wiretapping, known as the Terrorist Surveillance Program, by the National Security Agency (NSA). The shaky constitutional basis for this program was ultimately revealed in August 2006, when a federal judge in Detroit ordered the program ended immediately.

The use of unconstitutional wire taps to prosecute the war on terrorism was only one way the new threat challenged authorities in the United States. Another problem was deciding what to do with foreign terrorists captured on the battlefields in Afghanistan and Iraq. In traditional conflicts, where both sides are uniformed combatants, the rules of engagement and the treatment of prisoners of war are clear. But in the new war on terror, extracting intelligence about upcoming attacks became a top priority that superseded human rights and constitutional concerns. For that purpose, the United States began transporting men suspected of being members of al-Qaeda to the U.S. naval base at Guantanamo Bay, Cuba, for questioning. The Bush administration labeled the detainees "unlawful combatants," in an effort to avoid affording them the rights guaranteed to prisoners of war, such as protection from torture, by international treaties such as the Geneva Conventions. Furthermore, the Justice Department argued that the prisoners were unable to sue for their rights in U.S. courts on the grounds that the constitution did not apply to U.S. territories. It was only in 2006 that the Supreme Court ruled in *Hamdan v. Rumsfeld* that the military tribunals that tried Guantanamo prisoners violated both U.S. federal law and the Geneva Conventions.

32.2 The Domestic Mission

By the end of this section, you will be able to:
- Discuss the Bush administration's economic theories and tax policies, and their effects on the American economy
- Explain how the federal government attempted to improve the American public education system
- Describe the federal government's response to Hurricane Katrina
- Identify the causes of the Great Recession of 2008 and its effect on the average citizen

By the time George W. Bush became president, the concept of supply-side economics had become an article of faith within the Republican Party. The oft-repeated argument was that tax cuts for the wealthy would allow them to invest more and create jobs for everyone else. This belief in the self-regulatory powers of competition also served as the foundation of Bush's education reform. But by the end of 2008, however, Americans' faith in the dynamics of the free market had been badly shaken. The failure of the homeland security apparatus during Hurricane Katrina and the ongoing challenge of the Iraq War compounded the effects of the bleak economic situation.

OPENING AND CLOSING THE GAP

The Republican Party platform for the 2000 election offered the American people an opportunity to once again test the rosy expectations of supply-side economics. In 2001, Bush and the Republicans pushed through a $1.35 trillion tax cut by lowering tax rates across the board but reserving the largest cuts for those in the highest tax brackets. This was in the face of calls by Republicans for a balanced budget, which Bush insisted would happen when the so-called job creators expanded the economy by using their increased income to invest in business.

The cuts were controversial; the rich were getting richer while the middle and lower classes bore a proportionally larger share of the nation's tax burden. Between 1966 and 2001, one-half of the nation's income gained from increased productivity went to the top 0.01 percent of earners. By 2005, dramatic examples of income inequity were increasing; the chief executive of Wal-Mart earned $15 million that year, roughly 950 times what the company's average associate made. The head of the construction company K. B. Homes made $150 million, or four thousand times what the average construction worker earned that same year. Even as productivity climbed, workers' incomes stagnated; with a larger share of the wealth, the very rich further solidified their influence on public policy. Left with a smaller share of the economic pie, average workers had fewer resources to improve their lives or contribute to the nation's prosperity by, for example, educating themselves and their children.

Another gap that had been widening for years was the education gap. Some education researchers had argued that American students were being left behind. In 1983, a commission established by Ronald Reagan had published a sobering assessment of the American educational system entitled *A Nation at Risk*. The report argued that American students were more poorly educated than their peers in other countries, especially in areas such as math and science, and were thus unprepared to compete in the global marketplace. Furthermore, test scores revealed serious educational achievement gaps between white students and students of color. Touting himself as the "education president," Bush sought to introduce reforms that would close these gaps.

His administration offered two potential solutions to these problems. First, it sought to hold schools accountable for raising standards and enabling students to meet them. The No Child Left Behind Act, signed into law in January 2002, erected a system of testing to measure and ultimately improve student performance in reading and math at all schools that received federal funds (Figure 32.7). Schools whose students performed poorly on the tests would be labeled "in need of improvement." If poor performance continued, schools could face changes in curricula and teachers, or even the prospect of closure.

Figure 32.7 President Bush signed the No Child Left Behind Act into law in January 2002. The act requires school systems to set high standards for students, place "highly qualified" teachers in the classroom, and give military recruiters contact information for students.

The second proposed solution was to give students the opportunity to attend schools with better performance records. Some of these might be **charter schools**, institutions funded by local tax monies in much the same way as public schools, but able to accept private donations and exempt from some of the rules public schools must follow. During the administration of George H. W. Bush, the development of charter schools had gathered momentum, and the American Federation of Teachers welcomed them as places to employ innovative teaching methods or offer specialized instruction in particular subjects. President George W. Bush now encouraged states to grant educational funding vouchers to parents, who could use them to pay for a private education for their children if they chose. These vouchers were funded by tax revenue that would otherwise have gone to public schools.

THE 2004 ELECTION AND BUSH'S SECOND TERM

In the wake of the 9/11 attacks, Americans had rallied around their president in a gesture of patriotic loyalty, giving Bush approval ratings of 90 percent. Even following the first few months of the Iraq war, his approval rating remained historically high at approximately 70 percent. But as the 2004 election approached, opposition to the war in Iraq began to grow. While Bush could boast of a number of achievements at home and abroad during his first term, the narrow victory he achieved in 2000 augured poorly for his chances for reelection in 2004 and a successful second term.

Reelection

As the 2004 campaign ramped up, the president was persistently dogged by rising criticism of the violence of the Iraq war and the fact that his administration's claims of WMDs had been greatly overstated. In the end, no such weapons were ever found. These criticisms were amplified by growing international concern over the treatment of prisoners at the Guantanamo Bay detention camp and widespread disgust over the torture conducted by U.S. troops at the prison in Abu Ghraib, Iraq, which surfaced only months before the election (Figure 32.8).

(a)   (b)

Figure 32.8 The first twenty captives were processed at the Guantanamo Bay detention camp on January 11, 2002 (a). From late 2003 to early 2004, prisoners held in Abu Ghraib, Iraq, were tortured and humiliated in a variety of ways (b). U.S. soldiers jumped on and beat them, led them on leashes, made them pose naked, and urinated on them. The release of photographs of the abuse raised an outcry around the world and greatly diminished the already flagging support for American intervention in Iraq.

In March 2004, an ambush by Iraqi insurgents of a convoy of private military contractors from Blackwater USA in the town of Fallujah west of Baghdad, and the subsequent torture and mutilation of the four captured mercenaries, shocked the American public. But the event also highlighted the growing insurgency against U.S. occupation, the escalating sectarian conflict between the newly empowered Shia Muslims and the minority of the formerly ruling Sunni, and the escalating costs of a war involving a large number of private contractors that, by conservative estimates, approached $1.7 trillion by 2013. Just as importantly, the American campaign in Iraq had diverted resources from the war against al-Qaeda in Afghanistan, where U.S troops were no closer to capturing Osama bin Laden, the mastermind behind the 9/11 attacks.

With two hot wars overseas, one of which appeared to be spiraling out of control, the Democrats nominated a decorated Vietnam War veteran, Massachusetts senator John Kerry (Figure 32.9), to challenge Bush for the presidency. As someone with combat experience, three Purple Hearts, and a foreign policy background, Kerry seemed like the right challenger in a time of war. But his record of support for the invasion of Iraq made his criticism of the incumbent less compelling and earned him the byname "Waffler" from Republicans. The Bush campaign also sought to characterize Kerry as an elitist out of touch with regular Americans—Kerry had studied overseas, spoke fluent French, and married a wealthy foreign-born heiress. Republican supporters also unleashed an attack on Kerry's Vietnam War record, falsely claiming he had lied about his experience and fraudulently received his medals. Kerry's reluctance to embrace his past leadership of Vietnam Veterans Against the War weakened the enthusiasm of antiwar Americans while opening him up to criticisms from veterans groups. This combination compromised the impact of his challenge to the incumbent in a time of war.

Figure 32.9 John Kerry served in the U.S. Navy during the Vietnam War and represented Massachusetts in the U.S. Senate from 1985 to 2013. Here he greets sailors from the USS *Sampson*. Kerry was sworn in as President Obama's Secretary of State in 2013.

Urged by the Republican Party to "stay the course" with Bush, voters listened. Bush won another narrow victory, and the Republican Party did well overall, picking up four seats in the Senate and increasing its majority there to fifty-five. In the House, the Republican Party gained three seats, adding to its majority there as well. Across the nation, most governorships also went to Republicans, and Republicans dominated many state legislatures.

Despite a narrow win, the president made a bold declaration in his first news conference following the election. "I earned capital in this campaign, political capital, and now I intend to spend it." The policies on which he chose to spend this political capital included the partial privatization of Social Security and new limits on court-awarded damages in medical malpractice lawsuits. In foreign affairs, Bush promised that the United States would work towards "ending tyranny in the world." But at home and abroad, the president achieved few of his second-term goals. Instead, his second term in office became associated with the persistent challenge of pacifying Iraq, the failure of the homeland security apparatus during Hurricane Katrina, and the most severe economic crisis since the Great Depression.

A Failed Domestic Agenda

The Bush administration had planned a series of free-market reforms, but corruption, scandals, and Democrats in Congress made these goals hard to accomplish. Plans to convert Social Security into a private-market mechanism relied on the claim that demographic trends would eventually make the system unaffordable for the shrinking number of young workers, but critics countered that this was easily fixed. Privatization, on the other hand, threatened to derail the mission of the New Deal welfare agency and turn it into a fee generator for stock brokers and Wall Street financiers. Similarly unpopular was the attempt to abolish the estate tax. Labeled the "death tax" by its critics, its abolishment would have benefitted only the wealthiest 1 percent. As a result of the 2003 tax cuts, the growing federal deficit did not help make the case for Republicans.

The nation faced another policy crisis when the Republican-dominated House of Representatives approved a bill making the undocumented status of millions of immigrants a felony and criminalizing the act of employing or knowingly aiding illegal immigrants. In response, millions of illegal and legal immigrants, along with other critics of the bill, took to the streets in protest. What they saw as the civil rights challenge of their generation, conservatives read as a dangerous challenge to law and national security. Congress eventually agreed on a massive build-up of the U.S. Border Patrol and the construction of a seven-hundred-mile-long fence along the border with Mexico, but the deep divisions over immigration and the status of up to twelve million undocumented immigrants remained unresolved.

Hurricane Katrina

One event highlighted the nation's economic inequality and racial divisions, as well as the Bush administration's difficulty in addressing them effectively. On August 29, 2005, Hurricane Katrina came ashore and devastated coastal stretches of Alabama, Mississippi, and Louisiana. The city of New Orleans, no stranger to hurricanes and floods, suffered heavy damage when the levees, embankments designed to protect against flooding, failed during the storm surge, as the Army Corps of Engineers had warned they might. The flooding killed some fifteen hundred people and so overwhelmed parts of the city that tens of thousands more were trapped and unable to evacuate (Figure 32.10). Thousands who were elderly, ill, or too poor to own a car followed the mayor's directions and sought refuge at the Superdome, which lacked adequate food, water, and sanitation. Public services collapsed under the weight of the crisis.

Figure 32.10 Large portions of the city of New Orleans were flooded during Hurricane Katrina. Although most of the city's population managed to evacuate in time, its poorest residents were left behind.

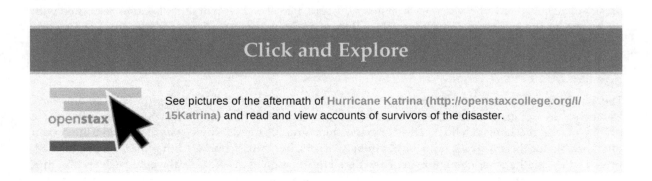

Click and Explore

See pictures of the aftermath of Hurricane Katrina (http://openstaxcollege.org/l/15Katrina) and read and view accounts of survivors of the disaster.

Although the U.S. Coast Guard managed to rescue more than thirty-five thousand people from the stricken city, the response by other federal bodies was less effective. The Federal Emergency Management Agency (FEMA), an agency charged with assisting state and local governments in times of natural disaster, proved inept at coordinating different agencies and utilizing the rescue infrastructure at its disposal. Critics argued that FEMA was to blame and that its director, Michael D. Brown, a Bush friend and appointee with no background in emergency management, was an example of cronyism at its worst. The failures of FEMA were particularly harmful for an administration that had made "homeland security" its top priority. Supporters of the president, however, argued that the scale of the disaster was such that no amount of preparedness or competence could have allowed federal agencies to cope.

While there was plenty of blame to go around—at the city, state, and national levels—FEMA and the Bush administration got the lion's share. Even when the president attempted to demonstrate his concern with a personal appearance, the tactic largely backfired. Photographs of him looking down on a flooded New

Orleans from the comfort of Air Force One only reinforced the impression of a president detached from the problems of everyday people. Despite his attempts to give an uplifting speech from Jackson Square, he was unable to shake this characterization, and it underscored the disappointments of his second term. On the eve of the 2006 midterm elections, President Bush's popularity had reached a new low, as a result of the war in Iraq and Hurricane Katrina, and a growing number of Americans feared that his party's economic policy benefitted the wealthy first and foremost. Young voters, non-white Americans, and women favored the Democratic ticket by large margins. The elections handed Democrats control of the Senate and House for the first time since 1994, and, in January 2007, California representative Nancy Pelosi became the first female Speaker of the House in the nation's history.

THE GREAT RECESSION

For most Americans, the millennium had started with economic woes. In March 2001, the U.S. stock market had taken a sharp drop, and the ensuing recession triggered the loss of millions of jobs over the next two years. In response, the Federal Reserve Board cut interest rates to historic lows to encourage consumer spending. By 2002, the economy seemed to be stabilizing somewhat, but few of the manufacturing jobs lost were restored to the national economy. Instead, the "outsourcing" of jobs to China and India became an increasing concern, along with a surge in corporate scandals. After years of reaping tremendous profits in the deregulated energy markets, Houston-based Enron imploded in 2003 over allegations of massive accounting fraud. Its top executives, Ken Lay and Jeff Skilling, received long prison sentences, but their activities were illustrative of a larger trend in the nation's corporate culture that embroiled reputable companies like JP Morgan Chase and the accounting firm Arthur Anderson. In 2003, Bernard Ebbers, the CEO of communications giant WorldCom, was discovered to have inflated his company's assets by as much as $11 billion, making it the largest accounting scandal in the nation's history. Only five years later, however, Bernard Madoff's Ponzi scheme would reveal even deeper cracks in the nation's financial economy.

Banks Gone Wild

Notwithstanding economic growth in the 1990s and steadily increasing productivity, wages had remained largely flat relative to inflation since the end of the 1970s; despite the mild recovery, they remained so. To compensate, many consumers were buying on credit, and with interest rates low, financial institutions were eager to oblige them. By 2008, credit card debt had risen to over $1 trillion. More importantly, banks were making high-risk, high-interest mortgage loans called **subprime mortgages** to consumers who often misunderstood their complex terms and lacked the ability to make the required payments.

These subprime loans had a devastating impact on the larger economy. In the past, a prospective home buyer went to a local bank for a mortgage loan. Because the bank expected to make a profit in the form of interest charged on the loan, it carefully vetted buyers for their ability to repay. Changes in finance and banking laws in the 1990s and early 2000s, however, allowed lending institutions to securitize their mortgage loans and sell them as bonds, thus separating the financial interests of the lender from the ability of the borrower to repay, and making highly risky loans more attractive to lenders. In other words, banks could afford to make bad loans, because they could sell them and not suffer the financial consequences when borrowers failed to repay.

Once they had purchased the loans, larger investment banks bundled them into huge packages known as collateralized debt obligations (CDOs) and sold them to investors around the world. Even though CDOs consisted of subprime mortgages, credit card debt, and other risky investments, credit ratings agencies had a financial incentive to rate them as very safe. Making matters worse, financial institutions created instruments called **credit default swaps**, which were essentially a form of insurance on investments. If the investment lost money, the investors would be compensated. This system, sometimes referred to as the securitization food chain, greatly swelled the housing loan market, especially the market for subprime mortgages, because these loans carried higher interest rates. The result was a housing bubble, in which the value of homes rose year after year based on the ease with which people now could buy them.

Banks Gone Broke

When the real estate market stalled after reaching a peak in 2007, the house of cards built by the country's largest financial institutions came tumbling down. People began to default on their loans, and more than one hundred mortgage lenders went out of business. American International Group (AIG), a multinational insurance company that had insured many of the investments, faced collapse. Other large financial institutions, which had once been prevented by federal regulations from engaging in risky investment practices, found themselves in danger, as they either were besieged by demands for payment or found their demands on their own insurers unmet. The prestigious investment firm Lehman Brothers was completely wiped out in September 2008. Some endangered companies, like Wall Street giant Merrill Lynch, sold themselves to other financial institutions to survive. A financial panic ensued that revealed other fraudulent schemes built on CDOs. The biggest among them was a pyramid scheme organized by the New York financier Bernard Madoff, who had defrauded his investors by at least $18 billion.

Realizing that the failure of major financial institutions could result in the collapse of the entire U.S. economy, the chairman of the Federal Reserve, Ben Bernanke, authorized a bailout of the Wall Street firm Bear Stearns, although months later, the financial services firm Lehman Brothers was allowed to file for the largest bankruptcy in the nation's history. Members of Congress met with Bernanke and Secretary of the Treasury Henry Paulson in September 2008, to find a way to head off the crisis. They agreed to use $700 billion in federal funds to bail out the troubled institutions, and Congress subsequently passed the Emergency Economic Stabilization Act, creating the Troubled Asset Relief Program (TARP). One important element of this program was aid to the auto industry: The Bush administration responded to their appeal with an emergency loan of $17.4 billion—to be executed by his successor after the November election—to stave off the industry's collapse.

The actions of the Federal Reserve, Congress, and the president prevented the complete disintegration of the nation's financial sector and warded off a scenario like that of the Great Depression. However, the bailouts could not prevent a severe recession in the U.S. and world economy. As people lost faith in the economy, stock prices fell by 45 percent. Unable to receive credit from now-wary banks, smaller businesses found that they could not pay suppliers or employees. With houses at record prices and growing economic uncertainty, people stopped buying new homes. As the value of homes decreased, owners were unable to borrow against them to pay off other obligations, such as credit card debt or car loans. More importantly, millions of homeowners who had expected to sell their houses at a profit and pay off their adjustable-rate mortgages were now stuck in houses with values shrinking below their purchasing price and forced to make mortgage payments they could no longer afford.

Without access to credit, consumer spending declined. Some European nations had suffered similar speculation bubbles in housing, but all had bought into the mortgage securities market and suffered the losses of assets, jobs, and demand as a result. International trade slowed, hurting many American businesses. As the **Great Recession** of 2008 deepened, the situation of ordinary citizens became worse. During the last four months of 2008, one million American workers lost their jobs, and during 2009, another three million found themselves out of work. Under such circumstances, many resented the expensive federal bailout of banks and investment firms. It seemed as if the wealthiest were being rescued by the taxpayer from the consequences of their imprudent and even corrupt practices.

32.3 New Century, Old Disputes

By the end of this section, you will be able to:
- Describe the efforts to reduce the influence of immigrants on American culture
- Describe the evolution of twenty-first-century American attitudes towards same-sex marriage
- Explain the clash over climate change

As the United States entered the twenty-first century, old disputes continued to rear their heads. Some revolved around what it meant to be American and the rights to full citizenship. Others arose from religious conservatism and the influence of the Religious Right on American culture and society. Debates over gay and lesbian rights continued, and arguments over abortion became more complex and contentious, as science and technology advanced. The clash between faith and science also influenced attitudes about how the government should respond to climate change, with religious conservatives finding allies among political conservatives who favored business over potentially expensive measures to reduce harmful emissions.

WHO IS AN AMERICAN?

There is nothing new about anxiety over immigration in the United States. For its entire history, citizens have worried about who is entering the country and the changes that might result. Such concerns began to flare once again beginning in the 1980s, as Americans of European ancestry started to recognize the significant demographic changes on the horizon. The number of Americans of color and multiethnic Americans was growing, as was the percentage of people with other than European ancestry. It was clear the white majority would soon be a demographic minority (Figure 32.11).

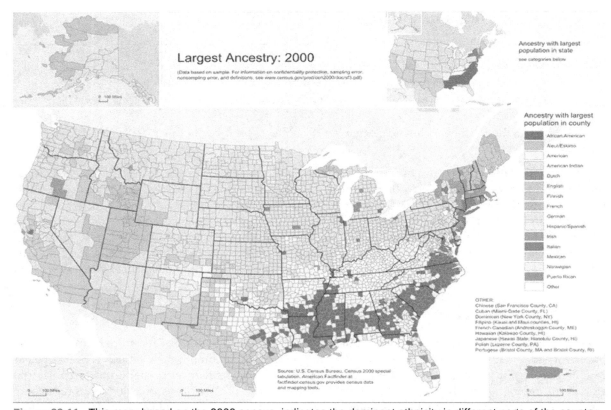

Figure 32.11 This map, based on the 2000 census, indicates the dominant ethnicity in different parts of the country. Note the heavy concentration of African Americans (dark purple) in the South, and the large numbers of those of Mexican ancestry (pink) in California and the Southwest. Why do you think so many in the Upper South are designated as simply American (light yellow)?

The nation's increasing diversity prompted some social conservatives to identify American culture as one of European heritage, including the drive to legally designate English the official language of the United States. This movement was particularly strong in areas of the country with large Spanish-speaking populations such as Arizona, where, in 2006, three-quarters of voters approved a proposition to make English the official language in the state. Proponents in Arizona and elsewhere argued that these laws were necessary, because recent immigrants, especially Hispanic newcomers, were not being sufficiently acculturated to white, middle-class culture. Opponents countered that English was already the *de facto* official language, and codifying it into law would only amount to unnecessary discrimination.

DEFINING "AMERICAN"

⬡ *Arizona Bans Mexican American Studies*

In 2010, Arizona passed a law barring the teaching of any class that promoted "resentment" of students of other races or encouraged "ethnic solidarity." The ban, to take effect on December 31 of that year, included a popular Mexican American studies program taught at elementary, middle, and high schools in the city of Tucson. The program, which focused on teaching students about Mexican American history and literature, was begun in 1998, to convert high absentee rates and low academic performance among Latino students, and proved highly successful. Public school superintendent Tom Horne objected to the course, however, claiming it encouraged resentment of whites and of the U.S. government, and improperly encouraged students to think of themselves as members of a race instead of as individuals.

Tucson was ordered to end its Mexican American studies program or lose 10 percent of the school system's funding, approximately $3 million each month. In 2012, the Tucson school board voted to end the program. A former student and his mother filed a suit in federal court, claiming that the law, which did not prohibit programs teaching Indian students about their culture, was discriminatory and violated the First Amendment rights of Tucson's students. In March 2013, the court found in favor of the state, ruling that the law was not discriminatory, because it targeted classes, and not students or teachers, and that preventing the teaching of Mexican studies classes did not intrude on students' constitutional rights. The court did, however, declare the part of the law prohibiting classes designed for members of particular ethnic groups to be unconstitutional.

What advantages or disadvantages can you see in an ethnic studies program? How could an ethnic studies course add to our understanding of U.S. history? Explain.

The fear that English-speaking Americans were being outnumbered by a Hispanic population that was not forced to assimilate was sharpened by the concern that far too many were illegally emigrating from Latin America to the United States. The Comprehensive Immigration Reform Act proposed by Congress in 2006 sought to simultaneously strengthen security along the U.S.-Mexico border (a task for the Department of Homeland Security), increase the number of temporary "guest workers" allowed in the United States, and provide a pathway for long-term U.S. residents who had entered the country illegally to gain legal status. It also sought to establish English as a "common and unifying language" for the nation. The bill and a similar amended version both failed to become law.

With unemployment rates soaring during the Great Recession, anxiety over illegal immigration rose, even while the incoming flow slowed. State legislatures in Alabama and Arizona passed strict new laws that required police and other officials to verify the immigration status of those they thought had entered the country illegally. In Alabama, the new law made it a crime to rent housing to undocumented immigrants, thus making it difficult for these immigrants to live within the state. Both laws have been challenged in court, and portions have been deemed unconstitutional or otherwise blocked.

Beginning in October 2013, states along the U.S.-Mexico border faced an increase in the immigration of children from a handful of Central American countries. Approximately fifty-two thousand children, some unaccompanied, were taken into custody as they reached the United States. A study by the United Nations High Commissioner for Refugees estimated that 58 percent of those migrants, largely from El Salvador and Honduras, were propelled towards the United States by poverty, violence, and the potential for exploitation in their home countries. Because of a 2008 law originally intended to protect victims of human trafficking, these Central American children are guaranteed a court hearing. Predictably, the crisis has served to underline the need for comprehensive immigration reform. But, as of late 2014, a 2013 Senate immigration reform bill that combines border security with a guest worker program and a path to citizenship has yet to be enacted as law.

WHAT IS A MARRIAGE?

In the 1990s, the idea of legal, same-sex marriage seemed particularly unlikely; neither of the two main political parties expressed support for it. Things began to change, however, following Vermont's decision to allow same-sex couples to form state-recognized **civil unions** in which they could enjoy all the legal rights and privileges of marriage. Although it was the intention of the state to create a type of legal relationship equivalent to marriage, it did not use the word "marriage" to describe it.

Following Vermont's lead, several other states legalized same-sex marriages or civil unions among gay and lesbian couples. In 2004, the Massachusetts Supreme Judicial Court ruled that barring gays and lesbians from marrying violated the state constitution. The court held that offering same-sex couples the right to form civil unions but not marriage was an act of discrimination, and Massachusetts became the first state to allow same-sex couples to marry. Not all states followed suit, however, and there was a backlash in several states. Between 1998 and 2012, thirty states banned same-sex marriage either by statute or by amending their constitutions. Other states attempted, unsuccessfully, to do the same. In 2007, the Massachusetts State Legislature rejected a proposed amendment to the state's constitution that would have prohibited such marriages.

Click and Explore

Watch this detailed documentary (http://openstaxcollege.org/l/15HolyWar) on the attitudes that prevailed in Colorado in 1992, when the voters of that state approved Amendment 2 to the state's constitution and consequently denied gay and lesbian Coloradans the right to claim relief from local levels of discrimination in public accommodations, housing, or jobs.

While those in support of broadening civil rights to include same-sex marriage were optimistic, those opposed employed new tactics. In 2008, opponents of same-sex marriage in California tried a ballot initiative to define marriage strictly as a union between a man and a woman. Despite strong support for broadening marriage rights, the proposition was successful. This change was just one of dozens that states had been putting in place since the late 1990s to make same-sex marriage unconstitutional at the state level. Like the California proposition, however, many new state constitutional amendments have faced challenges in court (Figure 32.12). As of 2014, leaders in both political parties are more receptive than ever before to the idea of same-sex marriage.

(a)   (b)

Figure 32.12 Supporters and protesters of same-sex marriage gather in front of San Francisco's City Hall (a) as the California Supreme Court decides the fate of Proposition 8, a 2008 ballet measure stating that "only marriage between a man and a woman" would be valid in California. Following the Iowa Supreme Court's decision to legalize same-sex marriage, supporters rally in Iowa City on April 3, 2009 (b). The banner displays the Iowa state motto: "Our liberties we prize and our rights we will maintain." (credit a: modification of work by Jamison Wieser; credit b: modification of work by Alan Light)

Click and Explore

Visit the Pew Research site (http://openstaxcollege.org/l/15GayMarriage) to read more about the current status of same-sex marriage in the United States and the rest of the world.

WHY FIGHT CLIMATE CHANGE?

Even as mainstream members of both political parties moved closer together on same-sex marriage, political divisions on scientific debates continued. One increasingly polarizing debate that baffles much of the rest of the world is about global climate change. Despite near unanimity in the scientific community that climate change is real and will have devastating consequences, large segments of the American population, predominantly on the right, continue to insist that it is little more than a complex hoax and a leftist conspiracy. Much of the Republican Party's base denies that global warming is the result of human activity; some deny that the earth is getting hotter at all. This popular denial has had huge global consequences. In 1998, the United States, which produces roughly 36 percent of the **greenhouse gases** like carbon dioxide that prevent the earth's heat from escaping into space, signed the **Kyoto Protocol**, an agreement among the world's nations to reduce their emissions of these gases. President Bush objected to the requirement that major industrialized nations limit their emissions to a greater extent than other parts of the world and argued that doing so might hurt the American economy. He announced that the United States would not be bound by the agreement, and it was never ratified by Congress.

Instead, the Bush administration appeared to suppress scientific reporting on climate change. In 2006, the progressive-leaning Union of Concerned Scientists surveyed sixteen hundred climate scientists, asking them about the state of federal climate research. Of those who responded, nearly three-fourths believed that their research had been subjected to new administrative requirements, third-party editing to change their conclusions, or pressure not to use terms such as "global warming." Republican politicians, citing the altered reports, argued that there was no unified opinion among members of the scientific community that humans were damaging the climate.

Countering this rejection of science were the activities of many environmentalists, including Al Gore, Clinton's vice president and Bush's opponent in the disputed 2000 election. As a new member of Congress in 1976, Gore had developed what proved a steady commitment to environmental issues. In 2004, he established Generation Investment Management, which sought to promote an environmentally responsible system of equity analysis and investment. In 2006, a documentary film, *An Inconvenient Truth*, represented his attempts to educate people about the realities and dangers of global warming, and won the 2007 Academy Award for Best Documentary. Though some of what Gore said was in error, the film's main thrust is in keeping with the weight of scientific evidence. In 2007, as a result of these efforts to "disseminate greater knowledge about man-made climate change," Gore shared the Nobel Peace Prize with the Intergovernmental Panel on Climate Change.

32.4 Hope and Change

By the end of this section, you will be able to:
- Describe how Barack Obama's domestic policies differed from those of George W. Bush
- Discuss the important events of the war on terror during Obama's two administrations
- Discuss some of the specific challenges facing the United States as Obama's second term draws to a close

In 2008, American voters, tired of war and dispirited by the economic downturn, elected a relative newcomer to the political scene who inspired them and made them believe that the United States could rise above political partisanship. Barack Obama's story resembled that of many Americans: a multicultural background; a largely absent father; a single working mother; and care provided by maternal grandparents. As president, Obama would face significant challenges, including managing the economic recovery in the wake of the Great Recession, fighting the war on terror inherited from the previous administration, and implementing the healthcare reform upon which he had campaigned.

OBAMA TAKES OFFICE

Born in Hawaii in 1961 to a Kenyan father and an American woman from Kansas, Obama excelled at school, going on to attend Occidental College in Los Angeles, Columbia University, and finally Harvard Law School, where he became the first African American president of the *Harvard Law Review*. As part of his education, he also spent time in Chicago working as a community organizer to help those displaced by the decline of heavy industry in the early 1980s. Obama first came to national attention when he delivered the keynote address at the 2004 Democratic National Convention while running for his first term in the U.S. Senate. Just a couple of years later, he was running for president himself, the first African American nominee for the office from either major political party.

Obama's opponent in 2008 was John McCain, a Vietnam veteran and Republican senator with the reputation of a "maverick" who had occasionally broken ranks with his party to support bipartisan initiatives. The senator from Arizona faced a number of challenges. As the Republican nominee, he remained closely associated with the two disastrous foreign wars initiated under the Bush administration.

His late recognition of the economic catastrophe on the eve of the election did not help matters and further damaged the Republican brand at the polls. At seventy-one, he also had to fight accusations that he was too old for the job, an impression made even more striking by his energetic young challenger. To minimize this weakness, McCain chose a young but inexperienced running mate, Governor Sarah Palin of Alaska. This tactic backfired, however, when a number of poor performances in television interviews convinced many voters that Palin was not prepared for higher office (Figure 32.13).

Figure 32.13 John McCain (on the far right) campaigns with his wife Cindy (in green), Sarah Palin (in black), and Palin's husband Todd. Palin was a controversial choice for running mate. The campaign never succeeded in erasing the charges that she was ignorant of foreign policy—an impression she enforced in her own ad-lib statements. (credit: Rachael Dickson)

Senator Obama, too, was criticized for his lack of experience with foreign policy, a deficit he remedied by choosing experienced politician Joseph Biden as his running mate. Unlike his Republican opponent, however, Obama offered promises of "hope and change." By sending out voter reminders on Twitter and connecting with supporters on Facebook, he was able to harness social media and take advantage of grassroots enthusiasm for his candidacy. His youthful vigor drew independents and first-time voters, and he won 95 percent of the African American vote and 44 percent of the white vote (Figure 32.14).

Figure 32.14 Barack Obama takes the oath of office as the forty-fourth president of the United States. Standing next to him is First Lady Michelle Obama. Like her husband, she graduated from Harvard Law School.

DEFINING "AMERICAN"

⊙ *Politicking in a New Century*

Barack Obama's campaign seemed to come out of nowhere to overcome the widely supported frontrunner Hillary Clinton in the Democratic primaries. Having won the nomination, Obama shot to the top with an exuberant base of youthful supporters who were encouraged and inspired by his appeal to hope and change. Behind the scenes, the Obama campaign was employing technological innovations and advances in social media to both inform and organize its base.

The Obama campaign realized early that the key to political success in the twenty-first century was to energize young voters by reaching them where they were: online. The organizing potential of platforms like Facebook, YouTube, and Twitter had never before been tapped—and they were free. The results were groundbreaking. Using these social media platforms, the Obama campaign became an organizing and fundraising machine of epic proportions. During his almost two-year-long campaign, Obama accepted 6.5 million donations, totaling $500 million. The vast majority of online donations were less than $100. This accomplishment stunned the political establishment, and they have been quick to adapt. Since 2008, nearly every political campaign has followed in Obama's footsteps, effecting a revolution in campaigning in the United States.

ECONOMIC AND HEALTHCARE REFORMS

Barack Obama had been elected on a platform of healthcare reform and a wave of frustration over the sinking economy. As he entered office in 2009, he set out to deal with both. Taking charge of the TARP program instituted under George W. Bush to stabilize the country's financial institutions, Obama oversaw the distribution of some $7.77 trillion designed to help shore up the nation's banking system. Recognizing that the economic downturn also threatened major auto manufacturers in the United States, he sought and received congressional authorization for $80 billion to help Chrysler and General Motors. The action was controversial, and some characterized it as a government takeover of industry. The money did, however, help the automakers earn a profit by 2011, reversing the trend of consistent losses that had hurt the industry since 2004. It also helped prevent layoffs and wage cuts. By 2013, the automakers had repaid over $50 billion of bailout funds. Finally, through the 2009 American Recovery and Reinvestment Act (ARRA), the Obama administration pumped almost $800 billion into the economy to stimulate economic growth and job creation.

More important for Obama supporters than his attempts to restore the economy was that he fulfill his promise to enact comprehensive healthcare reform. Many assumed such reforms would move quickly through Congress, since Democrats had comfortable majorities in both houses, and both Obama and McCain had campaigned on healthcare reform. However, as had occurred years before during President Clinton's first term, opposition groups saw attempts at reform as an opportunity to put the political brakes on the Obama presidency. After months of political wrangling and condemnations of the healthcare reform plan as socialism, the Patient Protection and Affordable Care Act (Figure 32.15) was passed and signed into law.

The act, which created the program known as **Obamacare**, represented the first significant overhaul of the American healthcare system since the passage of Medicaid in 1965. Its goals were to provide all Americans with access to affordable health insurance, to require that everyone in the United States acquire some form of health insurance, and to lower the costs of healthcare. The plan, which made use of government funding, created private insurance company exchanges to market various insurance packages to enrollees.

Figure 32.15 President Obama signs the Patient Protection and Affordable Care Act into law on March 23, 2010, as Vice President Biden, Speaker of the House Nancy Pelosi, Senate Majority Leader Harry Reid, and others look on. (credit: Pete Souza)

Although the plan implemented the market-based reforms that they had supported for years, Republicans refused to vote for it. Following its passage, they called numerous times for its repeal, and more than twenty-four states sued the federal government to stop its implementation. Discontent over the Affordable Care Act helped the Republicans capture the majority in the House of Representatives in the 2010 midterm elections. It also helped spawn the **Tea Party**, a conservative movement focused primarily on limiting government spending and the size of the federal government.

THE ELECTION OF 2012

By the 2012 presidential election, the Republicans, convinced Obama was vulnerable because of opposition to his healthcare program and a weak economy, nominated Mitt Romney, a well-known business executive-turned politician who had earlier signed healthcare reform into state law as governor of Massachusetts (Figure 32.16). Romney had unsuccessfully challenged McCain for the Republican nomination in 2008, but by 2012, he had remade himself politically by moving towards the party's right wing and its newly created Tea Party faction, which was pulling the traditional conservative base further to the right with its strong opposition to abortion, gun control, and immigration.

Figure 32.16 Former governor of Massachusetts Mitt Romney became the first member of the Mormon Church to run for president. He claimed his experience as a member of the Mormon lay clergy had made him sympathetic to the needs of the poor, but some of his campaign decisions contradicted this stance. (credit: Mark Taylor)

Romney appealed to a new attitude within the Republican Party. While the percentage of Democrats who agreed that the government should help people unable to provide for themselves had remained relatively stable from 1987 to 2012, at roughly 75 to 79 percent, the percentage of Republicans who felt the same way had decreased from 62 to 40 percent over the same period, with the greatest decline coming after 2007. Indeed, Romney himself revealed his disdain for people on the lower rungs of the socioeconomic ladder when, at a fundraising event attended by affluent Republicans, he remarked that he did not care to reach the 47 percent of Americans who would always vote for Obama because of their dependence on government assistance. In his eyes, this low-income portion of the population preferred to rely on government social programs instead of trying to improve their own lives.

Click and Explore

Read the transcript (http://openstaxcollege.org/l/1547percent2) of "On the 47 percent," the secretly recorded speech (http://openstaxcollege.org/l/1547percent) given by Mitt Romney at a Republican fundraiser.

Starting out behind Obama in the polls, Romney significantly closed the gap in the first of three presidential debates, when he moved towards more centrist positions on many issues. Obama regained momentum in the remaining two debates and used his bailout of the auto industry to appeal to voters in the key states of Michigan and Ohio. Romney's remarks about the 47 percent hurt his position among both poor Americans and those who sympathized with them. A long-time critic of FEMA who claimed that it should be eliminated, Romney also likely lost votes in the Northeast when, a week before the election, Hurricane Sandy devastated the New England, New York, and New Jersey coasts. Obama and the federal government had largely rebuilt FEMA since its disastrous showing in New Orleans in 2005, and the agency quickly swung into action to assist the 8.5 million people affected by the disaster.

Obama won the election, but the Republicans retained their hold on the House of Representatives and the Democratic majority in the Senate grew razor-thin. Political bickering and intractable Republican resistance, including a 70 percent increase in filibusters over the 1980s, a refusal to allow a vote on some legislation, such as the 2012 "jobs bill," and the glacial pace at which the Senate confirmed the President's judicial nominations, created political gridlock in Washington, interfering with Obama's ability to secure any important legislative victories.

ONGOING CHALLENGES

As Obama entered his second term in office, the economy remained stagnant in many areas. On average, American students continued to fall behind their peers in the rest of the world, and the cost of a college education became increasingly unaffordable for many. Problems continued overseas in Iraq and Afghanistan, and another act of terrorism took place on American soil when bombs exploded at the 2013 Boston Marathon. At the same time, the cause of same-sex marriage made significant advances, and Obama was able to secure greater protection for the environment. He raised fuel-efficiency standards for automobiles to reduce the emissions of greenhouse gases and required coal-burning power plants to capture their carbon emissions.

Learning and Earning

The quality of American education remains a challenge. The global economy is dominated by those nations with the greatest number of "knowledge workers:" people with specialized knowledge and skills like engineers, scientists, doctors, teachers, financial analysts, and computer programmers. Furthermore, American students' reading, math, and critical thinking skills are less developed than those of their peers in other industrialized nations, including small countries like Estonia.

The Obama administration sought to make higher education more accessible by increasing the amount that students could receive under the federally funded Pell Grant Program, which, by the 2012–13 academic year, helped 9.5 million students pay for their college education. Obama also worked out a compromise with Congress in 2013, which lowered the interest rates charged on student loans. However, college tuition is still growing at a rate of 2 to 3 percent per year, and the debt burden has surpassed the $1 trillion mark and is likely to increase. With debt upon graduation averaging about $29,000, students may find their economic options limited. Instead of buying cars or paying for housing, they may have to join the **boomerang generation** and return to their parents' homes in order to make their loan payments. Clearly, high levels of debt will affect their career choices and life decisions for the foreseeable future.

Many other Americans continue to be challenged by the state of the economy. Most economists calculate that the Great Recession reached its lowest point in 2009, and the economy has gradually improved since then. The stock market ended 2013 at historic highs, having experienced its biggest percentage gain since 1997. However, despite these gains, the nation struggled to maintain a modest annual growth rate of 2.5 percent after the Great Recession, and the percentage of the population living in poverty continues to hover around 15 percent. Income has decreased (Figure 32.17), and, as late as 2011, the unemployment rate was still high in some areas. Eight million full-time workers have been forced into part-time work, whereas 26 million seem to have given up and left the job market.

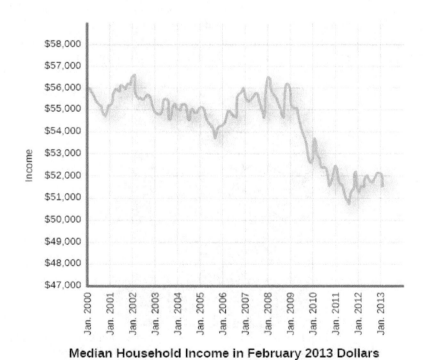

Median Household Income in February 2013 Dollars

Figure 32.17 Median household income trends reveal a steady downward spiral. The Great Recession may have ended, but many remain worse off than they were in 2008.

LGBT Rights

During Barack Obama's second term in office, courts began to counter efforts by conservatives to outlaw same-sex marriage. A series of decisions declared nine states' prohibitions against same-sex marriage to be unconstitutional, and the Supreme Court rejected an attempt to overturn a federal court ruling to that effect in California in June 2013. Shortly thereafter, the Supreme Court also ruled that the Defense of Marriage Act of 1996 was unconstitutional, because it violated the Equal Protection Clause of the Fourteenth Amendment. These decisions seem to allow legal challenges in all the states that persist in trying to block same-sex unions.

The struggle against discrimination based on gender identity has also won some significant victories. In 2014, the U.S. Department of Education ruled that schools receiving federal funds may not discriminate against transgender students, and a board within the Department of Health and Human Services decided that Medicare should cover sexual reassignment surgery. Although very few people eligible for Medicare are transgender, the decision is still important, because private insurance companies often base their coverage on what Medicare considers appropriate and necessary forms of treatment for various conditions. Undoubtedly, the fight for greater rights for LGBT (lesbian, gay, bisexual, transsexual) individuals will continue.

Violence

Another running debate questions the easy accessibility of firearms. Between the spring of 1999, when two teens killed twelve of their classmates, a teacher, and themselves at their high school in Columbine, Colorado, and the early summer of 2014, fifty-two additional shootings or attempted shootings had occurred at schools (Figure 32.18). Nearly always, the violence was perpetrated by young people with severe mental health problems, as at Sandy Hook elementary school in Newtown, Connecticut, in 2012. After killing his mother at home, twenty-year-old Adam Lanza went to the school and fatally shot twenty six- and seven-year-old students, along with six adult staff members, before killing himself. Advocates of stricter gun control noted a clear relationship between access to guns and mass shootings. Gun rights advocates, however, disagreed. They argued that access to guns is merely incidental.

Figure 32.18 A candlelight vigil at Virginia Polytechnic Institute and State University in Blacksburg, Virginia, in the wake of the 2007 murder of thirty-two people by a student. The incident remains the deadliest school shooting to date. (credit: "alka3en"/Flickr)

Another shocking act of violence was the attack on the Boston Marathon. On April 15, 2013, shortly before 3:00 p.m., two bombs made from pressure cookers exploded near the finish line (Figure 32.19). Three people were killed, and more than 250 were injured. Three days later, two suspects were identified, and a manhunt began. Later that night, the two young men, brothers who had immigrated to the United States from Chechnya, killed a campus security officer at the Massachusetts Institute of Technology, stole a car, and fled. The older, Tamerlan Tsarnaev, was killed in a fight with the police, and Dzhokhar Tsarnaev was captured the next day. In his statements to the police, Dzhokhar Tsarnaev reported that he and his brother, who he claimed had planned the attacks, had been influenced by the actions of fellow radical Islamists in Afghanistan and Iraq, but he denied they had been affiliated with any larger terrorist group.

Figure 32.19 Bystanders at the finish line of the Boston Marathon help carry the injured to safety after the April 2013 attack. Two bombs exploded only a few seconds and a few hundred yards apart, killing three people. (credit: Aaron Tang)

America and the World

In May 2014, President Obama announced that, for the most part, U.S. combat operations in Afghanistan were over. Although a residual force of ninety-eight hundred soldiers will remain to continue training the Afghan army, by 2016, all U.S. troops will have left the country, except for a small number to defend U.S. diplomatic posts.

The years of warfare have brought the United States few rewards. In Iraq, 4,475 American soldiers died and 32,220 were wounded. In Afghanistan, the toll through February 2013 was 2,165 dead and 18,230 wounded. By some estimates, the total monetary cost of the wars in Iraq and Afghanistan could easily reach $4 trillion, and the Congressional Budget Office believes that the cost of providing medical care for the veterans might climb to $8 billion by 2020.

In Iraq, the coalition led by then-Prime Minister Nouri al-Maliki was able to win 92 of the 328 seats in parliament in May 2014, and he seemed poised to begin another term as the country's ruler. The elections, however, did not stem the tide of violence in the country. In June 2014, the Islamic State of Iraq and Syria (ISIS), a radical Islamist militant group consisting of mostly Sunni Muslims and once affiliated with al-Qaeda, seized control of Sunni-dominated areas of Iraq and Syria. On June 29, 2014, it proclaimed the formation of the Islamic State with Abu Bakr al-Baghdadi as caliph, the state's political and religious leader.

Key Terms

al-Qaeda a militant Islamist group originally founded by Osama bin Laden

boomerang generation young people who must return to their parents' home in order to make ends meet

Bush Doctrine the belief that the United States has the right to protect itself from terrorist acts by engaging in pre-emptive wars or ousting hostile governments in favor of friendly, preferably democratic, regimes

charter schools elementary and secondary schools that, although funded by taxpayer money, are allowed to operate independently from some rules and regulations governing public schools

civil unions a civil status offered to gay and lesbian couples with the goal of securing the main privileges of marriage without granting them equal status in marriage

credit default swaps financial instruments that pay buyers even if a purchased loan defaults; a form of insurance for risky loans

Great Recession the economic recession that began in 2008, following the collapse of the housing boom, and was driven by risky and misleading subprime mortgages and a deregulated bond market

greenhouse gases gases in the earth's atmosphere, like carbon dioxide, that trap heat and prevent it from radiating into space

Kyoto Protocol an international agreement establishing regulations designed to reduce greenhouse gas emissions by the world's industrialized nations

Obamacare the Patient Protection and Affordable Care Act

subprime mortgage a type of mortgage offered to borrowers with lower credit ratings; subprime loans feature interest rates that are higher (often adjustable) than conventional mortgages to compensate the bank for the increased risk of default

Taliban a fundamentalist Muslim group that ruled Afghanistan from 1996 to 2001

Tea Party a conservative movement focused primarily on limiting government spending and the size of the federal government

WMDs weapons of mass destruction; a class of weapons capable of inflicting massive causalities and physical destruction, such as nuclear bombs or biological and chemical weapons

Summary

32.1 The War on Terror

George W. Bush's first term in office began with al-Qaeda's deadly attacks on the World Trade Center and the Pentagon on September 11, 2001. Shortly thereafter, the United States found itself at war with Afghanistan, which was accused of harboring the 9/11 mastermind, Osama bin Laden, and his followers. Claiming that Iraq's president Saddam Hussein was building weapons of mass destruction, perhaps with the intent of attacking the United States, the president sent U.S. troops to Iraq as well in 2003. Thousands were killed, and many of the men captured by the United States were imprisoned and sometimes tortured for information. The ease with which Hussein was deposed led the president to declare that the mission in Iraq had been accomplished only a few months after it began. He was, however, mistaken. Meanwhile, the establishment of the Office of Homeland Security and the passage of the Homeland Security Act and USA Patriot Act created new means and levels of surveillance to identify potential threats.

32.2 The Domestic Mission

When George W. Bush took office in January 2001, he was committed to a Republican agenda. He cut tax rates for the rich and tried to limit the role of government in people's lives, in part by providing students with vouchers to attend charter and private schools, and encouraging religious organizations to provide social services instead of the government. While his tax cuts pushed the United States into a chronically large federal deficit, many of his supply-side economic reforms stalled during his second term. In 2005, Hurricane Katrina underscored the limited capacities of the federal government under Bush to assure homeland security. In combination with increasing discontent over the Iraq War, these events handed Democrats a majority in both houses in 2006. Largely as a result of a deregulated bond market and dubious innovations in home mortgages, the nation reached the pinnacle of a real estate boom in 2007. The threatened collapse of the nations' banks and investment houses required the administration to extend aid to the financial sector. Many resented this bailout of the rich, as ordinary citizens lost jobs and homes in the Great Recession of 2008.

32.3 New Century, Old Disputes

The nation's increasing diversity—and with it, the fact that white Caucasians will soon be a demographic minority—prompted a conservative backlash that continues to manifest itself in debates about immigration. Questions of who is an American and what constitutes a marriage continue to be debated, although the answers are beginning to change. As some states broadened civil rights to include gays and lesbians, groups opposed to these developments sought to impose state constitutional restrictions. From this flurry of activity, however, a new political consensus for expanding marriage rights has begun to emerge. On the issue of climate change, however, polarization has increased. A strong distrust of science among Americans has divided the political parties and hampered scientific research.

32.4 Hope and Change

Despite Republican resistance and political gridlock in Washington during his first term in office, President Barack Obama oversaw the distribution of the TARP program's $7.77 trillion to help shore up the nation's banking system, and Congress authorized $80 billion to help Chrysler and General Motors. The goals of Obama's Patient Protection and Affordable Care Act (Obamacare) were to provide all Americans with access to affordable health insurance, to require that everyone in the United States had some form of health insurance, and to lower the costs of healthcare. During his second term, the nation struggled to grow modestly, the percentage of the population living in poverty remained around 15 percent, and unemployment was still high in some areas. Acceptance of same-sex marriage grew, and the United States sharply reduced its military commitments in Iraq and Afghanistan.

Review Questions

1. The prison operated by the U.S. military for the detention and interrogation of terrorist suspects and "enemy combatants" is located at _____.

    A. Kuwait City, Kuwait

    B. Riker's Island, New York

    C. Guantanamo Bay, Cuba

    D. Lahore, Pakistan

2. Unwarranted wiretapping in the United States was conducted by _____.

    A. the FBI

    B. the CIA

    C. the *New York Times*

    D. the NSA

3. In what ways did the U.S. government attempt to deny the rights of prisoners taken in Afghanistan and Iraq?

4. What investment banking firm went bankrupt in 2008, signaling the beginning of a major economic crisis?
   A. CitiBank
   B. Wells Fargo
   C. Lehman Brothers
   D. Price Waterhouse

5. A subprime mortgage is _____.
   A. a high-risk, high-interest loan
   B. a federal bailout for major banks
   C. a form of insurance on investments
   D. a form of political capital

6. What are the pros and cons of school vouchers?

7. A popular Mexican American studies program was banned by the state of _____, which accused it of causing resentment of white people.
   A. New Mexico
   B. California
   C. Arizona
   D. Texas

8. The first state to allow same-sex marriage was _____.

   A. Massachusetts
   B. New York
   C. California
   D. Pennsylvania

9. What was the result of the Bush administration's unwillingness to recognize that climate change is being accelerated by human activity?

10. The U.S. Supreme Court ruled the Defense of Marriage Act unconstitutional in _____.
   A. 2007
   B. 2009
   C. 2013
   D. 2014

11. Which of the following is *not* a goal of Obamacare (the Patient Protection and Affordable Care Act)?
   A. to provide all Americans with access to affordable health insurance
   B. to require that everyone in the United States acquire some form of health insurance
   C. to lower the costs of healthcare
   D. to increase employment in the healthcare industry

12. What has Barack Obama done to make college education more accessible?

Critical Thinking Questions

13. What factors led to the Great Recession?

14. How have conservatives fared in their efforts to defend "American" culture against an influx of immigrants in the twenty-first century?

15. In what ways are Barack Obama's ideas regarding the economy, education, and the environment similar to those of Bush, his Republican predecessor? In what ways are they different?

16. How successful has the United States been in achieving its goals in Iraq and Afghanistan?

17. In what ways has the United States become a more heterogeneous and inclusive place in the twenty-first century? In what ways has it become more homogenous and exclusive?

APPENDIX A

The Declaration of Independence

When in the Course of human events, it becomes necessary for one people to dissolve the political bands which have connected them with another, and to assume among the powers of the earth, the separate and equal station to which the Laws of Nature and of Nature's God entitle them, a decent respect to the opinions of mankind requires that they should declare the causes which impel them to the separation.

We hold these truths to be self-evident, that all men are created equal, that they are endowed by their Creator with certain unalienable Rights, that among these are Life, Liberty and the pursuit of Happiness. —That to secure these rights, Governments are instituted among Men, deriving their just powers from the consent of the governed, —That whenever any Form of Government becomes destructive of these ends, it is the Right of the People to alter or to abolish it, and to institute new Government, laying its foundation on such principles and organizing its powers in such form, as to them shall seem most likely to effect their Safety and Happiness. Prudence, indeed, will dictate that Governments long established should not be changed for light and transient causes; and accordingly all experience hath shewn, that mankind are more disposed to suffer, while evils are sufferable, than to right themselves by abolishing the forms to which they are accustomed. But when a long train of abuses and usurpations, pursuing invariably the same Object evinces a design to reduce them under absolute Despotism, it is their right, it is their duty, to throw off such Government, and to provide new Guards for their future security. —Such has been the patient sufferance of these Colonies; and such is now the necessity which constrains them to alter their former Systems of Government. The history of the present King of Great Britain is a history of repeated injuries and usurpations, all having in direct object the establishment of an absolute Tyranny over these States. To prove this, let Facts be submitted to a candid world.

He has refused his Assent to Laws, the most wholesome and necessary for the public good.

He has forbidden his Governors to pass Laws of immediate and pressing importance, unless suspended in their operation till his Assent should be obtained; and when so suspended, he has utterly neglected to attend to them.

He has refused to pass other Laws for the accommodation of large districts of people, unless those people would relinquish the right of Representation in the Legislature, a right inestimable to them and formidable to tyrants only.

He has called together legislative bodies at places unusual, uncomfortable, and distant from the depository of their public Records, for the sole purpose of fatiguing them into compliance with his measures.

He has dissolved Representative Houses repeatedly, for opposing with manly firmness his invasions on the rights of the people.

He has refused for a long time, after such dissolutions, to cause others to be elected; whereby the Legislative powers, incapable of Annihilation, have returned to the People at large for their exercise; the State remaining in the mean time exposed to all the dangers of invasion from without, and convulsions within.

He has endeavoured to prevent the population of these States; for that purpose obstructing the Laws for Naturalization of Foreigners; refusing to pass others to encourage their migrations hither, and raising the conditions of new Appropriations of Lands.

He has obstructed the Administration of Justice, by refusing his Assent to Laws for establishing Judiciary powers.

He has made Judges dependent on his Will alone, for the tenure of their offices, and the amount and payment of their salaries.

He has erected a multitude of New Offices, and sent hither swarms of Officers to harrass our people, and eat out their substance.

He has kept among us, in times of peace, Standing Armies without the Consent of our legislatures.

He has affected to render the Military independent of and superior to the Civil power.

He has combined with others to subject us to a jurisdiction foreign to our constitution, and unacknowledged by our laws; giving his Assent to their Acts of pretended Legislation:

For Quartering large bodies of armed troops among us:

For protecting them, by a mock Trial, from punishment for any Murders which they should commit on the Inhabitants of these States:

For cutting off our Trade with all parts of the world:

For imposing Taxes on us without our Consent:

For depriving us in many cases, of the benefits of Trial by Jury:

For transporting us beyond Seas to be tried for pretended offences:

For abolishing the free System of English Laws in a neighbouring Province, establishing therein an Arbitrary government, and enlarging its Boundaries so as to render it at once an example and fit instrument for introducing the same absolute rule into these Colonies:

For taking away our Charters, abolishing our most valuable Laws, and altering fundamentally the Forms of our Governments:

For suspending our own Legislatures, and declaring themselves invested with power to legislate for us in all cases whatsoever.

He has abdicated Government here, by declaring us out of his Protection and waging War against us.

He has plundered our seas, ravaged our Coasts, burnt our towns, and destroyed the lives of our people.

He is at this time transporting large Armies of foreign Mercenaries to compleat the works of death, desolation and tyranny, already begun with circumstances of Cruelty & perfidy scarcely paralleled in the most barbarous ages, and totally unworthy the Head of a civilized nation.

He has constrained our fellow Citizens taken Captive on the high Seas to bear Arms against their Country, to become the executioners of their friends and Brethren, or to fall themselves by their Hands.

He has excited domestic insurrections amongst us, and has endeavoured to bring on the inhabitants of our frontiers, the merciless Indian Savages, whose known rule of warfare, is an undistinguished destruction of all ages, sexes and conditions.

In every stage of these Oppressions We have Petitioned for Redress in the most humble terms: Our repeated Petitions have been answered only by repeated injury. A Prince whose character is thus marked by every act which may define a Tyrant, is unfit to be the ruler of a free people.

Nor have We been wanting in attentions to our Brittish brethren. We have warned them from time to time of attempts by their legislature to extend an unwarrantable jurisdiction over us. We have reminded them of the circumstances of our emigration and settlement here. We have appealed to their native justice and magnanimity, and we have conjured them by the ties of our common kindred to disavow these usurpations, which, would inevitably interrupt our connections and correspondence. They too have been deaf to the voice of justice and of consanguinity. We must, therefore, acquiesce in the necessity, which denounces our Separation, and hold them, as we hold the rest of mankind, Enemies in War, in Peace Friends.

We, therefore, the Representatives of the united States of America, in General Congress, Assembled, appealing to the Supreme Judge of the world for the rectitude of our intentions, do, in the Name, and by Authority of the good People of these Colonies, solemnly publish and declare, That these United Colonies are, and of Right ought to be Free and Independent States; that they are Absolved from all Allegiance to the British Crown, and that all political connection between them and the State of Great Britain, is and ought to be totally dissolved; and that as Free and Independent States, they have full Power to levy War, conclude Peace, contract Alliances, establish Commerce, and to do all other Acts and Things which Independent States may of right do. And for the support of this Declaration, with a firm reliance on the protection of divine Providence, we mutually pledge to each other our Lives, our Fortunes and our sacred Honor.

The 56 signatures on the Declaration appear in the positions indicated:

Column 1

Georgia:

Button Gwinnett

Lyman Hall

George Walton

Column 2

North Carolina:

William Hooper

Joseph Hewes

John Penn

South Carolina:

Edward Rutledge

Thomas Heyward, Jr.

Thomas Lynch, Jr.

Arthur Middleton

Column 3

Massachusetts:

John Hancock

Maryland:

Samuel Chase

William Paca

Thomas Stone

Charles Carroll of Carrollton

Virginia:

George Wythe

Richard Henry Lee

Thomas Jefferson

Benjamin Harrison

Thomas Nelson, Jr.

Francis Lightfoot Lee

Carter Braxton

Column 4

Pennsylvania:

Robert Morris

Benjamin Rush

Benjamin Franklin

John Morton

George Clymer

James Smith

George Taylor

James Wilson

George Ross

Delaware:

Caesar Rodney

George Read
Thomas McKean
Column 5
New York:
William Floyd
Philip Livingston
Francis Lewis
Lewis Morris
New Jersey:
Richard Stockton
John Witherspoon
Francis Hopkinson
John Hart
Abraham Clark
Column 6
New Hampshire:
Josiah Bartlett
William Whipple
Massachusetts:
Samuel Adams
John Adams
Robert Treat Paine
Elbridge Gerry
Rhode Island:
Stephen Hopkins
William Ellery
Connecticut:
Roger Sherman
Samuel Huntington
William Williams
Oliver Wolcott
New Hampshire:
Matthew Thornton

APPENDIX B
The Constitution of the United States

We the People of the United States, in Order to form a more perfect Union, establish Justice, insure domestic Tranquility, provide for the common defence, promote the general Welfare, and secure the Blessings of Liberty to ourselves and our Posterity, do ordain and establish this Constitution for the United States of America.

Article. I.

Section. 1.

All legislative Powers herein granted shall be vested in a Congress of the United States, which shall consist of a Senate and House of Representatives.

Section. 2.

The House of Representatives shall be composed of Members chosen every second Year by the People of the several States, and the Electors in each State shall have the Qualifications requisite for Electors of the most numerous Branch of the State Legislature.

No Person shall be a Representative who shall not have attained to the Age of twenty five Years, and been seven Years a Citizen of the United States, and who shall not, when elected, be an Inhabitant of that State in which he shall be chosen.

Representatives and direct Taxes shall be apportioned among the several States which may be included within this Union, according to their respective Numbers, which shall be determined by adding to the whole Number of free Persons, including those bound to Service for a Term of Years, and excluding Indians not taxed, three fifths of all other Persons. The actual Enumeration shall be made within three Years after the first Meeting of the Congress of the United States, and within every subsequent Term of ten Years, in such Manner as they shall by Law direct. The Number of Representatives shall not exceed one for every thirty Thousand, but each State shall have at Least one Representative; and until such enumeration shall be made, the State of New Hampshire shall be entitled to chuse three, Massachusetts eight, Rhode-Island and Providence Plantations one, Connecticut five, New-York six, New Jersey four, Pennsylvania eight, Delaware one, Maryland six, Virginia ten, North Carolina five, South Carolina five, and Georgia three.

When vacancies happen in the Representation from any State, the Executive Authority thereof shall issue Writs of Election to fill such Vacancies.

The House of Representatives shall chuse their Speaker and other Officers; and shall have the sole Power of Impeachment.

Section. 3.

The Senate of the United States shall be composed of two Senators from each State, chosen by the Legislature thereof, for six Years; and each Senator shall have one Vote.

Immediately after they shall be assembled in Consequence of the first Election, they shall be divided as equally as may be into three Classes. The Seats of the Senators of the first Class shall be vacated at the Expiration of the second Year, of the second Class at the Expiration of the fourth Year, and of the third Class at the Expiration of the sixth Year, so that one third may be chosen every second Year; and if Vacancies happen by Resignation, or otherwise, during the Recess of the Legislature of any State, the Executive thereof may make temporary Appointments until the next Meeting of the Legislature, which shall then fill such Vacancies.

No Person shall be a Senator who shall not have attained to the Age of thirty Years, and been nine Years a Citizen of the United States, and who shall not, when elected, be an Inhabitant of that State for which he shall be chosen.

The Vice President of the United States shall be President of the Senate, but shall have no Vote, unless they be equally divided.

The Senate shall chuse their other Officers, and also a President pro tempore, in the Absence of the Vice President, or when he shall exercise the Office of President of the United States.

The Senate shall have the sole Power to try all Impeachments. When sitting for that Purpose, they shall be on Oath or Affirmation. When the President of the United States is tried, the Chief Justice shall preside: And no Person shall be convicted without the Concurrence of two thirds of the Members present.

Judgment in Cases of Impeachment shall not extend further than to removal from Office, and disqualification to hold and enjoy any Office of honor, Trust or Profit under the United States: but the Party convicted shall nevertheless be liable and subject to Indictment, Trial, Judgment and Punishment, according to Law.

Section. 4.

The Times, Places and Manner of holding Elections for Senators and Representatives, shall be prescribed in each State by the Legislature thereof; but the Congress may at any time by Law make or alter such Regulations, except as to the Places of chusing Senators.

The Congress shall assemble at least once in every Year, and such Meeting shall be on the first Monday in December, unless they shall by Law appoint a different Day.

Section. 5.

Each House shall be the Judge of the Elections, Returns and Qualifications of its own Members, and a Majority of each shall constitute a Quorum to do Business; but a smaller Number may adjourn from day to day, and may be authorized to compel the Attendance of absent Members, in such Manner, and under such Penalties as each House may provide.

Each House may determine the Rules of its Proceedings, punish its Members for disorderly Behaviour, and, with the Concurrence of two thirds, expel a Member.

Each House shall keep a Journal of its Proceedings, and from time to time publish the same, excepting such Parts as may in their Judgment require Secrecy; and the Yeas and Nays of the Members of either House on any question shall, at the Desire of one fifth of those Present, be entered on the Journal.

Neither House, during the Session of Congress, shall, without the Consent of the other, adjourn for more than three days, nor to any other Place than that in which the two Houses shall be sitting.

Section. 6.

The Senators and Representatives shall receive a Compensation for their Services, to be ascertained by Law, and paid out of the Treasury of the United States. They shall in all Cases, except Treason, Felony and Breach of the Peace, be privileged from Arrest during their Attendance at the Session of their respective Houses, and in going to and returning from the same; and for any Speech or Debate in either House, they shall not be questioned in any other Place.

No Senator or Representative shall, during the Time for which he was elected, be appointed to any civil Office under the Authority of the United States, which shall have been created, or the Emoluments whereof shall have been encreased during such time; and no Person holding any Office under the United States, shall be a Member of either House during his Continuance in Office.

Section. 7.

All Bills for raising Revenue shall originate in the House of Representatives; but the Senate may propose or concur with Amendments as on other Bills.

Every Bill which shall have passed the House of Representatives and the Senate, shall, before it become a Law, be presented to the President of the United States; If he approve he shall sign it, but if not he shall return it, with his Objections to that House in which it shall have originated, who shall enter the Objections at large on their Journal, and proceed to reconsider it. If after such Reconsideration two thirds of that House shall agree to pass the Bill, it shall be sent, together with the Objections, to the other House, by which it shall likewise be reconsidered, and if approved by two thirds of that House, it shall become a Law. But in all such Cases the Votes of both Houses shall be determined by yeas and Nays, and the Names of the Persons voting for and against the Bill shall be entered on the Journal of each House respectively. If any Bill shall not be returned by the President within ten Days (Sundays excepted) after it shall have been presented to him, the Same shall be a Law, in like Manner as if he had signed it, unless the Congress by their Adjournment prevent its Return, in which Case it shall not be a Law.

Every Order, Resolution, or Vote to which the Concurrence of the Senate and House of Representatives may be necessary (except on a question of Adjournment) shall be presented to the President of the United States; and before the Same shall take Effect, shall be approved by him, or being disapproved by him, shall be repassed by two thirds of the Senate and House of Representatives, according to the Rules and Limitations prescribed in the Case of a Bill.

Section. 8.

The Congress shall have Power To lay and collect Taxes, Duties, Imposts and Excises, to pay the Debts and provide for the common Defence and general Welfare of the United States; but all Duties, Imposts and Excises shall be uniform throughout the United States;

To borrow Money on the credit of the United States;

To regulate Commerce with foreign Nations, and among the several States, and with the Indian Tribes;

To establish an uniform Rule of Naturalization, and uniform Laws on the subject of Bankruptcies throughout the United States;

To coin Money, regulate the Value thereof, and of foreign Coin, and fix the Standard of Weights and Measures;

To provide for the Punishment of counterfeiting the Securities and current Coin of the United States;

To establish Post Offices and post Roads;

To promote the Progress of Science and useful Arts, by securing for limited Times to Authors and Inventors the exclusive Right to their respective Writings and Discoveries;

To constitute Tribunals inferior to the supreme Court;

To define and punish Piracies and Felonies committed on the high Seas, and Offences against the Law of Nations;

To declare War, grant Letters of Marque and Reprisal, and make Rules concerning Captures on Land and Water;

To raise and support Armies, but no Appropriation of Money to that Use shall be for a longer Term than two Years;

To provide and maintain a Navy;

To make Rules for the Government and Regulation of the land and naval Forces;

To provide for calling forth the Militia to execute the Laws of the Union, suppress Insurrections and repel Invasions;

To provide for organizing, arming, and disciplining, the Militia, and for governing such Part of them as may be employed in the Service of the United States, reserving to the States respectively, the Appointment of the Officers, and the Authority of training the Militia according to the discipline prescribed by Congress;

To exercise exclusive Legislation in all Cases whatsoever, over such District (not exceeding ten Miles square) as may, by Cession of particular States, and the Acceptance of Congress, become the Seat of the Government of the United States, and to exercise like Authority over all Places purchased by the Consent of the Legislature of the State in which the Same shall be, for the Erection of Forts, Magazines, Arsenals, dock-Yards, and other needful Buildings;—And

To make all Laws which shall be necessary and proper for carrying into Execution the foregoing Powers, and all other Powers vested by this Constitution in the Government of the United States, or in any Department or Officer thereof.

Section. 9.

The Migration or Importation of such Persons as any of the States now existing shall think proper to admit, shall not be prohibited by the Congress prior to the Year one thousand eight hundred and eight, but a Tax or duty may be imposed on such Importation, not exceeding ten dollars for each Person.

The Privilege of the Writ of Habeas Corpus shall not be suspended, unless when in Cases of Rebellion or Invasion the public Safety may require it.

No Bill of Attainder or ex post facto Law shall be passed.

No Capitation, or other direct, Tax shall be laid, unless in Proportion to the Census or enumeration herein before directed to be taken.

No Tax or Duty shall be laid on Articles exported from any State.

No Preference shall be given by any Regulation of Commerce or Revenue to the Ports of one State over those of another: nor shall Vessels bound to, or from, one State, be obliged to enter, clear, or pay Duties in another.

No Money shall be drawn from the Treasury, but in Consequence of Appropriations made by Law; and a regular Statement and Account of the Receipts and Expenditures of all public Money shall be published from time to time.

No Title of Nobility shall be granted by the United States: And no Person holding any Office of Profit or Trust under them, shall, without the Consent of the Congress, accept of any present, Emolument, Office, or Title, of any kind whatever, from any King, Prince, or foreign State.

Section. 10.

No State shall enter into any Treaty, Alliance, or Confederation; grant Letters of Marque and Reprisal; coin Money; emit Bills of Credit; make any Thing but gold and silver Coin a Tender in Payment of Debts; pass any Bill of Attainder, ex post facto Law, or Law impairing the Obligation of Contracts, or grant any Title of Nobility.

No State shall, without the Consent of the Congress, lay any Imposts or Duties on Imports or Exports, except what may be absolutely necessary for executing it's inspection Laws: and the net Produce of all Duties and Imposts, laid by any State on Imports or Exports, shall be for the Use of the Treasury of the United States; and all such Laws shall be subject to the Revision and Controul of the Congress.

No State shall, without the Consent of Congress, lay any Duty of Tonnage, keep Troops, or Ships of War in time of Peace, enter into any Agreement or Compact with another State, or with a foreign Power, or engage in War, unless actually invaded, or in such imminent Danger as will not admit of delay.

Article. II.

Section. 1.

The executive Power shall be vested in a President of the United States of America. He shall hold his Office during the Term of four Years, and, together with the Vice President, chosen for the same Term, be elected, as follows

Each State shall appoint, in such Manner as the Legislature thereof may direct, a Number of Electors, equal to the whole Number of Senators and Representatives to which the State may be entitled in the Congress: but no Senator or Representative, or Person holding an Office of Trust or Profit under the United States, shall be appointed an Elector.

The Electors shall meet in their respective States, and vote by Ballot for two Persons, of whom one at least shall not be an Inhabitant of the same State with themselves. And they shall make a List of all the Persons voted for, and of the Number of Votes for each; which List they shall sign and certify, and transmit sealed to the Seat of the Government of the United States, directed to the President of the Senate. The President of the Senate shall, in the Presence of the Senate and House of Representatives, open all the Certificates, and the Votes shall then be counted. The Person having the greatest Number of Votes shall be the President, if such Number be a Majority of the whole Number of Electors appointed; and if there be more than one who have such Majority, and have an equal Number of Votes, then the House of Representatives shall immediately chuse by Ballot one of them for President; and if no Person have a Majority, then from the five highest on the List the said House shall in like Manner chuse the President. But in chusing the President, the Votes shall be taken by States, the Representation from each State having one Vote; A quorum for this Purpose shall consist of a Member or Members from two thirds of the States, and a Majority of all the States shall be necessary to a Choice. In every Case, after the Choice of the President, the Person having the greatest Number of Votes of the Electors shall be the Vice President. But if there should remain two or more who have equal Votes, the Senate shall chuse from them by Ballot the Vice President.

The Congress may determine the Time of chusing the Electors, and the Day on which they shall give their Votes; which Day shall be the same throughout the United States.

No Person except a natural born Citizen, or a Citizen of the United States, at the time of the Adoption of this Constitution, shall be eligible to the Office of President; neither shall any Person be eligible to that Office who shall not have attained to the Age of thirty five Years, and been fourteen Years a Resident within the United States.

In Case of the Removal of the President from Office, or of his Death, Resignation, or Inability to discharge the Powers and Duties of the said Office, the Same shall devolve on the Vice President, and the Congress may by Law provide for the Case of Removal, Death, Resignation or Inability, both of the President and Vice President, declaring what Officer shall then act as President, and such Officer shall act accordingly, until the Disability be removed, or a President shall be elected.

The President shall, at stated Times, receive for his Services, a Compensation, which shall neither be encreased nor diminished during the Period for which he shall have been elected, and he shall not receive within that Period any other Emolument from the United States, or any of them.

Before he enter on the Execution of his Office, he shall take the following Oath or Affirmation:—"I do solemnly swear (or affirm) that I will faithfully execute the Office of President of the United States, and will to the best of my Ability, preserve, protect and defend the Constitution of the United States."

Section. 2.

The President shall be Commander in Chief of the Army and Navy of the United States, and of the Militia of the several States, when called into the actual Service of the United States; he may require the Opinion, in writing, of the principal Officer in each of the executive Departments, upon any Subject relating to the Duties of their respective Offices, and he shall have Power to grant Reprieves and Pardons for Offences against the United States, except in Cases of Impeachment.

He shall have Power, by and with the Advice and Consent of the Senate, to make Treaties, provided two thirds of the Senators present concur; and he shall nominate, and by and with the Advice and Consent of the Senate, shall appoint Ambassadors, other public Ministers and Consuls, Judges of the supreme Court, and all other Officers of the United States, whose Appointments are not herein otherwise provided for, and which shall be established by Law: but the Congress may by Law vest the Appointment of such inferior Officers, as they think proper, in the President alone, in the Courts of Law, or in the Heads of Departments.

The President shall have Power to fill up all Vacancies that may happen during the Recess of the Senate, by granting Commissions which shall expire at the End of their next Session.

Section. 3.

He shall from time to time give to the Congress Information of the State of the Union, and recommend to their Consideration such Measures as he shall judge necessary and expedient; he may, on extraordinary Occasions, convene both Houses, or either of them, and in Case of Disagreement between them, with Respect to the Time of Adjournment, he may adjourn them to such Time as he shall think proper; he shall receive Ambassadors and other public Ministers; he shall take Care that the Laws be faithfully executed, and shall Commission all the Officers of the United States.

Section. 4.

The President, Vice President and all civil Officers of the United States, shall be removed from Office on Impeachment for, and Conviction of, Treason, Bribery, or other high Crimes and Misdemeanors.

Article III.

Section. 1.

The judicial Power of the United States, shall be vested in one supreme Court, and in such inferior Courts as the Congress may from time to time ordain and establish. The Judges, both of the supreme and inferior Courts, shall hold their Offices during good Behaviour, and shall, at stated Times, receive for their Services, a Compensation, which shall not be diminished during their Continuance in Office.

Section. 2.

The judicial Power shall extend to all Cases, in Law and Equity, arising under this Constitution, the Laws of the United States, and Treaties made, or which shall be made, under their Authority;—to all Cases affecting Ambassadors, other public Ministers and Consuls;—to all Cases of admiralty and maritime Jurisdiction;—to Controversies to which the United States shall be a Party;—to Controversies between two or more States;— between a State and Citizens of another State,—between Citizens of different States,—between Citizens of the same State claiming Lands under Grants of different States, and between a State, or the Citizens thereof, and foreign States, Citizens or Subjects.

In all Cases affecting Ambassadors, other public Ministers and Consuls, and those in which a State shall be Party, the supreme Court shall have original Jurisdiction. In all the other Cases before mentioned, the supreme Court shall have appellate Jurisdiction, both as to Law and Fact, with such Exceptions, and under such Regulations as the Congress shall make.

The Trial of all Crimes, except in Cases of Impeachment, shall be by Jury; and such Trial shall be held in the State where the said Crimes shall have been committed; but when not committed within any State, the Trial shall be at such Place or Places as the Congress may by Law have directed.

Section. 3.

Treason against the United States, shall consist only in levying War against them, or in adhering to their Enemies, giving them Aid and Comfort. No Person shall be convicted of Treason unless on the Testimony of two Witnesses to the same overt Act, or on Confession in open Court.

The Congress shall have Power to declare the Punishment of Treason, but no Attainder of Treason shall work Corruption of Blood, or Forfeiture except during the Life of the Person attainted.

Article. IV.

Section. 1.

Full Faith and Credit shall be given in each State to the public Acts, Records, and judicial Proceedings of every other State. And the Congress may by general Laws prescribe the Manner in which such Acts, Records and Proceedings shall be proved, and the Effect thereof.

Section. 2.

The Citizens of each State shall be entitled to all Privileges and Immunities of Citizens in the several States.

A Person charged in any State with Treason, Felony, or other Crime, who shall flee from Justice, and be found in another State, shall on Demand of the executive Authority of the State from which he fled, be delivered up, to be removed to the State having Jurisdiction of the Crime.

No Person held to Service or Labour in one State, under the Laws thereof, escaping into another, shall, in Consequence of any Law or Regulation therein, be discharged from such Service or Labour, but shall be delivered up on Claim of the Party to whom such Service or Labour may be due.

Section. 3.

New States may be admitted by the Congress into this Union; but no new State shall be formed or erected within the Jurisdiction of any other State; nor any State be formed by the Junction of two or more States, or Parts of States, without the Consent of the Legislatures of the States concerned as well as of the Congress.

The Congress shall have Power to dispose of and make all needful Rules and Regulations respecting the Territory or other Property belonging to the United States; and nothing in this Constitution shall be so construed as to Prejudice any Claims of the United States, or of any particular State.

Section. 4.

The United States shall guarantee to every State in this Union a Republican Form of Government, and shall protect each of them against Invasion; and on Application of the Legislature, or of the Executive (when the Legislature cannot be convened), against domestic Violence.

Article. V.

The Congress, whenever two thirds of both Houses shall deem it necessary, shall propose Amendments to this Constitution, or, on the Application of the Legislatures of two thirds of the several States, shall call a Convention for proposing Amendments, which, in either Case, shall be valid to all Intents and Purposes, as Part of this Constitution, when ratified by the Legislatures of three fourths of the several States, or by Conventions in three fourths thereof, as the one or the other Mode of Ratification may be proposed by the Congress; Provided that no Amendment which may be made prior to the Year One thousand eight hundred and eight shall in any Manner affect the first and fourth Clauses in the Ninth Section of the first Article; and that no State, without its Consent, shall be deprived of its equal Suffrage in the Senate.

Article. VI.

All Debts contracted and Engagements entered into, before the Adoption of this Constitution, shall be as valid against the United States under this Constitution, as under the Confederation.

This Constitution, and the Laws of the United States which shall be made in Pursuance thereof; and all Treaties made, or which shall be made, under the Authority of the United States, shall be the supreme Law of the Land; and the Judges in every State shall be bound thereby, any Thing in the Constitution or Laws of any State to the Contrary notwithstanding.

The Senators and Representatives before mentioned, and the Members of the several State Legislatures, and all executive and judicial Officers, both of the United States and of the several States, shall be bound by Oath or Affirmation, to support this Constitution; but no religious Test shall ever be required as a Qualification to any Office or public Trust under the United States.

Article. VII.

The Ratification of the Conventions of nine States, shall be sufficient for the Establishment of this Constitution between the States so ratifying the Same.

Done in Convention by the Unanimous Consent of the States present the Seventeenth Day of September in the Year of our Lord one thousand seven hundred and Eighty seven and of the Independance of the United States of America the Twelfth In witness whereof We have hereunto subscribed our Names,

G. Washington
Presidt and deputy from Virginia

Delaware
Geo: Read
Gunning Bedford jun
John Dickinson
Richard Bassett
Jaco: Broom

Maryland
James McHenry
Dan of St Thos. Jenifer
Danl. Carroll

Virginia
John Blair
James Madison Jr.

North Carolina
Wm. Blount
Richd. Dobbs Spaight
Hu Williamson

South Carolina
J. Rutledge
Charles Cotesworth Pinckney
Charles Pinckney
Pierce Butler

Georgia
William Few
Abr Baldwin

New Hampshire
John Langdon
Nicholas Gilman

Massachusetts
Nathaniel Gorham
Rufus King

Connecticut
Wm. Saml. Johnson
Roger Sherman

New York
Alexander Hamilton

New Jersey
Wil: Livingston
David Brearley
Wm. Paterson
Jona: Dayton

Pensylvania
B Franklin
Thomas Mifflin
Robt. Morris
Geo. Clymer
Thos. FitzSimons
Jared Ingersoll
James Wilson
Gouv Morris

Constitutional Amendments

The U.S. Bill of Rights (Amendments 1–10)

The Preamble to The Bill of Rights

Congress of the United States begun and held at the City of New-York, on Wednesday the fourth of March, one thousand seven hundred and eighty nine.

The Conventions of a number of the States, having at the time of their adopting the Constitution, expressed a desire, in order to prevent misconstruction or abuse of its powers, that further declaratory and restrictive clauses should be added: And as extending the ground of public confidence in the Government, will best ensure the beneficent ends of its institution.

Resolved by the Senate and House of Representatives of the United States of America, in Congress assembled, two thirds of both Houses concurring, that the following Articles be proposed to the Legislatures of the several States, as amendments to the Constitution of the United States, all, or any of which Articles, when ratified by three fourths of the said Legislatures, to be valid to all intents and purposes, as part of the said Constitution; viz.

Articles in addition to, and Amendment of the Constitution of the United States of America, proposed by Congress, and ratified by the Legislatures of the several States, pursuant to the fifth Article of the original Constitution.

Note: The following text is a transcription of the first ten amendments to the Constitution in their original form. These amendments were ratified December 15, 1791, and form what is known as the "Bill of Rights."

Amendment I

Congress shall make no law respecting an establishment of religion, or prohibiting the free exercise thereof; or abridging the freedom of speech, or of the press; or the right of the people peaceably to assemble, and to petition the Government for a redress of grievances.

Amendment II

A well regulated Militia, being necessary to the security of a free State, the right of the people to keep and bear Arms, shall not be infringed.

Amendment III

No Soldier shall, in time of peace be quartered in any house, without the consent of the Owner, nor in time of war, but in a manner to be prescribed by law.

Amendment IV

The right of the people to be secure in their persons, houses, papers, and effects, against unreasonable searches and seizures, shall not be violated, and no Warrants shall issue, but upon probable cause, supported by Oath or affirmation, and particularly describing the place to be searched, and the persons or things to be seized.

Amendment V

No person shall be held to answer for a capital, or otherwise infamous crime, unless on a presentment or indictment of a Grand Jury, except in cases arising in the land or naval forces, or in the Militia, when in actual service in time of War or public danger; nor shall any person be subject for the same offence to be twice put in jeopardy of life or limb; nor shall be compelled in any criminal case to be a witness against himself, nor be deprived of life, liberty, or property, without due process of law; nor shall private property be taken for public use, without just compensation.

Amendment VI

In all criminal prosecutions, the accused shall enjoy the right to a speedy and public trial, by an impartial jury of the State and district wherein the crime shall have been committed, which district shall have been previously ascertained by law, and to be informed of the nature and cause of the accusation; to be confronted with the witnesses against him; to have compulsory process for obtaining witnesses in his favor, and to have the Assistance of Counsel for his defence.

Amendment VII

In Suits at common law, where the value in controversy shall exceed twenty dollars, the right of trial by jury shall be preserved, and no fact tried by a jury, shall be otherwise re-examined in any Court of the United States, than according to the rules of the common law.

Amendment VIII

Excessive bail shall not be required, nor excessive fines imposed, nor cruel and unusual punishments inflicted.

Amendment IX

The enumeration in the Constitution, of certain rights, shall not be construed to deny or disparage others retained by the people.

Amendment X

The powers not delegated to the United States by the Constitution, nor prohibited by it to the States, are reserved to the States respectively, or to the people.

Amendment XI

The Judicial power of the United States shall not be construed to extend to any suit in law or equity, commenced or prosecuted against one of the United States by Citizens of another State, or by Citizens or Subjects of any Foreign State.

Amendment XII

The Electors shall meet in their respective states and vote by ballot for President and Vice-President, one of whom, at least, shall not be an inhabitant of the same state with themselves; they shall name in their ballots the person voted for as President, and in distinct ballots the person voted for as Vice-President, and they shall make distinct lists of all persons voted for as President, and of all persons voted for as Vice-President, and of the number of votes for each, which lists they shall sign and certify, and transmit sealed to the seat of the government of the United States, directed to the President of the Senate; — the President of the Senate shall, in the presence of the Senate and House of Representatives, open all the certificates and the votes shall then be counted; — The person having the greatest number of votes for President, shall be the President, if such number be a majority of the whole number of Electors appointed; and if no person have such majority, then from the persons having the highest numbers not exceeding three on the list of those voted for as President, the House of Representatives shall choose immediately, by ballot, the President. But in choosing the President, the votes shall be taken by states, the representation from each state having one vote; a quorum for this purpose shall consist of a member or members from two-thirds of the states, and a majority of all the states shall be necessary to a choice. [And if the House of Representatives shall not choose a President whenever the right of choice shall devolve upon them, before the fourth day of March next following, then the Vice-President shall act as President, as in case of the death or other constitutional disability of the President. —]* The person having the greatest number of votes as Vice-President, shall be the Vice-President, if such number be a majority of the whole number of Electors appointed, and if no person have a majority, then from the two highest numbers on the list, the Senate shall choose the Vice-President; a quorum for the purpose shall consist of two-thirds of the whole number of Senators, and a majority of the whole number shall be necessary to a choice. But no person constitutionally ineligible to the office of President shall be eligible to that of Vice-President of the United States.

Superseded by Section 3 of the 20th amendment.

Amendment XIII

Section 1.

Neither slavery nor involuntary servitude, except as a punishment for crime whereof the party shall have been duly convicted, shall exist within the United States, or any place subject to their jurisdiction.

Section 2.

Congress shall have power to enforce this article by appropriate legislation.

Amendment XIV

Section 1.

All persons born or naturalized in the United States, and subject to the jurisdiction thereof, are citizens of the United States and of the State wherein they reside. No State shall make or enforce any law which shall abridge the privileges or immunities of citizens of the United States; nor shall any State deprive any person of life, liberty, or property, without due process of law; nor deny to any person within its jurisdiction the equal protection of the laws.

Section 2.

Representatives shall be apportioned among the several States according to their respective numbers, counting the whole number of persons in each State, excluding Indians not taxed. But when the right to vote at any election for the choice of electors for President and Vice-President of the United States, Representatives in Congress, the Executive and Judicial officers of a State, or the members of the Legislature thereof, is denied to any of the male inhabitants of such State, being twenty-one years of age,* and citizens of the United States, or in any way abridged, except for participation in rebellion, or other crime, the basis of representation therein shall be reduced in the proportion which the number of such male citizens shall bear to the whole number of male citizens twenty-one years of age in such State.

Section 3.

No person shall be a Senator or Representative in Congress, or elector of President and Vice-President, or hold any office, civil or military, under the United States, or under any State, who, having previously taken an oath, as a member of Congress, or as an officer of the United States, or as a member of any State legislature, or as an executive or judicial officer of any State, to support the Constitution of the United States, shall have engaged in insurrection or rebellion against the same, or given aid or comfort to the enemies thereof. But Congress may by a vote of two-thirds of each House, remove such disability.

Section 4.

The validity of the public debt of the United States, authorized by law, including debts incurred for payment of pensions and bounties for services in suppressing insurrection or rebellion, shall not be questioned. But neither the United States nor any State shall assume or pay any debt or obligation incurred in aid of insurrection or rebellion against the United States, or any claim for the loss or emancipation of any slave; but all such debts, obligations and claims shall be held illegal and void.

Section 5.

The Congress shall have the power to enforce, by appropriate legislation, the provisions of this article.

Changed by Section 1 of the 26th amendment.

Amendment XV

Section 1.

The right of citizens of the United States to vote shall not be denied or abridged by the United States or by any State on account of race, color, or previous condition of servitude—

Section 2.

The Congress shall have the power to enforce this article by appropriate legislation.

Amendment XVI

The Congress shall have power to lay and collect taxes on incomes, from whatever source derived, without apportionment among the several States, and without regard to any census or enumeration.

Amendment XVII

The Senate of the United States shall be composed of two Senators from each State, elected by the people thereof, for six years; and each Senator shall have one vote. The electors in each State shall have the qualifications requisite for electors of the most numerous branch of the State legislatures.

When vacancies happen in the representation of any State in the Senate, the executive authority of such State shall issue writs of election to fill such vacancies: *Provided*, That the legislature of any State may empower the executive thereof to make temporary appointments until the people fill the vacancies by election as the legislature may direct.

This amendment shall not be so construed as to affect the election or term of any Senator chosen before it becomes valid as part of the Constitution.

Amendment XVIII

Section 1.

After one year from the ratification of this article the manufacture, sale, or transportation of intoxicating liquors within, the importation thereof into, or the exportation thereof from the United States and all territory subject to the jurisdiction thereof for beverage purposes is hereby prohibited.

Section 2.

The Congress and the several States shall have concurrent power to enforce this article by appropriate legislation.

Section 3.

This article shall be inoperative unless it shall have been ratified as an amendment to the Constitution by the legislatures of the several States, as provided in the Constitution, within seven years from the date of the submission hereof to the States by the Congress.

Amendment XIX

The right of citizens of the United States to vote shall not be denied or abridged by the United States or by any State on account of sex.

Congress shall have power to enforce this article by appropriate legislation.

Amendment XX

Section 1.

The terms of the President and the Vice President shall end at noon on the 20th day of January, and the terms of Senators and Representatives at noon on the 3d day of January, of the years in which such terms would have ended if this article had not been ratified; and the terms of their successors shall then begin.

Section 2.

The Congress shall assemble at least once in every year, and such meeting shall begin at noon on the 3d day of January, unless they shall by law appoint a different day.

Section 3.

If, at the time fixed for the beginning of the term of the President, the President elect shall have died, the Vice President elect shall become President. If a President shall not have been chosen before the time fixed for the beginning of his term, or if the President elect shall have failed to qualify, then the Vice President elect shall act as President until a President shall have qualified; and the Congress may by law provide for the case wherein neither a President elect nor a Vice President elect shall have qualified, declaring who shall then act as President, or the manner in which one who is to act shall be selected, and such person shall act accordingly until a President or Vice President shall have qualified.

Section 4.

The Congress may by law provide for the case of the death of any of the persons from whom the House of Representatives may choose a President whenever the right of choice shall have devolved upon them, and for the case of the death of any of the persons from whom the Senate may choose a Vice President whenever the right of choice shall have devolved upon them.

Section 5.

Sections 1 and 2 shall take effect on the 15th day of October following the ratification of this article.

Section 6.

This article shall be inoperative unless it shall have been ratified as an amendment to the Constitution by the legislatures of three-fourths of the several States within seven years from the date of its submission.

Amendment XXI

Section 1.

The eighteenth article of amendment to the Constitution of the United States is hereby repealed.

Section 2.

The transportation or importation into any State, Territory, or possession of the United States for delivery or use therein of intoxicating liquors, in violation of the laws thereof, is hereby prohibited.

Section 3.

This article shall be inoperative unless it shall have been ratified as an amendment to the Constitution by conventions in the several States, as provided in the Constitution, within seven years from the date of the submission hereof to the States by the Congress.

Amendment XXII

Section 1.

No person shall be elected to the office of the President more than twice, and no person who has held the office of President, or acted as President, for more than two years of a term to which some other person was elected President shall be elected to the office of the President more than once. But this Article shall not apply to any person holding the office of President when this Article was proposed by the Congress, and shall not prevent any person who may be holding the office of President, or acting as President, during the term within which this Article becomes operative from holding the office of President or acting as President during the remainder of such term.

Section 2.

This article shall be inoperative unless it shall have been ratified as an amendment to the Constitution by the legislatures of three-fourths of the several States within seven years from the date of its submission to the States by the Congress.

Amendment XXIII

Section 1.

The District constituting the seat of Government of the United States shall appoint in such manner as the Congress may direct:

A number of electors of President and Vice President equal to the whole number of Senators and Representatives in Congress to which the District would be entitled if it were a State, but in no event more than the least populous State; they shall be in addition to those appointed by the States, but they shall be considered, for the purposes of the election of President and Vice President, to be electors appointed by a State; and they shall meet in the District and perform such duties as provided by the twelfth article of amendment.

Section 2.

The Congress shall have power to enforce this article by appropriate legislation.

Amendment XXIV

Section 1.

The right of citizens of the United States to vote in any primary or other election for President or Vice President, for electors for President or Vice President, or for Senator or Representative in Congress, shall not be denied or abridged by the United States or any State by reason of failure to pay any poll tax or other tax.

Section 2.

The Congress shall have power to enforce this article by appropriate legislation.

Amendment XXV

Section 1.

In case of the removal of the President from office or of his death or resignation, the Vice President shall become President.

Section 2.

Whenever there is a vacancy in the office of the Vice President, the President shall nominate a Vice President who shall take office upon confirmation by a majority vote of both Houses of Congress.

Section 3.

Whenever the President transmits to the President pro tempore of the Senate and the Speaker of the House of Representatives his written declaration that he is unable to discharge the powers and duties of his office, and until he transmits to them a written declaration to the contrary, such powers and duties shall be discharged by the Vice President as Acting President.

Section 4.

Whenever the Vice President and a majority of either the principal officers of the executive departments or of such other body as Congress may by law provide, transmit to the President pro tempore of the Senate and the Speaker of the House of Representatives their written declaration that the President is unable to discharge the powers and duties of his office, the Vice President shall immediately assume the powers and duties of the office as Acting President.

Thereafter, when the President transmits to the President pro tempore of the Senate and the Speaker of the House of Representatives his written declaration that no inability exists, he shall resume the powers and duties of his office unless the Vice President and a majority of either the principal officers of the executive department or of such other body as Congress may by law provide, transmit within four days to the President pro tempore of the Senate and the Speaker of the House of Representatives their written declaration that the President is unable to discharge the powers and duties of his office. Thereupon Congress shall decide the issue, assembling within forty-eight hours for that purpose if not in session. If the Congress, within twenty-one days after receipt of the latter written declaration, or, if Congress is not in session, within twenty-one days after Congress is required to assemble, determines by two-thirds vote of both Houses that the President is unable to discharge the powers and duties of his office, the Vice President shall continue to discharge the same as Acting President; otherwise, the President shall resume the powers and duties of his office.

Amendment XXVI

Section 1.

The right of citizens of the United States, who are eighteen years of age or older, to vote shall not be denied or abridged by the United States or by any State on account of age.

Section 2.

The Congress shall have power to enforce this article by appropriate legislation.

Amendment XXVII

No law, varying the compensation for the services of the Senators and Representatives, shall take effect, until an election of Representatives shall have intervened.

APPENDIX C
Presidents of the United States of America

Table C1 Presidents of the United States of America

Order	Election Year	President
1	1788–1789	George Washington
2	1792	George Washington
3	1796	John Adams
4	1800	Thomas Jefferson
5	1804	Thomas Jefferson
6	1808	James Madison
7	1812	James Madison
8	1816	James Monroe
9	1820	James Monroe
10	1824	John Quincy Adams
11	1828	Andrew Jackson
12	1832	Andrew Jackson
13	1836	Martin Van Buren
14	1840	William Henry Harrison
15	1844	James K. Polk
16	1848	Zachary Taylor
17	1852	Franklin Pierce
18	1856	James Buchanan
19	1860	Abraham Lincoln
20	1864	Abraham Lincoln
21	1868	Ulysses S. Grant
22	1872	Ulysses S. Grant
23	1876	Rutherford B. Hayes
24	1880	James A. Garfield

Table C1 Presidents of the United States of America

Order	Election Year	President
25	1884	Grover Cleveland
26	1888	Benjamin Harrison
27	1892	Grover Cleveland
28	1896	William McKinley
29	1900	William McKinley
30	1904	Theodore Roosevelt
31	1908	William Howard Taft
32	1912	Woodrow Wilson
33	1916	Woodrow Wilson
34	1920	Warren G. Harding
35	1924	Calvin Coolidge
36	1928	Herbert Hoover
37	1932	Franklin D. Roosevelt
38	1936	Franklin D. Roosevelt
39	1940	Franklin D. Roosevelt
40	1944	Franklin D. Roosevelt
41	1948	Harry S. Truman
42	1952	Dwight D. Eisenhower
43	1956	Dwight D. Eisenhower
44	1960	John F. Kennedy
45	1964	Lyndon B. Johnson
46	1968	Richard Nixon
47	1972	Richard Nixon
48	1976	Jimmy Carter
49	1980	Ronald Reagan
50	1984	Ronald Reagan
51	1988	George H. W. Bush

Table C1 Presidents of the United States of America

Order	Election Year	President
52	1992	Bill Clinton
53	1996	Bill Clinton
54	2000	George W. Bush
55	2004	George W. Bush
56	2008	Barack Obama
57	2012	Barack Obama

APPENDIX D

U.S. Political Map

Figure D1   (credit: U.S. Department of the Interior, U.S. Geological Survey, The National Atlas of the United States of America/nationalatlas.gov)

U.S. Topographical Map

Figure E1

APPENDIX F

United States Population Chart

Table F1 United States Population Chart[1]

Census Year	Population		Census Year	Population
1610	350		1820	9,638,453
1620	2,302		1830	12,866,020
1630	4,646		1840	17,069,453
1640	26,634		1850	23,191,876
1650	50,368		1860	31,443,321
1660	75,058		1870	38,558,371
1670	111,935		1880	50,189,209
1680	151,507		1890	62,979,766
1690	210,372		1900	76,212,168
1700	250,888		1910	92,228,496
1710	331,711		1920	106,021,537
1720	466,185		1930	123,202,624
1730	629,445		1940	132,164,569
1740	905,563		1950	151,325,798
1750	1,170,760		1960	179,323,175
1760	1,593,625		1970	203,211,926
1770	2,148,076		1980	226,656,805
1780	2,780,369		1990	248,709,873
1790	3,929,214		2000	281,421,906
1800	5,308,483		2010	308,745,538
1810	7,239,881			

1. Population figures for the decades before the first U.S. census in 1790 are estimates.

APPENDIX G

Further Reading

THE PRE-COLUMBIAN WORLD AND EARLY GLOBALIZATION

Alchon, Suzanne Austin. 2003. *A Pest in the Land: New World Epidemics in a Global Perspective*. Albuquerque: University of New Mexico Press.

Brown, Kathleen M. 1996. *Good Wives, Nasty Wenches, and Anxious Patriarchs: Gender, Race, and Power in Colonial Virginia*. Chapel Hill: University of North Carolina Press.

Clendinnen, Inga. 1991. *Aztecs: An Interpretation*. Cambridge: Cambridge University Press.

Cook, Harold John. 2007. *Matters of Exchange: Commerce, Medicine, and Science in the Dutch Golden Age*. New Haven: Yale University Press.

Curtin, Philip D. 1990. *The Rise and Fall of the Plantation Complex: Essays in Atlantic History*. Cambridge: Cambridge University Press.

Leon, Portilla Miguel. (1992) 2006. *The Broken Spears: The Aztec Account of the Conquest of Mexico*. Boston: Beacon Press.

Mann, Charles C. 2005. *1491: New Revelations of the Americas Before Columbus*. New York: Knopf.

—. 2011. *1493: Uncovering the New World Columbus Created*. New York: Knopf.

Meltzer, David J. 2009. *First Peoples in a New World: Colonizing Ice Age America*. Berkeley: University of California Press.

Niane, Djibril Tamsir. 1965. *Sundiata: An Epic of Old Mali*. Translated by G. D. Pickett. London: Longmans.

Northrup, David. 2013. *Africa's Discovery of Europe*. Oxford: Oxford University Press.

Pagden, Anthony. 1995. *Lords of all the World: Ideologies of Empire in Spain, Britain and France c.1500–c.1800*. New Haven: Yale University Press.

Prescott, William Hickling. 1936. *History of the Conquest of Mexico, and History of the Conquest of Peru*. New York: Modern Library.

Seed, Patricia. 1995. *Ceremonies of Possession in Europe's Conquest of the New World, 1492–1640*. Cambridge: Cambridge University Press.

Taylor, Alan. 2002. *American Colonies*. New York: Penguin Books.

Thornton, John K. 1992. *Africa and Africans in the Making of the Atlantic World, 1400–1680*. Cambridge: Cambridge University Press.

Wey Gómez, Nicolás. 2008. *The Tropics of Empire: Why Columbus Sailed South to the Indies*. Cambridge, MA: MIT Press.

THE COLONIAL AMERICAS

Bailyn, Bernard. 2012. *The Barbarous Years: The Peopling of British North America: The Conflict of Civilizations, 1600–1675*. New York: Vintage Books.

Berlin, Ira. 1998. *Many Thousands Gone: The First Two Centuries of Slavery in North America*. Cambridge, MA: Belknap Press.

Calloway, Colin G. 2011. *First Peoples: A Documentary Survey of American Indian History*. Fourth edition, Boston: Bedford/St. Martin's Press.

Elliott, J. H. 2006. *Empires of the Atlantic World: Britain and Spain in America, 1492–1830.* New Haven: Yale University Press.

Fischer, David H. 1989. *Albion's Seed: Four British Folkways in America.* New York: Oxford University Press.

Gaustad, Edwin S. 1982. *A Documentary History of Religion in America.* Grand Rapids, MI: Eerdmans.

Gibson, Charles. 1964. *The Aztecs Under Spanish Rule: A History of the Indians of the Valley of Mexico, 1519–1810.* Stanford, CA: Stanford University Press.

Hatfield, April Lee. 2004. *Atlantic Virginia: Intercolonial Relations in the Seventeenth Century.* Philadelphia: University of Pennsylvania Press.

Liss, Peggy K. 1975. *Mexico Under Spain, 1521–1556: Society and the Origins of Nationality.* Chicago: University of Chicago Press.

Morgan, Edmund S. 1958. *The Puritan Dilemma: The Story of John Winthrop.* Boston: Little, Brown.

Rediker, Marcus. 2007. *The Slave Ship: A Human History.* New York: Viking Books.

Richter, Daniel K. 2001. *Facing East from Indian Country: A Native History of Early America.* Cambridge, MA: Harvard University Press.

Roberts, David. 2004. *The Pueblo Revolt: The Secret Rebellion that Drove the Spaniards Out of the Southwest.* New York: Simon & Schuster.

Spicer, Edward Holland. 1962. *Cycles of Conquest: The Impact of Spain, Mexico, and the United States on the Indians of the Southwest, 1533–1960.* Tucson: University of Arizona Press.

Twinam, Ann. 1982. *Miners, Merchants, and Farmers in Colonial Colombia.* Austin: University of Texas Press.

Weber, David J. 1992. *The Spanish Frontier in North America.* New Haven: Yale University Press.

REFORM, PROTEST, AND REVOLUTION

Anderson, Fred. 2005. *The War That Made America: A Short History of the French and Indian War.* New York: Viking Books.

Bailyn, Bernard. 1986. *The Peopling of British North America: An Introduction.* New York: Knopf Doubleday.

Breen, Timothy H. 2004. *The Marketplace of Revolution: How Consumer Politics Shaped American Independence.* Oxford: Oxford University Press.

Butler, Jon. 2000. *Becoming America: The Revolution before 1776.* Cambridge, MA: Harvard University Press.

Calloway, Colin G. 1995. *The American Revolution in Indian Country: Crisis and Diversity in Native American Communities.* Cambridge: Cambridge University Press.

Cook, Don. 1995. *The Long Fuse: How England Lost the American Colonies, 1760–1785.* New York: Atlantic Monthly Press.

Egerton, Douglas R. 2009. *Death or Liberty: African Americans and Revolutionary America.* Oxford: Oxford University Press.

Ellis, Joseph J. 2003. *Founding Brothers: The Revolutionary Generation.* New York: Random House.

Fischer, David Hackett. 2004. *Washington's Crossing.* Oxford: Oxford University Press.

Fleming, Thomas J. 1997. *Liberty! The American Revolution.* New York: Viking Books.

Holton, Woody. 1999. *Forced Founders: Indians, Debtors, Slaves, and the Making of the American Revolution in Virginia.* Chapel Hill: University of North Carolina Press.

—. 2007. *Unruly Americans and the Origins of the Constitution.* New York: Hill and Wang.

Isaac, Rhys. 1982. *The Transformation of Virginia, 1740-1790.* Chapel Hill: University of North Carolina Press.

Lovejoy, David S. 1972. *The Glorious Revolution in America*. New York: Harper & Row.

McCullough, David. 2005. *1776*. New York: Simon & Schuster.

Middlekauff, Robert. 1982. *The Glorious Cause: The American Revolution, 1763–1789*. New York: Oxford University Press.

Noll, Mark A. 2003. *The Rise of Evangelicalism: The Age of Edwards, Whitefield, and the Wesleys*. Downers Grove, IL: InterVarsity Press.

Norton, Mary Beth. 1980. *Liberty's Daughters: The Revolutionary Experience of American Women, 1750–1800*. Boston: Little, Brown.

Olwell, Robert. 1998. *Masters, Slaves & Subjects: The Culture of Power in the South Carolina Low Country, 1740–1790*. Ithaca, NY: Cornell University Press.

Rakove, Jack N. 2010. *Revolutionaries: A New History of the Invention of America*. Boston: Houghton Mifflin Harcourt.

Raphael, Ray. 2001. *A People's History of the American Revolution: How Common People Shaped the Fight for Independence*. New York: New Press.

Stout, Harry S. 1991. *The Divine Dramatist: George Whitefield and the Rise of Modern Evangelicalism*. Grand Rapids, MI: Eerdmans.

Webb, Stephen Saunders. 1995. *Lord Churchill's Coup: The Anglo-American Empire and the Glorious Revolution Reconsidered*. New York: Knopf.

Wood, Gordon S. 1992. *The Radicalism of the American Revolution*. New York: Knopf.

Young, Alfred Fabian. 1999. *The Shoemaker and the Tea Party: Memory and the American Revolution*. Boston: Beacon Press.

THE EARLY REPUBLIC

Appleby, Joyce Oldham. 2000. *Inheriting the Revolution: The First Generation of Americans*. Cambridge, MA: Belknap Press.

Dubois, Laurent. 2004. *Avengers of the New World: The Story of the Haitian Revolution*. Cambridge, MA: Belknap Press.

Ellis, Joseph J. 1997. *American Sphinx: The Character of Thomas Jefferson*. New York: Knopf.

Ferling, John. 2004. *Adams vs. Jefferson: The Tumultuous Election of 1800*. New York: Oxford University Press.

Hickey, Donald R. 1989. *The War of 1812: A Forgotten Conflict*. Urbana: University of Illinois Press.

Kamensky, Jane. 2008. *The Exchange Artist: A Tale of High-Flying Speculation and America's First Banking Collapse*. New York: Viking Books.

Langguth, A. J. 2006. *Union 1812: The Americans Who Fought the Second War of Independence*. New York: Simon & Schuster.

Litwack, Leon F. 1961. *North of Slavery: The Negro in the Free States, 1790–1860*. Chicago: University of Chicago Press.

Maier, Pauline. 1997. *American Scripture: Making the Declaration of Independence*. New York: Knopf.

Smith, Jean Edward. 1996. *John Marshall: Definer of a Nation*. New York: Holt.

Taylor, Alan. 2010. *The Civil War of 1812: American Citizens, British Subjects, Irish Rebels, & Indian Allies*. New York: Vintage Books.

INDUSTRIALIZATION AND TRANSFORMATION

Blackmar, Elizabeth. 1989. *Manhattan for Rent, 1785–1850*. Ithaca, NY: Cornell University Press.

Howe, Daniel Walker. 2007. *What Hath God Wrought: The Transformation of America, 1815–1848*. New York: Oxford University Press.

Igler, David. 2013. *The Great Ocean: Pacific Worlds from Captain Cook to the Gold Rush*. Oxford: Oxford University Press.

Johnson, Paul E. 1978. *A Shopkeeper's Millennium: Society and Revivals in Rochester, New York, 1815–1837*. New York: Hill and Wang.

Johnson, Walter. 1999. *Soul by Soul: Life Inside the Antebellum Slave Market*. Cambridge, MA: Harvard University Press.

Marx, Leo. 1964. *The Machine in the Garden: Technology and the Pastoral Ideal in America*. New York: Oxford University Press.

Rees, Jonathan. 2013. *Industrialization and the Transformation of American Life: A Brief Introduction*. Armonk, NY: M.E. Sharpe.

Sandage, Scott A. 2005. *Born Losers: A History of Failure in America*. Cambridge, MA: Harvard University Press.

JACKSONIAN DEMOCRACY

Allgor, Catherine. 2000. *Parlor Politics: In Which the Ladies of Washington Help Build a City and a Government*. Charlottesville: University of Virginia Press.

Deloria, Philip Joseph. 1998. *Playing Indian*. New Haven: Yale University Press.

Deyle, Steven. 2005. *Carry Me Back: The Domestic Slave Trade in American Life*. New York: Oxford University Press.

Dippie, Brian W. 1982. *The Vanishing American: White Attitudes and U.S. Indian Policy*. Middletown, CT: Wesleyan University Press.

Feller, Daniel. 1995. *The Jacksonian Promise: America, 1815–1840*. Baltimore: Johns Hopkins University Press.

Marszalek, John F. 1997. *The Petticoat Affair: Manners, Mutiny, and Sex in Andrew Jackson's White House*. New York: Free Press.

Meacham, Jon. 2008. *American Lion: Andrew Jackson in the White House*. New York: Random House.

Mihm, Stephen. 2007. *A Nation of Counterfeiters: Capitalists, Con Men, and the Making of the United States*. Cambridge, MA: Harvard University Press.

Saxton, Alexander. 1990. *The Rise and Fall of the White Republic: Class Politics and Mass Culture in Nineteenth-Century America*. London: Verso.

Sellers, Charles. 1991. *The Market Revolution: Jacksonian America, 1815–1846*. New York: Oxford University Press.

Steinberg, Theodore. 1991. *Nature Incorporated: Industrialization and the Waters of New England*. Cambridge: Cambridge University Press.

Watson, Harry L. 1990. *Liberty and Power: The Politics of Jacksonian America*. New York: Hill and Wang.

—. 1998. *Andrew Jackson vs. Henry Clay: Democracy and Development in Antebellum America*. Boston: Bedford/St. Martin's Press.

Wilentz, Sean. 2005. *The Rise of American Democracy: Jefferson to Lincoln*. New York: Norton.

THE ANTEBELLUM SOUTH

Berlin, Ira. 2003. *Generations of Captivity: A History of African-American Slaves*. Cambridge, MA: Belknap Press.

Clark, Emily. 2013. *The Strange History of the American Quadroon: Free Women of Color in the Revolutionary Atlantic World*. Chapel Hill: University of North Carolina Press.

Delfino, Susanna, and Michele Gillespie. 2002. *Neither Lady nor Slave: Working Women of the Old South*. Chapel Hill: University of North Carolina Press.

Fox-Genovese, Elizabeth. 1988. *Within the Plantation Household: Black and White Women of the Old South*. Chapel Hill: University of North Carolina Press.

Genovese, Eugene D. 1974. *Roll, Jordan, Roll: The World the Slaves Made*. New York: Pantheon Books.

Hall, Gwendolyn Midlo. 1992. *Africans in Colonial Louisiana: The Development of Afro-Creole Culture in the Eighteenth Century*. Baton Rouge: Louisiana State University Press.

Johnson, Walter. 1999. *Soul by Soul: Life Inside the Antebellum Slave Market*. Cambridge, MA: Harvard University Press.

McCurry, Stephanie. 1995. *Masters of Small Worlds: Yeoman Households, Gender Relations, and the Political Culture of the Antebellum South Carolina Low Country*. New York: Oxford University Press.

Potter, David Morris, and Don E. Fehrenbacher. 1976. *The Impending Crisis, 1848–1861*. New York: Harper & Row.

Rasmussen, Daniel. 2011. *American Uprising: The Untold Story of America's Largest Slave Revolt*. New York: HarperCollins.

Wyatt-Brown, Bertram. 1982. *Southern Honor: Ethics and Behavior in the Old South*. New York: Oxford University Press.

REFORM AND ABOLITION

DuBois, Ellen Carol. 1978. *Feminism and Suffrage: The Emergence of an Independent Women's Movement in America, 1848-1869*. Ithaca, NY: Cornell University Press.

DuBois, Ellen Carol, and Lynn Dumenil. 2005. *Through Women's Eyes: An American History with Documents*. Boston: Bedford/St. Martin's Press.

Heyrman, Christine Leigh. 1997. *Southern Cross: The Beginnings of the Bible Belt*. New York: Knopf.

Mayer, Henry. 1998. *All On Fire: William Lloyd Garrison and the Abolition of Slavery*. New York: Bedford/St. Martin's Press.

Mintz, Steven. 1995. *Moralists and Modernizers: America's Pre-Civil War Reformers*. Baltimore: Johns Hopkins University Press.

Rorabaugh, W. J. 1979. *The Alcoholic Republic, an American Tradition*. New York: Oxford University Press.

Stewart, James Brewer. 1976. *Holy Warriors: The Abolitionists and American Slavery*. New York: Hill and Wang.

CIVIL WAR AND RECONSTRUCTION

Alcott, Louisa May, and Bessie Zahan Jones. 1960. *Hospital Sketches*. Cambridge, MA: Harvard University Press.

Berlin, Ira, Joseph P. Reidy, and Leslie S. Rowland. 1998. *Freedom's Soldiers: The Black Military Experience in the Civil War*. Cambridge: Cambridge University Press.

Blight, David W. 2001. *Race and Reunion: The Civil War in American Memory.* Cambridge, MA: Belknap Press.

Catton, Bruce. 1962. *Mr. Lincoln's Army.* Garden City, NY: Doubleday.

Donald, David Herbert. 1960. *Charles Sumner and the Coming of the Civil War.* New York: Knopf.

Earle, Jonathan Halperin. 2008. *John Brown's Raid on Harpers Ferry: A Brief History with Documents.* Boston: Bedford/St. Martin's Press.

Egerton, Douglas R. 2014. *The Wars of Reconstruction: The Brief, Violent History of America's Most Progressive Era.* London: Bloomsbury Press.

Emberton, Carole. 2013. *Beyond Redemption: Race, Violence, and the American South After the Civil War.* Chicago: University of Chicago Press.

Faust, Drew Gilpin. 2008. *This Republic of Suffering: Death and the American Civil War.* New York: Knopf.

Fehrenbacher, Don E. 1978. *The Dred Scott Case, Its Significance in American Law and Politics.* New York: Oxford University Press.

Foner, Eric. 1970. *Free Soil, Free Labor, Free Men: The Ideology of the Republican Party Before the Civil War.* New York: Oxford University Press.

—. 2006. *Forever Free: The Story of Emancipation and Reconstruction.* New York: Vintage Books.

Gallagher, Gary W. 2011. *The Union War.* Cambridge, MA: Harvard University Press.

—. 2013. *Becoming Confederates: Paths to a New National Loyalty.* Atlanta: University of Georgia Press.

Gienapp, William E. 2002. *Abraham Lincoln and Civil War America: A Biography.* New York: Oxford University Press.

Goodwin, Doris Kearns. 2006. *Team of Rivals: The Political Genius of Abraham Lincoln.* New York: Simon & Schuster.

Guelzo, Allen C. 2013. *Gettysburg: The Last Invasion.* New York: Knopf

Hahn, Steven. 2003. *A Nation Under Our Feet: Black Political Struggles in the Rural South, from Slavery to the Great Migration.* Cambridge, MA: Belknap Press.

Holt, Michael F. 1978. *The Political Crisis of the 1850s.* New York: Wiley.

LaFantasie, Glenn W. 2007. *Twilight at Little Round Top: July 2, 1863—The Tide Turns at Gettysburg.* New York: Vintage Books.

Lemann, Nicholas. 2006. *Redemption: The Last Battle of the Civil War.* New York: Farrar, Straus & Giroux.

Levine, Bruce C., and Eric Foner. 1992. *Half Slave and Half Free: The Roots of Civil War.* New York: Hill and Wang.

Manning, Chanda. 2008. *What this Cruel War Was Over: Soldiers, Slavery, and the Civil War.* New York: Vintage Books.

McPherson, James M. 1994. *What They Fought For 1861–1865.* Baton Rouge: Louisiana State University Press.

Oates, Stephen B. 1970. *To Purge This Land with Blood: A Biography of John Brown.* New York: Harper & Row.

Richardson, Heather Cox. 2001. *The Death of Reconstruction: Race, Labor, and Politics in the Post-Civil War North, 1865–1901.* Cambridge, MA: Harvard University Press.

Stampp, Kenneth M. 1990. *America in 1857: A Nation on the Brink.* New York: Oxford University Press.

Thomas, Emory M. 1991. *The Confederacy as a Revolutionary Experience.* Columbia: University of South Carolina Press.

Vorenberg, Michael. 2001. *Final Freedom: The Civil War, the Abolition of Slavery, and the Thirteenth Amendment.* Cambridge: Cambridge University Press.

Williams, Heather Andrea. 2005. *Self-Taught: African American Education in Slavery and Freedom*. Chapel Hill: University of North Carolina Press.

WESTWARD EXPANSION

Brown, Dee. 1970. *Bury My Heart at Wounded Knee: An Indian History of the American West*. New York: Holt Rinehart Winston.

Dando-Collins, Stephen. 2008. *Tycoon's War: How Cornelius Vanderbilt Invaded a Country to Overthrow America's Most Famous Military Adventurer*. Philadelphia: Da Capo Press.

Greenberg, Amy S. 2012. *A Wicked War: Polk, Clay, Lincoln, and the 1846 U.S. Invasion of Mexico*. New York: Knopf.

Madley, Benjamin. 2012. "The Genocide of California's Yana Indians." In *Centuries of Genocide: Essays and Eyewitness Accounts*, edited by Samuel Totten and Williams S. Parsons, 16–53. New York: Routledge.

Mahon, John K. 1967. *History of the Second Seminole War, 1835–1842*. Gainesville: University of Florida Press.

Neihardt, John G. 1975. *Black Elk Speaks: Being the Life Story of a Holy Man of the Oglala Sioux*. New York: Pocket Books.

Richardson, Heather Cox. 2008. *West from Appomattox: The Reconstruction of America After the Civil War*. New Haven: Yale University Press.

Soluri, John. 2005. *Banana Cultures: Agriculture, Consumption, and Environmental Change in Honduras and the United States*. Austin: University of Texas Press.

Stephanson, Anders. 1995. *Manifest Destiny: American Expansionism and the Empire of Right*. New York: Hill and Wang.

White, Richard. 2011. *Railroaded: The Transcontinentals and the Making of Modern America*. New York: Norton.

FROM THE GILDED AGE TO THE PROGRESSIVE ERA

Addams, Jane, and Norah Hamilton. 1910. *Twenty Years at Hull-House: With Autobiographical Notes*. New York: Macmillan.

Bederman, Gail. 1995. *Manliness & Civilization: A Cultural History of Gender and Race in the United States, 1880–1917*. Chicago: University of Chicago Press.

Berg, A. Scott. 2013. *Wilson*. New York: Simon & Schuster.

Boyer, Paul S. 1978. *Urban Masses and Moral Order in America, 1820–1920*. Cambridge, MA: Harvard University Press.

Chauncey, George. 1994. *Gay New York: Gender, Urban Culture, and the Makings of the Gay Male World, 1890-1940*. New York: Basic Books.

Cronon, William. 1991. *Nature's Metropolis: Chicago and the Great West*. New York: Norton.

Dalton, Kathleen. 2002. *Theodore Roosevelt: A Strenuous Life*. New York: Knopf.

Dewey, John. 1915. *The School and Society*. Chicago: The University of Chicago Press.

Du Bois, W. E. B., David W. Blight, and Robert Gooding-Williams. 1997. *The Souls of Black Folk*. Boston: Bedford Books.

Fitzpatrick, Ellen F., Lincoln Steffens, Ida M. Tarbell, and Ray Stannard Baker. 1994. *Muckraking: Three Landmark Articles*. Boston: Bedford/St. Martin's Press.

Gilmore, Glenda E. 1996. *Gender and Jim Crow: Women and the Politics of White Supremacy in North Carolina*. Chapel Hill: University of North Carolina Press.

Goodwin, Doris Kearns. 2013. *The Bully Pulpit: Theodore Roosevelt, William Howard Taft, and the Golden Age of Journalism*. New York: Simon & Schuster.

Goodwyn, Lawrence. 1976. *Democratic Promise: The Populist Moment in America*. New York: Oxford University Press.

Hershkowitz, Leo. 1977. *Tweed's New York: Another Look*. Garden City, NY: Anchor Press.

James, William. 1975. *Pragmatism*. Cambridge, MA: Harvard University Press.

Kraditor, Aileen S. 1981. *The Ideas of the Woman Suffrage Movement 1890–1920*. New York: Norton.

Lears, T. J. Jackson. 2009. *Rebirth of a Nation: The Making of Modern America, 1877–1920*. New York: HarperCollins.

Lunardini, Christine A. 1986. *From Equal Suffrage to Equal Rights: Alice Paul and the National Woman's Party, 1910–1928*. New York: New York University Press.

Matthews, Jean V. 2003. *The Rise of the New Woman: The Women's Movement in America, 1875–1930*. Chicago: Dee.

Osofsky, Gilbert. 1971. *Harlem: The Making of a Ghetto. Negro New York, 1890–1930*. New York: Harper & Row.

Pegram, Thomas R. 1998. *Battling Demon Rum: The Struggle for a Dry America, 1800–1933*. Chicago: Dee.

Peiss, Kathy Lee. 1986. *Cheap Amusements: Working Women and Leisure in Turn-of-the-Century New York*. Philadelphia: Temple University Press.

Quammen, David. 2008. *Charles Darwin On the Origin of Species: The Illustrated Edition*. New York: Sterling.

Riis, Jacob A. 1971. *How the Other Half Lives: Studies Among the Tenements of New York*. New York: Dover.

Sinclair, Upton. 1971. *The Jungle*. Cambridge, MA: Bentley.

Von Drehle, David. 2003. *Triangle: The Fire That Changed America*. New York: Atlantic Monthly Press.

Washington, Booker T. 1963. *Up from Slavery, An Autobiography*. Garden City, NY: Doubleday.

Wiebe, Robert H. *The Search for Order, 1877–1920*. New York: Hill and Wang.

Woodward, C. Vann. 1957. *The Strange Career of Jim Crow*. New York: Oxford University Press.

IMPERIAL EXPANSION AND THE FIRST WORLD WAR

Barry, John M. 2004. *The Great Influenza: The Epic Story of the Deadliest Plague in History*. New York: Viking Books.

Eisenhower, John S. D. 2001. *Yanks: The Epic Story of the American Army in World War I*. New York: Simon & Schuster.

Fromkin, David. 2004. *Europe's Last Summer: Who Started the Great War in 1914?* New York: Knopf.

Hart, Peter. 2007. *Aces Falling: War Above the Trenches, 1918*. London: Weidenfeld & Nicolson.

Hoganson, Kristin L. 1998. *Fighting for American Manhood: How Gender Politics Provoked the Spanish-American and Philippine-American Wars*. New Haven: Yale University Press.

Kaplan, Amy. 2002. *The Anarchy of Empire in the Making of U.S. Culture*. Cambridge, MA: Harvard University Press.

Kennedy, David M. 1980. *Over Here: The First World War and American Society*. New York: Oxford University Press.

Lengel, Edward G. 2008. *To Conquer Hell: The Meuse-Argonne, 1918*. New York: Holt.

Maier, Charles S. 2006. *Among Empires: American Ascendancy and Its Predecessors*. Cambridge, MA: Harvard University Press.

McCullough, David G. 1977. *The Path between the Seas: The Creation of the Panama Canal, 1870–1914*. New York: Simon & Schuster.

Thomas, Evan. 2010. *The War Lovers: Roosevelt, Lodge, Hearst, and the Rush to Empire, 1898*. New York: Little, Brown.

Tooze, J. Adam. 2014. *The Deluge: The Great War and the Remaking of Global Order 1916–1931*. New York: Viking Books.

Twain, Mark. 2009. *Following the Equator A Journey Around the World*. Waiheke Island: Floating Press.

THE ROARING TWENTIES

Allen, Frederick Lewis. 1931. *Only Yesterday: An Informal History of the Nineteen-Twenties*. New York: Harper & Bros.

Bryson, Bill. 2013. *One Summer: America, 1927*. New York: Anchor Books.

Davison M. Douglas. 2005. *Jim Crow Moves North: The Battle over Northern School Desegregation, 1865–1954*. New York: Cambridge University Press.

Moore, Lucy. 2010. *Anything Goes: A Biography of the Roaring Twenties*. New York: Overlook Press.

Robinson, Thomas A., and Lanette R. Ruff. 2011. *Out of the Mouths of Babes: Girl Evangelists in the Flapper Era*. New York: Oxford University Press.

Russell, Francis. 1968. *The Shadow of Blooming Grove: Warren G. Harding in His Times*. New York: McGraw-Hill.

Shlaes, Amity. 2013. *Coolidge*. New York: Harper.

Watts, Steven. 2005. *The People's Tycoon: Henry Ford and the American Century*. New York: Knopf.

THE GREAT DEPRESSION AND THE NEW DEAL

Browder, Laura. 1998. *Rousing the Nation Radical Culture in Depression America*. Amherst: University of Massachusetts Press.

Cohen, Lizabeth. 1990. *Making a New Deal: Industrial Workers in Chicago, 1919–1939*. Cambridge: Cambridge University Press.

Domhoff, G. William, and Michael J. Webber. 2011. *Class and Power in the New Deal: Corporate Moderates, Southern Democrats, and the Liberal-Labor Coalition*. Stanford, CA: Stanford University Press.

Hamby, Alonzo L. 2004. *For the Survival of Democracy: Franklin Roosevelt and the World Crisis of the 1930s*. New York: Free Press.

Hofstadter, Richard. 1955. *The Age of Reform: From Bryan to F.D.R.* New York: Knopf.

Hurt, R. Douglas. 1984. *The Dust Bowl: An Agricultural and Social History*. Chicago: Nelson-Hall.

Katznelson, Ira. 2013. *Fear Itself: The New Deal and the Origins of Our Time*. New York: Norton.

Kennedy, David M. 1999. *Freedom from Fear: The American People in Depression and War, 1929–1945*. New York: Oxford University Press.

Lumley, Darwyn H. 2009. *Breaking the Banks in Motor City: The Auto Industry, the 1933 Detroit Banking Crisis and the Start of the New Deal*. Jefferson, NC: McFarland.

Poppendieck, Janet, and Marion Nestle. 2014. *Breadlines Knee-Deep in Wheat: Food Assistance in the Great Depression*. Berkeley: University of California Press.

Shindo, Charles J. 1997. *Dust Bowl Migrants in the American Imagination*. Lawrence: University of Kansas Press.

Shlaes, Amity. 2007. *The Forgotten Man: A New History of the Great Depression*. New York: HarperCollins.

Smith, Fred C. 2014. *Trouble in Goshen: Plain Folk, Roosevelt, Jesus, and Marx in the Great Depression South*. Jackson: University Press of Mississippi.

Solomon, William. 2002. *Literature, Amusement, and Technology in the Great Depression*. Cambridge: Cambridge University Press.

Terkel, Studs. 1970. *Hard Times: An Oral History of the Great Depression*. New York: Pantheon Books.

WORLD WAR, COLD WAR, AND AMERICAN PROSPERITY

Dobrynin, Anatoly. 1995. *In Confidence: Moscow's Ambassador to America's Six Cold War Presidents*. New York: Crown.

Doenecke, Justus D., and Mark A. Stoler. 2005. *Debating Franklin D. Roosevelt's Foreign Policies, 1933–1945*. Lanham, MD: Rowman & Littlefield.

Fischer, Conan. 2003. *The Ruhr Crisis, 1923–1924*. Oxford: Oxford University Press.

Homan, Lynn M., and Thomas Reilly. 2001. *Black Knights: The Story of the Tuskegee Airmen*. Gretna, LA: Pelican.

Kessler-Harris, Alice. 1982. *Out to Work: A History of Wage-Earning Women in the United States*. New York: Oxford University Press.

Mitchell, Greg. 1998. *Tricky Dick and the Pink Lady: Richard Nixon vs. Helen Gahagan Douglas—Sexual Politics and the Red Scare, 1950*. New York: Random House.

O'Sullivan, John. 2006. *The President, the Pope, and the Prime Minister: Three Who Changed the World*. New York: Regnery.

Overy, R. J. 1995. *Why the Allies Won*. New York: Norton.

Robinson, Jo Ann Gibson, and David J. Garrow. 1987. *The Montgomery Bus Boycott and the Women Who Started It: The Memoir of Jo Ann Gibson Robinson*. Knoxville: University of Tennessee Press.

Schweizer, Peter. 2002. *Reagan's War: The Epic Story of His Forty-Year Struggle and Final Triumph over Communism*. New York: Doubleday.

Sone, Monica Itoi. 1979. *Nisei Daughter*. Seattle: University of Washington Press.

Weinberg, Gerhard L. 1994. *A World at Arms: A Global History of World War II*. Cambridge: Cambridge University Press.

Wyman, David S. 1998. *The Abandonment of the Jews: America and the Holocaust 1941–1945*. New York: New Press.

FROM CAMELOT TO CULTURE WARS

Appy, Christian G. 2003. *Patriots: The Vietnam War Remembered from All Sides*. New York: Viking Books.

Branch, Taylor. 1988. *Parting the Waters: America in the King Years, 1954–63*. New York: Simon & Schuster.

Clendinen, Dudley, and Adam Nagourney. 1999. *Out for Good: The Struggle to Build a Gay Rights Movement in America*. New York: Simon & Schuster.

Clinton, Bill. 2004. *My Life*. New York: Knopf.

Cowie, Jefferson. 2010. *Stayin' Alive: The 1970s and the Last Days of the Working Class*. New York: New Press.

Delpla, Isabelle, Xavier Bougarel, and Jean-Louis Fournel, eds. 2012. *Investigating Srebrenica: Institutions, Facts, Responsibilities*. New York: Berghahn Books.

Dudziak, Mary L. 2000. *Cold War Civil Rights: Race and the Image of American Democracy*. Princeton, NJ: Princeton University Press.

Farber, David R. 1994. *The Age of Great Dreams: America in the 1960s*. New York: Hill and Wang.

Frank, Thomas. 2004. *What's the Matter with Kansas? How Conservatives Won the Heart of America*. New York: Metropolitan Books.

Friedan, Betty. 1963. *The Feminine Mystique*. New York: Norton.

Gitlin, Todd. 1993. *The Sixties: Years of Hope, Days of Rage*. New York: Bantam Books.

Goodwin, Doris Kearns. 1976. *Lyndon Johnson and the American Dream*. New York: Harper & Row.

Karnow, Stanley. 1983. *Vietnam, a History*. New York: Viking Press.

King, Martin Luther. 1986. *A Testament of Hope: The Essential Writings of Martin Luther King, Jr.* Edited by James Melvin Washington. San Francisco: Harper & Row.

Levy, Ariel. 2006. *Female Chauvinist Pigs: Women and the Rise of Raunch Culture*. New York: Free Press.

McCain, John, and Mark Salter. 1999. *Faith of My Fathers*. New York: Random House.

Meriwether, James. 2008. "'Worth a Lot of Negro Votes:' Black Voters, Africa, and the 1960 Presidential Campaign." *Journal of American History* 95(3): 737–63.

Murch, Donna Jean. 2010. *Living for the City: Migration, Education, and the Rise of the Black Panther Party in Oakland, California*. Chapel Hill: University of North Carolina Press.

Schlesinger, Arthur M. 1965. A *Thousand Days: John F. Kennedy in the White House*. Boston: Houghton Mifflin.

Selvin, Joel. 1994. *Summer of Love: The Inside Story of LSD, Rock & Roll, Free Love, and High Times in the Wild West*. New York: Dutton.

Stein, Judith. 2010. *Pivotal Decade: How the United States Traded Factories for Finance in the Seventies*. New Haven: Yale University Press.

Warren Commission. 1964. *Report of the Warren Commission on the Assassination of President Kennedy*. New York: McGraw-Hill.

X, Malcolm. 1992. *The Autobiography of Malcolm X*. Edited by Alex Haley. New York: One World/Ballantine Books.

TWENTY-FIRST-CENTURY PROBLEMS

Bravin, Jess. 2013. *The Terror Courts: Rough Justice at Guantanamo Bay*. New Haven: Yale University Press.

Cowen, Tyler. 2001. *The Great Stagnation: How America Ate All the Low-Hanging Fruit of Modern History, Got Sick, and Will (Eventually) Feel Better*. New York: Dutton.

Ehrenreich, Barbara. 2001. *Nickel and Dimed: On (Not) Getting by in America*. New York: Metropolitan Books.

Gerges, Fawaz A. 2011. *The Rise and Fall of Al-Qaeda*. Oxford: Oxford University Press.

Gordon, Joy. 2010. *Invisible War: The United States and the Iraq Sanctions*. Cambridge, MA: Harvard University Press.

John Cannan, 2013. "A Legislative History of the Affordable Care Act: How Legislative Procedure Shapes Legislative History." *Law Library Journal* 105(2): 132–73.

Keen, D. 2012. *Useful Enemies: When Waging Wars Is More Important than Winning Them*. New Haven: Yale University Press.

Lance, Peter. 2004. *1000 Years for Revenge: International Terrorism and the FBI*. New York: Regan Books.

Lewis, Michael. 2010. *The Big Short: Inside the Doomsday Machine*. New York: Norton.

Little, Douglas. 2002. *American Orientalism: The United States and the Middle East since 1945*. Chapel Hill: University of North Carolina Press.

Oreskes, Naomi, and Erik M. Conway. 2010. *Merchants of Doubt: How a Handful of Scientists Obscured the Truth on Issues from Tobacco Smoke to Global Warming*. New York: Bloomsbury Press.

Rivoli, Pietra. 2005. *The Travels of a T-Shirt in the Global Economy: An Economist Examines the Markets, Power and Politics of World Trade*. Hoboken, NJ: Wiley.

Simon, Bryant. 2009. *Everything but the Coffee: Learning About America from Starbucks*. Berkeley: University of California Press.

Wright, Lawrence. 2006. *The Looming Tower: Al-Qaeda and the Road to 9/11*. New York: Knopf.

Answer Key

Chapter 1

1. A 3. B 5. A 7. A 9. It was known that the Earth was round, so Columbus's plan seemed plausible. The distance he would need to travel was not known, however, and he greatly underestimated the Earth's circumference; therefore, he would have no way of recognizing when he had arrived at his destination. 11. D

Chapter 2

1. D 3. B 5. A 7. Luther was most concerned about indulgences, which allowed the wealthy to purchase their way to forgiveness, and protested the Church's taxation of ordinary Germans. Both wanted the liturgy to be given in churchgoers' own language, making scripture more accessible. 9. B 11. A 13. C

Chapter 3

1. C 3. As the Spanish tried to convert the Pueblo to Catholicism, the native people tried to fold Christian traditions into their own practices. This was unacceptable to the Spanish, who insisted on complete conversion—especially of the young, whom they took away from their families and tribes. When adaptation failed, native peoples attempted to maintain their autonomy through outright revolt, as with the Pueblo Revolt of 1680. This revolt was successful, and for almost twelve years the Pueblos' lives returned to normalcy. Their autonomy was short-lived, however, as the Spanish took advantage of continued attacks by the Pueblos' enemies to reestablish control of the region. 5. D 7. B 9. A 11. They encouraged colonization by offering headrights to anyone who could pay his own way to Virginia: fifty acres for each passage. They also used the system of indenture, in which people (usually men) who didn't have enough money to pay their own passage could work for a set number of years and then gain their own land. Increasingly, they also turned to African slaves as a cheap labor source. 13. A 15. Indians didn't have any concept of owning personal property and believed that land should be held in common, for use by a group. They used land as they needed, often moving from area to area to follow food sources at different times of year. Europeans saw land as something individuals could own, and they used fences and other markers to define their property.

Chapter 4

1. C 3. Since the proprietors of the Carolina colonies were absent, English planters from Barbados moved in and gained political power, establishing slave labor as the predominant form of labor. In Pennsylvania, where prospective servants were offered a bounty of fifty acres of land for emigrating and finishing their term of labor, indentured servitude abounded. 5. B 7. B 9. B 11. The Freemasons were a fraternal society that originated in London coffeehouses in the early eighteenth century. They advocated Enlightenment principles of inquiry and tolerance. Masonic lodges soon spread throughout Europe and the British colonies, creating a shared experience on both sides of the Atlantic and spreading Enlightenment intellectual currents throughout the British Empire. Benjamin Franklin was a prominent Freemason. 13. D

Chapter 5

1. D 3. The Currency Act required colonists to pay British merchants in gold and silver instead of colonial paper money. With gold and silver in short supply, this put a strain on colonists' finances. The Sugar Act curtailed smuggling, angering merchants, and imposed stricter enforcement. Many colonists feared the loss of liberty with trials without juries as mandated by the Sugar Act. 5. B 7. D 9. A 11. The Committees of Correspondence provided a crucial means of communication among the colonies. They also set the foundation for a colonial government by breaking away from royal governmental structures. Finally, they promoted a sense of colonial unity. 13. A

Chapter 6

1. C 3. D 5. B 7. C 9. In the eighteenth century, militaries typically fought only in the summer months. On December 25 and 26, 1776, Washington triumphed over the Hessians encamped at Trenton by surprising them as they celebrated Christmas. Shortly thereafter, he used this same tactic to achieve victory at the Battle of Princeton. 11. The British southern strategy was to move the military theater to the southern colonies where there were more Loyalist colonists. Slaves and Indian allies, the British hoped, would also swell their ranks. This strategy worked at first, allowing the British to take Charleston. However, British fortunes changed after Nathanael Greene took command of the southern Continental Army and scored decisive victories at the battles of Cowpens and Guilford. This set the stage for the final American victory at Yorktown, Virginia. The southern strategy had failed. 13. A

Chapter 7

1. A 3. Citizenship within a republic meant accepting certain rights and responsibilities as well as cultivating virtuous behavior. This philosophy was based on the notion that the success or failure of the republic depended upon the virtue or corruption of its citizens. 5. C 7. A 9. A group of farmers in western Massachusetts, including Daniel Shays, rebelled against the Massachusetts government, which they saw as unresponsive to their needs. Many were veterans

of the Revolutionary War and faced tremendous debts and high taxes, which they couldn't pay with their worthless paper money. They felt that they didn't have a voice in the Massachusetts government, which seemed to cater to wealthy Boston merchants. They wanted their debts to be forgiven and the Massachusetts constitution to be rewritten to address their needs, and when these demands weren't met, they rebelled. **11.** A

Chapter 8

1. B **3.** Federalists believed in a strong federal republican government led by learned, public-spirited men of property. They believed that too much democracy would threaten the republic. The Democratic-Republicans, alternatively, feared too much federal government power and focused more on the rural areas of the country, which they thought were underrepresented and underserved. Democratic-Republicans felt that the spirit of true republicanism, which meant virtuous living for the common good, depended on farmers and agricultural areas. **5.** D **7.** D **9.** A **11.** The election was considered a revolution because, for the first time in American history, political power passed from one party to another. Jefferson's presidency was a departure from the Federalist administrations of Washington and Adams, who had favored the commercial class and urban centers of the country. The Democratic-Republican vision increased states' rights and limited the power of the federal government, lowering taxes and slashing the military, which Adams had built up. **13.** B

Chapter 9

1. C **3.** Industrialization made manufactured goods more abundant and more widely available. All but the poorest Americans were able to equip their homes with cookstoves, parlor stoves, upholstered furniture, and decorations such as wallpaper and window curtains. Even such formerly expensive goods as clocks were now affordable for most. **5.** D **7.** The federal government passed laws allowing people to sell back land they could not pay for and use the money to pay their debt. States made it more difficult to foreclose on mortgages and tried to make it easier for people to declare bankruptcy. **9.** A **11.** D **13.** A successful northern manufacturer and inventor, Cooper valued hard work, thrift, and simplicity. He lived according to these values, choosing utilitarian, self-made furnishings rather than luxurious goods. Cooper's vision of hard work leading to respectability led him to found the Cooper Union for the Advancement of Science and Art; admission to this college, which was dedicated to the pursuit of technology, was based solely on merit.

Chapter 10

1. B **3.** A **5.** Northern manufacturers were expected to gain from the tariff because it made competing goods from abroad more expensive than those they made. Southern plantation owners expected the tariff would be costly for them, because it raised the price of goods they could only import. Southerners also feared the tariff represented an unwelcome expansion of federal power over the states. **7.** A **9.** The Petticoat affair divided those loyal to President Jackson from Washington, DC, insiders. When Washington socialite Peggy O'Neal's husband committed suicide and O'Neal then married John Eaton, a Tennessee senator with whom she was reportedly unfaithful to her husband, Jackson and those loyal to him defended Peggy Eaton against other Washington, DC, socialites and politicians. Martin Van Buren, in particular, supported the Eatons and became an important figure in Jackson's "Kitchen Cabinet" of select supporters and advisers. **11.** A **13.** Whigs opposed what they viewed as the tyrannical rule of Andrew Jackson. For this reason, they named themselves after the eighteenth-century British-American Whigs, who stood in opposition to King George. Whigs believed in an active federal government committed to internal improvements, including the establishment of a national bank. **15.** B **17.** D **19.** Tocqueville came to believe that democracy was an unstoppable force whose major benefit was equality before the law. However, he also described the tyranny of the majority, which overpowers the will of minorities and individuals.

Chapter 11

1. A **3.** Jefferson wanted Lewis and Clark to find an all-water route to the Pacific Ocean, strengthen U.S. claims to the Pacific Northwest by reaching it through an overland route, explore and map the territory, make note of its natural resources and wildlife, and make contact with Indian tribes with the intention of establishing trade with them. **5.** B **7.** C **9.** American slaveholders in Texas distrusted the Mexican government's reluctant tolerance of slavery and wanted Texas to be a new U.S. slave state. Most also disliked Mexicans' Roman Catholicism and regarded them as dishonest, ignorant, and backward. Belief in their own superiority inspired some Texans to try to undermine the power of the Mexican government. **11.** A **13.** The Chinese were seemingly more disciplined than the majority of the white miners, gaining a reputation for being extremely hard-working and frugal. White miners resented the mining successes that the Chinese earned. They believed the Chinese were unfairly depriving them of the means to earn a living. **15.** B

Chapter 12

1. A **3.** Some southerners believed that their region's monopoly over the lucrative cotton crop—on which both the larger American and Atlantic markets depended—and their possession of a slave labor force allowed the South to remain independent from the market revolution. However, the very cotton that provided the South with such economic potency also increased its reliance on the larger U.S. and world markets, which supplied—among other things—the food and clothes slaves needed, the furniture and other manufactured goods that defined the southern standard of comfortable living, and the banks from which southerners borrowed needed funds. **5.** Southern whites often used paternalism to justify the institution of slavery, arguing that slaves, like children, needed the care, feeding, discipline, and moral and religious education that they could provide. Slaves often used this misguided notion to their advantage: By feigning ignorance and playing into slaveholders' paternalistic perceptions of them, slaves found opportunities to resist their condition and gain a degree of freedom and autonomy. **7.** C **9.** B **11.** Many slaveholding expansionists believed that the events of the Haitian Revolution could repeat themselves in Cuba, leading to the overthrow of slavery on the island and the creation of an independent black republic. Americans also feared that the British would seize Cuba—which, since Britain had outlawed slavery in its colonies in 1833, would render all slaves on the island free.

Chapter 13

1. A **3.** They both emphasize the power of the individual over that of the majority. Evangelists of the Second Great Awakening preached the power of personal spirituality, whereas transcendentalists were more concerned with the individual soul. **5.** C **7.** B **9.** At first, temperance reformers, who were predominantly led by Presbyterian ministers, targeted the middle and upper classes. When the movement veered toward teetotalism instead of temperance, the movement lost momentum. However, it was reborn with a focus on the working class in the 1840s. **11.** C **13.** C

Chapter 14

1. A **3.** This federal law appeared to northerners to be further proof of a "Slave Power" conspiracy and elite slaveholders' disproportionate influence over U.S. domestic policy. Northerners also resented being compelled to serve as de facto slave-catchers, as the law punished people not only for helping fugitive slaves, but also for failing to aid in efforts to return them. Finally, the law rankled many northerners for the hypocrisy that it exposed, given southerners' arguments in favor of states' rights and against the federal government's meddling in their affairs. **5.** B **7.** C **9.** The Supreme Court decided that Dred Scott had not earned freedom by virtue of having lived in a free state; thus, Scott and his family would remain enslaved. More broadly, the Court ruled that blacks could never be citizens of the United States and that Congress had no authority to stop or limit the spread of slavery into American territories. **11.** B

Chapter 15

1. D **3.** Slavery was more deeply entrenched in the Deep South than it was in the Upper South or the border states. The Deep South was home to larger numbers of both slaveholders and slaves. Pro-Union sentiment remained strong in parts of the Upper South and border states, particularly those areas with smaller populations of slaveholders. **5.** D **7.** B **9.** C

Chapter 16

1. C **3.** The Thirteenth Amendment officially and permanently banned the institution of slavery in the United States. The Emancipation Proclamation had freed only those slaves in rebellious states, leaving many slaves—most notably, those in the border states—in bondage; furthermore, it did not alter or prohibit the institution of slavery in general. **5.** D **7.** B **9.** The Fifteenth Amendment granted the vote to all black men, giving freed slaves and free blacks greater political power than they had ever had in the United States. Blacks in former Confederate states elected a handful of black U.S. congressmen and a great many black local and state leaders who instituted ambitious reform and modernization projects in the South. However, the Fifteenth Amendment continued to exclude women from voting. Women continued to fight for suffrage through the NWSA and AWSA. **11.** C

Chapter 17

1. B **3.** During the first two years of the Civil War—when it appeared that the Confederacy was a formidable opponent—President Lincoln grew concerned that a Union defeat could result in the westward expansion of slavery. Thus, he hoped to facilitate the westward movement of white settlers who promoted the concept of free soil, which would populate the region with allies who opposed slavery. To encourage this process, Congress passed the Homestead Act and the Pacific Railway Act in 1862. The government also constructed and maintained forts that assisted in the process of westward expansion. **5.** Farmers who were able to invest a significant amount of capital in starting up large farms could acquire necessary supplies with ease. They also had access to new, technologically advanced farm machinery, which greatly improved efficiency and output. Such farmers hired migrant farmers to work their huge amounts of land. These "bonanza farms" were often quite successful, whereas family farms—unable to afford the supplies they needed for success, let alone take advantage of the technological innovations that would make their farms competitive—often failed. **7.** D **9.** In the cases of both mining and cattle ranching, diminishing resources played a key role. In mining, the first prospectors were able to pan for gold with crude and inexpensive materials, and therefore, almost anyone could head west and try his luck. Similarly, the quantity of cattle and the amount of grazing land meant that cowboys and would-be cattle barons had ample room to spread out. But as the easiest minerals were stripped away and large-scale ranchers purchased, developed, and fenced off grazing land, opportunities diminished.

It took significantly more resources to tunnel down into a mine than it did to pan for gold; instead of individual prospectors, companies would assess a site's potential and then seek investment to hire workers and drill deep into the earth. Likewise, as the cattle trails were over-grazed, ranchers needed to purchase and privatize large swaths of land to prepare their cattle for market. **11.** C **13.** B

Chapter 18

1. B **3.** New inventions fueled industrial growth, and the development of commercial electricity—along with the use of steam engines—allowed industries that had previously situated themselves close to sources of water power to shift away from those areas and move their production into cities. Immigrants sought employment in these urban factories and settled nearby, transforming the country's population from mostly rural to largely urban. **5.** C **7.** "Captains of industry" (such as Carnegie or Rockefeller) are noted for their new business models, entrepreneurial approaches, and, to varying degrees, philanthropic efforts, all of which transformed late nineteenth-century America. "Robber barons" (such as Gould) are noted for their self-centered drive for profit at the expense of workers and the general public, who seldom benefitted to any great degree. The terms, however, remain a gray area, as one could characterize the ruthless business practices of Rockefeller, or some of Carnegie's tactics with regard to workers' efforts to organize, as similar to the methods of robber barons. Nevertheless, "captains of industry" are noted for contributions that fundamentally changed and typically improved the nation, whereas "robber barons" can seldom point to such concrete contributions. **9.** B **11.** C

Chapter 19

1. D **3.** At the end of the nineteenth century, a confluence of events made urban life more desirable and more possible. Technologies such as electricity and the telephone allowed factories to build and grow in cities, and skyscrapers enabled the relatively small geographic areas to continue expanding. The new demand for workers spurred a massive influx of job-seekers from both rural areas of the United States and from eastern and southern Europe. Urban housing—as well as services such as transportation and sanitation—expanded accordingly, though cities struggled to cope with the surging demand. Together, technological innovations and an exploding population led American cities to grow as never before. **5.** D **7.** D **9.** Better public education and the explosion of high schools meant that the children of the middle class were better educated than any previous generation. While college had previously been mostly restricted to children of the upper class, the creation of land-grant colleges made college available on a wide scale. The curricula at these new colleges matched the needs of the middle class, offering practical professional training rather than the liberal arts focus that the Ivy League schools embraced. Thus, children of the emerging middle class were able to access the education and training needed to secure their place in the professional class for generations to come. **11.** A

Chapter 20

1. B **3.** The contested elections of the Gilded Age, in which margins were slim and two presidents were elected without winning the popular vote, meant that incumbent presidents often had only a weak hold on their power and were able to achieve little on the federal level. Some Americans began to establish new political parties and organizations to address their concerns, undermining the federal government further. Meanwhile, despite the widespread corruption that kept them running, urban political machines continued to achieve results for their constituents and maintain political strongholds on many cities. **5.** A **7.** A **9.** Women were able to play key roles in the alliance movement. The alliance provided them with political rights, including the ability to vote and hold office within the organization, which many women hoped would be a positive step in their struggle for national women's rights and suffrage. In the end, nearly 250,000 women joined the movement. **11.** D

Chapter 21

1. B **3.** The muckrakers played a pivotal role in initiating the Progressive Era, because they spurred everyday Americans to action. Unlike earlier sensationalist journalists, the muckrakers told their stories with the explicit goal of galvanizing their readers and encouraging them to take steps to address the issues. With photographs and descriptions of real-life scenarios of which many Americans were unaware, the muckrakers brought the tribulations of child factory workers, the urban poor, and others into the living rooms of the middle class. **5.** B **7.** D **9.** A **11.** D **13.** Wilson's actions were limited by his belief in his New Freedom platform, which promised voters a small government. Still, he took a number of steps in the first year of his presidency to shore up the economy and push back against destructive trusts. With those goals accomplished, he largely left the Progressive agenda alone. As the 1916 election season approached, however, Wilson realized that his hands-off policy was not endearing him to voters, and he ended his first term in a flurry of Progressive legislation that reminded the voting public of all he could do for them.

Chapter 22

1. B **3.** The Midway Islands provided a more stable path to Asian markets and a vital naval coaling station, which steamships needed in order to travel further afield. **5.** The Taft Commission introduced reforms to modernize and improve daily life in the Philippines. Many of these reforms were legislative in nature, impacting the structure and composition of local governments. In exchange for the support of resistance leaders, for example, the commission offered them political appointments. **7.** A **9.** The Open Door notes and the American foray into China revealed the power of economic clout. Given the unprecedented technological advances of the industrial revolution, American goods were often less expensive and of better quality than those produced in other countries, and they were highly sought after in Asia. Therefore, when Hay derided the spheres of influence model, wherein each country had its own room to maneuver in China, he was able to flood Chinese markets with American trade. Through these maneuvers, the United States was able to augment its global standing considerably without the use of its military forces. **11.** B **13.** B **15.** Taft's policies created some troubles that were immediate, and others that would not bear fruit until decades later. The tremendous debts in Central America created years of economic instability there and fostered nationalist movements driven by resentment of America's interference in the region. In Asia, Taft's efforts at China-Japan mediation heightened tensions between Japan and the United States—tensions that would explode, ultimately, with the outbreak of World War II—and spurred Japan to consolidate its power throughout the region.

Chapter 23

1. C **3.** Wilson's foreign policy goal was to minimize American involvement abroad and use a less imperialistic approach than the presidents before him. Rather than being guided by America's self-interest, he hoped to enact a policy based on moral decisions, acting only when it was morally imperative. In practice, however, Wilson found himself, especially in South and Central America, following the steps of other, more interventionist presidents. He sent troops into Haiti, the Dominican Republic, and Cuba, often to ensure that America's interests were met. In Asia and Mexico, Wilson also found it difficult to remain outside of world affairs without jeopardizing America's interests. **5.** C **7.** A **9.** The ban on alcohol did not take effect until one year after the war, when the public sentiments that had eased its passage began to wane. The law proved difficult to enforce, as ever-greater numbers of Americans began to defy it. Organized crime's involvement in the illegal liquor trade made enforcement even more difficult and the procurement of alcohol more dangerous. All of these elements led to the law's repeal in 1933. **11.** B **13.** B **15.** By the time of the 1920 election, the United States was tired and traumatized by the events of the past year. The nation had fought a brutal war, with veterans bringing home their own scars and troubles, and it had suffered domestically as well. Economic uncertainty and shortages, violent racial conflicts, fear of a Communist takeover, and a deadly flu pandemic had left Americans overwhelmed and unhappy. They did not seek new Progressive ideals, they did not want to be the world's policeman, and they did not want to destabilize what already felt unsteady. By choosing a reassuring-looking candidate who promised to bring things "back to normal," Americans squarely voted to hunker down, nurse their wounds, and try to enjoy themselves.

Chapter 24

1. C **3.** D **5.** B **7.** The reincarnated Ku Klux Klan championed an anti-black, anti-immigrant, anti-Catholic, and anti-Jewish philosophy, and promoted the spread of Protestant beliefs. The Klan publicly denounced the groups they despised and continued to engage in activities such as cross-burning, violence, and intimidation, despite their public commitment to nonviolent tactics. Women's groups within the Klan also participated in various types of reform, such as advocating the prohibition of alcohol and distributing Bibles in public schools. **9.** B **11.** The prohibition amendment failed due to its infeasibility. It lacked both public support and funds for its enforcement. It also lessened Americans' respect for law and order, and sparked a rise in unlawful activities, such as illegal alcohol production and organized crime. **13.** C **15.** B

Chapter 25

1. B **3.** At the outset of his presidency, Hoover planned to establish an agenda that would promote continued economic prosperity and eradicate poverty. He planned to eliminate federal regulations of the economy, which he believed would allow for maximum growth. For Americans themselves, he advocated a spirit of rugged individualism: Americans could bring about their own success or failure in partnership with the government, but remain unhindered by unnecessary government intervention in their everyday lives. These philosophies and policies reflected both the prosperity and optimism of the previous decade and a continuation of the postwar "return to normalcy" championed by Hoover's Republican predecessors. **5.** A **7.** D **9.** American films in the 1930s served to both assuage the fears and frustrations of many Americans suffering through the Depression and reinforce the idea that communal efforts—town and friends working together—would help to address the hardships. Previous emphasis upon competition and individualism slowly gave way to notions of "neighbor helping neighbor" and seeking group solutions to common problems. The *Andy Hardy* series, in particular, combined entertainment with the concept of family coming together to solve shared problems. The themes of greed, competition, and capitalist-driven market decisions no longer commanded a large audience among American moviegoers. **11.** D

Chapter 26

1. C **3.** Roosevelt recruited his "Brains Trust" to advise him in his inception of a variety of relief and recovery programs. Among other things, the members of this group pushed for a new national tax policy; addressed the nation's agricultural problems; advocated an increased role for the federal government in setting wages and prices; and believed that the federal government could temper the boom-and-bust cycles that rendered the economy unstable.

These advisors helped to craft the legislative programs that Roosevelt presented to Congress. **5.** D **7.** The National Recovery Administration (NRA) established a "code of fair practice" for every industry. Business owners were made to accept a set minimum wage and maximum number of work hours, as well as to recognize workers' rights to organize and use collective bargaining. While the NRA established over five hundred different codes, it proved difficult to adapt this plan successfully for diverse industries with very different characteristics and practices. **9.** A **11.** The Indian Reorganization Act, or Indian New Deal, of 1934 put an end to the policies set forth in the Dawes Severalty Act of 1887. Rather than encouraging assimilation, the new act promoted Indians' development of local self-government and the preservation of Indian artifacts and heritage. John Collier, the Commissioner on Indian Bureau Affairs, was able to use the law to push for federal officials' return of nearly two million acres of government-held land to various tribes.

Chapter 27

1. A **3.** D **5.** Many American women joined the armed forces, where they served as nurses, repaired and piloted airplanes, drove trucks, and performed clerical duties. Women in civilian life assumed occupations, often in the defense industries, that would have gone to men in times of peace. Women who did not take on wartime employment also contributed by recycling scarce materials, buying war bonds, planning meals using rationed foods, and generally making do with less. **7.** Roosevelt believed that his demand for an unconditional surrender from Germany and Japan would serve several purposes: It would provide reassurance to the Soviet Union of the nation's loyalty, prepare the Axis nations for a complete postwar transformation, and prevent any other nations from engaging in negotiations that would undermine the Big Three's plans for the defeated belligerents. **9.** B **11.** Truman wanted to end the war quickly and save lives by avoiding an invasion of the Japanese home islands. However, he might have achieved this by waiting for a definitive response from Japan following the bombing of Hiroshima. Truman may also have wanted to demonstrate America's power to the Soviet Union and hoped that the unleashing of his nuclear arsenal would send a strong message to Stalin.

Chapter 28

1. C **3.** The GI Bill provided returning veterans with a year of unemployment compensation, so they did not have to worry about finding jobs immediately. It allowed them to receive low-interest loans to buy homes or start businesses, and it paid for tuition for those who wished to attend college or vocational school. However, African American veterans could use their educational benefits only to attend schools that accepted black students, and some Mexican American veterans had difficulty gaining access to their benefits. Also, because those who had received a dishonorable discharge were not eligible, thousands of gay and lesbian servicemen and women who had been dishonorably discharged for their sexual orientation were unable to receive benefits. **5.** D **7.** D **9.** The construction of houses meant more work for people in the construction trades, including plumbers and electricians, and for those who worked in the lumber and appliance industries. The growth of the suburbs also led to a boom in the manufacture and sale of automobiles, which, in turn, created jobs for those in the steel, rubber, and oil industries. **11.** Antitrust lawsuits deprived studios of their theaters, and the careers of many actors, directors, and screenwriters were destroyed by Senator McCarthy's blacklist of suspected Communists. Meanwhile, the new technology of television drew audiences away from the movies by providing convenient at-home entertainment. **13.** C

Chapter 29

1. B **3.** Kennedy's economic development programs, supported by the Peace Corps, were intended to reduce poverty in developing nations so their citizens would be less attracted to Communism. After the Bay of Pigs invasion failed to overthrow the government of Fidel Castro, Kennedy demanded that the Soviet Union remove intermediate-range missiles from Cuba. He also increased support for the anti-Communist government in South Vietnam and sent advisors and troops to train the South Vietnamese army. **5.** D **7.** D **9.** D **11.** C **13.** The birth control pill enabled women to prevent or delay pregnancy, and thus marriage, and to limit the number of children they had. The freedom to control their reproduction also allowed women more opportunity to pursue higher education and work for pay outside the home.

Chapter 30

1. B **3.** Although hippie culture was not entirely homogenous, many hippies desired peace, rejected traditional social values, and sought to live a nonmaterialistic existence close to nature. Many also used drugs both recreationally and as a way to achieve greater spiritual insight. **5.** D **7.** C **9.** According to John Kerry's testimony, Vietnamese civilians were often subjected to shocking violence. Soldiers raped, mutilated, shot at, and brutally murdered civilians. Troops also intentionally destroyed Vietnamese villages, well beyond the destruction typically wrought by war. **11.** B **13.** D **15.** Carter succeeded in improving U.S. relations with China and engaged in talks with the Soviet Union regarding limiting nuclear weapons. He called attention to human rights abuses on the parts of foreign governments. Finally, he helped Menachem Begin and Anwar Sadat lay the groundwork for a peace treaty between Israel and Egypt.

Chapter 31

1. A **3.** Reagan planned to cut taxes for the wealthy in the hope that these taxpayers would then invest their surplus money in business; this, Reagan believed, would reduce unemployment. Reagan also sought to raise interest rates to curb inflation, cut federal spending on social programs, and deregulate industry. Finally, Reagan hoped—but ultimately failed—to balance the federal budget. **5.** D **7.** C **9.** After Congress ended support for the Nicaraguan Contras, President Reagan sought other sources of funding for them. Lt. Col. Oliver North then oversaw a plan by which arms would be sold to Iran and the money received from the sales would be sent to fund the Contras. **11.** A

Chapter 32

1. C **3.** The United States denied the rights of prisoners captured in Afghanistan and Iraq by imprisoning and interrogating them outside of the United States, where they were not protected by U.S. law. The U.S. also classified these prisoners as "unlawful combatants," so that they would not be entitled to the protections of the Geneva Conventions. **5.** A **7.** C **9.** The administration refused to ratify the Kyoto Protocol, and, as a result, the United States has not been required to reduce its greenhouse gas emissions. Meanwhile, climate scientists have experienced interference with their work. For critics of climate change, this hampering of scientific research and consensus has provided further evidence of the lack of agreed-upon conclusions about climate change. **11.** D

Index